W9-BRX-995

1,000 PLACES TO SEE BEFORE YOU DIE®

by **PATRICIA SCHULTZ**

WORKMAN PUBLISHING, NEW YORK

AN IMPORTANT NOTE
TO READERS

Though every effort has been made to ensure the accuracy and timeliness of the information contained in this book (and all the contact information and prices have been updated for 2010), it may change at any time for many reasons, including market forces, political and economic conditions, and weather. Readers should be sure to call or e-mail ahead for confirmation of information when making any travel plans. The author, editors, and publisher shall not be responsible for any travel conditions experienced by readers resulting from changes in information provided in this book. If you discover any out-of-date or incorrect information in the book, we would appreciate it if you would let us know via our website, www.1000BeforeYouDie.com.

Design by Paul Hanson

ISBN 978-0-7611-6102-8

Previously cataloged as:
Library of Congress Cataloging-in-Publication Data
Schultz, Patricia.
1,000 Places to See Before You Die / Patricia Schultz.
p. cm.
ISBN 978-0-7611-0484-1
1. Travel—Guidebooks. I. Title.
G153.4.S385 2003
910'.2'02—dc21   2003041148

Workman books are available at special discount when purchased in bulk for premiums and sales promotions as well as for fund-raising or educational use. Special editions or book excerpts also can be created to specification. For details, contact the Special Sales Director at the address below.

Workman Publishing Company, Inc.
225 Varick Street
New York, NY 10014-4381
www.workman.com

Printed in the United States of America
First Printing, updated edition: February 2010
10 9 8 7 6 5 4 3 2 1

*Life is not measured
by the number of
breaths we take but by
the places and moments
that take our breath away.*

—ANONYMOUS

DEDICATION

How important it is to pick the right parents.
For their unconditional love, support, and encouragement,
enabling me to make my life One Great Adventure,
to Leonard and in special memory of Mary

And to the late Sally Kovalchick,
whose spirit, integrity, and editorial expertise are still very
much felt at Workman Publishing

ACKNOWLEDGMENTS

First and foremost I want to thank my publisher, Peter Workman, whose vision and commitment to *1,000 Places* are the only reasons a project of this magnitude made it from concept to print. His enormous love for books and travel was the foundation upon which the Workman family created the best imaginable home for this guide.

Sharing his enthusiasm was the late Sally Kovalchick, a much-loved and highly respected editor and a kindred adventurer (she had sailed up Papua New Guinea's Sepik River and camped out in the Sahara Desert with Bedouin guides, for example). Completing the trio of enormous talents was Paul Hanson, whose tasteful design and sensitivity made beautiful visual sense of the reams of material put before him.

On a more daily basis, I must thank one thousand times my diligent and untiring editors Margot Herrera, Liz Carey, and Matt Hannafin. Professionally and emotionally, I turned to them again and again for coaching, for focus, and to slowly but surely make it through a project that confirmed to me just how huge the world is. Anne Cherry spent more than a year shepherding the book through many stages; Katherine Adzima's editorial talents were also indispensable. Cindy Schoen is anyone's idea of the bright and unflappable assistant from heaven. She never once refused nor questioned any of my requests, no matter how silly or time-consuming. Copyeditor Dan Geist helped keep my prose from veering into grammatical wildernesses, and Barbaralynn Altorfer and Barbara Peragine worked miracles with the layout and typesetting. With a keen eye and fierce determination, my dear friend Giema Tsakuginow hunted down photography for some of the most obscure destinations, as did Aaron Clendening at Workman.

Many thanks also to Nicki Clendening from Workman's crackerjack publicity department. She is determined that every travel-inclined individual on the planet knows about this book. Doug Wolff, in the production department, did a wonderful job in making the book a reality.

Special thanks to the conscientious team of researchers and factcheckers (Kelli Bagley, Brian Flegel, Yosefa Forma, Brad Plumer, Arielle Simon, and Jenny Whitcher) who learned more about patience, currency conversions, time zones, and language barriers than they knew existed.

Despite complications and detours down a road that seemed to have no end, everyone involved at Workman in this herculean collaboration was unflagging right up to the time we shipped our opus off to the printer. I thank them one and all, wholeheartedly.

I wouldn't know where to begin to thank everyone in the travel world for the impact they have had on me and, as a result, on this book. From the hotel owner in Bath who showed me the hidden corners of Somerset's countryside to the professional boards of tourism who patiently helped me make sense of their countries' countless possibilities, innumerable people shared their love and appreciation of the world's wonders with me. All those who opened their homes and hearts helped shape the impressions and opinions presented in these pages.

But at the end of seven years made up of very long days, those I really need to thank are my family in my hometown, Beacon, New York, and my friends both here and abroad. Without the knowledge that they were at my side to cheer me on, sympathize, and never question my resolve (though sometimes questioning my sanity), I could never have completed the project. They made *1,000 Places* possible. My sister, Roz; her husband, Ed; and their children, Star, Corey, and Brittany never wavered

in their support, nor did any of my long-time friends at the Adlon, the Manhattan building that is my nurturing base and the reason I always enjoy coming home after any trip. I hope that Despina, Michael, Nancy, Itzik, Jeannie, Nelson, and John and the doormen and neighbors who saw me always running to Federal Express or Kinko's minutes before closing time know the importance of their quiet support, small favors, and regular promises to help me celebrate when the book finally appeared. I intend to take them all up on that.

There are a few other friends to whom I'd like to give special thanks: Teddy Sitter Danilo, whose intelligence, integrity, humor, and strength have always encouraged me to be and do the best I can; Elizabeth Ragagli, whose gung-ho road-warrior spirit and love-the-country-you're-in approach to travel probably most closely reflects my own; Nick Stringas, because he is like a Rock of Gibraltar in any storm; Annie Brody, a fellow Manhattanite I met in Florence years ago, with whom I later co-authored *Made in Italy*. A psychic once told me a lady with red curly hair would have a great influence on my career. That's Annie.

Finally, to Bob Gilbert and Tad Gast—although they're no longer here on earth, their spirit never leaves me. And to Giovanni, whom I continue to see in every corner of Italy.

CONTENTS

THE UNITED STATES
OF AMERICA
AND CANADA • 561

From Alaska's Inside Passage to Savannah's Historic District,
the Art Institute of Chicago to the French Quarter in
New Orleans, the Las Vegas Strip to New York's Finger Lakes Region,
Monticello in Virginia to Jackson Hole in Wyoming,
Skating the Rideau Canal in Ottawa to Heli-Skiing in British Columbia

LATIN AMERICA • 777

From the Mayan Ruins of Palenque in Mexico
to Belize's Barrier Reef, the San Blas Archipelago
of Panama to Buenos Aires's Tango Bars,
Chile's Wine Region to the Otavalo Market in Ecuador,
Machu Picchu in Peru to the Penguin Rookeries of Antarctica

THE CARIBBEAN, BAHAMAS, AND BERMUDA · 849

From Cap Juluca in Anguilla to the Exuma Cays in the Bahamas,
Cuba's Jazz Festival to Sailing the Grenadines,
Old San Juan in Puerto Rico to Saba Marine Park

INDEXES · 895

INTRODUCTION

The Story of This Book

Is it nature or nurture that sends a person out onto the Road—that whispers in one's ear that it's time to take off and make for the horizon, just to see what's out there?

The urge to travel—to open our minds and move beyond the familiar—is as old as man himself. It's what drove the ancient Romans to visit Athens's Acropolis and Verona's amphitheater. It's what sent Marco Polo off on his momentous journey east, and what moved St. Augustine of Hippo to write, "The world is a book, and those who do not travel, read only one page." Whether we go to London for the weekend or to a place that's utterly alien, travel changes us, sometimes superficially, sometimes profoundly. It is a classroom without walls.

I can't speak for everyone, but I can tell you about my own wanderlust. Family legend (never proven) has it that we're somehow related to Mark Twain, America's great storyteller and also one of the preeminent globe-trotters of his day. How then to explain my mother's reaction when I had my own first Great Adventure?

It was the late 1950s, and Atlantic City was as exotic and unknown to me as Shangri-la—all sand and sea, hotels and boardwalk, and the intimation of greater things just beyond what I could see from the family beach blanket. I set off at the first opportunity, but after what seemed only a few precious minutes of intoxicating discovery (in fact several hours), I was snatched up by my apoplectic mother and a cadre of relieved lifeguards and brought back to the roost. This is my earliest memory: I had heard the siren call of the great, global beyond, and I had answered. I was hooked. I was four.

Fast-forward to college graduation. Campus buddies were heading straight for Wall Street apprenticeships, international banking programs, and family business obligations, but I made a bee-line for the airport and my own private Grand Tour through the marvels of Italy and its neighbors. Could one make a living off *la dolce vita*? I was amazed when my first articles got published, but then I realized: one could. Many guidebooks and innumerable articles later, I found myself at a round table facing publisher Peter Workman and his right-hand editor, the late Sally Kovalchick, who told me about their desire to compile the world's most enticing and intriguing treasures between two covers, and their belief that I was up to the challenge. I was on board.

When it came time to actually do it, though—to choose from the nearly bottomless grab bag of the world's possibilities, both legendary and unsung—I realized I was in for a lengthy battle with philosophy and methodology and all the questions anyone who flips through this book is bound to ask. How did I arrive at these particular destinations and events? What were my criteria? How to explain the wide range, from undeniably glorious far-flung mysteries to apparently mundane backyard beauties? The inclusion of the Taj Mahal and the Sistine Chapel makes sense, but why give the Pork Pit in Montego Bay the same weight as Paris's legendary Taillevent? Am I really implying that an agritourist B&B on a Tuscan wine-producing estate is just as worthy as Bangkok's storied Oriental Hotel, where Somerset Maugham and Rudyard Kipling were regulars? Does the weirdness of Roswell hold up against the magic of Tikal? Antoine de Saint-Exupéry's Little Prince had it easier when he asked the geographer,

"What place would you advise me to visit now?" and was told, "The planet Earth. It has a good reputation."

In the final analysis, the common denominator I chose was a simple one: that each place impress upon the visitor—and, I hope, upon the reader—some sense of the earth's magic, integrity, wonder, and legacy. That was the standard I applied, across every continent, from the conspicuous and predictable to the small and humble, from spiritual spots like Bagan in Myanmar to temporal ones like Hong Kong's shopping districts, from natural wonders like the Grand Canyon to man-made ones like Petra, Jordan's fabled "lost city"—life experiences all. To compile my list, I drew upon the decades of insatiable travel that followed my epiphany on the sands of Atlantic City. I pored over hundreds of travel books and glossy magazines and spoke to scores of tourism boards and PR agencies effusively loyal to their clients—then I sleuthed out the real story on my own. I picked the brains of travel colleagues and peripatetic friends, and queried anyone stepping off a bus, train, or plane who was smiling. At countless dinner parties, I listened while complete strangers scribbled the names of magical places on cocktail napkins, or swore me to secrecy and then whispered their favorite destinations in my ear.

In the seven years it took me to research and write this formidable project, I was reminded time and again that travel is always personal, and that no two people walk away from the same experience with the same memories. What it came down to, in the end, is that each of the places in this book is truly, completely, and undeniably inspiring—through the ages or to the modern world—often both—to the simply curious traveler as well as to poets, adventurers, painters, pilgrims, scholars, and travel writers.

"Travel," wrote my maybe-ancestor Twain in *The Innocents Abroad*, "is fatal to prejudice, bigotry and narrow mindedness, and many of our people need it sorely on these accounts." Travel dispels many of our bad impressions, confirms the positive, and promises innumerable surprises. It opens our eyes to exotic places like Zanzibar, Katmandu, Machu Picchu, and Lalibela—names familiar to us through films, books, and tales, but whose reality is so much more than they could ever explain. In the flesh, it shows us why even the most clichéd travel experiences—riding a gondola in Venice, taking a Turkish bath in Turkey, braving Times Square on New Year's Eve—are perennially popular. With travel, our minds become more curious, our hearts more powerful, and our spirits more joyous. And once the mind is stretched like that, it can never return to its original state.

The world today is a smaller place than it was even twenty years ago, and while the romantic concept of Ultima Thule—what *Webster's* describes as "any far-off, unknown region"—may still be found in the otherworldly landscapes of Namibia, the Himalayan kingdom of Bhutan, and the timeless Nadaam horse games of Mongolia's Ulaanbaatar, the fact remains that these places all lie only a day or two's journey away, thanks to today's monumental travel infrastructure. What does this do to our sense of adventure, of exploring the Other? For me, it comes down to a matter of viewpoint: As the Sherpa said to Edmund Hillary on the slopes of Mount Everest, some people travel only to look, while others come to see. Some road warriors can speed from New York to L.A. without registering a thing; I can walk around my mid-Manhattan block and come home with a carton of milk and stories to tell. In the end, the number of miles covered has nothing to do with the real pleasures of travel; the inherent beauty of the world and the discovery it promises are all around us.

In this time of global uncertainty, even the intrepid might feel inclined to stick closer to home base, or to retreat into armchair travel—and even this can be rewarding. I can shut my eyes and hear the sound of loons again on

Squam Lake, or the flutter of prayer flags outside a Tibetan monastery in Llasa. I can smell the spices of the market in the ancient medina of Fez, or the floating aroma of *fritto misto* in the cobbled backstreets of an Italian Riviera village. This is my moveable feast, the memories that sustain me until my next ticket is in hand, my next Great Adventure about to begin.

1,000 Places to See Before You Die is my own personal short list of dream trips. While the number daunted me at first, I came to realize there were a thousand times a thousand possibilities. . . . Perhaps I'll save them for a sequel, or for another life. Not every entry is for everybody, but show me someone who won't find enough between these two covers to keep busy for the next few decades. Never a travel snob, I confess I've never understood the appeal of certain must-do's (though I've happily included them), like playing the finest golf courses in Scotland or going bungee-jumping in New Zealand, but these activities may well figure into your own game plan. I know I'll raise eyebrows by including unconventional destinations such as Calcutta and Madagascar, arduous choices that some travelers might avoid, but I consider them deeply moving and insightful windows into the human experience. The same goes for Chicago's landmark Superdawg hot dog stand, whose inclusion will be questioned only by those who have never been there.

The number of hotels I've included might also need a brief explanation. A longtime hotel buff, my opinion about cities both large and small is always greatly influenced by where I hang my hat and unpack my bag. Can one even think of visiting London without enjoying high tea at the Ritz? Or, when in Singapore, having a Singapore Sling where it originated, at the legendary Raffles Hotel? Isn't Singita safari lodge on the periphery of Kruger National Park as inspirational as the game viewing? And isn't Sweden's Ice Hotel the ultimate hoot?

Other unforgettable memories I have not been able to re-create for this book, like the day my driver in Casablanca took me to his mother's home for Saturday lunch when I asked him who served the best couscous in town, or the time I somehow became the guest of honor at a stranger's four-day wedding celebration in Cairo. From experiences like these I learned that camel meat's not bad, and serendipity really is the best tour guide.

Any trip can be fraught with disappointment: Expectations are always high, and anything can go wrong. Here are a few suggestions for both first-time and inveterate travelers: More important than packing a bag full of money, pack a bag full of patience and curiosity; allow yourself—encourage yourself—to be sidetracked and to get lost. There's no such thing as a bad trip, just good travel stories to tell back home. Always travel with a smile and remember that you're the one with the strange customs visiting someone else's country. Relying on the kindness of strangers isn't naive—there are good people wherever you go. And, finally, the more time you spend coming to understand the ways of others, the more you'll understand yourself. The journey abroad reflects the one within—the most unknown and foreign and unmapped landscape of them all, the ultimate terra incognita. As Mr. Twain said, "Twenty years from now you will be more disappointed by the things you didn't do than by the ones you did. So throw off the bowlines. Sail away from the safe harbor. Catch the trade winds in your sails. Explore. Dream. Discover."

How the Book Is Organized

For the purposes of this book, I've divided the world into eight regions, which are then further subdivided geographically:

- EUROPE: Great Britain and Ireland, Western Europe, Eastern Europe, and Scandinavia
- AFRICA: Northern Africa, Middle and Southern Africa
- THE MIDDLE EAST
- ASIA: East Asia, South and Central Asia, Southeast Asia
- AUSTRALIA, NEW ZEALAND, AND THE PACIFIC ISLANDS
- THE UNITED STATES OF AMERICA AND CANADA: Subdivided by state or province
- LATIN AMERICA: Mexico, Central America, South America, Antarctica
- THE CARIBBEAN, BAHAMAS, AND BERMUDA

Within these divisions, entries are further divided by country (see the contents for a quick reference), and within each country they're organized alphabetically by region or town. In the back of the book are special indexes that allow you to find information by the type of experience, e.g., Gorgeous Beaches and Getaway Islands, followed by a general index.

At the end of each entry, the text describes practical information that will help you in planning a trip. But remember: Since travel information is always subject to change, you should confirm by phone, fax, or e-mail before you leave home. Even the contact numbers we give you have been found at times to vanish or change or merge. It's all part of the adventure of travel.

How the Listings Are Organized

Here's a run-through of what you'll see at the end of each entry.

WHAT

• TOWN: includes small towns as well as cities.

• ISLAND: used for destinations whose character depends on their *being* islands—Manhattan, Hong Kong, and Singapore don't count. Nor, of course, does England.

• HOTEL: from the world's coziest country inn to Vegas's largest resort to a safari camp on the Masai Mara.

• RESTAURANT: encompasses the highest haute cuisine, the lowest and most down-home local fare, plus bars, food festivals, and all other things gastronomic.

• SITE: any physical location that's not a town, island, hotel, or restaurant—such as a temple, museum, or archaeological dig, as well as larger destinations such as a city's historic district, a wine region, or a national park.

• EXPERIENCE: this category includes skiing and golf destinations, historic walks, mountain treks, and other activities.

• EVENT: covers regularly scheduled programming—music and theater festivals, Chinese New Year, the Pushkar Camel Fair, and the like.

WHERE

Distance from major cities or landmarks, address or general location, and as much contact information as we could get—phone, fax, e-mail, and web address.

A NOTE ON PHONE NUMBERS: All phone numbers in the book are listed with their country codes, so to call any of them from your home country, you simply have to dial your international access code (011 in the U.S. and Canada; 0011 in Australia; 00 in the U.K., Ireland, and New Zealand; etc.), then the listed number. U.S. and Canadian numbers are listed *without* the country code; to call these countries from outside their borders, simply add the number "1" at the beginning, after dialing your international access code. Listings of all world country codes and other dialing information are available on many websites, including www.travel.att.com/traveler/codes/index.jsp.

In many countries, you must add a 0 before the local number when calling within the borders. (Naturally, you do not need to dial the country code in these instances.)

HOW

"How" includes information on specific recommended outfitters or operators who offer tours, treks, safaris, and other package or customized travel to the particular destination.

WHERE TO STAY

Hotels and inns listed under this head, though not discussed in the entry text, are good choices located near the topic of the entry, and are always of at least acceptable quality.

COSTS

I've listed prices for all hotels, restaurants, attractions, and package trips discussed in the book, based on the following parameters:

HOTELS: Listed hotel costs are per room, for two people, unless noted otherwise. Where applicable, hotel entries include information for high and low season and for significant room categories discussed in the text. Amenities included in the rates are also listed, though complimentary breakfasts are not. Remember, though, that these prices are rack rates, and represent what a hotel charges when demand is at its peak. Hotels are almost always flexible with these prices, offering various discounts to keep occupancy high.

Some hotels—particularly in Europe—offer room-only rates in low season and much higher half-board rates (including breakfast and dinner for two) in high season. Where this is the case, I've listed both prices.

TRIPS/TREKS/EXCURSIONS: Trip costs are usually given in total, per person, based on double occupancy, with notes on what is included in the rate (accommodations, meals, transportation, amenities, etc.). If an operator offers several different lengths of trip (five-day, one-week, two-week, etc.), the cost is listed per person, per day, based on double occupancy—just multiply this by the number of nights to calculate total trip cost. Note that entries do not include airfare unless otherwise stated.

RESTAURANTS: Meal prices listed are per person and represent the approximate total cost of a meal (dinner, unless stated otherwise) without wine.

WHEN

For hotels, sites, and restaurants, "When" may not appear if the establishment is open year-round. Short seasonal closings (less than one month) are usually not noted. For package trips, "When" includes the months (and sometimes days of the week) that the outfitter offers a particular trip, or the times when a particular destination is and is not accessible due to weather conditions, etc.

Be sure to contact hotels, restaurants, and target attractions if traveling during holiday months, and bear in mind large local or cultural holidays at your destination. The Bank Holidays of the World website (www.bankholidays.com) maintains a worldwide database of public holidays.

BEST TIMES

For many entries, I've listed the best times to visit, taking into account weather, sports and leisure opportunities, peak tourist crowds, festivals, and other significant events. When no "Best times" are listed, the reason is "wonderful anytime."

Travel Safety

This book represents travel opportunities in an ideal, peaceful world. However, that's not the world we actually live in. Travelers will be perfectly safe visiting most of the destinations discussed, but a few places may pose some risk, either currently or in the future. Therefore, before making plans to travel to destinations with which you're not familiar, be sure to do your homework.

The U.S. Department of State maintains travel advisories on its website at www.travel.state.gov. Other information listed includes a general overview of each country, entry requirements for U.S. citizens, and information on health, safety, crime, and other travel issues.

The British Foreign & Commonwealth Office maintains similar information on its website, www.fco.gov.uk. On the theory that it never hurts to get a second opinion, I recommend going to this site after you've heard what the U.S. State Department has to say about a particular country. Click on "Travel and living abroad," then on "Travel Advice" to access travel information on all countries, including warnings on travel to dangerous areas.

Travel Documents

In addition to a valid passport, many countries listed in this book require that foreign citizens obtain travel visas in advance of their trip. Competent travel agents will be able to provide information on where visas are required, but you can also get it ahead of time from the U.S. Department of State, the U.K. Foreign & Commonwealth Office, or the relevant government ministry of your home country. U.S. citizens can look on-line at www.travel.state.gov, which notes the documentation required for each country and provides a link to the country's embassy. British citizens should go to www.fco.gov.uk, click on "Travel and living abroad," then on "Travel Advice by country," and scroll to "Entry Requirements," which provides a link to the relevant embassy.

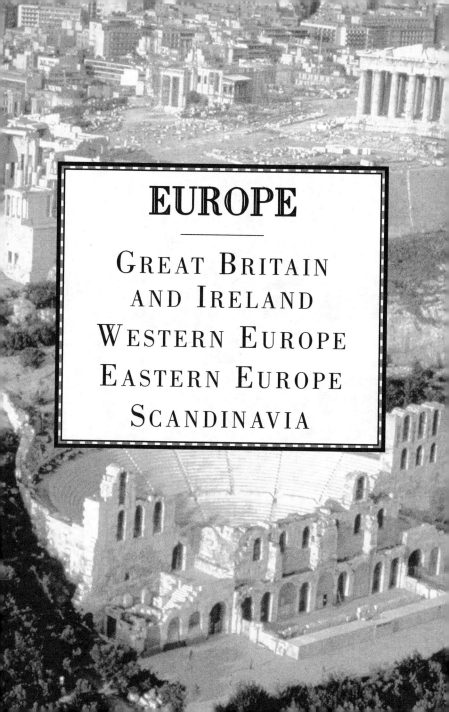

EUROPE

GREAT BRITAIN
AND IRELAND
WESTERN EUROPE
EASTERN EUROPE
SCANDINAVIA

GREAT BRITAIN AND IRELAND

Weekend Guests of the Astors

CLIVEDEN

Taplow, Berkshire, England

As surprisingly comfortable as it is overwhelmingly grand, this National Trust property is England's most majestic country-house hotel. Even adjectives like "spectacular" and "magnificent" seem inadequate amid the aristocratic proportions of the Italianate villa, much of whose present-day character reflects three generations of Astors (preceded by one Prince of Wales, among others), who lived here until 1966. (In the 1960s Cliveden was also the setting of the infamous Profumo scandal that led to the collapse of the Conservative government in 1964.) A dinner in the excellent restaurant Waldo's is reason enough to drive from London, though as an overnight guest you'll have the luxury of working it off on the hotel's 376 acres of riding paths or jogging trails. Overlooking the River Thames, 15-foot-high windows afford views of the hotel's antique boats, including Nancy Astor's silent electric canoe. Piloted by uniformed boatmen, these are available for pre-dinner Champagne cruises or picnics with large hampers of food furnished by the hotel. Take pleasure in the formal gardens, drawing-room fires, tailcoated footmen, chandeliered dining rooms, and palpable air of exclusivity, but what you may enjoy most is the royal treatment extended even to titleless guests.

WHAT: hotel, restaurant. **WHERE:** 10 miles/16 km northwest of Windsor. Tel 44/1628-668-561, fax 44/1628-661-837; reservations @clivedenhouse.co.uk; www.clivedenhouse.co. uk. **COST:** doubles from $500. Prix fixe dinner at Waldo's $95. **WHEN:** dinner only, daily.

Clivedon was built in 1666 by the Second Duke of Buckingham.

England's Most Visited Historic Site

WINDSOR CASTLE

Windsor, Berkshire, England

Standing at the very heart of the British national identity, Windsor is the oldest and largest castle in Britain and, with 1,000 rooms, the largest occupied castle in the world. The present queen, Elizabeth II, spent much of her

The view of Windsor Castle from the Long Walk

Highlights of a trip to Windsor Castle include the Changing of the Guard, which takes place even when the queen is not in residence (although with less pomp and regalia); the Queen Mary's Doll House, an exquisite gift in miniature designed in 1923 by architect Sir Edwin Lutyens; and the 16th-century architectural jewel of St. George's Chapel which, together with Westminster Abbey, shares the distinction of being a pantheon of many English monarchs. The flat tomb in the center contains the vault of Henry VIII and his third wife, Jane Seymour.

childhood here, so it is not surprising that her public felt her pain when a devastating fire partially destroyed 100 rooms in the state and private apartments in 1992, her *annus horribilis*. A magnificent $53 million restoration completed in 1997 employed a beehive of artisans using the same techniques as when the castle was begun under William the Conqueror, 900 years ago. It has been lived in by eight successive royal houses since then. In 1916, King George V assumed the name of the place out of fondness—and to disassociate the royal family from its Germanic origins.

WHAT: site. **WHERE:** 21 miles/34 km west of London. Tel 44/2077-667-304, fax 44/2079-309-625; windsorcastle@royalcollection.org.uk; www.royalresidences.com. **COST:** admission (to castle, doll's house, and chapel) $25. **WHEN:** daily, though hours and rooms open to the public are restricted in Apr, Jun, and Dec and on certain occasions when royal or state events take place.

A Walled City and Architectural Feast

CHESTER

Cheshire, England

In 1779, author James Boswell wrote of Chester: "It pleases me more than any town I ever saw." Important in Roman times (England's largest amphitheater is here), the Middle Ages, and during an 18th-century revival, Chester has much to show for its three historical heydays. A well-preserved fortified wall, one of the finest in England, surrounds much of the historic city: built during the Roman period, and rebuilt at different times after that, it is topped by a lovely 2-mile footpath. Parts of the wall bypass the city's important red sandstone cathedral on two sides and lead to the 19th-century Eastgate, where Chester's famous wrought-iron clock tower proudly stands. Chester's greatest attraction is the city itself: within the walls is one of England's best collection of black-and-white "magpie" buildings, some facades a riot of striped patterns. Anticipating today's high-rises, the two-tiered decoratively timbered buildings with a connecting walkway above street level make up the Chester Rows, a popular double-decker shopping area that is the city's most famous feature. After a day full of history and architecture (and the crowds they attract), repair to the serenity of the city's premier hotel, the Chester Grosvenor. This handsome 19th-century building in the heart of Chester's historic neighborhood can trace its origins to the reign of Queen Elizabeth I.

Chester's city center

It is owned by the Duke of Westminster's Grosvenor Estate, and as a sophisticated hotel featuring its own gourmet restaurant, the Arkle, the Grosvenor knows no competition in this area of the country.

WHAT: town, hotel, restaurant. **CHESTER:** 207 miles/333 km northwest of London, 43 miles/69 km southwest of Manchester. **THE CHESTER GROSVENOR:** Eastgate. Tel 44/1244-324-024, fax 44/1244-313-246; reservations@chestergrosvenor.com; www.chestergrosvenor.com. *Cost:* doubles from $335. Dinner at the Arkle $90. **BEST TIMES:** the classical Chester Summer Music Festival, last 2 weeks of Jul. The Chester Fringe Festival takes place simultaneously, offering every other kind of music from jazz to Cajun.

Where England Comes to an End

PENZANCE AND LAND'S END

Cornwall, England

The last town before Land's End, Penzance is famous for its pirates and for a climate so mild (courtesy of the Gulf Stream) that palm trees and subtropical plants are commonplace. As a favorite base for exploring the westernmost county in England, Jean Shrimpton's Abbey Hotel is the town's first choice and one of the most eclectic and charming hotels around. In the deft hands of the 1960s supermodel, this rambling row of 300-year-old townhouses built on the foundations of a 12th-century abbey is filled with antiques and a certain bohemian air.

Much of Penzance's importance is as the starting point for a trip to the castled island of St. Michael's Mount, attached to the mainland by nothing more than a cobbled causeway. For centuries it has been the subject and inspiration for the local artists' community, seeming to float ethereally just above the sea. It was originally created in 1135 as a sister abbey to the more famous Mont-Saint-Michel across the Channel in Normandy. From afar, the parapets and terraced cliff gardens of the monastery-castle-fortress create a romantic profile against skies of changing light and scudding clouds. The arduous climb to the top of the castle, rising 250 feet from the sea, is well worth it for the views.

Nearby Land's End is an obligatory day trip. Often called the "toe" of England, this is the southernmost and westernmost point in the ancient duchy of Cornwall with a distinctive flavor and coastal beauty. It is one of Britain's most visited natural attractions, since the craggy promontory's tip (more officially called Penwith) is where England ends—or begins. The ancient Cornish called it "Pen von Laz" meaning "end of the earth." For those seeking bleak end-of-the-world solitude or moved by geographical extremities, lonely heather moors that overlook the point where the Atlantic Ocean converges with the English Channel are a gull's cry away. Facing west, on a clear day you'll see the outline of the Isles of Scilly.

Of the group of 100-plus rocky islands (five inhabited but many more named) with exotic palms, rare seabirds, and some of the most beautiful beaches in Britain, Tresco, privately owned since 1834, is most visited—primarily for its world-famous gardens. With

Where the English Channel meets the Atlantic Ocean

more than 3,000 species of plants, they are considered the finest in the British Islands, a subtropical wonderland thanks to the Mediterranean-like climate provided by the Gulf Stream. The only place worth staying on the car-free island is also one of its highlights: The Island Hotel sits on its own little promontory, surrounded by gardens and open views of the sea and off-islands.

WHAT: town, hotel, island. **PENZANCE:** 280 miles/451 km southwest of London. *When:* castle on St. Michael's Mount open year-round, but days and hours change with the seasons and weather. **ABBEY HOTEL:** Abbey St. Tel 44/1736-366-906, fax 44/1736-351-163; www.theabbeyonline.com. *Cost:* doubles $175 (low season), $250 (high season). **LAND'S END:** 10 miles/16 km west of Penzance. **ISLES OF SCILLY:** ferry departure from Penzance. *When:* daily during high season. **ISLAND HOTEL:** Old Grimsby, Tresco. Tel 44/1720-422-883; www.tresco.co.uk. *Cost:* doubles from $215. *When:* Mar–Nov. **BEST TIMES:** Apr–Jun, Sept–Oct.

Britain's Most Famous and Influential Artists' Colony

ST. IVES

Cornwall, England

With 326 miles of dramatically contorted coastline (well over 100 of them protected as the ruggedly scenic Coastal Path, a must-hike choice for international trekkers), Cornwall also offers peaceful villages and deserted headlands. St. Ives is the most famous of the West Country's fishing villages, a Cubist tumble of well-kept white cottages falling over one another. The almost Mediterranean quality of light has attracted artists here; today's art galleries and artisans' shops prolong its role as Britain's most famous artists' colony with a holiday-resort air. That London bastion of British art, the Tate Gallery, opened an offshoot here in 1993 in a hand-

some rotunda above the sea with striking views from its rooftop restaurant. It includes works by the St. Ives school of artists, mostly from 1925 to 1975, drawn from the mother museum's rich collection. It also administers the small but special Barbara Hepworth Museum and Sculpture Garden, studio and home of St. Ives's leading artist who, together with her husband, painter Ben Nicholson, helped establish this port town as an outpost for avant-garde and abstract artists in the 1930s. This is also the land of ancient myth: according to legend, King Arthur was born and held court at nearby Tintagel Castle, its crumbling ruins crowning Cornwall's north coast, with Merlin's Cave at the foot of the rocky cliffs below.

What: town, site. **St. Ives:** 320 miles/ 515 km southwest of London, 21 miles/34 km northeast of Land's End. **Tate Gallery:** Porthmeor Beach. Tel 44/1736-796-226; www.tate.org.uk. *Cost:* admission $9. *When:* open daily, Mar–Oct, closed Mon, Nov–Feb.

One of Cornwall's beguiling coves

Seaside Delights on the Cornish Riviera

Hotel Tresanton and The Seafood Restaurant

St. Mawes and Padstow, Cornwall, England

An old yachting refuge, the once-dilapidated Hotel Tresanton has been reclaimed and reborn under the design-savvy auspices of new owners to become the best place to stay in this newly fashionable southwestern edge of Britain. Here on the Roseland Peninsula on Cornwall's temperate south coast in the picturesque and unspoiled fishing village of St. Mawes, Olga Polizzi (scion of England's most famous hotel dynasty, the Fortes) and her family have created a boutique hotel with a nautical motif, featuring breezy terraces, gorgeous views, and a simple but superb restaurant specializing in local ingredients with wisps of Mediterranean influence (one of the hotel's many aspects reminiscent of seaside resorts much farther south). This is the only place to be in Cornwall for Sunday lunch. The Tresanton can also plan your getaway picnic to the quiet coves and deserted beaches of the nearby Lizard Peninsula (the southernmost point in England and one of its most beautiful). Sail there on the family's 48-foot *Pinuccia*, the sloop-rigged racing yacht

originally commissioned by the Italian publisher Rizzoli for the 1939 World Cup.

Another worthy destination is Padstow's famed The Seafood Restaurant. The friendly little port of Padstow is one of Cornwall's oldest towns (founded in the 6th century) and quaint enough to attract stopovers by those en route to Land's End, but the devotees who book here months in advance hardly stumble upon this much-lauded eatery by chance. People come from all over the country ("foreigners" to home-bred Cornishmen) to eat in this light, airy, plant-filled restaurant housed in a former quayside grain warehouse, and thrill to classic dishes (grilled Dover sole, local oysters) and imaginative adaptations (spicy Goan fish curry, seafood ravioli) alike. Chef-owner, author, BBC food-series personality and seafood guru Rick Stein's careful and expert

Harborside shopping in Padstow

choice of local "gifts from the sea" is best showcased in his signature *fruits de mer* plate, handpicked off the trawlers and lobster boats bobbing outside.

WHAT: hotel, restaurant. **HOTEL TRESANTON:** Lower Castle Rd., St. Mawes (300 miles/483 km southwest of London, 55 miles/88 km northeast of Land's End). Tel 44/1326-270-055, fax 44/1326-270-053; info@tresanton.com; www. tresanton.com. *Cost:* doubles from $372 (low season), from $455 (high season). Dinner $70. *When:* open Feb–Dec; restaurant open daily for lunch and dinner. **THE SEAFOOD RESTAURANT:** Riverside, Padstow (275 miles/442 km southwest of London, 57 miles/92 km east of Land's End). Tel 44/1841-532-700, fax 44/1841-532-942; reservations@rickstein.com; www. rickstein.com. *Cost:* dinner $60. *When:* open daily for lunch and dinner. **BEST TIMES:** Apr–Sept for sailing and water sports.

One of the Greatest of All Great Houses

CHATSWORTH HOUSE

Bakewell, Derbyshire, England

Of the dozens of historic "Great Houses" enriching England's countryside, Chatsworth, the centuries-old home of the Duchess and the late Duke of Devonshire, is one of the most impressive. It has some 300 rooms open to the public, including lavish state apartments decorated with a wealth of art treasures. There are also important gardens landscaped by the ubiquitous Lancelot "Capability" Brown in the 1760s; the equally esteemed Joseph Paxton turned them into some of the most celebrated gardens in all of Europe a century later.

Set in the verdant folds of the Derwent Valley, this Baroque palace was built in the late 17th century, as were parts of the famous gardens, notably its striking Cascade House of forced waterfalls. Many generations of dukes have added to the prodigious art collection. Paintings by such masters as Tintoretto, Veronese, and Rembrandt are here, and the present duke and duchess have enhanced the

collection with more contemporary works, including that of their friend Lucian Freud. Visitors to the 100-acre garden (within a 1,000-acre parkland) should visit the chapel first, one of the finest Baroque interiors in all of England.

Chatsworth's painted hall

WHAT: site. **WHERE:** 150 miles/241 km north of London, 4 miles/6 km east of Bakewell. Tel 44/1246-582-204, fax 44/1246-583-536; visit@chatsworth.org; www.chatsworth.org. **COST:** admission. **WHEN:** open daily, year-round. **BEST TIMES:** May and Sept for the gardens.

Romantic Island Getaway Where History Lingers

BURGH ISLAND HOTEL

Bigbury-on-Sea, Devon, England

More than sixty years have passed since the Duke of Windsor and Wallis Simpson escaped the attention of the world and fled to this Art Deco retreat on its own 26-acre private island off the southern coast of Devon. Renovated with panache by new owners who mercifully left a whiff of its Deco decadence intact, Burgh Island is still the place to renounce life's pressing matters and revel in the island aura that inspired Agatha Christie (who was born in Devon) to pen *And Then There Were None* and *Evil under the Sun* during a visit in the early 1930s. It is not hard to conjure up the moment when Jazz Age Brits flocked here and Noël Coward sipped gin cocktails at this then-exclusive retreat built in 1929 by millionaire Archibald Nettlefold to host his world-weary friends. Reached by a kind of giant sea tractor during high tide, or by foot across the sands at low tide, it is an easy return to terra firma to visit some of the highlights of Devon's beautiful coastline (such as Dartmouth or Plymouth, both within forty minutes). But the whole idea is to enjoy the life of a privileged castaway: afternoon cream tea (this is, after all, Devon, where the tradition is sacrosanct) is served in the hotel's Palm Court.

WHAT: hotel. **WHERE:** 200 miles/322 km southwest of London. Depart from Bigbury-on-Sea, closest village on mainland. Tel 44/1548-810-514, fax 44/1548-810-243; reception@burghisland.com; www.burghisland.com. **COST:** doubles from $460, includes breakfast and dinner. Dinner $90. **BEST TIMES:** Apr–Sept.

In a Poetic Setting, Peaceful Beyond Imagination

GIDLEIGH PARK

Chagford, Devon, England

Buried deep in the wild country of Dartmoor National Park, secluded and elegant Gidleigh Park encourages bewildered guests with roadside signs reading "Keep Heart"—they're on the right track. It's well worth the single-lane drive to this Tudor-style manse, a stately 1929 tribute to other times, whose 45 magnificent acres of gardens, pastures, and woodland get lost within the untamed natural beauty of the encircling national preserve, Britain's second largest park. From the terraced patio, guests hear only the rushing

Built on a 16th-century foundation

waters of the North Teign River, the music of nature that will lull them to sleep at night and invite them for excellent trout fishing in the morning. Its setting is its glory, but only one of many. It is also one of the finest eating establishments (with an

unrivaled wine cellar) in this area of the country. Prices are memorable (if you have to ask, this isn't the place for you), but so is the singularly delightful experience Gidleigh Park offers. Of the impressive circuit of England's famous country manor houses, Gidleigh Park has been one of the prime destinations since it opened in 1977, rivaled by few others in culinary refinement or natural beauty.

WHAT: hotel, restaurant. **WHERE:** 220 miles/354 km southwest of London. Tel 44/1647-432-367, fax 44/1647-432-574; gidleigh park@gidleigh.co.uk; www.gidleigh.com. **COST:** doubles from $510, includes dinner. **BEST TIMES:** May–Jun, when the rhododendrons, azaleas, bluebells, and wildflowers are in bloom.

To the Sporting Life Born

ARUNDELL ARMS

Lifton, Devon, England

This old coach inn has been one of England's premier fishing hotels for more than half a century, with 20 miles of its own fish-rich water on the Tamar River and five of its tributaries that are home to wild brown trout,

sea trout, and salmon. With exclusive rights to private beats, gorgeous natural surroundings, excellent cuisine, and top-notch accommodations in an area of Old England where timeless rhythms rule and country customs are honored, the Arundell Arms is a standout among a vanishing breed of well-heeled sporting hotels. Four wild rivers—the Lyd, the Carey, the Wolf, and the Thrushel—descend from Dartmoor's granite peaks, becoming deep pools, gravelly runs, fast shallows, and open glides. Within a mile or so of the hotel, all these rivers join the Tamar, one of the best salmon rivers in England. Book in advance and fish alone all day on these private beats, where salmon average 10 pounds and your day's catch will be tonight's perfectly

prepared dinner. With a head bailiff who is a former Welsh Open fly-fishing champion, daily challenges offered for advanced fishermen, and beginners' courses for the Johnny-come-latelys, the Arundell Arms is a real fisherman's hotel. But countless other outdoor pastimes call: there is the neighboring National Park of Dartmoor with 400 square miles of moors to wander; Daphne du Maurier country to experience (the actual Jamaica Inn that inspired the eponymous novel is a half hour's drive away), famous country houses and gardens to visit, and inviting bridle paths to explore.

WHAT: hotel. **WHERE:** 250 miles/402 km southwest of London. Tel 44/1566-784-666, fax 44/1566-784-494; reservations@arundell arms.com; www.arundellarms.com. **COST:** doubles from $281 (low season), from $380 (high season), includes 5-course dinner. **BEST**

TIMES: May, Jun, and Sept are the nicest months (and the best for brown trout); Jul and Aug for sea trout; Sept and Oct for salmon.

An Inspiring Inn on the Edge of the Moors

THE RISING SUN

Lynmouth, Devon, England

On the wild "Heritage Coast" of England, the inseparable Lynmouth and Lynton (linked by a famous century-old train that uses cables and pulleys to service the twin towns) nestle in a dramatic and romantic corner of the West Country where Somerset becomes Devon, on the edge of Exmoor National Park. Richard Doddridge Blackmore found the inspiration for his classic novel *Lorna Doone* here, while staying as a guest at the old smugglers' inn, the Rising Sun. A quayside 14th-century inn of crooked beams, uneven floors, and thick walls, it oozed inspiration to the Romantic poet Percy Bysshe Shelley as well, who chose the inn's private thatched-roof cottage for his honeymoon in 1812. It is a cozy refuge with a four-poster bed, lovely views of the odd little harbor and its bobbing boats, and "a climate so mild," wrote Shelley, "that myrtles of immense size twine up our cottage, and roses bloom in the open air in winter." From here, one of countless footpaths makes the perfect starting point for forays into the sweeping moors of the bordering national park, or down the breathtaking descent across the face of Countisbury Cliffs, at 1,200 feet the highest in England. Enjoy bracing sea winds and breathtaking scenery before ambling back "home" to the lovely Rising Sun, whose smiling staff, creaky floors, and burning fireplace make the restaurant's freshly caught salmon and lobster taste particularly scrumptious.

WHAT: town, hotel. **LYNMOUTH (AND LYNTON):** 205 miles/330 km southwest of London. **THE RISING SUN HOTEL:** The Harbour. Tel 44/1598-753-223, fax 44/1598-753-480; risingsunlynmouth@easynet.co.uk; www.risingsunlynmouth.co.uk. *Cost:* doubles $150 (high season); Shelley's Cottage $182.

A Uniquely Capricious Pleasure Palace

ROYAL PAVILION

Brighton, East Sussex, England

The star attraction of Brighton, self-anointed "London-by-the-Sea," is the restored Royal Pavilion, a pseudo-Oriental pleasure palace built in the late 1700s by the Prince Regent, later King George IV. He lent his name to an era called the Regency, and his play-palace graphically demonstrates the excesses and extravagances of that period when Brighton became England's most fashionable—and one of Europe's first—seaside resorts. The fantasy structure of minarets and onion domes offers a whimsical interior to match, arguably one of Europe's most unusually ornate interiors. Victoria and Albert visited a number of times, but the queen was not enthralled with the bon vivant air of the seaside town and eventually packed her bag. By the early 1900s, Brighton was becoming passé and soon became known for its tatty,

decadent decay—nonetheless embraced by those who sought out the melancholy romance of out-of-fashion resort towns off-season. Always loved for its embracing breezes, architecture, once-royal patronage, and reliably memorable fish-and-chips while promenading along the 3-mile-long amusement-lined Palace Pier, Brighton's regentrification is well under way. Cafés, antiques shops, and galleries make up the trendy area of tight-knit alleyways called The Lanes. It's worth tracking down English's Oyster Bar and Seafood Restaurant, a long-time institution known for its no-fuss, super-fresh oysters on the half-shell, among other goodies, plucked from the English Channel. Ask for a table downstairs.

Enjoying Brighton's ambience

WHAT: town, site, restaurant. **BRIGHTON:** 52 miles/84 km south of London on the coast. **ROYAL PAVILION:** tel 44/3000-290-900, fax 44/3000-290-908; visitor.services @brighton-hove.gov.uk; royalpavilion.org.uk. *Cost:* admission $15. **ENGLISH'S:** 29-31 East St. Tel 44/1273-327-980, fax 44/1273-329-754; info@englishs.co.uk; www.englishs.co.uk. **BEST TIMES:** most of May is given over to the Brighton Festival, England's largest arts festival.

---

*A Bucolic Standout in
the European Circuit of Summertime Culture*

GLYNDEBOURNE FESTIVAL

Lewes, East Sussex, England

For true operatic pilgrims, summer in Europe remains a must, with no lovelier setting than at the renowned Glyndebourne Festival amid the green hills of the Sussex Downs. The cream of British society has been flocking

here since its 1934 opening, to a grand country estate whose small but charming old opera house was recently replaced by a much larger, modern theater with excellent acoustics. It opened in 1994 to everyone's delight (even skeptical old-timers love the new building),

and tickets are somewhat less difficult to come by. Serious opera aficionados know they'll find high standards in the festival's innovative repertoire that offers a little of everything for everyone, performed by international lyrical artists both established and emerging. For others it is the social season's highlight: there is the ritual evening picnic enjoyed on the garden-framed lawn that stretches before the graceful neo-Elizabethan country manor, private home of the festival founder's son. Sheep and cows graze within sight while musicians can be heard tuning up. To get there, hop on the train from London for the one-hour trip to Lewes. Or live the Sussex dream and book at the 400-year-old creeper-covered Gravetye Manor, Sussex's most baronial estate and one of Britain's first. Filled with comfortable furniture, surrounded by famously gorgeous gardens, offering one of the area's best chefs (who packs a mean gourmet picnic hamper for the opera), and a wine list rivaled by few in the nation, Gravetye is the perfect luxurious match for Glyndebourne.

WHAT: event, hotel, restaurant. **GLYNDE-BOURNE FESTIVAL:** 1.5 miles/2 km east of Lewes, 55 miles/88 km south of London. Tel 44/1273-813-813, fax 44/1273-814-686; www.glyndebourne.com. *Cost:* tickets $80–$325; standing room, $15. *When:* mid-May–Aug. Booking begins in Mar. May and Aug are best for finding tickets. **GRAVETYE MANOR:** in East Grinstead, 20 miles/32 km northwest of Glyndebourne in West Sussex; 30 miles/48 km southwest of London. Tel 44/1342-810-567, fax 44/1342-810-080; info@gravetyemanor. co.uk; www.gravetyemanor.co.uk. *Cost:* doubles $375. Dinner $85. *Best times:* May–Sept.

Gravetye Manor sits on 1,000 acres.

A Timeless Tableau of the English Countryside

THE COTSWOLDS

Gloucestershire and Worcestershire, England

Whether by car or by foot, to tour this area of countryside is to experience the quintessence of rural England. Wool, once Britain's biggest industry, was the key trade here in the Middle Ages. Almost every prosperous town in the region had a Sheep Street and an impressive church or cathedral built from the industry's profits. Most of the villages built from the local honey-colored limestone (and therefore aesthetically unified like few others) have preserved their character despite being unabashedly devoted to tourism. The pristine town of Chipping Campden has a showpiece main street and the famous 10-acre Hidcote Gardens (which first pioneered the idea of a garden as a series of "rooms"). Victorian arts-and-craftsman William Morris chose Bibury as the most beautiful village in England. Antiques shoppers make a beeline to picturesque Stow-on-the-Wold for its bucolic beauty and excellent browsing. Cheltenham boasts its Promenade, Burford its atmospheric 15th-century pub/inn The Lamb, a longtime charmer on—where else?—Sheep Street, and the nearby River Windrush is idyllic for afternoon strolls. Broadway deserves its popularity, given an architecturally striking High Street lined with interesting antiques stores. Broadway is also home to one of England's great old hotels, the celebrated Lygon Arms. Serving wayfarers since 1532, it is something of a tourist honeypot itself, but when the last bus pulls out of town, guests can indulge in this inviting, many-gabled hostelry that once hosted King Charles I and Oliver Cromwell and have the picture-perfect town pretty much to themselves.

Close to Broadway's hubbub, but so distantly removed, Buckland Manor hotel is an Elizabethan home that grew around a medieval core and was completed in the 19th century. Made from the locally quarried golden-hued stone, generously gabled and distinguished by mullioned windows outside, the house is impeccably furnished with choice antiques, and fresh flowers abound. Buckland is surprisingly unstuffy, a glimpse of the disappearing lifestyle of the landed gentry to the manor born, cocooned within an oasis of 10 acres of formal gardens. Part of the compound is a small 13th-century church whose bell sounds

occasionally. Grazing Highland cattle and Jacob sheep can be seen from the sumptuous upper-floor guest rooms. A superb dinner is elegantly served amid silver domes and candlelight. It's just 3 miles to Broadway Tower, the highest point around and a favorite picnic spot, where it is said you can see twelve shires on a clear day.

WHAT: site, hotel, restaurant. **COTSWOLDS:** west of London, stretching 100 miles/161 km north of Bath to Chipping Campden. **LYGON ARMS:** High St., Broadway. Tel 44/1386-840-318, fax 44/1386-841-088; sandra@lygon arms.co.uk; www.lygonarms.co.uk. *Cost:* doubles from $115. **BUCKLAND MANOR:** 2 miles/3 km south of Broadway. Tel 44/1386-852-626; enquire@bucklandmanor.com; www.buckland manor.co.uk. *Cost:* doubles from $540. 3-course dinner $80. *When:* restaurant open daily for lunch and dinner. **BEST TIMES:** May–Oct, with numerous town fairs. The Cheltenham Gold Cup Horseracing Festival every Mar.

Exquisite Country Digs and Dining in an Idyllic Setting

CHEWTON GLEN

New Milton, Hampshire, England

England's loveliest country getaway, Chewton Glen sits serenely surrounded by immaculate gardens and barbered lawns, on the fringe of the historic New Forest, a 100-square-mile wooded preserve first put aside by

William the Conqueror as his private hunting grounds in 1079. Volumes have been written about Chewton Glen, a neo-Georgian country manor hotel distinguished by an air of well-being: through forty years of ownership under the watchful eyes of Martin and Brigitte Skan, it has maintained the highest standards of service and quality. Nothing ruffles the polished feathers of the extremely congenial staff at this grand, green-shuttered, ivy-clad home where croquet on the front lawn is one of myriad amenities, including indoor and out-

door pools, tennis courts, and a 9-hole golf course. Guests needn't ever leave the 130 acres of private grounds, though the hotel's location itself is ideal for visits to Stonehenge, Salisbury, and Winchester, each no more than an hour's drive away. Or stick close to home and be pampered at the hotel's recently added full-service spa, then dine at the acclaimed Marryat Room—guests rarely miss the memorable meals here prepared by acclaimed chef Pierre Chevillard. In between there are hours spent lingering by the pool, in one of the many

Chewton Glen became a hotel after World War II.

peaceful sitting rooms or cozy nooks, or listening to the cocktail hour's pianist play a Noël Coward tune. Chewton Glen's relative proximity to London means a handsome and cultured weekend clientele, while its bucolic location and gorgeous surroundings make you feel as if the capital didn't quite exist at all. Wherever you come from, try not to come alone: this place is far too special not to share.

WHAT: hotel, restaurant. **WHERE:** Christchurch Rd. (20 miles/32 km west of Southampton, 100 miles/161 km southwest of London). Tel 44/1425-275-341, fax 44/1425-272-310; in the U.S., tel 800-344-5087; reservations@chewtonglen.com; www.chewton glen.com. **COST:** doubles from $535. Dinner $105. **BEST TIMES:** Apr–Oct.

A Medieval Wonder That Still Surprises

WINCHESTER CATHEDRAL

Winchester, Hampshire, England

Work first began on Winchester Cathedral in 1089 to create what would become the longest medieval cathedral in existence (526 feet): famous for its soaring twelve-bay nave, it is one of England's greatest, as lovely from without as within. It is proof of the former market town's prominence in the Middle Ages when, as capital of the Anglo-Saxon kingdom of Wessex, Winchester was a major religious and commercial center. The cathedral was built of Quarr stone from the nearby Isle of Wight on the ruins of a Saxon church. Literary buffs make a pilgrimage here to visit the tomb of Jane Austen (1775–1817), combining the excursion with a visit to Chawton Cottage, her pleasant country home 15 miles west of town, where many of her greatest works were penned. Much of the mood and spirit of the age immortalized in her six major novels, including *Sense and Sensibility* and *Emma*, is still within reach in Hampshire's hilly interior. This bucolic area was a lode mined for literary inspiration by a later titan, Thomas Hardy (1840–1928), who hailed from neighboring Dorset (known by its historical name Wessex in his work), one of England's smallest and most culturally rich shires.

WHAT: site. **WHERE:** 72 miles/116 km southwest of London.

A Christian church was first built on this site in the 7th century.

A Retreat Where Royals Relaxed

OSBORNE HOUSE

Isle of Wight, England

C harles Dickens was drawn to the sandy beaches and dramatic cliffs of this island off the southern coast of England. Today's most visited site is Osborne House, the cherished home of Queen Victoria and Prince Albert,

where they lived some of their happiest hours. Constructed at Victoria's own expense as a seaside retreat in 1845, it was here that the family managed to leave behind royal responsibilities, enjoying long walks and informal family dinners prepared by the couple's nine children. Grief-stricken at the early death of her consort, Albert, in 1865, Victoria requested that everything remain exactly as it had been in his final days. Today their spirit imbues every corner of the place, offering a unique insight into royal family life, from the cozy clutter of treasured family mementos to the bedroom where the queen died on January 22, 1901.

The island is a favorite summer destination of the British, one that attracted Alfred, Lord Tennyson, among other notables. The coastal Tennyson Down provided the poet and those who follow in his footsteps with outstanding views of the Needles, three offshore rock pinnacles battered by the waves of the English Channel. The Down is part of the 65-mile Coastal Path that encircles the diamond-shaped island. Don't skip the interior's highlight: the 11th-century Carisbrooke Castle. The best-preserved Norman castle in the kingdom provides spectacular views for those who climb to the top of the keep. A less enthusiastic visitor, Charles I, was held hostage here by Oliver Cromwell in 1647 pending execution: His attempt to escape was foiled when he got stuck between the window bars.

WHAT: island, site. **ISLE OF WIGHT:** 90 miles/145 km southwest of London off the mainland coast of Hampshire. Frequent car ferries and passenger catamarans leave from Southampton, Portsmouth, and Lymington year-round. **OSBORNE HOUSE:** 1 mile/1.6 km southeast of East Cowes. Tel 44/1983-200-022; www.english-heritage.org.uk. *Cost:* admission. *When:* open Apr–Oct. **BEST TIMES:** Cowes Week, the island's well-known yachting festival, takes place in early Aug.

The Mother Church of the Anglican World

CANTERBURY CATHEDRAL

Canterbury, Kent, England

T he present Canterbury Cathedral, greatly rebuilt in 1174 after fires destroyed earlier structures, was once England's—and northern Europe's—most sacred pilgrimage site. In 1170 one of the most important

View from Christ Church gate

12th- and 13th-century stained-glass windows. Much of Canterbury was destroyed during a 1942 WW II air raid, but the local people had removed the windows for safekeeping (the replacement windows were destroyed, but the cathedral itself remained unscathed). The original windows can once again be seen in place. The most important are considered to be those in the Great West Window, Bible Windows, and Miracle Windows. Located on the route from London to the port of Dover, Canterbury was already an important town in ancient Roman times. It gained further favor when, in A.D. 597, St. Augustine was sent by Pope Gregory the Great to convert the heathen Anglo-Saxons to Christianity; it would soon become the seat of the Primate of the Church of England, with St. Augustine its first archbishop. The great English poet Geoffrey Chaucer (1335–1400) wrote *Canterbury Tales* about a group of pilgrims who traveled from London to St. Thomas Becket's shrine in 1387, further immortalizing the town and cathedral.

incidents in British history took place here: Archbishop Thomas Becket was cruelly murdered in the northwest transept of the cathedral by four knights of Henry II. He would be canonized three years later, encouraging a repentant Henry II to establish the cathedral as the center of English Christianity. The cathedral is famous for its outstanding

WHAT: site. **WHERE:** 11 The Precincts (56 miles/90 km southeast of London). Tel 44/1227-762-862, fax 44/1227-865-222; visits @canterbury-cathedral.org; www.canterbury-cathedral.org. **COST:** admission $12. **WHEN:** open daily; services Mon–Fri 8 A.M., Evensong 5:30 P.M., Sat/Sun Evensong 3:15 P.M., Sun, Sung Eucharist 11 A.M.

A Magnificent Pile of Medieval Origin

LEEDS CASTLE

Maidstone, Kent, England

L ike a lady of the lake, Leeds appears as if a mirage, its buff-colored stone and crenellated towers reflected in the waters that surround it. Once described by Lord Conway as the loveliest castle in the world, it is

historically noteworthy as well as visually striking, a trip through the ages beginning with its earliest construction in the 12th

century (replacing a 9th-century wooden structure) until its recent bequest to a private foundation in 1975. It gained much favor as a royal residence, not unlike that of Balmoral today, beginning as early as 1278 when it was given to Edward I by a wealthy courtier seeking favor. It eventually passed along to Henry VIII, who loved spending time here, and who invested much effort and money in expanding and redecorating it to resemble more a royal palace and less a military fortress. For many years it was a dower castle: six queens called it their favorite residence.

In the 9th century, Leeds was known as Esledes.

The distinctive lake-like moat that encircles it is unlike any other water-defense setting in Britain.

Some of the 500-acre parkland is given over to gardens and includes an aviary opened in 1988 that is one of the best in the country. Then there is the unlikely Dog Collar Museum (dogs once played an important role in guarding the grounds): it sounds like an oddity, but winds up being a highlight for most visitors. Spanning a period of 400 years, some of the collars are veritable works of art.

WHAT: site. **WHERE:** 40 miles/64 km southeast of London (and not to be confused with the city of Leeds in the north). Tel 44/1622-765-400, fax 44/1622-735-616; enquiries@leeds-castle.co.uk; www.leeds-castle.com. **COST:** admission $27. **BEST TIMES:** open-air concerts take place late Jun–early Jul; Apr–Jun for the garden; Food and Wine Festival in May.

Eden on London's Doorstep

SISSINGHURST CASTLE GARDEN

Sissinghurst, Kent, England

"The Garden of England," fertile Kent lives up to its affectionate nickname—in May its apple orchards in blossom are an unforgettable sight. Its most renowned garden and one of the most beloved

(and in a nation besotted with gardens, the competition is tough) is Sissinghurst, created by Vita Sackville-West and Harold Nicolson, her diplomat husband. Sackville-West—Bloomsbury writer, journalist, and famed eccentric—added inspired gardener to her list of talents when she created these spectacular gardens in the 1930s around the great Elizabethan manor where she and Nicolson

lived. (At the same time, she became the contributing gardening columnist for the *Observer*.) She designed a series of gardens within gardens, each one devoted to a particular theme revolving around a family of plants or a single color. Most famous, and imitated around the world to this day, is her White Garden, which reaches its zenith in June. June and July are glorious in the Rose

Garden, whose old Bourbon, centifolia, and moss roses are world-renowned. The Herb Garden is full of both the familiar and the exotic throughout the summer, while the Cottage Garden filled with thousands of bulbs is at its best in the fall. Despite day visitors who take advantage of Sissinghurst's relative proximity to London, the gardens are still an oasis of serenity and beauty.

WHAT: site. **WHERE:** 53 miles/85 km southeast of London, tel 44/1580-710-700, fax 44/1580-710-702; sissinghurst@nationaltrust.org.uk; www.nationaltrust.org.uk/sissinghuurst. **COST:** admission. **WHEN:** open Fri–Tues, Mar–Nov.

Glorious Walking and Delicious Repasts

THE LAKE DISTRICT

Lancashire and Cumbria, England

William Wordsworth described England's Lake District as "the loveliest spot that man has ever known." The English understandably treat this far northwestern area with reverence. It is one of the country's most scenic areas, at once pastoral and wild, graced with some fifteen principal lakes, dozens of lesser ones, and clusters of grazing sheep everywhere in between. The largest of the eleven protected national parks in England and Wales, the Lake District consists of some 880 square miles with a great variety of natural beauty. Most of it is privately owned; the rest belongs to the National Trust. Naturalists return time and again to explore its 1,800 miles of footpaths. Immortalized on canvas and in literature, it is the birthplace and definitive landscape of English Romanticism. Poet laureate Wordsworth (1770–1850) lived at Dove Cottage in Grasmere with his sister (who felt Grasmere "calls home the heart to quietness") and is buried in the graveyard of the village church there.

Wordsworth was just as taken with nearby Ullswater, describing it as "perhaps . . . the happiest combination of beauty and grandeur, which any of the lakes affords"; it was on Ullswater's shores that he beheld his famous "host of golden daffodils." In summer a restored Victorian steamer plies the 9-mile length of the lake, the second largest in the district—the best way to enjoy the lakescape that inspired the giants of Romanticism. When summer crowds reach their peak and the world is too much with you, retreat to England's first Relais and Chateaux country house, Sharrow Bay, on the relatively secluded southern shore of Ullswater. Legendary for its exceptional views of the lake, the half-mile of waterfront it commands, its sumptuous teas, and a renowned six-course dinner (desserts are a grand tradition here), 19th-century Sharrow Bay Country House Hotel is also known for its heartfelt hospitality.

The Lakeland's other well-known luxury hotel-cum-restaurant is Miller Howe (in local dialect *howe* means "hill of"). Formerly owned and run by celebrity chef John Tovey, this small Edwardian-style hotel boasts a magical setting, with views over Windermere to the Langdale Pikes, that vies for attention with the hotel's much-celebrated five-course menu. The experimental British cuisine now under the eye of Tovey's successor protégée, Susan Elliott, is served in a flamboyant and theatrical manner beginning with dimmed lights and an expectant hush. The service is friendly and the air is that of a comfortable house party. Kudos are also plentiful for the prodigious wine list and lavish desserts.

A trek up to Orrest Head (the only way to walk off Miller Howe's sinfully abundant Lakeland Platter breakfast) offers one of the best panoramic views in the region. A high point of the unforgettable photo op is Sca Fell Pike: at 3,210 feet, the tallest peak in England.

WHAT: site, hotel, restaurant. **THE LAKE DISTRICT:** begins in northern Lancashire but falls mostly in Cumbria, 280 miles/451 km northwest of London. Lakeland is just 35 miles across, with Grasmere at its midpoint. **SHARROW BAY COUNTRY HOUSE HOTEL:** 2 miles/3 km outside of Pooley Ridge, 7 miles/11 km west of Penrith. Tel 44/17684-86301, fax 44/17684-86349; info@sharrowbay.co.uk; www.sharrowbay.co.uk. *Cost:* doubles from $575, includes English breakfast and dinner. Prix fixe 6-course dinner $115. *When:* open Mar–early Dec. *Best times:* Apr–Jun and Sept–Oct. Wordsworth's daffodils still bloom every spring. Many local shows and fairs, Jun–early Sept. **MILLER HOWE:** Rayrigg Rd., Windermere. Tel 44/15394-42536, fax 44/15394-45664; info@millerhowe.com; www.millerhowe.com. *Cost:* doubles from $175 (low season), from $255 (high season), includes breakfast and dinner. Dinner for nonguests $80. *When:* restaurant open daily for lunch and dinner. **BEST TIMES:** spring and fall for the most beautiful flowers (the area receives more rainfall than any other district in England).

A typical spring day in beautiful Cumbria

"The man who tires of London tires of life.
For there is in London all that life can afford."
—*SAMUEL JOHNSON*

LONDON

England

A city of contrasts, London is simultaneously the cradle of pomp, pageantry, and history and the birthplace of all things groundbreaking and cutting edge. Once the immutable capital of fish-and-chips, it's now a cheerful chameleon, brilliantly reinventing itself when no one is looking, then preening nonchalantly when the global spotlight turns its way.

THE TOP TEN SIGHTS

BRITISH MUSEUM—Unless you have a week to visit the 2.5 miles of galleries, head for the Elgin marbles (which once decorated the Parthenon in Athens), the Rosetta Stone, the Magna Carta, and the Egyptian mummies.

WHERE: Great Russel St.Bloomsbury. Tel 44/20-7323-8299; www.thebritishmuseum.ac.uk.

BUCKINGHAM PALACE—Official residence of the queen. When she's away in August and September, parts of the 600-room landmark (the state apartments, the throne room, and the Picture Gallery) are open to the public. The Changing of the Guard is done on alternate days at 11:30 A.M. **WHERE:** St. James's. Tel 44/20-7839-1377; www.royal.gov.uk.

HAMPTON COURT—Five hundred landscaped acres of gardens and a famous maze of tall hedges (the key is to turn left upon entering). For 200 years a royal palace: Henry VIII and five of his six wives lived here. Owes much of its present look to Sir Christopher Wren. **WHERE:** 13 miles/20 km west of London in East Molesey, Surrey. Tel 44/870-752-7777; www.hrp.org.uk.

HYDE PARK/KENSINGTON GARDENS—Hyde Park is London's largest park, and was once the favorite deer-hunting ground of Henry VIII. Well-manicured Kensington Gardens blends with Hyde, bordering Kensington Palace.

NATIONAL GALLERY—One of the world's best art collections, with works by every major European school from the 13th to the early 20th century. **WHERE:** Trafalgar Square. Tel 44/20-7747-2885; www.national gallery.org.uk.

ST. PAUL'S CATHEDRAL—The 17th-century masterpiece of Sir Christopher Wren (who is buried in the crypt) is located in the Wall Street–like area called The City. Encircling the great dome (which offers a wonderful 360-degree view of London) is the Whispering Gallery—be careful what you say. **WHERE:** The City. Tel 44/20-7246-8357; www.stpauls.co.uk.

TATE GALLERY—The largest repository of British art, divided into two separate museums. The Tate Britain houses the classics, while the Tate Modern (connected by a footbridge across the Thames) houses art from 1900 to the present. **WHERE:** Millbank (British); Bankside (Modern). Tel 44/20-7887-8000; www.tate.org.uk.

TOWER OF LONDON—Built in the 11th century by William the Conqueror, the Tower contains the Crown Jewels (including the 530-carat Star of Africa diamond and Queen Victoria's crown, studded with some 3,000 jewels, mostly diamonds), the macabre Execution Row (where Anne Boleyn, among others, met her fate), and many other exhibitions. **WHERE:** Tower Hill, The City. Tel 44/870-756-6060; www.hrp.org.uk.

VICTORIA AND ALBERT MUSEUM—The largest decorative arts museum in the world, with works from all periods and all corners of the world. Includes the largest collection of Italian sculpture outside Italy, and the best museum gift shop. **WHERE:** Cromwell Rd., South Kensington. Tel 44/20-7942-2000; www.vam.ac.uk.

WESTMINSTER ABBEY—This English Gothic cathedral has been the site of almost every British coronation since 1066. The Henry VII Chapel, built in 1503, is one of the most beautiful in Europe. The Poets Corner has monuments to and tombs of Chaucer, Thomas Hardy, Tennyson, Browning, and others. **WHERE:** Westminster. Tel 44/20-7222-5152; www.westminster-abbey.org.

OTHER MUST-DO'S

A NIGHT AT THE THEATER
In the WEST END (Trafalgar Square; listings at www.londontheatre.co.uk), fifty-plus theaters promise some of the best and most varied theatergoing in the world. SHAKESPEARE'S GLOBE THEATRE (Southwark; tel 44/20-7902-1400; www.shakespeares-globe.org), open since 1997, is a faithful re-creation of the original 1599 Elizabethan theater, complete with thatched roof and productions staged as they were during the Bard's lifetime (but not all in period costume). ROYAL SHAKESPEARE

Inside the Globe Theatre

COMPANY, Britain's national theater company, performs throughout the year at various theaters in London (tel 44/17-8940-3404; www.rsc.org.uk).

AN EVENING OF MUSIC ST. MARTIN-IN-THE-FIELDS (Trafalgar Square; box office tel 44/20-7839-8362; www.stmartin-in-the-fields.org) hosts frequent chamber music concerts, concerts by candlelight Thursday through Saturday, and evensong on Sunday in its elegant early 18th-century setting. Home of the famous choir of the same name. From mid-July to mid-September, the beautiful ROYAL ALBERT HALL (South Kensington; box office tel 44/20-7589-8212; www.royalalberthall.com) hosts the Promenade Concerts, a.k.a. the "Proms." Orchestras from around the world provide a varied program, but it is the Last Night of the Proms that's the hot ticket in town.

BIG EVENTS On a Saturday in early June, TROOPING THE COLOUR is the official celebration of the queen's birthday, with all the queen's horses and all the queen's men departing from Buckingham Palace. You want pomp? Look no further. For more tradition, head for the ROYAL ASCOT RACES, held in Berkshire in June, as famous for millinery finery and appearances by the royal family as for the races themselves (twenty-four over a four-day period). Even those not sitting in the Royal Enclosure wear their Sunday best. The WIMBLEDON LAWN TENNIS CHAMPIONSHIPS is the tennis world's most prestigious tournament. Most tickets disappear by December for the mid- to late-June event.

KEW GARDENS—London's vast 300-acre indoor/outdoor Royal Botanical Gardens boast 50,000 species of plants, including the world's largest orchid collection. **WHERE:** Richmond, Surrey, about 6.5 miles southwest of London. Tel 44/20-8332-5655 for recorded info, or 44-20-8332-5000; www.rbgkew.org.uk.

NATIONAL PORTRAIT GALLERY—An offshoot of the National Gallery next door, the Portrait Gallery is dedicated to collecting "the likenesses of famous British men and women," from Hans Holbein the Younger's Henry VIII portraits to Andy Warhol's silkscreen of Mick Jagger. **WHERE:** Trafalgar Square. Tel 44/20-7306-0055; www.npg.org.uk.

REGENT'S PARK—The most classically beautiful of London's parks, with hundreds of deck chairs that invite sunbathing. **WHERE:** Marylebone.

SHOPPING In Piccadilly, FORTNUM & MASON (tel 44/20-7734-8040; www.fortnumandmason.com) is the world's most elite grocery store, catering to the

Fortnum & Mason displays its edible wares.

carriage trade. FLORIS (Jermyn Street; tel 44/20-7930-2885; www.florislondon.com) has been London's leading perfumer and purveyor of toiletries since it opened in 1730. Today it's run by the eighth generation of the Floris family and is still in its original but expanded premises. TURNBULL AND ASSER (Jermyn Street; tel 44/20-7808-3000; www.turnbullandasser.com) is the place for custom-made shirts. As much cultural experience as shopping spree, HARRODS (Knightsbridge; tel 44/20-7730-1234; www.harrods.com) is the king of department stores, priding itself on selling everything except elephants—though they were once available too. The elaborate Food Halls sell "everything for everybody" and the fourth floor's Georgian Restaurant offers more than fifty esoteric blends at teatime. HARVEY NICHOLS (Knightsbridge; tel 44/20-7235-5000; www.harveynichols.com), London's most fashionable department store, also offers the best chance after a shopping marathon to recharge in its Fifth Floor Café and Restaurant and its famous food halls. On Regent Street, Soho, LIBERTY (tel 44/20-7734-1234; www.liberty.co.uk) sells housewares and furniture in unique Art Deco surroundings. Famous for its fine-patterned prints and fabrics.

HITTING THE MARKETS Located west of Notting Hill, PORTOBELLO MARKET (Portobello Road Antique Dealers Association, tel 44/20-7229-8354; www.portobelloroad.co.uk) is the granddaddy of all Saturday street markets. Thousands of stalls sell everything from antiques, collectibles, and vintage clothing to fruits and vegetables. In Camden, CAMDEN PASSAGE offers an unpredictable jumble where junk alternates with quality. Held Wednesday and Saturday. South of Tower Bridge, BERMONDSEY MARKET is a proper flea market, scoured early by dealers. Held every Friday.

SIR JOHN SOANE'S MUSEUM—Hogarth originals and Piranesi drawings hang in the charmingly chaotic home of the eminent early-19th-century architect, where time stands still. **WHERE:** Lincoln's Inn Field. Tel 44/20-7405-2107; www.soane.org.

THE WALLACE COLLECTION—Bequeathed to the nation by Lady Wallace in 1897, the collection is displayed in its founders' home. **WHERE:** Manchester Sq., Marylebone. Tel 44/20-7563-9500; www.the-wallace-collection.org.uk.

W H E R E   T O   S T A Y

CLARIDGE'S—The very bastion of tradition somehow manages to be unstarchy. So much a part of the old establishment that it functions as a kind of annex to Buckingham Palace, unflappably hosting all heads of state. Inhale lobby life, come for afternoon tea or a port in the Reading Room, or visit Gordon Ramsay's restaurant, among London's best and most popular. **WHERE:** Brook St., Mayfair. Tel 44/20-7629-8860; www.the-savoy-group.com. **COST:** high.

BLAKE'S—The standard by which all other boutique hotels are judged. Daring color schemes, stylish decor, an opulent atmosphere of privacy, a who's-who clientele, and top-drawer service—with prices to match. **WHERE:** Roland Gardens, South Kensington. Tel 800-926-3173 (from the U.S.) or 44/20-7370-6701; www.blakeshotels.com. **COST:** high.

PORTOBELLO HOTEL—A privately owned hotel with individually decorated rooms on an elegant Victorian terrace. You'll either love or hate the quirky style, made up of finds from the nearby Portobello market. **WHERE:** Stanley Gardens, between Notting Hill and Kensington. Tel 44/20-7727-2777; www.portobello-hotel.co.uk. **COST:** moderate.

JAMES HOUSE B&B—Among London's many B&Bs, the James House wins for convenient location, nice furnishings, and modest rates. **WHERE:** Ebury St., in the Victoria Station neighborhood. Tel 44/20-7730-7338; www.jamesandcartref.co.uk.

NOTE: At press time, this was closed for renovations.

EATING & DRINKING

BIBENDUM—An eclectic, modern, and consistently wonderful menu served in an Art Deco masterpiece of a building. A separate, tiny, but very popular Oyster Bar is at street level. **WHERE:** Fulham Rd. South Kensington. Tel 44/20-7581-5817; www.bibendum.co.uk.

THE CINNAMON CLUB—A favorite of MPs and others, the Cinnamon Club is the best of London's new Indian restaurants, located in the 1897 Old Westminster Library, around the corner from Westminster Abbey. **WHERE:** Great Smith St., Westminster. Tel 44/20-7222-2555; www.cinnamonclub.com.

THE GEORGE INN—London's only surviving galleried 17th-century coaching inn, now a pub. Charles Dickens was a frequent patron. **WHERE:** Borough High St., Southwark. Tel 44/20-7407-2056.

The view from Oxo Tower

THE GRENADIER—The oldest pub on Wilton Street, reputedly haunted, where Bloody Marys are the drink of choice on Sundays. Always crowded. Duke of Wellington Steak is a favorite: The duke's officers once hung out here. **WHERE:** Wilton Row, Knightsbridge. Tel 44/20-7235-3074.

GEALE'S—An old-time, no-fuss, neighborhood place that's your best bet for fish-and-chips.

WHERE: Farmer St., Notting Hill. Tel 44/20-7727-7969.

GORDON RAMSAY—Regularly called the best food in London; French cuisine served with attentive discretion. The dishes are innovative and complex, on the order of fillet of sea bass wrapped in basil leaves and steamed with new potatoes, celeriac puree, baby bok choy, crème fraîche, and caviar sauce. The trick is getting a reservation. **WHERE:** Royal Hospital Rd., Chelsea. Tel 44/20-7352-4441; www.gordonramsay.com. (There's a second location at Claridge's Hotel.)

THE IVY—One of the most difficult tables to book in town, with a glamorous 1930s decor, a high-energy buzz, great people-watching, and consistently excellent food—all at a reasonable price—from the reinvented fish-and-chips to the signature salmon fish cakes. **WHERE:** West St., Tel 44/20-7836-4751.

LE PONT DE LA TOUR—The French- and Italian-influenced British menu is the draw here, but who can remember that with views like these (overlooking Tower Bridge from the Butlers Wharf Building) and the chance to eat outdoors when the warm weather arrives? **WHERE:** Tower Bridge. Tel 44/20-7403-8403.

OXO TOWER RESTAURANT—Breathtaking views of St. Paul's and nighttime scenes of the illuminated Thames are the real attraction here. The modern British and European cuisine gets wavering reviews. **WHERE:** Barge House St., Blackfriar's Bridge. Tel 44/20-7803-3888; www.harveynichols.com.

THE RED LION—Built in 1821 and redesigned in the 1870s, this is the ultimate Victorian pub. Small and intimate. **WHERE:** Duke of York St., St. James's. Tel 44/20-7930-2030.

RULES—London's oldest restaurant, established as an oyster bar in 1798. Oysters are still a house specialty (along with game), with a setting that's very late-1700s. **WHERE:** Maiden Ln., Covent Garden. Tel 44/20-7836-5314; www.rules.co.uk.

The World's Most Famous Flower Show

CHELSEA FLOWER SHOW

London, England

I n a gardening-mad nation, the grand event of the season is this Olympics of gardening, a monumental four-day horticultural orgy. One enormous pageant of flowers is displayed with painstaking drama and imaginative precision by 700 juried exhibitors. The cream of British and international horticulturalists, they fill the 11 acres of the Christopher Wren–designed Royal Hospital grounds, 3.5 acres under state-of-the-art twin "marquee" tents. It is a quintessentially British celebration of gardening but with a natural appeal (and great people-watching opportunities) that easily reaches beyond obsessive gardeners to the steadfast nongardening public that doesn't know a dandelion from a magnolia. Existing in some form since 1827, it is a premier event organized by the Royal Horticultural Society and sets the global standard (the society also organizes the largest annual flower show in the world at Hampton Court, as well as the RHS Flower Show at Tatton Park in Cheshire). Tickets to Chelsea are restricted to 160,000 over the four-day period, with the first two days (Tuesday and Wednesday) reserved for RHS members only. Though many believe people-watching is best on public days (Thursday and Friday), the true gardener will want to see the exhibitions at their perky best before they wilt from the adoring gaze and scrutiny of so many fans. If you miss the Chelsea Flower Show, don't miss London's Royal Botanic Gardens (a.k.a. Kew Gardens), the world's most famous gardens. They will take your breath away.

WHAT: event. **WHERE:** tickets can be bought directly from the Royal Horticultural Society (RHS), tel 44/870-906-3781; www.rhs.org.uk/chelsea. To become an RHS member, tel 44/207-821-3000. **COST:** annual RHS membership for one, which includes 2 tickets, $122. Full-day ($70) and half-day ($43) tickets for admission on public days only. **WHEN:** the 4-day event is held during the last full week of May. Tickets become available late Nov and sell out by early Apr. Tickets cannot be purchased at the door.

The Standard Bearer
and Embodiment of England

THE CONNAUGHT HOTEL

London, England

T here are many top-drawer hotels in London, but the Connaught never strays far from first place. With a clientele and staff that are equally loyal, the Connaught exudes a refined clublike atmosphere that embodies

English luxury and Edwardian elegance. Considered a dignified bastion of white-glove hospitality since it opened deep in the heart of Mayfair, renovations and alterations are always undertaken with extreme discretion.

The famous mahogany staircase

Some things never change, and shouldn't: here at the Connaught, it's always 1897. Named after Queen Victoria's third son, the Duke of Connaught, this low-profile landmark hotel is clearly favored by a list of longstanding guests who choose to ignore the trends of fashion and avoid media glare. The service by its expert, dedicated staff is surprisingly low-key; the hotel's refined old-world charm is never effusive. With just ninety-two luxuriously appointed rooms and suites, the Connaught is a "baby grand" hotel in size and is home to the much-acclaimed restaurant Hélène Darroze at the Connaught. Recently transformed by Michelin-starred chef Hélène Darroze, a protégée of Alain Ducasse, and by Parisian designer India Mahdavi, the restaurant and its sister venue, Espelette, are very much at the forefront of London's vibrant dining scene. These warm yet modern spaces feature menus that lean toward authentic regional French cuisine and seasonal specialties. If you've never stayed at Buckingham Palace, stay (or break your fast) here for the next best thing.

WHAT: hotel, restaurant. **WHERE:** 16 Carlos Place, Mayfair. Tel 44/207-499-7070, fax 44/207-495-3262; info@the-connaught.co.uk; www.the-connaught.co.uk. **COST:** doubles from $625. Tasting menu at Hélène Darroze, $140.

A Civilized Ritual Steeped in Tradition

TEA AT THE RITZ

London, England

A rite of kings and commoners alike, tea is taken in every little hamlet across the British Isles. But nowhere is it served with more reverence or flair than at the Ritz, the grand old-world icon that sets the standard for Britain's most sacrosanct tradition. The quintessentially British rite can be traced back more than 150 years, to Anna, Seventh Duchess of Bedford, who would suffer from fainting spells from late-afternoon "pangs of hunger," and—well, the rest is history. Purists swear by the Ritz, whose dazzling Versailles-inspired setting (and queues) provide an unforgettable glimpse of life at the top. (Brown's and Claridge's run neck-and-neck for second place.) Promising as much pomp and circumstance as the changing of the guard, the etiquette and rules of afternoon tea appear at their stylized best in the Ritz's rococo Palm Court: tables are draped in crisp linen tablecloths and covered with fine bone china and a silver triple-tier stand of goodies. Dainty finger sandwiches complement warm scones, homemade strawberry jam, and clotted cream, as well as an array of bite-size tea cakes and fancy sweets that permit the pastry chefs to show off their talents. Finish it all and you'll understand why the thought of dinner is enticing—only if it's tomorrow's. Since its creation by the great impresario César Ritz in 1906, stepping into the Palm Court is like stepping back into Edwardian England—especially following renovations that have freshened up the grande dame's over-the-top gilt-and-mirrors glamour. They're not exaggerating when they suggest booking one month in advance for a Saturday afternoon table, and men dare not show up without jacket and tie—the Ritz still puts on the ritz.

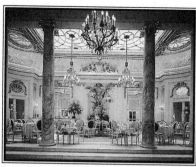

Louis XVI style in the Palm Court

WHAT: hotel, restaurant. **WHERE:** 150 Piccadilly. Tel 44/207-493-8181, fax 44/171-207-2687; for reservations only tel 44/207-300-2308; in the U.S. tel 877-748-9536; enquire@theritzlondon.com; www.theritzlondon.com. **COST:** doubles from $444 (low season), from $660 (high season). Afternoon tea $60. **WHEN:** 2 teatime sittings daily, 3:30 and 5 P.M. For those without reservations, show up at 2 P.M. for best shot at unbooked space.

Ancient Rome's Line in the Sand

HADRIAN'S WALL

Hexham, Northumberland, England

Where Roman legions once marched, sheep now peacefully graze along the remaining sections of a dividing wall that was constructed some 1,800 years ago as a political statement and no-nonsense proof of power to the contentious Scots. The demarcation line for Rome's northernmost border of a mighty empire that stretched 2,500 miles east to what is now Iraq and named after the 2nd-century Roman emperor (A.D. 76–138) who ordered its construction, Hadrian's Wall was built by some 18,000 soldiers and indentured slaves. Originally consisting of 800,000-odd bricks, it spanned 73 miles from Bowness-on-Solway in the west (beyond Carlisle) to Wallsend in the east (beyond Newcastle). Work was begun in A.D. 121 during a visit by Hadrian following repeated invasions from the north and was abandoned in 383 as the Roman Empire crumbled. The best-preserved remaining chunk, a 10-mile stretch in Northumberland north of England's much-visited Lake District, is Britain's largest classical ruin, and one of northern Europe's most impressive and important.

Set up camp in the nearby Langley Castle Hotel; built in 1350, it is far younger than Hadrian's Wall, but its turreted 7-foot-thick walls and original medieval stained-glass windows and spiral staircases still evoke a fascinating sense of history. Close to Northumberland Park, Hadrian's Wall, and a number of ancient Roman forts built as auxiliary garrisons, Langley is a pocket of contemporary luxury dressed in medieval clothes.

WHAT: site, hotel. **HADRIAN'S WALL:** Hexham, the most popular base for visiting the wall, is 27 miles/43 km west of Newcastle, 30 miles/48 km east of Carlisle (in Northumberland, a 5-hour drive north from London). **LANGLEY CASTLE HOTEL:** in Langley-on-Tyne, 7 miles/ 11 km west of Hexham. Tel 44/1434-688-888, fax 44/1434-684-019; manager@langleycastle. com; www.langleycastle.com. *Cost:* doubles from $230. **BEST TIMES:** Apr–Oct.

Langley Castle Hotel

The Thrill of the Hunt

THE NEWARK ANTIQUES AND COLLECTORS FAIR

Newark, Nottinghamshire, England

Think antiques-lover's paradise and you think of London. But how and where do the umpteen antiques dealers that fill the stalls and stores of Portobello and Camden Passage replenish their stock? Newark's Antiques Fair, open to the public, is Europe's largest, filling an 86-acre showground with up to 4,000 indoor and outdoor vendors' stands. Antiques hunters will find the two-day fair (held six times yearly) both a joy and an endurance test: the stalls stretch to infinity and parking can be a nightmare. Sellers arrive from all over Great Britain and Europe, attracting buyers and the merely curious from all over the world. Most dealers are savvy merchants and fantastic deals are not likely though by no means impossible. The early-bird axiom here is all important: the shows are held Monday and Tuesday, with a sub-stantially higher admission fee for Monday (those arriving Tuesday morning before gates open at 8 A.M. might still happen upon a choice worm). In addition to the hope of the ultimate find, the crowds come for the enor-mous range and variety. Those with little intention to buy will enjoy this as an enor-mous cultural outing. Since the British traveled so extensively during colonial days, shopping in England is like shopping the world.

WHAT: event. **WHERE:** 108 miles/174 km north of London. The fairgrounds are 2 miles/3 km north of Newark; regular 90-minute train service from London and a dealers' bus available to and from Newark's train station. Tel 44/1636-702-326, fax 44/ 1636-707-923; www.dmgantiquefairs.com. **COST:** admission $32 for Mon (allows entrance Tues), $8 for Tues only. **WHEN:** 5:30 A.M.– 7 P.M., Mon–Tues; 6 times yearly in Feb, Apr, Jun, Aug, Oct, and Dec.

LE MANOIR AUX QUAT'SAISONS

Great Milton, Oxfordshire, England

The extraordinary talents of Raymond Blanc draw food lovers to this *chef d'oeuvre* of the *art de vivre*. Fans and scrutinizing critics alike regard his celebrated manor-restaurant as one of the best in the nation, a niche of French perfection by a transplanted former waiter turned self-taught master chef. Built of mellow Cotswolds stone in the 15th century, this is a quintessentially perfect English country house used as a luxury venue for the gastronomic whims of its Gallic chef-proprietor. Although Blanc insists his touch is light and that he would not have his manor experienced as if it were a shrine or temple, there is still something that approaches reverence in the barely audible tones of diners in awe who make the hour's drive from London. Return patrons from Sydney or Los Angeles are as commonplace as in-the-know Europeans. For the uninitiated, prices are remarkably high, but so are the standards of the kitchen. The manor's head gardener—responsible for overseeing the 3-acre potager garden and its cornucopia of fresh bounty—holds such an important role that her name appears on the menu. Contented once-in-a-lifetime splurgers are advised to go the distance and fall into the enveloping luxury of one of the sumptuous rooms, such as the romantic round Junior Suite in the converted medieval dovecote, reached by spiral staircase. The Manoir's dining has always been its strong suit (wait until you sample breakfast), but the accommodations are just as noteworthy.

WHAT: restaurant, hotel. **WHERE:** Church Rd. in Great Milton, 40 miles/64 km northwest of London, 8 miles/13 km southeast of Oxford. Tel 44/1844-278-881, fax 44/1844-278-847; lemanoir@blanc.co.uk; www.manoir.co.uk. **COST:** dinner $195. Doubles from $675; dovecote suite, $1,100.

OXFORD AND CAMBRIDGE UNIVERSITIES

Oxfordshire and Cambridgeshire, England

Two almost equidistant day trips from London will steep you in the nation's ancient collegiate history. Although the city of Oxford predates the university, it is the university that draws visitors today and has given the city its identity and character since it first emerged as a formal center of learning around 1167. Don't go looking for the "campus." In fact, Oxford University is collectively formed of thirty-six colleges (all founded before the 16th century) that are inextricably linked with the town. The buildings are like a textbook of English architecture, creating a skyline of tall towers, pinnacles, and spires and making Oxford a visually fascinating city, one excellent for walking. Hook up with a walking tour led by a professor or student—they're chock-full of info about the twenty-four prime ministers and centuries worth of intellectual luminaries (from

All Soul's College, Oxford University

Graham Greene to Lewis Carroll and Percy Bysshe Shelley to Bill Clinton) that the university has produced.

Visit the history-steeped students' drinking halls (the well-known 13th-century Bear Inn on Alfred Street with its collection of thousands of clipped ties, for starters), then take a lovely stroll along the Thames. Later, stop at the Ashmolean Museum on Beaumont Street, a treasure trove of fine arts and antiquities that first opened in 1683, making it the oldest public museum in Britain. Looking as if it could very well be one of the university's hundreds of buildings scattered about town is the gabled 17th-century Old Parsonage Hotel. Ask for Room 26, where Oscar Wilde once lodged. In the very center of town but with a country inn ambience, the hotel has been extensively and beautifully restored.

The small, charming city of Cambridge hosts England's other great university, one of Europe's oldest (only forty years younger than Oxford) and most prestigious. Amid the town's narrow lanes and cluttered bookstores, the university—with its thirty-one colleges (sixteen of medieval origin)—has produced alumni as varied as John Milton, and Stephen Hawking. Darwin, Newton, and Cromwell lived here at different times. The King's College Chapel, called by Henry James "the most beautiful in England," was begun by an adolescent Henry VI in 1441 in the late-Gothic English style known as Perpendicular and remains the country's finest example. Rubens's 17th-century *Adoration of the Magi,* donated to the college in 1961, hangs behind the main altar softly lit by vast 16th-century stained-glass windows beneath an awe-inspiring fan-vaulted ceiling. The classic view of the chapel is enjoyed from the Backs, the strip of gardens and emerald-green lawns along the banks of the lovely River Cam where "punting" is a pastime not to be missed. Relive those carefree college days on a wooden, flat-bottomed boat slowly maneuvered by a pole-wielding university student beneath the weeping willows that line the embankments. Include a visit to the Fitzwilliam Museum, one of Britain's oldest and finest public museums, and alone worth a visit from London to Cambridge. Its prize collection centers around 17th-century Dutch art, enriched with masterpieces by everyone from Titian and Michelangelo to the French Impressionists.

WHAT: towns, sites, hotel. **OXFORD:** 54 miles/87 km northwest of London. **OLD PARSONAGE HOTEL:** 1 Banbury Rd. Tel 44/1865-310-210, fax 44/1865-311-262; info@oldparsonage.co.uk; www.oldparsonage-hotel.co.uk. *Cost:* doubles $313. **CAMBRIDGE:** 55 miles/88 km north of London, 80 miles/129 km northeast of Oxford. **KING'S COLLEGE CHAPEL:** King's Parade; www.kings.cam.ac.

uk/chapel. *Cost:* admission. *Best times:* the much-loved concert of Christmas carols is internationally broadcast from King's College Chapel; check for regularly scheduled choral services and the occasional concert by the famous Chapel Choir. **FITZWILLIAM MUSEUM:** Trumpington St; Tel 44/1223-332-900, fax 44/1223-322-933; fitzmuseum-enquiries@ lists.cam.ac.uk; www.fitzmuseum.cam.ac.uk. *When:* open Tues–Sun. **BEST TIMES:** spring and fall to avoid the biggest crowds; May–Sept for best weather.

Britain's Most Perfect Baroque Palace

BLENHEIM PALACE

Woodstock, Oxfordshire, England

O f England's countless country houses, Blenheim is justifiably the most celebrated. Its size and opulence are testimony to its wealth of history: it was a gift of a grateful Queen Anne to General John Churchill, First Duke of Marlborough, after his crushing defeat of the French in 1704 at Blenheim, a small Bavarian village on the Danube. Deserving of a victorious general, the lavish palace—impersonal in scale, but undeniably impressive—is England's answer to Versailles, and was where Sir Winston Churchill, Britain's WW II leader, was born in 1874. Regarded as the finest true Baroque manor in Britain, it stands amid 2,000 acres of what once were royal hunting grounds for the Saxon kings. Although the manor has changed little structurally since its completion in 1722, the park and gardens, originally laid out by Henry Wise, Queen Anne's gardener, were transformed in the 1760s by Lancelot "Capability" Brown, the great landscape gardener, who also added Blenheim Lake. Still spectacular, the grounds are a major drawing card and include the famous Marlborough Maze, the world's largest hedge maze. Within walking distance of Blenheim Palace, and predating it by many years, the timbered Feathers Inn promises an outstanding meal in atmospheric surroundings. Roaring fireplaces, beamed ceilings, and a lovely outdoor courtyard invite overnight stays in a lovely countrified setting that belies London's proximity.

WHAT: site, hotel, restaurant. **BLENHEIM PALACE:** 8 miles/13 km northwest of Oxford and 62 miles northwest of London. *Cost:* admission. *When:* open daily, mid-Mar–Oct. **FEATHERS INN:** Market St. Tel 44/1993-812-291, fax 44/1993-813-158; enquiries@ feathers.co.uk; www.feathers.co.uk. *Cost:* doubles from $275. Lunch $36, dinner $60.

Birthplace of Sir Winston Churchill

Perfection Itself

LUDLOW

Shropshire, England

Every country has a running list of contenders for the "prettiest little town" pageant. On every Anglophile's list, Ludlow is sure to make an appearance (Lacock and Lavenham also come to mind). In a quiet, mellow region of pastoral scenery along England's border with Wales, an area known as the Welsh Marches, Ludlow takes some patience in getting to—it has thus far blessedly escaped the blight of bus tours, urban sprawl, and shopping malls. Swans glide on the River Teme that encircles it, spanned by medieval bridges that were a frequent subject for Turner's paintings. Because of its proximity to the Welsh border, the imposing Ludlow Castle went up in 1094 upon orders from the Earl of Shrewsbury; it would later host the two young princes (the sons and heirs of Edward IV) who died in the Tower of London and Catherine of Aragon. Cobbled streets are distinguished by elegant Georgian and Jacobean timbered houses and, in recent years, a number of excellent restaurants—surprising for an unassuming country outpost of this size and location. Not the largest but considered by many the best is the intimate Merchant House, which blazed Ludlow's gastronomic trail. A respectful showcase for local Shropshire produce, just six small tables accommodate privileged diners who come from as far away as London to enjoy one of the region's most artfully presented, deliciously orchestrated meals. The perfect end to a perfect day.

WHAT: town, restaurant. **LUDLOW:** 160 miles/257 km northwest of London. **THE MERCHANT HOUSE:** Lower Corve St. Tel 44/1584-875-438; www.merchanthouse.co.uk. *Cost:* dinner $55. *When:* lunch and dinner Fri and Sat; dinner only Tues–Thurs. **BEST TIMES:** Shakespeare (along with much else) is the draw at the 2-week Ludlow Festival, late Jun–early Jul; Food Festival 2d weekend of Sept. Twice-monthly Sun flea market in town square, spring through fall; food market Fri, Sat, and Mon year-round.

Britain's Finest Georgian City and an Exquisite Country Retreat

BATH AND STON EASTON PARK

Somerset, England

A spa destination for centuries after the ancient Romans discovered Britain's only hot water springs here, Bath was later made fashionable by Queen Anne, who rediscovered its therapeutic waters in 1702, launching its rebirth as England's premier spa town. The flourish of 18th-century architecture that followed—sweeping crescents and terraces, noble squares, stately homes of honey-colored Bath limestone—transformed Bath into what is today Britain's most perfectly and beautifully preserved Georgian city. Relaxed, refined, and prosperous, the city is a gracious host: no one seems to come for the waters, but rather to relive the epitome of the 18th-century good life while enjoying a taste of today's best antiquing, shopping, and dining.

Bath's graceful Royal Crescent

The city's historical heart is at the Roman Baths, Britain's finest ancient Roman ruins. Overlooking them are the 16th-century Bath Abbey and the 18th-century Pump Room, a noted watering hole and restaurant, where you can still sample the mineral waters from a running fountain, and one of the greatest temples to old-fashioned teatime anywhere. The Circus is one of Bath's most spectacular sites, thirty-three subtly differentiated limestone houses forming a huge Colosseum-inspired circle designed by John Wood, the Elder, orchestrator of Bath's architectural golden days. In 1775 his son designed the nearby, equally spectacular Royal Crescent, a huge semi-ellipse of thirty identical stone town houses overlooking Royal Victoria Park on what is hailed as the most majestic street in Britain. Bath's most elegant hotel, the Royal Crescent, is housed in two Georgian town houses. Bath's heyday is celebrated here in all its patrician glory, so stop by, if only for tea.

After sightseeing in town, retire to Ston Easton Park, a stately Palladian mansion of ocher-colored Bath stone. With an Elizabethan shell gracefully rebuilt in 1740, Ston Easton has recently been exquisitely refurbished. It is a period gem of the highest order, a delight for those seeking an unforgettable country retreat reflecting the lifestyle described by Jane Austen. The nouvelle fare offered in the lovely restaurant overlooking the river valley is inspired, and the romantic 26-acre parkland was designed by Humphry Repton in the 18th century.

WHAT: town, hotel. **BATH:** 115 miles/185 km west of London. **ROYAL CRESCENT HOTEL:** 16 Royal Crescent. Tel 44/1225-823-333, fax 44/1225-339-401; info@royalcrescent.co.uk; www.royalcrescent.co.uk. *Cost:* doubles $320. **STON EASTON PARK:** 11 miles/18 km southwest of Bath in the village of Ston Easton. Tel 44/1761-241-631, fax 44/1761-241-377; enquiry@stoneaston.co.uk; www.stoneaston.co.uk. *Cost:* doubles from $295. Dinner $65. **BEST TIMES:** May–Sept. The important Bath International Music Festival features classical, pop, and jazz, 17 days late May–early Jun. Somerset Carnival first 10 days of Nov.

A Standout in England's Smallest City

CATHEDRAL CHURCH OF ST. ANDREW

Wells, Somerset, England

The cathedral town of Wells is a medieval gem. It reached its pinnacle of prestige in the late Middle Ages when the magnificent Cathedral Church of St. Andrew was built on the site of an 8th-century Saxon cathedral to reflect the town's affluence. The town gradually fell into a centuries-long slumber that would preserve its character and heritage for today's visitors. Although one of Britain's smallest cathedrals, St. Andrew dwarfs the perfectly preserved limestone town that spreads out in its shadow (Wells is England's smallest city: every town with a cathedral is considered a city). Its recently restored west facade is heavily ornamented with six tiers of 365 carved life-sized figures that comprise the most extensive surviving array of medieval sculpture in Britain. Completed in the early 13th century, they illustrated every imaginable biblical story for the illiterate masses. The facade's twin towers were not added until the late 14th century, yet look as if they were always meant to be part of the whole. Inside the quintessentially Gothic interior, the ingenious engineering solution of criss-crossed "scissor arches," added in 1338 to support the central tower, serve their purpose to this day. England's oldest clock, the second oldest in the world built in 1392, is found in the north transept, announcing the hour with a fanfare of tilting knights and their armored steeds. Facing the statue-studded west facade is Wells's most charming hotel, the Swan, a former coaching inn whose interior of baronial log fireplaces, beamed ceilings, and rich wood paneling evokes its 500 years of history.

WHAT: site, town, hotel. **CATHEDRAL CHURCH OF ST. ANDREW:** Wells is 120 miles/ 193 km southwest of London, 20 miles/32 km southwest of Bath. *Cost:* admission free (donation appreciated). **THE SWAN HOTEL:** 11 Sadler St. Tel 44/1749-836-300, fax 44/1749-836-301; info@swanhotelwells.co.uk; www.swanhotelwells.co.uk. *Cost:* doubles from $190 (high season). **BEST TIMES:** May–Oct.

Queens of the High Seas

CUNARD'S *QM2* AND *QE2*

Southampton, England

In 1840, Samuel Cunard secured the first contract to carry mail by steamship between Britain and North America, and to this day the line that bears his name remains the most recognized in the world. Flagship *Queen Elizabeth 2*, launched at the end of the 1960s, was the last great ocean liner built for the rough north Atlantic, and for more than 30 years was the only ship sailing that route on a regular schedule. The 1,791-passenger ship is a treasure, an anachronism of luxury, strength, and speed in an age of more proasaic cruise ships, delivering a nostalgic six-day crossing full of white-glove service, informal lectures, time spent in the spa or library, and much gazing out over the rail at the never-ending sea.

In 2003, *QE2* sailed her last transatlantic season, replaced on the route by younger sibling *Queen Mary 2*. Billed as the largest, longest, widest, tallest passenger ship ever— more than twice the size of *QE2* and more than three times the size of the legendary *Titanic*—*QM2* is also the first real ocean liner built in more than three decades. The onboard ambience she'll offer is more Y2K than *fin de siècle*, with a shipboard planetarium, a spa run by Canyon Ranch, and a restaurant overseen by chef/restaurateur Todd English. Expect a large dose of golden-age steamship aura mixed into the modernity, including a lounge designed to resemble London's Kew Gardens, wooden deck chairs and thick blankets, and one of the original *Queen Mary*'s whistles mounted on her funnel, audible up to 10 miles away. You can literally hear the future coming.

WHAT: experience. **WHERE:** departures from Southampton, 2 hours southwest of London. **HOW:** tel 44/2380-634-166; in the U.S., tel 800-7-CUNARD or 305-463-3000; www.cunard.com. **COST:** 6-night transatlantic crossings on the *QM2* from $1,000 per person, all-inclusive; some deals include one-way air between the U.K. and many U.S. cities. **WHEN:** Apr–Dec for transatlantic crossings. The *QM2*'s maiden voyage was April 2004 when the *QE2* began other itineraries from the Caribbean to the Baltic.

---

*Drama, the Bard,
and Ghosts at Shakespeare's Birthplace*

STRATFORD-UPON-AVON

Warwickshire, England

The timeless appeal and universality of William Shakespeare's work have made his hometown a point of pilgrimage. Already a flourishing market town in the Bard's lifetime, Stratford's half-timbered homes and air of historical prosperity would most likely draw visitors even without the fame of her native son. Although visits to his wife Anne Hathaway's cottage, to the house where he was born, or to the 13th-century Trinity Church where he and his family were buried make up the required circuit, tickets for a performance by the Royal Shakespeare Company will set your visit apart. Of the three theaters in town, most classics are performed at the Royal Shakespeare Theatre; there are weekly matinees for those heading back to London in time for dinner. The Elizabethan-style Swan Theatre was reconstructed along the lines of Shakespeare's original Globe Theatre, and The Other Place is a more intimate venue for experimental productions.

Unpack at the magnificent Ettington Park Hotel, a stately neo-Gothic home on the banks of the River Stour. Sitting on the same site where a manor was first accounted for in the Domesday Book of 1086, this 19th-century luxury country house has long been associated with the Shirley family (Shakespeare's Hal speaks of a "valiant Shirley" in Henry IV). The family ghosts linger still—the legendary Lady in Grey has quite a reputation in England. One of the more famed hauntings of the hotel has occurred here a number of times: the same book, Sir Walter

Anne Hathaway's cottage

Scott's *St. Ronan's Well*, has been known to fly off the shelf, always falling open to the same verse: "A merry place, 'tis said, in days of yore; But something ails it now—the place is cursed." Guests will be hard pressed to find anything less than blessed about this pampering Warwickshire escape nestled amid 40 acres of deer-inhabited parkland and manicured gardens.

What: town, hotel. **Stratford-upon-Avon:** 90 miles/145 km northwest of London. Bookings for theaters, tel 44/8701-607-930, fax 44/1926-485-089; in the U.S. contact Global Tickets, tel 800-223-6108; info@shakespeare-country.co.uk; www.shakespeare-country.co.uk. *When:* theater season is Mar–Nov. *Best times:* Apr 23, the day traditionally celebrated as Shakespeare's birth and death. **Ettington Park Hotel:** Alderminster is 5 miles/8 km south of Stratford-upon-Avon. Tel 44/1789-450-123, fax 44/1789-450-472; enquiries@handpicked.co.uk; www.ettingtonpark.co.uk. *Cost:* doubles from $160 (low season), from $215 (high season).

England's Finest Medieval Castle

Warwick Castle

Warwick, Warwickshire, England

For nine centuries at the heart of British history, the magnificent feudal fortress of Warwick is the country's finest medieval castle. Its commanding position on an escarpment above the River Avon was described as "the most noble site in England" by no less a connoisseur than Sir Walter Scott. Originally built to keep visitors out, it is more visited than any other English house in private hands, and the second most visited castle after Windsor. The guards at the gate keep the long lines moving within the monumental Norman walls. One of Europe's most important collections of medieval armor and weaponry is on display, together with paintings by such old masters as Rubens and Van Dyck. The castle's bellicose character is best viewed from outdoors, although it was tempered in the 18th century by 60 acres of grounds, landscaped by Lancelot "Capability" Brown, where preening peacocks have since taken up residence.

What: site. **Where:** 92 miles/148 km northwest of London. Tel 44/1926-495-421, recorded info 44/8704-422-000, fax 44/1926-406-611; customer.information@warwick-castle.com; www.warwick-castle.co.uk. **Cost:** admission $33. **When:** open daily.

The First Earl of Warwick was given his title in 1088.

A Masterpiece of Medieval Technology

SALISBURY CATHEDRAL

Salisbury, Wiltshire, England

The paintings of Turner and Constable long ago familiarized the world with Salisbury Cathedral and its remarkable 404-foot spire. The cathedral was begun in 1220 and was completed in a record thirty-eight years (the spire, the tallest structure then known in the world—and still the highest in England—was added toward the end of the 13th century). With many great cathedrals requiring centuries of construction, this was a remarkable engineering accomplishment not unlike that of 20th-century Manhattan's most daring skyscraper projects.

As a result of its quick completion, Salisbury is the most stylistically unified of all the great European cathedrals and the very pinnacle of what is known as the Early English or pointed Gothic style. Sir Christopher Wren measured an alarming 29.5-inch tilt of the spire in 1668, but no further shift has since been detected.

Those who trust architecture from 700 years ago can climb the spire's steps for a view across the small town of Salisbury and the Salisbury Plain in the direction of Stonehenge, Wiltshire's other significant and far more ancient site. The attractive and still lively market town of Salisbury was created by the cathedral, not the other way around, which often was the case.

Welcoming pilgrims and wayfarers since its earliest days, the 13th-century Rose and Crown Inn, with its hand-hewn beams and welcoming air still firmly intact, is an inviting place to spend the night. It's a lovely old inn whose lawn stretches down to the Avon River, where relaxed guests can dangle their feet and count the swans that glide by. The view is a Turner canvas come to life, the cathedral's soaring spire in full sight.

Salisbury Cathedral was a feat of 13th-century engineering.

WHAT: town, site, hotel. **SALISBURY:** 90 miles/145 km southwest of London, 8 miles/ 13 km south of Stonehenge. **SALISBURY CATHEDRAL:** admission $8; www.salisbury cathedral.org.uk. **ROSE AND CROWN INN:** Harnham Rd., 1.5 miles/2 km outside Salisbury center. Tel 44/1722-399-955, fax 44/1722-339-816; www.legacy-hotels.co.uk/legacy-roseand crown. *Cost:* doubles from $220. **BEST TIMES:** the cathedral's Choir School sings Evensong frequently (check for schedule). Town market held Thurs and Fri; 2-week cultural festival held late May–early Jun.

A Walk Through a Classical Painting

STOURHEAD

Stourton, Wiltshire, England

Inspired by the paintings of Claude Lorrain and Gaspard Poussin, Stourhead is arguably England's most fabled garden, and one that has long elicited superlatives. It is the most celebrated example of 18th-century English landscape gardening, confirmation that no country holds a candle to England's horticultural expertise. Stourhead's poetic vistas and landscapes punctuated with architectural highlights such as a neoclassical Pantheon, a grotto, and temples built to Flora and Apollo create a classical effect that is the finest of its genre in England, the prototype much mimicked around the world in private and public gardens alike. The 18th-century Palladian-inspired house, whose beautiful interior is also open to the public, was the home of a wealthy local banking family. "Henry the Magnificent" Hoare, inspired by a Grand Tour of the Mediterranean, decided to relandscape his estate's 100-acre grounds upon his return home. Although Stourhead is a garden for all seasons, perhaps among its most romantic walks would be one in early fall along the footpaths that wind around a chain of small manmade lakes, or in summer when its famous dells of rhododendrons and camellias are in full bloom. Within strolling distance of the gardens' main gate, the Spread Eagle Inn is a local institution, known for its Sunday lunches and leisurely dinners of simple, traditional cooking. Better yet, stop by on your way into the gardens: the inn packs a great box lunch for a picnic on the bucolic grounds, in a shady corner of your choice.

WHAT: site, restaurant. **STOURHEAD:** 112 miles/180 km southwest of London, 45 miles/72 km south of Bath. Tel 44/1747-841-152, fax 44/1747-842-005; stourhead@national trust.org.uk; www.nationaltrust.org.uk *Cost:* admission $19. *When:* open daily; house open Apr–Nov, Fri–Tues. **SPREAD EAGLE INN:** Tel 44/1747-840-587; www.spreadeagleinn.com. *Cost:* lunch $28.

One of the World's Great Mysteries

STONEHENGE

Wiltshire, England

Stonehenge can still be the magical, mystical, mysterious kind of place it was probably meant to be—but only if you catch it between tour bus caravans. No one knows who built Stonehenge or why (far-fetched theories credit aliens from outer space, King Arthur, Merlin, and the ancient people of Atlantis), although it is pretty certain this stunning collection of artfully placed rocks was used for

The outer ring was probably completed around 1500 B.C.

rituals or ceremonies pertaining to the sun. The massive trilithons—two upright stones with a cross lintel on top—were assembled some 4,000 years ago. Some of the standing stones weigh up to 50 tons—it is estimated that to drag each one into position took over 1,000 men. Scholars disagree about where the stones came from (some say southern Wales) and how they got to the windswept Salisbury Plain. In the 17th century, the widely held view that the circle was somehow connected to the Celtic druids took hold and has never died, even though it has since been proven that the site predates the Iron Age priestly cult by at least 1,500 years and probably more. Researchers believe the stones were to be put together in three distinct stages (two of which were never completed), in alignments made possible by sophisticated builders with a knowledge of astronomy, mathematics, and engineering unparalleled anywhere in Europe at that time. It was probably intended as a solar or lunar calendar, among other things; today, thousands gravitate here for the summer solstice.

WHAT: site. **WHERE:** 85 miles/137 km southwest of London. Tel 44/1980-623-108, fax 44/1980-623-465; www.english-heritage.org.uk. **COST:** admission $11. **BEST TIMES:** early morning or late afternoon to avoid crowds; during summer solstice.

Grand, Stately, Elegant

CASTLE HOWARD

York, Yorkshire, England

Although best known today as the location for the BBC's 1981 adaptation of Evelyn Waugh's *Brideshead Revisited*, Castle Howard has been respected for centuries as one of the most colossal privately owned palaces in the British Isles. This early 18th-century residence (not really a castle, though sitting on the former site of one) holds court amid its own grandiose 1,000-acre parkland and gardens. It's still lived in by the Howard family, whose ancestors saw in the then inexperienced architect Sir John Vanbrugh the talent that would later secure him the commission to create the lavish Blenheim Palace near Oxford. The main body of Castle Howard was completed in 1715, including its signature gilt Great Hall that rises 70 feet from floor to dome. The 160-foot aptly named Long Gallery is the castle's other highlight, lined with a large number of portraits of the Howard line by Holbein and others. Unless you're a relation, you won't be spending the night here. But you can happily unpack your

Castle Howard's Great Hall

bags at the handsome, nearby Middlethorpe Hall. Commissioned in 1699, the same year as Castle Howard, it has recently been converted into what most hold to be the grandest country hotel in northern England. Surrounded by 26 impeccable acres that border York's famous racecourse, the elegant William III–style hotel with its top-ranked restaurant is the perfect jumping-off point for a tour of Yorkshire's dales and moors. Explore the area's wealth of national parks and the countryside that inspired *Wuthering Heights* (Emily Brontë and her sisters hailed from nearby Haworth, now a revered literary site of pilgrimage).

WHAT: site, hotel. **CASTLE HOWARD:** 15 miles/24 km northeast of York (follow signs from A64 toward Malton/Scarborough). Tel 44/1653-648-444, fax 44/1653-648-501; contact @castlehoward.co.uk; www.castlehoward.co.uk. *Cost:* admission. *When:* open daily, mid-Mar–Oct. **MIDDLETHORPE HALL HOTEL:** Bishopthorpe Rd., 1.5 miles/ 2 km south of York. Tel 44/1904-641-241, fax 44/1904-620-176; info@middlethorpe.com; www.middlethorpe.com. *Cost:* doubles from $315 (high season). **BEST TIMES:** May for rhododendrons; late Jun–Jul for roses; Sept–Oct for fall colors. May–Oct is racing season.

The City's Crowning Glory

YORK MINSTER

York, Yorkshire, England

A must-visit on the cathedral city circuit, ancient York is surrounded by 3 miles of beautifully restored medieval walls built on Roman foundations: its walltop footpath is one of England's finest pleasures. Within lies an architecture-rich city that is a joy for strollers, with all paths leading to its famous showpiece cathedral, the Minster. A wonder of Gothic architecture, it is the largest medieval cathedral in Great Britain and the largest north of the Alps: a breath-sapping climb up the central tower's spiral 275-step staircase provides the chance to appreciate the scale of this massive building (offset by views of the Yorkshire Moors beyond) and the genius of the buttresses that hold it up—a sophisticated engineering feat completed before America was even "discovered." The present cathedral was begun in 1220 on a site where previous cathedrals and churches had stood, possibly as far back as 627. It is famous for its 128 intricate stained-glass windows, some of which date back to the Minster's earliest days as do the elaborately carved Choir Screen and the rich interior of the Chapter

The showpiece of an architecturally rich city

House. Churches, like castles, represented power and importance (the archbishop of York is second only to the archbishop of Canterbury in the hierarchy of the Church of England), but even prior to the Minster's construction, York was an important location. There was a major Viking settlement here from 867 and some streets still retain their Danish names; ruins dating to the 10th century are at the center of the extremely popular Jorvik Viking Center (Jorvik was the Nordic name for the city) in Coppergate, bringing you back to the year A.D. 975, long before the Minster's first block was laid.

WHAT: site, town. **YORK:** 203 miles/327 km north of London. **YORK MINSTER:** Deangate, tel 44/1904-557-216; visitors@yorkminster.org; www.yorkminster.org. *Cost:* admission. **JORVIK:** tel 44/1904-643-211, fax 44/1904-627-097; enquiries@vikingjorvik.com; www.vikingjorvik.com. *Cost:* $15.00. **BEST TIMES:** in Aug the city goes horserace-crazy—a plus or minus, depending on the visitor. The 2-week Viking Festival takes place in Feb.

Where Golf Was Born

SCOTTISH GOLF

Scotland

A pilgrimage to the courses where the game of golf was invented provides golf lovers with dozens of choices. Many of the links here are undisputedly some of the finest on earth. Officially recorded since 1552, golf is believed to have been a diversion for the bored Scottish aristocracy as early as the 14th century. You'll feel like aristocracy yourself at a handful of storied hotels whose raison d'être is to indulge guests with as much nonpareil golf as the long hours of daylight will permit—and luxury après-golf accommodations to boot. The Old Course at St. Andrews is the world's most legendary temple of golf, which explains why you sometimes need to reserve tee times up to a year in advance. An elegant Edwardian country house, Greywalls Hotel, exudes the warmth of a private home—one fortunate enough to overlook the fabled Muirfield Course. It's the world's oldest golf course, and visitors are permitted, with a little help from the Greywalls's concierge. Gleneagles, whose Queen's and King's courses are the oldest of five, is framed by

remarkable scenery. The magnificently situated Turnberry Hotel faces out to sea and has its own lighthouse; it has hosted the British Open three times on its two famous courses on the untamed Scottish coast. Neophytes at Carnoustie call its course treacherous, but world champions call it the best in Britain. At Royal Troon, only men can comment on

Sir Edward Lutyens designed the crescent-shaped Greywalls Hotel in 1901.

its old course; the club is so steeped in tradition that women are still not allowed to play it. Anyone can try their hand at Royal Dornach. At just 6 degrees short of the Arctic Circle, it is the most northerly of the world's great golf courses, though with a balmy climate thanks to the Gulf Stream. The list goes on and on—there are well over 500 courses in Scotland—but why not start at the top?

WHAT: experience. **HOW:** in the U.S., contact the British Tourist Authority, tel 877-899-8391, fax 212-986-1188; www.travelbritain.org. The pamphlet "Golf Britain—The Essential Guide" lists pertinent information on more than 150 locations.

Scotland's Loire Valley

THE CASTLE TRAIL

Grampian Highlands, Scotland

Some 600 castles dot the the Scottish countryside, with the highest concentration in the rugged Grampian Highlands, named for the hill range that bisects it. Many of these castles are dramatic ruins, such as Slains, said to have inspired Bram Stoker to write *Dracula*, and Dunnottar, where Zeffirelli chose to film *Hamlet*. (The Bard himself staged Macbeth's murder of Duncan in Castle Cawdor—home of the thane, or clan chief—northeast of Inverness, unofficial capital of the Highlands.) Others are beautifully restored, owner-occupied stately homes, such as Drum, Crathes, and Fyvie. Balmoral Castle, "this dear paradise" of Queen Victoria, is still the private summer residence of the British sovereign (with restricted visiting hours for both castle and gardens as a result). An eleven-castle circuit through the Grampians linked by blue and white signposts make up the Castle Trail, historic properties owned by the National Trust for Scotland (overnight accommodations can be arranged at privately owned castle/hotels in the area). Following the Dee, Don, or Spey Rivers (think excellent salmon and trout fishing), it is an excursion that blends beautifully (excuse the pun) with visits to the dozens of single-malt-whisky distilleries. More than half of the country's distilleries are in this area—the region's other claim to fame.

Quaint rural accommodations are not hard to come by, but few match Cawdor Cottages for history and style. Set within the 50-square-mile estate belonging to 600-year-old Cawdor Castle, five cottages have been done up in flawless taste by Lady Cawdor, a former fashion magazine editor.

WHAT: experience, site, hotel. **WHERE:** the trail, northwest of Aberdeen (main city of the Grampian Highlands), is about 150 miles/ 241 km long. **HOW:** contact the

Dunnottar Castle, near Stonehaven

Aberdeen and Grampian Tourist Board, tel 44/8452-255-121; info@visitscotland.com; www.aberdeen-grampian.com. **CAWDOR COTTAGES:** Cawdor, Nairn. Tel 44/1667-404-666; www.cawdor.com. *Cost:* Cottages sleep 2–6. Doubles from $495 (low season), from $667 (high season), 3-night minimum. **WHEN:** some but not all properties are open daily, year-round. Balmoral Castle on Royal Deeside open Apr–late Jan.

Gliding Through the Highlands and Islands

THE HEBRIDES

Scotland

The drama of Scotland's Hebrides ("islands at the edge of the sea"), created by earthquakes, volcanoes, and retreating glaciers, is topped only by the floating-country-manor luxury of the *Hebridean Princess*. This romantic five-star vessel carrying just fifty very cosseted passengers (with a crew of thirty-eight), glides through the 500-island archipelago, still relatively untrammeled by tourism, off the western coast of Scotland. The atmosphere of a house party prevails, with the terribly respectable guests lounging in the handsome chintz-draped cabins (some with private balconies), dining on excellent smoked salmon and Champagne (with eighteen varieties of Scotch whisky for sampling), and making daily calls on remote towns and little-visited lochs. Small tenders bring passengers ashore to ancient distilleries for a wee dram, a bracing ride on the ship's bicycles, or exhilarating treks through nature reserves without another soul in sight. One day may promise a visit to a long-abandoned castle sitting atop a lonely bluff or nothing more intense than an afternoon's stroll on deserted beaches or antiques-store hopping in a somnolent, waterfront town.

Rum, Mull, Colonsay, Staffa, Barra, Lewis—for those not familiar with the powerful, sometimes bleak, and often eerie beauty of the Hebrides Islands, a "Hebridean Sampler" is an enchanting temptation, from the moment the bagpiper welcomes guests on board through to the wafting strains of Mendelssohn's majestic "Hebrides Overture"

The island chain stretches 150 miles.

that warm the blanketed, sunset-gazing passengers as they linger on the deck.

WHAT: experience, site. **WHERE:** most embarkations from Oban (92 miles/148 km northwest of Glasgow, 124 miles/200 km northwest of Edinburgh). Various cruises visit the Hebrides, the Highlands and their hinterlands, and Ireland. **HOW:** Hebridean Island Cruises, tel 44/1756-704-747, fax 44/1756-704-794; reservations@hebridean.co.uk; www.hebridean.co.uk. **COST:** 7-night cruise from $2,530 to $14,830, includes meals, excursions, and gratuities. Cruises available from 4 to 12 days. **WHEN:** cruises offered Mar–Nov. **BEST TIMES:** May–Jun.

An Island Apart, with Lordly but Cozy Digs

ISLE OF SKYE AND KINLOCH LODGE

The Inner Hebrides, Scotland

A newish bridge has diluted some of its mystique and otherworldliness, but the Isle of Skye still remains a land apart in history and fantasy. The largest of the Inner Hebrides (50 miles long and from 3 to 25 miles wide), and one of the closest to the mainland, Skye is renowned for its unforgettable landscapes and as the hiding place for Scottish hero Bonnie Prince Charlie in 1746 after the infamous mainland defeat of his 5,000 Highlanders by the English Duke of Cumberland.

The wet and windy Hebrides, both Inner and Outer, have long been associated with tweeds, woolens, single-malt whiskies, edge-of-the-world landscapes—the very spirit of Scotland. Getting to Skye is half the fun when you follow the scenic 45-mile "Road to the Isles" from Fort William to Mallaig on Scotland's western coast, one of the main ferry ports for Skye. Tap deeper into the Scottish soul and linger a few days as (paying) houseguests at the family-owned and -managed Kinloch Lodge in the beautiful southern corner of the island. Built in 1680 as a hunting lodge for the Macdonald family, it is the elegant but unpretentiously comfortable home of Lord Macdonald, high chief of the Donald clan, his wife, Claire, and their four children. Lady Macdonald cheerfully confesses to never having had a cooking lesson in her life, but that hasn't stopped her from writing a dozen cookbooks and building a reputation as one of the leading authorities on Scottish cooking. Everything served at Kinloch is either from the island or the waters that surround it. Balmy weather and fertile land have made this waterfront area the Garden of Skye.

WHAT: island, hotel, restaurant. **SKYE:** off the northwest coast of Scotland. The Skye Bridge connects the island with Kyle of Lochalsh on the mainland. 176 miles/283 km northwest of Edinburgh, 146 miles/235 km northwest of Glasgow. **KINLOCH LODGE:** tel 44/1471-833-333, fax 44/1471-833-277; reservations@kinloch-lodge.co.uk; www.kinloch-lodge.co.uk. *Cost:* doubles from $70. Dinner $85.

Distillery Hopping in Pursuit of the Amber Elixir

SCOTCH WHISKY TRAIL

Highlands, Scotland

J ust as true Champagne can come only from the Champagne region in France, you must go to Scotland to find authentic Scotch whisky (spelled without the "e") on its native soil. The country boasts more than one "Whisky Trail," and a number of Lowland distilleries are an easy day trip southeast of Edinburgh. But the Highlands are the most celebrated home of Scotland's legendary "spirits," the malt whiskies (from the Gaelic *uisge beatha,* or water of life) that have been produced in this region for centuries. A signposted route through the scenic eastern (Grampian) Highlands—the whisky-making capital of the Western world—leads the traveler to some of the most memorable spots at which to discover "the mystery of the malt." Of the seven or eight world-famous distilleries located on this route, must-sees include Glenlivet (in Glenlivet) and Glenfiddich (in Dufftown), with Cardhu (in Archiestown) thrown in for good measure. Of the eighty-odd licensed single-malt distilleries in Scotland, these are some of the premier. Although the aforementioned all come from the secluded glens of the Spey Valley (where dozens of smaller and lesser-known distilleries make tempting detours), these world-acclaimed single malts all taste remarkably different, as a visit to a number of distilleries will prove. Water is key, and so is the quality of grain (barley) and the amount of peat used in the fire. Blended Scotch whisky, on the other hand, is the marriage of up to sixty single malts, and promises an identical character bottle after bottle. After a few wee drams of this water of life, designated passengers might feel the distinction between one amber elixir of happiness and the next getting a little cloudy.

WHAT: experience. **HOW:** contact the Scotch Whisky Association, Edinburgh. Tel 44/131-222-9200; enquiries@swa.org.uk; www.scotch-whisky.org.uk. The association can suggest Whisky Trail itineraries in different areas of Scotland, including those described above, to distilleries where visitors are welcome.

Tartans, Bagpipes, and Brute Strength

HIGHLAND GAMES

Braemar, Highlands, Scotland

Blazing with brightly colored tartans and ringing with the sound of bagpipes and ancient clans dancing and celebrating all things Scottish, these unique summer sporting events have their roots in the Middle Ages. Begun as county fairs for the exchange of goods and news, they provided clan chiefs the chance to witness the physical prowess of the area's most promising young lads. Of the nation's forty-some annual gatherings, those at Braemar are the most renowned. Queen Elizabeth usually pops in from nearby Balmoral Castle to cheer on the kilted Scotsmen. A breed of gigantic men called the "Heavies" engage in "throwing the hammer," "putting the stone," and the gathering's prime event, "tossing the caber"—a 20-foot tree trunk weighing over 130 pounds. There are all

A round of traditional tug-of-war

kinds of Highlands dancing and traditional music, and a bit of whisky to help the celebrations along.

WHAT: event. **WHERE:** throughout the Highlands; the most famous games are in Braemar's Princess Royal and Duke of Fife Memorial Park. Tel/fax 44/1339-755-377; info@braemargathering.org; www.braemar gathering.org. **COST:** tickets $13–$28. **WHEN:** late May–Sept; Braemar, 1st Sat in Sept.

Heaven on Earth, the Carnegie Club

SKIBO CASTLE

Dornoch, Highlands, Scotland

A waken to the sound of a strolling bagpipe player beneath your window, the same wake-up call that roused King Edward III, Rudyard Kipling, the Rockefellers, and Madonna on her wedding day. So begins an enchanting day for a select few at Andrew Carnegie's Skibo Castle, originally christened Schytherbolle in the 10th century by Celtic inhabitants, who believed it to be a gift from Gaelic fairies. When Carnegie returned to his homeland after making his millions in America as one of the world's most successful industrialists, he was so taken by this stunning site, he called it "heaven on earth." Carnegie would spend a stunning amount to build a baronial mansion on the ruins of the crumbling castle, creating a singularly magnificent "home at last." Recently purchased by an American entrepreneur, Skibo now opens its baronial doors to privileged club members who can live like steel tycoons in a nostalgic ambience of authentic 19th-century furnishings, a gracious tartan-kilted staff, and such amusing traditions as being led into the enormous candlelit dining hall by a lone piper in full dress. The estate's 7,500 acres teem with game and wild fowl, and there's a private, award-winning 18-hole waterfront golf course.

WHAT: hotel. **WHERE:** 40 miles/64 km north of Inverness. Tel 44/1862-894-600, fax 44/1862-894-601; www.carnegieclubs.com. **NOTE:** At press time, public access was restricted. Check before visiting.

Scenic Home of Scotland's Mascot

LOCH NESS

Highlands, Scotland

W hether you believe in the Loch Ness monster or not, the sight of the beautiful glacier-gouged Loch Ness and the crumbling ruins of Urquhart Castle, atop its own promontory, is not to be missed.

Allegedly first spotted in A.D. 565 by St. Columba, *Nessitera rhombopteryx*, better known as Nessie, has captured the world's imagination and remains the main draw to the

Highlands of Scotland, a beautifully scenic region that effortlessly holds its own in the nonmonster-related category.

With the loch measuring 24 miles in length and 755 feet deep, Nessie makes only rare appearances, and local folk aren't particularly keen on tracking her down: an ancient legend predicts a violent end for the region if the monster is ever captured. Sophisticated underwater technology and sonar-rigged mini-submarines continue their search nonetheless, egged on by would-be sightings as recent as 1961, when thirty visitors reported seeing her just before an explosion that sank their craft, and 1973, when a local monk claimed a viewing. Scotland's age-old love of whisky has also been mentioned as facilitating sightings.

Loch Ness, no monster in sight

For the multitudes who don't spot the long-necked animal or buy into the monster mania, Loch Ness can prove anticlimactic. But not if you take the less-trafficked road along the loch's eastern shore, explore the striking Falls of Foyers or the peaceful glens west of the Loch Ness's Visitor Center in Drumnadrochit, and—this is key—check into the Highland's finest hotel/restaurant. Guests at the handsome 18th-century Dunain Park Hotel begin their day with an exceptional Scottish breakfast, a mere prelude to the memorable local fare that makes dinners here a highlight of the Highlands.

WHAT: site, hotel, restaurant. **LOCH NESS MONSTER EXHIBITION:** Drumnadrochit, 13 miles/21 km from Inverness on the north shore of Loch Ness, 171 miles/275 km north of Edinburgh. **DUNAIN PARK HOTEL:** 2 miles/3 km southwest of Inverness on A82, in direction of Fort William. Tel 44/1463-230-512, fax 44/1463-224-532; info@dunainparkhotel.co.uk; www.dunainparkhotel.co.uk. *Cost:* doubles from $155, cottages from $125. Dinner $45. *When:* restaurant open for dinner daily. **BEST TIMES:** Highland Games end of Jul in Inverness.

A Baronial Bastion of Ease and Luxury

INVERLOCHY CASTLE

Fort William, Highlands, Scotland

"I never saw a lovelier or more romantic spot," wrote Queen Victoria, no stranger to the allure of the Highlands, who stayed at Inverlochy Castle in 1873 shortly after its completion. Set amid magnificent scenery, it is a grand baronial castle hotel of limited formality, cozy with roaring fireplaces and over-stuffed chairs, and set on 500 acres of private land on the shores of Loch Lochy. Its good taste and country opulence show up in a great profusion of flowers, fragrant toiletries reminiscent of grand luxe hotels, fresh herbs and just-picked vegetables from the walled gardens and local suppliers, and after dinner, a

Ben Nevis

single-malt whisky from a neighboring distillery. To enjoy this singular combination, wayfarers come from all over the world, elated at their own good fortune at having found a room (there are just seventeen available) at one of Britain's most special country retreats.

Against the backdrop of Ben Nevis, the highest peak in Great Britain (4,406 feet), the castle is the ideal base from which to experience the magic of Scotland's Highlands and off-shore excursions.

"There is still something of an Odyssey up there, in among the islands and the silent Lochs," wrote D. H. Lawrence, who visited the Highlands in 1926. "It is still out of the world, like the very beginning of Europe." The same awe will most likely be experienced by visitors a century later.

WHAT: hotel. **WHERE:** in Torlundy, 3 miles/5 km northeast of Fort William, 140 miles/225 km northwest of Edinburgh. Tel 44/1397-702-177, fax 44/1397-702-953; in the U.S., 888-424-0106; info@inverlochy.co.uk; www.inverlochycastlehotel.com. **COST:** doubles from $485 (low season), from $660 (high season). **WHEN:** open Mar–Dec.

The Full Flavor of Scottish Hospitality amid Highland Beauty

AIRDS HOTEL

Port Appin, Highlands, Scotland

Scotland wasn't united with England until 1707, and it has proudly held on to its individualistic character. It was also around that time that this large white-stucco inn on the filigree coastline of Argyll first started welcoming

ferryboat passengers on their way to the Isle of Lismore and others, plying them with haggis, whisky, and a warm fire. Fast-forward to today's gracious welcome by The Airds' amiable hosts Shaun and Jenny McKivragan, who guarantee an excellent stay at his family-owned and -run inn. The Airds has garnered countless accolades for its vista-rich location on the wildly beautiful Loch Linnhe, as well as its service, furnishings, and especially its kitchen and prodigious cellar, whose wine list runs fifty pages long. The impressive selection of Scotch single-malt and blended whiskies merits a mention, too. Since 2004,

award-winning chef J. Paul Burns has presided over the top-notch restaurant. The Airds could be known solely as a top-notch foodie shrine if not for the panoply of day trips this area of the northern Highlands offers. The castle town of Inverary (the ancient capital of Argyll) is one of Scotland's most handsome—and twice as inviting with the nearby 90-acre lush Crarae Gardens thrown in. This is also the area for Scotland's best lunch: stop in at the Loch Fyne Oyster Bar (Clachan Farm in Cairndow), whose famous blue-ribbon oysters are so fresh they've never known ice. But save room for dinner—always at 8:00—the event of the day back at The Airds.

WHAT: hotel, restaurant. **WHERE:** 27 miles/43 km south of Fort William, 100 miles/161 km north of Glasgow, 125 miles/201 km northwest of Edinburgh. Tel 44/1631-730-236, fax 44/1631-730-535; airds@airds-hotel.com; www.airds-hotel.com. **COST:** doubles from $400 (low season), from $430 (high season), includes dinner. 4-course dinner $80. **WHEN:** restaurant open daily for lunch and dinner. **BEST TIMES:** spring and late fall.

The Airds is an old ferry inn.

The Most Distinguished of Them All

BALMORAL HOTEL

Edinburgh, Scotland

You won't find a room at the inn in Scotland's Balmoral Castle, but great consolation can be found in the regal treatment lavished upon guests of its eponymous hotel. The Balmoral is a palatial old railway hotel—with

no official royal connection despite its name —built in 1902 at the east end of Princes Street, Edinburgh's premier retail strip. It has recently made a dazzling comeback in its bid for supremacy as the capital's hotel of choice. The city's most elegant landmark, with kilted doormen at its entrance, is as much a tourist attraction as the city's other icon, Edinburgh Castle. It draws guest-wannabes who daydream their way through afternoon tea or sample the bounty of Scotland's best distilleries in the high-ceilinged Palm Court Bar and leave with a taste of the high life, Scottish style. Outside, the mile-long Princes Street awaits, the city's main boulevard for designer everything, including Jenner's, the world's oldest department store, opened in 1838.

WHAT: hotel. **WHERE:** 1 Princes St. Tel 44/131-556-2414, fax 44/131-557-8740; reservations@thebalmoralhotel.com; www.roccofortehotels.com. **COST:** doubles from $515.

In the heart of Edinburgh

Impregnable and Most Famous Icon of Scotland

EDINBURGH CASTLE

Edinburgh, Scotland

One of Europe's loveliest capitals owes much of its character and good looks to its showcase landmark, Edinburgh Castle. Most of the city's history is clustered in and around the medieval castle and the Royal Mile, the west-east pedestrian thoroughfare from Castle Hill to High Street, that links it to Holyrood Palace, once occupied by Mary Stuart and royal residence to the present queen and Prince Philip for one week every year. Edinburgh Castle sits atop the collapsed crater of an extinct volcano, its earliest traces dating to the tiny 12th-century Chapel of St. Margaret, the oldest structure in Edinburgh. The sprawling castle has played many roles: fortress, military garrison, state prison. But its highlight was as royal palace, and today the Honours of Scotland (the Scottish crown jewels) are displayed here. The oldest regalia in Europe, they include the Scottish crown, scepter, and sword of state. In the palace, the royal chambers used until the king permanently moved to England in 1603 can also be visited (Mary, Queen of Scots, gave birth here to James VI of Scotland, who would rule England as James I). The Royal Mile and its offshoots were confined by the old city walls, so many tenements grew vertically; the back streets and winding passageways in this section of the Old Town are still redolent of the Middle Ages. Across the chasm that separates the high Old Town from the lower New Town sits the classic Caledonian Hotel, known for its own royal accommodations and views of the castle, most romantic when brightly illuminated at night. Dripping in Edwardian splendor, any rooms at "the Caley" with views of the medieval skyline and Gothic spires of the Royal Mile are something special. Its longtime friendly rival, the Balmoral Hotel, sits gracefully at the opposite end of mile-long Princes Street, Edinburgh's shop-lined Fifth Avenue.

WHAT: site, hotel. **EDINBURGH CASTLE:** Castlehill. *Cost:* admission. **CALEDONIAN HILTON HOTEL:** Princes St. Tel 44/131-222-8888; in the U.S., tel 800-774-1500; www.hilton.co.uk/caledonian. *Cost:* doubles from $340; with castle views, from $520.

The castle sits high above the city.

A Plethora of Scottish Culture

THE FESTIVALS OF EDINBURGH

Scotland

Every August this conservative city morphs into center stage for a world-class extravaganza of music, drama, dance, and alternative entertainment. Having recently celebrated its fiftieth anniversary, the Edinburgh International Festival has long been drawing first-rank names and talents. Garnering as much attention is the Fringe, the festival's amateur offshoot, where you can expect the unexpected from more than 650 diamond-in-the-rough troupes from all over the world, performing in 150-plus venues, from beer halls to school gyms. The Fringe is now the largest arts festival in the world, with no artistic vetting, and therefore open to anyone with a wish to perform. The nighttime performance of the Military Tattoo (the name comes from the closing-time cry "doe den tap toe" in Low Country inns during the 17th and 18th centuries, meaning "turn off the taps") is possibly the world's most outstanding military spectacle, augmented by its dramatic setting on a castle esplanade. The pipe-and-drum music and display of gymnastic skill may not be high art, but it's great entertainment. And if all this is not enough, the annual Edinburgh Film Festival (now the longest continually running film festival in the world) and Jazz and Blues Festivals add to the cultural logjam. Tickets for the principal performances should be bought in advance, but with such abundant choices, one can show up empty-handed and still be guaranteed a wonderful time, especially if you're still around for the last night's spectacular fireworks.

WHAT: event. **HOW:** tickets for main festival events, in the U.S. through Global Tickets; tel 800-669-8687. For general information on festivals, www.edinburgh-festivals.com. **COST:** tickets from free up to $80. **WHEN:** mid-Aug–early Sept.

A Traditional Frenzy of Good Fun at Year's End

HOGMANAY

Edinburgh, Scotland

This is *the* national holiday throughout Scotland, celebrated with special fervor in Edinburgh. It is the year's *ceilidh*, the Big Event, when parties go on in houses, pubs, and village halls. In Edinburgh, it is also Europe's greatest street party with song and dance carrying through the night and well into the morning. Its strongest tradition, inextricably linked to the good time enjoyed by all, is the consumption of great quantities of spirits (let's remember where Scotch whisky originated) that pushes an already boisterous holiday over the top. The famous Scottish dish the world loves to hate, haggis (a loosely packed mutton and oatmeal sausage boiled in a sheep's stomach), plays a major role in the evening's hours-long meal, often accompanied by dancing and the soulful wail of bagpipes. The meaning of "Hogmanay" has long been locked in controversy. It is said that it derives from either the Anglo-Saxon *Haleg Monath* (Holy Month) or the ancient Gaelic *Oge Maidne* (New Morning). In some towns, Hogmanay is still called Cake Day because children used to go from door to door collecting gifts of cake and confections. What has survived the centuries is the Scots' determination that the new year begin on a happy note.

WHAT: event. **WHERE:** celebrated throughout Scotland, most extravagantly in Edinburgh. **WHEN:** approximately 3 days, culminating Dec 31.

A Grand Hotel on Wheels

THE ROYAL SCOTSMAN

Edinburgh, Scotland

From the kilted piper who greets you as you board the restored vintage train to the magnificent scenery that rolls by your mahogany-paneled parlor car, there is no finer way to view the Scottish Highlands. Traveling through mountains and glens in romantic Edwardian elegance on little-used railway lines, stopping along the way to visit magnificent homes and private castles, this train is renowned as one of the world's most exclusive. Your five-star vantage point is like an elegant country house on wheels, with seamless service and cabins fitted out in rich wood with Scottish-motif marquetry. The kitchen produces excellent meals reflecting the local bounty, from full Scottish breakfasts to dinners featuring loch prawns, smoked salmon, or rack of lamb. The wine selection is surpassed only by the whisky tastings—you'll not be driving home tonight.

WHAT: experience. **WHERE:** departures from Edinburgh; optional departures from London. **HOW:** tel 44/131-555-1344; in the U.S., tel 800-524-2420; enquiries@royalscotsman.co.uk; www.royalscotsman.com; or contact Abercrombie & Kent, in the U.S., tel 800-323-7308, fax 630-954-3324; www.abercrombiekent.com. **COST:** from 2 nights, $3,600 per person, to 4-night tour, $6,620 per person, all-inclusive, single or double occupancy. Some 4-night tours include golf at Gleneagles. **WHEN:** round-trip Edinburgh loop, Apr–Oct.

The Scottish Highlands in style

Local Rebel and Master of Modern Design

THE MACKINTOSH TRAIL

Glasgow, Scotland

Glasgow's greatest architect-designer, Charles Rennie Mackintosh (1868–1928), earned Scotland's second city its reputation as a hub of creativity, but his name recognition was at a low ebb until 1996, when his House for

an Art Lover—designed for a competition in 1901—was finally built in Bellahouston Park, southwest of the city. His undisputed masterpiece, the Glasgow School of Art, has become a place of pilgrimage: when completed in 1899 it was heralded as Europe's finest example of Modernism. His restaurants and tearooms about town were also renowned; visit the Willow Tearooms, the only example still standing. Mackintosh ultimately became better known for his furniture designs than for his architecture—some of the furniture at the Willow may be reproduction, but the atmosphere is authentic: ask to be seated in the Salon de Luxe, an Art Nouveau fantasy. Viewing his designs in their original settings helps Mackintosh fans understand the aesthetic and social context that shaped his ideas. His inimitable style remains vividly alive throughout town, from designs found on the wrought-iron gates of a private garage to decorative motifs used on restaurant menus and the ubiquitous stylized rose that has become a kind of Glasgow logo.

WHAT: experience, restaurant. **CHARLES RENNIE MACKINTOSH SOCIETY:** 870 Garscube Rd. Tel 44/141-946-6600, fax 44/141-945-2321; info@crmsociety.com; www.crmsociety.com. Conducts tours of principal Mackintosh sites in and around Glasgow. *When:* upon request. **GLASGOW SCHOOL OF ART:** 167 Renfrew St. Tel 44/141-353-5500; info@gsa.ac.uk; www.gsa.ac.uk. **WILLOW TEAROOMS:** 217 Sauchiehall St. Tel 44/141-353-5500. *Cost:* tea $20.

Charles Rennie Mackintosh's Willow Tearooms

A Victorian City's Top Address

ONE DEVONSHIRE GARDENS

Glasgow, Scotland

If Leonard Bernstein found One Devonshire Gardens "inspirational" and "pure theater," imagine the effect it has on the average unsuspecting guest. You must ring the front doorbell upon arrival, but it is the last time you'll

Leave your cares at the door.

raise a finger here. Three exquisitely refurbished Victorian town houses dating to the late 1800s have been connected to create a chic jewel box whose superb service and much-touted restaurant may tempt one to see not a whit of Glasgow beyond these gorgeous walls. Critics have cited Glasgow as being the

greatest surviving example of a Victorian city, and here is prime proof. Millionaire guests will feel right at home; everyone else will feel like they've died and gone to heaven, cosseted by a genuinely thoughtful staff from the front door onward. Its quiet location in the leafy, fashionable West End area of town makes it feel just removed enough to add to its exclusive atmosphere; the sumptuously decorated rooms, many of them with plushly draped, rich mahogany four-poster beds and crackling fireplaces, also help. On a par with the best that Paris or London has to offer, accommodations in Glasgow took a quantum leap forward with the opening of this privately owned boutique hotel in 1986. Reason enough for a trip to the city.

WHAT: hotel, restaurant. **WHERE:** Glasgow is 40 miles/64 km west of Edinburgh. 1 Devonshire Gardens. Tel 44/141-339-2001, fax 44/141-337-1663; reservations@onedevonshire gardens.com; www.onedevonshiregardens.com. **COST:** doubles from $250. Dinner $55. **BEST TIMES:** Glasgow International Jazz Festival, 1 week in late Jun, early Jul (www.jazzfest.co.uk).

In the Middle of the Ocean:
Wildlife, a Victorian Castle, and Farm-Fresh Meals

BALFOUR CASTLE

Shapinsay, Orkney Islands, Scotland

The small, fertile island of Shapinsay, one of the northernmost of the sixty-seven islands that make up Scotland's remote Orkney archipelago, is even today given over mostly to cattle and sheep rearing and is small enough to

walk around in one day. Here you can get away from e-mail and tax collectors and reduce stress to zero; seal and bird watching (with some 300 species identified in the islands) are the highlight of the day, and your background music is the bleating of lambs and the sound of seagulls against the ocean waves.

The seven-spired Balfour Castle is a landmark of the windblown Orkney Islands. Built in 1848 around an existing 1793 house by Shipinsay's' most important benefactor, Balfour Castle was purchased in 1960 by a Polish officer, Captain Zawadski. His Scottish widow and her family run it today as a distinguished home and country manor. Meals are ample, simple, and delicious, with vegetables from the castle's gardens, locally grown meats and shellfish from the island's waters (guests are not likely to recall ever tasting sweeter lobster or scallops) and served when the gong is sounded from somewhere deep in the castle. If there's a TV on the premises no one ever requests it, and the only newspaper on the island is the *Orcadian*, which comes out every Thursday. The only pub in Shapinsay, found in the castle's old gatehouse, gives a unique spin to "island nightlife."

WHAT: island, hotel. **SHAPINSAY:** air connection daily (except Sun) from Inverness or Aberdeen to the neighboring island of Kirkwall in the Orkneys; connect from there by frequent 30-minute car and passenger ferry; www.orkneyferries.co.uk. **CASTLE BALFOUR:** tel 44/1856-711-282, fax 44/1856-711-283; info@balfourcastle.co.uk; www.balfourcastle. co.uk. *Cost:* doubles $140, includes 3-course dinner. *Note:* At press time the castle was closed for renovation. Check before visiting.

Cliffs of the Orkney Islands

BEST TIMES: Jun–Sept; midsummer for bird life. Puffins can be seen in May–early Jul.

A Manor Amid a Poetic Landscape That Never Ends

KINNAIRD ESTATE

Dunkeld, Perthshire, Scotland

Every country estate must have country, and Kinnaird is surrounded by 9,000 glorious acres of it. Even in Scotland's beautiful countryside, few of the many castles or manor houses accepting overnight guests can match this. Despite the breadth and enormity of the estate, and the growing reputation of its impeccable restaurant, Kinnaird, with just nine beautifully furnished rooms in the magnificent 1770 manor, is a place of great warmth and charm. Its welcoming ambience is due in large part to the smiling, house-proud staff and the easygoing outlook of the owner, the American-born Constance Ward. She ensures the well-heeled guests an authentic Scottish country-house atmosphere free of sti-

fling reserve, but with an infallible attention to the utmost detail more commonly found in five-star hotels.

Set above a bluff overlooking the fish-rich River Tay and with storybook views down the valley, Kinnaird was built as a hunting lodge for a local duke of obvious wealth. It still attracts a mostly field-and-stream clientele, though even the most unoutdoorsy types are lured by country walks through a contemplative and poetic landscape of woodlands,

The River Tay is a haven for anglers.

moors, lochs, ponds, and heather-covered hills.

WHAT: hotel, restaurant. **WHERE:** 7 miles/11 km from Dunkeld, 22 miles/35 km north of Perth, 65 miles/105 km north of Edinburgh. Tel 44/1796-482-440, fax 44/1796-482-289; enquiry@kinnairdestate.com; www.kinnairdestate.com. **COST:** doubles from $470 (low season), from $725 (high season), includes dinner. 3-course dinner $110. **WHEN:** closed Mon–Wed in Jan and Feb. **BEST TIMES:** Sept–Oct for salmon fishing; Jul–Oct for Pitlochry Theatre Festival.

Where the Lowlands Meet the Highlands

THE TROSSACHS

Callander, West Highlands, Scotland

The heather-clad hills of the Trossachs and their centerpiece, Loch Lomond, the largest and most famous of Scotland's fjordlike lakes, have enthralled travelers since novelist Sir Walter Scott's writings first popularized the area in the early 19th century. Here the Lowlands meet the Highlands of the north and west in an area rich in history thanks to Rob Roy (Red Robert), a real-life 18th-century Highlander, cattle dealer, and outlaw who became a Scottish folk hero akin to England's Robin Hood. In addition, there is Stirling Castle, the country's most significant stronghold—whoever held Stirling controlled the Scottish nation. Dating to the Middle Ages and second only to Edinburgh Castle in grandeur, it was the residence of Mary, Queen of Scots, as an infant monarch. Just north of Glasgow, the Trossachs envelop visitors in the sort of pristine wildness usually associated with the Highlands farther north. The "bonnie, bonnie banks" of Loch Lomond (dotted with thirty-some tiny islands) are bonnie indeed, but Sir Walter Scott also favored the fresh-water beauty of Loch Katrine, where he set his narrative poem "The Lady of the Lake" in 1810. Today a small Victorian steamer, the SS *Sir Walter Scott*, plies its serene waters that mirror wooded peaks and forested shores.

WHAT: site. **THE TROSSACHS:** the Rob Roy and Trossachs Centre, Ancaster Square,

Some of the inhabitants at the edge of the Highlands

Callander (east of both Loch Lomond and Loch Katrine), is the traditional base for touring the Trossachs. Tel 44/1877-330-342, fax 44/1877-330-784; callander@vs.com. *When:* open daily, year-round. **STIRLING**

CASTLE: 23 miles/37 km northeast of Glasgow. **BEST TIMES:** May–Sept. Stirling Highland Games are held on a Sun, first half of Jul; Callander World Championship Highland Games usually last weekend in Jul.

Muscle-Flexing English Icons of an Embattled Past

CAERNARFON CASTLE

North Wales, Wales

I t is said that no other country on earth has as many castles per square mile as Wales. From Roman garrisons and Norman strongholds to Saxon forts, the history of Wales has been written in stone. Visitors never have to search far

for the next tumbledown ruin or glowering medieval pile: Wales has some 300-odd castles to explore. A series of more than a dozen brooding castles in North Wales were built, beginning in 1277, by England's fearsome Edward I (1272–1307) to impress and ultimately (in 1282) subdue the fiery Welsh. Crenellated Caernarfon Castle, located on the Menai Straight, was built on a site famous since Roman times as the gateway to Snowdonia. It was the greatest of Edward's castles: the official royal residence in North Wales and the seat of government. Its octagonal 13th-century towers still dominate the town.

Caernarfon Castle is said to be modeled on the ancient walls and towers of Constantinople.

Edward II, born here in 1284, was also given the honorary title of Prince of Wales here in 1301 as a gesture to placate the Welsh people; it is a title conferred on the eldest son of the reigning English monarch to this day.

The castle has witnessed two investitures in the 20th century: Edward III, presented by his father George V in 1911, and HRH Prince Charles, the current Prince of Wales, in 1969 —the latter amid great pomp and ceremony.

For accommodations far less royal but oh so much more comfortable, Wales's best farm-house hospitality can be found in this attraction-packed corner of North Wales. Ty'n Rhos and its 70-acre farmstead is one of Wales's loveliest country hotels, a family-run inn whose exceptional kitchen plays no small role in its status as the best base from which to tour the many wonders of North Wales.

WHAT: site, hotel. **CAERNARFON CASTLE:** 8 miles/13 km southwest of Bangor. Tel 44/1286-677-617; www.caernarfon.com. *Cost:* admission $8. **TY'N RHOS:** 20 minutes by car from Caernarfon Castle. Tel 44/1248-670-489, fax 44/1248-670-079; enquiries@tynrhos.co.uk; www.tynrhos.co.uk. *Cost:* doubles $165.

A Garden and a Country Hall for All Seasons

BODNANT GARDEN AND BODYSGALLEN HALL

Conwy and Llandudno, North Wales, Wales

Wales's most beautiful garden is situated above the River Conwy, overlooking one of the country's loveliest valleys and against the postcard-perfect backdrop of the Snowdonia Mountains. Significant enough to have elicited the protection of the National Trust in 1949, Bodnant Garden is one of the finest in all the British Isles, and it's no secret that the English are tough competition in the botanical department. Here is a pleasure ground for all seasons, covering nearly 100 acres arranged in formal Italian-style terraces beginning at the manor house and leading down to a wild garden full of colorful flowers, exotic shrubs, magnificent trees, and rock ensembles. Depending on the time of year, visitors can enjoy dense dells of rhododendrons, camellias, or magnolias, old-fashioned bluebell woods, or the Laburnam Arch, a 180-foot-long tunneled walk where a mass of golden blossoms joins and meets overhead, best seen in late May and early June. Laid out in 1875, Bodnant is still the magnificent home of Lord Aberconway, president emeritus of the Royal Horticultural Society, who obviously could think of no finer place to retire.

Fancy yourself a peer of Lord Aberconway and check into Bodysgallen Hall in nearby Llandudno, often mentioned as the best country house in Wales. That this is a top-drawer operation is immediately apparent from the grand entranceway's enormous, flawless flower arrangements, the massive fireplaces, and the lovely selection of fine antiques. Tucked into the woods on the outskirts of Snowdonia National Park, the main house dates largely from the 17th century (incorporating a 13th-century lookout tower). Many of the guest rooms have gorgeous views of the mountains of Snowdonia and nearby Conwy, a small medieval town of perfectly preserved walls that grew up around an important 13th-century Edwardian castle. The small Victorian seaside resort town of Llandudno is just 1 mile away, its pastel hotels lining the promenade and along the ornate gingerbread pier. Resist the open-air restaurants promising fresh seafood for at least one

Bodysgallen Hall sits on 200 acres of wooded parkland.

dinner at Bodysgallen. Try Welsh lamb, Anglesey lobsters, and salmon from the River Conwy. After dinner, moonlit strolls can be enjoyed amid formal rose- and herb-scented boxhedge gardens re-created from 17th- and 18th-century archives. Carefully hidden on the 200 acres of beautifully tended grounds are sixteen small cottages, many with their own private courtyard gardens, for those who want to indulge the fantasy of owning a small stone bungalow in the Welsh countryside, if only for a night.

WHAT: site, hotel. **BODNANT GARDEN:** 8 miles/13 km south of Conwy and Llandudno on the northern coast of Wales; www.bodnant garden.co.uk. *Cost:* admission $12. *When:* daily, mid-Mar–Oct. *Best times:* spring–fall, but truly a garden for all seasons. **BODYSGALLEN HALL:** 20 miles/32 km east of Caernarfon Castle, 30 miles/48 km east of Snowdon. Tel 44/1492-584-466; info@bodys gallen.com; www.bodsgallen.com. *Cost:* doubles from $290, includes use of hotel spa. **BEST TIMES:** spring–fall; the Llandudno October Fair, 1 week mid-month, dedicated to music, poetry, and art.

Within the Embrace of Snowdonia

MAES-Y-NEUADD

Harlech, North Wales, Wales

This handsome granite and slate manor—whose name means "mansion in the meadow"—dates back to the 14th century, with more "recent" 16th- and 18th-century additions. It's the perfect jumping-off point for exploring Snowdonia's timeless grandeur, which is visible without leaving the hotel's beautiful landscaped grounds. It is also a first-class gastronomic destination and imaginative "Steam and Cuisine" joint venture with the nearby Ffestiniog Railway: a chance to dine royally while enjoying the narrow-gauge steam railway that travels an extremely scenic 14-mile route to and from the coast at Porthmadog up into the Snowdonia Mountains to the former mining town of Blaenau Ffestiniog.

Replacing a horse-drawn tramway that carried slate during the area's mid-19th-century heyday, it is one of many steam-powered "toy trains" still operating in Wales. Keeping alive the country's legacy of mining and a priority for train buffs, it connects towns with names like Dduallt, Tanygrisiau, and Tan-y-Bwlch that are still not accessible by automobile.

Meanwhile, the closest castle is never far away, and Maes-y-Neuadd is only 3 miles from 13th-century Harlech, one of the country's most important military bastions, known for its unique vistas over coastal sand dunes and its history as the last Welsh stronghold to fall to the English during the 17th-century civil war.

"Steam and Cuisine"

WHAT: hotel, restaurant. **WHERE:** within Snowdonia National Park. Tel 44/1766-780-200, fax 44/1766-780-211; maes@neuadd.com; www.neuadd.com. **COST:** doubles from $165. Dinner $80. **WHEN:** hotel and restaurant open year-round; train operates Mar–Oct. **BEST TIMES:** May–Jul.

Where King Arthur and His Knights Lie in Sleep

SNOWDONIA NATIONAL PARK

North Wales, Wales

Blessed though it is with picturesque towns and coastal hamlets, Wales is most famed for stunning interior landscapes, and the Snowdonia Mountains offer unparalleled grandeur and beauty. King Arthur's spirit

is said to watch over towering Mount Snowdon, where (according to legend) his Knights of the Round Table lie sleeping. At 3,560 feet, it is the second highest peak in Great Britain after Scotland's Ben Nevis. Unlike American national parks, Snowdonia is inhabited. One of the villages within its sprawling terrain, Llanberis, is the departure point for the steep one-hour trip (4–5 miles) aboard the Snowdon Mountain Railway (a three-hour trek by foot is a popular alternative); Britain's only rack-and-pinion railway has been making this run since 1896. It stops just 70 feet short of the summit, leaving the final stage a short and easy ascent for the weak of knee. From the top on a clear day you can see much of the park's 840 square miles of varied landscapes and as far as Ireland's Wicklow Mountains, 90 miles

away. This is some of the country's most spectacular scenery and there is the opportunity to walk windswept moorland, sail on mountain lakes, bicycle on marked routes, and enjoy a vast range of natural beauty and wildlife. Rugged peaks and wooded valleys join 27 miles of coastline, but place of honor goes to Mount Snowdon itself, the highest of the park's fifteen peaks over 3,000 feet. Its Welsh name, Yr Wyddfa, means "tomb," referring to the grave of Rhita Gawr, the legendary giant slain by King Arthur.

WHAT: site. **WHERE:** towns popularly used as bases to explore the park are Betws-y-Coed, Dolgellau, and Bala. Park information at tel 44/ 1766-770-274; www.eryri-npa.co.uk. **COST:** train round-trip $37. **WHEN:** train operates May–Oct. **BEST TIMES:** May–Jun and Sept–Oct.

Olympics of Welsh Culture

INTERNATIONAL MUSICAL EISTEDDFOD

Llangollen, North Wales, Wales

When a Welsh men's choir bursts into song, the audience bursts into tears. For reasons lost in time, Wales has long been known for the heavenly quality of its renowned male voice choirs, characterized by

polyphonic "hymn singing," a kind of aural waterfall of many rhythms and melodies. The

male choirs are a major attraction of the *eisteddfodau*, ancient Welsh festivals of music

Available for purchase
on this level only

To order,
call 800-845-0005
or visit americangirl.com

3 40407 36986 8

FFB50

and culture that stem from a 12th-century Celtic tradition of traveling singing bards. Many eisteddfods are held annually across the country but the two principal ones are the Llangollen International Musical Eisteddfod—considered the Welsh Olympics of poetry and song—with 12,000 performers of music, song, and dance from fifty different countries in colorful national costume, and the Royal National Eisteddfod, a totally Welsh festival (with headphone translation facilities available), held in a different town every year. Wales's rich tradition of choral singing, primarily by men, was integral in preserving the Welsh language and continues to play a big part in both festivals. In a country barely the size of Massachusetts (or half the size of Switzerland), there are more than 100 male choirs with 60 to 100 voices that rehearse and give concerts year-round to prepare and qualify for the national event: rehearsals can be just as enjoyable as the big show, and visitors are welcome at most. Welsh ballads and spirituals are standard fare, but Broadway tunes and pop ditties (in Welsh) often turn up on the programs.

A celebration of music, song, and dance

WHAT: event. **LLANGOLLEN INTERNATIONAL MUSICAL EISTEDDFOD:** Royal International Pavilion, Llangollen, 140 miles/225 km north of Cardiff, 25 miles/40 km west of Chester, England. Tel 44/1978-862-001, fax 44/1978-862-005; info@international-eisteddfod.co.uk; www.international-eisteddfod.co.uk. *When:* 1 week early to mid-Jul. *Cost:* tickets from $15 for unreserved seats, from $30 for concerts with world-renowned artists. **ROYAL (OR "NATIONAL") EISTEDDFOD:** takes place in a different town or city every year. For information, contact the Eisteddfod Office, 40 Parc Ty Glas, Llanishen, Cardiff. Tel 44/2920-763-777, fax 44/2920-763-737; www.eisteddfod.com. *When:* 1 week, early Aug. *Cost:* tickets from $25 for unreserved seats, from $65 for special performances.

One Man's Dream

PORTMEIRION

North Wales, Wales

O n a wooded hillside on its own little peninsula with romantic views of sand, sea, and mountains, the tiny town of Portmeirion is more redolent of southern Italy than of North Wales. Welsh architect Sir

Clough Williams-Ellis—inspired, it is said, by a trip to Portofino—built this unique Italianate folly of a town piecemeal, from 1925 until its completion in 1975 on his 90th birthday. Although predominantly Mediterranean in feel (think campanile, piazza, fountains, and arcaded loggia), the village's more subtle architectural influences range from Asian to traditional English, reflecting Sir Clough's light-opera approach. Down beside the sea,

The coastal, hillside town of Portmeirion

removed from curious day visitors, is the Hotel Portmeirion, one of the architect's early ventures. Inaugurated in 1926, it reopened in 1990 after a major fire, as exuberant as first envisioned. It is known for its spirited interior, both opulent and informal and something of a treasure chest: rooms might be done up in Indian—or Victorian Welsh. Some guests find it magically escapist (Noël Coward was inspired to write *Blithe Spirit*, his most ethereal play, while staying here); for others, it's a bit like visiting a dotty aunt.

WHAT: town, hotel. **PORTMEIRION:** 10 miles/16 km south of Snowdonia on the coast. **HOTEL PORTMEIRION:** tel 44/1766-770-228, fax 44/1766-771-331; hotel@portmeirion-village.com; www.portmeirion.com. *Cost:* doubles in Main House $335. **BEST TIMES:** May–Sept for best weather; Portmeirion Antique Fair usually 1st weekend in Mar and Nov.

The Land's End of Wales and a Food Lover's Mecca

PLAS BODEGROES

Pwllheli, North Wales, Wales

At a time when Wales was the last place to come to mind as a gastronomic destination, Plas Bodegroes (Rosehips Hall) arrived in the mid-1980s and changed all that. The handsome Georgian manor house is located on the west coast's Lleyn Peninsula, in a spot whose quiet is broken by little besides birdsong. The emphasis here falls firmly on the cuisine. Innovative, exciting, accomplished, using top-quality local ingredients without pretension, the kitchen never ceases to impress. In fact, it is arguably the best place to eat in the country. The enjoyment of a few days in this stylish, informal 18th-century manor house, overseen with friendly ease by owner and hostess Gunna Chown—her husband, Chris, reigns in the kitchen—is enhanced by its location on the wild and classically Welsh 24-mile-long outcrop of rock and green pastures, the Land's End of Wales. Parts of the untamed Lleyn Peninsula were without electricity until the late 1960s, and Welsh is still widely spoken in the area. Clifftop walks, birding, and exploring sleepy coastal towns that preserve the old ways fill serene, regenerating days that culminate with another brilliant dinner back at Plas Bodegroes in this little-known stronghold of Welsh culture.

WHAT: restaurant, hotel. **WHERE:** 20 miles/32 km west of Snowdonia on the southern coast of Lleyn Peninsula. Tel 44/1758-612-363, fax 44/1758-701-247; gunna@bodegroes.co.uk; www.bodegroes.co.uk. **COST:** dinner $70. Doubles from $180. **WHEN:** open Mar–Nov. Dinner Tues–Sun, lunch Sun only. **BEST TIMES:** May, Jun, Sept, and Oct for local festivals.

Two Oases for the Mind and Body

HAY-ON-WYE FESTIVAL AND LLANGOED HALL

Hay-on-Wye and Llyswen, South Wales, Wales

This compact little border town in the Black Mountains claims to be the world's capital of antiquarian and secondhand books and is a monument to British eccentricity. The farming community of 1,300 surrounded by sheep-grazed hills has anywhere from twenty to thirty-five bookstores (depending on whom you ask) that stock millions of titles. Its annual Festival of Literature is known to bibliophiles everywhere—writers and poets come from around the world to give readings and hold informal discussions of their work. It may be the most prestigious literary festival in Britain, and it certainly is the most interesting. The audiences at some of the 150 scheduled events, featuring more than 250 authors in ten days, are a discerning lot of vociferous readers and critics who relish interaction with authors of integrity in a charming rustic setting and as yet uncommercialized venue.

Stay nearby at Llangoed Hall, a longtime favorite of festivalgoers. The hotel has a well-heeled family feel, discreetly taking its direction from owner Sir Bernard Ashley, whose personal collection of *objets* and paintings is lavishly distributed throughout this comfortably grand country house dating back to the 1600s. With no reception desk, guests are treated like family friends and whisked directly up to gorgeously decorated chambers. The lodgings are graced with the unmistakable flair, originality, and good taste long associated with Laura Ashley, the company founded by Sir Bernard and his late wife. Situated on the grassy banks of the River Wye (which provides guests with some of the best salmon and trout fishing in the United Kingdom), it has garnered many accolades since opening in 1990, all

deserved, for the 10 acres of pristine gardens with views over the Black Mountains, the wonderfully professional staff who nurture Llangoed's just-like-home philosophy, the excellent food from a refined kitchen, the chance to stretch one's legs in the bordering 500-square-mile Brecon Beacons National Park, and the relaxed ambience of an Edwardian house party. It may well be here

An illustration of Llangoed Hall

that you'll first understand that the expression *Croesco y Cymru* ("Welcome to Wales") also means "Welcome home."

WHAT: town, event, hotel, restaurant. **HAY-ON-WYE FESTIVAL:** 15 miles/24 km east of Brecon, 20 miles/32 km west of Hereford, England. Tel 44/1497-821-299; www.hayfestival.co.uk. *When:* 10 days, late May, early Jun. **LLANGOED HALL:** in Llyswen, 9 miles/14 km west of Hay-on-Wye, 10 miles/16 km from Brecon, entrance to the National Park. Tel 44/1874-754-525, fax 44/1874-754-545; enquiries@llangoedhall.com; www.llangoedhall.com. *Cost:* doubles from $300. Dinner $65. **BEST TIMES:** Late May–early Jun for the Literature Festival. The Royal Welsh Show in Builth Wells is 4 days mid- to late Jul with agricultural and equestrian events. Brecon Jazz Festival, 3 days, mid-Aug.

A Shrine to Wales's Most Renowned Bard

DYLAN THOMAS'S BOATHOUSE

Laugharne, South Wales, Wales

U p on the hill in St. Martin's churchyard, in the refreshingly uncommercialized town of Laugharne, a simple white cross marks the grave of Dylan Thomas, Wales's most famous poet, and his wife, Caitlin. There are

still old-timers in town who remember him sitting in Brown's Hotel, the local pub where he would regularly enjoy a pint. The nearby boathouse where he lived with his wife for the last years of his life has become a shrine in miniature. Thomas devotees come in a steady stream, attempting to grasp something of the

Thomas's boathouse overlooks the Taf Estuary.

man. His writing shed and home are just as he left them, filled with his papers, manuscripts, and furnishings. It was here that he wrote some of his most famous works, including *Under Milk Wood*, his "play for voices" translated into the classic film in 1971 starring Welsh-born Richard Burton, Elizabeth Taylor, and Peter O'Toole and filmed in nearby Fishguard. The boathouse's quiet setting overlooking the Taf estuary is lyrically beautiful: it takes little to imagine the pull it exerted on Thomas, who died at the age of thirty-nine in 1953, at New York City's White Horse Tavern.

WHAT: site. **WHERE:** about 65 miles west of Cardiff, on the coast. **COST:** admission. **BEST TIMES:** Dylan Thomas Festival is 3 weeks, late Jul–Aug, in his birth city of Swansea.

Wordsworth's Beloved 12th-Century Ruins

TINTERN ABBEY

Monmouthshire, South Wales, Wales

" Y ou will find among the woods," wrote one of the residents of Tintern Abbey, "something you never found in books." Once a thriving center of religion and learning and the richest abbey in Wales, Tintern was

founded in 1131 by the Cistercian monks. Roofless and in ruins for centuries, Tintern Abbey has long been a destination for artists and poets. Enchanted by its sylvan setting in a steep gorge in the wooded Wye

Valley, poets such as Wordsworth were moved by its soaring arches and windows, and the abbey shell that stands open to the sky almost to its full height, an outstanding example of medieval Gothic. Before being dissolved in

Remains of the abbey

1536 by Henry VIII when the slate roof was destroyed, Tintern had grown to include the abbey church, chapter house, infirmary, and dining hall, their outlines still visible. Marked paths through the surrounding woodland lead up to Devil's Pulpit, a well-known lookout over the poignant grace of Tintern's remains, the vista that likely inspired Wordsworth's much-loved sonnet celebrating the greatness of God in nature: "And I have felt, A presence that disturbs me with the joy of elevated thoughts; a sense sublime. . . ."

WHAT: site. **WHERE:** 30 miles/48 km northeast of Cardiff at border with England. **COST:** admission.

Wales's Greatest Religious Monument

ST. DAVID'S CATHEDRAL

St. David's, South Wales, Wales

People still flock here in the thousands the way they did in the Middle Ages when St. David's Cathedral was one of the British Isles' most popular pilgrimage spots. Small by English standards, the medieval cathedral dedicated to Wales's patron saint is the largest in the country, overwhelming what is officially Britain's smallest city (the presence of a cathedral designates the village as a city despite its size). St. David founded a monastic community in this coastal corner of southwestern Wales around A.D. 550 that grew to great importance. The cathedral, begun in the 12th century, is believed to stand on that site, flanked by the once magnificent Bishop's Palace; then boasting lavish apartments, it now sits quietly in glorious ruins. Together they constitute Wales's most sacred site, and one of its most visually evocative—the setting is a remote and tranquil part of the valley of the River Alun barely inland from the coast whose jagged terrain protected it from marauding pirates. A number of ecclesiastical buildings grew up in the shadow of the centerpiece cathedral. Dating back to 1860, the Choir School is one of the more recent, and is the site of today's Warpool Court Hotel, whose manicured lawns lead down to the Irish Sea. It is all part of the 250 miles of unspoiled coastline whose inlets, coves, and huddled bays make up the Pembrokeshire Coast National Park, one of three national parks that cover Wales's most scenic landscape and the only one in Britain to include its balmy coastline. Its 182 miles of marked serpentine footpaths provide excellent walks in the company of wildflowers and seabirds.

WHAT: site, hotel. **ST. DAVID'S:** 100 miles/161 km west of Cardiff. *Cost:* free admission to cathedral. **WARPOOL COURT HOTEL:**

Construction of the present cathedral began in 1181.

tel 44/1437-720-300, fax 44/1437-720-676; info@warpoolcourthotel.com; www.warpool courthotel.com. *Cost:* doubles from $230.

BEST TIMES: Mar 1 commemorates the death of St. David. The Pembrokeshire County Show is held for 3 days mid-Aug.

Magnificent Microcosm of History

DROMOLAND CASTLE

Newmarket-on-Fergus, Clare, Ireland

Splendid ancestral home to one of the few native Gaelic families of royal blood, Dromoland Castle was built in 1543 by the O'Briens, barons of Inchiquin, direct descendents of the High King Brian Boru, valiant leader of a victory over the Danes in 1014. Today the eighteenth Baron of Inchiquin still lives on the grounds (but with 370 acres, don't expect to see him in the breakfast room or during afternoon tea). Imposing from outside, inside this massive pile is surprisingly intimate—a scrapbook of Irish history where the exemplary service demanded by the O'Briens still prevails. The grand elegance of Dromoland is most evident in the theatrical setting of its high-ceilinged dining room. House specialties such as Dromoland Estate venison with fig chutney give new sophistication to local cuisine. One could conceivably never leave the grounds, if not for the enticing vicinity of the fabled Ballybunion Golf Course, 70 miles away, and Lalhinch, the "St. Andrew's of Ireland" only 35 miles away. Dromoland's own 18-hole golf course serves nicely as a backyard alternative, and an on-site luxury spa, horseback riding, and shooting will placate nongolfers. One must-do day trip is the half-hour drive to the nearby Cliffs of Moher, one of Ireland's most dramatically beautiful natural attractions. Rising majestically up out of the Atlantic 700 to 1,220 feet, these dark walls of moss-covered limestone stretch for 5 miles between Hag's Head and O'Brien's Tower.

WHAT: hotel, restaurant. **WHERE:** 8 miles/ 13 km from Shannon. Tel 353/61-368144, fax 353/61-363355; in the U.S., 800-346-7007; sales@dromoland.ie; www.dromoland.ie. **COST:** doubles $235 (low season), $425 (high season). Dinner $85. **BEST TIMES:** May–Oct.

A Tale of Two Castles

BLARNEY CASTLE AND BUNRATTY CASTLE

Blarney (Cork) and Bunratty (Clare), Ireland

Visit Ireland and not kiss the Blarney Stone? Not if you want to obtain that precious "gift of the gab" acknowledged by Irish poet and playwright Oscar Wilde when describing his own people as "a nation of great failures but the greatest talkers since the Greeks." Hordes of people come from the most distant corners of the world, clamber up the 127 steep steps of 550-year-old Blarney Castle, lie on their backs over a sheer drop of 120 feet (strong-armed "holders" guarantee there are no mishaps, but no one seems to consider the germ factor), and contort themselves into unflattering positions to kiss a rock believed to have made its way here in 1314 from Scotland. Others claim the oblong block of limestone dates back to the Crusades. Regardless, and for inexplicable reasons, the stone was always believed to have special powers and continues to exercise much fascination. Elizabeth I is said to have introduced the word *blarney* into the English language in the 16th century when the silver-tongued lord of Blarney Castle plied her with one too many unfulfilled honey-sweet promises. "Blarney! It's all blarney!" the perturbed queen was said to have remarked.

Ireland's other must-see castle is the country's most authentic (and also highly trafficked). Built alongside the O'Garney River and today surrounded by a huge theme park of a 19th-century Irish village, the current Bunratty Castle was built in the early 1400s, although earlier fortifications may have dated back to the 13th century at this strategic site. This great rectangular edifice with square towers is Ireland's most complete and most impressive medieval stronghold. Its centerpiece Great Hall is where the resident earl held court and received emissaries under the 48-foot ceilings.

Deep coffers have furnished the castle today with a magnificent collection of period furniture, paintings, sculpture, and tapestries. Torchlit medieval-style banquets offer those who leave skepticism back at the hotel a most enjoyably raucous evening of traditional Irish music and eat-with-your-hands meals, flowing claret, and mugs of mead at long communal tables.

WHAT: site. **BLARNEY CASTLE:** 5 miles/ 8 km northwest of Cork. For information tel 353/21-4385252; www.blarneycastle.ie. *Cost:* $14. **BUNRATTY CASTLE:** 5 miles/8 km east of Shannon airport. For reservations tel 353/61-360788, fax 353/61-361020; reservations@ shannondev.ie; www.shannonheritage.com. *Cost:* admission $22. Banquet $85. *When:* medieval banquets daily. **BEST TIMES:** May–Sept.

Blarney Castle was built in 1446.

Heavenly Music and Food

CORK JAZZ FESTIVAL

Cork, Ireland

Ireland's number two city hosts the country's number one jazz festival during a fall weekend before settling in for a winter's respite. Cork is the south's sporting, commercial, and brewing center: Guinness's two contenders, the well-loved dry stouts Murphy's and Beamish, are both produced in County Cork. But it is Guinness—what James Joyce called "the wine of Ireland"—that sponsors this major music fest. Beer plays a big role in keeping the beat alive, though one overshadowed by the power, quality, and diversity of the music in a country in love with its musical heritage. The big-time international names perform in the Opera House and a number of other theaters around town, but the pubs and street corners can offer up some of the festival's most inspiring, and spontaneous, performances by up-and-coming talents. Nearby Kinsale (18 miles/29 km southwest of Cork; see below) has recently taken up the torch as a smaller, more intimate venue with a jazz fest all its own.

WHAT: event. **WHERE:** Cork is 160 miles/257 km southwest of Dublin, 76 miles/ 122 km south of Shannon. jazz@equestcom. lol.ie, www.corkjazzfestival.com. **COST:** tickets from $25. **WHEN:** late Oct.

A Charming Seaport as Culinary Capital

KINSALE

Cork, Ireland

In yesterday's gastronomically challenged Ireland of corned beef and cabbage, seaside Kinsale's role as the country's culinary capital may have been taken as a comical oxymoron. But since the so-called Irish cooking revolution,

this beautiful yachting and fishing town on the Irish Sea and its impressive (and still growing) profusion of excellent restaurants large and small has drawn pampered palates from near and far. The increasingly popular Kinsale International Gourmet Food Festival might include everything from a cooking demonstration by the Housewife of the Year to oyster husking. Unofficial headquarters is the hopping, much-loved Blue Haven Hotel. Situated on the site of the Old Fish Market in the center of Kinsale, a superb dinner at the Blue Haven's top-notch seafood restaurant doesn't leave guests with much room for the next morning's renowned seven-course Irish breakfast—you'll be tempted nonetheless if you've had the foresight to check into the recently refurbished guest rooms next door. Despite its growing popularity, Kinsale is still a fine town for strolling. Its cobblestoned streets are lined with pastel-painted 18th-century homes and there's a harbor full of bobbing boats, but you can pub-hop straight to The Spaniard Inn for hilltop views, simple food, and foot-tapping Irish music.

WHAT: town, event, hotel, restaurant. **KINSALE:** 18 miles/29 km southwest of Cork. **BLUE HAVEN HOTEL:** 3 Pearse St. Tel 353/ 21-477-2209; www.bluehavenkinsale.com. *Cost:* doubles from $155. Dinner $55. **THE SPANIARD INN:** tel 353/21-772-436, fax 353/21-773-303. **BEST TIMES:** Oct for 4-day Gourmet Festival and Jazz Festival.

Swans at Kinsale's picturesque harbor

A Garden Above Most Gardens

POWERSCOURT HOUSE AND GARDENS

Enniskerry, County Wicklow, Ireland

I n this bucolic country aptly known as the "Garden of Ireland," Powerscourt is arguably its finest garden and widely considered to be one of the world's greatest. Nestled in the foothills of the Wicklow Mountains are 45 acres of a richly textured landscape of formal flower beds, sweeping Italianate terraces, statuary, ornamental lakes, delightful strolls, and more than 200 varieties of trees and shrubs. There is a dolphin pond, displaying its fine fountain, and a Japanese garden that invites one to stroll its series of concentric paths and over brightly painted bridges.

Once an important site to guard against the Anglo-Normans, today's Powerscourt manor is based on a 13th-century castle. It was magnificently rebuilt in the 18th century, and further alterations were undertaken over the centuries when the terraces were designed, thousands of trees were planted, and statuary ironwork and decorative items collected by the family were introduced. The estate contains the highest waterfall in Ireland at 398 feet set in a beautifully wooded deer park where the Powerscourt lords introduced the first herd of Japanese sika deer to Europe. The current owners, the Slazenger family, purchased the estate from the 9th viscount Powerscourt in 1961 and were behind the addition of the 36-hole Powerscourt golf resort, ranked one of the finest in Ireland.

WHAT: place. **WHERE**: near Enniskerry, 12 miles/19 km south of Dublin, www.powerscourt.ie, tel 353/1-204-6000, fax 353/1-204-6900; golf information tel 353/1-204-6033. **COST**: admission to house and garden $11. **WHEN**: daily, 9:30 A.M.–5:30 P.M. in summer. Gardens close at dusk in winter.

Every Day a Homegrown Feast

LONGUEVILLE HOUSE

Mallow, Cork, Ireland

S ome claim chef William O'Callaghan is the most important force working in the Irish kitchen today. How appropriate that he is given carte blanche at Longueville House, his family's ancestral Georgian mansion. On the family's 500-acre ancient farmland estate, the O'Callaghans have created a veritable garden of plenty. Longueville is unique in that almost everything is homegrown, raised and made here, including the lamb, vegetables, herbs, fruit, salmon, cheese—even chocolate. For the odd things that must be purchased, the chef needn't wander far down the road. Until recently, Longueville boasted Ireland's only vineyard, making its own limited production of a fine Riesling-like wine in this land enamored of beer and whiskies. The entire O'Callaghan family is on hand to oversee a highly professional operation: Longueville is both smooth and casual. The hotel's award-winning Presidents' Room restaurant is lined with the portraits of Ireland's past heads of state; those still alive show up in person when in the area. The finger bowl set will not be disappointed, nor will those looking for the exceptional weekend or special occasion. The O'Callaghans have called this splendid man-sion home since 1720. Before that their ancestors, the Ua Ceallachains, resided in the 16th-century castle whose crumbling ruins can be seen on the grounds, at the foot of a grassy hill near the banks of the Blackwater River, the Irish Rhine.

WHAT: hotel, restaurant. **WHERE:** 3 miles/ 5 km west of Mallow, 21 miles/34 km northwest of Cork, 53 miles/85 km south of Shannon. Tel 353/22-47156, in the U.S., 800-323-5463; info@longuevillehouse.ie; www.longueville house.ie. **COST:** doubles $160. Dinner $50. **WHEN:** hotel and restaurant open mid-Mar to mid-Nov. **BEST TIMES:** Apr–May, Sept–Oct.

The Best of Irish Country Life and Good Eating

BALLYMALOE HOUSE

Shanagarry, Cork, Ireland

A rambling 19th-century house built into the ruins of a medieval castle draped in wisteria, Ballymaloe is the password for "coziest inn in Ireland." Myrtle Allen has lived here since 1947, raising her six children and slowly building a reputation—first national and then international—as an inspired self-trained cook, cookbook author, and born hostess. Most kitchen ingredients (except for the signature fresh fish offerings direct from nearby Ballycotton Harbor) are from Allen's famous orchards, gardens, and 400-acre work-ing farm that surround the country house. The ancient gatehouse and stables have been converted into large, comfortable guest quarters (Mrs. Allen tries to book guests into rooms that suit them best).

In a nearby converted apple barn, Darina, her ebullient daughter-in-law (herself a well-known cookbook author and leading authority on Irish food) runs the country's first and most important cooking school (more than thirty courses are offered yearly, from one day to several weeks each). Ballymaloe ("place of honey" in Gaelic) owes its special conviviality to the enveloping welcome of the extended Allen clan and family-like staff who create an elegant, but very unhotel-like atmosphere, "divorced from snobbery" as Myrtle Allen would say while describ-ing her simple country-house cooking.

Ballymaloe sits among rolling farmlands only 2 miles from the coast.

WHAT: restaurant, hotel. **WHERE:** 20 miles/32 km east of Cork, 150 miles/262 km west of Dublin, 80 miles/129 km south of Shannon. Tel 353/21-465-2531, fax 353/21-465-2021; res@ballymaloe.ie; www.ballymaloe.com. **COST:** doubles $155. Dinner $100.

Majestic Wilderness in the Island's Northernmost Fringe

GLENVEAGH NATIONAL PARK

Donegal, Ireland

Rural, isolated, rugged, and always breathtaking, Donegal—Ireland's northernmost county—has a distinctive, top-o'-the-world feel. Its 230-plus miles of sea-torn, largely uninhabited coastline define the northwestern corner of Ireland that faces the open sea toward Iceland. Slieve League, the tallest sea cliffs in Europe, are its dramatic highlight. But like a microcosm of Ireland, it also includes heather-covered moors, peat bogs, and the island's steepest mountains. A corner of Ireland that the bus caravans of Waterford shoppers and Blarney-kissing tourists never allot the time to visit, independent Donegal still clings proudly to Gaelic, Ireland's native language (it is the largest area where it is still widely spoken), and ancient customs. Deep within the county, far from its distinctive coastline, is Glenveagh National Park, considered Ireland's most beautiful (the concept of national parks is still rather new to Ireland) and one of the country's most important natural attractions. The park itself is closed to traffic, but a jitney from the Visitors' Center provides drop-off service at Glenveagh Castle, built in the 19th century, whose important exotic gardens flourished under its American owner, who left it to the Irish nation in 1983. Beyond the 4 acres of cultivated gardens of flora brought from Chile and Tasmania, the Far East and the Himalayas, the park gradually reverts to a wild lonely loveliness that takes many visitors by surprise.

WHAT: site. **WHERE:** Donegal Town is 138 miles/140 km northwest of Dublin, 176 miles/283 km northeast of Shannon, 112 miles/180 km west of Belfast. Glenveagh National Park is a 45-minute drive northeast of Donegal Town. Tel 353/74-913-7072; www.heritageireland.ie. **COST:** admission to park free, castle $4. **WHEN:** park open daily, year-round. **BEST TIMES:** mid-May.

A Wandering Homage to James Joyce, Dubliner Extraordinaire

BLOOMSDAY

Dublin, Ireland

In 1922, at the age of forty, revered Irish novelist James Joyce published his masterwork, *Ulysses,* which details a single memorable day in the life of Leopold Bloom, Irishman, Jew, and modern Odysseus. Today the quirky citywide Bloomsday festival celebrates that one day—June 16, 1904—with wandering Joyceans following Bloom's every footstep and seeking to relive the sights, smells, and sounds of turn-of-the-century Dublin. With much of the city little changed since then, this is not such a stretch. Davy Byrnes, the famous "moral pub" mentioned in *Ulysses*, is a case in point, drawing writers and poets since 1873 and still going strong. Devout Joyce lovers from Dublin and abroad, often dressed in Edwardian garb of boater hats, waistcoats, long skirts and parasols, retrace Bloom's day by ordering Gorgonzola sandwiches, sipping (much) Burgundy wine and Guinness stout, and buying cakes of lemon soap. The James Joyce Center, focal point for the popular ten-day festival (but one of many organizations involved), offers an extensive roster of activities such as lectures, walking tours, readings, and reenactments of the best-known scenes from *Ulysses*. Located in a beautifully restored Georgian town house, the center's archives, exhibits, and reference library are open year-round. Erratically scheduled but worth checking out: the chance of accompanying Joyce's nephew on a walking tour of neighborhood sites in local "Joyce Country."

WHAT: event. **WHERE:** at different venues around town. Check with Tourist Office or James Joyce Center, 35 North Great George's St. Tel 353/1-878-8547, fax 353/1-878-8488; info@jamesjoyce.ie; www.jamesjoyce.ie. Davy Byrnes is at 21 Duke St. **COST:** admission to center; some events may cost separately. **WHEN:** 8–10 days surrounding Jun 16 every year.

The World's Most Beautiful Tome

THE BOOK OF KELLS

Dublin, Ireland

Ireland's oldest university, Trinity College, is home to the 9th-century illuminated Book of Kells. Founded in 1592, Trinity (familiarly known as TCD, Trinity College, Dublin) boasts an impressive roster of alumni that includes Jonathan Swift, Bram Stoker, Oscar Wilde, and Samuel Beckett. But its most important role today is as privileged custodian for this early medieval manuscript, the most important—and the most beautiful—work of art to survive from the early centuries of Celtic Christianity. Each page is magnificently decorated with elaborate patterns and mythical animals, influenced by the hand-wrought metalwork traditions of that period. The illumination is unlike any other in the intricacy, complexity, and variety that cover every one of its 680 pages, rebound in the 1950s into four separate volumes. Such fanciful illumination by the scribes and monks of the monastery of Kells was called "a work not of men, but of angels" by a 13th-century chronicler. The Book of Kells is housed in the ground-floor Colonnades area of the college's Old Library, built in 1712 and enlarged in the 19th century. It still suffers from lack of shelf space to accommodate the quarter of a million volumes stacked floor-to-lofty-ceiling. It is one of eight buildings on the 40-acre site that collectively hold more than 4 million volumes: Trinity College has received one copy of every Irish or British book published since 1801.

WHAT: site. **WHERE:** Trinity College, College Green. Tel 353/1-608-2320, fax 353/1-608-2690; www.tcd.ie. **COST:** admission $12. **WHEN:** open daily. **BEST TIMES:** Spring and fall to avoid summer lines.

To Your Health: Slainte!

PUBS AND
ST. PATRICK'S FESTIVAL

Dublin, Ireland

Traditional or newly cosmopolitan, Dublin's greatest asset has always been its people, and their gifts of music and gab. The most entertaining ticket in town is a visit to any of the city's 1,000-some pubs, where the thick oil-black "Dublin gargle" (Guinness) continues to be the national drink and music is almost always a by-product. Dubbed "poetry in a glass" and brewed in Dublin since 1769, the brew was once accompanied by advertising slogans such as "Guinness is good for you!" and still inspires a kind of reverence that has little to do with the bottled stuff found around the globe. To get the head just right, a good bartender will pull it from the tap a little at a time, over two or three minutes.

By the middle of the prosperous 18th century, Dublin could count 2,000 alehouses, 300 taverns, and 1,200 brandy stores. Who serves the best stout in today's Dublin, where Guinness accounts for seven out of every ten pints of beer consumed? Start with a creamy pint of what James Joyce called "the wine of Ireland" at the lantern-lit Brazen Head, known as the oldest pub in town. Born as a coaching inn in 1198 and licensed as a pub in 1661, it has added a few new rooms that might have less character than the original ones, but offer live music as compensation.

Doheny & Nesbitt, a mere 130 years old, is a handsome Victorian specimen of carved wood, etched glass, spit-and-polish pride, and "snugs"—small semi-partitioned nooks where women could be served in the old days. Few wind up their pub crawl with the same impression as the acerbic Yeats, taken by a friend against his will to a local bar: "I've seen a pub. Now would you kindly take me home." Poor Yeats would not have fared well during the annual March fanfare that fills the pubs and streets of Dublin in celebration of the world's most famous Irish icon.

No other figure, sacred or profane, living or dead, is associated as closely with Ireland as its venerated patron St. Patrick. Born in Scotland and brought to Ireland as a slave in

Doheny & Nesbitt dates back to the late 1800s.

A.D. 432 (and never proved to have actually rid Ireland of serpents, as folklore goes), he is beloved among both the Irish diaspora and the Irish of the Emerald Isle itself.

March 17 is dear to every heart in every town, but the home of the largest annual celebration is Dublin and its pubs. While a number of U.S. cities hold large parades that are treasured by the Irish-American (and Irish-for-the-day) community, foreign celebrations pale in comparison to Dublin's: it's a four-day festival that has experienced the same zeal of renewal that much of the city's arts and cultural scene has enjoyed within the last few years. The parade that proudly marches down O'Connell Street is still the holiday's grand centerpiece, with drill teams, floats, and delegations from around the world.

WHAT: restaurant, event. **BRAZEN HEAD:** 20 Lower Bridge St. **DOHENY & NESBITT:** 5 Lower Baggot St. **DUBLIN LITERARY PUB CRAWL:** 2 hours of entertainment by actors featuring 4 pubs. Tel 353/1-670-5602, fax 353/1-670-5603; colm@dublinpubcrawl.com; www.dublinpubcrawl.com. *Cost:* $17. **ST. PATRICK'S FESTIVAL:** for event information tel 353/1-676-3205, fax 353/1-676-3208; info@stpatricksday.ie; www.stpatricksday.ie. Free events planned at different venues around town. *When:* 4 days surrounding Mar 17 (usually Mar 16–19); parade on Mar 17, preceded by a smaller one on Mar 16. Skyfest, one of Europe's largest fireworks displays, is on the final night.

Classic Irish with a French Twist

RESTAURANT PATRICK GUILBAUD

Dublin, Ireland

Dublin has every reason to be proud of the French-owned and -run Restaurant Patrick Guilbaud: It is the country's most acclaimed restaurant and had much to do with launching the image of the Irish capital as something more than a pub-grub-only destination. Lavish, classy, and sophisticated, this is Dublin's stellar proof that it is evolving into a gastronomic presence to be reckoned with. At first glance, with its ebullient French owner, chef, and staff, the menu might appear of a Gallic bent. But using the best of the local bounty—Connemara lobster, Dublin Bay prawns, plump Bantry Bay scallops, salmon straight from local rivers, and venison from the outlying Wicklow mountains—the menu deftly combines an otherwise French cuisine with Irish underpinnings.

After spending his first ten years across town, restaurant owner Guilbaud has happily ensconced his Franco-Gaelic eatery in these new, airy, and elegant quarters on the ground floor of the luxury Merrion Hotel. Composed of four conjoined Georgian townhouses lavishly furnished in a period decor, the hotel also features lovely formal gardens of box hedges and fountains.

WHAT: restaurant, hotel. **RESTAURANT PATRICK GUILBAUD:** Upper Merrion St. Tel 353/1-676-4192; www.restaurantpatrickguilbaud.ie. *Cost:* dinner $125. *When:* open Tues–Sat. **MERRION HOTEL:** tel 353/1-603-0600, fax 353/1-603-0700; info@merrionhotel.com; www.merrionhotel.com. *Cost:* doubles from $670.

In a Class by Itself

THE SHELBOURNE

Dublin, Ireland

Just as the once sleepy Dublin continues its renaissance, so does its favorite old dowager hotel, the Shelbourne. Not that it was ever out of style, but showing off its new renovation, the massive reddish Victorian building stands stately once again on the north side of the city's landmark St. Stephen's Green (Europe's largest garden square). Built in 1824, it is the last survivor of Dublin's great 19th-century hotels. Steeped in tradition, the Shelbourne holds on to much of its historic grandeur—the Irish Constitution was drafted here in 1922—with public areas replete with chandeliers, glowing fireplaces, and fine art. The Lord Mayor's Lounge is a great spot for a sumptuous tea: like William Thackeray, who took to the deep armchairs overlooking the green, Dublin's elite gather here to nibble finger sandwiches, pastries, and scones with thick preserves and cream. The famous Horseshoe Bar is the only place to be for August's prestigious Horse Show Week, or any Friday night, for that matter. The Shelbourne speaks more of the Dublin of literary legend (think *Ulysses*) than of the new Dublin, morphing into one of Europe's trendiest capitals. And though it has for years been a destination for those of wealth and pedigree, it remains both welcoming and unstuffy.

WHAT: hotel, restaurant. **WHERE:** 27 St. Stephen's Green. Tel 353/1-663-4500, fax 353/1-661-6006; www.theshelbourne.ie. **COST:** doubles from $265 (low season), from $345 (high season). Tea in the Lord Mayor's Lounge $45.

Windswept Outposts of Gaelic Culture and Language

ARAN ISLANDS

Galway, Ireland

With an ever-dwindling population (now about 1,500), the trio of wind-blown Aran Islands off Ireland's western coast is a pocket-sized window onto the hardscrabble life of centuries past. "Three stepping stones out of Europe" wrote poet Seamus Heaney, describing the stark scenario. Pony-drawn carts still outnumber cars here and English is spoken only to the few visitors who come for the moody, heart-stopping beauty that can be interpreted either as starkly romantic or monotonously bleak. Against all odds, the islanders have made do with the harsh elements—most notably on Inishmore, the largest island, which is nearly devoid of vegetation. Immortalized a century ago by Dublin-born playwright J. M. Synge (who set his play *Riders to the Sea* here), the Aran Islands represent, in Synge's words, "Ireland at its most exotic, colorful, and traditional. The weather often keeps everybody, visitors and residents alike, locked away in the pubs" where the murmur of Irish Gaelic (once steadily vanishing—before a recent revival—save in isolated outposts such as this) and the telling of tall tales will linger on in one's memories long after the return to terra firma.

A visit to the haunting ruins of the 11-acre Dún Aengus, a 4,000-year-old megalithic cliff fort, is a highlight for those who want to be alone with their thoughts and the haunting cries of wheeling seagulls. The islands, long known for their heavy homespun and handmade knits ("Irish" sweaters are called "Aran" sweaters in Ireland; each family knitted a distinctive pattern so that if a family member drowned at sea, the body could be identified

by its sweater), are a place of idle hours and daylong bike rides. Robert Flaherty, the American director of poetic documentaries, made *Man from Aran* here in 1934; it is often shown on the island. The smaller islands, Inishmaan and Inisheer, promise almost complete isolation with but a handful of ancient fortresses, churches, rooms for rent, and a couple of simple museums to visit.

WHAT: island. **WHERE:** 30 miles/48 km off the coast of Galway City. **HOW:** 90-minute ferries from Doolin (County Clare), a growing center of traditional Irish music, and 10-minute flights (high season only) from Galway City. For ferries, tel 353/65-707-4455; doolinferries@ eircom.net; www.doolinferries.com. For flights, tel 353/91-593034, fax 353/91-593238; info@ aerarann.com; www.aerarann.com.

A Cozy, Romantic Hideaway
in the Rugged Beauty of Connemara

CASHEL HOUSE HOTEL

Cashel, Galway, Ireland

A trip through the singular beauty of Connemara comes to a perfect conclusion at Cashel House, a gracious country estate with its own handsomely stocked pony stud farm and stables. Idyllic paths meander

past the estate's award-winning gardens and through 50 stream-crossed acres of rolling hills, shaded woodland, even a small private beach. No sooner did owners Dermot and Kay McEvilly purchase the 19th-century country house in 1968 than it achieved fame as the vacation spot of choice of President and Madame de Gaulle. So enchanted were they by the grounds, the hospitality of the McEvillys, and the little-promoted wonders of Connemara's natural beauty that they proposed to retire in this western region of Ireland.

The conservatory-style dining room is the relaxed setting for sophisticated but

unpretentious meals showcasing the fresh bounty of Connemara's lakes, hills, and coastal waters. Choose from dozing in front of peat fires; an afternoon of tennis, biking, or boating; or the glory of getting lost in a good book, topped off with wonderful dining.

WHAT: hotel. **WHERE:** Cashel Bay is 42 miles/68 km northwest of Galway, 95 miles/ 153 km north of Shannon, 15 miles/24 km southeast of Clifden. Tel 353/95-31001, fax 353/95-31077; res@cashel-house-hotel.com; www.cashel-house-hotel.com. **COST:** doubles $260 (low season), $380 (high season). Dinner $80. **WHEN:** open year-round. **BEST TIMES:** Apr–Oct.

CONNEMARA

Galway, Ireland

Connemara is difficult to pinpoint: it is not a town or a valley, but a ruggedly poetic area of Galway, a part of Ireland known for its romantic landscape. Making up the western third of County Galway, Connemara was once part of the biggest private estate in Ireland. Wild, lonely, and for the most part uninhabited, its peat bogs and rocky coasts conjure up Yeats's vision of "a terrible beauty," and are a main reason why so many artists and poets are drawn to this country (and this county).

The immensely scenic Sky Road is one of Western Ireland's most delightful (and less-trafficked) drives, a steep and narrow one-lane corniche that twists and turns along the coastline to offer glimpses of the Twelve Bens, a dozen sharp—often mist-enshrouded—gray peaks, culminating at 2,388 feet. This is the untamed heart of the Connemara National Park, 3,800 acres of heaths, grasslands, and some of Ireland's best hiking trails. Herds of red deer and Connemara ponies, the only horse breed native to Ireland, can sometimes be glimpsed roaming the park.

Within sight of the Twelve Bens and near the entrance to the park is Rosleague Manor, a wonderful supplement to the Connemara experience. Owned and run by the brother-and-sister team of Paddy and Anne Foyle, the two-story Regency home draws anglers who come for the excellent salmon, trout, and sea fishing. Everyone else comes for the comfortable country-house living and Paddy's renowned dinners of seafood and homegrown vegetables that epitomize the spirit of Connemara.

WHAT: site, hotel. **CONNEMARA:** Clifden is the "capital" of the region, 50 miles/80 km northwest of Galway. National Park Visitor Centre, Letterfrack. Tel. 353/95-41054; www.heritageireland.ie. *Cost:* admission to park is free. *When:* park open Easter–Oct. **ROSLEAGUE MANOR:** 7 miles/10.5 km north of Clifden in Letterfrack. Tel 353/95-41101, fax 353/95-41168; rosleaguemanor@eircom.net; www.rosleague.com. *Cost:* doubles $210 (low season), $295 (high season). Dinner $65. *When:* hotel and restaurant open Easter–Oct. **BEST TIMES:** Arts Festival in Clifden, mid-Sept; Connemara Pony Show in Clifden, 3d Thurs in Aug.

GALWAY

Ireland

Poised at the very edge of Europe and in the heart of one of Ireland's most beautiful counties, the city of Galway is "the most Irish of all Irish cities." The ancient Gaelic love for language and music flourishes here in Ireland's

Moran's Oyster Cottage is almost 300 years old.

unofficial arts capital, one of the fastest-growing cities in Europe, its energy level kept vibrant by the local university. The city can seem to be one big festival, particularly in the summer, emphasizing the people's love for all things Irish. It is also the country's most musical town, so those who come for the famous Oyster Festival (which launches the September–April season of the Galway Bay oyster, *Ostrea edulis*) will find the pubs and streets filled with the lilt of the Irish fiddle. An "Oyster Pearl" beauty queen reigns over the festival, which has spawned similar events in the neighboring fishing villages of Clarenbridge and Kilcolgan (usually in early September). Many make the short trip to Kilcolgan just to experience a meal at Moran's Oyster Cottage on the Weir, legendary oyster headquarters. Willie Moran is the sixth generation of his family to run this venerable thatched cottage pub serving award-winning oysters from the Morans' own private oyster beds.

WHAT: town, event, restaurant. **GALWAY:** 60 miles/97 km north of Shannon. **MORAN'S OYSTER COTTAGE:** The Weir, Kilcolgan (10 miles/16 km southeast of Galway). Tel 353/91-796-113, fax 353/91-796-503; www.morans oystercottage.com. *Cost:* a dozen oysters, $25. **BEST TIMES:** Galway International Oyster Festival, 4 days in Sept; Galway Arts Festival late Jul; Galway Races, late Jul–early Aug.

How Green Is My Valley

DELPHI LODGE

Leenane, Galway, Ireland

There are return guests who swear that the Delphi Lodge is the best salmon and sea trout fishery in the West—it certainly is its most gorgeously situated. Standing alone by a lake amid glorious mountain country,

its isolated setting in the middle of an unspoiled valley backed by green velveteen hills is like few others in Ireland or Europe. Built as the sporting playground of the Marquis of Sligo in the 19th century, Delphi is today owned by

Take a picnic lunch and explore the hills.

congenial Peter Mantle, himself a keen fly-fisherman. The ambience is that of a relaxed country estate, where dinners take place at a large table generally overseen by Peter, who has a knack for making the guest mix seem always perfect, as if at a country house party. Although an angler's heaven, Delphi is not for seasoned fishermen alone—complete novices can take advantage of weekend courses that run five or six times a year, and many nonanglers come for the solitude and the chance to unwind, taking long walks or leisurely drives along the little-trammeled Connemara coastline.

WHAT: hotel. **WHERE:** 45 miles/72 km northwest of Galway, 90 miles/145 km north of Shannon. Tel 353/95-42222, fax 353/95-42296; delfish@iol.ie; www.delphilodge.ie.

COST: doubles from $281. Dinner $69. **WHEN:** closed Dec–Jan. **BEST TIMES:** spring salmon, Feb–May; grilse Jun–Jul; sea trout Aug–Sept.

Golf Heaven

BALLYBUNION GOLF CLUB

Ballybunion, Kerry, Ireland

Fom Dublin to Donegal, Ireland is blessed with more than 250 golf courses, a kind of North Carolina of the European golf scene. Possibly the most scenic and charming golf destination on earth (and host of the 2006 Ryder Cup Championship), Ireland allows idyllic castle hotels to serve as a base for a number of courses within an hour's radius, and a drive through countryside that can be as enjoyable as the time spent on the fabled links. If you want to start at the top of the greenest of the greens in the south, the celebrated Ballybunion Golf Club is most golfers' vacation of choice. Stretched along the blustery gray coastline of County Kerry and facing the Atlantic, the Old Course opened in 1893 on superb terrain. Its closing stretch is still considered among the most difficult anywhere in the world, a "true test of golf," to quote Tom Watson, five-time British Open champion. Many flock to the challenging Portmarnock Golf Club, 6 miles north of Dublin, long considered Ireland's premier golf club, but the tried-and-true links of the Southwest remain the busiest and most visited destinations for golfers coming for the first time to Ireland. In addition to Ballybunion's Old Course, there are the scenic Waterville Links, the picturesque Killarney, outstanding Tralee, and the famed Lahinch—the St. Andrew's of Ireland.

WHAT: experience. **BALLYBUNION GOLF CLUB:** Sandhill Rd., Ballybunion is 45 miles/86 km from Limerick, 67 miles/107 km southwest of Shannon. Tel 353/68-27146; info@ballybuniongolfclub.ie; www.ballybuniongolfclub.ie. **HOW:** Irish Links in the U.S. specializes in custom-designed golf tours to all of Ireland's champion links. Tel 800-824-6538; info@irish-links.com; www.irish-links.com. **COST:** costs vary. **WHEN:** Apr–Oct for visitors, Nov–Apr for members only. **BEST TIMES:** May–Sept.

Last Stop Before Brooklyn

DINGLE PENINSULA

Dingle, Kerry, Ireland

The westernmost point in Europe juts out fiercely and dramatically into the Atlantic; "next parish, America" as the saying goes. The lilt of Irish Gaelic is still heard here, and Celtic monuments to ancient Christianity

The dramatic shores of the Dingle Peninsula

still litter the rugged and spectacularly scenic coastline. The windswept Dingle Peninsula is 30 miles long and from 5 to 12 miles across, providing hikers, cyclists, and motorists with a vast and visually complex expanse of water and shore. From here you can see the seven Blasket Islands—evacuated in 1953 and uninhabited since, they once gave rise to a unique body of literature and today make for a mysterious, near-mystical destination when the sea is not too rough.

Dingle is the prettiest town in all of County Kerry, still reliving its moment when, in 1969, Robert Mitchum (and a sizable Hollywood contingent) arrived to film *Ryan's Daughter*. In the cheerily painted town is a collection of pottery shops, alternative bookstores, and the country's highest pub-per-person ratio, plus the family-run Doyle's Seafood Bar, famous the world over for its straightforward cooking based on lobster and fresh fish served with minimal ceremony. When Doyle's opened thirty years ago, John Doyle would go down to the small port every day to cull from the local fishermen's daily catch; now the fishermen come to Doyle's. New owners have changed little. Doyle's signature mille-feuille of warm oysters with Guinness sauce is still the draw, as is the selection of deliberately understated seafood that relies upon quality and freshness for its success. This homey bar/restaurant with flagstone floors and eight simple guest rooms in the town house next door has helped attract attention to Dingle as a culinary outpost—the other reason to visit this remarkable corner of Ireland, last stop before Brooklyn.

WHAT: site, town, restaurant, hotel. **DINGLE:** 45 miles/72 km northwest of Killarney, 95 miles/153 km southwest of Shannon. **DOYLE'S SEAFOOD BAR AND TOWNHOUSE:** 4 John Street. Tel 353/66-915-1174, www.doylesofdingle.com. *Cost:* Dinner $60. *When:* hotel and restaurant open mid-Feb to late Nov. *Note:* At press time, Doyle's was undergoing a change in ownership. Check before visiting.

A Dream Drive and a Victorian Beauty

THE RING OF KERRY AND THE PARK HOTEL KENMARE

Kenmare, Kerry, Ireland

If Ireland is one big scenic drive, then the famed Ring of Kerry is the portion most sought out for its singular beauty. Though a secret no longer, there are plenty of views to go around. Beginning and ending in Killarney, a breath-

taking succession of gray-blue land- and seascapes unfolds along what is less glamorously known as N70 and N71, a 110-mile coast-

hugging road that follows the dips and bumps of the Iveragh Peninsula, providing some of Ireland's most extravagant scenery. Make one little detour, and you are in unchartered terrain with nary a tour bus to be seen—only traffic jams of the four-legged kind. Offshore the craggy outlines of the mystic Skellig Islands are visible. The steep barren slopes of Skellig Michael are the site of monastic cells dating back to the 7th century; cruises will bring visitors in close, but landings are not permitted.

Avoid the high-season tour bus congestion of Killarney and use tiny, picturesque Kenmare as your base. This 19th-century market town is made all the more delightful by the presence of Packie's, a cozy bistro-style place whose menu is known far and wide for both the simple (Irish stew, rack of lamb) and the imaginative (gratin of crab and prawns or the daily blackboard special).

Later you can check into the Park Hotel

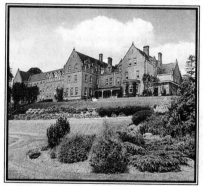

Park Hotel Kenmare overlooks terraced gardens.

Kenmare, one of Ireland's most exquisite country-house hotels. Built in 1897, the stern, gray stone house has become known for many things: its splendid eclectic collection of antiques, original paintings, and tapestries; a smiling no-task-is-too-small staff that perfects the irresistible combination of impeccable efficiency with Irish friendliness; a warm, welcoming atmosphere; a renowned restaurant serving Irish-Continental cuisine; and an adjoining 18-hole golf course with breathtaking views. The aforementioned gorgeous scenery has long made this corner of southwest Ireland one of the country's most alluring.

WHAT: experience, site, town, restaurant, hotel. **RING OF KERRY:** Killarney, often the starting point for the drive, is 84 miles/135 km southwest of Shannon, 192 miles/305 km southwest of Dublin. *Where to stay:* Shelburne Lodge, on the road to Cork. Tel 353/64-6641013, fax 353/64-6642135. *Cost:* doubles $140 (low season), $230 (high season). *When:* open Feb–mid-Dec. **KENMARE:** 20 miles/32 km from Killarney. **PACKIE'S:** Henry St. Tel 353/64-41508. *Cost:* dinner $50. *When:* open Mar–Oct, dinner, Tues–Sat. **PARK HOTEL KENMARE:** tel 353/64-6641200, fax 353/64-6641402; in the U.S., 800-525-4800; info@parkkenmare.com; www.parkkenmare.com. *Cost:* doubles $250 (low season), $295 (high season). Dinner $65. *When:* open mid-Apr–Nov; restaurant, lunch and dinner daily. **BEST TIMES:** May, Sept.

As Unique as Ireland Itself

SHEEN FALLS LODGE

Kenmare, Kerry, Ireland

For such a small, unassuming town, lovely Kenmare offers a very high standard of accommodations and eateries. One resort hotel that helped establish Kenmare's reputation is the graciously staffed Sheen Falls Lodge,

Sheen Falls was founded in the 18th century as a private fishing lodge.

cocooned within semitropical gardens and woodland walks beneath giant pine trees. Its breathtaking setting, at the head of Kenmare Bay, between the River Sheen and its cascading waterfalls, can be enjoyed from most of the spacious, beautifully appointed rooms—yet guests still spend most of their time out in nature's midst. The Gulf Stream warms the bay, accounting for the temperate climate and the profusion of ferns, palm trees, camellias, and fuchsia—is this Ireland? It's the kind of weather that encourages guests to take up the myriad amenities offered by the lodge,

including a 15-mile stretch of private salmon fishing on the River Sheen.

For those who venture beyond the lodge's 300 acres there are six championship golf courses within a 50-mile radius (including Waterville, regularly listed as one of Ireland's top five), or the lazy appeal of a motoring meander along the famously beautiful Beara Peninsula and Macgillycuddy's Reeks. But the day's climax is back at the lodge, seated at its wide-windowed La Cascade Restaurant overlooking the floodlit falls. Talented chef Philip Brazil oversees the all-Irish cuisine that has been repeatedly recognized for its use of ingredients from the immediate area. The end result is always exceptional, much like everything else at the Sheen Falls Lodge.

WHAT: hotel, restaurant. **WHERE:** 1 mile/ 2 km outside of Kenmare, 105 miles/168 km southwest of Shannon. Tel 353/64-41600, fax 353/64-6641386; in the U.S., 800-735-2478; info@sheenfallslodge.ie; www.sheenfalls lodge.ie. **COST:** doubles $440 (low season), $640 (high season). Dinner $91. **WHEN:** closed Jan; dinner daily. **BEST TIMES:** to avoid the crowds, Feb–Apr, Oct–Dec; Aug 15 for traditional local fair.

The Greenest Spot in a Very Green Country

KILLARNEY NATIONAL PARK

Kerry, Ireland

Perfectly situated as a base for the numerous drives, sites, and natural attractions this corner of County Kerry offers in spades, Killarney is as attractive for its village character as for the incredibly scenic hinterlands

that await beyond. Head on the road south for a visit to "the jewel of Killarney," Muckross House and its elegant lakeside gardens that burst with rhododendrons and azaleas in early summer. An ivy-covered Victorian mansion, built as a private home in 1843, it is now a handsome museum of County Kerry folklore

and history and serves as the entry point to the car-free 25,000-acre Killarney National Park, the county's centerpiece. Lakes, rivers, waterfalls, heather-covered valleys, woodlands, and the large variety of wildlife they support promise wonderful cycling, nature walks, and rides in two-wheel horse-drawn "jaunting cars," all of which can be arranged in Killarney. Large enough to let you escape sight of the other *Homo sapiens* who inundate the area in summer, the park possesses the grandeur of true wilderness, just minutes south of civilization. Here is found one of Ireland's most photographed panoramas, the Ladies' View (the ladies being Queen Victoria and her ladies-in-waiting) of Macgillycuddy's Reeks and across the lakes toward Killarney's other natural gem, the Gap of Dunloe, 9 miles west of town. Horseback tours can be arranged to explore the rugged glacial pass of craggy cliffs

and the rock-strewn gorge. The Gap's unoffical gateway is Kate Kearney's Cottage, a well-known former coach inn full of character and, on occasion, traditional Irish music.

WHAT: site, town. **KILLARNEY:** 84 miles/ 135 km southwest of Shannon, 192 miles/ 305 km southwest of Dublin. Tourist information office at Beech Rd., tel 353/64-6631633. **KILLARNEY NATIONAL PARK:** for information, tel 353/64-6635960; knpeducationcentre@eir com.net; http://homepage.eircom.net/~knp. **MUCKROSS HOUSE:** on N71, on the southern outskirts of Killarney. *Cost:* admission.

Golf and Riding in the Heart of Thoroughbred Country

HORSE COUNTRY AND MOUNT JULIET

Straffan (Kildare) and Thomastown (Kilkenny), Ireland

South of Dublin, counties Kildare and Kilkenny are home to many of Ireland's 300 stud farms, offering a poetic landscape of endless rolling green pastures. Think County Kildare and think thoroughbred, in particular

the Irish Stud Farm and the internationally famous Curragh Race Track (home of the Irish Derby the last week in June and often referred to as the Churchill Downs of Ireland). Some of the country's most famous horses have been born and raised on the impeccable grounds of the government-owned Irish Stud Farm, the standard for all other stud farms in the country, if not the world. Only in Ireland will you find such a passion for horses, a bond that can be traced back to ancient Celtic myths. On the farm's almost 1,000 acres are the delightfully surprising Japanese Gardens, laid out in 1910. Ireland's finest and arguably the most beautiful in Europe as well, they follow the soul's journey from oblivion to eternity. The same feeling of well-being can be found in the Kildare Hotel and Country Club, the "K Club." A 19th-century manor house is the hub

of this 330-acre deluxe sporting resort that looks every bit as gorgeous as the Irish Stud Farm, with miles of bridle trails for its own stable of beauties. But golf is the magic word here, as the K Club's 18-hole course is the only Arnold Palmer–designed golf course in Ireland and is consistently rated as one of the country's top twenty courses. The club is close enough to Dublin to lure day-trippers, but why not unwind in God's country for a few days and take up the club's private beats rich in salmon and trout?

Another luxurious horse-country and golf retreat is Mount Juliet; once the largest private estate in the country, its handsome, ivy-walled stone manor house was built by the Earl of Carrick more than 200 years ago. Its 1,500 acres include unspoiled woodland, pasture, formal gardens, and—the landmark for which it is acclaimed—a manicured 18-hole championship golf course designed by Jack Nicklaus. Dubbed the "Augusta of Europe," its world-class par-72 course has hosted the Irish Open three times. Indoors, cozy, handsomely appointed bedrooms with fireplaces and large windows overlook the rolling grounds that lead to the hotel's Ballyinch Stud Farm, where thoroughbreds graze idly in lush meadows. Riding stables provide mounts for forays on trails without end, private beats on the River Nore allow 4 miles of trout and salmon fishing, and spa facilities for the massage-inclined mean guests can indulge in everything or nothing at this premier sporting estate.

WHAT: site, hotel, experience. **IRISH STUD FARM:** in Tully, 30 miles/48 km west of Dublin. *Cost:* admission. *When:* open to public daily, mid-Feb to Dec. The Irish Derby is held at Curragh. Racing season is Mar–Oct. **KILDARE HOTEL AND COUNTRY CLUB:** 20 miles/32 km west of Dublin in Straffon. Tel 353/1-601-7200, fax 353/1-601-7299; www.kclub.ie. *Cost:* doubles from $345 (low season), from $485 (high season). **MOUNT JULIET:** 75 miles/121 km southeast of Dublin, 12 miles/19 km south of Kilkenny in Thomastown. Tel 353/56-73000, fax 353/56-73019; info@mountjuliet.ie; www.mountjuliet.ie. *Cost:* doubles from $220 (low season), from $500 (high season). Dinner $70. **BEST TIMES:** May–Oct.

A Castle Hotel in Ireland's Prettiest Village

ADARE MANOR

Adare, Limerick, Ireland

Adare Manor is an astonishing Gothic pile—with fifty-two chimneys, 365 leaded-glass windows, and turrets everywhere, it looks every bit the location for *The Hound of the Baskervilles.* Former home and

seat of the Earls of Dunraven, it is a self-contained 840-acre baronial haven for guests who relish being cosseted like descendants of royalty. Ushered into the present when it opened in 1988 as one of the country's most impressive castle hotels, it fulfills storybook standards with colossal halls, ornate fireplaces (seventy-five of them), enormous oil paintings of family ancestors, Waterford-crystal chandeliers, and grounds embellished with groomed box hedges and formal French parterre gardens. With a riverside location for vacationing anglers and an 18-hole golf course (including three lakes) designed by Robert Trent Jones Jr. in 1995, it is an outdoorsman's dream. Then there's the dining: stylish and sophisticated evenings in the oak-paneled dining room call for jacket and

Adare Manor's drawing room

tie and gourmand palates. Local produce, including many vegetables and herbs direct from the estate's gardens, create a culinary experience to match the setting. In the morning you can enjoy the ten-minute stroll from the wrought-iron front gates of the manse to the charming medieval town just beyond. Often called Ireland's prettiest village—certainly one of its most photographed—Adare's main street is lined with thatched-roof and Tudor-style houses, good restaurants and pubs, and a smattering of gift and craft shops.

WHAT: hotel, town. **ADARE:** 10 miles/ 16 km south of Limerick, 25 miles/40 km northwest of Shannon, 120 miles/193 km southwest of Dublin. **ADARE MANOR:** tel 353/61-605-200, fax 353/61-396-124; in the U.S., 800-GO-ADARE; adaremanor@aol.com; www.adaremanor.com. **COST:** doubles $335 (low season), $615 (high season). Dinner $95. **BEST TIMES:** spring–fall.

Checking In as a Guest of the Guinness Family

ASHFORD CASTLE

Cong, Mayo, Ireland

What is the fairest castle hotel of them all? "Hotel" is something of an understatement when applied to Ashford Castle, an imposing flight of fancy reflected in the waters of Lough Corrib, a 68-square-mile lake that is Ireland's second largest and its best for brown trout fishing. Think turrets, drawbridge, and battlements, then imagine this austere time capsule brimming with gracious service and appointed with canopied four-poster beds, cavernous armor-lined corridors, and crackling fireplaces in richly paneled drawing rooms. This is Ashford Castle's timeless magic. Dating from the 13th century, and serving as the private residence of the Guinness brewing family for nearly 100 years, world-famous Ashford Castle sits confidently on the short list of Ireland's dream hostelries. Traditional dining takes place in the elegant George V Room and the Connaught Room, both replete with vast windows, Waterford crystal engraved with Ashford's crest, and custom-made Wedgwood settings. Guests choosing to leave such plush trappings can stroll through some of the 350 wooded acres to reach Cong, a town that offers a cozy, intimate foil to Ashford's polished, grandiose image. The 1952 silver-screen classic *The Quiet Man*, directed by John Ford, was filmed in this sleepy hamlet and in the surrounding emerald countryside. Old-timers still talk about John Wayne (who plays an American boxer returning to his roots) and Maureen O'Hara (the local beauty he woos and weds), both guests of Ashford for ten weeks while filming, as if they left but yesterday. Westport, a half hour's drive away and often cited as everyone's favorite Irish town, is one of countless tempting excursions. It may someday grow up to be a proper city, but for centuries it has stayed small, picturesque, and friendly.

WHAT: town, hotel. **CONG:** 27 miles/ 43 km northwest of Galway City, 130 miles/ 209 km northwest of Dublin, 90 miles/145 km north of Shannon. **ASHFORD CASTLE:** tel 353/94-954-6003, fax 353/94-954-6260; in the U.S., 800-346-7007; ashford@ashford.ie; www.ashford.ie. **COST:** doubles from $160 (low season). Dinner $80. **BEST TIMES:** spring–fall.

Island Allure

WATERFORD CASTLE HOTEL AND GOLF CLUB

Ballinakill, Waterford, Ireland

Island-lovers looking to indulge in the Irish castle-turned-hotel fantasy have only one—remarkable—choice. Waterford Castle is situated on its own island: a spit of land in the River Suir, about 2 miles downstream from the crystal-famous southern Irish city of Waterford. Simply called The Island, its 300-acre spread is the castle hotel's private dominion. Amenities include boules, tennis, bicycle paths, and an 18-hole golf course designed by Irish pro Des Smyth, encouraging guests to leave mainland reality behind if only for a few days of other-worldly relaxation. And with just nineteen seignorial rooms and suites, guests share their lordly domain with only a handful of other castaways. Built on Norman foundations that date back some 800 years, the 18th-century castle comes complete with authentic turrets, gargoyles, and battlements. Pass through massive studded oak doors to the grand hallway where an enormous coat-of-arms has been woven into a circular carpet. Baronial sitting rooms and antiques-filled suites with soothing views over the grounds and water make guests feel very far indeed from the madding crowd.

The Island was most likely settled by monks in the 6th century.

WHAT: hotel. **WHERE:** 100 miles/161 km southwest of Dublin, 95 miles/153 km southeast of Shannon. Tel 353/51-878203, fax 353/51-879316; info@waterfordcastle.com; www.waterfordcastle.com. **COST:** doubles $260 (low season), $310 (high season). **BEST TIMES:** Mar–Aug.

Showcasing the Offbeat and Little Known

WEXFORD OPERA FESTIVAL

Wexford, Ireland

The best time to catch sleepy Wexford is in October, when the whole town turns out in full swing for its renowned Opera Festival. Wexford puffs up its chest with pride, as the over-fifty-year-old event grows in prestige and recognition, continuing to showcase lesser-known operas and sometimes world-class performers. Unsnobby, nonelitist, and often offbeat, it is the country's most important opera festival. Myriad other art exhibitions, concerts, and pub nights of traditional Irish music enthusiastically jump on board for the three-week period, creating a town-wide partygoing atmosphere.

Experience more of that spirit of both small-town pride and sophistication with a stay at County Wexford's most gracious and beautiful inn, the exquisite Regency-style Marlfield House. Set amid 36 acres of gardens and parkland that are as impeccably

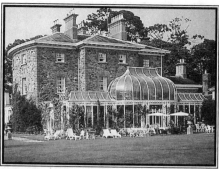

Marlfield House's kitchen gardens provide fresh herbs, vegetables, and fruit.

overseen as the inn itself, this 1820 seat of the Earls of Courtown (sold to the present owners in 1978) is an oasis of calm with its own lake and wild fowl reserve. Enjoy refined dining in the romantic, candlelit Victorian-style conservatory added by the current owners. Filled with plants, mirrors, and the aroma of delicately prepared seafood, an evening here makes for the perfect ending to a Wexford stay.

WHAT: event, hotel. **WHERE:** Wexford is 88 miles/142 km south of Dublin. **WEXFORD OPERA FESTIVAL:** The 19th-century Theatre Royal on High St. is the center of Opera Festival performances. Tel 353/53-912-2144, fax 353/53-912-4289; info@wexfordopera.com; www.wexfordopera.com. *Cost:* tickets from $16–$180. *When:* 3 weeks in Oct. **MARLFIELD HOUSE:** Courtown Rd., Gorey (half an hour north of Wexford, 90 minutes south of Dublin). Tel 353/55-21124, fax 353/55-21572; info@marlfieldhouse.ie; www.marlfieldhouse.com. *Cost:* doubles from $295. Dinner $95. *When:* closed mid-Dec–Jan; restaurant open daily for dinner. **BEST TIMES:** May–Sept.

An Emerald Isle Gem

TINAKILLY COUNTRY HOUSE

Rathnew, Wicklow, Ireland

I n a country known around the world for its verdant, coast-to-coast beauty, it says something that the Irish call Wicklow "the Garden of Ireland." The Wicklow Mountains, a major beauty spot, are located remarkably close

to the capital city. Hotel guests can be in downtown Dublin within forty-five minutes, though it will seem light-years away after they check into the Victorian Italianate Tinakilly House. This gracious 19th-century country manor was built for the captain of the *Great Eastern*, who laid the first successful transatlantic cable in 1866. His love for the sea is evident everywhere (the lobby's central staircase is a replica of the one on the captain's ship), and nautical memorabilia fill the public rooms and guest rooms, most of which are named after a famous ship. Adjacent to the tidal-lake Broadlough Bird Sanctuary,

The Great Entrance Hall promises a year-round log fire.

and surrounded by 7 acres of sylvan grounds, Tinakilly is serene, quiet, wonderfully romantic,

and offers an embarrassment of country pursuits (Wicklow offers twenty-three golf courses), though with a renowned and award-winning restaurant right on the grounds, one might be tempted just to live from one excellent meal to the next. Find a quiet view-filled corner, or an empty chair in front of the ever-burning fire in the great hall, and spend a few hours with a good book between epicurean feasts.

WHAT: hotel, restaurant. **WHERE:** 30 miles/ 48 km south of Dublin. Tel 353/404-69274, fax 353/404-67806; in the U.S., 800-525-4800; reservations@tinakilly.ie; www.tinakilly.ie. **COST:** doubles from $115. Dinner $50. **BEST TIMES:** hotel gardens best in spring, early summer, and fall.

Nature's Masterwork

GIANT'S CAUSEWAY

Bushmills, Antrim, Northern Ireland

"When the world was moulded and fashioned out of formless chaos," wrote William Thackeray, "this must have been the bit left over— a remnant of chaos." The scenery of Northern Ireland is its primary attraction, and few attractions are as notable as the grand, strange, and astonishing Giant's Causeway. Now under the attentive auspices of the National Trust, this honeycomb mass along the island's northern coast is made up of more than 40,000 volcanic basalt columns (each a foot or two across) created by volcanic eruptions some sixty million years ago. Things have changed considerably since early-17th-century travelers made the taxing trip to this wild edge of the island by horseback, with a stop for a tippling of the King's whiskey at Bushmills, the world's oldest distillery (licensed in 1608 but with historical references dating from 1276). The distillery is still there, but go easy on the amber elixir today if you want to hopscotch around the Causeway's tightly packed formations of mostly hexagonal pipes (some with four or five, others with as many as ten sides and reaching as high as 40 feet), or tool along the clifftop belvederes to marvel at the Causeway from afar. If modern-day

The stepping stones of the Giant's Causeway

visitors are struck with wonder at the sight, imagine the disbelief of the ancient Irish who attributed this geological wonder to the fabled giant Finn McCool. The legendary Ulster warrior of Irish myth was said to have created the Causeway as a bridge to his lady love on the Scottish island of Staffa.

WHAT: site. **GIANT'S CAUSEWAY:** 75 miles/ 120 km northwest of Belfast. Tel 44/28-207-31855, fax 44/28-207-32537; causewaytic@ hotmail.com; www.northantrim.com. **OLD BUSHMILLS DISTILLERY:** Main St., Bushmills. Tel 44/28-207-33218; www.bushmills.com. *Cost:* admission $6.

Spectacular Views and Daunting Challenge

ROYAL PORTRUSH

Portrush, Antrim, Northern Ireland

The only course in the country to have hosted the British Open Championship (1951), Royal Portrush is one of two distinguished golf courses in Northern Ireland that is consistently ranked in the world's top fifteen golf destinations.

It is the country's most spectacular and seductive and, together with its friendly rival Royal County Down in Newcastle (see entry below), it is considered one of the stiffest tests of just about every club in your bag.

One of three "Royal" courses in Northern Ireland, it was founded in 1888 and came under King Edward VII's patronage in 1893. Overlooking the fabled links are the romantic ruins of the 13th-century Dunluce Castle, the largest Norman castle in the North. Its colorful history includes the day in 1639 when its kitchen (and cooks) fell into the sea. Of Portrush's two 18-hole courses, Dunluce

Course gets the attention, ranking number three in the United Kingdom. Favorite holes are the fifth, "White Rocks," with its spectacular views of the sea and cliffs, and the aptly dubbed "Calamity Corner," one of the most daunting par-3s in the country.

WHAT: site, experience. **WHERE:** 64 miles/ 103 km north of Belfast (1 hour from Belfast International Airport). Tel 44/28-7082-2311, fax 44/28-7082-3139; info@royalportrush golfclub.com; www.royalportrushgolfclub.com. **WHEN:** open year-round to guests Mon, Tues, Thurs, and Sun all day; Wed and Fri mornings only; Sat after 3 P.M. **BEST TIMES:** May–Oct.

Wuthering Heights

MOURNE MOUNTAINS

Newcastle, Down, Northern Ireland

Made famous by the traditional Irish ballad in its lyrics, "Where the Mountains o' Mourne sweep down to the sea," this distinctive range of granite mountains is Northern Ireland's highest. In a county otherwise given over to gentle green countryside and associated with the later years of St. Patrick, the tightly packed Mournes are barely 7 miles across, with a dozen of the fifty-odd peaks (resembling "earth-covered potatoes," wrote C. S. Lewis) over 2,000 feet. This so-called Kingdom of Mourne is ringed by a road, with just one other that runs through it. A web of ancient footpaths through open moorland and upland pastures once used by smugglers and shepherds makes it a rambler's paradise. Head for the safe and relatively easy climb up the Mournes' highest peak, Slieve Donard (2,796 feet), where they say if the day is crystal-clear, you can see all the countries of the British Isles. The ascent begins near Bloody Bridge north of the lively seaside town of Newcastle. For gazing upon the Mournes and their wuthering beauty, the best accommodations can be found at the Slieve Donard Hotel, with hiking paths that start on the manicured grounds. Besides offering luxe rooms-with-a-view and classic Irish cuisine, the turreted, Victorian red-brick hotel is also the home base of choice for those who come from near and far to play the world-class links of the Royal County Down Golf Course, which is within walking distance.

WHAT: site, hotel experience. **SLIEVE DONARD:** Newcastle is 30 miles/48 km southwest of Belfast. **SLIEVE DONARD HOTEL:** Downs Rd., Newcastle. Tel 44/28-4372-1066, fax 44/28-4372-4830; res@sdh.hastingshotels.com; www.hastingshotels.com. *Cost:* doubles from $315. **ROYAL COUNTY DOWN GOLF COURSE:** borders the hotel grounds. tel 44/28-4372-3314; www.royalcountydown.org. **BEST TIMES:** May–Sept. Mournes Festival of music and dance, 1st week of Aug in many local towns.

WESTERN EUROPE

A Floating Arts Festival and Royal Hilltop Lodging

BREGENZ FESTIVAL

Austria

"If music be the food of love," wrote Shakespeare, "play on." The plays of Shakespeare and the music of Beethoven and Schubert are but a sampling of the dramatic and orchestral works that may be performed during the spectacular Bregenz Festival (Bregenzer Festspiele). The vast floating stage on the edge of Lake Constance (the Bodensee) is magical among the symphony of hills and starry nights.

For those who miss the one-month outdoor festival, the picturesque Lake Constance, which crosses the borders of Austria, Germany, and Switzerland, is the centerpiece of a resort area highly popular for fishing, boating, and hiking. The place to stay is the antique-filled 17th-century Hotel Deuring Schlössle, which sits high on a hill overlooking the lake and the charming city of Bregenz. The ivy-covered Baroque château in a park full of flowers offers just thirteen sumptuous rooms; the most requested is the octagonal tower suite with working fireplace. The hotel's restaurant has ranked among the country's top ten for years.

WHAT: town, event, hotel, restaurant. **BREGENZ:** 126 miles/200 km northwest of Innsbruck, 70 miles/110 km northeast of Zurich, Switzerland. **BREGENZ FESTIVAL:** tel 43/5574-4076, fax 43/5574-407400; ticket@bregenzerfestspiele.com; www.bregenzerfest spiele.com. *When:* late Jul–late Aug. **HOTEL**

DEURING SCHLÖSSLE: Ehre-Guta Platz. Tel 43/5574-47800, fax 43/5574-4780080; www. deuring-schlossle.at. *Cost:* doubles $305 (low season), $668 (high season); tower suite $530 (low season), $930 (high season). Dinner $70. **BEST TIMES:** Apr–mid-Oct.

Where Nature, Wine, and History Meet

DÜRNSTEIN AND THE MELK ABBEY

Austria

Wachau's exposure to the sun, and the beautiful, albeit not really blue, Danube that runs through the region make this one of Austria's most productive and scenic wine-growing areas. Fortified abbeys and castles crown the valley's rolling hills, on which steeply terraced vineyards alternate with forested slopes and orchards of apricot trees that bloom in late spring. The little walled town of Dürnstein—famous as the site where Richard the Lionhearted of England was imprisoned in 1192 following an altercation with Leopold V—is justly popular. For lovely accommodations, you needn't go any farther than the leafy terrace of the Schloss Dürnstein Hotel, featuring liltingly beautiful views of the river, excellent dining, and an attractive wine list. (Have a glass of the local läuner vetliner on the terrace.)

Dürnstein's hilltop Kuenringer Castle was destroyed and replaced in 1650; the ruins of the original structure can be reached by foot for some remarkable views of the surroundings, said to have inspired the tales of the magic kingdoms of the Brothers Grimm. Leave the charming castle grounds for a delightful side trip to Melk Abbey (Stift Melk), a recently renovated 1,000-year-old Benedictine monastery, filled with manuscripts and precious works of art, including the famous Melk crucifix. This particularly picturesque stretch of the Danube is a favorite for short boat cruises, a wonderful way to see the area.

WHAT: town, site, experience, hotel, restaurant. **DÜRNSTEIN:** 50 miles/80 km west of Vienna, 19 miles/30 km from Melk. **HOTEL SCHLOSS DÜRNSTEIN:** tel 43/2711-212, fax 43/2711-21230; hotel@schloss.at, www.schloss.at. *Cost:* doubles $275. Lunch $35. *When:* open Apr 1–Nov 5. **MELK:** 62 miles/100 km west of Vienna. *How:* cruises depart Krems (via Dürnstein and Spitz) to Melk daily. Contact DDSG Blue Danube Schiffahrt in Vienna. Tel 43/1-588-800, fax 43/1-588-80440; info@ddsg-blue-danube.at; www.ddsg-blue-danube.at. *Cost:* cruises between nearby Krems and Melk $27 one-way; Vienna to Dürnstein $29. *When:* mid-Apr–late Oct. Melk Summer Festival 1 week in late May. **BEST TIMES:** apricot trees usually blossom in early Apr. Grape harvest is usually mid–late Sept.

Schloss Dürnstein's terrace overlooks the Danube River.

A Well-Armed and Well-Preserved Old Town

Old Graz

Austria

Graz, the southeastern seat of the Hapsburgs as early as 1379, features one of Central Europe's best-preserved *Altstädte* (old towns). Just look around Graz and you'll see the ubiquitous motto "Austria rules the world" (A.E.I.O.U., or *Austriae est imperare orbi universo*) left behind by Friedrich III, King of Germany and Holy Roman Emperor, who resided here. The city boasts the empire's (and Europe's) largest armory: more than 30,000 pieces of every imaginable kind of armor and equipment used for war and jousting fill four floors of the 17th-century Landeszeughaus

Shining armor without knights in the Landeszeughaus Armory

Armory. The town's draw may be its magnificent architecture from the Middle Ages and the Renaissance, but the tone of Graz today is young and upbeat, thanks to three prominent universities (one offering the only faculty of jazz in all of Europe), the oldest founded in the 16th century. From spring until fall, a number of prestigious fairs and music festivals enliven the flagstone streets and squares, while students keep the atmospheric beer cellars, bars, and publike *beisls* buzzing. As capital of the agriculturally rich region of Styria, one of Graz's most enticing day trips is a meander out along any of the eight "wine roads" south of the city.

What: town. **Where:** 119 miles/190 km southeast of Vienna. **Landeszeughaus:** Herrengasse 16. Tel 43/316-8017-9810; fax 43/316-8017-9843. **Cost:** admission $10. **When:** open daily.

Alpine Driving at Its Most Beautiful

Grossglockner Road

Austria

Feast your eyes on the essence of alpine beauty and take the white-knuckle, breathtaking drive along Austria's lofty Grossglockner Road. Named after the country's highest peak and traversing some of Austria's most scenic regions, the road was an important trading route between Germany and Italy in the Middle Ages. The fantastic Grossglockner Road (now also Highway 107) was built between 1930 and

1935, and while most adventurers strike out today from Salzburg, the road actually begins farther south, in the heart of Hohe Tauern National Park. Almost 700 square miles in size, it boasts 300 mountains over 9,840 feet (3,000 meters), 246 glaciers, lush valleys, and dozens of pretty villages in which to seek a good meal and a simple overnight guesthouse. Spectacular vistas of the park's centerpiece, the towering Grossglockner, 12,460 feet tall, make it hard for drivers to keep their eyes on the hairpin turns. The 47-mile strip

Grossglockner from the Franz-Josephs-Höhe terrace

from Bruck to Heiligenblut is the most riveting, highlighted by the Edelweiss-Spitze and Franz-Josephs-Höhe, two awesome panoramic terraces at 8,500 feet and 7,800 feet respectively. Throw in the fantastic 6-mile sector called the "Road of the Glaciers" and you'll have an unforgettable journey.

WHAT: experience. **WHEN:** road open May–Nov. Lienz is a good jumping-off point from the south; Salzburg from the north.

To Ski or Après-Ski

LECH AND KITZBÜHEL

Austria

Some of the choicest downhill skiing (and après-ski) in the world can be found in the western reaches of the Austrian Alps. When other resorts go bare, Arlberg, a wonderfully picturesque niche well above the tree line,

ensures ample amounts of powder. The region encompasses Lech, its most charming village resort, as well as St. Anton, Zürs, St. Cristoph, and Stuben. In Lech-Zürs alone there are thirty-five lifts and cable cars serving a 65-mile ski circuit of groomed pistes and 75 miles of open, ungroomed runs, including the magnificent 12-mile Madloch tour. The home of modern ski technique, the revolutionary method named for Arlberg, is practiced today around the globe and the area's schools and instructors are among the world's best. Sharing Lech's indisputable air of exclusivity but lack of pretense is the village's smallest and best five-star hotel, the Gasthof Post. Run

by the gracious Moosbrugger clan for three generations, the former post house is known for its impeccable yet homey ambience and excellent restaurant.

Where Lech is sought out for its unspoiled character, Kitzbühel is beloved for its fashionable, glamorous atmosphere. The smoothed but mighty crags behind the medieval walled town provide mostly intermediate ski circuits (except for the difficult, world-famous Hahnenkamm downhill race), heart-stopping cable car rides, and 120 miles of awesome summertime hiking possibilities that set it apart from all those Kitzbühel wannabes. Those looking for a vibrant après-ski scene

An early photo of a ski instructor with his students at the bottom of the slope in Lech

will be drawn to the town's historic center of cobbled streets and pastel-painted medieval houses. There are trendy boutiques for shopping, lively casinos, and sophisticated clubs. Visitors can also relax with hot chocolate and pastries at the well-known Café Praxmair. Set high on the sunny side of the Kitzbüheler Horn is the elegant but friendly Tennerhof

Hotel, a quaint converted 17th-century farmhouse and a joy any time of the year. The eating is some of the best in town, so dine here even if you're lodging elsewhere.

WHAT: experience, town, hotel. **LECH:** 125 miles/201 km from Zurich. **GASTHOF POST:** tel 43/5583-22060, fax 43/5583-220623; info@postlech.com; www.postlech.com. *Cost:* doubles from $340 (low season), from $395 (high season), includes half board. *When:* open late Jun–late Sept, late Nov–late Apr. **KITZBÜHEL:** 55 miles/88 km southwest of Salzburg, 75 miles/121 km east of Innsbruck. **TENNERHOF HOTEL:** Griesenauweg 26. Tel 43/5356-63181, fax 43/5356-6318170; tennerhof@kitz.net; www.tennerhof.com. *Cost:* doubles from $330 (low season), from $380 (high season). *When:* open mid-Dec–Apr, late May–early Oct. **BEST TIMES:** Jan–early Feb for winter skiing; Mar for spring skiing; Jul–Aug for hiking.

Europe's Foremost Music Festival

SALZBURG FESTIVAL

Salzburg, Austria

Mozart's birthplace, and its glorious natural setting, is the appropriate venue for Europe's largest and most important annual musical event. More than 180 classic and contemporary performances, including operas, symphonies, major concerts, and recitals are scheduled around town—expect the banner events to be sold out well in advance (unless you're willing to pay your concierge top dollar for his scalper connections). It's easier to find tickets for the matinees—chamber music or church concerts, which can be no less enjoyable. During the festival—or indeed anytime you're craving luxury—stay at Salzburg's Hotel Schloss Mönchstein. This 14th-century turreted castle, built as the summer escape for the archbishops of Salzburg, sits atop a hill surrounded by gardens and 25 acres of parkland

and is a ten-minute elevator ride from the heart of Salzburg's historic center. Recently refur-

A scene from Mozart's Die Entführung aus dem Serail

bished, its parquet floors, Oriental rugs, leaded-glass windows, 18th-century furniture, and small chapel that dates back to at least 1500 convey the hotel's history; guests like Czar Alexander II of Russia and Mozart himself conducted many a dalliance here. But it's the modern amenities in the seventeen guest rooms that justify this theatrical setting's five-star hotel status. A stay in the Tower Suite will make you feel it deserves twice that.

WHAT: event, hotel. **SALZBURG FESTIVAL**

(**SALZBURGER FESTSPIELE**): Events held at various venues throughout Salzburg. Tel 43/662-8045500, fax 43/662-8045555. In the U.S., Global Tickets, tel 800-223-6108; www. salzburgfestival.at *Cost:* tickets $35–$410. *When:* 5 weeks, beginning last week of Jul. **HOTEL SCHLOSS MÖNCHSTEIN:** Mönchsberg Park. Tel 43/662-8485550, fax 43/662-848559; www.monchstein.at. In the U.S., tel 800-44UTELL. *Cost:* doubles from $390 (more during festival).

---

*"It stands at the far end of the Alps like
a grandiloquent watchman of history."*
—*JAN MORRIS*

VIENNA

Austria

The legacies of Beethoven, Freud, Klimt, and Mahler lure visitors to this gracious old-world city, the least frenetic yet one of the most compelling capitals of Europe. Famous for its *gemütlichkeit,* its trams, its cafés, and its pastry stores, it is a delightfully civilized and comfortable city and a timeless destination for art, music, and culture.

THE TOP TEN SIGHTS

A number of Vienna's top sights are at the HOFBURG (IMPERIAL HAPSBURG PALACE), the residence of the Hapsburg emperors until 1918. **WHERE:** tel 43/1-533-7570; www.hofburg-wien.at.

THE IMPERIAL APARTMENTS (KAISERAPPARTMENTS)—Emperor Franz-Josef I lived here in the late 19th and early 20th centuries. Visitors can see his opulent private rooms, the great audience hall, the court silverware and tableware room, and the dining rooms, richly decorated in rococo stucco work, tapestries, and Bohemian crystal chandeliers—Vienna at its most Viennese.

LIPIZZANER HORSES OF THE SPANISH RIDING SCHOOL—Founded in 1572, the Spanische Reitschule preserves classic dressage in its purest form, with presentations open to the public. Its horses were bred over the centuries from Spanish, Italian, and Arabian stock. **WHERE:** tel 43/1-533-9031; www.spanische-reitschule.com.

THE TREASURY (SCHATZKAMMER)— This superb collection includes the imperial crowns of the Holy Roman and Austrian empires and numerous treasures from the house of Burgundy and the Order of the Golden Fleece.

VIENNA BOYS' CHOIR AT THE HOFBURGKAPELLE—Linked with Vienna's musical life since 1498 and associated over the years with composers such as Mozart, Schubert, and Bruckner, the choir has performed internationally since 1926. **WHERE:** members of the choir perform Sunday Mass at the Imperial Chapel Jan–Jun and Sept–Dec. Reservations required: www.viennaticketoffice.com.

The Vienna Boys' Choir

ELSEWHERE IN VIENNA

ALBERTINA MUSEUM—Combining a 17th-century palace and a new fourteen-story building, the Albertina contains one of the world's largest collections of graphic art (from the Gothic to the contemporary), plus some 25,000 architectural drawings and a major new photography collection. **WHERE:** Albertinaplatz. Tel 43/1-534-830; www.albertina.at.

BELVEDERE PALACE (SCHLOSS BELVEDERE)—Actually two 18th-century palaces separated by landscaped gardens; the upper palace exhibits 19th- and 20th-century Viennese art (featuring works by Klimt), while the lower palace showcases the Gothic and Baroque. **WHERE:** Prinz-Eugen-Strasse. Tel 43/1-795-57-134; www.belvedere.at.

KUNSTHISTORISCHES MUSEUM—One of the richest fine-arts museums on the planet, with works from the ancient world and all over Europe, housed in palatial galleries. The Italian and Flemish collections are especially fine, as is the world's largest collection of paintings by Pieter Brueghel

the Elder. **WHERE:** Maria-Theresien-Pl. Tel 43/1-525-4031; www.khm.at.

ST. CHARLES CHURCH (KARLSKIRCHE)—One of Vienna's great buildings, the Karlskirche was built in the early 18th century. Its entrance is framed by huge freestanding columns, mates to Rome's Trajan's Column. There's a magnificent view from the roof. **WHERE:** Karlsplatz.

ST. STEPHEN'S CATHEDRAL (STEPHANSDOM)—Retaining its medieval atmosphere despite centuries of renovation and rebuilding, the Stephansdom dominates the city skyline with its towering Gothic spires. Inside, it's filled with monuments, sculptures, and paintings. Catacomb tours run regularly Mon–Sat. **WHERE:** Stephansplatz. Tel 43/1-515-52-3526; www.st.stephan.at (German only).

SCHLOSS SCHÖNBRUNN—Built by the Hapsburgs between 1696 and 1712, this 1,441-room palace (of which about 40 can be visited) is full of delicate rococo touches that set it in contrast to the starker Hofburg. Mozart performed here at age six for the Empress Maria Theresa, and Emperor Franz-Joseph was born here. The palace's park was opened to the public around 1779 and quickly became a popular recreational area, with a hedge maze, reproduction Roman ruins, botanical garden, and zoo. **WHERE:** Schönbrunner Schlossstrasse. Tel 43/1-81113-239; www.schoenbrunn.at.

OTHER MUST-DO'S

CHRISTMAS IN VIENNA—Vienna is Christmas: white with snow, adorned with traditional decorations, and beautifully noncommercial. There's midnight Mass at St. Stephen's, and at City Hall's huge Christkindlmarkt, hundreds of festive outdoor stands sell everything that smells and tastes of the holidays. "Silent Night" and other Viennese carols are sung by the Vienna Boys' Choir. Top it off with the extravagant New Year's Eve Kaiserball at the Hofburg.

THE MUSIKVEREIN—One of the greatest music halls in the world, built in the Baroque style in 1867, with nearly flawless acoustics. It's home to the Vienna Philharmonic, whose New Year's Eve Johann Strauss concert is broadcast around the world. The celebrated Vienna Mozart Concerts take place here and elsewhere in town, May–Oct. **WHERE:** Bösendorferstrasse. Tel 43/1-505-8190; www.musikverein-wien.at.

THE STAATSOPER (VIENNA STATE OPERA)— Built in 1887 as the imperial court opera, the green-domed opera house is one of the world's best, offering an incredibly long season (Sept–Jun) of mostly staples: Verdi, Mozart, and Strauss. **WHERE:** Opernring. Tel 43/1-514-44-2250; www.wiener-staatsoper.at.

WHERE TO STAY

THE PALAIS SCHWARZENBERG—Built in the early 18th century by an aristocratic family whose descendants still occupy about half of it and set on 18 bucolic acres in the heart of Vienna, it's more like a stately country home than an urban hotel. Despite ancestral portraits and other artworks (including Renoirs and Gobelins), public areas and rooms are inviting and unstuffy. The hotel's renowned restaurant has one of the most impressive settings (and chefs) in the city. **WHERE:** Schwarzenbergplatz. Tel 43/1-798-4515; www.palais-schwarzenberg. com. **COST:** high. **NOTE:** At press time, the Palais was closed for renovation.

THE KÖNIG VON UNGARN—Vienna's oldest hotel, tucked in the shadow of St. Stephen's cathedral and in operation since 1815. Simple and polished, with a lovely courtyard, it's a welcome respite from the city's opulence. **WHERE:** Schulerstrasse. Tel 43/1-515-840; www.kvu.at. **COST:** moderate.

EATING & DRINKING

DEMEL AND SACHER'S—Open since 1887, **Demel** is one of the reasons Vienna is known as Europe's pastry capital, setting up an Olympic-sized array of more than sixty pastries in its music-box-perfect front rooms. The five-layer chocolate Anna torte and the profoundly rich chocolate Sacher torte are house specialties. Sample the goods here and then trot over to the **Hotel Sacher**'s café to compare—both insist they have the original secret recipe, though Demel's usually wins out. Sacher's strudel, however ("mit Schlagobers"—with whipped cream), knows no rival. **WHERE:** *Demel:* Kohlmarkt. Tel 43/1-535-1717. *Sacher's:* Philharmonikerstrasse. Tel 43/1-514-560.

HAWELKA CAFÉ—Whole books have been written at and about this classic, unapologetically smoky café, the enduring prototype in the city that invented European café culture. Its superb coffee is dense, bitter, and fresh. **WHERE:** Dorotheergasse. Tel 43/1-512-8230; www.hawelka.com.

THE HEURIGER EXPERIENCE—At these alfresco wine taverns, sprinkled along the edge of the nearby Vienna Woods, large quantities of seemingly innocent wine are partially responsible for the atmosphere: alive with bonhomie, singing, and shameless Viennese accordion schmaltz. Beethoven lived at **Mayer am Pfarrplatz** in 1817; today it's a favorite Heuriger. **WHERE:** Heiligenstadt. Tel 43/1-370-3361; www.pfarrplatz.at.

STEIRERECK—Austria's finest restaurant and the birthplace of New Viennese Cuisine, served amid baronial trappings with elegance and flair. Find a table in the more intimate and romantic winter garden, a greenery-filled conservatory built against an outside wall. **WHERE:** Rasumofskygasse. Tel 43/1-718-0080.

ZU DEN DREI HUSAREN—Old Vienna's enduring monument to its school of haute cuisine. Tourists love it, but so do the locals, who know they can reliably find Viennese standards at candlelit tables in a plush romantic ambience of stag horns and tapestries. Sample Austria's finest labels from its enormous wine list. **WHERE:** Weihburggasse. Tel 43/1-512-1092.

Some Enchanted Evening

THE OPERA BALL AND HOTEL IMPERIAL

Vienna, Austria

Thousands of white-tied and elegant-gowned waltzers attend more than 300 formal balls with different themes that Vienna throws during the winter *Fasching* or carnival season. But the belle of all the balls is the legendary

Opera Ball. It is held in the Baroque Vienna State Opera House, minus the opera and its seats, which are removed by a beehive of workers who transform the ornate Staatsoper into a splendid, cavernous ballroom overnight. The *Opernball* opens with the grand entry of 200 graceful young debutantes (the daughters of rich and titled Austrian families), joined by 5,000 guests who come from all echelons of Viennese society and around the world to partake in the fairy-tale event first established by the Emperor Franz Josef in 1877. The dance floor becomes a kaleidoscope of color as dancers whirl to the sprightly strains of the Viennese waltz.

When three-quarter time winds down at 5 A.M., turn to the next page of the fairy tale by retiring to your room at the Hotel Imperial, Vienna's trophy hotel. Built in 1867 in the Renaissance style by Emperor Franz Josef for his niece and her husband, the Duke of Württemberg, it was used to house the duke's most distinguished guests and is still the official hotel for state visitors, just as when former guest Richard Wagner booked seven rooms and composed day and night. Many things remain unchanged, give or take a few multimillion-dollar renovations: priceless furnishings, marble floors, gilded balustrades, ceiling frescoes, glittering chandeliers. Guests will naturally feel as if they're being treated like Queen Elizabeth who uttered before leaving that it was "the most beautiful hotel we have ever stayed in."

WHAT: event, hotel. **VIENNA STATE OPERA:** Opernring 2. Opera Ball office, tel 43/1-514-44-2250, fax 43/1-514-44-2259; information@wiener-staatsoper.at; www.wiener-staatsoper.at. *Cost:* admission from $325. *When:* the Thurs before Ash Wed in Lent, traditionally mid-Feb or early Mar. **HOTEL IMPERIAL:** 16 Kärntner Ring. Tel 43/1-501-100, fax 43/1-50110-410; in the U.S., tel 800-325-3589; hotel.imperial@ luxurycollection.com; www.luxurycollection.com. *Cost:* doubles from $470.

First held in 1877, the Opernball *is little changed today.*

On the Rubens Trail

CATHEDRAL OF OUR LADY

Antwerp, Belgium

While Brussels and Bruges attract tourists, Antwerp carries on its business. If you bypass it, though, you will miss seeing what remains of the 16th- and 17th-century golden period, when Antwerp dominated the intellectual, commercial, and artistic life of the Low Countries. Antwerp's defining cultural landmark is the soaring 404-foot white stone lacework tower atop the Gothic Cathedral of Our Lady (Onze-Lieve-Vrouwekathedraal), with its famous carillon of forty-seven bells. In summer, Monday evening concerts at eight shouldn't be missed. The cathedral is the city's largest public building and the largest church in the Benelux countries with seven aisles and 125 pillars. Four masterworks by Peter Paul Rubens hang in the transept and in the choir, and are among the most emotional biblical scenes ever rendered. Although he was born in Germany, Rubens's parents were from Antwerp and the artist returned here as court painter and diplomat. Follow the Rubens trail by visiting the Koninklijk Museum voor Schone Kunsten (Royal Museum of Fine Arts), which holds one of the world's largest collections of his work. Then drop by the more intimate Rubenshuis (Rubens House Museum), a patrician mansion where the artist lived and worked from 1610 to 1640.

WHAT: town. **ANTWERP:** 32 miles/50 km north of Brussels. **CATHEDRAL OF OUR LADY:** Handschoenmarkt near Grote Markt. *Cost:* $3. **ROYAL MUSEUM OF FINE ARTS:** Leopold de Waelplaats 1–9. Tel 32/3-238-7809; www.kmska.be. *Cost:* admission $8. *When:* Tues–Sun. **RUBENS HOUSE:** Wapper 9. Tel 32/3-201-1555; info.rubenshuis@cs.antwerpen.be. *Cost:* admission $8. *When:* Tues–Sun.

Glories of Rubens in the Royal Museum of Fine Arts

The Seat of Flemish Painting Delicately Preserved

BRUGES

Belgium

Little disturbs the impression that the clock stopped in Bruges some centuries ago. The quaint city famed for the flowering of Flemish painting in the 15th century is ideally explored by open-top boats that slip past

Historical luxury at Die Swaene

gliding swans and through the meandering canals crossed by stone bridges (in Flemish, *brugge* means "bridges"), and you'll see why Bruges is called the "Venice of the North."

Stay at the romantic Die Swaene hotel (and restaurant) overlooking a canal, wander the tourist-free town at night, with many of its preserved gabled landmarks and canals

evocatively floodlit, and have the remarkable Memling Museum to yourself first thing in the morning. Within the 12th-century walls of the vast St. John's Hospice, there are six perfect paintings by the seminal Flemish master Hans Memling (c. 1430–1494), while other works by him and fellow Flemish artists make up the superb collection found at the city's other important museum, the Groeninge. In the Market Square, concerts are regularly played on the centuries-old carillon. Bruges can pack a lot of punch: the local Church of Our Lady (Onze-Lieve-Vrouwekerk) houses Michelangelo's *Madonna and Child.*

WHAT: town, hotel. **WHERE:** 55 miles/88 km northwest of Brussels, 57 miles/92 km west of Antwerp. **DIE SWAENE HOTEL:** Steenhouwersdijk 1. Tel 32/50-342798, fax 32/50-336674; info@dieswaene-hotel.com; www.dieswaene-hotel.com. *Cost:* doubles from $275. **BEST TIMES:** May's Procession of the Precious Blood on Ascension Day. Canal Festival, 1 week late Aug. Boats operate Mar–Nov. Sept generally has best weather.

Approaching Perfection—Just Like Home

COMME CHEZ SOI

Brussels, Belgium

The irony of the informal name chosen for this top-drawer restaurant ("Just Like Home") makes you wonder how master chef and owner Pierre Wynants dines at home, because dinner at his revered restaurant (if you've

remembered to book three months in advance) is an extraordinary event. The occasion is even more rarefied for those who manage to get a reservation for the table d'hôte in the kitchen, while all others repair to the bistro-size fifty-seat dining room whose Art Nouveau decor is an homage to the city's pioneer architect Victor Horta. Through-the-roof prices and polished service that impresses even the most discerning clients is

Pierre Wynants at Comme Chez Soi

daily fare here. Wynants's signature fillet of North Sea sole with a white wine mousseline of tiny shrimp approaches perfection.

WHAT: restaurant. **WHERE:** 23 Place Rouppe. Tel 32/2-512-2921, fax 32/2-511-8052; info@commechezsoi.be; www.comme chezsoi.be. *Cost:* dinner $205. **WHEN:** lunch and dinner, Tues–Sat. Closed Jul.

The Central Courtyard of the Continent's Capital

LA GRAND PLACE

Brussels, Belgium

Few great urban squares make the impact you'll find upon entering Brussel's gigantic one-of-a-kind Grand Place (Grote Markt). Louis XIV of France bombarded the entire city center in the 17th century, destroying more than 5,000 wooden buildings; what you see today is damage-turned-triumph. Most art historians agree with Jean Cocteau, who called it "a splendid stage." The ornate Baroque facades of the powerful (and competitive) guild houses and the Gothic Hôtel de Ville that dates to 1402, the only building to have survived the 1695 destruction, are the highlights. The heart of town since the 13th century, something's always going on: this is the incomparable setting for the Flower Carpet (Tapis de Fleurs), August 14 to 16 in even years only. The design each year is unique, a highly classified secret until the 700,000 begonias from the flower-growing district near Ghent are deposited to create an ephemeral carpet 80 by 250 feet. For a nominal fee, it can be viewed from the best vantage point: the second-floor balcony of the Town Hall. The square is equally captivating during the Ommegang pageant, the annual medieval pageant the first Tuesday and Thursday in July that reenacts a sumptuous 1549 procession honoring the Holy Roman Emperor Charles V.

In a building that once housed the butcher's guild, the renowned restaurant La Maison du Cygne is exquisite, with ancient wood paneling, gorgeous chandeliers, and original paintings by Pieter Brueghel the Younger and Arciboldo. The recently renovated Hotel Amigo, right behind the Town

Glorious flowers in the Grote Markt

Hall, is the hotel of choice for its Grand Place proximity and unerring old-world hospitality.

WHAT: site, restaurant, hotel. **RESTAURANT LA MAISON DU CYGNE:** 9 Grand Place. Tel 32/2-511-8244, fax 32/2-514-3148. *Cost:* dinner $90. **WHEN:** lunch and dinner Mon–Fri; Sat dinner only. **HOTEL AMIGO:** 1–3 Rue de l'Amigo. Tel 32/2-547-4747, fax 32/2-513-5277; hotelamigo@hotelamigo.com; www.rocco fortehotels.com. *Cost:* doubles from $900. **BEST TIMES:** bird market every Sun morning till 2 P.M.; flower market daily except Mon. Catch the kitschy but enjoyable Music and Light Show, just after nightfall, Apr–Sept.

Mussels and Fries, a National Passion

LÉON DE BRUXELLES

Brussels, Belgium

Belgium's excellent local *pommes frites* are not French fries at all—a grievous misnomer, as this universally known and loved side order is Belgian in origin. Although indulged at any time of day, smothered with

a healthy dollop of mayonnaise and wrapped in a cardboard cone, they are also the perfect compliment to Belgium's other much-heralded specialty, *moules* (mussels), a combination as beloved and ubiquitous as the American burger and fries. The well-known Léon de Bruxelles (until recently known as Chez Léon) is the quintessential mussels-and-fries joint. Having secured its fame over 100 years as it slowly expanded into a row of eight old houses and looking every bit the tourist trap, this venerable, old-fashioned restaurant is a warren of rooms filled with mussels-devouring Bruxellois. The *frites*—twice fried and light as a feather—

The best frites in town

have long been known as the best in town. The blue-shelled mussels are prepared fourteen different ways, although there are other regional specialties on the menu such as eel in green sauce (*anguilles au vert*) made with sorrel, chervil, and parsley.

WHAT: restaurant. **WHERE:** 18 Rue des Bouchers. Tel 32/2-511-1415, fax 32/2-514-0231. **COST:** dinner $35.

Seductive Sweets

MARY CHOCOLATIER

Brussels, Belgium

If Mary's handmade chocolates are the finest in a country that claims to make the world's best, does that make Mary's the best anywhere? One nibble and you'll join fourth-generation devotees, including the royal court, who think so.

With its blue velvet decor and Louis XVI furniture, this elegant shop looks like a refined jewelry store, and with royally rich bon-

Mary's bonbons are nonpareil.

bons beginning at $35 per kilogram we're in the same financial ballpark. All those artistic chocolate gems are made on the premises, including the famous Belgian pralines, seventy different kinds filled with everything from caramel to delicate liqueurs. It's enough to convert even the most chocolate resistant.

Heavenly Brews, Heavenly Digs

ABBAYE D'ORVAL

Orval, Belgium

In a country barely the size of New Jersey, the breadth of Belgium's beer-brewing tradition is astonishing—a rough count proclaims that hundreds of breweries produce 300 varieties within its borders, but more ambitious estimates approach 1,000. Many are local beers that are not found outside of Belgium, or of their towns of origin. Much has been made of the centuries-old tradition of unique, excellent ales and beers brewed by the Trappist monks: of the six Trappist breweries in the world, five are in Belgium (the sixth is over the border, in Holland). The breweries are generally not open to the public, but the monks' elixirs can be enjoyed at countless bars and taverns throughout Brussels and the countryside (and more and more frequently abroad).

In the forested hills of the Ardennes region (where the Battle of the Bulge was waged) is the famed Abbaye d'Orval. Its ruins date to the arrival of the Cistercians (from which the even stricter order of the Trappists broke off in the 17th century) in 1110; other buildings date to the 17th century. A community of monks carefully tend their beautiful grounds, medicinal herb garden, and dispensary, where the famous Orval beer is sold along with bread and cheese. Talk about heavenly picnics.

For the antithesis in accommodations, one of Belgium's top-ranked country restaurants and prettiest inns, the Auberge du Moulin Hideux, is just 16 miles away. Nestled in a beautiful setting of wooded hills that come right down to the converted stone gristmill, this rural inn is the very study of country chic. Miles of beautiful walking trails through leafy hardwood forests promise the chance to work off the meals that attract long-time loyalists who travel from Brussels, Paris, and beyond.

WHAT: site, hotel, restaurant. **ORVAL:** 100 miles/161 km south of Brussels. **ABBAYE D'ORVAL:** Villers-devant-Orval. Tel 32/61-311060. *Cost:* admission. **AUBERGE DU MOULIN HIDEUX:** Route du Moulin Hideux, Noir Fontaine, 16 miles/25 km from Orval. Tel 32/61-467015; info@moulinhideux.be; www.moulinhideux.be. *Cost:* doubles from $330. Dinner $95. *When:* open mid-Mar–Nov.

Monks have been brewing beer since the Middle Ages.

Queen of Resorts and the Resort of Kings

BIARRITZ

Aquitaine, France

Enamored of the town's wild beauty, Victor Hugo prayed in 1830 that Biarritz would "never become fashionable." His hopes were dashed when the newly married Napoleon III and his empress, Eugénie, arrived in 1855 and built the aristocratic pink-colored Villa Eugénie as a summer residence. Biarritz became a favored destination, and royal and noble travelers came to "take the waters" long after the imperial couple stopped visiting in 1870. They were later replaced by a more diverse group of artists, writers, and other glitterati. Still tinged with past glamour, Napoleon's villa now is the beautifully refurbished Hôtel du Palais, the focal and social point of this Atlantic-coast resort. Luckily for hotel guests today, Napoleon picked the choicest stretch of beachfront, La Grande Plage. Ask any of the young international surfing set, who first discovered the best waves in Europe along these same lovely beaches in the late 1950s and made Biarritz the unoffical surfing and windsurfing capital of the continent. The hotel's opulent, spacious guest rooms overlook the rugged coastline in this wild edge of the Basque country, where the mighty Pyrénées step into the Bay of Biscay. At the Palais, the delightful spirit of old Biarritz is much in evidence. Try your luck at the classic casino and enjoy the luxurious saltwater spa facility.

WHAT: town, hotel. **WHERE:** 118 miles/190 km southwest of Bordeaux, 20 miles/32 km from the Spanish border. **HÔTEL DU PALAIS:** 1 Avenue de l'Impératrice. Tel 33/5-59-41-64-00, fax 33/5-59-41-67-99; in the U.S., tel 800-223-6800; reception@hotel-du-palais.com; www.hotel-du-palais.com. *Cost:* garden-view doubles from $530 (low season), from $640 (high season); sea-view doubles from $710 (low season), from $815 (high season). **BEST TIMES:** May–late Oct.

An Ancient Corner of France Is Glorious Above and Below Ground

THE DORDOGNE AND THE CAVE OF LASCAUX

Aquitaine, France

Henry Miller called the lush green *département* of Dordogne a "country of enchantment." The walled market towns here—Domme, Brantôme, Sarlat, and Rocamadour—are some of France's most picturesque.

Hilly but not mountainous, the Dordogne is also perfect walking and biking country.

Deservedly associated with good food, such as duck and glorious foie gras, deep red Cahors wine, truffles, and wild cèpes mushrooms, this scenic corner of France is also rich with flower-strewn valleys, Romanesque churches, and medieval hamlets. Of the more than 1,500 châteaux, many are now hotels, often dramatically positioned along one of the tributaries flowing into the majestic Dordogne River.

This was some of the most fought-over land in Europe, but Dordogne's most significant history is truly ancient, as revealed underground in its painted caves. Discovered by four teenagers in 1940, the famous Cave of Lascaux (near Montignac) contains the world's most extraordinary repository of prehistoric wall paintings, executed by Stone Age artists some 17,000 years ago. Permanently closed to the general public in 1963 to prevent deterioration, it was re-created 200 yards away, in the form of Lascaux II. A dazzlingly accurate replica made in the 1980s by masters of the Beaux Arts in Paris, Lascaux II uses the same pigments that were available to Cro-Magnon man, and its limestone walls and 20-foot ceilings are covered with replicas of the original caves' stunning renderings of bison, horses, boars, and bulls. Arrive early—Lascaux II sells out.

This area of the Dordogne, a fertile river valley, is riddled with *grottes ornées,* some dating back nearly 25,000 years. The town of Les Eyzies-de-Tayac in the Vézère Valley is the perfect base for forays into the Valley of Man, one of the richest in the world in ancient sites and deposits. Don't miss the caves of Font-de-Gaume, whose Paleolithic artwork approaches that of Lascaux in importance.

WHAT: experience, site. **DORDOGNE:** as a base use Périgueux (the departmental capital), 79 miles/118.5 km northeast of Bordeaux. *How:* for biking and walking tours, contact Butterfield and Robinson in Canada, tel 866-511-9090, fax 416-915-8001; info@butterfield.com; www.butterfield.com. *Cost:* 8-day trips all-inclusive from $6,495. *When:* late May–Oct. *Best times:* May, Jun, Sept, and Oct. **LASCAUX:** 300 miles/480 km southwest of Paris near Montignac, 12 miles/19 km from Les Eyzies-de-Tayac (28 miles/45 km southeast of Périgueux). *How:* the original Lascaux Cave is virtually inaccessible: only 5 people may enter daily by special authorization. Exclusive tours, such as those offered periodically (usually once a year) by Discovery Tours, escort groups of 15 or less (with entry in groups of 5). Discovery Tours, a department of the American Museum of Natural History, tel 212-769-5700 or 800-462-8687, fax 212-769-5755; www.amnhexpeditions.org. *Cost:* 2-week trip including Spain's caves in Altamira, from $7,350, includes most meals, land transportation, guide. May departure. *Cost:* admission $7. *When:* open Feb–Dec.

The Pastoral Birthplace of Spa Cuisine

EUGÉNIE-LES-BAINS

Aquitaine, France

This tiny backwater village, whose thermal springs and pastoral setting enchanted the Empress Eugénie, after whom it was renamed, was ignored by time and tourism until the arrival of master chef Michel Guérard and

his wife, Christine. Guérard was the creator of every gourmand's pipe dream, *cuisine minceur* ("spa" cuisine, which helped spawn the nou-velle cuisine revolution of the 1970s, allowing diners to eat royally while staying trim). Those of the calories-to-the-wind school can opt for

A room at Couvent des Herbes, in Les Près d'Eugénie

Guérard's full-tilt *cuisine gourmande* menu. Either choice leaves visitors with unforgettable dining memories. The accommodations in this hamlet near Biarritz have a rustic but refined charm that's almost too good to be true. Eugénie-les-Bains consists almost entirely of the meticulously run Guérard fiefdom: two spas (the original operation plus the newer La Ferme Thermale), three hotels (one housed in the former imperial residence), and two restaurants (the complex as a whole is known as Les Près d'Eugénie). Many travelers come intending to use this drowsy hamlet as a base for exploring the beautiful Pyrénées and Basque region to the south or the Bordeaux area to the north, but they find it hard to leave the small town that once enchanted an empress and her coterie.

WHAT: town, restaurant, hotel. **EUGÉNIE-LES-BAINS:** 87 miles/140 km south of Bordeaux, 75 miles/121 km northeast of Biarritz. **LES PRÈS D'EUGÉNIE:** for reservations or information about any of the spas, hotels, or restaurants, tel 33/5-58-05-05-05, fax 33/5-58-51-10-10; in the U.S., tel 800-524-4800; guerard@relaischateaux.fr; www.michelguerard.com. *When:* open mid-Mar–early Dec. **BEST TIMES:** summer and autumn.

Basking in the Wine Culture of Bordeaux

St.-Emilion

Aquitaine, France

Bordeaux is an almost religious pilgrimage for oenophiles and gastronomes. At its heart is the refined city of Bordeaux, a wonderfully restored center of 18th-century architecture that serves as an elegant base for forays into vine-crossed districts with such revered names as Médoc, Graves, and Sauternes. There are more than 10,000 vineyards, but the lovely little medieval village of St.-Emilion lures one to linger. Sloping vineyards roll down to its 13th-century ramparts on all sides, enclosing cobbled medieval streets lined with wine stores and bakeries selling light-as-air macaroons. Châteaux Margaux and Mouton-Rothschild, and the *dégustation des vins* they offer, are day trips away in Médoc. But the small-parcel vineyards that fan out from St.-Emilion's town walls provide an intimate opportunity to sample some of

The Château Grand Barrail, admiring its own reflection

Bordeaux's most refined and complex red wines. The aristocratic 19th-century Château Grand Barrail estate has recently opened as a country hotel. Many of the spacious guest rooms overlook the endless vineyards, and the Belle Epoque restaurant's menu of regional specialties offers an impressive *carte des vins,* more than half from the cellars of St.-Emilion vintners.

WHAT: town, hotel, restaurant. **ST.-EMILION:** 22 miles/35 km northeast of

Bordeaux. **CHÂTEAU GRAND BARRAIL:** Route de Libourne, 14 miles/23 km northeast of Bordeaux; 1 mile/2 km from St.-Emilion. Tel 33/5-57-55-37-00, fax 33/5-57-55-37-49; in the U.S., tel 800-525-4800; hotelgrandbarrail @hotels-emeraude.com; www.grand-barrail. com. *Cost:* doubles from $410 (low season), from $450 (high season). Dinner $55. **BEST TIMES:** spring and fall except Sept harvest season, when the château vintners are closed to the public.

Art and Wine in a Glorious Setting

MUSÉE D'UNTERLINDEN AND THE WINE ROAD OF ALSACE

Colmar, Alsace, France

The serpentine ribbon of road that comprises Alsace's celebrated Route du Vin is studded with picturesque towns featuring glorious food and sites, many worth overnight stops. The attractive town of Colmar is home to the

popular Musée d'Unterlinden (Under the Linden Trees), housed in a 13th-century convent. The jewel in its remarkable collection is an immense altar screen with folding wing pieces. Considered one of the most exciting works in the history of German art, the Issenheim Altarpiece was created in 1512–16 by Würzburg-born Matthias Grünewald, "the most furious of realists." Grünewald's carved altarpiece was believed to have had miraculous powers to cure ergotism, a widespread disease of the Middle Ages. Entire books have been written about this masterwork, majestically displayed in the convent's Gothic chapel, and the museum's assemblage of religious art. Colmar itself is rich in medieval and Renaissance architecture and is the birthplace of Auge Bartholdi, designer of the Statue of Liberty.

The Route du Vin begins (or ends) south of Colmar and runs along the lush vineyard-covered slopes of the Vosges foothills. The

road zigzags and moseys along a string of post-card-perfect walled medieval towns of half-timbered houses with quirky roofs and balconies, overflowing with geraniums. Convivial *winstubs* (the Alsatian equivalent of pubs) serve wine from hundreds of local vineyards. Alsace's fine, fresh wines include Riesling, Sylvaner, Gewürztraminer, Muscat, and Tokay–Pinot Gris. Rich farmland and orchards attest to Alsace's reputation as "the pantry and larder of Europe," and the ambrosial pâté de foie gras—one of man's nobler creations and reason enough for the trip from Paris—is said to have originated here. Of the Wine Road's 100 or so gabled wine villages, Riquewihr and Kaysersberg share the prize for sheer quaintness, and fortified Turckheim is said to be the best-preserved town in France. To single out just one great inn is impossible, though a longtime favorite with Wine Road gastronomes and locals is the

Auberge de l'Ill, in an idyllic riverside setting. Another star is the Château d'Isenbourg, where the hotel's stellar Alsatian wine collection, stored in a vaulted 12th-century *cave*, complements a regional cuisine just as exceptional.

WHAT: town, site, experience, hotel, restaurant. **MUSÉE D'UNTERLINDEN:** Rue des Unterlinden, Colmar. Tel 33/3-89-20-15-50, fax 33/3-89-41-26-22; www.musee-unterlinden.com. *Cost:* admission $9. *When:* open daily

Château d'Isenbourg and surrounding vineyards

May–Oct; Wed–Mon, Nov–Apr. **WINE ROAD (ROUTE DU VIN):** runs from Marlenheim, west of Strasbourg, to Thann, south of Colmar: from 60–130 miles/97–209 km, depending on detours. *Best times:* the road is well traveled from Easter–Nov and especially crowded mid-Aug–Oct. **AUBERGE DE L'ILL:** Rue de Collonges, Illhaeusern (9 miles/14 km from Colmar). Tel 33/3-89-71-89-00, fax 33/3-89-71-82-83; auberge-de-l-ill@auberge-de-l-ill.com; www.auberge-de-l-ill.com. *Cost:* dinner $160. Doubles from $375. Hotel and restaurant closed 1st week of Jan. **CHÂTEAU D'ISENBOURG:** in Rouffach, 9 miles/14 km outside Colmar. Tel 33/3-89-78-58-50, fax 33/3-89-78-53-70; isenbourg@grandese tapes.fr; www.isenbourg.com. *Cost:* dinner $70. Doubles from $175. *When:* hotel and restaurant open mid-Mar–Jan. **BEST TIMES:** in Jul the Colmar International Music Festival brings classical musicians from around the world; wine harvest in Sept–Oct; Christmas markets in Dec.

A Triumph of Gothic Architecture Is a City's Crowning Glory

CATHÉDRALE NOTRE-DAME DE STRASBOURG

Strasbourg, Alsace, France

This ancient capital of Alsace is the modern-day headquarters of the Council of Europe and home of the European Parliament. There are those who associate Strasbourg with *choucroute* (an earthy, peasant-style dish made of sauerkraut, various sausages, bacon, pork, and potatoes), the hearty regional specialty, and those who think at once of its magnificent Gothic cathedral. The russet-colored sandstone structure, begun in the 12th century, is one of the largest buildings in the Christian world and one of the most architecturally harmonious Gothic structures to survive the Middle Ages. When completed in 1439, its 466-foot lacy openwork spire made it the tallest building in Christendom (it still ranks as the tallest dating from medieval times). Other showstoppers are the stained-glass windows, some dating back to the 12th century, and the 16th-century astronomical clock. Every day at precisely 12:31

P.M. it whirs into action as a parade of macabre allegorical figures enact Christ's Passion. Afterward, tourists make a beeline for the square's second-most-visited site in time for lunch: the richly carved Maison Kammerzell, a 16th-century merchant's house, is now a famous restaurant. Though it looks like a tourist trap, locals insist that its *choucroute à l'alsacienne* is *formidable*. Try any of the ten versions and cast your vote.

WHAT: town, site, restaurant. **STRASBOURG:** 306 miles/492 km east of Paris, 90 miles/145 km east of Nancy. **MAISON KAMMERZELL:** 16 Place de la Cathédrale. Tel 33/3-88-32-42-14, fax 33/3-88-23-03-92; info@maison-kammerzell.com; www.maison-kammerzell.com. *Cost:* 3-course *choucroute* dinner $55. **BEST TIMES:** Festival de Musique in Jun and Jul, some organ concerts are held in the cathedral; holiday market in the winter.

Doucement *by Barge and by Balloon*

BURGUNDY (BOURGOGNE)

France

Barging and ballooning in Burgundy give new meaning to the expression "living well is the best revenge." Both serene and leisurely modes of transportation guarantee the appropriate pace—*doucement*—to savor one

of France's most beautiful regions through the back door. Drift quietly along a centuries-old network of rivers and canals or let a lofty breeze waft your balloon over dozens of privately owned, forest-ringed castles that once housed the powerful dukes of Burgundy in the late Middle Ages. Glide over the world-class vineyards of Montrachet, Meursault, and Pommard in the heart of Burgundy's Côte d'Or, or "Golden Slope," which gives the world some of its finest red and dry white wines. This is the heart of viticultural Burgundy that stretches from Dijon to Santenay, whose celebrated vineyards provide idyllic days of wine tasting and châteaux touring. Colorful village markets offer fresh produce and delicious cheeses to accompany the humble *vin local*—which can assume the magic of a *premier cru* when enjoyed during earthbound *pique-niques* or special candlelight dinners in the vaulted chambers of a medieval château. Store up memories and insights into provincial life, with children who gleefully wave you on or a pasture full of

blasé Charolais cattle that barely acknowledge your passing.

Though its famous namesake chef died prematurely in 2003, Hôtel Bernard Loiseau (a.k.a. La Côte d'Or) still serves his daring *cuisine légère*, a healthy "light touch" cooking style that uses the very best of local produce and little or no cream or butter, and avoids the addition of extra flavors to basic combinations. The result—enhanced by any of the 20,000 bottles of wine in the restaurant's cellar—is sublime.

Enjoy the views from on high.

WHAT: site, experience, restaurant, hotel. **WHERE:** in the heart of Burgundy, midway between Paris (164 miles/264 km to the northwest) and Lyons (151 miles/243 km to the south). **BALLOON TRIPS:** Bombard Society in the U.S., tel 561-837-6610 or 800-862-8537, fax 561-837-6623; travel@bombardsociety.com; www.buddybombard.com. *Cost:* 4 nights/5 days from $8,940 per person (includes rapid TGV train from Paris to Dijon). *When:* late May–mid-Oct. **BARGE TRIPS:** Barge Lady in the U.S., tel 312-245-0900 or 800-880-0071, fax 312-245-0952; ellen@bargelady.com; www.bargelady.com. A choice of 6-night/7-day cruises from simple to luxury barges that can include all meals on board or many on land; ballooning trips are also offered. *Cost:* from $3,000 per person (includes rapid TGV train from Paris to Dijon), ballooning from $200 per person. *When:* Apr 15–Nov 1. **HÔTEL BERNARD LOISEAU:** 2 Rue Argentine, Saulieu. Tel 33/3-80-90-53-53, fax 33/3-80-64-08-92; in the U.S., tel 800-RELAIS-8; loiseau@relaischat eaux.fr; www.bernard-loiseau.com. *Cost:* lunch $140, dinner $210. Doubles from $205. *When:* lunch and dinner daily; closed Jan. **BEST TIMES:** May–Oct. May and Sept for ballooning; May, Jun, and Sept for barge trips.

A Showcase of Romanesque Architecture and Rural Hospitality

VÉZELAY AND L'ESPÉRANCE

Burgundy, France

Time takes a leap back to the Middle Ages in Vézelay, whose Basilica of Ste.-Madeleine attracted multitudes of pilgrims for centuries. Follow in their footsteps up the picturesque town's steep main street.

At its summit, the great Romanesque church has stood since the 11th century, when it was one of the focal points of Christendom. Relics of St. Mary Magdalene, Christianity's most beloved pardoned sinner, were credited with many miracles and drew an onslaught of devoted Christians, who stopped here on the way to Santiago de Compostela in northwestern Spain. After the relics were eventually declared false, Vézelay fell out of favor and the cathedral fell into ruins. It escaped demolition in 1840, was painstakingly restored, and is once again a showcase of Romanesque architecture, a masterpiece of light and space.

Located in the fertile heartland of one of the world's most prestigious wine-producing regions, Vézelay can be the perfect town from which to soak up Burgundy's magic if you have booked at the nearby 15th-century Château de Vault-de-Lugny. With just twelve sumptuous guest chambers and the personal attention of the warm owners, this is like staying at an old friend's dream château, replete with a 13th-century dungeon. Dinner is served by candlelight in the atmospheric old kitchen, or when weather permits, outdoors near the ancient moat and a family of preening peacocks. For a special off-site dinner, travel to St.-Père at the foot of Vézelay, birthplace of the world-lauded Marc Meneau, who modestly refers to himself as a "country chef." At L'Espérance, an old stone farmhouse with a glass-enclosed dining room, Meneau and his wife, Françoise, have combined an ambience of rural ease with world-class sophistication and a subtle menu of local game and produce.

WHAT: town, hotel, restaurant. **VÉZELAY:** 135 miles/217 km southeast of Paris.

Château de Vault-de-Lugny: 7.5 miles/ 12 km from Vézelay on the road to Avallon. Tel 33/3-86-34-07-86, fax 33/3-86-34-16-36; hotel@lugny.fr; www.lugny.fr. *Cost:* doubles from $250. *When:* open late Mar to mid-Nov. **L'Espérance:** in St.-Père-en-Vézelay, 1.5 miles/2 km from Vézelay. Tel 33/3-86-33-39-10; www.marc-meneau-esperance.com. *Cost:* dinner $135. Doubles from $215 (low season), from $435 (high season). **Best times:** spring; Jul 22 is the yearly Madelaine Pilgrimage; also delightful around wine harvest, Sept–Oct.

Drinking and Eating Stars

Champagne and Les Crayères

Reims, Champagne-Ardenne, France

om Pérignon, the local 17th-century Benedictine monk credited with the discovery of *la méthode champenoise,* is said to have exclaimed, "I am drinking stars!" after sampling the world's first bubbly. Sparkling wine can come from anywhere, but Champagne comes only from Champagne, a region of 68,000 vine-laden acres. The only large city in this hilly region is Reims, famous for the Cathédrale Notre Dame, where thirty-seven French kings were crowned and today most visited for its Chagall windows and richly sculpted, perfectly proportioned 13th-century facade.

Wine lovers soon head underground, to the chalky honeycomb of *caves,* or cellars, where patient *remuers* give millions of bottles of aging wine the requisite fraction of a turn each day (about 220 million bottles are produced annually). Of the 100-some Champagne houses, the most famous *grands marques* (Moët et Chandon, the largest producer; Taittinger; Seagrams-owned Mumm; Veuve Clicquot–Ponsardin; and Perrier-Jouët) offer guided tours and tastings that are instructive and fun. Pommery may be the most polished and impressive, with 11 miles of subterranean wine cellars. The spectacular galleries, carved out by the ancient Gallo-Romans, were used as hospitals, schools, and bomb shelters during the world wars.

While in Champagne you must save your budget and appetite for a meal at the world-famous Les Crayères (named after those centuries-old chalk pits where Champagne is aged). Leader of the restaurant renaissance in the region since his arrival in 1983, former Chef and owner Gerard Boyer with his wife, Elyane, founded and ran one of France's most special restaurant-hotel operations before his departure in 2004. The beautifully situated and landscaped, turn-of-the-century château is housed on the former estate of the Princess de Polignac (a Pommery ancestor). The acclaimed wine list, including more than 200 selections of bubbly, pays homage to Reims's

Pommery, the largest vineyard in the Champagne region

heritage. This is the stuff of special occasions, a fling with luxury, where ornate chandeliers suspended from the lofty ceilings magically light a setting befitting such lavish cooking. The elegantly appointed bedrooms—some with views of the spires of Reims's Gothic cathedral—are Les Crayères's ultimate luxury. They also mean "designated drivers" need not abstain.

WHAT: site, restaurant, hotel. **CHAMPAGNE:** the region begins 90 miles/145 km east of Paris, with Reims at the northernmost edge. To follow the Champagne Route, pick up a map in any local tourist office and look for signposted roads that mark the way. *When:* the Grandes Maisons de Champagne are open year-round for guided visits, although during the off-season they close 1 or 2 days weekly. The traditional time to visit Champagne is May–Oct. This area does not get as crowded during the summer months as other regions in France but is dismal in winter except on Jan 22, the Fête de St. Vincent, patron saint of wine growers. **LES CRAYÈRES:** 64 Boulevard Henry Vasnier, a few minutes outside Reims. Tel 33/3-26-24-90-00, fax 33/3-26-24-90-01; in the U.S., tel 800-RELAIS-8; www.gerard boyer.com. *Cost:* dinner $215. Doubles from $495. *When:* restaurant open Wed–Sun. **BEST TIMES:** harvest traditionally begins mid-Sept and lasts 2–3 weeks, but can change due to climatic influences.

A Hairpin Coastal Drive on Corsica, a Mountain in the Sea

LES CALANCHES

Ajaccio, Corsica, France

Except for its eastern coast's 200-mile stretch of white and gold sand beaches, Corsica resembles a mountain in the middle of the sea. The Greeks called it Kallisté, "the most beautiful." Les Calanches takes its name from the weathered granite pinnacles and phantasmagorical outcroppings whose colors shift from every shade of orange and pink to vermilion according to the day's light. With precipitous drops of up to 3,000 feet to the sparkling indigo sea below, their eroded formations were described by Guy de Maupassant as "a nightmarish menagerie petrified by the will of an extravagant god." Except for late July and August, when the island is inundated with European visitors, the roads remain blissfully uncrowded. Whether you take the narrow road that weaves through the Calanches archways or one that meanders deep into the empty, craggy interior, Corsica is a place of astonishing natural beauty. Its charm is evocative of the old Mediterranean, not French or even European in character. Hotels are small, individualistic, and rustic, except for the luxurious beachside Le Maquis, named for the thick underbrush of thyme, lavender, and sage that clothes the untamed interior like an aromatic mantle— giving Corsica its nickname, "the perfumed isle."

WHAT: island, site, hotel. **LES CALANCHES:** from Ajaccio, follow the coastal road north toward Calvi. Les Calanches begin 50 miles/ 80 km outside Ajaccio. **LE MAQUIS:** 11 miles/ 18 km south of Ajaccio in Porticcio. Tel 33/ 4-95-25-05-55, fax 33/4-95-25-11-70; in the U.S., tel 800-525-4800; info@lemaquis.com; www.lemaquis.com. *Cost:* doubles from $250 (low season), from $590 (high season). **BEST TIMES:** late spring, Sept, and Oct. Wildflowers carpet the island in Apr and May.

A Blooming Place of Pilgrimage for Art Lovers

GIVERNY

Haute-Normandie, France

Much of Claude Monet's love affair with natural light and color took place in this green-trimmed pink country house, where the artist lived and worked from 1883 to 1926. His greatest passion was his garden, and it has been meticulously re-created and planted to provide a glory of floral drama for the three seasons it is open to the public. Unlike formal French gardens, flowers and exuberant color spill over onto the gravel paths and hang from trellises like—well, a Monet canvas. It was here that Monet and his fellow Impressionists—Sisley, Cézanne, Pissarro, Manet, and Renoir—would set up their easels outdoors (in itself a radical act in the context of artistic tradition). The way they captured the changes in light and weather at different times of the day altered the course of 20th-century art. Even Monet did not grasp its inherent beauty right away. "It took me some time to understand my water lilies," he wrote. "And then, suddenly, I had the revelation of the magic of my pond. . . . Since then I have hardly had another model." Weekend crowds can be distracting here, but the famous water garden of lilies, Japanese bridges, and lithe willows still provides a contemplative escape.

WHAT: site. **WHERE:** 84 Rue Claude Monet (50 miles/80 km northwest of Paris). Tel 33/2-32-51-28-21, fax 33/2-32-51-54-18; contact@fondation-monet.com; www.fondation-monet.com. **COST:** admission $8. **WHEN:** open Apr–early Nov, Tues–Sun. **BEST TIMES:** each month has its own riot of color and blooms; water lilies appear end of Jun.

A Gothic Wonder Surrounded by Galloping Tides

MONT-SAINT-MICHEL

Basse-Normandie, France

Ranking among the wonders of the Western world, the fortified island-village of Mont-Saint-Michel is France's most-visited site, perched on a giant granite outcropping rising from a flat seabed. Its sheer audacity and engineering amaze those approaching it from the mile-long causeway (soon to be replaced by a bridge) that links it to the mainland. The perspective changes as one explores the narrow streets lined with souvenir and curio shops on this tiny island of 100 inhabitants. Much has been made of the dangerous "galloping" tides that can vary 50 feet between high and low tide. When the tide is out, 10 miles of sand are laid bare, leaving the Gothic and Romanesque abbey that sits 500 feet above sea level hauntingly isolated against a dramatic sky. Ramparts begun in the 13th century ring the mountain and the Benedictine abbey and gardens that mark the site where Michael the Archangel is said to have appeared in A.D. 708. In addition to the unique setting, what has drawn tourists over the centuries is the ensemble of 13th-century buildings within the abbey called La Merveille (The Marvel), a Gothic masterpiece. The islet's other masterpiece is La Mère Poulard's soufflé-like omelets, whose "secret recipe" has something to do with cooking in a copper skillet over an open oak fire. Since 1888, this restaurant/inn has been the best place to dine or spend the night. Here you can experience the silent magic of a near deserted Mont-Saint-Michel in the late evening hours.

WHAT: site, restaurant, hotel. **MONT-SAINT-MICHEL:** 200 miles/322 km west of Paris, 30 miles/48 km east of Saint-Malo. **LA MÈRE POULARD:** Grande Rue. Tel 33/2-33-89-68-68, fax 33/2-33-89-68-69; hotel@mere poulard.com; www.merepoulard.com. *Cost:* prix fixe menus begin at $50. Doubles from $275. **BEST TIMES:** spring and fall; dramatic and nearly empty in winter.

Where the Liberation of Europe Began

NORMANDY'S D-DAY BEACHES

Basse-Normandie, France

On June 6, 1944, the Allied Expeditionary Forces launched Operation Overlord, the largest military operation in history, and more than 5,000 ships and landing craft, 50,000 vehicles, and 11,000 planes set off across the English Channel's rough waters to begin an invasion that took the Nazis completely by surprise, and eventually led to their defeat. On beaches code-named Omaha, Utah, Gold, Juno, and Sword, the devastation cost the lives of some 4,900 Allied soldiers the first day alone, with the totals for the two-week invasion almost beyond imagination.

Time has erased most of the scars from this quiet 50-mile stretch of windswept coast, but many of the men remain, with 9,386 American soldiers buried under simple marble crosses and Stars of David at Colleville-sur-Mer's American Cemetery (on a cliff above Omaha Beach), and nearly 5,000 British, Canadian, Australian, and South African troops resting in the British Cemetery at Bayeux.

At Arromanches, concrete vestiges of the great prefabricated harbor known as Mulberry B (or "Port Winston"), designed to assist in landing Allied supplies, lie offshore. Several museums detail the D-Day invasion, the most important of them being the Musée du Débarquement (Normandy Landings Museum, close to Mulberry B), with its landing diorama, models, films, and photographs. About 30 miles to the south, the Caen Memorial is also moving and informative, with displays dedicated to the causes and consequences of WW II, and new exhibitions about the Cold War.

WHAT: site. **WHERE:** 170–185 miles/ 274–298 km northwest of Paris. **MUSÉE DU DÉBARQUEMENT:** Place du 6 Juin, Arromanches-les-Bains. Tel 33/2-31-22-34-31; www.normandy1944.com. **CAEN MEMORIAL:** Esplanade Dwight Eisenhower. Tel 33/2-31-060644; www.memorial-caen.fr. **HOW:** R. Crusoe & Son offers 8-night tours of Normandy visiting D-Day sites and museums. In the U.S., tel 800-585-8555 or 312-980-8000; www.rcrusoe.com. *Cost:* $6,490 per person, double occupancy, includes all transportation within France and most meals. *When:* May, Jun, Sept, and Oct.

*"'If one of us dies,' the husband told his wife,
'I shall move to Paris.'"—SIGMUND FREUD*

PARIS

Île de France, France

Paris nourishes the senses and feeds both intellect and soul. Tourists flock to its magnificent museums and exhibits, but the life of this culture-rich city revolves around its neighborhood cafés and bistros, where visitors can occasionally pull off the seemingly impossible feat of passing for Parisians. *Est-ce que c'est possible?* In the City of Light, the birthplace of romance and style, everything is magic, and anything can happen.

THE TOP TEN SIGHTS

ARC DE TRIOMPHE—The largest triumphal arch in the world (about 163 feet high and 147 wide) was erected by Napoleon in 1806 to commemorate his army's victories. Over the years it became the focal point for state funerals, and during WW II, both the invading Germans and the liberation of Paris parade passed beneath it. It's the site of France's Tomb of the Unknown Soldier, and it has an observation deck and exhibition hall at the top, with photos and lithographs depicting the arch's history. **WHERE:** Place Charles de Gaulle-Étoile, 8th arrondissement. Enter via the underground passage. www.monuments.fr.

BASILIQUE DU SACRÉ-COEUR—Planned as a votive offering to take France's mind off its loss in the Franco-Prussian War of 1870,

The names of major Revolutionary and Napoleonic victories are engraved on the Arc de Triomphe.

Sacré-Coeur was built between 1876 and 1914 in an ornate Romano-Byzantine style, after a design by Paul Abadie. Gleaming white and with a 273-foot central dome, the outside of the cathedral is almost confectionary. Inside is one of the world's largest mosaics, depicting Christ with outstretched arms. Owing to its hilltop location, the view from its dome is the second highest in Paris. **WHERE:** Place St.-Pierre, 18th arrondissement. Tel 33/1-53-41-89-00.

CENTRE GEORGES POMPIDOU—Looking like it were turned inside out so that all its brightly painted pipes and ductwork show, the bold Centre Pompidou opened in 1977 as a center for 20th- (and now 21st-) century art. Yes, its futurism is a bit dated today, but a late-'90s restoration freshened things quite a bit, adding 5,000 feet of exhibition space, improved dining options, and a number of new auditoriums for film screenings, music, and theater and dance performances. Attractions include the National Museum of Modern Art, with its 40,000-work collection (only about 850 are on display though). Outside, street performers are always doing their thing, and there's a great view of Paris from the rooftop. **WHERE:** Place Georges Pompidou, 4th arrondissement. Tel 33/1-44-78-12-33; www.centrepompidou.fr.

THE EIFFEL TOWER—Probably the most recognized structure in the world, the Eiffel Tower was built as a temporary, decorative centerpiece for the 1889 Universal Exhibition and was only saved from demolition because, as the tallest structure in Europe (at the time), it was useful as a radio tower. Today, of course, it's the very symbol of Paris, 1,056 feet high and providing a 40-mile view from its observation platforms. Two restaurants— Altitude 95 and Le Jules Verne—are located on the first and second levels, respectively. **WHERE:** Champ de Mars, 7th arrondissement. Tel 33/1-44-11-23-23; www.tour-eiffel.fr.

HÔTEL DES INVALIDES/NAPOLEON'S TOMB—Designed originally as a residence for disabled and aged French soldiers, the hotel eventually housed some 4,000 residents, who lived according to military and religious rules and worked in various manufacturing shops. Upon its completion, the structure boasted a huge martial building erected around a large courtyard as well as a church, whose gilded dome was designed by Jules Hardouin Mansart. During the French Revolution, a mob seized enough arms from the Invalides armory to storm the Bastille. In 1840, the body of Napoleon was laid to rest here after being buried first on St. Helena. In addition to the tomb, visitors today can see the Musée de l'Armée, full of weapons, uniforms, and equipment, and the Musée des Plans-Reliefs, with scale models of various French towns and monuments. **WHERE:** Place des Invalides, 7th arrondissement. Tel 33/1-44-42-37-72.

THE LOUVRE—This is the big one: once the largest palace in the world and now the largest art museum. Home of the *Mona Lisa* and the poor, armless *Venus de Milo*; home of I. M. Pei's controversial pyramid; and home, all told, of some 400,000 works of art—some 35,000 of which are on permanent display. Stretching for almost half a mile along the banks of the Seine, the palace began as a medieval fortress and was expanded over the centuries into a luxurious royal residence. The palace was designated a museum immediately after the revolution, and its collection was significantly expanded by Napoleon. Today the collections are divided into seven departments: Egyptian antiquities; Asian and Islamic antiquities and art; Greek, Etruscan, and Roman antiquities; sculpture; painting; prints and drawings; and objets d'art. Guided tours are available in English. **WHERE:** Quai du Louvre, 1st arrondissement. Tel. 33/1-40-20-53-17; www.louvre.fr.

MUSÉE DE CLUNY—Built in the 15th century as a residence, the mansion was seized during the revolution and later rented to Alexandre du Sommerard, who filled it with his collection of medieval artworks. Upon his death in 1842, the Gothic building was bought back by the government, along with its collection of tapestries, statues, medieval crosses and chalices, jewelry, coins, manuscripts, and more. The site also contains the ruins of second-century Roman baths. **WHERE:** Place Paul-Painlevé, 5th arrondissement. Tel 33/1-53-73-78-00; www.musee-moyenage.fr.

MUSÉE D'ORSAY—Carved from the neoclassical Gare d'Orsay railroad station, the Musée d'Orsay exhibits works from the years 1848 to 1914, a period that saw the rise of Impressionism, Symbolism, pointillism, realism, the Fauvists, and the late Romantics. Works on display in the arching, glass-roofed building include Daumier, Ingres, Delacroix, Manet, Monet, Courbet, Cézanne, van Gogh, Renoir, Whistler, and Matisse. Also on display are furniture, architectural models, photographs, and objets d'art. **WHERE:** Rue de Bellechasse, 7th arrondissement. Tel 33/ 1-40-49-48-14; www.musee-orsay.fr.

MUSÉE PICASSO—With 203 paintings, 191 sculptures, 85 ceramics, and more than 3,000 drawings, engravings, and manuscripts, the Picasso represents the greatest single collection of the artist's work in the world. Occupying the 17-century Hôtel Salé, the museum's collection also includes works by Cézanne and Matisse. **WHERE:** Rue de Thorigny, 3rd arrondissement. Tel 33/1-42-71-25-21; www.musee-picasso.fr.

NOTRE DAME—The Cathedral of Notre Dame—a "symphony of stone," according to Victor Hugo—is the historic and geographic heart of Paris. Its foundation stone was laid by Pope Alexander III in 1163, and construction was completed roughly two centuries later. A 387-step hike to the top of the south tower promises close-ups of the bestiary of gargoyles and a magnificent 360-degree view of one of the world's great cities beyond. **WHERE:** Place du Parvis Notre-Dame, 4th arrondissement. Tel. 33/1-42-34-56-10; www.notredameparis.fr.

OTHER MUST-DO'S

BASTILLE DAY (JULY 14)—On Bastille Day, French patriotism and passion for their history and heritage reaches fever pitch, commemorating the day the revolutionary mob stormed the Bastille. Numerous events across town culminate with a grand parade down the beautiful Champs-Elysées and fireworks over the Eiffel Tower.

A BATEAUX-MOUCHE CRUISE ON THE SEINE— Bateaux-mouches are to Paris what gondolas are to Venice—a wonderfully touristy way to see the city from a different perspective. These glass-enclosed boats ply the waters of the Seine and slip underneath its famous bridges to give you a glimpse of life along the quais of the refined Right Bank and the storied Left. **WHERE:** departures from the Right Bank, next to Pont de l'Alma. Tel 33/1-42-25-96-10; www.bateaux-mouches.fr.

AU LAPIN AGILE—Paris's oldest bar-cabaret and a Montmarte landmark, Au Lapin Agile was immortalized by Toulouse-Lautrec and Utrillo. A glimpse of Paris past, it has been the heartbeat of French folk music for decades, with lively singalongs that warm up after the tourists leave. As authentic as the cabaret

experience can be. **WHERE:** Rue des Saules, 18th arrondissement. Tel 33/1-46-06-85-87; www.au-lapin-agile.com.

ÎLE ST.-LOUIS—A small, romantic island in the middle of the Seine, featuring many 16th- to 18th-century mansions. Since the 17th century it's been largely residential, and exclusive. Search out Berthillon (Rue St.-Louis en l'Île, tel 33/1-43-54-31-61) for its well-known ice cream. **WHERE:** across from Notre Dame on the Pont St. Louis, 4th arrondissement.

JARDINS DES TUILERIES—Designed in 1664 by André Le Nôtre, planner of the grounds at Versailles, the Tuileries gardens form Paris's loveliest promenade, dotted with statues and fountains. **WHERE:** between the Place de la Concorde and the Louvre, 1st arrondissement.

MARCHÉ AUX PUCES DE CLIGNANCOURT— A must for every flea-market lover, with thousands of vendors selling everything under the sun, including one-of-a-kind finds for early birds with sharp eyes. One of the largest in Europe, held daily, and yes, that might be that famous American designer you see sleuthing around. **WHERE:** Avenue de la Porte de Clignancourt, 18th arrondissement.

MARMOTTAN MONET MUSEUM—Boasts more than 130 works from all stages of Claude Monet's creative life, as well as more than 300 Impressionist and Postimpressionist paintings, pastels, watercolors, and sculptures by Gauguin, Degas, Manet, Pissaro, Renoir, Rodin, and others; collections of illuminated manuscript pages and First Empire furniture and objets d'art; and works by German, Flemish, and Italian primitive painters. **WHERE:** Rue Louis-Boilly, 16th arrondissement. Tel 33/1-44-96-50-33; www.marmottan.com.

OPÉRA GARNIER—This rococo wonder, with one of the largest stages in existence, was completed in 1875, with a delightful ceiling added in 1964 by Marc Chagall. A serious recent renovation added air-conditioning, polished up the gilded statues and busts, and replaced the red damask.

Lavish performances put on here by the National Opera, the Paris Ballet, and others promise the ultimate night on the town. **WHERE:** Place de l'Opéra, 9th arrondissement. Tel 33/1-71-25-24-23; www.opera-de-paris.fr.

PLACE DES VOSGES—The small rose-brick Place des Vosges is the city's oldest and most beautiful square, planned by Henri IV in the early 17th century and entirely surrounded by arcades. Victor Hugo lived here, at no. 6. **WHERE:** the old Jewish quarter of the Marais, 4th arrondissement. Tel 33/1-42-72-60-46.

STE.-CHAPELLE—The walls of this small chapel, one of the supreme achievements of the Middle Ages, consist of more stained glass than stone—all told, it forms the largest expanse of stained glass in the world. There are candlelit classical concerts in this Gothic jewel box when the sun goes down. **WHERE:** Boulevard du Palais, 4th arrondissement. Tel 33/1-53-40-60-80; www.monuments.fr.

WHERE TO STAY

HÔTEL MEURICE—With many rooms overlooking the Jardins des Tuileries and a central location, the Meurice has hosted sultans and royalty for nearly two centuries. Check in and see why. **WHERE:** Rue de Rivoli, 1st arrondissement. Tel 33/1-44-58-10-10 or 800-650-1842 in the U.S.; www.meuricehotel.com. **COST:** high.

THE PLAZA ATHÉNÉE—At the newly refurbished Plaza, an army of discreetly professional staff provide the kind of service expected by the heads of state who stay here, as well as by more mortal guests. Its location is smack dab among the Avenue Montaigne's famous coutouriers and jewelers, and guests have special priority at the hotel's star-studded Alain Ducasse restaurant. **WHERE:** Avenue Montaigne, 8th arrondissement. Tel 33/1-53-67-66-65 or 800-650-1842 in the U.S. ; www.plaza-athenee-paris.com. **COST:** high.

A balcony at the Plaza Athénée provides a perfect view of the Eiffel Tower.

THE RITZ—The legendary Ritz boasts a pink marble Louis XV interior. Stay for a spot of tea, a relaxing aperitif, or a très haute dinner experience at L'Espadon. Big spenders can check in for the ultimate romantic stay. **WHERE:** in the elegant and historic Place Vendôme, 1st arrondissement. Tel 33/1-43-16-30-30 or 800-223-6800 in the U.S.; www.ritzparis.com. **COST:** high.

L'HÔTEL—For over a century, L'Hôtel was always the right address, and now, following its stylish but historically correct renovation, it's a chic, upscale address for a new generation of savvy travelers. **WHERE:** Rue des Beaux-Arts, in the heart of St.-Germain-des-Pres, 6th arrondissement. Tel 33/1-44-41-99-00; www.l-hotel.com. **COST:** moderate.

HÔTEL LE SAINTE-BEUVE—A very Parisian experience that won't break the bank, a five-minute walk to the Luxembourg Gardens. Rooms have antique furniture and face the quiet street. **WHERE:** Rue Sainte-Beuve, 6th arrondissement. Tel 33/1-45-48-20-07; www.paris-hotel-charme.com. **COST:** low.

EATING & DRINKING

ANGELINA—The decadent Mont Blanc dessert takes a backseat only to the richest hot chocolate imaginable, at Paris's most popular salon de thé. Its marble, gilt, and red-carpeted setting attracts everyone from grandmothers to the Agha Khan.

WHERE: Rue de Rivoli, 1st arrondissement. Tel 33/1-42-60-82-00.

BRASSERIE LIPP—Waiters still dress in black waistcoats and long, crisp white aprons, much as they have since the place opened in 1886. The atmosphere is lively and the profiteroles in hot chocolate sauce are reason enough to come, especially if preceded by the best choucroute-and-beer combination this side of Alsace-Lorraine. **WHERE:** Boulevard St.-Germain, 6th arrondissement. Tel 33/1-45-48-53-91.

THE CAFÉ SCENE—The Left Bank's St.-Germain-des-Prés is the traditional and still fashionable hub of the café scene, offering a glimpse of Paris from Hemingway's *A Moveable Feast.* The venerable **CAFÉ DE FLORE** (Boulevard St.-Germain, 6th arrondissement, tel 33/1-45-48-55-26; www.cafe-de-flore.com) and **LES DEUX MAGOTS** next door (tel 33/1-45-48-55-25) still draw ex-pats, homegrown intelligentsia, and the curious, generations after their WW II heyday as rendezvous of choice for the literary and artistic.

A new take on café society in an historical setting, the **CAFÉ MARLY** (tel 33/1-49-26-06-60) is discreetly housed in the Louvre's renovated Richelieu wing. The arcade terrace overlooks I. M. Pei's stunning glass pyramid in the theatrical Cour Napoléon.

FAUCHON—The city's, and perhaps the country's, most famous food emporium. Intricately prepared window and counter displays of picture-perfect food are scrutinized as carefully as this season's runway fashions. Coveted souvenirs are snatched up here for the packaging alone. **WHERE:** Place de la Madeleine, 8th arrondissement. Tel 33/1-42-68-36-45.

GUY SAVOY—One of Paris's finest and most innovative restaurants, owned by one of the city's finest and most innovative chefs. The menus change seasonally, and usually comprise nine courses; the decor is sophisticated and comfortable, featuring warm woods, leather, and stone. **WHERE:**

Rue Troyon, 17th arrondissement. Tel 33/1-43-80-40-61; www.guysavoy.com.

LA COUPOLE—Every meal is a sentimental journey at one of the most legendary scene-making brasseries in Paris. Loved by locals and tourists alike, its traditional seafood platters of oysters and mussels are served in a cavernous train-station–like Art Deco setting, festive and busy since the day it opened in 1927. **WHERE:** Boulevard du Montparnasse, 14th arrondissement. Tel 33/1-43-20-14-20.

LADURÉE—The quintessential French tea salon, the ornate Ladurée was established in 1862 and looks like something out of Versailles. The pineapple carpaccio with lime sorbet is a signature dessert, but order just about anything on the menu to experience a confectionary epiphany. **WHERE:** Avenue des Champs-Elysées, 8th arrondissement. Tel 33/1-40-75-08-75.

LE GRAND VÉFOUR—For an unforgettable visual and gustatory experience, have a once-in-a-lifetime meal in the over-the-top 18th-century setting of Le Grand Véfour. You'll walk away understanding why the French insist they can cook (and decorate) better than anyone else in the world. **WHERE:** Rue de Beaujolais, 1st arrondissement. Tel 33/1-42-96-56-27.

LE JULES VERNE—Set on the second platform of the Eiffel Tower, with a view so breathtaking it makes eating close to impossible. The skybound menu gives new meaning to the term haute cuisine. **WHERE:** Eiffel Tower, 7th arrondissement. Tel 33/1-45-55-61-44.

LES BOUQUINISTES—Fighting old-school conservatism, this contemporary bistro draws a polyglot crowd with its colorful modern interior and adventurous but unpretentious menu. It is owned by the untraditional Guy Savoy (see above). **WHERE:** Quai des Grands Augustins, 6th arrondissement. Tel 33/1-43-25-45-94.

WILLI'S WINE BAR—The bistro food is as tantalizing as the unmatched wine selection at this hugely popular bar, where the mingling of fashion types and foreigners in-the-know make for a buzzy atmosphere

that is both refined and relaxed. **WHERE:** Rue des Petits-Champs, 1st arrondissement. Tel 33/1-42-96-37-47.

Unique among the Palace Hotels of Paris

HÔTEL DE CRILLON

Paris, Île de France, France

The world's most-visited city has a noble share of grand hotels, but when you step from the busy Place de la Concorde into the quiet marbled lobby of the fabled Hôtel de Crillon, you'll see why this one stands apart.

The ancient Egyptian obelisk in front of the hotel

The only luxury palace hotel in France still French-owned (by the Taittinger family), the Crillon is a serious splurge but a guaranteed high point of a visit to the City of Lights. The 18th-century building is suitably grand and stylish for the crowned heads, famous entertainers, and celebrated VIPs who fill the hotel's *livre d'or*. Diplomats from nearby Embassy Row use the distinguished bar as an unofficial United Nations.

Tout Paris seems to stop by for a late afternoon tête-à-tête or a leisurely tea in the elegant Jardin d'Hiver. Just off the lobby, Paris's finest hotel restaurant offers inspiring views of the Place de la Concorde and its famous obelisk. The menu at the top-rated Les Ambassadeurs is presented with snap-to but friendly service beneath frescoed 20-foot ceilings with massive crystal chandeliers. Everything about this magnificent hotel and restaurant radiates quality and refinement, opulence and comfort.

WHAT: hotel, restaurant. **WHERE:** 10 Place de la Concorde. Tel 33/1-44-71-15-00, fax 33/1-44-71-15-02; in the U.S., tel 800-888-4747; crillon@crillon.com; www.crillon.com. **COST:** doubles from $750. Dinner at Les Ambassadeurs $295.

Superlative Cuisine Balances the Classic and the Nouvelle

TAILLEVENT

Paris, Île de France, France

Much of the glory of Paris has been its proliferation of world-famous gastronomic temples. Here is the country's highest concentration of starred restaurants and superstar chefs who offer that unique, flawless dinner, where guests are treated like royalty and clairvoyant service sparkles. At Taillevent, the polished, clublike, mid-19th-century setting is presided over by the third-generation owner and consummate host, Valerie Vrinat. Chef Alain Solivérès uses a solidly classic base sprinkled with imagination, a masterful mélange of the old and the new. In perfect harmony with the unimpeachable menu is Taillevent's legendary wine list—25,000 bottles! Its wine shop is considered one of Paris's finest. Choosing from the best of Paris's celebrated restaurants can involve hours of fervent discussion and guidebook perusal, but the same revered names always surface: L'Ambroisie, L'Arpège, Guy Savoy, Lucas Carton, Pierre Gagnaire, Michel Rostang, Grand Véfour, and Alain Ducasse. How to know who carries the edge? Book weeks in advance, try them all, and cast your vote.

WHAT: restaurant. **WHERE:** 15 Rue Lamennais. Tel 33/1-44-95-15-01, fax 33/1-42-25-95-18; resa@taillevent.com; www.taillevent.com. **COST:** dinner $185. **WHEN:** open Mon–Fri. Reservations for Fri night must be made at least 3 months in advance.

A Showcase of Gothic Expression

CATHÉDRALE NOTRE DAME DE CHARTRES

Île-de-France, France

Chartres's incomparable Gothic cathedral—the first to use flying buttresses and the third largest after Rome's St. Peter's and the Canterbury Cathedral in Kent, England—is known for its unrivaled stained-glass windows and the sculptures that decorate it inside and out. The magnificent stained glass, covering an expanse of more than 27,000 square feet, is an almost incomprehensible achievement. The stirring jewel-like windows created by 12th- and 13th-century master glass artists were saved from destruction in both world wars by being removed piece by piece and hidden for safekeeping. The kaleidoscopic colors—ruby reds, emerald greens, "Chartres blue," and rich golds —are once again brilliant and vibrant, as the windows undergo a lengthy, painstaking, and expensive restoration. For the illiterate masses they served as illuminated pages from the Bible, familiar narratives that could be read bottom to top—earth to heaven—and left to right. Chartres Cathedral is a showcase of Gothic architecture and continues to stagger even the most blasé modern-day observer. The sixth

A Gothic masterpiece of stained glass and sculptures

church built on this spot, it houses a tunic worn by the Virgin Mary. The nave, the widest in Europe, barely accommodated the hordes of pilgrims who came during the Middle Ages. Things are no different today.

WHAT: site. **WHERE:** 60 miles/97 km southwest of Paris. **BEST TIMES:** an international organ festival takes place in Jul and Aug.

Outrageous Opulence, Absolute Power

CHÂTEAU DE VERSAILLES

Versailles, Île de France, France

Home of the most flamboyant court since the collapse of ancient Rome, and indisputably France's most-visited château, Versailles was built by the French monarchy at the height of its glory—a century-long heyday lasting from 1682, when Louis XIV brought his court and entourage of 20,000 here from Paris until 1789 when Louis XVI and Queen Marie Antoinette were notified that revolutionary mobs were arriving. In 1662, on the site of his father's old hunting lodge, Louis XIV began construction of France's new seat of government, which became a symbol of royal excess. Its most memorable room is the restored 236-foot-long Galérie des Glaces (Hall of Mirrors), whose seventeen large arched windows are matched by as many sparkling beveled mirrors, which have witnessed many elaborate balls, Louis XVI marrying Marie Antoinette, and the signing of the Treaty of Versailles in 1919. The elaborately Baroque Grands Appartements (State Apartments) are equally extraordinary. After exploring the palace's interior, take a stroll through Versailles's famous 250-acre park; the formal gardens were designed by the well-known André Le Nôtre, and on Sundays the fountains are in full flow. Better yet, check into the neighboring turn-of-the-century Trianon Palace hotel for some royal pampering once reserved for guests of the Sun King. Woolly descendants of Marie Antoinette's sheep still graze in front of the château hotel.

WHAT: site, hotel. **CHÂTEAU DE VERSAILLES:** 13 miles/21 km southwest of Paris. Trains run regularly from Montparnasse station. Tel 33/1-30-84-74-00; www.chateauversailles.fr. *Cost:* admission $20. *When:* Tues–Sun. *Best times:* the Fêtes de Nuit are special light-and-fireworks shows held in Jun–Sep; contact local tourism office for schedule. **TRIANON PALACE HOTEL AND SPA:** 1 Boulevard de la Reine. Tel 33/1-30-84-50-00, fax 33/1-30-84-50-01; concierge.piano@hilton.com; www.trianonpalace.com. *Cost:* doubles from $325.

The Brilliant Works of Albi's Most Famous Son

TOULOUSE-LAUTREC MUSEUM

Albi, Languedoc-Roussillon, France

One of Europe's best single-artist museums, Musée Toulouse-Lautrec has the largest concentration of works by the eponymous artist. Born in 1864 in Albi la Rouge (whose nickname comes from the pink brick and terra-cotta produced locally), the crippled and tormented Henri de Toulouse-Lautrec was from an aristocratic family that was horrified when Henri took off to immerse himself in

A Toulouse-Lautrec poster from 1892

the nocturnal fringes of Paris's demimonde. Fans of Toulouse-Lautrec will want to spend hours with more than 1,000 of his paintings of the prostitutes, cabaret dancers, and café dwellers displayed within the austere Palais de la Berbie, a former bishop's residence built in 1265 as a fortress. An extensive representation of the famous posters that marked the beginning of an entirely new art form is also here, vicious caricatures of the pretensions of those days. The palais was dedicated to the Belle Epoque painter in 1922, following his death in 1901. Centuries of intermarriage and a form of dwarfism are believed to be the cause of Lautrec's physical suffering, but what colors and characters he produced!

WHAT: site. **WHERE:** Palais de la Berbie (just off Place Ste.-Cécile), Albi (47 miles/76 km northeast of Toulouse). Tel 33/5-63-49-48-70, conservation@museetoulouselautrec.com; www. mairie-albi.fr. **COST:** admission $4. **WHEN:** open daily, except Oct–Mar open Wed–Mon.

Wild Horses, Bulls, and the Gypsy Spirit

THE CAMARGUE AND THE GYPSY PILGRIMAGE

Languedoc-Roussillon, France

One of France's most enchanting country hotels lies on a 200-acre working ranch in the heart of the intriguing region known as the Camargue, along France's southern coast. A microcosm of the area's wild, rugged scenery, the ranch is both a government-protected bird sanctuary (known for its flocks of pink flamingos) and the final frontier for the *gardians*, some of the last cowboys in Europe. You can ride out on one of the 300 snow-white Camargue horses or help the herders gather the stocky black Camargue bulls, which are raised for races. At the heart of this wilderness stands Le Mas de Peint, an unassuming 17th-century stone farmhouse. Its spacious, uncluttered interior reflects the delightful style and restraint, relaxed simplicity and luxury of Camargue tradition. Antique pieces enhance the cool common areas and ten spacious guest rooms. There are plumped, overstuffed armchairs dresssed in natural fabrics; the crisp linen sheets are embroidered with the branding symbol of the ranch; and a young chef works sophisticated wonders from produce grown on the farm.

Try to visit the area at the end of May, in order to witness the annual Gypsy Pilgrimage in honor of their protectress, Sarah. During this festive *Grand Pélérinage*, the village of

Herding bulls at Le Mas de Peint

Stes.-Maries-de-la-Mer vibrates with the color and rhythms of more than 20,000 Gypsies (some from as far away as Hungary and Romania) as they sing and dance in homage to the servant girl believed to have come from Egypt, the alleged ancestral home of today's European *gitane* race. The legend goes that Sarah accompanied Mary Magdalene, Martha, Mary Jacobé, and Mary Salomé, all followers of Jesus, in A.D. 40, when they were exiled from ancient Judea. Their boat, without sails or oars, miraculously arrived on the shores of the town that now bears their names, and whose local church is said to hold their bones.

Although never canonized, Sarah became the object of adoration of all Gypsies. On May 24, the day dedicated to the Saintes Maries, guitars appear and flamenco bursts out wherever more than two or three Gypsies are gathered. Their soulful music accompanies the wooden statue of Sarah in its annual procession to the sea.

WHAT: site, hotel, event. **LE MAS DE PEINT:** in Le Sambuc, 20 miles/32 km southeast of Arles, 6 miles/10 km from the beach. Tel 33/90-97-20-62; www.masdepeint.com. *Cost:* doubles from $330. Dinner $80. **GYPSY PILGRIMAGE:** main festival day is May 24 in Stes.-Maries-de-la-Mer.

A Disneyesque Creation of Medieval Military Might

THE WALLS OF CARCASSONNE

Languedoc-Roussillon, France

An extraordinary example of early military architecture, Carcassone is the very image of a storybook medieval town. It is surrounded by the longest walls in Europe (nearly 2 miles), a fairy-tale concoction of turrets, watchtowers, battlements, and drawbridges begun in the 6th century. It would take thirteen centuries of alterations, additions, and embellishments by the Romans, Gauls, Visigoths, Arabs, Franks, and French royalty before the double ramparts encircling this prosperous fortified city, the largest in Europe, were completed. The *lices,* a path between the concentric inner and outer fortifications, offers views within the preserved citadel as well as the lush green countryside and the River Aude without. Its nighttime illumination provides high drama, though torchlight is no longer used. La Cité is the older part of town, sitting on a 1,500-foot hill that for centuries was the border between the present France and Spain. The 12th-century Cathédrale St.-Nazaire has the most interesting architecture in La Cité. If you're looking for an exquisite spot to check your bags, try next door at the Hôtel de la Cité, on the site of a former Episcopal palace. Built into the ancient ramparts and incorporating one of the fifty-two watchtowers, the newly renovated ivy-covered hotel is one of the finest in the area and boasts an elegant restaurant, La Barbacane.

Carcassonne and the Hôtel de la Cité overlook the Lauragais Valley.

WHAT: town, site, hotel, restaurant. CARCASSONE: 500 miles/805 km southwest of Paris, 55 miles/88 km southeast of Toulouse. HÔTEL DE LA CITÉ: Place de l'Eglise. Tel 33/4-68-71-98-71; in the U.S., tel 800-237-1236; reservations@hoteldelacite.com; www.hoteldelacite.com. *Cost:* doubles from $445 (low season), from $600 (high season). Dinner at La Barbacane, $100. *When:* hotel closed mid-Jan to early Mar. La Barbacane open Apr–Nov, dinner only. BEST TIMES: Jul 14 for Bastille Day fireworks over the ramparts; Medieval Festival early Aug. Festival de Carcassonne offers cultural events throughout Jul.

A Flawlessly Proportioned City Center

PLACE STANISLAS

Nancy, Lorraine, France

Nancy is one of the loveliest cities in Europe, with a remarkably pretty main square that is widely held to be France's—some say the world's—most beautiful urban monument. Although Nancy is also known for its Art Nouveau architecture, the Place Stanislas is its unparalleled legacy. Named after the twice-deposed king of Poland who, with his son-in-law, Louis XV, commissioned its construction in 1751–60, it is the epitome of rococo delicacy, as can be observed in the gilded wrought-iron gates and the integrated architecture of the Hôtel de Ville (Town Hall), its arcades, and surrounding buildings. Nancy flourished as capital of the duchy of Lorraine from the 12th to the 18th century, undergoing a program of town planning and beautification toward the end of that period. The square and its surrounding area were the elegant showpiece for the last ducs de Lorraine and remain today the symbolic heart of the city and its rich past.

Every bit as elegant as the square on which it stands, the 18th-century mansion housing the Grand Hôtel de la Reine is exceptional and has been designated a historical landmark. Check into one of the grand guest rooms overlooking the square or at least luxuriate in one of the cafés that share this incomparable setting.

WHAT: town, site, hotel. PLACE STANISLAS: the town is 230 miles/370 km southeast of Paris, 92 miles/148 km west of Strasbourg. *When:* closed to traffic Jun 1–Sept 15. GRAND

Place Stanislas is a rococo delight.

HÔTEL DE LA REINE: 2 Place Stanislas. Tel 33/3-83-35-03-01, fax 33/3-83-32-86-04; www.hoteldelareine.com. *Cost:* doubles from $170; Royal Suite overlooking square $385. BEST TIMES: Jul 14 for impressive Bastille Day parade.

Europe's Premier Shrine

LOURDES

Midi-Pyrénées, France

Every year millions of the faithful and devout flock to this mountain town to the spot where, in 1858, a local teenage girl named Bernadette had eighteen visions of the Virgin Mary in a riverside grotto. France's most-visited city after Paris, Lourdes has somehow managed to accommodate the crowds while still radiating a certain quiet and benevolent sanctity that disarms the most skeptical. Despite the building blocks of dormitorylike hotels and tawdry souvenir stands selling wind-up virgins and the like, Lourdes and the legions of pilgrims it attracts can still be a moving—at times unsettling—experience. More than 140 countries (many of them, such as Japan and Saudi Arabia, are not known for their Christian population) are represented by visitors who come mainly for the water they believe to have miraculous healing powers: During the visits by the Virgin Mary (never seen by anyone besides Bernadette), a spring welled up in the grotto and has been running ever since. Of some 2,500 "unexplained healings," the church has officially recognized sixty-five miracles since Bernadette's death in 1879 (she was canonized in 1933); about thirty such healings occur each year.

WHAT: site. **WHERE:** 497 miles/800 km southwest of Paris near the Spanish border in the mountainous Pyrénées region; 100 miles/161 km east of Biarritz in the direction of Carcassonne. **HOW:** contact Lourdes Tourist Office, tel 33/5-62-42-77-40, fax 33/5-62-94-60-95; www.lourdes-infotourisme.com. **WHEN:** 6 official pilgrimage dates yearly; the most important is Aug 15. **BEST TIMES:** early evening for the daily candlelight procession. The most popular season is Easter–early Nov; off-season there are fewer crowds.

The Playground of Kings and Country Home of a French Count

LOIRE VALLEY AND DOMAINE DES HAUTS DE LOIRE

Pays de la Loire, France

The winding Loire Valley has captured the hearts of travelers for centuries, as it did the nobility and royalty who built more than 1,000 châteaux and manors along France's "Royal River," each one a masterpiece of sumptuousness and excess. How to isolate the must-sees from the regretfully-must-pass-bys? Chambord and Chenonceau are the most renowned châteaux. With 440 rooms and 365 fireplaces, Chambord is the largest (and that's saying something) and François I's favorite hunting place. Chenonceau is an unsurpassed Renaissance masterpiece with ornamental gardens to match, gracefully spanning the river Cher. But many of the lesser-known châteaux are just as special for their majestic moats, bucolic riverine locations, lush parklands, isolation, and ancestral interiors chockablock with artwork and furniture. Ghosts and legends from the early days of the French Renaissance linger in them all.

Ironically, the best way to recuperate from château burnout may be to spend a few sumptuous nights in one. After touring the Loire Valley for a while, the urge is great to unpack your bags, even for just a night or two. The Domaine des Hauts de Loire is not as overwhelming as most of the castle-fortresses scattered across the valley of France's longest river. The gracious, vine-covered manor house was built in 1860 as the hunting lodge of the Count de Rostaing, and the aristocracy gathered to chase wild boar and stag in what was then the count's game-rich 1,000-acre park. The lodge, stables, and guardian's cottage now house charming, antiques-appointed gabled guest rooms. The quality of the service would have pleased the count's weekend aristo-

guests, but the Domaine's real attraction is the award-winning kitchen. Dinners served in the countrified restaurant before blazing log fires or on the candlelit terrace are memorable—worthy of their setting in the Valley of the Kings.

And bear in mind that few regions in this country that gave the world La Tour de France are more suited to biking trips in terms of beauty, history, and grandeur than the Loire Valley. A classic pedaling trip can include expert guides and gourmet picnics in the shade of royal castles.

WHAT: site, experience, hotel, restaurant. **LOIRE VALLEY:** usually refers to the area southwest of Paris between Orléans (about 80 miles/129 km from Paris) and Saumur. **DOMAINE DES HAUTS DE LOIRE:** midway between Blois and Tours in the heart of the Loire Valley. Tel 33/2-54-20-72-57, fax 33/2-54-20-77-32; in the U.S., tel 800-RELAIS-8. *Cost:* doubles from $185 (low season). Dinner $100. *When:* hotel open mid-Feb to Dec 1, restaurant closed Mon and Tues. **BIKE TRIPS:** in the U.S. contact Butterfield and Robinson, tel 800-678-1147; www.butterfield.com. **BEST TIMES:** mid-Apr to mid-Nov.

Nantucket with a French Accent

ÎLE DE RÉ

Poitou-Charentes, France

A recent mainland invasion of this small French outpost in the Atlantic— just 20 miles long and in some places only 200 feet wide—has done little to taint its unspoiled charm. You'll see mostly local island people and

in-the-know Parisians pedaling around the vineyards and potato fields, past oyster parks, vegetable gardens, and the local bird reserve. Genteel, old-fashioned, slow-paced, and surprisingly friendly, in this corner of France doors and bicycles are left unlocked, the bartender knows your name and preference, and

young families fill the uncrowded beaches digging for cockles and relishing the island's other *petits plaisirs*. The architecture is plain, the outdoor markets every morning's highlight, and irresistible seafood shacks serve mussels from their backyards, perfumed by a fire made with pine needles. Île de Ré's cover was temporarily blown a few years ago when the aging French rock star Johnny Halliday abandoned St.-Tropez for the scene-free low profile of Île de Ré; islanders were relieved when boredom soon drove him back where he came from. Outsiders will find characteristic blissful low-keyed do-nothingness at the Hôtel L'Océan. This small, simple, but stylish place offers the island's newest and most charming accommodations and has an excellent restaurant. Pick your lobster from the tank, sit outside, and make plans to extend your stay indefinitely.

WHAT: island, hotel. **ÎLE DE RÉ:** 300 miles/483 km from Paris to La Rochelle, then a 30-minute bus or cab ride across the bridge that connects the island to the mainland. **HÔTEL L'OCÉAN:** 172 Rue de St.-Martin, Le Bois-Plage-en-Ré. Tel 33/5-46-09-23-07, fax 33/5-46-09-05-40; info@re-hotel-ocean.com; www.re-hotel-ocean.com. *Cost:* doubles from $105. **BEST TIMES:** May–Oct.

The Quintessential Provençal Experience

AIX-EN-PROVENCE

Provence-Alpes-Côte d'Azur, France

Take a promenade beneath the sun-filtering canopy of plane trees, past the gurgling rococo fountains and stately 17th- and 18th-century buildings, the weekly open-air markets, and the outdoor cafés, then ask yourself:

is Aix-en-Provence's Cours Mirabeau not the most beautiful street in Europe? You may have to say yes. Ever since medieval ramparts were torn down to make room for this lovely avenue, it has been the center stage of Aix-en-Provence. It is the perfect main street in the perfect Provençal town; both remain unspoiled, despite the city's evolution and growth. Trail off down le Cours in the footsteps of Paul Cézanne. This is the landscape, including Mont Ste.-Victoire, that he loved to paint time and time again. Try to visit during the last two weeks in July, when the whole town is abuzz for the Aix-en-Provence Festival, also known as the International Festival of Lyrical Art and Music, and life whirls around the principal opera and many musical concerts. Tickets for any of the performances held in the open-air 1,200-seat Théâtre de l'Archevêché are understandably the first to go, but classical and chamber music concerts and recitals held all around the city are just as magical. The two-week Aix

en Musique precedes the festival with mostly classical performances beginning in late June, and jazz picks up when the festival leaves off for the better part of August.

While in Aix, stay in a tranquil country setting only a minute's walk from town. The bright and sunny 18th-century Hôtel La Villa Gallici embodies the charm and spirit of Provence. Every room proclaims an unwavering attention to detail: fresh flowers everywhere; an unerring choice of color and pattern for all the swags, swathes, covers, and drapes; the perfectly planned gardens and terraces. The plane trees that shade the breakfast terrace make it an oasis in which the glamorous garden pool gleams like a mirage. To complete the dream, you needn't go far for the perfect meal. Both the hotel's simple Provençal menu and the more gastronomic dining found at the nearby Le Clos de la Violette are the work of chef Jean-Marc Banzo. Both spots offer some of the most enjoyable dining in the south of France.

WHAT: town, site, event, hotel, restaurant. **COURS MIRABEAU:** for more information visit www.aix-en-provence.com. **AIX-EN-PROVENCE FESTIVAL:** Palais de l'Ancien Archevêché. Tel 33/4-34-08-02-17, fax 33/4-42-63-13-74; billeterie@festival-aix.com; www.festival-aix. com; *Cost:* opera tickets from $28; concerts or recitals from $21. *When:* approximately last 2 weeks of Jul. **HÔTEL LA VILLA GALLICI:** Avenue de la Violette. Tel 33/4-42-23-29-23, fax 33/4-42-96-30-45; www.villagallici.com. *Cost:* doubles from $325. Dinner $110. **LE CLOS DE LA VIOLETTE:** 10 Avenue de la Violette. Tel 33/4-42-23-30-71. *Cost:* dinner $125.

The Ultimate in Glamour

ANTIBES AND HÔTEL DU CAP EDEN-ROC

Provence-Alpes-Côte d'Azur, France

A visit to Antibes, one of the Riviera's great delights, must include a tour of the Musée Picasso, followed by the meal of a lifetime at the Restaurant de Bacon. Owned for more than fifty years by the same family—who don't accept the day's catch from local fishermen unless it's still moving—Bacon has long been known for its magnificant bouillabaisse, a hearty but refined fish stew. It's like the Mediterranean in a bowl, and it tastes even better if served on the outdoor terraces overlooking the colorful Vieux Port and bay of Antibes. In 1946, Picasso spent some of his happiest months in Antibes and Vallauris, the neighboring potters' and crafts center, where more than 100 small ateliers still thrive. Some of his prolific body of work is housed in the stone Château Grimaldi. The artist bequeathed close to 300 paintings, ceramics, drawings, and sculptures to the city with the stipulation that they never leave their birthplace.

Nearby, the glamorous ghost of F. Scott Fitzgerald lingers at the Hôtel du Cap Eden-Roc, an 1870 cliffside palace surrounded by 20 exquisite acres of scented gardens, pines, and century-old palm trees on one of the world's most exclusive coastlines. In *Tender Is the Night,* the place was immortalized as the Hôtel des Etrangers, the epitome of grand living. The international royalty of the movie industry hang their tuxes and gowns here during the Cannes Film Festival (when who you are is where you stay), by day wheeling and dealing around the beautifully situated swimming pool. Ever since its inauguration, princes and kings, dukes and duchesses, and all manner of other celebrities have been regular guests. Present-day development has not obliterated the past: the Hôtel du Cap is still one of the last great places to find the Riviera of 1920s literature and 1950s Brigitte Bardot films. The discreetly exclusive Madonna Suite, whose spacious sun-soaked terrace overlooks the Isles of Lerins and the Esterel Mountains, is one of the Riviera's most coveted accommodations. Bring along an extra

The Musée Picasso displays more than 3,500 of the artist's pieces.

suitcase and fill it with money: the Eden-Roc accepts no credit cards.

What: town, site, restaurant, hotel. **Cap d'Antibes:** 13 miles/21 km southwest of Nice, 9 miles/14 km from Cannes. **Musée Picasso:** Château Grimaldi, Place du Château. Tel 33/4-92-90-54-20; www.musee-picasso.fr. *Cost:* admission. *When:* open Tues–Sun. **Restaurant de Bacon:** Boulevard de Bacon. Tel 33/4-93-61-50-02, fax 33/4-93-61-65-19; contact@restaurantdebacon.com; www.restaurantdebacon.com. *Cost:* bouillabaisse dinner $105. *When:* open Feb–Oct. **Hôtel du Cap Eden-Roc:** Boulevard Kennedy. Tel 33/4-93-61-39-01, fax 33/4-93-67-76-04; reservation@hdcer.com; www.edenroc-hotel.fr. *Cost:* doubles from $665 (low season), from $905 (high season). Madonna Suite, $7,075. *When:* open mid-Apr to mid-Oct. **Best Times:** Jul–Aug.

Spectacle and Glory Without the Blood

AMPHITHEATER OF ARLES

Provence-Alpes-Côte d'Azur, France

Arles, the former capital of Provence and best known as the city of van Gogh's anguish, has bullfighting in its blood. Its extraordinarily well-preserved amphitheater, Les Arènes, dates from the 1st century B.C. and is marginally larger than that of Nîmes, the other bullfighting center in Provence. Arles's most famous monument (and the city's star attraction) maintains its links with the past by hosting bullfights and celebrations of the Confraternity of Gardians (herdsmen) whose feast day, the Fête des Gardians on May 1, is proudly celebrated by young and old.

In a departure from the Spanish-style *mise-à-mort*, in Arles and the Camargue region the bulls are feted and adored and attention focuses on the grace and spectacle of the corrida, where the bull is not

Originally host to gladiator fights and then used as a fortress, the amphitheater today is known for its bullfights.

killed. The bullfighters are as celebrated as the beasts; at the landmark Grand Hôtel Nord-Pinus, their signatures fill the guest book along with those of Hemingway, Edith Piaf, and Picasso. Although newly renovated, the delightfully eccentric hotel is still dedicated to the cult of the bull, with old corrida posters gracing the walls and glass-encased matador costumes on display. Try for Room 10, where nervous toreadors spent sleepless nights before their appearance in the Roman arena, which seats 26,000 vociferous aficionados. Napoleon III occupied Room 10 in 1856, undoubtedly enjoying the three wrought-iron balconies overlooking the animated Place du Forum. Today, the hotel's acclaimed restaurant sets up its tables there, beneath the shade of century-old plane trees.

WHAT: site, town, hotel. **ARLES:** 22 miles/ 35 km south of Avignon, 57 miles/92 km north-west of Marseilles. **GRAND HÔTEL NORD-PINUS:** Place du Forum. Tel 33/4-90-93-44-44, fax 33/4-90-93-34-00; info@nord-pinus.com; www.nord-pinus.com. *Cost:* doubles from $225. Dinner $45. **BEST TIMES:** period between the Sun after St. George's Day (Apr 23) and the May 1 Fête des Gardians marks the opening of the bullfighting season.

Lifestyle of the Rich and Papal

AVIGNON AND HÔTEL LA MIRANDE

Provence-Alpes-Côte d'Azur, France

The ancient papal city of Avignon protects many historic gems behind its 14th-century crenellated walls. It is known as the home of seven popes who broke with Rome, the first in 1309. Five popes lived and ruled for 100 years from the once-sumptuous fortress residence, the Palais des Papes. Pillaged during the French Revolution of all its original finery, the palace today needs a willing imagination to envisage the luxurious living that once went on. This is partially possible in the Chapelle St.-Jean, known for its beautiful 14th-century frescoes by Matteo Giovanetti, and in the huge banqueting hall with its famous ceiling. It is easiest to imagine the papal tenants in their private chambers, the loveliest being the Chambre du Cerf, the pope's private study, where the murals depicting hunting scenes were most likely the work of Giovanetti. The nearby Petit Palais, the former archbishop's palace begun in 1318, today houses a rich collection of 15th-century works from the Avignon School and 13th- to 16th-century Italian works whose highlight is the young Botticelli's *Madonna and Child.*

If you visit Avignon in midsummer, you can enjoy one of Europe's most important and exciting fetes, the Festival d'Avignon. Recognized as the country's foremost theater and dance festival, it has outgrown its original venue, the courtyard of the Palais des Papes, and "Off Avignon" (as the lively fringe scene is known) now involves the entire city. Any theater, church, cloister, square, or street corner may become the stage for national and visiting troupes that perform prose, comedy, opera, music, mime, and dance. The core of the festival continues to be theater, however; premieres by living playwrights intermix with the classics and occasional performances in English.

Meanwhile, do whatever you can to stay at Avignon's boutique-hotel gem La Mirande. Only superlatives could be used to describe its location (almost all the rooms overlook the Palais des Papes); history (the Louis XIV sunburst over the hotel entrance indicates a more recent facade, though the 15th-century structure was built on the foundations of an earlier cardinal's palace); taste (the look and feel of a genteel 18th-century home was deftly re-created by one of France's premier designers); and impeccable decor (many of the choice antique pieces are straight from the art-loving owners' family). The superlatives continue with the hotel restaurant—one of the city's best. A highly acclaimed chef is the creative force behind a softly lit dining room, with an Aubusson tapestry and double-coffered ceiling. These give way to a glass-topped central courtyard, the perfect spot for tea, and a garden color-splashed and scented with jasmine and honeysuckle. The effect is so sumptuous and theatrical, it brings to mind the make-believe quality of a Visconti movie set.

WHAT: site, event, town, hotel, restaurant. **WHERE:** 2½ hours by train from Paris. **FESTIVAL D'AVIGNON:** 8 bis Rue de Mons. Tel 33/4-90-14-14-60, fax 33/4-90-27-66-52; www.festival-avignon.com. *Cost:* tickets $28–$70, on sale beginning early Jun. *When:* early Jul–early Aug. **PALAIS DES PAPES:** Tel 33/4-90-27-50-00, fax 33/4-90-27-50-88; rmg@palais-des-papes.com; www.palais-des-papes.com. **HÔTEL LA MIRANDE:** 4 Place de la Mirande. Tel 33/4-90-14-20-20, fax 33/4-90-86-26-85; mirande@la-mirande.fr; www.la-mirande.fr. *Cost:* doubles from $440 (low season), from $550 (high season).

Epitome of Belle Epoque Luxury

INTERCONTINENTAL CARLTON CANNES

Cannes, Provence-Alpes-Côte d'Azur, France

It is impossible to visit the Riviera and ignore the allure of Cannes, and if you miss a visit to the grand doyenne Hotel Carlton, you've missed the spirit of this resort city. Best known as a glittering command post for the prestigious Cannes Film Festival, the elegant white-turreted Carlton presides over the Promenade de la Croisette—the palace- and palm-studded seafront boulevard that is the main focus of city life.

The Carlton's strip of beach is Cannes's nicest, and sautéed bodies have cavorted there since Coco Chanel first made sunbathing fashionable. The Carlton's lobby, bar, and beach are the ultrasophisticated magnets for the haut monde. You're apt to glimpse a face from *Paris Match*, a movie mogul, maverick, or nubile starlet. Unless you're related to Jack, Sharon, Mel, or Bruce, settle for a drop-in visit at the terrace bar or for tea, before or after the film festival frenzy. Even on an off month, this is the most colorful hotel in Cannes, your best shot at mingling with the Riviera's beautiful set.

WHAT: town, hotel. **CANNES:** 16 miles/26 km southwest of Nice, 100 miles/161 km east of Marseilles, 562 miles/904 km south of Paris. **INTERCONTINENTAL CARLTON CANNES:** 58 Boulevard de la Croisette. Tel 33/4-93-06-40-06, fax 33/4-93-06-40-25; in the U.S., tel 800-327-0200; cegha-resvn@interconti.com; cannes.france.intercontinental.com. *Cost:* doubles from $285. **BEST TIMES:** Cannes Film Festival takes place 12 days mid–late May.

The InterContinental Carlton Cannes opened its doors in 1912.

The Genuine Innocence of Old Provence

HOSTELLERIE DE CRILLON LE BRAVE

Crillon le Brave, Provence-Alpes-Côte d'Azur, France

For nostalgic Francophiles who haven't yet fulfilled their dream of a home in Provence, there is Hostellerie de Crillon le Brave, nestled in the hills of the Rhône Valley. Beside the local church a cluster of 16th- and 17th-century honey-colored stone buildings creates a village within a village. This quintessential Provençal country inn is comfortably and tastefully decorated with simple fruitwood antiques and luminous Cézanne-colored Souleiado fabrics. The main house once served as the local priest's home and village school. The flagstone terrace is shaded by cypress and fig trees, clematis and jasmine. In the distance, fields of lavender and olive trees stretch toward the dramatic contours of 6,000-foot Mont Ventoux. The hotel's terraced Mediterranean gardens lead down to quiet sun-dappled corners and the beautifully sited swimming pool. Crillon le Brave is out of the loop, a tranquil spot far from any hubbub, though a roster of tempting day trips might succeed in luring you away from your newfound home deep in the heart of Provence—temporarily.

WHAT: town, hotel. **CRILLON LE BRAVE:** 24 miles/38 km northeast of Avignon, 18 miles/29 km east of Orange, 65 miles/105 km north of Marseilles. **HOSTELLERIE DE CRILLON LE BRAVE:** Place de l'Eglise. Tel 33/4-90-65-61-61, fax 33/4-90-65-62-86; in the U.S., tel 800-RELAIS-8; reservations@crillonlebrave.com; www.crillonlebrave.com. *Cost:* doubles from $325. *When:* open mid-Mar–early Jan. **BEST TIMES:** lavender blooms in Jun; truffle hunting in Nov.

High-Altitude Views from a Favorite Aerie

EZE

Provence-Alpes-Côte d'Azur, France

As you approach Eze at 1,300 feet above the cobalt-blue Mediterranean, you may forget that this scrupulously restored medieval town was designed for military defense, not tourist dollars. It is the highest of Provence's perched villages and one of the most visited. An extraordinary sight, clinging to a cone of sky-born rock, Eze's stepped serpentine alleyways and flower-decked cobbled passageways are home to artisans and antiques dealers catering to the tourist trade. Eze's Jardin Exotique (Exotic Garden) boasts an exceptional collection of cacti—and everywhere, those views! High inspiration seems to come with the altitude. Friedrich Nietzsche, a

The Château Eza, high on a cliff above the Mediterranean

Eze, it is surprising to find a second extraordinary operation, namely the Château Eza, a 400-year-old building refurbished in the 1920s by Prince William of Sweden. Today it is a luxury hotel with a noted chef and an outdoor dining terrace so handsome that it can make you forget the wonderful food. (Dining is even finer at the Château de la Chèvre d'Or, although the restaurant is enclosed.)

WHAT: town, hotel, restaurant. **EZE:** 7 miles/11 km east of Nice, 5 miles/8 km west of Monte Carlo. **CHÂTEAU DE LA CHÈVRE D'OR:** Rue du Barri. Tel 33/4-92-10-66-66, fax 33/4-93-41-06-72; in the U.S., tel 800-RELAIS-8; reservations@chevredor.com; www.chevredor.com. *Cost:* doubles from $395 (low season), from $410 (high season). 7-course tasting menu $290. *When:* hotel and restaurant open early Mar–mid-Nov. **CHÂTEAU EZA:** Rue de la Pise. Tel 33/4-93-41-12-24, fax 33/4-93-41-16-64; in the U.S., tel 800-507-8250. *Cost:* doubles from $321. Prix fixe dinner from $92. *When:* hotel open Apr–Oct; restaurant open late Dec–Oct.

regular visitor, wrote *Thus Spoke Zarathustra* in Eze; a mule path wending down to the sea is now known as Sentier Nietzsche (Nietzsche's Path).

After the last day-tripper leaves, guests at the Château de la Chèvre d'Or have much of the tiny town to themselves. They will feel like pampered guests in the stunning home of a wealthy friend. Few pools have a view like this one, and if you've checked into the Medieval Suite, your private terrace and alfresco Jacuzzi share the same panorama.

In a postage-stamp-size enclave such as

A Splendid Medieval Citadel

LES BAUX-DE-PROVENCE

Provence-Alpes-Côte d'Azur, France

Cardinal Richelieu once called Les Baux-de-Provence a "nesting place for eagles." Framed by the sheer rock ravines of the Val d'Enfer (Valley of Hell), Les Baux's lonely position on a windswept plateau overlooks vineyards and thousands of olive trees (some planted by the Greeks and Romans) that produce some of the best limited-production wines and olive oil in the south of France. Les Baux's amazing collection of narrow, climbing streets and medieval and 16th- and 17th-century stone houses are now home to local craftsmen who sell their wares to a steady stream of tourists. In the 17th century, Cardinal Richelieu, under orders from Louis XIII, was responsible for the destruction of what remains of the Ville Morte (Dead City); the ruins of this 13th-century cliffside castle and ramparts outside the main town are a romantic vestige of Les Baux's glorious past.

Tucked between the crags below, the princely L'Oustau de Beaumanière restaurant is housed in an old Provençal manor house in a verdant oasis. Dining under the vaulted ceilings or on the terrace, overlooking the sylvan duck ponds and partaking of L'Oustau's fabled wine cellar are culinary experiences of a high order.

WHAT: town, restaurant, hotel. **LES BAUX-DE-PROVENCE:** 18 miles/29 km south of Avignon, 50 miles/80 km north of Marseilles. **L'OUSTAU DE BEAUMANIÈRE:** Maussane-les-Alpilles. Tel 33/4-90-54-33-07, fax 33/4-90-54-40-46; contact@oustaudebaumaniere.com; www.oustaudebaumaniere.com. *Cost:* dinner $215. Doubles from $280. *When:* hotel and restaurant open Mar–Dec. **BEST TIMES** spring and fall; appealingly tourist-free off-season.

Gastronomic Center of the Riviera

MOUGINS

Provence-Alpes-Côte d'Azur, France

Another idyllic day on the Riviera, another authentic "perched village," with wandering cobbled lanes and open-air markets that smell of fresh herbs and cut flowers. Mougins is particularly charming, despite having been discovered decades ago, and has remained surprisingly untrammeled. Today it has become a gastronomic center for the Riviera as the home of Le Moulin de Mougins, the internationally renowned restaurant of Roger Vergé, the master chef who helped put Provençal cuisine on menus around the world. (Picasso was the unrivaled local celebrity until Vergé arrived.) In an atmospheric 16th-century olive oil mill surrounded by palms and mimosas, Vergé creates what he calls his *cuisine du soleil;* a traditional, simple, but modernized cuisine using the aromatic herbs, spices, and sun-ripened vegetables of Provence, mostly from Vergé's own garden. After 35 years, the affable chef and his wife, Denise, passed the torch to the well-known Sébastien Chambru, who promises continued success. A handful of guest rooms are available for people who refuse to eat and run. The decor bears the infallible touch of Madame Vergé, whose aesthetic influence is evident everywhere in her husband's hilltop empire.

WHAT: town, restaurant, hotel. **MOUGINS:** 4 miles/6 km north of Cannes. **LE MOULIN DE MOUGINS:** Quartier Notre-Dame-de-Vie. Tel 33/4-93-75-78-24, fax 33/4-93-90-18-55; reservations@moulindemougins.com; www.moulindemougins.com. *Cost:* dinner from $135, lunch from $70. Doubles from $260. *When:* restaurant and hotel open mid-Jan–Nov.

Le Moulin de Mougin is a former olive oil mill.

A Beautiful Diva on the Sea

VIEUX NICE

Provence-Alpes-Côte d'Azur, France

O n balmy summer nights Vieux Nice—the medieval warren of the Old Town (called *babazouk* in the Niçois dialect)—and the popular Cours Saleya buzz with a mix of young and old, locals and tourists. Although Nice is the fifth largest city in France, it has a small-town ambience, and the main market, Tuesday through Sunday, evokes the colors, smells, and wonders of the Provençal countryside just outside town. The golden era when Nice was Europe's most fashionable winter retreat is reflected in the deep pinks and ochers of the town's elegant Italianate architecture (Nice, after all, belonged to Italy; it was ceded back to France in 1860). The wedding cake Hôtel Negresco, built in 1912 on the seafront in the grand style of a French château, is one of the Riviera's great hotels and deserves a lingering visit. Recently restored, this national landmark shimmers like a gem; the immense 19th-century Baccarat crystal chandelier in the Salon Royal was commissioned by a Russian czar. The Gobelin tapestries on the wall seem too big to be real, but they're the real thing. Rooms facing the Bay of Angels have balconies overlooking the fabled Promenade des Anglais, where a twilight stroll reminds you why the Côte d'Azur is still the coast with the most.

The Hôtel Negresco is filled with art and antiques.

WHAT: town, hotel. **NICE:** 19 miles/31 km from Cannes, 567 miles/912 km from Paris. **HÔTEL NEGRESCO:** 37 Promenade des Anglais. Tel 33/4-93-16-64-00, fax 33/4-93-88-35-68; in the U.S., tel 800-223-6800; reservations@hotel-negresco.com; www.hotel-negresco.com. *Cost:* doubles from $410 (low season), from $510 (high season). **BEST TIMES:** Festival de Jazz is 2d week in Jul; Carnival is held each year in late winter.

World-Class Art Collections in a Village Perché

LA FONDATION MAEGHT

St.-Paul-de-Vence, Provence-Alpes-Côte d'Azur, France

S t.-Paul-de-Vence is a gem of a medieval pedestrian-only hill town north of Cannes, whose ancient charm is not lost despite high-season crowds. Step inside the cool galleries of the Fondation Maeght and be transported by one of the world's most famous small museums of modern art, with views like no other. Founded in 1964, this low-lying gallery and its breezy pine-shaded, terraced gardens showcase world-class works by Giacometti, Miró, Calder, Braque, Matisse, Kandinsky, and others. Many of the major 20th-century artists represented either lived in or regularly visited St.-Paul-de-Vence, dining at the charming La Colombe d'Or and leaving behind their work to pay the bill. The restaurant and inn, once little more than an informal bistro, is now one of the region's most renowned, in part because it was the haunt of great artists and writers as well as for the original Chagalls, Picassos, and Légers that decorate the walls of the dining room. The rich and famous check in here, but to experience one of Provence's perfect stopovers, stay at another small hotel of enormous charm—Le Saint-Paul, right in the heart of town.

WHAT: town, site, restaurant, hotel. ST.-PAUL-DE-VENCE: 19 miles/30 km north of Cannes, 6 miles/10 km from Nice. LA FONDATION MAEGHT: tel 33/4-93-32-81-63, fax 33/4-93-32-53-22; contact@fondation-maeght.com; www.fondation-maeght.com. *Cost:* admission. LA COLOMBE D'OR: Place Général de Gaulle. Tel 33/4-93-32-80-02, fax 33/4-93-32-77-78; contact@la-colombe-dor.com; www.la-colombe-dor.com. *Cost:* dinner $55. Doubles from $410. *When:* hotel and restaurant closed Nov 3–Dec 19. HÔTEL LE SAINT-PAUL: 86 Rue Grande. Tel 33/4-93-32-65-25, fax 33/4-93-32-52-94; reservations@lesaintpaul.com; www.lesaintpaul.com. *Cost:* doubles from $355 (low season), from $465 (high season). *When:* open Feb 5–Jan 3. BEST TIMES: spring.

A Nostalgic Myth That Never Dies

ST.-TROPEZ

Provence-Alpes-Côte d'Azur, France

Brigitte Bardot lives. Since first arriving in 1956 to star in Roger Vadim's *And God Created Woman,* la Bardot has never left. A parade of nubile Bardot lookalikes, golden boys, and bon vivant wannabes fill the topless—and

sometimes bottomless—beaches, some of the nicest and sandiest on the Riviera. "The good old days" and their sybaritic hedonism have dimmed over the decades, but St.-Tropez has survived its fame, success, and ballooning summer crowds and has even become fashionable again. Its flirtatious charm remains evident, especially in the early-morning hours or off-months, when the light and innocence of this old fishing town can still be appreciated. On the other hand, this craziest of resorts is all about its eccentric habitués and impromptu street theater. Maybe Colette started it in the 1920s, when she scandalized the outside world by going around with bare legs.

It's not the place to get away from it all. For nonpareil people-watching, turn up for breakfast—or après-beach, when everyone has baked at the popular Plage Tahiti (where topless sunbathing is said to have originated) or at Pampelonne—at the portside Café Sénéquier command post on the Quai Jean Jaurès. This is the perennially "in" place to watch the parade of those in various aesthetic stages of beach and resort chic that they could never get away with back home. The St.-Tropez glamour quotient remains intact, with flair and dare aplenty.

WHAT: town, restaurant. ST.-TROPEZ: 45 miles/72 km southwest of Cannes. CAFÉ

SÉNÉQUIER: Quai Jean Jaurès, tel 33/4-94-97-00-90. **WHERE TO STAY:** Les Moulins de Christophe Leroy, about a mile away, Route des Plages, Ramatuelle. Tel 33/4-94-97-91-91; info@christophe-leroy.com; www.christophe-leroy.com. *Cost:* doubles from $295.

A Hinterland Escape Minutes from the Riviera

VENCE

Provence-Alpes-Côte d'Azur, France

A microcosm of the *arrière-pays*, the rolling backcountry beyond the coastal Riviera, Vence was long a Provençal magnet for artists and writers. Nestled in the hills covered with pines, cypresses, and olive

The Templars' fabled treasure may be buried beneath Château St.-Martin.

groves, it still attracts well-heeled visitors who want to escape the coast's *comme-des-sardines* crowds. Cognoscenti are attracted to the open-air market, regarded as one of the best in the region, and to Vence's unpretentious every-day feel. The Matisse Chapel here is a 20th-century tour de force. After recovering from a long illness in 1948, Henri Matisse promised a Dominican sister, who was one of his nurses and sometimes his model, that he would dec-orate the Dominican Oratory connected to the home. Brimming with enthusiasm, he began the Chapelle du Rosaire at seventy-seven and died three years after its completion. "Despite its imperfections, I think it is my master-piece," declared Matisse after five years of work, "the result of a lifetime devoted to the search of truth."

Visitors can prolong the experience by checking into the elite Château du Domaine St.-Martin, a handsome inn tucked away on a wooded hillside above the town. The secluded hostelry sits on the site of a 12th-century Crusader castle whose draw-bridge and chapel still remain. The present structure was built in 1936 and, with its hillside villas, encompasses 35 acres, with magnificent panoramas at every turn and a soothing pool area shaded by olive trees.

WHAT: town, site, hotel, restaurant. **VENCE:** 19 miles/31 km northeast of Cannes, 15 miles/24 km northwest of Nice. **CHAPELLE DU ROSAIRE (MATISSE CHAPEL):** 466 Avenue Henri-Matisse. Tel 33/4-93-58-03-26. *Cost:* admission. *When:* Mon–Fri, closed 2 weeks in mid-Dec. **LE CHÂTEAU DU DOMAINE ST.-MARTIN:** Avenue des Templiers (2 miles/3 km outside Vence). Tel 33/4-93-58-02-02, fax 33/4-93-24-40-93; in the U.S., tel 800-RELAIS-8; reservation@chateau-st-martin.com; www.chateau-st-martin.com. *Cost:* doubles from $330 (low season), from $705 (high season). Dinner $90. *When:* hotel and restaurant open Mar–Oct; restaurant open Thurs–Mon. **BEST TIMES:** Apr–Jun, Sept, and Oct.

A Lakeside Jewel in the Savoy Alps

ANNECY AND TALLOIRES

Rhône-Alpes, France

T his miniature Venice in an alpine setting is an unspoiled medieval and Renaissance treasure. Annecy is crisscrossed by the Thiou River—which creates numerous canals before joining with the Fier, confluent with the

Rhône—and sits on the northern shore of Lac d'Annecy. Of the region Paul Cézanne exclaimed, "What a superb vestige of times past!" In the delightful Vieille Ville (Old City), lovingly preserved churches and flower-bedecked quayside town houses are reflected in crystal-clear rivers and canals crossed by arched pedestrian bridges. (Environmentally conscious local governments have done much to keep the city and its environs pollution free.) In warm weather, boat excursions visit the shores of the pristine lake. Otherwise, window-shop along the lively, beautifully kept city streets, which contain an astounding number of food specialty shops and elegant antiques stores. Food fans say a visit to Annecy without a meal at the fabled Auberge de Marc Veyrat (still commonly known by its old name, "L'Eridan") is like going to Agra and missing the Taj Mahal. The virtuoso chef himself picks the rare alpine herbs and fresh wildflowers he uses. One must also make a visit to the Auberge du Père Bise, in nearby Talloires. This hotel-restaurant, a picture-book cluster of houses scattered along crystal-clear Lac d'Annecy, has long been a beacon in the French gastronomic world. Sophie Bise, the granddaughter of founder Père Bise, is one of France's most esteemed female chefs. Parisians think nothing of making a long trip here to lunch on lobster tail or *mousse de foie gras,* plus a sampling from the restaurant's world-class wine cellar, all served on the pergola-covered lakefront veranda. Sybarites will admire the tapestries and antiques that

Dining alfresco at Auberge de Marc Veyrat

have transformed the former monks' cells of this onetime 17th-century Benedictine abbey into luxury living quarters.

WHAT: town, restaurant, hotel. **ANNECY:** 334 miles/537 km southeast of Paris, 85 miles/137 km east of Lyons. *Best times:* Tues, Fri, and Sun are market days; flea/antiques market on last Sat of every month. **AUBERGE DE MARC VEYRAT:** 13 Vieille Route des Pensières, Veyrier-du-Lac (3 miles/5 km from Annecy). Tel 33/4-50-60-24-00; www.marcveyrat.fr. *Cost:* dinner $125. Lake-view doubles from $425. *When:* hotel and restaurant open May–Nov. *Note:* At press time this was closed temporarily. **AUBERGE DU PÈRE BISE:** Route du Port, Talloires (8 miles/13 km from Annecy). Tel 33/4-50-60-72-01, fax 33/4-50-60-73-05; in the U.S., tel 800-RELAIS-8; bise @relaischateaux.com; www.relaischateaux.com/bise. *Cost:* dinner $125. Doubles from $370. *When:* hotel closed mid-Dec to mid-Feb; restaurant open for lunch and dinner daily in high season.

Stepping into History in One of Europe's Most Exquisite Château Hôtels

CHÂTEAU DE BAGNOLS

Beaujolais, Rhône-Alpes, France

Everyone hopes to find an authentic corner of France overlooked by tourism, and here it is. The little-visited niche of Beaujolais is often compared to Tuscany, with vineyard after vineyard cloaking folds of rolling sunlit hills.

And lucky are those few who drive over the drawbridge to the magnificent Château de Bagnols, France's premier country home and a designated historic monument, one of some 150 baronial châteaux scattered throughout this viticultural backwater. English owners have painstakingly brought Bagnols back to its former glory with the help of more than 400 craftsmen and artisans. The walls are once again extravagantly decorated with Renaissance-inspired paintings, and the canopied beds are hung with period velvets and silks, the sumptuous fabrics that made nearby Lyons famous. The antique beds are the château's tour de force, each a theatrical work of art from the owner's personal collection. To choose among the twenty spacious rooms, museum-like but relaxed and cozy, is nearly impossible. In the morning, make a foray into la belle France, or head for Sunday lunch at the Auberge du Cep in nearby Fleurie, for Beaujolais cooking and wines at their best.

The Appartement aux Bouquets at the Château de Bagnols

WHAT: hotel, restaurant. **WHERE:** in Beaujolais, 20 miles/32 km north of Lyons. Tel 33/4-74-71-40-00, fax 33/4-74-71-40-49; www.bagnols.com. **COST:** doubles from $650 (low season), from $721 (high season). Dinner $115. **WHEN:** hotel and restaurant open Apr 4– Jan 2. **BEST TIMES:** May–Oct.

Premier Skiing and Hiking amid Mountain Scenery

CHAMONIX AND TOUR DU MONT-BLANC

Rhône-Alpes, France

No wonder Chamonix was chosen to host the first Winter Olympics in 1924. Long before it was heralded as Europe's best resort for advanced and expert skiers, Chamonix was a serious mountaineering center and summer capital for climbers. Glacier-wrapped Mont Blanc rears up straight over town, and on a clear day you can see the Matterhorn, 40 miles away. "I never knew—I never imagined what mountains were before," said Percy Bysshe Shelley after a visit in 1816. The Chamonix Valley cuts through Europe's highest mountains and glaciers, providing stunning views and terrain that make for peerless summer hiking and radical off-piste skiing that's steep, high, and long. The outstanding run—and not just for experts—is the celebrated Vallée Blanche, a rugged, uninterrupted 12-mile glacier run of breathtaking scenery. Even farther aloft is the 12,000-foot needle-pointed Aiguille du Midi, reached by the world's highest cable car ride, a heart-stopping experience for skiing and nonskiing altitude lovers. A cog train accesses the glorious 6,300-foot summit of the Mer de Glace (Sea of Ice), the second-largest glacier in the Alps, another alpine wonderland that must have held Shelley in thrall.

In the midsummer months, the region is host to seasoned hikers, many of whom undertake the lovely Tour du Mont-Blanc. The point of the tour is not to make it to the *top* of the highest mountain in western Europe, but rather to follow a circular route through France, Italy, and Switzerland and their ever-changing panoramas of glaciers, peaks, and meadows. Following roads once used by the Roman legions and crossing through a succession of seven valleys (each with its own scenery, cuisine, and culture), you encounter remote villages and customs unchanged for centuries. Take a picnic lunch for the wildflower-covered meadows.

WHAT: town, experience. **CHAMONIX:** 381 miles/613 km southeast of Paris, 51 miles/82 km southeast of Geneva, Switzerland. *When:* cable cars and cog trains run daily, year-round. *Best times:* Jan–Mar for skiing. **TOUR DU MONT-BLANC:** departure from and return to Chamonix. Hiking experience is required; climbing experience is not. *How:* Wilderness Travel in the U.S., tel 510-558-2488 or 800-368-2794, fax 510-558-2489; info@wildernesstravel.com; www.wildernesstravel.com. *Cost:* from $3,695 per person for 2-week trips, excluding airfare. *When:* Jul–Sept departures.

In the Heart of the Trois Vallées

COURCHEVEL

Rhône-Alpes, France

Host to the 1992 Winter Olympics and one of the highest, most attractive, and best-equipped ski locations in the French Alps, Courchevel sits in the confluence of three alpine valleys that make up the world's largest ski area. Many of its slopes are north facing, with some of the most immaculate grooming found anywhere. Courchevel's four "villages" are named after their varying altitudes, the best being the highest at 6,012 feet (1,850 meters). They are cosmopolitan but not intimidatingly chic, and the hundreds of trails, the extensive crisscrossing network of lifts, and the varied terrain (great for near beginners, and wonderful for all levels of intermediate skiers) make this one of the best ski establishments anywhere. Many travelers come to ski the Courchevel sector alone, but it is well linked to other resorts in the Trois Vallées, such as the attractive Méribel, or Val-Thorens, the highest ski resort in Europe.

Courchevel is known for its deluxe dining and luxury hotels. One of the finest is Le Mélézin, the first European property of

Terrace dining at Hôtel Le Mélézin

Amanresorts, whose exquisite Asian hotels have transformed the concept of five-star boutique accommodations in the Pacific. Its minimalist luxury is a warm and welcome change from the Tyrolian chalet theme so ubiquitous in these ultra-scenic parts.

WHAT: experience, town, hotel. **COURCHEVEL:** 393 miles/632 km southeast of Paris. *Best times:* mid-Jan–mid-Feb for skiing. **HÔTEL LE MÉLÉZIN:** Rue de Bellecôte. Tel 33/4-79-08-01-33, fax 33/4-79-08-08-96; in the U.S., tel 800-477-9180; lemelezin@ amanresorts.com; www.amanresorts.com. *Cost:* doubles from $1,035, suites from $2,690. *When:* open mid-Dec–mid-Apr.

Enclave of Medieval and Renaissance France

VIEUX LYONS

Rhône-Alpes, France

Recently restored and once again fashionable, the square-mile old quarter called Vieux Lyons showcases the glory days when Lyons was Europe's mercantile and financial center. A series of narrow streets form a picturesque labyrinth lined with more than 350 buildings, considered the country's most extensive and homogeneous grouping from the late Gothic period to the 17th century. Quaint *traboules* (covered passageways), unique to Lyons, hark back to the days when they helped people move precious bolts of silk during inclement weather. The *traboules* connect streets lined with arcaded galleries, antiques shops, charcuteries, Italianate courtyards, and La Cour des Loges, one of Lyons's most stylish hotels.

The dazzling concentration of some of Europe's highest-rated restaurants in and around Lyons have made it a magnet, second only to the gastronomic capital, Paris. Of the city's more than 700 dining establishments, a good number are casual *bouchons,* Lyons's traditional bistros. The homey, family-run Café des Fédérations, with its sawdust-covered floors and sausage-strung dining room, has been a longtime favorite for its wonderful, earthy fare. But it is stellar, innovative chefs like Jean-Paul Lacombe, whose family has run the renowned and charming Léon de Lyons since 1905, who have contributed to Lyons's fame as France's mecca of fine dining.

WHAT: site, hotel, restaurant. **VIEUX LYONS:** on the west bank of the Saône River, 287 miles/460 km southeast of Paris. **LA COUR DES LOGES:** 2468 Rue du Boeuf. Tel 33/4-72-77-44-44, fax 33/4-72-40-93-61; contact@courdesloges.com; www.courdesloges. com. *Cost:* doubles from $350. **CAFÉ DES FÉDÉRATIONS:** 8 Rue du Major Martin. Tel 33/4-78-28-26-00, fax 33/4-72-07-74-52; www.lesfedeslyon.com. *Cost:* dinner $30.

When: open Mon–Fri, Sept–Jul. **LÉON DE LYONS:** 1 Rue Pleney. Tel 33/4-72-10-11-12, fax 33/4-72-10-11-13; leon@relaischateaux. fr; www.leondelyon.com. *Cost:* dinner $95. *When:* open Sept–Jul. **BEST TIMES:** Easter– late Jul and Sept–late Nov.

France's Most Beloved Grand Chef

RESTAURANT PAUL BOCUSE

Lyons, Rhône-Alpes, France

Hailing from a family that has been running restaurants since 1767, Paul Bocuse has won the most accolades and awards in the culinary world since opening the restaurant that bears his now world-famous name in 1965. Elegantly attired food lovers flock to his gourmet temple from all corners of the globe, content to be in the deft hands of the chefs who run things smoothly in his frequent absence. Yet the larger-than-life spirit of Bocuse is always palpable. The first chef ever to be decorated with the Legion of Honor by a French president, Bocuse continues to offer the down-to-earth regional fare that he promotes during his world travels as ambassador of French cuisine. A handful of France's superstar chefs may come close to matching his celebrity status as a national treasure, but none surpasses him.

Since he led a second French revolution (of cooking) in the 1970s, which came to be called nouvelle cuisine, his message has been one of simplicity. Try the full-flavored black truffle soup or spit-roasted Bresse chicken with a glass of Beaujolais from Bocuse's own wine firm to understand the extraordinary success of the world's most famous living chef.

WHAT: restaurant. **WHERE:** 40 Rue de la Plage, Collonges-au-Mont-d'Or (5 miles/8 km outside Lyons, which is 287 miles/460 km southeast of Paris). Tel 33/4-72-42-90-90; www.bocuse.fr. **COST:** dinner $175.

A Pristine Alpine Town of Rustic Charm

MEGÈVE

Rhône-Alpes, France

When skiers think of a picturesque alpine village, they think Megève. Neighboring resorts dominated by Mont Blanc may offer higher-altitude skiing, but they are hard pressed to top tiny Megève for scenery, charm, and après-ski enjoyments. Designated a must for society's winter schedule by the Baroness de Rothschild in the 1920s, its colorful horse-drawn sleighs and traditional town center have kept this glamorous year-round destination popular among a privileged set that comes for the authentic and cozy rhythms of mountain-village life (albeit one with a casino) and low-key luxe. Set in a beautiful, wide valley, Megève may be too low to ensure snow all season long, but on a good day the excellent woodland terrain is ideal for gentle intermediate cruising. It is also known for its 47 miles of cross-country skiing, and the ski school is one of Europe's foremost. Regulars come back in warm weather for first-rate hiking, 18-hole golf, and a bevy of top-notch restaurants. Although not the most exclusive or expensive, surely the most charming hotel in town is Les Fermes de Marie, a *bijou* cluster of five century-old *mazots*, chalet-like farm buildings gathered from nearby hamlets and lovingly reassembled in the heart of town, beam by beam and stone by stone. There is an all-natural spa, called a health and beauty

farm; together with a mouthwatering menu of homemade ultrafresh mountain cuisine, this Megève hostelry gives new meaning to the term "mountain refuge."

WHAT: town, hotel. **MEGÈVE:** 372 miles/599 km southeast of Paris, 22 miles/35 km west of Chamonix, 43 miles/69 km southwest of Geneva, Switzerland. **LES FERMES DE MARIE:** Chemin de Riante Colline. Tel 33/4-50-93-03-10, fax 33/4-50-93-09-84; contact @fermesdemarie.com; www.fermesdemarie.com. *Cost:* doubles from $260 (low season), from $445 (high season), includes breakfast and dinner for 2. **BEST TIMES:** Dec–Mar, Jun–Sept.

Both Grand and Homey,
One of France's Most Revered Restaurants

LA MAISON TROISGROS

Roanne, Rhône-Alpes, France

Years after they've dined here, people speak reverently of La Maison Troisgros, as if it were a religious experience. Dinner at Troisgros—from the simple house specialty of *saumon à l'oseille* (salmon with sorrel sauce)

to the large rolling dessert cart—attracts diners who think nothing of driving down from Brussels to partake in the gastronomic celebration. The *menu dans la tradition*, a

Pierre Troisgros and son Michel

seven-course extravaganza, is a tribute to the kaleidoscopic produce of the countryside as interpreted by the unrivaled talents of Pierre Troisgros. When his co-chef and brother, Jean, died in 1983, his son, Michel, stepped in to help his father create some of the finest food anywhere in France. Yet despite its revered status, the dining room is surprisingly ordinary—somehow an appropriate foil for food that is nothing less than extraordinary. The restaurant also operates a small hotel with lovely rooms.

WHAT: restaurant. **WHERE:** Place de la Gare, Roanne (54 miles/87 km west of Lyons). Tel 33/4-77-71-66-97, fax 33/4-77-70-39-77; in the U.S., tel 800-RELAIS-8; info@troisgros.com; www.troisgros.com. **COST:** dinner $220. Doubles from $395. **WHEN:** open Thurs–Mon.

A Family Affair

PIC

Valence, Rhône-Alpes, France

I t all started in 1891 with Sophie Pic and a simple country café. Founder of the fabled Pic culinary dynasty, Sophie was the first of four generations to raise the traditional regional cuisine to a gastronomic art form. More than 100

years later, Sophie's great-grandchildren continue one of France's oldest and most respected family lines of *chefs du cuisine*. Anne Pic—daughter of the renowned Jacques Pic, who died in 1992—is currently the creative force in the kitchen. She runs one of the most provincial of France's grand restaurants and perhaps one of the least known of the great gastronomic shrines. The homey atmos-

One of Pic's fresh dishes

phere and local clientele blend seamlessly with the superlative food and a sophisticated ambience that is elegant without being overdone. Understand what all the fuss is about by ordering the Pic Generations Menu on a summer evening on the outdoor patio. It includes, among other wonders, the Pic family's classic, *filet de loup au caviar,* a delicate filet of bass with caviar. The wine cellar, stocked with more than 20,000 bottles, includes more than 400 different Côtes-du-Rhônes, the wine for which Pic has become the ambassador to the world. A small on-site hotel caters to traveling gourmands.

WHAT: restaurant. **WHERE:** 285 Avenue Victor Hugo, Valence (60 miles/97 km south of Lyons, 335 miles/539 km south of Paris). Tel 33/4-75-44-15-32, fax 33/4-75-40-96-03; info@pic-valence.com; www.pic-valence.com. **COST:** Dinner $155, Pic Generations Menu $450. Doubles from $410. **BEST TIMES:** Apr–Jun.

A Worthy Heir to a Famous Name

GEORGES BLANC

Vonnas, Rhône-Alpes, France

I t was chef Georges Blanc's grandmother who first put the tiny town of Vonnas on the gastronomic map. She was called the world's greatest cook by Curnonsky, a revered French gourmet of the early 20th century. Her equally celebrated daughter-in-law passed on her talent and passion to her son, Georges Blanc, and today the family restaurant on the banks of the River Veyle attracts diners from all parts of the world. The fanfare is easy to understand once the food arrives: it is simply some of the most sublime imaginable. It is not by chance that the dessert cart brims with dozens of concoctions to top off an already unbeatable meal: Blanc began his career as a pastry chef, and sweets still have a strong claim on his heart. The profusion of flowers and antiques spills over into attached hotel guest rooms, many of which have balconies and views of the river and blooming gardens.

WHAT: restaurant, hotel. **HÔTEL GEORGES BLANC:** Place du Maré, Vonnas (38 miles/60 km from Lyons, 259 miles/417 km from Paris, and 11 miles/18 km from Macon, the closest town). Tel 33/4-74-50-90-90, fax 33/4-74-50-08-80; www.georgesblanc.com. **COST:** dinner $170. Doubles from $325. **WHEN:** restaurant and hotel closed Jan 2–Feb 1. Restaurant open Wed–Sun.

A 19th-Century Landmark in a Fairy-Tale Principality

THE GRAND CASINO

Monte Carlo, Monaco

The tiny principality of Monaco, no bigger than London's Hyde Park, has catered to gamblers and the idle rich for the last 100 years. Both types can be found with all their over-the-top idiosyncracies at the legendary Grand Casino, the world's most renowned casino, and indisputably the most glamorous. This is one of the last places on earth to witness chaffeur-driven Rolls-Royces disgorging wealthy exiles, sun-baked yacht owners, and

Charles Garnier, architect of the Paris Opera House, also designed Monte Carlo's Grand Casino.

celluloid divas weighed down by serious jewelry. The sedate, even discreet, Belle Epoque setting was designed in 1863 by Charles Garnier, grand architect of the Paris Opéra. Black tie is no longer required, but jackets and ties are a must in the inner sanctum of high rollers, and many women wear long dresses. No Monégasque gambler sets foot in the casino without first stopping by the lobby of the Hôtel de Paris—a poker chip's toss across the impeccably groomed Place du Casino—to rub the left knee of the bronze statue of Louis XIV's horse for good luck. Facing the hotel and alongside the casino, the Garnier-designed Café de Paris is a de rigueur stop for a pre- or après-casino drink or a crêpe Suzette, invented here in the early 1900s and named after a friend of the Prince of Wales.

WHAT: site. **WHERE:** Place du Casino. Tel 377/98-06-21-21. **COST:** admission charged to some gaming rooms. **WHEN:** open year-round, from noon until the last customer leaves.

Dowager Queen of the Riviera

HÔTEL DE PARIS

Monte Carlo, Monaco

If you're not staying with the Grimaldis (the royal family that has ruled Monaco since the 13th century), try the palatial Hôtel de Paris. The regal stopping place of emirs and archdukes since its inception one year after the opening of the Grand Casino next door, the Hôtel de Paris looms over the main square, a must-see for curious tourists and destination for the fabulously rich and very famous.

Much of the hotel's acclaim owes to its highly rated restaurants, particularly the formal Le Louis XV, a dazzling jewel box that has been the domain since 1987 of Alain Ducasse, one of the world's most celebrated chefs. Here Ducasse prides himself on using humble Mediterranean ingredients of the finest quality and refining them into a superb, albeit simple, haute cuisine. The restaurant's opulent Louis XV decor includes Baccarat crystal, damask linens, gold-rimmed china, and silver service.

The new Centre Thalassothérapie de Thermes Marins, wedged into a cliff adjacent to the hotel, is reached through an adjoining walkway beneath the hotel. Time spent at this state-of-the-art spa is—like an evening at Le Louis XV—sheer heaven.

WHAT: hotel, restaurant. **MONTE CARLO:** 15 miles/24 km east of Nice. **HÔTEL DE PARIS:** Place du Casino. Tel 377/98-06-30-00, fax 377/98-06-59-13; in the U.S., tel 212-973-0099. For Le Louis XV, tel 377/98-06-88-64, fax 377/92-16-69-21; office@sbmny.com; www.montecarloresort.com. *Cost:* doubles from $595 (low season), from $740 (high season). Dinner at Le Louis XV $295. **BEST TIMES:** cultural and sports events in Monaco year-round; International Fireworks Festival every Jul and Aug; Formula One Grand Prix late May/early Jun.

The Summer Capital of Europe

BADEN-BADEN AND BRENNER'S PARK HOTEL AND SPA

Baden-Württemberg, Germany

Baden-Baden, located at the northern edge of the dense Black Forest, has been known as the "summer capital of Europe" since the mid-19th century, when Queen Victoria and Napoleon III basked in its curative springs.

Its dignified old-world glory can be found in the dripping elegance of the gilt-and-stucco casino, in the shaded Lichtentaler Allee, a lushly landscaped promenade along the Oos River, and in the pastel houses where Europe's royal families and high society made their second homes. Today Baden-Baden is once again living unashamedly on leisure and pleasure. The new palatial Caracalla baths have no fewer than seven pools. There are 300 miles of hiking paths on the periphery of the Black Forest, and a 13-mile bike path meanders through rich farm country.

The rich and royal now stay at the Brenner's Park Hotel and Spa. One of the few remaining grand spa hotels in Europe, the 125-year-old hotel commands a perfect location overlooking the Oos River. The columns and Pompeiian-style frescoed walls of the hotel's large heated glass-enclosed *schwimmbad* call to mind the ancient Roman general Caracalla, whose Roman legionnaires first discovered the curative powers of Baden-Baden's thermal springs in the 3rd century A.D. The hotel also offers sophisticated beauty and health care, and a nearby golf course that the Duke of Windsor called "a real pearl." In Baden-

Baden the Belle Epoque lives on; the pace is as unhurried as in bygone times, when one came to take the restorative cures of the ionizing springs. "I fully believe I left my rheumatism in Baden-Baden," wrote Mark Twain. "Baden-Baden is welcome to it."

WHAT: town, hotel. **BADEN-BADEN:** 100 miles/161 km south of Frankfurt. **BRENNER'S PARK HOTEL AND SPA:** Schillerstrasse 4116. Tel 49/7221-9000, fax 49/7221-38772; in the U.S., 800-745-8883; information@brenners. com; www.brenners.com. *Cost:* doubles from $480.

Brenner's Park Hotel and Spa

R&R Deep in the Heart of the Black Forest

HOTEL TRAUBE TONBACH

Baiersbronn, Baden-Württemberg, Germany

The Traube Tonbach is one of the Black Forest's great resorts: big, well equipped, excellently situated in a lush green valley in this fabled southwest corner of Germany. There are spa and beauty treatments and

sporting facilities galore, all of which pale next to the large hotel's famous restaurant Die Schwarzwaldstube (Black Forest Room). France and its gastronomic capital of Strasbourg are just over the border, and the French influence is reflected in the refined style of head chef Harald Wohlfahrt: witness his signature grilled

pigeon with chanterelle mushrooms. In the fifteen years he has held court here, Wohlfahrt has brought the kitchen from strength to strength. A few days of meandering through this ancient forest with such sublime food awaiting your return is the perfect scenario. Despite the density of its lofty fir trees, this southwestern corner of Germany is filled with sunny charm at every turn. The hotel, owned and run by the Finkbeiner family for more than 200 years, is within striking distance of dozens of different hiking, bike-riding, and motoring trails and a memorable historic railroad journey. Hitch up with the classic Schwartzwald Hochstrasse (the Black Forest Crest Road), from Baden-Baden in the northwest to Freudenstadt in the southeast for 41 miles of natural beauty.

WHAT: restaurant, hotel. **WHERE:** Tonbachstrasse 237 (50 miles/80 km east of Strasbourg, 63 miles/100 km southwest of Stuttgart, 31 miles/50 km southeast of Baden-Baden). Tel 49/7442-4920, fax 49/7442-492692; info@traube-tonbach.de; www.traube-

tonbach.de. **COST:** prix fixe 5-course dinner $190. Doubles from $195. **WHEN:** restaurant open Wed–Sun. **BEST TIMES:** fall.

The rustic and elegant hotel lobby

An Exotic Isle on Germany's Riviera

THE BODENSEE (LAKE CONSTANCE)

Konstanz, Baden-Württemberg, Germany

The Bodensee, also known as the "Swabian Sea," is Germany's largest lake and the closest it can come to the Riviera. In Germany's southernmost region and shared with Austria and Switzerland, it is best seen from the corniche road that follows the lake's northern German shore with its string of pretty resorts. Countless ferries crisscross the waters offering all kinds of excursions to the three different countries; most special is the "paradise island" of Mainau with its masses of riotous flowers and exotic vegetation. A scented isle that evokes balmy images of the Mediterranean, it was occupied in the 13th century by Teutonic knights who later built the island's Baroque castle in 1732. The Grand Duke of Baden took possession in 1853 and began bringing home rare plants from his travels abroad. His great-grandson and the present-day summer resident of the castle,

Count Lennart Bernadotte, has kept up the family passion for botany. The lake's neartropical, moist microclimate leads to spectacular foliage and flowers, including more than 1,000 varieties of roses. Konstanz is the lake's largest and liveliest resort town, with a beautiful medieval core perfectly intact (it avoided WW II bombing thanks to its position at the border of politically neutral Switzerland). On its own small island, tethered to town by a causeway, is the Steigenberger Inselhotel, which began life in the 13th century as a cloistered monastery. Reformer Jan Hus was held here before his execution, and Count Ferdinand von Zeppelin

The Steigenberger Inselhotel, just over the bridge from town

where fresh fish plucked from the lake land daily on the menu, and most of the spacious balconied rooms enjoy lovely views of the lake.

WHAT: site, hotel. **KONSTANZ:** 126 miles/200 km southwest of Munich, 41 miles/65 km northeast of Zurich, Switzerland. **STEIGENBERGER INSELHOTEL:** Auf der Insel 1. Tel 49/7531-1250, fax 49/7531-26402; konstanz@steigenberger.de; www.konstanz.steigenberger.de. *Cost:* doubles from $325 (low season), from $365 (high season). **BEST TIMES:** spring for the most beautiful flower displays.

of dirigible fame was born here when it was a private residence. The terraced restaurant,

---

A Drive Through Postcard-Perfect Beauty

THE ALPINE ROAD AND ZUGSPITZE

Bavaria, Germany

The German Alpine Road (Deutsche Alpenstrasse) is one of Europe's most ancient and scenic routes, winding along the Bavarian Alps, the spectacularly beautiful natural border between Germany and Austria. For 300

view-filled miles east of the Bodensee (Lake Constance), past ancient castles, quaint chalet-inns, and mountaintop villages with elaborately painted houses the Bavarians call *Lüftlmalerei*, the road gives travelers a look at some of the best of Germany. A good halfway stopping point is Garmisch, host of the 1936 Winter Olympics and home of the Zugspitze, Germany's highest mountain. It's an easy ascent to the top of this 9,731-foot peak with heart-stopping views, either by the cog railway, which departs from the center's train station for a leisurely seventy-five-minute ride, or, for those who know no fear, by the cable car, which leaves from Eibsee, just outside town.

Finally, there could be no greater finale to the Alpine Road than the lake, Königssee. With vertical escarpments of the Wartzman Mountains almost completely surrounding the lake, the most enjoyable—and only—way to see Königssee is by boat. Electric and quiet, the boats do not disturb the deep, cool waters as they drop visitors off at the pint-sized pilgrimage church of St. Bartholomä, wedged into a small cove. Originally constructed in the 11th century, Bartholomä was rebuilt some 600 years later. With the Königssee as its highlight, this gorgeous little slice of Germany that protrudes into Austria is the centerpiece of the stunning Berchtesgaden

National Park. The 120 miles of hiking trails are sprinkled with high-altitude restaurant-huts, and the region abounds with chaletlike guesthouses and rooms for rent.

WHAT: experience, site. **KÖNIGSSEE:** 15 miles/24 km south of Salzburg, Austria.

BERCHTESGADEN NATIONAL PARK: guided walks offered May to Oct; contact the local tourism office, tel 49/8652-1760, fax 49/8652-4050; tourismus@koenigssee.com; www.koenigssee.com. **BEST TIMES:** early summer or Sept for hiking.

Medieval Countryside, Restorative Wines, and a Gracious Inn

THE ROMANTIC ROAD

Bavaria, Germany

The Romantic Road (Romantische Strasse), stretching for 180 miles from Würzburg southward to Füssen, on the border with Austria, is more aptly named for the dozens of medieval towns, villages, and castles that line its way than for the scenery in between. Pity the people on the jam-packed tour buses who see it fleetingly in a day. They've missed the essence of what makes this road trip unique—the handful of towns forming a romantic chain of pearls must be appreciated slowly. Before you even set off, a visit to Würzburg and its glorious Baroque palace, the Residenz, sets the tone for the rest of your trip. Created when great wealth came together with the genius of architect Balthasar Neumann, the Residenz was commissioned in 1720 by the powerful and pleasure-loving prince-bishops who would make this their home and who apparently saw little conflict between religious service and flagrant ostentation. As you enter the Residenz, a monumental vaulted staircase, the largest in the country, is a not so subtle reminder that you are in one of Europe's most sumptuous buildings. To gild the lily, Giovanni Tiepolo was called in from Venice to cover the staircase ceilings—and others—with his colorful frescoes. The artist outdid himself in the already elaborate Throne Room, a profusion of delicate stucco and grandiose architecture enhanced further by his work, creating a space that is airy, opulent, and magical.

If your head is swimming, restore yourself with a sampling of the local white wines in the cozy tavern in the cellar of the Residenz, then move along to Rothenburg ob der Tauber (Red Castle on the Tauber), which is in love with its own image as the best-preserved medieval town in Europe. A tourist trap, yes, but a gorgeous one, with flowers spilling from window boxes, leaning half-timbered houses, cobblestone alleyways, city walls more than a mile long, and a 13th-century Rathaus.

The beauty, history, and charm of Rothenburg are echoed in the world-renowned Hotel Eisenhut—you may never want to leave the front lobby, where remnants of a 12th-century chapel can be found. The inn is maintained by the great-grandson of the original owner who first offered rooms to travelers in 1876, joining four 16th-century patrician homes on the ancient marketplace. The three-story, galleried dining hall is one of the best tickets in town—at least until the warm weather arrives and everyone heads out to the hotel's flagstone terrace on the Tauber River. It's just the place to stay on the Romantic Road, and many call it the best boutique hotel in Germany. The next day, head to Dinkelsbühl, a less touristy version of Rothenburg. Be in

Nördlingen in time to hear its town crier from high in the church tower, and visit Germany's best example of rococo architecture, the gemlike Wieskirche, which stands alone in its own alpine meadow. Begin and end your experience with a bang, touring Mad King Ludwig's two royal castles, Hohenschwangau and Neuschwanstein, which cap the southern end of the Romantic Road.

WHAT: experience, site, hotel. **ROMANTIC ROAD:** start at Würzburg, 74 miles/116 km southeast of Frankfurt. For information contact Romantic Road Association, tel 49/9851-551387, fax 49/9851-551388; info @romantischestrasse.de; www.romantische strasse.de. **RESIDENZ:** tel 49/9313-551712; www.wuerzburg.de. *Cost:* admission $10. *When:* Tues–Sun. **HOTEL EISENHUT:** Herrngasse 3-5, Rothenburg ob der Tauber. Tel 49/9861-7050, fax 49/9861-70545; hotel@ eisenhut.com; www.eisenhut.com. *Cost:* doubles from $190. *When:* Mar–Dec. **BEST TIMES:** Jun for the Mozart Festival in Würzburg; late Aug–early Sept for Imperial City Days; late Nov–late Dec for the Christmas Market in most towns.

A Treasure Chest of Architecture and Living Piece of History

BAMBERG

Bavaria, Germany

Set like Rome on seven hills and justly known as one of the most beautiful small towns in all of Europe, Bamberg's magic is inextricably linked to its rich history as capital of the Holy Roman Empire under Heinrich II, the town's most famous son. A treasure chest of architecture of all periods encased within a city that is by no means a static museum piece, Bamberg is a lively joy to visit for its

Bamberg's Rathaus

history, antiques stores, and nine breweries. It's been called a beer drinker's Eden, producing more than thirty varieties, one of them (the smoky Rauchbier), first brewed in 1536. Even Munich can't match that. The wonderfully picturesque Altes Rathaus (town hall) must be one of Europe's most photographed: half-timbered, frescoed, and built on its own little island in the middle of the River Regnitz. The imposing four-towered Kaiserdom, the city's great cathedral, built under Heinrich II and site of his coronation in 1012, is testimony to Bamberg's affluence as a powerful, ecclesiastical center and famous for its interior's elaborate sculptural decoration.

The spacious, sloping Domplatz square is a textbook illustration of the town's architectural evolution from Romanesque to Gothic and Renaissance to Baroque. There are more luxurious hotels in town, but for pure atmosphere, the classy Hotel St. Nepomuk wins out for its history as a former mill built in 1410, with many cozy rooms overlooking the river and the Rathaus, and a well-known restaurant specializing in regional cuisine.

WHAT: town, hotel. **BAMBERG:** 38 miles/ 60 km north of Nürnberg, 148 miles/238 km northwest of Munich. **HOTEL ST. NEPOMUK:** Obere Mühlbrucke 9. Tel 49/951-98420, fax 49/951-9842100; info@hotel-nepomuk.de; www.hotel-nepomuk.de. *Cost:* doubles with river view $265. **BEST TIMES:** spring, fall, and Christmas.

An Urban Legend Takes to the Hills

RESIDENZ HEINZ WINKLER

Chiemsee, Bavaria, Germany

Müncheners went into withdrawal when the country's finest chef left the kitchen of Tantris (and Munich) to set up a place of his own. Residenz Heinz Winkler is close enough for them to make the trip for a gastronomic fix; the chef has set up shop in a charming 600-year-old coaching inn in idyllic Bavarian country, with Austria just down the road. Diners can experience much of the alpine beauty the area has to offer without even leaving the dining room's magnificent open-air terrace, but there's no doubting that the best activity available is eating. Trailing his stars, toques, and accolades behind him, Winkler explores the frontiers of lighter German cooking still redolent of classical French principles, but enhanced with the Bavarian flourishes for which he is world-famous. A signature seasonal dish that embodies his philosophy in the kitchen is his venison soufflé with celery mousse. Plan to dip into Winkler's excellent collection of great wines, whether from Germany's Rhine Valley or farther afield. And save room for the iced Grand Marnier soufflé with fresh strawberries, knowing you needn't go far to sleep it all off (hope for a balconied room with mountain views). But keep in mind that Herr Winkler thinks that breakfast is the most important meal of the day. Once fortified, head out to explore the surrounding area. Germany's southeastern corner is famous for Ludwig II's sumptuous Schloss Herrenchiemsee, created in 1885 after his trip to France

Residenz Heinz Winkler is only a few short minutes from Chiemsee.

to mimic Versailles (in particular its Hall of Mirrors, reproduced here to scale and overlooking Ludwig's gardens) and built on its own island, one of three in the middle of beautiful Chiemsee, Bavaria's largest lake.

WHAT: restaurant, hotel. **WHERE:** Kirchplatz 1, Aschau (50 miles/80 km southeast of Munich, 38 miles/60 km west of Salzburg, Austria). Tel 49/8052-17990, fax 49/8052-179966; info@residenz-heinz-winkler.de; www.residenz-heinz-winkler.de. *Cost:* Dinner $140. Doubles from $350 (low season), from $410 (high season). **BEST TIMES:** spring and fall.

Mad Ludwig's Last Fantasy

COACHING IN BAVARIA AND NEUSCHWANSTEIN CASTLE

Germany

Turn back the clock and follow in the tracks of Germany's eccentric Ludwig II along the "King's Road" in a horse-drawn coach. Authentic 19th-century carriages hold up to nine passengers, who often choose to ride on leather-covered seats behind the uniformed coachman. The spectacular, unspoiled beauty of the Bavarian meadows, dense woodlands, mountains, and crystal-blue lakes is enhanced by the sound of cowbells and horses' hooves. Forgotten coach roads are practically traffic-free and lead you at a leisurely pace past isolated rural villages, historic *gasthof* inns, and country churches with onion-shaped domes, to the Mad King's flamboyant Neuschwanstein Castle and its fairy-tale alpine setting.

Neuschwanstein was one of three castles created by Ludwig, and by far his most ambitious and theatrical extravagance. Set on an isolated rock ledge amid heart-stopping scenery, it is the turreted prototype that inspired the castle in *Sleeping Beauty* and later at Disneyland. An expert at turning his will and whimsy into reality, Ludwig called upon the royal court's set designer rather than an architect for the creation of Neuschwanstein. (You can also visit the nearby castle of Hohenschwangau, where Ludwig lived while overseeing the work of Neuschwanstein.) It would take seventeen years and endless royal funds before it was finished—following Ludwig's mysterious death at age forty, days after he was forced to abdicate for reasons of insanity. Ludwig lived at the castle only 170 days before he died.

WHAT: experience, site. **COACH TRIP:** contact Coaching in Bavaria, tel 49/8808-386, fax 49/8808-1349; www.coaching-in-bavaria.com. Departures from Lake Starnberg (30 miles/48 km south of Munich). *Cost:* $425 per person for 2-day trip. *When:* departures every Fri and Sat, mid-May–Nov. **NEUSCHWANSTEIN CASTLE:** Füssen (74 miles/119 km southwest of Munich). *Cost:* admission $5. **BEST TIMES:** fall.

An Architectural Landmark and Its Masterpieces

ALTE PINAKOTHEK

Munich, Bavaria, Germany

Much of Munich's status as the nation's "secret capital" is due to its world-class museums. With room after room of Old Master and early northern European Renaissance masterworks in its collection, which range from the 14th to the 18th centuries, Munich's recently refurbished Alte Pinakothek (Old Picture Gallery) now rivals the Louvre for high-style display. Those running to catch the young Leonardo da Vinci's *Virgin and Child* or Titian's *Crowning with Thorns* might miss out on works by Memling, Brueghel, Hals, and Dürer (the *Four Apostles,* his final work, is another museum highlight). The picture gallery boasts one of the world's largest concentrations of 17th-century Flemish painter Rubens: of his sixty-two works here, *Self-Portrait with His Wife* and the huge *Last Judgment* are especially detour-worthy. Van Dyck, his most distinguished student, is also extensively represented here. The imposing brick building, constructed in Venetian Renaissance style, is itself an architectural treasure, built in the early 19th century to house the personal art collection of Ludwig I. Across the street is the Neue Pinakothek (New Picture Gallery), picking up with major 19th-

century works where its sister museum leaves off. For an odd but entertaining juxtaposition of experiences, spend a morning in the two picture galleries, and an afternoon on the Oktoberfest grounds.

WHAT: site. **ALTE PINAKOTHEK:** Barer Strasse 27. Tel 49/89-2380-50, fax 49/89-2380-5125. *Cost:* admission $10. *When:* Tues–Sun. **NEUE PINAKOTHEK:** Barer Strasse 29. Tel 49/89-2380-50. *Cost:* admission $10. *When:* Wed–Mon.

Admiring the paintings at the Alte Pinakothek

A Charmed Time of Year

CHRISTKINDLMARKT

Munich, Bavaria, Germany

The American novelist Thomas Wolfe concluded that Munich is "a German dream translated into life"—and the description seems especially apt during Advent, when the capital of Bavaria turns into a three-dimensional

Christmas card. Countless holiday markets crop up around Germany during the holiday season, selling handcrafted ornaments and crèche figures, candles, wood-carved toys, and traditional objects associated with the season, including the *Weihnachtspyramiden* (the "Christmas pyramid," a candle-powered merry-go-round found in every German home). Rivaled only by Nüremberg's picturesque market (famous for its gingerbread houses and ornaments made from spices), Munich's Christkindlmarkt is one of Germany's largest, oldest, and most enjoyable. Hundreds of brightly garlanded

stalls sprawl across the Marienplatz, the central square at the heart of Munich's Altstadt (Old Town), around an enormous fir tree. Decked with lights donated by a Bavarian town, it stands proudly before the Rathaus. This is the neo-Gothic town hall, with a forty-three-bell carillon; frequent concerts with accompanying dancing figures add to the Yuletide flavor.

WHAT: event. **HOW:** contact the Munich tourist office, tel 89/233-0300, fax 89/233-30233; www.muenchen-tourist.de. **WHEN:** Munich's Christkindlmarkt, like most in Germany, late Nov–Dec 24.

World Technology in a Nutshell

DEUTSCHES MUSEUM

Munich, Bavaria, Germany

T he largest, oldest, and most complete museum of its kind in the world covers every conceivable aspect of scientific and technical endeavor with demonstrations and interactive displays in fifty-five different departments,

including musical instruments, aeronautics, photography, physics, textiles, and everything in between. As absorbing for kids as for adults, it is a hands-on extravaganza of do-it-yourself chemistry experiments and buttons, gears, levers, and handles galore. Built on an island in the middle of the Isar River, a full day can easily be spent in the company of historical originals such as Germany's first submarine (built in 1906), the first electric locomotive (Siemens, 1879), the laboratory bench at which the atom was first split, dozens of automobiles, including the first Benz of 1886 and luxury Bugattis and Daimlers from the 1920s and 1930s. Other priceless

artifacts include a complete and eerily convincing replica of Spain's Altamira caves. Judging from the head count, aeronautics is a favorite department; its hangar-sized halls house pioneering planes, from the Wright Brothers' Type-A Standard, built in the U.S. in 1909, to military aircraft from the 1930s and 1940s. From here there is direct access to the section devoted to space travel, where the most recent Spacelab exhibits are not half as interesting as the displays of such earlier attempts as Hitler's V-2, code-named A4.

WHAT: site. **WHERE:** Museumsinsel 1. Tel 49/89-21791; www.deutschs-museum.de; info@ deutsches-museum.de. **COST:** admission $10.

Prost! Munich's Giant Party

OKTOBERFEST

Munich, Bavaria, Germany

I f you think that residents of Germany's "beer capital" are delightfully jolly, eat heartily, and drink plenty (beginning with beer quaffed at breakfast) on a normal day, wait till you see them in party mode during Munich's

sixteen-day bonanza, Oktoberfest. If this quintessentially Bavarian festival celebrated in the company of lots and lots of boisterous strangers from around the world sounds like your idea of a grand time, book now! The place to be is the Theresienwiese meadow (named after Princess Theresa, whose

betrothal to Crown Prince Ludwig in 1810 was the reason for the first-ever October celebration), where twelve huge tents—some holding up to 6,000 stein-hoisting drinkers each—are erected months in advance. This is the annual culmination of the city's love affair with the outdoors, and the last hurrah to the *biergarten* season. Oktoberfest opens with a colorful parade of 7,000 participants that wends through the main streets of Munich to the fairgrounds. Led by the steed-drawn beer wagons of Munich's major breweries (Bavaria boasts more than one sixth of the world's breweries), carriages follow with thirteen Bavarian big brass bands and hundreds of Oktoberfest waitresses in Bavarian costume. The fairgrounds are so huge they become a city of their own, filled

One of the huge Oktoberfest beer tents

with refreshment stands, side shows, open-air concerts, shooting galleries, gut-churning thrill rides, and merry-go-rounds. To the sound of unending oompah music, some 6 million people consume 5 million liters of a special "Wies'n" beer brewed especially for the annual festival, 400,000 sausages, and 600,000 chickens.

Those who arrive outside of festival time can still spend a few delightful hours at Hofbräuhaus am Platzl. Since 1589, it has been Munich's biggest and most beloved beerhouse, and the world's most famous. No place for the faint-hearted, this cavernous tourist destination is eternal Oktoberfest.

WHAT: event, restaurant. **OKTOBERFEST:** fairground on the west side of the city. *When:* 16 days, beginning on a Sat and ending the 1st Sun of Oct. Contact Munich Tourist Office, tel 49/89-233-96500, fax 49/89-233-30233; tourismus@muenchen.de; www.oktoberfest.de. *Cost:* admission free. *When:* open daily, 9 A.M.–midnight. **HOFBRÄUHAUS AM PLATZL:** Platzl 9. Tel 49/89-2901-3610, fax 49/8922-7586; hbteam@hofbraeuhaus.de; www.hofbraeuhaus.de.

A Centuries-Old Labor of Love

THE PASSION PLAY OF OBERAMMERGAU

Bavaria, Germany

This peaceful town in the Bavarian Alps comes alive every ten years to honor a vow made in 1633, when a plague devastated much of Europe, leaving behind only misery and hunger. To escape the plague,

the townspeople promised to reenact the life of Christ once every decade, in the year ending in zero, forever. The plague ended, and the original performance by peasants took place in a field in 1634. Since then the Passion Play has grown in sophistication

and length (5½ hours and sixteen acts). What has remained constant is the sincerity with which the entire town participates and holds its heartfelt promise sacred. Set amid breathtaking scenery, in a festive atmosphere that engulfs the town, citizens young and old turn out in handmade costumes. Despite its international fame, the natural performances somehow escape commercialism; the ancient vow is still the most important thing in these people's lives.

WHAT: event. **WHERE:** 50 miles/80 km south of Munich. **HOW:** Oberammergau Tours 49/8822-92310; in the U.S., tel 305-235-9165 or 877-235-9165; info@oberammergau tours.com; www.oberammergautours.com. Reserve well in advance. *Cost:* 4 days $1,398, land only, from Munich to Oberammergau. **WHEN:** in 2000, the play ran late May–late Sept.

A procession in Oberammergau's Passion Play

A Medieval Capital on the Danube

REGENSBURG

Bavaria, Germany

Capital of Bavaria before Munich and one of the most beautiful medieval cities in Germany, Regensburg and much of eastern Bavaria has remained an insider's secret even to Germans. During the years of Communist control, this area near the Czech border was considered a dead end. Much of the surviving architecture dating to its glory days between the 13th and 16th centuries (which moved Emperor Maximilian to say in 1517 that "Regensburg surpasses every German city with its outstanding and vast buildings") remains unchanged. Everything here is original, unlike many reconstructed German towns damaged by WW II air raids. Tourism authorities exaggerate little in listing no fewer than 1,300 buildings as being of historical interest, and Regensburg is known as "the city of churches" for good reason. The Dom St. Peter is held by many to be Germany's crowning Gothic example (housing what is likely to be the only extant statue of the Devil's grandmother) and is famous for both its 14th-century stained-glass windows and its internationally renowned boys' choir, the Domspatzen (Cathedral Sparrows). Situated at the northernmost navigable point of the Danube River, Regensburg was already an important river town when the Romans arrived in the 7th century. The Danube can best be observed at sunset from the 12th-century Steinerne Brücke (Old Stone Bridge), built with sixteen graceful arches. Call it a day at the nearby Historische Wurstküche, the town's oldest restaurant, where outdoor trestle tables on the Danube provide communal seating-with-a-view for a simple alfresco meal of Regensburg's famous grilled sausages and locally brewed beer.

WHAT: town. **REGENSBURG:** 76 miles/ 122 km northeast of Munich, 62 miles/ 100 km southeast of Nürnberg. **HISTORISCHE WURSTKÜCHE:** Thundorferstrasse 3, tel 49/ 941-466210. *Cost:* traditional meal $10. **BEST TIMES:** when not touring the world, the Domspatzen sing 9 A.M. Sun Mass in the Cathedral.

The Beat Goes On

BERLIN PHILHARMONIC

Berlin, Brandenburg, Germany

F or years, the classical music scene in Germany meant one man, one orchestra, one city: Herbert von Karajan and the Berliner Philharmoniker Orchester. Founded in 1882, with the arrival of von Karajan the

Philharmonic developed into the world's premier orchestra. Following the maestro's death in 1989, Italian-born Claudio Abbado stepped in, and in September 2002, the baton passed to Sir Simon Rattle. The orchestra's home is the Philharmonie am Kulturforum, a 1960s building designed by Hans Scharoun that has its share of avid fans and detractors. The regularly sold-out audience of 2,400, seated on nine levels surrounding the stage,

Conductor Sir Simon Rattle

enjoys unmatched visibility (no seat is more than 100 feet from the stage) and acoustics. Choice seats, understandably, are those with a head-on view of the conductor. During the heralded Berliner Festwochen (Berlin Festival Weeks), celebrating excellence in music and the arts, tickets are close to impossible to find. Concierges at first-class and deluxe hotels do their best to work miracles for guests.

WHAT: event. **WHERE:** Kemperplatz, Herbert-von-Karajan-Strasse 1 in the Tiergarten sector. For tickets, tel 49/25-488132, fax 49/25-614887; www.berlin-philharmonic.com. **WHEN:** Sept–Jun. **BEST TIMES:** Berliner Festwochen in Sept.

Symbol of a Country's Division and Unification

BRANDENBURG GATE

Berlin, Brandenburg, Germany

I n downtown Berlin today, it's hard to tell just where the demolished Berlin Wall once stood. But the Brandenburg Gate (Brandenburger Tor) still stands. Conceived in 1791 as a triumphal arch to celebrate a Prussian victory

and, ironically, as a "Gate of Peace," it was incorporated into the wall when it was built in 1961 at the height of the Cold War. The gate is an emotive icon of the country's reunification, and it still elicits a frisson of excitement and unease. Tourist vendors around town continue to sell what they claim are chunks of the

infamous wall. Once measuring 29 miles long and 13 feet high, with barbed-wire extensions that stretched across the countryside as a tangible Iron Curtain, large protected sections of *die Mauer* have been left standing in Berlin, designated as "historic landmarks." Before the wall came down, the Brandenburg Gate was within the eastern sector in a grim no-man's-land. Walk through its majestic arch today and you are in the former East Berlin, for forty-one years the Communist capital of the German Democratic Republic. This area was formerly the proud showpiece of Hohenzollern Berlin, and is again drawing visitors as the site of the city's most imposing monuments, which somehow escaped destruction. East of the gate rolls Unter den Linden (Under the Linden Trees), once the main east-west axis and one of the city's grandest boulevards. Revitalized, it is again the site of many embassies (relocated from Bonn) and renewed pulse point of the restored capital.

The quietly plush and superbly located Adlon Hotel was destroyed by the Soviets in 1945 and rebuilt in 1997. Its marble lobby, with the original grand staircase intact, shines with prewar glory and hums with top-flight service. The setting of the 1932 classic *Grand Hotel* was modeled after the Adlon Hotel; in a scene from that film, the divine Garbo first uttered "I vant

to be alone." The Presidential Suite promises a view of the awe-inspiring Brandenburg Gate.

WHAT: site, hotel. **HOTEL ADLON:** Unter den Linden 77, Mitte. Tel 49/30-22610, fax 49/30-2261-2222; in the U.S., 800-426-3135; hotel.adlon@kempinski.com; www.hotel-adlon.de. **COST:** doubles from $490; Presidential Suite $12,000. **BEST TIMES:** Jul–Aug, Dec–Jan, Mar.

The Brandenburg Gate illuminated at night

A Major Center of Art and Culture

THE MUSEUM SCENE

Berlin, Brandenburg, Germany

As the once-divided metropolis of Berlin fuses itself together in a flurry of urban renewal rarely seen before in European history, its inexhaustibly rich art collections have been shuffled, reorganized, and regrouped.

Pursuing its long-held dream of becoming the cultural and art capital not just of Germany but of Europe, investors and government have spent as much on the city's new museums as they have on new luxury hotels and extravagant shopping malls. The most impressive event was the 1998 reuniting of the Dahlem Museum in the West with the Bode Museum in the East, now under one roof again in the custom-built Gemäldegalerie am Kulturforum (the new Picture Gallery) in the Tiergarten

district. Of Berlin's array of more than 170 museums, this unrivaled compilation is in a class all its own for the breadth and depth of its collection of paintings by Europe's masters from the 13th to the 18th century. No fewer than twenty Rembrandts make up one gallery alone. Lovers of antiquities could spend days on the Museumsinsel (Museum Island), a cache of five museums whose lodestone is the Pergamonmuseum, built exclusively to house the colossal 2nd-century B.C. Pergamon Altar (a 40-foot-high colonnaded Greek temple with twenty-seven steps leading up to it), discovered in 1864 and brought here in 1902 from Turkey. The Ägyptisches Museum contains the sublime bust of Nefertiti—meaning "the beautiful one is here"—created well over 3,000 years ago and unearthed in 1912 by German archaeologists. Add to that the exciting new contemporary art museum, the Hamburger Bahnhof, housed in a brilliantly converted 19th-century railway station, and you will have barely scratched the surface of one of the world's most remarkable surveys of art, from the dawn of human culture to the avant-garde of today, in a city that is promising to be the country's showcase for the 21st century.

WHAT: site. **GEMÄLDEGALERIE AM KULTURFORUM:** in Tiergarten, Matthaeikirchplatz 8. **MUSEUMINSEL AND PERGAMONMUSEUM:** Bodestrasse 1-3. **ÄGYPTISCHES MUSEUM:** Schlossstrasse 70 in Charlottenburg. **HAMBURGER BAHNHOF, MUSEUM OF CONTEMPORARY ART:** Invalidenstrasse 50-51. All museums: tel 49/30-4242-42, fax 49/30-4222-90; service@smb.museum; www.smb.museum. **COST:** admission from $5. **WHEN:** Tues–Sun.

A Royal Rococo Palace Promising Carefree Escape

SANS SOUCI

Potsdam, Brandenburg, Germany

J ust outside his flourishing capital, Berlin, the enlightened Prussian ruler King Friedrich II—also known as Frederick the Great—in 1745, constructed a royal palace said to be the finest example of rococo architecture in Europe.

Here, amid the superb lakeland scenery, he was free to indulge in a flurry of cultural pursuits "sans souci"—without care (and preferably without his queen, Elizabeth Christine)—and surrounded by visiting guests such as the French writer and philosopher Voltaire (who stayed on for three years as a kind of personal mentor). Based on the king's own impeccable designs, Sans Souci was meant to rival Versailles in detail and extravagance, although it is modest in size and intimate by comparison. The long one-story building, crowned by a dome and flanked by two round pavilions, is surrounded by tiered terraces and carefully landscaped gardens spread out over 1 square mile. Other buildings, most notably the Neues Palais (the largest, with 400 rooms) and Schlosshotel Cecilienhof, were added over the following 150 years. The latter is a rambling, mock-

Elizabethan country home that was begun in 1913 as the home of Crown Prince Wilhelm of Hohenzollern and named after his daughter-in-law Cecilie. It would go down in history as the location for the history-altering Potsdam Conference that took place here between July 17 and August 2, 1945. It was here that the

The tiered terraces of Sans Souci

Allied statesmen Churchill (replaced mid-conference by Clement Atlee), Truman, and Stalin hammered out the division of postwar Germany agreed upon earlier that year at Yalta. Few of the visitors traipsing through the conference rooms of the 175-room house today realize that much of the manor (45 guest rooms) has been quietly functioning as a hotel and restaurant since 1960. For those checking in (lunch is a lovely option at the very least), the sense of "sans souci" is tangible once the

day's visitors taper off. Ask for the luxury Hohenzollern Suite, onetime lodging for the family of the last emperor.

WHAT: site, hotel. **SANS SOUCI:** 15 miles/ 24 km southwest of Berlin. **SCHLOSSHOTEL CECILIENHOF:** located in the nearby Neuer Garden. Tel 49/331-37050, fax 49/331-292498; potsdam.cecilienhof@relexa-hotel.de; www.relexa-hotel.de. *Cost:* doubles from $255; Hohenzollern Suite $370. **BEST TIMES:** spring shows off the gardens at their best.

A Baroque Pleasure Palace in the "Florence of the Elbe"

THE ZWINGER

Dresden, Saxony, Germany

Built during the city's 18th-century glory period, destroyed—like 80 percent of the city—in 1945 by one of WW II's most savage air raids, meticulously re-created in the late 1950s, and barely escaping the ravaging

floods of the summer of 2002, the Zwinger remains Dresden's—and one of Germany's—most famous Baroque buildings. The fabulous artwork that hangs in the museums found within the Zwinger Palace's complex of buildings was removed for safekeeping at the beginning of the war, hidden in the Soviet Union, and eventually returned to Dresden when still under Communist rule. The aptly named August the Strong (1694–1733), elector-king of Saxony, borrowed from brimming coffers to create this voluptuous pleasure palace and then filled it with such a remarkable art collection of old masters that art historians compare 18th-century Dresden to Florence or Venice, and even today it is considered one of Europe's most important art scenes. The Zwinger's showpiece museum is its Gemäldegalerie Alte Meister, awash with old masters: Raphael's *Sistine Madonna*, Giorgione's *Sleeping Venus*, and Titian's *Tribute Money* are just a few. The Zwinger's *Rustkammer* (arms room) is a stunning collec-

The Kempinski Hotel Taschenbergpalais

tion of ornamental armor and weaponry, while the famous *Porzellansammlung* is the world's most significant porcelain collection.

Before August the Strong began to collect great artwork, he collected women, and is known for his bevy of some 300 concubines. Perhaps the most famous was Cosel, and the august ruler commissioned E. M. Pöppelman, daring architect of the Zwinger, to build her the Taschenbergpalais. This great Baroque love nest (that could easily have accommodated his 299 former love interests as well) was also demolished by the saturation firebombing of 1945, although its smoldering shell was left standing. Countless deutschemarks later, the phoenixlike Kempinski Hotel Taschenbergpalais has risen on the spot, surely the most romantic and luxe hostelry in the area.

WHAT: town, site, hotel. **DRESDEN:** 123 miles/198 km south of Berlin, 158 miles/250 km northwest of Prague, Czech Republic.

Tourist office tel 49/351-4919-20; info@dresden-tourist.de; www.dresden-tourist.de. **THE ZWINGER:** Theaterplatz 1. *Cost:* 48-hour City Card gives admission to all museums and unlimited transportation, $30. *When:* Tues–Sun. **KEMPINSKI HOTEL TASCHENBERGPALAIS:** Taschenberg 3. Tel 49/351-49120, fax 49/351-4912812; in the U.S., 800-426-3135; www.kempinski-dresden.de. *Cost:* doubles from $295. **BEST TIMES:** Dresden Music Festival last 2 weeks of May.

A Bounty of Beautiful Music

SUMMER MUSIC FESTIVALS

Bayreuth (Franconia) and Schleswig-Holstein, Germany

For opera buffs, witnessing the performance of *Der Ring des Niebelungen* conducted by James Levine in the 18th-century Markgrafliches Opernhaus in Richard Wagner's hometown of Bayreuth is something akin to nirvana.

For five weeks every summer, Wagner lovers converge from all over the world, clutching hard-won tickets for Bayreuth's Wagner Festival. The rococo opera house shares the spotlight with the unadorned, intimidating Festspielhaus (festival house). Built and financed by Wagner, it is a high temple of music. The enormous stage is needed for the giant casts required to pull off his grand productions. The orchestra pit is sunken, so that the music seems to float toward you from nowhere and everywhere. Nearby, Wagner and his second wife, the daughter of composer Franz Liszt, are buried in the house where they lived.

For lovers of classical music in general, Germany's largest summer cultural event takes place in the province of Schleswig-Holstein, in the heart of the beautiful lake district between Hamburg and the Danish border. Ever since Leonard Bernstein launched the Schleswig-Holstein Music Festival, world-class artists have marked it on their summer schedules.

Some 125 performances are given in more than forty venues, including theaters, churches, barns, a riding academy, private manor houses, and candlelit castles. Most of the program relates to two themes: the music of a single nation (recent attention has been given to Israel and the Czech Republic), and an in-depth look at the work of an individual composer. Bernstein hoped to create a European equivalent of the Tanglewood Music Center, where the best of the up-and-coming generation of musicians profit from close contact with eminent performers; Bernstein conducted some of his last master classes here.

WHAT: event. **WAGNER FESTIVAL (WAGNER FESTSPIELE):** Bayreuth is 143 miles/230 km north of Munich. tel 49/921-78780; www.bayreuther-festspiele.de. *Cost:* tickets $20–$315. *When:* late Jul–late Aug. **SCHLESWIG-HOLSTEIN MUSIC FESTIVAL:** 40 Holzdamn, Hamburg. Tel 49/451-389-570, fax 49/451-389-5757; info@shmf.de; www.shmf.de. *Cost:* tickets $15–$225. *When:* mid-Jul to late Aug.

THE RHINE VALLEY

Germany

Cutting through 820 miles of European heartland from Switzerland to the North Sea, the Rhine River does not belong to Germany alone—but don't tell the Germans that. The span that runs through Germany—particularly

the 50-mile Middle Rhine or Rhine Gorge, running from Mainz to Koblenz—is where the river gained its historic importance and exhibits its greatest beauty, full of vineyard-clad banks, wooded forests, castle-topped crags, and tiny wine villages that put their best half-timbered faces forward.

The perennial question of how best to experience the Rhine—by river cruise or car—is best resolved by doing both. Scenic roads hug the river banks (the Rheingoldstrasse on the left bank, Lorelei-Burgenstrasse on the right) and river-cruise lines specialize in tours ranging from a few hours to a few days. For a side trip, the winding Mosel River (which flows into the Rhine at Koblenz) offers a magic all its own, with graceful, sleepy scenery that's the

polar opposite of the Rhine's powerful beauty, especially along the 85-mile stretch between Koblenz and the charming, ancient city of Trier, dating from 2000 B.C. Wines from both the Rhine and Mosel regions (mostly Rieslings) are well worth your time.

WHAT: experience, site. **WHERE:** Mainz is 200 miles/315 km northwest of Munich, 90 miles/140 km south of Cologne. Rhineland Tourist Board, Koblenz. Tel 49/261-915200; info@rlp-info.de. **VIKING RIVER CRUISES:** in the U.S., tel 800-304-9616; www.vikingriver.com. *Cost:* 8-day cruises Amsterdam to Basel, from $1,599 per person, double occupancy, includes meals and shore excursions. *When:* Mar–Nov. **BEST TIMES:** Sept for wine harvest time; Oct for foliage; Apr–May for smaller crowds.

COLOGNE'S CATHEDRAL QUARTER

Cologne, Rhineland, Germany

The 14th-century poet Petrarch thought Cologne's twin-towered Dom one of the finest cathedrals in the world. Take a 509-step hike to the windswept gallery high in the 515-foot south tower and you have climbed the highest

church tower in the world, in its day the tallest manmade construction of any kind. It took

more than 600 years to complete the Dom. Construction was begun over some Roman ruins after Frederick Barbarossa donated the relics of the Three Magi to Cologne, establishing the city as a major pilgrimage destination. They are still on display in their original 12th-century reliquary behind the high altar, which itself dates back to the early 14th century.

Head into the far more distant past at the nearby Germano-Roman Museum, just south of the Dom. While building an underground air-raid shelter in 1941, workers unearthed ancient Roman foundations, including a perfectly preserved mosaic floor from a Roman trader's villa. Once you surface, you can head back to the future at the Wallraf-Richartz Museum and the Museum Ludwig, on the other side of the Dom. Housed in a huge art complex, the Wallraf-Richartz contains paintings from the 14th to the 20th centuries. The

Cologne is Germany's oldest major city.

Ludwig is devoted exclusively to 20th-century art, its collection rivaled only by that of New York's Guggenheim. In effect, you can view 2,000 years of Western art and architecture without leaving the shadow of the cathedral.

At the end of the day, put your feet up at the Dom Hotel, nestled up against the great Gothic cathedral. The Dom Hotel proudly offers suave, old-fashioned, but friendly service that few hotels even aspire to anymore, with an almost one-to-one ratio of staff to indulged hotel guests. Deluxe rooms face the Dom Platz and have an angled view of the cathedral, which may also be admired from the glass-enclosed Atelier am Dom, the hotel's see-and-be-seen outdoor café. A view like that calls for a glass of the popular Kölsch beer, a light, clear local brew. Then you have an appointment with Petersglocke, the world's largest church bell, which tips the scales at 24 tons. When it rings out the hour, you'll know.

WHAT: site, hotel. **CATHEDRAL:** Dom Platz. **GERMANO-ROMAN MUSEUM:** Roncalliplatz 4. Tel 49/221-24438, fax 49/221-24030; roemisch-germanisches-museum@stadt-koeln.de. *Cost:* admission $6. **WALLRAF-RICHARTZ MUSEUM AND MUSEUM LUDWIG:** Bischofsgartenstrasse 1. Tel 49/221-21119, fax 49/221-22629; wrm@wrm.museenkoeln.de. *Cost:* admission $7. **DOM HOTEL:** Domkloster 2A. Tel 49/221-20240; in the U.S., 800-543-4300; www.starwoodhotels.com. *Cost:* doubles from $300.

In Germany's Oldest University City, a Romantic Icon

HEIDELBERG'S SCHLOSS

Heidelberg, Rhineland, Germany

In a magnificent hilltop setting of woodland and terraced gardens sits Heidelberg's magnificent, crumbling Schloss, probably the country's most famous castle. Sacked by French troops under Louis XIV in 1689, it has remained a dignified ruin ever since, only enhancing its romantic allure. Painters and poets from around the world have immortalized it in picture and verse. Mark Twain described it as "the Lear of inanimate nature—deserted, discrowned, beaten by the storms, but royal still, and beautiful." The Prince Electors had the red sandstone castle built over the course of three centuries (1400 to 1620), but it was already in ruins when "discovered" by the 18th-century Romantics who fell under its spell. For a vision of the castle to cherish, stroll along the Philosopher's Walk (Philosophenweg), a hillside wooded path above the Neckar River on the opposite (north) bank, where Goethe and Hegel wandered, or hop a sunset cruise on the Neckar and take in the famous scenery.

Nestled on a historic side street off the Philosopher's Walk is the only place you want to stay—Die Hirschgasse. The hotel dates back to 1472, and started as a tavern for the students of the local university (a tipsy Otto von Bismarck carved his name into one of the tables). The University of Heidelberg is Germany's oldest, founded in 1386. Mark Twain was smitten with picturesque Heidelberg, his first stop in Europe and the first he wrote about in his famous travelogue *A Tramp*

Heidelberg's Schloss and Old Bridge

Abroad. Guests will know how he felt after their first night at Die Hirschgasse, in the shadow of Germany's most romantic schloss.

WHAT: site, hotel. **THE SCHLOSS (HEIDELBERGER SCHLOSS):** Heidelberg is 55 miles/88 km south of Frankfurt. **DIE HIRSCHGASSE:** Hirschgasse 3. Tel 49/6221-4540, fax 49/6221-454111; info@hirschgasse.de; www.hirschgasse.de. *Cost:* doubles from $215 (low season), from $270 (high season). **BEST TIMES:** spectacular fireworks held over the castle 3 times a year, usually the 1st Sat of Jun and Sept and the 2nd Sat of Jul. Classical music concerts and opera (watch for *The Student Prince,* set in Heidelberg) held frequently in the castle's open-air courtyard in summer.

A Half-Timbered Fairy Tale

QUEDLINBURG AND HOTEL THEOPHANO

Sachsen-Anhalt, Germany

On the edge of the Harz, Germany's northernmost mountain range, lies the finest timber-framed townscape in the country, and perhaps in all Europe. Besides holding this distinction, Quedlinburg also boasts a treasure trove of medieval religious art, which is displayed in the town's hilltop Saxon-Romanesque cathedral. UNESCO has declared the entire town, which recently celebrated its 1,000th anniversary, a World Heritage Site. Quedlinburg was the cradle of the Ottonian dynasty, the first line of Saxon kings in what later became the Holy Roman Empire. (Heinrich I, the first German king, is buried in the cathedral.) As a preferred residence of the emperors, this small but flourishing town also grew as a cultural, spiritual, and religious center, and much attention and funds were lavished on the cathedral. The town's historic wealth is still visible everywhere, in the priceless gold and bejeweled sacred objects it exhibits and in the 1,300 hand-carved, half-timbered houses—the earliest, dating back to 1310, is the oldest in Germany. Architectural styles range from Gothic to Baroque to Quedlinburg's own idiom: facades accented with bright blues, reds, yellows, and greens. The town miraculously escaped both Allied bombing in WW II and the redevelopment plans of the former East German government.

On the town's main market square sits the lovely Hotel Theophano, a half-timbered landmark created from five historical buildings from the 17th century and dedicated to the memory of Theophano, a Byzantine princess who married Otto II, the Saxon pretender to the throne, in 972. The small hotel has been beautifully restored and decorated and it is run with warmth and ease by a young staff that aims to please. The hotel's Weinkeller (Wine Cellar) offers memorable meals in a handsome space of vaulted ceilings warmed by soft candlelight.

WHAT: town, hotel. **QUEDLINBURG:** a 3-hour drive southwest of Berlin. **HOTEL THEOPHANO:** Markt 13/14. Tel 49/3946-96300, fax 49/3946-963036; theophano@t-online.de; www.hoteltheophano.de. *Cost:* doubles from $125. Dinner $40.

Last of a Grand but Vanishing Breed

HOTEL VIER JAHRESZEITEN

Hamburg, Germany

This is the stuff of which grand hotels are made. Regularly hailed not only as Germany's best, but as one of the world's greats, the Vier Jahreszeiten has been the only place to stay in town since it was opened in 1897 by the Haerlin family. There are fresh flower arrangements the size of small forests and valuable Gobelin tapestries in the welcoming marble and rosewood lobby aptly called a "lounging hall." Despite the baronial size of the hotel that sits impressively on the Binnenalster, the smaller of Hamburg's lakes (ask for the higher lake-view rooms that come with a balcony), the hotel is run with the unflaggingly obliging service of a hotel half its size: the staff is known for greeting most guests by name within minutes of arrival. It has won every conceivable award, even after having unobtrusively passed, in 1989, from the private hands of the Haerlin family into a new corporate ownership. Hamburg, almost wiped

The hotel is in the heart of the historic district.

off the map by the 1940–44 bombing raids (the hotel miraculously escaped untouched), is once again a lively hub, with the highest per capita income in Europe. It is Germany's second-largest city: livable, lovely, and famous for its lofty standards and luxury hotels. The Vier Jahreszeiten stands proudly at the helm of top-flight accommodations with its stellar restaurant Haerlin, on the formal side and of excellent repute (as is its prodigious wine list), while the Condi café or *conditorei* (from which the name derives), decorated in perfect Biedermeier fashion, has long been one of the city's most popular institutions for lunch.

WHAT: hotel. **WHERE:** Neuer Jungfernstieg 9-14. Tel 49/40-34940, fax 49/40-34942601; vier-jahreszeiten@hvj.de; www.hvj.de. **COST:** doubles from $250.

Perfectly Intact, the Soul of Northern Germany

LÜBECK

Schleswig-Holstein, Germany

This Baltic river port has a glorious past. In the Middle Ages it was the capital of the Hanseatic League, a loose-knit association of independent merchant towns in northern Europe. Its canal-girdled, redbrick Altstadt (Old Town) is steeped in the city's rich medieval history, when it dominated the highly lucrative trading routes along the Baltic, and precious goods trickled down throughout Europe from here. Enclosed within walls of fortifications, gates, and a moat, Lübeck's Altstadt is so architecturally and historically significant that it was the first city in northern Europe to have the entire town center placed on the World Heritage list by UNESCO. One would never guess that a quarter of the center was

demolished by WW II bombings, because it has so skillfully and lovingly been rebuilt. What has been left untouched serves as a memorial; for example, the bells of the Gothic St. Mary Church (Marienkirche), which crashed during an air raid, lie in shatters where they fell.

Italy probably takes umbrage at Lübeck's centuries-old claim to originating marzipan (the town acknowledges that the sweet was first made with almonds imported from Italy). Check out the local delicacy in the celebrated old-world Café Niederegger, said to make the best marzipan in the world. In spite of all the town's beauty and history, one's most vivid recollection might be of an afternoon spent at the café, immersed in their famous *Nusstorte*, a cream-filled cake that hints of Italian almonds.

WHAT: town, restaurant. **LÜBECK:** 40 miles/ 65 km north of Hamburg. **CAFÉ NIEDEREGGER:** Breite Strasse 89, facing the handsome Gothic/ Renaissance Rathaus; info@niederegger.de; www.niederegger.de. **BEST TIMES:** the city provides many venues for the Schleswig-Holstein Music Festival, late Jun–mid-Aug; Christmas Market late Nov–Dec.

A gate to the city: Lübeck's Holstentor

A Former Whaling Island Becomes Germany's Playground

SYLT

Schleswig-Holstein, Germany

This breezy little barrier island off the northern tip of Germany where Denmark begins is the status destination for the fashionable and chic of Hamburg, which is obvious from the presence of enticing boutiques, excellent restaurants, and a tiny casino. This skinny, sandy island otherwise cherishes its traditions and fragile beauty. The largest island in the Friesian archipelago stretching from Denmark to the Netherlands, Sylt is just 1,800 feet wide at its narrowest point, its ever-shifting landscape of soft dunes and 40 miles of sandy coastline in danger of eroding right off the face of the map someday. It has a sizable gay and lesbian population, a famous nude beach (said to have begun the craze in the 1800s), and a relaxed lifestyle of just-caught seafood dinners in small fishing villages, summer days when yellow oilskin windbreakers are commonplace, invigorating air (often in the form of a bracing iodine-rich wind coming in off the North Sea) and restorative kick-back pastimes. Much is made of the quality of light and the sky, which turns all shades of pastels and grays at the end of the day. Sloping straw roofs and dollhouse-like brick cottages prove that the islanders intend to keep the modern world on the mainland; biking, horseback riding, and walking are the preferred means of transportation. With just twelve villages on the 38-square-mile island, quaint Keitum is at its "green heart," while the largest establishment is Westerland.

The latter is where you'll find the elegant 19th-century Hotel Stadt Hamburg, evocative of a stately country estate. In addition to the Stadt Hamburg's excellent restaurant, this small island is home to Restaurant Jörg Müller, one of the country's finest, and a more formal alternative to the homey oyster and shrimp joints across the island where everyone knows your name.

WHAT: island, hotel, restaurant. **SYLT:** 151 miles/240 km northwest of Hamburg. **HOTEL STADT HAMBURG:** Strandstrasse 2, Westerland. Tel 49/4651-8580, fax 49/4651-858220; www.relaischateaux.fr/stadthamburg. *Cost:* doubles from $370. **RESTAURANT JÖRG MÜLLER:** Süderstrasse 8, Westerland. Tel 49/4651-27788, fax 49/4651-201471; www.hotel-joerg-mueller.de. *Cost:* dinner $75. *When:* lunch and dinner daily. **BEST TIMES:** Jul and Aug best for swimming.

A Provincial City as Center Stage of German Classicism

WEIMAR

Thuringia, Germany

Home and inspiration to Cranach the Elder, Johann Sebastian Bach, Franz Liszt, Richard Strauss, and Friedrich von Schiller, Weimar is also closely associated with the much revered German poet Goethe, who lived here for close to sixty years (he penned most of his major works here, including his epic drama *Faust*) and is buried here. Nietzsche spent his last years here, and Walter Gropius founded the revolutionary Bauhaus movement of architecture here. Long marooned behind the Iron Curtain, its recent honoring as a European Capital of Culture has inspired a cultural and intellectual revival. All the traditions of the fine arts, music, literature, architecture, and philosophy are kept alive in Weimar in its small museums, institutes, theaters, and festivals. Long protected as a cultural jewel, it was largely untouched by WW II bombing and was kept intact during the decades of Communist rule. New life is now being breathed into the small cobblestoned city.

Local officials are divided about the other legacy Weimar left: the Buchenwald concentration camp, located 6 miles north of town. Ignore it and accentuate the positive? Embrace it, acknowledge it, and then move on? Certainly the city has seen the very best and the very worst of German history.

Stay in the historic Deco- and Bauhaus-decorated Elephant Hotel, on the stage-set Marktplatz; dating from 1696, no one can remember the origin of its name, but everyone from Richard Wagner to Hitler has found lodging here. From Weimar, wrote Goethe (who celebrated his 80th birthday at the Elephant), "the gates and streets lead to every faraway place on earth."

WHAT: town, hotel. **WEIMAR:** 190 miles/300 km southwest of Berlin, 176 miles/280 km northeast of Frankfurt. **HOTEL ELEPHANT WEIMAR:** Markt 19. Tel 49/36-438020, fax 49/36-43802610; in the U.S., 800-426-3135; elephant.weimar@arabellasheraton.com; www.starwoodhotels.com. *Cost:* doubles from $160. **BEST TIMES:** Aug 28 is the birthday of Goethe.

A Unique Island History and Culture

CRETE

Greece

The largest of the Greek islands is also one of its most fascinating. Crete was the birthplace of Minoan culture, Europe's first advanced civilization, and Knossos—discovered only in 1900—was its capital city. The reconstructed Palace of Knossos was once thought to have been the home of the legendary King Minos, whose wife bore the Minotaur—half bull, half man—which thrived on human sacrifice and lived in a secret labyrinth beneath the palace. The palace dates to 1700 B.C., although the brilliance and vibrancy of its frescoes and sophistication of its layout and organization make it seem almost contemporary. Knossos's restoration has been the source of heated controversy among archaeologists, who consider it, at best, the enlightened guesswork of the early-20th-century archaeologist Sir Arthur Evans. The Royal Apartments are without doubt the epitome of luxurious court living, four floors of rooms that illustrate Minoan life more than 3,000 years ago. Portraying a remarkably advanced and peaceful society, many of the Minoan treasures and frescoes (unsurpassed in the ancient world) have been removed and are now housed in Heraklion's Archaeological Museum (second only to that of Athens). Purists will prefer the nearby Palace of Phaistos. It was excavated at almost the same time and dates to the same period, but was left in a practically unreconstructed state.

Ruins of the Palace of Knossos

Meanwhile, the most spectacular natural wonder in Crete lies along the Samariá Gorge, the longest ravine in Europe. The popular but strenuous downhill hike through the White Mountains begins with a 3,000-foot drop during the first mile via the steep, zigzagging Xylóskalo (Wooden Stairs). A well-trodden 11-mile trail levels off after that, perfumed with mountain thyme and wild oregano. If you're lucky, you might glimpse the rare horned kri-kri (Cretan wild goat) known to live here. The hike's high point comes at Sidirósportes (Iron Gates), where trekkers squeeze through a 9-foot-wide space, the gorge's narrowest, between sheer rock walls soaring 2,000 feet on either side. The hike eventually leads down to a seaside village and a cool dip in the Libyan Sea some five to seven exhilarating hours later. The common jumping-off place is the coastal town of

Chania, known for its atmospheric historical port.

Not nearby, but worth the drive, is the polished Elounda Mare hotel, built into the side of a terraced slope graced by the natural beauty of the Mirabella Bay and views of the distant mountains. Half the suites come with their own wall-enclosed garden and small plunge pool, although the turquoise-blue sea is within easy reach. A deft balance between northern European sophistication and island simplicity, the Elounda Mare's Mediterranean aesthetics are reflected in its traditional but high-quality Greek furnishings and in its cuisine. The Elounda Mare boasts three acclaimed restaurants, all with outside dining, an excellent selection of fresh seafood, and extensive wine lists.

What: island, site, hotel. **Knossos:** 3 miles/5 km southeast of Heraklion. *Cost:* admission. **Phaistos:** 31 miles/50 km south of Heraklion. *Cost:* admission. **Samariá Gorge:** Chania is 85 miles/137 km west of Heraklion. *When:* gorge open May–mid-Oct. *Best times:* May and Sept. Crete's famous wildflowers bloom in May. **Elounda Mare:** 50 miles/80 km east of Heraklion. Tel 30/841-041102, fax 30/841-041307; mare@elounda-sa.com; www.elounda mare.gr. In the U.S., Relais and Chateaux, tel 212-856-0115. *Cost:* doubles with sea view from $415 (low season), from $765 (high season); bungalows with private pools from $645 (low season), from $1,190 (high season). **When:** open Apr–Oct.

White, White Cubist Homes Against a Blue, Blue Sea

MYKONOS AND DELOS

Cyclades, Greece

Mykonos has long been Greece's lively party island, and its image as a destination of attractive poseurs and young, dance-till-dawn Eurotravelers either lures or discourages potential first-timers. Chora, the picture-

The whitewashed Mykonos skyline

postcard capital, is clean, blindingly white-washed, and well maintained. Cosmopolitan clubs, gay bars, and wonderful (often nude) beaches populate a barren island where few of the old Greek traditions remain. The charm of the dry, rugged landscape dotted with retired windmills, some 400 churches, chapels, and shrines and the main town's stacked sugarcube houses with splashes of sky-blue doors and domes and brilliant red and pink bougainvillea can be all but obliterated by the high-season crowds. The warren of narrow streets was meant to defy the wind and confuse pirates, who plagued Mykonos in the 18th and 19th centuries; they still bemuse nonislanders, who enjoy getting lost among the tavernas, upscale boutiques, and Mykoniot homes. The resident pelican is a tame but curmudgeonly mascot who parades the waterfront and seems to have the run of things. The smallest of the Cycladic group, Mykonos is a mere 10 by 7 miles. You can escape the cruise ship crowds by heading to a secluded beach 2 miles out of town and checking in to the intimate Kivotos Clubhotel,

Mykonos's best. Or hop on a boat to the neighboring island of Delos.

The small, windswept island of Delos was the mythical birthplace of Apollo, god of truth and light, and his twin sister, the moon goddess Artemis. By 1000 B.C. the Ionians had inhabited the island and made it a religious center. Strategically positioned, and protected against attack by its sacred status, Delos flourished as the Aegean's major seaport and slave-trading center before gradually being abandoned around 70 B.C. Almost the entire island—a mere 1.5 square miles—is one large open-air archaeology museum, covered with ancient ruins, mosaics, and, in the spring months, wildflowers. Excavations begun in the late 19th century continue today. Its most photographed site is the famous Terrace of the Lions, where five of the original nine white-marble beasts (circa 7th century B.C.) remain. You may recall having seen one outside the entrance to Venice's Arsenal; Greece is still trying to get it back.

WHAT: island, hotel. **MYKONOS:** local airport has flights to/from Athens and, in season, some European cities; 5–7 hours by ferry, 3 hours by hydrofoil from Athens. **KIVOTOS CLUBHOTEL:** Ornos Bay, 2 miles/3 km from town. Tel 30/289-024094, fax 30/289-022844; kivotos@kivotosclubhotel.gr; www.kivotosclubhotel.gr. *Cost:* doubles from $310 (low season), from $340 (high season). *When:* open May–Oct. **DELOS:** accessible only by boat from Mykonos, 25 minutes away. *When:* morning departures daily in high season. **BEST TIMES:** May, Sept–Oct.

An Archetype of the Idyllic Greek Island

SANTORINI

Cyclades, Greece

As everyone's favorite Greek island, Santorini comes through with one of the Aegean's most unusual landscapes. The island's official name is Thira, although the medieval name—a corruption of St. Irene, left behind by the Italians—is far more commonly used. By any name, anyplace this gorgeous is bound to figure on every cruise ship's and island hopper's itinerary; large numbers of passengers, who fortunately never stay more than a few hours, take over the small island in the summer months. There is intense volcanic activity (there are two smoldering cones within the sunken 6-mile-wide caldera), and speculation is rife that Santorini is the remains of the mythical lost kingdom of Atlantis. Thirty-six varieties of grape grow in the rich volcanic soil, and Santorini produces delightful white wine, keeping everyone happy. The whitewashed cubical houses of tiny Oia—known as one of the most beautiful settlements in the Mediterranean—sit atop the 1,000-foot striated cliffs over the indigo waters of its partially sunken caldera (a "drinkable blue volcano," wrote Greece's Nobel Prize–winning poet Odysseus Elytis).

In Oia, maximize your visit with a stay at Perivolas, where the terraces provide the views that postcards are made of. Step out of your cool, cavelike apartment, and drink in a view similar to the scale of the Grand Canyon, only more beautiful. There may be more luxurious hotels on Santorini, but none provides sunset-viewing rights like the elegantly simple cave houses of the family-run Perivolas. The seventeen dazzlingly white-washed guesthouses have curved ceilings and walls; each terrace is the roof of the apartment below. One terrace is the site of a lipless pool, its Aegean blue identical to the real

thing beyond. Perivolas is a labor of love. The owner's handwoven, hand-dyed fabrics and rugs can be found throughout the elegantly spare rooms, where handmade Greek lace decorates windows and doors. It's a two-minute stroll down to the heart of the quiet town of Oia, and from there a twenty-minute ride to the tourist razzmatazz below in the island's main town, Thira. But for the daily ritual of sunset viewing, happiness is sitting on your own terrace with a glass of the local white wine in hand and the promise of fresh-grilled mussels for dinner in a nearby rooftop taverna.

A view from the cliffs of Santorini

WHAT: island, hotel. **SANTORINI:** 12 hours by ferry from Athens; a small airport services daily flights to Athens in high season. **PERIVOLAS:** in Oia, on the northwest tip of the island. Tel 30/286-071308, info@perivolas.gr; www.perivolas.gr. *Cost:* doubles from $595 (low season), from $735 (high season). *When:* open Apr–Oct. **BEST TIMES:** Apr–Jul and Sept–Oct.

Home to a Rich Religious and Artistic Heritage

PATMOS

Dodecanese, Greece

St. John the Divine was inspired to write the Book of Revelation during a two-year banishment to Patmos that began in A.D. 95. The small cave where St. John heard the voice of God (now known as the Sacred Grotto) is at the core of the Monastery of the Apocalypse. But the real draw is the tall, brooding Monastery of St. John the Theologian, an outstanding example of an 11th-century monastic complex of churches and courtyards, built as a fortress

The Monastery of St. John has been in continuous operation for more than nine centuries.

to protect its trove of religious treasures. From its inception, St. John was ornamented with outstanding paintings, carvings, and sculpture. Its rich tradition of learning established it as a renowned monastic center, a prestigious role it still enjoys today as the focal point of the Greek Orthodox faith in the Greek Isles.

St. John's extensive library and archives are important cultural treasures, second only to the collection of Mount Athos. Its 900th birthday was celebrated in 1988 to much fanfare. Patmos offers worldly satisfactions as well, with a hilly interior and stunning beaches that attract those who are less religiously inclined.

WHAT: island, site. **WHERE:** 150 miles/ 240 km from the mainland. **BEST TIMES:** the celebration of Holy Week and Greek Orthodox Easter on Patmos is unforgettable (usually in Apr).

Bridge Between Europe and the East

RHODES

Dodecanese, Greece

Thanks to its strategic location on ancient trade routes, Rhodes's economy was always a prosperous one. Little remains of the ancient past (the 100-foot bronze Colossus of Rhodes, one of the Seven Wonders of the World,

was sold off as scrap metal in the 7th century A.D. after being toppled by an earthquake). But the Middle Ages—a period on the island dominated by the crusading Order of the Knights of St. John—remain very much in evidence in the Old Town, the largest inhabited medieval town in Europe. The wonderfully preserved walls are one of the great medieval monuments in the Mediterranean, illustrating the engineering capabilities and financial and human resources available to the knights to keep out the infidels. Three miles long, up to 40 feet thick in some places, and encircled by a double moat, the walls encapsulate the Old Town,

an evocative framework for what is, in itself, a historical monument. The knights were divided into seven "tongues" or countries of origin, by which their "inns" were known— and still are, with plaques identifying such former lodges as the "Inn of the Tongue of Provence" and "Spanish House." Rhodes sits just 11 miles off the coast of Turkey, and even the mighty walls could not protect the knights from Suleiman the Magnificent and the Ottomans in 1522. The aesthetic influence of the 300-year Turkish presence can still be seen throughout the Old Town. The most delightful place to stay within the walls is the atmospheric, family-run San Nikolis, housed in a medieval building whose rooftop garden offers a fine breakfast with fantastic views.

WHAT: site, hotel. **OLD TOWN:** daily flights and a daily 16- to 18-hour ferry connect Athens and Rhodes in high season. **SAN NIKOLIS HOTEL:** 61 Hippodamou St. Tel 30/2241-034561, fax 30/2241-032034; nikoliss@hol.gr; www.s-nikolis.gr. **COST:** doubles from $170 (high season). **BEST TIMES:** Apr–Nov.

The Street of the Knights

The Most Beautiful Harbor Town in Greece

SYMI

Dodecanese, Greece

Symi's harbor town—an enchanting place—is a Greek treasure and a virtual museum of pastel late-19th-century neoclassical architecture. It showcases a brief period of fame and unmatched prosperity when this island of ship

builders and merchants built mansions and ornate churches before Symi drifted into obscurity. Today it bustles again, but only when day-trippers from nearby Rhodes sail in for lunch and a stroll. Some visitors are discouraged by the absence of sandy beaches and rarely venture into Symi's scenic interior of

The island, once home to 30,000 inhabitants, now has a population of approximately 2,500.

jagged rocks and pine and cypress woods. The coast, with its dramatic cliffs and small bays, is best reached by boat or on foot via a pleasant hike. Symi is an excellent island for any level of hiking. No walk is longer or more enjoyable than the 6-mile trek from beautiful Symi Town to the monastery of Panormitis (where overnight guests are welcome). Or, try the Hotel Aliki, housed in one of the most elegant of the old houses on the unspoiled waterfront, where the stars stayed when filming *Pascali's Island*. It is one of the nicest small hotels in Greece, restored with keen attention and rare good taste. Second-floor rooms afford views across the harbor. A few breakfast tables spill across the quay on the waterfront, where three steps lead down into the crystal-clear Aegean.

WHAT: town, hotel. **SYMI:** 13 miles/20 km north of Rhodes. **HOTEL ALIKI:** Akti G. Genimata. Tel 30/246-071665, fax 30/246-071655; info@simi-hotelaliki.gr; www.simi-hotel-aliki.gr. *Cost:* doubles from $100 (low season), from $185 (high season). *When:* open Apr–mid-Oct. **BEST TIMES:** May and Sept.

The Most Important Ancient Monument in the Western World

THE ACROPOLIS

Athens, Greece

A crowning achievement of Greek civilization's golden age, the astonishingly sophisticated Doric temple known as the Parthenon is the largest such structure built in Greece, and it has crowned the loftiest point of the city horizon (*acropolis* means "upper town") since the 5th century B.C. Dedicated to the patron goddess of the city, Athena Parthenos (Virgin Athena), it was originally so vividly painted (like all the other buildings on the Acropolis) that an alarmed Plutarch complained, "We are gilding and adorning our city like a wanton woman." Today it shimmers golden white in the sunlight, evidence of its subsequent incarnations as Byzantine church,

The Parthenon (top) and the Odeon of Herod Atticus

Frankish cathedral, and Ottoman mosque lost to history. Save the museum for last and see, among other superb statues, four of the original Caryatids, or maidens, formerly serving as columns, and the marble friezes that Lord Elgin did not manage to take back to England. Greece's primary artistic event, the summertime Athens Festival, presents ancient dramas, operas, music, and ballet performed by local and internationally acclaimed artists. The 2nd-century Odeon of Herod Atticus on the south slope of the Acropolis has legendary acoustics.

WHAT: site, event. **THE ACROPOLIS:** the 8-acre plateau of the Acropolis is easily reached by taxi or bus. **ATHENS FESTIVAL:** box office tel 30/1-0322-1459; www.greekfestival.gr. *Cost:* tickets $15–$85. *When:* festival is mid-Jun–Sept. **BEST TIMES:** once a month, during the full moon, the Acropolis opens at night. Otherwise, late afternoon, at sunset.

A Treasure House in Athens

NATIONAL ARCHAEOLOGY MUSEUM

Athens, Greece

T he National Museum holds more masterpieces of ancient Greek art and sculpture than any other museum in the world. Its unrivaled collection of Cycladic, Minoan, Mycenaean, and Classical Greek art is an essential part of any introduction to Greece. The star of the ground-floor sculpture rooms is the virile bronze of Artemision Poseidon, circa 5th century B.C.—the perfectly balanced body of an athlete about to launch his trident. Other magnets are the room dedicated to stunning ancient and Byzantine gold jewelry, the funerary mask of a bearded king once thought to be Agamemnon but now believed to date to the 15th century B.C. Save some of your strength for the outstanding Thira collection on the first floor, a range of pottery and artifacts rescued from the island of Santorini (Thira), dating to a Minoan civilization contemporary with that of Knossos on Crete. The Thira collection is known for its well-preserved frescoes, some of which have been returned to Santorini, where a new museum is being completed.

WHAT: site. **WHERE:** 44 Patission St. at Tissitsa St. Tel 30/1-0821-7724, fax 30/1-0821-3573; eam@culture.gr; www.culture.gr. **COST:** admission.

The Most Famous Oracle of Antiquity, Center of the Universe

DELPHI

Greece

For more than 1,000 years Delphi was the site of the most important oracle of ancient Greece, believed to be the mouthpiece of Apollo himself. On the seventh day of every month, a wise old Pythian priestess would go into a trance and utter her cryptic prophecies to the priests, who redelivered them as enigmatic riddles that could be taken in many ways. Lines would form days in advance, with supplicants arriving from beyond the Greek mainland. Peasants and world leaders alike consulted the oracle, bringing animals to be sacrificed and their questions to be answered, inscribed on stone tablets (many of which have survived). Delphi still resonates with mystery. Set in a spectacular location between two roseate rock faces and against the craggy peak of Mount Parnassus, it is said to have been founded by Zeus, leader of all gods, who determined that this spot was the center of the universe. A stone, the *omphalos*, still marks the spot that the ancients considered to be the navel of the world, where the priestess sat to receive the famous oracle. Above the remaining foundations of the Doric Temple of Apollo, the well-preserved 4th-century theater still stands, once site of the famous Pythian Festival, which, like the Olympic Games, was held every four years. Beyond, a path leads up to the stadium, the best preserved in all of Greece. Don't miss Delphi's on-site museum, a small but wonderful collection representing but a glimpse of ancient Delphi's once astounding treasure trove. Its celebrated bronze statue of a charioteer dates to the time of the amphitheater and stadium, a life-size symbol of the Pythian Games.

WHAT: site. **WHERE:** 117 miles/188 km northwest of Athens.

The oracle was probably last used in the late 4th century.

A Perfectly Preserved Ancient Greek Theater

EPIDAURUS

Peloponnese, Greece

T he perfectly preserved ancient theater at Epidaurus, built in the 4th century B.C., has acoustics that continue to astound modern-day authorities. The beauty of its setting and its harmonious proportions are without equal.

Restorations since its rediscovery in the last century have been minimal: the original stage of beaten earth has been kept, and the original fifty-four tiers of seats accommodate 14,000, with the red VIP seating in the front rows. Built with mechanical precision and an artist's eye for the natural backdrop of peaceful rolling hills, the theater at Epidaurus has become a popular venue for the productions of the Festival of Ancient Drama. It was also, understandably, one of Maria Callas's favorite places to perform. It's a magical place to watch the classics of Sophocles and Euripides, even if you don't understand the language in which they're performed. Epidaurus was the sanctuary of Asklepios, the Greek god of medicine, and it attracted the sick from near and far. Their treatments consisted of physical activity, relaxation, baths, and intellectual pursuits, and so it seems natural that this renowned theater was integrated with one of the world's first spas.

WHAT: site, event. **WHERE:** 25 miles/40 km from Nauplion. Tel 30/1-0322-1459, or contact Greek Festival S.A., tel 30/1-092-82900, fax 30/1-092-82933; www.greek festival.gr. **COST:** tickets $15–$40. **WHEN:** festival productions on weekends in Jul–Aug.

Barely Tethered to Reality

MONEMVASSIA

Peloponnese, Greece

M onemvassia's nickname, the Greek Mont-Saint-Michel, conveys some of the charm of this small medieval town that clings to the side of an islandlike rock jutting out of the southern Peloponnesian coast.

Like Gibraltar, Monemvassia once controlled the sea lines between medieval Western Europe and the Levant. Within this walled city, the houses and distinctly Byzantine churches are still occupied and connected by a long, narrow causeway to the mainland town of Gefira. Well-to-do Greeks have renovated once-crumbling ruins into vacation homes, but off-season, Monemvassia is nearly deserted, and the network of narrow side streets—sometimes just wide enough for two to pass—are yours alone. Three centuries-old buildings have been converted into the Hotel Malvasia, "the rock's" most atmospheric hotel, under government-controlled restoration. Each room is individually decorated with antiques; some have fireplaces, some have sea views.

WHAT: town, hotel. **MONEMVASSIA:** 60 miles/ 97 km southeast of Sparta. **HOTEL MALVASIA:** Old Town. Tel 30/732-061323; www.malvasia-hotel.gr. *Cost:* doubles with sea views from $110. **BEST TIMES:** Apr–Jun and Sept–Oct.

Spiritual Focus for the Eastern Orthodox World

MOUNT ATHOS

Northern Greece, Greece

The Byzantine Empire may have ended with the fall of Constantinople in 1453, but tell that to the monks of Mount Athos. Women (even female domestic animals) have not been allowed to set foot in this 140-square-mile semiautonomous monastic state since the 11th century, but male visitors with the appropriate permit can step back 500 years to the time of this theocracy's heyday, when more than forty monasteries housing 40,000 monks flourished. Today there are twenty monasteries. Most of them resemble fortified castles from the outside, reminders that the monks once had to fend off pirates, Christian crusaders, and the Ottoman Turks. Today's population of about 2,000 brothers carries on an unbroken 1,000-year tradition of study and liturgy. Priceless artwork and manuscripts have been amassed over the years, and the sacred clutter of relics and icons may be seen by visitors participating in morning and afternoon prayers. Visitors are also welcome to dine in the refectory with the monks (meals are vegetarian). Some monks are gregarious and welcoming, others oblivious to the limited but almost constant stream of guests during summer months, when it is most difficult to procure a permit. There is no land access to Athos, a heavily wooded area where wildlife abounds. Unrestricted numbers of Greek men may visit Mount Athos, but only ten foreign adult males per day may enter, spending no more than one night at any given monastery.

WHAT: site. **HOW:** the first, obligatory, step is to obtain a letter of recommendation from the consular section of your embassy in Athens to enter Athos on a specific date. They will then direct you to your next step—obtaining the permit—and you're on your way.

An Isle with Style

HYDRA

Saronic Gulf Islands, Greece

Your first sight of Hydra will be the lovely quasi-circular harbor town and many fine sea captains' houses fanning out and up into the rocky hills. All motor traffic (including kamikaze mopeds, thank goodness) is banned from this mountainous and barren island, where the people have always looked to the sea for their livelihood. Donkeys and horse-drawn carriages are the primary means of transportation. Once famous as a rendezvous spot for artists, writers, and the glitterati, Hydra still retains an image as one of the country's most stylish destinations. Tav-

The Hotel Bratsera's pool

ernas are rustic but frequented by a handsome crowd. The quietly chic Bratsera Hotel was created within the shell of an 1860 sponge factory; the doors, made from old packing crates, still bear the name of Athens's port, Piraeus. It is an unpretentiously elegant hotel, whose minimal nautical decor and spacious layout complement the local Hydriot character and history: exposed rich stonework, wooden beams, and relics of its former incarnation. On an island whose name mistakenly implies an abundance of water, the Bratsera's pool is a joy, and the only one on the island.

WHAT: island, hotel. **HYDRA:** less than 2 hours by hydrofoil from Athens. **HOTEL BRATSERA:** tel 30/298-053971, fax 30/298-053626; bratsera@yahoo.com; www.bratsera hotel.com. *Cost:* doubles from $185 (low season), from $215 (high season). *When:* open Mar–Oct. **BEST TIMES:** Apr–Jun and Sept–Oct.

A Rock Forest and Its Ancient Inhabitants

THE MONASTERIES OF THE METÉORA

Thessaly, Greece

Perched on seemingly inaccessible pinnacles of rock 1,000 feet above the Peneus Valley, what remains of a once-flourishing monastic community is as removed from earthly distractions as possible. The spikes, cones, and cliffs of this otherworldly landscape were created by the sea that submerged these plains 30 million years ago. Metéora méans, literally, "in the air," and there are more than sixty pinnacles, looking like chimney-top storks' nests. The earliest religious community was established here in the 10th century, and by the 16th century there were twenty-four monasteries and hermitages. Four survive essentially as museum pieces, while just two others function as religious outposts, with a handful of monks.

Of those that can be visited, Megálou Meteórou is the grandest and the highest, having held sway over the area since it was built of massive rocks on the highest peak (1,360 feet) in the 14th century. All the monasteries open to the public are worth visiting for the religious artworks collected over the centuries, the views, and the chance to observe the life of hermits and ascetics and some of the weirdest real estate on the planet. Until the 1920s the only way to reach them was by retractable ladders or nets. Since then steps to the monasteries have been hewn into the rocks. The adventure world has discovered Metéora's rock forest, and rock climbers can usually be spotted in the distance, looking like flies as they inch their way up the vertical pillars.

WHAT: town. **WHERE:** 110 miles/177 km southwest of Saloniki (Thessaloniki).

Welcome to Trulliland!

ALBEROBELLO

Apulia, Italy

I n the little-known but fascinating region of Apulia, the heel of the Italian "boot," is Alberobello, a town with a charm so peculiar that it's difficult to remember which country you're in, or which planet you're on. The city's *zona monumentale*

of conical whitewashed *trulli* takes visitors inside a child's storybook: imagine *Snow White and the Seven Dwarfs* as interpreted by Tolkien. There are more than 1,000 of these unique beehive structures in Alberobello and the rural area immediately surrounding it (twice that, by some accounts, in the area's Valle d'Itria). They crop up like clusters of mushrooms among the abundant olive trees. These whimsical, rather eerie hallmarks of Italy's southernmost region are found nowhere else in the country. Their primitive shape gives the impression that they are ancient, when in fact the oldest date to the 18th century. Today the *trulli* are used as homes, stores, storage space—even the local church of St. Anthony

(Sant'Antonio) is in the form of a *trullo*. If you fancy eating in one, look no further than Il Poeta Contadino, oddly formal for a centuries-old *trullo* but offering one of the area's best renditions of *cucina pugliese* (Apulia, or Puglia, is one of the country's richest agricultural regions and home of some of Italy's finest olive oil production). The wine selection at Il Poeta is one of the finest around.

WHAT: town, restaurant. **ALBEROBELLO:** 37 miles/60 km southeast of Bari. **IL POETA CONTADINO:** Via Indipendenza 21. Tel/fax 39/080-432-1917; info@ilpoetacontadino.it; www.ilpoetacontadino.it. *Cost:* four-course dinner $100. **BEST TIMES:** Apr–Jun and Sept–early Oct.

Glamorous Outpost of Roman Emperors and Modern-Day Sybarites

CAPRI

Campania, Italy

T his floating rough-cut gem of an island has been a favored summer playground since the Roman emperor Tiberius made it his ruling seat in A.D. 26. Almost every artist, designer, movie star, diva, politician, writer, royal, and financier of consequence since then has made an appearance in the island's stage-set Piazzetta, described by Noël Coward as "the most beautiful operetta stage in the world." An aphrodisiacal climate, lush Mediterranean gardens, and dramatic views from the car-free towns of Capri and Anacapri sustain the reputation of this 5-square-mile island Eden surrounded by emerald waters.

The sun, the sea, good wine, and great food come together gloriously on a sun-dappled terrace beneath the bamboo roof of La Fontelina. The view of Capri's signature *faraglioni*, three needlelike rocks—the tallest is almost 400 feet high—towering just minutes off this casual restaurant's coveted position on the rugged coast is unparalleled. La Fontelina also serves as Capri's most popular bathing spot, where diners can sunbathe and swim, before and after a lunch likely to include many rounds of the restaurant's signature fruit-filled sangria. Lunch may be a simple *insalata caprese*, the island specialty of superfresh mozzarella and sweet sliced tomatoes; it won't resemble anything you have ever tasted before.

Despite the endless roll call of glitterati, this is not a fancy island, and simplicity is valued. Pretensions are kept in check at the Hotel La Scalinatella, Capri's hideaway *in excelsis*. Demure sister of the far more extravagant Hotel Quisisana (and owned by the same family), La Scalinatella is intentionally understated but in many ways more stylish. It has the feel of relaxed luxury of a privately owned villa.

Dine at Da Paolino, one of Capri's most delightful restaurants: It's set in a lush lemon grove, where lantern-size fruits drip from the branches above your table. Those lemons have been adopted as a leitmotif; stylized versions appear on the plates, on the waiters' vests—and the real things garnish the fresh fish that swam in the local waters just hours before. Simple, good *cucina caprese* is served here in an ambience of *festa* and the celebration of the departure of the day's last boat

back to Naples. Don't head back to town for the obligatory late-night dalliance in the Piazzetta without sampling Paolino's signature dessert—you guessed it, a scoop of homemade lemon sorbet.

WHAT: island, hotel, restaurant. **CAPRI:** 45 minutes by hydrofoil from Naples, 20 minutes from Sorrento. **LA FONTELINA:** linked by a 10-minute boat ride to Marina Piccola across the bay, where guests are collected and

Soak up the sun at Hotel La Scalinatella.

left off at the pier. Otherwise, an enjoyable 45-minute walk to or from the Piazzetta. Tel 39/081-83-70-845. *Cost:* lunch $25. *When:* open Easter–Oct. **HOTEL LA SCALINATELLA:** Via Tragara 8. Tel 39/081-83-70-633, www.scalinatella.com. *Cost:* doubles with sea view from $425 (low season), from $610 (high season). *When:* open Easter–Oct. **DA PAOLINO:** Via Palazzo a Mare 11. Tel 39/081-83-76-102, fax 39/081-83-75-611; dapaolino @iol.it. *Cost:* dinner $45. **WHEN:** open Easter–Oct. **BEST TIMES:** avoid the heat and crowds of Aug.

A Fallen Empire's Spoils

NATIONAL ARCHAEOLOGICAL MUSEUM

Naples, Campania, Italy

I f you wondered where all the precious sculpture and artifacts excavated from Pompeii and Herculaneum wound up, they're here. One of the richest treasure troves of Greco-Roman antiquities in the world fills this large 16th-century cavalry barracks. An invaluable collection of antiquities amassed by Pope Paul III of the Farnese family during the excavations of Roman ruins are exhibited on the ground floor; Heracles is here, 10 feet tall, with an anatomy that would have made Michelangelo cry. The section dedicated to mosaics excavated from Pompeii reveals fascinating, intimate vignettes of life in that thriving, sophisticated city before it was extinguished forever by the eruption of Vesuvius in A.D. 79. The museum's Gabinetto Segreto (Secret Gallery) opened to much fanfare in 1999. Contained in two rooms are more than 200 frescoes, mosaics, and statues whose erotic attributes explain why they were never before made available to the public.

WHAT: site. **WHERE:** Piazza Museo Nazionale 19. Tel 39/081-544-0166, fax 39/081-544-0013; archeona@arti.beniculturali.it; www.marketplace.it/museo.nazionale. **COST:** admission $9. **WHEN:** Wed–Mon.

Joyously Chaotic Everyday Life, Neapolitan Style

SPACCANAPOLI

Naples, Campania, Italy

D ive into the laundry-festooned back alleyways of one of Italy's most vibrant and spirited cities for a glimpse of the histrionics and brio for which Neapolitans are known. Once an enclave of monumental palazzi and magnificent churches, the quarter called Spaccanapoli now bustles against a backdrop of time-battered tenements and workshops. The city's busiest neighborhood is slowly undergoing regentrification as Naples enjoys a cultural resurgence, and it is no longer dangerous to wander alone here. Narrow streets throb with local vendors, who hawk everything from contraband cigarettes to fried pizza and the mussels and clams brought in live from the Bay of Naples. The city's famous San Carlo Opera House may be one of Europe's largest and most splendid, but Spaccanapoli delivers the spontaneity of street opera, and the curtain never comes down. Enrico Caruso was born here and kept an apartment in the historic waterfront Grand Hotel Vesuvio from 1905 until his death in 1921. The hotel's rooftop Ristorante Caruso and its views of the marina and the 12th-century Castel dell'Ovo may well have been the setting where someone first exclaimed, "See Naples and die!"

WHAT: site, hotel, restaurant. **SPACCANAPOLI QUARTER:** west of the Duomo di San Genaro.

GRAND HOTEL VESUVIO: 45 Via Partenope. Tel 39/081-764-00-44, fax 39/081-764-44-83; in the U.S. and Canada, tel 800-223-6800; info@vesuvio.it; www.vesuvio.it. *Cost:* harborview doubles from $345. Dinner in Ristorante Caruso $90.

Ghost City of a Vanished Civilization

POMPEII

Campania, Italy

No matter how much you've read about Pompeii, nothing quite prepares you for the striking effect of some of the world's most famous ruins. It's as if the ancient Romans had departed only yesterday—the homes, wine shops public baths, and bordellos they left behind are windows on the life that flourished in this thriving port city at the foot of Vesuvius in the days of the Caesars. In A.D. 79 one of the most disastrous volcanic eruptions in history—recorded by Pliny the Younger, who observed it from a distance—buried the town under more than 20 feet of ash (not lava) that would preserve it until it was rediscovered at the end of the 16th century. It was not until the mid-18th century that large-scale excavations were launched, and two thirds of the city (some 60 acres) remain buried even now. The opulence of Pompeii can be seen in its intricate mosaic floors and richly frescoed villas, although many of the city's decorative and art objects were stolen long ago or carted off to the National Museum of Archaeology in Naples for safekeeping. Even though more than 1 million tourists visit yearly, Pompeii is large enough to provide quiet corners and elusive enough to be misunderstood without the help of a guide. Entire areas of the dead city are astonishingly intact, a haunting remnant of a place that seems as advanced and civilized as anything around today (or perhaps more so).

WHAT: site. **WHERE:** 15 miles/24 km southeast of Naples, 147 miles/237 km southeast of Rome; frequent 30-minute shuttles from Naples's main train station. **COST:** admission. **BEST TIMES:** avoid weekends and the hottest hours of a summer afternoon; fewer bus tours off-season.

Italy's Dream Drive

THE AMALFI COAST

Campania, Italy

It's hard to keep your eyes on the road while zipping along the dazzling landscape of the vertiginous Amalfi Drive, an improbable 30-mile stretch of hairpin curves south of Naples. After visiting the Amalfi coast, a giddy

André Gide wrote in *The Immoralist* that "nothing more beautiful can be seen on this earth." Vertical cliffs plunge into an impossibly blue Mediterranean, as a coastline of seaside towns unfolds among terraced olive and lemon groves, oaks, and umbrella pines. No longer as remote as when arrival was possible only by sea or pack animal, the cliff-hanging town of Positano is still the ultimate refuge. Mercifully closed to traffic, the town's jumble of converted whitewashed and pastel fishermen's homes spills down a maze of narrow alleyways to the pebbly umbrella-lined beach, the only flat strip in town.

It is here that tanned, handsome Sergio will pick you up and spirit you away to Da Adolfo in his family's motor launch (look for the boat with the big red fish), far from Positano's crowded beach scene and past the Hotel San Pietro so you can revel in an afternoon of sybaritic indulgence on a secluded slip of a beach. This is the region that gives the world fresh *mozzarella di bufala;* imagine how heavenly it tastes when it is grilled on a fragrant lemon leaf and served under the warm Neapolitan sun. Things only get better with the exquisite simplicity of spaghetti made with a sauce of plump baby clams and mussels. Getting to Da Adolfo is half the fun; lingering well after lunch in a sun-induced torpor prolongs this outing's delight. Pull up a beach bed and umbrella, and order an ice-cold *limoncello* liqueur squeezed from the area's uniquely sweet lemons, the size of grapefruits. It's enough to make you ignore the next boat back into town.

Hard to believe that tiny, picturesque Amalfi was once the heart of Italy's oldest and one of its most powerful maritime republics. As early as the 9th century, this microharbor at the mouth of a deep gorge was dominating commerce with the Orient, which helps explain both the Moorish influence and importance of the town's duomo, the Cathedral of Sant'Andrea. Planned and built during the peak of the republic's independence, it stands at the top of a steep flight of steps. The Baroque interior is reached through 11th-century bronze doors cast in Constantinople. The 13th-century Chiostro del Paradiso is a lovely Byzantine and Moorish cloister whose intoxicating aura of Arabian fantasy once infused much of the city's, and coastline's, architecture. Experience Amalfi or any of the neighboring towns along the marvelously scenic coast when they are not besieged by tour bus caravans and sense something of the lingering Middle Eastern influence.

The Amalfi coast as seen from a terrace garden

WHAT: experience, restaurant, town, site. **AMALFI DRIVE:** rent a car in Salerno (17 miles/27 km east of Positano), Naples (35 miles/56 km north), or Rome (174 miles/280 km north). Buses also leave regularly from these cities to Positano. *Best times:* May and Sept, when weather is mild and hotels less crowded. **DA ADOLFO:** Spiaggetta di Laurito, 10 minutes each way on the complimentary boat shuttle that leaves from the main jetty at the Positano beach every 30 minutes, 10 A.M.–1 P.M., and returns 4 P.M.–7 P.M. Tel 39/089-87-50-22. *Cost:* lunch $20. *When:* closed Oct–Apr. **AMALFI:** 11 miles/18 km east of Positano, 38 miles/61 km southeast of Naples. *Best times:* Feast of Sant'Andrea, the town's patron saint and patron of fishermen, is celebrated Jun 27 and Nov 30. **CATHEDRAL OF SANT'ANDREA:** on the Piazza Duomo.

Bastions of Elegance and Luxury

POSITANO'S HOTELS

Campania, Italy

I n 1953, John Steinbeck described the Hotel le Sirenuse as "a dream place . . . not quite real"—and so it remains, perched above the terraced homes of Positano and draped in fuchsia, bougainvillea, and honeysuckle. Vines insinuate themselves everywhere, the floors are paved in cool, hand-painted tiles, and a mingling of precious antiques enhances the hotel's elegant but comfortable personality. Run by a family whose summer villa this once was, a special feeling of welcome sets Le Sirenuse apart. So does a narrow lap pool-with-a-view and a small but exquisite spa and gym designed by the famous Milanese architect Gae Aulenti. The Pompeiian red 18th-century building was named for the sirens of Homer's *Odyssey,* those alluring demiwomen said to have inhabited the small Li Galli islands, which you can see from your terrace.

Slightly east of town, a tiny 17th-century chapel alongside the fabled coastal drive discreetly signals the presence of the Hotel le Sirenuse's longtime friendly rival, the multistoried San Pietro, carved into the precipitous cliff below and one of the world's most dramatically situated hotels, a triumph of human ingenuity and sheer extravagance. An elevator cut into solid rock whisks guests down to the airy lobby, terraced guest rooms, and, ultimately, the vest-pocket-size cove where guests can swim and sunbathe, even play tennis. Nonguests can idle away an afternoon at the bougainvillea-covered restaurant, 300 feet above the Tyrrhenian Sea, open to the breeze but protected from the sun. At sunset, have a leisurely drink on the tiled terrace: the view up and down the coastline is heart-stopping.

WHAT: hotel. **WHERE:** Positano is 35 miles/ 56 km southeast of Naples, 165 miles/265 km southeast of Rome. **HOTEL LE SIRENUSE:** Via Cristoforo Colombo 30. Tel 39/089-87-50-66, fax 39/089-81-17-98; info@sirenuse.it; www. sirenuse.it. *Cost:* doubles from $495. **HOTEL SAN PIETRO:** Via Laurito 2 (1 mile/2 km east of Positano). Tel 39/089-87-54-55, fax 39/089-81-14-49; www.ilsanpietro.it. *Cost:* doubles, all with private terrace and sea views, from $595. Lunch $65. *When:* open Apr–Oct. **BEST TIMES:** Apr–May and Sept–Oct.

Where Poets Go to Die

RAVELLO

Campania, Italy

P erched 1,100 feet above the tiny coastal town of Amalfi, Ravello has been described as closer to heaven than to the sea. Two irresistibly romantic gardens—the Villa Rufolo and the Villa Cimbrone—justify its reputation as "the place where poets go to die." Hotel guests can hope to experience breathtaking views of the cerulean sea from the Moorish-inspired Palazzo Sasso. Constructed in the 12th century, now a deluxe hotel, Sasso is all about the view. Richard Wagner found inspiration on this site in 1880, penning a part of *Parsifal* during a stay here. (Every summer an internationally renowned classical Wagner

Palazzo Sasso's sun deck with plunge pools

music festival takes place in the gardens of the Villa Rufolo.) This clifftop aerie looks east along the dramatic Lattari Mountains and their wild, contoured coastline toward Salerno, filling guest rooms and guests' hearts with warm sun and high romance. Its recent transformation into a modern-day hideaway left the spirit of the medieval structure unspoiled. Nine terraced acres of bougainvillea, roses, and mimosas fan out below the pink palazzo (sometimes overlooked by those hypnotized by the blending of the clear cobalt sky and sea beyond).

Follow the aroma of simmering tomato sauce and roast lamb that lead you to Cumpà Cosimo, the town's best trattoria. When most foreigners think of good, full-flavored Italian food, they think of Neapolitan cuisine, and that is what you'll find here. Ingredients grown in the rich volcanic soil around Naples, honest wines, and the deft hands of Netta Bottone (daughter of the original founder, Cosimo) make any meal here delicious. There is usually a marathon sampling of seven different pastas. Day-trippers don't often hang around Ravello for dinner, leaving the barebones Cosimo's to the local folk, who enjoy the excellent pizza and inexpensive conviviality.

WHAT: town, hotel, event, restaurant. **RAVELLO:** 3 miles/5 km from Amalfi, 16 miles/26 km west of Salerno. **PALAZZO SASSO:** Via San Giovanni del Toro 28. Tel 39/089-81-81-81, fax 39/089-85-89-00; info@palazzo sasso.com; www.palazzosasso.com. *Cost:* doubles with sea view from $425 (low season), from $530 (high season). *When:* open Mar–Dec. **WAGNER FESTIVAL:** tel 39/089-85-81-49, fax 39/089-85-82-49; info@ravello.info; www.ravelloarts.org. *When:* Mar–Oct, principal concerts Jun–Aug. *Cost:* tickets from $35. **CUMPÀ COSIMO:** Via Roma 44. Tel 39/089-85-71-56. *Cost:* dinner $30. *When:* open daily for lunch and dinner, Apr–Oct.

Some of the World's Oldest and Best-Preserved Temples

PAESTUM

Salerno, Campania, Italy

Discovered by accident in the 18th century, Paestum was inhabited for 700 years before falling along with the ancient Roman Empire in its final days. On a flat coastal plain that Percy Bysshe Shelley called "inexpressibly grand" are some of the ancient world's most glorious ruins, and possibly the oldest. Of the two sun-bleached limestone pièces de résistance here, the Basilica is one of Western civilization's earliest standing edifices. A temple dedicated to Hera, the wife of Zeus, it dates from the 6th century B.C and is one of Europe's best preserved. Next to it stands the famous Temple of Neptune, considered one of the ancient world's largest and most beautiful temples. Built around 450 B.C., it is one of the Mediterranean's most complete structures, with only its roof and parts of its inner walls missing and thirty-six Doric columns still vertical. See Paestum in the late afternoon, when a less harsh Neopolitan light warms their golden stone. Then head to the nearby agriturismo farm and inn of the Baronessa Cecilia Bellelli Baratta, whose 400 water buffalo supply Italy with some of its best *mozzarella di bufala*. Guests of her family-run

Tenuta Seliano can feast on fresh mozzarella and ricotta daily, as well as a whole cornucopia of products directly from the farm, prepared to perfection by the baroness herself and served family-style in the garden. This must be why Pliny the Elder referred to the region as Campania Felix—Happy Campania indeed.

WHAT: site, hotel. **PAESTUM:** 62 miles/ 100 km southeast of Naples, 19 miles/ 30 km south of Salerno. **TENUTA SELIANO:** 2 miles/3 km from Paestum, in Borgonuovo. Tel 39/082-872-4544; seliano@agrituris moseliano.it; www.agriturismoseliano.it. *Cost:* doubles from $106 (low season), from $135 (high season). *When:* open Mar–Oct, Dec–Jan 10. **BEST TIMES:** May, Jun, Sept, and Oct.

A Grand Hotel and Unsurpassed Restaurant

THE BEST OF SORRENTO

Campania, Italy

The hazy outline of Mount Vesuvius dominates the view from the terraces of the Grand Hotel Excelsior Vittoria. With mosaic floors, marble staircases, dwarf palm trees, hand-painted cherubs, and elaborate Art Nouveau frescoes decorating the hotel's lofty interiors, guests feel as bathed in luxury here as the ancient Romans who once played in ancient Sorrentum. (Remains of the villa of Caesar Augustus are believed to have been found beneath the hotel.) The Belle Epoque spirit of bygone luxury lives on in this grandest of Sorrento's 19th-century hotels. Five acres of lemon-scented gardens and white-gloved service create a refuge from the clamor of the day-trippers who descend from cruise ships and buses on their way to Pompeii. Its old-world, aging drama recalls the British travelers for whom the hotel was built atop the dramatic 150-foot cliff when Sorrento was still a small, genteel resort favored for its mild winters. If Luciano Pavarotti never fails to put heart and

soul into his signature rendition of "Return to Sorrento," it's because he often stays here. Book the Caruso Suite for that same inspiration; opera's greatest tenor, Enrico Caruso, vacationed here in 1921, just before his death.

In a food-enthralled country where cautious critics sing high praises only with great reluctance, Don Alfonso 1890 has long garnered recognition as possibly the finest restaurant in southern Italy. Its location augments the experience, gorgeously poised between earth and the sparkling gulfs of Naples and Salerno. The loyal clientele think nothing of driving in from Naples or Bari just for lunch. Alfonso Iaccarino and his wife, Livia, who have known each other since childhood, are fanatic in their commitment to quality local ingredients and herbs.

Much of the seasonal menu is selected and produced at their nearby 10-acre farm overlooking Capri, and their olive oil has been ranked as some of the best in the world. But the cuisine at Don Alfonso is far from simple country cooking: Mediterranean at heart, it surprises with unusual and delicious, vaguely Asian influences, served in a cool and elegant atmosphere. The restaurant's noted wine cellar—a three-tiered cavern carved into the volcanic rock in Roman times—contains more than 30,000 bottles.

The Grand Hotel Excelsior Vittoria is surrounded by orange and lemon groves.

WHAT: hotel, restaurant. **GRAND HOTEL EXCELSIOR VITTORIA:** Piazza Tasso 34 (Sorrento is 32 miles/50 km southeast of Naples on the Amalfi Peninsula). Tel 39/081-877-71-11; info@exvitt.it; www.exvitt.it. *Cost:* doubles with sea views from $410, Caruso Suite $830. **DON ALFONSO 1890:** 5 miles/8 km above Sorrento, in Sant'Agata Sui Due Golfi. Tel 39/081-878-00-26, fax 39/081-533-02-26; info@donalfonso.com; www.donalfonso.com. *Cost:* dinner tasting menu. $90. **BEST TIMES:** Apr and Oct.

Where Food Is a Magnificent Obsession

THE QUADRILATERO

Bologna, Emilia-Romagna, Italy

Being the preeminent culinary center of a food-conscious country is an imposing position that Bologna la Grassa (Bologna the Fat One) has shouldered proudly and insouciantly for centuries. Most trips to this handsome medieval city are devoted to the pursuit of gastronomic pleasures. Head straight for the Quadrilatero. The well-known food district lies within a medieval labyrinth whose narrow streets and porticoed arcades of family-run shops make up the city's oldest and best-preserved quarter. Bologna is the birthplace of mortadella sausage (the distant and infinitely more tasty granddaddy of American bologna), meat-stuffed tortellini pasta, and the exquisitely chunky *ragú alla bolognese*. The popular preoccupation with eating is happily played out amid some of Italy's most historically important architecture. The hungry and the plain curious will be in paradise in Tamburini, Italy's most lavish food empo-

rium, an amazing display of artistically packaged and prepared foods, pastas, meats, and salads. A visit here is more about cultural enhancement than shopping, but no one with a sense of sight or smell or taste leaves the store empty-handed. The recent addition of a self-service bistrolike corner is a godsend.

WHAT: town, site. **BOLOGNA:** 66 miles/ 106 km north of Florence, 131 miles/210 km southeast of Milan. **THE QUADRILATERO:** east of the Piazza Maggiore. **TAMBURINI:** Via Capraie 1. Tel 39/051-23-47-26, fax 39/051-23-22-26; tambinfo@tin.it; www.tamburini.com. **WHEN:** most food stores closed Thurs afternoon and Sun.

A City of Great Art and Refinement

PIAZZA DEL DUOMO

Parma, Emilia-Romagna, Italy

Although generally identified as the home of Arturo Toscanini and *parmigiano* cheese, Parma offers so much more, as confirmed by a visit to the Piazza del Duomo, one of the loveliest city centers in Italy.

The stunning octagonal Battistero (Baptistry) is clad in Veronese-colored pink marble and elaborately festooned with reliefs by the local sculptor and architect Benedetto Antelami (1150–1230). Much of Antelami's renown comes from works found within the Baptistry, one of the finest examples of Romanesque architecture in northern Italy. In the Duomo next door, a high point, quite literally, of a visit to this 12th-century cathedral is looking up toward the recently restored cupola at Antonio Correggio's famous *Assumption of the Virgin* (1522–1530). A master of light and color, the "divine" Correggio was one of Italy's greatest masters of the High Renaissance, although the concentric circles of figures were described as a "mess of frogs' legs" by the bishop who commissioned the piece. Parma is one of Italy's most prosperous cities, and a sense of well-being harks back to its days of splendor as capital of the Farnese dukes from the mid-16th to the early 18th century.

WHAT: town, site. **PARMA:** 60 miles/97 km northwest of Bologna, 75 miles/121 km southeast of Milan. **PIAZZA DEL DUOMO:** center of town. *Cost:* admission charge to Baptistry only.

Once the Western Capital of the Byzantine Empire

RAVENNA

Emilia-Romagna, Italy

Ravenna is the home of the most celebrated mosaics in Western art. The superb 5th- to 7th-century Byzantine mosaics are dazzling reminders of Ravenna's storied past as the last capital of the Western Roman Empire

after the fall of Rome in the 5th century. Today it is a sleepy town, nonchalant about the unparalleled artistic treasures that fill its museums and churches. For the art-loving visitor, this means no crowds, no lines, and an enjoyably slow, genuine rhythm in a place where tourism seems almost incidental. The city's red-brick buildings are unpretentious, an intense contrast to the brilliance and refinement of the mosaics that cover their interiors. Tiny pieces of glass, colored marble, and semiprecious stones have been painstakingly cut to fit drawn designs of epic proportion. There are six places to see these tapestries of mosaics, ordered by the Byzantine rulers in their attempt to have Ravenna outdo rival cities, but most visited is the 6th-century duo of the Tomb of Gallia Placidia and the adjacent Basilica di San Vitale, believed by many to be the crowning achievement of Byzantine art in the entire world.

WHAT: town, site. **RAVENNA:** 46 miles/ 74 km east of Bologna, 90 miles/145 km south of Venice. **BASILICA DI SAN VITALE:** Via San Vitale. The Tomb of Gallia Placidia is just behind the Basilica. *Cost:* joint admission. **BEST TIMES:** a distinguished music festival takes place every year, late Jun–late Jul.

Getty's Former Seaside Retreat

LA POSTA VECCHIA

Località Palo Laziale, Lazio, Italy

John Paul Getty, once the richest man in the world, isn't around anymore (he left Italy in 1975, one year before his death), but you'll still feel like one of his most coddled guests at La Posta Vecchia, the magnificent Villa that was once his palatial seaside home. The billionaire oil baron and art collector extraordinaire gave new meaning to the expression "there's no place like home," and much of the money-is-no-object luxury and quiet sense of privacy he demanded has been left intact.

Getty purchased the villa from his friend Prince Odescalchi, whose ancestors built it in 1640 for guests visiting the family's neighboring 15th-century castle—still inhabited today by descendants of the noble lineage. The wealthy American tycoon spent millions amassing an enormous collection of antiques and antiquities (Maria de' Medici's marriage chest and Gobelin tapestries are just some of the myriad museum-level pieces) still used to appoint this amazing seventeen-guest-room villa. It was only by chance that his architects discovered the ancient foundations of a Roman villa—perhaps two—upon which the 17th-century structure was built. In what is now a small informal museum located beneath the villa, intricate mosaic floors indicate the wealth and affluence of those ancient Roman landlords (some have even suggested that

the emperor Tiberius lived here). Modern-day guests enjoy the ultimate in civilized living, the same timeless serenity of an unparalleled alfresco meal on the glorious seaside terrace, light-years away from the glory that is Rome, *caput mundi.*

WHAT: hotel. **WHERE:** Via Palo Laziale, 23 miles/37 km from Rome. Tel 39/06-99-49-501, fax 39/06-99-49-507; info@laposta vecchia.com; www.lapostavecchia.com. **COST:** doubles from $450 (low season), $830 (high season). Dinner $120. **WHEN:** open late Mar–early Nov. **BEST TIMES:** Mar–Jun, Sept, and Oct.

The Medici Suite

"Rome welcomes you when you come and forgets you when you go."—FEDERICO FELLINI

ROME

Lazio, Italy

A republic was declared in Rome in 509 B.C., and all roads have led here ever since. A very busy city of leisurely citizens, Rome serves up a jolt of big-city life with the warmth of a small provincial town.

THE TOP TEN SIGHTS

BASILICA OF SANTA MARIA MAGGIORE—One of Rome's four major basilicas, built in the 5th century, then restored and extended between the 12th and 18th centuries. Its magnificent 5th-century mosaics are among the oldest and most beautiful in the city, and its 15th-century coffered ceiling is said to have been gilded with some of the first gold brought from the New World, a gift of the Spanish monarchy. **WHERE:** Piazza di Santa Maria Maggiore. Tel 39/06-446-5836.

BORGHESE GALLERY—Begun by Cardinal Scipione Borghese in the 17th century, the collection includes Titian's *Sacred and Profane Love*, Raphael's *Deposition*, Bernini's *Apollo and Daphne*, and Caravaggio's *David with the Head of Goliath*, among innumerable other masterpieces. **WHERE:** Piazzale Scipione Borghese. Tel 39/06-32810; www.galleria borghese.it. Reservations required.

THE COLISEUM—Once able to seat 50,000, the Coliseum was begun in A.D. 72 by Vespasian and inaugurated in A.D. 80 by his son, Titus. Combat was the usual entertainment—between men, between animals, between men and animals, and even between ships, as the whole thing could be flooded. Centuries of neglect and outright ransacking have left it a shell largely without floor or seats, but what a shell it is, with three tiers of columns—Doric, Ionian, and

The Coliseum has long been an icon of the glory that was Rome.

Corinthian. Renovation projects go on perpetually. **WHERE:** Piazzale del Colosseo, Via dei Fori Imperiali. Tel 39/06-399-67700.

ETRUSCAN MUSEUM AT THE VILLA GIULIA—This elegant 16th-century country villa built for Pope Julius III holds thirty-five rooms with Italy's largest and best collection of ancient Etruscan sculptures, terra-cotta vases, sarcophagi, and jewelry. Very little is known about the Etruscans, whose empire predated the Roman. **WHERE:** Piazzale di Villa Giulia. Tel 39/06-320-1951.

PIAZZA CAMPIDOGLIO AND THE CAPITOLINE MUSEUMS—Designed by Michelangelo in the 1550s, the Piazza Campidoglio is one of Rome's most elegant piazzas, and home to one of its greatest museums, inaugurated by Pope Clement in 1734. Its collection includes ancient Roman sculptures and

The Pantheon was built to honor the ancient Roman gods.

Renaissance paintings, including numerous works by Tintoretto and Reni. The famous statue of the wolf suckling Romulus and Remus is here, as is the original statue of Marcus Aurelius astride a horse, which once sat in the center of the piazza. Pollution led to its removal indoors; a copy remains outside. **WHERE:** Piazza del Campidoglio. Tel 39/06-399-67800 or 39/06-671-02475; www.museicapitolini.org.

THE PANTHEON—Built in 27 B.C. by Marcus Agrippa and reconstructed by Hadrian in the early 2d century A.D., the Pantheon is the most complete ancient Roman building remaining today and one of its architectural wonders: its dome is exactly as wide as it is high, supported by pillars hidden in the walls. Raphael's tomb is here. **WHERE:** Piazza della Rotonda. Tel 39/06-6830-0230.

THE ROMAN AND IMPERIAL FORUMS— The center of Roman life in the days of the Republic, the Roman Forum was a stone quarry and cow pasture before excavations began in the 19th century. You need a map and guide to put some meaning to the ruins, which include numerous temples, the Umbilicus Urbus, considered the center of Rome (and, by extension, of the empire); the Curia, the main seat of the Roman Senate; and the House of the Vestal Virgins, home of the young women who minded the Temple of Vesta's sacred fire. The Imperial Forum was begun by Julius Caesar to show the power of the emperors. You can see his forum, once

the site of the Roman stock exchange; the Forum of Augustus, built to commemorate the defeat of Caesar's assassins; the famous Trajan's Column, with bas-reliefs depicting the emperor's campaign against the Dacians; the Forum of Trajan; and much more. **WHERE:** Via dei Fori Imperiali. Tel 39/06-399-67700.

SPANISH STEPS—Designed by Francesco de Sanctis and built between 1723 and 1725, these wide steps ascend in three majestic tiers from the busy Piazza di Spagna to the French Trinità dei Monti church, one of Rome's most distinctive landmarks and the place to be at sunset, with a view of Rome's seven hills. The steps take their name from the Spanish Embassy, which occupied a nearby palace in the 19th century. The boat-shaped fountain in the piazza was designed in the late 16th century by Bernini or his father (the jury is still out). The house where John Keats lived and died sits beside the steps. **WHERE:** Piazza di Spagna.

TREVI FOUNTAIN—Designed by Nicolo Salvi and completed in 1762, the fanciful Baroque fountain features Neptune standing on a chariot drawn by winged steeds. **WHERE:** Piazza di Trevi. (See also Hotel Fontana, page 194.)

VATICAN CITY—The world's smallest independent state, Vatican City is accessed through St. Peter's Square, surrounded by an elliptical colonnade with some 140 saints on top. Straight ahead is the facade of St. Peter's Basilica, the center of world Catholicism. The Circus of Nero, where St. Peter was crucified, once sat on this spot, and in 324 the emperor Constantine commissioned a basilica to be built here in the saint's honor. The present structure dates from the 16th and 17th centuries and contains cream-of-the-crop statuary, the Michelangelo-designed dome and his famous *Pietà*, and so much more that it's overwhelming—exactly as it was supposed to be. To the north of the piazza, the Vatican Museums (tel 39/06-6988-4341; www.vatican.va) contain one of the world's greatest collections of art from antiquity and the Renaissance, including Raphael's famous *stanze* (several rooms containing many of the artist's masterpieces), housed in a labyrinth of palaces and galleries. The gem of the collection is the famous Sistine Chapel, with its ceiling painted by Michelangelo between 1508 and 1512 (see separate entry on page 196).

OTHER MUST-DO'S

BOCCA DELLA VERITÀ—Reenact the scene from the 1950s Audrey Hepburn classic *Roman Holiday:* Go to the atrium of the Church of Santa Maria in Cosmedin and stick your hand in the gaping Mouth of Truth—legend has it that if someone puts his hand in the mouth and tells a lie, the mouth will bite down. Be careful what you say! **WHERE:** Piazza della Bocca della Verità.

MARKET AT CAMPO DEI FIORI—One of Italy's great daily marketplaces, and some of its best theater. Shaded by canvas *ombrelloni*, stalls sell the freshest produce available—come before 9 A.M. or the city's chefs will have snatched up all the best. Insight into daily Roman life at its most authentic continues after the last stall disappears. Patrons of the popular hole-in-the-wall La Vineria wine bar spill out onto the piazza, wineglass in hand, to discuss the scandal of the week or the day's soccer score.

OSTIA ANTICA—As evocative as Pompeii and twice as well preserved, Rome's best-kept secret can even be reached by subway. Excavations of the ancient port of Rome reveal much of the history of the far-flung Roman Empire. **WHERE:** Viale dei Romagnoli, Ostia Antica (16 miles southwest of Rome). Tel 39/06-5635-8099.

PIAZZA NAVONA—The Eternal City's nightlife at its best. In warm weather, take a seat outdoors at Tre Scalini café for the people-watching and the specialty *tartufo*, a rich chocolate concoction named for its resemblance to the knobby truffle. Against the background of Bernini's Baroque Fountain of the Rivers, a host of Felliniesque characters from central casting mingle with German students, retired couples from Florida, and Roman residents of all shapes and inclinations.

VIA CONDOTTI—Via Condotti and its grid of cobbled offshoots at the foot of the Spanish Steps offers ultrasmart shopping and the ideal venue for the early evening *passeggiata* ritual. In this atmospheric, traffic-free neighborhood is Rome's oldest café, Caffè Greco, a centuries-old watering hole where Casanova, Goethe, Lord Byron, and Buffalo Bill all stopped for a coffee break.

WHERE TO STAY

D' INGHILTERRA—Rome's best boutique hotel, the small and centrally situated D'Inghilterra was a favorite of those following the Grand Tour long before Valentino and Gucci shops began springing up around it. It offers old-world polish and charm and (for those who request one of the top-floor suites) an unforgettable breakfast with a view from your flowered terrace. **WHERE:** Via Bocca di Leone (near the Spanish Steps). Tel 39/06-69-9811; www.hoteldinghilterra. warwickhotels.com. **COST:** high.

GRAND HOTEL—Closed for years to restore its formal glory, the Grand was built in 1894 and was the first hotel in the world to have electric lighting. Its 19th-century interiors are as ornate as you'd expect, with rooms appointed in a combination of Empire, Regency, and Louis XV styles. Even if you're not staying, go for an aperitif or tea in the bar, which is a real see-and-be-seen scene. **WHERE:** Via Vittorio Emanuele Orlando (close to the train station, the Spanish Steps, and the Trevi Fountain). Tel 39/06-47091; www.starwoodhotels.com. **COST:** high.

HOTEL FONTANA—Named for the Trevi Fountain (in which Anita Ekberg splashed in *La Dolce Vita*). A dozen of the hotel's front rooms are so close you could dive into the fountain from them, but by just throwing three coins, you guarantee a return visit. The view is especially bewitching after dark, when this flight of fancy is illuminated in all its Baroque grandeur. **WHERE:** Piazza di Trevi. Tel 39/06-678-6113. **COST:** moderate.

EATING & DRINKING

CAFFÈ SANT'EUSTACHIO—Always packed with locals who stream in for the best espresso—something about the water, they say. Or is it the fresh beans roasted on the premises? Home of the city's most delicious cappuccino, never ever ordered after 11 A.M. except by innocents abroad. **WHERE:** Piazza Sant'Eustachio. Tel 39/06-688-02048.

DA CHECCO ER CARRETTIERE—One of the last of Rome's classic trattorias. Half the joy of a stroll through the former artists' quarter of Trastevere, now well on its way to gentrification, is winding up with a coveted table on Checco's outdoor patio, with a sampling of its well-known antipasti. **WHERE:** Via Benedetta. Tel 39/06-580-0985.

DA FORTUNATO AL PANTHEON—A local favorite for decades. Simple, well-prepared Roman cuisine is served by jacketed, bow-tied waiters to a well-heeled crowd. Hours are spent lingering over some of the best meals in town—does no one work in Rome? **WHERE:** Via del Pantheon. Tel 39/06-679-2788.

DER PALLARO—Typical, authentic, no-frills, and in the characterful neighborhood of the Campo dei Fiori—who doesn't love this place? The flowers are plastic and there's no menu to speak of: Whatever four-course menu Signora Paola is cooking up in the kitchen that day arrives at your table. (Try for one outdoors.) **WHERE:** Largo del Pallaro. Tel 39/06-6880-1488.

GIOLITTI—The city's oldest gelateria, so you won't be the only one standing in line to sample their fifty-some homemade flavors. Where else will you find Champagne ice cream? Stake out a table and order the preposterously oversized Copa Olimpico, a sampling of just about everything they offer. **WHERE:** Via Uffici del Vicario. Tel 39/06-699-1243.

LA ROSETTA—Small and chic. Much of the reliably fresh seafood is flown in daily from the talented chef's native Sicily. Expensive but worth it, this is by now a beloved institution with a strong following of locals and in-the-know out-of-towners. **WHERE:** Via della Rosetta. Tel 39/06-686-1002.

TRIMANI WINE BAR—A wood-paneled, family-run operation in the unlikely neighborhood of the train station. Simple but sophisticated meals are the perfect complement to dozens of excellent, mostly Italian wines by the glass. The selection is even more prodigious at the Trimani family's *enoteca* around the corner. **WHERE:** Via Cernaia. Tel 39/06-446-9661; www.trimani.com.

A Roman Holiday atop the Spanish Steps

THE HOTEL HASSLER

Rome, Lazio, Italy

Never have hotel guests been so undeterred by 136 steps—consider them the grand entrance to one of Rome's great hotels. The fabled Hotel Hassler glories in its one-of-a-kind location above the capital's famous

The hotel is adjacent to the Trinità dei Monti church.

Spanish Steps. Being a coddled guest of the Hassler let Audrey Hepburn feel like a princess both on and off the set when filming *Roman Holiday*, and what was good enough for Audrey (and just about every other celebrity and crowned head on the planet) is good enough for most. Dozens of the rooms and suites are blessed with terraces and romantic and dazzling panoramas of the Eternal City. Established in 1885 in a palazzo

that was once the home of Napoleon's sister, the Hassler is one of the rare luxury hotels in Europe today that is privately owned and operated. Impervious to contemporary whims, the old-world hotel is impeccably run by fifth-generation hotelier Roberto Wirth, who believes in real keys, superlative service, messages delivered on silver trays—simple amenities quickly growing extinct in the homogenization of the world's five-star properties. If you must go elsewhere to hang your hat, at least stop in for an aperitif at the Hassler Bar (which moves to the Palm Court in warm weather) or try the popular Sunday brunch in the hotel's Rooftop Restaurant. The food, while good, takes a backseat to the view of Rome's seven hills.

WHAT: hotel. **WHERE:** Piazza Trinità dei Monti 6. Tel 39/06-699-340, fax 39/06-678-9991; in the U.S., 800-745-8883; booking@hotelhassler.it; www.hotelhassler.com. **COST:** doubles from $495, Presidential Suite with terrace $4,385. **BEST TIMES:** heat can be bad in Jul and Aug; the Spanish Steps are covered with azaleas mid-Apr–mid-May.

The World's Most Famous Ceiling

SISTINE CHAPEL

Rome, Lazio, Italy

The spellbinding frescoes that cover the ceiling and walls of the Sistine Chapel are among Western civilization's greatest achievements. Historians always knew Michelangelo to be a master painter (although, following his

success with *David*'s completion, he painted infrequently before being commissioned to create the ceiling by Pope Julius), but the biggest revelation of its fourteen-year restoration (the most controversial of all time) was his startling use of light and bright colors, which had been drastically muted over the centuries from accumulated dust, dirt, incense, and countless candles. Although he started off

with a team of assistants and apprentices, Michelangelo fired them all and worked alone for four years before unveiling his work to a speechless pope and public in 1512. After an international restoration team completed work on this brilliant extravaganza depicting biblical scenes from the Creation (the creation of Adam is the ceiling's focus), they turned their attention to the wall behind the main altar and Michelangelo's equally powerful *Last Judgment*. Its completion in 1541 brought Pope Pius III to his knees. Although Michelangelo is often associated with his birth town of Florence (where he is represented by *David* and the Medici Chapels), his presence is strongly felt in the Eternal City. The Sistine Chapel rightly caps any visitor's short list, but the *Pietà* in St. Peter's Basilica confirms Michelangelo's genius as a sculptor, while Rome's elegant Piazza del Campidoglio shows off his natural talent as architect and city planner: one of the world's most beautiful and copied squares (reinterpreted in New York City's Lincoln Center), it has been left essentially as he designed it.

WHAT: site. **WHERE:** part of the Vatican Museums in Vatican City, Viale Vaticano. Tel 39/06-69-88-38-60. For guided tours, reserve in advance through Il Sogno, tel 39/06-8530-1758, fax 39/06-8530-1756; ilsogno@romeguide.it; www.romeguide.it. **COST:** admission $20, $40 for guided tour. **WHEN:** open daily except for 1st 3 Suns of the month. **BEST TIMES:** always crowded; come early, before the 8:45 A.M. opening.

A Coastline Hike with Inspiring Seascapes

CINQUETERRE

Liguria, Italy

Collectively known as the Five Lands, hidden in tiny coves along the craggy southern stretch of the Ligurian Riviera, the Cinqueterre were once virtually unknown to outsiders. Only recently connected by road to the rest of Italy and each other, these five villages offer a glimpse of an elusive, pristine Mediterranean—Italy as it must have been a century or more ago. This is one of the country's most dramatic coastal settings, with cliffs so harsh and unyielding, that for centuries these fishing hamlets were linked to each other only by boat or a network of mule paths strung along the cliffs. These ancient *sentieri* are now paved for the most part, and considered one of the more gorgeously scenic and not-too-difficult hikes in Europe. A heavenly plate of pasta with pesto sauce is the payoff at the end of the day, followed by a cold bottle of the local white dessert wine called sciacchetrà. With poetic names such as the Via dell'Amore, these panoramic footpaths pass through an overgrown, fragrant mantle of *macchia*, the Mediterranean's slowly disappearing ecosystem, together with agaves, prickly pears, palms, olives, and everywhere the daringly carved stepped vineyards that produce wine renowned at least since the 14th century, when it was praised by Boccaccio. Monterosso is the first, northernmost town, with a handful of hotels and the only village with what might be called a stretch of waterfront, and thus a natural base. They say you can reach the fifth village, Riomaggiore, by foot in five or six hours—but what's the rush?

WHAT: site. **WHERE:** Monterosso 57 miles/90 km east of Genoa, 6 miles/10 km from Levanto. Local trains on the Genoa–La Spezia railroad line stop in all 5 villages. **WHERE TO STAY:** Hotel Porto Roca, built into a cliff above Monterosso al Mare, Via Corone 1. Tel 39/0187-81-75-02, fax 39/0187-81-76-92; portoroca@portoroca.it; www.portoroca.it Ask for a room with a sea view. *Cost:* doubles with sea view from $390. *When:* open mid-Mar–Oct. **BEST TIMES:** May, Jun, and Sept; avoid weekends.

Postcard of the Italian Riviera

PORTOFINO

Liguria, Italy

Portofino wins the beauty contest in Liguria, the crescent-shaped region known as the Italian Riviera. The town's perfect little harbor has been designated a historical landmark, and Portofino is said to be the most photographed village in the world. The facades of the fishermen's dwellings are painted in the rich colors for which Liguria is known—faded mustard, ocher, pink, and rust. A fishing village no longer, Portofino is now graced by swank villas nestled in the wooded hills above; the small boats bobbing in the marina (alongside glamorous 150-foot yachts) are no longer used for fishing but as pleasure craft.

This exceedingly pretty village lies at the end of an unspoiled peninsula that is a carefully guarded government preserve, crisscrossed by marked footpaths affording beautiful views of the coastline. Exhilaration of another kind is as easily found at the harborside restaurants, despite their tourist-trap location. Follow the heady perfume of pesto-flavored *trenette* pasta and grilled scampi to a disarmingly simple Ligurian meal.

Cunningly situated on a hillside above town is one of the world's most famous getaways, the Hotel Splendido. If the roster of world-famous VIP guests doesn't make you feel lightheaded (the Duke and Duchess of Windsor were the first to sign the visitors' book in 1952), the views from this Benedictine-monastery-turned-villa-turned-five-star-hotel will. The 4-acre garden of luxuriant semitropical vegetation is so entrancing that even the five-minute stroll down to Portofino's perfect stage-set harbor (and its recently opened sister hotel, the Splendido Mare) may not lure guests away. The simple joy of an *aperitivo* on the Splendido's terrace overlooking the romantic bay and its tree-covered peninsula makes any evening a grand event. Groucho Marx summed it up nicely: "Wonderful place, wonderful people."

WHAT: town, restaurant, hotel. **PORTOFINO:** 23 miles/38 km southeast of Genoa, 106 miles/171 km south of Milan. **HOTEL SPLENDIDO:** 6 Salita Baratta. Tel 39/0185-26-7801, fax 39/0185-26-7806; in the U.S., tel 800-237-1236; info@splendido.net; www.hotelsplendido.com. *Cost:* doubles with sea view from $940, Splendido Mare doubles with sea view from $865. *When:* open Apr–Dec. **BEST TIMES:** May, Jun, and Sept. Though closed to traffic, the congestion on the coastal road leading to it makes visiting in Jul and Aug a test of patience.

Dining alfresco in Portofino

The Finest Location of Any Lake Town

BELLAGIO

Lombardy, Italy

O n this sylvan promontory, where the fjordlike lakes of Como and Lecco join, those to the grand life born should check into any of the lakefront rooms at the Grand Hotel Villa Serbelloni and revel in the same alpine

magic that captivated Pliny the Younger in the 1st century A.D. The Belle Epoque hotel's coveted Royal Suite once hosted crowned heads, but every room has the same royal view of Lake Como, whose natural beauty attracted Goethe, Shelley, Byron, and many others. Wordsworth described Lake Como as "a treasure which the earth keeps to itself." Bellagio itself is one of the prettiest towns in Europe, even though it's no longer the exclusive, aristocratic address it once was. Life has mellowed, but the band still plays by the lake under the stars, and the bracing air and riot of gardens and lush flowers hint of something inherently Italian about this otherwise Swiss scenario. The dowager hotel's real charm is its palpable sense of the past and the luxury of its formal parkland. (Don't confuse it with the 50-acre terraced garden of the same name on a hill overlooking the lake, on the site of Pliny's villa.) This lakescape inspired music by Verdi, Rossini, and Bellini. You'll see why.

The neoclassic Grand Hotel Villa Serbelloni opened in 1973.

WHAT: hotel, town, site. **BELLAGIO:** 48 miles/77 km north of Milan, 18 miles/30 km northeast of Como. **GRAND HOTEL VILLA SERBELLONI:** Via Roma 1. Tel 39/031-95-02-16, fax 39/031-95-15-29; inforequest@villa serbelloni.com; www.villaserbelloni.com. **COST:** doubles from $530 (low season), from $630 (high season). **WHEN:** open Easter–Nov. **BEST TIMES:** spring and fall.

Luxury on the Shores of Lake Como

HOTEL VILLA D'ESTE

Cernobbio, Lombardy, Italy

O riginally a cardinal's private pleasure palace, now operating as a grand hotel from which all others take their inspiration, the Villa d'Este is unrivaled for its regal decor as well as its majestic position on the verdant banks

A fountain in the Renaissance garden of the Villa d'Este

of Lake Como. Crystal-dripping chandeliers and exquisite silk draperies and upholsteries made in the nearby town of Como are soothing and inviting, grand but never overpowering. Lakeside rooms have the added luxury of seductive views of the glacier-sculpted lake and its profusion of elegant villas. Marble-statued terraces and gardens drenched in flowers cascade down to the water and can only be viewed by boat—that is, if you ever choose to leave the hotel grounds. There are 10 acres of gardens, shady waterside terraces for sipping cool Bellinis, and the exceptional Veranda Restaurant, whose glass walls bring the lake to your dinner table. A freshwater outdoor pool offers views of the mountains from its spot at the edge of Lake Como. It is suspended on a floating redwood deck, gently rocked by the waves created by the lake's lazy buzz of activity.

WHAT: hotel. **WHERE:** Cernobbio is 35 miles/56 km from Milan. Tel 39/031-34-81, fax 39/031-34-88-44; info@villadeste.it; www.villadeste.it. **COST:** doubles from $690 (low season), from $975 (high season). **WHEN:** open Mar–mid-Nov. **BEST TIMES:** Apr–Oct.

A Celebration of Renaissance Splendor

PALAZZO DUCALE

Mantua, Lombardy, Italy

Mantua is a city locked in its past, richly endowed with art and historical memories of the 400 years when it flourished under the patronage of the powerful Gonzaga family, who were to Mantua what the Medicis were to Florence. Their 500-room, fifteen-courtyard Palazzo Ducale, built between the 13th and 18th centuries, is so sumptuously decorated that an afternoon's visit can induce a magnificent stupor. Vast gilded halls and huge galleries are filled with vibrant canvases by Renaissance masters, most notably Andrea Mantegna, whose fanciful *Camera delgi Sposi* (*Bridal Chamber*, 1472–1474) is the fortress-cum-palazzo's highlight.

A watershed in Renaissance imagination, it is Mantegna's masterpiece and his only remaining fresco cycle, an important part of the unrivaled legacy of art left by the Gonzaga dynasty.

After stumbling out of the splendor of the Palazzo Ducale, how to match the experience? You can eat like the dukes of Mantua beneath the frescoed ceilings of Trattoria Il Cigno, where recipes from the personal cookbook of the Gonzagas' court chef hold diners enthralled centuries later.

WHAT: town, site, restaurant. **PALAZZO DUCALE:** Piazza Sordello 40 (Mantua is 95 miles/153 km southeast of Milan, 90 miles/145 km southwest of Venice). *Cost:* admission $9. *When:* Tues–Sun. **TRATTORIA IL CIGNO DEI MARTINI:** Piazza Carlo d'Arco 1. Tel 39/0376-32-71-01, fax 39/0376-32-85-28. *Cost:* dinner $40. *When:* open Wed–Sun; closed Aug.

Cutting-Edge Shopping and a Restaurant Extraordinaire

THE MILANESE EXPERIENCE

Milan, Lombardy, Italy

A must-see for shopaholics, the incomparable Via Montenapoleone and its offshoots are at the heart of the single most fashionable retail acre in the world. Shopping this exclusive "golden triangle" of showcase-studded streets is heaven for those with deep pockets and purgatory for those reduced to window-shopping. The city's tireless preoccupation with fashion, interior design, architecture, and food is showcased in this chic neighborhood—from the sleek boutiques of the high priests and priestesses of *la moda italiana* to landmark 19th-century tearooms and gourmet food stores. Window displays are either over-the-top extravagant or Zen-like in their simplicity, ditto the stores' interiors—everything is up to the nanosecond in this city that sets the trends and blazes the trail.

Whether you're laden down with designer-labeled acquisitions or just plain exhausted by the day's visual overkill, the only place to park your bags is at Milan's Four Seasons Hotel, a quiet oasis at the very hub of Montenapoleone's shopping strip. The order of nuns that established this former convent in 1450 did not take leave until the late 18th century. The cloistered villa has been transformed into a top-class 21st-century hotel—a unique space both calming and luxurious. This means fragments of exposed frescoes, ancient columns, and vaulted ceilings, but also exquisite guest rooms with spacious marbled baths and heated floors, acclaimed restaurants, and the casually elegant lobby (the convent's former chapel) that attracts local Milanesi and hotel guests alike—both a mirror of the city and a haven from it.

Top off a stylish day with dinner at the delightful Aimo e Nadia, located in a non-descript corner of the city. The well-known husband-and-wife owners have been together since their childhood in a village near Tuscany's Lucca, and today they share the cooking and tending of the garden that provides the kitchen's wonderfully fresh and savory ingredients. Much of the daily-changing menu hints of their Tuscan roots, but to dine here is to experience Italian cuisine at its purest and dishes that keep the house full of loyal patrons.

WHAT: experience, hotel, restaurant. **FOUR SEASONS HOTEL MILANO:** Via Gesù 8, between Via Montenapoleone and Via della Spiga. Tel 39/02-77-088, fax 39/02-77-08-50-00; www.fourseasons.com/Milan. *Cost:* doubles from $775. **AIMO E NADIA:** Via Montecuccoli 6. Tel 39/02-41-68-86, fax 39/02-48-30-20-05; info@aimoenadia.com; www.aimoenadia.com. *Cost:* dinner $125. *When:* Mon–Sat.

The Four Seasons Hotel Milano

The Country's Masterpiece Gothic Confection

Il Duomo

Milan, Lombardy, Italy

For sheer size and shock value, few buildings surpass Milan's Duomo. It is the world's largest Gothic cathedral (the only larger cathedral in any style is St. Peter's in Rome), begun in 1386 under the Viscontis and not

The cathedral dominates Milan's main square.

completed until 100 years ago. Its 135 marble spires and 2,245 marble statues could keep you busy looking at it for days, though well-heeled Milanese women, Zegna-suited gents, and too-cool teens pass through the spacious piazza without giving this mad wedding-cake confection so much as a fare-thee-well. An ele-vator to the roof offers the chance to stroll amid the fanciful forest of white marble pinnacles (which take on a rose tinge if the light is right) and to study the flying buttresses up close. There are stunning views over Italy's most frenetic city, while a glimpse of the Swiss Alps 50 miles away can be had when the notorious Milanese fog and pollution aren't obliterating the view. The interior is spartan and almost always virtually empty despite the potential seating for 40,000—whom were they expecting? Shelley swore this was the best place anywhere to read Dante as it remains naturally cool even during the hottest of afternoons. True, if you can ignore the gruesome statue of St. Bartolomeo who, flayed alive, is depicted holding his own skin.

WHAT: site. **WHERE:** Piazza Duomo. **COST:** admission to roof and elevator.

One of Leonardo's Most Powerful Works

The Last Supper

Milan, Lombardy, Italy

Where else can you tell a taxicab driver the name of a painting as your destination, and expect to get there? Every self-respecting Milanese, cabbie or not, knows the location of Leonardo da Vinci's *Il Cenacolo*

(The Last Supper), one of the world's most famous images, tucked away in the Gothic church of Santa Maria delle Grazie. The entire country closely followed the painstaking twenty-year restoration that was completed in 1999. On a wall in what once was the refectory

of the church's adjacent convent, Leonardo created this powerful 28-foot mural. Capturing the emotion-packed moment of Judas's betrayal of Jesus, it began to deteriorate almost immediately following its completion in 1495. Its recent restoration was as controversial as that of the Sistine Chapel, with some historians claiming that precious little has survived of the original painting or coloring, having been re- (and mis-) interpreted a little too zealously over time by countless restorers (there have been seven restorations since 1726); others herald it as a milestone of patience and craftmanship. There is no dismissing that it is one of Leonardo's finest works, one whose every brushstroke revealed the "intentions of the soul." He searched for years among the city's criminals for Judas's face; the result, art historian Giorgio Vasari declared, was "the very embodiment of treachery and inhumanity."

WHAT: site. **WHERE:** Chiesa di Santa Maria delle Grazie, Piazza Santa Maria delle Grazie. **COST:** admission. **WHEN:** Tues–Fri.

The World's Favorite Opera House

LA SCALA OPERA HOUSE (TEATRO ALLA SCALA)

Milan, Lombardy, Italy

It is December 7, opening night at La Scala, and all of Milan is here, dressed to the nines: a well-heeled, passionate, and impossible-to-please audience as theatrical as the opera onstage. After 1,000 days of intensive and painstaking renovation, the world's most famous opera house reopened in 2004 to the astonishment and heartfelt approval of many, the uncontested star at its own reopening night. Designed by Giuseppe Piermarini and originally opened in 1778, the highlights of La Scala's $78 million renovation are the outstanding acoustics (already considered some of the finest anywhere) and the drastic recreation of the backstage area, now a showcase of twenty-first-century technology. This gilt-and-velvet jewel box has hosted the best of the opera world from its earliest days. Verdi's *Otello* and *Falstaff* premiered here, as well as Puccini's *Turandot* and Bellini's *Norma*. Maria Callas sang here more than anywhere else. Included in the top-to-toe renovation, the intimate Museo alla Scala, a must-see for opera lovers, has reopened in its original location (entrance is on Largo Ghiringhelli) and has weathered the recent departure of world renowned musical director Ricardo Muti.

WHAT: site, event. **WHERE:** Via Filodrammatici 2, Piazza alla Scala. Tel 39/02-720-037-44; www.teatroallascala.org. **WHEN:** Opera season runs from Dec 7 through July; ballet and concerts other months.

La Scala, in a splendid renovation

Lakeside Beauties

ROCCA SCALIGERA

Sirmione, Lombardy, Italy

Wait till the afternoon crowds thin, then cross the drawbridge to this fairy-tale *castello* almost entirely surrounded by the deep blue water of Lake Garda. All towers and fancy battlements, the 13th-century

castle was built by the powerful della Scala (or Scaligeri) princes of nearby Verona, 2 miles out into the lake. Garda is the largest in Italy and considered by many to be the most beautiful in the Lake District.

Just as Bellagio is known as Como's Pearl of the Lake, fans of Garda call Sirmione the Jewel of the Lake. Beyond the castle are the narrow streets of the boutique- and café-lined Old Town, a pedestrian island still redolent of medieval times. In ancient times, the Lake District served as the cool summertime destination of Rome's VIPs, in particular the hedonist poet Catullus, who was drawn to Sirmione as much for its natural sulfur baths as for the lovely setting. The panoramic Grotte di Catullo is said to be the ruins of his villa.

By comparison the 19th-century Villa Cortine Palace Hotel seems downright modern. Palatial, colonnaded, formidably decorative, and just this side of over-the-top, it is the area's finest hotel, with impeccable gardens, lapped by the lake's edge.

WHAT: site, hotel. **ROCCA SCALIGERA:** on the southwestern shore of Lake Garda, 145 miles/232 km east of Milan. **VILLA CORTINE PALACE:** Via Grotte 6, Sirmione. Tel 39/030-99-05-890, fax 39/030-91-63-90; info@hotel villacortine.com; www.hotelvillacortine.com. *Cost:* doubles from $395 (low season), from $605 (high season, includes half board for 2). *When:* open Apr–Oct. **BEST TIMES:** Jul and Aug are the busiest months, preferred by some, avoided by many.

A Diminutive Archipelago in a Picture-Perfect Lake

BORROMEAN ISLANDS

Stresa, Lombardy, Italy

The old-world hotel where Ernest Hemingway's tragic WW I hero Frederic Henry trysted with his goddess, Catherine Barkley, in *A Farewell to Arms* still dominates the banks of Lake Maggiore, in a setting that only grows

more gorgeous with age. The enormous 19th-century Grand Hotel et des Iles Borromées is as romantic and princely as in the days of the young American soldier, and the lobby bar still serves a stiff Hemingway martini to help

guests slip into that mood of being "faint with love." The views alone are enough to warrant a certain lightheadedness: ask for any of the lakeside rooms for a priceless view over the 40-mile sweep of water toward the snow-

The Belle Epoque hotel greeted its first guest in 1863.

dusted Swiss Alps and a glimpse of the four Borromean Islands. The tiny but fabled Borromeans are named after the aristocratic Lombard family that has owned them since the 12th century. They consist of two Baroque palaces, a tiny fishing village, and two lavish gardens, whose springtime display of rhododendrons, camellias, azaleas, resident peacocks, and golden pheasants is world renowned. "What can one say of Lake Maggiore, and of the Borromean Islands," wrote Stendhal, "except to pity people who do not go mad over them?"

WHAT: island, hotel. **STRESA:** 51 miles/82 km northwest of Milan; frequent ferry service to Borromean Islands. **GRAND HOTEL ET DES ILES BORROMÉES:** 67 Corso Umberto I, Stresa. Tel 39/0323-938-938, fax 39/0323-32-405; borromees@borromees.it, www.borromees.it. *Cost:* doubles from $390, with lake view from $605, Hemingway Suite $4,980. **BEST TIMES:** blooming season from Mar (camellias) to end of May (azaleas and rhododendrons); international music festival, the Settimane Musicali di Stresa, mid-Aug–mid-Sept.

Opera on Home Ground

ROSSINI OPERA FESTIVAL

Pesaro, The Marches, Italy

The great composer Gioacchino Rossini was so fond of his hometown, Pesaro, that he left an ample fortune to the municipality, which honored him by establishing a Rossini Foundation. From this grew the annual Rossini Opera Festival, devoted exclusively to his work (the rarely performed ones as well as the famous) and now one of Italy's most popular summer music festivals, a favorite among purists since it was founded in 1980. Even when the festival is not in town, life centers around—where else?—the animated Via Rossini. Pesaro is a popular, attractive seaside resort, and its piazzas and cafés are always full. For the quintessential festival experience, stay at the handsomely refurbished but still old-world waterfront Hotel Vittoria, the meeting place for the stars of the festival. Check out the culinary genius of Otello Renzi, a genuine scholar of food and wine whose restaurant, Da Teresa, is named after his mother, who oversees the kitchen. The house specialties of fresh pasta and fish draw the festival's performing artists annually.

WHAT: event, town, hotel, restaurant. **ROSSINI OPERA FESTIVAL:** Via Rossini 24. Tel 39/0721-38-001, fax 39/0721-38-00220; www.rossinioperafestival.it. *Cost:* tickets $14–$175. *When:* 2 weeks, mid-late Aug. **HOTEL VITTORIA:** Piazzale della Libertà 2. Tel 39/0721-34-343, fax 39/0721-65-204; vittoria@viphotels.it, www.viphotels.it. *Cost:* doubles $170. **RISTORANTE DA TERESA:** Viale Trieste 180. Tel 39/0721-30-096, fax 39/0721-31-636. *Cost:* dinner $50. *When:* Feb–Nov.

A Perfect Expression of the Early Renaissance

URBINO

The Marches, Italy

I f Urbino's National Gallery of the Marches (Galleria Nazionale delle Marche) were located in a city like Florence, there would be lines across the piazza waiting to get in. But this small, proud town of 15,000 people is an underrated

tourist destination, with a prodigious art collection that includes works by Raphael (a native son), Piero della Francesca (including *The Flagellation of Christ*, which Piero considered his finest work), Paolo Uccello, and Luca Signorelli. All the better for the few who do drop in to explore this

country town, which could easily share the spotlight for its history, art, architecture, and gastronomy with Italy's better-known places.

Sitting atop a steep hill, Urbino is the strongest magnet of the Le Marche region. The 500-year-old university is one of Europe's oldest, and Urbino is home

Urbino's Renaissance style remains largely intact.

to one of Italy's greatest treasures, the Palazzo Ducale, which houses the National Gallery. During the second half of the 15th century, Urbino was one of the most prestigious courts, almost without peer in all Europe, under the visionary direction of Federico da Montefeltro. He commissioned the finest artists and architects to build and embellish his immense home. The result, the Palazzo Ducale, is considered the perfect expression of the early Renaissance. The courtier Baldassare Castiglione called this imperious fortress "a city in the shape of a palace."

WHAT: town, site. **WHERE:** 119 miles/191 km east of Florence, 19 miles/31 km southwest of Pesaro. **GALLERIA NAZIONALE DELLE MARCHE:** in the Palazzo Ducale; entrance located in the Piazza Duca Federico. *Cost:* admission. **BEST TIMES:** the Festival Internazionale di Musica Antica, the most important Renaissance and Baroque music festival in Italy, 10 days late Jul.

Coastal Glamour and the Interior's Mystique

LA COSTA SMERALDA

Sardinia, Italy

A n ancient crossroads between East and West, Sardinia emerged from mystery and obscurity in the late 1960s. The Costa Smeralda, a 34-mile tract of pristine boulder-strewn coast, was wild and unblemished when it was purchased by a consortium of international businessmen headed by Prince Karim, the Aga Khan, whose goal was to create a Xanadu playground for the consortium's members and friends while maintaining the area's pristine beauty. The tasteful five-star development they created transformed the island's traditional economy of shepherding and agriculture. Sardinia is now considered one of the world's most glamorous spots for the super rich and world famous. Two sequestered deluxe hotel enclaves are landmarks, erected on the choicest stretch of coastline. The wonderfully romantic Hotel Pitrizza harmonizes beautifully with the rocky coast and is home for those seeking seclusion and serenity. On the other hand, the rustic-elegant Hotel Cala di Volpe is pure theater, a cross between a self-contained medieval village and a colorful Bedrock minus the Flintstones. Its largely Italian clientele epitomize *la dolce vita:* handsome, fashionable, bejeweled, suntanned, and exuberant, filling this private corner of the coastline with glamour and brio.

Elsewhere, in the island's harsh and wild interior, the once-persecuted Sardi—their island coveted by every major maritime power of the Mediterranean—still live and maintain their traditions, folkloric costumes, and a unique dialect (close to spoken Latin). This is the other Sardinia, light-years beyond cosmopolitan Costa Smeralda, where only intrepid travelers need venture. The rough mountainous interior is dotted with more than 7,000 mostly conical *nuraghi*, stone structures

Hotel Cala di Volpe was designed to resemble a village.

dating back to the Bronze Age that are unique to Sardinia. Little has changed here since D. H. Lawrence's 1921 visit when, astonished, he described the island as "lost between Europe and Africa and belonging to nowhere."

WHAT: island, hotel, site. **SARDINIA:** 112 miles/180 km west of mainland Italy. **LA COSTA SMERALDA:** located on the northeast coast of Sardinia, 7 miles/12 km north of Olbia, the principal arrival point for car ferries from Genoa, Livorno, Civitavecchia, and Naples. Regular air service also available. **HOTEL PITRIZZA:** tel 39/0789-930-111; www.luxurycollection.com/pitrizza. *Cost:* doubles from $1,350 (low season), from $3,085 (high season), includes all meals. **HOTEL CALA DI VOLPE:** tel 39/0789-976-111, fax 39/0789-976-617; in the U.S., 800-325-3589. *Cost:* doubles from $1,200 (low season), from $2,700 (high season), includes all meals. *When:* open May–Oct. **BEST TIMES:** Jun–Aug.

An Archipelago of Volcanic Gems and Barefoot Chic

AEOLIAN ISLANDS

Sicily, Italy

Named for Æolus, god of the winds, and also known as the Lipari Islands, the chain of Aeolian Islands (Isole Eolie) floats off Sicily's northeastern flank, mere specks on the map of the Mediterranean Sea. This necklace of seven small isles is blessed with grottoes, bays, hidden coves, simple ways, and still-active volcanoes. Though but baby sisters to Mount Etna on the eastern coast of nearby Sicily, the volcanoes on Stromboli and Vulcano (where legend says Æolus lived) have created melancholy, beautiful terrain and sandy black beaches. Lipari, the attractive capital island and the largest, has an animated old town dominated by a 17th-century *castello* that houses a noted archaeological museum. A pleasant road encircles the unchanged island of Salina and its two extinct volcanoes; its rustic scenery was the backdrop of the popular Italian movie *Il Postino (The Postman)*. But Panarea is the jewel of the archipelago, brilliantly retaining that quintessential Italian mix of simplicity and upscale chic. Created in the 1960s as a bohemian alternative to the overly fashionable resort of Capri, it is the summer destination of northern Italian fashion and design types, who come for the barefoot lifestyle and low-key pace. The only time to get even minimally glamorous is when dining at Hotel Raya, whose breezy open terraces and top-notch restaurant overlook spectacular volcanic offshore rocks and Iddu, Stromboli's always rumbling volcano.

WHAT: island, hotel. **AEOLIAN ISLANDS:** Vulcano is the island closest to Sicily, 22 miles/35 km off the north shore. Hydrofoils *(aliscafi)* and boats servicing different Aeolian islands leave from Naples (hydrofoil ride about 5 hours). From Sicily's northern coast, boat service from Palermo, Milazzo, and Messina. The archipelago is linked by inter-island service. Service drops considerably off-season. **HOTEL RAYA:** Panarea. Tel 39/090-983-013, fax 39/090-983-103; info@hotelraya.it; www.hotelraya.it. *Cost:* doubles from $450 (low season), from $765 (high season; includes half board for 2). *When:* open late Mar–Oct. **BEST TIMES:** least crowded in May, Jun, and Sept.

The Epicenter of Ancient Greek Archaeology

VALLEY OF TEMPLES

Agrigento, Sicily, Italy

The main reason to come to Agrigento—called "the fairest of all mortal cities" by the ancient Greek poet Pindar—is to meander through the Valle dei Templi (Valley of Temples), a unique series of golden-stone Doric temples strung out along a long ridge facing the sea. Also a must is a visit to its first-rate archaeological museum. The Greeks, having first arrived in Sicily in the 8th century B.C., began building these temples approximately 300 years later. Today they are one of the most photographed images in Sicily, and the largest concentration of early Greek architecture outside Greece. The Tempio della Concordia (Temple of Concord), built around 430 B.C., is one of the showpieces of the Hellenic world; with thirty-four exterior columns still standing, it is one of the two best-preserved Greek temples to be found anywhere. Three times its size is the gargantuan Tempio di Giove (Temple of Zeus—whose Roman analogue was Jupiter or Jove), the third largest Greek temple ever built. Archaeologists believe it was larger than St. Peter's in Rome. The valley at sunrise or sunset is particularly impressive, and you can view it in comfort from rooms 205 or 206 of the Hotel Villa Athena, a converted 18th-century villa with an exceptional location directly across from the Temple of Concord. In early February, fragrant white almond blossoms blanket the valley and its surrounding fields and the town turns out for its annual festival of floats, games, and marzipan in the shape of everything from *fichi d'India* (prickly pears) to dimpled lemons that look real enough to squeeze.

WHAT: site, hotel. **VALLEY OF TEMPLES:** in southwest corner of Sicily, 79 miles/127 km south of Palermo. **HOTEL VILLA ATHENA:** 33 Via Valle dei Templi, Agrigento. Tel 39/0922-59-62-88; www.hotelvillaathena.it. *Cost:* doubles from $295. **BEST TIMES:** Feb and Jun, before the sirocco blows in from Africa.

The God Volcano, the Pillar of Heaven

MOUNT ETNA

Sicily, Italy

Most visitors' first glimpse of Europe's highest and most active volcano—the ancient Greeks called it the Pillar of Heaven—is from the gorgeously sited Greek Theater in the resort town of Taormina. As long as white smoke rises from Mount Etna's snow-capped peak—visible from 150 miles away when not cloaked in mist—all is calm with the world. But too frequently it turns black, stirring restlessness among the area's 1 million residents. These locals continue the centuries-long love-hate relationship with *'a muntagna,* as they call her in dialect, building and rebuilding their homes perversely close to the volatile mountain. Etna has erupted 300 times since the first recordings 3,000 years ago, most recently in 2001. In one of the most violent eruptions, in 1667, rivers of lava destroyed much of Catania, 19 miles away. No other gardens in Sicily are as lush as the vineyards and groves of lemon, orange, almond, and olive trees that today cover the fertile lower slopes leading up to the volcano. But a bus trip that passes through this green belt and continues up to the crater's lip fast becomes a ride through a toasted lunar landscape—brooding, dark, and fascinating. A cable car carries visitors over pinnacles of frozen lava dunes, minor craters, smoke holes—this vision of petrified chaos makes the ascent to Etna's 11,000-foot summit one of Italy's most haunting day trips.

WHAT: site. **WHERE:** 19 miles/30 km north of Catania on the east coast of Sicily. Day trips are offered from Catania and Taormina. **WHEN:** ascents are possible Apr–Oct.

From the Sacred to the Profane

TWO GEMS OF PALERMO

Palermo, Sicily, Italy

Sicily's remarkable cultural diversity is the result of twenty-five centuries of tumultuous history, and no other city in Europe has hosted such a variety of civilizations and waves of conquerors as Palermo. The most breathtaking window on this unique heritage is nearby Monreale's 12th-century Cattedrale di Santa Maria la Nuova. Built of golden Sicilian stone by King William II on a mountaintop overlooking his sprawling capital, the cathedral combines Moorish and Norman styles and is famed for the matchless multicolored mosaics that glorify every centimeter of wall space. Most of the Old and New Testament stories you're likely to have heard are depicted here, dramatically visualized with a host of human and animal figures. A huge, majestic Christ the Pantocrator broods over it all in the central apse. From the incense-filled interior and its 6,000 square yards of dazzling mosaics, step into the blinding sunshine of the equally famous cloisters of the adjacent Benedictine abbey. None of its 216 slender pillars are alike, and the hush is broken only by the splash of a fountain reminiscent of ancient Araby.

Maintain the Middle Eastern illusion with a trip to La Vucciria, Sicily's greatest market. Its crowded, souklike passageways are another reminder that from Sicily, just "one hop and you're out of Europe," as D. H. Lawrence wrote. La Vucciria is not just about shopping—it is a vibrant spectacle, full of merchants screaming, yelling, shouting, arguing, and singing about their wares, vying for volume and ribaldry—if the local vernacular were not unintelligible (it's like no other on earth), outsiders would catch comparisons of succulent pomegranates to parts of the female anatomy. You can eat your way through (if you enjoy sandwiches stuffed with tripe, goat intestines, or sliced spleen) or just succumb to the heady smells, from briny octopus to anchovies and fresh mint, basil, saffron, capers, and oregano. This being an island, expect awesome displays of fish and unrecognizable sea creatures, and from the interior hills, the proudly displayed carcasses of goats, insides intact, attesting to their freshness. And who knew so many different kinds of olives existed?

WHAT: site. **CATTEDRALE DI SANTA MARIA LA NUOVA:** Piazza Guglielmo il Buono, Monreale (5 miles/8 km southwest of Palermo). For more information see www.palermotourism. com. *Cost:* admission charged for cloisters. **LA VUCCIRIA:** south of the Piazza and Church (Chiesa) di San Domenico. *When:* Mon–Sat. *Best times:* most bustling in the morning.

On Its Own Natural Balcony Overlooking Mount Etna

TAORMINA

Sicily, Italy

More than twenty-three centuries ago, when Sicily was part of Magna Graecia, this tiny mountain town was already famed for its sweeping views. As Sicily's most fashionable resort, Taormina was described by Guy de Maupassant as "all that seems made on the earth to entice eyes, spirit, and imagination." Its ancient Greek amphitheater, the Teatro Greco, enjoys one of the loveliest sites anywhere. Framed by the stage columns is the snowcapped summit of Mount Etna and, beyond, the Straits of Messina and the terra firma of Italy and Europe. The acoustics are just as impressive, and the theater, hewn into the rock face of Mount Tauro at an altitude of 675 feet, is still used every summer for a festival of the arts, film, and music. Attending one of the Greek classics performed just before sunset is an experience without peer. The city's favorite pastime is a leisurely *passeggiata* along its one bougainvillea-swathed strip of boutiques and curio and ceramic shops, interspersed with intimate piazzas and dramatic belvederes. Be sure to stop by one of the cafés and have a traditional Sicilian dessert of granita (flavored shaved ice) while you watch Etna puffing gentle plumes into the Sicilian sky.

Then retire to the hotel that proves an old saw: The church and the government always know how to pick the finest real estate. The Hotel San Domenico, a luxurious hotel with transfixing views of Mount Etna, was built as a Dominican monastery in 1430. Today it is Sicily's finest and one of Italy's most romantic hotels, its rooms the actual (albeit enlarged) cells of monks until the last century. The brothers would never recognize the cushy wrought iron or richly carved wooden beds, the crisply ironed linen sheets or the gracious service. Enjoy a cool pomegranate juice before dinner in the former chapel, now the atmospheric hotel bar. Dining in the main hall, once the refectory, is a culinary event. The vast garden is a serene jasmine-scented oasis with palms and lemon trees and a near-perfect view of the azure Ionian Sea.

WHAT: town, hotel. **TAORMINA:** 155 miles/ 249 km east of Palermo, 33 miles/53 km north of Catania. **SAN DOMENICO PALACE HOTEL:** Piazza San Domenico 5. Tel 39/0942-613-111, fax 39/0942-62-55-06; www.lhw.com. *Cost:* doubles from $370 (low season), from $495 (high season). **BEST TIMES:** Apr–May, Sept–Oct; arts festival of music, ballet, and opera late Jun to mid-Sept.

The Finest Frescoes of Piero della Francesca

CHURCH OF SAN FRANCESCO

Arezzo, Tuscany, Italy

The docile, neighboring regions of Tuscany and Umbria were home to the Renaissance's seminal masters, among them the much-beloved 15th-century Piero della Francesca, whose greatest cycle of frescoes covers the apse of Arezzo's 14th-century Church of San Francesco. *The Legend of the True Cross (La Leggenda della Vera Croce)* (1452–1466), begun when the master was in his early thirties, depicts a legend from a 13th-century manuscript, according to which a branch of the Tree of Life was planted on Adam's grave. The branch took root and was eventually used to make the cross on which Christ was crucified. Under wraps for close to fifteen years, the frescoes are once again on display, brilliantly restored.

Don't leave Arezzo without a visit to the city's delightfully lopsided Piazza Grande, rimmed with palazzi. Arezzo is transported back to the Dark Ages with its historical Giostra del Saracino (Jousting Tournament) held on the last Sunday in August and the first Sunday in September. An elaborate *corteo* (procession) wends through the narrow cobblestoned streets beforehand, the rich costumes and authentic armor on knights and horses alike overseen by Tuscan-born filmmaker Franco Zeffirelli, the joust's biggest fan.

WHAT: site, town, event. **CHURCH OF SAN FRANCESCO:** Piazza San Francesco (Arezzo is 47 miles/76 km east of Siena, 51 miles/82 km south of Florence). **JOUSTING TOURNAMENT:** for tickets contact the local Tourist Information Office in Piazza della Repubblica 22, just outside the train station. Tel 39/0575-37-76-78, www.apt.arezzo.it. **BEST TIMES:** Italy's best traveling antiques fair is held in the Piazza Grande, 1st Sat of each month.

*"The god who created the hills around
Florence was an artist. No! He was a jeweler,
engraver, sculptor, bronze founder and painter:
He was a Florentine."—*ANATOLE FRANCE

FLORENCE

Tuscany, Italy

Cradle and heart of the Renaissance, Florence is a proud, aristocratic city whose warren of cobbled streets and piazzas is lined with medieval towers, historic cafés, and fortress-like palazzi. Sensory overload is a real concern. Then there's the other problem: What to do for an encore?

THE TOP TEN SIGHTS

BARGELLO MUSEUM—Housed in a Gothic palazzo built as an arsenal and fortress in 1255, the Bargello later served as an administrative hall and a jail before being transformed into a museum in 1965. Today it houses Florence's greatest collection of Renaissance sculpture, with works by Michelangelo (among his earliest), Donatello, Cellini, Giambologna, and Luca and Giovanni della Robbia. Highlights include Michelangelo's *Apollo, Bacchus* (looking slightly tipsy), and Madonna-and-child *Pitti Tondo* and Donatello's *David* and *Saint George*. The museum also includes collections of medieval weaponry, Oriental rugs, ivory sculpture, 16th-century majolica porcelain, frescoes of the school of Giotto, and historic Renaissance medals. **WHERE:** Via del Proconsolo. Tel 39/055-238-8606.

CHURCH OF SANTA CROCE—Built by the Franciscans between 1294 and 1442 but with a 19th-century facade, cavernous Santa Croce is chockablock with 14th-century frescoes and the tombs of famous Florentines, including Michelangelo, Rossini, Machiavelli, and Galileo, as well as a memorial to Dante, who died in exile in Ravenna. In the right transept you'll find Giotto's frescoes in the Cappella Peruzzi and the Cappella Bardi, the latter famous as a setting in *A Room with a View*, and featuring *The Death of Saint Francis* and *Trial by Fire Before the Sultan of Egypt*, among Giotto's best-known works. In the left transept, you can see Donatello's famous crucifix. Taddo Gaddi's frescoes in the Cappella Baroncelli depict scenes from the life of the Virgin, while in the right transept, the Cappella Castellani, Gaddi's son, Agnolo, designed the stained-glass windows in the high altar sanctuary, and painted the saints and the *Legend of the True Cross* cycle on its walls. **WHERE:** Piazza Santa Croce. Tel 39/055-244-6105.

CHURCH OF SANTA MARIA NOVELLA— Built for the Dominican order in the late 13th and early 14th centuries, Santa Maria Novella is the only one among Florence's major churches to boast an original facade, a multicolored marble design that seamlessly mixes Roman and Renaissance styles. Frescoes fill its interior, executed by Domenico Ghirlandaio (the church's highlight, directly behind the main altar), Filippino Lippi, and Nardo di Cione. Other attractions include the pulpit from which Galileo was denounced for saying the earth orbited the sun; Masaccio's *Trinità*, the first painting created using

The original multicolored marble facade of Santa Maria Novella

perfect linear mathematical perspective; and two famous crosses—one by Giotto, hanging in the sacristy, and one by Brunelleschi in the Cappella Gondi (behind the main altar), carved as an example to Donatello after the latter unveiled his less traditional interpretation in the Church of Santa Croce. **WHERE:** Piazza Santa Maria Novella. Tel 39/055-282-187.

GALLERIA DELL'ACCADEMIA—Founded in 1784 as an artists' academy, the Accademia has been the home since 1873 of Michelangelo's famous *David*, sculpted between 1501 and 1504 and standing for almost four centuries as the centerpiece of the Piazza della Signoria. (A copy now stands in its place outdoors.) In addition to this masterwork, carved from discarded marble when the artist was twenty-nine, the museum also houses Michelangelo's *Saint Matthew* and the four unfinished *Prisoners*, their forms struggling to break free from the marble around them. No one knows if they are unfinished or intentionally left half emerging from the raw stone blocks. Pieces from the 14th through the 19th centuries fill the other galleries. **WHERE:** Via Ricasoli. Tel 39/055-238-8609.

IL DUOMO (THE CATHEDRAL OF SANTA MARIA DEI FIORI)—Designed originally in 1296 by Arnolfo di Cambio, Florence's Duomo

was actually the work of several architects, who overcame enormous technical challenges to design what is probably the central achievement of Renaissance architecture. Finally consecrated in 1436, the cathedral boasts Filippo Brunelleschi's enormous octagonal dome (the largest in the world when it was built and now the very symbol of Florence), whose interior features an enormous *Last Judgment* fresco by Vasari and Federico Zuccari; stained-glass windows by Lorenzo Ghiberti; and Paolo Uccello's huge clock in the entrance wall. The cathedral's red, white, and green marble facade was a late addition in the 19th century. To complete your trip, visit the piazza's other two landmarks: the baptistry, with its famous bronze *Doors of Paradise* by Ghiberti, and Giotto's slender bell tower, with a view of Renaissance Florence from the top of its 414 steps. **WHERE:** Piazza del Duomo. Tel 39/055-230-2885.

MEDICI CHAPELS—Forming part of the monumental San Lorenzo complex (the Medicis' parish church, worth seeing but largely ignored by tourists), the Cappelle Medicee were Michelangelo's first architectural projects, begun in the 1520s and designed to hold the remains of Lorenzo the Magnificent and three other members of the ruling clan. The chapels are famous for the reclining, allegorical statues of female Dawn and male Dusk that adorn the tomb of Lorenzo II, Duke of Urbino (grandson of Lorenzo Il Magnifico), and for the figures of male Day and female Night on the tomb of Giuliano, Duke of Memours. Ironically, Michelangelo didn't complete the two most important tombs—those of Lorenzo Il Magnifico and his brother, Giuliano, who lie in a plain tomb opposite the altar. Later (and lesser) tombs hold the remains of the Medici monarchs who ruled till the end of the line in 1737. **WHERE:** Piazza Madonna degli Aldobrandini (in the middle of the Mercato San Lorenzo), accessible via a separate entrance from the church of San Lorenzo. Tel 39/055-238-8602.

MUSEO SAN MARCO—The most celebrated friar of this 13th-century monastery (expanded in the 15th century) was Fra Angelico, and today San Marco holds the largest collection of his work in Italy. His 1442 masterwork *The Crucifixion* is found here, as are a number of painted panels, altarpieces, and a series of frescoes that grace many of the plain cells where the monks lived and prayed. (Savonarola, the fire-and-brimstone fundamentalist who won and then lost favor with the Medicis, was prior of the monastery and resided in cell eleven.) Of a half dozen beautiful Last Supper frescoes found in Florence's various monasteries, the one in San Marco's refectory, by Domenico Ghirlandaio, is one of the most important. Ghirlandaio taught a young Michelangelo the art of fresco painting, something that would serve him well decades later in the Sistine Chapel. **WHERE:** Piazza San Marco. Tel 39/055-238-8608.

PIAZZA DELLA SIGNORIA AND PALAZZO VECCHIO—The civic center of Florence for more than 700 years, the Piazza della Signoria is now a popular outdoor sculpture gallery, drawing tourists to its cafés and round-the-clock street life. Some of the sculptures are originals—such as Giambologna's bronze of Grand Duke Cosimo I on horseback—while others (notably Michelangelo's *David* and Donatello's *Marzocco* and *Judith Beheading Holofernes*) are replicas, their originals now residing in Florence's various museums, sheltered from the elements. In front of Bartolomeo Ammannati's *Neptune* fountain is a plaque marking the spot where Savonarola held his Bonfire of the Vanities in the 1490s, encouraging Florentines to burn their mirrors,

books, games, wigs, paintings, and other symbols of decadent irreligion. The Florentines' zeal for his brand of puritanism lasted only so long, and in 1498, after hanging Savonarola, they burned him on the very same spot.

Looming over one side of the piazza, the Gothic, Arnolfo di Cambio–designed PALAZZO VECCHIO (tel 39/055-276-8224) was built between 1299 and 1302 to house the Signoria (ministry of the city government) and to this day serves as Florence's town hall. Inside, the Sala dei Cinquecento was the assembly hall for the Florentine Republic's 500-man congress. Against one wall is Michelangelo's 1533–1534 statue *Victory*. On the second floor are the *Quartiere degli Elementi*, frescoed by Vasari; the apartments of Eleonora di Toledo, home of Duke Cosimo I dei Medici and his Spanish wife for ten years, until they moved into the Palazzo Pitti across the river; and Donatello's original *Judith and Holofernes* statue.

PALAZZO PITTI AND THE GALLERIA PALATINA—Built by wealthy Florentine merchant and banker Luca Pitti in the late 15th century, the Pitti Palace was bought by the Medicis in 1550 and substantially enlarged, becoming the official residence of the ruling dukes. Today it contains some of the most important Florentine museums, especially the PALATINE GALLERY (tel 39/055-294-883), whose twenty-six rooms display High Renaissance and later-era art, including Titian, Raphael, Rubens, Murillo, and Caravaggio. It's the most important museum in Florence after the Uffizi. Other museums include the Silver Museum, the Gallery of Modern Art, the Porcelain Museum, and the Costume Gallery. Most of the interior decoration seen today was created during the 17th century, including the Pietro da Cortona frescoes that adorn the Medicis' main apartments. Bring a picnic for après-viewing and head for the Medicis' famous 16th-century Boboli Gardens, which climb the hill behind the palazzo.

OTHER MUST-DO'S

IL PONTE VECCHIO—Built in 1345 by Taddeo Gaddi, the Ponte Vecchio is the oldest and most famous bridge across the Arno River. Its classic overhanging shops were occupied by butchers until the Medici dukes objected to the stench and had them replaced by the goldsmiths and silversmiths who still occupy the premises today, selling everything from museum-quality Italian-made baubles to more affordable pieces. The bridge's fame saved it from being blown up by the retreating Germans during WW II. It was the only Arno bridge that survived. **WHERE:** connecting Via Por Santa Maria on the north bank with Via Guicciardini on the south.

MAGGIO MUSICALE FIORENTINO—As a capital of culture, Florence is a fitting host for one of the largest and most anticipated annual celebrations of classical music, opera, and dance in Europe. Inaugurated in 1933 and held annually since 1937, the prestigious festival has been under the direction of maestro Zubin Mehta since 1985, and attracts both rising stars and world-class performers. It begins in early May, with free open-air closing extravaganzas usually held in the Piazza della Signoria in late June or early July. **WHERE:** tel 39/055-2779-350 or 39/055-287222; tickets@maggiofiorentino.com; www.maggiofiorentino.com.

MERCATO NUOVO—Before you leave town, take a trip to the "New Market," in business since the 16th century. There may not be much to capture your interest among the merchandise, but stop by to rub the nose of the brass *porcellino* (wild boar), which legend says will ensure a rapid return to Florence. **WHERE:** on Via por Santa Maria at Via Porta Rossa.

MERCATO SAN LORENZO—Touristy to the core, Italy's largest and best daily open-air market comprises hundreds of white canvas-topped stalls filling the streets around the Medici's Church of San Lorenzo and the covered Mercato Centrale (both worth stopping into). This is one-stop shopping for those long lists of the don't-forgets back home, as well as plenty of local color. **WHERE:** side streets between the train station and the Duomo.

SUNSET AT PIAZZALE MICHELANGIOLO—The postcard-worthy views from Florence's hilltop square inspired more than one Renaissance master. Popular with the tour bus set during the day and with local youths and bikers at night, it's the perfect Lovers' Lane, centered around one of the two copies of Michelangelo's *David*. Or make the trip up for the summertime watermelon stands and the always crowded Gelateria Michelangiolo. **WHERE:** Viale Michelangiolo.

VESPERS AT CHURCH OF SAN MINIATO—Florence's oldest church, this much-beloved 11th-century Romanesque structure dominates the city's highest hill. Its romantic setting, full of birdsong and with panoramic views, makes it a favorite venue for weddings, and its daily program of Gregorian chant makes it the best place in town for time travel right back to the Middle Ages. **WHERE:** Via del Monte alle Croci, near Piazzale Michelangiolo. Tel 39/055-234-2731.

WHERE TO STAY

HOTEL HELVETIA AND BRISTOL—Travelers from Stravinsky to the Danish royal family have lodged in this grandly revamped 19th-century palazzo, a plush mix of British-style comfort and Italian elegance. It's nestled on a side street between tony Via Tornbuoni's incomparable shopping and the Duomo, the heart of Florence, just a half-minute's walk away. **WHERE:** Via dei Pescioni, near the Palazzo Strozzi. Tel 800-203-3232 (in the U.S) or 800-46-34-41-00 (within Italy). **COST:** high.

TORRE DI BELLOSGUARDO—A world away (but only ten minutes by cab) from the heart of Florence's historic district is this elegantly frescoed 14th-century hilltop villa, whose

7th-century tower suite offers eagle's-nest views of Florence and the surrounding hills. Similar vistas can be enjoyed from the lovely pool. Dante is said to have found respite here. **WHERE:** Via Roti Michelozzi, in the hills above the old Porta Romana gate. Tel 39/055-229-8145. **COST:** moderate to high.

PENSIONE LA SCALETTA—The rooms aren't the draw at this family-run top-floor pensione. Instead, repair with your cappuccino to the two-tiered rooftop terrace, whose 360-degree views encompass its stalwart neighbor, the Pitti Palace, the verdant Boboli Gardens, and the surrounding terra-cotta roofscape—succor for the weary and overshopped. **WHERE:** Via Guicciardini, near Piazza Pitti. Tel 39/055-283-028. **COST:** low.

EATING & DRINKING

CAFFÈ RIVOIRE—It's cozy inside when cold weather dictates this historic café's specialty of bittersweet hot chocolate (with a de rigueur dollop of fresh whipped *panna*). But in nice weather the outdoor tables on the renowned Piazza della Signoria supply the best front-row seats in town for people- and piazza-watching. Even on a slow day, there's the wonder of the life-size copy of Michelangelo's *David* and other statuary. **WHERE:** Piazza della Signoria. Tel 39/055-214-412.

ENOTECA PINCHIORRI—Gourmands genuflect at the mention of this temple to high gastronomy. In a region long known for simple, rustic trattorie, this elegant ristorante has found a loyal clientele of the rich and famous by offering imperial service, theatrical silver-domed presentations, and a wine list widely regarded as one of Italy's finest—and that's saying something. The experience won't soon be forgotten, nor will the evening's bill. **WHERE:** Via Ghibellina. Tel 39/055-242-777; www.enotecapinchiorri.it.

FUORI PORTA—Florence's most popular wine bar is found just outside the city's 14th-century ramparts and the San Niccolò gate, on the way up to or down from the Piazzale Michelangiolo. The best of the Tuscan reds are here by the glass, along with a whole host of crostini and savory snacks that would make any palate sing. **WHERE:** Via del Monte alle Croci. Tel 39/055-234-2483.

LA TRIPPERIA—Just a handful of these vendors are left, selling sandwiches stuffed with tripe (cow's stomach), a much-loved local delicacy that earns high points with both blue- and white-collar Florentines. If you want to just look and leave the lip-smacking to the locals, make your way to the well-known "Trippaio" pushcart, a commisary on wheels that sells mounds of gleaming viscera, parked daily outside the main American Express office. **WHERE:** Via Dante Alighieri.

Grab a bite at one of Florence's legendary tripe stands.

NERBONE—Roll up your sleeves and join the market merchants and shoppers who stop by this popular no-lingering lunch counter within the covered 19th-century Mercato Centrale. The simple down-home menu follows the market's whims, and it doesn't get any fresher than this. **WHERE:** stall 292 in the Mercato Centrale. Tel 39/055-219-949.

OMERO—After taking in the view from the outdoor terrace, head inside for a traditional Tuscan-style meal. Everyone is here for the pasta, plus just about the best and most tender *bistecca alla fiorentina* around, and (in artichoke season) the deep-fried batterless *carciofini* wedges. Eight different first courses leave no room for a proper entree, but most diners usually find room for a sampling from the nine-dessert menu. **WHERE:** Via Pian dei Giullari, Arcetri (15 minutes by taxi from the center of Florence). Tel 39/055-220-053; www.ristoranteomero.it.

OSTERIA DEL CAFFÈ ITALIANO—With the inviting combination of a casual wood-paneled wine bar in front and slightly more serious dining in back, this handsome osteria, housed in a landmark early Renaissance palazzo, is the best place in town for a self-styled *degustazione* by the glass. Beneath vaulted ceilings and wrought-iron chandeliers, its old wooden tables, display of first-rate salami and cheeses, and interesting mix of habitués feels just right. **WHERE:** Via Isola delle Stinche, near Piazza Santa Croce. Tel 39/055-289-368; www.caffeitaliano.it.

VIVOLI—Ice cream purists may insist it's no longer the city's best, but don't tell that to the crowds always loitering outside, tucking into flavors that run the gamut from familiar but delicious vanilla to whiskey, rice, or fig. Besides, the Piazza Santa Croce is just one cobblestone block away, with stone benches on which to sit and pause. **WHERE:** Via Isola delle Stinche, near Piazza Santa Croce. Tel 39/055-292-334; www.vivoli.it.

A Showcase of the Renaissance's Glory Days

THE UFFIZI GALLERIES

Florence, Tuscany, Italy

Here, in a palace designed in 1560 by architect Giorgio Vasari for Grand Duke Cosimo de' Medici, are some of the most recognized and oft-reproduced masterworks of Western civilization. It is the largest such holding of Renaissance paintings anywhere and is widely regarded as one of the most important picture galleries in the world. Collected by the Medicis themselves over time, the superb collection of Italy's unparalleled artistic heritage spans six centuries: the crowds confirm that the Botticelli rooms *(Allegory of Springtime, The Birth of Venus)* are some of the most popular. There are also earlier wonders of the Renaissance from such trailblazers as Cimabue and Giotto; Michelangelo, native son of Florence, is represented here by his only extant painting on canvas, the *Doni Tondo.* Add to them equally seminal work by artists like Leonardo da Vinci, Piero della Francesca, Filippo Lippi, Raphael . . . the list goes on and on. Stendhal swooned from the sensory overload of walking the streets of Florence (and no doubt stopping in at many of the city's sixty-six museums); visitors to the Uffizi will likely experience something of "Stendhal's Syndrome." The U-shaped galleries can easily (and probably should) be divided into more than one visit. Each should be capped off with a *caffè* at the museum bar overlooking the Piazza della Signoria, the heart of the city past and present.

WHAT: site. **WHERE:** Piazzale degli Uffizi off the Piazza della Signoria; tel 39/055-238-8651, fax 39/0-55-238-8694; info@uffizi.firenze.it; www.uffizi.firenze.it. **COST:** admission $9. **WHEN:** Tues–Sun.

VILLA SAN MICHELE AND VILLA LA MASSA

Florence, Tuscany, Italy

I f you're looking for the comforts of a luxurious home, head for the spectacular Villa San Michele, in the cool hills of Fiesole above Florence. Its stunning ocher-colored facade is believed to be the design of Michelangelo.

Things are decidedly sumptuous inside. A 1602 fresco of the Last Supper graces the former refectory, now a lounge, but in warm weather everyone—guest or visitor—gravitates to the open-air loggia, whose sunset and twilight views of Brunelleschi's Duomo and the surrounding terra-cotta rooftops make it one of the loveliest venues anywhere in Europe. Luxuriant and fragrant, terraced gardens engulf the villa and the converted Limonaia, a winter garden where citrus trees were kept by the monks in the cold weather. Today it's home to the villa's two most exclusive suites. The notoriously hot and humid summers of Florence and the Arno Valley are virtually a world away from the grassy terrace, where the region's most beautifully situated pool offers Piero della Francesca views.

Until recently, the San Michele was Florence's villa-hotel supreme, but competition has arrived on the other side of town at the Villa La Massa, a sumptuously renovated 16th-century property of Como's Villa d'Este Hotel. Located on the banks of the Arno, fifteen minutes from the center of Florence, it offers a glimpse of Tuscan life as the Florentine aristocracy must have enjoyed it.

WHAT: hotel. **VILLA SAN MICHELE:** Via Doccia 4 (Fiesole is 5 miles/8 km from the center of Florence). Tel 39/055-567-8200, fax 39/055-567-8250; in the U.S., tel 800-237-1236; reservations@villasanmichele.net; www.villasanmichele.com. *Cost:* doubles from $1,215. *When:* mid-Mar–mid-Nov. **VILLA LA MASSA:** 4.5 miles/7 km from the center of Florence, in Candeli. Tel 39/05-562-611, fax 39/05-563-3102; in the U.S., tel 800-735-2478; www.villalamassa.com; info@villalamassa.it. *Cost:* doubles from $490 (low season), from $680 (high season). *When:* open late Mar–early Nov. **BEST TIMES:** mid-May to mid-Oct.

LUCCA

Tuscany, Italy

B lessedly bypassed by mass tourism and protected within its perfectly preserved Renaissance walls, this is the archetypal Tuscan hill town—minus the hill. Lucca is actually quite flat, all the better to grab a bike and coast around its timeless cobblestone side streets and to visit the ancient palazzi that today house handsome antiques shops and food stores. Of its dozens of medieval churches, the most important are the elaborate San Michele in Foro (begun in 1143) and the stately 11th-century Duomo. Relax with a gelato in the atmospheric wood-paneled Antico Caffè di Simo, where Giacomo Puccini, Lucca's most famous son, once whiled away his afternoons. And don't even think about leaving town without having lunch at the deservedly popular trattoria Da Giulio in Pelleria, one of Tuscany's most authentic and beloved eating destinations.

Later, jump back on your wheels and follow the 3-mile oak-shaded path atop the city walls for a bird's-eye view of the ancient groves of olive trees that unfold beyond the town's *centro storico:* the *lucchesia* area gives the world its finest *olio di oliva.*

WHAT: town, restaurant. **LUCCA:** 45 miles/ 72 km west of Florence. **DA GIULIO IN PELLERIA:** Via delle Conce, 45, Piazza San Donato. Tel/fax 39/0583-55-948. *Cost:* dinner $25. *When:* lunch and dinner, Tues–Sat. **BEST TIMES:** Sept–Oct, the local opera season, always features some Puccini operas; there is an outdoor antiques market the 3d Sun of every month.

A Wine Town and Its Showpiece

MONTALCINO

Tuscany, Italy

Local legend attributes the founding of the Abbazia di Sant'Antimo to the Holy Roman Emperor Charlemagne (742–814), though the present building dates back only to 1118. Sitting alone in an olive grove along

the old pilgrimage road linking Rome to Santiago de Compostela in Spain, it was built of local travertine and luminous, honey-colored alabaster from nearby Volterra. The abbey is most beautiful when warmed by the late-afternoon Tuscan sun, a glowing example of medieval Romanesque architecture, one of the finest in Italy. The seven monks of the Norbertini order, who live in a nearby farm-house, fill the cavernous church daily with etherial Gregorian chants at regular intervals, evoking a sense of history and mystery that transports visitors back to the Middle Ages. Is it by some divine chance that all seven monks sing like cherubim? They'll convince you it's the acoustics: they're perfect. After vespers, it's just a ten-minute walk to Il Molino, an ancient stone mill turned hotel that most likely dates back to the abbey's 12th-century

The label art for Brunello di Montalcino wine

origins. Rebuilt in 1606, it worked as a water mill until its 1998 restoration. Overnight guests settle into beautifully refurbished rooms on peaceful grounds shaded by olive and fruit trees.

The next day, venture into the town of Montalcino for sightseeing and for tasting the premier DOCG Brunello wine and its lighter-weight cousin Rosso di Montalcino. Montalcino is a small, sleepy, but well-to-do hill town that is little changed since the 16th century. At 2,000 feet above sea level, it offers lovely vistas over faded terra-cotta roof tiles, a timeless landscape covered with vineyards yielding the sangiovese grosso grapes used for the Brunello wine, one of the most distinguished reds produced in Italy. Hike up to the 14th-century Fortezza that moonlights as the town *enoteca* for Brunello tasting by the glass or sit for hours in the Piazza del Popolo's 19th-century Caffè Fiaschetteria Italiana. The local tourist office will supply you with lists and maps of the dozens of local wine producers, world-recognized and not, whose rolling estates make up much of this idyllic 12-square-mile corner of southern Tuscany.

If you have time, consider staying at a dream villa: the exquisitely refurbished 18th-century stone farmhouse Poggio di Sopra sits grandly on a hilltop amid the extensive vineyard belonging to the new but highly regarded wine-producing estate Castello Romitorio.

WHAT: town, site, hotel. **MONTALCINO:** 26 miles/41 km south of Siena, 134 miles/213 km north of Rome. **ABBAZIA DI SANT'ANTIMO:** 7 miles/11 km south of Montalcino (follow the signs for Castelnuovo dell'Abate), Tel 39/0577-83-56-59. *When:* Mon–Sat vespers at 5 P.M.; Sun vespers at 6:30 P.M. Check for schedule of other daily times. **IL MOLINO DI SANT'ANTIMO:** tel 39/331-6797-713; info@molinosantimo. com; www.santantimo.com. Can accommodate a maximum of 8 guests. *Cost:* weekly rates from $2,830 (low season) to $4,670 (high season), includes maid and miscellaneous utilities. **POGGIO DI SOPRA:** 6 miles/9 km from Montalcino. Tel 39/0577-847-212, fax 39/0577-847-110; info@castelloromitorio. com; www.castelloromitorio.com. Divided into 2 apartments that can accommodate a maximum of 4 and 6 guests. *Cost:* weekly rates from $1,.415 (low season) and $2,475 (high season), includes maid and utilities. **BEST TIMES:** May–Oct.

Testimony to a Renaissance Pope's Vision and Ambition

PIENZA

Tuscany, Italy

The Renaissance Pope Pius II dreamed of creating the perfect urban gem. In 1458 he commissioned the famed architect Bernardo Rossellini to raze his humble hometown, Corsignano, and re-create it as Pienza (renamed after himself, Pio) as a papal annex and summertime retreat—the ideal High Renaissance city. Money ran out and the pope died, but not before the collaboration resulted in "the Pearl of the Renaissance" you see today, the only town center in Italy to survive the centuries almost perfectly intact—so much so that when director Franco Zeffirelli chose to film his 1968 *Romeo and Juliet* here (eschewing the more predictable choice of Verona), every stone was already in place. The core of town is the embodiment of Pius's dream, the grand Piazza Pio II, flanked by noble palazzi and an imposing cathedral set on a cliff's edge. Walk around behind the cathedral for picture-perfect views of the Val d'Orcia, dominated by Monte Amiata, a dormant volcano. These same vistas can be enjoyed during breakfast by guests of Il Chiostro di Pienza, a 15th-century Franciscan convent-turned-hotel. The old monks' cells are larger now, but the calm cloister remains untouched.

WHAT: town, hotel. **PIENZA:** 33 miles/ 55 km southeast of Siena, 75 miles/125 km south of Florence. **HOTEL IL CHIOSTRO DI PIENZA:** Corso Rossellino 26. Tel 39/0578-748-400, fax 39/0578-748-440; info@relaisil chiostrodipienza.com; www.relaisilchiostrodi pienza.com. *Cost:* doubles from $170. **BEST TIMES:** May, Jun, and Sept. Local fair celebrating Pecorino di Pienza, the area's superb sheep's-milk cheese, 1st Sun in Sept; flower market 1st Sun in May.

Tuscany's Perfect Coastal Corner

IL PELLICANO

Porto Ercole, Tuscany, Italy

Il Pellicano is one of the Mediterranean's most wonderful seaside resorts, born of a love affair between an Englishman and an American woman when it opened in 1965 with a guest list that included Charlie Chaplin. While most think of rolling vineyards and medieval hill towns when conjuring up Bertolucci-induced images of Tuscany's interior, the seaside-savvy

Relax by the heated seawater swimming pool.

will yearn instead for this tiny peninsula in the southwest coastal corner of Tuscany that juts out into the eye-dazzling waters of the Tyrrhenian Sea. The exclusive 8-acre compound is composed of stone cottages scattered down a dramatic cliff face of Monte Argentario, covered with pine and olive trees around the hotel's own private cove. Brilliant white umbrellas and deck chairs the color of the water line the stone seawall "beach." You can dive directly into the sea here, and guests paddle about idly waiting for the afternoon barbecue, held on a shaded terrace.

Despite its relaxed, villa-meets-country-club atmosphere, Il Pellicano matches the standards of a much larger world-class hotel. The service is excellent, as are the wine list and the fresh, unstuffy food, with fish straight out of the sea. The rooms are airy, first-rate, and extremely tasteful, and most have private balconies. And everywhere are gentle breezes and the vast expanse of the sea.

WHAT: hotel. **WHERE:** Località lo Sbarcatello in Porto Ercole, 100 miles/161 km north of Rome. Tel 39/0564-858-111, fax 39/0564-833-418; info@pellicanohotel.com; www.pellicanohotel.com. **COST:** doubles from $620 (low season), from $835 (high season), sea view extra. **WHEN:** open late Mar–early Nov. **BEST TIMES:** May and Sept.

Wine and Landscapes to Make You Swoon

CHIANTI AND SAN GIMIGNANO

Tuscany, Italy

Chianti is Italy's most beautiful wine region and its most important, producing premier red wines whose reputation today could not be finer. In Tuscany's heartland, it stretches between Florence and Siena.

Wine production in the area goes back to the pre-Roman Etruscans. The serendipity of lazy vineyard-hopping drives and spontaneous wine-tasting stops is heightened by the region's postcard-perfect landscape. Even designated drivers will swoon. The old Via Chiantigiana links a string of wine towns that dot a history-rich area of forested hills, medieval castles, stone farmhouses, and wine-producing estates—both small, unsung wine producers and renowned names like Antinori, Fresco-baldi, and Ricasoli. Producing first-rate wines in a setting that could not be more pictur-esque, the tiny, family-owned 14th-century village of Castello di Volpaia welcomes a lim-ited number of guests to it's unique *agritur-ismo* establishment. Optional meals prepared exclusively for guests highlight the region's seasonal best, as well as the family's own olive oil, honey, preserves, and aromatic vinegar. But meals here, good as they are, are just something to accompany Volpaia's finest vin-tages, all of which manage to somehow taste better when consumed next to the vine-clad hill where the grapes are grown.

Just over another of those hills is San Gimignano, a name long synonomous with "Tuscan hill town." San Gimignano has cap-tured the traveler's imagination for centuries. Its distinctive skyline bristles with fourteen medieval towers dating back to the 12th and 13th centuries—a mere fraction of the original estimated seventy. Try to arrive late in the after-

The hilltop town of Montereggione in Chianti

noon, when the tour bus caravans have pulled out and given the town back to the people. Climb to the top of the Palazzo del Popolo's 117-foot Torre Grossa, the highest of San Gimignano's towers, for a bird's-eye view of the town, its towers, and the Val d'Elsa beyond. Then settle in at the Bel Soggiorno's rustic and spacious restaurant, where the menu shares the spotlight with the glorious Tuscan countryside framed by the oversized windows. Wild game from the surrounding wood-covered hills is the house specialty, and a selection of Chianti's best offerings completes the ticket. Nearby, in two adjoining piazzas, there is an ambitious summer program of everything from alfresco ballet to opera. Imagine the plaintive strains of *Tosca* wafting up and over San Gimignano's medieval skyscrapers.

WHAT: hotel, town, restaurant, event. **CASTELLO DI VOLPAIA:** 35 miles/55 km south of Florence, 4 miles/7 km north of Radda in

Chianti. Tel 39/0577-738-066, fax 0577-738-619; info@volpaia.com; www.volpaia.com. Apartments and villas accommodating 2–11 guests are available year-round. *Cost:* double-occupancy apartments with kitchen from $850 per week (low season), from $1,380 (high season). *Best times:* Aug 10 is feast day of Castello di Volpaia's patron saint, Lorenzo, with fireworks and a festival. Grape harvest is usually mid–late Sept. **SAN GIMIGNANO:** 35 miles/56 km southwest of Florence. *Best times:* summer music and dance festival, mid-Jun–Aug. **BEL SOGGIORNO:** Via San Giovanni 41. Tel 39/577-94-31-49. *Cost:* dinner $55.

Center Stage in Siena

PIAZZA DEL CAMPO AND THE PALIO

Siena, Tuscany, Italy

Aerial shots of the Piazza del Campo, ringed with 13th- and 14th-century palazzi, reveal its unusual scallop shape, but they don't prepare you for its size or beauty. Built at the point where Siena's three hills converge,

Il Campo is divided into nine marble-trimmed strips, which represent the city's ancient Government of Nine and are also said to imitate the folds in the cloak of the Virgin Mary. Looming on one side is the Palazzo Pubblico, with its sky-scraping 320-foot bell tower, the Torre del Mangia, the second highest in Italy. If you climb its 505 steps, you will be rewarded with a vertigo-inducing view of idyllic Chianti countryside that stretches toward Florence, but your view is probably better—and certainly less strenuous—from any café table below. The piazza has always been the city's center stage and location for the raucous bareback horse race known as the Palio.

Hysteria and excitement fuel this twice-yearly event, which culminates in ninety seconds and three hair-raising laps around the earth-covered piazza. But first, a remarkable procession, the *corteo storico*, unfolds. Each of the seventeen *contrade*, the historical divisions of the town (with names like Giraffe, Tower, Wolf, and Wave), are represented by dozens of pages, drummers, and banner bearers dressed in the *contrada*'s heraldic colors and elaborate historical costumes, including knightly armor. A highlight of the parade is synchronized flag throwing, which Sienese youths practice from their earliest days.

This reenactment of the pomp and pageantry of Siena's medieval past is motivated not by tourism dollars, but rather by the participants' deeply felt emotions about their *contrade*, the city, and its history—not to mention centuries-old feudal rivalries (the race dates to the 12th century). Only ten of the *contrade* compete in each race, a selection determined by lot before the festival. In this freewheeling, treacherous race, with (padded) death-defying corners, the first horse to cross the finish line (even without a rider) wins. The prize? A banner of cloth painted with the image of the Virgin Mary, plus official bragging rights for the year.

Unless you live in Siena, obtaining tickets can be frustrating. The alternative is spending hours under the Tuscan sun, standing in the packed square with 50,000 new best friends.

WHAT: site, town, event. **PIAZZA DEL**

CAMPO: Siena is 21 miles/34 km south of Florence. **PALIO:** Siena Tourist Office, Piazza del Campo 56. Tel 39/0577-28-05-51, fax 39/0577-281-041; infoaptsiena@terresiena.it; www.terresiena.it. *Cost:* $215 for bleacher seats. *When:* Jul 2 and Aug 16.

Piety in Paradise

BASILICA OF SAN FRANCESCO

Assisi, Umbria, Italy

St. Francis's humanity, humility, and love for nature somehow survive the unashamed commercialization of this small pink-hued Umbrian hill town: The spirit of the young, barefoot monk—Assisi's favorite son—lives on.

The enormous basilica built in his honor (which would have mortified him) was a medieval architectural feat and is still considered one of the engineering marvels of that period. In the early 13th century, Giotto covered much of the upper and lower basilica with remarkable frescoes, the first to break with the static icons of the Byzantine school. His masterpiece depicts the life of St. Francis in twenty-eight scenes. A devastating earthquake in 1997 caused extensive damage not only to the structure itself but to the priceless artwork. A remarkable degree of restoration was accomplished in time for Italy's Jubilee celebration in 2000, but painstaking repair will continue for years. Most tourists visit Assisi in an afternoon; the stillness and beauty that so moved the young St. Francis are most apparent in the evening and early morning. Consider spending the night at the comfortable family-run Hotel Umbra. Housed in a 15th-century building that rests on ancient Roman foundations, its back rooms afford serene views of the Umbrian Valley and the charming sound of birdsong.

WHAT: site, town, hotel. **ASSISI:** 110 miles/ 177 km northeast of Rome. **HOTEL UMBRA:** Via degli Archi 6. Tel 39/075-81-22-40, fax 39/075-81-36-53; info@hotelumbra.it; www. hotelumbra.it. *When:* mid-Mar to mid-Jan. *Cost:* doubles from $170 **BEST TIMES:** spring and fall.

Una Villa Stupenda

PALAZZO TERRANOVA

Città di Castello, Umbria, Italy

High up in the hills of Umbria sits a stately Palladian-inspired palazzo. It is the "dream for all seasons" of a very special British couple, Umbrian by adoption, who have opened a lovingly run jewel-like country hotel to

a few extremely privileged guests. This is every Italophile's fantasy made real; the unrivaled site 1,800 feet above the Tiber Valley commands heart-stirring views, especially from the 18th-

La Traviata Suite takes its colors from an artist's palette.

century villa's turret, and there are 30 acres of idyllic countryside perfect for quiet strolls. The verdant, unspoiled region of Umbria is known for its clear light and vibrant spectrum of colors that inspired the palettes of Raphael, Luca Signorelli, and Piero della Francesca. The large and airy guest quarters consist of eight magnificent suites named after favorite composers and operas. La Traviata is the most splendid—its romantic bathroom includes an enormous travertine tub carved from one solid block of stone. The oversized windows of La Bohème open on to storybook views, as does the front terrace from beneath white canvas umbrellas. This is truffle and wild mushroom country, thick with forests that offer wild game that may show up on the palazzo's menu when in season. The elegant cuisine shows a sophisticated, albeit unpretentious, hand.

WHAT: hotel. **WHERE:** Località Ronti, Morra (82 miles/132 km southeast of Florence). Tel 39/075-857-0083, fax 39/075-857-0014; info@palazzoterranova.com; www.palazzoterranova.com. **COST:** doubles from $435 (low season), from $595 (high season); La Traviata Suite $820. **BEST TIMES:** for mild weather, spring and fall; mountain views Dec–Feb.

*Umbria's City of Silence,
Forgotten in the Passage of Time*

GUBBIO

Umbria, Italy

An austere, proud mountain outpost, the tiny no-nonsense stone town of Gubbio hangs on to its medieval charm and authentic flavor. Despite its growing popularity with off-the-beaten-trackers looking for a classically picturesque hill town minus day-tripping hordes, Gubbio remains a sleepy backwater stop. Its lack of big-time tourist attractions and out-of-the-way location are responsible for much of its appeal—and the reason it retains its nickname, City of Silence. Set into the rugged, steep slope of forest-clad Mount Ingino, Gubbio was a modestly prosperous Roman settlement, Iguvium, as is obvious from the ancient Roman amphitheater that sits at the foot of today's town. But it is the Eugubium of the Dark Ages, when this was a busy little market center, that one senses most here. All roads lead to the much-photographed central square, the Piazza Grande, whose austere grandeur makes it easy to imagine the harsh atmosphere of medieval life. From 1387 to 1508, the Montefeltro counts of nearby Urbino ruled the town, putting up visiting emissaries at their aristocratic guest quarters. They have recently been reborn as the Hotel Relais Ducale, offering the same vistas of the Piazza Grande and the Umbrian plains that must have dazzled the dukes' guests of yore.

WHAT: town, hotel. **GUBBIO:** 28 miles/45 km northeast of Perugia, 105 miles/170 km southeast of Florence. **HOTEL RELAIS DUCALE:** Via Ducale 2. Tel 39/075-922-0157, fax 39/075-922-0159; info@reslaisducale.com; www.relaisducale.com. *Cost:* doubles from $185. **BEST TIMES:** Apr–Oct; May 15 for the Corsa dei Ceri, a raucous race of huge wooden "candles."

High in the Sky, a Romanesque Jewel

IL DUOMO

Orvieto, Umbria, Italy

O
rvieto, one of Italy's most dramatically situated hill towns, commands a position atop a high, flat column of tufa stone more than 1,000 feet above sea level. It can be seen from a great distance when the sunlight

catches the Gothic facade of its famous cathedral. The perfect centerpiece of this ancient town, the Duomo is as amazing outside as it is inside. Beginning in the late 13th century, artists and architects from all over Italy took more than 300 years to finish this fascinating hybrid of Romanesque, Gothic, and High Renaissance styles. But the Duomo's undisputed main draw is the cycle of frescoes portraying the end of the world, begun by Fra Angelico in 1447 and completed in 1499–1503 by Luca Signorelli.

The unique twelve-sided tower of La Badia

These important Renaissance frescoes were probably the inspiration for Michelangelo's *Last Judgment* in the Vatican's Sistine Chapel nearly half a century later. (An unimpressed Leonardo da Vinci, however, said the figures reminded him of sacks "stuffed full of nuts.") The frescoes cover almost 10,000 square feet of the walls and ceiling of the Duomo's San Brizio chapel. At the base of the vertical city walls is La Badia, a beautifully preserved 12th-century abbey, now a first-class hotel.

WHAT: town, site, hotel. **IL DUOMO:** Orvieto is 60 miles/97 km northwest of Rome, 53 miles/85 km south of Perugia. **HOTEL LA BADIA:** 2 miles/3 km from the town center on the main road into town. Tel 39/0763-30-19-59, fax 39/0763-30-53-96; info@labadia hotel.it; www.labadiahotel.it. *Cost:* doubles from $255 (low season), from $350 (high season), $415 for 2 with half board. *When:* open Mar–Dec.

Seeing and Being Seen Since Time Immemorial

LA PASSEGGIATA

Perugia, Umbria, Italy

M
aybe because it's the only flat strip of land in an exceptionally hilly town, or maybe because a vibrant international student population has kept this prosperous city humming since 1270, but when it's time for

the late-afternoon *passeggiata*, Perugia's Corso Vannucci ("il Corso") is the place to be. Every American town has its Main Street, and every Italian town its main *corso*, and some innate alarm system sends every ambulatory Perugino, young and old, heading for this venue like clockwork.

Nowhere can the timeless ritual of the see-and-be-seen evening walk be experienced more fully than in Perugia. Trade and the arts flourished here in the Middle Ages, and much of the imposing backdrop—the Fontana Maggiore, the Palazzo dei Priori, and the Palazzo del Cambio—date from Perugia's golden medieval period. Observe the elegance and character of the Perugini who turn out to stop, chat, gesticulate, argue soccer scores, union wage increases, or political scandals, and to check out the latest fashions, store window displays, new grandchildren, or each other. Then it's time for dinner: the broad Corso Vannucci empties out, and Perugia slips back into its quiet time warp—at least until tomorrow, same time, same place.

WHAT: town, experience. **WHERE:** 112 miles/180 km north of Rome, 96 miles/154 km southeast of Florence.

Music Under the Umbrian Stars

SPOLETO FESTIVAL

Spoleto, Umbria, Italy

The world-class Spoleto Festival (formerly known as the Festival of Two Worlds) brought Spoleto back into the limelight in 1957 after centuries of historical obscurity. Such obscurity kept the medieval town virtually untouched, making Spoleto an inimitable setting for three weeks of high-quality dance, music, art, and drama courtesy of world-renowned artistic talents, including Luciano Pavarotti, the Paul Taylor Dance Company, and many, many others.

Come for the grand finale where an enraptured audience sits on the graduated steps that lead up and out of the Piazza Duomo. The day's last light illuminates the gold mosaics of the church's 12th-century facade while sparrows dart about before sunset to the strains of Beethoven or Mozart. Italian-American founder and composer Gian Carlo Menotti visited more than thirty hill towns in Tuscany and Umbria before succumbing to Spoleto's perfect charms.

WHAT: event. **WHERE:** 80 miles/129 km north of Rome. Box office, tel 39/0743-47967; www.festivaldispoleto.com. **WHEN:** 3 weeks, beginning end of Jun.

The Romanesque facade of Spoleto's Duomo

Riding the Glaciers

CROSSING THE MONT BLANC MASSIF

Courmayeur, Valle d'Aosta, Italy

Courmayeur is one of the most popular ski resorts in Europe, nestled at the base of Monte Bianco (Mont Blanc), Europe's highest mountain, and stunningly situated in the middle of a dozen other peaks above 13,000 feet.

The cable car ride that originates here at La Palud and carries steel-nerved adventurers up and over the Mont Blanc Massif into Chamonix, France (bring your passport) is one of the most breathtaking of its kind in the Alps. Aptly called "Riding the Glaciers," it is a three-part trip whose most impressive moment is spent dangling over the Vallé Blanche and a sea of glacial snowfields more than 2,000 feet below before arriving at the viewing station high above Chamonix (where the bar's sunbathing terrace offers some of the world's most sensational views).

Meanwhile, back down on earth, visitors will enjoy the old-fashioned but stylish alpine town of Courmayeur. The tiny nearby hamlet of Entreves is the home of La Maison de Filippo, one of the most famous restaurants in the Alps. An avalanche of appetizers that make up the bulk of a seemingly endless meal in a festive all-you-can-eat atmosphere has earned the barnlike tavern the nickname "Chalet of Gluttony" among hungry skiers.

WHAT: experience, town, restaurant. **CABLE CAR RIDE:** originates at La Palud, 2 miles/3 km north of Courmayeur, 22 miles/35 km northwest of Aosta. *Cost:* round-trip $50. *When:* close to a dozen departures daily. Cable car to Chamonix runs Apr–Sept; to halfway point year-round. *Best times:* early morning, when views are clearest. **LA MAISON DE FILIPPO:** 2 miles/3 km north of Courmayeur in Entreves. Tel 39/0165-869-797 or 39/0165-869-705; www.lamaison.com. *Cost:* dinner $65. *When:* open Wed–Mon, Dec–May.

City of a Thousand Horizons

ASOLO

Veneto, Italy

Robert Browning pronounced this Renaissance town "the most beautiful spot I ever was privileged to see" and spent most of his final years there. Nestled in the gentle green hills of the Veneto, and within breathtaking

view of the pink snowcapped Dolomite mountains, the English poet's "delicious Asolo" was a cool, favorite retreat of nearby Venice's noble and patrician families who came here to escape the suffocating heat and ennui of the city's summers. A 15th-century doge bequeathed the jewel-like town to Caterina Cornaro, Venetian-born queen of Cyprus—she relinquished her rule of the island in exchange for a golden exile here. Due to her patronage of the arts, Asolo became, and remains today, a hilltop oasis of culture and social life and an enchanting asylum for foreign writers, artists, and intellectuals lured by

a countryside lush with fruit orchards, cypresses, and vineyards. Over the years, most of them lodged at the Palladian-styled villa purchased by Browning, the home of today's perfectly faded Villa Cipriani Hotel. One of Europe's most seductive country hotels, it is particularly known for its top-notch dining and its fragrant garden, filled with roses, pomegranates, and birdsong. Pampered guests occasionally venture beyond the garden's walls for the idyllic 4-mile drive to Maser to visit Palladio's 16th-century masterpiece, the elegant Villa Barbaro, abounding with trompe l'oeil frescoes by Paolo Veronese.

Hotel Villa Cipriani

WHAT: town, hotel. **ASOLO:** 40 miles/ 64 km northwest of Venice. **HOTEL VILLA CIPRIANI:** Via Canova 298. Tel 39/0423-52-34-11, fax 39/0423-95-20-95; villa cipriani@HO10.net; www.villacipriani asolo.com. *Cost:* doubles from $235. **BEST TIMES:** Apr–Jun and Sept–Oct. Local music festival in Aug or Sept. Asolo's famous Antiques Fair 2d weekend of every month except Jul and Aug.

The Dolomite Drive

CORTINA D'AMPEZZO

Veneto, Italy

The drive through the majestic beauty of the sawtoothed peaks and needles of the Dolomite Mountains in the northern reaches of alpine Italy is to mountain lovers what the cliff-hugging Amalfi Coast is to fans of cerulean blue sea. The 68-mile white-knuckle drive linking Bolzano and the premier ski resort town of Cortina is a study in road engineering, through an awe-inspiring mountainous landscape that comes as a shock to those who think of Italy as rolling vineyards and olive groves. With the Passo del Pordoi (Pordoi Pass)—the heart of the mountain range—as its apogee, the road ends in Cortina, anointed

the "Pearl of the Dolomites." At close to 4,000 feet, it is Italy's number one ski area and one of the best in Europe. Given world-class status when the 1956 Winter Olympics were held here, it is actually an advanced intermediate's paradise, with 95 miles of ski runs. But this is a sophisticated year-round resort where the *bella gente* of Rome and Milan come not only to ski and hike through

The Miramonti Majestic Grand Hotel has stunning alpine views.

lodge set in a magnificent mountain valley location on the outskirts of town. Most of the rooms have balconies and captivating views, while inside, amid the alpine decor, a blazing hearth and cozy bar offering eighteen different kinds of hot chocolate keep things inviting.

WHAT: experience, town, hotel. **CORTINA D'AMPEZZO:** 258 miles/411 km from Milan, 100 miles/161 km north of Venice. **MIRAMONTI MAJESTIC GRAND HOTEL:** Via Pezie 103, Cortina. Tel 39/0436-42-01, fax 39/0436-867-019; www.miramontimajestic.it. *Cost:* per person double occupancy from $245 (low season), from $440 (high season; 1-week minimum), includes breakfast and dinner. *When:* open late Dec–late Mar and Jun–Aug. **BEST TIMES:** Feb, Mar, Jul, and Aug.

the bracing, rugged countryside, but also to practice the art of *il dolce far niente*, the sybaritic pleasure of doing nothing. Those who come to relax, shop, sleep late, enjoy two-hour lunches, people-watch—and perhaps squeeze in a little leisurely skiing—can do no better than to stay at the celebrated 100-year-old Miramonti Majestic Grand Hotel, a former Austro-Hungarian hunting

---

Giotto's Legacy in Brilliant Technicolor

SCROVEGNI CHAPEL

Padua, Veneto, Italy

Giotto's frescoes were instrumental in transforming late medieval and Renaissance painting because of the breadth of the Biblical storytelling, the realism and emotion depicted in the many characters, and the power of the colors. Covering every centimeter of the 13th-century Scrovegni Chapel, these frescoes are some of the most important not only in Italy but in the entire world. Giotto and his students labored from 1303 to 1306 to create thirty-eight scenes. Easily read in typical medieval storybook form, they illustrate the lives of the Virgin Mary and Jesus Christ. Together with the remaining frescoes depicting the life of St. Francis in the Basilica of Assisi, this fresco cycle constitutes the greatest body of work of the Tuscan-born artist (1267–1337). After the 1997 earthquake in Assisi that permanently damaged some of Giotto's frescoes, the Paduan frescoes were laboriously restored to their original brilliance, dominated by the famous cobalt blue.

WHAT: site. **WHERE:** Piazza Ermitani, off Corso Garibaldi (26 miles/42 km west of Venice). Reservations required, tel 39/0492-01-00-20, fax 39/0492-01-00-21; www.cappel ladegliscrovegni.it. **COST:** admission $17.

*"When I went to Venice,
my dream became my home."*
—MARCEL PROUST

VENICE

Veneto, Italy

Here it is, the Venice of your dreams, wooing, intriguing, disorienting, and exhilarating visitors like no other city on earth. Misty and mystical bridge between East and West, straddling both yet belonging to neither, Venezia is like a faded, once great queen that still manages to enchant and beguile. The never-ending stream of tourism began well over 1,000 years ago, and no wonder: As Henry James said, a visit to Venice becomes a perpetual love affair.

THE TOP TEN SIGHTS

GALLERIE DELL'ACCADEMIA—Venice's largest museum, the Accademia contains the most extensive collection of Venetian masters in the world, spanning the 13th to the 18th centuries and all the major painters, including Titian, Tintoretto, Giorgione, Veronese, Bellini, and Carpaccio. Viewing 15th-century depictions of the city, it's amazing to see how little has changed. **WHERE:** Campo della Carità, Dorsoduro. Tel 39/041-520-0345.

CA' D'ORO AND THE GALLERIA GIORGIO FRANCHETTI—Created by early-20th-century philanthropist Baron Giorgio Franchetti, the Ca' d'Oro comprises two joined palaces (the opulent 15th-century Ca' d'Oro—one of the city's most famous and beautiful canalside palazzi—and the smaller Ca' Duodo) and contains the baron's private collection of paintings, sculpture, and furniture, which he donated to the Italian government during World War I. Among the masterpieces on display are Titian's *Venus* and Mantegna's *St. Sebastian.* **WHERE:** directly on the Grand Canal, Cannaregio. Tel 39/041-520-0345.

CHIESA DEI FRARI (CHURCH OF THE FRIARS)—In a city filled with churches, this immense Franciscan bastion—built in the 13th and 14th centuries—stands out as the home of several masterworks, including Titian's *Assumption,* depicting the ascension of the Virgin Mary into heaven; Donatello's wood-carving *St. John the Baptist;* and Bellini's 1488 triptych *The Madonna and Child Enthroned.* **WHERE:** Campo dei Frari, San Polo. Tel 39/041-522-2637.

CHIESA DEI SANTI GIOVANNI AND PAOLO (CHURCH OF SAINTS JOHN AND PAUL)— Also built during the 13th and 14th centuries, this massive Gothic church—the largest in Venice after St. Mark's—contains the tombs of twenty-five doges, plus works by a number of Venice's greatest painters, including Bellini and Veronese, whose ceilings depict New Testament scenes. To the right of the church is Andrea del Verrocchio's famous 15th-century bronze statue of the mercenary Bartolomeo Colleoni astride a horse, one of the great masterworks of early Renaissance sculpture. **WHERE:** Campo SS. Giovanni e Paolo, Castello. Tel 39/041-523-5913.

PALAZZO DUCALE (DOGE'S PALACE)—
Between the Basilica di San Marco and
St. Mark's Basin sits the palace from which
the dukes ruled La Serenissima (the Most
Serene Republic) and much of the eastern
Mediterranean for 1,000 years, with each
doge elected for life. Filled with paintings
by the greatest Venetian artists, including
Veronese and Tintoretto, the present pink-
and-white marble structure is the cumulative
work of many architects over the centuries,
meant to impress Venice's wealth and power
upon visitors arriving by ship. Highlights
include the doge's private apartments, the
assembly room of the Council of Ten, and
the Bridge of Sighs (Ponte dei Sospiri),
which links the palace with the Palazzo delle
Prigioni, where prisoners were held after
being judged by the council. The Romantic
poets gave it its name. Take an English-
language tour or a self-guided audio tour
to really understand the palace and the
maritime empire that was governed from
its halls. **WHERE:** Piazzetta San Marco,
San Marco. Tel 39/041-271-5911.

*Experience the city from a uniquely Venetian
perspective.*

THE GRAND CANAL—Venice's Main Street,
its 2-mile aquatic thoroughfare, is lined with
hundreds of weather-worn Byzantine and

Gothic palazzi and abuzz with canal life.
For a nominal fee, jump on the number 1
vaporetto (water bus), which plies the full
length of the S-shaped "Canalazzo," for a
cruise through 1,000 years of local history,
dodging errant gondolas and delivery boats.
Starting at either Piazza San Marco or the
Santa Lucia train station, savor it once by
day for rush-hour stimulus and once at night
for the quiet, unmatched romance of it all.

PEGGY GUGGENHEIM COLLECTION—One
of the world's great collections of modern art,
housed in a palazzo on the Grand Canal that
was once the home of Peggy Guggenheim,
patron to many of the greatest 20th-century
artists, including Jackson Pollock and her
husband, Max Ernst. Her collection includes
works by Duchamp, Picasso, Léger, Klee,
Magritte, Rothko, Chagall, Mondrian, and
many others. A sculpture garden contains
works by Giacometti, Claire Falkenstein,
and Mirko. Interestingly, Ms. Guggenheim's
palace is an unfinished work, begun in the
1750s and intended to rise two stories taller
than it ended up. **WHERE:** Calle Venier dei
Leoni, Dorsoduro. Tel 39/041-240-5411;
www.guggenheim-venice.it.

BASILICA DI SAN MARCO—Sitting at the
eastern end of the Piazza San Marco, the
basilica was originally built as the final
resting place of St. Mark, whose body was
smuggled by two merchants out of Alexandria
in 828. The current structure is the third
church built on the site, and dates from the
11th century. Byzantine, almost mosquelike
in style, it is one of the world's most richly
embellished and distinctive Roman Catholic
churches, surmounted by replicas of the
Quadriga, the four famous bronze horses
looted from Constantinople in 1204. (The
originals are currently in St. Mark's Museum,
inside the basilica.) Other "appropriations"
from around Venice's once huge merchant
empire decorate the structure inside and out.
Byzantine mosaics cover the dimly lit ceilings
of the interior. The sarcophagus of St. Mark

sits beneath four columns in the presbytery, while behind the altar is the Pala d'Oro altar screen, one of the basilica's greatest treasures, comprised of more than 2,000 precious stones and enameled panels. **WHERE:** Piazza San Marco, San Marco. Tel 39/041-270-8334.

PIAZZA SAN MARCO—The heart of Venice then and now, St. Mark's is one of the world's most beautiful public squares, full of cafés, shops, tourists, and, of course, flocks of overfed pigeons. At its wider end, the not-so-square square is crowned by the beautiful St. Mark's Basilica (see above) and the famous Campanile, the tallest structure on the Venice skyline. The current tower is a 20th-century re-creation of the 8th-century original, which collapsed without warning in 1902. Ascend to its summit for a miraculous view. On a clear day you may be able to see the faint outline of the Dolomite Mountains.

When Napoleon arrived in 1797 he called the square "the finest drawing room in Europe," and so it may very well remain today, with its throngs of visitors staring in wonderment at the elegant colonnades and at the Basilica's ornate facade, sipping espresso at the Caffè Florian (see below) or Caffè Quadri while the orchestras play, or simply sitting in the sun, chatting. Every sixty minutes, two bronze Moors atop the 15th-century Torre dell'Orologio strike the hour. To get the full effect, go several times: in the early morning to have it all to yourself, in the afternoon for the spectacle of the crowds, and at night for intense romance.

SCUOLA GRANDE DI SAN ROCCO—Built in 1515 as the home of a religious and social confraternity (one of many in Venice at the time), this structure is by far the most renowned of them all, gaining lasting fame because of its collection of works by Tintoretto, who painted some fifty works for the *scuola* over thirty years from 1564 to 1594. It's the largest collection of his dark and dramatic work anywhere. The top floor contains scenes from the New and Old Testaments, including

the enormous *Crucifixion,* considered Tintoretto's masterpiece. **WHERE:** Campo San Rocco, San Polo. Tel 39/041-523-4864.

OTHER MUST-DO'S

GONDOLA, GONDOLA!—Yes, they're touristy and overpriced and the Venetians won't go near them, but they're also the most enjoyable and romantic way to see the hidden corners of this unique city whose streets are filled with water. The gondolier won't sing, and can often be taciturn, but it's best anyway to glide in silence through the enchanting web of more than 150 sleepy back canals, immersed in your own fantasy of traveling back 500 years to the heyday of the Most Serene Republic. **WHERE:** gondoliers congregate at all the main tourist spots, including the Doge's Palace and the Rialto Bridge areas.

TORCELLO—You won't want to follow Katharine Hepburn into the waters of a Venetian canal (as in the 1955 classic *Summertime*), but find a Rossano Brazzi lookalike and head for the green, quasi-deserted island of Torcello for an idyllic picnic, far from the crowds of tourists and pigeons in the Piazza San Marco. Forgot your picnic hamper? The country-cozy Trattoria al Ponte del Diavolo (tel 39/041-730-401) is the best option among slim dining pickings, its garden tables promising a perfect lunch. Let dessert be a viewing of Torcello's ancient cathedral and its breathtaking 12th- and 13th-century Byzantine mosaics, some of the most important in Europe. **WHERE:** at the northeast end of the Venetian lagoon, accessible via the vaporetto (departing from Ponte della Paglia and the Fondamenta Nove terminal) or via an "outer islands" tour, which includes the lace-making island of Burano and the glass-making island of Murano.

VIVALDI'S CHURCH—Officially called the Church of La Pietà, this was the site where local Baroque maestro Antonio Vivaldi worked as choirmaster for an orphanage and conservatory from 1703 to 1741, while composing some of his masterworks. Today, those works (and others, by the Red Priest's contemporaries) are performed here by candlelight on a regular basis. There's nothing like hearing a performance of *Le Quattro Staggioni* (The Four Seasons) beneath Tiepolo's luminous ceiling fresco. Or is it the excellent acoustics? **WHERE:** Riva degli Schiavoni, Castello. Tel 39/041-522-2171; www.pietavenezia.org.

WHERE TO STAY

HOTEL DANIELI—Ranked as one of the world's most historically endowed hotels, the Danieli occupies the 14th-century canal-front home of a former doge. Its enclosed courtyard is now the hotel's spectacular lobby, with its inviting Bar Dandolo. It is an intriguing respite for hotel guests and curious drop-ins alike—the former happily repairing to the magnificent suites that look out onto the Grand Canal. (A tip: Rooms without the canal view aren't worth the ducal rates.) **WHERE:** Riva degli Schiavoni, Castello. Tel 39/041-522-6480; www.venice-hotel-danieli.com. **COST:** high.

HOTEL FLORA—Even before you enter through the glass doors of this cozy, atmospheric hotel you can see the lush patio courtyard that gives it its name. Guests spend most of their time in this small green oasis during the warm weather months, taking breakfast, tea, or an *aperitivo* amid the delightful calm created by thick climbing vines and flowering plants. Lucky rooms look out on this enclosed secret garden, but the most coveted view is from the top-floor corner room, which overlooks what is said to be the palazzo of Desdemona of *Othello* fame. Isn't Venice romantic? **WHERE:** Calle Larga XXII Marzo, San Marco. Tel 39/041-520-5844. **COST:** moderate.

HOTEL AI DO MORI—A five-star address and upper-story rooms within poking distance of the onion-shaped Byzantine cupolas of St. Mark's Basilica. Its pièce de résistance is the top-floor Artist's Room, whose private terrace is so close to the bronze Moors of the Piazza San Marco's clock tower that you could reach out and help them strike the hour. Be sure your knees are up to the climb, though: The hotel has no elevator. **WHERE:** Calle Larga San Marco, San Marco. Tel 39/041-520-4817; www.hotelaidomori.com. **COST:** low.

EATING & DRINKING

THE CAFÉS OF PIAZZA SAN MARCO—During the cold months, the 18th-century interior of the CAFFÈ FLORIAN (tel 39/041-528-5338) makes this the café of choice in the magnificent Piazza San Marco. But when the warm weather arrives and the tables are moved outdoors and the *orchestrine* are playing their timeless tunes into the moonlit hours, any of the outdoor cafés will do just fine. You might even rebel and set up camp in the less known CAFFÈ CHIOGGIA (tel 39/041-528-5011) around the corner, facing the lacy pink-and-white marble facade of the Doge's Palace. The jazz quartet here is the best, and you can contemplate the flotilla of parked gondolas bobbing in the waters of the fabled lagoon to your right, or watch the Moors strike the hour from atop the clock tower to your left. **WHERE:** Piazza San Marco, San Marco.

CANTINA DO MORI—Pretension-free and brimming with bonhomie, Cantina do Mori is Venice's most beloved *bacaro* (wine bar). Jostle through the crowd of regulars four-deep at the bar, order a glass of the regional red wine for a song, and graze on a variety of *cichetti* (finger foods in the style of Spanish tapas). Professors and well-heeled palazzo owners banter with store clerks and merchants from the nearby fish market in an old-time setting so authentic you'd expect Casanova to tap you on the shoulder. There are countless other neighborhood *bacari* around town: try them all. **WHERE:** Calle due Mori, Castello. Tel 39/041-522-5401.

CLUB DEL DOGE—Tethered by a thread of reality to the magnificent 16th-century Gritti Palace, the hotel's superbly positioned summer terrace restaurant can't be beat for a magical setting on the Grand Canal. Directly across is Venice's solitary Baroque pearl, the Chiesa della Salute (Church of Good Health), its graceful flutes even more beautiful when illuminated at night. If you can't afford the Gritti's sumptuous Venetian-style rooms, save up for a candlelit dinner or sunset *aperitivo* on the open-air terrace, still the place to be, especially if you're a head of state or want to feel (or spend) like one. **WHERE:** Gritti Palace Hotel, Campo Santa Maria del Giglio, San Marco. Tel 39/041-794-611; www.venice-hotel-gritti.com.

DA FIORE—In a city of fine fish restaurants, Da Fiore is generally regarded as the best, with few competitors able to match its all-around excellence or the passion and expertise of its owners, chef Mara Martin and her husband, Maurizio. An accommodating English-speaking wait staff patiently explains the intricacies of an inspired menu that showcases the Adriatic's rare delicacies, all prepared to perfection. **WHERE:** Calle del Scaleter, Campo San Polo, San Polo. Tel 39/041-721-308; www.dafiore.net.

HARRY'S BAR—At the other end of the gamut from Cantina do Mori wine bar is the small, almost nondescript Harry's, which also happens to be perhaps the best-known bar in the world. An international crowd comes to see what all the hoopla is about, most of them ordering the signature Bellini and club sandwiches. You may leave without having understood what drew Hemingway back time and again, or you may add your name to the endless list of veteran regulars, some of whom venture upstairs to the revered restaurant, more known, perhaps, for its cosmic prices than for its classically good, often excellent, menu. **WHERE:** Calle Vallaresso, San Marco. Tel 39/041-528-5777.

THE RIALTO MARKETS—An eye-popping stroll through the lively canalside Rialto Markets will bring you back a few centuries, when these *erberia* (produce) and *pescheria* (fish) markets were some of the largest and most important in the Mediterranean. Galleys unloaded their exotic wares from the far-flung outposts of the Venetian Republic along these same quays, and a babel of tongues hawked a bewildering variety of goods—spices, coffee, silks, ivory. The produce market is slowly giving way to stands selling gondolier hats and Chinese lace masquerading as Burano-made, but the daily seafood market still bustles, with all shapes and sizes of fish, crustacea, and exotic creatures that don't resemble anything you've ever seen before. See it here first before it winds up on your dinner plate tonight. **WHERE:** near the Rialto Bridge, San Polo.

Where All the World's a Mesmerizing Stage

CARNEVALE

Venice, Veneto, Italy

Until the expiring 1,000-year-old Venetian Empire fell to Napoleon in 1797, it seemed that it was holding on solely for the hedonistic annual Carnevale, when the well-heeled came from Europe's courts to partake

Dressed up for one of Carnevale's many costume parties

Countless concerts and events wrestle Venice out of its wintertime hibernation, filling the piazzas, churches, and Byzantine palazzi with masquerading revelers. Off-limits to all but the luckiest invitation holders are the candlelit masked balls hosted by the descendants of the ancient doges and Venice's once powerful noble families. One of the rare exceptions is also one of the city's most sumptuous: book in advance to attend Il Ballo del Doge (the Doge's Ball), held in the privately owned 15th-century frescoed Palazzo Pisani Moretta on the Grand Canal. It's an evening filled with extravagant banquets and strolling minstrels, all in a magical atmosphere illuminated by a thousand candles, re-creating that moment when La Repubblica Serenissima still held sway and life in Venice really was as if a dream.

in unbridled and licentious festivities that went on for weeks, sometimes months. Carnevale in Venice was resuscitated in 1980 and took off as if it had never skipped a beat. Leave the havoc and hedonism to Rio: Carnevale here is a reenactment of that final swan song of the Most Serene Republic, of rich damasks and powdered wigs, cascades of lace, costumes borrowed from the 18th century and reminiscent of the days of Casanova, dandies, and everywhere the characters and masks from Italy's Commedia dell'Arte theater troupe.

WHAT: event. **CARNEVALE:** last 10 days prior to Shrove Tues (the day before Ash Wed). **BALLO DEL DOGE:** held the Sat before Shrove Tues. Tel/1 39/041-523-3857; www.ballodeldoge.com. *Cost:* $1,415 per person, includes dinner, drinks, and the evening's entertainment.

A Floating Oasis a Motor Launch Away

CIPRIANI HOTEL

Venice, Veneto, Italy

Like a private estate or country club in the middle of Venice, the Cipriani Hotel is marvelously removed from the taxing hubbub of tourist-overrun Venice. But the city's magnificent Piazza San Marco is never more than

a sleek motor launch away—one of the best arrivals you're ever bound to make. Set on the tip of the peaceful island of Giudecca, the Cipriani's flower gardens and Olympic-sized pool (both a luxury in land-starved Venice) and silk Fortuny wall coverings in the discreetly gorgeous guest rooms make it a veritable sanctuary with unrivaled levels of service and unabashed comfort. When room

rates aren't an issue, check into the jewel-like annex, the restored 15th-century Palazzo Vendramin or Palazzetto, where the good life gets even better: of the twelve exquisite apartments with personal butlers, the best have heart-stirring views of the canal and the Doge's Palace beyond. The Cipriani's restaurant is one of the city's finest and most sophisticated. Like the lobby itself, it is not grand or overbearing, but there's no mistaking its polished and easy elegance. The "Cip," the hotel's floating pontoon bar, is the city's newest spot to while away an idyllic hour and order a perfect Bellini made from Prosecco and fresh white peach puree available only in season (May through August). Much of the hotel's relaxed perfection is owed in no small measure to its doting and famously charming general manager, Natale Rusconi, regarded with supreme respect in the hotel world.

WHAT: hotel, restaurant. **WHERE:** Giudecca Island. Tel 39/041-520-7744, fax 39/041-520-3930; in the U.S., tel 800-237-1236; info@hotelcipriani.it; www.hotelcipriani.com **COST:** doubles from $1,230, Palazzo Vendramin from $1,105. Dinner at Cip $145. **WHEN:** main building closed Nov to mid-Apr.

The Train of Kings, the King of Trains

VENICE SIMPLON-ORIENT-EXPRESS

Venice, Veneto, Italy

The first Orient-Express pulled out of Paris for Istanbul in 1883 for the 1,700-mile trip across Europe. Suspended in 1977, it is now on a roll again as the Venice Simplon-Orient-Express (VSOE) and still the journey of a lifetime. The legendary original rail cars of inlaid marquetry and polished brass have had their original 19th-century splendor impeccably restored and once again offer the most advanced and luxurious rail travel available, albeit minus the spies, silent film stars, and royalty of yesteryear. Much of the 1920s glamour and mystique of Agatha Christie still lingers, the dining and white-gloved service as faultless as one could hope from the world's most famous train ride, a kind of grand hotel on wheels. The train now offers a network of routes across the continent (connecting Rome, Prague, and Istanbul, for example) but the traditional thirty-two-hour Venice to London trip is still the most commonly booked. And though there are a number of stops and ever-changing scenery along the way, the Orient-Express is about the train itself. As rail travel becomes increasingly about high-velocity records and service that is perfunctory at best, here is the chance to travel back in time to the Golden Age of Rail.

WHAT: experience. **WHERE:** Venice–London and vice versa. A widening selection of other overnight routes (including Florence and Rome in Italy) also available. In the U.S., tel 800-524-2420, fax 630-954-3324; www.orient-express.com. **COST:** Venice–London $2,340 per person, double occupancy, includes all meals plus tea on board (shorter sectors, such as Venice–Paris, can be booked). **WHEN:** mid-Mar–late Nov.

The Venice Simplon-Orient-Express in the Austrian Alps

Home of Romeo, Juliet, and Aïda

VERONA

Veneto, Italy

Suspend all disbelief and immerse yourself in the romance of Verona. Local officials, determined to keep the *Romeo and Juliet* myth alive, have designated a 14th-century palazzo—complete with requisite balcony—as the residence of the Capulets. Millions of the curious and lovelorn come here to breathe the air that Shakespeare's star-crossed lovers once did. The graffiti and love notes left behind are innocent, humorous, and sometimes bittersweet, scribbled in every language. Don't leave the simple courtyard without rubbing the right breast of a nubile bronze Juliet—a peculiar tradition no one can seem to explain.

If it's summertime, join your fellow romantic pilgrims for a night of opera in the impeccably preserved 2,000-year-old Roman amphitheater. The perfect acoustics have survived the millennia, making this one of the most fascinating venues for live (and microphoneless) performances today. Since 1913, when it was first performed to commemorate the 100th anniversary of Verdi's birth, *Aïda* has been the one constant in each year's changing schedule, and tickets to it are the most cherished. José Carreras may seem an inch tall from the highest and cheapest seats in the house (which you'll be lucky to get, as all 20,000 seats regularly sell out), but his voice will be as crystal clear as the cool night air, and the view of the surrounding hills of the Veneto is thrown in at no extra cost. Even the opera-challenged will take home the memory of a lifetime when hundreds of cast members fill the stage during *Aïda*'s Triumphal March. Post-opera, head to the historic Caffè Dante and sit outdoors in Verona's most beautiful square, the Piazza dei Signori.

WHAT: town, site, event. **VERONA:** 71 miles/114 km west of Venice. For information contact iatverona@provincia.vr.it; www.tourism.verona.it; tel 39/045-806-8680. **CASA DI GIULIETTA (JULIET'S HOUSE):** Via Cappello 23. *Cost:* admission. **OPERA PERFORMANCES:** Arena di Verona. *How:* box office located in Via Dietro Anfiteatro 6/B. Tel 39/045-80-05-151; www.arena.it for ordering tickets, schedules, and directions. *Cost:* from $34. *When:* late Jun–early Sept.

Palladio's Masterpiece of Scale, Perspective, and Trompe l'Oeil

TEATRO OLIMPICO

Vicenza, Veneto, Italy

Vicenza is the hometown of Andrea di Pietro della Gondola, or Andrea Palladio, who helped define Western architecture, and of his last and possibly greatest work, the Teatro Olimpico. Begun in 1580, the year of his death, and completed five years later by his student Vicenzo Scamozzi, the Teatro Olimpico was inspired by the theaters of antiquity, with a backdrop representing ancient Thebes. Cunningly designed trompe l'oeil makes the stage appear far deeper than its actual 14 feet. The first theatrical production here took place in 1585, and plays are still performed today. Before arriving at the Teatro Olimpico, a walk along the length of Corso Palladio leaves no doubt that its namesake was the greatest architect of the High Renaissance. He designed two churches in Venice and a number of country villas on the outskirts of Vicenza (his most famous, Villa la Rotonda, is a substantial but enjoyable walk from the city center) and along the Veneto's Brenta Canal. But Vicenza boasts the highest concentration of his urban palazzi and is a magnet for architecture buffs.

WHAT: town, site. **VICENZA:** 46 miles/74 km west of Venice. **TEATRO OLIMPICO:** Piazza Matteotti (at Corso Palladio). *Cost:* admission.

A Precious Piece of History Preserved

ANNE FRANK HOUSE

Amsterdam, Netherlands

With her moving diary translated into more than sixty languages, Anne Frank is one of the world's most beloved teenagers, and her hiding place is one of Amsterdam's most visited sites. As vivid as the world's recollections of her concealment from the Nazis during WW II may be (who hasn't read the book or seen the movie or the play?), a visit to the attic of this modest 1635 canal house is so powerful that it comes as a surprise to many. Amsterdam has long harbored a climate of tolerance, a fact that makes a reflective visit to the shelter all the more poignant.

After two years of living with her parents and the family of an employee of her father in cramped quarters in silence, unable to open a window for a breath of fresh air, the two families were turned in to the police and sent to concentration camps. The fifteen-year-old Anne, together with 100,000 other Amsterdam Jews, never returned. Her father survived and was presented with the diary upon his return; it is on display downstairs as part of a permanent collection. The swinging bookcase that hid the secret door to the attic is still there; so are the black-and-white pictures she clipped from movie magazines and pasted on her wall.

WHAT: site. **WHERE:** Prinsengracht 267, just below Westerkerk. Tel 31/20-556-7100, fax 31/20-620-7999; www.annefrank.nl. **COST:** admission $12.

Prinsengracht 263

Neighborhood Living Rooms and an Art Deco Treasure

CAFÉ SOCIETY

Amsterdam, Netherlands

Amsterdammers are very attached to the old-time concept of *gezelligheid*, which means more to them than just "coziness" or "homeyness." It is what draws locals to the ubiquitous so-called brown cafés *(bruine kroegen)*, a name taken either from their smoke-stained interiors (the result of tobacco or hashish) or, more appetizingly, from the time-burnished wood paneling found in many of them. Amsterdammers come alive here and conversation flows like (or as a result of) the unfailingly great Dutch brews and the popular *jenever*, a smooth but potent Dutch gin, served ice cold but never on the rocks, and often followed with a beer chaser. There are said to be more than 1,000 of these social sanctuaries—including one that supposedly has not closed its doors since it first opened in 1574. Unless you have time to check them all out, simply wander the elegantly funky Jordaan district, or head for the Café 't Smalle, a favored watering hole since it first opened in 1786 as a liquor distillery and "tasting house." Its splendid waterside terrace is a heaven-sent alternative to the murky, smoke-filled interiors of some old-time brown favorites.

If you're looking for old-world glamour, try the decidedly unbrown Café Americain, built as part of a canal-cornered grand hotel in 1880. Mata Hari would still recognize its ornate albeit faded Art Deco interior as the location for her wedding reception. It's a venerable favorite among the local café society, and after a performance at the Stadsschouwburg (Municipal Theater) just next door, it's impossible to get a table. But in the late afternoon a quiet, cozy hour can be enjoyed as the waning daylight illuminates the stained-glass windows.

WHAT: restaurant. **CAFÉ 'T SMALLE:** Egelantiersgracht 12, in the Jordaan district. Tel 31/20-623-9617. *When:* open from late morning until the last customer goes home, usually around 1 A.M. **CAFÉ AMERICAIN AT THE AMERICAN HOTEL:** Leidsekade 97, just off the Leidseplein. Tel 31/20-556-3000. *When:* 7 A.M.–1 A.M.

Classic History and Blooming Beauty by Boat

CANAL CRUISES AND TULIP TIME

Amsterdam and Lisse, Netherlands

Think it's too touristy to see Venice by gondola? Then you probably won't be inclined to experience Amsterdam by boat either, but you'll miss seeing this City of Canals the way it was meant to be seen. The canalside town houses and warehouses built by merchants in the 17th century were high (four or five stories) and narrow (land was at a premium, and property taxes were steep), each distinguished by its fanciful gables, every one of them different. Of the five concentric semicircles of elm-lined canals and the 160 smaller canals connecting them to create a fanlike historic center, Herengracht is lined with the largest and most stately of the canal houses. The "Gentlemen's Canal," it was the most stylish address during Amsterdam's golden age. But the smaller houses on other canals (especially in the Jordaan neighborhood) can be more interesting architecturally. Amsterdam takes pride in its trim brick homes, and has designated a great portion of them as protected landmarks. Many facades are illuminated at night, and so are the city's 1,281 characteristic arched bridges. Add that to the glow of old-fashioned streetlamps reflected in the glimmering canals and a candlelight cruise makes for a romantic evening along the dark waters of time.

In the spring, riverboats and barges take to the canals to view the largest flower spectacle on earth, offering three- to seven-night cruises that sail through and past the country's patchwork, rainbow-colored countryside. Almost all put in at the Keukenhof Gardens, a historic, once-royal park where more than 6 million tulips, daffodils, and hyacinths cover 70 acres. Ten miles of footpaths wind past imaginatively manicured flower beds, fountains, tree-shaded ponds, and large greenhouses that showcase some 500 tulip varieties, among them the pur-

plish "black" tulip. Other cruise stops include the remarkable auction house at Aalsmeer (the world's largest, with 17 million cut flowers on the block daily) and some of the country's major nurseries.

A Bulb Route (Bloemen Route) originating in Amsterdam encourages the independent traveler to "do it yourself" *(doe het zelf)*, whether by bike, train, or car. Those who avoid the spring crowds will also miss the tulips, but for a consolation prize, visit Amsterdam's daily year-round floating Bloemenmarkt (Flower Market) along the Singel Canal. For 200 years, barges have come here laden with cut flowers and potted plants.

WHAT: experience, site, event. **CANAL CRUISES:** Rederij Lovers is one of many companies offering daytime and candlelight cruises. Tel 31/20-530-1090, fax 31/20-530-1099; www.lovers.nl. All cruises leave from the Central Station. *Cost:* from $17 for a simple daytime cruise to $98 for luxurious 5-course dinner cruises, per person. Candlelight cruise without dinner $42. *When:* frequent departures daily. **KEUKENHOF GARDENS:** 20 miles/32 km from Amsterdam in the direction of The Hague. *Cost:* admission. *When:* tulip display from late Mar to late May. **TULIP CRUISES:** Barge Lady, in the U.S., tel 800-880-0071, fax 312-245-0952; www.bargelady.com. *Cost:* 6-night cruise during tulip time, from $6,986 to $8,772 per person, all-inclusive. *When:* Apr–mid-May. *Best times:* mid-Apr to early May. The Queen's Birthday (Koningindag) Apr 30, a national holiday, falls during Tulip Time.

The Oldest Singing Tower

OUDE KERK

Amsterdam, Netherlands

Together with neighboring Belgium, the Netherlands gave the world its largest musical instrument, the carillon, a bronze chorus of multiple bells that grace an untold number of church towers across the Low Countries.

During the so-called 17th-century golden age, as the Dutch empire expanded, Amsterdam became one of the richest cities in the world, and merchants donated large sums to their local churches. Today Amsterdam's churches have more carillons than any other Dutch city (nine in total, of which four give weekly concerts), and the joyful sound of their music cascading down cobblestoned streets and rebounding across the canals and squares makes astonished visitors (and the occasional unjaded Amsterdammer) stop and smile. The

Some of the church's stained glass dates to 1555.

Rolls-Royces of carillons are those cast by the 17th-century French Hemony brothers, whose state-of-the-art technology produced an exceptional sound quality that has never been matched. Amsterdam's oldest church, the Oude Kerk (Old Church), dating from about 1300 (well before the small red-light district that ironically grew up around it), promises the best venue for weekly concerts with a magnificent, restored forty-seven-bell Hemony carillon. The Oude Kerk's delightful location in a linden tree–shaded square means outdoor cafés and ringside seats from which to listen to Amsterdam's oldest "singing tower." The Netherlands is also famous for its organs, and the Old Church proudly owns three of the most sophisticated extant in the country; their summertime concerts are one of the season's greatest pleasures. One 18th-century model is said to be one of the world's finest. If the concerts don't take your breath away, hike up the 230-foot tower for the best view of this unique City of Canals.

WHAT: site. **WHERE:** Oudekerksplein. Tel 31/20-625-8284, fax 31/20-620-0371; info@oudekerk.nl; www.oudekerk.nl. **COST:** admission $7. **WHEN:** carillon concerts Sat 4 P.M., year-round; frequent organ concerts in summer.

Rambling and Romantic, a Poetic Canalside Hotel

PULITZER HOTEL

Amsterdam, Netherlands

L ocated on one of Amsterdam's prettiest canals and cleverly created by internally adjoining more than twenty landmark merchants' homes, the Pulitzer Hotel could only be found in Amsterdam. Four and five stories

high, most of the Pulitzer's narrow, whimsical buildings of diamond-paned windows and gabled roofs are at least 200 years old: some line the Prinsengracht (Princes Canal), then curve around on a small side street before lining the parallel Keizergracht canal, creating

a U-shape that encloses an interior courtyard and garden. The great-grandson of press magnate Joseph Pulitzer rescued the hotel's decaying, canalside merchant homes in 1971, creating an environment whose timeless charm reflects the character of this civilized old-world city, an impression underscored by the hourly bells of nearby Westerkerk, chiming away since 1631.

Half the rooms have extraordinary water views—who needs to stay on a houseboat?—made even more magical at night, when the arched bridges are illuminated by tiny white lights. Rambling and romantic, the hotel offers plenty of private, cozy corners to sit and catch your breath or pass an hour on a late afternoon, as the light that the Dutch landscape painters made famous filters through the leaded windows. Pulitzer's, the new and immediately trendy café/bar/ restaurant, is further reason to be held captive within these welcoming walls.

The Sheraton Hotel Pulitzer brings together twenty-five restored 17th-century canal houses.

WHAT: hotel. **WHERE:** Prinsengracht 315-331. Tel 31/20-523-5235, fax 31/20-627- 6753; in the U.S., 800-325-3535; pulitzer. amsterdam@luxurycollection.com; www. starwoodhotels.com. **COST:** deluxe doubles with canal view $388, with garden view $338.

A Walk on the Wild Side

RED-LIGHT DISTRICT

Amsterdam, Netherlands

What so fascinates visitors to Amsterdam about its red-light district (De Walletjes) that a nocturnal stroll through this medieval heart of downtown ranks on most tourists' agenda up there with the museum shrines to Rembrandt and van Gogh? The world's oldest profession, practiced by the businesswomen (and some men) who give new meaning to the expressions "window dressing" and "window shopping," is here on display, in an architecturally interesting (and only marginally seamy) warren of quaint gabled buildings and narrow canals. Amsterdam has long been known as an "open city" and these denizens of the night are registered, regulated, and taxed, and represented by a union since 1984. The proud Dutch housekeeper's penchant for window display takes a most peculiar twist here. You won't see much going on; it's infre-

quent that you'll even get a beckoning "come hither" look from any of the rose-lit windows and their generally impassive inhabitants. But maybe that's what makes it all the more remarkable, to see these ladies of the night patiently await their next assignation, braiding their hair, doing their nails or the crossword puzzle, reading Dostoyevsky, while showing off their wares to sailors, foreign businessmen, and assorted innocents abroad.

WHAT: site. **WHERE:** behind Dam Square, the area in between Oudezijds Voorburgwal (near the Oude Kerk) and Oudezijds Achterburgwal.

An Ode to Rembrandt and the Dutch Golden Age

RIJKSMUSEUM

Amsterdam, Netherlands

This is the Netherlands' greatest museum and, for lovers of the 17th-century Old Dutch master Rembrandt van Rijn (1606–1669), guardian of the country's finest works. If you want to cut to the chase through more than 150 rooms full of beauties, head for Rembrandt's magnificent *The Night Watch* (1642) on the upper floor (Room 224). The enormous king-size canvas is the artist's best-

Vermeer's The Kitchen Maid

known painting, one of the world's most famous, and has a grand hall all to itself. It is the pivotal point around which this turreted neo-Gothic museum was designed in 1885 by P. J. H. Cuypers. It houses the largest and finest collection of Dutch paintings anywhere in the world. Adjoining rooms showcase Rembrandt's sensitive *Jewish Bride* (1662) and *Self-Portrait as the Apostle Paul*

(1661); there are twenty-one of his works in all. Other rooms on the top floor are no less impressive, with works by Jan Vermeer, Frans Hals, and Jacob van Ruisdale, among many others.

Dating from a decree in 1808 by Louis Bonaparte, brother of Napoleon, the astonishing collection of the 17th-century Dutch golden age has long been the uncontested drawing card of "The Rijks." But it is strong in other areas as well—it has an impressive collection of delftware, and its extensive Asian art collection (with some 100 Buddhas from all over the East) gets the attention it merits thanks to a 1996 face-lift of the South Wing.

WHAT: site. **WHERE:** Stadhouderskade 42. Tel 31/20-674-7000, fax 31/20-674-7001; info@rijksmuseum.nl; www.rijksmuseum.nl. **COST:** admission $16. **NOTE:** Museum under renovation until 2009; portions may be closed.

Shrine to a 19th-Century Native Son

VAN GOGH MUSEUM

Amsterdam, Netherlands

A major refurbishment of the main building of the van Gogh Museum and a dramatic new annex designed by Japanese architect Kisho Kurokawa unveiled in June 1999 confirmed the Netherlands'—and the world's— steadfast Vincent worship. Vincent van Gogh (1853–1890) was the 19th century's most important Dutch artist, and what an outstanding home his 200 paintings, 500 drawings, and 700 letters now have. Visitors and architects call the new annex, clad in gray stone and titanium steel, both striking and welcoming. In the light-filled space of the annex's fusion of Japanese and European sensibilities, all of van Gogh's paintings in the collection can now be displayed for the first time, from his earliest work, done in 1881 in the Netherlands, to those done just days before his suicide in France at the age of thirty-seven. "I should like to do portraits which will appear as revelations to people in a hundred years' time," the prolific artist wrote to his sister Wil just before his death.

You may agree with some of the Amsterdammers who find the architecture jarring, but after you've seen the vibrant colors and dazzling landscapes of this visionary genius, all you'll remember is the art. You may not have known their names, but you'll recognize the images: *The Potato Eaters, Sunflowers,* and *Wheatfield with Crows.* Van Gogh's anguished life is easily detectable, its abrupt end readily foreseeable in some of his more turbulent paintings. Works by dozens of artists who influenced him, or whom van Gogh influenced in turn, are also on display.

Detail of Self-Portrait with Felt Hat, *1887*

WHAT: site. **WHERE:** Paulus Potterstraat 7. Tel 31/20-570-5200; info@vangoghmuseum.nl; www.vangoghmuseum.nl. **COST:** admission.

At the Heart of a Nature Reserve, a Magnificent Obsession

KRÖLLER-MÜLLER MUSEUM

Otterlo, Netherlands

J ump on one of the free white bicycles left about for public use, and make your way to the center of the vast De Hoge Veluwe nature and game reserve, Holland's largest national park, to see the remarkable art collection housed

in the Kröller-Müller Museum. Both park and art collection were left to the Dutch state in 1938 by industrialist Anton Kröller (the

13,000 acres of woodland served as his private hunting grounds), whose wife, Helene, spent her life and fortune amassing 278 works by Vincent van Gogh. These are the highlights of the museum's display but by no means all there is to see. Together with the collection in Amsterdam's newly refurbished van Gogh Museum, this constitutes nearly the entire oeuvre of the 19th-century Dutch artist, including one of the *Sunflowers, The Bridge at Arles,* and *L'Arlesienne.* Kröller-Müller went on to collect work by other major artists, predominantly of the 19th and 20th centuries: Courbet, Seurat, Picasso,

Vincent van Gogh's Still Life with Four Sunflowers, *1887*

and Mondrian, to name a few. Surrounding the museum is one of Europe's largest outdoor sculpture gardens, 47 acres studded with works by 20th-century sculptors such as Henry Moore, Richard Serra, and Claes Oldenburg.

If there are enough hours in the day, trade your white bike in for your car and drive to visit Het Loo near Apeldoorn. The recently restored royal palace and gardens were built in the late 17th century by the prince and princess of Orange, who would thereafter go on to take over the throne of England as William and Mary. A small-scale Versailles, the palace houses a recently organized museum celebrating the history of the House of Orange, but the formal Baroque gardens are the jewel in this royal crown.

WHAT: site. **KRÖLLER-MÜLLER MUSEUM:** at the center of De Hoge Veluwe National Park (Otterlo is 50 miles/80 km southeast of Amsterdam). Tel 31/31-859-1241, fax 31/31-859-1515; info@kmm.nl; www.kmm.nl. *Cost:* admission to park $10, admission to museum $10. *When:* park open daily; museum open Tues–Sun. **HET LOO:** 14 mile/22 km northeast of Otterlo. Tel 31/555-772-400; www.paleishetloo.nl. *Cost:* admission. *When:* Tues–Sun.

Home of the Royal House of Orange

DELFT

Netherlands

Step into this 17th-century Dutch town whose quaint tree-lined canals and graceful humpbacked bridges were captured so perfectly in the canvases of Jan Vermeer and Pieter de Hoogh. Perhaps more so than in any other city in the country, the 16th and 17th centuries are preserved in this town whose name is known worldwide for its characteristic blue-and-white china. Still made and hand-painted here and widely available, delftware's timeless patterns and color scheme have survived the passage of centuries and collectors' trends. When the sea of day-trippers heads back to Amsterdam or The Hague, the town returns to the townspeople and the serenity that so inspired Vermeer settles back in. Located on the attractive market square is the 14th-century Gothic Nieuwe Kerk (New Church), where William I, the Silent (1533–1584), founder of the royal House of Orange and a kind of Dutch George Washington, lies in a magnificent marble and alabaster mausoleum surrounded by twenty-two columns; most monarchs since him have been brought here for burial as well. A marvelous panoramic view from the church tower provides

Float down the Oude Delft canal on your way to the market square.

a glimpse of The Hague on a clear day. The nearby "Old Church," founded around 1200, is the resting place of Vermeer. A stroll along the tree-lined Oude Delft, possibly the first city canal (and certainly the prettiest) anywhere in the Netherlands, brings you to the town's most famous site: the Prinsenhof, a former 15th-century convent-turned-royal residence where William lived and was assassinated in 1584 (the bullet hole is still visible). Today it houses a museum dedicated to the history of the Dutch Republic. In the former storerooms of the Prinsenhof, with an entrance from a small alleyway off the Oude Delft canal, is a quiet and sedate little restaurant, De Prinsenkelder, promising the end to a perfect day in the town that so understandably inspired some of Holland's greatest artists.

WHAT: town, restaurant. **DELFT:** 9 miles/ 14 km southeast of The Hague, 45 miles/ 71 km from Amsterdam. **DE PRINSENKELDER RESTAURANT:** Schoolstraat 11. Tel 31/15-212-1860, fax 31/15-213-3313; www.deprinsenkelder.nl. *Cost:* dinner $40. **BEST TIMES:** market day is Thurs in central square. Flower market along canals Thurs; flea market along canals on Sat, May–Sept.

A Small Feast of a Collection from the Golden Age

HET MAURITSHUIS

The Hague, Netherlands

Vermeer's famous *View of Delft* moved the French writer Marcel Proust to call it the most beautiful painting in the world. Together with other gems such as Rembrandt's graphical *Anatomy Lesson of Dr. Nicolaes Tulp*

(the first canvas to bring him recognition), it forms the core of a small but splendid collection from the great 17th-century Dutch masters. Long acknowledged as one of the world's finest small museums, the Mauritshuis occupies the beautiful, Palladian-inspired mansion of Maurits van Nassau-Siegen, 17th-century Dutch governor-general of Brazil. Inside, it's almost like viewing a private collection, while outside a small, tree-shaded pond is crisscrossed by resident swans. Tour groups are uncommon, and most art lovers linger on the upper floor, where other works by Vermeer (including his celebrated *Girl with a Pearl Earring*), Rembrandt, and Jan Steen can be found.

As the seat of government for the Netherlands, home to Queen Beatrix and the International Court of Justice, The Hague is a powerful and dignified city. Some of its regal past can easily be recaptured at high tea in the magnificent lounge of the city's historical Hotel des Indes, built in 1856 for the private adviser to King William III. Formerly a lavish baronial town house, it was here that Mata Hari practiced her subtle subterfuge while the hotel was used as Allied headquarters during the dark days of WW I.

WHAT: site, hotel, restaurant. **WHERE:** The Hague is 31 miles/50 km southwest of Amsterdam. **HET MAURITSHUIS:** Korte Vijverberg 8. Tel 31/70-302-3456, fax 31/ 70-365-3819; www.mauritshuis.nl. *Cost:* admission $17. **WHEN:** open Tues–Sun. **HOTEL DES INDES:** Lange Voorhout 54–56. Tel 31/70-361-2345, fax 31/70-361-2350; www.hoteldesindesthehague.com. *Cost:* doubles from $250. High tea $50.

The Very Embodiment of Country-Inn Gezellig

MANOIR INTER SCALDES

Kruiningen, Netherlands

Inter Scaldes is its own destination. People find their way from all parts to the dramatic thatched-roof farmhouse cum inn-restaurant and English-style garden created by a local husband-and-wife team. They come for the oysters

and mussels, some of Europe's tastiest, and for conversation-stopping preparations of lobster and langoustine. The showcase lamb is raised down the road, grazing on seaside pastures beyond the dikes. Travelers to Amsterdam who leave the Netherlands without experiencing a foray into the Low Country for a glimpse of the polder farms reclaimed from wetlands, and countless lakes, connected islands, and estu-

aries and for a taste of culinary offerings from the North Sea are missing out on a veritable Dutch treat.

WHAT: restaurant, hotel. **WHERE:** Zandweg 2 (Kruiningen is 69 miles/110 km from The Hague). Tel 31/11-338-1753; info@ interscaldes.nl; www.interscaldes.eu. **COST:** doubles from $275. 4-course dinner $120. **WHEN:** dinner Wed–Sun.

Holland's Mecca for the Good Life

EUROPEAN FINE ART FAIR

Maastricht, Netherlands

The museum-quality offerings of the most prestigious art market on the international calendar make their much-awaited appearance at Maastricht's annual European Fine Art Fair (TEFAF). Poor Maastricht barely has time

to catch its breath after its late-winter Carnival celebration (one of the most famous in Europe) with parades of elaborate floats, parties, and fancy dress, when more than 150 art and antiques dealers from a dozen countries arrive to show thousands of paintings and works of art to art lovers, collectors, and curators. Major museums from around the world are regularly represented among the expert buyers at the fair, assured by the crackerjack team of international experts who examine all objects for authenticity, quality, and condi-

tion. The ancient Roman town of Maastricht is the perfect host city because of its charm, sophistication, high-end shopping, dining, and newfound bon vivant ambience. Here at Holland's southernmost point, wedged in between Belgium and Germany, languages, customs, and trends flow freely across borders. Worldly Maastricht and its lively cafés and restaurants brim with high-rolling fairgoers who come to town every March to pick up an extra Rembrandt etching or add to their collection of Gobelin tapestries.

Ideally located in the traffic-free historical center on the city's most beautiful tree-shaded square is the Hotel Derlon. Not only is this hotel of choice the next-door neighbor to the beloved Onze Lieve Vrouwebasiliek (or Basilica of Our Lady, a great pilgrimage church even today), but it boasts the ruins of a Roman forum in its cellar.

Alternatively, stay outside the city at one of Holland's most luxurious country hotels, Château St. Gerlach, located in the southeastern hill-and-dale region of Limburg, in the lovely Geuldal River Valley. Local hotelier and restaurateur Camille Oostwegel took on a herculean restoration project with this 1,000-acre estate. The exceptional 97-room château has been reborn with handloomed Venetian fabrics and opulent silks; Provençal, Spanish, and Italian antiques; a contemporary glass winter garden; and restored Baroque Austrian frescoes in the estate's church that are among the country's most important. Surrounded by Baroque gardens that blend into a natural preserve grazed by Scottish Highland cattle and Koniks horses, the quiet beauty of the setting may make the trip into nearby Maastricht less of a temptation.

WHAT: town, event, hotel. **MAASTRICHT:** 130 miles/207 km southeast of Amsterdam. **TEFAF:** tel 31/411-645-090, fax 31/411-645-091; www.tefaf.com. *Cost:* $80. *When:* 1 week mid-Mar. **HOTEL DERLON:** Onze Lieve Vrouweplein 6. Tel 31/43-321-6770, fax 31/43-325-1933; info@derlon.com; www.derlon.com. **CHÂTEAU ST. GERLACH:** 1 Joseph Corneli Allée, Valkenburg (8 miles/13 km east of Maastricht). Tel 31/43-608-8888, fax 31/43-604-2883; info@stgerlach.com; www.stgerlach.com. *Cost:* doubles from $395. **BEST TIMES:** the Preuvenement, a prominent 4-day food fair, takes place mid–late Aug.

Part of the St. Gerlach estate

A Veritable Jazz Woodstock

NORTH SEA JAZZ FESTIVAL

Rotterdam, Netherlands

The wow-power of the prestigious sixteen-day Montreux Jazz Festival in Switzerland is condensed here into a three-day weekend whose smorgasbord of thirteen round-the-clock concert venues and a legion of world-class artists packs the same punch. For more than twenty-five years, the North Sea Jazz Festival has been the largest annual gathering of jazz in Europe, spanning the spectrum of blues, fusion, gospel, and soul. Legendary names and nascent talents from around the globe perform side by side: the first year the festival featured jazz legends like Sarah Vaughan and Count Basie. It has since introduced such new talent to European audiences as a young Shirley Horn. In 2006, the festival moved from its longtime home in The Hague to Ahoy' Rotterdam. Despite the change in venue, the festival still promises jazz lovers the same rich experience it always has.

WHAT: event. **NORTH SEA JAZZ FESTIVAL:** info@northseajazz.com; www.northseajazz. com. *Cost:* Full festival ticket $475; 1-day ticket $105. For travel packages from the U.S., contact Ciao! Travel, tel 800-942-CIAO or 619-297-8112; jazz@ciaotravel.com; www. ciaotravel.com. *Cost:* from $1,249 per person, double occupancy for 3-night package, land only. **WHEN:** annually, 2d full weekend in Jul.

Queen—or King—for a Day

POUSADA RAINHA SANTA ISABEL

Estremoz, Alentejo, Portugal

O f the forty-six government-owned *pousadas* (inns) scattered throughout the Portuguese countryside, the Rainha Santa Isabel, luxuriously housed in a historically significant edifice, is one of the most highly rated.

Sensitively integrated into this hill town's 13th-century Estremoz castle (largely rebuilt in the 18th century, following a fire), the *pousada* was originally the home of King Dinis and his wife, the sainted Queen Isabel. Vasco da Gama came here in 1498 to accept gifts from King Manuel I for the ruler of Calcutta before sailing for India. The views that entranced Portuguese royalty remain, and visitors will find museum-quality antiques and tapestries and grandiose public areas with 22-foot ceilings, monumental staircases, wide marble corridors, and massive furniture. The banquet hall is cavernous, warmed up by an attentive staff and the promise of an excellent meal of regional specialties, accompanied by offerings from the *pousada*'s well-known wine cellar. Rugs from nearby Arraiolos and canopied four-poster beds lavishly decorate the thirty guest rooms. The room where Saint Isabel died in 1336 escaped the fire and is now a small chapel open to the public.

WHAT: hotel, town. **ESTREMOZ:** 90 miles/ 145 km east of Lisbon. **POUSADA RAINHA SANTA ISABEL:** Largo Dom Dinis. Tel 351/ 268-332-075; in the U.S. and Canada, tel 800-223-1356; recepcao.staisabel@pousadas.pt; www.pousadasofportugal.com.. *Cost:* doubles $215 (low season), $355 (high season). **BEST TIMES:** Sat for the market, where you can pick up Estremoz's famous earthenware pottery.

An Open-Air Museum of Portuguese Architecture

ÉVORA

Alentejo, Portugal

E ach age has left its trace on Évora. Today it is protected as a national treasure. A panoply of mansions and palaces whose architecture ranges from medieval to the local Gothic-to-Renaissance transitional style

The Pousada dos Lóios seen through the columns of a Roman temple

called Manueline to the Renaissance, Évora is especially evocative when floodlit at night. Although it has been compared to Florence and Seville, the town is wonderfully Portuguese, with Moorish overtones in its pierced balconies, attractive whitewashed homes, and cool tiled patios. When the Moors were ousted in the 12th century after 450 fruitful years in residence, Évora became a favored destination of the kings of Portugal and flourished as a center of learning and the arts in the 15th and 16th centuries, after which it lapsed into obscurity. The core of the Old City within the medieval walls contains most of the places of interest, including the Gothic cathedral and the 16th-century Church of dos Lóios, dedicated to São João and famous for its *azulejos*, the traditional hand-painted blue-and-white tiles of Portugal. Adjacent to the church, and next to the ruins of a 2nd-century Roman temple dedicated to Diana, is a former 15th-century baronial mansion (later the Convent of dos Lóios) that is now the Pousada dos Lóios. Following in the footsteps of the monks who offered hospitality to many a passing monarch, it is now one of Portugal's more luxurious state-owned inns. The former refectory serves as the dining room, but hope for pleasant weather, when meals can be enjoyed in the vaulted cloister.

WHAT: town, hotel. **ÉVORA:** 86 miles/138 km southeast of Lisbon. **POUSADA DOS LÓIOS:** Largo Conde de Vila Flor. Tel 351/266-730-070; recepcao.loios@pousadas.pt; www.pousadasofportugal.com. In the U.S. and Canada, tel 800-223-1356. *Cost:* doubles $215 (low season), $355 (high season). **BEST TIMES:** most festive last 10 days of Jun, during the Feira de São João, dedicated to St. John the Evangelist.

A Medieval Castle and Cozy Inn That Looks Down on Eagles

MARVÃO

Alentejo, Portugal

Three thousand feet below the hilltop town of Marvão spreads the Alentejo heartland of Portugal. Huddled within fortified 13th-century ramparts, Marvão is one of the country's most charming castle towns, with a population of just 300. It is intimate enough for you to quickly absorb its strong medieval character and small-town quaintness.

Check into the cozy Pousada de Santa Maria. It doesn't pretend to have the landmark grandeur or imposing facade of other *pousadas*, and that is much of its charm. It has been converted from adjoining 18th-century village houses, with red-tile floors, beamed ceilings, and stone fireplaces decorated with *azulejo* tiles.

Spectacular views from the restaurant over the distant mountains to Spain, nearly 4 miles away, explain why Marvão was such a vital piece in the military chess game played out over the centuries between Spain and

Portugal. This enchanting castle-inn is a good place to be alone with your thoughts and "look down on the eagles," as one Portuguese poet put it.

WHAT: town, hotel. **MARVÃO:** 140 miles/ 224 km northeast of Lisbon. **POUSADA DE** **SANTA MARIA:** Rua 24 de Janeiro 7. Tel 351/245-993-201; in the U.S., tel 800-223-1356; recepcao.stamaria@pousadas.pt; www.pousadasofportugal.com. *Cost:* doubles $170 (low season), $280 (high season). **BEST TIMES:** Apr–May and Sept–Oct.

A Sylvan Setting for a Pleasure Palace Turned Hotel

BUSSACO FOREST

Coimbra, Beiras, Portugal

The secluded Bussaco Forest (Floresta do Bussaco) isn't really a forest, but an enormous walled arboretum carefully tended by local monks for centuries. As the Portuguese empire grew, exotic trees were brought from all corners of the globe, and eventually the monks achieved a botanical splendor of such renown that a 17th-century papal bull threatened excommunication to anyone who tampered with the trees. Not long after religious orders were supressed in 1834, King Carlos I commissioned an Italian theater set designer to create a summer pleasure palace—the last summer residence built by the Portuguese monarchy—in the midst of the 250-acre forest. The result is an extravagant pastiche bristling with pinnacles, turrets, and arched windows. Inside, the fantasy continues with stained-glass windows, hand-painted murals and tiles, suits of armor, and views that once seduced royalty. It was the Portuguese monarch's last hurrah: it was completed in 1907 and King Carlos was assassinated in 1908. His son used the palace before fleeing to England and a life of exile after his 1910 abdication. The palace's latest incarnation is as the Palace Hotel do Bussaco, one of Europe's most special hotels, a turn-of-the-century jewel of romance and royal luxury.

WHAT: site, hotel. **BUSSACO FOREST:** 137 miles/220 km north of Lisbon, 69 miles/111 km from Porto. **PALACE HOTEL DO BUSSACO:** Mata do Bussaco. Tel 351/231-937-970, fax 351/231-930-509; bussaco@almeidahotels.com; www.jpmoser.com/palacedobussaco.html. *Cost:* doubles from $95 (low season), $240 (high season). **BEST TIMES:** May–Sept.

The Town That Belonged to the Queens of Portugal

ÓBIDOS

Estremadura, Portugal

Wrapped in a Moorish wall, the tiny whitewashed village of Óbidos was deemed so lovely that it became a queen's dowry. In 1282 King Dinis presented Queen Isabel with the fief as a wedding present, and for the next 600 years, every Portuguese monarch would do the same, perpetuating its name, Casa das Rainhas, the House of Queens. Óbidos is a museum of a town, a national monument so picturesque it can convince any visitor—and they are legion—that he or she can be a great photographer. The town features ramparts built by the Moors as crenellated battlements, which are almost ⅗ of a mile in circumference, and a stroll along the wide walkway at the top provides spectacular views of Óbidos and the countryside beyond. The imposing 15th-century castle was built as a fortress, and converted into a royal palace in the 16th century. Now one wing has been transformed into a nine-room *pousada*, and you can be a knight for a night in one of Portugal's most atmospheric hotels. The baronial hall is filled with suits of armor, and one can imagine the visiting queens of the past and their royal retinues. The restaurant serves food

The Pousada do Castelo

for a more plebeian palate, but you can feast on the views alone, and best of all, overnight guests have the town to themselves before the tour buses arrive and after they depart.

WHAT: town, hotel. **ÓBIDOS:** 50 miles/80 km north of Lisbon (close enough to guarantee tour bus caravans). **POUSADA DO CASTELO:** tel 351/262-955-080, fax 351/262-959-148; in the U.S. and Canada, tel 800-223-1356; recepcao.castelo@pousadas.pt; www.pousadasofportugal.com. *Cost:* doubles $215 (low season), $355 (high season). **BEST TIMES:** May–Jun and Sept–Oct.

A Billionaire's Art Collection in Its Own Museum

MUSEUM CALOUSTE GULBENKIAN

Lisbon, Portugal

When Calouste Gulbenkian, an unashamedly rich Armenian oil tycoon, died in 1955, he bequeathed one of the world's greatest private art collections to Portugal, which had been his home since WW II. Art

One of Calouste Gulbenkian's Lalique pieces

Nouveau jewelry and objets by Gulbenkian's friend René Lalique are some of the highlights of this remarkable collection of more than 6,000 pieces amassed during fifty years of astute and passionate collecting. Many of these spectacular works were purchased from the Hermitage in St. Petersburg in the 1920s, when the Soviet Union needed hard currency. The collection spans the period from 2700 B.C Egypt to the early 20th century and represents Gulbenkian's wide interests and deep pockets. Star works by Ghirlandaio,

Rembrandt, Renoir, and Manet are displayed cheek by jowl with countless exquisite objects that captivated this connoisseur's eye—including illuminated medieval manuscripts, ancient Greek coins, and Middle Eastern carpets.

WHAT: site. **WHERE:** Avenida de Berna 45A. Tel 351/21-782-3000, fax 351/21-782-3032; museu@gulbenkian.pt; www.museu.gulbenkian.pt. **COST:** admission $6; free Sun. **WHEN:** open Tues–Sun. **BEST TIMES:** Apr, Sept, and Oct.

Summer Resort of Portuguese Royalty

SINTRA

Lisbon, Portugal

Lord Byron had already seen his fair share of the Continent when he wrote to his mother from Sintra, calling it "perhaps the most delightful [village] in Europe." Today the same cool, gentle climate and garden setting that made this a favorite summer residence for the Portuguese kings for more than 500 years provides city dwellers and tourists an idyllic respite from the heat and hustle of Lisbon. Commanding the highest peak are the dramatic 8th-century ruins of a Moorish citadel, the Castelo dos Mouros, with a heavenly view to the sea.

Stay in a castle of your own at the Palacio de Seteais, a dreamy 18th-century palace built by the Dutch consul to Portugal that looks down across vineyards and orange groves to the sea mist. Common areas and some of the older guest rooms are graced with antiques; gold leaf and crystal chandeliers anchor ballroom-high ceilings. The name *Seteais* refers to the seven sighs said to have been the reaction to a peace treaty signed here during the Napoleonic wars—a reaction shared by many guests today, enthralled by the palace's spell.

WHAT: town, hotel. **SINTRA:** 18 miles/ 29 km northwest of Lisbon. **HOTEL PALACIO DE SETEAIS:** 8 Rua Barbosa do Bocage. Tel 351/21-923-3200, fax 351/21-923-4277; reservas.hps@tivolihotels.com; www.tivolihotels.com. *Cost:* doubles from $395. **BEST TIMES:** Apr–May and Aug–Sept.

Pearl of the Atlantic

MADEIRA

Portugal

With a subtropical climate warmed by the Gulf Stream, this volcanic outcrop off the coast of Africa is Portugal's own floating garden. The early 15th-century discovery of Madeira by Prince Henry the Navigator launched Portugal's golden age. It was "discovered" again by the vacationing winter-weary British in the 19th century. Anglo loyalty became almost legendary, so taken were the British by the lush, vertical landscapes; the wild terrain terraced and farmed by gentle people; the dark, sweet wine—and "days of perpetual June."

Dramatic peaks and a crisscross network of signposted walking paths encourage forays into the verdant countryside. A longtime favorite hike follows the old *levadas*—a manmade web of irrigation channels that carried water from the mountaintops down through the farms to the fields and villages below. The 36- by 14-mile island (70 percent is national park) packs more into its chaotic terrain than most areas five times its size. A corkscrew drive into the dramatic interior up and over its razorback spine, the Serra de Agua, is a white-knuckle thriller, with rewarding views of Pico Ruivo—at 6,109 feet, Madeira's highest mountain.

The distinguished Reid's Palace is the undisputed queen of Funchal, Madeira's capital, created to accommodate every visiting aristocrat's need since opening in 1891. High on a promontory that commands a sweeping panorama of the harbor city and the craggy, verdant mountains beyond, Reid's is enveloped in acre upon flowering acre of tended gardens, a fragrant riot of flowers, palms, and birds of paradise. Winston Churchill, George Bernard Shaw, and countless other dignitaries and celebrities have made this turn-of-the-century hotel the roosting spot of choice. The hotel's Les Faunes restaurant is considered the best on

A dragon tree at Reid's Palace

the island, and late-afternoon high tea—like most things at this Mediterranean villa—is something of an island institution.

WHAT: island, hotel. **MADEIRA:** 400 miles/644 km south of Lisbon, 300 miles/483 km west of Casablanca, Morocco. **REID'S PALACE:** Estrada Monumental 139, Funchal. Tel 351/291-71-71-71, fax 351/291-71-71-77; reservations@reidspalace.com; www.reidspalace..com. *Cost:* doubles from $545 (low season), from $705 (high season). Dinner at Les Faunes $100; afternoon tea $40. *When:* Les Faunes is closed Jun–Sept. **BEST TIMES:** grape harvest at its peak in mid-Sept, when the 3-day Festa do Vinho Madeira (Madeira Wine Festival) takes place.

Home Base for Andalusia's Pueblos Blancos

ARCOS DE LA FRONTERA

Andalusia, Spain

The views from the cliff-hanging terrace in the historic center of this old Arab town may be some of the most riveting in Spain. Dramatically perched on a crag crowned by a Moorish castle and overlooking the

gorge of the Guadalete River that surrounds it on three sides, Arcos was built in the form of a natural amphitheater. Its winding streets—some no more than a few feet wide, some disappearing into steps—evoke its Arabian past. The monumental view that moved Charles de Gaulle to write his memoirs while staying at the spectacularly sited Parador de Arcos de la Frontera—the 18th-century palace and seat of the king's magistrate—may make you stay put as well. But then you'd miss excursions to the dozen or so whitewashed villages along the Ruta de los Pueblos Blancos, a popular scenic drive. Also famed for its spectacular position and views is Ronda, the picturesque home of bullfighting and a favorite haunt of Hemingway. As a bullfighting aficionado, he was drawn to Ronda's bullring, built in 1784—the oldest and one of the most beautiful in Spain.

WHAT: town, hotel. **ARCOS DE LA FRONTERA:** 19 miles/31 km east of Jerez. Ronda is 43 miles/68 km east of Arcos, on the Ruta de los Pueblos Blancos. **PARADOR DE ARCOS DE LA FRONTERA:** Plaza del Cabildo. Tel 34/956-700500, fax 34/956-701116; arcos@parador.es; www.parador.es. **COST:** doubles in the historic wing from $130. **BEST TIMES:** Apr–Jun and Sept–Oct.

Iberia's Greatest Mosque

LA MEZQUITA

Córdoba, Andalusia, Spain

The Mezquita's 900 columns create a forest of onyx, jasper, marble, and granite, topped by horseshoe arches of candy-striped red-and-white marble. Add decorative mosaics and plasterwork, and you have one of Europe's most breathtaking examples of Spanish Muslim architecture. The Mezquita was constructed as a mosque by a succession of emirs between the 8th and 10th centuries, when Córdoba was the seat of the Western Caliphate and Europe's largest city. Later it was partially destroyed and, in 1236, rebuilt

The Mezquita's columns and arches

as a cathedral. In its day, La Mezquita was the crowning Muslim architectural achievement in the West, rivaled only by the mosque in Mecca. The cathedral that sits awkwardly in its center today pales by comparison, although its 18th-century Baroque mahogany choir stalls are some of Europe's most elaborate. Even the Holy Roman Emperor Charles V regretted having destroyed something "unique" to make way for something "commonplace." The Moorish minaret-turned-church-spire provides a fine view of the ancient Arab and Jewish quarters below, and a short respite in the Courtyard of the Orange Trees is as fragrant and refreshing as when it was first enjoyed by the caliphs.

WHAT: site. **WHERE:** Calle Cardenal Herrero (Córdoba is 260 miles/418 km southwest of Madrid). Tel 34/958-225226; info@mezquitadecordoba.org; www.mezquita decordoba.org. **COST:** admission $11.

THE ALHAMBRA AND PARADOR DE GRANADA

Granada, Andalusia, Spain

"Nothing in life could be more cruel than to be blind in Granada," reads an inscription within the walls of the Alhambra, the greatest expression of Spanish Muslim art and architecture. With sections that date back to the 9th century (begun by the Caliphate), the wonder you see today was created mainly under the reigns of Yussuf I (1333–1353) and Mohammed V (1353–1391). Although austere and unassuming on the outside, nearly every surface inside is covered with fantastically ornate geometric and flowing arabesque patterns.

For almost 250 years the "Red Fortress" served the Moorish rulers of Granada as palace, harem, residence for court officials, and, once, as a garrison for 40,000 soldiers. With the

The Parador de Granada mixes Christian and Arabic styles.

Christians' ultimate victory in 1492, the last Moorish ruler, Boabdil, and his entourage left Spain forever, and the Catholic monarchs moved into the Alhambra. It is in the great Hall of Ambassadors that Ferdinand and Isabella supposedly met with Columbus in 1492 before his first voyage. Here, as everywhere, is the soothing murmur of water, coming from the tiled pools, fountains, and channels that are an integral part of the architecture. The dramatic use of exquisite webs and lacy filigree is showcased in the Hall of the Two Sisters, whose intricately honeycombed ceiling somehow escapes gaudiness, managing to be simply beautiful.

The most famous and perhaps the most beautiful of Spain's eighty-some government-run inns, the Parador de Granada enables guests to sleep within the enchanted walls of the Alhambra. Itself a former Moorish palace converted into a Franciscan convent by the newly arrived Catholic monarchs in 1492, the parador offers privileged views of the Alhambra gardens and Nasrid palaces, the ancient Moorish Albaicín quarter and the countryside beyond. A better location can hardly be imagined, and a long waiting list attests to its popularity. The rooms in the richly appointed original building are filled with antiques and character, plus the opportunity to meander about the Alhambra patios and magnificent gardens after closing hours. More ordinary and less-expensive rooms are available in the new wing, For those who didn't book far enough in advance, an outdoor lunch might suffice: the parador's terrace offers romantic views of the Alhambra's rose gardens while you dine on regional Andalusian specialties.

If you visit in early summer, you can enjoy Granada's annual seventeen-day International Music and Dance Festival, which begins in late June and features everything from classical music to bewitching flamenco.

WHAT: site, hotel, event. **ALHAMBRA:** Granada is 160 miles/256 km east of Seville. *Cost:* admission. **PARADOR DE GRANADA:** Real de la Alhambra. Tel 34/958-221440, fax 34/958-222264; granada@parador.es; www.parador.es. *Cost:* doubles in the historic wing, from $440. Lunch or dinner $45. **INTERNATIONAL MUSIC AND DANCE FESTIVAL:** contact Festival Internacional de Musica y Danza de Granada, tel 34/958-221-844, fax34/958-220-691; info@ granadafestival.org; www.granadafestival.org. *Cost:* tickets $3–$40. *When:* late Jun. **BEST TIMES:** Apr–Jun and Sept–Oct.

In the City of Carmen

SEVILLE

Andalusia, Spain

Seville is lovely at any time of the year, but it is worth rearranging your entire itinerary and booking far in advance to be there in spring. Semana Santa (Holy Week) is celebrated throughout the Mediterranean and Christian world, but nowhere as it is in Seville. Each evening of the week before Easter, members of the city's sixty *cofradías* (brotherhoods), many of them hooded, barefoot, and dragging chains, slowly parade through the darkened streets. There are candlelit processions of elaborate gilt and bejeweled floats bearing the image of Mary or Christ. Haunting, deeply devotional songs give way, two weeks later, to the throbbing beat of the flamenco dancing and music that swirls around the flamboyant round-the-clock revels of Feria de Abril, a one-week hiatus from the worries of the real world. Women dressed in multicolored flounced flamenco gowns ride horseback behind their *caballeros*, who wear the elegant, short-jacketed suits and broad-rimmed hats of the region.

Try to stay in the Alfonso XIII, perhaps the most exotic hotel in Spain, evoking Moorish opulence of old. Built to accommodate visiting royalty during Seville's 1929 World's Fair, it took its inspiration from the local *mudejar* architecture and decorative arts to create an

A float in the Easter procession of the Semana Santa

exuberant Spanish palace around a central patio that would fool even a skeptical caliph. Panels of Moorish *azulejo* tilework, cool marble floors, and inlaid columns and archways offer an oasis from the heat and the traffic of its central location between the Alcazar and the cathedral, the city's must-see landmarks. Check out the Alfonso's lobby and courtyard where *toda* Sevilla goes for tapas or an evening sherry-sipping rendezvous at the piano bar.

Tapas are believed to have originated in Seville, and the unpretentious, no-frills, deliciously authentic tradition of tapas grazing remains strong here. The idea is to always stay a little bit hungry, and to eat your way around town at the city's myriad neighborhood bars. Small and succulent portions of finger foods are classically paired up with the region's famous fortified wines and sherries from nearby Jerez. One needn't look far for the ingredients— cured green *sevillano* olives from the gnarled groves of the surrounding hills, and paper-thin slices of Jabugo ham, which locals insist is the world's best. There are slices of omelettes, deep-fried squid, slabs of spicy salami, and chunks of aged manchego cheese. There's usually sawdust on the floor and hams hanging from the rafters; sailors mix with the upscale young set—a *copa* of wine is the great leveler. La Albariza uses empty, upended sherry casks as tabletops to accommodate a rather tony crowd, while Las Teresas is exactly how you'd imagine the quintessential tapas bar. Either way, you're bound to walk away with newly forged friendships and tomorrow's hangover.

WHAT: town, event, hotel, restaurant. **SEVILLE:** 90 miles/144 km southwest of Córdoba. **HOLY WEEK:** Palm Sun to Easter Sun. **FERIA DE ABRIL:** 6 days, beginning 2 weeks after Easter Sun (on a Tues). **HOTEL ALFONSO XIII:** Calle San Fernando 2. Tel 34/954-91-7000, fax 34/954-91-7099; www.starwoodhotels.com. *Cost:* doubles from $425. **LA ALBARIZA:** Calle Betis 6. Tel 34/954-332016. **LAS TERESAS:** Calle Santa Teresa 2. Tel 34/954-213069. *Cost:* tapas $3–$10.

A Masterwork of Architectural Sculpture

GUGGENHEIM MUSEUM BILBAO

Basque Country, Spain

The dazzling titanium- and stone-covered edifice that dominates this shipbuilding and steel center is one of the century's most talked-about museums—the Guggenheim Museum Bilbao. The bizarrely shaped structure is described by its architect, American Frank O. Gehry, as a ship run aground on the Nervión River. Art lovers visiting Europe now include Bilbao as an essential part of their itinerary. The strikingly unusual building has jump-started the city's desire to create a new image of cultural and economic revival and an openness to the world after its long history of Basque separatism. The New York–based Solomon R. Guggenheim Foundation manages the operation, rotating parts of its own permanent collection and helping to organize temporary exhibitions. The vast, free-form Bilbao museum is almost twice as large as its New York sibling. The Basque regional government has covered the $100 million construction costs and created an acquisition fund. Resembling a huge, spectacular sculpture

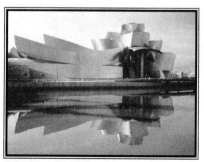

Frank Gehry's Spanish masterpiece

from afar, this is one museum that will never serve as a mere backdrop. Its eighteen galleries promise an interaction between structure and contents, so that the building remains sympathetic to its rotating exhibits, never overwhelming the artwork. It is, declared Philip Johnson, "the greatest building of our time."

WHAT: site. **WHERE:** Avenida Abandoibarra 2 (Bilbao is 72 miles/116 km east of Santander). Tel 34/944-35-9000; www.guggenheim-bilbao.es. **COST:** admission $14.

A Coastal Belle Epoque Setting Fit for a Queen

SAN SEBASTIÁN

Basque Country, Spain

Along with Biarritz, its French counterpart across the border, San Sebastián is the great Belle Epoque resort of the Basque coast. The potential of the lovely city and its crescent-shaped La Concha beach must have been obvious to the Spanish queen-regent María Cristina when in 1866 she decided to make it her summer residence and the royal court's summer capital, thus raising it to the pinnacle of fashion. Most of the turn-of-the-century architecture has remained intact, though its function may have changed: the classic horseshoe-shaped opera house is now home base for the well-known San Sebastián Film Festival, held in late September.

During the festival, the aristocratic Hotel María Cristina, which sits like a queen on the west bank of the Urumea River, serves as headquarters for the film-world aristocracy. Once the destination of every titled head in Europe, the 1912 landmark still dazzles with its opulent lobby of ormolu, intricate marquetry, onyx columns, and Carrara marble floors.

For dinner, guests should make every effort to secure a table at Arzak, the gastronomic star of Basque country. A notoriously independent people of distinct ancestry, the Basques are fascinated with food, and their culinary traditions are a source of deep regional pride, as a visit to the awesome La Brecha food market will confirm. The Basque region (Euskadi, in the Basque tongue) is home to one third of Spain's top-rated restaurants. And no one is more beloved for his culinary genius than Juan Mari Arzak. This local celebrity began garnering stars in the early 1970s, and is credited as the originator of the *nueva cocina vasca*—a revolutionary movement that changed fine dining throughout Spain in the 1980s the way nouvelle cuisine did in France. From heavy and traditional to innovative and light, from roasts to seafood, cooking is a masculine art in the Basque region, passed on from father to son. So it is curious and refreshing to see Arzak now sharing his kitchen and legend with his daughter, Elena. After an unforgettable repast at

Chef Juan Mari Arzak in his kitchen

Arzak's, you'll want to hug them both and exclaim, *"Eskarrikasko!"*—Basque for *gracias.*

WHAT: town, hotel, restaurant. **SAN SEBASTIÁN:** 57 miles/92 km from Bilbao, 12 miles/21 km from the French border, 300 miles/483 km north of Madrid. **HOTEL MARÍA CRISTINA:** Calle Oquendo 1. Tel 34/943-437600, fax 34/943-437676; hmc@luxurycollection.com; www.starwoodhotels.com. *Cost:* doubles from $230. **ARZAK:** Alto de Miracruz 21. Tel 34/943-285593, fax 34/943-272753; www.arzak.info. *Cost:* prix-fixe menu $205. *When:* open Tues–Sun. **BEST TIMES:** jazz festival in Jul, film festival in Sept.

Fragile and Invaluable Link to the Ice Age

THE CAVES OF ALTAMIRA AND SANTILLANA DEL MAR

Cantabria, Spain

Forbidden to all but a chosen few, the Caves of Altamira (las Cuevas de Altamira) are often described as the Sistine Chapel of prehistoric art. Together with Lascaux Cave in France (also closed except by special permission), they contain the best Upper Paleolithic cave paintings in Europe. Discovered in perfect condition by a local hunter in 1879, the red-and-black bison, bulls, horses, and boars demonstrate early man's love of beauty and astonishing artistic skill. The cave paintings date back to between 20,000 and 15,000 B.C and range from 4 to 8 feet high. Unfortunately, a century's worth of tourism has resulted in serious bacteria-caused deterioration, and the number of visitors has been drastically curtailed. Preference is given to those with legitimate scholarly interests. For flexible travelers planning a trip to Spain a year in advance, a fax to the local museum and a lot of patience may result in the coveted letter of admission that will allow you into the cave. Next door at the Museo de Altamira, a remarkable replica cave re-creates the same setting and paintings (including before-and-after photos that show the damage done), but lacks some of the excitement of visiting the real thing.

In town, you can still capture the medieval spirit of Santillana del Mar's small cluster of perfectly preserved mansions and palaces. Jean-Paul Sartre called it "the prettiest little village in Spain." Despite its name, Santillana del Mar lies 3 miles inland from the sea. This rural community does not live by tourism alone. Local dairy farmers sell fresh milk and cheese from their stable doors. Stroll through town to the 12th-century church of St. Juliana, the burial place of the 3d-century martyred saint. Over time her name was corrupted and transformed to Santillana. At the other end of the main street is the 400-year-old Convent of the Poor Clares, whose museum contains a surprisingly rich assemblage of religious paintings and statues.

If you've fallen under the spell of this tiny town, end your stroll at the Plaza de Ramón Pelayo, where the Parador Santillana Gil Blas has been created within the elegant but countrified 17th-century ancestral residence of a local family. A more recently built and less expensive annex absorbs the overflow of guests. A visit to Santillana is incomplete if there's no room at this inn.

WHAT: site, experience, town, hotel. **CAVES OF ALTAMIRA:** an easy 1.5-mile/ 2-km walk from the village of Santillana del

Mar. *Note:* At press time, the caves had been temporarily closed due to conservation issues. For status, contact the Museo de Altamira. **MUSEO DE ALTAMIRA:** Tel 34/942-818005; fax 34/942-840157; informacion@maltamira. mcu.es; www.museodealtamira.mcu.es. *Cost:* admission \$4. **SANTILLANA DEL MAR:** 21 miles/34 km west of Santander. *Best times:* May–Oct. **PARADOR SANTILLANA GIL BLAS:** Plaza de Ramón Pelayo 11. Tel 34/942-028028, fax 34/942-818391; santillanagb@parador.es; www.parador.es. *Cost:* doubles \$205 (low season), \$240 (high season).

The dining room of Parador Santillana Gil Blas

A Saint's Birthplace Conveys a Vivid Sense of the Past

ÁVILA

Castile and León, Spain

The near-perfect 11th-century walls of Ávila are a protected national treasure. Ten feet thick and 40 feet high, they took more than 2,000 workers ten years to build. For a mile and a half they wend around this

Ávila was once a popular pilgrims' destination.

played a role in Spain's religious and spiritual history, particularly as the hometown of St. Teresa, who was born here in 1515. A frail, witty Carmelite nun from a wealthy local family of Jewish descent, she would become one of the most famous of all Catholic saints and the female patron saint of Spain. (St. James the Apostle is Spain's male patron saint.)

hilltop town and include 90 semicircular guard towers, 9 narrow arched gates, and more than 2,300 embattlements. The results still look astonishingly new. A walkway around the top allows you to envision an approaching army of Moors. Even the city's plain, rugged 12th-century cathedral—half fortress, half church—was built as part of the walls and served a military function. Ávila has long

A stay at the Hotel Palacio Valderrábanos puts you in the spiritual and geographic heart of Ávila. It was built in the early 1300s as a bishop's residence, with rooms overlooking the cathedral. Try for a suite in the fortified lookout tower for an extra special view of the past.

WHAT: town, hotel. **ÁVILA:** 68 miles/ 110 km northwest of Madrid. **HOTEL PALACIO VALDERRÁBANOS:** Plaza de la Catedral 9. Tel 34/920-211023, fax 34/920-251691; reservas@palaciovalderrabanoshotel.com; www.palaciovalderrabanoshotel.com. *Cost:* doubles $165, tower suite $225. **BEST TIMES:** Mar–Oct; feast day of St. Teresa is Oct 15.

A Most Unusual Cathedral and a Shelter for Knights

LEÓN

Castile and León, Spain

Begun in 1205, the walls of León's Gothic cathedral were built more with glass than stone. One hundred twenty-five stained-glass windows, three giant rose windows, and fifty-seven oculi fill the lofty interior with bejeweled shafts of light. In the cathedral-building mania of the Middle Ages, European cities strove to outdo each other with the highest steeples, the biggest rose windows, the largest churches. León's contribution was certainly the boldest, amazing even modern-day critics and architects with its illusion of weightlessness and the profusion of light. Some of the windows soar as high as 110 feet and are the original 13th-century glassworks; cumulatively, they cover more than 18,000 square feet.

Designated the capital of Christian Spain in 914, León is now a charming provincial town that retains the aura of its regal past. Some of the country's most important and interesting sacred art can be found in the Cathedral Museum. Once an important stopover for pilgrims on the historical Road to Santiago, it is an obligatory stop today for anyone who is at all interested in medieval architecture.

The Parador de León deserves a prize for its entrance alone—a sumptuous "plateresque" facade (so called because of its resemblance to lacy silver plate work) that seems to stretch forever. The entrance hall is replete with an elaborate coffered ceiling and a 16th-century grand staircase. Awed visitors might even miss the 10-foot-high cast-iron chandelier overhead. One of León's principal attractions and one of Spain's finest examples of Renaissance architecture, it is also Spain's largest *parador* since the addition of a modern annex.

Its original wing was completed in 1549 upon the earlier orders of King Ferdinand to shelter knights and weary pilgrims on their way to Santiago de Compostela. Only 30 of the 250 rooms are housed in the historic wing, as is the regional restaurant with views of the Rio Bernesga. Both the Antiguo Monasterio de San Marcos and Museo Arqueológico, all part of the same landmark edifice, are open to the public. Vast common areas are distinguished by precious antiques, a remarkable *mudejar* ceiling, tapestries, and museum-quality artwork, creating high drama that is carried over in the suites.

WHAT: town, site, hotel. **LEÓN:** 200 miles/320 km north of Madrid. **CATHEDRAL DE LEÓN:** Plaza de Regla. Tel 34/987-875-770, fax 34/987-241-216; catedral@catedraldeleon.org; www.catedraldeleon.org. *Cost:* admission. **PARADOR DE LEÓN:** Plaza de San Marcos 7. Tel 34/987-237300, fax 34/987-233458; leon@parador.es; www.parador.es. *Cost:* doubles $235 (low season), $490 (high season), suites $490 (low season), $895 (high season). **BEST TIMES:** Apr–Oct.

Spain's Most Beautiful Square

SALAMANCA'S PLAZA MAYOR

Castile and León, Spain

No nation has as many World Heritage Cities as Spain, and of its six municipalities so designated by UNESCO, Salamanca may be the most delightful. Visitors naturally gravitate to the heart of the town, the lovely

18th-century Baroque Plaza Mayor. All the ancient city's other attractions are within walking distance, but linger awhile here to take in the spirit of Salamanca. What was once Europe's most important university was founded here in 1218 by Alfonso IX, and its current population of 15,000 students keeps the city young and vibrant. They fill the café tables that pour

The Spanish Baroque plaza was designed by Alberto Churriguera.

out from the plaza's shaded arcades—no one seems to be studying. Visitors and locals alike wind up here in the Plaza Mayor at some point, often serenaded by the roving groups of caped student minstrels. A "new" 16th-century cathedral stands cheek by jowl with an older and smaller Romanesque sibling. Both are must-see sites. So is the Hotel Rector, formerly the private mansion of a wealthy family. They now live upstairs, and leave fourteen faultlessly decorated rooms below for travelers in the know.

WHAT: town, site, hotel. **SALAMANCA:** 127 miles/204 km northwest of Madrid. **HOTEL RECTOR:** Paseo del Rector Esperabe 10. Tel 34/923-218482, fax 34/923-214008; info@hotelrector.com; www.hotelrector.com. *Cost:* doubles from $195. **BEST TIMES:** Mar–Oct.

King of Spain's Culinary Gem

MESÓN DE CÁNDIDO

Segovia, Castile and León, Spain

For sheer atmosphere and the best roast suckling pig *(cochinillo asado)* in a country that prides itself on roast suckling pig, this 100-year-old eatery is the place. In what may be the most beautiful city in Spain, many

generations of the gregarious Cándido family have entertained everyone from Hemingway to Salvador Dalí. Their restaurant has become a culinary pilgrimage for royalty, politicians,

bullfighters, and artists. No one leaves without the conviction that a more delightful and quintessentially Spanish repast cannot be found. The *cochinillo* is rivaled only by the *cordero asado* (roast baby lamb), another exquisitely prepared regional delicacy.

It's siesta time after a memorable meal here, so before savoring Cándido's outstanding food, savor Segovia's monumental sights. It is believed that Walt Disney took the castle-palace Alcázar as inspiration for the castle in *Snow White and the Seven Dwarfs*. It is one of Spain's most photographed and beloved sites, built during the 12th and 13th centuries on a high crag visible from afar. The equally well-preserved Acueducto Romano (Roman Aqueduct) is one of Europe's finest surviving examples of Roman architecture, its 166 double-tiered arches constructed without mortar more than 2,000 years ago. Make time for a retreat to the cool interior of the graceful 16th-century cathedral, the last and most elegant to be built in the Gothic style at a time when the rest of Europe was well into the Renaissance.

WHAT: town, restaurant. **SEGOVIA:** 57 miles/91 km west of Madrid. **MESÓN DE CÁNDIDO:** Plaza de Azoguejo 5. Tel 34/921-425911, fax 34/921-429633; www.meson decandido.es. *Cost:* prix fixe dinner $50. **BEST TIMES:** spring and Jun 21–29, the feast days of the local patron saints, John and Peter.

Fascinating Confluence of Three Cultures

LA CATEDRAL DE TOLEDO

Toledo, Castile La Mancha, Spain

B ecause of its artistic riches, the city that so inspired El Greco makes for a rather frantic day trip from Madrid—the average time unsuspecting tourists allot. Better to spend a little more time. But any visit, brief or leisurely, should start at Toledo's famous cathedral. Ranked among the world's greatest Gothic structures, it was built between the 13th and 15th centuries on the site of an old Arab mosque. This layering and juxtaposition of the artistic, architectural, and historic legacies of Toledo's Catholic, Moorish, and Jewish communities are what make the city fascinating.

After Alfonso VI captured Toledo from the Moors in 1085, a cosmopolitan tolerance endured for five centuries, encouraging intellectual exchange and trade. The ensuing prosperity and Toledo's role as a center of culture and learning filled the city with master craftsmen, whose superb talents can be admired in the cathedral's exquisite details. El Greco's most famous painting, *The Burial of Count Orgaz*, hangs in the nearby Iglesia de Santo Tomé (Church of St. Thomas), but the sacristy here has close to thirty of his paintings as well as works by Velázquez, Titian, and Goya.

Toledo's best restaurant, Hostal del Cardenal, is housed in an elegant 18th-century cardinal's palace, which is also the most charming place to spend the night, guaranteeing the luxury of seeing this intriguing city before and after the daily deluge of day-trippers.

WHAT: town, site, hotel, restaurant. **LA CATEDRAL DE TOLEDO:** Plaza Mayor Toledo, 45 miles/89 km south of Madrid. **HOSTAL DEL CARDENAL:** Paseo de Recaredo 24. Tel 34/925-224900, fax 34/925-222991; cardenal @hostaldelcardenal.com; www.hostaldel cardenal.com. *Cost:* doubles from $125. Dinner $65. **BEST TIMES:** during the celebration of Corpus Christi (often falling in Jun), a 500-pound gold reliquary said to be made from gold brought back by Columbus from the New World is paraded through the streets.

An Unsurpassed Collection of Romanesque Art

CATALAN NATIONAL ART MUSEUM

Barcelona, Catalonia, Spain

Housed in the imposing Palau Nacional (National Palace), the Museu Nacional d'Art de Catalunya houses the world's finest treasure trove of Romanesque and Gothic paintings, sculpture, and metalwork. More than twenty-five works have been transferred here from churches and monasteries in Catalonia and displayed in simple settings that re-create their original locations. The sobriety of Romanesque churches often contrasted with the richness of the art within. Exhibited in sequential order, the master artworks offer a fascinating journey through the evolution of primitive Romanesque style to

A Cardet altar frontal from the second half of the 13th century

its zenith between the 11th and 13th centuries and the early stages of Gothic art that followed. A highlight is the Pantocrator from the main apse of the Church of San Clemente de Taüll, dating from 1123. Installation of these magnificent frescoes—which depict a majestic Christ holding a book with the Latin inscription "Ego sum lux mundi" ("I am the light of the world")—was overseen by the director of the Sistine Chapel restoration. The austere setting and overall effect here are no less powerful. Built for the 1929 World's Fair and reopened in 1995 after a major renovation overseen by Milanese architect Gae Aulenti, the imitation Renaissance-Baroque National Palace is often referred to as the Prado of Romanesque art.

WHAT: site. **WHERE:** Parc de Montjuïc. Tel 34/936-220376; www.mnac.es. **COST:** admission $12. **WHEN:** open Tues–Sun.

One of Spain's Most Extraordinary Buildings

LA SAGRADA FAMILIA

Barcelona, Catalonia, Spain

To finish or not to finish? The enormous Sagrada Familia remains the incomplete, roofless masterpiece of the eccentric genius Antoni Gaudí. The Catalan architect, a national hero, was run over and killed by a tram in 1926 before he could complete his most bizarre, controversial creation. The most famous proponent of *modernismo* (the Catalan avant-garde style, unique to the region, that flourished from 1890 to 1920), Gaudí put Barcelona on the architectural map. The Sagrada Familia is his most emblematic and idiosyncratic work, Art Nouveau with a twist.

Gaudí tapped into the same playful Catalan spirit one sees in the work of Picasso, Miró, and Dalí, and more often than not avoided straight lines in favor of flowing, organic forms. He created a number of other surreal works, such as Parc Güell, the apartment and office building of Casa Batlló, and several private homes. But the fantasist is best known for the Sagrada Familia, a melted sand castle frozen in mid-creation. Only the crypt, apse, and facade were completed before his death. Gaudí is buried in the crypt, where a museum displays scale models showing how he envisioned the church. Authorities say it may not be completed until well into the 21st century—if ever.

The Sagrada Familia's apse was completed in 1894.

WHAT: site. **WHERE:** Plaça de la Sagrada Familia. Tel 34/932-080414; www.sagrada familia.org. **COST:** admission $16.

Tracing the Evolution of Genius

MUSEU PICASSO

Barcelona, Catalonia, Spain

Adjoining 13th- and 19th-century palaces provide a handsome setting for one of Spain's most interesting museums, a must for Picasso lovers. Beginning with the boyhood sketchbooks and marginal doodlings of the nine-year-old artist (born in Málaga in 1881), the museum provides the rare opportunity of following Picasso's evolution as an artist, particularly in his earlier works. There are paintings that hint of his Blue Period and studies for his seminal *Guernica* as well as *The Maids of Honor,* forty-four Cubist variations done in the 1950s on the classic *Las Meninas,* the famous Velázquez painting hanging in Madrid's Prado Museum. Although this may not be the finest assemblage of Picassos, it is the largest, with 3,600 paintings, drawings, engravings, and ceramics. Dating from 1890 to 1967, many pieces were donated by the artist before his death in 1973, and the majority of ceramics were given by Jacqueline Picasso in 1982. This modern collection is found on a narrow street along the outskirts of Barcelona's Barri Gótic (Gothic Quarter), a quiet warren of medieval buildings and byways containing most of the city's historic and artistic treasures along with numerous tapas bars to sustain one's energy.

WHAT: site. **WHERE:** Carrer de Montcada 15-19. Tel 34/932-563000; www.museupicasso. bcn.es. **COST:** admission $13. **WHEN:** Tues–Sun.

---

*Quaint and Charming Haunts
of Artists and Intellectuals*

CADAQUÉS AND FIGUERES

Catalonia, Spain

The simple, whitewashed fishing village of Cadaqués is often called the most painted village in the world. Picasso, Dalí, Utrillo, Miró, Max Ernst, Man Ray, and the filmmaker Luis Buñuel took inspiration from its simplicity and classic Catalan beauty. The last resort town on the Spanish coast before the French border, Cadaqués, and its horseshoe-shaped bay, is hugged by the mountains of the Costa Brava. Despite its century of popularity with those who braved the narrow switchback road (only recently paved), Spain's easternmost town hasn't changed much since Salvador Dalí and Marcel Duchamp played chess at Bar Meliton. The lazy, do-nothing pace continues, the bars and cafés filling after siesta and staying open till dawn.

If Cadaqués has escaped exploitation it is because of its lack of sandy beaches. An authentic working-class character persists, with a smattering of outdoor portside restaurants serving the simple dinners of grilled sardines and dorado brought in daily by the town's last working fishermen. No-frills hangouts like Dalí's favorite haunt, Casa Anita, continue to serve fresh seafood to new generations of artists. Locals love to watch newly arrived outsiders look around, soak in the atmosphere, and then declare the place too boring. Better they head for Ibiza.

From Cadaqués, take a day trip to Figueres, home of the Teatre-Museu Dalí. An ode to madness, it may enchant, fascinate, or annoy, but it leaves no visitor indifferent. It is fully in keeping with the eccentric artist, who was born in Figueres in 1904. Today the Teatre-Museu Dalí, built in and around the 19th-century theater where his first exhibition took place in 1919, is the principal draw for this town in the heart of Catalonia. From the plastic store mannequins to the pile of rubber tires out front, the entire display is best described as odd. "The museum cannot be considered to be a museum," Dalí himself said. "It is a gigantic surrealist object

The Dalí Theater-Museum has works spanning the artist's entire career.

in which everything is coherent, nothing is beyond my understanding." Many of his principal works are here, together with paintings by El Greco and Mariano Fortuny from Dalí's private collection. Dalí lived and worked here until his death in 1989 and is buried in the inner court, beneath the museum's dome.

The protean artist also designed sets for theater and film, dabbled in literature, and wrote his own cookbook. That he and his wife, Gala, became loyal habitués of the local Restaurant Empordà is not surprising: although ordinary on the outside, it is Catalonia's best eatery. Some of Dalí's sketches and lithographs grace the walls, but patrons come for the artistry in the kitchen, which produces excellent game and seafood specialties in the haute Catalan manner.

WHAT: town, restaurant, site. **CADAQUÉS:** 122 miles/196 km north of Barcelona. **CASA ANITA:** Calle Miguel Roset 16. Tel 34/972-258471. *Cost:* dinner $35. **FIGUERES:** 88 miles/140 km north of Barcelona, 25 miles/40 km north of Girona. **TEATRE-MUSEU DALÍ:** Plaça de Gala-Dalí 5. Tel 34/972-677500, fax 34/972-501666; www.dali-estate.org. *Cost:* admission $16. *When:* open daily, Oct–Jun. **RESTAURANT EMPORDÀ:** Avenida Salvador Dalí. Tel 34/972-500562; hotelemporda@hotelemporda.com; www.hotelemporda.com. *Cost:* prix fixe dinner $65.

The Oldest Tourist Route in Europe

THE WAY OF ST. JAMES AND THE CATHEDRAL OF SANTIAGO DE COMPOSTELA

Galicia, Spain

Follow in the footsteps of El Cid, Louis VII of France, and St. Francis of Assisi along the 1,000-year-old Way of St. James (also called the Road to Santiago). Along with Rome and the Holy Land, the city of Santiago de Compostela is one of Christendom's three principal pilgrimage destinations. Since the 9th century, millions have come from all over Europe and the British Isles to the cathedral, said to house the relics of Sant Iago (St. James, the Apostle), Jesus' cousin (St. John the Divine), and Santiago Matamoros (Slayer of the Moors). As with their medieval predecessors, the motives of those making the "route of forgiveness" today can be spiritual or not, but all say it is a trip that stays with them for life.

Modern pilgrims can pick up the Camino de Santiago at Roncesvalles, in the Spanish foothills of the Pyrenees, the most popular of the eight routes that make up the Way of St. James. They travel 500 miles through the vineyards of the Rioja and the former kingdoms of northern Spain. Those who don't have the time or stamina for the four-plus-week journey by foot walk the final 90 miles through the green and enchanting region of Galicia. Tired but elated travelers typically get their first glimpse of Santiago's cathedral and its twin towers from Monte de Gozo, 2 miles from the finish line.

Construction of the extravagant Cathedral of Santiago de Compostela was begun in 1078 on the site of a 9th-century basilica that had been destroyed by the infidels (who took the

Destination of pilgrims: the Cathedral of Santiago de Compostela

pilgrims who were pouring in from all corners of Europe. The hotel is the oldest building on the square, and if you're lucky enough to get a room overlooking the cathedral, you'll feel like one of the *reyes católicos* yourself. If not, console yourself with a lovely view over one of the four cloistered courtyards, with original fountains and open loggias, formed by the building's cross-shape design. This is one of Spain's most glorious *paradores* (historical sites transformed into government-owned hotels). If it's all too grand in proportion and price for the pilgrim in you, you can still drop in for a simple but excellent dinner.

bells back to Córdoba as a souvenir). The cathedral's elaborate, two-towered Baroque facade was added in the 18th century, covering and protecting the original Door of Glory, which becomes visible as you enter; pilgrims press their fingers into the holes made in the stone by a millennium of their predecessors. The impact of the cavernous interior, as plain and simple as the facade is ornate, is heightened by the golden-cloaked, bejeweled statue of St. James in its place of honor above the main altar.

Outside, the spacious Plaza del Obradoiro ("work of gold") and the magnificent 16th- to 18th-century buildings that flank it evolved around the cathedral. The plaza is also home to the Parador de Santiago de Compostela (formerly called the Hotel Reyes Católicos)—allegedly the oldest hotel in the world—with what must be the world's most beautiful hotel doorway. In 1499 King Ferdinand and Queen Isabella founded the Royal Hospice in Santiago to serve as a respite for the countless

WHAT: experience, town, site, hotel. **WAY OF ST. JAMES:** final leg is across the northern regions of Spain, from east to west. *How:* numerous biking tours are operated Jun–Sept by Bravo Bike, tel 34/91-559-5523, fax 34/91-638-0642; www.bravobike.com. *Cost:* 8 days/7 nights guided trip, $2,115 per person double occupancy. Walking tours and tours by coach in Apr–Oct operated by Saranjan, Inc. In the U.S., tel 800-858-9594, fax 206-720-0623; info@saranjan.com; www.saranjan.com. *Cost:* 2-week coach tour, $8,450 per person double occupancy, all-inclusive 11 day/10 night walking tour, $5,250 per person double occupancy, all-inclusive. **CATHEDRAL OF SANTIAGO DE COMPOSTELA:** Plaza del Obradoiro. Santiago de Compostela is 45 miles and 72 km south of La Coruña. **PARADOR DE SANTIAGO DE COMPOSTELA:** Plaza del Obradoiro 1. Tel 34/981-582200, fax 34/981-563094; santiago@parador.es; www.parador.es. *Cost:* doubles $315. **BEST TIMES:** Jul 25, the feast day of St. James, is celebrated with fireworks, music, and processions.

> *"Nobody goes to bed in Madrid*
> *until they have killed the night."*
> —ERNEST HEMINGWAY

MADRID

Spain

Madrid these days is Europe's liveliest capital. Your first thought, and your parting one, may be that no one sleeps in this town—visit any of the neighborhood restaurants, *mesones,* or tapas bars around midnight for a loud and friendly confirmation.

THE TOP TEN SIGHTS

BULLFIGHTS AT LA PLAZA DE LAS VENTAS—Bullfighting has become a controversial sport, but it is an inextricable part of Spanish history, culture, and national identity. Aficionados and the merely curious can experience a Sunday-afternoon *corrida* at La Plaza de las Ventas and understand something of the Spanish soul, old and new. **WHERE:** Calle Alcalá. Tel 34/91-356-22-00. Bullfighting each Sun in season, Mar–Oct. Fights daily during festivals in May and Sept.

CENTRO DE ARTE REINA SOFIA—Home of Picasso's *Guernica,* Madrid's contemporary arts museum occupies an 18th-century former hospital building located near the Prado. Its collection, separated into two floors—one pre-1939 and one post-, marking the end of Spain's civil war—includes works by Spanish artists such as Miró, Dalí, Juan Gris, and Antoni Tàpies, as well as Alexander Calder, Man Ray, Jean Dubuffet, and others. **WHERE:** Calle Santa Isabel. Tel 34/91-774-1000; www.museoreinasofia.es.

FLAMENCO AT CORRAL DE LA MORERÍA— Catering mostly to tourists but respected as the best flamenco nightclub north of Andalusia, Corral de la Morería is flashy, colorful, and drenched in tradition, reflecting the flamenco resurgence that's been going on since the 1980s. Every night is an event, with first-rate performances and foot-stomping passion that never dissipates. **WHERE:** Calle de la Morería. Tel 34/91-365-8446.

EL RASTRO FLEA MARKET—Sleep late on Sunday morning and you'll miss the bargains at the famous, sprawling, five-century-old El Rastro flea market, teeming with hawkers and gawkers selling everything imaginable. Everyone eventually winds up at the market's most famous tapas bar, Los Caracoles—try the delicious snail specialty. **WHERE:** Plaza Cascorro and Ribera de Curtidores.

MUSEO SOROLLA—The restored, elegant home of Valencian artist Joaquín Sorolla, Spain's foremost Impressionist painter, maintains a lived-in feel (right down to his used paintbrushes) while displaying a collection of his works, including portraits of aristocrats and paintings of Spain's common people. **WHERE:** Paseo de General Martínez Campos. Tel 34/91-310-1584.

PALACIO REAL—Begun in 1738 on the site of the old Moorish Alcázar fortress, the Palacio Real was the royal residence from 1764 until King Alfonso XIII abdicated the throne in 1931, and today functions as the king's official residence, though he doesn't actually live there. State business takes up much of the palace, but the rooms occupied by Alfonso and his family are open to the public, as are the Throne Room, the Reception Room, the Painting Gallery (with works by Caravaggio, Velázquez, Goya, and others), the Royal Armoury, and the Royal Pharmacy, all of them chock full of treasures. **WHERE:** Plaza de Oriente, Calle de Bailén. Tel 34/91-454-8700; www.patrimonionacional.es.

THE PRADO—The key component of the "Golden Triangle of Museums" (with Reina Sofia and Thyssen), the refurbished Prado is a treasure house that could keep Madrid on the European cultural map all by itself. Sculptures, drawings, and works in other media are displayed, but the museum is primarily known for its collection of more than 8,600 paintings by El Greco, Goya, Murillo, Rubens, Titian, Bosch, Raphael, Botticelli, Fra Angelico, and many others. Eighty percent of Velázquez's paintings are here, including his *Las Meninas*, the most visited among the 2,000 works the museum can display at any one time. **WHERE:** Paseo del Prado. Tel 34/91-330-2800; www.museodelprado.es.

SUNDAY IN EL RETIRO PARK—A stroll through El Retiro Park is a Sunday morning ritual for many a Madrileña family. Laid out in the 1630s and once reserved for royals and their guests, the 350-acre park is full of fountains and statues, plus a lake, the Cáson del Buen Retiro (housing the Prado's modern works) and the Palacio de Velázquez and Palacio Cristal exhibition halls. **WHERE:** Plaza de la Independencia (just behind the Prado).

THE TAPAS CRAWL—If you want to act like a Madrileño, you must move from *tasca* to *tasca*, nibbling as you go, leading up to dinner around 11 P.M. The possibilities are endless, from *albondigas* (meatballs) to *zamburiñas* (small scallops). **WHERE:** the greatest concentration of tapas bars is in the Villa y Corte area, the oldest part of town. The streets that branch out from the Plaza Mayor are lined with grazing possibilities.

THYSSEN-BORNEMISZA MUSEUM—Fills in the Prado's gaps with more than 800 paintings from the 13th through the 20th centuries, including works by El Greco, Goya, Velázquez, Rembrandt, Caravaggio, Kandinsky, Pollock, and Picasso. The collection was amassed by Baron Hans Heinrich Thyssen-Bornemisza of Switzerland and acquired by Spain in 1993. **WHERE:** Paseo del Prado. Tel 34/91-369-0151; www.museothyssen.org.

OTHER MUST-DO'S

THE PLAZA MAYOR—The huge cobblestone square was completed in 1619 in the Castillian-Baroque style, and has seen its share of bullfights, hangings, riots, wild carnivals, and the nasty doings of the Inquisition. Today it remains one of the city's great meeting places, the heartbeat of Viejo Madrid. Choose any of its nine arched exits that lead into streets filled with *tabernas*, tapas bars, and *mesones*, sometimes one on top of each other. Listen for the *tunas*, the wandering troupes of singing students dressed as medieval minstrels. **WHERE:** bounded by Calle Mayor on the north and Cava de San Miguel on the west.

A waiter pours wine at the La Taurina Tapas Bar in Madrid.

WHERE TO STAY

PALACE—Three times the size of the Ritz (see below), the Palace is Madrid's other upmarket splurge and Belle Epoque beauty, where guests are also treated like royalty. Opened by King Alfonso XIII in 1912, it covers an entire city street just one block from the Prado and features grand public spaces and a stunning glass-roofed lobby. **WHERE:** Plaza de las Cortes. Tel 34/91-360-8000, fax 34/91-360-8100; in the U.S., tel 800-937-8461; www.palacemadrid.com. **COST:** high.

REINA VICTORIA—Not glamorous but comfortable, the Reina Victoria was frequented for generations by famous bullfighters and those, like Hemingway, who followed them. Today it remains one of the city's most historic and beloved hotels. **WHERE:** Plaza Santa Ana 14. Tel 34/91-701-6000, fax 34/91-522-0307. **COST:** moderate.

RITZ HOTEL—Madrid's Ritz Hotel is the ritziest of all the Ritzes, built in 1919 by order of King Alfonso XIII, who needed proper accommodations for the royal guests arriving for his wedding. It has remained the choice of the celebrated and aristocratic ever since. **WHERE:** Plaza de la Lealtad. Tel 34/91-701-6767, fax 34/91-701-6776; in the U.S., tel 800-225-5843; www.ritzmadrid.com. **COST:** high.

EATING & DRINKING

CASA BOTÍN—Possibly Spain's oldest restaurant, this folkloric tavern in the shadow of Plaza Mayor has been an obligatory stop for passing luminaries since it opened in 1725. It looks like a tourist trap and it is, but is still loved by discerning locals for its atmosphere and a typically Castillian cuisine. **WHERE:** Calle Cuchilleros. Tel 34/91-366-4217.

CAFÉ GIJÓN—Madrid's after-hours nightlife, or *movida*, knows no rival. Just turn up on Calle de las Huertas around midnight for a wide selection of tapas bars and smoke-filled hangouts. For a more reflective moment, find a window seat or barside stool at the old-world Café Gijón, since 1888 Madrid's definitive literary café. **WHERE:** Paseo de Recoletos. Tel 34/91-521-5425.

CASA LUCIO—Tucked into the side streets spilling out from the Plaza Mayor, this is the most reliable of the old timers, and one that, despite its location, somehow escaped the tourist crowds that fill up Botín. **WHERE:** Calle Cava Baja. Tel 34/91-365-3252.

CASA PATAS—A loud, informal bar-restaurant and meeting place for musicians and artists who come for the tapas and stay for the flamenco. Traditional and classic flamenco names fill the bill, but it is most exciting for the impromptu *nuevo flamenco* performances that fill the back room. **WHERE:** Calle Cañizares. Tel 34/91-369-0496.

EL CENADOR DEL PRADO—Fashionable but not formal, El Cenador is a perennial favorite for enjoying *cocina nueva* amid the conservatory decor. Much is made of their signature *patatas con almejas* (potatoes with clams)—turns out they're right. **WHERE:** Calle del Prado. Tel 34/91-429-1561.

LA TRAINERA—Landlocked Madrid has long boasted some of the best seafood in the country, and for close to forty years this large, friendly restaurant has offered the best lobster, crab, crayfish, prawns, and other seafood. **WHERE:** Calle Lagasca. Tel 34/91-576-8035.

ZALACAÍN—Often considered Spain's best restaurant, and awarded many stars by food critics, Zalacaín offers an elegant decor, perhaps the most refined wine list in town (try any of the vintage riojas), and superb Basque-influenced dining. Jacket-and-tie formality doesn't keep Madrid's glitterati from filling this dark venue, which recalls a Velázquez painting. **WHERE:** Calle Álvarez de Baena. Tel 34/91-561-4840.

A Self-Contained Island Haven

LA RESIDENCIA

Deià, Mallorca, Spain

Deià was beloved by both Frédéric Chopin and the English poet Robert Graves, who believed that the simple town possessed spiritually uplifting qualities. Artists and writers continue to be drawn to its quiet, unspoiled beauty, which has so far escaped the tour buses and overbuilding rampant elsewhere in the Balearic Islands. Sheer mountains loom behind, and Mediterranean coves lie below.

La Residencia, one of the islands' finest hideaways, is surrounded by 30 acres of flowering gardens, set among terraced olive and citrus groves between sea and the slopes of a 4,000-foot mountain. Consisting of two creeper-covered 17th-century manor houses, La Residencia is aptly named. Luxurious but decidedly unglitzy, it's like the impeccable Mallorcan home of a wealthy, art-loving, and flawlessly refined friend. Low-keyed despite its fame as one of Spain's best, the hotel's restaurant, El Olivo, is a cozy place that was once an olive oil press. Indoors, exceptional Mediterranean cuisine is served in a candlelit, romantic setting. In warm weather, dining moves outside to a palm- and bougainvillea-scaped terrace. An old mule track provides a delightful three-hour trek through mountainside lemon and olive groves to the nearby village of Soller, although most guests prefer to experience nature through the pampering indulgence of algae and herb treatments and massages at the hotel's new beauty center.

WHAT: town, hotel, restaurant. **DEIÀ:** northern coast of Mallorca, 40 minutes from Palma de Mallorca's airport, 17 miles/27 km northwest of Palma. **LA RESIDENCIA:** tel 34/971-639011, fax 34/971-639370; reservas@hotel-laresidencia.com; www.hotel-laresidencia.com. *Cost:* doubles from $385 (low season), from $805 (high season); suites with private pool from $1,060 (low season), from $2,960 (high season). 5-night minimum during high season. Dinner at El Olivo $90. **BEST TIMES:** spring and fall for hiking, walking, and cycling; Jun–Aug for swimming.

With Shoes to Fill and a Culinary Torch to Carry

RESTAURANT STUCKI BRUDERHOLZ

Basel, Switzerland

Master chef Hans Stucki was one of Switzerland's culinary giants until his premature death in 1998. Those in the food world reverently dropped his name the way aspiring artists do that of Picasso. Good news:

the torch was picked up by one honored enough to have worked under his tutelage in the kitchen for close to a decade. At the forefront of Switzerland's (and Europe's) new guard of stellar chefs, Jean-Claude Wicky effortlessly maintained the standards of Stucki, before passing this Michelin-starred restaurant to chef/owner Tanja Grandits in 2008. Under Grandits—a rising star in the culinary world—the decor, mood, and menu have lightened up, but the culinary style remains assertive and the international clientele—although a tad younger—is savvy enough to know that the wonder and genius of Stucki continues to rule. Grandits carries her rendition of that legacy into the future with ease.

WHAT: restaurant. **WHERE:** Bruderholzallee 42. Tel 41/61-361-8222, fax 41/61-361-8203; info@stuckibasel.ch; www.stuckibasel.ch. **COST:** dinner $90. **WHEN:** open Tues–Sat.

A Royal Playground Above the Clouds

GSTAAD

Bernese Oberland, Switzerland

At the confluence of four alpine valleys, Gstaad is the pearl of the magnificent Bernese Oberland, one of the world's best winter playgrounds. Make that summertime playground as well. With its 155 miles of downhill runs, 60 miles of cross-country trails, and a host of year-round activities, this is where royalty and the world's celebs ski, but who knew it could be so unspoiled and unpretentious. It has almost the air of a country village, albeit a very affluent one: those stores are mighty expensive and none of the gorgeous hotels are catering to the have-nots.

Gstaad is so low-key and quiet you might even find it a tad boring, unless you're staying at the Palace Hotel Gstaad, one of the most sought-after hideaways in the world. Towering over tiny Gstaad like a neomedieval castle dreamed up by Mad Ludwig, this 107-room hotel, built in 1912, bills itself as Switzerland's largest family pension, but don't let the cozy and rustically decorated rooms fool you: this hotel is the epicenter of the local

Though it looks like a castle, the Palace Hotel was built as a resort.

social scene. Guests check into this splendid fantasyland for extended periods of time, drawn by the management's motto that "Every king is a client, every client is a king." In addition to great service, great food is also readily available, but for real local alpine *gemütlichkeit* (homeyness) take the cable car to the mountaintop terraced Berghaus Eggli restaurant for raclette or fondue and a view you'll never forget.

WHAT: town, experience, hotel. **GSTAAD:** 42 miles/67 km southwest of Interlaken. **PALACE HOTEL GSTAAD:** tel 41/33-748-5000, fax 41/33-748-5001; info@palace.ch; www.palace.ch. *Cost:* doubles from $605 (low season), from $930 (high season). *When:* open mid-Jun–mid-Sept, mid-Dec–Mar. **BEST TIMES:** annual Musiksommer founded by Yehudi Menuhin takes place from mid-Jul to early Sept.

Staggering Views Riding the World's Highest Railroad

JUNGFRAUJOCH

Bernese Oberland, Switzerland

T he scenic wonders of Switzerland all come into focus in the central region called the Bernese Oberland, and the rail trip up to the Jungfraujoch is the acme of all high-altitude excursions. At 11,400 feet, the Jungfraujoch terminus has been the highest railroad station in the world for more than a century and, as one of the most popular excursions in Switzerland, it can often seem like Grand Central Station at rush hour. Come early or late in the season to avoid the worst of the crowds, and treat yourself to some of the most staggering mountain scenery anywhere in the world. There are stops along the way and things to do once you arrive, including a visit to the chilled depths of the famed Eispalast (Ice Palace), a cavernous area carved out of a glacier and featuring permanent ice sculpture on display. Check out the Sphinx Terrace, from which the views of the Mönch and Jungfrau peaks are topped only by that of the 14-mile icy expanse of the Aletsch Glacier, Europe's longest.

Head to the Top of Europe restaurant for a lunch break that gives new meaning to "haute" cuisine (the food is definitely not the point here). Vary your return trip by taking the route to the traditional mountain village of Grindelwald, which shares its first-class ski area with equally adorable Wengen. It is one of the region's most picturesque year-round resorts (especially favored for its high-terrain hiking), dramatically set beneath the towering north face of the Eiger peak. In Interlaken, stay at the Victoria-Jungfrau Grand Hotel and Spa. With refinement and service as lightweight as an eiderdown quilt and as efficient as a Swiss-made watch, the hotel is a monument to luxury, seemingly untouched (thanks to frequent but seamless renovations) since it was built in 1865.

WHAT: experience, hotel. **JUNGFRAUJOCH RAIL TRIP:** full-day round trips offered daily from Interlaken (36 miles/58 km southeast of Bern, 90 miles/145 km southwest of Zurich) and Grindelwald (17 miles/27 km east of Interlaken). *Cost:* $160 (second class) from Interlaken. *When:* Jun–Sept. *Best times:* check with Interlaken Tourism, tel 41/33-826-5301, fax 41/33-826-5375; reservations@interlaken tourism.ch; www.interlakentourism.ch, for daily-changing weather conditions; don't bother going on a cloudy day. **VICTORIA-JUNGFRAU GRAND HOTEL AND SPA:** Höheweg 37, Interlaken. Tel 41/33-828-2828, fax 41/33-828-2880; interlaken@victoria-jungfrau.ch; www.victoria-jungfrau.ch. *Cost:* doubles from $645, includes use of most spa facilities; deluxe doubles with mountain view $740.

Walking on Top of the World

KANDERSTEG

Bernese Oberland, Switzerland

Of all the images of Switzerland, the most enduring is that of a snow-dusted winter paradise. But early-19th-century visitors put it on the map as an aristocratic summer destination prescribed for its invigorating and bracing alpine air. Today's summer visitors are lured by the network of high-terrain foot trails and marked walking paths that make the Alps among the world's finest locations to rejuvenate the body and nourish the soul.

With the country's concentration of glorious mountain scenery, the choice of where to start can be daunting. The steep-sided ravines of charming Kandersteg (population 1,000) in the canton of Bernese Oberland has long been known as a rambler's (and cross-country skier's) paradise. Visit its tiny 16th-century church, then head for the cablecar that lifts walkers to the historically important Gemmi Pass connecting Kandersteg with Leukerbad in Valais, or to Lake Oeschinen, one of Switzerland's most striking natural wonders. Color-coded signposts throughout town point hikers on their way, indicating the time needed roundtrip.

The town's handsome chalet-style lodges have been welcoming Alps-lovers for decades. In the same family since 1893, the Royal Park Hotel is well-known as Kandersteg's finest, offering excursions such as to the two-hour scenic drive to Aletsch Glacier, Europe's largest, and a rejuvenating spa that awaits weary hikers at the end of the day. Half board is optional, though loyal return guests wouldn't think of eating elsewhere.

WHAT: town, experience. **WHERE:** 28 miles/45 km southwest of Interlaken. **HOW:** For walking trail and cable car information, contact Kandersteg Tourism, tel 41/33-675-8080; info@kandersteg.ch; www.kandersteg.ch. **ROYAL PARK HOTEL:** Tel 41/33-675-8888, fax 41/33-675-8880; royal@rikli.com; www.royalkandersteg.ch. *Cost:* doubles from $400 (low season); from $500 (high season). **BEST TIMES:** Jun–Jul for alpine flowers, Sept–Oct for cooler weather.

Stupendous Scenery and the
World's Most Dramatically Sited Revolving Restaurant

MÜRREN

Bernese Oberland, Switzerland

The Bernese Oberland is no secret: the most popular destination in Switzerland merits the year-round tourism it receives thanks to mountain villages such as the tiny, traffic-free Mürren. Facing the dramatic Jungfrau massif from its perch on a balcony-like ledge above the Lauterbrunnen Valley, it is the highest year-round inhabited village in the canton. Its high-altitude location is accessible only by cog railway or cable car.

Mürren is considered the birthplace of downhill racing in its modern form (beginners, go elsewhere); the first-ever slalom race was organized here in 1924. The local Arlberg–Kandahar race is now regarded as the unofficial world championship of the alpine countries. Nothing rivals the challenging 9-mile run with staggering views from the Schilthorn. It's just as popular with nonskiers who hop on the

Each rotation of the restaurant takes fifty-five minutes.

cable car for the 360-degree panorama of peaks, lakes, and year-round snowfields from its 9,742-foot summit, Piz Gloria.

The summit's eponymous revolving restaurant was made world-famous by the 1969 James Bond thriller *On Her Majesty's Secret Service*, and its incomparable eagle's-nest setting is said to take in some 200 peaks. Designed like a big-windowed alien spaceship (who else could have built it up there?) anchored to the alpine bedrock, Piz Gloria offers an incomparable panoramic vista, and the James Bond pasta special and 007 dessert made with five scoops of ice cream do their best to live up to the view.

WHAT: town, experience, restaurant. **MÜRREN:** 19 miles/31 km south of Interlaken. Round-trip cable car from Mürren to Piz Gloria, $85. For more information, contact Switzerland Tourism. In the U.S. tel 877-794-8037, fax 212-262-6116; www.myswitzerland. com. **RESTAURANT PIZ GLORIA:** Schilthorn. Tel 41/33-856-2156. *Cost:* dinner $45. **BEST TIMES:** Jan and Feb for best skiing; surrounding meadows are covered with wildflowers mid-Jun–Aug.

The Queen of Resorts and the Alps' Most Famous Rail Excursion

St. Moritz and the Glacier Express

Engadine, Switzerland

St. Moritz is not only for those who appreciate the "ritz" in this world-class ski resort's name. Despite the cosmopolitan mix of socialites, bluebloods, and tanned movie stars that helped create this celebrated (and, yes, pricey) resort's image of glamour and fashionability, St. Moritz is not as ultra-exclusive or snooty as its popular image leads one to expect. St. Moritz can be a generally sporty place with superb downhill skiing on all levels and ideal cross-country skiing. At an altitude of 6,000 feet,

annual snowfalls are dependable. Intermediate skiers will enjoy hopping the cable car to Piz Corvatsch, almost 11,000 feet above sea level.

There is lots of nonskiing activity, including the famous British-made Cresta Run, the world's first sleigh and toboggan run, where women are not allowed, so risky is the head-first, white-knuckle ride. Consider a summertime holiday here, or at lovely Pontresina, just 4 miles east of St. Moritz: it is one of the Engadine's—and Europe's—best hiking bases and mountaineering centers.

In St. Moritz, the enduring place to be seen is the very Hollywood faux-Gothic Badrutt's Palace Hotel. But today's more discreet set gravitates to the glitz-free Suvretta House, with Christmas-card views of the mountains. A triumph of subdued luxury, from here it's an easy walk to Jöhri's Talvo. Classy but creative, this is one of the country's very best eating experiences, delightfully set in a charming 17th-century Engadine farmhouse (*talvo* means "hayloft" in Romansh, the archaic tongue of the Engadine Valley).

At the end of your stay, ride the rails to Zermatt in the east. The Glacier Express is advertised as the slowest express train in the world (averaging 25 miles an hour), but the little-red-engine-that-could passes through the heart of the Swiss Alps and offers an up-close look at riveting scenery on its roller-coaster journey (gradients can approach 110 percent). Proudly painted the colors of the Swiss flag, it passes over 291 bridges and through 91 tunnels, and crosses the Oberalp Pass at 6,706 feet—the 7½-hour, 169-mile trip's highest point. Serious rail buffs can consider Switzerland's other great rail excursion, the Bernina Express. A four-hour rail trip from Zurich to Lugano (also doable by car), it

The Glacier Express on one of the route's 291 bridges

is the only train route in Switzerland that crosses the Alps without the benefit of tunnels en route.

WHAT: town, hotel, experience. **ST. MORITZ:** 125 miles/201 km southeast of Zurich. **SUVRETTA HOUSE:** Via Chasellas. Tel 41/81-836-3636, fax 41/81-836-3737; info@ suvrettahouse.ch; www.suvrettahouse.ch. *Cost:* doubles from $360 (low season), from $450 (high season) in winter; from $253 (low season), from $286 (high season) in summer. *When:* open Jul–mid-Sept, early Dec–mid-Apr. **GLACIER EXPRESS:** from St. Moritz to Zermatt and return. Reservations are necessary and must be made in advance. They can be booked online, or book locally upon your arrival at any Swiss rail station. In the U.S., contact Rail Europe, tel 800-622-8600; in Canada, tel 800-361-RAIL; www.raileurope. com. *Cost:* one-way first class $235, second class $150. **BEST TIMES:** Jul–Sept and end of Dec–Mar.

A Pure Swiss Country Hideaway

SCHLOSSHOTEL CHASTÈ

Tarasp, Engadine, Switzerland

Hidden in one of eastern Switzerland's most beautiful and least trammeled corners, this Swiss country inn is a place where old traditions flourish, and hospitality is reflected in the heartfelt greeting *"Allegra!"* (from the ancient Romansch language still spoken in these parts). Run by the Pazeller family since 1480 and just a short drive from the Austrian border, this lovely sgraffito-covered (scratched stucco) farmhouse commands the center of a tiny hamlet named for the fantasy-like feudal castle that looms on a nearby hilltop. The area boasts countless hiking paths and high mountain trails through enchanted woodlands, alpine meadows carpeted with wildflowers, old villages (nearby Guarda is uncontestedly one of the country's most photogenic). Switzerland's only national park, Parc Naziunal Svizzer, is just 13 miles away, a pristine sanctuary of 65 square miles with sixteen hiking circuits.

The best finish to a vacation-perfect day in these bracing elements would be your return to Chastè, a rural retreat of cosmopolitan luxury highlighted by the presence of host and chef Rudy Pazeller. His talents shine in the kitchen's small but sophisticated menu and throughout the inn's impeccable guest rooms.

WHAT: hotel. **WHERE:** 8 miles/13 km east of Guarda, 132 miles/210 km southeast of Zurich. Tel 41/81-861-3060, fax 41/81-861-3061; chaste@relaischateaux.com; www.relaischateaux.com. **COST:** doubles from $295 (low season), from $310 (high season). **WHEN:** open late May–late Oct, Christmastime–late Mar. **BEST TIMES:** Jun, Aug, and Oct.

Some of the Finest Skiing Anywhere

DAVOS-KLOSTERS

Graubünden, Switzerland

Davos shares its popularity as a supreme ski destination with its smaller and lower (barely) twin city of Klosters. Offering top-of-the-line skiing for all levels, Davos is Europe's largest ski resort. At 5,120 feet, it is also its highest city, great for cold-weather sports even in warm winters. Long, scenic valley trails make it second only to Switzerland's Engadine for cross-country skiing.

Davos shares a sweeping network of lifts and slopes with nearby Klosters, whose more

Hotel Chesa Grischuna and its restaurant

attractive alpine village is where you want to unpack your bags (Swedish and British royalty return here faithfully). Almost intimate compared to Davos, Klosters still nurtures its sobriquet of "Hollywood on the Rocks" because of the international movie people it attracts. VIP or not, they all come for the exemplary Parsenn-Weissfluh ski area, which many experts agree is the finest in Europe. Its famous descent from Weissfluhgipfel (9,330 feet) to Küblis (2,670 feet) is a must for the very good skier, a magnificent 9-mile piste over vast, open snowfields.

You won't need royal connections to be treated as such at the atmospheric Chesa Grischuna. Housed in a handsome wooden chalet in the very center of town, it is Klosters's most preferred hotel with the area's finest restaurant.

WHAT: town, experience, hotel, restaurant.

KLOSTERS: 100 miles/161 km southeast of Zurich. Davos is 7 miles/11 km north of Klosters. **HOTEL CHESA GRISCHUNA:** Bahnhofstrasse 12, Klosters. Tel 41/81-422-2222, fax 41/81-422-2225; hotel@chesagrischuna.ch; www. chesagrischuna.ch. *Cost:* doubles from $215 (low season), from $305 (high season). Dinner $60. *When:* open mid-Dec–late May and early Jul–mid-Oct. **BEST TIMES:** Mar for skiing; Jul for alpine flowers; Aug–Sept for hiking.

Extraordinary Music Making in a Deserving Setting

LUCERNE FESTIVAL

Switzerland

I f judged by quality rather than by glamour, turnout, or hype, the Lucerne Festival would be hard to beat. It is one of Europe's oldest (inaugurated by Toscanini in 1938), most eclectic, and most appealing, usually mentioned in the same breath as the other major summer music events: Salzburg, Bayreuth, Aix-en-Provence, and even Glyndebourne. A veritable Who's Who of big-name conductors, orchestras (sometimes more than a dozen), soloists, and chamber ensembles perform at a variety of interesting locations, including the new, ultra-modern Culture and Convention Center. Positioned on the Lido-like banks of the gracious Lake Lucerne, it makes for a dramatic departure from the city's medieval storybook setting.

Lucerne is a tourist favorite in part because it embodies everyone's image of a Swiss town. Wagner, who knew this area well, wrote, "I do not know of a more beautiful spot in this world!" and when in town stayed at the large 19th-century Schweizerhof Hotel (pristine after a 1999 renovation). Its guest book is filled with the signatures of more recent festival folk like Pinchas Zukerman, Mstislav Rostropovich, and, hopefully, you.

WHAT: event, hotel. **LUCERNE FESTIVAL:** Hirschmattstrasse 13 (Lucerne is 36 miles/57 km southwest of Zurich). Tel 41/41-226-4400, fax 41/41-226-4460; www.lucernefestival. ch. For tickets tel 41/41-226-4480, fax 41/41-226-4485; info@lucernefestival.ch. *Cost:* tickets $30–$270. *When:* 4 weeks, mid-Aug to mid-Sept. **HOTEL SCHWEIZERHOF LUZERN:** Schweizerhofquai 3. Tel 41/41-410-0410, fax. 41/41-410-2971; www.schweizerhof-luzern.ch. *Cost:* doubles from $305 (low season), from $400 (high season).

The Quintessential Alpine Movie Set

PARK HOTEL VITZNAU

Vitznau, Lucerne, Switzerland

N abbing a terraced room with a lake view is crucial, though guests might wonder if the Park Hotel Vitznau is nothing more than a stage set the general manager strikes at the end of each idyllic day. The elegant Belle

Epoque hotel's immaculately tended lawns reach right down to the shimmering edge of the gorgeous Lake Lucerne (whose German name is Vierwaldstättersee, the Lake of the Four Forest Cantons). Three full-time gardeners make the hotel's flower-filled grounds one of its most attractive attributes.

Since opening in 1902, the lavish Park Hotel has been the stronghold of the tiny lakefront community of Vitznau on the Lucerne Riviera. Its towering neighbor Mount Rigi is mirrored in the calm waters of the lake, and the climax of many a traveler's visit to the area is watching the sun rise over the Alps from the mountain's 5,896-foot summit. Many say it is Switzerland's most beautiful mountain view.

Built in 1871, the cog railway to Rigi-Kulm is Europe's oldest, one of many railways and aerial tramways that string the surrounding

mountains permitting similar views. But most guests have a hard time budging from the hotel's lakefront sun terrace or, when hunger beckons, the open-air terrace of the hotel's well-known Quatre Cantons restaurant. Its French menu often includes perfectly prepared fish plucked that morning from the lake.

WHAT: hotel, experience, restaurant. **PARK HOTEL VITZNAU:** Kantonstrasse. Tel 41/41-399-6060, fax 41/41-399-6070; info@park hotel-vitznau.ch; www.parkhotel-vitznau.ch. *Cost:* doubles with lake view $595 (low season), $645 (high season). Dinner at Quatre Cantons $110. **COG RAILWAY:** shuttles leave directly from the hotel; or call Lucerne tourist information, tel 41/41-227-1717. **WHEN:** hotel open late Apr to mid-Oct; restaurant open year-round. **BEST TIMES:** Jun and Sept.

No Longer Revolutionary, but Still Brilliant Fusion

RHEINHOTEL FISCHERZUNFT

Schaffhausen, Switzerland

Jaded palates will agree with those who originally heralded André Jaeger— he is the virtuoso chef instrumental in creating Europe's first great fusion cuisine. Twenty years ago, after his grounding as food and beverage manager

at Hong Kong's prestigious Peninsula Hotel, Jaeger returned to his picturesque, lively hometown of Schaffhausen. Here he became a

It won't be hard to get a room with a view.

pioneer in the highly traditional food world: the first to marry East and West. Fast forward to the present: His European and Asian cuisine is still thrillingly unique, a blend of widely disparate tastes and textures with a natural sophistication that continues to garner kudos from Europe's harshest critics. This fresh, modern-day cuisine with a nod to Eastern sensibility is presented in a perfectly preserved 15th-century fishermen's guild house, directly on the Rhine River near Switzerland's border with Germany.

Overnight guests at Die Fischerzunft can while away a few hours in between degustations strolling Schaffhausen's pedestrian-only

Altstadt (historic quarter) of fountains and Gothic, Baroque, and rococo facades, or make the trip to the nearby site of the Rhine Falls, the most powerful waterfall in Europe (Goethe called it the "ocean's source"). Then follow the broad and peaceful river east to Stein am Rhein, just before the river empties into the enormous Bodensee (Lake Constance). Dating back to the 11th century, the town's flamboyant frescoes and half-timbered homes put it on Switzerland's short list of most charming photo ops.

WHAT: restaurant, hotel, town. **WHERE:** Rheinquai 8 (Schaffhausen is 29 miles/ 47 km north of Zurich; Stein am Rhein is 12 miles/19 km east of Schaffhausen). Tel 41/ 52-632-0505, fax 41/52-632-0513; info@ fischerzunft.ch; www.fischerzunft.ch. **COST:** doubles from $195. Dinner $105. **WHEN:** open Wed–Sun.

La Dolce Vita, Swiss Style

LUGANO'S SPLENDID VILLAS

Ticino, Switzerland

One of Lugano's special pleasures is a walk along the shady lakefront promenade and up to the magnificent 17th-century Villa Favorita. Built by Prince Leopold of Prussia, it is now the home of the prestigious Thyssen-Bornemisza Museum. In 1992 there was a much-publicized sale of a staggering 800 Old Masters to Madrid's Villahermosa Museum (at the behest of the Spanish-born wife of the late owner, Baron Hans Heinrich Thyssen-Bornemisza). A powerful Swiss industrialist with a passion for art, the baron was the son of the original founder of this eclectic, remarkable collection of more than 150 "leftover" major works from 19th- and 20th-century European and American masters such as De Chirico, Munch, Hopper, Schiele, Wyeth, and Pollack. The oldest part of the collection includes imposing pieces of furniture from the 16th and 17th centuries.

The villa's seductive lakeside views are augmented by the famous garden, a meticulous masterpiece in itself. An artistically groomed arrangement of almost 100 species of native and exotic flowers and trees intermingled with classical statues, it is a horticultural legacy carried on by the Thyssen-Bornemisza family, who still resides here.

By now you might want your own villa. For a liberal dose of *la dolce vita*, check into the formerly private red-ocher Italianate Villa Principe Leopoldo. Built by the aristocratic Prussian von Hohenzollern family in 1868, it still speaks of princely grandeur inside and out, uniquely set atop the Collina d'Oro (Golden Hill), with spectacular views of the mountain-fringed Lake Lugano from most suites and one of the area's most stylish dining rooms and outdoor terraces. After lunch, it's an easy one-hour walk from the hotel to the wonderfully picturesque lakeside town of

The Villa Principe Leopoldo, named after Prince Frederic Leopold

Gandria, which spills down the wooded flank of Monte Brè. There, a funicular lifts you 3,000 feet to the moutain's summit. For the uncontested best view in these parts, take in the vista from atop the 5,581-foot peak of the aptly named Mount Generoso.

WHAT: town, site, hotel, restaurant. **LUGANO:** 143 miles/230 km south of Zurich, 45 miles/72 km north of Milan. **VILLA FAVORITA AND THE THYSSEN-BORNEMISZA FOUNDATION:** Strada Castagnola, Via Rivera 14. Tel 41/91-972-1741, fax 41/91-971-6151. *Cost:* admission. *When:* Thurs–Sun, Apr–Oct. **VILLA PRINCIPE LEOPOLDO AND RESIDENCE:** Via Montalbano 5. Tel 41/91-985-8855, fax 41/91-985-8825; info@leopoldohotel.com; www.leopoldohotel.com. *Cost:* doubles from $355. Dinner $80. **BEST TIMES:** May–Jun and Sept–Aug; Blues-to-Bop Music Festival and Worldmusic Festival in Sept.

The Pearl of the Alps

SAAS-FEE

Valais, Switzerland

Everyone falls for Saas-Fee in a big way. Then again, nearly everything in these parts is big: the mountain village (nicknamed "Pearl of the Alps") is surrounded by a majestic arena of thirteen peaks towering over 13,120 feet (including the nearby Matterhorn and Dom; the latter—at 14,908 feet—is the highest mountain entirely on Swiss soil). This is stunning scenery, indeed. And although one naturally expects extensive skiing to match, the steep terrain, tight ring of dramatic peaks, and extensive glaciers have limited development. But Saas-Fee offers some of the best snow conditions in Europe, and its Felskinn-Mittelallalin ski area is Switzerland's premier *summer* ski destination. The area's high-terrain walking paths also draw summertime visitors.

Given the quaint atmosphere (visitors must leave their cars outside town and rely upon a few select electric cars in town), the other big draw in town may seem somewhat incongruous: award-winning chef Markus Neff, the king of the Hotel Fletschhorn. What is such a sophisticated culinary personality doing high on a forested hill, in a chalet-like hotel-restaurant just outside town? He's continuing the legacy of famed chef Irma Dutsch, who first made the restaurant a destination for international gourmands. His French-based seasonal cuisine blends local flavors with smatterings of the exotic and poetic that would be a standout anywhere.

WHAT: town, experience, hotel, restaurant. **SAAS-FEE:** 161 miles/255 km east of Geneva (and just east of Zermatt), close to Italian border. **HOTEL FLETSCHHORN:** tel 41/27-957-2131, fax 41/27-957-2187; hotel.info@fletschhorn.ch; www.fletschhorn.ch. *Cost:* doubles from $305. Dinner $120. *When:* open Jun to mid-Oct, mid-Dec to May.

Chalets are surrounded by glorious scenery in Saas-Fee.

Upbeat and Fun, but Mighty Serious About Skiing

VERBIER

Valais, Switzerland

With some of Europe's steepest and best off-piste skiing and very lively nightlife, Verbier, in the French-speaking region of Valais ("valley"), is one of the Alps' great ski destinations. The nexus of more than 250 miles of pistes connecting four valleys, it is a magnet for young, adventurous ski buffs, who consider this stylish but relaxed town nothing short of heaven. Advanced (and aspiring expert) skiers will have their field day, enjoying wonderful top-to-bottom off-piste runs in the company of a guide. Early risers can sidestep the drawback of long lines at lifts that are being modernized and improved one by one.

The slopes aren't the only thing in town that are steep—hotel and restaurant rates are consistently high, but that doesn't seem to keep away the young *beau monde* who eschew the glitz of St. Moritz but not its luxuries. In the very heart of this remote but tres chic town (it will feel like the French-speaking town's social hub) is the Hotel Farinet. Overlooking the main square and the slopes beyond, it is just a few minutes walk from the chair lifts. You don't need to be a hotel guest to enjoy its vibrant après-ski scene at the bar or at the Casbah lounge, always abuzz with a healthy-looking and fashionable crowd, many of them young professional types from nearby Geneva.

WHAT: town, experience, restaurant, hotel. **WHERE:** 100 miles/161 km east of Geneva. **HOTEL FARINET:** Place Centrale. Tel 41/27-771-6626, fax 41/27-771-3855; www. hotelfarinet.com. *Cost:* doubles from $250 (low season), from $350 (high season). **BEST TIMES:** Jan, Jul, and Sept are least crowded; mid-July for the Verbier Festival (www. verbierfestival.com).

Magic Mountain and Unparalleled Skiing

ZERMATT

Valais, Switzerland

The granite profile that launched a million postcards, the distinctive snaggletooth form of the awe-inspiring Matterhorn rears above the bustle of the popular resort town of Zermatt. Despite its contained size, traffic-free quaintness, and music-box chalets, Zermatt is all business: An international mix of intermediate and advanced skiers flock here for the wonderful ski runs. Its three ski areas go up to well over 9,600 feet, and the famous Kleine Matterhorn cable car offers the highest piste skiing in Europe: count on good snow and good skiing into spring and early summer. Zermatt is also the Alps' biggest heli-skiing center: the most epic run is from Monte Rosa, at almost 15,000 feet, through remarkable glacier scenery. Zermatt is known as well for its large and varied array of restaurants in uniquely beautiful locations, and a very healthy après-ski nightlife.

English explorer and mountaineer Edward Whymper was the first to scale the 14,685-foot Matterhorn (Mont Cervin to the French-speaking Swiss) in 1865, departing from Zermatt. You may not be following in his footsteps all the way up the mountain, but you can lodge in the same hotel he did: the Hotel Monte Rosa, considerably more luxurious today than when it opened in 1839. Then the town's only inn, it accommodated the few British who were the first to "discover" Zermatt and the beauty of its environs. You'll want a room with a view.

WHAT: town, experience, hotel. **ZERMATT:** 150 miles/241 km east of Geneva on the border with Italy; reachable only by rail either from Brig or Visp (both about 30 miles/48 km distant) where most visitors leave their cars. **HOTEL MONTE ROSA:** Bahnhofstrasse. Tel 41/27-966-0333, fax 41/27-966-0330; in the U.S., 800-223-6800; www.monterosazermatt.ch. *Cost:* doubles from $410 (summer), from $730 (winter) includes breakfast and dinner. *When:* open mid-Jun to mid-Oct, mid-Dec to mid-Apr. **BEST TIMES:** Feb, Mar, and Jul–Oct.

A Bird's-Eye View of Mountain Majesty

WINTER ALPINE BALLOON FESTIVAL

Château d'Oex, Vaud, Switzerland

Hot-air balloon festivals are no longer a conversation-stopping novelty, but ballooning through the Alps in the middle of winter? At the annual Winter Alpine Balloon Festival, as many as sixty-five balloons from more than fifteen countries ascend gracefully as a carnival ambience takes over the popular resort town below, with organized dinners held each evening. If you miss the festival, alternative weeks offer wintertime flying that is no less awesome, among majestic peaks and through snow-covered alpine valleys. Elegant in-flight luncheons are served while passengers drift serenely over Christmas-card settings.

Summertime ballooning in Switzerland takes place in the softer rolling hills of the Emmental valley, in the otherwise dramatic Bernese Oberland. The precise geometric patterns of Swiss farmland and picture-perfect, flower-decked rural wooden chalets create the perfect "aerial nature walk," according to Buddy Bombard, who leads one of the world's most reliable ballooning outfitters.

WHAT: experience, event. **WHERE:** 40 miles/64 km east of Lausanne in the vicinity of Gstaad. **HOW:** In the U.S., contact The Bombard Society, "Buddy Bombard's Private Europe," tel 561-837-6610 or 800-862-8537; www.buddybombard.com. **COST:** 9-day festival trip $17,990 per person, double occupancy, all-inclusive. Nonfestival trip is 8 days, $16,510 per person. Summertime trip is 5 days, $8,940 per person. **WHEN:** 2 festival departures in mid-Jan. Nonfestival departures in Feb. One summer departure in 1st week of Sept.

In the Fabled Footsteps of a Legendary Mentor

RESTAURANT DE L'HOTEL DE VILLE

Crissier, Vaud, Switzerland

There was a time when Frédy Girardet was regarded not only as Switzerland's chef par excellence, but one of the world's best—even his Parisian peers reluctantly named him Chef of the Century in 1989. After years of threatening to retire to pursue other interests, the legendary "Pope of Swiss Cuisine" finally shocked the gastronomic world by doing just that in 1996. The world did not collapse nor stop. In fact, his associate chef and star protégé of seventeen years, Philippe Rochat, orchestrated a seamless transition and continues to serve a full house of Chez Girardet's loyal patrons, who book two months in advance and drive the 38 miles from Geneva for a weekend table. Rochat eventually changed the name of the gourmet shrine and brought the formality—but not quality—of the service down half a notch. However, he has kept a number of his mentor's all-time favorite signature dishes alive and as exquisitely executed as in the past. Here in the canton of Vaud, Switzerland's Francophone heart, Rochat, like Girardet before him, comfortably balances the French and the German, the high and the low, the folksy and the sublime. This canton is home to the outstanding white wines of the surrounding Lavaux area and the excellent cellar features both these and French wines.

WHAT: restaurant. **WHERE:** 1 Rue d'Yverdon (Crissier is 4 miles/7 km west of Lausanne). Tel 41/21-634-05-05, fax 41/21-634-2464; www.phillipe-rochat.ch. **COST:** dinner $280. **WHEN:** open Tues–Sat.

The Hills Are Alive with the Sound of Music

MONTREUX JAZZ FESTIVAL

Montreux, Vaud, Switzerland

Since 1967, the Montreux Jazz Festival has been Europe's leading jazz event, but it has never locked itself into just one format, presenting blues, reggae, funk, soul, rap, rock, and pop as well as its namesake style. Always ahead of the curve, the festival features both new and known talent, exclusive jams, and the finest sound system and halls, with the big-time acts performing in the principal venues and the lesser-knowns toughing it out on the streets—no surprise that the latter can be just as enjoyable. Beginning as a three-day event, the fest has grown to sixteen days, adding much to the strong musical tradition of this ever-popular town that sits on the banks of the lovely Lake Geneva.

Since the 19th century, artists, writers, and musicians have been attracted to this resort city with its distinct French accent and worldly atmosphere, ambitiously compared to that of Cannes. You'll

understand why Lake Geneva is called the Swiss Riviera when you see the palms, cypresses, and magnolias that flourish here (thanks to the mountains that protect the city from the harsh winter winds)

B.B. King at Montreux

and the cafés that line the marvelous lakeside walks. Cannes can only covet the Château de Chillon, just down the coast and within sight of Montreux. Switzerland's most important and most photographed castle, parts of it date back 1,000 years. It moved Lord Byron to write his famous poem *The Prisoner of Chillon*, and has undoubtedly lent inspiration to the music making that brings Montreux alive each July.

WHAT: town, event. **MONTREUX:** 62 miles/ 100 km east of Geneva on Lake Geneva. **MONTREUX JAZZ FESTIVAL:** tel 41/21-966-4444; info@mjf.ch; www.montreuxjazz.com. *How:* in the U.S., contact Ciao! Travel, tel 619-297-8112 or 800-942-2426, fax 619-297-8114; jazz@ciaotravel.com; www.ciaotravel.com. *Cost:* 6-night package from $2,550 includes air from New York, hotel, breakfast, tickets for 5 principal concerts. *When:* 16 days that include the first 3 full weekends of Jul.

Swiss Cuisine Steps to the Forefront

PETERMANN'S KUNSTSTUBEN

Küsnacht, Zurich, Switzerland

What's good enough for the Swiss president, a regular patron, is good enough for most. And now that two thirds of the Swiss triumvirate of master chefs is gone (Frédy Girardet is retired and Hans Stucki has passed on), Horst Petermann reigns in a league of his own, continuing to inspire chefs who are making a significant place for Swiss cuisine on the gastronomic map. In a relentlessly elegant, flower-filled dining room in a 19th-century lakeside house on the outskirts of Zurich, Petermann wows his international clientele with a menu that is almost compulsively inventive, every mouthful a revelation. In warm weather a small but delightful outdoor garden is the place to be. The ever-evolving and market-based offerings include fish dishes he keeps as fresh and natural as possible and various preparations of filet mignon and foie gras that underline his brilliance. Those with a sweet tooth will never forget Petermann's

Kunststuben *means "art parlors."*

signature hot mint soufflé on a "carpaccio" of thinly sliced peaches. The wine cellar lives up to expectations, including a small but particularly good selection of labels from Ticino, the Italian-speaking canton of southern Switzerland.

WHAT: restaurant. **WHERE:** Seestrasse 160 (Küsnacht is 6 miles/10 km south of Zurich on the lake's eastern shore). Tel 41/44-910-0715; www.kunstsuben.com. **COST:** 5–8 course lunch from $75, dinner from $125. **WHEN:** open Tues–Sat.

Impeccable Swiss Comfort

DOLDER GRAND HOTEL AND KRONENHALLE

Zurich, Switzerland

Pitted against some tough local competitors, including Zurich's prestigious lakeside Hotel Baur au Lac and the neoclassical Eden au Lac, the Dolder Grand Hotel manages to outshine them all—and in fact, for many five-star-hotel connoisseurs, is among the handful of Europe's finest. With spires and turrets in the style of the German Art Nouveau called Jugendstil, the extraordinary building sits in an equally extravagant 125-acre park high above Zurich, reached by funicular.

Its acclaimed restaurant faultlessly serves an excellent traditional Mediterranean menu; Sunday lunch buffet is also justifiably renowned. From the hotel's understatedly elegant guest rooms (many with balconies) to the gorgeous 9-hole golf course, pool (with a wave-making machine), and skating rink, everything at the Dolder shares the same remarkable views of Switzerland's most commercially and financially powerful city. The century-old main wing is the favorite of return guests; don't miss the Gobelin Room, which houses an enormous 18th-century tapestry.

Down below, in town, everyone who is anyone turns up at Kronenhalle at one time or another. Tradition is everything in Zurich, and it reigns supreme at this well-loved classic. Kronenhalle's animated scene is something to behold, and

its traditional Swiss and French cooking is very good. But the decor is the highlight. Every inch of burnished wood paneling is covered by 20th-century paintings and drawings, including originals by Klee, Chagall, Braque, Picasso, Matisse, and Kandinsky. They were collected by longtime owner Hulda Zumsteg, whose portrait still hangs here as well. Since her passing in 1985, her son carries on in the tradition that drew regulars like James Joyce, Richard Strauss, and Thomas Mann. In the likely event that there's no available table

The Dolder celebrated its 100th anniversary in 1999.

when you arrive without reservations, head to the genial adjoining bar, ask for the signature Ladykiller, and take in the scene. Perhaps a cancellation will provide a table. Even if you order nothing more than the standard sausage and favorite *rösti* potatoes, it will be delicious, you'll be full (for the next couple of days), and the evening will be consummately Swiss.

WHAT: hotel, restaurant. **DOLDER GRAND HOTEL:** Kurhausstrasse 65. Tel 41/44-456-6000, fax 41/44-456-6001; info@thedoldergrand.com; www.thedoldergrand.com. *Cost:* doubles from $605. Dinner at The Restaurant $90; Sun lunch buffet $80. **KRONENHALLE:** Rämistrasse 4. Tel 41/44-262-9900; www.kronenhalle.com. *Cost:* dinner $85.

EASTERN EUROPE

A Trio of Bohemian Spas

CARLSBAD

Bohemia, Czech Republic

"I feel as if I'm in some paradise of innocence and spontaneity," wrote Goethe, who spent sixteen summers in Karlovy Vary, more commonly known abroad by its German name, Carlsbad. That Beethoven, Brahms, Bach, Liszt, and many others all found inspiration during frequent visits to this spa town speaks volumes. Thanks to the Czech Republic's geological fault lines, there are more than thirty spa towns in the area still in operation. Carlsbad is the largest and most renowned. Only its centuries-old competitor Marianske Lazne (Marienbad) comes close to rivaling its fame. For more than 400 years, the world's rich and famous have come to "take the waters" of Carlsbad's twelve natural thermal springs, which range from 76 to 161 degrees Fahrenheit. (The "thirteenth spring" is Becherovka, a well-known locally produced herb-and-mineral liqueur, also said to be curative.) Situated in a beautiful and wooded valley, Carlsbad retains an elegant, important air, dominated by handsome 19th-century architecture.

Dating from 1701, the starred Grand Hotel Pupp was once one of Europe's most famous hotels, with countless celebrities, including Goethe, Paganini, and Freud, filling its guest

Mineral springs were discovered here in the 1300s.

register. Use this as your regal base, and drive forty-five minutes south to the smaller, quieter Marienbad, whose thirty-some mineral springs were the favorite choice of Kafka, Chopin, and England's King Edward VII. Given its rather lazy ambience, the fact that the town boasts a top-ranked golf course (the country's finest) may come as something of a surprise. For the curious with time and wheels, the third and smallest of the local trio of well-known spa towns is Frantiskovy Lazne (Franzenbad), almost at the German border.

WHAT: town, hotel. **CARLSBAD:** 76 miles/ 120 km west of Prague. **GRAND HOTEL**

PUPP: Mírové námesti 2. Tel 420/35-3109111, fax 420/35-3224032; pupp@pupp.cz; www.pupp.cz. *Cost:* doubles from $435. **BEST TIMES:** fall. International Film Festival Karlovy Vary is in early Jul.

An Exquisite Medieval Jewel, No Longer Unknown

CESKY KRUMLOV

Bohemia, Czech Republic

Cesky Krumlov has an impressive history, but it is a living town, and provides an interesting window on genuine Bohemian village life, particularly in the off-season, when the ever-increasing tourist crowds subside.

Most notable among the impressive amalgam of medieval, Renaissance, Baroque, and rococo buildings is the splendid castle (Krumlov hrad, also called the Schwarzenberg Castle). Czech castles are a dime a dozen, but with 300 rooms, this is the second largest in the Czech Republic after Prague's. For some 300 years, it was the official residence of the Rozenberk dynasty, the powerful noble family that ruled southern Bohemia from 1316 to the 16th century. You can also fill your days exploring the countless nooks and crannies of this pristine, fairy-tale river town, meandering through twisting and cobbled alleyways, some so narrow you must walk sideways.

The Czech Republic is famous for its beers (although brewing is a millennium old, lager was invented in the Bohemian town of Pilsen, or Plzen, in 1842) and Cesky Krumlov has its own brewery, the Eggenberg. The cavernous Beer Hall at 27 Latrán is the place to sip its tasty dark beer on tap.

Park your bags at the Hotel Rüze, the

city's most romantic hotel, recently refurbished. A 16th-century Renaissance building used as a Jesuit monastery, it offers lovely rooms (some with gorgeous views of the historical center and the castle) and an excellent restaurant specializing in traditional Czech dishes.

WHAT: town, hotel. **CESKY KRUMLOV:** 113 miles/180 km south of Prague (35 miles/ 56 km from Austrian border). *When:* castle and château open Apr–Oct. **HOTEL RÜZE:** Horní 154. Tel 420/380-772100, fax 420/ 380-713146; info@hotelruze.cz; www.hotel ruze.cz. *Cost:* doubles from $205 (low season), from $315 (high season). **BEST TIMES:** spring and fall. International Music Festival, 3 weeks in Aug; Festival of Early Music, last week of Jul.

The Vltava (Moldau) meanders through and around Cesky Krumlov.

Religious and Political Symbol of Might and Glory

CASTLE DISTRICT

Prague, Bohemia, Czech Republic

High atop the hilly West Bank of this "Golden City" is one of the most beautiful sights in Europe: Prague Castle (Prazsky hrad) perched above the curving Vltava (or Moldau) River that flows below it, with the Gothic masterpiece of St. Vitus Cathedral (Chrám svatého Vita) soaring behind it. This was the site of early Prague, and everything that evolved from it lay in its proverbial shadow. An amble through this picturesque hilltop town-within-a-town provides breathtaking views of the river and the Gothic-style Charles Bridge. The fabled skyline of spires and turrets of the lower Old Town (Staré Mesto) rises above the

The Charles Bridge with Prague Castle in the background

ancient rooftops of the right, or east, bank. Prague Castle is a monumental fortresslike collection of buildings and courtyards spanning the millennia from the 10th to the 20th centuries. Its spiritual core is the 14th-century cathedral, not completed until 1929. Of its twenty-one chapels, the most lavish is dedicated to "Good King" Wenceslas, patron saint of Bohemia; others honor Czech princes and kings from the 11th to the 13th centuries.

Adjacent is the Royal Palace (Krávlovsky palác), residence for the lords of Bohemia from the 11th to the 16th centuries. This is where, in 1990, the dissident writer Václav Havel was inaugurated as president of what was then Czechoslovakia. Prague's two most important art galleries are the highlight for many: the deconsecrated St. George's Basilica houses a unique collection of ancient Czech art, while six centuries of European art is found in the Sternberk Palace. If the rich 1,000-year heritage of the castle complex makes your head swim, escape to the small and intimate Hotel U Páva (the name means "peacock"), with its excellent location on a charming gaslit street. The homey rooms in the front of the house have unforgettable nighttime views of the illuminated Prague Castle.

Just 100 yards from the Charles Bridge is the riverside Four Seasons, Prague's first bona fide luxury hotel. Much of the hotel comprises three classic 18th- and 19th-century buildings (one of which served as King Charles IV's laundry), with suites that promise romantic views of the river and the hilltop castle.

WHAT: site, hotel. **CASTLE DISTRICT:** on Prague's west bank. **THE HOTEL U PÁVA:** U Luzického semináre 32 (Malá Strana). Tel

420/2-575-33360 upava@romantichotels.cz; www.romantichotels.cz. *Cost:* doubles $140 (low season), $155 (high season); with castle view $166 (low season), $180 (high season).

FOUR SEASONS: Veleslavinova 2a. Tel 420/2-2142-7000, fax 420/2-2142-6000; www.fourseasons.com. *Cost:* from $520; suites with castle view $1,530.

Europe's Longest and Most Beautiful Medieval Bridge

CHARLES BRIDGE

Prague, Bohemia, Czech Republic

Much of Prague's present architectural beauty was achieved during its 14th-century glory days under Charles IV, king of Bohemia and Moravia and Holy Roman Emperor. It was Charles who established a university in the city and commissioned his namesake Charles Bridge in 1357, Prague's most beloved and recognized icon. There are fourteen other bridges that span the swirling Vltava River (which overflowed its banks in the unprecedented floods of 2002), but the view from the foot of this pedestrian bridge on the east bank is nothing short of wondrous, encompassing the remarkable mélange of architecture on the hilly slope of the Malá Strana (Lesser Town) that leads up to Prague Castle on the opposite bank. Thirty-six Baroque saints, the majority added in the 17th century, line the bridge's graceful sixteen-arched crossing.

The ritual of visiting the landmark bridge at many different times of day is a must. Early morning on the swan-studded Vltava means having the bridge to yourself while the guardian statues hover like ghosts shrouded in the lifting mist. Midday brings on a mass of residents, tourists, buskers and other street performers, and T-shirt vendors ("Czech 'em out!"). At night, the spirit of an ongoing block party winds down and the bridge becomes magical, even spellbinding.

Within arm's reach of the bridge, the romantic boutique inn U Trí Pstrosu (At the Three Ostriches) offers oak-beamed guest rooms and excellent dining with a view. Formerly Bohemia's first coffeehouse, its massive centuries-old walls keep out the noise of the crowds. Ask for a corner room for the best views.

WHAT: site, hotel. **U TRÍ PSTROSU:** Drazického námestí 12. Tel 420/2-5728-8888; info@hotelutripstrosu.cz; www.utripstrosu.com. **COST:** doubles from $100.

A flood swept away the Charles's predecessor, Judith Bridge.

Mozart Lives On in This City of Music

ESTATES THEATER

Prague, Bohemia, Czech Republic

P rague has enjoyed an unparalleled cultural renaissance since the end of the forty-year Communist regime. For centuries a magnet for classical musicians ("Whoever is Czech, is a musician," asserts a local proverb),

it is again a dream for music lovers, with prestigious international festivals and an embarassment of choices for those looking to hear the music of Bedřich Smetana and Antonín Dvořák, 19th-century local boy wonders. Wolfgang Amadeus Mozart loved this city and called the people "my Praguers." He basked in their veneration, a welcome change from the lack of appreciation in his native Austria. The spirit of Mozart's genius is almost tangible in the cherubim-filled Estates Theater (Stavovské divadlo), the site of the premier performance of his opera *Don Giovanni*, conducted by the composer himself in 1787. Restored to its neoclassical pale green elegance, and reopened in 1991 on the 200th anniversary of Mozart's death, this is a jewel case of tiered boxes that is spectacular inside and

out. Concertgoers may recognize the Estates from scenes in the film *Amadeus* by Czech director Milos Forman; fees from the film-making generated the seed money for the theater's sumptuous eight-year renovation. Any lucky modern-day audience would be likely to agree with Gustave Flaubert's dec-laration that "the three most beautiful things ever created in this world are the sea, *Hamlet*, and Mozart's *Don Giovanni*."

WHAT: site, experience. **WHERE:** Ovocny trh 6. Tel 420/2-2490-1448 (information), fax 420/2-2493-1544; info@narodni-divadlo.cz; buy tickets online at www.narodni-divadlo.cz. **WHEN:** concert and opera season Sept–Jun (*Don Giovanni* performed often). **BEST TIMES:** Prague Spring Music Festival concerts (3 weeks beginning early–mid-May); expect crowds.

The Heart and Soul of the City of Spires

OLD TOWN SQUARE

Prague, Bohemia, Czech Republic

T he glorious architectural confusion of the oldest segment of Prague city lies on the east bank of the meandering Vltava River just off the Charles Bridge. The city's first settlements appeared here in the 10th century when

a bustling marketplace grew from its strategic riverside location at the mercantile crossroads of Central Europe. One thousand years later

the Old Town Square (Staromestské námestí) is still the very heart of Prague. This was the haunted neighborhood of Franz Kafka, but don't expect an air of melancholy and paranoia. Today the square is a veritable stage set with bright outdoor café umbrellas; store windows that are a paean to *kapitalismus;* young entrepreneurial types glued to their cell phones; musicians, mimes, and tarot readers; and a milling crowd of tourists who come to witness the hourly procession of apostles and allegorical figures on the famous 600-year-old astronomical clock (Staroměstská radnice). A climb to the top of the 200-foot tower of the former Town Hall above it gives a dazzling panorama of this "City of One Hundred Spires"—surely the spires and turrets number twice that. Like many of the capital's architectural gems, the 14th-century Church of Our Lady of Tyn (Tynky chrám) glows from a recent cleaning, its magnificent Gothic facade and elegant twin gables one of the city's most recognizable silhouettes.

A view with Town Hall on the left

WHAT: site. **BEST TIMES:** the annual Christmas Fair early Dec–early Jan: open-air festivities and musical performances take place around a giant Christmas tree. There's also an Easter market.

Raucous and Rowdy, the Czech Beer Experience

U FLEKU

Prague, Bohemia, Czech Republic

"Wherever beer is brewed, all is well. Whenever beer is drunk, life is good" goes one Czech proverb. After an evening at Prague's oldest and most famous beer hall, you won't have any trouble believing that Czechs consume more *pivo* (beer) per capita than any other nationality—except that all these hundreds of beer-swilling, fun-making stein wielders are speaking and singing in every language except Czech. Everyone complains about the noise and the food, but the place has been packed for centuries: records show that a license to make beer on this spot dates back to 1499, and the original Budweiser was a Czech beer. U Fleku neither exports nor even bottles its famously pungent brew—and there doesn't appear to be a need to, since the whole world comes here. Six large tavernlike rooms of communal tables, outside gardens, and shade trees make the capacity crowd seem less astounding than it is; the place is downright cozy during cold and dark winter evenings. A Czech brass oompah band plays traditional drinking music most summer weekends and if you've never experienced Munich's Oktoberfest, you won't have to after this. The rich, dark home-brewed beer with its creamy head may not be to everyone's liking, but 46,000 hectoliters of the elixir (about 2.15 million gallons) are said to be consumed yearly. Little wonder that any complaints about the goulash and dumplings are halfhearted.

WHAT: restaurant. **WHERE:** Kremencova 11. Tel 420/2-2493-4019, fax 420/2-2493-4805; ufleku@ufleku.cz; www.ufleku.cz. **COST:** dinner $15.

Where History and Scenery Vie for Attention

CASTLE HILL

Budapest, Hungary

Buda, on the left bank of the Danube River, is the hilly, older part of Budapest. From its highest point—the lovingly reconstructed Buda Castle (or Royal Palace)—the views of the Danube and Pest's monumental buildings are gorgeous. Getting there can be no less dramatic: from Pest, stroll across the Danube on Budapest's graceful, landmark Chain Bridge, and grab the steep-climbing funicular that connects you with Castle Hill and its cobbled streets and restored buildings from the Hapsburg era. The immense Buda Castle commands the most strategic location in town. Here the Hungarian kings set up an imposing showpiece residence they would call home for

Fisherman's Bastion

seven centuries. Now it boasts four museums, including the Hungarian National Gallery, and some of the 9 miles of medieval underground tunnels used during WW I (parts of which today house the tacky Buda Wax Works). Views from the seven-turreted Fisherman's Bastion are inspiring, especially in the evening. Something of the area's bohemian character lingers in the cozy coffee houses and bookstores, but the regentrified UNESCO-protected neighborhood of twisting alleyways and handicrafts shops thrives on tourism and hasn't seen an aspiring artist in years.

The neighborhood's premier lodging site is the Hilton, the only hotel in this quietly elegant part of town. Its historically sensitive, award-winning design incorporates the ruins of a 13th-century church; the Baroque facade of a 17th-century Jesuit college serves as the contemporary hotel's main entrance. The hotel's small casino is the nicest in town (among more than a dozen), but you might find the summertime classical concerts in the former church's Dominican courtyard more interesting.

WHAT: site, hotel. **BUDA CASTLE:** Budvári Palota Disztér 17. **BUDAPEST HILTON HOTEL:** Hess Andras ter 1–3. Tel 36/1-889-6600, fax 36/1-889-6644; in the U.S., tel 800-221-2424; info.budapest@hilton.com; www.budapest.hilton.com. *Cost:* doubles from $170.

Blue It's Not, Beautiful It Is—and How

THE DANUBE BEND

Budapest, Hungary

N orth of where it divides Buda from Pest, the wide Danube (Duna to the Hungarians) twists through a narrow valley that many consider the loveliest stretch of its entire 1,890-mile course from the Black Forest to

the Black Sea. This is the celebrated Danube Bend (Duna Kanyar), famous for its historic towns and scenic beauty, and a classic day trip for city-weary foreigners and Hungarians alike, by boat, car, or train. The most popular of the riverside towns (and suffering from peak-season crowds and commercialization) is Szentendre, settled in medieval times by Serbs escaping the Turkish invasion to the south, a charming artist colony since the 1920s. It still counts a dozen Orthodox churches within its boundaries, as well as a surprising number of galleries and museums, most notably an expansive museum dedicated to the work of Hungarian ceramicist Margit Kovács. Visitors more interested in handicraft shopping, dallying in cafés, and strolling along back streets lined with yellow, orange, and green houses will also be rewarded.

A bit farther north is Esztergom, seat of the Magyar kingdom in the 12th and 13th centuries. As the center of the Hungarian Catholic Church, it is the nation's most sacred

Inside Esztergom Cathedral

city, dominated by Hungary's largest cathedral, built in the mid-19th century.

WHAT: experience, town. **DANUBE BEND:** boat service from Budapest mid-Apr to mid-Oct. **SZENTENDRE:** 13 miles/21 km north of Budapest, 1½ hours by boat. **ESZTERGOM:** 40 miles/64 km north of Budapest, 4 hours by boat (hydrofoils cut time to 1 hour, 10 minutes).

Grandeur of a Once Opulent Temple of Delectables

GERBEAUD

Budapest, Hungary

T he final eastbound stop in the sweet-tooth triathlon (after Angelina's in Paris and Demel's in Vienna), Budapest's famous Gerbeaud coffeehouse is a neo-Baroque throwback to imperial times, and an oasis of relaxation

Just one of the salons where customers can enjoy coffee and a sweet

in a city reinventing itself at breakneck speed. But then, that's nothing new. In the late 19th century, Budapest was one of the fastest-growing cities in the world and the city's coffeehouses became second homes for writers, artists, politicians, journalists, and even a bit of royalty in the person of Empress "Sissi" Hapsburg. Opened in 1858 and at its current site since 1870, Gerbeaud survived the bleak period of Communism and is now back on the tourist circuit—ensuring its survival, but making it impossible to find a late afternoon table in the vast, mansionlike interior, with its heavy velvet curtains, silk wallpaper, crystal chandeliers, and marble-topped tables.

Throughout its history, Gerbeaud has been a nirvana for chocoholics. Astounded by the dozens of ultra-rich confections made daily on the premises, wide-eyed, sweet-toothed, first-time patrons are hard pressed to choose between delicacies such as Gerbeaud's signature seven-layer chocolate cake (the original Hungarian rhapsody?) and its famous cherry or apple strudel.

WHAT: restaurant. **WHERE:** Vörösmarty tér 7 (Pest). Tel 36/1-429-9000 or 429-9021; gerbeaud@gerbeaud.hu; www.gerbeaud.hu.

Big, Grand, and Traditional, Re-creating Its Glory Days

GUNDEL

Budapest, Hungary

Budapest's fanciest and most famous restaurant is also widely considered the country's—and maybe Eastern Europe's—best. Reopened to much fanfare in 1992 after restoration by Hungarian-born American restaurateur George Lang (owner of New York's Café des Artistes), the aristocratic magic of its 1894 debut can still be felt, from the era when Budapest was the Paris of Eastern Europe. The menu is delightfully old-fashioned, with many classic dishes prepared as they were in Gundel's glory days. Some of Hungary's best wines never leave the country, and they can be found on the extensive wine list, the city's most impressive, including a noble Tokay dessert wine, one of many under the Gundel house label. Just next door is Gundel's popular sister establishment, Bagolyvár (The Owl's Castle), whose menu is less extensive, less expensive, and more homestyle—owner Lang wants visitors and Hungarian diners alike to have a choice between a grand evening, complete with wandering Gypsy violinists, and a cozy down-home alternative.

WHAT: restaurant. **WHERE:** Allatkerti ut 2 ut City Park (Pest). Tel 36/1-468-4040, fax 36/1-363-1917; info@gundel.hu; www.gundel. hu. **COST:** dinner at Gundel's $50; at Bagolyvár $20.

Taking the Waters in the Style of the Ottoman Pashas

HOTEL GELLÉRT

Budapest, Hungary

The Turkish occupation of Hungary from 1541 to 1686 is still detectable in the revered tradition of public bathing, a form of leisure that the Hungarians take mighty seriously. Budapest's many bathing establishments survived Communism, but none so brilliantly as those of the Hotel Gellért. This dowager of the capital's hotels, an Art Nouveau gem, was built in the early 1900s over eighteen generous hot springs with pools (open to the public) modeled after the ancient baths of Caracalla. Beneath the Gellért's spectacular florid stained-glass domes and mosaics inlaid with gold, locals quietly play chess on floating boards, socialize in hushed tones, or paddle about at their leisure in the elaborately tiled pools. Visitors loll about swathed in Turkish towels (or much less) awaiting their massage appointments. The city's more than thirty spas offer the chance to partake in the ancient ritual of these restorative waters. It is said there are more than 1,000 underground hot springs in Hungary, 80 beneath Budapest alone, but the historic Gellért's is the Taj Mahal of baths, the most colorful and fascinating way to soak up the local Eastern European culture, even if just for a few hours.

Construction of the indoor pools began in 1916 and was completed two years later.

WHAT: hotel, experience. **WHERE:** Szent Gellért Ter 1 (Buda). Tel 36/1-889-5500, fax 36/1-889-5505; gellert.reservation@danubius hotels.com; www.danubiusgroup.com. **COST:** doubles from $135, includes entrance to baths. Entrance to baths for nonguests $18.

Europe's Largest Medieval Market Square

RYNEK GLOWNY

Kraków, Poland

Kraków remained in a dismal Rip Van Winkle sleep during forty-four years of Communism. When it awoke in the early 1990s, a new vitality quickly resuscitated its core, the Rynek Glowny, the largest and most authentic medieval market square on the continent. All roads lead to it, and all of Kraków sooner or later passes, shops, or congregates here. Ringed by Gothic, Renaissance, and Baroque facades that belie its 1257 origin, the center is dominated by the Sukiennice, an arcaded pale yellow "cloth hall" (a clearinghouse and marketplace for textiles) built in the 14th century and updated during the Renaissance. It still serves as a commercial hub, its bottom floor taken over by stalls selling kitsch items relating to Pope John Paul II (once archbishop of Kraków), folk art, and Eastern European crafts.

In the square's northeast corner is St. Mary's, one of the most magnificent Gothic churches in Europe, founded in 1222 and rebuilt in 1355. Every Polish child knows the story behind the bell tower's trumpeteer, who sounds each hour with a simple broken-off

The Sukiennice has been rebuilt and renovated several times over the centuries.

solo, reenacting the fate of the 13th-century hero who received an arrow in his throat midnote while warning of a Tatar invasion.

Within Old Town's traffic-free district and just two blocks from the square is arguably the city's finest historical hotel, the Hotel Francuski, first opened in 1912. Though fully refurbished, it still offers old-world charm and original Art Nouveau atmosphere and decor. Also on the square is the historic restaurant Wierzynek, the best place to enjoy courtly European service and traditional Polish specialties. Said to be one of the oldest operating restaurants in Europe, its history goes back to 1364, when innkeeper Mikolaj Wierzynek created a banquet served on gold and silver plates for the guests of King Casimir the Great, including Holy Roman Emperor Charles IV. Wierzynek restaurant has hosted every visiting head of state ever since. Experience 500 years of history at the elegant café downstairs or the venerable upstairs salon, where seasonal game, mountain trout, and mushroom-sauced delights are served amid decorative reminders of the establishment's storied past.

WHAT: site, hotel, restaurant. **RYNEK GLOWNY:** flea market in the square every Sat near Grzegórzecke St. Annual fairs sprawl across the square at Easter and Christmastime. **HOTEL FRANCUSKI:** Ulica Pijarska 13. Tel 48/12-627-3777, fax 48/12-627-3700; rez.francuski@orbis.pl. *Cost:* doubles from $215. **WIERZYNEK:** Rynek Glowny 15. Tel 48/12-424-9624; www.wierzynek.com.pl. *Cost:* dinner $35.

Symbol of the Nation's Identity

WAWEL HILL

Kraków, Poland

The majestic complex of Gothic and Renaissance buildings that make up Wawel Hill—the Royal Palace and Cathedral—preside over the city from a high rocky hill above the Vistula River. This was the Polish royal residence for more than 500 years, until the end of the 16th century, when Warsaw became Poland's capital. Wawel Hill is a symbol of the Polish kingdom: though it was ransacked by the Nazis when they used it as their local headquarters during WW II, room after room is still filled with rare, enormous tapestries (the largest collection of its kind in Europe), gilded and painted ceiling scenes, and lavish Baroque furniture. You'll likely be surrounded by groups of reverent Polish schoolchildren being instructed about their glorious past, when Kraków—*totius Poloniae urbs celeberrima*, "the most celebrated Polish city"—was the envy of Europe.

The famous 1364 cathedral, called "the sanctuary of the nation," was the seat formerly held by Archbishop Karol Wojtyla from 1963 until his election as Pope John Paul II in 1978. For centuries the Polish kings were crowned and buried here; heroes and martyrs were also entombed here, amid its endless chapels and artworks.

Unlike Warsaw, Kraków was spared destruction during WW II and its grand history and remarkable concentration of architecture are evident everywhere. From the castle (and, particularly, the cathedral's Sigismund Tower) you can see much of the

The 14th-century Wawel Cathedral

Old Town (Stare Miasto), about 4 square miles of preserved streets and centuries-old buildings and monuments that are some of Europe's most graceful and authentic.

WHAT: site. **HOW:** for inquiries and booking, contact the Tourist Service Office, tel 48/12-422-5155 (ext. 291), fax 48/12-422-1697; www.krakow-info.com/wawel.htm. **COST:** for Royal Palace, admission $5; free Mon. For Cathedral, admission $3.

A Tribute to Poland's Musical Genius

CHOPIN'S BIRTHPLACE

Zelazowa Wola, Poland

Frédéric Chopin was born to a French father and Polish mother in this tiny village west of Warsaw in 1810. He lived in Poland for his first twenty years, acquiring a reputation mostly as a pianist before leaving for Paris

and international fame. Although he was buried in Paris, music lovers find the journey to his Polish birthplace (now a museum) and the shady park that surrounds it a poignant pilgrimage. Schedule your day trip from

Warsaw for a summer Sunday morning beginning in May for concerts by virtuoso pianists who perform in the parlor where Chopin created his early waltzes, polonaises, mazurkas, and nocturnes. The rapt audience is seated on the terrace in front of the house. With the strains of Chopin still in the air, head for Kampinos National Park. The well-marked green trail originates in the town of Zelazowa

The piano Chopin played during the last two years of his life

Wola and makes its way through thick forests and flower-strewn meadows—a setting that most likely fueled Chopin's creative fires. If you choose not to leave the urban confines of Warsaw, check the schedule of summer Chopin concerts that take place in the city's wonderful Park Lazienki near the impressive Frédéric Chopin Memorial, unveiled in 1926.

WHAT: site, event. **ZELAZOWA WOLA:** 33 miles/53 km west of Warsaw. **CHOPIN MUSEUM:** tel 48/22-826-5935; muzeum@nifc.pl; www.chopin.nifc.pl. **COST:** admission to Chopin Museum and park in Zelazowa Wola. **WHEN:** concerts May–Sept; often scheduled for Oct 17, anniversary of Chopin's death. In Warsaw, same months. Chopin International Piano Competition held in Warsaw every 5 years (2005, 2010, etc.). **NOTE:** At press time, the museum was closed for renovation.

The Sistine Chapels of the East

THE PAINTED MONASTERIES OF MOLDAVIA

Suceava, Moldavia, Romania

A handful of vividly painted monasteries are the highlight of this dramatically remote corner of Moldavia in northeastern Romania, one of Europe's most scenic and unspoiled areas. Most of the monasteries are painted inside and out, top to bottom, with elaborate frescoes—promises of redemption, warnings of damnation—remarkably fresh in color and quality despite 500 years of exposure to the elements and the whims of many rulers.

Acclaimed as masterpieces of art and architecture of the 15th and 16th centuries, when this area was under the threat of invasion from the Turks, the fortified monasteries were covered with biblical scenes to educate the illiterate faithful in the ways of Orthodox Christianity. A kind of poor man's Bible, these late medieval billboards are brilliant examples of a Byzantine aesthetic infused with the vitality of local folk art, mythology, and historical references to the Turks and past battles won and lost. Arguably the most striking is the 15th-century monastery of Voronet, known by Romanians as the Sistine Chapel of the East. Its unique cerulean blue is obtained from lapis lazuli. Nearby are the painted monasteries of Sucevita, Moldovita, and Humor, all inhabited by small communities of nuns who keep their brand of Orthodox Christianity fervently alive in this dramatic mountain outpost where life has obliviously resisted the passing of the last few centuries.

WHAT: site. **WHERE:** 280 miles/451 km north of Bucharest. The monasteries are spread out over an area 45 miles/72 km or so directly west of Suceava (Voronet, the closest monastery to Suceava, is 25 miles/40 km away), capital of the region and the jumping-off point, accessible by air and train from Bucharest. **HOW:** for prearranged customized travel or group tours, contact Romantic Travel in Bucharest, tel 40/21-326-0438, fax 40/21-326-3036; contact@romantictravel.ro; www.romantic.ro. **BEST TIMES:** summer and fall, when weather is best and local festivals are numerous.

Voronet, built in the late 1400s, is dedicated to St. George.

In a Lost Corner of Central Europe

COUNT DRACULA'S CASTLE

Bran, Transylvania, Romania

The figure of Count Dracula that captured the imagination of 19th-century author Bram Stoker did exist. Prince Vlad Dracula of Walachia (c. 1431–1476), who allegedly lived in Bran Castle in the wild and raw region of Transylvania, was never known in his lifetime for drinking blood—that was something born of Stoker's fantasy as he researched the vampire-related tales prevalent in the folklore of eastern and southeastern Europe. However,

*Vlad's father was a member of the Order of the Dragon (*dracul *is Romanian for dragon).*

he was known for his ruthless cruelty, including his habit of having his perceived enemies impaled alive on enormous stakes—a practice from which he derived the nickname Tepes (the Impaler). No one's all bad, though, and in his native land Vlad is remembered as a hero for his battles with the Ottoman Empire. There is no proof that the prince actually ever lived at the medieval Bran Castle, but that hasn't stopped the steady trickle of thrill-seekers, who find in this "land beyond the forest" (the Latin meaning of Transylvania) one of the last great European wildernesses, a time-locked country that seems never to have felt the 20th century's touch, never mind the 21st's. Among the forest-blanketed Carpathian Mountains bordering Transylvania are ancient Saxon towns where farmers drive ox-drawn carts and maintain a simple life that by no means curbs the sense of hospitality for which they have long been known.

WHAT: site. **WHERE:** in Brasov County in the town of Bran, 130 miles/209 km from Bucharest. In Bucharest, contact Paralela 45 for customized trips, tel 40/21-311-1959, fax 40/21-312-2774; secretariat@paralela45.ro. **BEST TIMES:** May–Jun, Sept–Oct.

Romancing the Rails

THE TRANS-SIBERIAN EXPRESS

Russia

The world's longest continuous rail line and one of its greatest train journeys, the Trans-Siberian Express stretches almost 6,000 miles—one third of the distance around the globe—and crosses eight time zones between Moscow and Vladivostok on the Pacific coast, an area closed to all foreigners and most Russians throughout the Soviet era. One of the truly heroic engineering marvels in the last 100 years, the network of routes crosses taiga, steppe, desert, and mountain. It was once an arduous voyage of several months, but this epic rail ride can now be enjoyed in luxurious comfort during two-week journeys in the company of expert guides.

Three slightly different routes travel in both directions from Moscow and St. Petersburg in Western Russia across Siberia to the Far East, with the option of including Mongolia and ending up (or beginning) in Beijing. Each trip affords in-depth, in-style exploration of regional capitals, remote towns, and villages.

WHAT: experience. **WHERE:** eastbound departures from Moscow and St. Petersburg or westbound from Vladivostok on the Pacific coast, Beijing or Ulaan Baatar in Mongolia. **HOW:** in the U.S., contact MIR Corporation, tel 800-424-7289 or 206-624-7289, fax 206-624-7360; info@mircorp.com; www.mircorp.com. In the U.K., contact Trans-Siberian Express, tel 44/1619-289-410, fax 44/1619-416-101; mail @gwtravel.co.uk; www.gwtravel.co.uk. **COST:** 13–15-day all-inclusive (land only) trips from $6,195 per person, double occupancy. **WHEN:** limited departures late May–mid-Sept.

Within the Fortress Walls of the Kremlin

THE ARMORY MUSEUM AND RED SQUARE

Moscow, Russia

Once you get over the fact that you're actually standing inside the fortified walls of the Kremlin, head to the Armory Museum for a dizzying crash course on the lifestyles of the rich and famous czars. It includes more than 4,000 objects from the 12th century to 1917. Fortunately, some of the premier pieces are displayed first (in Hall II), so you can see them while you still have your wits about you. There's a stunning collection of ten Fabergé eggs, intricate mini-worlds created as tributes to the czars by genius jeweler Peter Carl Fabergé, who became court goldsmith in 1885. The pièce de résistance here is a delicate silver egg engraved with a map of the Trans-Siberian Railroad. The obligatory "surprise" inside was a golden clockwork model of a train with crystal windows and a tiny red ruby for a headlight.

You'll have to buy a separate ticket to view the dazzling crown jewels of the Romanovs in the poorly indicated Almazny Fond (Diamond Vaults). There are no written explanations, but it won't take you long to gravitate to the scepter of Catherine the Great—topped by the Orlov Diamond, a gift from her lover Count Orlov—and her diamond-encrusted crown. Be sure to see the Shah Diamond, given to Czar Nicholas I by the Shah of Iran.

No photos or guidebooks can prepare you for the sensation of standing at the center of the vast, magnificent Red Square. In Russian, *krasnaya* (red) is closely related to *krasivaya*, the word for "beautiful," but for years to come, Red Square will be associated with Communism and the Soviet military parades of tanks and hardware that took place there regularly. It is bordered on the west by the Kremlin, within whose shadow is the Lenin Mausoleum, where Lenin's eerily embalmed body has been lying in state since his death in 1924. At the far end of the square loom the multicolored pinnacles and onion domes of St. Basil's Cathedral, one of Moscow's best-known landmarks, commissioned by Ivan the Terrible in the mid-1500s. Opposite the Kremlin, an enormous steel-frame and glass construction recalls the great old train stations of London or Paris; it is GUM, whose initials stand for State Department Store. Since the dust of *perestroika* has settled, it is curious to see how unbridled capitalism and the proliferation of slick new franchises chockablock with Western goods abut old-world, poorly stocked Russian shops that seem on their way to extinction.

WHAT: site. **WHERE:** the Armory Museum is located in the southwest corner of the Kremlin. For more information, contact the Russian National Group, tel 877-221-7120, fax 212-575-3434; info@russia-travel.com; www.russia-travel.com. *Cost:* admission to Kremlin $11, additional $10 for the Armory. **WHERE TO STAY:** Le Royal Meridian National Hotel sits in its original Art Nouveau splendor across the street from Red Square, 15/1 Mokhovaya St. Tel 7/495-258-7000; jwww.national.ru. In the U.S. and Canada, Le Meridien Hotels, tel 800-543-4300; www.lemeridian.com. Ask for Lenin's room, or one of the 30 rooms with full or partial views of the square and the Kremlin. *Cost:* doubles from $580, suites with view of Red Square from $950.

Russia's Most Famous and Influential Cultural Institution

THE BOLSHOI

Moscow, Russia

For decades the Bolshoi was a sacred artistic institution, flourishing under czars and Soviet leaders alike. After the fall of Communism, Russia's perilous economy gave rise to the rumor that the Bolshoi had exhausted

The Metropole Hotel offers old-world opulence.

itself and was now simply rehashing past glories. But the excitement is back as one of the world's great ballet and operatic companies evolves into a creative force once again, deserving of its majestic, gilded 19th-century theater. Although tradition remains sacrosanct—the repertory still consists primarily of the Russian classics—innovation, reform, and new blood are bringing the Bolshoi into the 21st century. Not all performances are sold

out, but that doesn't mean that tickets are easy to come by.

Check in across the street at one of the finest hotels in Russia, and be assured of top ballet seating (for which you'll pay top dollar) while you enjoy a stay at a five-star landmark you may recognize from *Doctor Zhivago*. The Metropole Hotel, run by an efficient British-Russian joint venture, offers the opulence of the late 19th century. Even if you're not taking a room here, stop by for a drink before the ballet or come for an extravagant caviar breakfast in the posh glass-domed salon, where Lenin used to deliver impassioned speeches.

WHAT: event, hotel. **BOLSHOI BALLET AND OPERA:** Bolshoi Theater, 1 Teatralnaya Ploshchad. Tel 7/095-392-9270; sales@bolshoi.ru; www.bolshoi.ru. *Cost:* tickets $50–$150. Performance information and ticket buying easiest through your hotel. *When:* no set ballet or opera season. Theater closed Jul–Aug. **METROPOLE HOTEL:** Teatralny Proyezd 1/4. Tel 7/499-501-7841, fax 7/499-501-7810. In the U.S., tel 7/499-501-7800, www.metropol-moscow.ru. *Cost:* doubles from $490. Breakfast buffet $30.

The Subway That Stalin Built

THE MOSCOW UNDERGROUND

Moscow, Russia

Y ou may have imagined that an evening at the Bolshoi followed by some celebratory caviar and vodka would surely be your most vivid memory of Moscow. But don't even think about leaving the city without venturing

deep into its subterranean passageways on the least expensive subway ride (about 30 cents!) you're ever likely to take. The first stop of the very safe 140-station system was completed in 1935. The older the station, the more elaborate the decor—we're talking crystal chandeliers, gold leaf, mosaics, and faux

Roman statues. The most beautiful and interesting stations are Mayakovskaya, Kievskaya, and Komsomolskaya. Some escalator descents are so steep, you'll think you're on your way to the center of the earth. Each station is announced—though that may not help you much. While rush hour is not recommended for claustrophobes, others may find it provides the most insightful moments. And they said New Yorkers were the champions at scowling and avoiding eye contact.

WHAT: experience. For more information, in the U.S. contact the Russian National Group, tel 877-221-7120, fax 646-473-2205, info@russia-travel.com; www.russia-travel.com.

The Most Important Repository of Russian Art

TRETYAKOV GALLERY

Moscow, Russia

Home to the world's largest and most important collection of 19th- and 20th-century Russian art, the Tretyakov Gallery underwent almost ten years of renovation and expansion. Even with twice the exhibition space, only 5 percent of the colossal collection can be displayed at any one time. The basis of this astounding assemblage of art was bequeathed to Moscow by the wealthy merchant P. M. Tretyakov in 1892. Here, 19th-century works predominate, added to by subsequent state acquisitions. In the early decades of the 20th century, Russian painters were in the vanguard of European art, and the work of Kandinsky, Chagall, and Malevich are on display here. An exceptional group of 11th-century icons is another principal attraction. The main gallery dates to the early 1900s, a fanciful building in the Russian Art Nouveau style, which incorporates Tretyakov's home. A visit here is an intimate experience compared to St. Petersburg's daunting Hermitage.

WHAT: site. **WHERE:** .6 miles/1 km south of the Kremlin, Lavrushinsky Pereulok 10. **COST:** admission $8. **WHEN:** open Tues–Sun.

Cruising from Moscow to St. Petersburg

WATERWAYS OF THE CZARS

Moscow, Russia

Follow the song of the Volga boatman on a cruise from Moscow to St. Petersburg, sailing the Volga and Svir rivers, trolling the shores of lakes Onega and Ladoga, and exploring some of the villages that make up Moscow's "Golden Ring," with monasteries and churches dating from the 11th century. Just outside Moscow is Sergeiev Posad, the capital of the Russian Orthodox Church, and the small town of Uglich, founded in 1148. Uglich retains much of its charm and original wooden architecture, including the famed Tsarevitch Church, built in memory of Ivan the Terrible's

Cruising the Volga River

son, who died mysteriously on this spot.

In Lake Onega—the second largest lake in Europe—the island of Kizhi is filled with extraordinary examples of ancient wooden architecture, a highlight being the 18th-century twenty-two-domed Church of the Transfiguration, built entirely without nails.

Your vantage point is a serviceable though not luxurious German-built, Swiss-managed river cruise boat, where European chefs interpreting local cuisine add to the quintessentially Russian experience.

WHAT: experience. **WHERE:** departures from Moscow and St. Petersburg. **HOW:** in the U.S., contact Exeter International, tel 813-251-5355 or 800-633-1008, fax 813-251-6685; info@exeter international.com; www.exeterinternational.com. **COST:** 13-day tours/cruises all-inclusive from $4,200 per person, double occupancy.

Dining in the Garden of the Yusupov Princes

NOBLEMAN'S NEST

St. Petersburg, Russia

Half the fascination of visiting the amazing Yusupov Palace, once owned by one of the richest families in Russia, is dining at the elegant restaurant, Dvorianskoye Gnezdo, which means Nobleman's Nest. Housed in a glass pavilion in a corner of the palace garden, it is the dining venue of choice for visiting heads of state and those who wish to recapture the romance of St. Petersburg past. Candlelit and chic, its menu offers Europeanized Russian cuisine, though the occasional detractor complains of erratic quality. But who can concentrate on the food when you are in the middle of the perfect Anna Karenina moment? The restaurant's proximity to the Mariinsky Theater (formerly the Kirov) makes it an ideal après-theater choice.

Find time to visit the palace itself. Its private gilt and velvet rococo theater is as precious as a Fabergé egg, but it's the infamous cellar that draws many tourists and history buffs. This is where Rasputin, the Siberian mystic who wielded a sinister influence over the last czar, Nicholas II, met his grisly end at the hands of Nicholas's good friend Prince Yusupov, in 1916. When cyanide-laced wine didn't work, Yusupov shot him, tied him up, and threw him into the Neva River—while still alive, many believe. A wax statue of the "mad monk" now sits at a table in the shadows of the palace cellar.

WHAT: restaurant. **WHERE:** 21 Ulitsa Dekabristov. Tel/fax 7/812-312-3205. **COST:** dinner $100.

THE WHITE NIGHTS FESTIVAL AND THE GRAND HOTEL EUROPE

St. Petersburg, Russia

N amed after the season when the sun never sets, the relatively new White Nights festival of music has been thrilling audiences with various performances and cultural events highlighted by St. Petersburg's superb opera and ballet company and the five-tiered theater that gives the company its name—the Kirov during the Soviet era, now (as in czarist times) the Mariinsky. The one-month cultural festival provides an international audience the chance to see gala productions ranging from classical Russian ballets to concerts by the St. Petersburg Philharmonic and visiting world-class artists.

The primary venue, the 19th-century Mariinsky Theater, together with the Bolshoi in Moscow, has produced some of the world's greatest ballet dancers. Attending a performance here should be a top priority even when the long summer nights have come and gone. Dress to the nines, have some Champagne during intermission, and blend in with those elated to relive a bygone era.

Continue your historical itinerary by staying at the Grand Hotel Europe. An international joint venture, this miracle of a hotel is a heavily restored reincarnation of the former Europeiskaya, opened in 1875 and thus St. Petersburg's oldest hotel. Much of the old-school aristocratic ambience is gone. In its stead—to the delight of international visitors following in the footsteps of Gorky, Strauss, and Debussy—is the sort of Europeanized five-star service and white-glove sophistication not yet a common commodity among Russia's aspiring hotels.

Just barely off the Nevsky Prospekt, St. Petersburg's Champs-Elysées, the Europe was once a gleaming symbol of the City of the Czars' prosperous days as Russia's capital from 1712 until 1918. Now, once again, it is the pulse of a reawakened city: the elegant Caviar Bar is the rendezvous of choice for the New Russians, with their cell phones and cigars, and the prestigious Restaurant Europe offers a level of luxury and fine dining not seen in the city during Communism. If you don't stay here, stop by for the buffet breakfast under the Europe's exquisite Art Nouveau stained-glass ceiling or the Sunday morning jazz brunch.

WHAT: event, hotel. **WHITE NIGHTS FESTIVAL:** at the Mariinsky Theater, Teatral'naya Ploshchad 1/2, and other venues in St. Petersburg. *How:* in the U.S., contact Exeter International, tel 813-251-5355 or 800-633-1008, fax 813-251-6685; info@exeterinternational.com; www.exeterinternational.com. *Cost:* from $6,650 per person for a 7-day tour includes air and land. *When:* last 2 weeks in Jun. **GRAND HOTEL EUROPE:** Mikhailovskaya Ulitsa 1/7. Tel 7/812-329-6000, fax 7/812-329-6001; res@grandhoteleurope.com; www.grandhoteleurope.com. *Cost:* doubles from $455 (low season), from $855 (high season). Dinner in the Restaurant Europe $110.

Looted Booty Finds a Home

THE HERMITAGE

St. Petersburg, Russia

It would take approximately nine years to cast even a brief glance at each of the museum's 150,000 works on display (and that's only 5 percent of the museum's collection!) in the never-ending maze of the Hermitage Museum's

1,000 rooms. The unrivaled bounty of the collection (twenty-four Rembrandts, forty Rubenses—just for example) is enhanced by the immensely beautiful salons themselves: the Hermitage was the Winter Palace of every czar and czarina since Catherine the Great.

One of the world's finest collections of Italian Renaissance art can be found on the second floor, an artist's who's who that culminates with two works by Leonardo da Vinci and the museum's only Renaissance sculpture: Michelangelo's *Crouching Youth*. The top floor houses prominent works by Picasso and Matisse and a host of Impressionists and Post-Impressionists. The rooms themselves are so busy with patterned parquet floors, crystal chandeliers, inlaid marquetry, molded and painted ceilings, gold leaf, objets of jasper, lapis lazuli, and amber, they almost upstage the art collection. It's easy to imagine the gala balls, power meetings, and declarations of war that took place in the State Rooms. The Malachite Room, fashioned almost entirely from the rich green stone mined in the Ural Mountains, is a masterwork in itself.

WHAT: site. **WHERE:** 32 Dovortsovaya Naberezhnaya (Palace Embankment). Tel 7/812-710-9652, fax 7/812-312-1550; www. hermitagemuseum.org. **COST:** admission. **WHEN:** open Tues–Sun.

Intimacy and Grandeur in Russia's Finest Palace

PAVLOVSK

St. Petersburg, Russia

The gold-and-white summer palace that Catherine the Great built for her son, Paul I (whose name in Russian is Pavel, hence Pavlovsk), has been painstakingly preserved and looks exactly as it did in the late 1700s

when the young grand duke arrived with his grand duchess and their brood of ten royal children. This masterpiece of neo-Palladian style was built on a bluff overlooking a 1,500-acre estate. The former royal hunting grounds now make a lovely park of ponds, lime-tree-lined allées, rolling lawns, pavilions, and woodlands popular with residents of St. Petersburg. Most palaces and estates of the period were built as symbols of Russian imperial might—venues for state occasions, royal balls, and entertaining on a scale surpassing anything seen in the West. But Pavlovsk was conceived as a home. By palace standards, its rooms (numbering approximately forty-five) are intimate (and exquisite), their contents precious and personal. Although Pavlovsk seems miraculously untouched by the ravages of history, it is in fact an extraordinary replica. Hitler's troops used the place as Gestapo headquarters before setting fire to it and the gardens in 1944. It took a virtual army of Russia's finest artisans twenty-five years to re-create the finest architectural monument to Russia's prerevolutionary past, following detailed logs, plans, prints, and correspondence. A loyal palace staff somehow managed to bury, warehouse, hide, and protect a large number of the original furnishings and artworks that once again grace Pavlovsk.

WHAT: site. **WHERE:** 16 miles/26 km south of St. Petersburg, outside Pushkin. Tel 7/812-452-1536; www.pavlovskmuseum.ru. **COST:** admission. **WHEN:** Sat–Thurs.

A Czar's Summer Palace to Rival Versailles

PETRODVORETS

St. Petersburg, Russia

To get a taste of the mind-boggling opulence of imperial St. Petersburg, take the boat service from the riverside Winter Palace (The Hermitage) and motor on the Neva River to the Gulf of Finland to Petrodvorets,

Peter the Great's Grand Palace. Just as St. Petersburg was built as a powerful combination of both East and West—too Russian to be European, too European to be Russian—Petrodvorets was Peter's "window on Europe." He built it in the early 1700s to rival the architecture and glittering court life of Versailles, and to show European royalty that he could keep up with the best of them. Peter personally drew up the plans for the extravagant summer palace and 300 acres of gardens, where 66 fountains, 39 gilded statues, and 12 miles of manmade canals were constructed by the finest French and Italian architects and engineers. St. Petersburg experienced near annihilation during the 900-day German siege in World War II, but the czar's pet project, completed after his death by Catherine the Great, was painstakingly rebuilt according to Peter's original plans.

WHAT: site. **WHERE:** 20 miles/32 km from St. Petersburg on the southern shore of the Gulf of Finland. Forty-minute hydrofoil service departs from the Winter Palace embankment in St. Petersburg, May–Sept. **COST:** admission. **WHEN:** closed Mon and the last Tues of every month.

The Grand Palace and the Grand Cascade of Petrodvorets (formerly known as Peterhof)

A Glimpse of Traditional Seafaring Life

AEROSKOBING

Aero, Denmark

Folks from relatively stress-free Copenhagen go to Funen to relax; to *really* get away from it all, they go to Aero, its offshore little-sister island with picture-perfect villages, rolling hills, and patchwork farms. It's a popular

sailing center south of the island of Funen, which is ringed by some ninety smaller neighboring islands, many privately owned. Low-key life in Aero centers around salty, perfectly preserved Aeroskobing, a market town in the 1300s that reached prosperity as a sea captains' town in the late 1600s. The principal pastime is browsing its small shops and viewing the cobblestone streets lined with winsome, sometimes gently listing, half-timbered houses decorated with red geraniums and lace curtains. Although lively and lived in, Aeroskobing is a heritage town, the only one in Denmark to be protected in its entirety. Denmark is a nation of bicycle riders, and touring by bike is understandably popular on both Aero and Funen, where more than 580 miles of marked bike paths crisscross the gentle curves of the islands' topography. Aero's empty country roads, sometimes single-laned, meander past old windmills and thatched houses whose painted, decorative doors are unique to the island. The last two weeks of July, a small but well-known music festival jazzes things up considerably, jolting Aeroskobing forward into the 21st century, if only for a few summer afternoons.

WHAT: island. **WHERE:** 46 miles/74 km south of Odense, Funen's principal town. In high season, frequent 1-hour car ferries leave from Svendborg.

The Best and the Best

HOTEL D'ANGLETERRE AND NOMA

Copenhagen, Denmark

Visiting celebs and seasoned sybarites have always headed straight for Copenhagen's main square to the Hotel d'Angleterre for grand-style Danish hospitality. Step into a world of sparkling chandeliers, marble

floors, and an aristocratic air that reflect the hotel's origin as a 1594 manor house. A recent renovation has helped it reclaim the preeminent status it held for decades after its opening in 1775, and it is again the premier address in Copenhagen, impeccably run, old-world elegant, and exuding a sense of restrained warmth.

Much of the hotel's appeal is its excellent location, steps from the Stroget, the capital's famous miles-long pedestrian shopping boulevard (the longest and oldest in Europe), and at the top of the Nyhavn harbor area with its café- and restaurant-lined canal. Here tall ships, working fishing boats, and pleasure craft

The Hotel d'Angleterre is on the main square, Kongens Nytorv.

creak and bob in the city's most picturesque corner. Try the afternoon tea in the hotel's glass-domed Palm Court. At night, you needn't go far for the best meal in town. In fact, Noma's fare is regularly voted as one of the most exciting meals in Scandinavia. This world renowned modern Nordic restaurant is a food lover's gem, its chef and owner Rene Redzepi revered as a high-priest for his masterful innovation of ingredients from the North Atlantic. In a minimalist, understated space housed in an 18th-century warehouse in Christianhavn, Noma's experimental gas-

tronomy leaves some unimpressed and others (such as Danish royalty and countless mere mortals who book months in advance) enamored. Local and seasonal are key words in the Noma universe. So are high prices. This great dining experience does not come cheap.

WHAT: hotel, restaurant. **HOTEL D'ANGLETERRE:** Kongens Nytorv 34. Tel 45/33-12-00-95, fax 45/33-12-11-18; dangleterre @dangleterre.dk; www.dangleterre.com. *Cost:* doubles from $590. **NOMA:** Strandgade 93, Christianhavn. Tel 45/3296-3297, www. noma.dk. *Cost:* dinner $174.

Northern Europe's Largest Repository of Art

NY CARLSBERG GLYPTOTEK

Copenhagen, Denmark

When the Danes recently toasted the impressive renovation and new extension of their most important museum, we can only hope they did so with beer, since the Ny Carlsberg Glyptotek was founded by the

world-famous Carlsberg Brewery. Bequeathed to the country a century ago by beer baron Carl Jacobsen (who also gave Copenhagen its statue of the Little Mermaid in 1913), the Glyptotek has grown to become northern Europe's largest and most important repository of ancient statuary, mosaics, and artifacts. It also owns an

unrivaled collection of thirty-five works by Paul Gauguin (briefly married to a Dane), which are displayed alongside other 19th-century French and Danish masterworks by artists such as Manet, Monet, and Cézanne. The museum also houses the largest collection of Rodin sculptures outside of Paris, and one of only three complete sets of Degas bronzes. The airy 1996 wing, designed by the esteemed Danish architect Henning Larsen, was unveiled during Copenhagen's successful stint as Cultural Capital of Europe. Contemporary and cool, it holds its own against the museum's two original late-19th-century and early-20th-century buildings with their great skylit galleries, decorative moldings, painted panels, and richly tiled floors. In the city's highly civilized and perfectly stylized manner, the buildings are linked by a lovely glass-domed winter garden and attractive café for the weary of foot.

WHAT: site. **WHERE:** across the street from the Tivoli Gardens. Entrance at Dantes Plads 7. Tel 45/33-41-81-41; info@glyptoteket.dk; www.glyptoteket.dk. **COST:** admission $11; free on Sun. **WHEN:** Tues–Sun.

Delectible and Artistic Sandwiches in Mind-Boggling Variations

RESTAURANT IDA DAVIDSEN

Copenhagen, Denmark

Those who think a sandwich by any other name is still a sandwich should make a quick stop at this Copenhagen institution, a showcase of the national open sandwich called *smørrebrød*. Ida Davidsen ("the smørrebrød queen of Copenhagen") runs this fifth-generation family restaurant, now more than a century old. The menu of 178 variations, said to be the largest in Scandinavia, is the size of the Copenhagen telephone directory. The sandwiches are displayed in a glass case, and like everything in this aesthetically sensitive country, each is carefully and artfully prepared. Quantity is important, but quality and freshness are paramount. The choices are delectable, if somewhat improbable: tongue with fried egg, pigeon with mushrooms, and pureed smoked salmon head the more imaginative offerings. More pedestrian palates will pick up at the choice of shrimp, liver paté, roast beef, and chicken. Even the Queen of Denmark has her hankerings for the occasional takeout and has had royal occasions catered by Ida Davidsen at her residence, Amalienborg Palace.

WHAT: restaurant. **WHERE:** Store Kongensgade 70. Tel 45/33-91-36-55, www.idadavidsen.dk. **COST:** sandwich $15. **WHEN:** Mon–Fri, Aug–Jun.

Keeping the Magic Alive in Scandinavia's Fun Capital

TIVOLI GARDENS

Copenhagen, Denmark

If you're looking for "wonderful, wonderful Copenhagen," you're guaranteed to find it in the capital's fabled Tivoli Gardens. No one enjoys this classic amusement park more than the Danes themselves; since the day it opened in 1843, a visit here has been a much-loved summertime tradition. More than 100,000 twinkling white Christmas lights and 400,000 flowers set the fun-filled (and in the evening, romantic) scene. The park's 20 leafy acres feature carnival games, marching bands, and amusement rides (the creaky 1914 roller coaster is the same vintage as the merry-go-round of tiny Viking ships). Dance halls, beer gardens, and a full schedule of mostly free open-air stage performances keep young and old entertained and coming back. There are dozens of restaurants and food pavilions—some of them very elegant but pricey (traditional Tivoli fare of pølser hot dogs with fried onions is usually heaven enough for most). Divan 2 is the most renowned restaurant in the gardens, in operation since they were first built in an area well outside the city center by

King Christian VIII. It is Tivoli's most refined (read: expensive) dining venue with an impeccable French menu. Its less-expensive and more informal sister establishment, Divan 1, leans more toward local cuisine. Tivoli, said to have inspired Walt Disney to create Disneyland, is light years removed from the archetypal American amusement park.

WHAT: site, restaurant. **TIVOLI GARDENS:** entrance at Vesterbrogade 3. Tel 45/33-15-10-01; www.tivoligardens.com. *Cost:* admission. *When:* open daily late Apr–mid-Sept; mid-Nov–Christmas with limited attractions. **DIVAN 2:** tel 45/33-75-07-50, fax 45/33-75-07-30; restaurant@divan2.dk; www.divan2.dk. *Cost:* dinner $45. **BEST TIMES:** Tivoli is at its most magical at night; visit May–early Jun to see 100,000 tulips in bloom. Fireworks just before midnight Wed, Fri, and Sat.

To Be or Not to Be at Hamlet's Elsinore

KRONBORG SLOT

Helsingor, Denmark

So Elsinore Castle's real name is Kronborg Slot, and so it was built centuries after the time of the Danish prince on whom Shakespeare based his tormented, brooding Hamlet. But this fortified Nordic icon of secret passages, with

its suitably gloomy dungeon and canon-studded battlements, could not have been a better backdrop for Shakespeare's dark tragedy. After several miles of sleepy fishing villages along the coastal road north of Copenhagen, the great moat-encircled castle rises above the town of Helsingor that grew up around it. Filling its vast coffers via "400 years of legal piracy," Helsingor Castle (as it is also called) collected tolls paid to the Danish crown from passing ships, until the taxes were abolished in 1857.

Originally built in 1420 and enlarged in 1574, Kronborg had all the trappings of a great regal Renaissance residence. Its starkly

furnished Knights Hall is one of the largest and oldest in northern Europe; the luxurious castle chapel is still the dream wedding location for many a lucky Danish couple. Occasional performances of *Hamlet* are staged in the torch-lit courtyard, where audiences can envision the inky fog and the tormented prince agonizing over the "slings and arrows of outrageous fortune." Meanwhile, somewhere off in a dark and dank chamber reposes the spirit of Viking chief Holger Danske, a mythic Charlemagne-era hero: legend has it that as long as he sleeps, the kingdom of Denmark will be safe.

WHAT: site. **WHERE:** Helsingor is 28 miles/

45 km north of Copenhagen, connected by 45-minute rail service. Tel 45/49-21-30-78, fax 45/49-21-30-52; kronborg@ses.dk; www.kronborgslot.dk. **COST:** admission from $6.

A Remarkable Day Trip and Not Just for the Art

LOUISIANA MUSEUM OF MODERN ART

Humlebaek, Denmark

Follow one of Zealand's most picturesque drives north of Copenhagen to this exceptional museum situated at a stunning site on the "Danish Riviera." Since opening in 1958, the Louisiana Museum has brought together art, nature, and architecture in perfect harmony. Its highly regarded exhibitions of modern classics of the post–WW II era as well as the (sometimes controversial) vanguard of contemporary art are displayed in spacious, natural-light-flooded halls that embody the very essence of Danish modernism. No less impressive is its permanent collection, including an extensive collection of the fragile and spindly sculptures of Alberto Giacometti and works by Picasso, Andy Warhol, Robert Rauschenberg, Francis Bacon, and Georg Baselitz. The sparkling waters of the Oresund that separate Denmark from nearby Sweden vie for your attention from every window, and the open-air sculpture garden boasts work by such artists as Alexander Calder, Henry Moore, and Jean Arp. The origin of the museum's name is a curious one: the original landowner had a succession of three wives, all named Louise.

WHAT: site. **WHERE:** 22 miles/33 km north of Copenhagen. Tel 45/49-19-07-19; mail@louisiana.dk; www.louisiana.dk. **COST:** admission $17. **BEST TIMES:** chamber music concerts in Jul and Aug.

Fairy Tales Do Come True

EGESKOV CASTLE AND STEENSGAARD HERREGAARDSPENSION

Kvaerndrop and Millinge, Funen, Denmark

If something is rotten in the state of Denmark, it certainly isn't the garden island of Funen. Nor is it the island's regal and privately owned Egeskov Castle, widely held to be Europe's best preserved Renaissance island castle.

Constructed in 1554, it passed into the hands of the current owners' ancestors in 1784. A Victorian-era suspension drawbridge links the castle to a grand forecourt where white peacocks roam: beyond are some of the 1,500 acres of working farmland that has long been Egeskov's commercial side. But the 30 manicured acres enveloping the castle given over to some of Denmark's most important private gardens (including Europe's largest collection of fuchsias) are the highlight. A recently constructed bamboo maze re-creates the castle's 18th-century maze, believed to be the largest in Europe and older than that of England's Hampton Court. This castle, too, has a colorful tale: a 16th-century lord locked his daughter away in one of the turrets for five years after he discovered that she and her boyfriend were "each other so near, so she by accident bore a son."

With rich, aristocratic decor and a main house whose history dates back to 1310, the Steensgaard Herregaardspension is an easy drive from Egeskov. Set in its own shady 25-acre park and surrounded by manicured English gardens, this half-timbered country manor-turned-inn lies at the end of a tree-lined entryway, past a swan-filled pond. It's a scenario ennobling enough to have enticed Danish Prince Henrik to spend the night upon occasion. The candlelit dining room is renowned enough that meals are often reserved for guests of the inn only, as if one needed any further reason to check in here. Seasonal game specialties—pheasant, fowl, and wild boar—are raised on the manor's private 1,600-acre preserve. There are just eighteen spacious rooms, some located in "newer additions" dating to the 16th century.

Steensgaard Herregaardspension boasts a history and resident ghost that date back centuries.

Don't be put off by the tale of the manor's resident ghost: one night in July 1594, the third wife of the lord of the castle Otte Emmiksen, a.k.a. "The Evil One," conspired with the cook to eliminate her husband. The cook did him in with a meat cleaver, was arrested and drawn and quartered, and the wife escaped free. But legend has it she returns regularly after midnight, attempting to scrub the (imaginary) bloodstains from the floorboards of the library (originally the lord's bedroom) where the crime took place. This seems only fitting for Hans Christian Andersen's island (see Odense, next page)—one would surely be disappointed not to find the countryside so rich with local lore.

WHAT: site, hotel, restaurant. **EGESKOV CASTLE:** Egeskov Gade 18, Kvaerndrup (a 20-minute drive from Odense, Funen's biggest town, 97 miles/156 km west of Copenhagen). Tel 45/62-27-10-16; info@egeskov.dk; www.egeskov.com. *Cost:* admission $35. *When:* daily, May–Oct for grounds and some rooms in castle. **STEENSGAARD HERREGAARDSPENSION:** 4 Steensgaard, Millinge (22 miles/35 km from Odense). Tel 45/62-61-94-90, fax 45/63-61-78-61; steensgaard@herregaardspension.dk; www.herregaardspension.dk. *Cost:* doubles from $260. Dinner $100.

Scandinavian Perfection

FALSLED KRO

Millinge, Funen, Denmark

Located in a picture-perfect farming village on the southern coast of Funen, Falsled Kro consists of a charming complex of elegant but rustic buildings with thatched roofs and large open fireplaces. But the charm of this quintessential Scandinavian country inn isn't the reason patrons travel here from afar: it's Falsled Kro's stellar restaurant. Together with suppliers and gatherers from neighboring castles and manor houses, chef and co-owner Jean-Louis Lieffroy breeds, fishes, grows, hunts, and smokes much of what winds up on your plate. The result is breathtaking.

Some of the restaurant's crops include asparagus, strawberries, raspberries, hazelnuts, plums, and pears.

WHAT: restaurant, hotel. **WHERE:** 513 Assensvej, 2-hour drive from Copenhagen. Tel 45/62-68-11-11, fax 45/62-68-11-62; info@falsledkro.dk; www.falsledkro.dk. **COST:** doubles from $318. Dinner $125. **WHEN:** Tues–Sun.

A Pilgrimage for Fairy-Tale Lovers

ODENSE

Funen, Denmark

The island of Funen is known to the world as the birthplace of Hans Christian Andersen. Possibly the world's most esteemed storyteller, Andersen's work—including beloved classics like "Thumbelina" and "The Ugly Duckling"—is more widely translated and read than anything except the Bible and the writings of Karl Marx, and his Little Mermaid is Copenhagen's world-recognized icon. Odense, his hometown, is Denmark's third-largest city. With a charming medieval core, it attracts fairy-tale lovers from all over. Born in 1805 to a local shoemaker and washerwoman, both illiterate, Andersen was an inveterate traveler whose battered suitcases are on display at the museum adjoining his childhood home, as is the fire rope he never traveled without, hanging it outside his hotel window. Visitors can view original manuscripts (officials still await the return of "The Emperor's New Clothes," which disappeared some years ago) and letters to his close friend Charles Dickens. Also make time to enjoy the island's bucolic rolling countryside, dotted with thatched-roofed farmhouses, orchards, country manors, and inns called *kros*.

WHAT: town, site. **ODENSE:** 97 miles/156 km west of Copenhagen. An 11-mile suspension bridge connects Copenhagen, on the island of Zealand, to Funen. **HANS CHRISTIAN ANDERSEN MUSEUM:** Hans Jensensstraede 37-45. Tel 45/66-13-13-72. *Cost:* admission $11. *When:* daily mid-Jun–Aug; Thurs–Sun in winter. **BEST TIMES:** in Jul, plays are held 3 times a day, intermittently in English.

A Stroll Back Through Danish History in a Former Royal Capital

ROSKILDE

Denmark

A onetime ecclesiastical seat and the royal capital of Denmark until 1455, fjord-side Roskilde recently marked its 1,000th anniversary, and some of the jubilee air lingers on. The city's hallmark edifice is its 13th-century Gothic cathedral, a kind of Westminster Abbey of Denmark. It is the burial place for thirty-eight Danish kings, whose royal marble and alabaster tombs reflect the changing styles of the times. Enjoying centuries of commercial prominence as a trading center, Roskilde has never lost its identity as that handsome and pleasant town long favored by royalty. It has a lively student population, and a large colorful market still transforms the town every Wednesday and Saturday.

The nation's best Viking ship museum, the Vikingeskibshallen, displays five perfectly preserved longships discovered and reconstructed in 1957. Dating from approximately 1000, they were presumably sunk in the Roskilde Fjord to stop the passage of enemy ships. It's worth jumping on the old wooden steamer that sails out of Roskilde to cruise this lovely fjord. For four days in late June or early July, an international twenty-something crowd descends upon Roskilde for northern Europe's largest rock music festival, during which more than 100 bands play at seven venues around the ancient town.

WHAT: town, site, event. **ROSKILDE:** 20 miles/32 km west of Copenhagen. **VIKINGESKIBSHALLEN:** Vindeboder 12. Tel 45/46-30-02-00; www.vikingeskibsmuseet.dk. *Cost:* admission $7. **ROSKILDE ROCK FESTIVAL:** Havsteensvej 11. Tel 45/46-36-66-13, fax 45/46-32-14-99; www.roskildefestival.dk. *Cost:* $395, includes camping. *When:* late Jun or early Jul.

The "Land's End" of Denmark

SKAGEN

Denmark

T he Danes consider this something of a Riviera, while Americans liken it to Cape Cod. At the Jutland peninsula's—and mainland Europe's—north-ernmost tip pointing into the North Sea, the small weather-hardened fishing communities who for centuries inhabited these heathered moors and sea-swept coastline have been joined by a thriving artists' colony—and the tourists who followed. All were lured by Skagen's simple life—the characterful town and the unspoiled dunes.

The small but excellent Skagen Museum illustrates works of the local, late-19th-century impressionist movement that was inspired by the land- and seascapes, and the shifting colors and quality of the light here. Writers have been equally moved: Isak Dinesen wrote much of *Out of Africa* while a guest at the wonderfully charming, gabled Brøndums Hotel. Creaking floors and antique-furnished sitting rooms make this feel like a private home, one distinguished by a number of old paintings given in exchange for lodging. The 150-year-old inn's intimate dining room produces exceptionally fresh and delicious meals, with a predictable accent on seafood. Every morning at dawn, the local townfolk have the pick of the best at the wharf's barn-like fish-auction house before the day's catch is spoken for and shipped off to markets all over northern Europe.

WHAT: town, hotel. **SKAGEN:** 300 miles/ 482 km northwest of Copenhagen. **BRØNDUMS HOTEL:** Anchersvej 3. Tel 45/98-44-15-55; www.broendums-hotel.dk. *Cost:* doubles with shared bath $250. **BEST TIMES:** Jun–Sept.

Again the Center of the Society Life

HOTEL KÄMP

Helsinki, Finland

After a thirty-year hibernation when it was earmarked for demolition, the Hotel Kämp has been reborn after a breathtaking, full-fledged, no-expenses-barred restoration. Sitting proudly on the elegant Esplanade in the very heart of the city, the Kämp was as much a standout for its unparalleled splendor when it opened in 1887 as it is today, a true gold standard in the five-star, last-word-in-luxury category, unequaled anywhere else in Scandinavia. Since its inception, the Kämp has served as the capital's central meeting place for aristocrats, politicians, journalists, artists, and celebrities. The hotel also proved to be artistic inspiration for the composer Jean Sibelius, who visited it as often as possible and dedicated a song to it, and to the Swedish artist Victor Andren, whose painting *A Party at Kämp* still holds its position of importance in the exclusive Restaurant Kämp. Capturing the spirit of fin-de-siècle Helsinki, the hotel stands comfortably behind its motto "You have to be something special to be born twice."

The Mirror Room is the largest of the hotel's meeting rooms.

WHAT: hotel. **WHERE:** Pohjoisesplanadi

29. Tel 358/9-576-111, fax 358/9-576-1122; in the U.S., 800-325-3589; hotelkamp@hotel kamp.fi; www.hotelkamp.fi. **Cost:** doubles from $280.

A Tribute to Design, History, and Finnish Cuisine

THE SAVOY

Helsinki, Finland

Three things explain why the Savoy is one of Finland's most important eating establishments. First, its very beautiful and elegant design commissioned in 1937 from Alvar Aalto (1898–1976), one of Finland's most famous sons. He designed everything from the service stations to the lighting fixtures. Second, it was the favored haunt of the beloved "Marski," the country's revered national hero, Carl Gustav Mannerheim—architect of Finland's independence and president of the first republic from 1944 to 1946. Follow in his footsteps and order his favorite cocktail: the Marskin Ryyppy (a schnapps made with vodka, aquavit, dry vermouth, and dry gin—known throughout Finland as a "Marski," and said to have been consumed in large quantities by the general during those trying times). He also loved *vorschmack*, a stew made of ground beef and mutton with minced herring that is simmered for two days and served with potato puree, pickles, beetroot, and sour cream. By now a traditional national dish, some say the recipe originated with Mannerheim himself, and

(here's reason number three) the Savoy's is still considered the best around.

Diners who have their eye on the restaurant's famous, freeform flower vase will be happy to know that the nearby store Artek is known for its inventory of Alvar Aalto–designed furniture, ceramics, and objects. But to understand the breadth of Aalto's genius and his influence as the leading light of 20th-century Scandinavian design, visit Finlandiatalo (Finlandia Hall). Completed in 1971, it is Finland's main symphonic concert hall, and the oldest symphony orchestra in Scandinavia performs here from September to May.

What: restaurant, site. **The Savoy:** Eteläesplanadi 14. Tel 358/9-684-4020, fax 358/9-628-715. *Cost:* dinner $100. *When:* Mon–Fri. **Artek:** Eteläesplanadi 18. Tel 358/9-613-252-77, fax 358/9-613-252-65. **Finlandiatalo:** Mannerheimintie 13e. Tel 358/9-402-4211.

A Shrine to Jean Sibelius

AINOLA

Järvenpää, Lake District, Finland

Jean Sibelius was Finland's greatest composer, and the streams of pilgrims who come from all parts of the world to visit his home, named after his wife, Aino, are a testimony to the reverence in which he is held. Although born in

1865 in nearby Hämeenlinna, Finland's oldest inland town (founded in 1639), Sibelius lived in this modern villa in the south for half a century until his death in 1957. Considered avant-garde at the time of its construction, the house was designed by Finnish architect Lars Sonck, who was already known for his design of the summer residence of the president of Finland. Both Sibelius and his wife are buried on the grounds.

The museum is not conducive to concerts, but try not to leave Finland without hearing his work performed by the Helsinki Philharmonic Orchestra in Finlandia Hall during the winter season (September through May). Helsinki's late summer arts (and music-intensive) festival is Scandinavia's largest and one of its most important. Originating as Sibelius Week in the 1950s, it has grown to include all forms of dance and music, from jazz to pop, with the performance of Sibelius's music always a much-awaited highlight.

WHAT: site, event. **WHERE:** 24 miles/ 39 km from Helsinki. Tel 358/9-287-322; www.jarvenpaa.fi. **COST:** admission. **WHEN:** open Tues–Sun. **BEST TIMES:** Helsinki Festival last 2 weeks of Aug and into early Sept.

An Island Castle Offers
Opera Under the Stars—and the Midnight Sun

SAVONLINNA OPERA FESTIVAL

Lake District, Finland

Finland is a land of lakes (with close to 188,000 of them), coastal inlets, and rivers, from the Saimaa Lake District near the Russian border to the gulf of Bothnia in the west. It is also one of the most heavily wooded regions

Olavinlinna Castle

on earth—the interlocking network of lakes, surrounded by dense forests of pine and birch trees, creating a vision of pristine nature rarely seen anywhere.

Set amid gorgeous scenery, the town of Savonlinna occupies three islands in Lake Saimaa, on the eastern edge of the Lake District. Long a spa destination for the Russian czars and their retinues, since 1912 the town has been more famous for its opera festival, the most important in northern Europe, held annually in the courtyard of the 15th-century Olavinlinna Castle. A well-preserved island fortress built to repel attacks from the east, and now connected by a bridge to the mainland, the castle provides one of the most evocative settings of any outdoor music festival, enhanced by the long hours of shimmering late-day light.

For atmosphere and setting today, there is just one choice of lodging for those seeking to prolong the magic of an evening's opera performance: the Hotel Rauhalinna. Built in 1897 by a general in the czar's army, it was a lacy Moorish/Victorian fantasy gift for his wife. Set on the lake and reachable by road or boat from Savonlinna harbor, it is a deservedly popular treat. Try its well-known "Buffet of the Czars" lunch or, at the very least, find respite at its café with lovely lake views.

WHAT: town, event, hotel. **SAVONLINNA:** 214 miles/340 km northeast of Helsinki. **SAVONLINNA OPERA FESTIVAL:** Olavinkatu 27. Tel 358/15-476-750, fax to order tickets 358/15-476-7540; info@operafestival.fi; www.operafestival.fi. *Cost:* tickets $50–$110. *When:* Jul–early Aug. **HOTEL RAUHALINNA:** 10 miles/16 km by road (30 minutes by boat) from Savonlinna. Tel 358/15-739-5430, fax 358/15-272-524. *Cost:* doubles from $200 during opera season. "Buffet of the Czars" lunch $28 (offered in Jul only). **WHEN:** hotel open early Jun–late Aug.

A Winter Adventure Amid the Nordic Ice Floes

ICEBREAKER CRUISE

Kemi, Lapland, Finland

The *Sampo* is one of the world's few tourist icebreakers, offering a one-of-a-kind experience on the frozen Gulf of Bothnia, the northernmost tip of the Baltic Sea. The four-hour cruise departs from Kemi, just south of the Arctic Circle, and ventures out into Europe's largest continuous ice field. Once out at sea, passengers are invited to don bright-orange watertight survival suits and float among the newly broken ice, sometimes 3 feet thick. They can alight from the *Sampo* onto the rock-hard sea for ice fishing or be whisked away by snowmobiles or husky-driven sleds. Either way, it is an exhilarating ride through splendid solitude that is both heart stopping and surreal as the midwinter half-light reflects off the white solid surface of the sea. Finland holds claim to being the world's number one builder of ice-breaking ships, so passengers are in good hands. The captain leads a fascinating tour of the ship from bridge to engine room.

Tours that include the icebreaker often include land activities in or around Kemi such as winter safaris (snowmobile or dogsled rides, reindeer mushing, and exploration of Sami/Lapp settlements). Created every winter since

The 3,900-ton Sampo

1996, Kemi's fantastic SnowCastle grows larger and more inventive every year. The three-story-tall wintry stronghold is composed of a courtyard, ice-sculpture exhibitions, a chapel, café, and auditorium where performances are often staged. Guests can overnight at the "World's Largest SnowCastle"—preferably in the Honeymoon Suite.

WHAT: experience, hotel. **WHERE:** on the Bay of Bothnia, in the northern Lapland

region that covers one third of Finland, 1-hour flight from Helsinki. *SAMPO:* book through Sampo Tours, tel 358/16-258-878, fax 358/16-256-361; sampo@kemi.fi; www.sampotours.com. *Cost:* $335 for 1-day winter adventures, includes half-day on the *Sampo.* Longer winter-safari adventures in Lapland available.

When: departures daily, end of Dec–mid-Apr. **SNOWCASTLE:** tel 358/16-259-502, fax 358/16-259-708; info@snowcastle.net; www.snowcastle.net. *Cost:* doubles from $195, Honeymoon Suite $450. *When:* open Feb–end of Apr. **BEST TIMES:** Jan and Feb for the Northern Lights.

The Real Winter Wonderland

SANTA'S VILLAGE

Rovaniemi, Lapland, Finland

Yes, Virginia, there is a Santa Claus, and this is where he lives. Rovaniemi is considered the gateway to Lapland—known for its indigenous, formerly nomadic Sami (once commonly known as Lapp) people—and

to Finland's Arctic Circle, Santa's home turf. You can have your photo taken with one foot planted on either side of the Arctic Circle. Santa's Village is how every child always imagined it to be, a snowy winter wonderland with a wonderfully jovial Santa in attendence every day. His busy workshop and helpers show how he keeps up, while the post office displays some of the 600,000 letters received every year from all over the world, about a third of which get answered. An irresistible gift shop provides myriad Yuletide presents that can be shipped back home with a Santa's Village postmark, or, for a nominal fee, add your child's name to a list to receive a post-

card from Santa. A nearby reindeer farm provides the chance for a Magic Sleighride (though one that never leaves the ground) drawn by Rudolph, Dancer, and Prancer lookalikes (a snowmobile alternative is also available). Rovaniemi was nearly razed by the Germans in 1944 and largely rebuilt following plans that the famous Finnish architect Alvar Aalto laid out in the shape of reindeer antlers.

Although there are only 6,500 Sami living in northern Finland now, and their nomadic days of herding roaming reindeer are diminishing, their cultural identity and customs are proudly kept alive at the fascinating, award-winning Arktikum Science Center, depicting life above the Arctic Circle. The lovely Restaurant Oppipoika promotes Lappish cuisine: the standard salmon and fresh fish are ever present, but sample the unusual reindeer pepper steak and elk stew, with a dessert made of local cloudberries. Who knew you could eat so well in the Arctic Circle?

WHAT: town, site, restaurant. **ROVANIEMI:** 536 miles/850 km north of Helsinki. **SANTA'S VILLAGE:** 5 miles/8 km north of Rovaniemi, tel 358/16-356-2096; aija@arcticcircle-information.fi; www.santaclausvillage.info. **RESTAURANT**

Santa takes his reindeer for a practice run.

OPPIPOIKA: Korkalonkatu 33. Tel 358/20-798-4609, fax 358/20-798-4697; www.lao.fi/apprentice. *Cost:* lunch $17. *When:* lunch, Mon–Fri. **BEST TIMES:** special events during Christmas season mean big crowds but no one seems to mind.

The Island of Ice and Fire

THE RING ROAD

Iceland

Amerca's closest European neighbor, vast, volcanic Iceland is sadly misnamed. In fact it is about 89 percent ice free, and boasts one of the planet's most incredible landscapes, full of contrasts and extremes.

Medieval Europeans popularly believed it to be the threshold of the underworld, and Jules Verne chose a volcano here as the entranceway for his *Journey to the Center of the Earth*. The word *geyser* was coined here, named after Geysir, the largest of the island's many spouting hot springs. There are also lava fields, bubbling mud pools, and steam vents, but look in another direction and you'll see plenty of ice, including the dramatic glacial lagoon at Jokulsarlon, famous for icebergs that break off from

One of Iceland's swimmable volcanic craters

the glacier face and form an ever-changing maze for chugging tour boats. In yet another direction, you'll see pristine farms and extraordinarily green grasslands, mostly along the coast.

The two-lane Ring Road (or Route 1—the only show in town) runs in an 860-mile circuit around much of the island, taking in everything from ocean scenery to the empty, treeless tundra to the fire and ice of the interior. Motorists may feel as if they've returned from a trip to the moon when they return to Reykjavik, the world's northernmost capital.

Icelanders tend to be very hospitable, and if you befriend any of the cosmopolitan residents, ask them to take you to the city's fabled Blue Lagoon, thirty-five minutes outside town, one of a dozen public thermal

swimming pools that are said to be Iceland's health and beauty secret. The natural swimming area is filled with silica-rich water whose milky turquoise color comes from blue-green algae. With temperatures near 102 degrees Fahrenheit sending up billowing white steam, and a geothermal power plant just next door, the scenario seems almost surreal—much like the entire island.

WHAT: experience, island. **WHERE:** Reykjavik is only 5 hours by plane from Washington, Boston, or New York. The Ring Road begins and ends in Reykjavik. For information in the U.S., contact the Iceland Tourist Bureau, tel 212-885-9700; www.icelandtouristboard.com. **BEST TIMES:** summer, when average temperature in Reykjavik is 50 degrees Fahrenheit. Jul sunset is about 1 A.M.

Immersed in the Beauty of the Sognefjord

KVIKNE'S HOTEL

Balestrand, Norway

Norway's unique beauty lies in its fjords, and the Sognefjord is not only the longest and deepest, but also one of the most dramatic. After a four-hour sail from Bergen along a spectacular landscape, you'll see the rambling Victorian carved-wood frame of Kvikne's Hotel on a small peninsula jutting into the 127-mile-long fjord. Dating back to 1752, the

The Kvikne family has owned the hotel since 1877.

hotel has been the destination of poets and monarchs for the four generations that the Kvikne family has been at the helm. A modern wing has been added, but ask for a room in the original house, where some rooms have balconies and unforgettable fjord views. Though it is full of day-trippers and tourists, the hotel maintains a family-run base-camp ambience, encouraging treks and bike rides into the extravagantly beautiful countryside. A sail up the gorgeous little Fjaerlandfjord north of Sognefjord to see the Jostedals Glacier is a wonderful day trip.

WHAT: hotel. **WHERE:** Balestrand on the Sognefjord, 4 hours by steamer from Bergen, daily departures. Tel 47/57-69-42-00, fax 47/57-69-42-01; www.kviknes.no. **COST:** doubles in new wing $255, in original house $340. **WHEN:** open early May–Oct.

Where Nature, Commerce, and Culture Collide

BERGEN AND TROLDHAUGEN

Norway

Founded in 1070 and the capital of the Kingdom of Norway during the Middle Ages, Bergen was an outpost of the powerful Hanseatic League of Baltic merchant communities organized in the 12th century. At that time the wharfside district of Bryggen (the Quay) was its bustling trading center. It is still a remarkable collection of timbered warehouses and hostelries that today are home to artisan workshops, cafés, and the interesting Hanseatic Museum. Although most were destroyed by a series of devastating fires over the centuries (the museum building is one of the few that survived), many of the structures were painstakingly (and repeatedly) re-created until the league was phased out in the 18th century. The beautiful Romanesque St. Mary's Church (Mariakirken) is an original 12th-century gem, which served as the spiritual hub of the Hanseatic merchants for three centuries. Bryggen is the only surviving neighborhood of these gabled wooden buildings. Their dis-

Until the 1830s, Bergen was Norway's largest town.

tinctive red-brick and ocher color scheme appeared all over northern Europe during the era of Hanseatic influence, and they are much of the reason behind Bergen's tourist moniker—the Wooden City.

Just south of Bergen is Troldhaugen (Troll's Hill), the 19th-century summer villa of musician and composer Edvard Grieg (1843–1907), born in Bergen and buried at Troldhaugen with his wife. Try to catch a concert here in the summer or fall—visit in early summer for the acclaimed Bergen International Festival, which features a wide variety of music and performing arts but is always dominated by the work of the native maestro performed by Bergen's Philharmonic Orchestra.

Bergen is surrounded by seven mountains (the funicular to Floyen climbs 1,000 feet to the steepest of them for gorgeous views), making it not only a naturally picturesque base but also the most practical gateway to Norway's unique fjord lands. A day trip from Bergen encapsulates the best of this breathtakingly beautiful corner of the country. Start with a bus trip through steep switchback roads to Stalheim for a view of the valley below. At Gudvangen, you board a boat to sail through the Naerøyfjord (the narrowest in Norway) and the Aurlands Fjord, some of the loveliest branches of the dra-

matic Sognefjord. After that astounding panorama of natural beauty comes the train ride from the town of Flam 2,850 feet up and over the side of a gorge to Mydral. For 12 miles and forty-five harrowing minutes, your train darts in and out of twenty tunnels maneuvering twenty-one hairpin turns past countless waterfalls. The conductor's reassurance that the train is fitted with five sets of standby brake systems—plus a shot (or two) of aquavit back at a Bergen café after the twelve-hour round trip—should calm any jangled nerves.

WHAT: town, site, event, experience. **BERGEN:** 347 miles/558 km west of Oslo. Bergen Tourist Information Office, Vaagsallmenningen 1. Tel 47/55-55-20-00, fax 47/55-55-20-01. **TROLDHAUGEN:** 5 miles/8 km south of Bergen. Tel 47/55-92-29-92, fax 47/55-92-29-93; info@troldhaugen.no; www.troldhaugen.com. *Best times:* concerts held at Troldhaugen from end of Jun–mid-Nov and as one of the venues of the Bergen International Festival, 11 days in late May and early Jun. Jun 15 is Grieg's birthday. **SOGNEFJORD CRUISE:** in U.S., contact Scantours, Inc., tel 800-223-7226 or 310-636-4656, fax 310-390-0493; info@scantours.com; www.scantours.com. *Cost:* all-day cruise excursion $200. *When:* daily morning departures. Advance purchase suggested in summer months.

Where the Joy of the Midnight Sun Is Infectious

NORWEGIAN COASTAL VOYAGE AND NORTH CAPE

Bergen, Norway

Norway's legendary Hurtigruten cruise steamers sail along its intricate Gulf stream–warmed coastline, a region of exquisite fjords, glaciers, mountains, and in the summer months, a sun that never fully sets.

The lifeline for the remote towns of northern Norway—some still accessible only by sea—this fleet of workboats stops in some thirty-five ports between Bergen and the Arctic Circle near the Russian border for a 1,500-mile, twelve-day round trip. A Hurtigruten ship is not a luxury cruiser, but with this kind of scenery, the comfortable cabins and straightforward food are part of the adventure as you sail in and out of large and small ports. Some stops—such as North Cape (Nordkapp), a sheer, granite cliff rising 1,000 feet out of the frigid Norwegian Sea—are long enough for optional land excursions. Due to the cape's location, farther north than Alaska and most of Siberia, the sun stays above the horizon from May 12 to August 1 and below it from November 19 to January 25. The cape's plateau, 800 miles from the start of the Arctic ice cap, is a largely uninhabited place of wild and romantic moonscape—nothing grows on this tundra. This is a site that visitors either love or hate, but it elates adventurous tourists—just check out the festivity in the clifftop observatory's Champagne bar, where you feel as if you're about to fall off "the World's very end," as one Italian pilgrim wrote in 1664.

WHAT: site, experience. **COASTAL CRUISE:** in Bergen, see any travel agency. In the U.S., contact Hurtigruten, tel 866-552-0371, fax 954-486-9340; retailsales@hurtigruten.us; www.hurtigruten.us. One-way north, 7 days; one-way south, 6 days; round-trip, 12 days. **COST:** round-trip high season rates begin from $3,709 per person. **WHEN:** departures from Bergen and Kirkenes daily year-round. **BEST TIMES:** Jun–Aug nicest though busiest months.

An Isolated Archipelago of Striking, Rugged Beauty

LOFOTEN ISLANDS

Norway

Nature is powerful in Norway, perhaps nowhere more so than in the Lofoten Islands, 123 miles north of the Arctic Circle. This 118-mile-long archipelago of small fishing communities set against a dramatic wall of towering snow-patched peaks—granite formations that date back several billion years—has drawn increasing numbers of mainlanders (and foreign artists) attracted to its seclusion, special light, bracing air, and unpolluted waters. The traditional *rorbu* (fishing cottage) was traditionally built on the docks extending out over the water; today they are popular as rentals for their simplicity (and the insight into the local way of life). This steep island-world is bathed in summer nights of eight-hour dusk, with the midnight sun shining from June until late July. Svolvaer (population 4,000), the main town for the islands, has a thriving summer art colony. Ferries arrive here from mainland Bodø, where Edgar Allan Poe spent a number of years writing *A Descent into the Maelstrom*, describing the unique phenomenon of immense volumes of water flushed through deep, narrow gorges with the outgoing tide. A maelstrom—the word, of Dutch origin, means "grinding stream"—is a furious, natural whirlpool (also known as a "kettle") that creates a goose-bump-inducing howl. Before catching the ferry to the Lofoten, visit Saltstraumen Eddy on the mainland to see what mesmerized Poe.

WHAT: island. **WHERE:** Bodø is 466 miles/ 750 km north of Trondheim, 890 miles/1,432 km north of Bergen, 810 miles/1,303 km north of Oslo. Ferries from Bodø to the Lofoten take 4–6 hours; flights from Bodø take 30 minutes. **BEST TIMES:** Jun–Jul.

The warm Gulf Stream ensures mild winters and cool summers in the Lofoten Islands.

At Home Amid a Wealth of Tradition and Quality

MUNCH MUSEUM AND HOTEL CONTINENTAL

Oslo, Norway

Edvard Munch (1863–1944) remains hugely popular today, the only Nordic painter whose influence is recognized on a global level. That he was not terribly successful during his lifetime (he was posthumously hailed as the father of Expressionism) is evident from the fact that he was able to hold on to much of his work: more than 22,000 pieces in his possession were bequeathed to the city of Oslo in 1940 shortly before his death. As if these weren't enough, the collection has been augmented over time by gifts from individuals, filling the Munch Museum, opened in 1963, to the rafters. It now includes paintings, drawings, watercolors, prints, sculptures, and personal possessions such as books and letters, an edited portion of which is exhibited and rotated regularly.

Munch lost his mother at age five, and was often ill as a child. His lifelong struggle with malaise and mental torment colors much of his work, which ranges from realism to latter-day Expressionism. His most famous work, *The*

Scream, was stolen from the museum in August 2004 and recovered two years later. Also on view is *Night* (like *The Scream,* painted during the same prolific period in the 1890s when he had achieved a certain renown). Despite the massive number of works on display, representing the artist at every age and under the sway of a variety of aesthetic impulses, there is a constant current of melancholy and loneliness.

Hotel Continental, the capital's finest accomodations, is privately owned and faultlessly operated by four generations of the Brochmann family, who built it in 1900. It features Norway's largest collection of Munch graphics—the family's own—used to decorate the public areas. Right across the street from the National Theater (and excellently situated in the privileged shadow of the Royal Palace), it has long enjoyed a bond with the theater, hosting performers and playgoers as hotel guests or at its famous Theatercafeen. The most authentically re-created Viennese café in northern Europe, the Theatercafeen has been legendary since the day it opened. Lively and always full, it is eclipsed only by its more formal sister establishment, the much touted Annen Etage, an elegant venue for some of the city's most refined dining. It's a more casual scene at Dagligstuen, a bar and restaurant that offers the best spot for viewing the hotel's large collection of Munch's work.

WHAT: site, hotel, restaurant. **MUNCH MUSEUM:** Toyengata 53. Tel 47/23-49-3500; info@munch.museum.no; www.munch.museum.no. *Cost:* admission $12. *When:* open daily Jun–mid-Sept, open Tues–Fri mid-Sept–May. **HOTEL CONTINENTAL:** Stortingsgaten 24-26. Tel 47/22-82-40-00, fax 47/22-42-96-89; booking@hotel-continental.no; www.hotel-continental.no. *Cost:* doubles from $490. Dinner at Theatercafeen $50; at Annen Etage $95.

Remarkable 1,000-Year-Old Relics

VIKINGSKIPHUSET

Oslo, Norway

The Age of the Vikings, when Norsemen terrorized the coasts of Europe, lasted approximately from 800 to 1050 (the bold explorer Leif Ericsson is said to have discovered America in 1001). Little was written down of their vivid sagas and legends, embellished over the ages by word of mouth. The single best place to experience the wealth of their heritage is at the cathedral-like Vikingskiphuset or Viking Ship Museum, built in 1936 to house three incredibly well-preserved 9th-century Viking burial ships discovered at the turn of the century in the nearby Oslo Fjord. Considered the country's most important archaeological cache, the three vessels contained the royal

Graceful Viking ships and their burial treasures are housed here.

bodies of Viking chieftains and one queen (believed to be the grandmother of Harald Fairhair), all entombed with their servants, pets, and countless artifacts meant to serve them in the afterlife in the royal manner to which they were accustomed. Together, they constitute the largest Viking find ever recorded, and have shaped the understanding of Norway's distant maritime past. The artistry and craftsmanship confirm that the Vikings excelled at more than sailing.

WHAT: site. **WHERE:** Huk Aveny 35, Bygdøy. Tel 47-13-52-80; postmottak@khm. uio.no. **COST:** admission $8.

Norway at Its Most Dramatic

GEIRANGERFJORD

Øye, Norway

Enthralled by the unmatched countryside and in search of perfect salmon and trout fishing, Europeans (particularly the British) "discovered" Norway's fjords in the late 1800s. The vertical cliff-walled Geirangerfjord,

10 miles long, was—and still is—held as the ne plus ultra: Norway at its most dramatic. View it from the remarkable Ornevegen (Eagles' Road), from Andalsnes to Geiranger, with its eleven hairpin, hair-raising turns—completed in 1952, it remains an astonishing feat of engineering. Stop at the Eagle's Turn to take in the unforgettable view of the fjord winding through the valley. From Andalsnes to Valldal is another of Norway's audacious serpentine roadways, the Trollstigveien (Trolls' Path), which crosses one of Norway's most desolate regions.

Not the most accessible of the fjords but arguably the most popular, tourists can choose from numerous attractions—half-day cruises, excellent salmon fishing, hiking, bicycling, visits to poignantly deserted farming hamlets inaccessible by road, and excursions to Jostedalsbreen, Europe's largest glacier, and spectacular waterfalls with names like Seven Sisters and Bridal Veil. A great base for enjoying the Geirangerfjord area and neighboring Norangsfjord is the Union Hotel. It's one of the old-time "fjord castles" so popular at the end of the 19th century. Today renovated and modernized, the hotel still holds sway in the area: Norway's King Harald and Queen Sonja chose

Seven waterfalls make up Sju Søstre (the Seven Sisters).

to celebrate their silver wedding anniversary here in 1993. You can even bathe in German Kaiser Wilhelm's original bath (he returned no fewer than twenty-five times) if you can wrangle Room 12.

WHAT: site, hotel. **GEIRANGERFJORD:** approximately 7 hours from Oslo on the Serpentine Road. **UNION HOTEL:** Øye, on the banks of the Norangsfjord (234 miles/373 km from Bergen, 269 miles/427 km from Oslo). Tel 47/70-06-21-00; www.unionoye.no. *Cost:* doubles $245. *When:* open late Apr–mid-Oct. **BEST TIMES:** May–Sept.

Winter's Best and Brightest Spectacle

THE NORTHERN LIGHTS

Tromsø, Norway

The same extreme reaches of northern Europe that provide endless days of summer sunshine promise something just as remarkable during the otherwise daunting winter months: the Aurora Borealis ("dawning of the north")

or Northern Lights, an eerie, silent display of dancing lights in the heavens above. On most clear winter nights, Arctic winds collide with the electron-charged atmosphere of the earth, creating an aurora of these swirling apparitions around the magnetic North Pole. The predominant color is green, but, during major nighttime

Tromsø is Norway's largest city north of the Arctic Circle.

shows, the skies also take on fleeting pink and gray curls along the edges, with a glimmer of lilac in the center. To learn the cold, hard scientific facts, the Northern Lights Planetarium in Tromsø, gateway to the Arctic and Norway's self-dubbed "Paris of the North," has the technology and film documentaries. But city lights can lessen the intensity of the spectacle: local Sami (Laplander) guides take visitors by snowmobile, dogsled, or reindeer sled to the frozen inlands of northern Norway. The once nomadic Sami are concentrated in inland towns such as Karasjok (305 miles/485 km east), capital of the Sami region, and Kautokeino (263 miles/418 km southeast).

WHAT: experience. **WHERE:** Tromsø is 1,084 miles/1,744 km north of Oslo. **WHEN:** cloudless nights, late Nov–early Apr. **BEST TIMES:** Jan or Feb, around 11 P.M. or midnight. Tromsø holds an annual Northern Lights Festival of classical and contemporary music for 4 days mid–late Jan.

On the Blossoming Banks of the Queen of Fjords, Norway's Oldest Inn

HARDANGERFJORD

Utne, Norway

Of the countless fjords that create Norway's lacework coastline, Hardanger—the Garden Fjord—is generally considered one of the most beautiful. Terraced fruit orchards cover its fertile banks as it stretches

113 miles inland. Particularly famed as a destination during apple and cherry blossom time, it transforms into an undulating blanket of pink and white blooms in the late spring when visitors flock here in annual pilgrimage not unlike Washington, D.C.'s.

The perfect base for exploring this exquisite corner of western Norway is found at the foot of the steep banks of the Hardangerfjord: the small Utne Hotel, accommodating guests from all over the world since 1722. Norway's oldest, the inviting inn was run by the same family for five generations before being purchased by a cultural foundation in 1996, thus ensuring that its beautiful historic furnishings and textiles (not to mention its hospitality and charm) would continue uninterrupted well into the future.

Its ever-present amiable innkeepers keep it cozy, snug, and country-fresh. The traditional Norwegian interior of painted wood and decorative arts is the simple, airy backdrop for family antiques and photos and works left behind by the artists who have favored this spot since the late 1800s.

Nearby is the Hardanger Folk Museum, the town's excellent open-air cultural attraction, featuring a cluster farm made up of 19th-century buildings.

WHAT: site, hotel. **UTNE:** 25 miles/40 km south of Voss, 87 miles/140 km southeast of Bergen, 233 miles/370 km from Oslo. **UTNE HOTEL:** tel 47/53-66-64-00, fax 47/53-66-69-83; reception@utnehotel.no; www.utne hotel.no. *Cost:* doubles from $235. *When:* open Apr–Oct. **BEST TIMES:** May–Sept.

Journey to the Top of the World

THE NORTH POLE

Norway

J ust a century ago, no man had ever stood at latitude 90 degrees north. Today the North Pole, a spot that fascinated generations of explorers, is a tourist destination, albeit a rarefied one, and officially part of Norway.

Sailing from the mountainous, heavily glaciated Norwegian island of Spitsbergen or from Murmansk, Russia's northernmost port, special nuclear-powered icebreaker ships negotiate the Arctic Basin's ever-changing panorama of wind-polished ice, navigating at speeds of up to 20 knots. Aboard ship, a series of lectures and presentations by on-board specialists punctuate days when the sun never sets, and passengers stay on the alert for sightings of polar bears, seals, walruses, and Arctic birds. Inflatable expedition boats and helicopters are used for the reconnaissance essential to icebreaker navigation, and also to give passengers the chance to experience the area up close. When the ship reaches 90 degrees north it finds

a suitable parking space, lowers the gangway (ice conditions permitting), and allows passengers to descend for a walkabout, a barbecue,

Few other vessels are powerful enough to ply such icy waters.

Polar bear sightings are a North Pole highlight.

and, for the truly hardy, a quick plunge into the Arctic Sea. Champagne flows, dancing and celebrating begin, a crew member rides his bike across an ice floe, another begins a game of

Arctic golf (using Day-Glo golf balls), and everyone remembers the great names who came to this place through so much adversity. "The Pole at last!" wrote Robert E. Peary on April 6, 1909. "The prize of three centuries, my dream and ambition for 23 years. Mine at last."

WHAT: experience. **WHERE:** the ship's departure point at Spitsbergen is approximately 1,250 miles/2012 km from Oslo and 600 miles/966 km south of the North Pole. **HOW:** in the U.S., contact Quark Expeditions, tel 866-961-2961 or 203-803-2888; enquiry @quarkexpeditions.com; www.quarkexpeditions. com. **COST:** 13-night expeditions $22,690 per person, double occupancy, departing via Oslo, includes all flights within Norway and the Arctic, accommodations, meals, and activities. **WHEN:** Jul.

Gliding Through Sweden's Scenic Heartland

GÖTA CANAL

Götaland, Sweden

This four-day cruise among the 100,000 lakes of Sweden's lake district is a highlight for boat lovers and those who fancy the chance to see Sweden at the romantic pace of times gone by. The Göta Canal, the "Blue Ribbon" connecting Göteborg on the North Sea and Stockholm on the Baltic, was dug out by almost 60,000 soldiers, who removed more than 200 million cubic feet of earth and rock, creating fifty-eight locks. Century-old ships brimming with character traverse the 322 nautical miles via a series of canals and lakes and even a stretch of inland sea. Canalside towpaths serve as bicycle paths, and land excursions to a number of small towns alternate on east- and westbound trips, encouraging round-trip journeys. Gliding along, you'll pass well-tended farms, monasteries, castles, and medieval churches. The old-fashioned Soderkopings Brunn Inn makes it tempting to jump ship and stay a few days. The picturesque town of Soderkoping, a bustling trading center 1,000 years ago, was issued a royal charter in 1774 for its curative springs. Spa services are still available, but most guests seem more enticed by the rambling hotel's famous waffles and punch served on the long Victorian-style veranda.

WHAT: experience, hotel. **CANAL CRUISE:** in the U.S., contact Nordic Saga Tours Inc., tel 800-848-6449; www.nordicsaga.com. *Cost:* 2–6-day cruises from $595 per person, double occupancy, includes all meals and tours. *When:* May–Sept. **SODERKOPING:** 113 miles/ 180 km south of Stockholm. **SODERKOPINGS BRUNN INN:** tel 46/121-10900, fax 46/121-13941. *Cost:* doubles from $245. **BEST TIMES:** Jun–Aug.

An Island Retreat Rich in Medieval History

VISBY

Gotland, Sweden

It takes very little time to fall in love with Gotland, a mysterious sea-swept island in the middle of the stony gray Baltic off the southeast coast of Stockholm. The largest of Sweden's islands (78 miles long), it is definitely not typically Swedish, although it officially became part of the nation in 1679. Once a strategic hub of Hanseatic trade in the Baltic Sea, Gotland today offers serenity and a landscape of lush meadows that are tapestries of orchids (thirty-five different varieties thrive here), poppies, and wildflowers. You'll also find desolate moorlands, stone walls, close to 100 unspoiled medieval country churches, and pristine farmlands that date back to the 6th-century Vikings (nowhere else in Sweden have so many Viking or medieval treasures been discovered). Dramatic stone pillars, the island's monumental "sea stacks" carved out of soft limestone by the wind and waves, dot a coastline marked by long empty beaches, tiny fishing villages, and steep cliffs. Gotland's highlight is the once prominent Hanseatic town of Visby, a living shrine to the island's 14th-century heyday when it was a country all its own and Visby boasted sixteen churches. Its defensive walls, more than 2 miles long with forty-four lookout towers, are some of the best preserved in Europe, often compared to those in Ávila, Spain, and Carcassonne, France.

During the summer, festivals come thick and fast, and Gotland finds itself at the forefront of Sweden's artistic and cultural life (Ingmar Bergman lived and filmed here, on Gotland's ancillary island of Farö in the north). Book much in advance (preferably into the restored 19th-century Wisby Hotell, the nicest place on the island, located in the historic center) for August's annual Medieval Week, when the townspeople go about their business in colorful gowns and velvet doublets, and minstrels and street theater bring the city back to its Hanseatic trading days when it was as vibrant, rich, and powerful as London or Paris.

A medieval wall encloses the ancient town of Visby.

WHAT: island, town, hotel. **VISBY:** 60 miles/97 km from the Swedish mainland. The nearest port from Stockholm is Nynäshamn, a 5-hour ferry trip to Visby. There are daily 40-minute flights as well. **WISBY HOTELL:** Strandgatan 6. Tel 46/498-257500, fax 46/498-257590; cl.wisby@choice.se; www.wisbyhotell.se. *Cost:* doubles $125 (low season), $300 (high season). **BEST TIMES:** in the short summer season, Visby can be crowded though the countryside remains relatively empty. May and Sept are nice, too, but less likely to invite swimming. Midsummer Eve, Jun 23; Medieval Week, 1st week in Aug.

The World's Largest Igloo

THE ICE HOTEL

Jukkasjärvi, Norrland, Sweden

Is this the coolest place to stay in the world? You bet. The Ice Hotel is a magically translucent palace with guest rooms (there's even a Honeymoon Suite), a cinema, a 45-foot vodka bar using "glasses" crafted from ice, galleries, and a futuristic-looking colonnaded reception hall whose pure ice chandeliers are lit by fiber optics. Built every November since 1990 out of 4,000 tons of densely packed snow and ice, the hotel disappears each spring when it melts into the River Torne on whose banks it is constructed. The surreal ice building is a marvel in itself, but the interior trappings can be even more amazing: the furniture, art, and sculptures in the public rooms are the work of engineers and well-known ice carvers. Things can be surprisingly toasty (well, maybe that's an exaggeration): your ice-block "bed" is lavishly draped with layers of reindeer hides beneath your high-tech sleeping bags. You can roast in the sauna before a hearty breakfast, then set off for a day full of fun (but remember you're north of the Arctic Circle and the sun doesn't shine for six weeks from December to January): choose from snowmobile (or reindeer) safaris, dogsledding, ice fishing, experiencing the eerie patterns of the Northern Lights, cross-country skiing, helicopter tours, or visits to native Sami (the once nomadic people formerly called Laplanders who herded reindeer for a living) villages. For those who get their share of been-there-done-that kicks after just one night of chilling out in a freezer whose internal temperature hovers around 25 degrees Fahrenheit, nearby conventional chalets (featuring creature comforts like central heating) offer alternative accommodations.

The Ice Hotel's architecture changes from year to year.

WHAT: hotel. **WHERE:** daily 90-minute flights from Stockholm. The Ice Hotel is 8 miles/12 km from airport in Jukkasjärvi. Transport to and from hotel by conventional taxi is available, but ask for the dogsled or snowmobile to pick you up. Tel 46/980-66800, fax 46/980-66890; info@icehotel.com; www.icehotel.com. **COST:** doubles from $175, including guided tour, thermal sleeping bag, and breakfast. **WHEN:** mid-Dec–late Apr, temperatures permitting. **BEST TIMES:** Jan for the Northern Lights. The important Sami festival and market (the Marknad) in Jokkmokk, 126 miles/200 km away, is the first week of Feb.

The Versailles of the North

DROTTNINGHOLM PALACE AND COURT THEATER

Lake Mälaren, Svealand, Sweden

C learly inspired by the style of Versailles, the official year-round home of Sweden's present-day King Carl XVI and Queen Silvia is widely held to be one of the most delightful European palaces. On its own tree-covered island (Drottningholm means "queen's island") in Lake Mälaren, the many-windowed rococo palace is open to the public even when the royal family is in residence. Built in 1622 for Sweden's Queen Eleonora, the interior still dazzles with its collection of opulent 17th- to 19th-century art and furniture, gilt ceilings, and magnificent chandeliers. Fountains and formal gardens further encourage comparisons to the real Versailles.

Visit the unforgettable Drottningholm Court Theater, the world's most perfectly preserved 18th-century theater, where performances are still given using original sets and stage machinery. Originally lit by 400 candles, today it is illuminated by as many flickering flame-shaped electric bulbs. The wooden theater was built in 1766 by the mother of King Gustav III for an intimate audience of his friends and courtiers. The 18th-century operas and ballets performed today by some of Europe's premier talents (and by an orchestra playing original period instruments) transport audiences back in time.

WHAT: site. **WHERE:** 7 miles/11 km west of Stockholm. Frequent 1-hour steamboat service (with guided tour along the way) leaves from Stadshusbron in Stockholm. For information about performances at the Court Theater, tel 46/8-660-8225, fax 46/8-566-93101; dst@dtm.se; www.dtm.se. **COST:** admission to palace; theater tickets $22–$91. **BEST TIMES:** the theater holds performances during the Drottningholm Festival, Jun–Aug.

A Castle, a Special Inn, a Picture-Perfect Town

GRIPSHOLM CASTLE

Mariefred, Svealand, Sweden

T his endearing lakeside village, with its main attraction, the impregnable redbrick Gripsholm Castle, is Stockholm's perfect day trip. Throw in an excellent lunch at the acclaimed country manor Gripsholms Värdhus

Hotel, Sweden's oldest inn, and this is anybody's idea of a perfect day. It's about the journey as much as the destination when you arrive by a nostalgic little coal-fired steamboat, the *Mariefred*, then return by narrow-gauge steam train. The day in Mariefred revolves around the 16th-century onion-towered castle, attentively watching over the town from its position on Lake Mälaren. The castle was occupied until 1864 and is still considered one of the five royal palaces of Sweden. But it's principally known as the national portrait gallery, with one of the finest collections in the world (and, with 1,200 of its 4,000 portraits on display, Europe's largest).

Reserve a table for a wonderful lunch on the lakeside glassed-in veranda of the Gripsholms Värdshus & Hotel. It first welcomed guests in 1609 when it was just a hospice built on the site of an earlier monastery (ceiling beams date back to 1507 and the wine cellar, where tastings can be arranged, was used by the monks as early as 1493). The staff here is a delight, so are the romantic guest rooms and lakeview suites beautifully decorated in country style. It all makes for a wonderful and easy getaway and day-trippers often regret their haste: bring your toothbrush and check in.

WHAT: town, site, hotel, restaurant. **MARIEFRED:** 40 miles/64 km southwest of Stockholm. Boats leave from Stockholm mid-May–Sept. Trains leave daily year-round. **GRIPSHOLMS CASTLE:** admission. **GRIPSHOLMS VÄRDSHUS & HOTEL:** Kyrkogatan 1. Tel 46/159-34750, fax 46/159-34777; info@gripsholms-vardshus.se; www.gripsholms-vardshus.se. *Cost:* doubles from $290. Dinner $50. **BEST TIMES:** Jun–Aug; local festival 1st Sat in Jun.

The Local Specialty as Art

ULRIKSDALS WÄRDSHUS

Solna, Svealand, Sweden

Famous throughout the country for its unrivaled smörgåsbord, Sweden's great culinary art form, there could be no lovelier setting than this country inn within its own royal park, built in 1868 upon request of the Swedish

Crown. Most other restaurants serve smörgåsbords only during summer months and again at Christmas (when it's called a Yule Table or Julbord), but guests come to Ulriksdals Wärdshus at all times of the year (the present-day king and queen have been known to appear) to tuck into the groaning table of more than seventy-five different offerings. According to unofficial smörgåsbord etiquette, one visits the food-laden table five times, the first for herring (there are twenty variations), the last for desserts. In between are a panoply of Nordic specialties such as smoked eel, sweet Baltic

shrimp, reindeer, those famous Swedish meatballs, pork chops with the ubiquitous lingonberry sauce, and the much-loved national specialty, Jansson Temptation—a delectable quiche of anchovies, potatoes, onions, and heavy cream—that no self-respecting smörgåsbord or Swede goes without. The typical drink to accompany such indulgence is Swedish aquavit with a beer chaser or schnapps. But the inn also has one of the finest wine cellars in the country, and all except the most expensive are available by the glass. If you're still lucid at sunset (which is not until 9 P.M. in July), the country's blue and yellow flag is ceremonially lowered out on the lawn, and everyone stands to sing the national anthem, one of the inn's more delightful traditions.

WHAT: restaurant. **WHERE:** in Ulriksdals

Royal Park, 5 miles/8 km north of Stockholm. Tel 46/8-850815, fax 46/8-850858; info@ ulriksdalswardshus.se; www.ulriksdalswards hus.se. **COST:** smörgåsbord $48; Julbord $75; dinner $70. **WHEN:** open daily.

Bastions of Hospitality for Nobel Winners and the Noble of Budget

THE GRAND HÔTEL AND OPERAKÄLLAREN

Stockholm, Svealand, Sweden

During the second week in December, the Grand Hôtel hosts the Nobel Prize winners and their entourages, but everyone can enjoy the same elite hospitality year-round at Sweden's best hotel, standing proudly on the

waterfront and in the very center of town. Nonguests too should stop at this 1874 landmark of old-world ambience, if only for a meal in the glassed-in Grand Veranda overlooking the harbor (known for its legendary smörgåsbord and homemade pastries) or a tipple at the classic Cadier Bar. The Grand is privately owned—a fact that seems underlined by the personable ambience and the management's sacrosanct credo that each arrival be treated as a "holy guest." Some of Europe's most demanding palates return regularly to the hotel's refined Franska Matsalen (French Dining Room), whose candelabra-lit setting is pure magic. Magnificent nighttime views across the water to the illuminated Royal Palace accompany an over-the-top dinner and Sweden's most impressive wine cellar. If you still have any kroner left, ask for a room with a waterside view, then book your next meal at the nearby Operakällaren.

Unabashedly luxurious in its location within the Royal Opera House, right across

The Grand Hôtel has a view of the harbor, the Old Town, and the Royal Palace.

from the Royal Palace, the Operakällaren is one of Scandinavia's most famous restaurants, a landmark since it opened in 1787 by decree of King Gustav III (whose 1792 assassination in the Opera House during a fancy dress ball was the inspiration for Verdi's *Un Ballo in Maschera*). It has since evolved into a complex of many restaurants that vary in formality and price, but the main Belle Epoque dining room is the draw, overseen by co-owner Stefan Catenacci, culinary adviser to the king and queen of Sweden. This is the city's most theatrical venue for an evening's repast, featuring plush Oriental rugs, carved oak wall and ceiling panels, once-risqué murals, extravagant crystal chandeliers, and service as impeccably polished as the silverware. A fillet of tender young reindeer and seasonal game dishes highlight the Swedish and international cuisine. The wine list is excellent, but consider toasting the long summer days with Stenborgare, the restaurant's own schnapps.

WHAT: hotel, restaurant. **GRAND HÔTEL:**

Södra Blasieholmshamnen 8. Tel 46/8-6793500, fax 46/8-6118686; info@grand hotel.se; www.grandhotel.se. *Cost:* doubles with waterfront view $495, without $455; suites from $1,015. Smörgåsbord at Grand Veranda $56; dinner at Franska Matsalen $85. **OPERAKÄLLAREN:** entrance from the Kungsträdgarden (Royal Garden), Karl XII.s Torg 2. Tel 46/8-6765800, fax 46/8-6765872; info@operakallaren.se; www.operakallaren.se. *Cost:* dinner $85.

Island-Hopping in the Capital's Front Yard

STOCKHOLM ARCHIPELAGO

Svealand, Sweden

There are a number of ways to see Sweden's archipelago, a latticework of some 24,000 islands and smooth glacier-polished outcroppings that dot a 150-mile stretch off its eastern coast. You can travel by ferry, vintage steamer, three-mast schooner, private sailboat, or yacht. But the most important thing is not to miss them: they are one of the country's most important natural attractions and its wild frontier. Only 6,000 people live on 1,000 islands; the rest are uninhabited.

Sweden's summer is brief but glorious and this is the place to celebrate it—kayaking, picnicking, biking, and walking the unpaved island roads. Take a thirty-minute ferryboat ride from Stockholm out to the well-known restaurant Fjaderholmarnas Krog, accessible only by boat, for a leisurely lunch of just-caught fish, perfectly prepared. Alternatively, stay on board one of the steamers for the scenery: skerries (*skärgärden*, the Swedish word for archipelago, means "garden of skerries"), islets, flower-bedecked fishing cottages, landing stages, meadows, farms, beaches, and a late evening sky of changing pastels. Writers and artists have traditionally been drawn to Vaxholm, while the boating crowd firmly favors Sandhamn, hub for the prestigious annual Royal Regatta.

The archipelago has two environments—the wooded, protected inner part and the barren, wild outer archipelago, the latter home to seabirds, seals, and a few very hardy fishermen. Take a leisurely, blissful sail and you'll understand a lot more about Stockholm, built on fourteen of the archipelago's islands, and its connection to the sea.

WHAT: experience, restaurant. **ARCHIPELAGO TOUR:** for a sea and land journey, in the U.S., contact Scantours, tel 800-223-7226 or 310-636-4656; info@scantours.com; www. scantours.com. *Cost:* 6-day "Taste of Stockholm Archipelago" tour from $1,112 per person (double occupancy), includes hotels and all boat tickets. *When:* departures Jun–Aug. **FJADERHOLMARNAS KROG:** Fjaderholmarna (Feather Islands). Tel 46/8-7183355. *Cost:* lunch $40. *When:* open May–Sept 15. *Best times:* Aug is crayfish season.

The World's Oldest Preserved Man-of-War

VASAMUSEET

Stockholm, Svealand, Sweden

On August 10, 1628, the magnificent royal warship *Vasa* sank on her maiden voyage in front of thousands of horrified onlookers before she even left the Stockholm harbor (sudden gusts of wind and not enough ballast are the most popular explanations). Built at vast expense to be the largest and most powerful battleship ever constructed, the 226-foot, 64-cannon man-of-war was supposed to become the pride of the Swedish war fleet. She took two years to complete on the site where the Grand Hôtel now stands.

Salvaged 333 years after her demise, and since then painstakingly restored, she can now be seen with her complete lower rigging at the Vasa Museum, the only maritime museum of its kind in the world. Large enough to dwarf even the wondrous museum especially built around her at enormous cost and completed in 1990, she is the oldest fully preserved warship in the world. Elaborate wooden carvings cover the exterior of the boat; of the 700 sculptures, 500 are figure sculptures, all of which had been stripped of their original paint and gilt. Almost as interesting was the ship's cargo, which included 4,000 coins, medical equipment, and a backgammon set.

A video is shown regularly, illustrating the painstaking five-year resurrection of the ship upon its discovery in 1961. The Vasa is the most visited museum in Scandinavia, and an immediate favorite for anyone visiting Stockholm.

WHAT: site. **WHERE:** Galärvarvsvägen 14, Djurgården. Tel 46/8-51954800; www.vasa museet.se. **COST:** admission $12.

The Fleeting Return of Long Summer Days and a Pagan Celebration of Nature

MIDSUMMER EVE

Tallberg, Svealand, Sweden

All of Scandinavia celebrates the Nordic festival of Midsummer (Midsommar), but perhaps nowhere as enthusiastically as in Sweden. This ancient Germanic custom honoring life itself has ancient pagan roots—a fertility rite, it was held at the exact time the sun and earth were considered at the peak of their reproductive powers. Everyone takes to the countryside, often dressing in colorful local costumes, resuscitating old-world traditions, eating favorite foods, and imbibing substantial amounts of aquavit, resulting in folks of all ages and sorts singing and dancing. Young girls believe they will dream of their future husbands if they sleep with a freshly picked bouquet of nine different wildflowers under their pillows. But who can tell when it's time to sleep during the long hours of the midnight sun, when even the birds are confused?

One of the best places to celebrate Midsommar is in Sweden's central rural province of Dalarna around the beautiful Lake Siljan, a hilly area often referred to as Sweden's "folklore district." Traditions and customs are lovingly kept alive, thanks in great part to local old-time families such as the Åkerblads. Experience it by visiting their eponymous 15th-century red-framed farmstead, which they converted to an inn in 1910. The mix of antiques (think canopied beds and grandfather clocks) and decorative paintings and carvings found throughout enhances the old-fashioned country atmosphere for which Dalarna is famous. Don't miss the chance to eat here: Swedes come from all parts to do just that.

WHAT: event, hotel, restaurant. **TALLBERG:** 176 miles/283 km northwest of Stockholm. **ÅKERBLADS HOTEL:** tel 46/247-50800, fax

Hotel Åkerblads sits on a hillside above Siljan Lake.

46/247-50652; info@akerblads.se; www.akerblads-tallberg.se. *Cost:* doubles $130. Dinner $38. *When:* restaurant open for lunch, dinner daily. **BEST TIMES:** May–Sept; midsummer falls on the summer solstice, usually Jun 21, but for Scandinavia's Lutheran Church it falls on St. John the Baptist's feast day, Jun 24, and is generally celebrated on the Fri closest to that day.

AFRICA

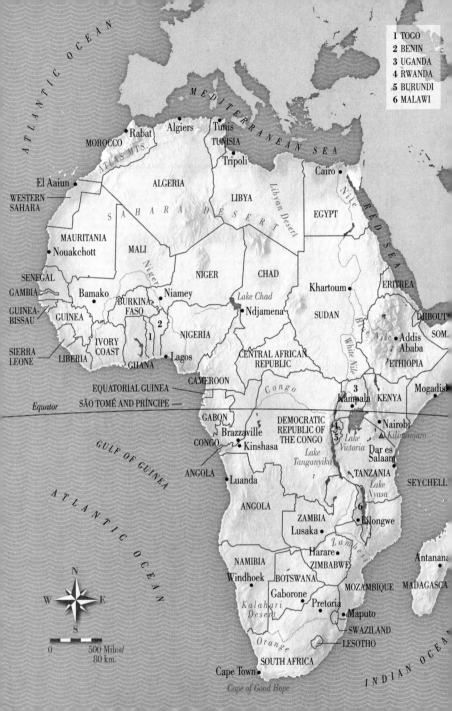

ATLANTIC OCEAN

MEDITERRANEAN SEA

| 1 TOGO |
| 2 BENIN |
| 3 UGANDA |
| 4 RWANDA |
| 5 BURUNDI |
| 6 MALAWI |

MOROCCO
Rabat
Algiers
Tunis
TUNISIA
Tripoli
Cairo

ATLAS MTS.

El Aaiun
WESTERN
SAHARA
ALGERIA
LIBYA
EGYPT

SAHARA DESERT

Libyan Desert

Nile
RED SEA

MAURITANIA
Nouakchott
MALI
Niger
NIGER
CHAD
Khartoum
ERITREA
DJIBOUTI

SENEGAL
GAMBIA
Bamako
Niamey
Lake Chad
SUDAN
SOM.
Addis
Ababa
ETHIOPIA

GUINEA-
BISSAU
GUINEA
BURKINA
FASO
2
NIGERIA
Ndjamena
Blue Nile

SIERRA
LEONE
IVORY
COAST
1
Lagos
CENTRAL AFRICAN
REPUBLIC
White Nile

LIBERIA
GHANA
CAMEROON
Mogadishu

EQUATORIAL GUINEA
SÃO TOMÉ AND PRÍNCIPE
Congo
3
Kampala
KENYA

Equator
GABON
DEMOCRATIC
REPUBLIC OF
THE CONGO
Nairobi
Kilimanjaro

GULF OF GUINEA
Brazzaville
CONGO
Kinshasa
5
Lake
Victoria
Dar es
Salaam

ANGOLA
Luanda
Lake
Tanganyika
TANZANIA
SEYCHELLES

ATLANTIC OCEAN
Lake
Nyasa

ANGOLA
6
Lilongwe
Antananarivo

ZAMBIA
Lusaka
MADAGASCAR

N
W   E
S
NAMIBIA
Harare
ZIMBABWE
Zambezi

Windhoek
BOTSWANA
MOZAMBIQUE

Gaborone
Pretoria
Maputo

Kalahari
Desert
SWAZILAND

0   500 Miles/
80 km.
Orange
LESOTHO

SOUTH AFRICA

Cape Town
Cape of Good Hope
INDIAN OCEAN

NORTHERN AFRICA

Eternal Wonders of the Ancient World

THE GREAT PYRAMIDS OF GIZA

Cairo, Egypt

Since their logic-defying construction, the Pyramids at Giza have embodied antiquity, mystery—and far-fetched speculation. "From the summit of these monuments," cried Napoleon, "forty centuries look upon you!"

The pyramids are the only wonder of the ancient world to have survived nearly intact. The funerary Great Pyramid of Cheops (or Khufu) is the oldest at Giza and the largest in the world, built circa 2500 B.C. with some 2.3 million limestone blocks, weighing an average 2.75 tons each, and moved by a force of around 20,000 men. Two smaller pyramids nearby belonged to Cheops's son and grandson. The Sphinx (Abu 'l-Hol, "Father of Terror") sits nearby, a strange figure with a lion's body, a human face, and a royal beard. The booming sound-and-light show that takes place every evening after sundown is a melodramatic display, yet a surprisingly entertaining crash course in pharaonic history. As Cairo's population passes the 15 million mark, the pyramids' former isolation in the desert has been infringed on by the suburbs that continue to grow around them.

Touts and persistent camel drivers offer their horses and knackered "ships of the desert" to see the pyramids as they were meant to be experienced. They are most magical at dawn and dusk, or when bathed in moonlight and silence.

Giving new meaning to the real estate dictum "Location, location, location," the elegant 19th-century Mena House is just a stone's throw from the Great Pyramids. Set within 40 acres of lush parkland and gardens on the edge of the Sahara, this veritable oasis of escape from the amusement-park atmosphere that now often surrounds the pyramids was once the rest house and hunting lodge of the empire-building Khedive Ismail. The omnipresent pyramids loom in full, unobstructed view from your hotel room, the breakfast terrace (Evelyn Waugh thought it was "like having the Prince of Wales at the next table"), the hotel's 18-hole golf course, and the garden-enveloped swimming pool.

Prior to 1870, the Mena House was the king's hunting lodge.

Maintaining much of its colonial air, the Mena House's original wing was home to the 1943 "Big Three" conference attended by Franklin Roosevelt, Winston Churchill, and Chiang Kai-shek, and was the site where plans for D-Day were initiated, as well as the formal signing of the peace treaty between Israel and Egypt in 1978. The old, refurbished suites that command a view of the pyramids are far more interesting than rooms in the new annex. The Moghul Restaurant offers the finest Indian cuisine in Egypt, a culinary reminder of the hotel's membership in the prestigious, Indian-based Oberoi hotel chain.

WHAT: site, hotel, restaurant. **THE PYRAMIDS:** 11 miles/18 km southwest of central Cairo. *Cost:* admission. **MENA HOUSE:** Pyramids Road, Giza; 45 nerve-racking, white-knuckle minutes by cab from central Cairo. Tel 20/2-383-3222, fax 20/2-383-7777; reservations @oberoigroup.com; www.oberoimenahouse. com. *Cost:* doubles from $190, from $270 for rooms with a pyramid view. Dinner at Moghul Restaurant $40. **BEST TIMES:** Nov–Mar.

For the Intrepid Visitor: Plunge Right In

ISLAMIC CAIRO

Egypt

An amble through this overwhelming medieval microcosm, with what must be the greatest population density in the Middle East, is a remarkable passage through the Cairo of six or seven centuries ago. This ancient quarter of Cairo assails the senses, confounds, and confuses. Amid barely contained pandemonium, oddly coupled with both intense poverty and one of the world's lowest crime rates, lies the legendary hospitality of the Egyptian people. Meanwhile, chickens, horses, and sheep walk the narrow, potholed streets, further congested with men on donkey carts collecting garbage, itinerant street vendors, and people going about life as they always have. The dust and rubble offset the faded architectural grandeur of a city that was once the intellectual and cultural center of the Arab world.

Given a daunting number of sites, start at the spectacular 12th-century Citadel of Salah al-Din; its founder was known throughout Christendom as Saladin, the Crusaders' chivalrous foe. Perched on a steep spur, this heavily fortified bastion offers a matchless panorama of Cairo's minaret-punctuated skyline and endless sprawl. The holiest and most awe-inspiring of the city's places of worship is the 9th-century Mosque of Ibn Tulun, notable for both its grand scale and extreme simplicity. The Islamic Art Museum's collection, the most extensive of its kind in Egypt, spans the 7th to 19th centuries. The Khan el-Khalili's maze of bazaars is another mind-boggler for its sheer size alone. The richly ornamented Qualawun el-Nasir complex includes a *madrasa*, or theological school, and mausoleums. Built by three of the most important Mamluk sultans, it is considered a large-scale masterwork of their lavish architectural style. The list of Islamic Cairo's highlights goes on, but culture shock may have caught up with even the most intrepid visitor, who by this point has likely had his or her fill of noise, belching bus fumes, and ornery livestock demanding the right of way.

WHAT: site. **WHERE:** start off at the foot of the Citadel in the Midan Salah al-Din (Saladin Square).

A 14th-Century Caravansary in Old Cairo: Africa's Largest Souk

KHAN EL-KHALILI

Cairo, Egypt

Noisy, wonderful, chaotic, and awash with the smells of spices, incense, and leather, Khan el-Khalili is one of the world's great bazaars— a sprawling, confusing, enclosed city-within-a-city first set up as a caravansary in 1382. Everyone here wants your business, your money, your time for a glass of mint tea. Whether you're shopping or not, bypass the tiny stalls and workshops on the most trammeled pathways (which have become highly touristed) and penetrate deep into the bewildering warren of back alleys, where Cairenes still shop for their dowries, cotton *galabiyas*, fezzes, and *sheehas*, or hooka water pipes. This is the place to practice your haggling technique, but don't expect to win against merchants with thousands of years of practice in their blood. Almost everything is available here. Mini bazaars within the bazaar specialize in such goods as carpets, gold, fabrics, perfume, and cosmetics (where the tiny pots of eye-lining kohl, Cleopatra-style, are made from burned, crushed olive pits). Open round-the-clock since 1752, El Fishawy is still the Khan's most famous coffee and tea house, immortalized by Lawrence Durrell. In a rich 19th-century European ambience of gilded mirrors, hammered brass, and cracked marble-topped tables, puff on a water pipe, have your fortune told, people-watch, and order what is said to be the best coffee in the city, delivered in little brass pots.

WHAT: site, restaurant. **WHERE:** in the heart of Cairo, bordered by Midan Hussein (Hussein Square), Sharia el-Muizz, and Sharia el-Muski. El Fishawy is a few steps west of Midan Hussein—just ask. **WHEN:** every day, but many shops are closed Sun.

Storehouse of a Great Civilization

MUSEUM OF EGYPTIAN ANTIQUITIES

Cairo, Egypt

Most tour groups head straight upstairs for the gallery dedicated to the mind-boggling treasures of boy-king Tutankhamen. Others make a beeline for the mummy room, only recently reopened after fifteen years. Regardless of your viewing strategy, the museum houses such an unparalleled collection of treasures (arranged chronologically from the Old [2700–2200 B.C.], to Middle [2100–1800 B.C.], and New [1600–1200 B.C.] Kingdoms) that, allowing just one minute to

examine each of its 136,000 pharaonic artifacts, it would take a visitor nine months to
see it all. Another astounding 40,000 items
remain crated in the basement, evidence of
the chronic space shortage that has plagued
Egypt's greatest museum since it was founded
in 1858. A visit here is overwhelming, to say
the least; so are the crowds. After viewing
the 1,700 objects unearthed in 1922 in the
small tomb of the relatively insignificant
pharaoh Tut and the two rooms of twenty-
seven mummified royal pharaohs and their
queens, the rest of the museum's exhibits can
seem lackluster. A more relaxed return visit
can do justice to these other masterworks.

Egyptian gods Anubis, Horus, and Isis

WHAT: site. **WHERE:** at the eastern end of Midan Tahrir (Liberation Square). Tel 20/
2-579-6974; www.egyptianmuseum.gov.eg.
COST: admission $9.

"Corridor of Marvels"

DIVING IN THE RED SEA

Sinai, Egypt

Ranking with Australia's Great Barrier Reef as the world's best place to
dive, the Red Sea was described by no less an expert than Jacques
Cousteau as "a corridor of marvels—the happiest hours of my diving
experience." The sea is famed for its diverse
marine life and the spectacular clarity of the
water, with visibility often in excess of 150
feet. (The lack of rain in the surrounding
desert means no runoff to degrade visibility.)
Much of the uniqueness of a Red Sea dive
derives from the dramatic juxtaposition of the
stark beauty of the Sinai Desert above and the
veritable Garden of Eden below. About 10
percent of Red Sea species are found nowhere
else on earth.

At the southernmost tip of the Sinai
Peninsula, dive resorts such as Sharm el-Sheik
offer a range of day boats out to the spectacular
dive sites of Ras Mohammed, Egypt's first
national marine park. But live-aboard boats
can bypass the underwater crowds and head
for even more pristine reefs, steep drop-offs,
sea mounts, and wrecks.

WHAT: site, experience. **WHERE:** the M.Y.
Juliet departs from Sharm el-Sheik weekly,
year-round. **HOW:** Juliet Divers, tel 20/
12-218-2668; info@julietdivers.com; www.
julietdivers.com. **COST:** $6-day tour $1,360,
includes full board, diving gear not included.

The unusual and poisonous lionfish

A Desert Wilderness of Mystical Places and Camel Races

THE SINAI

Nuweiba, Egypt

Those who head to the mountain-lined coast of the Red Sea for diving and snorkeling holidays should consider an unprogrammed off-road segue into the Sinai's desert wilderness with a Bedouin guide. On the Gulf of Aqaba, Nuweiba is the best jumping-off point for treks by foot, jeep, or camel. It's near the ancient Byzantine monastery of Santa Katerina, located on the slopes of Mount Sinai, from whose summit God is said to have delivered the Ten Commandments to Moses, and Colored Canyon, where the rock strata contain an outstanding spectrum of colors that change with the light. Members of some of the fourteen indigenous tribes of nomadic Bedouins have chosen to take up the opportunities offered by tourism, most commonly as guides for overnight (and longer) trips to oases and nomadic camps. There you can experience life as the Bedouins have known it since biblical times. Book your trip to Nuweiba for mid-January, in time for the annual camel races at Wadi Zalaga, when tribes converge from across the southern Sinai. Anywhere from 60 to 100 camels race 12.6 miles, while honking jeeps and fellow dromedaries race alongside to cheer on their favorite mounts. The barbecue and party the night before rivals the post-race celebration. Nuweiba, long a popular ferry departure point for Muslim pilgrims en route to Mecca, is now aiming at more of a resort and diving village atmosphere. The nicest top-end hotel option is the beachfront Hilton Coral Resort, which can arrange any of your Bedouin fantasies.

WHAT: site, experience, hotel. **NUWEIBA:** 296 miles/476 km southeast of Cairo. Air and bus service from Cairo and Sharm el-Sheik. **WADI ZALAGA:** 3 hours by 4-wheel drive from Nuweiba. **HILTON NUWEIBA CORAL RESORT:** tel 20/69-520320, fax 20/69-520327; www.hilton.com. *Cost:* doubles from $150. **BEST TIMES:** Nov–Mar.

The desert of prophets and saints

A Unique Cruise to Awesome and Irreplaceable Monuments

ABU SIMBEL

Lake Nasser, Upper Egypt, Egypt

More than 3,000 years ago, on the 34th anniversary of his reign, the never modest Pharaoh Ramses II ordered the colossal Sun Temple of Abu Simbel to be carved into the side of a cliff—with four 65-foot-high seated statues of himself as a young pharaoh on the exterior and an equally awesome interior. The immense monument took an unknown number of men thirty-six years to complete. In the 1960s an ingenious UNESCO rescue operation saved this and twenty-two other temples from being submerged forever when a high dam was built at Aswan. The $40 million effort entailed moving and rebuilding both the temple and the statues on higher ground. Engineers even aligned the relocated temple to reproduce a semiannual phenomenon on February 22 and October 22, thought to be the anniversaries of Ramses's birth and coronation: When the first rays of the sun reach 180 feet deep into the temple's sanctuary, they illuminate murals of the deified pharaoh and his fellow gods.

The result of the Aswan High Dam is Lake Nasser, or the "Nubian Sea"—the largest freshwater man-made lake in the world. Long unvisited and forgotten, it was a blind spot on the Egyptian map for decades. But the first cruise ship (and still without question the handsomest) parted the waters for tourists on this 300-mile-long lake in 1990: the fifty-four-cabin M.S. *Eugénie*, a faux steamboat appointed in homage to the opulent comfort enjoyed by wealthy, fin-de-siècle Egyptophiles. While the majority of foreign cruise passengers today sail north on the Nile from Aswan to crowded Luxor and its legendary sites, travelers heading south to Lake Nasser on the M.S. *Eugénie* may feel they have the lake's temple-dotted shores almost to themselves. The empty desert beyond is like a moonscape, its wind-hewn natural pyramids and bluffs a quiet source of fascination. The steamboat was named after the French empress who opened the Suez Canal in 1869; the *Eugénie*'s pièce de résistance is the Imperial Suite, six times the size of the average spacious cabin. It would have pleased Her Majesty, indeed.

WHAT: site, experience. **ABU SIMBEL:** on the west bank of Lake Nasser, 176 miles/283 km south of Aswan, 25 miles/40 km north of the Sudanese border. A small airport services daily flights from Aswan, making day trips easier. **M.S. *EUGÉNIE:*** departures from Aswan or Abu Simbel. *How:* M.S. *Eugénie* is owned by Belle Époque Travel in Cairo. Tel 20/2-516-9656, fax 20/2-516-9646; eugenie @eugenie.com.eg; www.eugenie.com.eg. *Cost:* 3-, 4-, and 7-night cruises from $460 (low season), from $760 (high season) per person per night, all-inclusive from Aswan or Abu Simbel. Imperial Suite from $650 per night (low season), $950 (high season). *When:* departures year-round. **BEST TIMES:** Nov–Mar, and during the biannual festivals of Feb 22 and Oct 22 for huge fairs offering music, dancing, and entertainment.

Where Egypt Ends: The Exotic Promise of Africa and An Edwardian Hollywood Set

ASWAN AND THE OLD CATARACT HOTEL

Upper Egypt, Egypt

Toward the south of Egypt, near the Sudanese border, the Nile becomes increasingly dramatic; the desert closes in and palm-studded islands and elephantine granite boulders lend a natural beauty and sense of occasion to Egypt's (and once the Roman Empire's) southernmost town. Since time immemorial, Aswan's position at the crossroads of important caravan routes gave its markets a flourishing trade in gold, slaves, and ivory. The souk still brims with spices, perfumes, and produce; it's Egypt's most evocative and colorful marketplace after Cairo's.

Aswan has long been a favored winter destination for foreigners, a restful yet exciting town, where idleness and sightseeing mingle effortlessly. Sail into antiquity aboard a traditional *felucca* in the late afternoon, or arrange a five-day float downstream to Luxor. Or book into Aswan's Old Cataract Hotel, on a picturesque bend in the Nile. Agatha Christie was so captivated by this timeless scenario that she staged and wrote much of *Death on the Nile* here. When the movie adaptation was filmed, the Old Cataract Hotel was given a plum part. Everything about it suggests a marriage of Edwardian and Oriental elegance, a magical ambience that lured Aga Khan III to honeymoon here and return regularly. He even chose to be buried in Aswan, and his simple mausoleum, one of the town's most-visited sites, can be seen from some of the guest rooms. While any of the refurbished rooms in the original wing will do, the individualistic suites have added drama and history. Agatha Christie's favorite suite has a small balcony

The Old Cataract Hotel overlooking the Nile

from which she could watch the sunset in privacy and retreat to a small writing room at will to pen her Nile romances. And speaking of Nile romances, the Suite of a Thousand and One Nights (now known as the Winston Churchill Suite) will make you want to stay at least that long, or maybe longer.

WHAT: town, hotel. **ASWAN:** 133 miles/ 214 km south of Luxor, 550 miles/885 km south of Cairo. **OLD CATARACT HOTEL:** Abtal El Tahrir Street. Tel 20/97-316-000, fax 20/97-316-011; in the U.S. and Canada, tel 800-221-4542; www.sofitel.com. *Cost:* Nile-view doubles from $287 (low season), from $327 (high season); *Note:* At press time, the Old Cataract Hotel was closed for renovations. **BEST TIMES:** Nov–Mar.

Watery Lifeline of Ancient and Modern Civilizations

A NILE CRUISE

Aswan, Upper Egypt, Egypt

Although tamed by the construction of the Aswan High Dam, the Nile has not changed much since the distant days when Ramses was a boy. In the 5th century B.C., the Greek historian Herodotus described Egypt as "the gift of the Nile," and to sail along the river's ageless green shores is to understand why the ancient Egyptians worshipped it. The river remains the lifeblood of Egyptian civilization, the heart and soul of its people. The languid tempo of huddled riverside settlements is timeless. Pajamaed children run to the shore to wave you on, men waist-deep in water wash their oxen, lateen-sailed *feluccas* glide by—the same riverine scenes that inspired Plato, Alexander the Great, Julius Caesar, and Napoleon and that are portrayed in the simple murals of the ancient tombs. A Nile cruise to or from Upper Egypt's Aswan and Luxor area, with its matchless concentration of ancient ruins, valleys of funerary monuments, and an entire metropolis of royal tombs, is the centerpiece of any

Temple of Sobek and Horus

journey to Egypt. Among a fleet of more than 200 ships that ply the Nile's calm waters, Abercrombie & Kent's four Sun Boats are among the most spacious and luxurious, like a rich friend's elegantly fitted yacht. They never carry more than eighty like-minded passengers, who are coddled and enfolded in an ambience of mild old-world decadence and flawless service. Open top decks are perfect for viewing blood-orange sunsets, pondering the wonders visited that day, and watching Egypt drift by.

WHAT: experience. **WHERE:** passengers typically fly from Cairo to Aswan or Luxor to board any of the 4 Sun Boats. **HOW:** in the U.S. and Canada, contact Abercrombie & Kent, tel 800-323-7308 or 630-954-2944, fax 630-954-3324; info@abercrombiekent.com; www.abercrombiekent.com. **COST:** 5- to 8-day cruises are typically part of longer, all-inclusive tour package: 11 days (from $2,990 per person) to 14 days ($7,290 per person, Royal Suite), airfare extra. **WHEN:** departures year-round, except for June, when ships are in drydock. **BEST TIMES:** Nov–Mar.

Capital of Ancient Egypt's New Kingdom and
A Victorian Respite in the Grand Manner

LUXOR AND THE OLD WINTER PALACE

Luxor, Upper Egypt, Egypt

The Temple of Karnak, built over a period of 1,500 years, is one of the greatest architectural achievements ever executed. That St. Peter's basilica in Rome and St. Paul's cathedral in London could easily fit inside its

100-acre site with room for eight other buildings of equal size becomes evident when you stand in the middle of its awesome 60,000-square-foot Hypostyle Hall, where 134 columns tower 80 feet high and measure 33 feet around. The greatest religious shrine of

antiquity, Karnak is linked by a 2-mile Nile-side promenade (once entirely lined with sphinxes) to its twin shrine to the south, the Temple of Luxor. The city of Luxor stands on the site of ancient Thebes, the flourishing capital of Egypt's New Kingdom, when it had more than a million inhabitants. While the Nile's east bank, where the sun rises, holds the crowning achievements of ancient Egyptian architecture, Luxor's fascination continues across the river on the west bank. There Thebans built their City of the Dead, the largest and most famous necropolis of ancient Egypt. Of the many royal tombs excavated in the Valley of the Kings, only that of Tutankhamen was found intact. Visitors can only speculate sadly about what must have disappeared from the plundered tombs of more powerful pharaohs such as Ramses II. The seven-chambered tomb of Ramses' consort Nefertari —reopened in 1995—in the nearby Valley of the Queens, is believed by art historians to be the finest now on view to the public, a vividly and intricately painted labor of love by the pharoah for the favorite of his forty wives.

Sightseeing in Luxor can be taxing: Wake-up calls at the crack of dawn will help you achieve some degree of solitude by the ruins before the hordes and the heat arrive. After a long, dusty day, repair to the Old Winter Palace. Bypass the new wing and ask for a room in the original wing of the hotel (founded in 1886) for nostalgia's sake.

Old Winter Palace in the heart of Luxor

Its high ceilings, giant armoires, Oriental carpets, and ornate crystal chandeliers hark back to the early days of British imperialism. The garden at the Old Winter Palace, the largest and most beautiful in Luxor, has a dozen full-time gardeners who ensure that this is the coolest place in town for tea.

WHAT: town, hotel. **LUXOR:** 415 miles/668 km south of Cairo on the Nile; 133 miles/214 km from Aswan. **OLD WINTER PALACE:** Cornich El Nile Street. Tel 20/95-380-422, fax 20/95-371-192; in U.S. and Canada, tel 800-221-4542; www.sofitel.com. *Note:* At press time, the Old Winter Palace was temporarily closed for renovation. **BEST TIMES:** Nov–Mar.

Desert Tempo in an Oasis Stuck in Time

SIWA OASIS

Siwa, Western Desert, Egypt

Covering two thirds of Egypt and the very antithesis of the green Nile Valley, the Western Desert (an extension of the Sahara) is punctuated by only a handful of exotic oases. Picturesque Siwa, located near the Libyan border on a centuries-old caravan route, is famous for its dates and olives. Despite the recent arrival of television and a steady trickle of adventure tourism, this lush oasis remains an intriguing desert outpost, where the unique Siwan culture and customs continue much as they did when Alexander the Great passed through in 331 B.C. (the dis-covery of his alleged tomb here made international headlines in 1995). Siwi, a Berber tongue, is spoken instead of Arabic. Women veiled in raven black still wear the traditional complex braids and cover themselves with Egypt's largest, most ornate silver jewelry—a local craft whose examples have become coveted collector's items. The oasis is sustained by 300 life-giving springs and freshwater streams. More than 300,000 palm trees and 70,000 olive trees attract an amazing bird population.

Within this biblical setting, the magical Adrère Amellal Oasis hotel lies within a lush grove of ancient date palms. The lodge is the brainchild of a Cairene businessman bent on proving that luxury and return to nature are not mutually exclusive. There is no electricity, no phones, and no nightlife; instead, there are

rock salt houses, candlelit alleys, exquisite meals from the hotel's organic garden, and fascinating excursions into the Great Sand Sea of Egypt's Western Desert.

WHAT: town, hotel. **WHERE:** 7 hours by car from Alexandria via Mersa Matrouh, both northeast of Siwa on the Mediterranean coast. **ADRÈRE AMELLAL OASIS:** tel 20/27-367-879; info@siwa.com; www.adrereamellal.net. *Cost:* doubles from $550, includes all meals and excursions. **BEST TIMES:** Nov–Mar.

A Windsurfer's Paradise

ESSAOUIRA

Morocco

The colorful little port town of Essaouira is a stone's throw from Morocco's best beach, a wonderful swath that curves for miles to the south. When you're souked out from visits to Marrakech, Fez, and Tangier, this is the

place to park your bag for some R and R, Moroccan style. Within Essaouira's walled fortifications, designed by a French architect for Sultan Sidi Mohammed in the 18th century, is the central medina, a hurly-burly whose narrow lanes teem with the craft shops and artisans for which this city is known, as well as friendly cafés in a relaxed atmosphere of a small-town neighborhood. Since the 1980s Essaouira has

been a secret (on everybody's lips) as an excellent surfing and windsurfing destination because of the strong Atlantic winds, so its image as a hassle-free tourist-friendly town may soon be a thing of the past. Go now and check into the simple, serene, and stylish Villa Maroc. The renovated hotel has twenty-two rooms with blue-painted balconies and shutters wrapped around an open courtyard filled with jasmine and bougainvillea. Some have fireplaces, others have antique canopied beds. The best part is breakfast on the open-air roof terrace, and dinner featuring aromatic spices from the local markets and served indoors by the soft light of wrought-iron chandeliers.

WHAT: town, hotel. **WHERE:** 100 miles/161 km west of Marrakech. **VILLA MAROC:** 10 Rue Abdellah Ben Yassin. Tel 212/524-473-147, fax 212/524-

Outdoor cafés line the lively streets of Essaouira.

475-806; hotel@villa-maroc.com; www.villa-maroc.com. **COST:** doubles from $280, includes

dinner for 2. **BEST TIMES:** Mar–May and Sept to mid-Dec. World Music Festival late June.

Symbolic and Spiritual Heart of Morocco

FES EL BALI AND THE FESTIVAL OF WORLD SACRED MUSIC

Fez, Morocco

The intellectual, cultural, and religious center of Morocco for the last 1,200 years, Fez offers countless wonders. If you want to get totally immersed in the flavor of Old Morocco, Fez's old town, Fes el Bali, will give you the chance

of a lifetime. An almost perfectly preserved medieval town whose donkey-wide, winding alleyways and covered bazaars are encircled by an unbroken line of magnificent ramparts and gates, Old Fez is the largest, and most confusing, medina in the Maghreb area of North Africa, once so large it was subdivided into twenty smaller medinas. Crammed with every conceivable sort of workshop, market, and restaurant, it is a delirious assault of sights, sounds, and smells you are not likely to forget. Fes el Bali and its dye pits, tanneries, butcher shops, tiled fountains, mosques, and spice markets is best seen with a local Fassi guide. Even they sometimes lose their way amid the maze of narrow streets—but it's better than getting lost alone.

Apart from electricity, everything in the sacred city of Fez seems to belong to another century. You can keep the Ali Baba dream alive if you check into the Palais Jamaï, a princely palace built in 1879, the only hotel within the walls of the medina. During the Fez Festival of World Sacred Music, another dimension is added. Still in its nascent stage—and refreshingly uncommercial and movingly sincere for that reason—this unique music festival confirms that if music is the world's universal language, sacred music is the universal language

of the soul. You may hear local ritual Berber music, the whirling dervishes of Konya, choirs from Harlem performing gospel music, female Gregorian chanting from France, or ancient Judeo-Spanish lullabies. The weeklong festival schedules at least two concerts a day in different outdoor venues in and around the magnificent city—Morocco's oldest imperial capital—which include a 15th-century Moorish palace and the ancient Roman ruins of Volubilis, 35 mi/70 km outside of town. Fez is the perfect setting for evening concerts, which are interrupted only by the Muslim call to prayer and the song of swallows.

WHAT: town, site, hotel, event. **WHERE:** concerts held throughout Fez. **HOW:** in the U.S., contact Sarah Tours, tel 703-619-0777 or 800-267-0036, fax 703-619-9399; sarahtur @erols.com; www.morocco-fezfestival.com. **COST:** Sarah Tours can book your stay anywhere from a 5-star hotel to the home of a Moroccan family. For $3,185 per person double occupancy, during the festival week, you get full board, a 4-star hotel, 2 concerts daily, and round-trip airfare from New York. **WHEN:** 2 weeks, end of May. **PALAIS JAMAÏ:** Bab Guissa. Tel 212-535-634331, fax 535-635096; H2141@sofitel.com. *Cost:* doubles from $235.

The Berbers' Singles Scene

IMILCHIL BETROTHAL FAIR

Imilchil, Middle Atlas Mountains, Morocco

S cattered among the remote villages of the Atlas Mountains, the nomadic Berber tribes maintain the ancient customs of their ancestors. The most emblematic ritual is the betrothal ceremony at the annual Imilchil fair.

Having spent spring and the hot summer days in the mountains with their flocks, neighboring clans return to the verdant plain of Imilchil every September to settle in for the winter and to celebrate with this much-awaited social gathering, a kind of marriage mart. Singles come to find and be found: young men dressed in white *djellabahs*, dis-

Will these young people find their soul mates?

playing their most precious silver daggers; girls wearing modest dresses and *handiras* capes, heavily hand-embroidered and accessorized with as much jewelry as befits their family's position. It is the girls who do the browsing, making small talk; a young girl may take the hand of a handsome young man and lead him about, giggling and asking questions. If she decides he's a kindred soul, they walk to the scribes' tent, the two families close in to negotiate, and that evening the couple is married. The fair lasts just three days, and the music and dancing make it feel like one large wedding reception.

WHAT: event. **HOW:** in the U.S., contact Sarah Tours, tel 703-619-0777 or 800-267-0036, fax 703-619-9399; sarahtur@erols.com; www.sarahtours.com. **COST:** $2,695 per person, all-inclusive 10-day air/land journey originating in New York. **WHEN:** early Sept.

Cultures and Vistas Untouched by Time

TREKKING THE HIGH ATLAS

Morocco

T he Moroccans believe that the High Atlas Mountains are as close as you can get to heaven without leaving earth. This majestic, often snowcapped mountain range can be glimpsed from different vantage points in and

around Marrakech, and its beauty is arresting whether seen from a distance or up close. It

was here that John Huston shot the breathtaking "Tibetan" sequences of *The Man Who*

Would Be King. Reasonably flat terrain can be alternated with a more challenging trek at heights averaging 13,000 feet, determined by individuals or Berber-guided groups that join

up with U.S.-run Sarah Tours. Owned by a Moroccan-born native of the Atlas Mountains who is a twenty-year veteran of Moroccan expeditions, Sarah Tours knows their turf: "from the lofty crags and screes of the Toubkal, to the cedar

Meet denizens of the Atlas range.

forests of Michlefen and the plunging gorges and karsts of the Mgoun Valley." Amid the highest Atlas peaks, move through vast panoramas untouched by modern times. The promise of contact with the unchanged Berber and Moorish mountain people—shepherds, nomads, remote villagers—only enhances the expedition.

WHAT: experience. **WHERE:** customized and packaged tours usually depart from Marrakech. **HOW:** in the U.S., contact Sarah Tours, tel 703-619-0777 or 800-267-0036, fax 703-619-9399; sarahtur@erols.com; www.sarahtours.com. **COST:** $1,850 per person, all-inclusive 10-day air/land trip originating in New York (all accommodations—hotels, camping, and stays with indigenous Berbers—and meals, and jeep, mule, or camel, according to terrain). **WHEN:** Mar–Oct. **BEST TIMES:** May and Sept.

A Historic Oasis of Luxury

HOTEL LA MAMOUNIA

Marrakech, Morocco

When Truman Capote advised, "Before you go to Marrakech, make sure you say goodbye to all your friends and draw your savings from the bank," he must have been booked at La Mamounia. It is one of Morocco's (and North Africa's) most special hotels, the jewel in the crown of her many exotic hostelries. Built in the 1920s on the revered site of a sultan's palace within the ancient walls of the old city, it is a curious mix of Art Deco and traditional Moroccan. The original gardens, laid out in the 16th century, are still maintained—32 aromatic acres of orange, lemon, and banana trees, palms, mimosas, roses, jasmine, and ancient garden walls covered with bougainvillea.

If you really have drawn your savings from the bank, you might stay in Winston Churchill's favorite suite, facing the city and its mosques. Dedicated to the great statesman, it is decorated with some of Churchill's oil paintings of these very gardens. But if you want to feel like the pasha whose palace once

Porters in fezzes and pointed yellow slippers at the arched entrance

stood here, request the Moroccan Suite for the full effect of the exotic local atmosphere. Whatever room you choose, dine at Le Marocain, the hotel's traditional restaurant and one of the best in the city, perhaps the country. The open-air terrace lets in the sound of the fountains and birds, while the scent from the garden mingles with the spices on your plate.

WHAT: hotel, restaurant. **WHERE:** Avenue Bab Djedid (10 minutes from Marrakech airport). Tel 212/524-388-600, fax 212/524-444-660; information@mamounia.ma; www. mamounia.com. **COST:** doubles from $500 (low season), from $565 (high season); the Winston Churchill Suite and the Moroccan Suite from $1,200 (low season), from $1,350 (high season). Dinner at Le Marocain $125. **BEST TIMES:** Mar–May, Oct, and late Dec–early Jan.

An Impromptu Circus Where the Curtain Goes Up at Sunset

PLACE DJEMAA EL-FNA

Marrakech, Morocco

According to Paul Bowles, a Moroccan at heart, Marrakech without the huge Djemaa el-Fna would be just another Moroccan city. This is where it all happens, an impromptu medieval circus enacted around the clock.

The snake charmers, performing monkeys, and souvenir sellers may be there for the foreigners, but the dentists, barbers, storytellers, acrobats forming human pyramids, cartwheeling dancers, and scribes writing wills and bills are surrounded by small crowds of locals. From the countless food stalls, aromas of sizzling kebabs, couscous, and sheep brains cooked in their own skulls fill the square. Maybe fresh-squeezed orange juice will do. Dusk is the bewitching hour, when lanterns around the square are lit, the cast of fire swallowers, healers, shoe shiners, and soothsayers reaches a climax, and the Place Djemaa crawls with humanity well into the night. A number of outdoor rooftop cafés ring the square, where you can take in the colorful scenario at a distance with a glass of sugared mint tea. Could this have been the very spot that Winston Churchill had in mind when he advised, "If you have only one day to spend in Morocco, spend it in Marrakech"?

WHAT: site. **WHERE:** Djemaa el-Fna Square.

Romancing the Palate

YACOUT

Marrakech, Morocco

The great chef Paul Bocuse once announced, "There are only three cuisines in the world: French, Chinese, and Moroccan." And not necessarily in that order, one is inclined to believe, after dinner at Yacout. Deep in the heart of the medina, through the massive, unmarked door of a sumptuous 200-year-old house, visitors cross carpets strewn with rose petals to enter rooms that are almost too romantic, with hundreds of flickering candles, tiles and mosaics, and fireplaces. In the air, there's a scent of jasmine and the delicate music of a zither. Yacout, which means "sapphire" in Arabic, has created a visual mise-en-scène that enchants all the senses. Rapt guests succumb to the arrival of a feast (sans menu) redolent of ancient caravans and the foreign nations that shaped Moroccan history and food. The elaborate variety showcases the breadth of traditional Moroccan food, but even a simple couscous dazzles. Repair to the gloriously tiled, beautifully lit courtyard for après-dinner mint tea and desserts sweeter than honey served next to a splashing fountain and a narrow pool.

WHAT: restaurant. **WHERE:** in the medina, Marrakech's old quarter; 79 Sidi Ahmed Soussi. Tel 212/443-82929, fax 212/443-82538. **COST:** $85. **WHEN:** open Tues–Sun for dinner only.

Desert Beauty and Mystique

THE GREAT SAHARA

Morocco

N o roads, no people, total silence, and at night, an ocean of stars, uncannily clear and bright. Spending a few days in the quiet expanse of the Sahara is a magical odyssey. Local Berber guides bring alive the traditions, romance, and history of their extraordinary environment. After penetrating deep into the Sahara by jeep, in and around the shifting sands and undulating waves of towering golden dunes, your tented campsite appears like a mirage against the Erg Chebbi sand dunes, the highest in Morocco. Walks are arranged in the cool, early hours of the morning; jeeps convey you to desert towns, fortresses, ruins, and cool oases where foreigners rarely venture. Camel- and goat-herding Tuareg nomads drop by your camp with their tales and musical instruments. Delicious campfire meals are enjoyed in the dining tent or under the stars that have guided caravans since ancient times. You'll see enough shooting stars to last a lifetime—have your wishes ready.

WHAT: site, experience. **HOW:** off-road Sahara expeditions are typically part of a longer 15-day trip through Morocco, originating in Casablanca. In the U.S., contact Overseas Adventure Travel, tel 800-493-6824; www.oattravel.com. **COST:** from $2,795 per person, all-inclusive air-land package featuring 3 nights camping in the Sahara. **BEST TIMES:** Jan–Apr and Sept–Dec.

Follow ancient caravan routes through the Great Sahara.

A Lush, Remote Hideaway

LA GAZELLE D'OR

Taroudant, Morocco

Deservedly famous as one of the most exclusive and opulent retreats in northern Africa, this former hunting lodge is surrounded by its own luxurious oasis in the middle of the desert. Snuggled amid the jasmine,

rose bushes, and towering lilies and hibiscus are thirty flower-covered stone cottages in as many acres. Beyond them stretches a citrus plantation thick with gnarled olive trees. Beyond that lies the desert, and on the horizon, the snowcapped Atlas Mountains. There is a riding stable on the grounds for sunset forays, but most of the well-heeled British and French guests luxuriate in doing nothing. A famous poolside lunch buffet of numerous Moroccan salads and specialties draws nonhotel visitors. The dining hall is an opulent Moorish tentlike space, where a five-course Moroccan-European dinner is

served by gracious waiters exotically dressed as if for some royal feast. The hotel is a ten-minute drive from the ancient market town of Taroudant, once magnificent enough to be called "Little Marrakech." Hidden behind 4 miles of red, crenellated, 20-foot-high walls, the town has an excellent souk for some animated bargaining and trinket shopping.

WHAT: hotel, restaurant. **WHERE:** 1 hour from Agadir, transfer arranged. Tel 212/488-52039, fax 212/488-52737; reservations@gazelledor.com; www.gazelledor.com. **COST:** doubles from $495, includes half board for 2. **WHEN:** open mid-Sept to mid-Jul.

Africa's Ancient Mosaics

BARDO MUSEUM

Tunis, Tunisia

Tunisia's national museum, a fine complex of 13th- to 19th-century buildings that includes the Beylical Palace, houses the continent's largest selection of ancient mosaics, arguably the finest in the world. Almost

too well endowed, the Bardo's collection of colorful and vivid objects is of such exuberant quantity that visitors run the risk of overkill. Tunisia was the heartland of Roman Africa, so it is ironic that the earliest true mosaic in the world (dating to the 5th or 4th century B.C.) was discovered in nearby Carthage, indicating that the Carthaginians, not the Romans, invented

the art form. Mosaics were soon being used to create "tapestries" of richly colored landscapes and portraits, where volume was conveyed through gradation of colors, and compositions became more and more complex. Rural, hunting, agricultural, marine, and urban life are represented in elaborate scenes of abundance and sensual gratification. To quote from an inscription on a piece found at an archaeological site in Algeria, "To hunt, to bathe, to gamble, to laugh, that is to live."

WHAT: site. **WHERE:** Rue Monju Slim; 3 miles/5 km outside of central Tunis. **COST:** admission. **WHEN:** open Tues–Sun.

On a Clifftop, a Coastal Village of Great Charm

SIDI BOU SAID

Tunisia

Its very name makes you smile. Sidi Bou Said is a painting-perfect blue-and-white Tunisian village that has drawn tourists for two and a half centuries, yet one whose silent back streets retain their simple charm. The view of the indigo-blue Mediterranean below blends with an immaculate blue sky and the town's brass-studded, sky-blue wooden doors. It's almost too intense against the dazzling whitewashed, domed houses smothered in bougainvillea. Discovered by wealthy French and other European expats at the turn of the 19th century, and again in 1942 by André Gide, Sidi could have been overbuilt had not the government issued orders in 1915 to preserve its character. They have been surprisingly effective: very little here is not wonderfully Tunisian, except the tourists. The irony is that non-Muslims were not permitted to roam these streets until 1820, when followers of Abu Said lifted a centuries-old ban. Abu Said (who died here in 1231 and is buried in the local mosque) was a teacher of Sufism and was adopted by the anti-Christian Corsair pirates as their protector against the European infidels—the very ones that now flock here for the almost obligatory mint-tea-with-a-view on the open terrace of the much-vaunted Café des Nattes.

WHAT: town. **WHERE:** 13 miles/21 km east of Tunis. **BEST TIMES:** spring and fall.

MIDDLE AND SOUTHERN AFRICA

The Four Corners of Southern Africa

CHOBE NATIONAL PARK

Botswana

At Chobe National Park, in a corner of Africa still redolent of the game-rich continent of old, four countries come together: Botswana, Zambia, Namibia, and Zimbabwe. Although it's home to some of Botswana's most varied wildlife, the park is best known for its huge resident elephant population—in the dry season it boasts Africa's highest concentration of elephants. The Chobe River at the park's northern reaches is its lifeline and perennial water supply. Sunset boat rides float you by yawning hippos, herds of elephants, and flocks of myriad waterfowl lining the riverbanks; the floodplains are filled with grazing herds of buffalo and big game. Arrange to stay at the Chobe Chilwero Lodge. Secluded and sitting

Catching sight of Chobe's elephants

high on a hill, the fifteen luxurious thatched-roof bungalows of the lodge, whose name means "riveting view," afford the best lookout over the park and the river.

WHAT: site, experience, hotel. **WHERE:** 15 minutes from Kasane airport, or 1½ hours by car from Victoria Falls. **CHOBE CHILWERO LODGE:** in the U.S., contact Abercrombie & Kent, tel 800-554-7016; info@abercrombie kent.com; www.abercrombiekent.com; southern africa@sanctuarylodges.com; www.sanctuary lodges.com. **COST:** $590 per person per night (low season), $900 (high season), includes day activities in Chobe National Park. **BEST TIMES:** Jun–Nov.

The Kalahari's Best-Kept Secret

JACK'S CAMP

Kalahari Desert, Botswana

Ostrich Jack—hunter, explorer, bush hero—fell in love with the magic of this remote corner of Botswana in the 1960s, pitched camp, and never left. Today an old-fashioned permanent safari camp run by Jack's son, Ralph Bousfield, sits on the edge of the Makgadikgadi salt pans in the middle of the Kalahari Desert. Ralph has inherited his father's passion for this eerie lunar landscape and he and his partner, Catherine, share it with their guests. Even for those who have seen it all, the light, silence, solitude, and sheer vastness of the space here guarantee an uncommercial and unusually authentic safari experience. A Bushman tracker escorts guests on walks, opening their urban eyes to the subtle vagaries of the unique and delicate ecosystem. But Jack's Camp has a double life. When the rains come, the salt pans, once the bed of a lake the size of Lake Victoria, sprout green and create a vast water source for enormous flocks of flamingos. It becomes one of the last open migration routes in Africa; wildebeest and zebra arrive by the thousands, with lions, cheetahs, and hyenas fast on their heels. This is unblemished, wild Africa at its best, evocative of other times. So are the five classic 1940s canvas tents set up in a palm oasis and furnished with the iron beds and worn Persian carpets that once belonged to Ralph's grandparents. There are clouds of mosquito netting, chambray sheets, silver tea service—altogether an incomparable romanticism that's hard to resist.

WHAT: hotel, experience. **WHERE:** 50-minute air charter transfers arranged from Maun. **HOW:** Contact Jack's Camp office in Johannesburg, tel 27/447-1605, fax 27/447-6905; reservations@unchartedafrica.com; www.unchartedafrica.com. **COST:** from $1,000 per person, per night land only. **WHEN:** Feb–Dec. **BEST TIMES:** May–Sept, after the rainy season.

Elephant-Back Safaris in the Bush

ABU'S CAMP

Okavango Delta, Botswana

The beloved Abu was big, strong, sensitive, and intelligent. At 13 feet high and weighing 5½ tons, he was the most popular means of conveyance at this exclusive elephant-back safari camp in the magnificent Okavango Delta, the largest inland delta in the world. Abu, alas, passed on in 2004, but other elephants still provide transportation. Transportation by elephant through the delta's crystalline waterways provides access to areas that are otherwise impossible to reach. And because the elephants' smell masks your own, you can get close to wildlife unthreatened by these gentle herbivores. This is some of Africa's best game-viewing territory, but your safari is also about being adopted ever so briefly by this ragtag family of five venerable elephants and seven younger ones—themselves adopted by your host, American conservationist Randall Moore. Like the hero of a Disney movie, he rescued this bunch of unrelated misfits and orphans who had spent their lifetimes in zoos abroad and reintroduced them to the land where they were born. Moore's rapport with his elephant "family" is something to witness, as is that of the *mahout* (trainer or driver) who straddles the wide-as-a-horse neck of his mount, his legs tucked behind the huge flapping ears, directing his charge with verbal commands. Back at camp, there are five luxury-style tents and three-course gourmet meals, served with fine napery under a giant fig tree. Tomorrow you can leave your maharaja fantasies back at camp and walk alongside the herd, an incredible experience.

Abu's extended family

WHAT: hotel, experience, site. **WHERE:** 30-minute private charter from Maun. Tel 267/661-260. **HOW:** in the U.S., contact Esplanade Tours, tel 617-266-7465 or 800-426-5492; info@esplanadetours.com; www.esplanadetours.com. **COST:** 3-night/4-day package $7,720 per person, all-inclusive; never more than 10 guests; includes private charter transfer from Maun. **WHEN:** open Feb–Nov.

An Incomparable Wildlife Oasis

OKAVANGO DELTA

Botswana

This inland delta, where the Okavango River meets the Kalahari Desert, has been called the world's largest oasis. The Okavango, a tributary of the mighty Zambezi, creates a unique "water in the desert" ecosystem the size of Switzerland, forming floodplains, lagoons, channels, and islands where, as a local brochure says, "if you see 10 percent of what sees you, it's an exceptional day." A magnet for wildlife since time immemorial, it is also a magnet for safari connoisseurs who—like the European explorer David Livingstone in 1849—come for the chance to travel deep into the continent in search of untamed Africa. The bird life is second to none, and there are legions of elephants, zebras, buffalos, giraffes, and hippos. As you glide through a labyrinth of papyrus-fringed and lily-covered waterways in the traditional *mokoro* dugout canoe or explore its islands and islets on foot, you're immersed in a lush, otherworldly environment of teeming colors and sounds. On the delta's eastern fringes is the Moremi Wildlife Reserve, whose remarkable landscapes are some of the most scenic in southern Africa. Together they are a magical environment, understood by no one so well as Soren Lindstrom, the area's safari guide extraordinaire. His comfortable mobile camp stays one step ahead of you (moving to strategic sites with names like Xaxanaxa, overlooking a hippo pool) as you float, walk, and jeep around one of the leading wildlife areas of southern Africa.

WHAT: site, experience, hotel. **WHERE:** 3 hours by car from Maun; air transfers can be arranged. **HOW:** Bushbuck Safaris, tel 44/1669-630-386, fax 44/1669-630-385; info@bushbucksafaris.com; www.bushbucksafaris.com. **COST:** largest party—12 people, $500 per person per day, all-inclusive, land only; smallest party—one person, $850 per person per day. **WHEN:** open Mar–Oct. **BEST TIMES:** Apr to mid-Oct.

The Surviving Castles and Churches of a Fallen Empire

GONDER

Amhara Region, Ethiopia

At its strategic position at the foothills of the Simen Mountains, one of the highest ranges in Africa, Gonder became the capital of the Ethiopian empire in the 17th century under Emperor Fasil, and remained so for 250 years. Surrounded by high stone walls, the Royal Enclosure lies at the heart of the

Gonder is the castle capital of Africa.

town and is a one-stop visit for the most important imperial buildings. No fewer than five castles can be found there, the oldest attributed to Fasil and the most recent dating to the mid-18th century. In addition to being the empire's administrative and commercial center, Gonder was also its religious center. Of the dozens of churches that once populated the city, seven were built during Fasil's reign. The most important standing today is Debre Birhan Selassie, famed for its 17th-century ceiling fresco of eighty cherubic faces.

WHAT: town, site. **WHERE:** 471 miles/ 758 km north of Addis Ababa. **HOW:** Experience Ethiopia Travel (EET) in Addis Ababa includes Gonder in customized trips or organized tours, minimum of 12 days, with rates according to size of group. Tel 251/1-519-291, fax 251/1-519-982; EET@ ethionet.et; www.experienceethiopia.com; in the U.S., contact Safari Experts, tel 435-649-4655; safari@safariexperts.com; www.safari experts.com. **COST:** for 4, $390 per person per day, all-inclusive (lower rates for larger groups). **WHEN:** mid-Sept to mid-Jun. **BEST TIMES:** Ethiopian Christmas and Epiphany are in Jan; Gonder is at its most colorful during Epiphany (Jan 19).

The Mystery of Subterranean, Rock-Hewn Churches

LALIBELA

Amhara Region, Ethiopia

The mysterious subterranean, monolithic rock-hewn churches of Lalibela have been in continuous use by Orthodox priests since the 12th and 13th centuries, when this remote mountain town was the capital of the important Zagwe Dynasty. The purpose of each church has eluded modern-day historians. Each building is unique in size, shape, and execution, precisely and painstakingly carved out of solid bedrock (some say by tens of thousands of workers), and some are ornately decorated. Legend has it that at least one of the churches was built by angels in a single day; another legend holds that the churches came to the Zagwe king in a dream.

All of the eleven churches are carved below ground level, some reaching more than 30 feet high. They are ringed by courtyards and trenches that interconnect and become a tangled maze of tunnels and passages between one building and the next. The churches are as treasured in Ethiopia as the Great Pyramids are in Egypt. The town of Lalibela itself, set amid craggy, dramatic escarpments more than 8,000 feet high, is a delight.

WHAT: site, town. **WHERE:** 454 miles/730 km north of Addis Ababa. **HOW:** Experience Ethiopia Travel (EET) in Addis Ababa includes Lalibela in customized trips or organized tours, minimum of 12 days, with rates according to size of group. Tel 251/1- 519-291, fax 251/1-519-982; eet@ethionet.et; www.experienceethiopia.com; in the U.S., contact Safari Experts, tel 435-649-4655 or 435-649-3554; safari@safariexperts.com; www.safariexperts.com. **COST:** for 4, $315 per person per day, all-inclusive (lower rates for larger groups). **WHEN:** mid-Sept to mid-Jun. **BEST TIMES:** Ethiopian Christmas and Epiphany are in Jan.

Religious artifacts

An Unspoiled Corner of Kenya

OL DONYO WUAS

Chyulu Hills, Kenya

Set amid a quarter of a million acres of the open plains of Masai land and offset by the dramatic Chyulu range of volcanic mountains, this privately owned property offers exclusive access to one of Kenya's few remaining wilderness areas. The owner and occasional resident personality, Richard Bonham, who was born in Kenya, chose the site of his stunningly situated home for its view of rolling wooded grassland and the snow-capped peak of Mount Kilimanjaro looming across the Tanzania border. The lodge is perched high on a ridge, and seven double-thatched rondavel-style (circular) cottages, some on stilts, offer privacy and verandas with views of Kilimanjaro. Beds with a view make for an unforgettable afternoon siesta. This is Africa as it was in the early 20th century. The vast, mainly uninhabited panoramas are broken only by the sight of young Masai herders with their cattle, serenely at home among the wild animals. Bonham himself occasionally pops up, happy to head out with guests on horseback, by foot, or in an open-top Land Rover for day safaris, bringing along his wealth of experience and inimitable style.

WHAT: hotel, experience. **WHERE:** Regularly scheduled 50 minute air taxi flights run from Nairobi. **HOW:** Richard Bonham Safaris, in Nairobi, tel 254/20-600457, fax 254/20-605008; reservations@bush-and-beyond.com; www.oldonyowuas.com. **COST:** $530 per person per night, all-inclusive. Air transfer extra. **WHEN:** closed Apr, May, and Nov. **BEST TIMES:** Dec–Mar.

In the Shadow of Mount Kenya

PRIVATE WILDLIFE RESERVES

Isiolo, Central Highlands, Kenya

In the foothills of Mount Kenya in the Central Highlands, a few fortunate guests can revel in spellbinding views of ridge after ridge and the freedom to see wild game on boundless private properties—vast herds of everything from elephant and giraffe to zebra and antelope. Borana Lodge and Lewa Wilderness, two neighboring cattle ranches comprising more than 100,000 acres in northern Kenya, offer game drives led by excellent native trackers and guides; you'll rarely see another vehicle, an almost unheard-of luxury in the comparatively crowded national parks of East Africa these days. Both offer horseback expeditions on patient steeds that allow very close encounters with the resident wildlife, and exhilarating night game drives under a canopy of stars to spot what you may have missed during the day. The conservation-minded Craig family, owners of the sprawling 60,000-acre Lewa Wilderness at Lewa Downs, has transformed a parcel of their farm, along with some adjacent government land, into the Ngare Sergoi Rhino Sanctuary for that endangered species. Thirty-six black rhinos and white rhinos are now protected from poachers by guards with walkie-talkies. Neighboring guests at Borana Lodge are welcome visitors.

WHAT: experience, hotel. **WHERE:** 4 hours north of Nairobi by car; air transfers from Nairobi to Nanyuki can be arranged, followed by a 1-hour drive to either ranch. **WILDERNESS**

TRAILS AT LEWA DOWNS: contact Bush and Beyond: in Nairobi, tel 254/2-600-457, fax 254/2-605-008; info@bush-and-beyond.com; www.bush-and-beyond.com; in the U.S., tel 888-995-0909, fax 505-795-7714; travel@unchartedoutposts.com; www.unchartedoutposts.com. *Cost:* $325 per person per day (double occupancy), all-inclusive, does not include conservation fees. **BORANA LODGE:** tel 254/2-567-251; www.borana.co.ke. *Cost:* $325 per person per day (double occupancy), includes meals. **BEST TIMES:** mid-Jul to Nov and mid-Dec to Mar.

Locked in Time on the Swahili Coast

ISLAND OF LAMU AND THE PEPONI HOTEL

Lamu Town, Lamu, Kenya

Not quite undiscovered, but still relatively unspoiled, the tiny island of Lamu is Kenya's oldest living city and a fascinating place in which to explore the country's ancient Swahili and Islamic cultures. There is

just one car on the island—its streets are too narrow to accommodate any conveyance other than donkeys. You are in the Indian Ocean, but much is redolent of the Middle East—this was once Africa's link with Arabia. Like Mombasa and Malindi, farther south, Lamu is one of a string of port towns founded by Arab traders in ivory, spices, and slaves. The men still wear full-length white robes and caps; the women are draped in the Islamic black purdah; and travel is by dhow, the traditional wooden sailing vessels that ply the waters off the coast. You can rent one of these boats (be sure to negotiate) for a romantic day trip around the Lamu archipelago, with a fresh grilled-fish lunch thrown in.

Most of the hippies have gone, replaced by younger European backpackers and a growing

Buildings along the Lamu waterfront

mix of the curious and the beautiful. The latter invariably check into the charming Peponi Hotel, located on a 12-mile strip of virgin beach.

Full of international eccentrics, villagers, and Nairobi ex-pats, the hotel's public bar hums with life and color. There is deep-sea fishing and windsurfing, but you can also just relax in one of the whitewashed, open-terraced beach bungalows, which are separated from each other by flame trees and tangles of bougainvillea. The breezy rooms exude a faint colonial feel; there are revolving fans, mosquito netting, and colorful Zimbabwe-print throw pillows on the traditional Lamu-legged wooden beds. The Danish family that has owned and run Peponi for thirty years has created a spe-

cial, intimate hotel known as much for the spontaneity of the staff's smiles as the sophistication of its simple, market-fresh menu that hints of Swahili influence. The trade winds rustle the palm trees and carry the call from the minaret of the town's 19th-century mosque.

WHAT: island, hotel. **LAMU:** 90-minute daily flights from Nairobi; frequent flights from Mombasa, Malindi, and Nairobi to neighboring Manda Island; transfer by boat. **PEPONI HOTEL:** 20 minutes by dhow or donkey from Lamu Town. Tel 254/42-463-3421, fax 254/42-463-3029; peponi@peponi-lamu.com; www.peponi-lamu.com. *Cost:* doubles from $285. Dinner $20. *When:* open Jul–Apr. **BEST TIMES:** Sept–Mar.

The Great Animal Migration Like No Other

THE MASAI MARA

Kenya

The Masai Mara is nature's stage for what must be the most spectacular wildlife pageant on earth. Each year when the rainy season ends in May, hundreds of thousands of wildebeests mass together, moving in search

of greener pastures and vital sustenance from the Serengeti (Masai for "endless plains") in Tanzania north to the wide-open grasslands of Kenya's Masai Mara, where they arrive in July and August. Along with migrating herds of zebra, antelope, and gazelle, there are at times more than a million animals on the move, and a horseback safari affords you a remarkable vantage point to view an animal kingdom unrivaled anywhere in Africa. (The core of the Masai Mara Game Reserve is closed to those on horseback, but you can reach it in a four-wheel-drive for a glimpse of lions, cheetahs, hyenas, giraffes, and elephants.) Riding through the unspoiled Loita Hills and the great rolling plains of the Mara, you'll pass through *manyattas* (villages) of the nomadic Masai people, who protect the game

they believe to be "God's cattle." Some ascents will reach 8,600 feet, providing spectacular views and open vistas. And while you marvel at the views, the staff proceeds ahead to set up camp in a lovely setting and has dinner and a hot shower ready for your arrival. They also keep watch throughout the sound-filled night to keep the wildlife at bay.

You can also view the endless expanse of the Masai Mara from God's perspective—in a hot-air balloon safari. Nothing can compare with sailing above the rolling plains of Africa in a hot-air balloon. At dawn, you ascend into a sky all shades of rose and orange. Masai villagers stand rooted as they watch you drift across the still sky. Skim over an enormous herd of skittish wildebeest that dodge the shadow of your balloon; a toy-size chase vehicle fast upon their trail leaves a flurry of dust. The awesome, magical stillness, punctuated by the erratic blasts of the hot-air burner, envelops you. Only the promise of a delicious Champagne breakfast in the bush can take the edge off the disappointment of your return to earth.

WHAT: site, event, experience. **THE MASAI MARA:** southeastern Kenya at the Tanzania border, about 150 miles/241 km from Nairobi. *How:* Equitour hosts 13-day riding safaris, tel 800-545-0019; sarah@equitours.com; www. ridingtours.com. *Cost:* from $5,515 per person, includes all meals and accommodations. *When:* annual trips and upon request. **BALLOON SAFARIS:** usually arranged through your safari company. Can also be booked through The Safari Company, Ltd., in Nairobi, tel 254/72-391-4094 or 254/73-374-7555;

Masai greet travelers on horseback.

safaris@thesafaricoltd.com; www.thesafarico ltd.com. *Cost:* 1-hour flights in the Masai Mara Reserve $435 per person. **BEST TIMES:** Jul–Sept to view migration in Kenya's Masai Mara Game Reserve; May–Jun across the border in Tanzania's Serengeti National Park.

An Authentic Safari Camp That Keeps the Excitement Alive

LITTLE GOVERNOR'S CAMP

Masai Mara, Kenya

The Governor's family of camps is known as the doyen of all safari camps, the first to open in the legendary Masai Mara in 1972 on a romantic spot reputed to have been one of Teddy Roosevelt's favorite campsites. Soon

after, something a little more intimate and even more remote was created: Little Governor's Camp. It remains a favorite old-

Unconcerned elephants wander into camp.

fashioned canvas-tent safari camp; built around a small lake teeming with birds and wildlife, it is accessible only by boat. In such a rough bush setting—epitomizing the landscape that inspired Hemingway and adventurers the world over—the high level of professionalism, quality, and luxury is rather amazing. There are a few things you won't find at the Ritz, such as giraffes wandering into camp or the wake-up call of a hippopotamus. Surrounded by the Masai Mara, the "theater of the wild," you are guaranteed an abundance of game viewing in wide-open vistas where the grasslands seem to roll on forever. Can the Ritz match that?

WHAT: hotel, experience. **WHERE:** the western section of the Masai Mara Game reserve in western Kenya, at the Tanzania border (45-minute small aircraft transfers arranged from Nairobi). In Nairobi, tel 254/2-734-000, fax 254/2-734-023; info@governors camp.com; www.governorscamp.com. **COST:** $521 per person per night (double occupancy), includes game runs, full board, and transfers to and from Masai airstrip. **BEST TIMES:** Jul–Sept, during the Great Migration. Many babies are born Dec–Mar, the next best months.

Unashamed Luxury in the Shadow of Mount Kenya

MOUNT KENYA SAFARI CLUB

Nanyuki, Kenya

The up-country Mount Kenya Safari Club has been a Kenyan tradition since American movie star William Holden fell in love with its blend of romance, history, and extraordinary scenery and bought it, with two friends, in 1959. Built directly on the equator (the tennis court crosses the line) and along a dramatic ridge 7,000 feet above sea level, the hotel boasts a magnificent view of Mount Kenya, Africa's second highest mountain. Peacocks, ibis, cranes, and marabou parade across the sweeping green lawns; forested foothills extend from the impeccably manicured 100-acre property. Its casual elegance harks back to earlier days as a private club, when its roster of celebrity members was as impressive as that of today's guests. Of the wide range of accommodations—almost all with verandas, views, and wood-burning fireplaces—the ones with the most character are the older William Holden Cottages; the most luxurious, the new riverside villas. Distractions include game viewing, horseback riding, and golf. But the hotel—a microcosm of Kenya's majestic beauty—is itself worth the trip.

WHAT: hotel. **WHERE:** near Nanyuki, a 3-hour drive north of Nairobi (arranged by hotel). Tel 254/2-216-940, fax 254/2-216-796; in the U.S., tel 800-845-3692; www.fairmont.com/kenyasafariclub. **COST:** doubles from $299; William Holden and Riverside Suites from $450, includes full board. **BEST TIMES:** avoid the rainy month of Apr.

A Sea Angler's Paradise

PEMBA CHANNEL FISHING CLUB

Shimoni, Kenya

Hemingway wannabes leave the inland wildlife to others and happily head for this coastal mecca, famous for exhilarating, record-breaking fishing safaris. This small, delightful, and exclusive club near the Tanzania border

Together the crews have over 150 years of experience.

offers glorious days aboard five state-of-the-art boats in the fabled corridor that separates the southeastern Kenyan coastline and Pemba Island. The channel is widely known as home to the biggest fish that Kenya—even the whole of Africa—has to offer. These are the waters said to have inspired Ernest Hemingway to write *The Old Man and the Sea*. In their translucent depths live marlin (three types), sailfish, swordfish, wahoo, and yellowfin tuna, not to mention the vicious mako shark and its cousin, the tiger shark. It is not unusual in the course of a thrilling and exhausting day to reel in a 100-pound tuna or 300-pound marlin; the club has set national records for each fish, at 193 pounds and 800 pounds, respectively. (The club holds 70 percent of all marlin records in Kenya.) There are photographs throughout the club of 700-pound monsters being hauled into the boat, but most are tagged and released—it's the memory that stays with you. If you're more intrigued by the prospect of scuba-diving, the club's 67-foot M.Y. *Kisiwani* live-aboard yacht is at your disposal for viewing the spectacular tropical reefs and pristine waters surrounding the spice island of Pemba, part of the Zanzibar archipelago.

WHAT: experience, hotel. **WHERE:** 50 miles/80 km from Mombasa. Tel 254/722-205020, fax 254/414-91265; in U.K., 44/128-574-0452, fax 44/128-574-0014; info@pembachannel.com; www.pembachannel.com. **COST:** hotel, $180 per person, includes all meals; boat, from $780, 9-hour day, all-inclusive; M.Y. *Kisiwani* live-aboard, minimum 7 days $1,980 per person, all-inclusive. **WHEN:** open Aug–Mar. **BEST TIMES:** Dec to mid-Mar for best fishing.

A Land as Exotic and Magical as Its Name, and the River That Runs Through It

RAFTING THE MANGOKY RIVER

Madagascar

With limited and primitive roads and almost no tourist facilities, the best way to experience Madagascar is by paddling down the calm waters of the Mangoky River to the island's remote and seldom visited southwest corner—a beautiful, untrammeled region of wild country. The mini-continent of Madagascar is an isolated land that became a laboratory for evolution. Strange creatures and plants are everywhere on the 100-mile stretch of the river from Beroroha to Bevoay: more than 30 species of lemurs and 8,000 species of plants found nowhere else on earth, 3,000 species of butterflies, 7 species of baobabs, and half the world's chameleons.

Floating past a baobab tree

wildlife sanctuary an ecologist's dream).

At the end of each of the eight wonder-packed days of rafting along the river, sandbar camps are set up under the evening sky. Being so close to the Tropic of Capricorn ensures that the spectacular sunsets linger the whole length of your first rum-and-lime.

WHAT: experience. **WHERE:** departing from and returning to Madagascar's capital, Antananarivo. Madagascar is 250 miles/402 km off the southeast coast of Africa. **HOW:** Remote River Expeditions: tel 261/20-95-52347, fax 261/20-95-52790; info@remoterivers.com; www.remoterivers.com. 3-week trip, of which 8 days are spent rafting and camping on the Mangoky River. **COST:** $3,795 per person, double occupancy, all-inclusive except for international flights. **WHEN:** May only.

Enthusiastic, knowledgeable, and passionate guides are indispensable. You can trek through rain forests and nature reserves, shop the colorful local markets, meet the gracious Malagasy people in their riverside villages and settlements, and have close encounters with the ringtail, indri, and sifaka lemurs (to name but a few of the animals that make this bizarre

The Warm Heart of Africa

LAKE MALAWI

Malawi

Teaming with more species of tropical fish than any other place on earth, snorkeling or diving in Lake Malawi is like swimming in the most exotic, warm-water aquarium imaginable. David Livingstone called this the

Lake of Stars, the Malawians call it Lake Malawi, the Tanzanians and Mozambicans (who share its border) call it Lake Nyasa. The third largest of all Africa's lakes and the most southern of the East African Rift Valley, Lake Malawi is a vast 365 miles long and 52 miles across and has depths plunging to well below sea level at 2,300 feet in the north. The clear, warm water supports over 1,000 species of tropical fish (including over 500 species of brightly colored cichlids) with only one river,

the River Shire, flowing into it before its water spills into the Indian Ocean via the Zambezi River.

On the eastern shore of the lake, lying in Mozambican waters but belonging to Malawi and overlooking the wilderness and mountains of Mozambique, lies the beautiful, remote Likoma Island, home to approximately 9,000 people, a handful of cars (although no more than 5 work at any one time), a few quadbikes and motorcycles and a huge Anglican church the size of Winchester Cathedral dedicated to Saint Peter and built in 1903. And the beautiful little lodge built completely from local materials by local islanders called Kaya Mawa, meaning "maybe tomorrow." The lake supports many traditional fishing villages scattered along the lakeshore and on its islands. The locals, amongst the friendliest people in Africa, welcome you to their villages and way of life.

Further south of Likoma Island, on the western shores of the mainland Nankumba Peninsula, is the newly opened Pumulani, with ten exquisite villas spread out along a lush hillside overlooking the lake, and

offering the mainland version of Kaya Mawa, and the crystal clear waters of Lake Malawi.

WHAT: site, hotel. **WHERE:** Short charter flight (about one hour) from Lilongwe, Malawi's capital city (serviced by many international airlines) to Kaya Mawa or Pumulani. **KAYA MAWA ON LIKOMA ISLAND:** Tel 265/931-8359; www.kayamawa.com; *Cost:* from $320 per person per day (double occupancy), all meals and most activities included. **PUMULANI:** Tel 260/216-246-090; www.pumulani.com. *Cost:* From $340 per person per day (double occupancy), all meals and most activities included. **BEST TIMES:** Jun-Oct.

What's in a Name?

TIMBUKTU

Mali

Settled by Tuaregs (the original "Blue Men of the Sahara") in the early 12th century, Timbuktu carries one of those fabled names that conjures up images of elusiveness and mystery, of a far corner of the world that's

impossible to reach or, once you've arrived, to penetrate. The city became famous in the 16th century, when its location on the ancient trans-Saharan caravan routes—and the precious salt and gold mined nearby—made it a thriving metropolis, known in Europe for its material and intellectual wealth and for its ardent Muslims. Today the city is little visited in spite of the Djingareyber, Sankoré, and Sidi Yahia mosques (all of them on UNESCO's World Heritage List) sitting amid the city's adobe buildings and the desert's shifting sands. Its fortunes reflect that of Mali as a whole, which has gone from being one of the most powerful nations in Africa to being one of the poorest in the world.

Timbuktu's precious cargo passed through its sister city of trade, Djenne, which lies 220 miles southwest. Affluent and powerful, it became even more renowned as a center of

Islamic learning, and children were sent here from all of West Africa to be educated. It has survived as one of the world's most beautiful mud-brick towns. Its superb Great Mosque (touched up each year after the heavy rains) is the largest and most elaborate mud structure in the world. South of here is the geographically isolated Dogon country, homeland of an intriguing civilization that has so far resisted both Christianity and Islam, preserving the traditions and customs of its animist ancestors, who came here 700 years ago, perhaps from Libya.

WHAT: site, town. **HOW:** Wilderness Travel, tel 800-368-2794 or 510-558-2488, fax 510-558-2489; www.wildernesstravel.com. **COST:** from $6,295 per person (double occupancy) for a 20-day trip. **WHEN:** 3 departures annually in Nov, Dec, and Jan. **BEST TIMES:** Nov–Mar.

Heaven's Prototype

MAURITIUS

Mark Twain wrote, "Heaven was copied after Mauritius." Thanks to an enlightened policy of ecotourism and preservation, this tiny, pear-shaped speck of an island smack in the middle of the Indian Ocean

remains unspoiled and intriguing. Independent since 1968, Mauritius is a 28-mile-wide microcosm of European colonialism and cultural diversity, an exotic mosaic of Indian, African, British, continental, and Chinese influences. Long a favorite of European sunseekers, it boasts sugar-white beaches, dramatic mountains, volcanic lakes, a gracious, Creole-speaking population, and a number of exquisite resort hotels—most of them sensitive to and respectful of the island's natural beauty. Foremost is the secluded Oberoi, on the island's less-developed northwest coast. Grand without being glitzy, with 20 lush, tropical acres and a world-class spa, it exudes such an air of intimacy and calm that it might as well have a Do Not Disturb sign at its discreet entrance.

The island's culinary treat is Spoon des Îles, the trump card of the island's glitterati magnet, Le Saint Géran Hotel, Spa & Golf Club, located on 60 acres at the tip of the Belle Mare Peninsula on the island's east coast. The first of chef Alain Ducasse's star-spangled restaurants to open outside Europe, it draws

from the island's Creole, French, and Asian elements, infallibly showcasing the area's renowned seafood.

For all the amenities available to visitors at the luxury hotels, the best beaches are the public ones, especially on weekends when Mauritian families turn up for reunions and food fests where all are welcome.

WHAT: island, hotel, restaurant. **WHERE:** 1,300 miles off the African coast. **THE OBEROI:** Baie aux Tortues, Pointe aux Piments. In Mauritius, 230/204-3600, fax 230/204-3625; in the U.S., tel 800-562-3764; reservations@oberoigroup.com; www.oberoi-mauritius.com. *Cost:* from $770 (low season), from $950 (high season). **LE SAINT GÉRAN HOTEL, SPA & GOLF CLUB:** Belle Mare. In the U.S., tel 866-522-0001; in Mauritius, 230/401-1688, fax 230/401-1777; www.one andonlyresorts.com. *Cost:* from $985 per person. Dinner at Spoon des Îles $120. **BEST TIMES:** temperature is pretty standard year-round. For diving, seas are clearest Mar–May and Sept–Nov.

Southern Africa's Big Wild

ETOSHA NATIONAL PARK

Namibia

Despite its harsh climate, Namibia has some of the world's most compelling and untrammeled scenery, with a diverse and plentiful wildlife that has adapted to the rigors of its desertlike conditions. The Etosha

National Park in the north, a semiarid savanna grassland ten times the size of Luxembourg, is the third largest game reserve in the world. With 144 species of mammals and well over 300 species of birds depending on its water holes, game sighting is relatively easy here. At the Etosha Pan, the flat depression at the heart of the park, the variety and profusion of species found at the water holes at any one time make for a veritable arkful. You may see spectacular numbers of elephants, zebras, giraffes, blue wildebeests, springboks, and the endangered black rhino. For a few days each year after the rains, when the pan fills with water, flamingos and pelicans descend by the tens of thousands.

There are three lodges within the park, but if you go the extra distance beyond the park's confines to the 19,800-acre Huab Lodge, a private reserve on the Huab River with game-viewing similar to Etosha's, you'll find the warmest welcome, the finest guides, and the most stylish comfort in the country. A swimming pool and natural thermal springs pass as your own private watering holes. There are excellent meals, and barking geckos will lull you to sleep—or is it the free-flowing South African wines?

WHAT: site, hotel, experience. **WHERE:** Huab Lodge, 6-hour drive north of Windhoek, 3-hour drive from Etosha. Air transfers can be arranged. Tel 264/67-687-058, fax 264/67-687-059; info@huab.com; www.huab.com. **HOW:** in the U.S., contact Namibia specialist Africa Adventure Co., tel 800-882-9453 or 954-491-8877, fax 954-491-9060; safari@africanadventure.com; www.africanadventure.com. Customized safaris arranged for small groups and private tours for all destinations in southern and eastern African wildlife countries and beyond.

Haunting Beauty and Unconfined Space

SKELETON COAST

Namibia

When the world is too much, this is the safari to consider—not to view game (which is a bonus) but to experience the strange solitude of one of the world's most unusual and scenic areas. Namibia's Skeleton Coast is a little-explored desert paradise of wide-open spaces, undeveloped, unpeopled, and far from civilization. Its name refers to the treacherous, barren shoreline where shipwrecks and whale bones litter the fog-shrouded beaches. The Cape Cross Seal Reserve is a breeding ground for tens of thousands of Cape fur seals; they lounge on the rocks and beaches, and their blue-eyed pups arrive in late November or early December. Light aircraft is the ideal way to visit much of this desolate land, which at times resembles a harsh moonscape, at other times a vast sea of shifting sand dune mountains, reputed to be the highest on earth. This is the Sossusvlei area of the Namib Desert, one of the world's oldest and driest, whose 1,000-foot-high

An ever-changing sandscape

apricot-colored dunes are shaped and driven like waves by the sea winds. Especially magnificent at sunrise or sunset when the colors of the dunes shift kaleidoscopically, the vastness of the region is best experienced by climbing a dune and listening to the roar of the sand grains spilling over the surface. You may even spot a rare desert elephant.

WHAT: site, experience. **WHERE:** safaris

depart from and return to Windhoek. **HOW:** in Namibia, through Skeleton Coast Safaris, tel 264/61-224-248, fax 264/61-225-713; info@skeleton coastsafaris.com; www.skeletoncoastsafaris.com. In the U.S., contact Safari Experts for customized trips throughout Namibia, tel/fax 435-649-4655; safari@safariexperts.com; www.safariexperts. com. **COST:** $5,495 per person, 4 days/3 nights all-inclusive. **BEST TIMES:** Apr–Nov.

The Galápagos of the Indian Ocean

ALDABRA ISLAND

Aldabra Islands, Seychelles

A t the center of Aldabra, the world's largest raised coral atoll, lies one of the world's largest lagoons, like a sea within a vast tropical ocean. This 50-square-mile atoll encompasses an ecosystem so isolated that the wildlife is in many cases considered unique. It is the last remaining natural habitat for giant Aldabra tortoises, the unofficial and much-beloved national icon of the Seychelles; 150,000 of these enormous antediluvian creatures roam the harsh terrain. With huge eyes, wrinkled necks, and an odd expression reminiscent of E.T.'s, some tip the scales at 600 pounds. Nature in its purest state reigns on Aldabra, observed biologist Sir Julian Huxley in 1970, who declared it a unique "living natural history museum" that should belong to the whole world. Open to the public only

since 1991, the island has become a nirvana for divers, naturalists, and ornithologists. Jacques Cousteau described it as the most spectacular drift dive anywhere. Lying closer to Mombasa, Kenya, than the principal Seychelles island of Mahé, Aldabra is the most distant of the Seychelles' outlying islands: The very distance that enabled the flora and fauna to survive human encroachment also makes it difficult to reach the hotel-free island. The only crowds you'll find are of the tortoise kind.

WHAT: island, experience. **WHERE:** 700 miles/1,126 km from Mahé; accessible by organized boat trips only. **HOW:** for the most knowledgeable and experienced diving program, book the custom-designed *Indian Ocean Explorer* live-aboard yacht. Contact Bushbuck Safaris in the U.K., tel 44/1669-630-386, fax 44/1669-630-385; info@bushbucksafaris.com; www.bushbucksafaris.com. **COST:** from $325 per person per night, all-inclusive, 7–14 nights. Air charter from Mahé to departure point on Assumption Island, from $1,200 per person round-trip. **WHEN:** Mar–Apr and Oct–Dec.

Coral "trees"

Exquisite Languor on Empty White Beaches

DESROCHES ISLAND
AND LODGE

Amirantes Island, Seychelles

The shallow lagoons and perfect beaches of this small, untouched island offer a slice of paradise in a forgotten corner of the world. And, like paradise, Desroches is difficult to reach—some 1,000 miles off the East African coast and only recently opened to tourists in a deep escape mode. It is a pristine, low-lying sand cay of shockingly white beaches (in the wild Amirantes archipelago of twenty-eight islands named after Admiral Vasco da Gama), barely half a mile wide and 3 miles long, and banded by concentric circles of aquamarine and turquoise waters of incredible visibility. You can walk the 10-mile palm-fringed, white-sand circumference in three hours or bicycle along paths through the giant coconut planta-

A remote and pristine beach

tion that covers the interior. Although it's far removed from the pretensions of civilization, the only hotel is, ironically, the very epitome of civilized hospitality. Desroches Island Lodge's ten sea-facing villas house twenty deluxe suites, and the dining is simple and excellent. The island's protective reef offers world-class deep-sea fishing and the best water activities in the Indian Ocean, but the inclination to tuck into a bestseller on your breezy veranda may be just too great to resist.

WHAT: island, hotel. **WHERE:** 45 minutes south of Mahé by air. **HOW:** in Mahé, contact Travel Services Seychelles, tel 27/13-737-6626, fax 27/13-737-6628; reservations@ desroches-island.com; www.desroches-island. com. **COST:** doubles from $700 per night, includes all meals. **WHEN:** open year-round. **BEST TIMES:** late Feb–Apr and late Oct–Nov for diving.

A Photographer's Nirvana

LA DIGUE ISLAND

Inner Islands, Seychelles

The huge, artfully weathered granite boulders that distinguish this most popular Seychelles island are actually the peaks of Gondwanaland, submerged millions of years ago midway between Africa and India.

Simplicity and a slow-moving serenity mark life for the 2,000 hospitable Digueois. On this traffic-free island, dancing school-children of a beguiling ethnic mix run to greet the oxcarts that plod through thick vegetation along unpaved roads to different points of interest.

Anse Source d'Argent is La Digue's most brilliant beach, divided into one incredibly beautiful hidden cove after another; its sculpted pink- and rust-colored boulders have eroded into sculptural forms that bring the work of Henry Moore to mind. The warm, luminescent waters are a spectrum of pastel blues and greens, so clear you could submerge a (waterproof) book and read it effortlessly. Arguably the most beautiful beach of the Seychelles' 115 islands, it is also one of the world's most photographed and rec-

ognizable; but, ironically, it's often blissfully empty. The rare black paradise flycatcher, an endangered bird whose population hovers around seventy-five, can be found only on this island, and might be seen flitting about the aviary reserve, unmistakable with its irides-cent blue-black feathers and trailing tail plume. Succumb to the island's sleepy, old-fashioned charm and stay on indefinitely at the island's principal hotel, the beachside La Digue Island Lodge.

WHAT: island, site, hotel. **WHERE:** half-hour boat ride twice daily from Praslin, 3 hours from Mahé. **HOW:** all arrangements can be made through La Digue Island Lodge, tel 248/292-525, fax 248/234-132; reservation@ ladigue.sc; www.ladigue.sc. **COST:** beachside suite and half-board for 2 at La Digue Lodge $525. **BEST TIMES:** Oct–Jan.

Underwater Drama

STE. ANNE MARINE NATIONAL PARK

Mahé, Inner Islands, Seychelles

The first marine park in the Indian Ocean and perhaps its most beautiful, Ste. Anne consists of six little islands within easy reach of the archi-pelago's principal island of Mahé, and the teeming waters that

surround them. Organized tours will bring you to the park and show you why the local gov-ernment had the foresight to protect this remarkable aquatic environment. A fasci-nating underwater theater can be viewed from a semisubmersible "sub-sea viewer," to the delight of nonsnorklers. But even the latter throw on a mask and flip over the side when introduced to the science-fiction seascape of multicolored coral gardens below. A deli-cious Creole lunch is arranged on uninhabited Round Island, under the shade of giant tamarind trees and never far from the park's

A marine-park inhabitant

magnificent beaches. You can disembark on lovely Cerf Island and check into one of Cerf Island Resort's villas built into a lush green hillside. A handful of families live on the traffic-free island, and there's a fine Creole restaurant. A frequent shuttle boat departs for Victoria on nearby Mahé, but castaways here are hard-pressed to find any reason to leave.

WHAT: site, island, hotel. **WHERE:** 15 minutes by boat east of Mahé. **STE. ANNE INFO:** Tel 248/22-51-14; info@scmrt-mpa.sc; www.scmrt-mpa.sc. **CERF ISLAND RESORT:** Tel 248/294-500, fax 248/294-511; info@cerf-resort.com; www.cerf-resort.com. *Cost:* from $410 for hillside villa. **BEST TIMES:** Oct–Jan.

Round-the-Clock Splendor

ELLERMAN HOUSE AND MOUNT NELSON HOTEL

Cape Town, Western Cape, South Africa

Sitting high on a hill in Bantry Bay and enjoying views of what must be one of the most beautiful coastlines in the world, the Ellerman House is South Africa's finest boutique hotel. Enormous picture windows in each of the

seven sumptuously furnished guest rooms keep the views center stage while letting in streams of sunshine. The hotel was built in 1912 as the private home of a British shipping magnate; a maximum of fourteen fortunate guests are pampered in exquisite settings and with top-notch dining. The feeling is something akin to that of a French Riviera hideaway, although here the artwork is by a virtual who's who of prominent South African painters. Patios and impeccably groomed terraces lead down to a pool whose color matches the dazzling sea.

Ellerman House, overlooking the sea

Cape Town is a ten-minute cab ride away, so head for high tea in style at the city's Mount Nelson Hotel. Ever since it opened its doors in 1899, this pink stucco grande dame has been welcoming Cape Town's most illustrious, colorful, and preeminent clientele. Mount Nelson is the hub around which the city's social life traditionally revolves, and if you have only one high tea in the country, have it here. Tea is served indoors or on the gracious garden veranda. It's a bacchanalia of pastries, cakes, and dainty nibbles in surreal quantities. The English ambience remains delightfully intact and, despite its central urban location, you are luxuriously surrounded by 6 acres of gardens, full of lush rose beds and hibiscus the size of trees.

WHAT: hotel, restaurant. **ELLERMAN HOUSE:** 180 Kloof Rd., Bantry Bay. Tel 27/21-430-3200, fax 27/21-430-3215;

info@ellerman.co.za; www.ellerman.co.za. *Cost:* doubles from $520; top-floor Ellerman Suite from $1,395. **MOUNT NELSON HOTEL:**

76 Orange St. Tel 27/21-483-1000, fax 27/21-483-1001; www.mountnelson.co.za. *Cost:* doubles from $555. Tea $20.

End-of-the-World Views and Lodging to Match

TABLE MOUNTAIN

Cape Town, Western Cape, South Africa

More than 3,500 feet above the fair city of Cape Town, the view from Table Mountain captures the mountains, city, and ocean, as well as virtually unspoiled wilderness, all in one breathtaking panorama. A cable car ride takes just five minutes to reach the flat "tabletop" summit that gave the landmark mountain its name, and which is visible to sailors 40 miles out at sea. Most of the Cape Peninsula's 2,200 species of flora can be found on the mountain, which is ablaze with blooms, including more than 100 species of iris, between September and March. Capetonians are understandably fond of coming up with picnic hampers and a bottle of wine from one of the celebrated vineyards nearby. Sunset here is the quintessence of romance. Fortunately, Table Mountain's cable car system runs frequently, so you don't have to face the only alternative: a two- to three-hour hike to the top. Some of the less strenuous routes begin in the magnificent Kirstenbosch National Botanical Gardens, on the eastern slope. There's such a rich display of South Africa's indigenous plants there that you may forget about making it to the top at all.

With Table Mountain as its backdrop, and on the exciting Victoria & Albert Waterfront, the tony Cape Grace Hotel is one of the continent's top-ranked accommodations for its near perfect service, beautiful guest rooms, and stunning views, either of the harbor or the mountain—or both.

WHAT: site, hotel. **TABLE MOUNTAIN CABLE CAR:** Lower Cableway, tel 27/21-424-8181; www.tablemountain.net. *Cost:* $11. **CAPE GRACE HOTEL:** West Quay, Victoria & Albert Waterfront. Tel 27/21-410-7100, fax 27/21-418-0495; reservations@capegrace.com; www.capegrace.com. *Cost:* from $620 (low season), from $745 (high season). **BEST TIMES:** Sept–Apr for sunny weather.

A Surf-and-Turf Safari

PHINDA RESOURCE RESERVE

KwaZulu-Natal, South Africa

This relatively new private reserve in northern Zululand is a winner not only for the seven different African ecosystems that meet within its 35,000 acres, but for its novel approach to safaris. Days are full, with a medley of boat and canoe trips for close-up looks at the bird life, crocs, and hippos of ancient waterways, or tracking the elusive black rhino by foot. Then there is big-game fishing, diving the world's southernmost reefs off the deserted coast of Maputaland, game drives delivering elephants, leopards, and rhinos, or visiting the highest vegetated sand dunes in the world.

While there's no doubt that such rare biodiversity is central to your safari experience, your attention will be riveted by the accommodations as well. The Mountain Lodge is set atop a hill with endless views of the Lebombo Mountains and Maputaland coastal range. Or you can opt for the contemporary Forest Lodge, a masterpiece of glass-walled units built around twisted trees and set on stilts within a rare sand forest. The Zen-like design is deliberately spare and vaguely Oriental, allowing the great outdoors in. You can relax in bed while birds sing and butterflies flutter outside your window.

WHAT: experience, hotel. **WHERE:** 185 miles/300 km north of Durban on Indian Ocean, shuttle service from Johannesburg airport upon request. Bookings should be made through the CCAfrica Central Reservations Office. In the U.S., tel 888-882-3742, fax 305/221-3223; usa@andbeyond.com; www.ccafrica.com. **COST:** Mountain Lodge or Forest Lodge from $425 (low seaon), from $750 (high season) per person per day, all-inclusive. **BEST TIMES:** Oct–Feb.

A Journey to Middle Earth, and Flying Through God's Window

THE DRAKENSBERG MOUNTAINS

Mpumalanga, South Africa

Few places in the world match the Mpumalanga for physical beauty; it is believed to be the inspiration behind the phantasmagorical setting for *The Lord of the Rings*, written by South African–born J.R.R. Tolkien.

South Africa's highest mountains, with panoramic passes, valleys, rivers, waterfalls, and forests, characterize the landscape of what was formerly known as the Eastern Transvaal. The entire area offers opportunities for hiking, horseback riding, bird-watching, golfing, and fishing. Visit the magnificent Blyde River Canyon, a gigantic gorge 15 miles long carved out of the face of the Transvaal escarpment, where deep cylindrical holes have been formed by river erosion, or God's Window, the canyon's unsurpassed lookout point. And if touring the spectacular Eastern Transvaal by car or on foot affords remarkable scenery, imagine taking it all in from an eagle's perspective. Smooth jet-powered helicopters swoop over the dramatic rock formations of the Blyde River Canyon and through lush valleys bursting with vegetation

You can see why the view onto Blyde River Canyon is called God's Window.

and color. Hover over river rapids and cascading waterfalls and land on a remote mountaintop on an otherwise unreachable grassy clearing. Lunch with a view takes on a new meaning, if the adrenaline rush hasn't obliterated your appetite. The Veuve Clicquot is popped, and eagles soar above you—and below. Divide your time in the mountains between the area's two outstanding lodges, the Cybele Forest Lodge and the Blue Mountain Lodge. Each provides a magnificent setting, breathtaking scenery, renowned dining, a stable of horses, fishing gear, and five-star service. In addition, there is a historic gold-rush town and a restored Ndebele tribal village to visit, and the world-famous Kruger National Park is an easy day trip away.

WHAT: site, experience, hotel. **WHERE:** 3½-hour drive east of Johannesburg; 10 miles/16 km from Nelspruit airport. **CYBELE FOREST LODGE:** tel 27/13-764-9500, fax 27/13-764-9510; wwew.cybele.co.za. *Cost:* doubles from $165. **BLUE MOUNTAIN LODGE:** tel 27/13-737-8446; bmlres@foreversa.co.za; www.bluemountainlodge.co.za. *Cost:* suites from $150, includes dinner for 2. **HOW:** in the U.S., contact Premier Tours, tel 800-545-1910; info@premiertours.com; www.premiertours.com. **HELICOPTER SAFARI:** in South Africa, book tours through your hotel or Regency Exclusive Safaris, tel 27/82-490-8202. *Cost:* from $360 per person, 3-hour trip, includes meal. **BEST TIMES:** Sept–Oct and Mar–Apr.

The Beauty and the Beasts

SABI SAND GAME RESERVE

Mpumalanga, South Africa

Some of the country's best game-viewing and splendor-in-the-bush accommodations can be found in the Sabi Sand Game Reserve. Sharing a fenceless border with the enormous Kruger National Park, this collectively

owned and managed private reserve welcomes the coming and going of wildlife but not the human traffic that comes with it; as one of few

Lunch at Londolozi's Tree Camp

guests you can enjoy the same game density as at Kruger, but with sumptuous amenities, and very likely never share the terrain with more than one or two other jeeps in the course of an exhilarating game drive. The animals are not tame, but they have become habituated to the sight of vehicles and will let them approach within a short distance. Rangers and trackers at the Sabi Sand Reserve are educated, charming, and entertaining, with a wealth of experience and a passion for the bush. Among the many private parks that make up the 163,000-acre reserve are the exalted trio of Londolozi, MalaMala, and Singita. Of Londolozi's three camps, the top of the line is the Tree Camp, directly on the banks of the Sabi River, a glorious contrast of raw bush and unashamed luxury shared by just eight privileged guests. MalaMala's most favored and romantic campsite is Kirkman's Kamp, built around a 1920s homestead. Singita features two luxurious lodges (Ebony and Boulders), both with spas and suites with private pools, and is generally considered the standout.

WHAT: site, experience, hotel. **WHERE:** 1-hour flight/5-hour drive from Johannesburg along SW boundary of Kruger National Park.

LONDOLOZI: tel 27/11-280-6655, fax 27/11-280-6656; www.londolozi.com. *Cost:* $710 per person, per day, all-inclusive. **MALAMALA:** tel 27/11-442-2267, fax 27/11-442-2318; www.malamala.com. *Cost:* $575 per person, per day, all-inclusive. **SINGITA:** tel 27/121-683-3424, fax 27/21-671-6776; reservations@singita.com; www.singita.com. *Cost:* $1,285 per person, per day, all-inclusive. **HOW:** in the U.S., contact Premier Tours, tel 800-545-1910; info@premiertours.com, www.premiertours.com. **BEST TIMES:** Mar–Oct.

An Oenophile's Odyssey

THE CAPE WINELANDS

Paarl, Western Cape, South Africa

A wine safari combines two of South Africa's greatest treasures: the spectacular Cape wine region and its excellent regional cuisine, a mix of the culinary skills of the Dutch, French, British, Portuguese,

Germans, and Malays. Within easy reach of Cape Town, the major estates and the small, sophisticated, fabled towns of Stellenbosch, Paarl, and Franschhoek have roots deep in the Dutch and French Huguenot chapter of the country's history, dating back to the mid-1600s. The gracious Cape Dutch homesteads are set against a bold backdrop of granite-peaked mountains, forests, and rolling vineyards. They are often centuries-old family-run concerns, whose private cellars can be visited and sampled by special arrangement. A visit to Groot Constantia, the oldest wine estate in the country—originally owned by Simon Van Der Stel, the first governor of the Dutch Colony here—offers the chance to experience some of the world's finest wines as well as a rich historical and architectural tradition. Stay in Paarl at Grande Roche, one of South Africa's uncontested jewels. The cluster of historical gabled buildings (whose

nucleus is the Dutch manor house dating to 1707) and house-proud hotel-of-the-year staff create a delightful atmosphere in this enviably scenic location. The hotel's sophisticated restaurant, Bosman's, draws Cape Town's epicures, who think nothing of helicoptering in to enjoy one of the country's best dining experiences.

WHAT: site, hotel, restaurant. **WHERE:** begins 25 miles/40 km east of Cape Town. **HOW:** in the U.S., contact Maxim Tours, tel 800-655-0222 or 973-927-0760, fax 973-927-1417; info@maximtours.com; www.maximtours.com; customized tours available. **COST:** $4,860 per person, all-inclusive air/land 10-day wine safaris. **WHEN:** departures year-round. **GRANDE ROCHE:** tel 27/21-863-5100, fax 27/21-863-2220; reserve@granderoche.co.za; www.granderoche.com. *Cost:* doubles from $255 (low season), from $365 (high season). 4-course prix fixe dinner $75. **BEST TIMES:** Sept–May.

Opulent, Gargantuan, and Extravagant Beyond Imagination

THE PALACE OF THE LOST CITY

Sun City, Northwest Province, South Africa

In the middle of dry bushveld and surrounded by the ersatz glitz and Las Vegas glamour of the entertainment and resort complex called Sun City stands the regal Palace of the Lost City, on a scale that is almost inconceivable.

Not everyone agrees on what is the world's finest hotel, but no one disagrees that this $190-million African fantasy extravaganza dazzles and astounds. A gambling casino, four hotels, two award-winning 18-hole golf courses, and a 136,000-acre game reserve were not enough to satisfy the young entrepreneur who created Sun City in 1979. He concocted a myth of a lost civilization that would be anchored by the magnificent Palace Hotel, a pleasure dome supposedly built upon its ruins. The hotel's attention to detail in architecture, service, and furnishings is mind-boggling. There are more than 300 rooms (for an extraordinary experience, book the King Suite); graceful reminders of African heritage and ethnic motifs greet visitors at every turn. Fifty-five groomed acres of man-made jungle and rain forest are studded with convincing remnants of the legendary Lost City civilization. It's one part Walt Disney, one part Xanadu, and one part Cecil B. DeMille.

WHAT: hotel. **WHERE:** 115 miles/185 km northwest of Johannesburg; connected to major cities in South Africa by air. Tel 27/14-557-4301; central reservations tel 27/11-780-7800; in the U.S., tel 954-331-8135; fax 954-331-3252; nat sales@sunint.co.za; www.suninternational.co.za. **COST:** doubles from $825; King Suite $6,625.

The Golden Age of Train Travel, Past and Present

ROVOS RAIL AND THE BLUE TRAIN

South Africa

Relive the glory days of steam travel in the lap of Edwardian luxury as you huff and puff with Rovos Rail through the heart of the bush and some of the continent's most magnificent scenery. A menu of train itineraries can

be mixed and matched according to the time and budget of rail and romance enthusiasts. Take the twenty-five-hour Cape Town to Knysna round-trip route through the fabled Hottentot Holland Mountains and along the lake district and dramatic coastline. Or plan ahead for the once-a-year no-holds-barred fourteen-day Cape Town to Dar es Salaam journey, which passes through Zimbabwe and Zambia with excursions to and stopovers in places such as Victoria Falls along the way. Some of the vintage steam trains used by Rovos Rail date back to the late 1800s. All prewar carriages are spacious, richly paneled cars, and a posh 1924 dining car is perhaps the handsomest of all. Exceptionally large suites are outfitted with queen-size beds and deluxe amenities. Dressing for dinner seems appropriate, when entrees like Cape rock lobster are paired with South Africa's best wine selection. It's red-carpet treatment all the way on the aptly named "Pride of Africa."

The Blue Train first took to the rails in 1946, and as elegant, stylish, and comfortable as the original trains were, passengers will certainly appreciate the new generation of railcars, introduced in the late 1990s. The fresh and sophisticated contemporary decor is accented by an African aesthetic—the most visible difference in this updated breed of luxury travel, whose runs from Cape Town to Pretoria (one night on board) and from Pretoria to Victoria Falls, Zimbabwe (two nights), are the most popular among a number of choices.

WHAT: experience. **HOW:** numerous itineraries for both trains are available. Information for both can be obtained in U.S. through Premier Tours, tel 800-545-1910; info@premiertours.com; www.premiertours.com. **ROVOS RAIL:** in South Africa, tel 27/12-315-8242, fax 27/12-323-0843; marielle@rovos.co.za; www.rovos.co.za. *Cost:* deluxe suite for 2 from $880. **BLUE TRAIN:** in South Africa, 27/12-334-8459, fax 27/12-334-8464; info@bluetrain.co.za, www.bluetrain.co.za. *Cost:* deluxe suite for 2 from $1,308.

Quench Your Thirst and Satiate Your Hunger in Style

CONSTANTIA WINE REGION

Western Cape, South Africa

Twenty minutes but light-years away from downtown Cape Town, Constantia offers an idyllic taste of wine country that obviates the need to venture east to the more extensive wine lands near Paarl. Day trippers will

regret not having reserved a stay at Cellars-Hohenort, a historical country hotel nestled against the forested eastern slopes of Table Mountain and housed in the 18th-century cellars of the former Cape governor's wine estate and triple-gabled manor house. Guests find a stylish rural retreat here, surrounded by orchards, vineyards, and beautifully landscaped gardens of roses, petunias, and caladiums. Although the ambience is understated and relaxed, everything is first class, and a dinner at The Cellars, the hotel's noted restaurant, may well be one of your most memorable in South Africa. Drawing on French and English inspiration, the young chef utilizes the Cape's bounty of fresh seafood, game, and produce.

The sweeping grounds of Cellars-Hohenort

Another excellent destination for epicures in Constantia is Buitenverwachting. The tongue-twisting name of this well-known wine-producing estate and its eponymous restaurant is Old Dutch for "beyond expectations"—but who thought to have such high expectations for antelope, ostrich, and springbok? Excellent Italian or French cuisine may be had elsewhere in the country, but if you want to be wonderfully reminded that you are in South Africa—where the South Atlantic and Indian Ocean meet, where the karoo lamb is redolent of the herbs and grasses on which it feeds, and where the African rock lobster is justly famous—then come to Buitenverwachting. Window-side seats look out over acres of vineyards, towering oak trees, and the crags of the Constantiaberg mountains. If you arrive earlier in the day for a wine tasting, buy one of the restaurant's picnic hampers and have a glorious lunch on the estate's gorgeous lawns.

WHAT: site, hotel, restaurant. **GROOT CONSTANTIA:** for general info, www.groot constantia.co.za. **CELLARS-HOHENORT:** 15 Hohenort Avenue, 8 miles/10 km south of Cape Town. Tel 27/21-794-2137, fax 27/21-794-2149; www.cellars-hohenort.com. *Cost:* doubles from $465. Dinner $41. **BUITENVERWACHTING:** Klein Constantia Road. Tel 27/21-794-5190; info@buitenverwachting.com. *Cost:* dinner $40. *When:* open Tues–Sat. **BEST TIMES:** Sept–May.

Africa's Southernmost Coast

THE GARDEN ROUTE

Western Cape, South Africa

This 130-mile stretch east of Cape Town runs along the coastal terrain of lakes, mountains, forests, and golden beaches. The waters are full of penguins, dolphins, and migrating whales. Its year-round beauty is enhanced between July and October, when multitudes of blooming wildflowers create a nonpareil diversity of flora due to unique climatic and soil conditions. The floral kingdom of the Southern Cape is the most varied in the world, as hiking among hundreds of miles of trails and leisurely drives through forests and parkland will illustrate. The famous Otter Trail in the Tsitsikamma National Park is a five-day hike through some of the country's most spectacular scenery; half-mile trails descend from the Visitor's Center for those without much time or stamina.

The charming town of Knysna is a must-see. While you're there, sample some of the area's renowned oysters. Every July visitors flock here for the Knysna Oyster Festival, a jam-packed week of sports, entertainment, and of course oysters. Follow the town's walking trails out along the coast to view the Heads, rock sentinels that stand guard at the mouth of the lagoon.

On a gorgeous sweep of beach lies the Plettenberg, the coastline's most exclusive hotel and an enchanting place to stop. Built around an 1860 manor house, a more contemporary addition has airy rooms that overlook

The Heads, just outside Knysna

the pool and ocean. Come at least for a wonderful lunch on the open terrace and whale-watch as you dine.

WHAT: experience, restaurant, hotel. **WHERE:** east of Cape Town, from Mossel Bay to Storms River. **KNYSNA OYSTER FESTIVAL:** www.oysterfestival.co.za. **PLETTENBERG HOTEL:** Look Out Rocks, tel 27/44-533-2030, fax 27/44-533-2074; reservations@collection mcgrath.com; www.plettenberg.com. *Cost:* doubles from $465. Lunch $20. **BEST TIMES:** Jul–Oct for wildflowers.

The Coast of Whales

HERMANUS

Western Cape, South Africa

Other bays along the coastline of South Africa's Western Cape attract migrating whales, but most of them return yearly to the waters of Walker Bay and the coastal town of Hermanus. The months of June to November see hundreds of courting, mating, and calving whales, particularly the southern right whale, with a few Bryde's and humpbacks thrown in for good measure. Hermanus sits atop a ledge where a 7-mile cliff walk is the prime vantage point for whale-watching; a roaming whale-crier, complete with sandwich board and bullhorn, keeps you apprised of approaching activity. Even on a rare whaleless day, you might be happily compensated with white sharks, jackass penguins, and seals in a naturally beautiful setting. Nearby, Grootbos Lodge offers the area's loveliest stay. This privately owned 295-acre nature reserve gives a limited number of guests the chance to meander on horseback or on foot over hills draped with wild lilies and fynbos, the predominant flora of the Cape, and through milkwood forests full of bird life. The young European owner and manager finds time to excel as a chef as well, and arranges beach barbecues along the coastline, where sunset is a bonus.

WHAT: site, hotel. **WHERE:** 2-hour drive east of Cape Town. **GROOTBOS LODGE:** tel 27/28-384-8000, fax 27/28-384-8040; reservations@grootbos.co.za; www.grootbos. com. **COST:** from $255 per person per day, includes dinner. **BEST TIMES:** Jun–Nov.

The Snow-Covered Roof of Africa

CLIMBING MOUNT KILIMANJARO

Kilimanjaro National Park, Tanzania

"Wide as all the world, great, high, and unbelievably white in the sun," wrote Ernest Hemingway in his famous short story "The Snows of Kilimanjaro." Few mountains offer the majesty and mystique of Kilimanjaro, at 19,340 feet the highest mountain in Africa, dwarfing the region's other peaks. The nine-day trek to the mountain's oddly flat top is 25 miles round-trip, if you ascend by way of the more remote, seldom used Shira Plateau. By avoiding the shorter, five-day, overcrowded Marangu Trail, or "tourist route," a few days are added on for proper acclimatization, the trek's biggest obstacle. One third of Marangu trekkers never make it past Gillman's Point, 600 feet below

An ocean of clouds surrounds the peak of Kilimanjaro.

the summit, because they have not allotted enough time to adjust to the low level of oxygen—approximately half of what humans normally breathe at sea level. No technical skills, ropes, or crampons are called for, and though it's no walk in the park, the grade is generally a gentle one. A battalion of porters bolts ahead to pitch tents and set up camp at spectacular sites by the time everyone straggles in. At the summit, your lightheadedness may be a reaction to the thrill and satisfaction of the surreal views—on a clear day the plains of Tanzania and Kenya spread out for hundreds of miles, 3½ miles below you.

WHAT: experience, site. **WHERE:** 6 hours by car from airport in Nairobi, Kenya; in Tanzania it's a 2-hour drive from Arusha's Mount Kilimanjaro Airport. **HOW:** in the U.S., contact Mountain Madness, tel 206-937-8389, fax 206-937-1772; info@mountain madness.com; www.mountainmadness.com. **COST:** $4,975 per person, all-inclusive, land only. **WHEN:** monthly departures, except during short rainy season in Apr–May and Nov.

Africa's Garden of Eden

NGORONGORO CRATER

Ngorongoro Conservation Area, Tanzania

The volcanic Ngorongoro Crater, the world's largest unflooded, intact caldera, is acclaimed as one of the natural wonders of the world, both for its unique topographical beauty and for the staggering concentration

of animals that live there. This natural amphitheater is the Serengeti in miniature, with wildebeests, zebras, and gazelles migrating from one side of the 12-mile-wide crater to the other as the seasons change. Elephants, buffaloes, hippos, and lions are also plentiful, and Ngorongoro is possibly the best place on earth to see the rare black rhino. In the middle of the crater is the mirrorlike Lake Magadi, a year-round supply of fresh

water that makes this a spectacular wildlife oasis. Most of the time the lake is ringed with masses of flamingos. Unabashed comparisons with Noah's Ark and the Garden of Eden are inevitable. The compact presence of so many animals also makes it a predator's paradise: safari goers couldn't ask for more. The human species is beginning to outnumber the wildlife, but reputable outfitters can furnish you with deluxe mobile tents and a crackerjack staff with encyclopedic knowledge and a knack for avoiding herds of fellow gazers.

Alternatively, stay at Ngorongoro Crater Lodge, one of East Africa's most luxurious permanent camps. It's owned and run by the Conservation Corporation, a respected South African safari company. Check into any of the thirty thatched cottages perched at the crater's edge, ask your butler to draw your bath in time for a firelit dinner of pan-African cuisine and Cape wines, and watch from your tub as the sunset's magic unfolds.

The crater is approximately 2,000 feet deep.

What: site, experience, hotel. **Where:** northern Tanzania; transfers from Nairobi or Mount Kilimanjaro airports can be arranged. **How:** in the U.S., contact Tanganyika Safari Company, Ltd., tel 800-882-6788; tangsafari@ aol.com; www.tangsafari.com. **Cost:** custom-designed safaris vary depending on size of group and length of trip. **Ngorongoro**

Crater Lodge: contact central reservations, Johannesburg, South Africa, tel 27/11-809-4300, fax 27/11-809-4400; safaris@and beyond.com; www.ccafrica.com. *Cost:* doubles from $655 (low season), from $1,450 (high season), all-inclusive. **When:** year-round, except rainy season Apr–May.

The Quintessential East African Wilderness

SELOUS GAME RESERVE

Tanzania

N amed after Frederick Courteney Selous (conservationist, hunter, explorer, and author) and famed for its large portered walking safaris, the Selous Game Reserve is Africa's largest protected area that is uninhabited by man. Here Tanzania's greatest population of elephants wander in an area bigger than Switzerland. Over three times the size of South Africa's Kruger Park and twice the size of the Serengeti, the Selous is the second largest game reserve in Africa (the largest being the central Kalahari Desert Game Reserve). Its 21,000 square miles are home to over a million animals, the Great Rufiji River, and Stiegler's Gorge, a canyon that measures over 300 feet deep and 300 feet wide.

Modernized portered walking safaris (with just a few porters, not the long lines of Roosevelt days) are still a highlight, and if you want to go whole hog they'll take you on a 2-week adventure. But nowadays most people prefer to set off from a luxurious lodge or campsite to explore deep into the remote parts of the Reserve, on foot or by boat. Most of the lodges in the northern area offer fly camping for a night or two. Porters carry your lightweight fly-camps—which are basically mosquito net tents set up on the ground, albeit with fine linen sheets, a shared hot shower and wonderful meals—giving you the luxury of sleeping safely in the open under the stars. For those who prefer more deluxe accommodations, Sand Rivers Selous (5 standard rooms, 2 suites, or a private honeymoon cottage) and it's new sister lodge, Kiba Point (with 4 open-fronted cottages) have built their utterly luxurious lodgings with wide open rooms or tents, putting barely anything between you and nature, except for the privacy of your en-suite bathrooms.

WHERE: 1 hour flight (scheduled or charter) southwest of Dar es Salaam. **HOW:** In the U.S., contact Africa Adventure Company, tel 954-491-8877; www.africanadventure. com. **SAND RIVERS SELOUS AND KIBA POINT:** both are on the banks of the Rufiji River. *Cost:* $450 per person per day (double occupancy), all inclusive (except air and park fees). **BEST TIMES:** Jun–Oct.

Island Outpost of Old Araby in the Indian Ocean

STONE TOWN

Zanzibar, Tanzania

The very name Zanzibar conjures up images of romantic spice islands, and—like legendary Timbuktu or Kathmandu—the name alone is almost reason enough to make the trip. For decades overlooked by Western

capitalism, Zanzibar is now at the brink of development. Wide-bodied jets, deluxe cruises, and package tours can greatly improve an island economy while destroying its delicate historical fabric: Now is the time to visit Stone Town's maze of narrow streets, crooked passages, and crumbling houses with overhanging balconies. Arab traders built homes here after they amassed their wealth by trading in gold, ivory, cloves, and—most lucratively—slaves destined for Arabia and Persia. Zanzibar was once the largest slave market on Africa's east coast. Today a 19th-century Anglican church stands on the spot of the old slave market, the main altar built where the whipping post once stood. The intricately carved doorways, some inlaid with brass, are all the luxury that's left of the lavish traders' homes.

A number of these dilapidated homes have been rescued by entrepreneur Thomas Green together with other partners. His restored historical hotel, 236 Hurumzi, captures the romance of this island, boasting antiques, local wood carvings, four-poster beds swathed in mosquito netting, and Zanzibari art. The

rooftop alfresco tea-room and restaurant serves food of a quality to match the decor. 236 Hurumzi is a former Persian home with ten rooms altogether; a hike up the steep teak staircase leads to four unique top-floor guest rooms open to the breezes and a mag-

A Stone Town tower

nificent view of the old city's minarets and the Indian Ocean. Beyond lie the African coast and the glaciers of Kilimanjaro, which, according to some guests, are visible on exceptionally clear days.

WHAT: island, town, hotel. **WHERE:** 22 miles/35 km off eastern coast of Tanzania; 2-hour boat crossing or daily half-hour flight from Dar es Salaam. **236 HURUMZI:** in Zanzibar, tel 255/77-7423266, fax 255/77-7429266; 236hurumzibookings@zanlink.com; www.236hurumzi.com. *Cost:* doubles from $125. **BEST TIMES:** Dec–Mar and Jun–Oct.

Through the Eye of a Needle

MURCHISON FALLS NATIONAL PARK

Uganda

Winston Churchill described Uganda as "the pearl of Africa." In a country on the mend from past political upheaval, you'll sometimes feel you have it all to yourself. Murchison Falls are uncontested as one

of the world's great natural wonders and were once described as the most exciting thing to happen to the Nile in its 4,200-mile stretch. Unlike the massive 5,600-foot expanse of the Zambezi cataracts at Victoria Falls, here the mighty Nile narrows from nearly 1,000 feet and explodes through a rock cleft barely 20 feet wide before plunging 130 feet with incredible force. It is a mesmerizing sight, whether approached on foot or by boat. A water launch on the Nile quietly approaches the base of the falls, slipping past numbers of massive animals—sometimes 100 hippos around one

bend, and everywhere some of the world's largest crocodiles, immobile, watching. There are few concessions to the 21st (or even the 20th) century here, and it takes little to imagine yourself a 19th-century explorer in search of the source of the Nile.

WHAT: site. **WHERE:** northwest Uganda; transfers arranged from Kampala. **HOW:** in Uganda, contact Let's Go Safari, tel 256/41-346-667; main office in Kenya, tel 254/20-444-7151; info@letsgosafari.com; www.lets-go-travel.net. *Cost:* 2-night trips from $515 per person. **BEST TIMES:** Dec–Mar.

Primate Watch in the Impenetrable Jungle

TRACKING THE MOUNTAIN GORILLA

Bwindi National Park, Uganda

The chance for an encounter of the closest kind with a rare mountain gorilla in its last remaining habitat is here in Bwindi National Park. The numbers of this powerful but gentle creature have been gravely reduced by

poaching, while the political unrest in neighboring Rwanda has curtailed the great strides that were made by the late Dian Fossey at the Karisoke Research Center. Today, half of

the dwindling population of about 600 beasts lives peacefully in Uganda, a country that is once again courting tourism. Small, controlled numbers of visitors accompanied by authorized guides are permitted to track the gorillas through what was formerly called the "impenetrable" jungle.

The trail through the tropical rain forest is challenging and exciting, and while there is no guarantee that you will see the gorillas, the local guides are experts at interpreting every broken twig and second-guessing the animals' daily routines. Different family groups of gorillas have been partially habituated to the human presence and eventually come in close to investigate their visitors—first the mighty silverbacks, the leaders of the groups, then the younger ones, followed by mothers carrying or nursing their babies. The guides, many of whom are affiliated with the Dian Fossey Gorilla Fund, are primate specialists—adding an invaluable element to these trips.

WHAT: site, experience. **WHERE:** southwestern Uganda, on the edge of the western Rift Valley. **HOW:** in the U.S., contact Natural Habitat Adventures, tel 303-449-3711 or 800-543-8917, fax 303-449-3712; www.natural habitatadventures.com. **COST:** $8,795 per person, 12-day safari, all-inclusive. **WHEN:** open year-round but call for availability. **BEST TIMES:** May–Aug and Dec–Feb.

So Close and Yet So Far

TONGABEZI SAFARI LODGE

Livingstone, Victoria Falls, Zambia

Just 10 miles or so downstream from the Tongabezi Safari Lodge are the thundering Victoria Falls; although you cannot hear their roar, you are somehow aware of their powerful presence. Yet Tongabezi itself is a

place of tranquility, built along the banks of the still-gentle Zambezi so that each guest cottage and its veranda enjoys award-winning sunsets. The lodge is no bush camp: There's a tennis court and riverside swimming pool, four-poster beds, and sunken baths (loos with views!). Tasteful natural furnishings one could describe as "high bush" decorate the Tree House, or open-air Honeymoon House, atop a cliff. This is the perfect roman-

Victoria Falls

tic base for your Zambezi experience, whether for invigorating morning bush walks and bird walks, or for gentle canoe trips with the option of overnighting on the river's many private islands. You can also choose to soar over the falls in the lodge's private plane or take a wild white-water rafting trip at their base.

WHAT: experience, hotel. **WHERE:** 10 miles/16 km upriver from Victoria Falls, Zambia. Transfers arranged. Tel 260/213-327468, fax 260/3-323-224; reservations@ tongabezi.com; www.tongabezi.com; in the U.S., contact Safari Experts, tel 435-649-4655; safari@safariexperts.com; www.safari experts.com. **COST:** $450 (cottages), $550 (houses) per person per night, all-inclusive. Rafting and flight over Victoria Falls extra. **BEST TIMES:** Mar–Sept.

Game Viewing at Its Best

HWANGE NATIONAL PARK

Hwange, Zimbabwe

Hwange is Zimbabwe's largest, best-known, and most accessible national park. It boasts more than 100 different species of animal and 400 species of birds, putting it in the front ranks of the world's wildlife centers. It is also one of the few great elephant sanctuaries left in Africa; herds of up to a hundred can be seen finding their way to the watering holes at dusk. Of the 300-mile network of game-viewing roads, the most popular is the 10-Mile Drive, a loop through and around the most wildlife-packed areas of the park and past the major watering holes, such as Nyamandhlovu Pan with its raised viewing platform.

One of the country's best permanent safari camps, the Hide, is ideally located on the eastern boundary of Hwange Park. Its name derives from the many hidden viewing spots, some underground and others unobtrusively constructed above, from which you can watch the wealth of wildlife without ever leaving camp. The Camp Pan, a fossilized riverbed that has long been a popular and busy watering hole, is located just paces from the guests' dining area. But the Hide's excellent guides lure guests away from the backyard action and comfortable accommodations with promises of even better viewing in the bush on organized walks and drives.

WHAT: site, experience, hotel. **WHERE:** 2-hour drive from Hwange Airport in Zimbabwe. **THE HIDE:** tel 263/4-498-835, fax 263/4-498-480; info@thehide.co.zw; www.thehidesafaris.com. In the U.S., contact Safari Experts, tel 435-649-4655; safari@safariexperts.com; www.safariexperts.com. *Cost:* from $220 (low season), from $295 (high season) per person, per day, all-inclusive. *When:* year-round. **BEST TIMES:** dry season, Jun–Oct, is best for game viewing; in the wet season, Nov–Apr, wildlife drop their young and the bush is full of wildflowers.

Canoeing the Zambezi River

MANA POOLS NATIONAL PARK

Zimbabwe

A canoe safari on the mighty Zambezi River, through ancient floodplains toward the Indian Ocean, is a trip through primeval Africa and some of its most remote and beautiful riverine scenery. Leaving the heart-stopping white-water rapids upriver at Victoria Falls, all is serene as canoers glide along channels and pools and past countless islands. Hippos and Cape buffalo wallow beneath the low-hanging branches of trees full of bird life. The Ruwesi Canoe Safari, a four-day trip, covers the most interesting stretch of the Middle Zambezi, and beautifully sited camps are set up as you progress downstream. Guides make sure you're canoe-bound just before sunrise, the river's most bewitching hour.

For the less peripatetic, the permanently sited Chikwenya Safari Lodge is beautifully situated at the confluence of the Sapi and Zambezi rivers, facing one of the Zambezi's largest islands. The Chikwenya's guides strike off on bush walks with guests in

Sunset on the Zambezi

tow—an activity allowed in very few of the national reserves. You'll get back to camp in time for the obligatory sunset river ride along the Zambezi, an end to another perfect day in the bush.

WHAT: site, experience, hotel. **WHERE:** northern Zimbabwe; air transfers can be arranged from Victoria Falls. **RUWESI CANOE SAFARI:** in the U.S., contact the Africa Adventure Company, tel 954-491-8877; safari@ africanadventure.com; www.africanadventure. com. *Cost:* $1,550 per person, all-inclusive 3-night/4-day canoe trip. *When:* May–Oct. **CHIKWENYA SAFARI LODGE:** Tel 263/4-499-165; www.chikwenyasafaris.com. *Cost:* all-inclusive doubles $350 (low season), $500 (high season). **BEST TIMES:** Jun–Oct.

A Landscape Wild and Weird

MATOBO NATIONAL PARK

Matobo Hills, Zimbabwe

Huge granite masses—seamed, split, shaped, and sculpted by time and the elements—form an array of giant whalebacks, fanciful castles, and knobbly outcrops that extend for thousands of square miles through the

Matobo Hills (aka the Matopos). This bizarre landscape so bewitched Cecil J. Rhodes (after whom Zimbabwe took its former name of Rhodesia), he arranged to be buried here. No one leaves the park without spending an awe-inspiring moment at the site of his hillside grave, named by Rhodes "View of the World." The area has deservedly been considered a center of spiritual power since the first hunters and gatherers decorated their homes with rock art some 30,000 years ago. Cave paintings can still be seen, their quality and quantity as impressive as the wildlife. Many paintings depict the white and black rhinos that still live here in great numbers. So do

leopards, cheetahs, and more than 300 species of birds, including the world's largest

The imposing granite "mountains"

number of raptors: eagles (the park is in fact shaped like a giant eagle), hawks, and owls. Lost amid this vast, natural rock garden is the Big Cave Camp, which accommodates just sixteen guests in a 2,000-acre wilderness on the border of the national park. Anything your hosts don't know about the area's geography, art, and wildlife isn't worth knowing. Dinner is served around a traditional outdoor fire, and if you're lucky enough to be there when a full moon illuminates the rock configurations, you'll understand why Rhodes could never leave.

WHAT: site, hotel. **WHERE:** Big Cave Camp is 28 miles/45 km from Bulawayo; transfers can be arranged by the camp. In Zimbabwe, tel 263/82-579-8811; res@prideof places.co.za; www.bigcave.co.za. **COST:** $215 per person, all-inclusive. **WHEN:** year-round. **BEST TIMES:** Sept–Nov, Mar–Jun.

The Smoke That Thunders

VICTORIA FALLS

Zimbabwe and Zambia

The falls are every bit as monumental and magnificent as you imagined, their noise greater than a million migrating wildebeests, their mists visible from 40 miles away. Dr. David Livingstone, who in 1855 became the first European to set eyes on them, named them after his queen (who unfortunately would never see them); they were soon widely recognized as one of the natural wonders of the world. A fantasy destination of every adventure traveler, the falls are a mile wide, spanning the entire breadth of the Zambezi River. As they crash 400 feet to the gorge below, they create a delicate, endless shower of rain, rainbows, and—if the moon is bright and full enough—lunar rainbows that drift in and out of view. At dawn and dusk the sky, water, and mist take on hues of pink and orange, especially during the wet season from March to May, when the cascades are at their greatest capacity and the opaque spray is kicked 1,000 feet into the sky. It is easy to imagine Dr. Livingstone's awe as he wrote: "On sights as beautiful as this, Angels, in their flight must have gazed." So was named today's 15-minute heart-stopping "Flight of the Angels" over the falls, which rates as one of the world's most scenic plane trips.

At the foot of the falls, the white-knuckle rapids provide some of the best rafting in the world. This is where the Zambezi plummets through the narrow basalt gorges separating Zambia and Zimbabwe—a mighty corridor of rushing, boiling white water interspersed with welcome havens of calm. The Zambezi's classic passages—with names like Ghostrider and Moemba Falls—are rated IV and V on a scale of I-VI (you'll walk around the *really* bad ones). Yet they are also some of the safest, in large part due to deep water and an absence of rocks midstream. The first day out following the put-in at Victoria Falls is the most adrenaline-packed: You bounce through ten of the world's biggest drops, reminiscent of those in the Colorado River in the Grand Canyon. Some local operators offer short-term, "crash" trips of one to three days, but it's a shame to travel such a distance only to shortchange the Mighty Z. Nothing tops it.

WHAT: site, experience. **HOW:** The "Flight of the Angels" and rafting are both offered by numerous local operators and can be booked through your hotel, safari outfitter, or a

Victoria Falls tour operator. **Cost:** "Flight of the Angels" about $110 per person. Rafting from $110 per person for half day; overnight trips are available.

In the Footsteps of Dr. Livingstone

VICTORIA FALLS HOTEL AND LIVINGSTONE ISLAND

Victoria Falls, Zimbabwe and Zambia

When it first opened in 1904, the Victoria Falls Hotel was an outpost of British civilization in the middle of nowhere. In the decades since, a number of hotels and lodges have sprung up near the falls,

as has a small tourist-trap city hawking souvenir paraphernalia galore. But this hotel will always be the elegant grand dame, a lovely and refurbished survivor of the colonial era following the falls' "discovery" by Dr. Livingstone. His presence, and that of his sometime co-explorer, Henry Stanley, is still tangible throughout the hotel. The invisibility of the falls from any area of the hotel only augments their aura of mystery and magic. As you walk past the hotel's green terraces and through gardens lush with bougainvillea and frangipani, you are drawn out of this shelter of human scale toward the raw power and roar of the nearby cataracts. As a hotel guest, you have the unmitigated luxury of visiting the falls repeatedly and at different times of the day; a dawn visit is a must. So is a trip to Livingstone Island, where Dr. Livingstone first set up camp; it is just one-half mile but an entire country away (you'll cross the border into Zambia en route).

A boat brings you to this World Heritage Site, a big chunk of island that splits the falls in two: No permanent structure can be built on the island, nor is there electricity; still, you'll be much better off than Livingstone, with a three-course lunch with a view, and sound effects you won't soon forget.

What: hotel, island. **Victoria Falls Hotel:** tel 263/13-44751, fax 263/13-44762; reservations@tvfh.africansun.co.zw; www.africansunhotels.com. *Cost:* doubles from $300. **Livingstone Island:** in Zambia, .5 mile/1 km upriver from Victoria Falls. In Zambia, contact Tongabezi Lodge, tel 260/3-327-450, fax 260/3-324-282; reservations@tongabezi.com. *Cost:* from $60. *When:* Jun–Nov. **Best times:** late Mar to mid-Nov.

Stanley and Livingstone didn't sleep here, but you can.

THE
MIDDLE
EAST

The Style and Charm of an Old Pasha's Palace

THE AMERICAN COLONY HOTEL

East Jerusalem, Israel

More than 100 years ago a wealthy landowning pasha built this fortress-like villa, including summer and winter rooms for his four wives. Today, as the American Colony Hotel, it is the city's most evocative and atmospheric hostelry. A well-known meeting place for international diplomats, correspondents, British and American expats, and—if one can believe the rumors—spies, it's as suggestive of romance and intrigue as *Casablanca*'s Rick's Café. Moorish arches, hand-painted tiles, and painted wooden-coffered ceilings adorn some of the more exotic guest rooms. The cool enclosed courtyard, complete with splashing fountain and lemon trees, is an inviting oasis for a drink or the Colony's famous Saturday buffet lunch of Middle Eastern and continental choices. English-owned, Swiss-managed, and with a predominantly Palestinian staff, a stay here is worth the splurge, especially for those checking into the Pasha's Style rooms, traditionally furnished and located in the original buildings.

Pasha-style elegance in Jerusalem

WHAT: hotel. **WHERE:** Nablus Road. Outside the old walls, a 10-minute walk from the Old City's Damascus Gate. Tel 972/2-627-9777, fax 972/2-627-9779; www.americancolony.com. **COST:** doubles $350, Pasha's Style rooms $425. Saturday buffet lunch $35. **BEST TIMES:** Apr–Sept.

A Timeless Tradition in a Biblical Town

CHRISTMAS IN BETHLEHEM

Palestinian Territories

Hope for peace springs eternal in Bethlehem, a Christian-Arab town caught in an eternally volatile valley. Now overcommercialized, Bethlehem was long the experience of a lifetime for Christians on Christmas

Eve, when international choirs filled Manger Square and the importance of being at Jesus' birthplace caused a real case of goose bumps. Pilgrims have been drawn to this site for more than sixteen centuries, since A.D. 326, when Queen Helena, mother of the Roman emperor Constantine the Great, searched out the grotto of Christ's birth, now marked by a fourteen-pronged silver star. Completed in A.D. 333, the Church of the Nativity is the oldest surviving church in the Holy Land and one of the most sacrosanct sites in Christianity. It is shared by the Greek Orthodox, Catholic, and Armenian churches, while the adjoining St. Catherine's Church is under the auspices of the Roman Catholic Franciscan Order. During less turbulent times, services were tradition-ally held on December 24 and 25 for Catholics, January 7 for Greek Orthodox, and January 19 for Armenians (these last two change slightly with each year's calendar). After December 24's special midnight Mass, Mass-goers lingered in the crowded Manger Square for a lively rendition of "Jingle Bells" and Christmas carols—in Arabic.

WHAT: site, event. **WHERE:** 6 miles/10 km west of Jerusalem. **HOW:** contact the English-speaking Franciscan Pilgrims' Office, Jaffa Gate, Jerusalem, as far in advance as possible for the status of Christmas activities. Tel 972/2-627-2697; fpo@cicts.org.

(Please note that tensions in the area have caused temporary suspension of these celebrations.)

A Mud Bath and a Good Soak for Whatever Ails You

THE DEAD SEA

En-gedi, Israel

Like a gondola ride in Venice or a camel ride at the Great Pyramids of Giza, a good bob in this famously buoyant body of water and a post-dip roll in the mud is the ultimate travel cliché—and, like many travel clichés, it is

not to be missed. At 1,305 feet below sea level, the Dead Sea is the lowest point on the face of the earth (Death Valley, in California, is America's lowest point at 282 feet below sea level), and its waters contain the highest concentration of salt anywhere. Join the tourists, grab a newspaper, and bob about like a human cork in—more specifically, on—waters with

If Le Méridien's spa can't relax you, the view will.

a salt concentration seven times greater than the Mediterranean's. Dead Sea mud has been part of the Holy Land's restorative and beauty regimen since the Queen of Sheba (Cleopatra was also known to come and take the cure). The mineral-rich area and its hot springs have spawned a treasure trove of spa facilities in and around the shoreside kibbutz En-gedi, a florid green oasis on a hillside of red desert rock. For years, the kibbutz's inn was the only place to stay, but more recent arrivals, such as the luxurious Le Méridien now fill out the spectrum. Le Méridien's supermodern spa treatments include facials and baths using mud, and rubdowns with Dead Sea salt crystals mixed with the scents of ancient oils.

WHAT: site, hotel. **EN-GEDI:** 1 hour east of Jerusalem by car. **LE MÉRIDIEN:** 20 miles/30 km from En-gedi. Tel 972/8-659-1234, fax 972/8-659-1235; info@fattal.co.il; www.star woodhotels.com. *Cost:* doubles from $430. Spa treatments extra.

A National Showcase for History, Anthropology, Art, and Culture

ISRAEL MUSEUM

Jerusalem, Israel

Even if you had no time at all to pause, an amble through the 20-acre Israel Museum would still give you a sense of the mother lode of Israel's history and heritage. The complex itself, opened in 1965, is an outstanding example of modern Israeli architecture, and it houses the world's most complete collection of Judaica, emphasizing the Ashkenazi and Sephardic cultures. Interiors of centuries-old synagogues from Germany, Italy, and most recently India, have been dismantled and reconstructed here. The Shrine of the Book is the subterranean home of a number of the fascinating Dead Sea Scrolls from the 1st century B.C.; its white onion-shaped dome was contoured to resemble the lids of the earthenware containers that held the scrolls when they were discovered by a shepherd in 1947. An archaeology wing displays a huge collection of important objects found throughout Israel. The 20-acre Billy Rose Sculpture Garden is the most exciting of the many outdoor exhibits; landscaped by the renowned Japanese American artist Isamu Noguchi, it contains classical and modern sculpture by major and lesser-known Israeli and international artists.

WHAT: site. **WHERE:** Ruppin Street, south of the Knesset. Tel 972/2-670-8811, fax 972/2-563-1833; www.imj.org.il. **COST:** $9. **WHEN:** Mon–Sat.

High-Status Choice of Presidents and Kings

THE KING DAVID HOTEL

Jerusalem, Israel

Symbol of a bygone era, the venerable King David Hotel has been compared to London's Savoy and Singapore's Raffles Hotel for its quality, style, and sense of traditional grandeur. Exceptional, uninterrupted views of Jerusalem's Old City from its gardens and terrace and the not-to-be-missed breakfast buffet are but two of many attributes that have secured this Israeli landmark's position as the country's highest-rated hotel. Whether ending your day with a sense of awe as the setting sun softly illuminates the yellow stone of one of the world's great cities, or beginning it with the justifiably famous *sabra* extravaganza that boasts as many as 100 deliciously fresh breakfast offerings, there's no place like the King David. Built in the 1930s, during the period of the British Mandate, the King David's ambience and history (and its consistently high-profile roster of famous guests) have survived a recent face-lift directed by theatrically inclined Adam Tihany. If only to dally until you can stand up again after breakfast, seek out a corner of the grand Art Deco, Egyptianesque lobby for some excellent people-watching.

The King David hosts many official dinners and state receptions.

WHAT: hotel. **WHERE:** 23 King David Street. Tel 972/2-620-8888, fax 972/2-620-8882; in the U.S., tel 800-223-7773; www.danhotels.com. **COST:** doubles from $420 (low season), from $480 (high season). Breakfast buffet for nonguests $35. **BEST TIMES:** Apr–Sept.

Sunrise and Heroism at a Legendary Mountain Fortress

MASADA

Israel

The haunting rock fortress of Masada is on a sheer-sided plateau surrounded by desert as desolate and dramatic as a moonscape. A palace complex and fortress built by Herod the Great 1,440 feet above the shores

Masada's excavation helped archaeologists re-create the famous battle between the Romans and the Jews.

of the Dead Sea, it was all but abandoned after his death. Eventually it became the stronghold of Jewish partisans in a battle against Rome in A.D. 73, when 967 Jewish men, women, and children defied their Roman attackers here for three years. When it was clear that they would be taken by more than 15,000 troops camped at the foot of the mountain, the Jews committed mass suicide.

It is a national tradition to make the ascent on foot to pay homage to one of the most tragic and heroic incidents in Jewish history. It is also a beautiful location from which to watch the sunrise. Arrive as early as possible if attempting either of the two footpaths, a must if you intend to beat the desert heat, or watch the sun levitate over Jordan and the Dead Sea. (You can descend by cable car.) An evening sound-and-light show at the foot of the mountain is as dramatic as you might expect.

WHAT: site, experience. **WHERE:** 1½-hour drive from Jerusalem, 2½ hours from Tel Aviv. Tel 972/7-6508-4207; www.parks.org.il. **COST:** admission $13 (includes cable car). **BEST TIMES:** Apr–Sept.

Genealogy of a People
Scattered Around the Globe

MUSEUM OF THE DIASPORA

Tel Aviv, Israel

A fascinating window into the world community of the Jewish people, this museum illuminates Israel's collective history and heritage. As Jerusalem embraces its millennia of history, the younger metropolis of

Tel Aviv looks to the future: A museum with modern-day, state-of-the-art methods used to weave the story of a people scattered around the globe could be found only here. That Jewish customs, costumes, music, and traditions are so diverse is enlightening but not surprising; the real surprise is the realization that all these communities stem from the same tribes. Though the recurring theme of "uniformity with variety" is explored in a number of educational and absorbing ways, this museum

is also fun. If you've never been to a Jewish wedding, you can experience one by using the many interactive multimedia exhibits here. Other exhibits offer intriguing glimpses of Jewish life in eighty different nations around the world, where Jews now speak 100 different languages.

WHAT: site. **WHERE:** Tel Aviv University campus. Tel 972/3-745-7800, fax 972/3-745-7831; bhmuseum@post.tau.ac.il; www.bh.org.il. **COST:** admission $9. **WHEN:** open Sun–Fri.

An Ancient Casbah by the Sea and an Underground City

OLD AKKO

Israel

L ocked within massive Ottoman-era walls, Old Akko (Acre) is genuine. It has not been gentrified, tidied up, reconstructed, or reborn as an artists' quarter. St. Francis and Marco Polo dropped by when Akko was the

regional seat of the Crusaders in the Holy Land. The present Old Akko was built in the 18th century on top of the Crusaders' city. The veritable warren of underground corridors, recently excavated, was once the home of 50,000 knights and inhabitants. Aboveground, the silhouettes of mosaic-adorned mosques, towering minarets, a Turkish bath, and caravansaries are monuments to the Ottoman influence and evoke the *Arabian Nights*.

18th-century Old Akko rests on more ancient sites.

Old Akko teems with real life, not tourists; the souks sell spices and household wares, not souvenir tchotchkes and postcards. The importance of Akko as a principal Mediterranean port can be traced to records dating from A.D. 1. Enjoy dinner at one of the many waterfront restaurants and admire the muscular seawalls. Hope for a table on the reed-shaded terrace of Abu Christo and order a feast of Middle Eastern appetizers and grilled fish fresh off the boat.

WHAT: site, restaurant. **OLD AKKO:** 14 miles/23 km north of Haifa. **ABU CHRISTO, OLD PORT:** tel 972/4-991-0065, fax 972/4-991-5653. *Cost:* dinner about $25. **BEST TIMES:** spring and fall.

Earth's Spiritual Center: Ancient Sites and Sacred Places

THE OLD CITY

Jerusalem, Israel

For many visitors, the Old City *is* Jerusalem, a vessel of more than 4,000 years of human experience. For the three great religions of the Western world, Judaism, Christianity, and Islam, it is one of the holiest of cities.

Punctuating the massive 16th-century city walls that Suleiman the Magnificent built atop ancient Roman ruins, eight fortified gates provide access to the Old City. The two most

The Dome of the Rock glitters inside and out with gilding, calligraphy, and elaborate mosaics.

important, the Jaffa and Damascus gates, lead into a warren of alleys and the distinctive sights, sounds, and scents of four ethnic districts and their markets: the Muslim Quarter (the largest and most full of character), the Christian Quarter, the Armenian Quarter, and the Jewish Quarter. Here in the heart of ancient Jerusalem there are no physical borders, but neighborhood divisions are hard to miss.

Many of the principal sites are practically on top of one another. The sumptuous, silver-domed El-Aksa Mosque is the largest and the most important place of Islamic prayer after Mecca and Medina. Revered by Muslims, the Temple Mount, the biblical Mount Moriah, is marked by the 24-karat-gilded Dome of the Rock, built *circa* A.D. 690 on the site where the prophet Mohammed ascended to heaven on a winged horse. It is also revered by the Jews as the site where Abraham was called upon by God to sacrifice his son (Isaac to Jews and Christians, Ishmael to Muslims), and is believed to have been the site of the altar of the first and second Temples of Judaism, since destroyed by invaders. Nearby is the Western (more descriptively, the Wailing) Wall, the last remnant of the walls that enclosed and supported the Temple Mount, and the holiest place of prayer in the Jewish world. Jews were barred from the area while it was under Jordanian control from 1949 to 1967. Try to be here when Orthodox Jews welcome Shabbat with prayer, song, and dance as the sun sets every Friday evening and it becomes an open-air synagogue. Each year tens of thousands of Christian pilgrims follow the Via Dolorosa past the Stations of the Cross on the route Christ is believed to have taken as he carried his cross to his crucifixion. Standing above Calvary (biblical Golgotha), the Church of the Holy Sepulcher is Christianity's holiest place, covering the sites of Jesus' crucifixion, burial, and resurrection.

After a day spent wandering the densely packed maze of the Christian Quarter's souk, rich in the scents of spices and sizzling *shashlik*, there is no better respite than to collapse at one of the Formica tables of Abu Shukri for a sampling of his hummus. Everyone in Israel begins a meal with hummus (mashed chickpeas seasoned with tahini, a sesame seed paste) and no one tires of something so simple and delicious. After mopping up your plate with warm pita bread (bring your own napkins), you'll understand why. The new Israeli cuisine may be poised to take off, but basic Arabic street fare has been a Middle Eastern favorite for a few thousand years. The best dishes are the *mezes*, or appetizers, which invariably include the celebrated hummus.

WHAT: site, restaurant. **THE OLD CITY:** a scenic 90-minute train ride from Tel Aviv. **ABU SHUKRI:** 63 Al-Wad Street, in the Old City near the Fifth Station of the Cross on the Via Dolorosa. Tel 972/2-627-1538. *Cost:* hummus $3, full meal $5. **BEST TIMES:** Apr–Sept.

Horseback Tours amid the Blooming Tapestry of the Galilee

VERED HAGALIL

Galilee, Israel

The Galilee is Israel's most fertile region, a historically rich parcel of rolling land blanketed by an ocean of wildflowers and blossoming trees in February and March. The terrain is rough and wild and best explored by horseback along ancient trails. But human endeavors have left patchworks of orange groves, rich vegetation, fruit orchards, and vineyards. On a scenic ridge enjoying wide vistas across the blue, freshwater Sea of Galilee and the Golan Heights beyond, is Vered Hagalil, the privately owned farm and ranch of Yehuda and Yonah Avni. Their twenty Arabian and quarter horses can be rented for guided trail rides by the hour and day; or take a weeklong guided pack trip around the harp-shaped lake or off into the hills to biblical sites such as Nazareth and the Mount of the Beatitudes, staying in a kibbutz, in an Arab village, or with some of the Avnis' friends. Although this is the best-organized riding operation in Israel, not everyone comes for the riding. (There are also jeep tours and, for the truly stationary, pool lounging.) Most guests try to be back in time for the home-cooked meals, an eclectic mix of Middle Eastern and American cuisine. Three generations of the affable Avni family and a young, personable staff imbue their working ranch with an informal hospitality and heartfelt love of the Galilee. It's a side of Israel that the package tourist rarely sees.

Riding through ancient ruins and wild landscapes

WHAT: site, hotel, experience. **WHERE**: 3 miles/5 km from the northwestern shores of the Sea of Galilee; 100 miles/161 km from Tel Aviv; 54 miles/87 km from Haifa. Tel 972/4-693-5785, fax 972/4-693-4964; vered@ veredhagalil.co.il; www.veredhagalil.co.il. **COST**: doubles from $135 (weekdays); 2-night minimum requested for weekends. $30 for 1-hour trail rides; prices vary for longer rides. **BEST TIMES**: Feb–Jun and Oct–Dec.

Splendid Remnants of a Golden Age

JERASH

Jordan

Widely held to be the best-preserved Roman provincial city in the Middle East—if not the world—Jerash (ancient Gerasa) is an archaeological masterpiece framed by the fertile hills of Gilead. Founded by the soldiers of Alexander the Great during the 4th century B.C., Jerash later joined the affluent and cosmopolitan cities of the Roman Decapolis, reaching its zenith around A.D. 150. Its prosperity was based on caravan trade, agriculture, and mining, and its citizens spent lavishly, erecting splendid buildings in a distinctive "Oriental Baroque" style. Its golden age was during the 2nd and 3rd centuries A.D., and the town's impressive array of fifteen churches dates back to the centuries just after. The Roman ruins include a triumphal arch, an unusual oval-shaped forum, a stadium, a monumental fountain, hot and cold baths, and numerous temples. A wide street of columns leads to the city's most splendid monument: the Temple of Artemis, patron goddess of Jerash, which still dominates the town center. If you time your trip for July or August, you may stumble upon the popular three-week Jerash Festival, when performances of music, dance, and drama take place in timeless open-air venues such as the Forum and the South Theater.

WHAT: site. **WHERE**: 30 miles/48 km north of Amman. **HOW**: Wilderness Travel offers a twice-annual trip throughout Syria and Jordan. In the U.S., tel 800-368-2794 or 510-558-2488, fax 510-558-2489; www.wildernesstravel.com. *Cost*: 16-day all-inclusive land package from $4,995 per person. *When*: Apr, Sept, and Nov. **BEST TIMES**: Mar–Jun, Jul and Aug for Jerash Festival, and Sept–Nov.

A City Half as Old as Time

PETRA

Jordan

The rose-red city of Petra, one of the wonders of the ancient world, has parts that are miraculously preserved and others that have been eroded and sculpted by floods and the elements. Until Swiss explorer Johann Ludwig

The Palace Tomb is thought to be modeled on a Roman palace.

Burckhardt "rediscovered" it in 1812, Petra had been forgotten for centuries. It can be reached on foot by the Siq Gorge, a narrow, winding passageway at times no wider than 6 feet, with rock faces on either side as high as a four-story building. At the end of this eerie, mile-long passageway, a magical sight looms through the fissure ahead: the Khaznah or Treasury, a soaring, classical Greek–style temple hewn right into the sheer face of a 130-foot cliff. It dates back to 56 B.C. and is one of the best-preserved of Petra's wonders. Petra, which means "rock," was a fortress city and thriving trade center whose inhabitants carved houses, temples, and tombs, sometimes with extremely elaborate and columned facades, out of the natural canyon walls. The area, 2 square miles in size, is as

remarkable for the number and variety of the rock-cut monuments as it is for the myriad hues of the rock and the ever-changing play of light as the desert sun makes its way across the sky.

The most desirable times to see this extraordinary city—dawn or dusk—are next to impossible unless you are a guest at the miragelike Hotel Taybet Zaman on the ancient road to Aqaba. Once a small Bedouin village, it grew over the centuries until, deserted and partially destroyed by an earthquake, it was transformed into a welcoming desert hostelry under the auspices of Jordan's then-queen Noor. Happily, its traditional Bedouin charm and character have survived intact. The original stone bungalows have been appointed with locally made carvings and carpets; the simple architecture and gardens evoke a desert-locked oasis; and the gracious local staff offer Arab specialties with traditional hospitality in the bakery and restaurant.

WHAT: site, hotel. **PETRA:** 3 hours by car from Amman. **HOTEL TAYBET ZAMAN:** 5 miles/8 km from Petra in Wadi Moussa. Tel 962/3-215-0111, fax 962/3-215-0101. **COST:** doubles $150. **HOW:** in the U.S., contact Frosch Travel (specializing in all of Jordan's highlights), tel 866-841-3555; travelwithus@frosch.com; www.froschvacations.com. **BEST TIMES:** Mar–May, Sept–Nov, and whenever the late-afternoon sun turns the city a deep pink.

Newest of Destinations in the Oldest of Nations

AL BUSTAN PALACE HOTEL

Muscat, Oman

Consistently voted one of the best hotels in the Middle East, the Al Bustan Palace is as favored by oil tycoons used to sheiklike pampering as by Western travelers merely hoping for such. The Sultanate of Oman has a

rich heritage of hospitality, and the Middle East–meets-West marriage of Arab romance and snap-to efficiency is seamless in this

country only recently opened to outside influence. It is a fascinating harmony not easily achieved in a nation enamored of its ancient

Complete with a private cove

for a Gulf summit meeting, Al Bustan was the dream of the nation's leader, Sultan Qaboos bin Said. The hotel's natural setting includes a dramatic mountain backdrop and its own cove on the Gulf of Oman. Indoors, the awesome lobby soars with the Islamic lines and graceful opulence of Omani architecture at its most regal. At the very least, stay for high tea. Those with deep pockets should check into the Arabic Suite to experience life as an emir.

traditions as well as its nascent oil-based wealth. *Bustan* means "garden," and there are 200 acres of them here—an oasis created by royalty for royalty. Built in 1985 as the venue

WHAT: hotel. **WHERE:** 6 miles/10 km from Muscat's downtown commercial area. Tel 968/799-666, fax 968/799-600; in the U.S., tel 888-424-6835; albustan@interconti.com; www.interconti.com. **COST:** sea-view doubles $366, Arabic Suite $513. **BEST TIMES:** Oct–Apr.

A Microcosm of Oman's Early Days

NIZWA

Oman

While coastal Oman was involved in lucrative sea trade with Zanzibar, India, and China in medieval times, inland Nizwa was the seat of the imams who ruled much of the interior for centuries. Renowned as a center of learning and famous for its ancient poets (and as the birthplace of Sinbad the Sailor), the city is also blessed with an imposing circular 17th-century fort. A recent restoration of the fort and neighboring historical dwellings has garnered international awards. Nizwa sits on a scenic road from Muscat that skirts two of the country's major mountain ranges, affording visitors views of some of the most diverse and beautiful countryside in the Gulf nations. As the center for Oman's jewelry and crafts industries, Nizwa draws shopping-minded visitors here on whirlwind day trips from Muscat. The curved *kanjar* daggers are manufactured here—prized symbols of Omani masculinity, they are now worn mainly in ceremonies. The city's large blue-domed mosque marks the site of a souk whose silver merchants by now are accustomed to today's souvenir-hunting Westerners.

The Nizwa Fort was built in the 17th century.

A more genuine air is found in the tourist-free byways, where the haggling and touting continue with an area reserved just for dates, another only for goats.

WHAT: town. **WHERE:** 108 miles/174 km southwest of Muscat. **WHERE TO STAY:** Although generally done as a day trip from Muscat, a reliable hotel choice in Nizwa is The Golden Tulip. Tel 968/2543-1616, fax 968/2543-1619; www.goldentulipnizwa.com. *Cost:* doubles from $180. **BEST TIMES:** Oct–Apr, Fri for livestock market.

Sentinels of the Past

OLD FORTS ROUTE

Muscat, Oman

Many of Oman's stalwart forts are reminders of the years 1507–1650, when the Portuguese controlled Muscat (a rich and thriving port since the dawn of Islam) and Oman's 1,000-mile coastline on the cusp of the Arabian Peninsula. Forts built by the Omani before or after this period (when Omani rule stretched from Zanzibar to Pakistan) are Arabic in design, with a Persian influence. Many served as a combination royal residence and seat of government, sometimes containing a mosque, school, or prison. Oman's forts are so much a part of its heritage that the image of the fort is seen everywhere, influencing the design of contemporary buildings and even the public telephone booths in Muscat, the sultanate's capital city. One need only look up on the way in from the airport to see the twin forts of Jalali and Merani, built by the Portuguese to guard the ancient trade and caravan routes and fend off rival foreign powers who scented profit in the Gulf of Oman. The Portuguese were never able to penetrate the interior, due to the hostility of the Omani as well as the mountain barriers.

WHAT: site. **HOW:** in Muscat, Zahara Tours organizes customized trips to the forts and other sites. Tel 968/2440-0844, fax 968/2440-0855; www.zaharatours.com. **COST:** prices vary depending on itinerary and size of group. **BEST TIMES:** Oct–Apr.

Remnants of Past Glory Endure

MADA'IN SALEH

Saudi Arabia

Comparisons to Jordan's pink-stone city of Petra are inevitable, although Mada'in Saleh is more compelling in many ways. Less known, less accessible, and therefore less visited than Petra, Mada'in Saleh, carved out of large outcrops of rock in the Arabian Desert, is known for tombs dating back to 100 B.C. Though their design is considered less spectacular than those in Petra, the local stone is more resistant to the elements, so the tombs are slightly better preserved. However, erosion has resulted in some bizarre formations, and multicolored mineral strata are revealed and warmed by the changing light of the day. Due north of the Wadi Hadhramamawt in what is now Yemen, Mada'in Saleh was a stopover on the famous frankincense route for caravans transporting the precious cargo and other aromatics and spices to the Mediterranean ports of Syria. But Mada'in Saleh's heyday was short-lived (the last tomb was built in A.D. 76); the Romans, always ingenious, began to ship their cherished incense by boat on the Red Sea directly to Egypt.

WHAT: site. **WHERE:** 208 miles/330 km north of Medina. **WHERE TO STAY:** The Mada'in Saleh Hotel offers accommodations and

Qasr Al Farid is Mada'in Saleh's largest tomb.

tour packages. Tel 966/4-884-2888, fax 966/4-884-2515; info@mshotel.com.sa; www.mshotel.com.sa. Cost: doubles from $70 (low season), $75 (high season). Packages of 3–5 days require a minimum of 4 people. **BEST TIMES:** Oct–Apr.

A Gateway to Mecca Holds On to Its History

OLD JEDDAH

Jeddah, Saudi Arabia

The timeless stream of Muslims en route to Mecca, Islam's holiest of cities, long ago transformed the Red Sea gateway of Jeddah into a thriving metropolis. It is the Rome of Arabia in terms of pilgrim traffic and trade.

Unlike much of the Arab world, Jeddah has managed to build around, instead of on top of, its history. In the Old Jeddah district, where silk route merchants would still feel pretty much at home, the original walls have been torn down, though the gates were left standing. The rest remains a protected urban area; many of the houses

The 106 rooms of Nassif House are now a cultural center.

are made of coral quarried from reefs in the Red Sea. The more impressive homes, of traditional carved wooden architecture, belonged to the merchant clans who filled their coffers from the pilgrim trade. Today some of these houses are museums; others are crumbling because their successful owners have moved their families to modern highrises. Old Jeddah's souk is considered the best left in Saudi Arabia; with most souks having morphed into shopping malls hawking Western-made goods and fashions, this vibrant place has retained much of its traditional flavor.

WHAT: site. **WHERE:** on the Red Sea, 44 miles/71 km west of Mecca.

The World's First Shopping Mall

THE COVERED SOUKS OF ALEPPO

Syria

Since Roman times, Aleppo has been a major trading center between Asia and the Mediterranean, with a strong corps of European merchants wheeling and dealing in the local bazaars. A timeless energy of commerce and a vaguely European spirit linger on in the fabulous labyrinth of the city's covered souks. This may be one of the best places in the Middle East to experience the exuberant bazaar life of a bygone era. The souks in this ancient crossroad still peddle cinnamon, saffron, cumin, coriander, carcasses of goats and lambs, roasted nuts, and the delicious pistachios for which Aleppo has been renowned for centuries. Beneath a stone vault built by the Ottomans, close to 20 miles of covered passages are abuzz with the hubbub of everyday shopping and the interactions of Arabs, Kurds, Armenians, Turks, and Iranians. When the *Orient Express* used to terminate in Aleppo, there was only one place to stay: the Baron Hotel, opened in 1909. The terrace is still a great place to recharge after a morning in the world's first shopping mall. An illustrious clientele used to do just that—Lawrence of Arabia's unpaid bill is on display in the lobby.

WHAT: site, hotel. **BARON HOTEL:** Baron Street, west of the clock tower, near Yarmouk Street. Tel 963/212-110-880, fax 963/212-218-164; hotelbaron@mail.sy. *Cost:* doubles from $80. **BEST TIMES:** Mar–May, Aug–Nov.

A Lonely Crusader Outpost Impervious to the Onslaught of Time

KRAK DES CHEVALIERS

Syria

In 1909, before he was Lawrence of Arabia, twenty-year-old T. E. Lawrence toured dozens of the Holy Land's Crusader castles and described Krak des Chevaliers as "the finest castle in the world. Certainly the most picturesque I have ever seen—quite marvelous." Sitting alone like a vast battleship on an impenetrable spur above a vast plain, it remains today the grandest and one of the best-preserved medieval castles in the world. Most of it was superbly constructed and expanded by the Knights of St. John from A.D. 1144 onward. They chose as their site the only significant break in the mountain range between Turkey and Lebanon, on an age-old caravan route between Damascus and inland Syria. So mighty was this moated bastion, whose fortified walls are studded with thirteen watchtowers, that it was never penetrated. Two of the era's greatest warriors, including the feared but chivalrous Saladin, were said to have taken one look and retreated without attempting an attack. In the early 1800s Swiss explorer Johann Ludwig Burckhardt, who would go on to discover Petra

and Abu Simbel, described Krak as "one of the finest buildings of the Middle Ages I ever saw." It remains in an impressive state of preservation, thanks to some light restoration carried out by the French in 1936.

WHAT: site. **WHERE:** a long but doable day trip from Damascus in the direction of Aleppo. **COST:** admission. **BEST TIMES:** spring and fall.

A Jewel of Islamic Architecture

OMAYYAD MOSQUE

Damascus, Syria

Getting lost in the backstreets of its Old City is reason enough to spend a few days in Damascus. Anchoring the evocative quarter and its covered streets of stalls is the magnificent Omayyad Mosque, one of Islam's greatest architectural monuments. It is an exotic and intriguing Syrian microcosm, a sacred place of worship for women whose veils may conceal smart European fashions, and men in *jelabiyyehs* or managerial types between meetings. As one of the claimants to the title "oldest continuously inhabited city," Damascus can trace its history back to the 3rd millennium B.C. from excavations carried out in the courtyard of the Omayyad Mosque. On a more contemporary note, this cool marble courtyard is the loveliest respite in town from

the day's heat and bustle. It was once the site of the Basilica of St. John the Baptist (the saint's head is believed to be buried in the mosque's sanctuary) until the Muslims arrived in A.D. 636. The mosque is ideally situated for a quiet, reflective moment after you've meandered about Souq al-Hamadiyyeh, the main market street just to the west: the perfect place for time travel.

WHAT: site. **WHERE:** male and female tourists welcome to enter the mosque by the gate in the northern wall at Bab al'Amarah.

Queen of the Desert

PALMYRA

Syria

Even if you have seen enough historical sites to last you a lifetime, Palmyra ("City of Palms") amazes. "It is lovely and fantastic and unbelievable," enthused Agatha Christie, who penned *Come, Tell Me How You Live*

A colonnaded street in Palmyra

while living in Syria. Palmyra has been mentioned in historical records as far back as the 19th century B.C., when it was known as Tadmor. An essential watering hole on the Silk Road and a vital link between the Mediterranean and China, Palmyra became fabulously wealthy by levying heavy tolls on caravans transporting precious cargo on their way to and from the Arabian Gulf and beyond. The incomparable ruins that spread across the 100-acre site today date to its zenith as a 2nd-century A.D. city with a population of 200,000 that prospered and mimicked Rome in grandeur. Since excavations began in 1924, the Temple of Baal (circa A.D. 32) and the amphitheater have been partially reconstructed. The Great Colonnade, Palmyra's main street and backbone, is almost a mile long and is lined with more than 300 standing columns. An onsite museum houses an excellent collection of artifacts, mosaics, and statuary found at the site. The natural beauty of Palmyra is enhanced by the almost complete absence of modern buildings.

WHAT: site. **WHERE:** 135 miles/217 km from Damascus. **HOW:** Wilderness Travel offers a tour of Syria and Jordan in Apr and Oct. In the U.S., tel 800-368-2794 or 510-558-2488, fax 510-558-2489; info@wildernesstravel.com; www.wildernesstravel.com. **COST:** 9-day all-inclusive land package from $4,295 per person. **BEST TIMES:** Mar–Nov and late Dec–early Jan.

An Oasis with One Foot in Abu Dhabi, One in Oman

AL-AIN

Abu Dhabi, United Arab Emirates (UAE)

Al-Ain/Buraimi straddles the border of the United Arab Emirates and the sultanate of Oman, and the halves of the oasis reflect the overnight wealth of the former and the more reticent conservatism of the latter.

The place is a favorite weekend escape for local emiratis and expats of Abu Dhabi and Dubai as well as visiting businessmen curious to see life beyond the oil-rich capitals, where nothing seems more than thirty years old. A peek into oasis life—where black-masked and -veiled women trailed by barefoot children slip through the cool, winding, unnamed dirt roads of the palm-shaded town—could be a vignette from 400 years ago. A camel racetrack, daily camel market, and livestock souk add character and draw a colorful following of Bedouins and people from faraway towns. The souk is a good spot for buying Omani goods and handmade silver crafts from Muscat—or maybe you're in the market for a goat. Like a 21st-century mirage in the midst of the desert, the Al-Ain Hilton offers modern-day amenities plus a luxurious pool and sports facilities that are appreciated after a morning visit to the dusty, boisterous marketplace. An in-house agency organizes safaris to archaeological sites accessible only by camel, and overnight trips that let you sleep under the stars or in Bedouin tents.

WHAT: site, hotel. **AL-AIN:** a 1½-hour drive from Abu Dhabi. Equidistant from Abu Dhabi and Dubai (82 miles/132 km). **AL-AIN**

HILTON: tel 971/2-681-1900; alain@hilton.com; www.hilton.com. *Cost:* doubles $200. **BEST TIMES:** Oct–Mar.

The Queen of Arabia and Her Tower of Wonder

BURJ AL ARAB

Dubai, United Arab Emirates (UAE)

The fifty-six-story Burj Al Arab ("The Arabian Tower") is the world's tallest hotel, shaped like the billowing sail of a traditional Arab dhow and rising out of the Arabian Gulf on its own man-made island, an homáge to Dubai's

seafaring heritage. Petrodollars paid for the five-year construction of this technical and engineering marvel, which upon its completion in 1999 immediately became the icon of tiny but confident Dubai, the most progressive, aggressive, and dynamic of the United Arab Emirates' seven sheikdoms—a kind of Arabian Hong Kong, with the design sense of Miami and the flash of Las Vegas. Conceived to pamper and amaze jillionaire sheiks and jaded international execs, the Burj al Arab is a cool oasis of unfathomable luxury, part James Bond and part glory-days Hollywood. It creates an over-the-top impression from the moment you enter its atrium lobby (at 600 feet the world's tallest) to the moment you step aboard the luxury submarine that takes you to its glass-walled seafood restaurant, submerged beneath the gulf. Rare multicolored

marble and 21,500 square feet of 22-karat gold leaf embellish this symbol of the New Arabia. Its enormous suite-only duplex guest quarters are some of the largest and most opulent in the world, outfitted with the latest technical wizardry and a private butler to show you how it all works. The *ne plus ultra* are the two 8,400-square-foot Royal Suite penthouses, two floors with their own private cinemas, meeting rooms, dining rooms, dressing rooms, rotating beds, and private elevator. They can be yours for a cool $7,000 a night.

WHAT: hotel. **WHERE:** Jumeirah Beach Rd., 10 miles/15 km south of Dubai. Tel 971/4-301-7777, fax 971/4-301-7000; BAA reservations@jumeirah.com; www.jumeirah.com. *Cost:* double suites from $1,350. **BEST TIMES:** Dec–Mar, when the heat is most tolerable; Fri mornings for the camel races.

Fort Knox on Sale—Arabia's Gold Rush

THE GOLD SOUK

Dubai, United Arab Emirates (UAE)

You've got to see this place to believe it. Even die-hard nonshoppers must visit Dubai's Gold Souk as part of their cultural experience if not for a shopping spree. Probably the largest such market in Arabia—and that

says a lot, given the local penchant for bauble buying—this
gold souk has held out after most
souks have gone the way of the
modern boutique-filled shopping
mall. Even seasoned souk-goers of

prepared
le-dazzle
here are
women
t elabo-
fted for
Expect *Window-shopping with the sheiks*
imaginable design
(and price) never

....uoms that make up the
United Arab Emirates, Dubai was the only
one to become wealthy through trade rather
than oil (although the discovery of oil in the
1960s sped up the modernization of an
already booming country). Bearing in mind
that trade was originally built on gold smug-

gling, it is not surprising that an anything-
goes spirit of capitalism flourishes here. And
here's the best news: The prices are actually
reasonable.

WHAT: site. **WHERE:** along Sikkat Al-Khail
St., near the Suq Deira. **HOW:** in the U.S.,
Worldview Travel can arrange any trip to Dubai,
customized to your interests and budget. Tel
714-540-7400, fax 714-979-6040; shahla@
worldviewtravel.com.

The Pearl of Arabia Felix:
A Time-Warped Capital, for Centuries Closed to Foreigners

OLD SANA'A

Sana'a, Yemen

Sana'a claims to be the oldest inhabited city on earth, and although other
cities clamor for the same title, visitors are convinced. Yemen's capital,
said to have been founded by a son of Noah, is bewitching, and its highlight

is the ancient medina (non-European) quarter,
Old Sana'a. Extraordinarily ornate mud-brick
houses—often four or five stories tall and
some believed to be more than 400 years
old—are built in a unique 1,000-year-old
high-rise style. Colored-glass windows and
intricate gingerbread facades embellished or
covered with brilliant white gypsum lend a
whimsical wedding-cake appearance to the
city. Shutters and doors are painted blue, and

some of the older windows are made with
panes of paper-thin alabaster. The narrow
streets seem straight out of the *Arabian
Nights*. More than forty souks are found within
the Suq al-Milh, where frankincense and
myrrh are still sold, together with roasted
locusts, sticky dates, sequined fabrics, and
the spices that make the local cuisine one of
the most delicately delicious in the Middle
East.

All 106 of the city's mosques were built before the 11th century.

WHAT: site. **WHERE TO STAY:** the Taj Sheba, Ali Abdolmoghini Street, is the best situated of the capital's hotels, a 10-minute walk from the old section of town; its Golden Oasis Restaurant has some of the best Yemeni cuisine in town. Tel 967/1-272-372, fax 967/1-274-129; info@tajshebahotel.com; www.tajsheba hotel.com. *Cost:* doubles from $135 (low season), from $175 (high season). Dinner at Golden Peacock $35. **BEST TIMES:** Sept–Apr.

Manhattan of the Desert

SHIBAM

Wadi Hadhramawt, Yemen

Yemen's ancient Incense Route ran through Wadi Hadhramawt, a remote but spectacular oasis of fertile fields and orchards framed by arid, stony desert plateaus. It is the largest *wadi* (oasis) in the Arabian Peninsula.

The region prospered throughout the ages as caravans laden with frankincense—the most valuable currency of its time, more valuable than gold—and myrrh gave rise to wealthy cities that flourished along their routes. In its heyday Shibam was the most celebrated Arabic Islamic city in Yemen. Like giant sand castles, nearly 500 clay-tower buildings of up to eight stories are crammed into less than a third of a square mile. Most date from the 16th century, but many are hundreds of years older. They are only marginally distinguishable to the outsider from those that were built only 50 to 100 years ago, thanks to strictly enforced codes that dictate the use of traditional materials.

Shibam is encircled by town walls made from the same baked-clay bricks. It has been the capital of Wadi Hadhramawt since the 3rd century A.D., and is believed to look today much as it did in the 1500s. Women veiled in black and wearing tall witchlike caps of straw slip along the shaded back alleyways. Accommodations in Shibam are limited to the small, simple, and lovely Shibam Guest House. Most visitors head down the road to Say'un, the valley's largest town, worth seeing in its own right, with some of the most beautiful mosques and minarets in all Yemen.

WHAT: town. **WHERE:** 1-hour flight followed by 30-minute drive from Sana'a; 6 hours by car. **HOW:** in Sana'a, Universal Touring Company specializes in customized itineraries to Wadi Hadhramawt. Tel 967/1-272-861, fax 967/1-272-134; touring@utcyemen.com; www. utcyemen.com. **BEST TIMES:** Mar and Oct.

ASIA

EAST ASIA

SOUTH AND CENTRAL ASIA

SOUTHEAST ASIA

EAST ASIA

From the Humble to the Theatrical

CLASSIC RESTAURANTS OF BEIJING

Beijing Province, China

L eaving Beijing without having experienced Peking duck is tantamount to bypassing bistecca alla fiorentina in Florence. Head for Quanjude Roast Duck Restaurant. It is one of the oldest restaurants in Beijing (dating back

to 1864) and the most popular place to experience China's culinary gem. The centuries-old procedure begins at special farms on the outskirts of town, where white-feathered Beijing ducks are raised on grain and soybeans to fatten them up. Once in the kitchen, the ducks are hung to dry and later lacquered with molasses, filled with air, hung on hooks, and slowly roasted over an open fire—which diners can watch through a glass wall. The entire duck is ceremoniously served in stages—first the plump boneless meat and crispy skin with side dishes of shallots, plum sauce, and crepes.

Foreigners will feel pretty proud of themselves for having ventured outside their hotel's safe, tame restaurants . . . until they catch a glimpse of what the local family at the next table has ordered: duck's gizzards, tongues, wings, hearts— everything from the web to the quack.

If your visit to the Forbidden City has fostered a fas-

Enjoy cuisine and architecture from centuries past at Fangshan.

cination with things imperial, dine at Fangshan Restaurant. Since 1925 this prestigious restaurant has been preserving the extravagant cuisine of the Qing dynasty (1644–1911), using the favored recipes of the 19th-century imperial court. In a lavish theatrical setting, the staff (in full vintage imperial garb) shows travelers what it might have been like to dine with the last Dowager Empress, who had 128 cooks. The kitchen still produces over-the-top banquets, and traditional delicacies such as shark's fin or bird's nest soup are fit for a royal palate. Fangshan's setting couldn't be more appropriate: an ancient pavilion on an island in the middle of Bei Hai Lake, just past the Bridge of Perfect Wisdom.

For a similar yet less theatrical, more intimate experience, try the Family Li Restaurant, where six family members work around the clock to duplicate the royal recipes of the Qing dynasty for eight to twelve extremely lucky diners. Handed down by a great-grandparent who worked at the imperial court, hundreds of these ancient recipes were destroyed during the Cultural Revolution in the 1960s but have been recalled to the best of the Li family's ability. The results are worth the two-month wait for dinner reservations. Visiting diplomats, local expats, the occasional Rockefeller, and ardent food lovers from around the world all make their way to this tiny restaurant, where they dine at the lone table lit by a single fluorescent bulb.

WHAT: restaurant. **QUANJUDE ROAST DUCK RESTAURANT:** 32 Qianmen Dajie, at the end of a maddeningly elusive alleyway. Tel 86/10-6511-2418. *Cost:* duck dinner $20. **FANGSHAN RESTAURANT:** Bei Hai Park, northwest of the Forbidden City. Tel 86/10-6401-1879. *Cost:* dinner $25. *Best times:* in late summer, for Bei Hai Lake's famous lotus blossoms. **FAMILY LI RESTAURANT:** 11 Yangfang Hutong, De Nei Dajie; Xicheng District in western Beijing. Tel 86/10-6618-0107. *How:* in the U.S., Geographic Expeditions helps with special requests for lunch or dinner for clients of their customized trips. Tel 800-777-8183 or 415-922-0448, fax 415-346-5535; info@geoex.com; www.geoex.com. *Cost:* about $50.

Where Mere Mortals Dared Not Enter

THE FORBIDDEN CITY

Beijing, Beijing Province, China

The magnificent Forbidden City, so named because it was off-limits to commoners for 500 years, was the imperial court for twenty-four emperors from the early days of the Ming dynasty in the 15th century until the fall of the Qing dynasty in 1911. It is the largest, most complete, and best-preserved cluster of ancient buildings in China, representing the work of battalions of laborers. Fires and lootings over the years have left a largely post-18th-century shell that mimics its original layout, and much of its storied wealth and opulent furnishings are long gone. Nonetheless, this vast complex of halls, pavilions, courtyards, and walls is a masterwork of architectural balance, monumental but never oppressive. A self-guiding tape narrated by Roger Moore helps bring it alive, with tales of eunuchs, concubines, ministers, priests, court intrigues, and terrific excesses. Occupying more than 183 acres, the expansive complex earns the title of "city." It was not unusual for emperors and servants alike never to venture beyond the moat-surrounded 35-foot walls and formidable gates—ever. That they believed themselves to be at the cosmic center of the universe is a fantasy visitors can readily appreciate today.

WHAT: site. **WHERE:** also called the Imperial Palace (Gugong) or the Palace Museum, the Forbidden City is adjacent to Tiananmen Square, at the center of the city. **COST:** admission. **BEST TIMES:** May to mid-Jun and late Aug to early Nov.

The tiled rooftops of the Forbidden City

Ancient China's Work of Genius

THE GREAT WALL

Beijing Province, China

Long a symbol of the country's strength, the Great Wall of China—Wan Li Chang Cheng, or the Long Wall of Ten Thousand Li—has captured the imagination of people worldwide throughout its history. Said to be the only manmade structure visible from the moon, it was built piecemeal over a period of 2,000 years as a defense against marauding nomadic tribes from the north. Some sections may have been constructed as early as the 8th century B.C., but it was not until the unification of the empire in 221 B.C. that the various sections of the wall were linked up to span some 3,750 miles. Over a million workers—peasants, soldiers, and prisoners—were involved in the construction, building it wide enough to allow ten soldiers or five horses to travel abreast between the 10,000 battlements and watchtowers. The wall was primarily built to keep foreigners out, but today it's a primary draw that lures them in. Only one third of the original wall remains, and on the average day its restored viewing points are barely able to accommodate the hordes of tourists and the carnival of kitsch souvenir vendors and T-shirt stands. Despite the zoolike atmosphere, a glimpse of the wall, serpenting its way across the serene mountains and valleys like an imperial ridge-backed dragon, is the only real way to understand what a colossal human feat it represents.

WHAT: site. **WHERE:** the traditional viewing spot is the restored mile-long section at Badaling, 50 miles/80 km northwest of downtown Beijing. The slightly less touristy alternative is Mutianyu, 57 miles/91 km northeast of Beijing. Simatai, 69 miles/111 km northeast of Beijing, is the least congested, for the moment. **BEST TIMES:** late afternoon, after bus tours have left.

A showcase of superb engineering

A Pedicab into the Vanishing Alleyways of Old Peking

THE *HUTONGS* OF BEIJING

Beijing Province, China

The bustling, polluted Chinese capital of American fast food, traffic jams, and aesthetics-free architecture is one of Beijing's two sides. The other can be glimpsed by taking a pedicab trip through narrow, labyrinthine alleyways *(hutongs)* where only the awning-covered vehicles can maneuver. In quiet corners of Beijing, far from the Forbidden City and Tiananmen Square, honking horns give way to the occasional ding of bicycle bells and the sound of chickens and ducks from inside walled courtyards—the lingering vestiges of traditional everyday life in a city projected to reach a population of 15 million by the year 2040. Go soon: The simple single-story houses in these pre-Communist urban villages are quickly being torn down and replaced by sterile high-rise monoliths and Western-style shopping malls, and in the process, traditional neighborhoods and lifestyles that go back to the Qing dynasty and beyond are being lost.

WHAT: experience. **WHERE:** guided tours leave from the north gate of Bei Hai Park. **HOW:** contact the local tourist office, tel 86/10-6615-9097, or book through your hotel. **COST:** $30 per person. **WHEN:** twice daily.

The Magical China of Poets and Painters

THE LI RIVER

Guilin, Guangxi, China

Reputed to possess the most beautiful mountains and rivers under heaven, Guangxi Province has been eulogized for thirteen centuries by painters and writers who tried to capture its unearthly karst formations on paper.

A cruise down the Li River is like entering a classic Chinese scroll painting of mist, mountains, and rivers. From Guilin, the jade-green Li wends its way through spectacular, almost surreal scenery of humpbacked and eroded shapes with whimsical names like Bat Hill, Five Tigers Catch a Goat, and Painting Brush Peak. The timeless riverside landscape seems oblivious to the constant stream of tour boats that ply single-file past picturesque villages where young boys bathe the family water buffalo, women wash their clothes, and farmers plow the rice fields. Some fishermen on skinny bamboo rafts still employ cormorants that are trained to dive and trap fish in their beaks. A ring placed around their necks stops them from swallowing the catch.

The small town of Yangshuo is the southern terminus of the cruises, and though it may not be the "real China"—cybercafés, B&Bs, and cafés offering "American Brunch" have sprung up to cater to foreign tourists—prices are cheap, the locals are friendly, and everyone speaks English. A bike ride through the surrounding green plains and the forest-covered limestone peaks allows you to see some of China's most remarkable scenery. Some of the peaks can even be climbed: From the summit at Moon Rock, a dramatic army of jagged peaks goes marching off into the distance. For back-lane scenes of traditional China and even more remarkable scenery, the rustic riverside village of Xingping is an hour's bike ride away past emerald-green rice paddies and striking landscapes.

WHAT: experience. **WHERE:** cruises begin in Guilin and end 50 miles/81 km downstream in Yangshuo; it's 1½ hours by bus back to Guilin. Guilin is an easy 1-hour flight north of Hong Kong, or 2½ hours from Beijing. **WHEN:** boat departures are year-round, but visibility is greatly reduced during the May–Sept rainy season. **BEST TIMES:** Oct–Apr, though the water level can be too low for boats to pass all the way downstream from Dec–Feb.

Cutting-Edge Elegance on the Kowloon Waterfront

HOTEL INTERCONTINENTAL

Hong Kong, China

Perched at the tip of Kowloon Peninsula and actually built out over the harbor's edge, the InterContinental isn't just the city's haute hotel, it's the social vortex, the ultimate see-and-be-seen scene. The heart-stopping views from its 40-foot windows make this one of the most visually stunning hotel lobbies in the world. The Intercontinental shares this 180-degree uninterrupted view of Hong Kong's skyline and unceasing water traffic with its newly refurbished Lobby Lounge, and the InterContinental's famed Chinese restaurant, Yan Toh Heen, is lauded as one of Asia's—and the world's—finest. Traditional Cantonese cuisine is served on exquisite table settings of hand-carved jade and ivory. NOBU InterContinental is the hotel's newest addition, presenting Chef Matsuhisa's world famous Japanese fusion fare.

The outdoor Jacuzzis boast views of the city.

Guest rooms share the same recurring view, one of the most exciting in the world at any time of day, and the deluxe terrace suites have their own outdoor Jacuzzis. Hong Kong boasts some of the world's most opulent, service-minded hotels, and the Intercontinental is one of the best places to be coddled and pampered, to revel in white-glove service and treat your palate and eye to meals with views you didn't think existed, hoping your business expense account is picking it all up.

WHAT: hotel, restaurant. **WHERE:** 18 Salisbury Rd., Kowloon. Tel 852/2721-1211, fax 852/2739-4546; in the U.S., tel 800-327-0200; www.intercontinental.com. **COST:** harborview doubles from $735. Dinner at NOBU $100; at Yan Toh Heen $96.

The Grand Duchess of the Far East

TEA AT THE PENINSULA

Hong Kong, China

If it's late afternoon in Hong Kong, what better way to absorb the city's colonial past than beneath the gilded, coffered ceiling of the Peninsula's exquisite lobby? A virtual shrine to past empires, it has been the venue of

Afternoon tea

choice for a sedate afternoon tea for lucky hotel guests, and those who wish they were, since its doors opened in 1928. Everyone is here: international businessmen, frazzled shoppers, impeccably groomed *tai tais* from Hong Kong's old-moneyed families, the wide-eyed and curious. Cognoscenti know to order the traditional Peninsula tea of trimmed finger sandwiches, delicate French pastries, and scones with clotted cream, which arrive on three-tiered silver servers carried by waiters in starched uniforms. The graciousness and grandeur are palpable, keeping the blunt and impatient city at bay. This is a cool oasis of civilization, in both the neoclassical landmark building or its new thirty-story state-of-the-art tower topped with the theatrical Philippe Starck–designed restaurant Felix, as cutting-edge and high-energy as the lobby is dignified and resplendent. In between, classically appointed rooms-with-a-view are some of the most inviting accommodations anywhere.

WHAT: restaurant, hotel. **WHERE:** Salisbury Rd., Kowloon. Tel 852/2920-2888, fax 852/2722-4170; pen@peninsula.com; www.peninsula.com. **COST:** traditional afternoon tea $21. Doubles in original building from $390, harbor-view suites in new tower from $1,170. **BEST TIMES:** Sept–Dec, and during the 2-week food festival in Aug.

Hong Kong by Ferry and Funicular

VICTORIA HARBOUR AND VICTORIA PEAK

Hong Kong, China

At any given hour, it looks like a round of bumper boats in the crowded waters of Victoria Harbour as the Star Ferry threads its way through a melee of tugs, barges, commuter boats, and the occasional junk, sampan, and gleaming cruise ship. The busy deepwater harbor, China's most important, is the soul and centerpiece of this dynamic port city and the place for which it was named: In Old Chinese, Hong Kong means "fragrant harbor." Since 1898 the two-tiered green-and-white ferries have been transporting visitors and commuters from Kowloon to Hong Kong Island and back. It is one of the world's most unforgettable ten-minute ferry rides, not only for the drama of the round-the-clock aquatic rush hour, but to view Hong Kong's granite forest of skyscraping banks and trading companies that stand as expressionless monoliths by day, illuminated towers of energy by night. Go first class—the upper deck guarantees a better perspective. Then again, second class promises better people-watching. Even better views are to be had via the world's steepest funicular railway, which has been making the climb to the 1,805-foot Victoria Peak and its relative peace and quiet since 1888. Up top you can marvel at the world's busiest harbor, some of the 235 outer islands dotting the South China Sea, and, when the weather is clear, the distant coast of mainland China. Landscaped gardens and paved paths such as Governor's Walk provide solitude and greenery.

Each time of day has its own magic, but dusk may be the most special as an orgy of neon

The pace of the harbor matches that of the city.

begins to grip the city, the Manhattan of Asia. Dining is available (as, unfortunately, are the kind of souvenir hawkers you hoped to leave below), but it's really all about the view.

WHAT: experience, site. **STAR FERRY:** sails from Tsim Sha Tsui in Kowloon to Central District on Hong Kong Island (and the reverse); www.starferry.com/hk. *Cost:* upper deck 30 cents, lower deck 25 cents. **PEAK TRAM:** terminus is between Garden Rd. and Cotton Tree Dr. in the Central District. *When:* daily. *Cost:* from $4 one-way. **BEST TIMES:** Sept–Dec.

Landscape Art That Still Casts a Spell

GARDEN OF THE HUMBLE ADMINISTRATOR

Suzhou, Jiangsu, China

An ancient Chinese proverb remains true today: "In Heaven there is paradise; on earth, Suzhou." Known as the Venice of the East, and with more than 100 gardens and as many silk factories, Suzhou was one of the oldest and wealthiest cities in the empire during the Ming dynasty, and was mentioned by Marco Polo when he wrote about the fabulous cities of the East. Suzhou's gardens are the very embodiment of Chinese landscape design, with every rock, plant, path, stone lantern, and pond carefully placed so that each step frames another impeccable vista. The Lingering Garden and Garden of the Humble Administrator enjoy special designation and government protection as two of China's four most important gardens. The latter is the largest, built on 10 acres of marshy lakes and pools connected by graceful arched bridges and stepping-stone pathways. Your impression is that the entire middle section of the garden is floating on water.

The city, with dozens of silk factories still in operation, is fascinating in itself. Detractors of Venice will see the same decrepitude and decadence here, but for others this photogenic, canal-threaded city still casts its spell effortlessly.

WHAT: site. **WHERE:** 52 miles/84 km by car or train east of Shanghai. **BEST TIMES:** spring and fall for the gardens at their best; early fall coincides with Suzhou's famous Crab Feast.

SHANGHAI MUSEUM

Shanghai, Shanghai Province, China

I n the 1930s Shanghai was known as the Paris of the Orient, and today, after a grim, revolutionary half-century, it's once again a glittering boomtown and ready for business. The spectacular, award-winning Shanghai Museum

reopened in 1995. Created through a combination of Western expertise, overseas Chinese benefactors, and government funds, and designed by well-known local architect Xing Tonghe, it's the world's finest showcase of Chinese art and antiquities. More than 120,000 cultural relics—from paintings, sculpture, and calligraphy to furniture, jade and ivory carvings, ceramics, and minority arts—trace 5,000 years of China's history, from the Neolithic Age through the Ming (1368–1644) and Qing (1644–1911) dynasties until modern times.

The beautifully configured, high-tech, and user-friendly space is three times larger than the original museum (which opened in 1952) and exhibitions are far superior to the old displays, which were dusty, poorly lit, and had Chinese-only descriptions. In a growing city with a population of 14 million, convoys of well-scrubbed schoolchildren in brightly colored uniforms are commonplace sights here, filling the lobby and pouring down the outside steps in cultural overdrive. As a capper, the museum shop and antiques store are each among the city's best.

WHAT: site. **WHERE:** 201 Ren Min Ave., People's Square. Tel 86/21-6372-5300, fax 86/21-6372-8522; www.shanghaimuseum.net/en. **COST:** free admission.

THE TERRA-COTTA WARRIORS OF XI'AN

Xi'an, Shaanxi, China

O ne of the more qualified contenders for the Eighth Wonder of the World (and regarded by many as the most sensational archaeological discovery of the 20th century), Xi'an's army of 2,200-year-old terra-cotta soldiers is

one of China's supreme cultural treasures, a life-size funereal honor guard standing in ranks near the tomb of Emperor Ch'in Shih Huang-ti, who died in 210 B.C. The soldiers were first discovered in 1974 by a local peasant who was digging a well, and so far three vaults have been excavated, the first alone containing more than 6,000 soldiers and horses arranged in an imposing formation of 38 columns, 16 feet deep. They have been left in situ; a protective hangar constructed over them now comprises the Museum of Qin Pottery Figures. The second vault contains an additional 1,000 soldiers and 500 horses, while the highlight of the third is an elaborately detailed war chariot. Every soldier, varying from 5 feet 10 inches to 6 feet 2 inches, differs in facial features and expressions. Most carry actual weapons of the day, and originally were painted.

Xi'an, the current capital of Shaanxi Province, was the homeland of eleven dynasties, including the powerful Qin, the first dynasty to rule over all eastern China. It was the easternmost city on the fabled Silk Road, which first linked East and West in the 2nd century B.C., providing a route for merchant caravans traveling between the route's remote kingdoms, exotic cities, and trading outposts. The resulting exchange of precious cargo, philosophy, religions, and technology transformed every culture along its route, to the doorstep of Europe and beyond.

WHAT: site. **WHERE:** included in most multiple-city tours of China. The Museum of Qin Pottery Figures is 20 miles/32 km north of Xi'an. **WHERE TO STAY:** the Shangri-La Golden Flower is located at 8 Chang Le Rd. West. Tel 86/29-323-2981, fax 86/29-323-5477; in the U.S. and Canada, tel 800-942-5050; www.shangri-la.com. *Cost:* doubles from $75. **BEST TIMES:** Apr–May, Sept to mid-Nov.

The Yangtze River: A Natural Art Gallery

THE THREE GORGES

Chongqing, Sichuan, China

The Three Gorges—Qutang, Wu, and Xiling—rank with the panda bear and the Great Wall as China's most globally recognized icons, showing up everywhere from classical poetry to modern postcards. For sheer scenic beauty, they can be topped by little else in China. So it made headlines when work began in 1995 on the world's largest dam and hydroelectric project, a multibillion-dollar effort that resulted in the relocation of more than a million people. Completed in 2009, it has partially submerged the gorges' vertical cliffs, rapids, and dozens of cultural sites and ancient temples, not to mention hundreds of villages and cities. Environmental and civil rights groups protested, but the Chinese government wasn't swayed, so the time for viewing the area is now.

Varying from some 1,000 feet to just 330 at their narrowest point, the Three Gorges is a special 126-mile stretch of the mighty, 4,000-mile-long Yangtze River, the third longest in the world (after the Amazon and Nile). At one point, most boats stop to shift passengers to smaller, more maneuverable, custom-built boats for a detour to the Three Little Gorges along the Daning River, even narrower and more dramatic, the highlight of most trips.

The Yangtze, also known as Chang Jiang (Long River)

WHAT: site, experience. WHERE: Chongqing is the stepping-stone for most ferries and many cruise ships. Connecting flights are to/from the provincial capital of Chengdu. The most popular stretch is from Chongqing to Wuhan. HOW: 3-night/4-day cruises are offered by Victoria Cruises. In the U.S., tel 800-348-8084 or 212-818-1680; www.victoriacruises.com. COST: doubles from $450 per person (low season), from $760 (high season). Shore excursions extra. Longer cruises are available. BEST TIMES: Apr, May, Sept, and Oct.

Tibet's Most Sacred Shrine and
the Fortress Palace of the Dalai Lamas

LHASA

Tibet, China

Lhasa, which in Tibetan means "the Holy City" or "Place of the Gods," is the vortex of Tibetan spirituality, a city that mystifies and intoxicates, despite the present-day Chinese presence. The vast hilltop Potala, the empty thirteen-story fortress that was once the winter palace and seat of the god-king, the Dalai Lama, is the most recognizable of the city's landmarks. Its white-and-red walls and golden roofs rise above the holy city, seeming to grow out of the hill on which it has stood since the 17th century. It is now a museum, an empty shell of its former self, its central figure and his government having taken its life with them when they fled to India in 1959 following the Chinese occupation. And yet, as 20th-century Chinese-born novelist Han Suyin wrote, "No one can remain unmoved by the sheer power and beauty of the structure, with its thousand windows like a thousand eyes." The Dalai Lamas, each of whom is believed to be the reincarnation of Avalokitshvara, the Buddhist embodiment of compassion, ruled Tibet as spiritual and temporal overlords from 1644; the current Dalai Lama, the fourteenth reincarnation, was just sixteen when Tibet was occupied by China. His private apartments have been left untouched, and surprisingly the building, said to have as many as 1,000 rooms, has been left undamaged by the Chinese; in fact, they are restoring it—reportedly for the purpose of luring tourism.

Though the Potala will be your first sight in Lhasa, the Jokhang Temple is actually the spiritual heart of the city, as well as the busy hub of the main market district, known as the Barkhor. Founded more than 1,300 years ago, the golden-roofed Jokhang is a mixture of Tibetan, Indian, Nepalese, and Chinese architecture and is Tibet's holiest shrine. Tibetan Buddhists express devotion to a holy site by walking clockwise around it, and here the circumambulation, or holy path of transformation, runs right around the marketplace and goes on from dawn until dusk. At the temple's entrance, devout worshippers repeatedly prostrate themselves to gain religious merit, while inside, a million butter candles softly illuminate the most important statue of Buddha, one of more than 200 in the temple. You may feel as if you have stepped back in time as you listen to the chanting of holy scriptures—a sensation that may last until long after you have walked back out into the bustling jamboree of the surrounding Barkhor marketplace.

WHAT: town, site. WHERE: reachable by plane from a number of cities, including Hong Kong, Beijing, and Chengdu. The "Friendship Highway" from Kathmandu, Nepal, takes 2 rough days but offers spectacular vistas. **WHERE TO STAY:** best in town is a former Holiday Inn at 1 Minzu Lu. Tel 86/891-683- 2221, fax 86/891-683-5796; www.lhasahotel. com. *Cost:* doubles from $100. **BEST TIMES:** May–Oct, but Aug is the rainy season.

Sacred Circuit Around the Mystical Home of the Gods

MOUNT KAILAS

Tibet, China

Though at 22,028 feet it's not among the highest peaks of the Himalayas, Kailas is one of the most beautiful. More important, though, it's the most sacred mountain in Asia, revered in the Hindu, Buddhist, and Bon faiths (the latter, Tibet's ancient indigenous religion). The devout believe that Kailas is the home of the gods and the center of the cosmos. For more than 1,000 years, they have come here on pilgrims' paths from all over Tibet and beyond to perform a *kora*, a 32-mile clockwise circumambulation around the mountain to pay homage to the deities. Some even prostrate their way around the peak. One circuit is said to erase the sins of a lifetime, and 108 assures Nirvana, the ultimate spiritual enlightenment.

Intrepid trekkers and travelers have picked up the custom, circling the mountain in the company of avid pilgrims and experiencing the austere beauty and silence of the landscape, visiting far-flung monasteries overlooked by the Chinese authorities, and encountering the occasional nomad family or yak herder. There is no mistaking the holiness of Mount Kailas, whence originates the sacred Ganges River. The mountain itself is off-limits to people; it has never been climbed, because that would disturb the gods.

WHAT: experience, site. **WHERE:** western Tibet. **HOW:** in the U.S., Mountain Travel-Sobek organizes monthlong trips for groups to Nepal and Tibet, departing from Kathmandu and including the Mount Kailas circuit. Tel 888-831-7526 or 510-594-6000; info@mtsobek. com; www.mtsobek.com. **COST:** from $8,000 per person, airfare not included. **WHEN:** Jun–Jul departures. **BEST TIMES:** May–Aug.

The Crossroads of the Silk Road

SUNDAY MARKET

Kashgar, Xinjiang, China

At the foot of the Pamir Mountains, where it's hard to remember you're still in China, much less the 21st century, the remote city of Kashgar hosts a mind-boggling Sunday market that is any photographer's dream. By most accounts it is Asia's (and arguably the world's) largest market. Estimates of 100,000 to 150,000 people sound right—a remarkable statistic considering that it's held weekly, and

From herbs to carpets, you are sure to find what you are looking for at the Kashgar market.

sell, and haggle over sheep, cattle, horses, dowry chests, fur hats, spices, fruit, daggers, and carpets in a scene not unlike what Marco Polo must have witnessed when he passed through in the 13th century, heading east. Although the Silk Road that once made Kashgar prosperous died out around the 15th century, when sea routes won most of the lucrative trade, try to explain that to these folks. Kashgar is just east of the Kyrgyzstan and Tajikistan borders, and its culture has more in common with the Central Asian republics than with Beijing, 2,000 miles east.

has been for probably well over 1,000 years. The Muslim Uighurs are the majority population in China's Alaska-size Xinjiang Province, and bearded Uighur men and women hidden behind veils of brown gauze come to trade,

WHAT: event. **WHERE:** in far western China. Many tours that follow the Silk Road include the Xi'an-to-Kashgar segment. The flight from Kashgar to Urümqi, the provincial capital, is about 2 hours; Urümqi is connected to most major Chinese cities by regular flights.

Life Among the Hill Tribes of Southern China

XISHUANGBANNA

Yunnan, China

The remote agricultural province of Yunnan is the perfect destination for relaxed travel through rural China. Bordering on Myanmar (formerly Burma) and Laos, its biggest draw is the Xishuangbanna region's small towns, which are home to more than one third of China's ethnic minorities. Market days, holidays, and festivals attract a veritable A-to-Z constellation of more than twenty-five hill tribes, from the Aini to the Zhuang, with the Buddhist Dai being one of the most prominent. They still wear their traditional clothing, colors, headwear, and body art, and sell handicrafts that have not changed in centuries. Among other attractions in Xishuangbanna are: Mount Jizu (a sacred Buddhist site to which many pilgrims come to watch the sunrise); boating on lovely Lake Erhai; the 200-acre Lunan Stone Forest of weirdly shaped eroded rocks; Dali, a town in a beautiful

mountain setting where backpackers come, stay, and tune out; and the Yangtze River's dramatic Tiger Leaping Gorge—one of the deepest in the world—where a challenging trek offers unparalleled adventure. Xishuangbanna is a tongue-twisting approximation of the original Thai name Sip Sawng Panna (Twelve Rice-Growing Districts), and there's an exotic and kick-back feel of tropical Thailand and Southeast Asia here.

WHAT: site. **WHERE:** the capital of Yunnan, China's southernmost province, Kunming is connected by air to most other major Chinese cities. From Kunming you can arrange for a driver to bring you to Xishuangbanna.

The Most Famous Beauty Spot in All China

WEST LAKE

Hangzhou, Zhejiang, China

Described by Marco Polo as "the finest and most beautiful city in the world," Hangzhou still offers a glimpse of old China, although what hasn't changed over the centuries or been destroyed by revolution is today obscured by the hordes of Chinese and foreign tourists. But during off-season or a quiet moment at sunrise, the city's West Lake is still one of the loveliest sights you will find in China. Its mist-shrouded shores are lined with landscaped gardens, pagodas, teahouses, shaded walkways, and classic pavilions with names like Autumn Moon on a Calm Lake. It may be at its most beautiful (and crowded) in July and August, when it's covered with a mantle of lotus flowers. The ubiquitous willow creates the perfect Chinese vignette, joined by groves of peach blossoms in spring, orange-scented acacia in autumn, and plum in winter. By hired boat, float up to the Three Pools Mirroring the Moon, the stone pagodas on the Island in the Little Ocean or, opposite this, the Island of the Hill of Solitude, whose excellent 150-year-old Louwailou Restaurant is one of many reasons to come ashore.

WHAT: site. **WHERE:** daily 2-hour flights connect Hangzhou to Hong Kong and Beijing; flights are also available from other major Chinese cities. Hangzhou is 3 hours southwest of Shanghai by train. **WHERE TO STAY:** the Shangri-la Hotel enjoys an enviable position on the northwest bank of West Lake, at 78 Beishan Rd. Tel 86/571-8797-7951, fax 86/571-8707-3545; in the U.S., tel 800-942-5050; slh@shangri-la.com; www.shangri-la.com. **COST:** lake-view doubles from $160. **BEST TIMES:** spring and fall.

Highlights of an Imperial City

OLD KYOTO

Japan

To stroll through Kyoto is to walk through eleven centuries of Japan's history. Once the home of the imperial court, the city was also a center of Japanese religion, aesthetics, music, theater, and dance, and reached its height as a center for crafts during the Muromachi Period (1334–1568). Spared by Allied bombing during WW II, the city is said to hold 20 percent of all Japan's national treasures, including more than 1,700 Buddhist temples and 300 Shinto shrines, all dispersed, often hidden, amid its modern cityscape. Kyoto's beauty can be elusive, but thoughtful visitors can still glimpse the Japan of the past in its temples and gardens, each a compound of several buildings, like a small village. The two-story, pagoda-roofed

Ginkakuji (Temple of the Silver Pavilion) is surrounded by gardens designed by a master landscape architect for meditative strolling; the nearby cherry-tree–lined, mile-long Path of Philosophy follows a narrow canal that is beautiful year-round. The Ginkakuji was inspired by the 14th-century Temple of the Golden Pavilion, which was destroyed by arson in 1950. Today, a three-story replica built soon after anchors the moss-covered grounds of its former site. A lovely half-hour walk from here leads to the Ryoanji Temple, whose small garden of raked white gravel and fifteen rocks has become a symbol of the essence of Zen wisdom. The Kiyomizu-dera temple, built on a steep hillside, offers sensational views of Kyoto from its wooden platform.

At one time, entire neighborhoods in Kyoto grew up around specific crafts; the country's finest artisans worked in the city, serving the imperial court and the feudal lords. Today the workshops of their descendants can be found on the quiet backstreets of Kyoto's historic districts, and the city's wares—including woodblock prints, silk and textile goods, lacquerware, dolls, and paper goods—are still known for their refinement, elegance, and artistry. To this day, the prefix *kyo-* before a craft is synonymous with fine work.

There's no better time to visit Kyoto than during any of its annual *matsuri*, or festivals. The three most important, the Jidai, the Aoi,

and the Gion, are worth juggling your itinerary for and making hotel reservations well in advance. Proud Kyotoites by the thousands participate in the Jidai festival on October 22—one of the newest, having started just over a century ago. A theatrical procession of costumes from the dynasties of the 8th through 19th centuries snakes its way through town, beginning at the Imperial Palace.

The cherry blossoms will be gone when the Aoi festival floats through town on May 15, but spring will still be at its loveliest as hundreds of participants wearing the costumes of imperial courtiers parade to the Shimogamo Shrine to pray for the city's prosperity. The Aoi dates back to the 6th century and is believed to be the world's oldest surviving festival.

On July 16 and 17, make way for thirty-one huge floats that make up the popular Gion festival, a procession that asks for the protection of Kyoto. It was first held in the 9th century, when the ancient capital was ravaged by a plague.

WHAT: site, event. **WHERE:** 2½ hours by bullet train from Tokyo. The largest concentration of small specialty stores is in the Gion district. For the time-pressed, the Kyoto Handicraft Center offers one-stop shopping or just a browse: Heian Jingu Kita, Sakyo-ku; tel 81/75-761-8001. **BEST TIMES:** April for cherry blossoms. Jidai festival, Oct 22; Aoi festival, May 15; Gion festival, Jul 16–17.

In the Footsteps of Shoguns and Samurai

WALKING THE NAKASENDO,
VISITING THE TAWARAYA

Kyoto, Japan

In the 17th century the 315-mile Nakasendo—literally "the road through the central mountains"—was the principal inland route between the capital, Kyoto, and Edo, a growing political and commercial center better known these days as Tokyo. Today "Walk Japan" covers the most enjoyable, most scenic, and best-preserved section of the Nakasendo, a 63-mile stretch that affords a glimpse of medieval and rustic Japan even the Japanese rarely see. Luggage goes by car while walkers put in a moderate 14 to 16 miles a day, staying in old post towns like Tsumago and family-run inns, many of which date from the early 1600s. These inns are a highlight of the trip, providing excellent meals, the ambience of Hiroshige feudal woodblock prints, and the occasional soak in a hot springs bath (*onsen*). Japanese-speaking American or British academic specialists accompany you and provide running commentaries on both the Edo period (1603–1867), when the road traffic of feudal lords, itinerant merchants, and pilgrims was at its height, and contemporary issues. It's worth a year back in the classroom.

For a luxurious stay at the beginning or end of your trip, don't miss the Tawaraya, a 300-year-old family-run *ryokan* (inn) now in its eleventh generation. Elegance and refinement pervade every aspect of the operation, from the almost starkly decorated accommodations (where the hand-painted scrolls change with the seasons) to the small, Zen-like private gardens off most of the eighteen rooms.

The gardens are an important part of the Tawaraya experience, each a harmonious blend of red maple, bamboo, ferns, stone lanterns, moss rocks, and water, revealing the serene spirit of Japanese culture. A restorative soak in the searing water of a perfumed cedar tub is followed by dinner, an elaborate, artistic, multi-course, *kaiseki*-style affair served in your room by a kimonoed attendant. After that the shoji screens are drawn and a plump futon is brought out and covered with fine starched linen sheets.

WHAT: experience, hotel. **NAKESENDO:** beginning or ending in Kyoto. *How:* Tours are offered by Walk Japan. Tel 81/90-5026-3638; www.walkjapan.com. *Cost:* $3,755 per person, based on double occupancy, though many inns require multiple sharing, Japanese style. Includes all costs except lunches and drinks. *When:* Mar–Nov departures. **TAWARAYA:** Fuyacho Oike, Kyoto. Tel 81/75-211-5566, fax 81/75-211-2204. *Cost:* doubles from $500. **BEST TIMES:** Apr for the cherry blossoms, May for azaleas, late Oct–Nov for fall foliage.

Towering Temples, the Great Buddha, and Roaming Deer

NARA KOEN

Nara, Japan

The highlight of the parkland called Nara Koen is a colossal bronze image of a sitting Buddha housed in Todai-ji (the Great Eastern Temple), which is believed to be the world's largest wooden structure. Nara's most-visited site has drawn Buddhist pilgrims and foreign visitors for centuries. The 53-foot Daibutsu Buddha, the largest in Japan, was originally commissioned in 743, not long after Nara was founded as the capital of a newly united Japan. (The court was moved to Kyoto in 794, where it remained for over 1,000 years.) Buddhism, imported from China in the 6th century, flourished, and so did Nara as a center of politics and culture. Nara remains more intimate in scale, and its ancient buildings and temples more intact and authentic than in neighboring Kyoto, where ancient neighborhoods are being encroached upon as the city's unplanned development continues. Nara Park's 1,300 acres of ponds, grassy lawns, trees, and temples are home to the famous deer believed to be sacred emissaries of the temples' gods. More than 1,000 roam the grounds, unintimidated by human visitors

and endearing—until they start to eat straw handbags, schoolchildren's lunches, even your paper map of the city.

WHAT: site, town. **WHERE:** 26 miles/42 km south of Kyoto. **COST:** admission charged for temple. **BEST TIMES:** Apr for the cherry blossoms, May for azaleas, late Oct–Nov for fall foliage.

A Winter Extravaganza

SAPPORO SNOW FESTIVAL

Sapporo, Japan

The Japanese talent for reshaping nature is unmatched. Small wonder, then, that the country that has raised *ikebana* (flower arranging) and garden design to an art form has also transformed this winter festival into

a world-famous show where hundreds of mammoth snow and ice sculptures depict such universal forms as Michelangelo's *Pietà* and

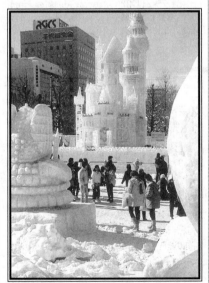

The Snow Festival was established after local high school students sculpted six snow statues in 1950.

the even more familiar Minnie Mouse. Ice palaces are large enough for families to walk through, and a host of other fantasy shapes are created from packed snow and shaved ice, for which more than 38,000 tons of snow are trucked in from the nearby mountains. Some sculptures that can reach more than 130 feet in height and 80 feet in width are begun weeks before the festival's February opening. The festival was established in the 1950s after the dismal years following WW II but really caught on in 1972 when Sapporo, Japan's newest major city, was chosen as the site for the Winter Olympics. Today the snow rides and entertainment transform the town into a wintertime outdoor theater and make Sapporo an excellent base from which to explore Hokkaido's wild, dramatic interior and ski resorts. Don't leave town without sampling the ramen noodles and Sapporo beer for which the city is famous.

WHAT: event. **WHERE:** 731 miles/1,176 km northeast of Tokyo, 177 miles/285 km northeast of Hakodate. Daily flights and overnight trains from Tokyo. www.showfes.com. **WHEN:** beginning of Feb, for 1 week.

Japan's Sacred Mountain, and a Rejuvenating Soak

CLIMBING MOUNT FUJI AND RESTORING THE SOUL

Shizuoka, Japan

Hailed as a goddess, revered as a sacred mountain and the country's national symbol, 12,390-foot Mount Fuji is Japan's highest peak, a perfectly symmetrical volcanic cone that's spellbinding when not shrouded in clouds, and is particularly beautiful when reflected on the mirror-calm surface of Lake Ashi-no. Famous throughout the world, the dormant volcano has always exuded a strong pull on the Japanese, who believe that to experience *goraiko* (sunrise) on its summit is one of the most moving of all natural experiences. They also admit that while everyone should climb Fuji-san once, only a fool would climb it twice. Still, judging by the huge number of gung-ho climbers who show up every summer—an impressive number of grandparents in their seventies and older among them —a good many of them must be return contenders. Six mountain paths, each with ten stations, lead to the summit, but most climbers begin a five- to six-hour climb to the top from the fifth station (8,250 feet), at either Gogome on the north side or Shin-Gogome on the south. The descent is a breeze.

The name Fuji means "fire" in the Ainu language, and in the resort area of Hakone, within the Mount Fuji National Park, intense volcanic activity can be observed from the funicular that passes above the Valley of Great Boiling (or Ojigoku, Big Hell) and its steaming sulfurous gorge. Public baths tap into searing-hot, mineral-rich *onsen* (hot springs, which abound throughout Japan) and promise to cure everything from stress to rheumatism to muscles sore from climbing the mountain. Despite the modernization and Westernization of Japanese cities, *onsen* are a tradition that refuses to die, and on weekends the wonderfully scenic area of Hakone fills with Tokyoites who come for a long, hot soak. Of the handful of traditional *ryokan* inns with their own indoor and outdoor *onsen,* Gôra Kadan, the former summer residence of the Kan-In-No-Miya imperial family, is one of the nicest in the country. The renowned Hakone Open-Air Museum houses sculptures by Henry Moore.

WHAT: site, experience, hotel. **MOUNT FUJI:** 44 miles/71 km south of Tokyo. *Best times:* Jul and Aug. After 9 A.M., clouds obscure most of the view from the summit. **GÔRA KADAN:** 57 miles/92 km southwest of Tokyo. 1300 Gôra, Hakone-machi. Tel 81/460-23331, fax 81/460-23334; in the U.S. and Canada 800-735-2478 or 212-856-0115; www.gora kadan.com. *Cost:* doubles with private open-air *onsen* from $1,005, includes dinner for 2. **BEST TIMES:** May, when the azaleas are in bloom.

The "goddess" of Japan, Mount Fuji

An Avant-Garde High-Tech Aerie

THE PARK HYATT TOKYO

Japan

You've never seen anything like this ultramodern hotel (unless you've seen the award-winning *Lost in Translation,* which was filmed here) occupying the top floors above Tokyo's busy nightlife district in a futuristic fifty-two-story skyscraper, one of the city's most dramatic. The largest guest rooms in Tokyo are equipped with every gadget and infinite amenities, including huge bathrooms, some with superlative views of Mount Fuji. The numerous restaurants offer soaring spaces with unmatched views. The starkly beautiful Kozue restaurant and the stylish, super-trendy top-floor New York Grill/New York Bar—the latter with two-story windows, an amazing 1,600-bottle wine cellar, an open kitchen, and fabulous original art—have brought an unprecedented level of sophistication to Tokyo. Together, they're the city's uncontested power scene. The gym and pool area are housed in a three-story glass-enclosed pyramid, making sunset and the neon-lit evening hours the perfect time to work out. The gorgeous, understated East-meets-West ambience in every facet of the design captures the trail-blazing essence of Tokyo better than any other city hotel—and that says a lot.

WHAT: hotel, restaurant. **WHERE:** 3-7-1-2, Nishi-Shinjuku. Tel 81/3-5322-1234, fax 81/3-5322-1288; in the U.S. and Canada, tel 800-233-1234; tokyo.park@hyatt.com; www.tokyo.park.hyatt.com. **COST:** doubles from $425. Dinner at New York Grill $115. **BEST TIMES:** late Mar–May and Oct–Nov.

A Predawn Institution—
Bring Your Galoshes!

TSUKIJI FISH MARKET

Tokyo, Japan

Jet lag can be a wonderful thing. If you find yourself wide awake at 5 A.M. and in the mood for some predawn action, the cavernous wholesale Tsukiji Fish Market seethes with activity, as you would expect of a place that supplies 90 percent of the fish consumed in Tokyo. Wander this staggering market's side aisles; you won't believe some of the things considered edible, much less prized delicacies. In a country where fresh seafood reigns supreme, maguro (tuna) is king: fresh and frozen, torpedo-size tunas are hauled in from the fishing boats alongside the market's riverside piers or flown in from as far away as Africa. At any of the lightning-fast auctions that begin the day, as many as 190 tons of tuna can be sold, and one fish alone can weigh more than

1,000 pounds. If you've worked up an appetite wandering the 50-acre market and are considering sashimi or sushi for breakfast, no one guarantees fresher fish nor a wider variety than the market's no-frills sushi bars, such as Sushi Dai. They get high marks for local color too.

WHAT: site, experience, restaurant. **TSUKIJI MARKET:** between Shin Ohashi-Dori Ave. and the Sumidagawa River. www.tsukiji-market.or.jp. *When:* open Mon–Sat; best hours are 5 A.M.–7 A.M. **SUSHI DAI:** building 6. Tel 81/3-3547-6797. *Cost:* sushi $3–$10 per piece. *When:* open Thurs–Tues.

The chaotic and cavernous fish market

A Venerated National Pastime

CHERRY BLOSSOM VIEWING

Yoshino, Japan

Every year after the bleak winter skies disappear, tens of millions of Japanese flock to the parks and temple gardens in pursuit of *hanami*, or cherry blossom viewing. When a gentle breeze carries snowflake-size

Petals and people carpet the ground.

pink-and-white petals fluttering to the ground on a spring day, it is easy to understand how the Japanese passion for these ephemeral blossoms is an almost spiritual thing. In Tokyo, city-dwelling office workers make do with nighttime *hanami*, sake-drinking parties in the large Ueno Park or along the moat encircling the Imperial Palace. But purists and *hanami* connoisseurs who aim to get as much as possible out of the one- to two-week-long season head for Yoshino Mountain in the Yoshino-Kumano National Park, not far from Nara and Kyoto, Japan's first capital cities. The mountain is virtually covered with tens of thousands of centuries-old white mountain cherry trees divided into groves (called Hitome-Sembon, or One Thousand Trees at a Glance) that, according to their altitude, bloom at different times, usually beginning in early April. Marked pathways, scattered temples, a predominantly Japanese blossom-viewing crowd, and the shops and teahouses in the pleasant town of Yoshino promise an unforgettable experience.

WHAT: event, experience, site. **WHERE:** the park is 21 miles/34 km south of Nara,

42 miles/68 km south of Kyoto. **WHEN:** usually in Apr, with lowest grove blossoming in early Apr. **BEST TIMES:** Hanakueshiki, the annual Yoshino cherry-blossom festival, is held each year on Apr 11–12, although some years this can be on the early side for peak viewing.

Hauntingly Beautiful and Vast

THE GOBI DESERT

Mongolia

Gobi simply means "desert," and of all the world's arid lands, this remote region—lying between Siberia to the north and the Tibetan Plateau to the south—has the greatest air of mystery. Stretching for 1,000 miles west to east, the Gobi is divided politically into two sections: half in Mongolia proper and half in the area of northern China called Inner Mongolia. Either side can be visited, but the Mongolian side has a little more romance and several million fewer people.

Contrary to the sterile sameness that the word "desert" may suggest, the Gobi holds many fascinations, and not just paleontological. It is a place of subtle colors that change with the day's light, of stark skies and vast spaces, an utterly silent landscape punctuated by the occasional *ger* (yurt), the Mongolians' round, white, tentlike homes. These cheerful people, who subsist on the animals they herd, are naturally generous, feeding and feting foreign guests who show up at their door unannounced. Their simple lifestyle continues in quiet, unspoiled isolation, much as it has for thousands of years.

WHAT: experience, site. **WHERE:** jeeps and interpreters can be hired in Ulaanbaatar, capital of Mongolia.

Air service is to Dalandzagad in the Gobi. **HOW:** contact Nomadic Expeditions. In Ulaanbaatar, tel 976/11-313-396, fax 976/11-320-311; in the U.S., tel 800-998-6634 or 609-860-9008, fax 609-860-9608; info@nomadic expeditions.com (U.S. office); mongolia@ nomadicexpeditions.com (Ulaanbaatar office); www.nomadicexpeditions.com. Both organized group tours and customized guided individual travel are available. **BEST TIMES:** May–Sept.

Light and shadows appear to alter the landscape.

Following the Trail of Genghis Khan in an Untamed Land

Horseback Riding in Mongolia

Mongolia

E ver since Genghis Khan encouraged his people to live by the sword, not the plow, Mongolians have been nomadic herders, holding to their horse-based culture and leaving vast tracks of ruggedly beautiful countryside virtually untouched over the centuries. To experience the land and spirit of this fiercely independent but traditionally hospitable nation, which has been autonomous since the 1920s, get on a horse yourself and take a ride through a land that betrays virtually no sign of the modern world. Organized treks head for one of Mongolia's best-kept secrets, Lake Hovsgal. A hundred miles long and 12 miles wide, it is one of the deepest and sweetest freshwater lakes in the world. West of Hovsgal lies the Darhat Valley, a huge basin surrounded by rugged mountains on three sides, resembling Jackson Hole, Wyoming. And within miles of the Russian border, visit the summer camp of the Tsaatan, or Reindeer People, an ethnic minority that raises, milks, eats, and rides reindeer.

The horse's role in Mongolian life is brought into colorful focus during the Naadam Festival, held each July. Herdsmen and women of all ages from all over Mongolia—many on horseback—come to the capital of Ulaanbaatar for two raucous days of socializing and unbridled competition in the age-old sporting events of horse racing, archery, and wrestling. The equestrian events are the festival's highlight, held on the rolling, grassy steppe outside the city. The sight and sound of 600 horses charging in a headlong gallop over a 10-mile course is a heart-stopping sensation, and only the celebration that follows—with its open-hearted Mongolian hospitality, drinking, and food—can match it.

A quiet moment on the Mongolian plains

WHAT: experience, event. **WHERE:** Naadam Festival in Ulaanbaatar. **HOW:** Boojum Expeditions offers equestrian trips originating from Ulaanbaatar. In the U.S., tel 800-287-0125 or 406-587-0125, fax 760-454-7407; info@boojum.com; www.boojum.com. *Cost:* from $2,180 per person for a 13-day trip. Nomadic Expeditions offers a 12-day itinerary including the Naadam Festival. In Ulaanbaatar, tel 976/11-313-396, fax 976/11-320-311; in the U.S., tel 800-998-6634 or 609-860-9008, fax 609-860-9608; info@nomadicexpeditions.com (U.S. office); mongolia@nomadicexpeditions.com (Ulaanbaatar office); www.nomadicexpeditions.com. *Cost:* from $3,885 per person, not including airfare. *When:* first 2 weeks in Jul, coinciding with the festival. **BEST TIMES:** Jul–Sept.

A Whirling Spectacle of Tradition and People-Watching

PARO FESTIVAL

Paro, Bhutan

N ow that Bhutan has ended its historic isolation from the outside world, its colorful traditional festivals, called *tshechus,* are the perfect window from which to view its heritage. These festivals traditionally take place in the courtyards of the great *dzongs*—the fortified monasteries that remain the centers of religion, education, and local government in each district of the kingdom. They are not staged for the benefit of visitors, who can consider themselves privileged witnesses to these events, which have remained unchanged for centuries.

The springtime celebration in Paro is the country's best-known annual dance festival. Throngs of joyful Bhutanese townspeople in traditional woven robes gather from all over the valley, while dancers (monks or trained laymen) in magnificent masks and costumes take on the aspects of peaceful or wrathful deities, demons, and animals, reenacting the legends of Himalayan Buddhism in the Dragon Kingdom. The dances, known as *cham,* are performed to bring blessings upon all onlookers, be they from across the valley or across the globe, to protect them against misfortune.

WHAT: event. **WHERE:** Paro Dzong, 34 miles/55 km west of the capital, Thimbu. **HOW:** in the U.S., contact Bhutan Travel, tel 800-950-9908 or 516-378-3805, fax 516-868-1601; bhutantravel@earthlink.net; www.bhutan travel.com. **COST:** 12-day ground package (with 2 days spent at the festival) $2,970 per person, double occupancy, all-inclusive. **WHEN:** 5-day festival usually falls in late Mar or early Apr, according to the Buddhist lunar calendar.

Untrammeled Terrain at a Sacred Mountain

CHOMOLHARI TREK AND THE TIGER'S NEST

Paro Valley, Bhutan

T he last independent Buddhist mountain kingdom in the Himalayas, Bhutan (Druk Yul, the Land of the Thunder Dragon) is one of the most remote and tantalizing corners of Asia. Seventy percent of its 18,000 square miles is forested, and the nation treats nature with admirable respect—its king is young and environmentally sensitive, and many of the country's higher regions remain nearly free of the footprints of man, untouched examples of the fast-disappearing Himalayan environment.

The nine-day trek to Chomolhari, Bhutan's sacred and highest mountain, at the border with Tibet, offers outsiders a rare opportunity to experience its unspoiled mountain wilderness and varied terrain, not to mention its almost complete lack of other trekkers (Bhutan heavily restricts tourism). Climbing beside terraced farms and verdant rice paddies, through meadows and low forests, travelers venture beyond the tree line into a world of glaciers and rock, where the legendary snow leopard prowls. Campsites are set up in high alpine pastures where yak herders bring their shaggy animals to graze by pristine mountain lakes.

Clinging to a sheer mountain ledge about 3,000 feet above the terraced Paro Valley, Taktsang, the Tiger's Nest, is a destination of treks long and short, and of reverent Buddhist pilgrims. The greatest of all Bhutanese monuments, it was founded in A.D. 747 by a Tibetan missionary venerated as the second Buddha and called Guru Rinpoche (Precious Teacher). Legend says he landed on this spot from neighboring Tibet astride a flying tiger, bringing the tenets of Buddhism with him. It's startlingly scenic, with nothing breaking the silence except a waterfall, the call of a raven, the fluttering of the prayer flags, and the chanting of a few monks. The stone monastery suffered

Taktsang is the greatest and most revered of all Bhutanese sites.

from a major fire in 1998, but it is slowly being restored.

WHAT: experience, site. **WHERE:** 8-day treks begin at Drukgyel Dzong in the Paro Valley. The city of Paro is the closest to the Tiger's Nest, which can be reached only by horse or on foot—it's about a 4-hour climb to the top. **HOW:** in the U.S., contact Bhutan Travel, tel 800-950-9908 or 516-378-3805, fax 516-868-1601; bhutantravel@earthlink.net; www.bhutantravel.com. **COST:** 9-day treks (typically part of a longer ground package) from $3,690 per person, double occupancy, all-inclusive. **WHEN:** Apr, May, and Oct departures. **BEST TIMES:** spring for the mountain flowers and the Paro Festival; fall for the popular Thimbu Festival.

The Private Toy Train of the Maharajas

PALACE ON WHEELS

New Delhi, Delhi Territory, India

Modeled after the luxurious private railway cars of the former rulers of Gujarat and Rajasthan, the Palace on Wheels is the subcontinent's answer to the Orient Express, replete with service-proud captains and

staff outfitted in crisp tunics and brilliant turbans straight out of *The Jewel in the Crown.* Each of the fourteen wagons (or "saloons")

is named after a former princely state and decorated in its most representative colors and fabrics. Rich veneered wood paneling and custom-designed furniture with inlaid motifs lend a further touch of class. The train travels mostly through the desert corners of Rajasthan, usually at night to allow full days of sightseeing in such magical cities as Jaipur, Udaipur, Jaisalmer, and Jodhpur. Guests are treated like royalty onboard and on land as well, with musicians and richly harnessed elephants meeting and greeting the train's arrival. Luncheons are arranged at former maharajas' palaces, and camel treks and tiger photo-safaris fill out the

exciting week on wheels, culminating in a grand finale visit to—where else?—the Taj Mahal, before heading back to New Delhi.

WHAT: experience. **WHERE:** round-trip from New Delhi. **HOW:** Sita World Travel, tel 800-421-5643 or 818-990-9530; sitatours @sitatours.com; www.sitatours.com. **COST:** 8-day trips $375 per person, double occupancy (low season), $500 (high season), includes all train and land costs. **WHEN:** Wed departures, Aug–Apr. **BEST TIMES:** Oct–Mar.

For the Palates of Princes and Peasants

TOP TABLES

New Delhi, Delhi Territory, India

India has one of the world's great cuisines, and the country's luxury hotel restaurants have become social hubs and gastronomic destinations for local businessmen and families as well as visiting foreigners. New Delhi's ITC Maurya Hotel has no rivals, offering the day-and-night selection of two of India's best-known restaurants. DumPukht's elegant and airy decor reflects the cuisine's royal origins as the refined court food of the 18th-century nawabs of Avadh. This little-known, delicate cuisine uses steam to slowly cook sealed vessels of finely cut meats and vegetables until they're ready to melt in your mouth. The Bukhara restaurant is radically different, offering robust and informal food and a hunting-camp atmosphere of stone walls, wooden-trestle tables, and a glassed-in kitchen that's always good for a show. The food is no less exquisite, but the emphasis is on perfectly prepared tandoori—originally made for peasants but fit for a king.

WHAT: restaurant. **WHERE:** ITC Maurya Hotel, Diplomatic Enclave. Tel 91/11-611-2233, fax 91/11-611-3333. **COST:** dinner at DumPukht $30; Bukhara $20.

In a Former Summer Capital, a Relic of the Raj

CHAPSLEE

Simla, Himachal Pradesh, India

In the 19th century, the British may have ruled India, but the real arbiter of day-to-day life, even for them, was the heat, which Kipling called "the central fact of India." To carry on business during the summer months, British officials would take to the northern hills of Simla, where melting snows kept the temperature tolerable and Victorian architecture, gardens, and entertainment re-created the sceptered isle they'd left behind. Chapslee, a stately, decidedly British ivory-colored manor house, was built in 1835, in the lap of the Himalayas at 7,000 feet. From the start, it offered the kind of princely living and grand hospitality demanded by the sahibs of yore and still found today, and a decor of Gobelin tapestries, Venetian chandeliers, Persian carpets, and an imposing portrait of the present owner's great-grandfather, the former maharaja of the state of Kapurthala. Today, Simla is one of India's most venerated British-built hill stations, and provides an imperial starting point for visitors exploring one of India's most beautiful states, Himachal Pradesh, a rural landscape dotted with remote Hindu and Buddhist temples and communities whose ceremonies, fairs, and festivals liven the summer months.

WHAT: town, hotel. **SIMLA:** regular direct flights to and from New Delhi, 230 miles/370 km; daily overnight train from New Delhi to Kalka connects with the "Toy Train," a narrow-gauge railway (an engineering marvel commissioned in 1903) that passes through beautiful hill country and 103 tunnels in a span of 63 miles/101 km. **CHAPSLEE:** on Lakkar Bazar. Tel 91/177-2658663, fax 91/177-2650921; chapslee@vsnl.com; www.chapslee. com. *Cost:* doubles from $260, includes meals. *When:* hotel open mid-Mar to late Dec. **BEST TIMES:** Apr–May and Oct–Nov.

A Glimpse of Tibet Against a Lunar Landscape

LADAKH

Leh, Jammu and Kashmir, India

Also known as Little Tibet and Moon Land, the awe-inspiring high-altitude plateau of Ladakh is tucked between the world's two highest mountain ranges, the Karakoram and the Great Himalayas. Politically Indian but geographically Tibetan, it shares age-old cultural and religious ties with the latter, and though it was closed to tourism until 1974, it's now attracting visitors who are drawn to the region but put off by the troubles in Tibet to the north and east and in the Kashmir Valley to the west.

The flight to Leh, the region's capital, is one of the most spectacular in the world of aviation sightseeing, and graphically illustrates the area's otherworldly remoteness. Likewise the 305-mile ride from Leh south to Manali, in the state of Himachal Pradesh, is a hard-to-forget trip that crosses four mountain passes on the world's second-highest motorable road. This can only be topped (literally) by the newly opened Nubra Valley, Ladakh's "Valley of Flowers," which requires a journey over Khardungla Pass—at 18,383 feet, it is the world's highest drivable road.

WHAT: site. **WHERE:** 75-minute flight from New Delhi to Leh. **HOW:** Geographic Expeditions in the U.S. offers 3 different touring and trekking itineraries to the Ladakh area, originating from New Delhi and traveling over the spectacular Trans-Himalayan Highway. Tel 800-777-8183 or 415-922-0448, fax 415-346-5535; info@geoex.com; www.geoex.com. **COST:** from $4,295 for 11-day trips to $5,695 for 15-day trips. **WHEN:** Leh–Manali road is usually open Jun to mid-Sept. Geographic Expeditions departures mid-Jun to Sept. **BEST TIMES:** the colorful Ladakh Festival, featuring dancing, sports, and ceremonies, is held mainly in Leh during first 2 weeks in Sept.

An Exotic Labyrinth of Canals and Lagoons

THE BACKWATERS OF KERALA

Kochi, Kerala, India

I solated, peaceful, and staggeringly beautiful, the southern coastal state of Kerala is one of India's unpromoted treasures, a gentle, floral alternative to the harsher Himalayas or the Rajasthan desert in the north. The twisting *kayals*, the jungle-shrouded backwater canals and lagoons that lie inland, connect sheltered villages and are often just wide enough for your canoe. They're the only way to reach secluded Coconut Lagoon Village, an enclave of thirty gracious *tarawads* (traditional carved wooden bungalows made without nails, some of them more than 400 years old) that were painstakingly dismantled and moved here along the cool banks of the backwaters. This is a place for lazy R&R in the shade of a nutmeg tree. Few cultural sites demand your attention, and the Ayurvedic health clinic offers restorative treatments and massages incorporating herbal oils made from the exotic spices that first drew Vasco da Gama to Kerala's shores in 1498.

A stopover in Kochi (formerly known as Cochin) is a must. The fascinating capital has been a trading port for more than 1,000 years, and is composed of a cluster of islands surrounded by a network of rivers, lakes, and estuaries. It is home to a unique culture and a courteous people. Be sure to have dinner at the Fort Cochin Restaurant in the Casino Hotel, considered one of the finest eateries in southern India.

WHAT: site, hotel, restaurant. **COCONUT LAGOON VILLAGE:** regular flights from Mumbai to Kochi; car service to Lake Vembanad, then boat trip to the village is arranged by hotel. Tel 91/484-301-1711, fax 91/484-266-8001; www.cghearth.com/coconut_lagoon. *Cost:* doubles from $120, private pool villas from $226. **CASINO HOTEL:** Willington Island, Kochi. Tel 91/484-301-1711, fax 91/484-266-8001; www.cghearth.com/casino_hotel. *Cost:* doubles from $95 (low season), from $120 (high season). Dinner $25. **BEST TIMES:** Nov–Feb. The area's largest and most colorful cultural festival, the Great Elephant March, is held in Trissur and Kovalam over 4 days in early Jan.

The local means of transportation

Erotic Tableaux in the Middle of Nowhere

THE TEMPLES OF KHAJURAHO

Madhya Pradesh, India

I n this sleepy little town a long way from anywhere, a century-long burst of creativity during the dynasty of the Chandela kings (around A.D. 1000) resulted in the construction of more than eighty-five temples, of which

twenty-two remain, decorated with long running friezes that intersperse day-to-day scenes with military processions. Khajuraho is most renowned, however, for its profusion of sensual and erotic friezes and sculptures, in which celestial maidens pout and pose while other figures engage in every imaginable position of the *Kama Sutra*. These sculptures are great jubilant paeans to life, with an extraordinary explicitness that makes them as remarkable today as they must have been when they were first unveiled.

WHAT: site. **WHERE:** on the way from nowhere to nowhere, the city is usually slotted between a trip to the Taj Mahal in Agra and a visit to the holy city of Varanasi. All 3 cities are connected with daily flights that originate in New Delhi. **WHERE TO STAY:** Hotel Chandela is about half a mile from the temples. Tel 91/7686-72355; www.tajhotels.com. *Cost:* doubles from $90 **BEST TIMES:** Oct–Mar. During a 7-day cultural festival in Mar, some of the country's best classical dancers perform on the temple grounds.

An Architectural Achievement of Mysterious Power

THE CAVE TEMPLES OF NORTHERN MAHARASHTRA

Ajanta and Ellora, Maharashtra, India

M umbai (Bombay) may be the pulsating commercial heart of Maharashtra, but its soul lies in the interior around Aurangabad and its astonishing hand-hewn cave temples, which offer riches comparable to those of the

Taj Majal. Dozens of *chaityas* (temples) and *viharas* (monasteries) were carved from solid rock faces; some were decorated with lavishly painted frescoes and statues, others with breathtaking architectural intricacy and detail. The thirty Buddhist temples of Ajanta date from around 200 B.C. to A.D. 650 but were virtually forgotten until the 19th century, which

probably accounts for their excellent state of preservation.

Whereas the Ajanta caves are known for their paintings, the thirty-four rock-cut temples of nearby Ellora are sculptural masterpieces. Their creation was a feat equivalent to carving an entire cathedral—interior and exterior, roof to floor—out of solid rock. It is

Exploring the cave temples of Ellora is sure to bring out the archaeologist in all of us.

believed that the Buddhist creators of Ajanta moved here after their work was finished there: of Ellora's thirty-four caves, the twelve earliest, begun in A.D. 600, are Buddhist. They are followed by seventeen Hindu and five Jain temples. The pièce de résistance is the Kailash Temple, whose dimensions and complexity astound: At almost 10,000 square feet, it covers twice the area of the Parthenon in Athens and is half again as tall. It has been estimated that approximately 200,000 tons of rock were removed to create this single cave temple.

WHAT: site. **WHERE:** Aurangabad, 230 miles/370 km northeast of Mumbai, is the most practical base; from there it is 60 miles/100 km northwest to Ajanta and 15 miles/25 km northeast to Ellora. *Cost:* 1-day excursion to caves $62. **WHERE TO STAY:** in Aurangabad, the Taj Residency offers full-day excursions to the caves daily. Tel 91/24-038-1106, fax 91/24-038-1053; in the U.S., tel 866-969-1825; residency.aurangabad @tajhotels.com; www.tajhotels.com. *Cost:* doubles $80. **WHEN:** Ajanta caves open Tues–Sun, Ellora caves open Wed–Mon. **BEST TIMES:** Oct–Mar. The Ellora Festival, 3d week in Mar, features classical Indian music and dance against the backdrop of the caves.

A Bewitching Landmark

TAJ MAHAL PALACE & TOWER

Bombay (Mumbai), Maharashtra, India

A Mumbai landmark since 1903, the Taj Mahal Palace & Tower is India's most famous hotel and probably its best, a Victorian extravaganza that faces the Arabian Sea and was in its day a rival of Singapore's Raffles Hotel, welcoming luminaries such as Mark Twain. ("A bewitching place, a bewildering place, an enchanting place," he wrote.)

The Mumbai elite tend to use the Taj as a private club, with splendidly uniformed doormen ushering locals and guests into the deliciously cool, gleaming white marbled interior of the elegant Old Wing. The high staff-to-guest ratio and white-glove service make this an ideal escape from the throbbing, whirling realities of the hot and humid city, with its population of 12 million. Balconied rooms on the high floors of the Old Wing are the place to stay, with calming views of the sea, the Gateway of India (the arched monument built by the British to welcome King George V in 1911), the bay, and the hills beyond. The hotel's many restaurants offer some of the best meals in town. This was the first hotel in the Taj Group, which now owns more than seventy hotels in India and abroad. An adjoining thirty-story modern wing built in 1972 lacks the historical ambience but offers the same views.

WHAT: hotel, restaurant. **WHERE:** Apollo Bunder, Colaba. Tel 91/22-6665-3366, fax 91/22-6665-0323; in the U.S., tel 866-969-

1825; tmhresv.bom@tajhotels.com; www.taj hotels.com. **Cost:** seaview doubles in Old Wing from $345, in New Wing from $275. Dinner $30. **Best times:** Nov–Mar.

Where Royal Concubines Watched the World Go By

PALACE OF WINDS

Jaipur, Rajasthan, India

Pink is the Rajput color of hospitality, and Jaipur, India's "Pink City," is a worthy home for Hawa Mahal, the five-story, salmon-pink "palace of winds," adorned with delicate floral motifs and filigree windows. It's really nothing more than an elegant facade, just one room thick, from which the ladies of the royal household could enjoy the breeze while viewing state processions or the parade of everyday life below. Visitors today can climb to the top for a view of the Old City's main street from any of Hawa Mahal's myriad honeycombed windows. In the late afternoon light, variations of pinks, oranges, and the salmon-rust color of the sandstone palace take on a special glow, complemented by the colorfully dressed Rajasthanis. It is part of the City Palace complex, a rambling, exotic blend of Rajasthani and Mughal architecture executed by master craftsmen, and is a fascinating place to wander, made all the more evocative by the presence of the former maharaja, who lives on a high floor.

To escape the teeming carnival of street life, repair to the exquisite Rajvilās hotel, where the fantasy of Rajasthan's princely life lives on. This 30-acre oasis of exotic pavilions, gardens, pools, and fountains with a pink fortress at its heart looks as if it has always been here, although it only opened in 1998. The use of ancient crafts and skilled workmanship supports the illusion of India as it was. Try one of the teak-floored, ultra-luxury desert tents.

What: site, hotel. **Where:** 175 miles/282 km from New Delhi. In the Old City on Siredeori Bazaar. **Cost:** admission. **Rajvilās:** 4 miles/6 km outside town on Goner Rd. Tel 91/141-268-0101, fax 91/141-268-0202; in the U.S., tel 800-562-3764; reservations@oberoigroup.com; www.oberoihotels.com. *Cost:* doubles from $640, luxury tents from $755. **Best times:** Sept–Mar, and sunrise, when the palace glows in the morning light.

A Giant Sand Castle in the Heart of the Great Indian Desert

JAISALMER

Rajasthan, India

Known as the Golden City, this former caravan center on the route to the Khyber Pass rises from a sea of sand, its 30-foot crenellated walls and medieval sandstone fort sheltering carved spires and palaces that soar into the sapphire sky. With its tiny winding lanes and hidden temples, Jaisalmer is straight out of *The Arabian Nights*, and so little has life changed here that it's easy to imagine yourself back in the city's early days, in the 13th century. It's the only fortress city in India still functioning, with one quarter of its population living within the original walls, and it is just far enough off the beaten path to have been spared the worst ravages of tourism. The city's wealth originally came from the heavy levies it placed on camel caravans that passed through, and merchants and townspeople built handsome *havelis* (Rajput mansions elaborately carved from the local golden stone). Stay at the

aptly named Hotel Pleasant Haveli and share a Kingfisher beer with the amiable owner Dilip on the rooftop terrace. With spacious, clean, and thoughtfully decorated rooms, this small hotel's never-say-no staff can help arrange everything, including a camel or jeep safari into the surrounding Thar Desert for the quintessential Jaisalmer experience.

WHAT: town, hotel. **WHERE:** 6 hours by car from Jodhpur. **HOTEL PLEASANT HAVELI:** Chainpura Street, Gandhi Chowk. Tel 91/2992-253253; reservations@pleasanthaveli.com; www.hotelpleasanthaveli.com. *Cost:* doubles from $50. **BEST TIMES:** Oct–Jan for camel safaris.

A Mammoth Pink Monument
to the Twilight Days of the Maharajas

UMAID BHAWAN PALACE

Jodhpur, Rajasthan, India

India's most colorful state, Rajasthan isn't called the Land of Kings for nothing. Rambling palaces and forts are everywhere, most converted into intriguing hotels after the maharajas were stripped of their regal stipends but

allowed to keep their real estate. After a while many of them begin to blur together in the minds of travelers, so if you begin to feel a bit blasé—"another day, another palace"— refresh yourself by pulling up to the most imposing of them all: the Anglo-Indian Umaid Bhawan Palace, one of the largest private residences ever built. This last of the royal palaces employed 3,000 artisans and laborers for fifteen years as a famine-relief project organized by Maharaja Umaid Singh for his subjects. The current maharaja, grandson of Umaid Singh, keeps one extensive wing for his family, leaving the rest for a museum of glorious paintings and armor and setting

aside 55 of the palace's 347 grandest rooms as a deluxe hotel, opened in 1971. The building, extravagant even by maharaja standards, is unique for its Art Deco details, which reflect both the period and the British architect's

Construction of the palace began in 1929.

tastes. The pink buff sandstone was chiseled and interlocked without the use of mortar—something to ponder while standing beneath the palace's lofty 135-foot-high central dome.

WHAT: hotel. **WHERE:** within the city limits of Jodphur, 3 miles/5 km from airport. Tel 91/291-510101, fax 91/291-510100; umaidbhawan.jodhpur@tajhotels.com; www.

tajhotels.com. **COST:** doubles from $544, Maharani and Maharaja suites from $835. **BEST TIMES:** the maharaja's birthday is celebrated every year from Dec 15–Jan 15, when extended family and residents of the state (who, despite what their government tells them, still consider him their king) come in full regalia to offer their best wishes.

A Tribal Gathering Unlike Any Other

THE PUSHKAR CAMEL FAIR

Pushkar, Rajasthan, India

In Rajasthan, livestock breeding flourished under the maharajas, who maintained legions of camels for warfare. The departure of those bellicose rulers and the arrival of the automobile largely sidelined the camel, but you can still see the legacy of those times at the annual Pushkar Camel Fair. It is one of the largest animal markets in Rajasthan's Thar Desert, and it's unequaled for color, music, costume, and festivities.

Rajasthan has the largest concentration of tribal people in India, and they converge by the tens of thousands on the small town of Pushkar each November before the full moon (coinciding with the religious Kartik Poornima festival) to parade, race, trade, and sell their prized dromedaries, which have been groomed and festooned for the occasion.

Rajasthanis are known for their love of brilliant colors, so the human participants outshine the steeds with their jewelry and brilliantly colored saris and turbans, which helps to explain the festival's popularity with foreign tourists, filmmakers, and photographers. More like a nonstop carnival, with acrobats, bazaars, and dancing under the stars, it is one of the most important annual fairs in this desert state.

For Hindus, Pushkar is an important pilgrimage center; the lake is said to have sprung from the spot where the god Brahma dropped a sacred lotus, and more than 1,000 temples now line its banks. At dawn on the day of the full moon, pilgrims gather to bathe in the lake.

WHAT: event, experience. **WHERE:** about 220 miles/354 km from New Delhi. **HOW:** Equitours offers annual November horse safaris in the Thar Desert to coincide with the Pushkar Camel Fair; trip originates in New Delhi. In the U.S., tel 800-545-0019 or 307-455-3363, fax 307-455-2354; www.riding tours.com. *Cost:* $6,785 per person, double occupancy for 18-night equestrian safari; includes domestic airfare and most meals. Geographic Expeditions offers jeep safaris through Rajasthan, with a 3-day stay at Pushkar. In the U.S., tel 415-922-0448, fax 415-346-5535; info@geoex.com; www.geoex. com. *Cost:* from $10,495 per person for 17-day trip, land travel only, all-inclusive. **WHEN:** 2-week festival almost always in Nov.

Country Palace, City Mansion

SAMODE HOTELS

Samode, Rajasthan, India

Y ou won't be the first to think the exquisite Samode Palace Hotel would make a perfect film set: Hollywood used it in *The Far Pavilions* and so have numerous Hindi movies. This jewel box of a palace was built in

Samode Haveli's dining room walls are hand-painted.

the 18th century as a luxurious country retreat in the farming village of Samode, outside Jaipur. The elaborately painted and enameled public rooms and sumptuous Diwan-i-Khas Hall may make you welcome the less opulent guest rooms for their comparatively plain decor.

Less palatial and overwhelming than its country sister, the stately Samode Haveli, tucked away in a quiet corner of bustling

Jaipur, was built as a city residence for a prime minister of the royal court. Retreat to any of its three amazing suites, with their original colored windows, mirror inlay, archways, and frescoes of flowers and idle court life scenes, for a taste of the princely pleasures of Old Jaipur. Both hotels are privately owned and run by the Samode Royal family, descendants of the aristocrats who built the Samode Palace. Their two remarkable properties offer a complete town-and-country idyll.

WHAT: hotel. **SAMODE PALACE:** 26 miles/ 42 km north of Jaipur. Tel 91/14-126-32370 or 91/14-232-40014, fax 91/14-126-31397; reservations@samode.com; www.samode.com. *Cost:* doubles from $200. **SAMODE HAVELI:** at Gangapole, in the heart of Jaipur's walled city. Tel 91/14-126-32370; www.samode.com. *Cost:* doubles from $165 (low season), from $275 (high season). **BEST TIMES:** Oct–Apr.

Twin Palaces in a City of Dreams

THE CITY PALACE AND THE LAKE PALACE

Udaipur, Rajasthan, India

U daipur has a profusion of palaces, temples, and cenotaphs, ranging from the modest to the extravagant. But nowhere are the power, pride, and wealth of the local maharanas (outside Udaipur called maharajas) more

One of Shiv Niwas's imperial suites

evident than at the immense City Palace. Onetime residence of Udaipur's princely ruler and the largest palace complex in Rajasthan, this is a conglomeration of elaborately decorated buildings and private apartments with additions by subsequent maharanas. Sitting high on the banks of artificial, mountain-ringed Lake Pichola, the palace's balconies, towers, and cupolas offer excellent views. There is a small museum, but it is the rambling, honey-colored palace itself that is worth seeing; the present maharana still resides in a private corner, but you can live royally in what once was the guesthouse, now the deluxe Shiv Niwas Hotel. Spacious accommodations with views of the lake once welcomed the Shah of Iran, the King of Nepal, and Roger Moore, who lived here for several months while filming the James Bond movie *Octopussy* in 1982. The antique fixtures and furnishings in the imperial suites are from the maharana's private collection, and the enormous beds match their scale within the pampering walls of this magical hotel.

The maharana of Udaipur's summer residence, the white marble Lake Palace, is now entirely leased out as a hotel, having been converted (so rumors say) at the suggestion of Jacqueline Kennedy. Other hotels may be grander and have flashier accoutrements, but none moves the spirit like this one. Built in the 18th century on a small island in the middle of Lake Pichola, it's one of the world's most romantic escapes, decorated with multicolor mosaics, mirror work, and inlaid tiles, and embellished with gardens, lily ponds, courtyards, and fountains. The most romantic rooms are those facing the City Palace across the lake. The location weaves its spell, whether at breakfast on an open veranda or while having a nightcap while the moon illuminates the water. A sunset cruise on one of the hotel's private launches glides past another palace, the Jag Mandir. Built in 1624 for a young Shah Jahan, future emperor and creator of the Taj Mahal, it now sits uninhabited, hinting of past splendors and royal ghosts.

WHAT: site, hotel. **UDAIPUR:** the airport, 16 miles/26 km (45 minutes) outside of town, offers daily flights to and from all major Indian cities (from New Dehli to Udaipur takes about 90 minutes). **SHIV NIWAS HOTEL:** tel 91/294-528-016; crs@hrhhotels.com; www.eternalmewar.in. *Cost:* doubles $155. **LAKE PALACE HOTEL:** tel 91/294-242-8800, fax 91/294-252-8700; in the U.S., tel 866-969-1825; lakepalace.udaipur@tajhotels.com; www.tajhotels.com. *Cost:* lake-facing doubles from $650, historical suites from $700. **BEST TIMES:** Oct–Mar.

The Lake Palace seems to float on the water.

Isolated Splendor No Longer Off-Bounds

TREKKING IN SIKKIM

Gangtok, Sikkim, India

O ne of the least touristed of India's twenty-two states, Sikkim is bordered by Nepal, Tibet, and Bhutan. Sikkim is still regarded as one of the last Himalayan Shangri-las, a place where ancient Buddhist gompas (monasteries) are perched on almost every outcrop of the awesome mountain landscape. The last Namgyal Chogyal (king) made headlines in 1963 by marrying an American; their daughter, Hope, has chosen to return to the country she loves and to operate TrekSikkim out of Gangtok, the provincial capital. Hope has trekked since the age of five and leads most of the trips through these foothills of the eastern Himalayas, where mountains aren't even named unless they're over 20,000 feet.

Straddling the border of Nepal and Sikkim is the sacred Mount Kanchenjunga (its Tibetan name means "Five Treasure Houses of the Great Snow Mountain" for its five peaks), rising to 28,146 feet—the third highest mountain in the world and worshipped as a guardian deity. The land is a botanist's fantasy: during a typical trek, you can pass from subtropical jungle to alpine meadow within hours. There are 454 species of orchids and 46 varieties of rhododendrons here, and magnolias and luxuriant forests abound.

WHAT: experience. **WHERE:** northeast corner of India. Daily flights from New Delhi or Calcutta to Bagdogra airport, 70 miles/ 113 km from Gangtok. **HOW:** TrekSikkim (treksikkim@namgyal.com; www.treksikkim. com) offers treks that originate in Bagdogra. *Cost:* 7- or 11-day treks from $150 per person per day, all-inclusive, land-only. **WHEN:** scheduled departures and customized travel late Mar–early Jun, Sept–early Dec.

Locals say the mountains are the "altar of the gods."

The World's Greatest Monument to Love

THE TAJ MAHAL

Agra, Uttar Pradesh, India

N othing can adequately prepare the visitor for his or her first glimpse of the Taj Mahal. It may be a visual cliché, the Niagara Falls of architecture, but it's also the embodiment of grace and romance, of balance and symmetry, an architectural icon revered for three and a half centuries as the most beautiful building in the world. The great Moghul emperor Shah Jahan built the white marble Taj as a tomb to honor his beloved queen, Mumtaz Mahal, who died while giving birth to their fourteenth child in nineteen years. One of their progeny would eventually dispose of the emperor, imprisoning him in the nearby Agra Fort. From his chambers he could gaze across at the Taj Mahal, mourning the loss of his wife and his empire. Perhaps the best time to visit is at night during the full moon when the Taj Majal is now open. Whenever you go expect to find local families illuminating the grounds with the flowerlike colors of their saris and turbans.

Thanks to the opening of the Amarvilās (Sanskrit for "eternal haven"), there's finally another reason to linger overnight in this otherwise unlovely city. The classic terraced gardens, bubbling fountains, marble pool, elegant tea lounge, excellent Mughlai and Indian restaurant, and Ayurvedic spa-with-a-Taj-view would make

One of the world's most famous symbols of romance

a fitting 21st-century home for any Mughal emperor. Every one of its 100-plus rooms has an unobstructed view of India's most beloved national monument, a mere 650 yards away.

WHAT: site, hotel. **WHERE:** 123 miles/198 km southeast of New Delhi, 3–4 hours by car or bus, 2 hours by the luxury Taj Express train. **AMARVILĀS:** Taj East Gate Rd. Tel 91/562-223-1515, fax 91/562-223-1516; in the U.S., tel 800-562-3764; reservations@oberoigroup.com; www.amarvilas.com. *Cost:* doubles from $640. **BEST TIMES:** mid-Oct–Mar.

An Eternal City on the Banks of the Sacred Ganges

THE GHATS OF VARANASI

Varanasi, Uttar Pradesh, India

Every Hindu yearns to visit Varanasi at least once in his or her life. Once called Kashi ("resplendent with divine light") and later Benares by Britain's empire builders, Varanasi has been the religious center of Hinduism throughout recorded time. The earliest settlement of this 3,000-year-old city (one of the world's oldest) began on the west bank of the Ganges River, believed by Hindus to hold salvation in every drop. Boats for hire take you along the revered waterway at dawn, when the light and the scenario are the most magical. One hundred or so broad *ghats* (stairs) lead down to the river, where it might seem that the better part of this city of one million people heads every morning for daily ablutions. Most of the bathers are old, since devout Hindus come here hoping to die, thus achieving instant nirvana and freeing the soul from the normal cycle of birth and rebirth. Hindus bathe in the river, drink from it, wash their clothes in it, and perform their contortionist yoga positions along its banks, which are lined with hundreds of temples and pilgrimage houses. Their bells and gongs only add to the surreal atmosphere as the sound of the conch shell welcomes the sun's first rays reflecting off the Ganga Ma, Mother Ganges.

WHAT: site. **WHERE:** daily flights to Varanasi from New Delhi (481 miles/774 km), Bombay (Mumbai) (950 miles/1,529 km), and a number of other major domestic cities. **WHERE**

TO STAY: best is the Taj Ganges, Nadesar Palace Grounds. Tel 91/542-250-3001, fax 91/542-250-1343; in the U.S., tel 866-969-1825; gateway.varanasi@tajhotels.com; www.tajhotels.com. *Cost:* doubles $165. **BEST TIMES:** Oct–Mar. Festivals throughout the year; Diwali, the Festival of Lights, is held Oct or Nov.

Echoes from the Paris of Asia

THE MARBLE PALACE

Calcutta (Kolkata), West Bengal, India

L eave the bewildering maelstrom of Calcutta's (now Kolkata) street life and step into the cool interior of the Marble Palace for a spin back to the 19th century. Making lavish use of Italian marble, the deep-pocketed Raja

Rajendra Mullick Bahadur created his personal folly, typical of the period's ostentation and the rajas' expensive emulation of haute Western civilization. Maintenance is not the strong suit of this crumbling city, where decrepit but stately buildings are clothed in moss and mildew, and this cavernous, once-grand mansion is no exception. It's now a ghostly stage set (often used by Indian film crews) that only hints at splendors and gala dinners from the days when Calcutta was the capital of the Raj, the second city in the British Empire after London. Descendants of the original owners live in the upper quarters, leaving the lower floors—chockablock

with inlaid mirrors, paintings, and memories— open to the public. One can only imagine the heirlooms that have been sold off here and there, but look what remains: a Reynolds, a Rubens, crystal chandeliers the size of elephants, enormous Baroque ballrooms and billiard rooms, Uffizi-like corridors with marble statuary and inlaid-mosaic floors, and an empty throne room where an errant peacock roams.

WHAT: site. **WHERE:** 46 Muktaram Basbu St., off Chittaranjan Ave. **COST:** Entrance free with a permit from the government tourist office. **WHEN:** open Tues, Wed, and Fri–Sun. **BEST TIMES:** Nov–Feb.

Where the Glory of the Raj Lingers

THE DARJEELING HIGHLANDS

West Bengal, India

G uarded by the awe-inspiring Himalayan peaks that rise out of the mist, the 7,000-foot summer resort of Darjeeling was founded by the British as a scenic escape from the searing heat of Calcutta and the low-lying

Bengali plains. During British rule, it became an exotic outpost that lured socialites, diplomats, and explorers bound for the Himalayas, just 30 miles to the north. From here, the thrill of watching the sun's first rays gild the snowy peak of Mount Everest is second only to the more reliable appearance of nearby Mount Kanchenjunga, the world's third-highest peak, and considered sacred by Buddhists. The British established Darjeeling as a major tea-growing center, and dozens of plantations can still be seen on all sides. Every afternoon a

The Darjeeling Toy Train made its first trip in 1881.

proper English tea is served at the cozy, old-fashioned Windamere Hotel, a gem left over from the days of the viceroys. The Windamere's profusely flowering gardens, mountain views, and simple, rustic rooms lure connoisseurs of classic comfort and excellent service, who warm to the idea of hot-water bottles tucked between the sheets and an after-dinner brandy in front of the fire that crackles in the salon in lieu of central heating.

WHAT: town, hotel. **DARJEELING:** the famous steam-engined Darjeeling Toy Train corkscrews up a narrow-gauge track (at an average 6 mph) for a 9-hour trip from Siliguri. It's a steep and winding 3-hour drive from Bagdogra—the nearest airport, 60 miles/97 km away—where flights arrive from New Dehli, Bombay (Mumbai), and all major Indian cities. **WINDAMERE HOTEL:** Observatory Hill. Tel 91/35-454-041 or 91/35-454-042, fax 91/35-454-211; reservations@windamerehotel.net; www.windamerehotel.com. *Cost:* doubles from $180. **BEST TIMES:** mid-Sept–Apr.

A Former Capital's Visual and Architectural Legacy

THE ROYAL SQUARE

Isfahan, Iran

With the finest concentration of Islamic monuments in the country, Isfahan is probably the most beautiful of Iranian cities. Shah Abbas the Great moved his capital here in 1598 and rebuilt an already

thriving trade center as a showcase for the wealthy Safavid dynasty; even today, many of the city's mosques, palaces, bazaars, bridges, wide avenues, and public parks reflect the glory days of his thirty-year supervision—one of the world's great experiments in city planning. The symbolic center of the Safavid dynasty and its Persian Empire was the immense Maidan-e-Imam (Imam Square, formerly known as Royal Square, and traditionally as Maidan-e-Naghsh-e-Jahan, the Square of the World's Image), one of the largest and most stunning public spaces in the world. Colorful tiled mosques and other 17th-century buildings—considered by the shah to be his masterpieces—form a glorious perimeter. Nearby, the complex and magnificent Friday Mosque (Masjed-e Jomeh) was built over a period lasting from the 11th to the 18th centuries (which included a period of Mogul influence on Persian architecture brought on by Genghis Khan's son, Olgedi, who lived here as a shah). Considered one of the world's greatest mosques, it has 476 domes.

Today's visitors can get a somewhat less lavish taste of the welcome granted to guests of the Safavid court by staying in the Abbasi Hotel, created in the shell of a 16th-century caravansary.

WHAT: site, hotel. **ISFAHAN:** 320 miles/ 515 km south of Tehran. **ABBASI HOTEL:** Anadegah Ave. Tel 98/311-222-6010, fax 98/311-222-6008; hotelabbasi@gmail.com; www.abbasihotel.com. *Cost:* doubles from $135. **HOW:** in the U.S., Distant Horizons specializes in small-group tours to Iran (including Isfahan and Persepolis) with a guest scholar. Tel 800-333-1240 or 562-983-8828, fax 562-983-8833; info@distant-horizons.com; www.distant-horizons.com. **COST:** 19-day trip $5,890 per person, double occupancy; includes airfare from New York, land package, all meals. **WHEN:** departures spring and fall. **BEST TIMES:** spring and fall.

Ceremonial Center of an Ancient Empire

PERSEPOLIS

Iran

In 512 B.C., Darius the Great chose to build a massive and magnificent palace complex on this spot, one worthy of the vast and far-flung Persian Empire, which knew no rival in the ancient world. Darius demanded the highest level of artistic and architectural achievement, and excavated tablets recount how, over a

The moody magnificence of Persepolis

period of sixty years, he had cedar brought from Lebanon and precious woods, stone, and gold imported from distant provinces to embellish the city, which became known as one of the wonders of the ancient world. In 330 B.C. it was captured by Alexander the Great and subsequently burned to the ground, though it's unclear whether the fire was deliberate or accidental (Alexander was not in the habit of destroying the cities he conquered). Persepolis sits on a plateau that rises 30 feet from the plain below, and even though the ruins today reflect but a shadow of its former glory, visitors to the approximately fifteen buildings that have been re-erected can imagine the grandeur of Darius's dream. Many scholars believe that the emperor never lived in Persepolis but used it exclusively during new-year rituals in the spring, when delegations came from all over his empire to present precious gifts to their mighty ruler.

WHAT: site. **WHERE**: 36 miles/58 km from Shiraz, or 400 miles/640 km south of Tehran. **HOW**: in the U.S., Distant Horizons specializes in small-group tours to Iran (including Isfahan and Persepolis) with a guest scholar. Tel 800-333-1240 or 562-983-8828, fax 562-983-8833; info@distant-horizons.com; www.distant-horizons.com. **COST**: 19-day trip $5,890 per person, double occupancy; includes airfare from New York, land package, all meals. **WHEN**: departures spring and fall. **BEST TIMES**: spring and fall.

Astounding Scenery Above the Clouds

JALJALE HIMAL

Nepal

Adventurers arriving en masse since the 1960s have indelibly altered Nepal's most popular treks, but unforgettable hill cultures and breathtaking scenery (minus the Coca-Cola signs and yellowed Rambo posters) can still be found on alternative, less-traveled routes. The Jaljale Himal High Ridge Trek in eastern Nepal remains something of a hidden jewel, offering some of the most pristine wilderness in the Himalayas today. There are regular views of four of the world's five tallest and most majestic peaks (Everest, Kanchenjunga, Lhotse, and Makalu) and some of the friendliest people in Nepal. Except for a handful of trekkers on the final three days, you'll see few non-Nepalese faces—most of the picturesque villages on this trek rarely see foreigners, so travelers can still experience authentic medieval Nepal and the daily life of its three ethnic groups (Hindus, tribals, and Tibetan Buddhists). But beware: This trip will spoil you. After Jaljale Himal, everything else will seem tame and commercialized by comparison.

A hillside vista

WHAT: experience. **WHERE**: trek departs from Tumlingtar, a 45-minute flight east of capital Kathmandu (included in rates below). **HOW**: a knowledgeable trekking operator is indispensable. In the U.S., Above the Clouds, tel 800-233-4499 or 802-482-4849, fax 802-482-5011; info@aboveclouds.com; www.aboveclouds.com. **COST**: 31 days from $3,800 per person, double occupancy, all-inclusive land package, includes 23-day moderate/strenuous trek and domestic air. Less-expensive and less-arduous 6-day treks cover a segment of the Jaljale Himal trail. **WHEN**: early/mid-Oct departure (shorter treks offered weekly Sept–May). **BEST TIMES**: mid-Oct to Dec and mid-Feb to Mar, for shorter trek.

The Heart of Old Kathmandu

DURBAR SQUARE

Kathmandu, Nepal

Since Nepal first opened to foreign tourism in 1951, legions of flower children have lingered in Kathmandu's history-rich Durbar Square (*durbar* means "palace"). With an astounding concentration of more than fifty temples, shrines, and old palaces within a few blocks, the square still has its moments of magic when not overrun with tourist groups, touts, and bicycle rickshaws. The sights, sounds, and smells can lead to sensory overload, and hours can be spent taking it all in from the platform steps of the triple-roofed Maju Deval temple. On the south side of the square is Kumari Ghar, the three-storied residence of the Kumari Devi (Living Goddess). Around the square, teeming modern consumerism

A quiet morning in Durbar Square

obliterates much of Kathmandu's medieval character as it rushes heedlessly toward the future. But it's still a great thrill to meander the tangle of back alleyways a bit farther from the square, reeking with incense and spices and full of hole-in-the-wall shops. Here, one can peek at a lifestyle that remains relatively oblivious to the arrival of Western visitors.

The Hotel Yak & Yeti is still one of the best in the area; it's also one of the most original and historically interesting. Ask for a room in the original wing, the royal 19th-century home of a former *rana* (prime minister).

WHAT: site, hotel. **WHERE:** Hotel Yak & Yeti is on Durbar Marg, just east of the Royal Palace, 4 miles/7 km from airport. Tel 977/1-248999, fax 977/1-227781; reservation@yakandyeti.com; www.yakandyeti.com. **COST:** doubles from $185. **BEST TIMES:** spring, autumn, and the end of Oct or beginning of Nov, during the Tihar Festival, a Hindu holiday honoring Lakshmi.

A Faded Medieval Time Capsule in the Kathmandu Valley

BHAKTAPUR

Kathmandu Valley, Nepal

Much of the area around Bhaktapur's magnificent Durbar Square is magically evocative of Kathmandu, Nepal's nearby capital, in the days before trekkers arrived bound for the Annapurna circuit and the Everest trail. Unlike rapidly developing Kathmandu, however, Bhaktapur (also called Bhadgaon, the City of Devotees) is still a small town of medieval tableaux that has nearly escaped creeping Western tourism. Its impressive architecture and recent townwide preservation (the most extensive in Nepal, thanks to a German-funded project initiated in the 1970s) is due to its prestige as a former capital, beginning in A.D. 1200, of one of the four independent kingdoms in the Kathmandu Valley. (They were united in the late 1700s.)

Durbar Square is bounded by the royal palace, with its seven courtyards; a sequence of pagoda-style Hindu temples; and the Golden Gate—made entirely of brass, it is one of Nepal's proudest artistic achievements. A short walk in any direction from the square brings you into the twisting backways where the town's potters and craftsmen, for centuries a source of the city's renown, carry on their unchanging traditions.

WHAT: town. **WHERE:** 9 miles/14 km east of Kathmandu. **BEST TIMES:** Oct–Mar.

Chomolungma, "Mother Goddess of the Universe"

MOUNT EVEREST

Nepal

The summit of Everest, the world's tallest mountain, is an epic goal that few mountaineers ever reach. But trekkers don't need to reach the top, nor even the overly popular base camp area, to experience the might of

Chomolungma, "Mother Goddess of the Universe," as Everest is known to the Sherpas. Many encounter Everest through a journey to the beautiful Khumbu Valley to view the magnificent scenery, with its fascinating high-altitude Sherpa villages, spectacularly sited Buddhist monasteries, and unique wildlife. A visual feast for mountain lovers, Everest-

Awe-inspiring Mount Everest

area treks are highlighted by breathtaking close-up views of the 29,028-foot peak as well as of heavyweight runners-up such as Lhotse, Makalu, and Cho Oyu. Balancing all this grandeur are the friendliness and cheerful good nature of the Sherpa people, whose hospitality provides a cultural experience as memorable as Everest itself.

WHAT: site, experience. **WHERE:** east of capital Kathmandu on the Tibet border. **HOW:** in the U.S., contact Mountain Travel Sobek, tel 888-831-7526 or 510-594-6000, fax 510-594-6001; info@mtsobek.com; www.mtsobek.com. **COST:** from $3,295 per person for 14-day trip (9-day trek). **WHEN:** treks depart Apr, Oct–Dec. **BEST TIMES:** spring and fall.

The Last Forbidden Buddhist Kingdom

THE KINGDOM OF MUSTANG

Mustang, Nepal

Surrounded by Tibet on three sides and governed by a Tibetan royal family, Mustang—a kingdom within a kingdom—survives as one of the last remnants of ancient Tibet. Although nominally integrated into the kingdom of Nepal in the early 1950s, it remains largely autonomous, and much of its medieval cultural fabric has survived. In fact, Mustang is said to be more like Tibet before the Chinese occupation than Tibet itself, filled with ancient walled fortress-villages and monasteries hewn from the rock, displaying a muted natural palette of grays and variegated rusty reds. Like much of the Tibetan plateau, the landscape is rugged and austere, a dramatic high-desert terrain flanked by towering peaks, including the snow-capped Annapurnas to the south. Though Nepal opened to tourism in the 1950s, Mustang's sensitive position along the Tibet border kept it off-limits until 1992, when the Nepali government began admitting a trickle of foreign tourists. Ironically, Mustang was well traveled in the past, its ancient trade routes dating back more than 1,000 years. Its treeless vistas must have appeared distant and extraordinary to European traders returning from China with their precious cargo. They would have been as hard pressed as today's trekkers to explain the otherworldliness of it all.

WHAT: experience. **WHERE:** northwest of Kathmandu and north of Pokhara. Treks depart from Jomsom. **HOW:** all travel to Mustang is restricted and must be made through a licensed trekking company; all treks are accompanied by a government liaison officer. In the U.S. and Canada, contact Asia 360 Travel, tel 877-274-2360 or 303-449-3712; fax 303-449-3712; info@asia360travel.com; www.asia360travel.com. *Cost:* 11-day custom package departing Kathmandu $2,195, includes guide, accommodations, meals, and airport transfers. **WHEN:** Mustang open to visitors Mar–Dec. Snow Lion departures twice yearly, Apr–May and Sept–Oct. **BEST TIMES:** spring trip coincides with Tigi, a Tibetan Buddhist festival.

Rooms with a View

FISH TAIL LODGE

Pokhara, Nepal

The only hotel with the good fortune to sit on the south side of Lake Phewa (royal ownership may have something to do with that), the Fish Tail Lodge has guest rooms with heart-stopping views framing all 22,946 feet of

Machhapuchhare (Fish Tail Peak). Its backdrop is nothing less than the Annapurna massif and some of the youngest mountains in the world, more than 26,000 feet high. The only way to reach the hotel is by rope ferry, manually operated by a round-the-clock raftsman.

If you have the clout of such former guests as Prince Charles or the emperor of Japan, you can ask for Room 17—the view doesn't get any better. Otherwise, loll in a hammock in the gardens that bloom year-round by the lake (the country's second largest), head out in a boat for some lazy drifting, and on cloudless days gaze into the calm water for a mirror image of these Himalayan Matterhorns. A glassed-in restaurant offers nonguests the same sensory experience, even if they can't be around for the unmatched sunrise spectacle for which the lake setting is famous. Undoubtedly a tourist town, Pokhara's rhythm is peaceful and slow. Many visitors here are gearing up for (or recovering from) short and long treks on some of Nepal's most popular trails.

WHAT: town, hotel. **POKHARA:** 125 miles/ 201 km west of Kathmandu, which can take as long as 5 hours by car due to the poor road; many choose to take 30-minute flight. **FISH TAIL LODGE:** tel 977/61-465071, fax 977/61-465072; in Kathmandu, tel 977/1-422-9647; info@fishtail-lodge.com; www.fishtail-lodge.com. **COST:** lake-view doubles from $150. **BEST TIMES:** Oct–Apr.

In Search of the Bengal Tiger in Asia's Richest Wildlife Sanctuary

CHITWAN NATIONAL PARK

Nepal

Chitwan, 360 square miles that were once the private hunting grounds of the king of Nepal and his guests, is now one of the finest protected forests and grassland regions in Asia. Boat and jeep safaris and treks by foot, led by naturalists and expert guides, explore the river kingdom and its prolific wildlife and bird species, said to number more than 500. But the best treks are a more traditional affair: A cadre of gentle elephants and their skilled mahouts are ready to take you in search of the great one-horned rhinoceros or the near-extinct royal Bengal tiger—of the hundred breeding adults left in Nepal, about fifty live in Chitwan and the adjacent Parsa Wildlife Reserve.

Tiger Tops Jungle Lodge, a cluster of stilted treetop-level thatched huts, sits within the parklands. In the early morning, it's like a chapter out of Kipling's *The Jungle Book;* at night, candlelit dinners (Tiger Tops has no electricity aside from solar-powered fans and reading lights) are simple, reminiscent of the safaris of Nepalese aristocrats and the Raj's great white hunters, who didn't confine their shooting to photographs. Elephant polo matches—once the sport of maharajas and kings and today an eccentric relic of colonial days—are resurrected during Tiger Tops' annual international tournament in December.

WHAT: experience, site, hotel. **WHERE:** 75 miles/121 km southwest of Kathmandu. Daily 30-minute flight from Kathmandu can be booked through Tiger Tops; the 40-minute car-and-boat connecting trip is arranged by the hotel and included in rates below. In Nepal, Tiger Mountain, tel 977/1-361-500, fax 977/1-361-600; info@tigermountain.com; www.tigermountain.com. In the U.S., contact Abercrombie & Kent, tel 800-554-7016 or 630-725-3400; info@abercrombiekent.com; www.abercrombiekent.com. **NOTE:** At press time, Tiger Tops Jungle Lodge was temporarily closed.

Tiger Tops is home to a large stable of elephants.

WHEN: open Sept–Jun. **BEST TIMES:** Mar and Apr.

For a Spot of Ceylon Tea at the Source

THE GALLE FACE HOTEL

Colombo, Sri Lanka

Connoisseurs of Raj-era hotels seek out the Galle Face, one of the few remaining colonial hotels not yet homogenized by heavy-handed renovations that leave them theme-park shadows of their former selves. Yes, the

A time capsule of Victorian architecture and grace

hole during British rule, when Ceylon was synonymous with tea. The vintage suites here are large enough to host a cricket match, with polished creaking teak floors, ceiling fans, and ocean views. A ubiquitous butler delivers breakfast with a smile and a certain cobwebbed quality of graciousness that the British must have been loath to leave behind.

Galle Face shows its age, but also its historical character and pride as Colombo's superior establishment during the British era. The glitzy five-star establishments in town can't pretend to duplicate its delightful 19th-century atmosphere, where barefoot waiters serve tea on a wide-open veranda swept by sea breezes—the prized watering

WHAT: hotel, restaurant. **WHERE:** 2 Galle Rd., in the south end of Galle Face Green in the historic section of town. Tel 94/1-541-010-16, fax 94/1-541-072; reservations@gallefacehotel.net; www.gallefacehotel.com. **COST:** doubles $55, royal suites from $130. **BEST TIMES:** Dec–Feb.

Honoring the Buddha's Tooth

ESALA PERAHERA

Kandy, Sri Lanka

The cultural stronghold of Kandy in Sri Lanka's lush hill country is well worth a visit any time of year, but visitors who arrive during Esala Perahera will experience one of Asia's greatest spectacles. For centuries this elaborate procession has honored the sacred tooth of Buddha, smuggled into Sri Lanka in A.D. 301, and eventually enshrined in the Dalada Maligawa (Temple of the Tooth), one of Buddhism's most revered pilgrimage sites. During the procession, the relic sits within its golden box atop an elephant, colorfully decked out from trunk to toe. A bright white linen carpet is unfurled before him so that his feet do not touch the bare ground. He is preceded by a show-stopping parade of dozens of other elephants and a frenzied cast of thousands of Kandyan dancers and drummers. Kandy's beloved Maligawa Tusker died in 1988 after fifty years of faithful service; his taxidermed remains are lovingly displayed in the Temple of the Tooth. A young Thai-born elephant specially trained for the role has taken his place.

It's hard to imagine Sri Lanka without its beloved elephants, an essential part of any *perahera*, or procession. From Kandy it's a fairly easy trip to the Pinnewala Elephant Orphanage, where some fifty-odd too-cute-to-be-true youngsters, some no more than a few weeks old, are already accustomed to being bottle-fed by visiting onlookers. Each drinks up to ten gallons of milk a day.

WHAT: event, town. **WHERE:** about 72 miles/115 km inland from capital Colombo, in the hill country. Pinnewala Elephant Orphanage is about 1½ hours by car west of Kandy, on the road to Colombo. **WHEN:** annual 10-day Esala Perahera festival peaks at the full moon of Esala, in either Jul or Aug. **BEST TIMES:** climate in Kandy is good year-round, due to its lakeside setting and altitude.

An Ancient Imperial Capital and a Restorative Seaside Resort

THE ROMAN RUINS OF EPHESUS

Turkey

One of the best-preserved ancient cities on the Mediterranean, Ephesus is Turkey's showpiece of Aegean archaeology. Although it is 3 miles away from the sea today, Ephesus was once one of the wealthiest trading port cities of the Greco-Roman era, ideally situated between the Near East and the Mediterranean ports of the West. Settled as early as 1000 B.C. by the Ionians, its extensive and impressive

The Library of Celsus

ruins testify to its ancient role as capital of the Roman province of Asia—in the time of Augustus Caesar, it was the second-largest city in the eastern Mediterranean, after Alexandria. Today, a mile-long marble-paved street grooved by chariot wheels leads past partially reconstructed buildings, such as the Great Theater (which held 25,000 spectators) and the beautiful two-story Celsus Library (built in A.D. 135), one of the largest libraries and most graceful surviving buildings of antiquity. The Temple of Artemis (known by the Romans as Diana, twin sister of Apollo) was considered one of the wonders of the ancient world. Only the foundation remains, but during Ephesus's heyday in 356 B.C., it was four times the size of the Parthenon in Athens, with a forest of 127 marble columns supporting a 60-foot roof. Ephesus continued to flourish until the 3rd century A.D., when it was razed by Goth invaders from Northern Europe. Hundreds of columns and statues disappeared from the site over the ensuing centuries; some showed up in Constantinople and were used to build and embellish its Byzantine cathedrals. Nevertheless, the Ephesus Museum has one of the best collections of Roman and Greek artifacts to be found in Turkey.

Kusadasi (Bird Island), a major Aegean resort, is the jumping-off place for Ephesus and a variety of other wonders, including the nearby Greek island of Samos. But while such proximity partially explains this formerly sleepy fishing town's metamorphosis into a coastal playground, its inherent pleasures stand on their own. At the end of the wide bay, now linked by

a causeway, an august Byzantine fortress still stands guard. The area is a popular destination for cruise ships and pleasure craft, and first-rate seafood restaurants around the harbor and a lively bazaar still offer the occasional find. On a small promontory in the bay, the eighty-four-room Kismet Hotel could get by on charm alone. Its personable owner, Hümeyra Ozbas, is a descendant of the last Ottoman sultan, Muhammed VI. Together with her husband, Halil, and their children, she runs the Kismet on a grand scale. Surrounded on three sides by the sea, with gardens of palms, pines, and night-blooming jasmine, the hotel manages to suggest a private Mediterranean villa complex and is the perfect place for a sundowner made with raki, the local anise-flavored liquor.

WHAT: site, town, hotel. **EPHESUS:** 12 miles/19 km north of Kusadasi, and about 107 miles/172 km north of Bodrum. *Cost:* admission. **HOTEL KISMET:** Akyar Mevkii, Türkmen Mah, Kusadasi. Tel 90/618-1290, fax 90/618-1295; info@kismet.com.tr; www.kismet. com.tr. *Cost:* doubles $185. *When:* Apr–Nov. **HOW:** in U.S., INCA arranges comprehensive deluxe tours of Turkey that include special after-hours entry to Ephesus and exclusive visits to mosaic- and mural-embellished apartments rarely open to the public. Tel 510-420-1550, fax 510-420-0947; info@inca1.com; www. inca1.com. *Cost:* 14-day itinerary from $8,295 per person, double occupancy (international airfare not included); longer tours available. *When:* INCA tours May and Sept to mid-Oct. **BEST TIMES:** spring and fall for sightseeing, Jun and Jul for beach weather. Music and dance performances during weeklong Ephesus Festival of Culture and Art in early May.

Pleasure craft fill one of Kusadasi's picturesque harbors.

Bazaar, Bath & Beyond

THE COVERED BAZAAR AND CAGALOGLU HAMAM

Istanbul, Turkey

I n the market for a flying carpet? Rugs galore, and everything else imaginable, can be had in Istanbul's great Kapali Çarsi (Covered Bazaar), a mini-city that sprawls across sixty-five streets and 50 acres and includes some 4,000 shops,

tiny cafés, and restaurants—all surrounded by a wall, and entered through any of eleven gates. Originally built by Mehmet the Conqueror in the 1450s, it's been substantially rebuilt over the years due to fires, though its original style of arched passageways and tiled fountains has been maintained. One of the largest (and oldest) shopping malls in the world, it offers a sea of choices for local curios and souvenirs: carpets, jewelry, icons, leather, water ewers, meerschaum pipes, ceramics, bronze, and copperware. Take a deep breath and plunge into the maze of twisting byways, where merchants offer small glasses of tea to discombobulated tourists in search of the elusive bargain. The occasional Istanbullu still comes here to buy a few meters of fabric or a gold bracelet for a special occasion, and, as is often the case, the side streets are the most authentic and evocative of the old days.

Once you're shopped out, a traditional Turkish bath is just the thing to help you decompress. There are still more than a hundred to choose from, but the best place to take the plunge after a long and dusty day of bargaining is the Cagaloglu on Yerebatan Caddesi. The Cagaloglu was a gift to the city in 1741 from Sultan Mahmud I, and it is believed that King Edward VIII, Kaiser Wilhelm II, Franz Liszt, and Florence Nightingale have all visited its magnificent white-marble domed steam room— Tony Curtis unquestionably did. Public baths were originally founded by the Romans, who

Get lost in the city of markets that stretches for 50 acres.

passed the tradition on to the Byzantines and from them to the Turks. Baths were a public utility because of water shortages, and provided a perfect marriage between the Koran's demand for cleanliness and the pleasure of corporal indulgence in a beautiful setting. Although most Turkish homes (especially in the cities) have adequate plumbing today, the baths remain a social institution.

Incidentally, the penalty for a man discovered in the women's baths used to be death; these days, you can escape with your life, but expect to find the men's and women's baths separately housed in interiors that have not changed much since Ottoman days.

WHAT: site, experience. **COVERED BAZAAR:** Yeniçeriler Caddesi and Fuatpasa Caddesi. *When:* open Mon–Sat. **CAGALOGLU HAMAM:** on Yerebatan Caddesi at Babiali Caddesi near Cagaloglu Square (near Hagia Sophia). *Cost:* admission.

Byzantium's Greatest Legacy

HAGIA SOPHIA

Istanbul, Turkey

The massive dome and four elegant minarets of the Hagia Sophia (Church of Holy Wisdom) rise above the chaos and hubbub of downtown Istanbul, for more than a millennium forming the most impressive silhouette on Asia's skyline. But step out of the relentless sun and find its essence in the haunting beauty of its dimly lit interior, one of the largest enclosed spaces in the world. The Byzantine capital of Constantinople was fast approaching its zenith as religious, commercial, and artistic center of the Roman Empire when, in the 6th century A.D., Justinian began work on this site on the Bosporus, which over time rose to become the greatest church in all of ancient Byzantium, symbolizing the power and wealth of its emperors. Sadly, much of the church's original gold and marble, and its 4 acres of intricate mosaics, were plundered during the Crusades in 1204 and carried off as booty. In 1453 Constantinople fell to the Ottoman Turks, and the church was converted to a mosque. In 1934 it was stripped of all religious significance and function, but it will always be a spiritual oasis, remaining as the single finest structure to have survived late antiquity.

Nearby, the rooms and restaurants of the Four Seasons Hotel offer views of the site as well as of the elegant Blue Mosque and its six minarets, built by Sultan Ahmet I beginning in 1609. Ironically, the Four Seasons building served for years as a prison where, beginning in 1917, dissident Turkish writers and politicians were incarcerated in far less sumptuous quarters than you'll find today. They might appreciate the irony, though they'd never recognize the spacious rooms, elegant appointments, and certainly not the seductively sybaritic baths. The courtyard, now filled with plants and birdsong, is a cool greenhouselike oasis where a restaurant offers meals that bear no resemblance whatsoever to prison fare. A Turkish coffee or a sunset cocktail on the rooftop terrace overlooking the spires of Istanbul creates a captivating moment . . . and then the lights come on, illuminating Istanbul's treasures against the inky night sky, and you find yourself a prisoner of pleasure, this time detained by the lure of romance and a staff the sultans would have envied.

WHAT: site, hotel. **HAGIA SOPHIA:** on Sultanahmet. *When:* Tues–Sun. *Cost:* admission $13. **FOUR SEASONS HOTEL:** Tevkifhane Sokak 1, Sultanahmet-Eminonu. Tel 90/212-402-3000, fax 90/212-402-3010; in the U.S., tel 800-819-5053; www.fourseasons.com/istanbul. *Cost:* doubles from $565. **BEST TIMES:** Apr–Oct.

Looking out to the Four Seasons courtyard and the Blue Mosque beyond

A Curiously Neglected Treasure

KARIYE MUSEUM

Istanbul, Turkey

A visit to this little-known mosque-turned-museum leaves visitors floored. It occupies what was originally the Church of the Holy Savior in Chora ("the country"), an out-of-the-way location on Istanbul's western edge.

It was first erected in the 5th century, then rebuilt numerous times. Much of the present-day structure and magnificent interior decoration was completed in 1321 by Theodore Metochites, the prime minister and leader of the artistic and intellectual renaissance that transformed late Byzantium. The Kariye Museum houses dazzling 14th-century mosaics and frescoes depicting biblical scenes from Adam to the life of Christ, as well as some of the most important and extensive Byzantine paintings in the world. Nevertheless, visitors often have the place to themselves, adding to the atmosphere of awe. Collect your thoughts afterward at the garden terrace, where tea is offered. A number of historic Ottoman houses nearby form an evocative pocket of Old Stamboul in the shadow of the

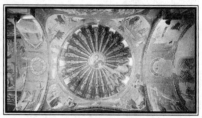

Experience one-of-a-kind mosaics and frescoes.

city's 5th-century walls (built less than 100 years after Constantine), which are several stories high, with walls up to 20 feet thick in spots.

WHAT: site. **WHERE:** by the Edirne Gate, Old City. Tel 90/212-631-92-41. **COST:** admission. **WHEN:** closed Wed. **BEST TIMES:** spring and fall.

*The Largest and Most Beautiful
Imperial Mosque*

MOSQUE OF SULEIMAN THE MAGNIFICENT

Istanbul, Turkey

K nown for its graceful minarets, stained-glass windows, and excellent acoustics, the Mosque of Sultan Suleiman the Magnificent (Süleymaniye Camii) is the largest and considered the most beautiful in all of mosque-

filled Istanbul. Crowning a hill with its looming, unmistakable silhouette, it is Istanbul's most

identifiable landmark, which is just what the builder had in mind. Suleiman I, the greatest,

Süleymaniye Camii is older and even more magnificent than the famous Blue Mosque.

richest, and most powerful of the Ottoman sultans, created this monument to himself between 1550 and 1557, and was buried here (together with his favorite wife, known in the West as Roxelana, "the Russian") just nine years after its completion. Near their elaborately tile-embellished octagonal tombs (ask for the *türbeler*) is the modest tomb of Mimar Sinan, Turkey's greatest architect, who was responsible for this extraordinary structure. Although the Süleymaniye is the most sumptuous (and, as it turned out, most famous) of the many tributes he designed for his patron, Sinan considered his masterpiece to be the Selimiye Mosque in Edirne, northwest of Istanbul, near the borders of Bulgaria and Greece.

WHAT: site. **WHERE:** Hesapçesme Caddesi, Beyazit. **COST:** admission. **BEST TIMES:** spring and fall.

A Rendezvous for Spies and Celebrities

THE PERA PALAS

Istanbul, Turkey

Stop by for tea in this century-old hotel, which drips with history and nostalgia. The Pera Palas was built in 1892 to accommodate predominantly European guests arriving in Constantinople on the Orient Express (and carried to the hotel in sedan chairs). Its guest book reads like a fantasy *Who's Who*, where the ghost of Mata Hari keeps company with that of Agatha Christie, who wrote much of *Murder on the Orient Express* in Room 411 in the 1930s. Turkey's national hero, Mustapha Kemal Ataturk (who would become the country's first president when it became a republic in 1923), preferred Room 101, which has been left just as he used it and is now a small museum. At present a much-needed renovation and restoration effort is underway which will preserve the building's cultural history while providing more modern amenities for guests. Visitors from the hotel's early days will still recognize the original elevator, which looks like a gilded birdcage, and the lobby's 20-foot walls of coral marble. The slightly faded atmosphere of the wonderfully Art Deco interior makes it a favorite with the British, and of film crews trying to capture an aura that only reality can exude. But guests pay a premium for nostalgia here, so many stay elsewhere and content themselves with a coffee in the grand salon or a drink at the bar.

WHAT: hotel, restaurant. **WHERE:** Mesrutiyet Caddesi, 89-100, Tepebasi. Tel 90/212-243-0737; www.perapalas.com. **NOTE:** At press time, the hotel was temporarily closed for renovation. **BEST TIMES:** spring and fall.

Treasures from the Sultanate and Tales from the Harem

TOPKAPI PALACE

Istanbul, Turkey

Over nearly four centuries, twenty-five sultans ruled the vast Ottoman Empire from the sprawling 175-acre Topkapi Palace complex, built on a promontory overlooking the Bosporus. Today many of the rooms and exhibits are dazzling and the legends so exotic that it is easy to imagine the time when the palace accommodated a community of 40,000 people and was like a city in itself. Most of the treasures of the sultanate have long since disappeared, but the pieces that remain on display in the Treasury are enough to jolt your imagination into envisioning what other baubles and trinkets were used by the likes of Suleiman the Magnificent. The famous Topkapi dagger is encrusted with enormous emeralds, as is the throne of Selim I, made with more than 25,000 precious stones. The Spoonmaker's Diamond, the fifth largest in the world, made its first public appearance on the coronation turban of Mehmet IV in 1648.

The other source of fascination in the palace is the harem (meaning "forbidden" in Arabic). The number of odalisques increased steadily with the decline of the Ottoman Empire, numbering more than 800 in the mid-19th century, when Sultan Abdulmecid I traded in Topkapi for the Versailles-like Dolmabahçe Palace up the Bosporus, equally ostentatious, though in a French, not Turkish, style.

If you want to try on the pasha lifestyle for yourself, consider the Sultan's Suite at the Çirağan Palace Hotel, which for a short time in the 19th century was the home of Sultan Abdulaziz. Majestically situated on the banks of the Bosporus, about 1½ miles north of Topkapi, the palace has been meticulously restored to its former state of unbridled opulence, with lush gardens, outdoor terrace restaurants, and a waterfront café. Guests not occupying the largest suite in Europe must content themselves with the standard rooms of the newer building next door, which are nothing short of regal. The hotel's much-respected Tuğra restaurant, on a terrace overlooking the Bosporus, treats everyone like royalty, serving classic Ottoman dishes while Turkish musicians perform.

WHAT: site, hotel. **TOPKAPI:** Sultanahmet. Entrance at the end of Babuhümayun Caddesi, behind Hagia Sophia. Tel 90/212-512-0480. *Cost:* admission $6. *When:* Wed–Mon. **ÇIRAĞAN PALACE HOTEL:** Çirağan Caddesi 32, Besiktas. Tel 90/212-326-4646, fax 90/212-259-6687; reservationoffice.ciraganpalace@kempinski.com; www.kempinski-istanbul.com. *Cost:* doubles from $495, Sultan Suite $28,300. **BEST TIMES:** spring and fall.

The original Çirağan Palace was built in the 17th century.

An Annual Event Is a Spiritual High

THE WHIRLING DERVISHES OF KONYA

Konya, Turkey

Konya is Turkey's most important center of Sufism, a mystical sect of Islam, and for nearly 700 years has been home to the Whirling Dervishes of the Mevlevi order. Their Mevlana Tekke (Mevlana Monastery) was founded by the 13th-century poet and philosopher Mevlana (master) Jalaluddin Rumi, who believed that an ecstatic, trancelike state of universal love could be induced by the practice of whirling around and around, in the manner of all things in the universe. Each year in mid-December his followers celebrate his *shebi Arus* ("day of union"—the day he died) by performing the *sema*, the whirling dance, one of the world's most mesmerizing spectacles. With their right palms up to the sky as if to receive God's grace, their left palms down as if to distribute it to the earth, the dervishes whirl around the room, directed by a dance master and accompanied by an orchestra of traditional instruments, and eventually assume a whirling position around the sheik, a senior dervish who represents the sun. In whirling away their earthly ties, the dervishes effect their union with God.

Following Mustapha Kemal Ataturk's overthrow of the Ottoman Empire in 1924, the Mevlevi order was banned as an obstacle to Turkey's modernization. After an interruption of twenty-five years, a group of dervishes convinced the local Konya government to once again allow the performance of "the Turn" as a cultural performance. It has continued annually to this day. The Mevlana Monastery—now a museum—is visited by more than a million Turks each year.

WHAT: event. **WHERE:** 160 miles/258 km south of Ankara. **WHEN:** Mevlana Festival held annually mid-Dec, culminating on Dec 17, the day of Mevlana's death in 1273.

Sailing the Turquoise Coast

THE BLUE VOYAGE

Bodrum and Marmaris, Lycian Coast, Turkey

A sailing odyssey along the "Turkish Riviera," where the Aegean and Mediterranean meet, unveils the glories of Turkey's ancient cultures. Whether chartered by a group or family, or individually rented by the cabin, a fully crewed wooden gulet, the two-masted diesel-propelled boat of traditional design, is the perfect way to explore the 230-mile serpentine Lycian coast, much of which is inaccessible by car. Here the waters take on a luminous blue that can be found nowhere else in Europe (hence the names Turquoise Coast and *mavi yolculuk*, or Blue Voyage) and provide the perfect backdrop to Greco-Roman ruins, sun-drenched beaches, simple lunches of fresh fish at cheerful dockside cafés, and even a small island given to Cleopatra as a gift by Marc Anthony.

Cruises usually cast off from the ancient port cities of Marmaris, Antalya, and Bodrum, the latter a former fishing village and charming seaside resort whose harbor is dominated by the striking Petronion, or Castle of St. Peter, built by the Knights Hospitaller of St. John of Jerusalem in 1402. Surrounded on three sides by water, it is one of the last and finest examples of Crusader architecture in the East, and was built from the remains of one of the Seven Wonders of the Ancient World: the marble 4th century B.C. tomb built for King Mausolus by his sister and wife, Artemesia. As grand a tomb as has ever been

built, it gave the English language the word "mausoleum" and stood for 1,500 years before being felled by an earthquake.

Bodrum has changed considerably in the last decade and is best known today as the yachting center of the Aegean. These are supreme cruising waters, with no fewer than eighty anchorages listed between Bodrum and Antalya. Most gulet cruises are booked for a week, but even a day trip south to the gorgeous mountain-rimmed Gökova Körfezi (Gökova Gulf) is worth it for the pleasures of a secluded cove and a simple fish lunch prepared by your crew. Generally speaking, cruises east of Marmaris take in classical sites, mixed in with some spectacular scenery, while the Aegean voyage west of Marmaris has a less ancient bent.

WHAT: town, experience. **WHERE:** southwest coast of Turkey. **WHEN:** Apr–Oct. **BEST TIMES:** mid-May–Jun, late Aug–Sept (avoiding the big tour groups that arrive in Jul and Aug).

A Cotton Castle of Curative Powers Since Roman Times

PAMUKKALE

Turkey

A freak of nature and a geological fairyland, Pamukkale (Cotton Castle) resembles a series of bleached rice terraces as you approach. The white travertine tiers, joined together like huge water lilies by petrified cotton-

candy waterfalls and gleaming white stalactites, are the result of hot mineral springs whose calcium-rich deposits have been accumulating for millennia. A popular resort since Roman times, Pamukkale still draws tourists, who are put in a festive mood by the bizarre formations and otherworldly weirdness. It is as dazzling during the day, when they appear pure white, as at sunset, when they pick up the muted pink and purple pastel colors of the sky.

Although proven harmful to the pools—and despite a ruling that will sooner or later

be enforced—wading in the 97°F. water is permitted for the time being, though anything other than a splash, a wallow, or a footbath is pretty much out, owing to the fact that most of the pools are only shin-deep. The otherwise unremarkable Pamukkale Motel is on the site of an ancient sacred Roman bath; sunken pillars and architectural fragments litter the bottom of the pool, which is deep enough for swimming.

WHAT: site. **WHERE:** 12 miles/19 km north of Denizli, 139 miles/220 km east of Kusadasi. **BEST TIMES:** spring and fall for sightseeing.

For Those Who Think They've Seen It All, Think Again

CAPPADOCIA

Ürgüp, Turkey

A trip to the steppes of Central Anatolia is the next best thing to intergalactic travel, at a fraction of the cost and inconvenience. Centuries of wind and water have sculpted a surrealistic landscape from the soft

volcanic terrain: minarets, cones, spires, "fairy chimneys," and rocky pinnacles in shades of pinks and russet-brown soar as high as five-story buildings and cover an area of about 50 square miles. Ancient inhabitants of Cappadocia hollowed out the tufa cones and cliffs to create troglodyte-style cave dwellings that are still lived in today. A major trade route between East and West, Cappadocia was home to a dozen different civilizations. The early Christians arrived in the 4th century, sculpting from the rock domed churches, complete with vaulted ceilings, columns, and pews. The open-air museum is the site of an ancient monastic colony, once said to have had more than 400 churches, hermitages, and small monasteries. Today fifteen are open to the public. Some of the simple frescoes date back to the 8th century, but it's the rich Byzantine frescoes of the 10th and 13th centuries that are the most astonishing.

Modern-day troglodytes must head for the utterly unique and charming Yunak Evleri

The eerie landscape of Cappadocia

hotel, a romantic web of tastefully restored connecting caves dating back as far as the 5th century.

WHAT: site, hotel. **WHERE:** Ürgüp, 279 miles/450 km southeast of Ankara. **YUNAK EVLERI:** Tel 90/384-341-69-20, fax 90/384-341-69-24; yunak@yunak.com, www.yunak.com. *Cost:* doubles from $150. **BEST TIMES:** Apr–Jun and Sept–Oct.

The World's Premier Carpet Marketplace

TOLKUCHKA BAZAAR

Ashkhabad, Turkmenistan

A ll color seems to have drained from Turkmenistan's dusty post-Soviet capital, but the Sunday market in Ashkhabad (the City of Love), an archetypal Asian bazaar as Cecil B. de Mille would have created it, is filled with a cast of thousands. It's a throwback to the marketplaces that for millennia have dotted this area, which was once crisscrossed by the ancient network of trade routes collectively known as the Silk Road. Most foreigners now come for the sheer entertainment value—you can buy anything here, but the draw for centuries has been carpets. Marco Polo wrote home about these beauties, commenting on their intricacy, quality, and rich colors. The Tolkuchka Bazaar is still one of the world's premier sources of rugs for serious buyers with a trained eye. Most are handwoven locally in the age-old tradition, but factory-produced alternatives with synthetic dyes have recently made an appearance. Although the style of carpets prevalent here draws its name from Uzbekistan's city of Bukhara, these rugs have always been made in Turkmenistan and were traditionally used to cover the floors and walls of the nomadic Turkmen's yurts.

WHAT: event, experience. **WHERE:** flights from Istanbul, Frankfurt, and Moscow. **HOW:** in the U.S., Geographic Expeditions includes Ashkhabad and the Sunday market on many of its trips to Central Asia. Tel 800-777-8183 or 415-922-0448, fax 415-346-5535; info@geoex.com; www.geoex.com. **COST:** from $7,995 per person, double occupancy, for 22-day trip through Central Asia, all-inclusive. **WHEN:** departures spring and fall.

An Authentic Living Museum

OLD BUKHARA

Uzbekistan

The 20th century hasn't yet arrived in Bukhara's Old Town, let alone the 21st, and even though the city's origins are lost in time, that didn't stop local authorities from arbitrarily choosing 1997 to celebrate Bukhara's 2,500th anniversary. Like Samarkand and Khiva, Bukhara was one of the legendary Silk Road caravan cities, but unlike its neighbors, it has avoided growing into a modern city (like Samarkand) or being so overpreserved that it's had the life squeezed out of it (like Khiva). Instead, Old Bukhara has a lived-in center. Close to 150 buildings are protected architectural sites, and overzealous restoration has been kept at bay so far. The 12th-century Kalan Mosque and Minaret and the 1,000-year-old Ismael Samani Mausoleum are some of the architectural highlights, but much of the Old City's present appearance dates to the 16th century, when Bukhara was capital of the Bukhara khanate. Of the dozens of caravansaries and bazaars, 100 madrassas (Islamic colleges), and 300 mosques that filled the desert city in those days, many remain, in various states of dilapidation and preservation.

Once you've seen Bukhara's famous monuments, take time to wander its backstreets, where goats have unofficial right of way, children romp, and old men fill the teahouses playing the backgammon-like game *shishbesh*. It's a precious glimpse of Central Asian life and culture on a more personal scale.

WHAT: town, site. **WHERE:** 5-hour drive west of Samarkand; closest airport is Tashkent. **HOW:** in the U.S., contact Geographic Expeditions. Tel 800-777-8183 or 415-922-0448, fax 415-346-5535; info@geoex.com; www.geoex.com. **COST:** from $7,795 per person, double occupancy, for 20-day Uzbekistan trip. **WHEN:** 6-day trips available year-round. **BEST TIMES:** spring and fall.

*Crossroads of the Living and
the Dead in Tamerlane's Capital City*

THE REGISTAN AND SHAH-I-ZINDA

Samarkand, Uzbekistan

U zbekistan has the most interesting historical and architectural legacy of all the Central Asian republics freed from Soviet domination in 1991. Its pinnacle is Samarkand, the navel of the vast empire held by Timur,

a.k.a. Tamerlane (1336–1405), one of history's greatest and cruelest conquerors. A fabled city that fired European imaginations with tales of its legendary beauty, it was built and embellished by architects, artists, and craftsmen abducted by Tamerlane and his descendants from faraway conquered territories. For 2,000 years, the city was one of the most important stops on the Silk Road, its bazaars thronged with merchants and shoppers.

Since its construction between the 14th and 16th centuries, Samarkand's Registan has been considered by many to be the noblest public square in the world, a breathtaking showcase of a civilization that placed supreme value on tangible beauty. A courtyard the size of a football field, it is surrounded on three sides by the soaring arches, towering minarets, and fluted turquoise domes of three madrassas (Islamic colleges).

Another of the most visually stunning sights in this city of superlatives is Shah-i-Zinda, a complex of mausoleums dating mostly from the 14th and 15th centuries. Exceptional masterworks of terra-cotta, majolica, and intricate tilework, they were created by master Persian and Azerbaijani craftsmen, and together form a showpiece of ceramic art that remains unrivaled in Central Asia. Some of the earliest mausoleums are those of Tamerlane's wives, his beautiful young niece, and his sisters, but it's the grave of Qusam

ibn-Abbas, believed to have been a cousin of the Prophet Mohammed, that is Shah-i-Zinda's most famous. An air of holiness surrounds the tomb, and three pilgrimages to it are deemed the equivalent of one to Mecca. Qusam ibn-Abbas is the "living king" who gave the complex its name, though ironically it's come to be known as the City of the Dead.

WHAT: town, site. **WHERE:** southeast Uzbekistan. **HOW:** U.S.-based travel agency MIR Corp., with an office in Tashkent, Uzbekistan, specializes in small-group tours and independent travel to Central Asia. Tel 800-424-7289 or 206-624-7289, fax 206-624-7360; info@mircorp.com; www.mircorp.com. **COST:** 15-day group tours from $3,995. **BEST TIMES:** Apr–Sept.

Wander around Samarkand's Registan, one of the grandest public squares in the world.

SOUTHEAST ASIA

Khmer Treasures in a City Rediscovering Itself

THE SILVER PAGODA

Phnom Penh, Cambodia

Once considered the loveliest of the French-built cities of Indochina, Phnom Penh has managed to preserve much of its charm through the violence of Cambodia's recent history; let's hope the same can be said after the current invasion of foreign investors and joint ventures. The best way to savor this fascinating city as it rediscovers itself is to stroll its wide, bicycle- and pedicab-jammed avenues, which are lined with colonial architecture in various stages of repair, and stop in at one of the sidewalk restaurants that are springing up around town. In the midst of it all, the sprawling Royal Palace is off-bounds to visitors except for a magnificent consolation prize, the Silver Pagoda compound. This is one of the country's rare showcases for the brilliance and exuberance of Khmer art and civilization. Pol Pot destroyed most of it, but he overlooked masterpieces like the life-size gold Buddha, weighing close to 200 pounds and adorned with over 9,500 diamonds, the largest approaching 25 carats. One can only wonder what the Royal Palace is holding back.

WHAT: site. **WHERE:** Silver Pagoda, M.V. Samdach Sothcaros and V. Oknha Chun. **WHERE TO STAY:** The Raffles Hotel Le Royal is the best of the city's historic hotels, at 92 Rukhak Vithei Daun Penh. Tel 855/23-981-888, fax 855/23-981-168; www.raffles.com. *Cost:* doubles from $300. **BEST TIMES:** Nov–Feb.

A Temple City Reborn

ANGKOR WAT

Siem Reap, Cambodia

Angkor, spread out over an area of about 40 miles in northwestern Cambodia, was the capital of the Khmer Empire from A.D. 800 to approximately 1200, and was abandoned in 1431, following the conquest of the Khmer kingdom. After decades of war and strife, its temples and monuments are once more open to travelers, and are among the world's premier architectural sites. The city's highlight, Angkor Wat, is a temple complex built at the beginning of the 12th century by King Suryavarman II. It took 25,000 workers over thirty-seven years to complete the construction, but after the fall of the empire, the complex remained unknown to the outside world until 1860, when French botanist Henri Mahout stumbled upon it deep in the jungle.

Angkor Wat is surrounded by a 570-foot-wide moat.

mysterious play of light and shadows joins nature's work to man's, evoking an *Indiana Jones and the Temple of Doom* atmosphere.

Now restored to its 1930s colonial splendor by Raffles International, the Grand Hotel Angkor is the ideal home base in the area, with a state-of-the-art spa and 14 acres of gorgeous gardens.

WHAT: site, hotel. **ANGKOR WAT:** 3.5 miles/6 km northeast of Siem Reap, which is connected by daily flights with Phnom Penh, 150 miles/241 km south. *How:* in the U.S., contact Asia Transpacific Journeys, tel 800-642-2742 or 303-443-6789, fax 303-443-7078; travel@asiatranspacific. com; www.asiatranspacific.com. *Cost:* 6-day land tour within Cambodia from $1,950, includes hotels, guide, and meals. Customized trips available. *When:* departures upon request. **GRAND HOTEL ANGKOR:** tel 855/63-963-888, fax 855/63-963-168; in the U.S., tel 800-769-9009; siemreap@raffles.com; www. raffles.com. *Cost:* from $180. **BEST TIMES:** Nov–May (dry season).

Constructed in the form of a central tower surrounded by four smaller towers, it was dedicated to the Hindu god Vishnu, and is embellished throughout with exquisite statues, carvings, and bas-reliefs depicting scenes from Hindu mythology.

Though considered a less-stellar attraction, the nearby fortified city of Angkor Thom boasts at its heart the Bayon, the last great temple built at Angkor. The Bayon is surrounded by fifty-four small towers that are now, like all of this magnificent religious complex, entangled in the dense growth of the implacable Cambodian jungle. The steamy undergrowth and

---

Beyond the Beaches on the Island of the Gods

THE HEART OF BALI

Indonesia

Package-deal tourists to Bali seem happy to stay in the Fort Lauderdale–like area of Kuta or to cocoon themselves in Sanur's toney hotels, but it's in the countryside—where Bali is vibrant with the theater of dance, prayer,

and mystery—that you'll really be able to absorb the island's magic. Here it is still possible to imagine that the October 2002 bombing—which shook Asia as the earlier September 11 attacks did America—never happened. Serendipity will lead you to the haunting rhythms of a practicing village gamelan orchestra, past a procession of lithe women carrying

impossibly high baskets of fruit offerings on their heads to the local temple, to preparations for a celebration that turns out to be a cremation. Bali's people are gracious and beautiful, a mix of Malay, Polynesian, Indian, and Chinese, and believe they are the chosen guardians of the Palau Dewata, the Island of the Gods, whose hilly terrain is peppered with temples (Ulu

Danu, beside Lake Bratan, is the most picturesque) and punctuated by constant temple festivals. Locals will direct you to tonight's
tooth-filling ritual or tomorrow's performance of
the kecak monkey dance. Visit the mist-
shrouded Mount Agung, at the island's heart,
considered by the Balinese to be the navel of the
world. Rent a jeep (or better, bicycles) to explore
the rest of the island, an abstract jigsaw of towns
and stepped rice terraces still cultivated by
water buffalo, with occasional harvest houses
built on stilts. Many of the towns specialize in
age-old crafts—to really understand Balinese
silver works, you must visit Celuk; for umbrellas, Sukawati and Mengwi; for wood carvings,
Mas and Tegallalang; for stone carving,
Batubulan; for traditional Ikat fabric, Tenganan.

WHAT: island, experience. **HOW:** for
biking or hiking tours, in the U.S., contact
Backroads, tel 800-GO-ACTIVE or 510-527-
1555, fax 510-527-1444; goactive@backroads.
com; www.backroads.com. **COST:** land costs for
6-day/5-night biking trip from $3,700 per
person, includes all inns, most meals. Bike
rental extra. **WHEN:** Oct–Dec departures. **BEST
TIMES:** Apr–Oct (dry season). The Hindu holiday Galungan celebrates the victory of good
over evil, with homes and temples decorated in
flowers and ornaments. It's held every 210 days.

See Bali at a leisurely pace by bicycle.

A Beachside Temple to Romance and Pampering

FOUR SEASONS RESORT AT JIMBARAN BAY

Bali, Indonesia

I t doesn't get any more romantic than this award-winning resort, disguised
as a traditional Balinese *banjar*, or village. Breezy, bougainvillea-covered
guest pavilions are strewn like so many frangipani petals across the resort's

The Resort Temple at the Four Seasons

terraced hillside, leading down to a private
4-mile crescent of white-sand beach and
turquoise waters. Privacy is paramount in these
sprawling three-roomed pavilions, despite their
open-air showers and sliding partitions that
broach the boundaries between indoor and outdoor. Each has a secluded, garden-surrounded
plunge pool, and if you arrange a *lulur* treatment—an exotic combination of Javanese
beauty ritual and age-old Balinese ceremonial
preparations—sarong-wrapped goddesses will
come to your pavilion to massage and exfoliate

you with sandalwood and spices from head to toe, splash you with cold yogurt, and soak you in masses of fragrant rose petals. With an introduction like that, you'll likely not resist any of the other intoxicating spa treatments, which—along with the resort's myriad water sports and nightly moonlit banquet—will be your rationale for never leaving this enchanting 35-acre oasis, your own little Balinese village. The Jimbaran's younger sister, the Four Seasons Resort at Sayan, is located about 22 miles north in the lush hills near Ubud, on 18 lovely acres on the banks of the sacred Ayung River.

WHAT: experience, hotel. **FOUR SEASONS JIMBARAN:** southern Bali, 15 minutes from Denpasar airport; $35 one-way transfer arranged by hotel. Tel 62/361-701-010, fax 62/361-701-020; fsrb.jimbaran@fourseasons.com. **FOUR SEASONS SAYAN:** near Ubud. Tel 62/361-977-577, fax 62/361-977-588; fsrb.sayan@fourseasons.com. For both resorts: in the U.S., tel 800-332-3442; www.fourseasons.com/locations/bali. **COST:** pavilions from $460, villas from $550; "Ocean and River" packages offer combined stays at both resorts. *Lulur* treatment (2 hours) $140. **BEST TIMES:** Apr–Oct (dry season).

Island Hub of Painting, Music,
and Dance, and a Temple of Hospitality

UBUD AND THE AMANDARI

Bali, Indonesia

T he Balinese have always believed that the gods live in the mountains, one reason to leave the teeming beach area of Kuta or Sanur behind and head north into the hills. For years Ubud has been known as the harborer of

Bali's artistic heritage—a significant distinction on an island where art is everywhere and everyone lives to create and embellish as a means of "making merit" and honoring the gods. It is useless to dwell on what Ubud was like before today's streams of tourists and foreign artists. The off-road town still possesses much of the allure that first drew European painters and sculptors in the 1920s, and their spirit lives on in the programs and schools for young artists they founded. Jump onto a ramshackle *bemo* packed with locals and chickens, and get off somewhere beyond the reach of Ubud's motorbike- and four-by-four congested main strip to find yourself among its fabled rice fields. Under the cone of an extinct volcano, farmers still cultivate these terraced paddies by hand, using a complex irrigation system dating back to the

9th century. You may see those same farmers perform in tonight's temple dance, and this morning's waiters from your hotel may show up as members of the local gamelan orchestra.

Sitting serenely among these terraced rice paddies, the Amandari resort (a name that roughly translates as "peaceful angel") is more retreat than hotel, a luxurious, idealized adaptation of a traditional walled Balinese village, built with native materials by local craftsmen. It is one of Asia's loveliest destinations. The reception area, an open thatched-roof building, recalls a *wantilan*, the meeting hall of all Balinese villages, while its pool hugs the contours of the surrounding emerald-green rice paddy terraces, overlooking the Ayung River and the valley beyond. With the gracious and ever-smiling Amandari staff (four to each guest), who come

A thatched-roof suite

from the nearby village of Kedewatan, visitors needn't go beyond the hotel's lush, temple-like, frangipani-scented grounds to immerse themselves in the magic of the Balinese spirit. For those who do venture out, the staff will share their knowledge about festivals, celebrations, and dance and music performances on the island.

WHAT: town, hotel. **WHERE:** about 1 hour's drive north of Denpasar's airport. The Amandari is located 2 miles/3 km outside Ubud; car transfer from Denpasar airport included in hotel rates. **AMANDARI:** tel 62/361-975-333, fax 62/361-975-335; in the U.S., tel 800-477-9180; www.amanresorts. com. **COST:** accommodations range from $20-a-night stays with local families to the Amandari, where double suites range from $750 per night. **BEST TIMES:** Apr–Oct (dry season).

One of the World's Last Frontiers

BALIEM VALLEY

Irian Jaya (Papua), Indonesia

Irian Jaya (now called Papua) is Indonesia's most distant province, and we're not just talking geographically. Adjectives like "tribal," "primitive," and "primeval" best describe the "lost world" of the former Dutch West New Guinea, just west of Papua New Guinea, with which it shares a disputed border. This journey explores trading paths that link local villages to the cool, green highlands or the vast lowland home of the Asmat people, known for their artistic wooden carvings and cultural rituals. There's even feasting and dancing around a roaring fire with aboriginal Dani tribesmen, best known to the outside world as the warriors of the Baliem Valley. They wear only their ornamental headdresses, war paint, and penis sheaths fashioned from dried-out gourds, which come in different sizes and lengths according to the occasion. These materially poor but culturally rich, gentle people teeter between the Stone Age and the 21st century.

You'll witness the former by leaving the valley's main town of Wamena, accessible only

One of the tribesmen in traditional attire

by air, and its fascinating marketplace to strike out on foot for some of the remote Dani villages. You'll know the local folk by the pig tusks the men wear through their noses.

WHAT: site. **WHERE:** daily flights from Jakarta or Bali to the provincial capital of Jayapura; continuing flight to Wamena in the heart of the valley. **HOW:** for organized land

tours contact Asia Transpacific Journeys, in the U.S., tel 800-642-2742 or 303-443-6789, fax 303-443-7078; travel@asiatranspacific. com; www.asiatranspacific.com. **COST:** 17-day expeditions from $6,995 per person (airfare not included); 24-day excursions also available. **WHEN:** 2 departures yearly: summer and early fall.

---

*The World's Largest Buddhist Monument,
and Lodging for Peaceful Souls*

BOROBUDUR AND THE AMANJIWO

Java, Indonesia

For those in search of spiritual secrets, the hour-long clockwise hike to the top of the massive pyramid-shaped Buddhist monument of Borobudur represents the timeless journey of man. Ideally, the journey ends with

complete detachment from the here and now—a concept that's not hard to grasp when you're suspended in space and hit with the powerful 360-degree panorama of Borobudur's four surrounding volcanoes. (Indonesia has more than a hundred active peaks, with sixty on the island of Java alone.) Built around A.D. 800, Borobudur was abandoned only 200 years later, possibly as a result of its being partially buried in ash from the eruption of nearby Mount Merapi in 1006. The well-preserved site was "discovered" by the British in the early 19th century. Over the course of a $25-million, ten-year international collaboration under the direction of UNESCO that was completed in 1983, Borobudur was painstakingly dismantled and reassembled. More than 3 miles of hand-carved reliefs representing the Buddhist universe of worldly, spiritual, and heavenly spheres wrap around its ten terraces. Gradually decreasing in size, the higher levels are studded with 72 bell-shaped stupas and more than 400 Buddhas, which give

Borobudur its prickly-porcupine silhouette. This is the world's largest Buddhist monument; it's ironic that it's located in a predominantly Muslim country.

Five minutes by car from Borobudur, the Amanjiwo resort echoes the circular layout of the monument, which is visible from most of the lushly landscaped grounds. There is no mistaking the Javanese spirit of Amanjiwo: It is as sensitive to the sacred setting as possible, yet it is also innovative and contemporary. Thirty-five freestanding domed suites—all with terraces and sunken tubs, many with private plunge pools—are arranged in half-moon terraces around the central stupalike main building. Such indigenous materials as teak, coconut wood, and local textiles have been reinterpreted with flair but in a restrained palette that keeps your attention on the setting. One of Amanjiwo's greatest draws is the chance it offers to visit Borobudur at dawn. Watching the mist rise off the rice fields and densely packed coconut plantations, revealing the silhouettes of distant volcanoes in the distance, is sheer magic.

WHAT: site, hotel. **WHERE:** on the island of Java, 26 miles/42 km northwest of Yogyakarta, 370 miles/596 km southeast of Jakarta. Amanjiwo is about 1 hour from both Yogyakarta and Yogyakarta airport and 2 hours from Solo. **AMANJIWO:** tel 62/293-88333, fax 62/293-88355; in the U.S., tel 800-477-9180; www.amanresorts.com. **COST:** doubles from $700. **BEST TIMES:** Apr–Oct (dry season).

Keeper of the Javanese Heritage

YOGYAKARTA

Java, Indonesia

I t is impossible to escape the pulse of Java and all things Javanese in the ancient village-cum-city of Yogyakarta, the island's flourishing art center. Visitors leave shopped out, enlightened, and entertained to their hearts' content. Rich in history,

"Yogya" and the nearby city of Solo, long havens of cultural refinement, are still ruled by sultans, whose sprawling *kratons* (palaces) are fascinating to visit. This is especially true when they become the venues for gamelan concerts, described as "the sound of moonlight." Exquisite classical dance performances, which originated in these very palaces, are still attended by members of the royal family and their batik-uniformed court retainers.

Royal patronage also keeps alive the inherent artistry of the Javanese, whose workshops are everywhere. Intricate silverwork, leather wayang shadow puppets, and colorful batik in every quality level and price range make shopping the city's many *pasars* (bazaars)

a herculean study in resistance. What doesn't tempt your eye will tantalize your palate—Yogya's street eats are ubiquitous and renowned. A visit to the nearby Buddhist monument of Borobudur is a must, as is the Hindu site of Prambanan, a 9th-century complex of 224 temples and shrines, 8 of which have been restored. During the full moon in the dry season (April through October), Prambanan becomes the floodlit backdrop for a cast of hundreds that performs the Ramayama ballet; it leaves even the most jaded international audience transfixed.

WHAT: town, event. **WHERE:** 370 miles/595 km southeast of Jakarta. **BEST TIMES:** Apr–Oct (dry season).

Twenty Minutes and Twenty Years from Bali

LOMBOK

Indonesia

A s Bali continues to suffer from tourist development and traffic jams, travelers in search of that island's lost innocence have moved on to Lombok, its unspoiled, unhurried neighbor to the east, where the population largely continues to live a traditional rural life. There is a saying: "You may find Bali in Lombok, but you'll never find Lombok in Bali." True, the island may not have Bali's Hindu temples, colorful festivals, and parades, but its people's smiles and welcome are just as warm, and in parts of Lombok Westerners are still something of a rarity.

The Three Gilis—small, sparsely inhabited islands off the northwest coast—are the current backpackers' meccas-of-the-moment, quiet spots known for their natural beauty and awesome snorkeling. In the north of Lombok, the three-day trek to the top of volcanic Mount Rinjani is touted to be one of the very best climbs in the area. Less-athletic visitors settle for a guided four-hour trek through farming villages along pathways that follow the contours of terraced rice paddies to 150-foot waterfalls.

With the exception of a tiny cluster of upmarket hotels on the western beach of Senggigi, accommodations are for the most part limited, rustic, and as a result incredibly inexpensive (as are the local handwoven textiles). The Oberoi Lombok is an exception, a shining star spread luxuriously across 24 beachside acres on Medana Beach, offering twenty thatched-roof Lombok-style villas with their own private pools (which are not to be confused with their oversize marble sunken baths). Pampering, seclusion, and privacy are the order of the day in this gorgeous microcosm of Indonesian style and grace, where (among other things) you can partake of the Oberoi Spa's special Mandi Lulur treatment, which combines relaxing steam heat with aromatherapy essences and the therapeutic effects of mud.

WHAT: island, hotel. **WHERE:** daily flights and ferry service connect Bali and Lombok. The Oberoi is on the island's northwest coast, on Medana Beach. **HOW:** tel 62/361-730-361, fax 62/361-730-791; in the U.S., tel 800-562-3764; reservation.tobi@oberoihotels.com; www.oberoihotels.com. *Cost:* terrace pavilions from $320, luxury villas with private pools from $620. **BEST TIMES:** Apr–Oct (dry season).

A Luxury Nature Camp in the Back of Beyond

AMANWANA

Moyo, Indonesia

Located east of Bali, the tiny island of Moyo is inhabited almost exclusively by butterflies, crab-eating monkeys, and rusa deer—plus a handful of cosseted barefoot visitors from this luxury nature camp, carved into a secluded cove amid lush jungle. The Amanwana gets its share of high-profile guests, but you needn't be trying to elude paparazzi to relish being both a million miles from civilization and within hailing distance of an excellent kitchen, superb water sports, and a hotel staff that lives to serve you. The twenty beachfront "tent" accommodations are actually spacious, canvas-roofed, teak-floored bungalows replete with camouflaged modern amenities, where the absence of TVs, telephones, and a daily newspaper will make reality seem like a bad dream.

Most of the island is a protected wildlife reserve, so guests eventually set off on a series of nature walks inland, jeep trips to a waterfall (where you can dive in from overhanging trees), or boat excursions to pristine bays and secluded coral coves. Amanwana is one of Indonesia's prime dive resorts, and

A tent with all the trimmings

its 1,000-foot vertical drop is home to giant lobster, turtles, and white-tip reef sharks. At 5 o'clock, everyone's aboard the hotel's wooden outrigger for a sunset cruise on the Flores Sea, the evening send-off to another fine day in paradise.

WHAT: island, hotel. **WHERE:** from Bali, transfer by air and private boat is $150 per person, round-trip. **HOW:** in Moyo, tel 62/371-22233, fax 62/371-22288. In the U.S., tel 800-477-9180; amanwana@amanresorts.com; www.amanresorts.com. **COST:** jungle tents from $700, ocean tents from $800, includes all meals and some activities. **BEST TIMES:** Apr–Oct (dry season).

Elaborate Funerals and Eloquent Architecture

TORAJALAND

Sulawesi, Indonesia

O nce known as the Celebes, Sulawesi is a fascinating island destination for exploring one of Indonesia's most distinctive cultural groups. Tanah Toraja, or Torajaland, located within mountainous folds north of the popular port city Ujung Pandang, is famous for its unusual and elaborate death feasts. A visitor hits the jackpot if he or she arrives in time for a local funeral ceremony, to which outsiders are enthusiastically welcomed. Joyous celebrations of the soul's departure for the hereafter go on for days, and are marked by flowing palm wine, music, dancing, colorful dress, and the sacrifice of a pig or water buffalo or two—or dozens, depending on the family's means. Wooden coffins and earthly goods are buried in caves hewn into the limestone cliffs. The Toraja profess Christianity, but instead of crosses, carved and painted wooden effigies—lifelike figures of the deceased called *tau tau*—line the cliffs. Although grave-visiting is the draw (there are cemeteries for the nobility, cemeteries for babies . . .), the island itself is a marvel to explore, for the templelike architec-ture of its *tongkonan* homes (bamboo-roofed structures that resemble the prow of a sailing ship), clove and banana plantations, bamboo villages floating on beautiful Lake Tempe, and remote mountain enclaves accessible only by foot. Unlike their policy in other parts of Indonesia, the colonial Dutch encouraged the Toraja to preserve their rich architectural and cultural traditions—with the exception of human sacrifice, a custom extinguished some time ago.

WHAT: event, experience, site. **WHERE:** daily flights to Ujung Pandang from Jakarta, Bali, and other Indonesian cities. It's a breathtaking 8-hour drive from Ujung Pandang north to Rantepao, in the heartland of the Toraja. **HOW:** for organized tours, contact NELL, tel 62/411-928-0999; info@sulawesi-adventure.com; www.nelltours.com.

Khmer Sanctuary with a View

WAT PHOU

Champassak, Laos

Built in stages between the 6th and 14th centuries—and thus predating Cambodia's Angkor Wat by 200 years—the hilltop temples of Wat Phou contain some of the best Khmer art in Southeast Asia. Even though centuries of abandonment left little of the original temples intact (they were only rediscovered in 1866), the scale and age of the complex is breathtaking, as is the hike up the massive stairs to the ruins of a 9th-century temple dedicated to the Hindu god Shiva. From this fantastic setting against the majestic mountain Linga Parvata, you can view the spectacular landscape—on a clear day as far as Vietnam and Cambodia. Below, the broad expanse of the Mekong River with its narrow fishing boats winds through fertile lowlands dotted by small villages.

Farther downstream, and often included in the same organized tour, is the Oum Moung, a less-elaborate Khmer temple that was probably used as a station for pilgrims on their way to Wat Phou. Little more than a romantic ruin, with less extensive and brilliant carvings than those at Wat Phou, Oum Moung is most interesting for the jungle walk that takes you there, beginning at a riverside settlement where life seems not to

Wat Phou as seen from a nearby hill

have changed since the 13th or 14th century, when the temple is believed to have been built.

WHAT: site. **WHERE:** travel by boat down the Mekong River from Pakse. **HOW:** in the U.S., contact Geographic Expeditions, tel 800-777-8183 or 415-922-0448, fax 415-346-5535; info@geoex.com; www.geoex.com. **COST:** all-inclusive 11-day tour of southern Laos (minimum of 2 people) from $3,500, includes domestic air. **BEST TIMES:** Nov–Feb.

Sleepy Backwater Town and Ancient Imperial Capital All in One

LUANG PRABANG

Laos

Most places in Laos are apt to take you back in time, but this is especially true in somnambulant, temple-filled Luang Prabang (City of the Buddha of Peace) in the mountainous north. With a population of just 15,000, it is Laos's second-largest city, still untouristed despite its former role as royal capital and the center of Laotian Buddhism. More than 600 saffron-clad monks inhabit its thirty pagodas, of which the most exceptional is the 16th-century Wat Xieng Thong, the Golden City Temple, built by royalty who held court in Luang Prabang until 1975, when the monarchy was abolished. Its many Thai-influenced structures, containing impressive images of Buddha, escaped an 18th-century invasion by Chinese pirates, making it the oldest in town.

Beyond the temples, visitors will find the city's unpaved back streets exude the same kind of Buddhist calm, with roosters roaming and children at play, while the main streets are lined with handsome French colonial architecture, including the former villa of Crown Prince Khampha. Now a hotel owned by the prince's daughter, it offers eleven simple but attractive rooms, a lovely courtyard, and an inviting upstairs veranda, but the Villa Santi Hotel's chief draw is its surprisingly sophisticated open-air restaurant, which serves full-course Laotian dinners. It's the most animated spot in town, but even here things are relaxed. Settle in for dinner after a stroll through the daily Nauvengkhan Market.

WHAT: town, hotel. **LUANG PRABANG:** 130 miles/209 km northwest of Vientiane. **VILLA SANTI HOTEL:** Sakkarine Rd. Tel 856/71-252157; www.villasantihotel.com. *Cost:* doubles from $120 (low season), from $180 (high season). **HOW:** in the U.S., contact Asia Transpacific Journeys, tel 800-642-2742 or 303-443-6789, fax 303-443-7078; travel@asiatranspacific.com; www.asiatranspacific.com. **COST:** 9-day tours of Laos, land cost from approximately $325 per person per day, includes guide, meals, hotels. Longer stays available. **WHEN:** departures Nov–Feb. **BEST TIMES:** Nov–Feb.

Carried Away on the Mother of Water

SAILING THE MEKONG RIVER

Laos, Cambodia, and Vietnam

Laos, Cambodia, and Vietnam share ancient and contemporary histories of war and French colonial influences, but it's the Mekong River that both links them and in many places separates them geographically, running along much of Laos's border with Myanmar (Burma) and Thailand, then through Cambodia and Vietnam and into the South China Sea. The river was once the major artery of the Angkor Empire, and remains an omnipresent symbol and lifeline of Indochina, along which its principal sites and cities were built and flourished. Today, glimmering Khmer temples, forgotten villages, and bustling markets line its timeless banks and dot the rich countryside.

A three-day Mekong cruise aboard *Vat Phou*—a handsome refurbished barge with just twelve cabins—provides a fascinating crash course on the hypnotic and little-visited Laotian segment of the river, viewable from the vessel's rich varnished-wood deck, which has the inviting charm of a wide veranda. But shore excursions call, including some of Laos's most imporant sites: the pre-Angkorian temple of Wat Phou, the roaring waterfalls of Phapheng (the largest in Southeast Asia), and the 4,000 islands that sprinkle the lower Mekong near the Cambodian border. The intricate network of tributaries that make up the 15,000-square-mile maze of the lush Mekong Delta in southwest Vietnam is a different experience from the river's broad upper reaches. Its rich fertile land provides three rice crops a year (making it the second largest rice exporter in the world), and communities of Khmer, Cham, and Kinh line the busy river banks. One-day trips from Ho Chi Minh City (Saigon) visit floating markets and enterprising farm communities and provide an insightful glimpse of Vietnam's "Rice Bowl."

Longer stays, with nights spent on riverboats, in simple guest houses, or with local families bring you deeper into another world little touched by the centuries.

WHAT: experience. **VAT PHOU:** the departure town of Pakse is linked with regular flights from the capital, Vientiane. *How:* in the U.S., contact Protravel, tel 212-755-4550; www.protravelinc.com. In Laos, contact Mekongcruises, tel 856/71-252-553, fax 856/71-252-304; www.mekongcruises.com. *Cost:* 2-night cruise from $435 per person (including shore excursions and meals). Packages including transfers from Bangkok or Vientiane (or abroad) available. *When:* departures from Pakse every Tues and Sat, Jul–Apr. **How:** Ann Tours has offices in Ho Chi Minh City (Saigon) and Hanoi. In HCMC, tel 84/8-3925-3636, fax 84/8-3832-3866; www.anntours.com. *Cost:* $70 per person (for groups of two) for one-day tour from HCMC to Delta; 2- to 8-day tours available. *When:* departures year-round. **BEST TIMES:** Nov–Mar.

Sleep in one of Vat Phou's *twelve staterooms.*

Epic Diving That Rates Among the Best

SIPIDAN ISLAND

Sabah, Borneo, Malaysia

"I have seen other places like Sipidan—forty-five years ago—but now, no more. Now we have found again an untouched piece of art," said Jacques Cousteau, thereby placing this speck of an island on every diver's

dream list. The tiny limestone island off the coast of Borneo offers little of interest, but walk 15 feet out from the shore's soft white sandy beach, stick your head in the water, and be prepared for the treat of a lifetime. Incredibly clear and calm waters enable even beginning snorkelers to experience the wonders of this underwater kingdom. Scuba

divers will find unparalleled wall diving, with a drop-off that falls 2,800 feet into a deep blue abyss, plus other, equally awesome dive experiences, all less than a five-minute boat ride away.

Sipidan's turtle population, one of the world's greatest concentrations, is indicative of the outstanding marine life that held

Cousteau in thrall. Until 1989, the only accommodations were in tents, but the rustic Sipidan Island Dive Lodge now offers a few dozen thatched-roof beachfront bungalows. This spot won't stay unhurried and unspoiled for long.

WHAT: island, experience. **WHERE:** 12 miles/19 km off northeast coast of Borneo. **HOW:** Asia Transpacific Journeys in U.S. includes Sipidan in their 16-day trip through Borneo. Tel 800-642-2742 or 303-443-6789, fax 303-443-7078; travel @asiatranspacific.com; www.asiatranspacific.com. **COST:** $325 per person per day, all-

Underwater visibility is greater than 100 feet.

inclusive except air. **WHEN:** trips offered in spring, summer, and fall (dryest months). **BEST TIMES:** May–Jun and Sept–Oct. High turtle concentration mid-Aug to mid-Oct.

In the Footprints of the Wild Men of Borneo

HEADHUNTERS' TRAIL

Sarawak, Borneo, Malaysia

For centuries the jungle area now called Sarawak was closed to outsiders and shunned for fear of its cannibal "wild men of Borneo." Its exotic rain forests are what most people imagine when they think of Borneo, and its communal longhouses, once home to notorious headhunters, now welcome outside visitors for the night. Retrace the original trail of the feared tribesmen, partially by longboat along the Baram River, partially by short treks through the dense jungle. Organized tours explore the Sarawak Chamber, the world's largest cave system, located in Gunung National Park; so far, twenty-seven interconnecting caves and 64 miles of passages have been discovered. You'll visit only choice areas, and stay to see the resident bats' evening departure in search of dinner. Gifts and food to share are brought to the Iban headman, the *tuai rumah*, whose longhouse will be your digs for the night. The river rides and primeval beauty of the encroaching jungle make this the adventure of a lifetime; sharing homemade hooch with your new Iban best friend isn't something you'll soon forget either.

WHAT: experience, island. **WHERE:** Borneo is the large island east of mainland Malaysia, its landmass shared by Malaysia, Indonesia, and Brunei. **HOW:** in the U.S., contact Asia Transpacific Journeys, tel 800-642-2742 or 303-443-6789, fax 303-443-7078; travel@ asiatranspacific.com; www.asiatranspacific. com. **COST:** from $325 per person per day for 9 nights, land only. **BEST TIMES:** Mar–Oct (dry season).

Luxury at the Jungle's Edge

THE DATAI

Langkawi Island, Malaysia

The Langkawi is an archipelago of ninety-nine islands called the Land of the Eagles. Located northwest of mainland Malaysia, where the Andaman Sea meets the Straits of Malacca, it is a tropical paradise of the purest white sand, magical sunsets, and idyllic sun-filled days. Just three of the islands are inhabited, and one is home to the discreet Datai, undoubtedly one of Malaysia's most beautiful resorts. Inspired by the local Malay kampong-style structures, and using native balau wood and local white marble, the Datai snuggles unobtrusively into an ancient rain forest. Aesthetic influences are at times Thai and Indonesian, at times hinting of Japanese or even Aztec.

The rain forest resort also has its own white-sand beach.

Lovely guest rooms, connecting corridors, lobbies, and the elevated Thai restaurant are all open-sided, letting in the jungle and creating a cool, exotic cocoon that ensnares and envelops guests, who are happy to stay within the exquisite grounds—except, perhaps, for those who make it to the hotel's adjacent 18-hole championship golf course, not your average rain forest attraction.

WHAT: island, hotel. **WHERE**: regular flights from Bangkok, Kuala Lumpur, and Penang. Hotel can arrange 30-minute transfer from Langkawi airport to resort ($20). **HOW**: tel 60/4-959-2500, fax 60/4-959-2600; datai@ ghmhotels.com; www.ghmhotels.com. **COST**: doubles from $435. **BEST TIMES**: Nov–Apr.

A Sultan's Island Escape

PANGKOR LAUT RESORT

Perak, Pangkor, Malaysia

They say Luciano Pavarotti cried when he saw how beautiful God had made this island—and Pavarotti has seen his fair share. Covered by a lush rain forest that's home to crab-eating macaque monkeys and more than 100 species of exotic birds, the island has escaped commercialization because it was the private domain of the Sultan of Perak until his death just a few years ago. The Pangkor Laut

Resort, the island's only hotel, resembles a Malay village, with dozens of simple bungalows built on stilts over the sea; it's one of Asia's most luxurious and beautifully situated hotels. As befits its five-star status, the resort offers a host of amenities and facilities, including sandy white beaches (with perfectly appropriate names like Emerald Bay) and handsome yachts and cruisers for visiting neighboring islands in the storied Straits of Malacca. Less peripatetic guests spend their entire vacation on their private balconies overlooking the water, completely disconnected from the world. Others prefer the hillside villas lost amid the ancient treetops. The resort's excellent restaurants serve everything from Chinese and Malaysian to East-meets-West cuisines in a number of handsome open-air pavilions or alfresco, under a canopy of a billion stars. Who wouldn't cry from joy?

WHAT: island, hotel. **PERAK:** off the western coast of Perak State. **HOW:** 45-minute private boat from the mainland port of Lamut, which is 150 miles/241 km north of Kuala Lumpur (one-way limo costs $155). **PANGKOR LAUT RESORT:** tel 60/327-831-000, fax 60/5-699-1200. In the U.S., tel 011/800-9899-9999; www.pangkorlautresort.com. *Cost:* villas from $350. **BEST TIMES:** pleasant temperatures year-round; Jun and Jul least rainy.

Pearl of the Orient

PENANG

Malaysia

No sun-and-fun island (though it does have palm-fringed, casuarina-shaded beaches on its northern coast), Penang has been a vibrant cultural crossroads since the first permanent Western settlement in the Far East was established here in 1786. At the time, the port cities on the Straits of Malacca were strategic way stations on European traders' lucrative routes from Madras to Canton. Today it's one of the most colorful, multiethnic communities in Asia, with Muslim Malays, Indians of various religions, and Buddhist Chinese successfully coexisting. The island recognizes and shows off its heritage in a more authentic manner than does Singapore, for instance. In the main city of Georgetown, a ride on a man-pedaled trishaw is a classic way to enjoy some of the best-preserved English colonial architecture in Southeast Asia. Colonial-era shops, temples, and clan houses make Penang's Chinatown authentic.

Follow the English of yore and jump on the funicular for a joyride up 2,720 feet through dense jungle and bamboo groves to the top of Penang Hill, where you can escape the heat and enjoy a panoramic view of the island and its harbor. And don't leave the island without stepping into the recently refurbished E&O—the Eastern & Oriental Hotel. Sister hotel to Singapore's Raffles and the Strand in Yangon, Myanmar, it was built in 1884 and stands today as a grand reminder of colonial days, when visitors like Noël Coward, Rudyard Kipling, and Somerset Maugham dallied over gin slings on the breezy veranda.

WHAT: town, hotel. **PENANG:** 250 miles/402 km northwest of Kuala Lumpur. Daily flights from Bangkok, Singapore, and Kuala Lumpur. **E&O HOTEL:** 10 Farquhar St. Tel 60/4-222-2000 or 60/4-261-8333, fax 60/4-261-6333; reservations@e-o-hotel.com; www.e-o-hotel.com. *Cost:* doubles from $225. **BEST TIMES:** Sept–Feb.

Floating Islands and Jumping Cats

INLE LAKE

Myanmar (Burma)

Inle Lake's quiet magic is worlds away from the congested capital Yangon, offering a time-warp setting of serene waters, gentle light, and warm smiles. The tribal people subsist on fishing and farming their man-made floating islands,

which are anchored to the lake's shallow bottom by bamboo poles that eventually become rooted. Settled centuries ago by the Intha, or "sons of the lake," Inle is roughly the size of Manhattan, so motorized boats are used for long stretches, but most trips through the maze of canals at the lake's edge are by flat-bottomed canoes. Of the twenty-some simple villages—some no more than a small cluster of fragile bungalows sitting gingerly on stilts—Ywama is the best known because of its floating market, which takes place every five days. The hardworking Intha pile their canoes high with leafy greens, rice, melons, bright flowers, and the plump, tasty tomatoes for which Inle is known. By 9 A.M. the market is winding down for the locals, and when the canoes show up bearing curious Westerners, all attention swings to the animated sale of bamboo hats, bundles of Burmese cigars, woven shoulder bags, traditional silk and cotton sarongs, and carved wood

Buddhas. If you miss the market in Ywama, make sure you go looking for it: It travels to other villages on other days of the week.

Of the many teakwood temples and monasteries on stilts, Nga Phe Kyaung is the most curious. Known as the "Jumping Cat Monastery," its monks have trained their cats to do various tricks, demonstrating that maybe they have just a little too much free time on their hands.

WHAT: site. **WHERE:** daily flights connect Inle Lake to Yangon in the south and Mandalay in the north. Inle Lake's Heho airport is 45 minutes by car to the lake. **WHERE TO STAY:** the lake's premier location is the lovely Inle Princess Resort. Tel/fax 95/1-211-226 or 95/1-210-972 in Yangon; princess@yangon.net.mm; www.inleprincessresort.com. *Cost:* doubles from $65; bungalows from $100. **BEST TIMES:** Sept–Mar (Sept–Oct for lake holidays and Nov for fairest weather).

Sailing Through a 2,500-Year-Old Civilization

THE ROAD TO MANDALAY RIVER CRUISE

Mandalay, Myanmar (Burma)

Mandalay—one of the most evocative names on the globe. Kipling immortalized it (though he never visited) and Sinatra sang the tune. The capital of Burma (now Myanmar) prior to British rule (which lasted from the mid-19th century until 1948), and known as the Golden City, Mandalay was built in the 19th century by the last of the royal leaders and is still redolent of its royal past as the heartland of Burmese culture and religion. Its huge market is a thriving phantasmagoria of earthy smells and a polyglot mixture of cultures.

Mandalay is the starting point for a cruise down the Ayeyarwady (Irrawaddy) River, the country's great natural highway and the focal point of Burmese life. The urban centers of its 2,500-year-old civilization line the banks, including the city of Bagan (formerly Pagan), where, along 8 miles of riverbank, some 2,200 Buddhist pagodas nestle so close together that they resemble a forest of spires and pinnacles. Founded by a Burmese king in A.D. 849, Bagan reached its apogee about 1000 and was abandoned in 1283 when Kublai Khan, in control of northern India, swept south with his soldiers. It was believed that building religious structures gained merit for a king and his people, so an army of skilled artisans embellished this spiritual center with what may originally have been more than 10,000 religious monuments. Much has disappeared—perishable teak burned by fires, all else eroded or destroyed by earthquakes and the passage of time. Nevertheless, what remains is one of the world's great archaeological sites, which some believe surpasses those of Indonesia's Borobudur and Cambodia's Angkor Wat. Shwezigon Pagoda, the most important of those you can see today, is said to house the collarbone and

The deluxe river cruiser passes the temples of Bagan.

a tooth of the Buddha. For an almost sacred experience, watch the sunset from the crumbling terraces of the Gawdawpalin Pagoda.

Your deluxe floating hotel, the *Road to Mandalay* (owned and operated by Orient-Express), is a microcosm of Burmese hospitality and European efficiency. In an enchanting country emerging after forty years of self-imposed isolation, where hotels, transport, and infrastructure are only now being developed and the people couldn't be more gracious, it's the only way to visit many of the special sites, which are often accessible only by water.

WHAT: town, site, experience. **WHERE:** departures from Bagan or Mandalay, from 3 days. **HOW:** contact Orient-Express Trains and Cruises, tel 800-524-2420; www.orient-express.com. **COST:** from 3-night cruise $2,200 per person, double occupancy; includes all meals. **WHEN:** year-round except Jun-Jul. **BEST TIMES:** Nov–Feb.

The Soul of Yangon

SHWEDAGON PAGODA

Yangon (Rangoon), Myanmar (Burma)

Rudyard Kipling wrote: "The golden dome said: 'This is Burma, and it will be quite unlike any land you know about.'" Stunned by the size and richness of the Shwedagon Pagoda, Kipling might well have been struck speechless had he ever actually made it inside the temple area. Sheathed in gold worth some $90 million, the glowing bell-shaped stupa stands at the center of the 14-acre Shwedagon complex. Tradition dictates that devotees and visitors walk clockwise as they pass a profusion of mosaic-covered columns, spires, ornate prayer pavilions, images of Buddha, seventy-eight smaller filigreed pagodas, and everywhere those who have come to pray, meet, meditate, chat, and watch their children at play. Bells tinkle. Incense burns. The perfume of flower offerings, the brilliant colors of the traditional *pasos* and *longi* (sarongs worn by men and women, respectively), the deep-saffron robes of the Buddhist monks, and the sound of gentle chanting and prayer create a sensual melange. The radiant thirty-two-story stupa rises ever upward, topped by a golden orb that is studded with 4,350 diamonds and precious stones, including a 76-carat diamond on its tip. To Buddhists, this is the most revered site in the country, said to house relics from the four Buddhas who have so far appeared on earth. It is most resplendent at sunset.

At the Savoy, a historical colonial-style hotel, ask for accommodations that overlook the pagoda, or take in the view from the hotel's appropriately (if too obviously) named Kipling's restaurant. After a day of battling tropical humidity and the dilapidated, fume-belching buses on Yangon's wide, tree-lined boulevards, first-world trappings such as air-conditioning and Yangon's only wine bar are a comfortable joy.

WHAT: site, hotel. **SHWEDAGON PAGODA:** on Singuttara Hill. **SAVOY HOTEL:** 129 Dhammazedi Rd. Tel 95/1-526-289, fax 95/1-524-891; res-savoy@myanmar.com.mm; www.savoy-myanmar.com. *Cost:* doubles from $95. **BEST TIMES:** Oct–Feb.

Earth Art, Millennia Old

BANAUE RICE TERRACES

Banaue, Luzon, Philippines

Banaue's rice terraces were carved out of the Cordillera Central mountain range more than 2,000 years ago and are still maintained as a way of irrigating the area's steep slopes, which rise to more than 5,000 feet above

sea level. Access is difficult, since the roads are roughly paved, but the effort rewards you with gorgeous views of one of the lesser-known wonders of the ancient world, covering more than 4,000 square miles. Bring a sweater, plenty of film, and good hiking boots, as Banaue is the perfect base from which to visit the villages of the Ifugao, the region's tribal people. The quality of light, the mountain air, and the drama of the ancient earthworks may make you leave your heart in the

Ancient terracing preserves precious topsoil.

highlands. The modest Banaue Hotel is the nicest operation in the area, offering balconied rooms and commanding views of the rice terraces. Staff can organize trips by car or by foot into the surrounding country.

WHAT: site, hotel. **BANAUE:** 220 miles/ 354 km north of Manila. **BANAUE HOTEL:** tel 63/74-386-4087, fax 63/74-386-4088; www. philtourism.com. *Cost:* doubles from $48. **BEST TIMES:** Oct–May (dry season).

A Lake Within a Volcano Within a Lake Within an Island

TAAL VOLCANO

Tagaytay, Luzon, Philippines

P ack a picnic lunch and head south out of traffic-jammed Manila to Taal Volcano, one of Asia's most beautiful panoramas. Among the world's lowest and smallest volcanoes, Taal is filled with water, creating a lake,

yet the volcano itself is located within a larger lake. (As the tour guides are wont to chant, "a lake within a volcano, within a lake, within the island of Luzon.") The blues and greens of the vista from forested Tagaytay Ridge have for generations made this a favorite getaway from the heat and chaos of downtown Manila. Boat trips across the crater lake and to Volcano Island are easily arranged, and there's horseback riding and a lovely hotel and casino too.
WHAT: site. **WHERE:** 40 miles/64 km south of Manila. **WHERE TO STAY:** rooms with a view can be booked at the Taal Vista Lodge.

Tel 63/886-4325; www.taalvistahotelcom, fax 63/812-1164. **COST:** doubles from $135. **BEST TIMES:** Feb–Apr.

Taal's first recorded eruption was in 1572.

Garboesque Isolation on a Private Isle

AMANPULO

Pamalican Island, Philippines

O f the Philippines' 7,000-odd islands, Pamalican is a very special getaway, a minuscule speck in the Sula Sea on which has been created a sibling of the Aman Resort, the archetypal luxury Asian getaway. Roll out of your

immense bed, pad across your enormous private casita, and awaken with the day on the

Amanpulo's footprint-free talcum-powder beach, surely the most dazzling in the Philippines.

Leaving your airy home will be the day's biggest challenge; the forty exquisite casitas are modeled after traditional bahay kubo houses, built of local materials, and decorated with gallery-quality crafts. If you do make it outside, you can engage in a host of enticing water activities including windsurfing, sailing, fishing, and most especially scuba diving—a coral reef encircles the 220-acre island only about 1,000 feet from shore, in some of the purest water you'll ever see. The hillside swimming pool seems to have no edges, a trademark of the Aman aesthetic, and it commands spectacular views of the surrounding islands, all framed by the multiple aquamarine, peacock, and turquoise blues of the sea.

Lazy days beckon.

WHAT: hotel. **WHERE:** 90-minute flight from Manila ($400 round-trip). In the Philippines, tel 632/759-4040, fax 632/759-4044; in the U.S., tel 800-477-9180; amanpulo@aman resorts.com; www.amanresorts.com. **COST:** beach casitas from $750 a night. **BEST TIMES:** Nov–May.

Life on the Slow Track

THE EASTERN & ORIENTAL EXPRESS

Singapore

Its pace as leisurely as life in the region's kampong villages, the luxurious Eastern & Oriental train travels from Singapore, the Lion State, up the Malay Peninsula through historical rubber plantations all the way to Bangkok, Thailand's frenzied City of Angels, then back again. Tea estates and hilltop pagodas roll by your window as you travel mile after mile through the jungle, its smell heavy and damp. From the observation car, glimpses of country life are precious snapshots: rice paddies dotted with toiling farmers, plows drawn by water buffalo, children in thatched-roof villages waving as the train passes by. Inside, your time machine on wheels is an indulgent world of opulence, its small but elegant compartments evocative of another era, its dining cars decorated with Chinese lacquer, Malaysian motifs, and Thai silks, and serving exquisite Eurasian meals. After making the 1,200-mile, forty-

Step into a dining car from another era.

hour journey, you'll have an urge to stay on and repeat the entire romantic and much-too-short experience in the opposite direction—if only to maintain the illusion that you're in the movie *Shanghai Express* and Marlene Dietrich is about to step into the coach.

WHAT: experience. **WHERE:** Singapore to Bangkok or the reverse. In Singapore, tel 65/6392-3500, fax 65/6294-0645, in the U.S., tel 800-524-2420; www.orient-expresstrains. com. **COST:** 2-night/3-day journeys from Singapore to Bangkok or reverse from $2,210 per person, includes all meals and some ground excursions. **WHEN:** weekly departures. **BEST TIMES:** Mar–Oct.

A Colonial Grand Dame of Literary Tradition

RAFFLES HOTEL

Singapore

This famed white elephant, landscaped with rustling palms and frangipani trees, its public rooms strewn with Asian period pieces and Oriental carpets, "stands for all the fables of the exotic East"—or so wrote Somerset Maugham. After an extensive restoration that managed to leave its 100-year-old soul and history intact, Raffles Hotel, one of Asia's great colonial landmarks, is once more the theatrical magnet for well-heeled travelers and the merely curious. It's as much a tourist attraction as it is a luxury hotel. In its spacious suites, teak floorboards, 14-foot ceilings, and overhead fans recall Raffles's first heyday, when Singapore was known as "the crossroads of the East."

As is true in most Asian cities, some of Singapore's best restaurants can be found in its hotels, and of the many at Raffles, the Empress Room is a standout, serving some of the best Chinese cuisine and dim sum in a city that is a food-lover's paradise. As for bars, Maugham liked his Million Dollar Cocktail in the hotel's Writers Bar (watering hole for the likes of Joseph Conrad and Rudyard Kipling), though the average visitor today heads for the Long Bar, where the Singapore Sling was invented in 1915; more than 2,000 are concocted here on a good day.

WHAT: hotel, restaurant. **WHERE:** 1 Beach Rd. **HOW:** tel 65/6337-1886, fax 65/6339-7650; in the U.S., tel 800-768-9009 or 506-870-6794; raffles@raffles.com; www. raffles.com. **COST:** doubles from $375. **BEST TIMES:** Mar–Oct.

A Grand Buffet in a Great Eating City

SINGAPORE'S STREET FOOD

Singapore

Food-crazed Singapore is probably the best place on earth for sampling the astonishing variety of Asia's many cuisines. There are formal restaurants galore, but what you're looking for is the city's wealth of street food, where

Singapore offers some of the most delicious street food in the world.

visiting dignitaries bond with cabdrivers at all hours of the day. And so what if it's not exactly on the street: This being tidy Singapore, street vendors have been confined to government-regulated "hawker centers." Locals and visitors alike can take advantage of these concentrated spots, where seemingly hundreds of stalls and booths prepare a staggering variety of food, all under stringent health inspection. Here among the din of clanging trays, the shouted orders, the tropical heat, and the smells of fermented fish paste, ginger, and

curry is a gastronomic and cultural experience that can be had only in Singapore. Malaysian, Indonesian, Indian, and Chinese cuisines are blended and reblended into Pacific Rim fusion at its most glorious. Even Hong Kong runs a distant second.

Every Singaporean has his or her own favorite hawker center, though they're often located out of town in large housing developments. There have been rumors that the Newton Circus hawker center, the most famous and the most touristy, will be torn down soon, though it remains as popular as ever. The noisy and confusing Chinatown Food Center is essential as much for its sights and smells as for the chance to sample every conceivable variety of Chinese food.

WHAT: experience, restaurant. **NEWTON CIRCUS:** Newton Rd. at Scotts Rd., near the MRT station. **CHINATOWN FOOD CENTER:** Smith St., between New Bridge Rd. and Trengganu St. **COST:** an assortment of dishes from various stalls, plus beer, should run between $10 and $20. **WHEN:** daily, late morning to late night. **BEST TIMES:** Mar–Oct.

Cruising the River of Kings to Siam's Ancient Capital

AYUTHAYA

Thailand

Once "the pearl of the east," the artistic, spiritual, and military center of Southeast Asia, Ayuthaya was the capital of Thailand from A.D. 1350 until its destruction by marauding Burmese four centuries later. Thirty-three kings of various dynasties built hundreds of temples and thousands of images to Buddha in a city-state that archives claim was one of the richest and fairest in Southeast Asia. The city's destruction in 1767 was so complete that rather than rebuild, the heartbroken king chose to relocate his court to Bangkok, 50 miles downriver. Today its ruins and canals (which are slowly being restored

and reclaimed) still speak of the city's former splendor, and visitors with a good imagination—and a good guide—will have no difficulty grasping its onetime grandeur and importance.

The royal way of visiting Ayuthaya today is via the Chao Phraya River, the River of Kings. Snaking 227 miles from Thailand's northern highlands to the Gulf of Siam (though technically speaking, everything above the lower 160 miles is known by a different name), it is Bangkok's lifeline. The *Manohra Song*, a lovingly restored, fifty-year-old, 50-foot rice barge made entirely of teak and rare woods, is the most luxurious vessel on the river, built to world-class yacht standards, with just four staterooms outfitted with Thai tapestries, sumptuous fabrics, carvings, and sophisticated crafts and antiques evocative of the ancient kingdom of Siam. The candlelit dinner served aboard is one of the best in Thailand. The *Manohra* is available for private charters, but its most popular cruise is the two-day overnight trip to Ayuthaya, a 50-mile trip that passes houses built on stilts, children splashing, bathing, and washing in their "front yard," and the timeless bustle and activity of watercraft plying the muddy river.

WHAT: site, experience. ***MANOHRA SONG:*** departures from the Bangkok Marriott. In Bangkok, tel 66/2-2477-0770, fax 66/2-476-1120. *Cost:* 2-night "Ayuthaya Adventure" from $2,026 per person, includes meals and excursions. **BEST TIMES:** Nov–Feb.

The Manohra Song *with Wat Arun in the background*

Temples of Pampering That Promise Nirvana

ANCIENT THAI MASSAGE

Bangkok, Thailand

Massage, Thailand's oldest form of medicine, is an ancient Eastern practice long considered the ultimate restorative experience. On every Bangkok corner, neon-lit parlors offer a red-light "modern" massage experience, but the authentic practice that can leave you rejuvenated, de-jet-lagged, and feeling like a warm bowl of Jell-O is found elsewhere. Traditionally viewed as a spiritual and healing art closely linked to the teachings of Buddhism, massage was for centuries practiced exclusively at temples, and Thailand's oldest and largest temple and university, Wat Po (also called Chetuphon Temple), is still famous for its bustling massage school. Unlike with other forms of massage, you keep your street clothes on for this while you're bent, stretched, pulled, tugged at, sat upon, and walked over. The pressure points in your body (there are twenty-nine in your feet alone) are given a rigorous workover. For a considerable amount more (consider it your ticket to heaven), the tranquil spa at the venerable Oriental Hotel is a temple of another sort, a beautifully simple space that has been created to immerse guests in total pampering. The Thai-influenced method practiced here (called "Oriental" after the hotel) is nothing less than miraculous, especially when preceded or followed by skin-smoothing treatments, such as being smeared with papaya puree or mud from the Mae Hong Son Valley—take your pick.

WHAT: experience. **WAT PO:** on Sanamchai Rd. next to the Grand Palace. Tel 66/2-221-2974; www.watpomassage.com. *Cost:* $11 for a 1-hour massage. **ORIENTAL SPA AT THE ORIENTAL HOTEL:** 48 Oriental Ave. Tel 66/2-659-9000; in the U.S., tel 800-526-6566; mobkk-spa@mohg.com; www.mandarinorien tal.com. *Cost:* $105 for a 90-minute traditional Thai massage.

The Granddaddy of All Bangkok Markets

CHATUCHAK WEEKEND MARKET

Bangkok, Thailand

Y ou'll be able to explore only a small part of Chatuchak's 30 jam-packed awning-covered acres before your head starts to swim from cultural overload. One of the world's largest outdoor markets, with an estimated 5,000 merchants ready for business every Saturday at 6 A.M., Chatuchak is the ultimate Bangkok market experience—a one-stop shopping extravaganza where the rare, the costly, and the unusual are sold side by side with pushcart food, computers, tribal crafts, genuine counterfeit everything, spices, orchids, pirated CDs, souvenirs, and pets (or are they?) that range from Siamese kittens to Siamese fighting fish. Silk garments and hand-painted china sell for a song, but Chatuchak is as much a sociologist's dream as a bargain hunter's paradise. It's a crowded, sense-numbing carnival, teeming with saffron-robed monks, ancient crones, mothers shopping for toys with their children, and pinstripe-suited businessmen buying provisions for dinner. Its exotic sights, smells, and sounds will stay with you for a lifetime.

WHAT: experience. **WHERE:** Chatuchak Park off Phahonythin Rd. on the highway to the airport; any cabdriver will take you from downtown or jump on the new Sky Train. **WHEN:** Sat and Sun.

The Fairy-tale City That Inspired The King and I

THE GRAND PALACE

Bangkok, Thailand

O nce upon a time, the Grand Palace was the walled residence of the Thai monarch, its monumental, phantasmagorical excess created some 200 years ago by the revered Chakri dynasty of the Kingdom of Siam. With 5 million tourists a year visiting one of Thailand's must-see sites, it's not surprising that current King Rama IX has moved down the road to nearby Chitralada Palace, closed to the public. No matter—it could not possibly be more gilded, decorated, and inlaid, more ornate and fantastical than the maze of more than 100 Eastern/Western buildings and courtyards at the Grand Palace, which remains the greatest single display of traditional Thai arts and architecture. The most famous of Bangkok's 400-odd temples is found within these walls: the Wat Phra Kaeo, popularly known as the Temple of the Emerald Buddha. Adjoining the original royal palace, the temple will be the grand finale of your visit, symbolically linking Thailand's spiritual heart with the former seat of its temporal power. Here sits the most venerated religious object in Thailand, a 26-inch seated Buddha carved from a solid block of semiprecious jade, which was lost and then discovered in the 15th century. Guarded by ancient bronze lions and precious beyond measure, it is perched serenely atop a gilded throne 34 feet high. As protector of the country, the Buddha presides over the only area of the Grand Palace where incense-burning Thai worshippers outnumber awestruck tourists.

WHAT: site. **WHERE:** Naphralan Rd. **COST:** admission $6. **BEST TIMES:** Oct–Mar.

Bangkok's Other Grand Palace

THE ORIENTAL

Bangkok, Thailand

Often rated as one of the world's best hotels, and buried under accolades for its large, can-do staff's perfect service, the riverside Oriental Hotel is a legend, as visited as Bangkok's Grand Palace and nearly as venerable:

The Somerset Maugham suite

It celebrated its 125th anniversary in 2001. Joseph Conrad was a guest in 1888; the Prince and Princess of Wales checked in a century later. Guests indulge in the romance and history of this Bangkok landmark in the Authors' Residence, housed in the only part of the original 1876 building still standing. Elaborate suites with names such as Somerset Maugham, Noël Coward, and James Michener are decorated as if the novelists were still in residence. Relive a period of the hotel's history during high tea in the Authors' Lounge, a gracious oasis from the smoggy, traffic-clogged metropolis of Bangkok. Few visitors travel halfway around the world just to stay at a hotel, but the Oriental offers many temptations within the enclave of its prime property on the banks of the Chao Phraya River. A Thai cultural program includes daily afternoon lectures by leading Thai scholars, who explore local customs, dance, art, and architecture. A renowned in-house cooking school shares the subtle secrets of the culinary arts of Siam, while the spa introduces you to the ancient Thai tradition of pampering and massage. Some of the best classical dance performances in town take place every evening in the Oriental's lavish riverside Sala Rim Naam. Despite a bevy of high-rise hotel competitors, the Oriental's raffish past and stylish present are unlikely to be eclipsed.

WHAT: hotel. **WHERE:** 48 Oriental Ave. Tel 66/2-659-9000, fax 66/2-659-9284; in the U.S. and Canada, tel 866-526-6567; mobkk-reservations@mohg.com; www.mandarinoriental. com. **COST:** doubles from $299, Authors' Suites from $1,390. Each class at cooking school $120 (4 classes available per week). Each lecture at Thai culture program $120. 90-minute massage at Oriental spa $105. **BEST TIMES:** Oct–Mar.

A Modern Temple of Ancient Thailand's Golden Age

THE SUKHOTHAI

Bangkok, Thailand

Bangkok does not lack for five-star international hotels of pan-Asian decor heavy on Western aesthetics, but the Sukhothai has become the hotel of choice for discerning guests looking for an elegant ambience where they can nevertheless wake up and know they're in Thailand.

A palm-lined drive and 6 acres of flower gardens and lily ponds recapture the serenity of the 13th-century kingdom of Sukhothai, from which this striking hotel takes its name and inspiration. Despite its size (there are some 200 exquisitely appointed rooms with oversized teak-floored bathrooms), the hotel evokes the air of a Buddhist retreat, with Sukhothai-style stupas reflected in pools of lotus blossoms and illuminated at night. Native craftsmanship is evident in the artful use of wood, granite, ceramic, and fabrics that recall the palatial salons of the ancient capital. This quintessential Thai experience crescendos on the open terrace of the Celadon, where traditional piquant cuisine mingles occasionally with the modern in dishes that are a feast for palate and eyes alike.

WHAT: hotel, restaurant. **WHERE:** 13/3 South Sathorn Rd. Tel 66/2-344-8888, fax 66/2-344-8899; in the U.S. and Canada, tel 800-226-6800; reservations@sukhothai.com; www.sukhothai.com. **COST:** doubles from $295. Dinner $30. **BEST TIMES:** Oct–Mar.

Settlements Long Lost to the World

THE HILL TRIBES OF NORTHERN THAILAND

Chiang Mai, Thailand

Chiang Mai is usually the jumping-off point for treks into the surrounding jungles, where a dozen or so hill tribes live much as they have for centuries, without electricity and plumbing—not to mention schools and

Local craftspeople

clinics. Until recently, these villages harbored opium-growing operations, which were their sole source of revenue. Today the Thai royal family has taken an interest, encouraging the cultivation of alternative agricultural crops, which the people are slowly accepting. The Karen people have lived in the region since ancient times. Others—Hmong, Akha, Lisu, and Lahu—began migrating in the 19th century and continue to cross from the nearby borders of Myanmar (Burma) and Laos. A village-to-village trek through the mist-blue mountains offers fascinating interactions with

a variety of cultures, and often includes overnight stays in simple settlements. Western visitors may be considered either commonplace or exotic, depending on the village's previous experience and accessibility, and on your local guide's personal connections.

The older women proudly dress up in full regalia to welcome visitors from abroad, layering on colorful embroidered and handwoven traditional clothing and silver-bangled headdresses. Get there before MTV does.

WHAT: experience. **WHERE:** Chiang Mai (400 miles/644 km north of Bangkok) and Chiang Rai (slightly farther north) are the most popular departures for hill-village treks. Both are connected to Bangkok and other cities by numerous daily flights. **HOW:** any local hotel or travel agency can arrange for treks of 1 day or longer, with overnight stays in remote villages. In the U.S., Asia Transpacific Journeys organizes small groups led by a Karen guide as part of a longer trip through Thailand. Tel 800-642-2742 or 303-443-6789, fax 303-443-7078; travel@asiatranspacific.com; www.asiatranspacific.com. **COST:** 14-day "Best of Thailand" from $6,295 per person, includes land travel and meals. **WHEN:** monthly departures Jan–Mar and Oct–Dec. **BEST TIMES:** Oct–Mar.

The Land That Time Forgot

THE FOUR SEASONS RESORT

Chiang Mai, Thailand

Once the budget purview for backpackers on their way north to the notorious Golden Triangle, Chiang Mai is now blessed with the incomparable Four Seasons Resort, which looked to the Lanna kingdom (founded in

1296) for spiritual and aesthetic inspiration. Incorporating traditions from neighboring Myanmar (Burma), Laos, and China, the gorgeously landscaped 20-acre resort resembles a Thai village in the northern foothills, right

down to the family of water buffalo that helps harvest the hotel's own rice paddies three times a year. Raft down a calm river on bamboo floats. Scale jungle-canopied mountains. Mountain-bike through lush forests to hidden waterfalls. Spend the afternoon atop an elephant's back, trekking with your personal mahout in the driver's seat, straddling your mount's massive neck. Afterward, have an aromatic Oriental massage with herbal oils extracted from ginger and lemongrass in the luxury of your spacious guest pavilion or in the new spa, one of the most tastefully designed in Asia, using the lush colors, scents, and fabrics of northern Thailand. Drop in at the Elephant Bar at day's end for sunset views of your hotel's mosaic of working rice paddies. Then settle in for dinner: Culinary wonders are produced nightly in the temple-like dining *sala,* where vistas of the misty Doi Suthep mountains soon fade into the darkness of night.

WHAT: hotel. **WHERE:** in the rural Mae Rim Valley; complimentary shuttle service to and from Chiang Mai (10 miles south). Chiang Mai is 400 miles/644 km north of Bangkok and is connected by numerous daily flights and trains. **HOW:** in Chiang Mai, tel 66/53-298-181, fax 66/53-298-190; in the U.S. and Canada, tel 800-819-5053; www.fourseasons.com/chiangmai. **COST:** from $455 for pavilion suites. **BEST TIMES:** mid-Oct to late Mar.

The resort reflects the traditional style of northern Thailand.

What's in a Name? Island Beauties

KOH PHI PHI

Thailand

Although devastated by the tsunami of December 2004, Koh Phi Phi (called Pee Pee Island in English), remains a textbook version of the ultimate dream isle. It was Hollywood's pick for the Leonardo DiCaprio sand-seeking-vagabond dud *The Beach.* Against a backdrop of steep, jungled limestone cliffs, a few simple bungalow resorts dot crescents of palm-shaded bleached-white sand. Day-trippers from nearby Krabi or Phuket are transported by boat to the beaches of Koh Phi Phi Don (Big Pee Pee Island), while those who hop a long-tailed boat can visit the even more spectacular Koh Phi Phi Le (Little . . .). Here you can visit unspoiled coves, crystal-clear waters, and nearly undeveloped beaches; Maya Bay, surrounded by soaring cliffs, is particularly beautiful. Snorkeling is excellent. About the only other thing to do, besides waiting for a simple grilled-fish lunch at an open-air beachside spot, is to visit the immense, cathedral-like caverns, where Sea Gypsies harvest edible birds' nests, a delicacy prized by Chinese gourmets for their nutritional value. That simple grilled-fish lunch sounds better and better.

WHAT: island. **WHERE:** day trips can be arranged from any hotel in Phuket or Krabi, both about 1½ hours by boat. Phangnga Bay is just north. **WHERE TO STAY:** The nicest and newest resort on the island, the Holiday Inn Resort Phi Phi Island, has 77 beachfront bungalows snuggled in a coconut plantation. Tel 66/75-627-300; reservation@phiphi.holidayinn.com; www.phiphi.holidayinn.com. **COST:** doubles from $112. **BEST TIMES:** Jan–May.

An Escapist Island in the Gulf of Siam

KOH SAMUI

Thailand

The backpacker brigade that popularized such idyllic havens as Ibiza, Goa, and Bali first stumbled upon Koh Samui in the 1970s. The island changed considerably once word got out—an airport was built in 1989 and Western tourists, drawn by talk of dazzling beaches and a kick-back vibe fill the growing number of upscale hotels—but much of its early appeal remains. So far. (According to a local ordinance, a hotel can be no higher than the palm trees—roughly three stories.)

Long sweeps of empty white beaches encircle the island, while the middle of the island remains dense with thick coconut plantations. Coconut palms have long been the mainstay of Koh Samui's economy, and 2 million coconuts are shipped to Bangkok each month. Beachside bars, tattoo parlors, $15 bungalow rentals, and "life's a beach" T-shirts testify to the island's somewhat receding tie-dyed character.

At the other end of the spectrum there's the Baan Taling Ngam resort, which proves that you can spoil guests—with an idyllic, secluded, exclusive setting—without spoiling the island. Nestled on one of the best spots on the island's western coast, Baan Taling Ngam (whose name translates as "home on a beautiful cliff") offers uncommonly lovely views from its guest rooms and terraces, revealing small islands and jungle-clad outcroppings scattered across the Gulf of Siam. Most of the humpbacked islets seen from any of the deluxe rooms of this cliff-edge aerie, or the breezy beachside restaurant and villas, are part of the Ang Thong National Marine Park, a popular destination for world-class diving and snorkeling. Eighty islands litter the surrounding blue-green waters of the Gulf of Siam. The largest inhabited island, Koh Pha Ngan (7 miles north and connected by daily boats), draws budget travelers and scuba lovers the way Samui once did.

WHAT: island, hotel. **WHERE:** southeast of Bangkok, numerous 75-minute flights daily. **BAAN TALING NGAM:** Taling Ngam Beach. Tel 66/77-429-100, fax 66/77-423-220; www. baan-taling-ngam.com. *Cost:* doubles from $275, villas from $400. **BEST TIMES:** Nov–May.

An Obstacle Course of Limestone Monoliths

PHANGNGA BAY

Krabi, Thailand

James Bond fans might recall Phangnga Bay as the spectacular island setting for *The Man with the Golden Gun*, much of which was filmed on Koh Phing Kan, and which Westerners have ever since referred to as James Bond Island.

Cinematic fame aside, this spectacular profusion of sheer limestone mountain peaks rising from the Andaman Sea's pistachio-green waters is one of the world's most beautiful natural phenomena. Located just off the southern Thai coast, near Krabi, the bay's sharp outcroppings reach up 1,000 feet, many covered by dense mounds of jungle and some shaped like animals (Koh Ma Chu, or Little Dog Island) or other familiar objects (Koh Khai, or Egg Island). On a gray day, these islands, with their tiny lagoons and mangrove swamps, have the mystical aura of Chinese watercolors.

Waking up from a nap at Phra Nang beach, you might think you're still dreaming.

Many of the humped and jagged islets are riddled with caves and caverns embellished with stalactites and stalagmites. Idyllic beaches and fishing villages built on stilts can be explored by sea canoe or long-tailed boats.

Accessible only by boat through the bay's towering karst outcroppings, the Rayavadee Premier Resort is nestled within a tropical rain forest on Cape Phra Nang, populated by wild monkeys and exotic bird life. It's one of the world's most unusual hotel locations. The resort was built on a shady coconut plantation, which was left virtually undisturbed during the eco-sensitive construction of 100 hexagonal two-story pavilions. No less than three beaches, lapped by the Andaman Sea, surround the property, and are its uncontestable highlight. One of them, the powder-white Phra Nang beach, has been declared by cognoscenti to be one of the most beautiful in the world, and certainly one of the nicest in Asia.

WHAT: site, hotel. **WHERE:** on the west coast of Thailand's Southern Peninsula, near Phuket. Memorable 90-minute boat ride from Phuket's international airport. **HOW:** day trips or canoe rentals can be arranged at any of the hotels in Krabi or on the islands of Phuket and Kho Phi Phi. **RAYAVADEE:** tel 66/75-620-740-3, fax 66/75-620-630; info@rayavadee.com; www.rayavadee.com. *Cost:* pavilions from $570. **BEST TIMES:** Oct–Apr.

Thailand's "City of Mist"

MAE HONG SON

Thailand

After five minutes in Bangkok's snarled, snail-paced, fume-belching traffic, you'll be more than ready to escape to Mae Hong Son, up in the hills 595 miles to the northwest. Increased tourism has left precious

few Thai towns that can claim to be unspoiled, free of Western impact, but Mae Hong Son, a lovely town on the border with Myanmar

(Burma) that the Thai call the City of Mist, fits the bill better than most. Situated in a province that's more rugged jungle than typical rice paddy, it was founded as an elephant training camp in the 1830s and remained cut off from the world until the late 1960s, when a paved road was built from Chiang Mai, 160 miles away.

Local guides can send you rafting down the gentle Pai River, bush trekking atop your very own pachyderm, or hiking to tribal villages in the hills. The only real excitement in town is the early morning market, when the hill-tribe women come down to buy and barter with the locals. Things have calmed down again by breakfast time, and the swirling mists that give the town its name lift by late afternoon. Motorbike to the top of Doi Kong Mu hill and the 19th-century Wat Phra That temple for a spectacular view of the Pai Valley and the surrounding mountains.

WHAT: town. **WHERE:** it takes 8 hours to drive 160 miles/257 km from Chiang Mai over numerous mountains and through some of Thailand's most beautiful countryside. A half-hour flight links Chiang Mai and Mae Hong Son with connections to and from Bangkok. **WHERE TO STAY:** the Rim Nam Klang Doi Resort is the nicest of the town's few hotels, with charming riverside bungalows. Tel 66/53-612-142; rimnamklangdoi@hotmail.com. *Cost:* doubles from $20. **BEST TIMES:** Nov–Feb. In early Apr a colorful local festival, Poi Sang Long, celebrates the initiation of young boys into the Buddhist monkhood.

Twin Havens Offer Thai Heaven

PHUKET

Thailand

Known as the Pearl of the Andaman Sea, Phuket and its gorgeous beaches and resorts were left remarkably untouched by the 2004 tsunami. Although much of the island's innocence and personality was lost in the tourist boom of the 80s and 90s, visitors now look to the resorts for signs of its former character. At Amanpuri, they need look no further. The firstborn of the Aman hotels and still considered to be the

Amanpuri *means "place of peace."*

most special, it's the premier vacation spot on the island, with secluded pavilion-suites that spill down a coconut-palmed hillside on a promontory overlooking beautiful Pansea Beach. The decor is one of ethnoluxe simplicity and Zen-like aesthetics: what appears to be a series of Thai temples are forty open-sided teak guest pavilions with many-curved roofs, intricate gables, and vaulted ceilings.

Inspired by Thai Buddhism, these centers of calm create an atmosphere many Western visitors at first find unsettling, but ultimately irresistible. Solitude is the special quality Amanpuri has to offer, and it is by blissful design.

Elsewhere on the island, the Banyan Tree is Southeast Asia's first and largest spa resort, offering an aromatic, hedonistic, near-religious experience that promises to salve your mind, body, and soul using the ancient methods of the East. No sunrise hikes or aerobics before breakfast here. This is about handing over your jet-lagged body for indulgent spa treatments whose names alone soothe and assuage: oasis of harmony, voyage of bliss, dream elixir. The Lomi Lomi massage promises to leave you "with fond memories"; manicures and pedicures are described as "royal"; and other treatments "polish" and "anoint" your body. The one-day program is called Vision of Serenity—and that is just what guests look like when they have finished with the massaging, body wraps, and pampering and wander back to their house-size beachfront villas.

WHAT: hotel, experience. **WHERE:** 70 minutes by plane southwest of Bangkok; air connections with other principal Asian cities. **AMANPURI:** tel 66/76-324-333, fax 66/76-324-100; in the U.S., tel 800-477-9180; amanpuri@amanresorts.com; www.amanresorts.com. *Cost:* pavilions from $925. **BANYAN TREE PHUKET:** tel 66/76-324-374, fax 66/76-324-375; in the U.S., tel 800-591-0434; phuket@banyantree.com; www.banyantree.com. *Cost:* private villas from $250; spa services from $60 per treatment. **BEST TIMES:** Oct–Apr.

An Eternal Honeymoon in le Petit Paris

DALAT

Vietnam

A cool retreat from the sweltering heat of Vietnam's coastal plains, Dalat became the hill station of choice for the French, who created here their own Petit Paris on a plateau close to 5,000 feet above sea level. Enjoying mild, springlike weather year-round, Dalat is called the City of Love because of its longtime popularity with Vietnamese honeymooners, who come for the high-country magic and a landscape dotted with clear lakes, waterfalls, evergreen forests, and flower gardens. Traditional French elegance blends with Vietnamese graciousness in the loveliest hotel in town, the Sofitel Dalat Palace. Overlooking Xuan Huong Lake, it was built in 1922, when Dalat was still Indochina's premier mountain resort. The hotel's world-class 18-hole golf course is a rarity in Vietnam, for the moment the only one of its kind.

WHAT: town, hotel. **DALAT:** 200 miles/322 km northeast of Ho Chi Minh City; daily flights available, but those with time should go by road—the 4-hour ride takes you through some of the most scenic landscape in the country. **SOFITEL DALAT PALACE:** 12 Tran Phu St. Tel 84/63-825-444; in the U.S., tel 800-SOFITEL; sofitel.reservations@dalatresorts.com; www.sofitel.com. **COST:** doubles from $200. **BEST TIMES:** Oct–Mar.

The Dalat Palace hotel has retained its French colonial charm.

The Mythical Bay of Dragons

HALONG BAY

Vietnam

I t's said that dragons once descended from heaven and spouted streams of jade droplets that fell into the waters of Halong Bay, forming thousands of islands and islets to protect the bay and its people from invading marauders.

Today this mysterious body of water, with its nature-sculpted limestone islands and outcroppings that resemble (and are named for) dogs, elephants, toads, monkeys, and other animals and shapes, has the surreal quality of classical Chinese and Vietnamese paintings, especially when the sails of sampans and junks are silhouetted against the horizon like giant butterflies. More than 100 miles in length, Halong is home to sandy unpeopled beaches and centuries-old floating fishing villages, whose boat people still honor the deities of these timeless waters. A ragtag fleet of tourist boats and inexpensive personality-free hotels have sprung up around Bay Chai and Hong Gai, but the only way to really experience the hidden lagoons and caves of stalagmites and fantastic rock formations is by

Kayak through the bay's outcroppings.

joining a kayaking trip and zigzagging your way through the maze of jagged isles.

WHAT: site, experience. **WHERE:** 100 miles/ 161 km east of Hanoi. **HOW:** in the U.S., custom tours can be arranged through Mountain Travel-Sobek, tel 888-831-7526 or 510-594-6000, fax 510-594-6001; info@mtsobek.com; www.mtsobek.com. **COST:** prices vary depending on the size of your group. **WHEN:** departures Apr–Nov. **BEST TIMES:** Mar and Nov.

A Hole-in-the-Wall Legend on Fried Fish Street

CHA CA LA VONG

Hanoi, Vietnam

F or more than seven decades, Cha Ca La Vong's dedicated clientele has been on to something: namely, *cha ca*, the restaurant's most famous—and only—dish. This succulent fried-fish masterpiece, whose recipe has been in the Doan family for generations and whose name translates roughly as "curried Red River fish," has become so entrenched in Hanoi's epicurean mythology that the city renamed the lane out front in its honor. *Cha ca* is an informal and entertaining affair. A rickety flight of wooden stairs leads to the unremarkable second-floor restaurant full of equally rickety chairs, where patrons cook chunks of seasoned garoupa fish themselves on a charcoal clay brazier, stirring in chives and dill. The rich, oily stew is then spooned into bowls of vermicelli rice noodles and enlivened by the addition of shrimp sauce, fried peanuts, and pickled vegetables. But the real secret ingredient? If you can believe the rumors, two drops of an essence extracted from the perfume gland of the ca cuong beetle.

WHAT: restaurant. **WHERE:** 14 Cha Ca St. Tel 84/4-825-3929. **COST:** about $5.

A Colonial Flavor Evocative of Indochine

THE FRENCH QUARTER OF HANOI

Vietnam

T he venerable French Quarter and its faded colonial charm is what sets Hanoi apart from Saigon (Ho Chi Minh City), its onetime rival in the south. Built by the French when Hanoi was the capital of French Indochina

(1887–1954), most of the area's once hand-some buildings are sorely in need of repair—even a coat of paint would be welcome—but the wide, tree-lined, still-elegant boulevards, and sprawling tumbledown villas afford visitors a glimpse of a proud, albeit struggling country's European legacy harmoniously blended with Chinese and Vietnamese architecture. Visit the 900-year-old Temple of Literature (the country's oldest university) and the Ho Chi Minh Mausoleum, a pedicab ride

The Sofitel Metropole in the heart of Hanoi

away. Better catch it soon: While city officials decide what to do with this potentially potent tourist attraction, historic structures are being modified with modern additions and satellite dishes, or even being razed—not unlike what the French did in the name of modernization upon their arrival.

For accommodations in the Quarter, the Metropole hotel, recently restored to its original 1920s style, is once again a standout in Vietnam's limited hotel market, recalling the days when it was operated by the French and was a gathering place for artists, writers, and government bigwigs. A modern wing has been added, but you'll be happiest in the original building, where architects have carefully preserved the buffed hardwood floors, green-shuttered windows, and other elements that give European distinction to the white stuc-coed facade. No hotel has a better address: guests are just one block from the enchanting Hoan Kiem Lake, where smiling women twice your age and three times as supple encourage you to join their crack-of-dawn t'ai chi classes.

WHAT: site, hotel. **WHERE:** Sofitel Metropole, 15 Ngo Quyen St. Tel 84/4-826-6919, fax 84/4-826-6920; in the U.S., tel 800-SOFITEL; sofitelhanoi@hn.vnn.vn; www.sofitel.com. **COST:** doubles from $259. **BEST TIMES:** Oct–Mar.

A Street for Every Ware

HANOI'S OLD QUARTER

Vietnam

L ocated between the green oasis of Hoan Kiem Lake and the Red River, the mazelike Old Quarter of Hanoi has been a shopping venue since the 15th century. Nearly forty of its narrow, crowded streets are named after

the goods once sold along them: Rice Street, Silk Street, Pots and Pans Street, Gold Street—there's even a Gravestone Street. It remains to be seen if names like Pirate Video Street or T-shirt Street will follow. Open dilapidated storefronts give new meaning to "window shopping." These cubbyholes are sometimes just large enough to hold a wizened old merchant amid goods stacked to the ceiling. After decades of suppression, every square inch of the Old Quarter is once again alive with capitalistic fervor. Noodles, flowers, antiques, and handicrafts are yours for the bargaining.

WHAT: site, experience. **WHERE:** main access is by Silk St. (Pho Cau Go).

Gather in all the sights and smells as you ride through Hanoi's Old Quarter.

Simple National Dish or Art Form?

PHO HOA

Ho Chi Minh City (Saigon), Vietnam

O ne of the most memorable attributes of Vietnam is its gastronomic tapestry of Asian and French-influenced cuisine, in which beef, fish, rice, and produce from the fertile Mekong River delta are infused with

explosive flavors and complex but delicate seasonings. Owing to this mix, the simple national dish of pho, a rice noodle soup eaten by rich and poor at breakfast and at every other hour of the day, can be almost lyrical. If you've only sampled it elsewhere, prepare yourself: The pho you have here will be like nothing you've tasted before.

Jump into a pedicab and make your way to Pho Hoa, perhaps the best known of the country's thousands of noodle restaurants. Pasteur Street is pho heaven, lined with nondescript storefront shops and stalls selling this specialty, but for twenty years Pho Hoa has been considered the best. The soul of pho is the broth, and an enormous cauldron at the Pho Hoa boils the seasoned and flavorful brew for five hours before your steaming bowl arrives, chock-full of slippery and soft chewy noodles and thin slices of beef or chicken. Go for breakfast so you can come back for lunch and dinner, too.

WHAT: restaurant. **WHERE:** 260C Pasteur St. Tel 84/8-297-943. **COST:** a full menu highlighted by pho about $2. **WHEN:** open daily 6 A.M.–midnight.

Rooftop R&R and Shopping Therapy in Go-Go Saigon

THE REX BAR AND THE BEN THANH MARKET

Ho Chi Minh City (Saigon), Vietnam

Nostalgia rules at the Rex Hotel's rooftop bar, once a home away from home for expats and wartime journalists, who gathered here around the clock to nurse a scotch and swap scoops. Old habits die hard, and the newly redecorated bar continues to be the city's most popular watering hole, embellished with year-round Christmas lights, singing birds, and topiary shrubs. There's a great view of downtown Saigon, where artillery has been replaced by the lights and cacophony of a perpetual traffic jam of bicycles, cars, motor scooters, and three-wheeled cyclos. Posh it isn't, but the Rex is dripping with history, and few Westerners pass through town without an obligatory tipple. The standard rooms are not the city's most luxurious, but fit the bill for visitors in search of the Saigon Experience and must be booked well in advance. Although it recalls earlier times, the Rex is also the hub of modern-day Saigon. There's a real international buzz here. You'd never know you're in a Communist country.

Ditto for your inevitable reaction to the Ben Thanh Market, the French-built municipal marketplace that lies to the west on Le Loi Street. An explosive wave of entrepreneurship has hit Vietnam, and Saigon has become one big selling game, with over forty markets spread around the city. Ben Thanh, the traditional alternative for vendors who can't afford the high commercial rents charged elsewhere in town, is *the* market. Enjoy it: Hundreds of vendors create a narrow maze of stalls touting everything from the latest Japanese gadgets to bolts of silk, cobra wine, and Coca-Cola. The traditional is stacked up alongside the modern and the fierce haggling is eternal. Go for the color and the exotic chaos, but realize that no matter how honed your negotiating skills, you're still going to pay twice as much as a local customer.

WHAT: hotel, restaurant, experience. **REX HOTEL:** 141 Nguyen Hue Boul. Tel 84/8-829-2185, fax 84/8-829-6536; rexhotel@hcm.vnn.vn; www.rexhotelvietnam.com. *Cost:* doubles from $105. **BEN THANH MARKET:** Le Loi St. **BEST TIMES:** Oct–Feb.

Exotic Time Machine of European Influences

HOI AN

Vietnam

Nowhere has Vietnam's charm and history endured longer than in the ancient port city of Hoi An, which for centuries was a major center for Japanese, Portuguese, Dutch, Arab, Chinese, and French merchants and

seafarers. A miracle left the city and its more than 800 historic structures unscathed by the Vietnam War, and today its people are understandably proud of their architectural heritage. You'll find many homes, temples, wells, pagodas, bridges, and stores in varying

The residential quarter

degrees of preservation, many of which are open to the public free of charge, allowing visitors to stroll in and out of the centuries. A

contemporary of Malaysia's port town of Malacca, Hoi An has so far escaped the overzealous tourism-incited preservation that's given that city something of a theme-park look, and the beautiful stretch of beach at Cua Dai, just outside town, is still blissfully free of resorts and hawkers. Development is in the wind, though, so make this your first stop.

WHAT: town. **WHERE:** on the coast, 18 miles/29 km south of Da Nang. **WHERE TO STAY:** the French colonial–style Hoi An Hotel, 6 Tran Hung Dao St., was home base for the U.S. Marines during the war. Western civilians now fill its simple rooms and sprawling gardens. Tel 84/510-861-445, fax 84/510-861-636; hoianhotel@dng.vnn.vn; www.hoian tourist.com. *Cost:* doubles from $85. **BEST TIMES:** Dec–Apr.

Vietnam Through the Back Door

THE MEKONG DELTA

Vietnam

From its origin high in the Tibetan Plateau, the Mekong River journeys through China, Myanmar (Burma), Laos, and Cambodia before flowing through Vietnam and splitting into the many waterways that form the Mekong River

delta, south of Saigon. Referred to as "Vietnam's rice bowl," it is one of the most fertile areas in southern Asia, supplying the country with most of its rice, fruit, and seafood

and affording foreign visitors a wonderful insight into the real Vietnam. In addition to viewing a countryside little changed by the centuries, and riverside villages accessible only by boat, you can experience the warmth and friendliness of the local people, who are forever offering fresh fruit, a glass of potent rice wine, coconut milk, and a smile. The

Floating markets are a common sight.

delta is home to a number of different peoples, including Vietnamese, Chinese, Khmer, and Cham. Year-round guided tours visit riverboat and city markets that showcase the area's bounty and travel into the heartland to see floating houses, villages built on stilts, and the popular beaches of Ha Tien, just miles from the Cambodian border.

WHAT: experience. **WHERE:** first towns of interest after Ho Chi Minh City (Saigon) are about 50 miles/80 km to the south, reachable by car. **HOW:** in Saigon, Saigontourist, tel 84/8-829-8914, fax 84/8-822-4987; www.saigon tourist.net. **COST:** 7-day tours along the Mekong River from $740 per person, double occupancy. **BEST TIMES:** Dec–Feb.

A Feast of Ethnicity in the Vietnamese Alps

SAPA

Vietnam

It's a long and bumpy ride north from Hanoi to Sapa, the country's most picturesque hill resort, perched at 5,000 feet in an incredibly beautiful mountain area that the French used to call the Tonkinese Alps, near the

Laotian and Chinese borders. The area is home to a wealth of hill tribes—collectively known as the Montagnard ("mountain people")—who come to the Sapa marketplace on Saturdays to sell their homegrown fruit and vegetables and handicrafts and to share news. Of the thirty-odd ethnic groups that live in distant villages on the mountainsides or deep valleys, the friendly Black Hmong and Red Dao dominate. You might get a good deal on a water buffalo. Sapa is the perfect base for day trips or over-night treks to Mount Fansi Pan (Vietnam's highest peak) or to the Montagnard villages, where the natural beauty of steep, terraced vegetable gardens and crystal-clear streams are easy on the eyes and refreshing to the spirit.

WHAT: town, event. **WHERE:** northwestern Vietnam at Chinese border. **HOW:** Hanoi is the

A bird's-eye view of the city

departure point for tours arranged by Global Spectrum. In the U.S., tel 800-419-4446; globalspectrumtravel@gmail.com; www.asian passages.com. **COST:** 12-day trek through Sapa, all-inclusive from Hanoi $1,945 per person. **BEST TIMES:** mid-Mar–May and Oct–Nov.

AUSTRALIA,
NEW ZEALAND,
AND
THE PACIFIC
ISLANDS

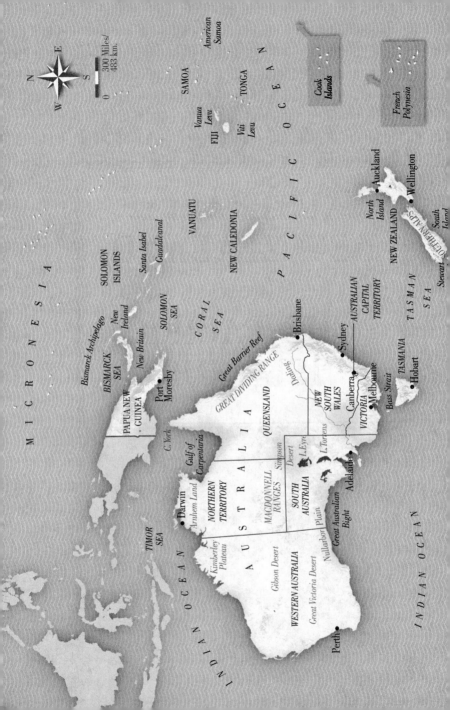

Magnificent Scenery and Lodging to Match

THE BLUE MOUNTAINS AND LILIANFELS

New South Wales, Australia

Microscopic droplets of oil from the leaves of dense eucalyptus forests hang in the air, refracting the sunlight to create the misty blue haze that gave this park its name. Just ninety minutes from Sydney, the Blue Mountains are a glorious playground of twenty-six small townships that offer everything from antiques shopping to bushwalking. The mountains are not even really mountains but a vast sandstone tableland whose dramatic eroded scenery is best enjoyed from lookouts like Govett's Leap. Echo Point is the best place to view the park's famous sandstone pillars, the Three Sisters. Just west of here are two of the park's highlights: The Scenic Skyway, Australia's only gondola ride, travels 1,000 feet above the canyon, and the Katoomba Scenic Railway, an open-sided cog-rail incline, descends at 52 degrees but feels twice as steep. If they're not hairy enough for you, there's still the Zig-Zag railway near the town of Lithgow, an engineering marvel of switchbacks and bridges built in the 1860s.

You can catch a highlight or two on a day trip from Sydney, but the area really deserves a longer stay, and for that, the 19th-century Lilianfels hotel is hard to beat. It's one of Australia's best getaway destinations, with a fantastic setting, magnificent panoramas, and Darley's, a smart, award-winning restaurant where the ingredients of your traditional meal come from the surrounding country. Looking every bit like a gracious European home, the hotel is perched 3,300 feet above sea level, almost at the edge of the cliff at Echo Point, with the canyons and ravines of the Jamison

Valley below. After all the outdoor adventure, you can sit by one of the hotel's inviting fireplaces (even on summer evenings the air is crisp), or enjoy a proper afternoon tea served on a veranda overlooking acres of English gardens and the misty eucalyptus forests. Full spa facilities further tempt one to cocoon.

WHAT: site, hotel, restaurant. **BLUE MOUNTAINS:** approximately 75 miles/122 km west of Sydney. **LILIANFELS:** in Katoomba. Tel 61/247-801-200, fax 61/247-801-300; U.S. bookings 800-237-1236; www.lilianfels.com.au. *Cost:* doubles from $355. **DARLEY'S:** about $105 for 3-course meal à la carte. **BEST TIMES:** Mar and Apr, when the mountains change to fall colors; spring (Sept and Oct).

Jamison Valley—showcasing nature's enduring beauty

Premier Vineyards Down Under

THE HUNTER VALLEY WINE REGION

New South Wales, Australia

The Hunter Valley conjures up visions of horse and cattle breeding and of mining, but for the most part Australians associate it with the grape, since the area is home to more than fifty wineries and dozens of restaurants.

Visitors may recognize such international labels as Rosemount or Lindemans, while smaller, limited-production operations are much respected at home. An easy two-hour drive from Sydney—making it the most popular and well-known of Australia's four wine regions—Hunter Valley is best avoided on weekends; on weekdays you'll find the roads quiet and dinner reservations easy to come by.

Gourmands who like charming country hotels should head for Peppers Convent, a magnificent complex in the heart of the valley. Hotel-restaurant combinations don't get any more idyllic: lovely accommodations are in a turn-of-the-century former convent, where your elegant suite may be a former kinder-garten or music room. The hotel's multiple-award-winning Robert's restaurant serves long and leisurely meals in an 1876 settler's cottage, accompanied by vintages from vines you can reach out and touch. Even if you don't stay for dinner, stop by to pick up a gourmet hamper for a lunch under the trees down by the creek.

WHAT: site, hotel, restaurant. **HUNTER VALLEY:** approximately 125 miles/200 km north of Sydney. **PEPPERS CONVENT:** Halls Rd., Pokolbin. Tel 61/2-4993-8999, fax 61/2-4998-7739; convent@peppers.com.au; www.peppers.com.au/convent. *Cost:* doubles from $304. 8-course dinner at Robert's $125. **BEST TIMES:** winter (Jun–Aug) and spring (Sept–Oct).

A Beloved Icon and a Luxe Hotel Overlooking the Waterfront

SYDNEY OPERA HOUSE AND THE HARBOR

New South Wales, Australia

Sydney is Australia's largest, oldest, liveliest and brashest city, and its Opera House—initially reviled for its startlingly modern design (resembling a cluster of billowing white "sails")—has come to be as emblematic of the city

as the Eiffel Tower is of Paris. Chosen from more than 200 designs submitted in 1957 by the world's most prominent architects, the project was instantly controversial. The building took fifteen years to complete, during which time its disillusioned Danish creator, Joern Utzon, removed himself from the project, never to see it finished. Today the opera house, perfectly situated on Sydney's busy and picturesque harbor, is the cultural heartbeat of the city. Numerous opera, symphony, ballet, and theater productions take place in its Opera Theater and Concert House (both of which pride themselves on perfect acoustics). If you want the experience without the music, the Opera House's Bennelong Restaurant, located in one of its most dramatic spaces, offers an elegantly spare menu amid magnificent harbor views.

For a view from the outside, you can't do better than the elegant Four Seasons Hotel, from whose upper floors you can view the Opera House to your right, the Harbour Bridge to your left, and the glistening expanse of the harbor filling out the vista all around. Its marble lobby isn't a bad spot for other kinds of views, either: Nearly every celebrity who visits Sydney passes through at some point. The hotel's coveted waterside location—near the spot where Australia was born—is the nucleus of the most popular tourist attractions: Circular Quay is the spot from which hundreds of ships zigzag their way across Sydney Harbour, and the 70-acre green oasis of the Royal Botanic Gardens offers some of the finest walks in town. If you want opera tickets, the Four Season's concierge is almost guaranteed to find you a seat.

Sydney's historical waterfront district, The Rocks, is close by, nestled next to the Harbour Bridge. Once the haunt of brawling sailors and ex-convicts, it has now been gentrified and made respectable, with restaurants, shopping, galleries, and exhibition spaces. Only the Lord Nelson, the city's oldest continuously operating pub, evokes the area's early days.

WHAT: site, hotel, restaurant. **SYDNEY OPERA HOUSE:** Bennelong Point. Box office, tel 61/2-9250-7777, fax 61/2-9251-3843; bookings@sydneyoperahouse.com; www.sydneyoperahouse.com. *Cost:* tickets from $20. *When:* performances year-round; the opera season usually runs Jan, Feb, and Jun–Oct. **BENNELONG RESTAURANT:** tel 61/2-9241-1999; www.guillaumeatbennelong.com.au. *Cost:* dinner $65. **THE FOUR SEASONS HOTEL SYDNEY:** 199 George St.; tel 61/2-9250-3100; in U.S., tel 800-332-3442; in Canada, tel 800-819-5053; www.fourseasons.com/sydney. *Cost:* opera house and harbor-view rooms on floors 6–23 from $263, standard city-view rooms $222. **THE ROCKS:** located between the harbor, Kent St. to the west, and Grosvenor St. to the south; www.rocksvillage.com.

Guests in an Ancient Land

ARNHEM LAND

Northern Territory, Australia

A vast area five times the size of Great Britain, Arnhem Land is a special place of pristine bush, eucalyptus forests, coastal wilderness, and abundant wildlife, owned and managed by the Gummulkbun Aboriginal people, whose home it has been for 65,000 years. It is one of Australia's most restricted areas, only recently opened to tourism (via Aboriginal-owned and -operated tour agencies). Cultural safaris allow small groups of visitors to share the wonders of the rich indigenous heritage, and to understand the meanings and mythology behind the ancient rock art that adorns the walls and ceilings of the caves and rock shelters throughout the area. Your hosts are Brian Rooke, an Aborigine from the Bass Strait Islands, and his wife, Phyllis. He has lived in the Arnhem Land region for twenty-five years and has an intimate knowledge of the country and culture. Home is a traditional safari-style tent deep in the Mudjeegarrdart bush, a quarter of a million acres that belongs to Phyllis's tribal family. The seasons and guests' interests determine your activities, whether it's a short trip or an extended camping tour. Identify traditional foods and medicines, visit the sites of cave paintings, explore the abundant bird life, cool off with a swim in a *billibong* (a natural water hole), or go fishing or crab

spearing and have your catch prepared for dinner. The operative word is "tradition," which you will observe and appreciate in the company of local guides with a natural affinity for their ancestral homeland and its people.

WHAT: experience, site, hotel. **WHERE:** reachable only by light aircraft, 1 hour from Darwin; transfers can be arranged. **How:** tours are offered by Umorrduk Safaris at Brookes Australia Tours, tel 61/8-8948-1306, fax 61/3-8660-2143; bbrookes@ozemail.com.au; www.brookesaustralia.com.au. In the U.S., contact Safari Experts, tel 435-649-4655; safari @safariexperts.com; www.safariexperts.com. **COST:** 3-day tours from $2,180, all-inclusive; 5-day tours from $5,145, all-inclusive. **WHEN:** park year-round; overnight trips May–Dec. **BEST TIMES:** Jun–Aug.

Spiritual Shrines of the Aborigines

AYERS ROCK AND THE OLGAS

Northern Territory, Australia

Never mind how many times it's appeared in movies or on postcards, the great red monolith of Ayers Rock, the world's largest, still stirs the spirits of those who visit it. Revered as a spiritual center of power by the

Aborigines, whose ancestors are believed to have lived here as much as 20,000 years ago, Ayers Rock constantly changes color, and at sunrise and sunset becomes such an amazing

The humbling majesty of Ayers Rock

visual experience that you'll soon understand why a world of mythology has been woven around it. Otherwise known by its Aboriginal name Uluru, "Giant Pebble," the rock rises 1,142 feet above the featureless plain and has a circumference of about 5 miles. Rich deposits of iron are the source of its orange-red color—Ayers Rock actually rusts when it rains. Climbing it is not prohibited, although because of its religious significance it is quietly discouraged by the Aborigines, who have managed the surrounding 511-square-mile national park since 1985. The strenuous one-hour trek up a single path is not for the faint of heart nor weak of knee. Many prefer the walk around it, at the base.

About 30 miles west of Ayers Rock are the Olgas, thirty-six gigantic rock domes, some reaching 1,800 feet, separated by chasms and valleys and spread out over an area of 15 square miles. Even more significant to today's Aborigines than Uluru, the area's name in their language is Kata Tjuta, or Many Heads. Public access is limited to the "Valley of the Winds" walk, a 4-mile loop best experienced in the absence of afternoon tour-bus caravans.

WHAT: site. **WHERE:** at the geographical center of the continent, 200 miles/322 km southwest of Alice Springs, near the town of Yulara. Flights from all major Australian cities. **WHERE TO STAY:** Ayers Rock Resort is located in Yulara, 12 miles/19 km from Ayers Rock. In Sydney, contact Voyages Hotels and Resorts, tel 61/2-8296-8010, fax 61/2-9299-2103; www.ayersrockresort.com.au. *Cost:* doubles from $178 for a budget lodge, from $400 for a 5-star room. **BEST TIMES:** Mar–May, Sept–Nov.

A Top-End Juxtaposition of Wilderness and Luxury

SEVEN SPIRIT BAY

Cobourg Peninsula, Northern Territory, Australia

With thousands of acres of untouched bush, mangrove, and jungle behind it and gorgeous waters and deserted beaches in front, this exceptional wilderness habitat is located in northern Australia's "Top End" within the 50,000-year-old homeland of some of the last Aboriginal tribes still leading a traditional life. Vast tracts of their land have been leased to the state to be managed as Gurig National Park, except for this resort and the land that surrounds it on the tip of the Coburg Peninsula, a finger of land pointing north toward Indonesia.

Accessible only by air, this remote pocket of comfort and civilization demonstrates an environmental sensitivity everywhere—the simple buildings, for example, are made of natural materials. Resident guides take guests fishing, and

The resort's lagoon pool

on bush walks and coastal tours. Or take a predawn hike to celebrate something as simple and magical as a sunrise. Seven Spirit Bay takes its name from the cycle of seven seasons in northern Australian Aboriginal tradition: lightning, thundering, rainmaking, greening, wind storming, fire raging, and cloudless blue. If you're lucky, every day will be cloudless blue.

WHAT: site, experience, hotel. **WHERE:** 1-hour air charter northeast of Darwin followed by half-hour 4-wheel-drive ride arranged by Spirit Bay. Tel 61/8-8979-0281, fax 61/8-8979-0284; www.peppers.com.au/seven-spirit-bay. **COST:** 2-night packages (with accommodation, all meals, round-trip air and transfers, and guided walks) $1,300 per person. **WHEN:** Apr–Oct (dry season).

Over the Top Down Under

KAKADU NATIONAL PARK

Northern Territory, Australia

On the world radar of superior wilderness areas, the 8,000-square-mile Kakadu National Park is a small but significant blip, still remote and little known despite its use as the outback location for *Crocodile Dundee*.

For now, its frontier freshness remains intact, and the resident population of 15-foot "saltie" and "freshie" crocodiles (the latter unique to these parts) still laze undisturbed in the shallows of the pristine river and marshland ecosystem.

In 1981 Kakadu received the rare double honor of being named a UNESCO World Heritage Site for its natural wonders as well as for the 5,000 rock paintings that grace its sandstone caves—"the greatest body of rock art in the world," according to the local museum. The paintings can be classified into three distinct periods of Aboriginal history, and date back from 30 to more than 25,000 years. Ubirr, 27 miles north of park headquarters, is one of the most visited outcrops; in its cavelike "galleries," images record life from the Stone Age to the 20th century.

WHAT: site. **WHERE:** 150 miles/241 km east of Darwin on northern coast. **HOW:** contact Ozhorizons, tel 61/7-4124-9943, www.ozhorizons.com.au. **COST:** 6-day all-inclusive land tours from Darwin from $720 per person. **WHEN:** departs once a month. **BEST TIMES:** Apr–Oct (dry season).

Over the Top: Hunting and Gathering in Prehistoric Forests

THE TIWI ISLANDS: BATHURST AND MELVILLE

Northern Territory, Australia

All but unknown to the outside world, Bathurst and its sister island, Melville, are the ancestral home of Australia's Tiwi Aborigines and provide the most fascinating cultural experience Australia has to offer.

Tiwi means "chosen people," and for 40,000 years this culture developed separately from other Aboriginal groups, escaping the colonization suffered by those on the continent just 50 miles away—even the early Catholic missionaries were culturally lenient, allowing many Tiwi beliefs to coexist with the newly imposed religion. Today, non-Tiwi can visit the islands only as part of Tiwi-owned and -operated tours. Local guides assist in total immersion: four-wheel-drive forays into Bathurst bushland in search of traditional "tucker" for lunch may turn up bandicoot, wallaby, some nice carpet snake, or—why not?—mangrove worms. After a rib-rattling jeep ride to the very edge of Australia, pull up on a magnificent beach facing the Timor Sea and Indonesia. The nearby Indonesian archipelago is reflected in the local textile crafts, with batik patterns still being created by local cooperatives.

WHAT: experience, island. **WHERE:** 50 miles/80 km off the coast of Australia's Top End. Half-hour flights depart from Darwin. **HOW:** in Darwin, contact Tiwi Tours, tel 61/8-8923-6523, fax 61/8-8923-6543; res@aussieadventure.com.au; www.aussieadventure.com.au. **COST:** 1-day tours $365, include air. **WHEN:** Mar–Nov. **BEST TIMES:** May–Nov.

Aboriginal artistry

Where the Oldest Living Rain Forest on Earth Meets the Great Barrier Reef

CAPE TRIBULATION

Queensland, Australia

Two of Australia's World Heritage sites, the Wet Tropics Rainforest and the Great Barrier Reef, come together at Cape Tribulation, so named in 1770 by a peeved Captain James Cook "because here began all my troubles"

when his ship hit a coral bed. Protected within the Cape Tribulation and Daintree National Parks and believed to have been the evolutionary cradle for much of Australia's unique wildlife, the cape's rain forest contains trees that are 3,000 years old, and many can be traced back over 120 million years. Dinosaurs have disappeared, but little else seems to have changed.

To immerse yourself entirely in this jungle exotica, choose from two outstanding ecotourism properties that comfortably coexist within miles of each other. Progressive forerunners in the design of environmental lodges, both Silky Oaks and Daintree Eco Lodge are swathed in their own private jungle. Naturalists on staff will point out the unique ecology, and a concentration of flora and fauna species that has no parallel on earth.

WHAT: site, hotel. **CAPE TRIBULATION:** 60 miles/97 km north of Cairns. **DAINTREE ECO LODGE:** tel 61/7-4098-6100; info@daintree-ecolodge.com.au; www.daintree-ecolodge.com.au. *Cost:* doubles from $445. **SILKY OAKS LODGE:** tel 61/7-4098-1666, fax 61/7-4098-1983; www.silkyoakslodge.com.au. *Cost:* doubles from $485, includes most activities. **BEST TIMES:** May–Sept.

A Romp on the World's Most Beautiful Highway

FRASER ISLAND

Queensland, Australia

On the world's largest sand island, you can swim in forty freshwater dune-surrounded lakes, walk through the ancient Valley of the Giants rain forest, join rangers to track down some of the island's 350 species of birds, or just enjoy the uninterrupted 75 miles of broad coastal beach—the world's most beautiful highway. Rent a jeep from the island's award-winning ecotourism hotel, the Kingfisher Bay Resort, and realize those macho dreams of Man Against the Outback. With the Pacific Ocean on one side and 40-foot cliffs patterned like Gothic towers on the other, spend the day cruising the beach without another vehicle in sight. You'll feel like Lawrence of Arabia at Sandy Cape, on the island's northern tip, where huge sand mountains roll down to a vibrant blue sea. Come August, the hotel's *Kingfisher I* catamaran is the perfect vehicle to sail amid the 2,000 migrating whales that return annually on their way south to the Antarctic.

WHAT: island, hotel. FRASER ISLAND: at

The resort was awarded a top architectural prize.

the southern end of the Great Barrier Reef, a 35-minute boat ride from Hervey Bay. KINGFISHER BAY RESORT: tel 61/7-4120-3333, fax 61/7-4127-9333; reservations@kingfisherbay.com; www.kingfisherbay.com. *Cost:* doubles from $165. BEST TIMES: Aug–Sept for whale watching.

Australia's Masterpiece

THE GREAT BARRIER REEF AND THE CORAL SEA

Queensland, Australia

The Australians call it the Eighth Wonder of the World, but that may actually be an understatement. The Great Barrier Reef is the only living organism on the planet that's visible from outer space. Stretching for more than 1,200 miles at between 10 and 50 miles off the coast of Queensland, it's not in fact one coral reef but an association of 2,900 smaller reefs, with some 300 stepping-stone islands sprinkled among them. The largest marine preserve in the world, it's home to a stupefying profusion of sea creatures, including 500 species of brilliantly colored hard and soft coral, 1,500 varieties of fish, and 4,000 kinds of mollusks.

Nature's treasures are abundant in the Great Barrier Reef.

You can sail it, snorkel it, and fly over it, but only by diving the depths of this extraordinary realm can you really grasp its diversity. Luckily, there's no shortage of agencies promising you the ultimate reef experience. *Quicksilver* is a high-tech, wave-piercing, turbo-powered catamaran that makes the ninety-minute trip to an anchored glass-bottomed platform, where you can swim, snorkel, or scuba dive; or travel in a semi-submersible vessel and listen to your guide's running commentary explaining the underwater extravaganza outside your window.

Those wanting a more prolonged experience can opt to spend four days aboard the luxurious mini–cruise ships *Coral Princess* or *Coral Princess II*. The 115-foot ships offer snorkeling, guided coral-viewing excursions in small glass-bottom boats, reef fishing, and evening presentations by trained marine biologists. If you've always dreamed of learning how to scuba dive, the ships' qualified PADI instructors will have you logging your first underwater hours.

Most people think the Great Barrier Reef is the last word in deep-sea diving, but beyond it the waters of the lesser-known, less-dived Coral Sea may be even more wonderful. Highlights of this pristine wilderness of crystal-clear waters and uninhabited coral atolls include huge perpendicular drop-

offs and 200- to 300-foot visibility. Imagine giant clams up to 7 feet across, 300-pound groupers, and innumerable turtles and sharks, along with an outstanding variety of hard corals and reef fish of all descriptions. Some live-aboard trips include a visit to the wreck of the *Yongala*, a 363-foot wonder said to be home to the greatest concentration and diversity of marine life in the world—a mind-boggling underwater experience.

WHAT: site, experience. **QUICKSILVER:** tel 61/7-4087-2100, fax 61/7-4099-5525; central_qsc@quicksilvergroup.com.au; www.quicksilver-cruises.com. *Cost:* $110 per person, includes smorgasbord lunch and equipment. *When:* daily departures Jul–Dec from Port Douglas. **CORAL PRINCESS CRUISES:** tel 61/7-4040-9999, fax 61/7-4035-5995; in the U.S., tel 931-924-5253; cruise@coralprincess.com.au; www.coralprincess.com.au. *Cost:* 4-day cruise from $1,210, all-inclusive except diving lessons and equipment. *When:* 4 weekly departures from Cairns and Townsville. **CORAL SEA TRIPS:** Coral Sea departures from Cairns and Townsville. *How:* in the U.S., contact Trip-n-Tour Pacific, tel 800-348-0842 or 760-451-1001, fax 760-451-1000; info@trip-n-tour.com; www.trip-n-tour.com. *Cost:* 7-night itinerary from $2,300 per person, all-inclusive. *When:* departures Jul–Dec. **BEST TIMES:** Oct–Nov for best sea conditions.

The Quicksilver's *underwater observatory*

Isle of Luxury in the Great Barrier Reef

HAYMAN ISLAND RESORT

Queensland, Australia

Sitting on its own private 900-acre island—one of the seventy-four Whitsunday Islands in the sapphire waters of the Great Barrier Reef—Hayman is one of the world's most opulent resorts. Of the many island resorts off Queensland's Golden Coast, it has no rival in natural attractions and man-made amenities. Travelers with the wherewithal come here for the isolation, lush tropical landscaping, choice of five restaurants, smiling service, otherworldly network of saltwater and freshwater swimming pools, and a priceless location just 27 nautical miles from the Great Barrier Reef. With the relaxed elegance of a very posh private club, Hayman offers a maximum of 400 guests a roster of water sports, one-day-or-more rental of a 40-foot Beneteau yacht, a 5-mile wilderness trail—even a nightclub. At the rarefied height of the resort's accommodations are the Lagoon Wing's eleven penthouse suites, each individually decorated with priceless antiques and artwork in Art Deco, Moroccan, or Japanese themes. The North Queensland Penthouse, an Australiana fantasy of a colonial homestead on the range (complete with butler service), will help remind you where you are.

Ponds, pools, and puddles abound.

WHAT: island, hotel. **WHERE:** flights from most mainland cities arrive at the neighboring island of Hamilton, connecting with a complimentary 50-minute scenic cruise to Hayman. Tel 61/7-4940-1838, fax 61/7-4940-1567; reservations@hayman.com.au; www.hayman. com.au. **COST:** doubles from $480, suites from $2,140, penthouses from $2,265. **BEST TIMES:** Oct–Nov for best sea conditions.

Pink Snowstorms on the Great Barrier Reef

HERON ISLAND

Queensland, Australia

Unlike many of the other islands near the Great Barrier Reef, Heron Island is a coral cay—literally part of the reef itself. To see the reef, all you have to do is walk down to the beach and bend over. The island's only resort organizes reef walks during low tide, and there's also diving and snorkeling in the crystal-clear waters that teem with multicolored fish and coral. The coral spawns each

November, when the polyps emit billions of pink-and-purple bundles of eggs and sperm. It's like being inside a pink snowstorm, and the phenomenon attracts divers from all over the world. Situated on the Tropic of Capricorn and only about 30 acres in size (of which half is a national park), Heron is more a summer camp for naturalists and divers than a glitzy reef resort. Hundreds of green sea turtles come in October and November and lay their eggs. They hatch in January and February. The humpback whales migrate north in June and July, and swim with their calves in October.

WHAT: island, site, event, hotel. **HERON ISLAND:** daily launches from Gladstone, 40 miles/64 km away. **HERON ISLAND RESORT:** tel 61/7-4972-9055, fax 61/7-4972-0244; reservations@poresorts.com; www.heronisland. com. *Cost:* 5 ranges of accommodations start at $317 per person per day, includes non-motorized water sports and island activities. **HOW:** in the U.S., contact Safari Experts, tel 435-649-4655; safari@safariexperts.com; www.safariexperts.com. **BEST TIMES:** Oct–Dec. Coral spawns immediately following first full moon in Nov.

An Embarrassment of Beaches

LIZARD ISLAND

Queensland, Australia

O f the dozen or so island resorts amid the emerald and turquoise waters of the Great Barrier Reef, this one, located farthest north, is the most beach-endowed. With just forty homestead-style bungalows, a justly

famous Blue Lagoon, and twenty-four secluded white-sand, palm-fringed coves, there's a good chance you'll have a beach to yourself—and reason to stay for a few weeks to check them all out individually. Uninhabited save for resort staff and guests, Lizard Island is a 2,500-acre national park, and the descendants of the 3-foot-long monitor lizards—after which Captain James Cook named the island in 1770—can be found sunbathing on the palm-studded green lawn in front of your bungalow. Being so far offshore and nearer the outer reef, Lizard has some of the clearest and bluest waters and some of the best diving of the islands. Cod Hole, a hot spot just 12 miles away, has long been a must-do diving site; dozens of giant potato codfish expect to be stroked and fed by hand—which may explain why they grow to 6 feet in length and weigh more than 400 pounds.

Things really jump on this otherwise relaxed and informal island when the black marlin are running, and 1,200-pound catches are not rare. Fishermen from all over the world descend on the island from August to November, and at the annual Black Marlin Classic in October, they reminisce about the seven world and two Australian records (as of this writing) that have been set here.

WHAT: island, event, hotel. **LIZARD ISLAND:** less than an hour's flight from Cairns over beautiful stretches of rain forest and the Great Barrier Reef. **LIZARD ISLAND RESORT:** tel 61/2-8296-8010, fax 61/2-9299-2103; www.lizardisland.com.au; travel@voyages. com.au. *Cost:* from $2,700 per room for 2 nights, includes all meals and activities. **BEST TIMES:** Oct–Nov for best sea conditions; the Black Marlin Classic is in Oct. Aug–Nov for best fishing.

Great Wine, Great Food

BAROSSA VALLEY

South Australia, Australia

The picturesque Barossa Valley is Australia's lodestone for all things gastronomic, and along with the nearby (and lesser-known) Clare Valley, produces close to 60 percent of Australia's wines. Maximize your wine-and-food experience with a stay at The Lodge Country House, a charming former homestead built in 1903 for one of Australian wine pioneer Joseph Seppelt's thirteen children. The handsome bluestone country-house inn is framed by 3 acres of gorgeous rose and flower gardens and stands just across the road from the Seppelts' sprawling showpiece vineyard, which dates back to the mid-1850s. The Lodge's shaded veranda is the gathering spot where the inn's eight privileged guests come to watch the sunset. A memorable candlelit dinner follows, accompanied by an excellent selection of Barossa's best. Some fifty wineries are within a half hour's drive (including Peter Lehman, Stanley Brothers, Henschke, Penfolds, and Richmond Grove), and many of them are represented on The Lodge's wine list.

From The Lodge it's a lovely ten-minute drive to Tanunda, the most important, lively, and charming of Barossa wine towns. Its blend of antique shops, wine stores, and cafés will fill an afternoon pleasantly, but your final destination should be the smart but casual 1918 Bistro and Grill, with its straightforward and memorable menu of modern Australian specialties. Locals in the know order from the extensive list of unlabeled Barossa wines, available to patrons at a substantial savings over the officially labeled versions. But you have to ask.

WHAT: site, hotel, restaurant. **BAROSSA VALLEY:** 45 miles/72 km northeast of Adelaide. **THE LODGE COUNTRY HOUSE:** Main Rd., Seppeltsfield. Tel 61/8-8562-8277, fax 61/8-8562-8344; stay@thelodgecountryhouse.com; www.thelodgecountryhouse.com.au. *Cost:* doubles $270; with breakfast and dinner for 2, $380. **1918 BISTRO AND GRILL:** Murray St., Tanunda. Tel 61/8-8563-0405; www.1918.com.au. *Cost:* dinner $60. **BEST TIMES:** Mar–Apr (harvest time) and Oct–Dec. In odd-numbered years only, the 1-week Vintage Festival takes place following Easter.

A Microcosm of All Things Australian

KANGAROO ISLAND

South Australia, Australia

Australia's third-largest island is uncrowded and uncomplicated and boasts a treasure trove of unique animal life amid a variety of unspoiled scenery. Sheep outnumber residents 300 to 1, but it's the armies of wild

Nature imitates art, Salvador Dalí style

kangaroos, koalas, Tamar wallabies (nearly extinct on the mainland), and fairy penguins that astound. They live among some of the whitest sand dunes on the planet, surf-sculpted boulders resembling abstract art (aptly called the Remarkable Rocks), sparkling seas, and a natural bridge carved from lime-stone called Admiral's Arch. Seal Bay is home to one of the world's rarest species of sea lions; they can be seen lounging on the white beach by the hundreds. They seem unper-turbed by *Homo sapiens,* who take advantage of an up-close-and-personal experience rarely possible in the wild. The sea lions' cousins, the New Zealand fur seal, frequent pretty coves at the island's southwestern tip. Visitors who sign up only for Adventure Charters of Kangaroo Island's whirlwind one-day excursions usually underesti-mate the island's size (90 by 40 miles) and invariably long to stay on at one of the charming local B&Bs—farms and home-steads that welcome guests with true Australian hospitality. Hope for availability at the Stranraer Homestead, a 3,500-acre working farm run by the Wheaton family since 1911.

WHAT: island, experience, town. **WHERE:** 75 miles/121 km south of Adelaide; daily fer-ries and air links available. **HOW:** Adventure Charters of Kangaroo Island, tel 61/8-8553-9119, fax 61/8-8555-9122; info@exceptional kangarooisland.com; www.adventurecharters. com.au. In the U.S., contact Safari Experts, tel 435-649-4655; safari@safariexperts.com; www. safariexperts.com. *Cost:* 1- to 3-day visits from $580 per person, all-inclusive (with air transfer). **BEST TIMES:** Sept–Feb.

A Walk on the Wild Side

CRADLE MOUNTAIN NATIONAL PARK AND THE OVERLAND TRACK

Tasmania, Australia

L ying 150 miles south of Australia, mountainous, Virginia-size Tasmania seems like the end of the earth even to mainland Aussies, and because of its isolated location, much of its flora and fauna exist nowhere else on

earth. Still, most of the island is green and civilized, much like England's Surrey—except, that is, for the 3 million largely wild acres set aside as parkland, encompassing some of Australia's most spectacular alpine scenery. The jewel in this natural crown is Cradle Mountain National Park, whose rugged peaks and high moorlands make up a large, untamed portion of the area. The 53-mile Overland Track, linking Cradle Mountain

Park with Lake St. Clair, is the country's most famous trail and one that every Aussie vows to do at least once in his or her life. Penetrating much of the rain forest, a boardwalk protects the environment from human impact.

There are basic huts along the way, but they're often full. Rather than carry camping equipment for the duration of the six-day hike, sign up with a reputable trekking agency that operates private huts with hot running water and private guest rooms. They'll supply an experienced Tasmanian guide who accompanies a group at a ratio of one per five guests (groups are never larger than ten); he or she will double as cook at the end of each glorious day of walking, during which you'll cover between 6 and 11 miles. The last day includes a walk through a dense eucalyptus forest to the shores of Lake St. Clair, Tasmania's most beautiful, carved out by glacial ice over the past couple million years; the 10-mile boat cruise that follows augments the magic of your Cradle Mountain experience.

If walking the Overland Track is about 50 miles more than your average vacation undertaking, the Cradle Mountain Lodge is a stationary alternative. Rustic and cozy, it's not a luxury operation (unless you count the huge breakfast of prime Tasmanian bacon and local free-range eggs). Rather, it's the kind of informal inn where a glass of Tasmanian cabernet is nursed in front of a roaring fire while swapping hiking stories. It's a good base from which to plan some days of horseback riding, canoeing, and hiking through lush rain forests and along alpine lakes. A popular tradition is the nightly "leftover extravaganza," when the kitchen's scraps are put out on a nearby platform for the forest's nocturnal wildlife, which includes the occasional Tasmanian devil (and we don't mean Errol Flynn).

WHAT: site, experience, hotel. **OVERLAND TRACK:** treks depart from and return to Launceston. For guided treks, contact Cradle Mountain Huts, tel 61/3-6392-2211, fax 61/3-6392-2277; bookings@cradlehuts.com.au; www.cradlehuts.com.au. *Cost:* from $2,025 per person sharing double bunk for 6-day hike, includes all meals and guide services. *When:* daily departures Oct–Apr. **CRADLE MOUNTAIN LODGE:** 50 miles/80 km south of Devonport. Tel 61/3-6492-2103, fax 61/3-6492-1309; www.cradlemountainlodge.com. *Cost:* $95 per person (double occupancy). **BEST TIMES:** Oct–Feb.

A Natural Playground of Limitless Choice

FREYCINET NATIONAL PARK AND FREYCINET LODGE

Tasmania, Australia

Freycinet is Tasmania's oldest coastal park, a dramatic combination of red granite mountains, white-sand beaches, and lapis-blue ocean. Unobtrusively nestled within its confines is the ecosensitive Freycinet, "the disappearing lodge," so carefully constructed that it is barely visible from even a few feet away. Luxurious cabins with red-wood terraces have been harmoniously integrated with the attention-stealing environment. Guests pick and choose from a host of nature-oriented activities including whale watching, visits to the breeding grounds of fairy penguins and black swans, and guided walks through forests populated by marsupials, brilliant-colored parrots, and laughing kookaburras. A self-guided nature walk through fields of wildflowers and up and over a spine of mountains leads to the trek's grand finale: Wineglass Bay, one of Australia's most beautiful panoramas. The Freycinet coastline is famous for its seafood—a chef doesn't need to do much to the local lobster-size crayfish to create an award-quality dinner at a window table overlooking Great Oyster Bay at sunset.

Tasmania's famous Wineglass Bay

WHAT: island, site, hotel. **FREYCINET LODGE:** 2 hours from both Hobart and Launceton, tel 61/3-6257-0101, fax 61/3-6257-0278; info@freycinetlodge.com.au; www. freycinetlodge.com.au. In the U.S., contact Austravel, tel 212-972-6880, fax 212-983-8376. **COST:** doubles from $235. **BEST TIMES:** Feb–Mar; May–Sept for whale watching.

An Inspirational Ride with the Twelve Apostles

THE GREAT OCEAN ROAD

Victoria, Australia

This long coastal highway, often compared to California's Pacific Coast Highway, ranks among the world's top scenic drives, cliff-hugging its way west of Melbourne along the rugged southern coast of the Australian

continent. Every bend of the 180-mile journey reveals another awesome scene of jagged bluffs, windswept beaches, old whaling and fishing towns, inventive restaurants, sweet B&Bs, and protected rain forest and national parkland populated by koalas and kangaroos. The timeless battle between the relentless waves of the Southern Ocean and the shoreline has resulted in prime surf beaches such as world-famous Bell's and such extraordinary rock formations as Loch Ard Gorge, the Bay of Islands, and, most famous of all, the Twelve Apostles. In the 19th century, these limestone pillars were known as the Sow and Piglets. The ocean has claimed four of the brood in the intervening years; of the remaining eight, some reach as high as 180 feet.

It's not hard to see why the Twelve Apostles stretch is also known as the Shipwreck Coast,

since the waters claimed hundreds of ships during colonization in the 1800s, when the journey from England took three to four months. This is the most spectacular segment of the Great Ocean Road, often broody and romantic during windy and stormy weather. It's best to drive the road round-trip, since the rugged sea views are different depending on your direction. If you're up to it, biking or walking with a small organized group is the best way of seeing it all. Be sure to take advantage of the lookout points along the way at sunset, and don't forget to visit nearby Coonawarra's best winemakers while you're in the area.

WHAT: experience, site. **WHERE:** 180 miles/290 km long, starting at the surf-center town of Torquay (62 miles/100 km southwest of Melbourne) and ending at Warrnambool.

How: Both Feet Walking Lodge offers 3-, 4-, and 6-day walking trips, tel 61/3-5334-0688; www.bothfeet.com.au. **Cost:** 3-day walking trip from $1,215 per person, all-inclusive. **When:** mid- to late Mar. **Best times:** May when the southern right whales arrive.

Glorious Isolation on the Edge of the Continent

CABLE BEACH

Broome, Western Australia, Australia

The Australians take their beaches seriously, so when they claim that Cable Beach is the continent's most beautiful, take notice. Large and lustrous South Sea pearls (from the world's biggest pearl oysters) put Broome on the map in the early 1900s, but today it's the epic 14-mile beach, almost half a mile wide when the tide is out, that draws connoisseurs. The Indian Ocean's waters are crystal clear, and pearly shells mingle with the sun-bleached sand, making it gleam and shimmer. In the small frontier town of Broome, the spirit of the pearling era is still evident among the Japanese, Chinese, Malay, and Aboriginal population. The pearling masters' indigenous architecture of wooden latticework screens, corrugated-iron bungalows, and colonial verandas is reflected in the luxurious Cable Beach Club, the only hotel adjacent to the beach. It's a long way from anywhere, and most guests come starved for the laid-back atmosphere, though everyone should be able to shake off their torpor long enough to take a sunset camel ride along the beach.

A leisurely camel ride along the water

What: site, town, hotel. **Broome:** town center is 3 miles/4.5 km from a new international airport. **Cable Beach Club:** tel 61/8-9192-0400, fax 61/8-9192-2249; www.cablebeachclub.com. *Cost:* from $255. **Best times:** Mar–Nov.

The Ultimate Outback Experience

EL QUESTRO STATION

Kimberly, Western Australia, Australia

You may feel a sense of discovery, as if you are the first to arrive, when you reach this million-acre working cattle ranch in the middle of Kimberly, just a dot on the map of massive, sparsely populated Western

Australia. El Questro Station is the ultimate outback experience, in a wonderful five-star incarnation. Saunter on over and offer to join the cowboys mustering 1,000 head of Brahman cattle in the bush, explore one of the property's many tropical gorges or remote water holes, or go on horse, camel, foot, or four-wheel-drive treks with resident rangers, who will introduce you to the station's thermal springs, waterfalls, and religious rock art. At pricey Homestead cabins, cantilevered over the Chamberlain River, you can cast your line from your private veranda and hope for a record-breaking barramundi, Australia's premier sport fish. Each airy suite is tastefully decorated with Asian and tropical Australian artifacts, a sign that you are closer to Indonesia than to Sydney.

Those whose wallets dictate Foster's instead of Champagne can choose one of the station's four less-expensive accommodation options, right down to bare-bones camping sites under the stars.

WHAT: experience, hotel. **WHERE:** 2 hours by light aircraft from Darwin. About 62 miles/100 km from Kununurra. **HOW:** tel 61/8-9169-1777, fax 61/8-9169-1383; www.elquestro.com.au; in the U.S., contact Safari Experts, tel 435-649-4655; safari @safariexperts.com; www.safariexperts.com. **COST:** Homestead $765 per person, includes all meals and most activities; other accommodations: doubles from $218; camping, $13 per person. **WHEN:** Apr–early Nov. **BEST TIMES:** Apr–Oct.

Wildflowers and Vineyards

MARGARET RIVER

Western Australia, Australia

In the last twenty years, Australia's sophisticated wine industry has given a cosmopolitan veneer to this remote and beautiful corner of the world, with its dazzling landscape of stunning surf beaches, manicured vines, and awesome forests. Prestigious wines produced by the Vasse Felix, Cape Mentelle, Cullens, and the venerable Leeuwin Estate are world renowned. The latter hosts the Leeuwin Estate alfresco concerts, a heralded summer event in January attracting world-class performers and ever-growing crowds. Blessed with a Mediterranean climate, the Margaret Valley area is also graced with the annual spring wildflower season in September and October, when the countryside is filled to the horizon with a kaleidoscope of color. More than 1,000 wildflower species have been identified, including almost 70 species of orchid. Eighty percent of its plant species are found nowhere else on earth, making it one of the

34 "biodiversity hotspots" in the world, and the only one in Australia.

Happily, Cape Lodge, one of Australia's most tasteful and relaxing country retreats, is located right in the middle of the region. The Dutch Cape–inspired main house is surrounded by rolling lawns and magnificent gardens, and overlooks a lovely lake, where guests can swim or paddle about in a canoe. Morning wake-up calls come from a chorus of kookaburras—so no one misses the gourmet breakfasts in the sun-drenched glass conservatory. It's a short drive to Margaret River, a delightful town full of antiques stores and crafts shops. Local restaurants with young and innovative chefs make this a culinary corner of Australia to be reckoned with.

WHAT: site, event, hotel. **MARGARET VALLEY:** 250 miles/402 km south of Perth. **LEEUWIN ESTATE CONCERTS:** tel 61/9-430-4099, fax 61/9-430-5687; info@leeuwinestate.com.au; www.leeuwinestate.com.au. **COST:** ticket prices vary. **CAPE LODGE:** in Yallingup, tel 61/8-9755-6311, fax 61/8-9755-6322; stay@capelodge.com.au; www.capelodge.com.au. *Cost:* doubles from $640, includes dinner. **BEST TIMES:** Sept–Oct (wildflower season).

In the Wake of Captain Cook

THE BAY OF ISLANDS

North Island, New Zealand

O ff the irregular coast of New Zealand's North Island, more than 150 smaller islands of varying size hopscotch across the deep blue waters, their tall Norfolk pines growing side by side with subtropical banana plants and fan palms in an ideal climate that adds to the bay's allure as a recreational playground. The area is world-famous for big-game fishing—author Zane Grey, a leading sportsman of his time, caught as many as five marlin here in a single day, including a 450-pound world-record striped marlin. (Grey's Hemingwayesque *Tales of the Angler's Eldorado, New Zealand* was instrumental in establishing the bay as a game-fishing hotspot.)

But the fishing-averse can have their own adventure, experiencing the Bay of Islands as Captain James Cook did, with the wind in your hair and the flapping of sails overhead as you slip past hundreds of hidden coves and secret beaches aboard the schooner *R. Tucker Thompson.* Alternatively, a 70-foot private charter boat like the ultra-stylish *Sirdar* can take you to an island all your own. For a trophy-size marlin to go with it, call on veteran fishing personality Dudley Smith, skipper and owner of the 32-foot *Triple B.*

For accommodations on shore, bask in the views from one of the luxurious suites dotted along the breathtaking par-72 championship golf course The Lodge at Kauri Cliffs. Set on 6,500 acres of a working sheep and cattle farm, Kauri Cliffs offers an array of activities to keep you busy: Take a stroll or a golf cart to one of three private beaches or make the 90-minute drive to the charming historic town of Russell, formerly a rowdy whaling port and New Zealand's first capital, with wooden-facade colonial buildings lining its picturesque waterfront. Linger at Sally's Café for tea and scones and the daily newspaper, or join the yachting fraternity on the veranda of the venerable old Duke of Marlborough Hotel for a sundowner (the hotel held the country's first liquor license).

WHAT: island, experience, hotel. **BAY OF ISLANDS:** 160 miles/257 km north of Auckland. *R. TUCKER THOMPSON:* in Paihia. Tel 64/9-402-8430; www.tucker.com.nz. *Cost:* daily 7-hour cruise with lunch $85. *SIRDAR* **YACHT CHARTERS:** in Auckland. Tel 61/2-9669-3627; www.sirdarcharters.com.au. *Cost:* hourly rate with crew $810; 4-hour minimum. **DUDLEY SMITH:** in Russell. Tel/fax 64/9-403-7200; www.tripleb.co.nz. *Cost:* hourly rate with crew $485; 4-hour minimum for 6 people. Day charter rates available. **THE LODGE AT KAURI CLIFFS:** Matauri Bay. Tel 64/9-407-0010; www.kauricliffs.com. *Cost:* doubles from $720 (low season), from $1,190 (high season). **BEST TIMES:** Nov to Mar for nicest weather.

A Paradise for Rainbow Trout and Those They Lure

LAKE TAUPO AND HUKA LODGE

North Island, New Zealand

Bumper stickers call Lake Taupo the Rainbow Trout Capital of the Universe, and they're not exaggerating: Even by New Zealand standards, these trout are monsters, with the average catch weighing in at 4 pounds and 10-pounders causing barely a stir. The nation's largest lake, measuring 20 miles by 25 miles (with a depth of 600 feet in some places), Taupo is the crater of an ancient volcano and is located near the center of the North Island, framed by three active volcanoes in nearby Tongariro National Park. All kinds of craft, from vintage steamers to modern catamarans, are available to take fishermen and sun-seekers out onto its cool, clear waters, and in the town of Taupo, your hotel's chef will prepare your catch to your liking.

Located 3 miles south of Taupo, Huka Lodge is the ne plus ultra of European-flavored country sporting lodges—it's where James Michener found the inspiration for parts of *Return to Paradise*. With its proximity to Lake Taupo, and with the frisky Waikato River running through its serene, parklike grounds, Huka's name is spoken with reverence in anglers' circles around the world. Spacious private villas are located along the serene, willow-draped banks of the river, redwoods tower over the glass roof of your bathroom, and sliding glass doors bring the outdoors in. You can ask for a gourmet lunch hamper and make an afternoon at mighty Huka Falls. As New Zealand's most exclusive hideaway, the quality of wining and dining is never less than superb.

WHAT: site, hotel. **LAKE TAUPO:** 190 miles/306 km south of Auckland. **HUKA LODGE:** 3 miles south of Taupo. Tel 64/7-378-5791, fax 64/7-378-0427; reservations@hukalodge.co.nz; www.hukalodge.co.nz. *Cost:* doubles from $495 (low season), from $930 (high season), includes 5-course dinner. **CHRIS JOLLY BOATS LTD.:** operates a small fleet of 4 charter boats with crew, fishing guides, and catering. Tel 64/7-378-0623, fax 64/7-378-9458; chrisj@chrisjolly.co.nz; www.chrisjolly.co.nz. *Cost:* boats from $135 per hour or $12 per person per hour, according to size of group. *When:* open fishing season year-round. **BEST TIMES:** May–Sept for fly fishing; Sept–Apr for troll fishing.

Huka Lodge on the Waikato River

The Ultimate Sheep Station Experience

WHAREKAUHAU COUNTRY ESTATE

Palliser Bay, North Island, New Zealand

A dramatic and remote coastal setting is not the first thing that comes to mind when you think "sheep station," and sheep station is not the first thing that comes to mind when you think "luxurious getaway," but Wharekauhau is all about confounding expectations. A sprawling 5,000-acre farm that includes miles of secluded black volcanic sand beaches, emerald green pastures, and dense forests rich with red deer, wild boar, and mountain goats, Wharekauhau provides a true New Zealand experience and exudes a genuine tradition of rural hospitality. Guests can roll up their sleeves and help with the dipping, shearing, and docking, ride horses or stroll along the beach, do a little surf casting, visit nearby seal rookeries, and explore historic Maori sites and local wineries—then recount it all over dinners of simple but elegantly presented home-cooked country fare. In the Maori language, Wharekauhau means "the place where the gods meet." They, too, must have loved the spirit of the place.

WHAT: experience, hotel. **WHERE:** 66 miles/ 105 km southeast of Wellington by car on the winding coast road (takes about 2 hours). Tel 64/ 6-307-7581, fax 64/6-307-7799; reservations @wharekauhau.co.nz; www.wharekauhau.co.nz. **COST:** doubles from $730 per person (double occupancy), includes 4-course dinner. **BEST TIMES:** Nov–Apr.

Wharekauhau *is a Maori word pronounced* forry-ko-ho.

An Eerie, Primeval Sci-Fi Show

BUBBLING ROTORUA

North Island, New Zealand

A t steamy Rotorua, center of the intense thermal field of the Taupo Volcanic Plateau, mud pools bubble and sulfurous fumaroles hiss up through crevices in the earth's surface, creating a bizarre geothermal spectacle that George Bernard Shaw called "the most hellish scene" he had ever witnessed.

There are bubbly "Champagne cauldrons," hot and cold rivers, otherwordly-looking natural silica terraces, and the unpredictable Pohutu Geyser, which sprays up to 100 feet in the air—sometimes for just a few minutes, sometimes for several hours at a time. Rotorua is home to one third of New Zealand's Maoris, whose legends explain the geothermal activity as a gift of fire from the gods. The area first boomed as a spa town in the 1840s, and although it's become commercialized and unashamedly touristy, visitors have been drawn to its sometimes frightening natural wonders ever since. If the ubiquitous smell of sulfur becomes too much, escape to the astonishingly beautiful countryside or to Solitaire Lodge, one of New Zealand's most beautifully sited hotels: It's built on the elevated tip of a forested promontory overlooking the magnificent, rainbow trout–rich Lake Tarawera and an extinct volcano of the same name.

The Taupo Volcanic Plateau is an especially mystical spot.

WHAT: site, hotel. **ROTORUA:** 135 miles/ 217 km southeast of Auckland. **SOLITAIRE LODGE:** tel 64/7-362-8208, fax 64/7-362-8445; solitaire@solitairelodge.co.nz; www.solitaire lodge.com. *Cost:* from $435 per person, double occupancy, includes all meals. **BEST TIMES:** Oct–Feb; Nov–Apr for fishing.

On the Trail of the Grape, with a Manor at Day's End

MARLBOROUGH WINE REGION

Blenheim, South Island, New Zealand

Unlike most of the world's revered wine-growing regions, which are celebrated for their grapes alone, the Marlborough region of the South Island combines two distinctive reasons to visit: the grandeur of the unspoiled

coastal Marlborough Sounds, with dozens of secluded bays and beaches, and to the south, the vineyards encircling the town of Blenheim. Surrounded by mountains, this rolling area of former sheep farms became a wine district little more than twenty years ago, but today it's one of the country's largest and best known, with fifteen area vineyards producing sauvignon blanc and chardonnay that are making their mark internationally. The area is still dominated by industry giant Montana, but the wineries of Cloudy Bay and Hunters are also recognizable names, and worth a visit.

Eight lucky guests will call Timara Lodge their home while here; the elegant but cozy

Tudor-style manor house was built in the 1920s, and its English-style gardens and small lake (complete with two black swans) make as lovely a setting as one could wish to find. Excellent food is, of course, complemented by an excellent cellar stocked with the best local and national wines, all passionately overseen by your delightful hosts.

WHAT: experience, hotel, restaurant. **BLENHEIM:** northeast corner of the South Island. **TIMARA LODGE:** off Dog Point Rd., tel 64/3-572-8276; timaralodge@xtra.co.nz; www.timara. co.nz. *Cost:* from $505 per person (double occupancy), includes dinner and airport transfers. *When:* closed Jun–Jul. **BEST TIMES:** Nov–Feb.

High-Country Farming in the Southern Alps

GRASMERE LODGE

Canterbury, South Island, New Zealand

Once the base for a high-country station covering 43,000 acres, this traditional homestead in New Zealand's Southern Alps now welcomes twenty-four guests, who can take part in seasonal farming activities among the cattle and fine-wool Merino sheep that still roam the rugged range. Most visitors are happy just to sit around the dinner table and listen to farming stories over a five-course meal of New Zealand produce that may include venison, beef, or lamb fresh from the farm or trout caught that same day by an elated guest. Grasmere encompasses more than four rivers, eight streams and creeks, and eight lakes, all of which may yield trophy trout. You can also fish for salmon at certain times of year. Your hosts will pile you into a four-wheel drive and share their love for this beautiful land, or arrange for you to see it from a horse or a helicopter. At an altitude of 2,200 feet, Grasmere is still dwarfed by the 5,783-foot mountain behind: just part of the beauty that makes a stay at Grasmere a cut above the rest.

WHAT: hotel. **WHERE:** 75 miles/121 km west of Christchurch, 75 miles/121 km east of Greymouth. Tel 64/3-318-8407; www.grasmere.co.nz. **COST:** from $420 per person (double occupancy) includes dinner and some activities. **BEST TIMES:** Jan–early Apr.

Superb Walks on the Routeburn and Greenstone

THE GRAND TRAVERSE

South Island, New Zealand

In a country where nature is king, it is no surprise that tramping is the national pastime—and what remarkable scenery there is to tramp through. Together, the Routeburn Track (which trekking connoisseurs compare favorably with the fabled Milford Track) and the Greenstone Valley Walk become the Grand Traverse, New Zealand's premier trek. The 24-mile Routeburn Track crosses the Southern Alps by means of the breathtaking Harris Saddle Pass at 3,900 feet and descends through a world of abundant forest, ferns, mountain streams, lakes, and waterfalls within the appropriately named Mount Aspiring National Park. Following an ancient Maori trail through Fiordland National Park, the 25-mile Greenstone Valley Walk crosses the main divide of the Southern Alps, within a beautiful river valley encircled by towering mountains. The six-day trek is not strenuous; the only thing that takes your breath away is the scenery. Guided treks offer a number of obvious advantages, not least being the use of private lodges with hot running water. Solo hikers stay in more rudimentary accommodations and must register with the local authorities. The number of hikers is strictly controlled, accompanied or not, so book well in advance.

WHAT: experience, site. **WHERE:** southwest corner of the South Island. Departure and return via Queenstown. **HOW:** contact Ultimate Hikes for guided tours. Tel 64/3-450-1940; info@ultimatehikes.co.nz; www.ultimatehikes.co.nz. **COST:** 3-day Routeburn Track Walk or 3-day Greenstone Walk from $710, all-inclusive; 6-day Grand Traverse from $950, all-inclusive. **WHEN:** Nov–Apr.

Cruising and Trekking in Fiordland National Park

MILFORD SOUND AND DOUBTFUL SOUND

South Island, New Zealand

The Australians may claim the Great Barrier Reef as the Eighth Wonder of the World, but Rudyard Kipling gave the honor to New Zealand's Milford Sound. Kiwis disagree with both—they rank it first or second. Milford is the most famous of more than a dozen grand fjords that make up majestic Fiordland National Park on the South Island's southwestern coast. The 10-mile-long inlet is hemmed in by sheer granite cliffs rising up to 4,000 feet, with waterfalls cascading from the mountain ridges. Playful bottlenose dolphins, fur seals, and gulls call its waters home, and crested penguins nest here in October and November before leaving for Antarctica. Mitre Peak is the centerpiece, a 5,560-foot pinnacle whose reflection in the mirror-calm water is one of the Pacific's most photographed sites. Flightseeing here is a great option, and boats leave frequently for two-hour cruises through the quiet beauty of the sound. On land, the Milford Track was once called by a flushed hiker "the finest walk in the world," a description that has deservedly stuck. It is a five-day, 32-mile trek most serious hikers around the world dream of undertaking, despite the sand flies, at least an inch of daily rainfall, and strenuous stretches demanding as much attention as the awesome scenery. (And don't miss the scenic 75-mile Milford Road from Te Anau to Milford Sound.)

Getting farther into Fiordland National Park requires four modes of transportation, culminating in your arrival by boat at Doubtful Sound, the deepest and, some say, most beautiful of New Zealand's fjords. The engines are turned off and you are enveloped in the centuries-old silence of one of the world's most remote and magical places. Captain Cook wasn't even sure these waters were a sound, hence its name. Ten times larger than Milford Sound and less known, Doubtful Sound retains an element of mystery and is void of the aerial tours and boat traffic that can mar a visit to Milford. Just two boats operate on the sound, at opposite ends and out of each other's line of sight, giving visitors the sensation of being alone in this exquisite pocket of primeval nature. Rainfall is 300 inches a year and up, but even a rainy day has its beauty, as spontaneous waterfalls sprout out of nowhere, their sound cloaked in mist and intrigue.

WHAT: site, experience. **MILFORD TRACK GUIDED WALKS:** in New Zealand, contact Ultimate Hikes, tel 64/3-450-1940; info@ultimatehikes.co.nz; www.ultimatehikes.co.nz.

Cost: 5-day/4-night tours from $1,185 per person; departure from Queenstown. *When:* Nov–Mar. **DOUBTFUL SOUND CRUISES:** Fiordland Travel, tel 64/3-442-7509, fax 64/ 3-442-7365; info@fiordland.co.nz; www.fiord land.co.nz. In the U.S., contact Mount Cook Line, tel 800-446-5494. *Cost:* day trip from Queenstown $115, from Te Anau $93.

On Top of the World Down Under

MOUNT COOK NATIONAL PARK AND THE TASMAN GLACIER

South Island, New Zealand

A third of New Zealand's most dazzling national park consists of permanent snow and ice. It boasts seventy-two named glaciers and twenty-seven mountain peaks that top 10,000 feet, including Mount Cook, which stands head and shoulders above its neighbors. It's not quite what one expects to find in the South Pacific, on the same island that gives us groves of palm trees and hibiscus plants. This is the place to splurge on unforgettable flightseeing in, around, and through the Southern Alps. Flights include a snow landing on the 19-mile-long Tasman Glacier, the longest river of ice outside the Himalayas; in the deep silence of the roof-of-the-world panorama, you can occasionally hear the rumble from within as the glacier shifts ever so slightly.

Skiing is the other activity of choice in this entirely alpine park, with heli-skiing, an exhilarating 8-mile-long glacier run (the southern hemisphere's longest ski run), and downhill ski touring available. A number of guided and unguided walks take anywhere from thirty minutes to three days for the well-known Copland Track. New Zealander Sir Edmund Hillary used this high-altitude park to train before his record-setting ascent of Mount Everest. The Hermitage, one of the world's best-sited hotels, offers this magnificent scenery from most of its picture windows.

WHAT: site, experience, hotel. **THE HERMITAGE:** 160 miles/ 257 km northeast of Queenstown in Mount Cook Village, tel 64/3-435-1809, fax 64/3-435-1879; reservations@hermitage.co.nz; www.mount-cook.com. **COST:** doubles from $215. **BEST TIMES:** Jan–Mar.

One of the park's red tarns—small mountain lakes formed by glaciers. The color is due to the abundance of red pond weeds.

The South Island's Action Capital

THE HOME OF BUNGEE JUMPING AND JET-BOATING

Queenstown, South Island, New Zealand

Beneath that Kiwi calm and reserve must throb a vein of derangement. How else to explain why New Zealand is the recognized home of both bungee jumping and jet-boating? The former act of madness originated eons ago as a coming-of-age ritual on the islands of Vanuatu, east of Australia. You may not have realized you had a burning desire to attach a thick rubber cord around your ankles before diving headfirst off a bridge into an apocalyptic void, but Queenstown's high-energy fun is infectious, and so far—with a 100 percent safety record—everyone has lived to tell about it, including an eighty-four-year-old grandfather. For an added fee, you can have the escapade filmed and bring the video home to relive your fleeting moment of lunacy. The world's first bungee site is the Kawarau Suspension Bridge, a 143-foot plunge that has hosted more than 300,000 jumps. But an alternative four-wheel drive to Skippers Canyon Bridge—a soul-shattering 229-foot descent into a rocky gorge—is just as memorable as the jump itself.

For those who'd rather be on the water than over it, the Shotover River's steep rock walls and white-water rapids are the scene for heart-stopping jet-boat trips that fly you over the shallow waters—sometimes only inches deep—negotiating huge boulders and rushing waters. Flat-bottomed boats perform 360-degree pirouettes within inches of canyon walls. Native New Zealander Sir William Hamilton first created a revolutionary propulsion jet that allowed navigation in shallow or difficult waters where others dared not go, and versions of Hamilton's jet are now used around the world, though only Shotover Jet

Tandem jumpers

is licensed to operate here, guaranteeing a traffic-free experience.

WHAT: experience. **BUNGEE JUMPING:** from the Kawarau Bridge, 14 miles/23 km outside Queenstown on State Highway 6. *How:* in Queenstown, A. J. Hackett (synonymous with bungee jumping since his historic leap from the Eiffel Tower in 1987), tel 64/3-442-4008; bungycentre@bungy.co.nz. *Cost:* $115 per person, includes transport to Kawarau. **JET BOATS:** on the Shotover River, a 4-mile/6-km drive from Queenstown. *How:* Shotover Jet, tel 64/3-442-8570; info@shotoverjet.co.nz; www.shotoverjet.co.nz. *Cost:* $75 per person, includes transportation from Queenstown. **BEST TIMES:** Jan–Mar.

THE PACIFIC ISLANDS

Blissfully Remote, Breathtakingly Beautiful

AITUTAKI

Cook Islands

It is ironic that of the many islands Captain James Cook sailed to in his quest for paradise, he missed Aitutaki, the one perhaps most qualified—and, as it happens, in the island group that was later named for him. Instead, Aitutaki was "discovered" by Captain William Bligh in 1789, just days before the mutiny aboard his H.M.S. *Bounty*. Today the only mutiny you'll find is among those resisting the return to Rarotonga, which seems downright raucous compared to this sleepy little island. Aitutaki doesn't profess to be the most stunning of all Pacific islands, but it may well be—at least according to the many seasoned travelers who have sailed these incredible waters before arriving here, speechless. Gorgeous at ground level, Aitutaki is also (like the rugged Tahitian island of Bora Bora, to which it is often compared) spectacular from the air, where its 30-mile protective reef resembles a scalloped turquoise carpet spread out on an indigo sea. The reef's necklace of twenty-one tiny *motus* (small islands) and their empty white beaches are perfect destinations for picnics, lolling, and snorkeling in the startlingly clear water.

WHAT: island. **WHERE:** 155 miles/249 km north of Rarotonga; 1 hour by plane. **WHERE TO STAY:** the island's best hotel is Aitutaki Lagoon Resort, tel 682/31-203, fax 682/31-202; www.aitutakilagoonresort.com. *Cost:* doubles from $395. **BEST TIMES:** Nov–Feb.

A Week of Beating Drums and Swaying Hips

ISLAND DANCE FESTIVAL

Rarotonga, Cook Islands

The Cook Islanders are considered the best dancers in the South Pacific, but their nightly hotel shows are usually the most authentic displays of traditional skills many travelers will see. True dance lovers and those wanting to see something more than pretty beaches should plan their Cook Islands trip around the annual Island Dance Festival, for which the crème de la crème of the islands' village and school dance troupes travel to "mainland" Rarotonga for a week of song and dance. The lusty, hip-swinging *tamure* is much like what you might see in Tahiti, though the drum-induced enthusiasm and spirit of the Cook Islanders will convince you that the dance belongs to them. It's second nature to male and female, young and old, part of the cultural glue that binds these fifteen far-flung islands. It is amusing to imagine the alarm of the early missionaries, just barely off the boat from dank, temperate England, encountering such decidedly unreserved behavior.

WHAT: event. **WHERE:** the principal venue in Rarotonga is the National Auditorium.

HOW: for information, contact the Board of Tourism, tel 682/29-435, fax 682/21-435; in the U.S. tel 888-994-2665; headoffice@ cookislands.gov.ck; www.cookislands.travel. **WHEN:** last week in Apr; National Grand Finals take place Sat night.

Underwater Garden of Eden

BEQA LAGOON

Beqa Island, Fiji

The legendary Beqa Lagoon is surrounded by one of the world's largest unbroken barrier reefs—90 miles of spectacular coral whose dazzling colors and kaleidoscopic marine life make for one of the Pacific's premier dive and snorkeling sites. For game fishermen, blue marlin, wahoo, swordfish, and black marlin will provide you with the fight of your life. Ashore, the roadless Beqa Island offers as many delights as its lagoon has colors, and even the been-there, seen-that traveler will delight in observing the sunset from a hammock strung between two coconut trees, or taking in a Fijian fire-walking show in which islanders walk across 1,200-degree red-hot stones. The Beqa Lagoon Resort is the island's only hotel, and while guests are drawn here first by the lagoon's fame, they're apt to return for the food and hospitality. With snorkeling just 150 feet from the twelve private *bure* bungalows and more than 100 dive sites just five to twenty minutes away by boat, its location can't be beat.

WHAT: experience, island, hotel. **BEQA:** boat (6 miles/10 km) from Pacific Harbor on the south coast of Viti Levu (a 90-minute taxi ride from Nadi's international airport). **BEQA LAGOON RESORT:** tel 679/330-4042, fax 679/330-4028; in the U.S., 800-542-3454, fax 949-646-8097; www.beqalagoonresort.com. *Cost:* double-occupancy *bure* bungalows $185, includes all activities except scuba ($80 per 2-tank dive) and game fishing. **BEST TIMES:** Sept–Nov; May–Dec for best diving.

Long, Lazy, White Beaches,
a Romantic Treehouse, and World-Class Diving

HORSESHOE BAY BEACH

Matangi Island, Fiji

This gorgeous, horseshoe-shaped, 240-acre island is all that remains of an ancient volcano that fell away into the sea, leaving behind one of the finest beaches in Fiji. Palm-fringed, it wraps around the submerged crater, now filled with deep sapphire waters, beside which you'll find the island's only accommodations, the Matangi Island Resort. Built by the island's owners to host just twenty-eight guests in fourteen circular Polynesian-influenced *bures*, this island retreat includes three

The island was the owners' private home until 1986.

Honeymoon Treehouses, each perched off the ground in enormous almond trees, offering complete privacy and romance, as well as superb views of the Tasman Straits. Paradoxically, children are actually welcome at the Matangi—a rarity among South Pacific resorts.

WHAT: island, hotel, experience. **MATANGI ISLAND:** from the airport on Taveuni Island, complimentary 40-minute bus/boat trip northeast to resort. **MATANGI ISLAND RESORT:** tel 679/880-0260, fax 679/880-0274; in the U.S., 888-628-2644; www.matangiisland.com. **COST:** doubles $610, includes all meals and most activities except scuba. **BEST TIMES:** Sept–Nov; May–Dec for best diving.

Island Sanctuary for Humans and Boobies

MOODY'S NAMENA

Namenalala Island, Fiji

A three-hour boat ride drops you off on the dragon-shaped island of Namenalala, whose name—loosely translated as Uninhabited Island—is accurate but for the ten guests of a small retreat on the edge of a jungle.

The tribal owners of this natural reserve named Tom and Joan Moody as honorary wildlife wardens, allowing the American couple and their few guests to live their island fantasy here. Namenalala has no television, no electricity, and a delicious do-whatever-you-like and when-you-like philosophy. The five unobtrusive treehouse *bures* are perched high on a wooded ridge to catch the ocean breeze and are unexpectedly luxurious, with romantic gaslights, his and her baths, canopied king-size beds, and wraparound decks with million-dollar views. But the mile-long island's true luxury is the feeling of being shipwrecked and forgotten, with no newspapers and no phone, just lazy picnics on any of the six beaches (guests who want the beach to themselves can post an "occupied" sign at the foot of the path) and walks through lush forests whose silence is bro-

ken only by exotic bird calls. Namenalala is home to a colony of red-footed booby birds, a giant variety of albatross, and orange-breasted honeyeaters, and is also the nesting ground for Hawkesbill and green turtles, who lay their eggs on the beaches between November and March. Namena Barrier Reef creates an unbelievable walk-in aquarium, with more than 100 varieties of brilliantly colored coral and clouds of gemlike fish that make for excellent snorkeling and diving. Namenalala and its reef belong to Mother Nature; its human interlopers are just temporary guests.

WHAT: island, hotel. **WHERE:** Moody's Namena can be reached only by boat from either of Fiji's 2 largest islands: Lautoka on Viti Levu or Savusavu on Vanua Levu. Tel 679/828-0577, fax 679/828-0901; moodysnamena@connect.com.fj; www.moodysnamenafiji.com.

In the U.S., contact McCoy Travel, tel 800-588-3454; www.mccoytravel.com. **COST:** from $1,505 per person for 5-night stay includes all meals and all activities except scuba. **WHEN:** hotel open May–Feb. **BEST TIMES:** Sept–Nov; May–Dec for best diving.

Heaven, Above and Below Water

JEAN-MICHEL COUSTEAU FIJI ISLANDS RESORT

Savusavu, Vanua Levu, Fiji

Unless you've been living on another planet, you'll recognize Jean-Michel Cousteau as the son of world-famous explorer and oceanographer Jacques Cousteau; you may surmise—correctly—that his resort offers an experience exceptional for its environmental consciousness. Settled in a 17-acre ocean-front coconut grove and resembling a traditional local village, the Cousteau resort is a progressive ecosensitive operation that, in addition to its undersea world, offers luxury, leisure, and languor thanks to a joint venture with California's Post Ranch Inn. For divers and nondivers alike, the South Seas experience served up here will be significantly different from that of other resorts. Staff naturalists lead hikes through tropical rain forests and to neighboring Fijian villages; or enjoy a massage followed by a candlelit dinner delivered straight to your private bungalow veranda. Still, this is essentially a scuba-diver's utopia. Jean-Michel designed the resort's 37-foot, state-of-the-art dive boat *L'Aventure*, whose captains and marine biologists guarantee you the best dive experience possible in one of the most diverse and populous marine habitats on earth. Jean-Michel is around often—who knows, you may go down under with Cousteau *fils* himself.

WHAT: hotel, island, experience. **WHERE:** Savusavu Bay, Vanua Levu, 1 hour northeast of Nadi. Daily flights from Nadi to Savusavu Bay. Tel 679/885-0188, fax 679/885-0340. In the U.S., for reservations, tel 800-246-3454 or 415-788-5794, fax 415-788-0150; info@fijiresort.com; www.fijiresort.com. **COST:** bungalows from $670, includes all meals for two. Dives aboard *L'Aventure* extra. **BEST TIMES:** Sept–Nov; May–Dec for best diving.

A Garden Island and the Soft Coral Capital of the World

TAVEUNI ISLAND

Fiji

A coconut plantation in the 19th century, Taveuni, Fiji's lushest and third largest island, earns its nickname as the Garden Island, boasting the largest population of indigenous plants and animals in the South Pacific.

Bures overlooking the Somosomo Straits

The towering spine of peaks reaches 4,000 feet, some of the highest in Fiji, and its fertile volcanic soil supports and explains the thick tropical flora. Flying north from Fiji's more populated and developed island of Viti Levu is like flying back fifty years in time. A string of small, traditional villages along the western side is home to easygoing, friendly Fijians, who greet Western visitors (no longer a novelty) with a warm, heartfelt welcome. But it's the world-famous dive sites in the narrow Somosomo Straits separating Taveuni and Vanua Levu that have put this area of Fiji on the travel map, offering a riotous profusion of soft coral reefs and the endless varieties of fish they attract. Premier diving sites are the 20-mile-long Rainbow Reef and the Great White Wall—Taveuni's Mount Everest of reefs—but local dive operators will take you farther afield to sites with no names that can be even more magnificent.

Taveuni Island Resort, a small hotel run by New Zealand couple Ric and Do Cammick, is the island's top land operation. Their seven bluffside *bures* command a magnificent view of the straits, but nothing compared to what you'll see down under. Every day, divers can gear up at one of the nearby dive operations for the dive of a lifetime. An afternoon return leaves time for a trip to the island's 180th meridian—the international date line—where you can stand with one foot in today and one in tomorrow.

WHAT: island, experience, hotel. **WHERE:** in Fiji's northern island group. Daily flights connect Taveuni with Viti Levu's airports of Nadi (90 minutes) or Suva (60 minutes) and other islands. **HOW:** contact Taveuni Island Resort, tel 679/888-0441, fax 679/888-0466. In the U.S., tel 877-828-3864; enquiries@taveunibooking.com; www.taveuni islandresort.com. Dives can be arranged thru hotel or at www.taveunidivers.com. **COST:** doubles from $415, includes all meals and airport transfer; scuba from $80 (1-tank dive). **BEST TIMES:** Sept–Nov; May–Dec for best diving.

A South Pacific Idyll as Seen with a Filmmaker's Eye

VATULELE ISLAND RESORT

Vatulele Island, Fiji

Vatulele is the movie-set result created when an award-winning Australian television producer teamed up with a Fiji-born hotel manager with top-drawer experience. Other island resorts may have locations of similar

natural beauty (reef-ringed azure-blue lagoons, powdery white beaches, swaying coconut palms), but where they strain to respect your privacy, here the house policy assumes you've come to this laid-back barefoot hideaway to relax and socialize, not necessarily in that order. Excellent dinners are enjoyed in the company of the resort's other eighteen couples, champagne flows like lemonade, and if you haven't met a dazzling gaggle of interesting, discerning Australian, American, and European types during your first couple of days, it's probably because you've been hiding in your *bure*. Attention to detail is the word of the day: Armloads of ephemeral frangipani blossoms decorate and scent the spacious, airy bungalows, while a Do Not Disturb sign (for those catnaps before cocktail hour) is fashioned out of a cowrie-shell necklace.

Fiji's diving possibilities are legion, and Vatulele is known as a five-star hotel with five-star diving. But unlike most of the dive-oriented resorts in the Pacific, nondivers here can chose from an embarrassment of activities topside while waiting for their diving Other to come up for air.

WHAT: island, hotel, experience. **WHERE:** 30 minutes by light aircraft from Nadi airport ($500 round-trip per person). Tel 679/ 672-0300; reservations@vatulele.com; www. vatulele.com. **COST:** from $1,375 per couple, per day, includes all meals and alcohol and all activities except scuba and game fishing (4-night minimum). **BEST TIMES:** Sept–Nov; May–Nov for best diving.

Barefoot Luxury in a Private Shangri-La

THE WAKAYA CLUB

Wakaya, Fiji

Of Fiji's more than 300 islands, very few are privately owned, but Canadian entrepreneur David Gilmour was so taken with the islands' beauty that he acquired this 2,200-acre slice of paradise in the 1970s and built his

dream home, which represents everything that's special about Fiji. The ruggedly forested, mountainous interior teems with wild horses, fallow deer, pigs, massive banyan trees, and soaring 600-foot cliffs, while thirty-two deserted shell-strewn beaches ring the perimeter. Gilmour's good taste is obvious everywhere, especially in the nine ultra-spacious plantation-style cottages. Indigenous natural materials prevail throughout: thatched roofs, distinctive handwoven bamboo walls, and lustrous yaka wood floors. At the open-air restaurant pavilion, whose cathedral ceiling soars more than 60 feet, muffled lali drums announce the superb meals, which are prepared by four resident chefs utilizing fresh-grilled seafood, local game, and organic vegetables planted from a backyard garden. Dinners are followed by nightly songfests performed by the warmhearted and ever-smiling Fijian staff, the very soul of this resort. You'll

Each bure has a private stretch of beach.

feel like David Gilmour's incredibly lucky personal guests—until you get your bill.

WHAT: island, hotel. **WHERE:** Tel 679/344-8128, fax 679/344-8406; in the U.S., 800-828-FIJI or 970-927-2044, fax 970-927-2048; www.wakaya.com. **COST:** doubles $1,900 per night, 5-night minimum, includes all meals and all activities except deep-sea fishing. Air transfer aboard the hotel's private aircraft $960 round-trip per couple from Suva, $960 round-trip from Nadi. **BEST TIMES:** Sept–Nov; May–Dec for best diving.

Faraway Beauties in a Hollywood-Perfect Location

THE YASAWA ISLANDS

Fiji

I f you feel like you're on a movie set, you are: The undeveloped and relatively inaccessible Yasawas were used for both the 1949 and 1980 versions of *The Blue Lagoon*, two Hollywood films most memorable for their remarkable

Pacific scenery. First charted by a U.S. exploring expedition in 1840, the Yasawas haven't changed much in the intervening century and a half: You'll still find many of the same small villages nestled beneath palm trees along some of the South Pacific's loveliest beaches. The Yasawa Island Lodge is everything you could hope for in the mythic South Pacific, commanding a romantically isolated spot on the northernmost island and boasting a stylish, informal blend of Western comfort and Fijian aesthetics. Days are unstructured and uncomplicated except for a few pressing questions: the hotel's white-sand beach or a five-minute walk to a number of deserted, spectacular alternatives dotting the 12-mile-long island? Grilled fresh lobster or fruit salad picked this morning? The exhilaration of light-tackle game fishing or dozing off to the music of rustling palms and lapping waves?

Those interested in seeing more of the islands can book aboard one of the four Blue Lagoon Cruises ships, which ply the islands' waters on one-, four-, and seven-day cruises. Most of the line's handsome Fijian crew call these volcanic islands home and are proud to share their knowledge of local customs and

Plying the Fijian waters

offer snorkeling tips. Sunset sailing leaves each day free for a visit to a different island and local village, for lunchtime barbecues, and for sunning on isolated beaches where the only tracks will be those left by you and the odd crab. Blue Lagoon began its operation in the 1950s with a single WW II ship; 1996 saw the maiden voyage of its most luxurious vessel, the *Mystique Princess*, a 180-foot, 72-passenger ship that's able to reach some of the area's more remote islands.

WHAT: island, hotel, experience. **YASAWA ISLANDS:** northeast of the main island of Viti Levu. **YASAWA ISLAND LODGE:** on the island of Viti Levu. The 35-minute flight from Nadi is arranged by the hotel. Tel 679/672-2266, fax 679/672-4456; reservations@yasawa.com. fj; www.yasawa.com. In the U.S., tel 877-828-

3864, fax 604-687-3454. *Cost:* doubles from $890, includes all meals and most activities. **BLUE LAGOON CRUISES:** depart from Lautoka, 25 minutes north of Viti Levu's Nadi airport. Tel 679/666-1626, fax 679/666-4098; reservations@blc.com.fj; www.blue lagooncruises.com. In the U.S., tel 877-252-3454; enquiries@blcfiji.com. *Cost: Mystique Princess* 4-day cruise from $2,710, includes all meals, activities, and land excursions. 3- and 7-day cruises available. **BEST TIMES:** Sept–Nov; May–Dec for best diving.

An Untainted World Apart

THE MARQUESAS ISLANDS

French Polynesia

For years the wild beauty of the little-visited Marquesas Islands—the most remote inhabited islands on earth, located 1,000 miles from anywhere—has drawn literary personalities and artists. One of the most scenic places in all French Polynesia, this is the untainted tropics, where forest-cloaked cliffs plunge into the rocky sea and eerie volcanic spires that Robert Louis Stevenson once likened to "the pinnacles of some ornate and monstrous church" are often lost in the clouds. Of the six inhabited islands (out of ten total), Fatu Hiva is said to be the most beautiful, due in large part to the beautiful Bay of Virgins, whose steep sides are ringed with lush groves of mangoes, oranges, and guavas. Paul Gauguin intended to live out his days here, but instead disembarked on the neighboring island of Hiva Oa. Herman Melville and Captain James Cook were just as captivated by the Marquesas's allure, believing them to be even more beautiful than the Tahitian islands. The largest town, with 1,500 handsome, tattooed, brightly smiling inhabitants and a bay that rivals the Bay of Virgins, moved Jack London to write, "One caught one's breath and felt the pang that is almost hurt, so exquisite was the beauty of it."

The 343-foot freighter/passenger ship *Aranui* is the lifeline that links the far-flung Marquesas with the outside world, delivering everything from cement to medicine to sugar. Entire towns—sometimes entire islands—turn out to greet the ship's monthly arrival, bartering *copra* (pressed and dried coconut meat) for basic supplies. *Aranui* passengers make landfall in the same whaleboats that transport cargo, and once ashore can make excursions to see lush valleys populated by wild horses and the volcanic basalt peaks that inspired Melville, London, and Stevenson. There are few roads,

The majestic rock formations at the Bay of Virgins

but follow the trails through steamy jungles to abandoned stone-carved tikis (Polynesian images of supernatural powers) or visit one of the world's most movingly beautiful cemeteries, where you'll find the frangipani-shaded graves of Gauguin and the Belgian singer Jacques Brel. A cruise ship could replicate the *Aranui*'s route, but not the experience. You'll come back from this cruise with much more than just a tan.

WHAT: island, experience. **WHERE:** 700 miles/1,126 km northeast of Tahiti. For air travel info, visit www.airtahiti.aero. *Aranui* departs from Papeete. **HOW:** in Papeete, Tahiti, Compagnie Polynesienne de Transport Maritime, tel 689/426-240 or 689/434-889; in the U.S., tel 800-972-7268; fax 650-574-6881; cptm@aranui.com; www.aranui.com. **COST:** 14-day cruises average $2,080, includes all meals and land excursions. **WHEN:** 16 departures spaced throughout the year. **BEST TIMES:** May–Nov.

South Pacific Beauty and an Idyllic Lagoon

BORA BORA

Society Islands, French Polynesia

Grab a seat on the left side of the plane for your first glimpse of the island that mesmerized Captain James Cook some 225 years ago. James Michener called it "the most beautiful in the world" and "the South Pacific at its unforgettable best"—so beautiful it's said to have been the inspiration for Bali H'ai in his *Tales of the South Pacific*. Four miles long and 2½ miles wide, Bora Bora rises as an oasis in the deep indigo sea, its circular palm-covered barrier reef of semiconnected *motu* islets embracing a wide lagoon whose palette of blues and greens defies description. The lagoon, in turn, surrounds the high green island, whose renowned, twin-peaked volcanic cones rise nearly a half mile above the water.

When the original owners of the Hotel Bora Bora arrived to build the first resort on this beautiful isle in the 1960s, they had their pick of locations and so secured the prime spot: exquisite, sugar-white Matira Beach, possibly the most idyllic in the Pacific. On it, they built a series of thatched bungalows, some on the beach and some out over the water, with two-tiered sundecks and steps that lead directly into the beautiful lagoon. A group of beach- or garden-sited *farés* (villas), some with their own private pools and Jacuzzis, are some of the largest accommodations on the island. The atmosphere is one of elegant South Pacific charm and simplicity, designed to blend harmoniously with the tropical splendor of the setting. With the powdery palm-studded beach at your fingertips, the blue lagoon at your door, and Mounts Otemanu and Pahia looming over your shoulder, you'll be effortlessly lulled into

The Hotel Bora Bora's over-water bungalows

the torpor of the island's kick-back rhythm. But some of the Pacific's best inshore snorkeling calls, offering underwater traffic jams of trumpet fish, angelfish, parrot fish, and the curiously named Pinocchio and Napoleon fish. Shark feeding is one of the hotel's more dramatic activities: Willing guests submerge themselves amid dozens of 5-foot blackfin lagoon sharks, which are regularly hand-fed by local divers. A four-wheel-drive journey that jounces and rattles you through the lush interior terrain is worth it for the cliffside views, which are as heart-stopping as the morning's nose-to-nose shark encounter.

WHAT: island, hotel, experience. **BORA BORA:** 145 miles/233 km northwest of Papeete, Tahiti. Daily 45-minute flights. The 20-minute transfer by hotel motor launch from Bora Bora airport through the lagoon to the hotel is a gorgeous introduction to the island. **HOTEL BORA BORA:** tel 689/604-460, fax 689/604-466; central reservations tel 689/604-411, fax 689/604-422; in the U.S., tel 800-477-9180; hotel borabora@amanresorts.com; www.amanresorts.com. *Note:* At press time, Hotel Bora Bora was closed for a complete renovation. Please check website for information on reopening dates. **BEST TIMES:** May–Nov.

Old Polynesia and a Room with a View

HUAHINE

Society Islands, French Polynesia

Steeped in tradition and a standout for its varied scenery, splendid beaches, proliferation of ceremonial temples *(maraes)*, picturesque main town, and tiny, charming villages, Huahine is one of the few Polynesian islands

Captain James Cook might recognize if he were to return today. Tourism has been late in arriving on this island, which is still largely agricultural and is often compared to Bora Bora before the luxury hotels arrived, so there's not much going on—but that's the point. Take advantage of the island's South Seas charm while you can, since it seems to be going extinct elsewhere in Polynesia.

Arriving by air will make you catch your breath, so brilliant are the waters within the protective coral reef that surrounds the island. Small motu islets lie inside the reef, providing sheltered land for watermelon and cantaloupe gardens. These and other goods arriving by boat turn the waterfront quay into a bustling impromptu marketplace. Otherwise life on the island is pretty quiet, but that's the reason you've come.

WHAT: island, hotel. **WHERE:** 40 minutes by air from Papeete, Tahiti. **WHERE TO STAY:** Te Tiare Beach Resort, tel 689/606-050; in the U.S., tel 888-600-8455 or 310-313-0797; www.tetiarebeachresort.com. *Cost:* garden bungalows from $510. Over-water bungalows available. **BEST TIMES:** May–Nov. In mid-Oct, Huahine is the starting point for the annual Hawaiki Nui Va'a Outrigger Race, which ends in Bora Bora.

A traditional meal and entertainment

Sleeping Beauty in the South Pacific

MAUPITI

Society Islands, French Polynesia

If you've seen one too many flame-lit, hip-gyrating "authentic Tahitian show" and dream of sleepy Bora Bora fifty years ago, Maupiti fits the fantasy bill. Guidebooks hesitate to include this untrammeled gem, so most travelers have never heard of the island—and that's good news. For the moment, at least, the Last Great Secret of French Polynesia remains blessedly quiet and laid back, delivering the languor of a real tropical paradise. The Bank Lady only makes an appearance twice a month, arriving by boat: If you want to change traveler's checks, just hope she knows the exchange rate. Otherwise you'll have to rely upon the kindness of strangers—what this small island of staggering beauty is all about.

Many of the private homes that rent rooms, or the small pensions that have a bungalow or two, don't even have telephones, so you'll just have to show up and knock on the door. Long *motu* islets offshore are home to watermelon and cantaloupe plantations.

You can help your innkeeper fish for tonight's lobster dinner or take a leisurely walk through the island's beautiful country-side along a crushed-coral road lined with fruit trees and hibiscus. Guides are available to take you to the island's 1,220-foot volcanic summit, or you can paddle an outrigger to an unpeopled cove for a picnic lunch. Or, you can just relax in your hammock, hypnotized by the rustle of palm fronds. Either way, Maupiti will never disappoint.

WHAT: island. **WHERE:** 25 miles/40 km east of Bora Bora; 4 flights weekly from Papeete (Tahiti) via Bora Bora. **WHERE TO STAY:** Pension Auira (also called Edna's), tel/fax 689/678-026. *Cost:* bungalows $190. **BEST TIMES:** May–Oct.

A Monument to the Bounty of Nature

MOOREA

Society Islands, French Polynesia

Perhaps the only thing more awesome than the incomparable view from Moorea's Belvédère lookout is Moorea itself. Contending with Bora Bora for the World's Most Gorgeous Island title, Moorea's jagged, dinosaur-scale peaks and spires have been the backdrop to numerous Hollywood films set in the South Seas. The paved circle-island road can be traveled by bicycle, scooter, car, or foot, but no matter how you go, you'll find it hard to keep your eyes on the road for most of its 36 scenic miles. The climax is the Belvédère, in the interior of the island at the highest point accessible by car, commanding one of the South Pacific's most incredible views: the deep blue Cook's and Opunohu bays cutting into the island's lush green interior and the dramatic Mount Rotui that separates them. As an awed James Michener put it, "To describe it is impossible. It is a monument to the prodigal beauty of nature."

The Hotel Sofitel Ia Ora's Polynesian bungalows sit on Moorea's most beautiful coconut-grove-shaded beach. Beyond is the cobalt blue Sea of Moon, and beyond that a postcard view of the green, cloud-topped mountains of Tahiti. At sunset, watch the whole sky ablaze with pinks, purples, and reds as you sip a sundowner at the Ia Ora's bar, built on stilts overlooking the lagoon. To maintain the day's high, head over to Te Honu Iti on picturesque Cook's Bay for dinner at a thatched-roof snack bar (also called Chez Roger), whose casual dockside atmosphere belies some of French Polynesia's best cuisine. You're in luck if chef-owner Roger Iqual's blackboard menu includes

A glorious vista of Cook's Bay

mahi mahi mousse, an island favorite; you'll find out why.

WHAT: island, hotel. **WHERE:** 12 miles/ 19 km northwest of Tahiti; 10 minutes by air, 1 hour by boat. **HOTEL SOFITEL IA ORA:** tel 689/551-212, fax 689/551-200; in the U.S., tel 800/763-4835; www.sofitel.com. **COST:** beach bungalows from $470. Circle island tours (approximately $25 per person) and car or bike rentals can be arranged by any of the island's hotels. **BEST TIMES:** May–Nov.

A Celebration of All Things Polynesian

HEIVA I TAHITI

Papeete, Tahiti, Society Islands, French Polynesia

A t this seven-week mother of all French Polynesian festivals, locals from many of the country's 115 islands converge upon Tahiti for singing, dancing, and sports competitions rooted in their common heritage.

The excitement is palpable, and colorful traditional costumes are worn by contestants and local spectators alike. When the dancing contests begin, be there! Although not heavily attended by visiting foreigners, this is the local culture so sorely missing from many of the glitzy resorts that sometimes manage to misplace, overlook, or dilute the spirit of this proud Polynesian race. Some of the contests are as timeless as fire walking, stone lifting, and outrigger canoe racing, but the present day also makes an appearance in the form of golf tournaments. Missionaries suppressed

the region's suggestive *tamure* dancing in the early 19th century, but it has been resuscitated with a vengeance; check with the local board of tourism to get times for the main dance playoffs and the emotionally charged finals that determine the year's best individuals and troupes. The winners often tour some of the principal hotels in August, in case you miss the boat.

WHAT: event. **WHERE:** different venues throughout Papeete. **WHEN:** beginning late Jun through Jul; Bastille Day, Jul 14, is always a highlight.

Island Refuge for Polynesian (and American) Royalty

TETIAROA VILLAGE

Tetiaroa, Society Islands, French Polynesia

Tetiaroa remains one of Polynesia's least-hyped destinations, despite the cachet that comes with being the private domain of the late great Marlon Brando and his Tahitian former wife Tarita, who costarred with him in

Mutiny on the Bounty. A mere fifteen minutes by air from Papeete, these gorgeous islands and their swimming-pool-blue lagoons were once the home of Polynesian royalty. In 1966 Brando purchased the island and developed its fourteen bare-bones, native-style, palm-frond-roofed farés, the only accommodations on the island. Following his death, new plans have been made to reincarnate the island's only accommodations into The Brando; a small, luxe but eco-friendly resort.

Air-conditioning is courtesy of the sea breeze that wafts through your windows, and sunsets and dinner are the island's only entertainment. It's heaven for many, hell for some, who cut their reservations short once island ennui sets in. You'll be sharing your island sanctuary with the spirit of the larger-than-life actor, as well as thousands of sea birds that come here to lay their eggs on the white powdery sands of the beaches. Their cries, and the sound of the sea as it breaks on the coral reefs around the atoll, are the only sounds you'll hear.

WHAT: island. **WHERE:** 26 miles/ 42 km north of Tahiti. **BEST TIMES:** May–Oct.

God's Aquarium

THE CORAL ATOLLS OF RANGIROA

Tuamotu Islands, French Polynesia

The world's second-largest atoll, comprised of 240 palm-covered islets that form a protective 100-mile oval around a turquoise lagoon, Rangiroa has been called "God's aquarium." It's a favorite of divers and snorkelers for

its bountiful aquatic population, while swimmers love its placid breeze-brushed waters and sun worshipers head for its gorgeous pink-hued beaches. Unlike the vertical profiles of Bora Bora and its neighboring volcanic islands, Rangiroa's is flat, though lush.

An unexpected dose of style and comfort is found at the chic Kia Ora Village, with its ten luxury overwater bungalows, excellent restaurant specializing in fresh fish and seafood caught right in its backyard, and nearby Blue Dolphins Club, a sophisticated scuba center available to hotel guests. For those who aspire to withdraw even farther from civilization, the ultimate Robinson Crusoe experience is an hour's boat ride away at Kia Ora Sauvage, a deserted 10-acre *motu* islet in the middle of nowhere. At this self-imposed exile for ten castaway guests, there's no electricity, no phone, no air-conditioning, and no problems.

WHAT: island, hotel, site. **WHERE:** 1-hour flight, 218 miles/351 km northeast of Papeete, Tahiti. Tel 689/931-117 or 689/931-111, fax 689/960-220; resa@hotelkiaora.pf; www.hotel kiaora.com. **COST:** Kia Ora Village garden bungalow $380, over-water bungalow $805, all meals extra at $135 per person per day. Kia Ora Sauvage beach bungalow $475,

includes all meals ($50 per person round-trip boat transfer extra). **BEST TIMES:** May–Nov.

The over-water bungalows

The Greatest Underwater Museum in the World

CHUUK LAGOON'S GHOST FLEET

Chuuk, Micronesia

On February 17, 1944, American Task Force 58 engaged in Operation Hailstorm, dropping over 500 tons of bombs on the Japanese Imperial Navy's Fourth Fleet in a surprise attack second only to Pearl Harbor in size and significance. Today Chuuk Lagoon (a.k.a. Truk Lagoon, its older and still commonly used name) holds the wrecks of sixty Japanese ships, the largest concentration of sunken ships in the world and the standard by which all other wreck dives are measured. A combination of unusually warm tropical water, prolific marine life, and lagoon currents has acted as a natural incubator, transforming the lifeless WW II hulks into magnificent artificial reefs with brilliant coral displays. These remarkable war ruins, left undisturbed with their guns, trucks, silverware, and sake bottles were brought to light by a fledgling dive industry in the 1970s. The 437-foot *Fujikawa*

Maru is the most famous relic, a Japanese aircraft carrier that sits upright in 40 to 90 feet of water, a gaping torpedo hole in her starboard side.

WHAT: experience, site, island. **WHERE:** almost all air connections to Chuuk are through Guam. **HOW:** in Chuuk, the best dive operation is the Blue Lagoon Dive Shop, tel 691/330-2796; www.truk-lagoon-dive.com. *Cost:* 2-dive boat trip $105 per person. **WHERE TO STAY:** the first and best hotel directly on the lagoon is the Blue Lagoon Dive Resort, tel 691/330-2727, fax 691/330-2439; blresort@mail.fm; www.blue lagoondiveresort.com. *Cost:* doubles from $125. **BEST TIMES:** Dec–Feb (dry season).

A High-Voltage Water World and First-Class Island Life

PALAU

Micronesia

One of many island constellations in the Pacific galaxy that is Micronesia, Palau's 343 islands are surrounded by spellbinding waters that many cognoscenti say offer the best diving in the world. The meeting place of

three major ocean currents, these waters support more than 1,500 species of fish and four times the number of coral species found in the Caribbean, and are known for their extraordinary drop-offs and wall diving: the Negemelis Drop-off is widely considered the world's best, a technicolor reef that begins at 2 feet and plummets vertically to more than 1,000 feet. The legendary Blue Corner is one of the planet's most exciting sites for the sheer abundance, variety, and size of its fish life—and those schooling gray reef sharks! More than fifty WW II shipwrecks—the remnants of an aircraft carrier attack—rare and exotic marine species, and visibility that can exceed 200 feet add to divers' wonderment.

Sprouting like emerald mushrooms along a 20-mile swath of transparent turquoise waters, the 200 Rock Islands are Palau's other crowning glory. Covered with palms and dense jungle growth, some of these low limestone mounds are rimmed with white-sand beaches and are home to a rich bird life, including cockatoos, parrots, kingfishers, and reef herons. Beach potatoes will find the perfect place to lose the rest of the world, and snorkelers will find the surrounding waters teeming with fish. The islands are uninhabited and have no electricity, but campers are rewarded with star gazing that is second to none.

In Palau, the world-class Palau Pacific Resort offers a first-class land-based dive operation called Splash. For nondivers, the island's best snorkeling is just feet from

A few of the countless varieties of coral

the hotel's chaise lounges. Carp Island Resort, on one of the outer Rock Islands, has rustic but welcoming beach cottages that are filled mostly with young international divers who appreciate its proximity to Palau's famed dive sites.

WHAT: island, experience, hotel. **PALAU**: in the westernmost reaches of Micronesia. Almost all flights connect in Guam. **PALAU PACIFIC RESORT**: 10-minute drive from Palau's capital city, Koror. Tel 680/488-2600, fax 680/488-1606. In the U.S., contact World of Diving & Adventure Vacations, tel 800-900-7657, fax 310-322-5111; ppr@palaunet.com; www.palauppr.com. *Cost:* doubles from $280; 2-tank dive $140 per person. **CARP ISLAND RESORT**: 15 miles/24 km south of Koror, 1 hour by boat. Tel 680/488-2978; carp corp@palaunet.com; www.carpislandpalau.com. *Cost:* doubles from $55; all-inclusive diving packages available. **BEST TIMES**: Dec–Feb (dry season); diving is good year-round.

Grass Skirts, Stone Money, and the Home of Gentle Giants

YAP, THE DARLING
OF MICRONESIA

Micronesia

Y ap doesn't even make it onto most maps, but it nevertheless stands out among Micronesia's 2,000-plus islands as the nation's cultural store-house—and also as the world's best destination for swimming with

1,000-pound manta rays in their natural habitat. On land, visitors may observe one of the Pacific's last island cultures still resistant to modern Western ways. Bare-breasted women wear traditional grass skirts, and men and women alike chew betel nuts day in and day out. A subtle narcotic, they produce a mild high that disappears as soon as the chewing stops—so why stop? Giant stone money units line the roads, still used but too heavy to trans-port. Their value is determined by size, shape, and the difficulty of acquisition. Yap was first discovered by divers who came to swim with the manta rays, gentle giants with wingspans of 10 to 20 feet that return to the same spot every day and accept the divers' nonthreatening presence. Mating season (late November through March) is a dramatic time, during

which females pirouette and soar through the waters, leading trains that can include fifteen or more males—a haunting spectacle. But the mantas are only one of many attractions. To discover them all, contact Bill Acker, a Texas-born Peace Corps worker who came to Yap twenty years ago. Today, he's proprietor of the harbor-front Manta Ray Bay Hotel, the first and best dive operation in the islands.

WHAT: island, experience, hotel. **MANTA RAY BAY HOTEL:** tel 691/350-2300, fax 691/350-4567, in the U.S. tel 800-348-3927; yapdivers@mantaray.com; www.mantaray.com. In the U.S., Trip-n-Tour Micronesia, tel 800-348/0842, fax 760-451-1000; info@trip-n-tour.com; www.trip-n-tour.com. **COST:** doubles from $120; 2-tank dive $115. **BEST TIMES:** Dec–Feb (dry season).

Man as Art in the Greatest Show on Earth

THE HIGHLAND
SING-SING FESTIVAL

Mount Hagen, Papua New Guinea

D uring the incomparable Highland Festival, drums thunder and the earth trembles as brilliantly painted bodies stomp and chant in friendly inter-tribal "sing-sing" competition. Hundreds of men and women travel for days on foot or by boat, bus, or truck to gather for this annual traditional event, and spend hours applying lavish face and body paint and elaborate headdresses before the shows begin. Anthropologists, journalists, and visitors mingle with locals representing many of Papua's 700 tribal groups, most of which have their own style of body decoration that shows their powerful sense of tribal kinship. In an effort to halt centuries-old tribal rivalry and warfare—euphemistically called "Highlands football"—the government instituted these annual shows so that traditional enemies could meet on neutral territory under peaceful circumstances. Although the shows have inevitably become more commercial since their early days in the 1960s, there's still nothing like them anywhere. Ornate wigs are made from human hair and translucent plumes; wild pigs' tusks adorn pierced noses; and masks painted in vivid primary-color striped and dotted patterns continue to excite the senses, defy description, and exhaust film supplies.

WHAT: event. **WHERE:** in the highland towns of Mount Hagen (mid-Aug). **HOW:** in the U.S., Asia Transpacific Journeys, tel 800-642-2742 or 303-443-6789; travel@asiatranspacific.com; www.asiatranspacific.com. *Cost:* $8,595 for 2-week land-only package, includes 3-night Sepik cruise (see below). *When:* mid-Aug departure for Sing-Sing; other departures May and Oct.

Cultural Heartland and River of Art

SEPIK RIVER

Papua New Guinea

L ong a lure for anthropologists, naturalists, and adventure seekers, the mysterious Sepik River inspires the same reverence to Papua New Guineans as the Congo does to Africans and the Amazon to South Americans. Today,

The MV Sepik Spirit travels to remote Middle Sepik.

an expedition up the river is an exploration of one of the world's last unspoiled reservoirs of nature, culture, art—and even humanity itself. Some native peoples here are only just emerging from complete isolation, and their riverside villages are so unique in their customs and artistic traditions that many collectors consider the Sepik Basin one of the world's best sources of primitive art. Unlike Papua New Guinea's Highland tribes, who express themselves in face and body painting, the proud Sepik people's contact with the spirit world is through their creative wood carving—their sacred *tambaran* spirit houses, embellished with intricately carved wooden posts and gables, are living museums of their tribal past.

River trips are available on the expeditionary, nine-cabin *MV Sepik Spirit*, launched in 1989 as the first vessel bringing visitors to much of the Middle Sepik. For a more grounded experience of the area, the handsomely rustic Karawari Lodge is located on the jungle-fringed Karawari River (a tributary of the Sepik and the only way to reach the lodge), in the middle of Arambak country, one of the most remote and unspoiled parts of Papua New Guinea. Dugout canoe is still the favored means of transportation (shades of the European adventurers who first explored this area little more than 100 years ago), but the lodge's canopied motor launch also makes forays to nearby villages, where you can see firsthand the collision of ancient and modern cultures. A young bare-breasted woman recently bought as a bride for five pigs may be wearing a digital wristwatch. The bird-watching alone makes a late-afternoon boat ride unforgettable: cormorants, cockatoos, hornbills, kingfishers, and parrots are regularly sighted on the otherwise quiet waterways.

Breakfast on the open veranda and listen as the Sepik Basin comes alive.

WHAT: experience, hotel. **WHERE:** *MV Sepik Spirit* makes weekly departures from Karawari and Timbunke, both accessible by air only. The Karawari Lodge is 20 minutes by boat from nearest airstrip; transfers are arranged by the lodge. **HOW:** in Papua New Guinea, Trans Niugini Tours, tel 675/542-1438, fax 675/542-2470; service@pngtours.com; www.pngtours.com. In the U.S., Unirep Ltd., tel 310/636-1400, fax 310/636-1314; unirep@earthlink.net. **COST:** *MV Sepik Spirit*, 4-day/3-night cruise $2,000 per person, includes all meals and tours. Karawari Lodge, doubles from $460, includes all meals and tours. **BEST TIMES:** Jul–Nov.

---

*Wigmen, Birds of Paradise, and
Luxury in the Wilderness*

AMBUA LODGE

Tari Valley, Papua New Guinea

This modest luxury lodge would surprise a discerning traveler anywhere; in Papua New Guinea, it astounds. Nestled at an altitude of 7,000 feet in the Southern Highlands, it offers a bird's-eye view of the lush rain forest

of the Tari Valley, a secluded Ireland-green region that has only recently opened to the outside world. Built with natural materials, decorated with local Sepik carvings, and sporting large picture windows everywhere to take in the sweeping view, the Ambua is the ultimate luxury wilderness accommodation, offering fine dining, excellent Australian wines, and, to take off the highlands chill, open fireplaces in the lounge and electric mattress pads and fluffy down comforters in each of the thatched, round bungalow units. Just a few minutes down the road from all this civilization live the Huli people, only a

few years removed from the Stone Age and known as the Wigmen for their flamboyant

The lodge is surrounded by dense green jungle.

headdresses. There is a good chance of encountering a sing-sing—a show of hopping, vocalizing, and drumming that reenacts the courtship of the male bird of paradise so revered in these parts. Thirteen species of the bird inhabit these lush green jungles, together with hundreds of species of high-altitude orchids and miniature tree kangaroos. The Ambua's network of nature trails will lead you to all these and more.

WHAT: hotel, experience. **WHERE:** 90 minutes by car from the Tari airstrip; transfer arranged by lodge. **HOW:** in Papua New Guinea, contact Trans Niugini Tours, tel 675/542-1438, fax 675/542-2470; service@pngtours.com; www.pngtours.com. In the U.S., Unirep, Ltd., tel 310/636-1400, fax 310/636-1314; unirep@earthlink.net. **COST:** doubles from $300, includes all meals and tours. **BEST TIMES:** May–Dec.

A Royal Birthday Party

HEILALA FESTIVAL

Nuku'alofa, Tongapatu, Tonga

This tiny island kingdom's beloved King Taufa'ahau Tupou IV passed on in 2006 at the age of 88. Today, his son King George Tupou V—the 44th direct descendent of Tonga's first absolute ruler—reigns over the last pure Polynesian chiefdom in the Pacific, and you are invited to his birthday celebration. Unlike other South Pacific nations, the Kingdom of Tonga was never claimed, nor even invaded, by a Western power, and the affection and pride the Tongan people feel for both their king and cultural heritage is everywhere evident during the Heilala Festival, named after the national flower, held for one week around August 1st. The capital city of Nuku'alofa on Tonga's main island of Tongatapu brims with festivities, which include dance and beauty contests, military parades, float contests, concerts, yacht regattas, sporting events, and parties. The entire country turns out for the fun, and a large diaspora of Tongans living overseas often returns home for the event. Everyone seems to be caught up in some competition—whether in nabbing the scale-tipping dogtooth tuna or in vying for the Bartender of the Year award—or at least using friendly rivalry as an excuse to hoist another Royal (the local Tongan beer) to another year of health and happiness for Polynesia's last surviving monarch.

WHAT: event. **WHERE:** most events take place in Nuku'alofa, the capital, although festivities are celebrated throughout the islands. See www.tongaholiday.com for information. **WHEN:** 1 week surrounding August 1.

A float at the annual Heilala Festival

Paddling through Paradise

KAYAKING THE VAVA'U ISLANDS

Tonga

he Pacific's best kayaking destination is Tonga's enchanting Vava'u group, some fifty reef-encircled, bush-clad islands separated by narrow waterways and protected within an emerald lagoon measuring about 13 by

15 miles. Vava'u's unsullied beauty is a prime destination for water sports and yachting, but the best way to visit the hidden marine caves, secluded coves, and turquoise waters lapping sugar-white sand beaches is by guided kayak trip. Guides will introduce you to both the local Polynesian environment and culture, visiting small outer-island villages and the traditional *umu* feast, where suckling pig is steamed in a covered underground pit to the accompaniment of Tongan song and dance.

Spend mornings kayaking between islands.

Vava'u's protected channels and coral reefs afford glorious opportunities for snorkeling and spotting dolphins and whales, which head from Antarctica to these shallow, warm waters June through November to bear their young. You won't be the first to abandon your kayak to slip into the water and swim with them. Uninhabited islands are the ideal spot for beachside barbecues or pitching camp under waving palms and the Southern Cross.

WHAT: experience. **WHERE:** 150 miles/ 240 km north of the principal island of Tongapatu and linked by several daily flights. **HOW:** in Tonga, Friendly Islands Kayak Co., tel/fax 676/70-173; tours@fikco.com; www. fikco.com. **COST:** 6-, 8-, and 10-day trips that include 4, 6, and 8 days of kayaking from about $1,370 per person, includes 3 nights hotel/resort, camping, all meals. No previous kayaking experience required. **WHEN:** May–Jan.

Total Immersion in Fa'a Samoa

SAFUA HOTEL

Savai'i, (Western) Samoa

ravelers looking for the fa'a Samoa—the Samoan way of life—will find it at the Safua, where they're likely to wind up lending a hand with the hotel's daily shopping at the local market, helping the village kids with their homework, or attending rafter-ringing Sunday services with the host's family. The unspoiled volcanic island of Savai'i is one of the most "old Polynesia" islands of any in the Pacific, and the small, charming Safua Hotel is owned and operated by its most informative, knowledgeable, and charismatic character, Vaasili Moelagi Jackson. Enveloping guests in Polynesian warmth, Moelagi, a female talking chief in her community's otherwise male council, is a leading force in the island's movement to preserve its indigenous culture and environment, which makes her an ideal guide to local customs. At her hotel, every day

is a chance to laze about, join an organized jaunt to gorgeous waterfalls or a nearby village ceremony, or even pick up a Samoan tattoo. A high point of the week is Safua's legendary *umu* feast; beginning at dawn a suckling pig is steamed in a pit oven and the lavish results are enjoyed by Moelagi and her guests after church services.

WHAT: island, hotel, experience. **SAVAI'I:** a 90-minute ferry ride from the capital city of Apia, though it feels far more remote. **SAFUA HOTEL:** tel 685/51-271, fax 685/51-272; safuahotel@lesamoa.net. *Cost:* $120 for a double bungalow. **BEST TIMES:** Apr–Oct.

The "Teller of Tales"
Finds His Own Treasure Island

VAILIMA, ROBERT LOUIS STEVENSON'S HOME

Apia, Upolu, (Western) Samoa

The 19th-century Scottish author Robert Louis Stevenson loved Samoa, and the Samoans—themselves great orators and storytellers—loved him, calling him Tusitala, "the teller of tales." Samoa has barely acknowledged the arrival of modern times, so when visiting Stevenson's Western-style mansion on the lush slopes of Mount Vaea, it's easy to imagine him still here. As he saw it, Upolu was "beautiful beyond dreams," a place that caused him to undergo a spiritual change during his five final years, and write that here, "My bones are sweeter to me." The obligatory pilgrimage up the winding trail to Stevenson's grave on a secluded knoll is a challenging but rewarding half-hour climb, leading to a view that overlooks his home and the mountains and sea he had come to love. It's one of the loveliest vistas in the South Pacific. Stevenson wrote his own poignant epitaph, even though his

death from a cerebral hemorrhage (and not the tuberculosis that plagued him all his life and caused him to leave Scotland) was sudden:

> *This be the verse you grave for me:*
> *"Here he lies where he longed to be;*
> *Home is the sailor, home from the sea,*
> *And the hunter home from the hill."*

WHAT: site. **WHERE:** 3 miles/5 km south of the capital city of Apia. Robert Louis Stevenson Museum, tel 685/20-798, fax 685/25-428; in the U.S., tel 801-225-1929, fax 801-225-5046. **COST:** admission. **WHEN:** open Mon–Sat. **BEST TIMES:** Apr–Oct.

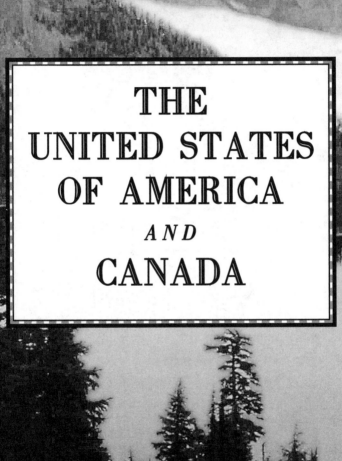

THE
UNITED STATES
OF AMERICA
AND
CANADA

One of America's Greatest Natural Wonders

MOUNT MCKINLEY AND DENALI NATIONAL PARK

Alaska, U.S.A.

T he tallest peak in North America at 20,320 feet, Mount McKinley and its regal reflection in the aptly named Wonder Lake are the primary attractions of Alaska's Denali National Park, but they're not the only draws. Visitors return from the 6-million-acre wildlife reserve (larger than the state of Massachusetts) with excited tales of sighting grizzlies, wolves, caribou, moose, Dall sheep, and golden eagles cruising the skies. And then there are the views, sweeping vistas of subarctic tundra and taiga, glaciers and deeply gouged valleys, and a good number of massive mountain peaks that almost—almost—compete with McKinley, which was named after the twenty-fifth U.S. president but is always referred to among Alaskans by its Athabascan Indian name: Denali, "the high one."

Mount McKinley/Denali is often wreathed in clouds, but your best shot at a clear and close-up view is from a hillside in the very heart of the park, where you'll find the rustic Camp Denali, founded by two female ferry pilots (and one of their husbands) in 1951 when they homesteaded land not yet designated national parkland. If you stay at the camp's cluster of seventeen log cabins you'll be one of forty happy campers who not only enjoy the wonderful and knowledgeable staff and excellent cooking, but the chance to experience the park on naturalist-guided hikes, or during evening educational programs, and explore wildlife-sighting possibilities at a relaxed pace. (Otherwise, touring and tent-camping are widely restricted to protect the park's fragile ecology; there is only one 90-mile road, of which only the first 15 miles are paved, and it is closed to private vehicles.) Summer brings long northern days, with sixteen to twenty hours of light in which to take in the scenery.

WHAT: site, hotel. **DENALI NATIONAL PARK:** 237 miles north of Anchorage. Tel 907-683-2294; www.nps.gov/dena. *Cost:* $10. *When:* park road closed Oct–late May due to snow; May–Sept access is by official bus, $25–$47 depending on destination within park. **CAMP DENALI:** within the park, 89 miles from the entrance. Tel 907-683-2290, fax 907-683-1568; info@campdenali.com; www.campdenali. com. *Cost:* $505 per person, double occupancy, all-inclusive, with round-trip transfer to/from gate. *When:* open early Jun–early Sept. **BEST TIMES:** Jun for wildflowers and birding; Jun 21 for the summer solstice, when almost-24-hour sunlight provides a unique wildlife-viewing experience; Aug–Sept for autumn foliage.

Mount McKinley and Nugget Pond as seen from Camp Denali

Nature Rules in This Microcosm of Alaska

KENAI PENINSULA

Alaska, U.S.A.

The Kenai Peninsula is a nature-packed area about the size of Vermont and New Hampshire put together, where all of Alaska's big-country wonders are available in microcosm: massive glaciers (Portage and Exit), a filigreed coastline of inlets perfect for kayaking, and prolific wildlife and marine life. From Anchorage, it's a scenic 125-mile drive on the Seward Highway to Resurrection Bay and the town of Seward, named for the secretary of state who in 1867 purchased Alaska from Russia for $7.2 million (less than 2 cents an acre), a move derided as "Seward's Folly" until gold was discovered thirty years later. A fishing and timber town, it's the jumping-off point for kayaking and sightseeing cruises of Kenai Fjords National Park, which abounds with whales, waterfalls, brown bears, and calving tidewater glaciers.

The highway ends 100 miles south at tiny Homer, a funky, artsy-craftsy town at the end of the peninsula. Sitting on a stunning 5-mile finger of land called "the Spit," the little town fancies itself both a cultural hub and the "Halibut Capital of the World." (Another fish town, Halibut Cove, is one of the peninsula's prettiest corners, reachable only by boat.) Drop into Homer's landmark Salty Dawg Saloon, an old trapper's hut where tourists hoist their beers with local cannery workers and fishermen.

From here, a leisurely boat trip across gorgeous Kachemak Bay provides glimpses of terns, puffins, cormorants, and mischievous sea otters. On the bay's distant shore is enchanting Kachemak Bay Wilderness Lodge, the ultimate escape-cum-classroom, where six luxurious private cabins blend with the landscape. Some guests come to fish, others to explore the wilderness in the company of the staff naturalists, others for the Dungeness crab, clams, shrimp, oysters, salmon, and, of course, halibut, all prepared to perfection.

WHAT: site, town, hotel. **WHERE:** Kenai Peninsula Tourism, tel 907-262-5229; www.kenaipeninsula.org. **KACHEMAK BAY WILDERNESS LODGE:** tel 907-235-8910; www.alaskawildernesslodge.com. *Cost:* 3-night package from $2,400, all-inclusive (includes boat to/from Homer). **BEST TIMES:** May and Sept for smaller crowds.

Mush, Balto, Mush! The Last Great Race

THE IDITAROD

Anchorage, Alaska, U.S.A.

For the ultimate experience of the Last Frontier, show up for the Iditarod, a grueling sled-dog race across the Alaskan wilderness from Anchorage all the way to Nome on the coast of the Bering Sea. Dogsledding as transport was all but eclipsed by airplanes and snowmobiles when, in 1973, the first Iditarod was organized to resuscitate the tradition and commemorate such events as when, during the 1925 diphtheria epidemic in Nome, twenty mushers and a sled team led by the legendary dog Balto crossed the frozen landscape to bring serum to the town.

Today an average of sixty-five mushers and their teams come from all over the country and from as far away as Japan and Russia to compete for a share of the $600,000 purse, traversing 1,149 miles in eight to fifteen days. Nicknamed the "Mardi Gras of the Arctic," the Iditarod has become the largest spectator event in Alaska, with crowds showing up for the pre-start party and camping out along the first few days' worth of trail. Along the way, entire towns turn out to cheer on the mushers and their teams. To get into the race yourself as an "Iditarider," place a bid for a spot on one of the mushers' sleds for the first 11 miles (the auction begins in November). Or contact musher extraordinaire Raymie Redington, son of Iditarod founder Joe Redington. Three generations of the family have participated in the legendary race dozens of times, and today they offer half-hour (or longer) sled rides or overnight wilderness trips. Raymie's place is also home to hundreds of huskies, all of them seemingly as game as their owner. The remote, fly-in Winterlake Lodge sits directly on the Iditarod Trail and becomes Dog Central when the first teams arrive on the race's third or fourth day. Guests who get the bug can take a ride on the trail on nonrace days with the lodge's own team of twenty-four Alaskan huskies. The lodge's three guest cabins offer a quintessential Alaskan wilderness experience, and the dinner menu is as remarkable as its wintry surroundings.

WHAT: event, hotel. **IDITAROD HEADQUARTERS:** in Wasilla, 40 miles north of Anchorage. Tel 907-376-5155; www.iditarod.com. The Iditariders Auction begins in Nov (minimum starting bid $500), tel 800-566-SLED. *When:* early Mar. **RAYMIE AND BARB REDINGTON:** Wasilla. Tel/fax 907-376-6730; redingtons@yahoo.com. *Cost:* half-hour dogsled ride $50. *When:* beginning with 1st snow in Nov. In dry months the dogs are hitched to wheeled sleds. **WINTERLAKE LODGE:** tel 907-274-2710; info@withinthewild.com; www.withinthewild.com. *When:* open year-round. *Cost:* $2,130 per person for 2 days/2 nights includes 50-minute scenic flight.

Power and Beauty Beyond Breathtaking

THE INSIDE PASSAGE AND GLACIER BAY

Alaska, U.S.A.

Southeastern Alaska is a kingdom of water and ice, a natural masterpiece in progress, "a solitude of ice and snow and newborn rocks, dim, dreary, mysterious," as naturalist John Muir wrote during his visit in 1879. Just 100 years

before, the area was completely choked with ice, and now the massive glaciers continue to advance and recede at their leisure, and boats are still the main way of getting around. In this sea wilderness, the whale is king. Schools of humpbacks feed here before swimming thousands of miles to winter in the warm waters of Hawaii, while orcas can be spotted here year-round. Seal pups frolic on passing ice-berg bits and bears roam the shoreline and streams, hunting for salmon.

One third of visitors to Alaska come for the cruise on the 1,000-mile Inside Passage, a route through the narrow strip of mainland and islands that make up Alaska's panhandle. Almost twenty cruise lines sail these waters each summer, oper-ating ships that range from small expedition vessels to floating cities that carry 2,000-plus passengers. Departing generally from Vancouver, British Columbia, at the route's southern end, Alaska's easygoing capital city of Juneau at its northern end, or Seward on the Gulf of Alaska, they cruise the panhandle's calm crystal waters and dramatic fjords, visiting touristy ports such as Ketchikan or (if you're lucky enough to be on one of the small ships) untouristy ones such as Haines and Petersburg. Sitka, known as the "Paris of the Pacific" during the 19th cen-tury, is still redolent of its days as trading outpost of the Russian empire.

The far northern end of the Inside Passage is capped off by the beautiful Glacier Bay National Park, a branching 65-mile fjord that's home to eleven glaciers and abundant wildlife. It's accessible by boat from the main-land town of Gustavus, which stands right at the head of the bay, where it meets Icy Strait. In such raw country, the genteel and wel-coming Gustavus Inn seems wonderfully incongruous and makes a great base from which to experience the Glacier Bay area, if you're not the cruising type.

WHAT: site, experience, hotel. **CRUISES:** small-ship lines (with vessels that carry 40–140 passengers) are the way to go in Alaska if you want to really experience the wilderness. Among them, the better operators are Lindblad Expeditions (tel 800-EXPEDITION or 212-765-7740; www.expeditions.com), Cruise West (tel 888-851-8133; www.cruisewest.com), Regent Seven Seas Cruises (tel 877-505-5370; www.rssc.com). *When:* cruise season runs May–Sept. Cruise lengths are generally 7 nights. **GUSTAVUS INN:** at the mouth of Glacier Bay. Tel 800-649-5220 or 907-697-2254, fax 907-697-2255; dave @gustavusinn.com; www.gustavusinn.com. *Cost:* $205 per person per night, double occu-pancy, includes all meals, airport transfers, afternoon nature walks, use of bikes and fishing poles. *When:* open mid-May–mid-Sept. **BEST TIMES:** May and Jun get the least rain; Jul and Aug are warmest; Jun–Aug for peak whale viewing; snow in Sept is not uncommon.

A High-Desert Resort Where Golf Rules

THE BOULDERS RESORT AND GOLDEN DOOR SPA

Carefree, Arizona, U.S.A.

Arizona is a paradise for golfers, and among its more than 250 courses The Boulders is a true standout, with two 18-hole Jay Morrish–designed courses standing green against the dramatic high-desert terrain. House-size, 12-million-year-old granite boulders surround the property, with Flintstones-like buildings nestled ingeniously among them. But it's not all about golf and spectacular location: The

Boulders is also one of the Southwest's most lavish hotel resorts, and since its opening in 1985 has regularly been voted one of North America's best. With the recent addition of the world-renowned Golden Door Spa, guests can now be pampered and rejuvenated in its glorious 33,000-square-foot sanctuary. Awesome

Ancient boulders surround the resort.

views fill the picture windows of the 160 one-bedroom casitas that look over the cacti-studded Sonoran Desert. Bridle trails that crisscross the hotel's 1,300 acres of unspoiled terrain promise John Wayne outings. The hotel—located in the whimsically named town of Carefree (with street names like "Why Worry Lane")—is tended to by a staff that is both warm and can-do efficient. In the evening, after the last hole is played, the good times continue with sunset balloon rides, excellent dining in eight different restaurants, and a chance to jump aboard a jeep tour with

a local astronomer to view the stars as you've never seen them before—all amid the aroma of juniper branches being burned in open-air hearths. The silence of the desert is broken only by the occasional howl of a lone coyote.

WHAT: hotel. **WHERE:** 34631 N. Tom Darlington Dr. (Carefree is 33 miles north of Phoenix and 13 miles north of Scottsdale). Tel 888-579-2631 or 480-488-9009; www.the boulders.com. **COST:** casitas from $129 (low season), $399 (high season). **BEST TIMES:** Jan–May, with a moonlight concert series Apr–Jun.

Sacred Outdoor Museum of the Navajo Nation

CANYON DE CHELLY NATIONAL MONUMENT

Chinle, Arizona, U.S.A.

Though it can't compare with the awesome immensity of the Grand Canyon, a four-hour drive away, Canyon de Chelly (pronounced "d'Shay" and derived from the Navajo *tsegi*, "rock canyon") serves as a showcase for

2,000 years of Native American history with a quiet magic and spirituality all its own. Sheer sandstone walls tower 600 feet and more above the 130-square-mile canyon, whose shapes and colors change in degree of breathtaking beauty according to the day's light. The canyon is best known, though, for its multistoried cliffside dwellings made of sun-dried clay and stone and built by the Anasazi

people between A.D. 700 and 1300. Mysteriously abandoned in the 1300s, they are the oldest houses in the United States. The Navajo (one of fifteen tribes that live in Arizona) became full-time canyon residents in the 1700s, and a population of 500 or so still till the fields, tend their goats and sheep, and act as your tour guides, since unaccompanied or unauthorized visits of the canyon floor are

Spider Rock in Canyon de Chelly

prohibited. Located in northeastern Arizona, the canyon is part of the vast Navajo Indian Reservation, the largest in North America. With a population of more than 200,000, it is considered a sovereign nation, where Navajo is still the native tongue. Canyon de Chelly is one of the tribe's holiest places, and despite the summer tourism, it is easy to find silence and solitude in this mysterious stone expanse. Some of America's finest pictographs (rock art) grace the desert walls, left behind by the Navajo, the Anasazi, and, even earlier, the Basketmakers, whose presence in the canyon dates back to the 4th century A.D. At the mouth of the canyon, the all-Navajo staff of the Thunderbird Lodge (on the grounds of an old trading post and the only accommodations officially within the park) offers Native American hospitality, as well as open-jeep "Shake and Bake" tours that take their name from the bumpiness of the dirt roads and the summer heat.

WHAT: site, hotel. **CANYON DE CHELLY:** 345 miles northeast of Phoenix. The Canyon de Chelly Visitors Center in Chinle is open year-round. Tel 928-674-5500; www.nps.gov/cach/. **THUNDERBIRD LODGE:** Chinle. Tel 800-679-2473 or 928-674-5841, fax 928-674-5844; www.tbirdlodge.com. *Cost:* doubles from $69 (low season), from $109 (high season). **BEST TIMES:** May–Oct. The Navajo Nation Powwow (Jul 4th weekend) and the annual Navajo Nation Fair and Rodeo (late Aug/early Sept) are both held in nearby Window Rock, capital of the Navajo Indian Reservation.

Nature's Masterpiece

THE GRAND CANYON

Flagstaff, Arizona, U.S.A.

Few things in this world produce such awe as one's first glimpse of the Grand Canyon. The mesmerized John Muir wrote, "It will seem as novel to you, as unearthly in color and grandeur and quantity of its architecture as if you had found it after death, on some other star." It took nature more than 2 billion years to create the vast chasm—in some places 17 miles wide—through a combination of shifting uplift, erosion, and the relentless force of the roaring Colorado River, which runs 277 miles along its length, a mile beneath its towering rims. Each year more than 4 million visitors flock to experience the wonder of its constantly changing pastel hues and unpredictable play of light and shadow, but 90 percent of them never make it past the visitor center, exhibits, museums, and gift shops at the popular (and congested) South Rim, at an elevation of 7,000 feet.

Book at least a year in advance (or pray for last-minute cancellations) at the uniquely sited El Tovar Hotel, built here by Hopi workers in 1905 of native stone and ponderosa pine logs. It is considered the crown jewel of all the national park hotels, and guests will find out why during a quiet moment in a wicker rocking chair on its wide porch, with edge-of-the-world views.

Mule trips leave from the South Rim for one-day trips down to Plateau Point, about halfway to the canyon floor; overnight mule-riders and hikers can check into the Phantom Ranch, a rustic, bare-bones former working ranch from the early 1900s, and the only accommodation below the canyon's rim.

From the South Rim it's a scenic 235-mile drive through mighty impressive country to the more tranquil, remote North Rim. At an elevation of 8,000 feet, it is only open mid-May through October. One of the most poetic ways to experience the canyon is to see it from the bottom up, white-water rafting the Colorado River, whether in kayaks, rafts, or motor-driven pontoon boats. One of America's greatest adventures, it's a guaranteed keeper on anyone's short list.

WHAT: site, hotel. **GRAND CANYON:** the South Rim is 230 miles north of Phoenix, 80 miles north of Flagstaff. The North Rim is 352 miles north of Phoenix, 210 miles north of Flagstaff. Tel 928-638-7888; www.nps.gov/grca.

Cost: park admission $25 per car. **EL TOVAR HOTEL, PHANTOM RANCH, MULE TRIPS, AND RIVER RAFTING:** for all, contact Grand Canyon National Park Lodges, tel 888-297-2757, fax 303-297-3175; www.grandcanyonlodges.com. *Cost:* El Tovar Hotel, doubles from $174 year-round (3 canyon-view suites $321); reservations are accepted 23 months in advance. Phantom Ranch, $42 per person when arriving on foot, with accommodation in 10-person dorms. Mule trips $421 per person year-round, includes all meals and an overnight stay in a cabin. Easy 4-hour rafting trips $184 per person, includes lunch. **MULTIPLE-DAY WHITEWATER RAFTING TRIPS:** Wilderness River Adventures, tel 800-992-8022; www.riveradventures.com. **WHEN:** Park, hotels, and treks year-round. **BEST TIMES:** May–Aug draw the greatest crowds, so consider Mar, Apr, Sept, or Oct. Off months of Nov–Feb have a beauty of their own.

Color, light, and shadow at the Grand Canyon

A Grand Canyon Filled with Water

LAKE POWELL

Page, Arizona, U.S.A.

Imagine the best of the West—its gnarled buttes, red-rock walls, surreal spires, and otherworldly, erosion-sculpted landscapes—then add water. That's Lake Powell: a 186-mile-long artificial lake, created by construction of the

Glen Canyon Dam, which was proposed in the 1920s, begun in the 1950s, and completed in the 1960s, though it wasn't until 1980 that enough of the Colorado River's glassy blue-green water was trapped to fill the lake to capacity. It's the nation's second largest artificial lake after Lake Mead, in Nevada's Mojave Desert. Named for Major John Wesley Powell, who first charted the area in 1869, the lake sprawls in a southwest-to-northeast crescent across the Arizona/Utah borderland, encompassing more than ninety offshoot canyons (some up to 10 miles wide) that together create a shoreline of almost 2,000 miles—longer than the entire Pacific coast of the United States. It's road-free along its zigzagging rim, so exploration by boat is not only the most rewarding and enjoyable but also the only real way to experience the lake's wealth, which includes countless isolated sandy coves where boaters can picnic or camp. Boat tours and canyon cruises leave from three of the lake's five marinas, and houseboats are rented easily—this is America's houseboat heaven, with some 400 available, sleeping eight to twelve.

Much was submerged by the (still) controversial creation of the lake, but fortunately Glen Canyon's most visited sight survived: Rainbow Bridge, called by the Navajo "The Rainbow Turned to Stone," a massive but delicate stone arch 290 feet high and 275 feet wide, 50 lake miles from Wahweap Marina. Now a national monument, it is the world's tallest known natural stone bridge, and is but one of the lake's myriad confirmations that nature creates the earth's most sublime art.

WHAT: site, experience. **WHERE:** Lake Powell is part of the Glen Canyon National Recreation Area, a 5-hour drive north of Phoenix; commuter flights connect Phoenix with Page, the area's largest town. Wahweap Marina (7 miles north of Page) is the best-equipped of the lake's settlements. For houseboat rentals and other info, contact Lake Powell Resorts & Marinas, tel 888-896-3829; www.lakepowell.com. *Cost:* 3-day rental, 6-person houseboats from $1,315 (low season), from $2,195 (high season). Larger boats and longer rental available. **WHERE TO STAY:** Lake Powell Resort, tel 888-896-3829 or 928-645-2433, fax 928-645-1031. *Cost:* lake-view doubles from $130 (low season), from $198 (high season). **BEST TIMES:** Jun–Oct for water sports; Apr, Jun, and Oct–Nov for fishing. Hottest and busiest in Jul, Aug.

Lake Powell is awash in color—red-rock walls, rose-colored sand, and blue-green water.

A Wrightian Legend

ARIZONA BILTMORE RESORT & SPA

Phoenix, Arizona, U.S.A.

The only surviving hotel in the world in whose design Frank Lloyd Wright participated, the Arizona Biltmore is a historic temple to good times. It's one of America's oldest resort hotels (it opened in 1929, just minutes

The Arizona Biltmore is known as the "Jewel of the Desert."

before the stock market crash), built by Albert Chase McArthur, an Oak Park apprentice to Frank Lloyd Wright, to whom its design is often erroneously credited. In fact, Wright acted only as a consultant on the project, but the spirit of the master designer is so evident, and so powerful, that it no longer really matters who built it.

Set in 39 lush acres (groomed by some thirty full-time gardeners) and now surrounded by Phoenix sprawl, this historic hotel garners high marks with modern-day trend seekers. A large hotel that feels intimate, the Biltmore is luxury all the way, lying at the end of a palm-lined drive that breathes with unforced relaxation. The staff is a joy, too. Wake-up calls are made by real human beings, and room service is delivered by a smiling attendant riding a three-wheel bicycle. Harpo Marx and his bride honey-mooned here; so did Ronald and Nancy Reagan. And it's not hard to imagine one-time guest Marilyn Monroe frolicking in the original Hollywood-esque cabana-lined Catalina Pool, built when Chicago chewing-gum king William Wrigley Jr. owned the place.

WHAT: hotel. **WHERE:** 2400 East Missouri Ave. Tel 800-950-0086 or 602-955-6600; reservations@arizonabiltmore.com; www.arizonabiltmore.com. **COST:** doubles from $129 (low season), from $299 (high season). **BEST TIMES:** Sept–Apr for good weather.

An Enchanting High-Desert Terrain and Its Oasis of Luxury

RED ROCK COUNTRY

Sedona, Arizona, U.S.A.

Local tale spinner Zane Grey introduced the spectacular Red Rock Country as the show-off backdrop for his 1924 classic *Call of the Canyon*. Most visitors experience déjà vu when they arrive thanks to more than eighty

Westerns that found their perfect cowboys-and-Indians' locations here—among them *Johnny Guitar, Broken Arrow,* and *Tall in the Saddle*—and in neighboring Utah.

It is of little wonder that the striated "layer-cake" terrain and sandstone skyscraper formations have drawn a community of artists (beginning with Max Ernst in the 1950s) to Sedona, where rock-watching and gallery hopping are both major pastimes. New Agers

gravitate here for the electromagnetic centers —vortexes from which healing powers and natural energies emanate, they say (think Machu Picchu and Stonehenge). True or not, there's no mistaking Sedona's specialness: The Yavapai-Apache tribe consider this sacred ground their Garden of Eden, believing this is where the first woman mated with the sun to begin the human race.

The unique 70-acre Enchantment Resort

has perfectly insinuated itself into this desert milieu, sitting at 4,500 feet (and so escaping the ovenlike summers) amid an ancient, peculiarly eroded landscape that varies from pink and orange to sienna and vermillion, depending on the day's mood and the sun's position. Strike out from the front door of your adobe-style casita for an early morning's hike or an open-jeep tour into the fantastical Boynton Canyon, and be back within the hotel's luxurious cocoon in time for a poolside barbecue. Be a humble witness to some of the West's most ravishing sunsets, whether from your private patio or from the open terrace of the resort's excellent Yavapai Restaurant.

WHAT: site, hotel. **WHERE:** Sedona is 120 miles north of Phoenix and 110 miles south of the Grand Canyon. **ENCHANTMENT RESORT:** 525 Boynton Canyon Rd. Tel 800-826-4180 or 928-282-2900, fax 928-282-9249; info@enchantmentresort.com; www.enchantment resort.com. *Cost:* doubles from $350 (low season), from $450 (high season). **BEST TIMES:** many arts and music festivals take place Jun–Aug, though these are also the hottest months (if dry); Jazz Festival in Sept.

A World-Class Wellness Center

CANYON RANCH HEALTH RESORT

Tucson, Arizona, U.S.A.

A pioneer among co-ed fitness resorts in the United States, Canyon Ranch opened in 1979 and has gone on to become one of North America's most famous health and well-being meccas. Set amid a gorgeous 150-acre spread of Sonoran Desert landscape in the foothills of the Santa Catalina Mountains, it consistently garners top ratings from travel and spa magazines. The nonstop roster of complimentary (but optional) programs, classes, and pursuits can seem intimidating at first, until you figure out that, if you want, you can do nothing more than laze by any of the three outdoor pools all day. Workouts are aimed at fitness of body, mind, and soul: In addition to more than fifty fitness classes daily, activities range from invigorating 6 A.M. 8-mile power hikes through saguaro-studded hills to evening discussions led by guest lecturers who explore an endless variety of topics. Buff, traffic-stopping bodies are far outnumbered by more average types who come to escape high-stress lives and unhealthy habits. Spa treatments are a paramount ingredient of the ranch's all-around approach to good health—who can resist the massage with crushed pearls or deep-moisturizing goat butter?—and the Southwest-accented cuisine is memorable, with daily demos that prove you, too, can reproduce the chef's specialties. In fact, the philosophy behind Canyon Ranch is that it provides guests with a vacation they can bring home with them—though that doesn't stop many guests from coming back for a return visit. For East Coasters who don't want to go west, the spa also has a beautifully sited and equally lauded sister facility in the Berkshire Mountains of Massachusetts.

WHAT: hotel, experience. **WHERE:** 8600 E. Rockcliff Rd. (30 minutes from the Tucson airport). Tel 800-742-9000 or 520-749-9000, fax 520-239-8535; www.canyonranch.com. **COST:** 4-night all-inclusive package from

$2,760 per person, double occupancy (low season), from $3,770 (high season). **BEST** **TIMES:** rates drop 25–40 percent during the hottest months, Jun–Sept.

As Low as You Can Get

DEATH VALLEY NATIONAL PARK

California, U.S.A.

Located in the heart of the Mojave Desert, Death Valley National Park enjoys the dubious distinction of being the lowest, driest, and hottest spot in America, with scorching summers that can reach 120 degrees—and in 1913 topped out at 134. Its fearsome name draws folks from all over the world, but what strikes them upon arrival is not just the area's brutality, but its spectacular and varied beauty, with parched Deadman Pass and Dry Bone Canyon standing in contrast to the dramatic hills and mountains, such as 11,000-foot Telescope Peak. Under the desert sun, hundreds of species of plant and animal life are indigenous to this parched environment, forty of them found nowhere else on earth.

The Valley is actually not a valley at all, but a block of land that has been steadily dropping between two mountain ranges that are slowly rising and sliding apart. More than 10,000 years ago a vast freshwater lake once filled Death Valley to a depth of 600 feet. Today, after thousands of years of dry, hot weather, only crusty salt flats remain. Within the long and narrow park confines (140 miles from one end to the other—about the size of Connecticut), one of the most popular sights is Artist's Palette, where mineral deposits have caused swathes of red, pink, orange, purple, and green to color the hills. Others are Zabriskie Point, with its views of wrinkled hills, and 14 square miles of perfectly sculpted Sahara-like sand dunes. Find the dead-end road that leads to the mile-high (and aptly named) Dante's View, from which you can see 360 degrees for 100 miles, taking in both the highest and lowest points in the Lower forty-eight: Mount Whitney, at 14,494 feet, and Badwater, at 282 feet below sea level.

Air-conditioned cars and luxury inns have improved on the experience that led 19th-century pioneers to give the valley its name. Among the latter, the luxurious Furnace Creek Inn is a veritable oasis of natural springs and palm gardens, with a lush 18-hole golf course thrown into the bargain. Built in 1927, the stone-and-adobe Mission-style inn is historic, and, with its less expensive motel-style ranch next door, a longtime favorite weekend getaway for weary Angelenos. You'll hear every language in the world around the spring-fed pool, a floating vantage from which to watch the changing colors of the Panamint Mountains in late afternoon. At night, gaze up in wonder as the desert sky is filled with a sea of brilliant stars.

WHAT: site, hotel. **DEATH VALLEY NATIONAL PARK:** at the California/Nevada border, 290 miles northeast of Los Angeles, 120 miles northwest of Las Vegas. Tel 760-786-3200; www.nps.gov/deva. *Cost:* $20 per car (good for 7 days). **FURNACE CREEK INN:** tel 800-236-7916 or 760-786-2345; www.furnacecreekresort.com. *Cost:* doubles from $305 (low season), from $320 (high season). **BEST TIMES:** Oct–May; dawn and late afternoon for the visual power and play of light.

The Spa of All Spas

THE GOLDEN DOOR

Escondido, California, U.S.A.

Check your skepticism at the door and leave behind your eight-day weeks of cell phones, business dinners, nannies, deadlines, and insomnia. Founded in 1958 by spa doyen Deborah Szekely of Mexico's Rancho La Puerta spa,

the Golden Door was the first wellness retreat to combine nascent American fitness concepts with European body treatments that have since become the gold standard. Consistently rated among the finest spas in the land, the Golden Door's 344 gorgeous acres accommodate just forty guests and are designed in a Japanese style, with meticulously trimmed greenery, meditative sand gardens, elevated wooden paths, and koi ponds. Guests (women only except during four annual co-ed weeks and five for men only) spend almost all their time outdoors communing with nature while blissfully tuning out for the duration of their Sunday-to-Sunday stay.

All accommodations in the elegantly rustic ryokan-style Japanese inn are spare, serene, single occupancy to honor personal space. Four staff members to every guest ensure serious pampering. Each guest is assigned a personal fitness trainer who tailors a daily schedule according to individual preferences and fitness and health needs. Begin your day with a sunrise hike or breakfast in bed, then relax at midafternoon with an hour-long massage in your room. A highlight of the week's stay is the trailblazing cuisine. The Golden Door's menu is low in fat and salt, yet sacrifices nothing in flavor with most of its ingredients picked from their own organic garden. Before you turn in, take a soak in a hot tub, followed by ki-atsu massage, the Golden Door's own version of watsu.

WHAT: hotel, experience. **WHERE:** 8 miles north of Escondido, 30 miles northeast of San Diego, 100 miles south of Los Angeles. 777 Deer Springs Rd. Tel 800-424-0777 or 760-744-5777; www.goldendoor.com. **COST:** $7,750 per person per week, all-inclusive except for tennis lessons. **BEST TIMES:** Sept–May.

A Futuristic Shrine to Art of the Past

THE GETTY CENTER

Los Angeles, California, U.S.A.

Masterpiece of famed architect Richard Meier, the 110-acre, six-building Getty Center was fourteen years and one billion dollars in the making, opening in 1997 as a modern Acropolis perched atop a Santa Monica

mountain ridge and looking out over L.A. to the Pacific. Designed to house the ever-expanding | Getty collection of pre-20th-century art and a library of more than 1 million books on art history, the hilltop citadel is a work of art itself, done in gleaming off-white travertine marble and glass. Luminous, sometimes soaring galleries rely heavily on natural light and are interspersed with courtyards, fountains, connecting walkways, and windows that frame views of the Robert Irwin–designed gardens and beyond. Van Gogh's *Irises* and five Cézannes (including his *Still Life with Apples*) are the Getty's magnets to the masses, but the museum's real strength remains its esoteric specialty collections, from Renaissance to Impressionism and 18th-century European decorative arts.

A hilltop acropolis houses one man's collection of art.

There is no more wonderful place to watch the sun set over the Pacific than from the wraparound terrace of the center's restaurant, whose cuisine of Californian, Asian, and Mediterranean flavors is attracting as much attention as the art. The same innovative kitchen oversees a simpler menu at the popular café. Food is a big part of the Getty's charms, exemplifying the attention the center devotes to atmosphere and all-around experience.

Among the other museums that add art to L.A.'s pop culture identity are the Los Angeles County Museum of Art (LACMA), Pasadena's small but excellent Norton Simon Museum, San Marino's Huntington Gardens and Galleries, and the Getty's sister museum, the Getty Villa in Malibu. This Pompeii-inspired home was commissioned from afar by the expatriate American oil billionaire John Paul Getty, ranked among the richest men of modern times. It was completed two years before his death in 1976, and although he never visited it, he chose to be buried there. Today it is devoted to his estimable survey of Greek and Roman antiquities. After being closed for years of renovations, in 2005 the Getty Villa reopened.

WHAT: site, restaurant. **WHERE:** 1200 Getty Center Dr. Tel 310-440-7300; www.getty.edu. **COST:** admission free; parking $15 (free after 5 P.M.). Dinner $50. **WHEN:** open Tues–Sun.

Where America Invents Itself

HOLLYWOOD

Los Angeles, California, U.S.A.

Ever since show-biz pioneers Cecil B. DeMille and Jesse Lasky were drawn to the climate-blessed West Coast in 1911, Hollywood ceased being a real place and became a concept, a glittering Tinseltown synonymous with fantasy, glamour, and ambition. It has long been true that the only stars you'll see on Hollywood Boulevard are at the local wax museum, but Hollywood is in the midst of a Times Square–like renaissance as it attempts to re-create the excitement of the industry's heyday. A major catalyst in the area's rebirth is the brand-new home of the L.A. Philharmonic, the $274 million Walt Disney Concert Hall, designed by celebrated architect Frank Gehry. At Grauman's Chinese Theatre you can literally walk in the footsteps of Charlie Chaplin, Marion Davies, Mary Pickford, and some 160 other stars of the silver screen from 1927 to the present, who have been immortalized in footprints, handprints, and the odd noseprint (Jimmy Durante's). Nearby, the mile-long Hollywood Boulevard Walk of Fame honors more than 2,000 stars from 1960 on.

Visit Universal Studios for a glimpse of the film world.

Most of the studios moved away long ago, and today only Paramount remains physically in Hollywood. For a glimpse of how movies are made, head over the Hollywood Hills to the San Fernando Valley and Universal City. In addition to its decades of history as a film-producing studio, Universal Studios has become a major tourist destination and its popular tour of the world's largest television and movie studio is fun for the whole family, skeptics included. Special effects rides let you experience an avalanche, an earthquake, and a freak encounter with a 30-foot King Kong.

If you're looking to rub shoulders with the likes of Harrison, Goldie, Meg, and Mel, then you're in the right town. Scandia, Chasen's, and the Brown Derby are no longer, but Musso & Frank Grill remains. It's one of the oldest restaurants in L.A., a watering hole for the industry's hoi polloi since 1919. In burnished-wood and leather booths, industry types nurse

Ketel One martinis and relish a defiantly 1920s menu fixed in time: chicken à la king, corned beef and cabbage, grilled calf's liver and onions, and eleven kinds of potatoes. A little less retro in ambience, the casual-chic Ivy provides a rare outdoor-lunch opportunity with great star-spotting potential, and they're even nice to tourists. Along the same lines is the perennially popular Spago Beverly Hills, where neck twisting detracts from Wolfgang Puck's consistently great signature pizzas.

For a show-biz experience extraordinaire, the city's finest and most nostalgic venue is the Hotel Bel Air, where stars young and old seek out anonymity and subtle service, blending unobtrusively into its 12-acre refuge of flowering native and sub-tropical flora. Shaded pathways meander past swan ponds to hideaway Mission-style bungalows—Marilyn Monroe's was recently transformed into a gym.

WHAT: site, hotel, restaurant. **HOLLYWOOD:** Los Angeles Convention and Visitors Bureau, tel 213-624-7300; www.lacvb.com. **WALT DISNEY CONCERT HALL:** 111 S. Grand Ave. Tel 213-972-7211; www.musiccenter.org. **GRAUMAN'S CHINESE THEATRE:** 6925 Hollywood Blvd. Tel 323-464-8111; www.manntheatres.com. **UNIVERSAL STUDIOS HOLLYWOOD:** 100 Universal City Plaza, Universal City (5 miles from Hollywood); www.universalstudioshollywood.com. *Cost:* $67. **MUSSO & FRANK GRILL:** 6667 Hollywood Blvd. Tel 323-467-7788; www.mussoandfrank.com. *Cost:* dinner $40. **IVY:** 113 N. Robertson Blvd., West Hollywood. Tel 310-274-8303. *Cost:* $65. **SPAGO BEVERLY HILLS:** 176 N. Canon Dr., Beverly Hills. Tel 310-385-0880; www.wolfgangpuck.com. *Cost:* Dinner $75. **HOTEL BEL AIR:** 701 Stone Canyon Rd., Bel Air. Tel 800-648-4097 or 310-472-1211; www.hotelbelair.com. *Cost:* from $345. Dinner at the Terrace $65. **BEST TIMES:** early Jul–mid-Sept, the outdoor Hollywood Bowl (in Griffith Park; www.hollywoodbowl.org) hosts the L.A. Philharmonic performing a repertoire that ranges from jazz to pop to classical; avoid "June Gloom" and hot Aug.

Sacred Golf, Nature's Wonderama, and All That Jazz

MONTEREY PENINSULA

California, U.S.A.

Mother Nature worked overtime on the rugged Monterey Peninsula. Pacific Grove (a.k.a. Butterfly Town, U.S.A., famous as the resting stop for tens of thousands of migrating monarch butterflies) and the too-charming-for-words artsy town of Carmel-by-the-Sea are big attractions, but the old fishing town of Monterey remains the peninsula's biggest draw. Forever immortalized by Nobel Prize winning novelist John Steinbeck, it hosts the Monterey Jazz Festival, a huge three-night affair that attracts more than 500 greats from around the world and is the oldest ongoing jazz festival in the nation.

Once famous for whaling and sardine-canning, Monterey was also California's first capital and retains more than forty buildings built before 1850. The incredible marine life of the region is best experienced today at the world-class Monterey Bay Aquarium on Cannery Row, a street made famous by Steinbeck's 1945 novel. A magical "indoor ocean," it's home to 700 varieties of marine animals from the Monterey Bay, including fish, sea otters, sharks, penguins, and the mesmerizing and improbably beautiful jellyfish. To complete your Monterey experience, check into the Old Monterey Inn, a beautifully renovated half-timbered Tudor built in 1929 with just ten perfectly appointed rooms.

One of the most stunning roads on either U.S. seaboard, the celebrated 17-Mile Drive connects Monterey to its peninsular neighbor Carmel, and is the only private toll road west of the Mississippi. A microcosm of the ragged coastline's romantic beauty, it's sheathed in rare wind-sculpted cypresses and dotted with ocean-sprayed outcroppings where hundreds of harbor seals and sea lions laze. Man-made highlights of the famous drive are the hard-to-believe multimillion-dollar homes, the legendary Pebble Beach Golf Links, and five neighboring championship courses. Sacred ground for golfers, Pebble Beach's ocean-hugging links are reminiscent of the demanding and windy courses of Scotland and Ireland, and are regularly ranked as one of the most spectacular (and expensive) tournament-class public courses in the world.

The tree-lined streets of the pretty, prosperous, and pampered town of Carmel are filled with art galleries, jewelry and gift shops, and cafés, with a crescent of beautiful sandy beach just minutes away. The 1770 Carmel Mission served as the headquarters for the entire mission system in California (under

Overlooking the bay at the Monterey Aquarium

Father Junipero Serra, who is buried here). The town's most high-profiled resident, Clint Eastwood, still makes his presence known. The Hog's Breath Inn (once owned by Eastwood) is fun for a Dirty Harry Burger or a night-cap near one of the outdoor patio's fireplaces. For something more substantial, head out of town to the venerable 1850s Mission Ranch, a 22-acre seaside dairy farm that the actor rescued in 1986 (the same year he was elected mayor of Carmel) and turned into a rustic inn. Check into one of its thirty-one rooms, or at least stay for dinner at the ranch dining room, popular with locals.

WHAT: site, experience, event, hotel, restaurant. **WHERE:** Monterey is 125 miles south of San Francisco, 345 miles north of L.A. Monterey County Convention and Visitors Bureau, tel 877-666-8373; www.seemonterey.org. **MONTEREY JAZZ FESTIVAL:** tel 925-275-9255 or 831-373-3366; www.

montereyjazzfestival.org. *Cost:* tickets $35–$110. *When:* 3d full weekend in Sept. **MONTEREY BAY AQUARIUM:** 886 Cannery Row, Monterey. Tel 831-648-4800; www.mbayaq.org. *Cost:* $30. **OLD MONTEREY INN:** 500 Martin St., Monterey. Tel 800-350-2344 or 831-375-8284; www.oldmonterey inn.com. *Cost:* from $270–$450. **PEBBLE BEACH GOLF LINKS:** tel 800-654-9300; www.pebblebeach.com. **HOG'S BREATH INN:** San Carlos and Fifth Sts., Carmel. Tel 831-625-1044. *Cost:* lunch $15. **MISSION RANCH:** Dolores St., Carmel. Tel 800-538-8221 or 831-624-6436; www.missionranchcarmel.com. *Cost:* from $120. Dinner $40. **BEST TIMES:** 4 days mid-Aug for the Pebble Beach Concours d'Elegance, to see some of the most beautiful antique cars ever made; Jul/Aug for the 3-week Carmel Bach Festival; Jan for prime whale watching; Jan/Feb for monarch butterflies.

Highway to Heaven

THE PACIFIC COAST HIGHWAY

California, U.S.A.

Also known by those not from these parts as Route 1, the Pacific Coast Highway is America's dream drive. You can head south from L.A. to San Diego, or take the traditionalist's route north to San Francisco and even

beyond, past the 19th-century fishing-town-turned-artist-colony of Mendocino in the direction of Oregon, whose own coastal stretch is often no less magnificent.

From the heart of L.A., head west to Santa Monica, then follow the coast to Malibu where you'll already feel a world away. The laid-back community's beachfront promenade, the famed Santa Monica Pier, and the weekend Farmer's Market (considered by many food professionals to be one of the best in the country) might cause a moment's dalliance as you pursue your motoring route to points north.

Temptation is no less alluring as you skirt the environs of neighboring Santa Barbara, about 100 miles north of L.A. at the foot of the dramatic Santa Ynez Mountains. This idyllic town, built originally around the 1786 Santa Barbara Mission (queen of California's many Spanish outposts), remains a quiet throwback to the golden land of the California myth and is sometimes called the American Riviera. The town's fine wineries are often compared to those of Napa of twenty years ago, while its dining options range from fresh produce at its enviable farmers' market to the funky,

Julia Child–blessed Super-Rica Taqueria on North Milpas Street, home to what many swear is the world's finest corn tortilla. More than a dozen sprawling rancho-type hotels provide rest and relaxation, among them the 500-acre San Ysidro Ranch, a rustic getaway for the rich and famous since opening in 1893, and where JFK and Jackie honeymooned.

About 50 miles north of Santa Barbara, the fabled PCH begins to unfurl at its most majestic, carving an awesome ribbon of highway 500 to 1,000 feet above the roaring Pacific. Extolled as America's road trip extraordinaire, with a host of don't-miss braking points, the wild and rugged 90-mile stretch from San Simeon past Big Sur and on to the Monterey Peninsula is the uncontested high point of the coastal drive.

Situated atop what he called "Enchanted Hill," publisher William Randolph Hearst's 115-room San Simeon mountaintop mansion is a Spanish-Moorish hodgepodge that strikes horror into the souls of architectural purists. The "castle" and its 127 manicured garden acres are an homage to the romance, eccentricity, and extravagance that cost Hearst thirty years of his life and much of his family's fortune, and remains to this day the most expensive private home ever built in America, an over-the-top billionaire's Disneyland from a time of unashamed spending. Hearst's feeding frenzy, in which he and his agents bought up and dismantled entire cloisters, ceilings, mantelpieces, choir stalls, and tapestries from around the world and reassembled them here, resulted in a mishmash of styles and periods, occasionally offset by subtle details of taste and refinement. A highlight of the tour (the only way to visit the grounds) is the home movies taken during the decades when Hearst's mistress, Marion Davies, made the castle a playground for such Hollywood pals as the Marx Brothers, Clark Gable, Cary Grant, and Charlie Chaplin.

After such an excessive dose of man-made extravagance, the natural masterpiece of Big Sur appears, a coastal wilderness located where the Santa Lucia Mountains encounter the roaring Pacific. It's a poem of crashing surf and rugged scenery you'll never forget: Henry Miller, called it "a place of grandeur and eloquent silence." The area is still widely undeveloped and has a dramatic loneliness about it, with angry ocean breakers on one side and a narrow curving road that snakes along the edge of the mountains. Pfeiffer Beach is breathtaking—in fact, there's precious little around here that's not. Stop to take it all in with a drink or dinner at the well-known Nepenthe, with its outdoor patio suspended 800 feet above the surf. Owned briefly by Orson Welles and Rita Hayworth, it's a traditional stopover for motorists seeking a stupendous vantage from which to view the sunset.

"Ventana" means window in Spanish, and Big Sur's stunningly sited Ventana Inn, perched 1,200 feet above the Pacific, is your window to vast 50-mile vistas of dramatic ocean and mountains, visible both from your room's private deck and from the inn's many public windows. Across the road, the Post Ranch Inn offers the same laid-back luxury and middle-of-nature feel, but with an environmentally conscious twist. Everything from your terrace is meant to be romantic, soothing, and relaxing, though you can also stretch your legs on the numerous nearby hiking trails, which take you out among the area's grassy meadows, deep canyons, and towering redwoods.

WHAT: site, experience, hotel, restaurant. **WHERE:** San Simeon is 250 miles north of

Miles of dramatic vista from the Ventana Inn

L.A., 215 miles south of San Francisco. Big Sur is 150 miles south of San Francisco. **SAN YSIDRO RANCH:** Montecito. Tel 888-767-3966 or 805-565-1700; www.sanysidroranch.com. *Cost:* doubles from $399. **HEARST SAN SIMEON STATE HISTORICAL MONUMENT:** Hearst Castle Rd., San Simeon. Tel 800-444-4445 or 916-414-8400; www.hearstcastle.org. *Cost:* tours $24. **NEPENTHE:** Highway 1, Big Sur. Tel 831-667-2345; www.nepenthe

bigsur.com. *Cost:* dinner $40. **VENTANA INN:** Highway 1, Big Sur. Tel 800-628-6500 or 831-667-2331, fax 831-667-0573; www.ventana inn.com. *Cost:* doubles from $400. **POST RANCH INN:** Highway 1, Big Sur. Tel 800-527-2200 or 831-667-2200, fax 831-667-2512; www.postranchinn.com. Cost: doubles from $550 (low season), from $750 (high season). **BEST TIMES:** Dec–Feb for whale watching.

A Beachside Dowager

HOTEL DEL CORONADO

San Diego, California, U.S.A.

It is eternal spring on the curved isthmus of Coronado, famous for its broad, family-friendly, and almost impossibly white beach—one of the nicest in a state that knows its beaches and gets to enjoy them 365 days a year. This is

the home of the Hotel Del Coronado (a.k.a. the Del, a.k.a. the Grand Lady by the Sea), which sits like a Victorian wedding cake on 26 lovely beachfront acres, the largest oceanfront resort on the Pacific Coast. Open since 1888, the Del has hosted every American president since Lyndon Johnson, plus countless celebrities and film crews—most importantly director Billy Wilder, who chose the hotel as the

principal setting of his 1958 film *Some Like It Hot,* starring Marilyn Monroe. Rumor has it that the big, white hotel with red gables was where the visiting Prince of Wales first met American widow Wallis Simpson in 1920, and where author and neighbor L. Frank Baum allegedly found his inspiration for the Emerald City in his *The Wizard of Oz.*

Simply put—you can't come to Southern California without staying here. Rent a bike at the hotel for a tool around the golf course, under the bridge that links Coronado with downtown, and along the harbor for the best view of San Diego.

Nor can you come to San Diego without visiting its world-famous zoo, one of the first in the world to display animals in naturalistic habitats free of cages or bars. Nearly 4,000 exotic animals (from pandas to Sumatran tigers) representing 800 species roam the park's 100 hilly acres. There's even summer nighttime viewing for

In 1888, the hotel was designed to be "the talk of the western world."

those who'd rather spend sun-drenched afternoons lolling on the beach. However you spend your day in this archetypal Southern California town, be back at your Oz-like home for a poetic Pacific sunset on wave-swept Coronado Beach, where there is nothing between you and Honolulu.

WHAT: hotel, site. HOTEL DEL CORONADO: 1500 Orange Ave., Coronado (120 miles south of Los Angeles, 16 miles north of Tijuana, Mexico). Tel 800-468-3533 or 619-435-6611, fax 619-522-8262; www.hoteldel.com. *Cost:* doubles from $250. SAN DIEGO ZOO: 2920 Zoo Dr. Tel 619-231-1515; www.sandiegozoo. org. *Cost:* adults $35. BEST TIMES: between late Dec and mid-Mar some 15,000 whales migrate along the coast to Baja California in Mexico.

Poetry in Motion

A TOUR ON SAN FRANCISCO'S CABLE CARS

San Francisco, California, U.S.A.

A s clichéd but charming as the gondolas of Venice and the double-decker buses of London, San Francisco's cable cars are a key component of the city's unique character and the only national historic landmark that moves.

With an unmistakable "ding! ding! ding!" announcing their arrival on sunny and foggy days alike, the cars are a throwback to the late 1800s, when they were the best transportation up and down the forty-three hills of America's most topographically endowed city. Today they still bustle along at a constant 9½ miles per hour (running by cable, not motor), their three lines comprising the world's only surviving cable car system.

The Powell-Hyde and Powell-Mason lines begin downtown below the busy high-end shopping area of Union Square and climb to the lofty neighborhood of Nob Hill, one of the city's most elegant addresses and hilltop home to two of its most important hotels, The Ritz-Carlton, widely considered the city's (and one of the world's) best, and the landmark Fairmont. Rebuilt in an extravagant manner after the 1906 earthquake, this was where Tony Bennett gave his first public performance of "I Left My Heart in San Francisco," back in 1962. The Powell-Hyde line ends at Fisherman's Wharf, the famous waterfront tourist destination that still holds on to a good dose of charm. It's worth joining the teeming humanity just to graze on take-away cracked crab and fish-and-chips from the harborside stands, and gaze at the spectacular views of Alcatraz prison—"The Rock"—and the majestic 2-mile-long Golden Gate Bridge, which you can also traverse for an exhilarating, wind-blasted walk and great views. Who knows who decided to paint it orange, but god love 'em.

If it's Saturday, head for the nearby Embarcadero and the wildly popular Ferry Plaza Farmers' Market, the city's best and biggest. The vibrant markets of Chinatown are no less remarkable, packed with people (it's the country's second largest Chinese enclave), fresh vegetables, and things you didn't know existed (or could be eaten).

In the heart of North Beach (the most enjoyable neighborhood to stroll around), Telegraph Hill offers some of the best vistas in town, particularly from the top of Coit Tower, where you can see the bay, bridges, and islands. You'll want to amble around Haight-Ashbury as well, a kind of retirement zone for '60s hippies. Angle yourself atop Alta Vista Park, overlooking downtown, for the postcard view of the "painted ladies"—a row of brightly painted Queen Anne Victorians on the 700 block of Steiner Street. San Francisco's wealth of architecture is one of its myriad treasures.

WHAT: experience, hotel. **SAN FRANCISCO:** San Francisco Convention and Visitors Bureau, tel 415-391-2000; www.sfvisitor.org. *Cable car ride* $5. **THE RITZ-CARLTON:** 600 Stockton St. Tel 415-296-7465; www.ritzcarlton.com. *Cost:* doubles from $299. **FAIRMONT:** 950 Mason St. Tel 415-772-5000; www.fairmont. com. *Cost:* doubles from $189. **BEST TIMES:** the famous fog is most prevalent in summer, and can make things chilly; spring (when Golden Gate Park is glorious) and fall are nicest; Chinatown's Chinese New Year generally falls in Feb, with festivities lasting 2 weeks. The 2-week International Film Festival is in Apr–May. The Gay Pride Parade is held the last week of Jun in the openly gay Castro district. Check listings year-round for the city's flourishing art and poetry scene.

The Restaurant That Changed the Way America Eats

CHEZ PANISSE

Berkeley, California, U.S.A.

In 1971, eating out meant beef Wellington and iceberg-lettuce salads with thousand island dressing—but that was before a young Alice Waters took an enlightening trip through France, where she was struck by the bold flavors of vegetables fresh from the garden, fruit right off the branch, and fish straight from the sea. Returning to the United States, the idealistic Berkeley grad opened Chez Panisse, in the process creating "California cuisine," turning San Francisco into one of America's best restaurant cities, and setting off a change in the way America eats. If it weren't for her, our local restaurants might never have discovered mesclun salad, wood-fired pizza, wild mushrooms, domestic goat cheese, and organic produce.

Identified the world over with pure, super-fresh local ingredients, simple preparation, and gorgeous presentation, Chez Panisse (named for a character in a film trilogy by Marcel Pagnol) is still going strong thirty years later. It's still as difficult to book, still serves a single prix fixe three- or four-course menu every day, and never offers the same meal twice. Some sixty local farms supply the kitchen, and if a farmer's got a new kind of pomegranate or cheese, it will show up on tonight's menu and inspire the entire meal. If you want to remember how food should taste, eat here.

Upstairs, the lively, more informal Chez Panisse Café offers the same unfussy sensibility in a less expensive à la carte menu. Elsewhere in San Francisco, you can find restaurants whose owners and chefs were mentored by or took their inspiration from Waters, such as the superlative and ever popular Zuni Café.

WHAT: restaurant. **WHERE:** Berkeley is 10 miles northeast of San Francisco. 1517 Shattuck Ave. Tel 510-548-5525; www.chez-panisse.com. **COST:** prix fixe dinner from $60; upstairs à la carte $40. **WHEN:** downstairs dinner only; upstairs lunch and dinner; both closed Sun.

Napa and Sonoma: America's Premier Vineyards

CALIFORNIA'S WINE COUNTRY

California, U.S.A.

If America has an answer to Tuscany as a locus for wine, food, and the good life, Napa and Sonoma are it. Consistently beautiful and gently landscaped, these fraternal twins, separated at birth by the Mayacamas Mountains and

distinctly different in character, produce about 7 percent of the world's wines, many of them of international caliber.

The 35-mile-long arc of Napa is the better known and more densely populated, with some 280 wineries (up from 20 in 1975) producing the region's signature cabernet and many other varieties. Among the more high-profile are the renowned Domaine Chandon in picturesque Yountville and the powerhouse Robert Mondavi Winery in Oakville.

The 250-acre Meadowood resort was built in the 1960s as a private country club and still has that old-money feel, with a hint of country club formality permeating the rambling main lodge and the cottage-style suites scattered in the hills above. A resident wine tutor oversees a cellar with wines from nearly every vintner in the valley.

Meadowood is host of the wine region's most important event, the three-day Napa Valley Wine Auction in early June, the largest and most prestigious charity wine event in the world; events take place valley-wide, but Meadowood is command central.

In addition to the resort's two dining venues—commonly held to be among Napa's best—the valley has a dizzying number of excellent eateries, from take-out markets and truck stops to The French Laundry, lauded by many in the food world as America's finest restaurant. In a simple, almost austere 100-year-old stone cottage, self-trained chef Thomas Keller astounds diners, taking French-inspired California cuisine to riveting heights.

The Napa Valley Wine Train's Champagne Vista Dome car—almost alfresco

For a multisensory experience, hop aboard the luxury Napa Valley Wine Train, which runs from Napa to St. Helena past twenty-seven vineyards. Guests wine and dine during a blissful three-hour, 36-mile round-trip gourmet journey aboard handsomely restored 1915-era Pullman coaches. You won't have to worry about drinking and driving.

On looks alone, the smaller Sonoma County appears more rustic and laid-back, but don't be misled by the folksy, unfussy character of its 200 wineries: Sonoma wines —principally cabernet, chardonnay, and zinfandel—often outpace those of Napa, while its fertile orchards and vegetable farms supply the kitchens of the area's finest restaurants. Sonoma's many inns and restaurants are as diverse as its wines. Small Healdsburg, on the banks of the Russian River Valley, is the center of the action, its late-19th-century Madrona Manor setting the standard for period elegance. The Victorian dowager's esteemed restaurant also sets it apart, with a cuisine based on Sonoma's cornucopia of produce and wines, with much of the best coming from the gabled inn's own extensive kitchen garden.

WHAT: site, hotel, restaurant, experience. **NAPA AND SONOMA VALLEYS:** 50–60 miles north of San Francisco. Napa Valley Conference and Visitors Bureau, tel 707-226-7459; www.napavalley.com. Sonoma County Convention and Visitors Bureau, tel 707-996-1090; www.sonomavalley.com. **MEADOWOOD NAPA VALLEY:** 900 Meadowood Ln., St. Helena, Napa. Tel 800-458-8080 or 707-963-3646, fax 707-963-3532; www.meadowood.com. *Cost:* doubles from $450 (low season),

$575 (high season). **THE FRENCH LAUNDRY:** 6640 Washington St., Yountville, Napa. Tel 707-944-2380; www.frenchlaundry.com. *Cost:* nine-course tasting menus $240. *When:* dinner daily, lunch Fri–Sun. Reservations must be made 2 months in advance. **NAPA VALLEY WINE TRAIN:** tel 800-427-4124 or 707-253-2111; www.winetrain.com. *Cost:* 3-hour ride from $49.50. **MADRONA MANOR:** 1001 Westside Rd., Healdsburg, Sonoma. Tel 800-258-4003 or 707-433-4231; www.madronamanor.com. *Cost:* doubles from $220 (low season), from $275 (high season). **BEST TIMES:** spring for wildflower season; fall for harvest season, when numerous festivals are held.

A High Sierra Beauty

YOSEMITE NATIONAL PARK

California, U.S.A.

"No temple made with hands can compare with Yosemite," wrote naturalist John Muir, whose efforts led to the establishment of Yosemite National Park in 1890. Most of the millions who converge in high season on this temple of nature head for the awesome beauty of the mile-wide, 7-mile-long Yosemite Valley, the park's "Main Street," cut by a river and guarded by sheer granite cliffs and domes that rise 2,000 to 4,000 feet. Avoid the park's notorious summertime people-jams by exploring the backcountry—the wilder 95 percent of the 750,000-acre domain, roughly the size of Rhode Island.

Most of the park's natural attractions have become icons of the American landscape, immortalized by the photographs of Ansel Adams. Who doesn't recognize the bald image of Half Dome, Yosemite's 8,842-foot trademark peak? Or El Capitan, the largest single granite rock on earth, rising 350 stories from the valley floor (twice the size of the Rock of Gibraltar) and drawing rock climbers from all over the world? The magnificent Yosemite Falls are the highest on the continent at 2,425

The sparkling waterfalls of Yosemite

feet. The cascade—divided into Upper Yosemite Fall (1,430 feet), the middle cascades (675 feet), and Lower Yosemite Fall (320 feet)—is at its most dramatic in spring and early summer, but dries to a trickle by the end of summer.

Hiking is a favored activity in the park, with 800 miles of trails that can be covered by horse, mule, or on foot. One of the most popular is the moderately strenuous Mist Trail, offering a close-up view of 317-foot Vernal Fall and the 594-foot Nevada Fall. For those who prefer to remain in the car, 196 miles of paved roads will get you to Glacier Point for spectacular views of the valley below. In Mariposa Grove, a refuge of 500 massive sequoias, the 2,700-year-old Grizzly Giant is believed to be the oldest.

Yosemite Valley's 1927 Ahwahnee Hotel, named after the Native American inhabitants of the park (in whose language "Yosemite" means "grizzly bear"), is the perfect park accommodation, and one of the national park system's most prestigious. A showpiece of stone and native timber, its views are heart stopping. Inside, decorative motifs reflect Ahwahnee Indian crafts, while the massive chandeliers look as if they were meant for a castle, and the fireplaces are large enough to walk into. Guests and nonguests alike can take lunch in the cavernous dining room, whose 25-foot windows frame the park's best assets.

South of Yosemite, Erna's Elderberry House and its exquisite 19th-century-style guest house, the Château du Sureau, offer European sophistication, gracious service, and an air of romance you don't expect to find in such a tiny hamlet. Erna, the Viennese-born virtuoso chef (and ebullient proprietor), is so inspired by the local market that she changes the menu almost daily, creating French-influenced meals that draw foodies the way El Capitan lures rock climbers.

WHAT: site, hotel, restaurant. **YOSEMITE NATIONAL PARK:** 190 miles east of San Francisco, 380 miles northeast of Los Angeles. Tel 209-372-0200; www.nps.gov/yose. *Cost:* $20 per car for a 7-day visit. **AHWAHNEE:** tel 209-372-1407; www.yosemitepark.com/accomodations.aspx. *Cost:* doubles from $299. **CHÂTEAU DU SUREAU:** Oakhurst (16 miles from Yosemite's south gate). Tel 559-683-6860, fax 559-683-0800; www.chateausureau.com. *Cost:* doubles from $385. 5-course dinner $95. **BEST TIMES:** mid-Aug for spectacular Perseid meteor shower; late Oct–early Nov for peak fall foliage; Nov–Mar for the smallest crowds. The Ahwahnee's Christmastime Bracebridge Dinner is a lovely tradition, so reserve early.

The Place to Ski and Be Seen,
with a Stimulating Cultural Life to Boot

ASPEN

Colorado, U.S.A.

Colorado is Rocky Mountain ski central, with more than two dozen resorts. Among them, Aspen is inarguably the most famous and sophisticated, and is the wintertime destination of choice for Hollywood celebs and those that

follow them. The 11,000-foot Aspen Mountain ("Ajax" to the locals) is a strong skier's mountain and no place for novices, but the area's 12-mile span of summits is also known for three other, less challenging resorts: Snowmass, Buttermilk, and Aspen Highlands as well as for its lively après-ski nightlife. In total, they offer 281 trails over 4,315 acres of terrain and generally excellent skiing conditions, all linked by free shuttle service and a transferable lift ticket.

You can match the beauty of the great outdoors with that of the great indoors at the Little Nell, Aspen's unpretentiously elegant (and only) ski-in/ski-out hotel, located on Aspen's flagship mountain. Reminiscent of a European ski chalet, it's located a snowball's throw from the sleek Silver Queen, the world's longest single-stage gondola, which hoists skiers up 3,257 feet in just thirteen minutes. The Nell has a busy bar and award-winning restaurant that are a scene both in winter and during the snowless months.

When the skiing life quiets down, Aspen's other charms come to the fore: a rich sense of community, and beautifully preserved late-19th-century gingerbread homes built during the town's silver-mining boomtown years, all set against the natural splendor of the Colorado Rockies. Paramount among the year-round array of cultural and performing arts events is the summertime Aspen Music Festival, an eight-week mini-Tanglewood known for the variety and breadth of its musical activity.

WHAT: town, experience, hotel, event. **ASPEN:** 200 miles southwest of Denver, connected by air service. For ski information, contact Aspen Skiing Company, tel 800-525-6200; www.aspensnowmass.com. *When:* first day of skiing is usually Thanksgiving; season closes mid- to late April. **LITTLE NELL:** 675 E. Durant St. Tel 970-920-4600; www.thelittlenell.com. *Cost:* doubles from $330 (low season) to $810 (high season). **ASPEN MUSIC FESTIVAL:** tel 970-925-3254; www.aspenmusicfestival.com. *When:* mid-Jun to mid-Aug. **BEST TIMES:** ski conditions optimal mid-Dec through Mar. Oct is least congested. You may want to avoid the "mud months," late Apr to mid-May.

How the West Was Wonderful

HOME RANCH

Clark, Colorado, U.S.A.

If you have more of a hankerin' to be a cattle baron than a cowpoke, and gourmet grub and wide-open vistas of a million acres of cedars, aspens, and pines fit the picture (the Routt National Forest is just next door) then there's

no place like Home. Here you can spend a few (or many) exhilarating hours in the saddle, riding though open meadows of wildflowers and deep valleys, then happily mosey back to marinate in your cabin's private outdoor Jacuzzi before an award-deserving dinner. You can choose from a long roster of year-round activities or just laze about and commune with nature. But you'd better be friendly, because this place is all about Western hospitality, something the gregarious owner (who writes, sings, and plays cowboy music) has raised to an art form. Repeat guests come back for the camaraderie and family-style atmosphere, where superb but laid-back meals are served at communal tables, or occasionally around the campfire. There are no more than fifty other guests, whom you may chose to see or not to see during the day. Guest quarters are aspen-shaded cabins paneled in wood and tastefully decorated with western antiques, woven Indian rugs, and wood-burning stoves—stylish, but in a cozy and comfortable way. You almost forget that this is an authentic working cattle ranch, until the sound of the triangle on the porch rings out across the valley. "Come and get it" never sounded so good.

WHAT: hotel. **WHERE:** 4-hour drive north from Denver, 18 miles from Steamboat Springs.

Tel 970-879-1780, fax 970-879-1795; www.homeranch.com. **COST:** doubles from $460 (low season, 2-night minimum); 1-week stays mandatory in summer, doubles from $5,280, all inclusive. **BEST TIMES:** Jan–Feb for skiing; May–Jun for wildflower blooming.

Cliff Dwellings of a Mysterious People in the Four Corners

MESA VERDE NATIONAL PARK

Cortez, Colorado, U.S.A.

O f the more than 300 national parks in the United States, 52,000-acre Mesa Verde ("Green Table," so named because of its pine and juniper forests) is the only one devoted exclusively to archaeology. Here, the Anasazi people (recently rebaptized as the "ancestral Puebloans") flourished from approximately A.D. 600, reaching the apex of their culture between the 11th and 13th centuries, by which time they'd begun building intricate multistoried dwellings of adobe or stone within the shelter of the rocky canyon walls. By the 14th century they had deserted the area for reasons that remain unclear. White men weren't widely aware of their dwellings until the 1870s, but within ten years the area was being mentioned as a potential national park. Exploration began in 1888, and to date more than 4,000 archaeological sites have been identified, of which approximately 600 are cliff dwellings. Only a few have been excavated, among them the park's highlights: the 156-room Cliff Palace and Balcony House, both on Chapin Mesa, and Long House on Wetherill Mesa. Admission is tightly controlled, and many sites (including these three) can only be visited in the company of a park ranger guide. The two 6-mile Mesa Top Loops (until recently called Ruins Road Drive) provide a motorist's tour with dozens of overlooks.

Mesa Verde is located in Four Corners country, where Utah, Colorado, New Mexico, and Arizona come together; from Park Point, the park's highest elevation (8,572 feet), you can

Mesa Verde is the largest archaeological preserve in the United States.

see all of them. The only place to hang your hat within the park is the modest but aptly named Far View Lodge, which is remarkable only for the fact that all its rooms offer Four-Corner views of up to 100 miles.

WHAT: site, hotel. **WHERE:** 35 miles west of Durango and 10 miles east of Cortez, in the extreme southwest of Colorado. Visitors Center in Cortez, tel 970-529-4465; www.nps.gov/meve. *Cost:* admission $10 per car. *When:* park can be entered year-round, but certain

sites only open Apr–Oct. **FAR VIEW LODGE:** across from Visitors Center, tel 800-449-2288 or 970-564-4300, fax 970-564-4311; www.visit mesaverde.com. *Cost:* doubles from $116. *When:* Apr–Oct. **BEST TIMES:** Apr–Jun and late Aug–Oct for fewer crowds. The Intertribal Arts and Crafts show is usually (but not always) held the last weekend in Jul and the annual Mesa Verde Country Indian Arts and Western Culture Festival is held on Memorial Day weekend.

Heaven via Road or Steam Engine

THE MILLION DOLLAR HIGHWAY AND THE DURANGO AND SILVERTON

Durango, Colorado, U.S.A.

In this southwestern pocket of Colorado, where desert meets mountain, the goal is the mountaintop panoramas, but getting up there is half the fun. Many roadsters herald the San Juan Skyway as the most beautiful drive in

the continental United States. An officially designated scenic byway, it links the old boom-or-bust mining towns of Ouray and

The Durango and Silverton's vintage locomotive puffs its way to heavenly heights.

Durango, the latter a charming, caught-in-time place that makes a great base for exploring the area. Besides exceptional, nonstop Rocky Mountain panoramas, the trip offers a nostalgic journey back to the early years of Colorado's statehood and its gold-mining days: A section of its length is known as the Million Dollar Highway, alluding (some say) to the value of the low-grade gold ore present in its road bed.

Train fans should hop on board the Durango and Silverton's puffing, vintage steam locomotive, which makes several trips a day (in season) along the 3½-hour, 45-scenic-mile route from Durango to Silverton, climbing a 3,000-foot ascent through glacier-carved valleys, along narrow canyon ledges, and through impassable stretches of the dense San Juan forest and mountains (the "newest" of the Rockies). After a two-hour layover, it makes the return trip to Durango. The Silverton once hauled mine workers, supplies, and precious ore along its narrow-gauge tracks (36 inches apart, versus the standard 56.5 inches) from one isolated mining camp to another. But today's precious cargo is wide-eyed visitors, the lucky ones getting off halfway at a designated flagstop in dense evergreen wilderness. This is Tall Timber Resort, now home to Soaring Tree Top Adventures, an all-but-hidden forest retreat that can only be reached by the steam engine train (or its 21st-century alternative: helicopter). A river runs through the secluded 180 private acres—virgin territory that knows no roads. Here in the middle of nowhere, you can experience the forest from the air, via a series of 24 zip lines that cover a mile and a quarter. A 4-course lunch is served on a platform overlooking the river.

WHAT: experience, town. **DURANGO AND SILVERTON NARROW GAUGE RAILROAD:** Durango. Tel 877-872-4607 or 970-247-2733; www.durangotrain.com. *Cost:* Durango–Silverton round-trip $49 winter, $79 summer. *When:* to Silverton, late May–Oct; to Cascade Canyon and return, Thanksgiving to early May. **TALL TIMBER RESORT:** tel 970-259-4813; www.talltimberresort.com. *Cost:* $399, for a full-day adventure, including lunch and round-trip first-class train transport. *When:* mid-May through mid-Oct. **BEST TIMES:** Jul–Oct.

A Natural High

ROCKY MOUNTAIN NATIONAL PARK

Estes Park, Colorado, U.S.A.

Rocky Mountain National Park boasts 191 craggy peaks within its 415 square miles—113 of them more than 10,000 feet and 78 above 12,000 feet. The granddaddy of them all, Longs Peak (14,255 feet), most likely inspired the well-known lyrics that celebrate America's purple mountains' majesty. Views of these peaks are unsurpassed on the Trail Ridge Road, billed as the highest continuous highway in the United States, raising to over 12,000 feet at its apex. Built in 1932 along the route of an old Indian path across the Continental Divide, this is a road trip extraordinaire, offering unsurpassed, sometimes dizzying vistas.

More than 350 miles of gentle nature trails give visitors the opportunity to get off the always busy Trail Ridge Road and into the solitude of the park's splendid backcountry, with its cool, dense forests, rushing streams, glacier-gouged lakes, and alpine meadows. The entire park is a wildlife refuge, with some creatures proving to be elusive (like the bobcat and mountain lion), while others are more commonplace—like elk, mule deer, and the bighorn (or Rocky Mountain) sheep, which has become the park's emblem.

There are no accommodations within the park, but 3 miles from the eastern entrance is Estes Park and the well-known Stanley Hotel, inspiration for Stephen King's spine-tingling thriller *The Shining*, much of which was written by the vacationing author in room 217. Built in 1909 by F. O. Stanley, who coinvented the Stanley Steamer automobile, this neoclassical-Georgian member of the National Register of Historic Places is all about its gorgeous setting, rich historic ambience, and sweeping views of Lake Estes and the Continental Divide.

WHAT: site, hotel. **ROCKY MOUNTAIN NATIONAL PARK:** Estes Park (the eastern entrance to the park) is 80 miles northwest of Denver; western entrance to park is through Grand Lake. Both have park information and visitor services. The 45-mile Trail Ridge connects these two entrance points. Park info, tel 970-586-1206; www.nps.gov/romo. *Cost:* admission $20 per car good for 7 days. *When:* park open year-round; Trail Ridge Road open Memorial Day to mid-Oct. Light midsummer snowfall is not uncommon. **STANLEY HOTEL:** 333 Wonderview, Estes Park. Tel 800-976-1377 or 970-586-3371; www.stanleyhotel.com. *Cost:* doubles from $159 (low season), from $199 (high season). **BEST TIMES:** May–Sept (which is also the park's busiest season). The Stanley Hotel hosts an old-fashioned July 4th celebration.

Festival Capital of the Rockies

TELLURIDE

Colorado, U.S.A.

Isolated in a box canyon surrounded by the highest concentration of 14,000-foot peaks in the United States, Telluride has a well-earned reputation among high-octane vertical ski buffs, vacationing celebs seeking a low-profile hiding place, and Victoriana-seekers looking to experience the charm of its gold- and silver-rush days. It's one of the best preserved of the old Western ski towns, with a smattering of dirt roads, a laid-back local population, and a main street that seems little changed since the day when Butch Cassidy robbed his first bank here, on June 24, 1889. Still, things are happening in Telluride. For one, the town is known as the festival capital of the Rockies, with more than twenty-five events planned between May and September, including the Bluegrass Festival (June), the Jazz Festival (August) and the Film Festival (Labor Day weekend). For another, the budget for ski improvements and maintenance year-round is obvious everywhere. Of the eighty-five ski trails and 2,500 acres of gorgeous Rockies terrain, more than two-thirds are given over to beginners and intermediates, while experts rank the steeps among the toughest in the country. The See Forever trail (the name may not be completely accurate, but close enough) is Telluride's longest, with views of Utah from its 360-degree starting point. For the town's (and maybe America's) best freebie, take the breathtaking 12-minute ride aboard the Gondola, connecting Telluride with neighboring Mountain Village.

Outside town, the Wyndham Peaks Resort & Golden Door Spa offers unmatched views of southwest Colorado's San Juan Mountains, as well as of the hotel and spa's own 42,000-square-foot mountain enclave. The latest in lap-of-luxury comfort tempts guests to just stay in and skip the slopes, or at least to rush back happily at day's end.

WHAT: town, experience, event, hotel. **TELLURIDE:** 65 miles south of Montrose, 125 miles north of Durango, 325 miles southwest of Denver. A small airport is located 5 miles outside of town. For ski and festival information, contact Visitors' Services, tel 888-605-2578 or 970-728-3041; www.visittelluride.com.

THE PEAKS RESORT: tel 866-282-4557 or 970-728-6800, fax 970-728-6175; www.the peaksresort.com. *Cost:* doubles from $139 (low season), from $199 (high season). **BEST TIMES:** Jun–Sept for cultural events; ski season late Nov to early Apr.

America's Big Ski

VAIL

Colorado, U.S.A.

With 193 exhilarating trails crisscrossing 10 square miles (5,289 ski-able acres) of majestic, snow-draped landscape, Vail is America's largest single-mountain ski resort and one of its favorites, perfect for all levels. You can ski for a week here and never repeat a run, nor tire of the remarkable variety of terrain, which includes the legendary Back Bowls, an immense, wide-open span of snow on the mountain's south side, stretching 7 miles across at its widest. Its open space astounds most first-time arrivals, and offers varying levels of difficulty (but mostly intermediate).

There's big money, top-notch technology, and plenty of action and activity here, including the world's largest network of high-speed quad lifts on a single mountain, the world's largest ski school (with more than 850 instructors), and more than 100 restaurants and twice as many stores in its pseudo-Tyrolean pedestrian-only village, set at a base altitude of 8,120 feet.

Vail's newest addition, and the first of its kind on the American ski scene, is the Blue Sky Basin, which was designed to give the intermediate and advanced skier a back-country experience. There are no conventional trails per se, just 645 acres of gorgeous territory and virgin powder. Not enough? A comprehensive user-friendly ski ticket is also valid at Beaver Creek, Breckenridge, and Keystone, all located within a 40-mile radius and linked by shuttle service.

When Vail opened in 1962, The Lodge at Vail was built as a dormitory for resort workers, and since it was the only game in town at that point, it had first dibs on the best location: slope-side and in the heart of Vail Village. Vail now boasts some of skidom's most elegant hostelries, but top-of-the-list luxury-seekers still go to The Lodge, which long ago retooled itself as a deluxe ski-in/ski-out property, possibly one of America's ultimate ski lodges, with the old-world charm of an alpine chalet.

On a busy day, Vail averages three people per acre.

WHAT: town, experience,

hotel. **VAIL:** 100 miles west of Denver; the Vail/Eagle County Airport is 35 miles west of town. Contact Vail activities desk for general and ski information, tel 877-204-7881 or 970-476-5601; www.vail.snow.com. *When:* ski season is mid-Nov–mid-Apr. **THE LODGE AT**

VAIL: 174 E. Gore Creek Dr. Tel 877-528-7625 or 970-476-5011, fax 970-476-7425; www.lodgeatvailrockresorts.com. *Cost:* doubles from $99 (low season), from $599 (high season). **BEST TIMES:** mid-Jan–mid-Mar for optimal ski conditions; Jun–Sept for summer activities.

*The Perfect Small American Town and
Its Oldest Inn*

ESSEX

Connecticut, U.S.A.

Essex is a mint-condition one-traffic-light river town where the dignified revolutionary-era spirit still lingers—and there's not a fast food joint in sight. The town boasts some of the nation's best examples of early colonial and federal architecture, built when the town was famous and prosperous for shipbuilding, a trade that was first established here in 1645, and flourished until the advent of the railroads in the mid-1800s. On Main Street and its narrow back roads, white picket fences frame many landmark buildings that even today remain private homes, while others have been turned into antique and specialty stores.

One of the most celebrated buildings in town is the Griswold Inn, the oldest continuously operating inn in Connecticut and one of the oldest in America. First opened in 1776 (and the first three-story building constructed in the state), the Griswold's heart is its famous, must-visit Tap Room, originally the town's first schoolhouse, built in 1738 and later relocated here from across town. A potbellied stove sits at its center, and its wood-paneled walls are lined with a prodigious collection of maritime memorabilia and original Currier and Ives prints, the largest such collection in private hands today. Much of the inn's buzz (not to mention Dixieland jazz and banjo music) emanates from here, a perennial magnet for locals, riverboat folks, yachtmen from Long Island Sound, and nostalgia-seeking landlub-

bers alike. Overnighters can hang their hats in any of the handsome guest rooms; many guests stay for the weekend just to be first in line for the inn's well-known Sunday Hunt breakfast, an enormous affair said to have been initiated by the British who commandeered the inn during the War of 1812. Guests come for the table-groaning buffet (the inn's sausages are made from a historical recipe), but also for the especially inviting camaraderie that envelopes the inn and reflects the key role the Gris has long played in Essex.

WHAT: town, hotel, restaurant. **ESSEX:** 100 miles northeast of New York City, 35 miles southeast of Hartford, 20 miles southwest of Mystic. Connecticut's Heritage River Valley, tel 860-244-8181; www.enjoycentralct.com. **GRISWOLD INN:** 36 Main St. Tel 860-767-1776, fax 860-767-0481; www.griswoldinn.com. *Cost:* doubles from $99 (low season), $115 (high season). Dinner $35, Sunday Hunt breakfast $19. **BEST TIMES:** among many local holidays is the Loser's Day Parade, first Sat in May, to commemorate the unsuccessful British attack on Essex in 1814. The Griswold Inn and Essex are also particularly charming when dressed up for the Christmas holidays.

Home and Inspiration for a Beloved American Icon

THE MARK TWAIN HOUSE

Hartford, Connecticut, U.S.A.

L iterary fans come from around the world to visit the home of one of America's most famous and beloved authors, Samuel Clemens, a.k.a. Mark Twain, a pen name he derived from the term used by Mississippi River pilots to indicate a water depth of two fathoms. "To us," Twain said, "our house . . . had a heart, and a soul, and eyes to see us with. . . . It was of us, and we were in its confidence, and lived in its grace and in the peace of its benediction." Twain commissioned his custom-designed High Victorian mansion from the well-known New York architect Edward Tuckerman Potter, and lived here with his wife, Olivia (and, eventually, three daughters), from 1874 to 1891, during which period he penned some of his most acclaimed works, including *The Adventures of Tom Sawyer, The Adventures of Huckleberry Finn, The Prince and the Pauper,* and *A Connecticut Yankee in King Arthur's Court.* The beautifully restored nineteen-room mansion features decorative work by Louis Comfort Tiffany (it's one of only two remaining domestic interiors of his design in the United States) and an immense collection of nearly 10,000 Victorian-era objects. Guided tours point out personal items that belonged to Twain and his family: his beloved billiards table, where he would spread out his manuscript when editing; the three-ton Paige typesetter, an ill-fated invention in which Twain invested, leading (along with a bad investment in suspenders) to his bankruptcy; the ornately carved 19th-century master bed, purchased during travels in Italy, at whose foot Twain and Olivia would sleep so they could admire the elaborate headboard.

Directly across from the Mark Twain House is a Gothic cottage that once belonged to writer Harriet Beecher Stowe, whose antislavery novel *Uncle Tom's Cabin* is regarded as the first international bestseller. Her home, though less ambitious, is also open to the public.

WHAT: site. **WHERE:** 351 Farmington Ave. (Hartford is 110 miles northeast of New York City, 45 miles north of New Haven). Tel 860-247-0998; www.marktwainhouse.org. **COST:** admission $14, includes guided tour. **WHEN:** closed Tues during Jan–Apr and Nov. **BEST TIMES:** Christmastime, when decked out in Victorian style.

A labor of love for Twain; beloved icon of Hartford

America's Maritime Museum

MYSTIC SEAPORT

Mystic, Connecticut, U.S.A.

Mystic is one of the Northeast's most visited tourist destinations, primarily due to Mystic Seaport, the Museum of America and the Sea. America's leading maritime museum, it houses the largest collection of historic boats and ships in the world. Much of its 17-acre riverfront site is taken up by a re-created coastal village complete with a schoolhouse, church, and dozens of homes, stores, and workshops that bring salty 19th-century maritime America to life. A number of fully rigged sailing ships docked here are open for visits, among them the *Charles W. Morgan* (1841), America's last surviving wooden whaleship (complete with "blubber room"), and the 1882 Danish vessel *Joseph Conrad*. The Seaport's most ambitious exhibit ever, "Voyages: Stories of America and the Sea," examines our nation's connection to its oceans, rivers, and lakes. The area's other major site, the important Mystic Aquarium and Institute for Exploration, offers more than forty live exhibits of sea life, including more than 4,000 specimens and the 1-acre "Alaska Coast,"

one of the world's largest beluga whale exhibits.

Take to the hills for a sweeping view of the harbor (and crowds), and follow privacy-seeking Lauren Bacall and Humphrey Bogart to The Inn at Mystic: The couple honeymooned here in what is now The Inn's main house, a regal Colonial Revival mansion built in 1904. A new annex has increased the number of rooms, all enjoying the same acclaimed kitchen and lovely views of the Long Island Sound, but hold out for the more atmospheric rooms of the original main house.

WHAT: town, site, hotel. **MYSTIC:** 127 miles northeast of New York City, 47 miles southeast of Hartford. **MYSTIC SEAPORT:** 75 Greenmanville Ave. (Rte. 27). Tel 888-973-2767 or 860-572-5315; www.mysticseaport.org. *Cost:* admission $24. **MYSTIC AQUARIUM:** 55 Coogan Blvd. Tel 860-572-5955; www.mysticaquarium.org. *Cost:* admission $26. **THE INN AT MYSTIC:** junction of Routes 1 and 27. Tel 800-237-2415 or 860-536-9604; www.innatmystic.com. *Cost:* doubles with fireplace and Jacuzzi from $115 (low season), from $195 (high season). **BEST TIMES:** May for Lobster Fest; Jun for Sea Music Festival; the 5-day Antique and Classic Wooden Boat Rendezvous late Jun; Chowder Fest, Columbus Day weekend; Lantern Light Evening Tours, during the Christmas holidays.

Handling the sails of the Charles W. Morgan

Preserved Colonial Architecture and Beauty, a Gift of Nature

LITCHFIELD HILLS AND THE MAYFLOWER INN

Connecticut, U.S.A.

The notion that quintessential New England is an endless drive from the urban chaos of New York City is dispelled upon approaching the Litchfield Hills, a bucolic, 1,000-square-mile horse-breeding enclave

tucked into the foothills of the Berkshire Mountains in northwestern Connecticut. Unfolding beyond every bend of the area's meandering roads is a classic Currier and Ives landscape of 18th- and 19th-century saltbox farmhouses, red barns, imposing white clapboard mansions, stone walls, and quiet lakes (including Bantam Lake, the largest natural lake in the state). Charming, picturesque hamlets and towns dot the area, with steepled Congregational churches rising next to tidy, emerald green town squares. Litchfield, Norfolk, and Salisbury are particular standouts in this regard.

Antiques hunters should head for Woodbury (known as Connecticut's antiquing capital) and its quiet and charming neighbors, Kent and New Preston. In nearby Washington, in the vicinity of the slender 5-mile long Lake Waramaug ("good fishing place"), the elegant 1894 Mayflower Inn is justifiably known as one of New England's most opulent, with spacious interiors filled to the rafters with English and French antiques (and prices to match). The inn began life as a private boys' school, and sits on grounds

crisscrossed with well-groomed trails and streams. Meals are memorable, romantic, and surprisingly unfussy. Expect the freshest and purest of the area's bounty: think game, freshwater trout, and the season's tastiest vegetables, as interpreted by the inn's expert chef. For dessert there are sweet dreams in four-

Litchfield Hills' historic communities are connected by scenic byways.

poster featherbeds with Frette linens, and the promise of tomorrow's sumptuous breakfast. In an area endowed with many gracious country inns, this one's the tops.

WHAT: site, hotel, restaurant. **LITCHFIELD HILLS:** 66 miles west of Hartford, 110 miles north of New York City. Litchfield Visitors Bureau, tel 860-567-4506; www.litchfieldhills.com. **MAYFLOWER INN:** 118 Woodbury Rd./Route 47, Washington. Tel 860-868-9466, fax 860-868-1497; www.mayflowerinn.com. *Cost:* doubles from $550 (year-round). Dinner $50.

BEST TIMES: weekends from mid-Mar–Dec for The Elephant's Trunk Bazaar, billed as New England's largest outdoor flea market, held every Sun in nearby New Milford, 20 minutes from the inn. For info tel 860-355-1448.

A Celebration of One Man's Taste:
His Gift to America

WINTERTHUR MUSEUM

Winterthur, Delaware, U.S.A.

Take one relatively modest twelve-room du Pont family home in the lush Brandywine Valley, massively increase its size, add the artistic passion and altruistic vision of its last owner, Henry Francis du Pont (1880–1969), and you wind up with the world's premier museum of 17th- through 19th-century American antiques and decorative arts. Opened officially in 1951, the connoisseur's obsessive collection of more than 60,000 items (later acquisitions have brought the figure to nearly 85,000) range from silverware to spiral staircases, from furniture to almost 200 period rooms and galleries, most of which you can visit in the company of exceptionally knowledgeable guides, on various "theme" tours.

The estate's garden, however, was H. F. du Pont's first love: Well before he began to collect, he was a passionate gardener, and today some 60 of the estate's remaining 979 acres (down from 2,500 at its height in the early 20th century) are given over to magnificent naturalistic gardens planted with native and exotic plants. The gardens are located close to the museum, and are accessible via the Garden Tram. Insatiable garden-lovers should take a trip just across the Pennsylvania border to Kennett Square and the Longwood estate's more formal and refined 1,000-acre gardens, the fancy of H. F.'s cousin Pierre S. du Pont. Overnight visitors can also give Pierre a nod of thanks for the gilded, Italianate Hotel du Pont, which he opened in 1913 in nearby Wilmington as grand lodging for his family's visiting business guests. A paean to European craftsmanship, this gracious Renaissance palazzo evokes the captains-of-industry era and the du Ponts' penchant for collecting: More than 700 original paintings hung throughout the hotel capture the rural beauty of their beloved Brandywine Valley.

WHAT: site, hotel. **WINTERTHUR:** 6 miles northwest of Wilmington on Route 52, 36 miles southwest of Philadelphia. Tel 800-448-3883 or 302-888-4600; www.winterthur.org. *Cost:* admission $18. **LONGWOOD GARDENS:** Route 1, Kennett Square, PA. Tel 800-737-5500 or 610-388-1000; www.longwoodgardens.org. *Cost:* admission $16. **HOTEL DU PONT:** 11th and Market Sts., Wilmington (a 20-minute drive from Winterthur). Tel 800-441-9019 or 302-594-3100, fax 302-594-3108; www.hoteldupont.com. *Cost:* doubles from $159 (low season), $259 (high season). **BEST TIMES:** the Winterthur Point-to-Point Steeplechase Races take place every May on the Sun of the 1st full weekend; the Azalea Woods generally peak on or around Mother's Day weekend.

Bypassed by Time, Sweetened by Modern-Day Luxury

AMELIA ISLAND

Florida, U.S.A.

O n tiny Amelia Island, the past and present coexist in a very unusual way. At its northern end, Fernandina Beach, the island's only town, revolves lazily around a fifty-block nucleus that is listed in the National Register

of Historic Places, and features some of the nation's finest examples of Queen Anne, Victorian, and Italianate mansions. In total, more than 450 historic buildings were built here before 1927, testimony of the island's glory days when it played vacation home to wintering socialites with names like Goodyear, Pulitzer, and Carnegie. The cobbled (and aptly named) Centre Street is the island's most appealing stretch, lined with galleries, bed-and-breakfasts, and turn-of-the-century eateries, and is reason-

The Ritz-Carlton sprawls along Amelia's east coast.

ably free of tourist kitsch. The wonderfully atmospheric Palace Saloon stands along this street; built in 1878, it bills itself as Florida's oldest watering hole and is still a perennial favorite with local fishermen and visiting golfers alike. It's one of the town's unofficial headquarters during the yearly Shrimp Festival, the island's biggest and most enjoyable event.

The 13-mile long island is one of the few places left in Florida where you can still ride horseback on the beach—an exhilarating experience of wind, surf, and ospreys. One of the choicest and most pristine stretches of beach belongs to The Ritz-Carlton, Amelia Island, whose guest rooms all enjoy enviable views and perfect sunrises. Considered by many to be one of the finest resorts in the South, The Ritz-Carlton offers golf, tennis, Southern hospitality,

and exceptional dining in its award-winning restaurant, The Grill, proving that Amelia Island is, once again, the ultimate playground for island lovers with cash to spare.

WHAT: island, town, hotel. **AMELIA ISLAND:** 25 miles north of Jacksonville International Airport, 105 miles south of Savannah, Georgia. Amelia Island Tourism Development Council, tel 800-2-AMELIA; www.ameliaisland.org. **THE RITZ-CARLTON, AMELIA ISLAND:** 4750 Amelia Island Parkway. Tel 800-241-3333 or 904-277-1100, fax 904-261-9063; www.ritzcarlton.com. *Cost:* oceanfront doubles from $259 (low season), from $399 (high season). Dinner at The Grill $70. **BEST TIMES:** for beach fun, spring, summer, and fall; for golf and tennis, spring, fall, and winter; the Shrimp Festival is held on the 1st weekend of May.

A Window on History, a Glimpse of the Future

KENNEDY SPACE CENTER

Cape Canaveral, Florida, U.S.A.

Even the most blasé visitors become transfixed with pride and patriotism at Kennedy Space Center, a living monument to America's indomitable will and technological prowess. Set amid 150,000 acres of marshland and mangrove swamps, this has been the headquarters of American rocketry and space exploration since 1950, when Bumper 8 was launched from the Cape. This is where Alan Shepard lifted off in 1961 to became the first American to be sent into space, where the first men left for the moon in July 1969 aboard Apollo 11, and where the crew of the ill-fated Space Shuttle *Columbia* left the Earth in January 2002. Security is a lot tighter now than before September 11, with more sensitive areas off-limits to the public, but there is still plenty to be seen and experienced through multi-media shows, hands-on experiences, and a Q & A with a real live astronaut that leaves adults and kids alike galvanized to strive for excellence. Begin at the Visitors Complex, where the Rocket Garden traces the evolution of America's space program, featuring eight authentic rockets including a Mercury Atlas, similar to the one used to launch John Glenn into space in 1962. At the other end of the plaza, twin IMAX 3-D theaters with six-story screens and seat-shaking sound systems immerse audiences in the exhilaration of a true journey of discovery, while a mock-up of the space shuttle sits near the launch control center where you can attend talks on current missions.

From the complex, grab a narrated bus tour that passes by the world-famous LC-39 launch pad and on to the Apollo/Saturn V Center to experience a narrated simulation of the Apollo 8 launch and marvel at a 363-foot Saturn V moon rocket, the most powerful ever built. Top off your adrenaline high with a visit to the Astronaut Hall of Fame, 6 miles west,

Despite two major shuttle tragedies, the United States space program continues to be a source of pride for many Americans.

where astronaut wannabes can buckle up in a G-force simulator, a space-station shuttle simulator that flips you 360 degrees, and a simulator that mimics the moon's light gravity—thrill rides that are the only thing the Kennedy Space Center lacks.

WHAT: site. **WHERE:** 45 miles east of Orlando, 220 miles north of Miami. Tel 321-449-4444; www.kennedyspacecenter.com. **COST:** admission \$38 (Astronaut Hall of Fame separate admission \$17.). **BEST TIMES:** to see a Space Shuttle launch, go to www.ksc.nasa.gov and click on "Next Shuttle Launch" for an update.

A Face-to-Face Encounter with Pseudo-Mythical Creatures

SWIMMING WITH MANATEES

Crystal River, Florida, U.S.A.

Gentle and endearingly playful, with puppy-dog faces attached to 2,000-pound potato-sack bodies that only their mothers could love, manatees (a.k.a. West Indian sea cows or *Sirenia*, "sirens") were often mistaken for

mermaids by ancient sailors—who presumably liked their mermaids plus-plus Rubenesque. Graceful and wonderfully charismatic, they're known to nudge and nuzzle their snorkeling visitors, and in recent decades have become a major cause célèbre, with their status on the critically endangered list focusing worldwide attention on them as never before.

The U.S. population of some 3,000 manatees lives almost exclusively in the warm-water bays, estuaries, and rivers of Florida's eastern and western coasts, wintering particularly in Citrus County, in the west-central part of the state. This is the only place in the world where you can have a face-to-face encounter with these gray-blue marine mammals. A number of outfitters in the small city of Crystal River equip visitors with snorkeling equipment (scuba diving is not permitted, nor is it necessary in these shallow waters) and provide a boat trip to nearby Kings Bay, where 100 to 250 of the area's population of about 400 tend to be on hand.

Federal laws prohibit certain behavior: snorkelers cannot pursue the animals, for instance, but must wait for the manatees to approach on their own—which they almost always do.

WHAT: experience. **WHERE:** 80 miles west of Orlando, 95 miles north of Tampa. **HOW:** Crystal Lodge Dive Center (located at the Best Western Hotel), 525 N.W. 7th Ave. Tel 352-795-6798, fax 352-795-9510; www.manatee-central.com. *Cost:* $32, includes all equipment. **BEST TIMES:** Nov–Feb; best time of day is 8 A.M.–noon, when the water is clear.

Manatees spend up to twelve hours per day resting.

America's Big Swamp

EVERGLADES NATIONAL PARK

Florida, U.S.A.

Nature lovers and the eco-curious will have a field day in the largest protected wetlands in the United States. The Everglades is a 1.5 million-acre subtropical freshwater marshland and the third largest national park in the lower forty-eight states after Death Valley and Yellowstone. Conveniently located down at Florida's southern tip, in Miami's backyard though atmospherically a million miles from South Beach, this is Florida as it existed before the Spanish explorers—or man in general—arrived. Half land and half water, the Everglades is a complex and fragile ecosystem, an endangered home to thousands of animal, bird, and plant species, a land full of tangled mangrove thickets crisscrossed by shallow, labyrinthine channels with names like Shark River, Hells Bay, Graveyard Creek, and Lostmans River. Wooden walkways, bicycle trails, and airboats (the latter not allowed within the park proper) give a glimpse of the peripheral marshland's flora and fauna, but penetration of the Everglades' mystery and history is best accomplished by kayak or canoe, ideally in the company of a guide.

Informative naturalists point out the park's residents—manatees, ibis, egrets, ospreys, bald eagles, alligators, turtles, more than fourteen native species of snakes, and, if you're exceedingly lucky, one of the ten remaining Florida panthers that reside in the park. Bird-watching can be outstanding when the winter's migratory guests swell the park's usual community of 347 species, and plant fanciers have more than

1,000 species to study beyond the ubiquitous sawgrass, so common here that the area is often referred to as the "river of grass." The beautiful, constantly shifting light across the Everglades landscape is quite unlike anything else, underscoring its endangered fragility.

WHAT: site, experience. **WHERE:** the 2 main entrances are both approximately 40 miles from downtown Miami: one 10 miles west of Homestead/Florida City, and the other (Shark Valley) along U.S. 41/Tamiami Trail. Closest to Naples is the park's western entrance, on Highway 29 in Everglades City. For general information, tel 305-242-7700; www.nps.gov/ever. **COST:** park admission $10 per car. **HOW:** North American Canoe Tours outfits visitors with canoes and kayaks for do-it-yourself tours or arranged adventures ranging from 1–14 nights, with accompanying guides. Tel 239-695-3299, fax 239-695-4155; www.evergladesadventures. com. *Cost:* $35 a day canoe rental, $45+ a day kayak rental; from $119 per person for 1-day guided canoe/kayak trip (min. 4 people); overnight guided trips starting at $500 per person (min. 4 people). **WHEN:** park open year-round; outfitter operates Oct–May. **BEST TIMES:** Jan–Mar, when the climate is comfortable, the bugs minimal, and the wildlife is abundant. Unfortunately, these are also the most crowded months.

The Charm and Color of America's Last Resort

KEY WEST

Florida, U.S.A.

D angling at the end of a 113-mile, 42-bridge ocean-skimming highway that tethers 51 of the 822 Florida keys to the mainland, Key West is famously billed as the southernmost point of the continental United States, and

enjoys its reputation as an eccentric, wacky, barefoot and carefree bohemian island town. It's a tropical melting pot of Caribbean, Latin American, and U.S. culture, populated by locals (known as "Conches"), writers, artists, retirees,

and a large gay community, all living in restored, Bahamian-influenced pastel Victorian homes or quaint, white-framed "Conch" cottages. Many eschew cars in favor of bicycles or foot power, as the island is flat coral-rock and small, easy to navigate by either means. Almost daily (at least in high season), the island's population is swelled by cruise ship passengers, who descend in the thousands in search of the requisite drink at the legendary Sloppy Joe's on mile-long Duval Street, which starts at the Atlantic Ocean and ends at the Gulf of Mexico.

Those who escape Duval Street's cavalcade of tourist tchotchke shops can find a more historical Key West at Hemingway House, where during a quiet moment you can still sense the aura of the Nobel Prize–winning author, who came to Key West in the 1930s, succumbed to its charm, and spent the next decade writing, drinking, and fishing prolifically. Papa helped put the island on the map as a quintessential party town where the margarita is the national drink and the attitude is anything goes. Soak up the atmosphere at the outdoor picnic tables at Schooner Wharf during the sunset cocktail hour, when patrons, local and tourist alike, contemplate the gorgeous sky, a unique Key West finger painting the color of coral. Those wanting a bit of pagan hoopla with their sunset can head for Mallory Square pier, where the daily sunset-watching ritual is augmented by a cast of jugglers, fire-eaters, and buskers.

For an oasis of civility at the end of a loopy day, book a room at the Gardens Hotel, named for the passion of former owner Peggy Mills, who from 1930 until her death in 1979 chose the living garden as an art form, and as her own private paradise and life's work. If not for the meandering footpaths of centuries-old bricks from Cuba and Central America (once used as ballast for sea-going galleons), one could get lost in the otherworldly beauty of the bougainvillea, orchids, and ferns blooming beneath a verdant canopy of hardwoods and palms. The restored, two-story, West Indian plantation-style main building (the former home of the original owner, dating from 1870) as well as two similarly styled new buildings hide behind thick walls in the heart of Key West's historic Old Town district. While salsa and reggae spill out of the bars that line Duval Street just a few steps beyond the front gates, the only music within is the rhythmic splashing of the fountains, the lazy whir of a ceiling fan, and birdsong. This is music to enjoy breakfast by, on the open-air brick porch where Key lime beignets almost steal the show.

WHAT: island, hotel. **KEY WEST:** 155 miles southwest of Miami. Tourist info: tel 800-FLA-KEYS; www.fla-keys.com. **THE GARDENS HOTEL:** 526 Angela St. Tel 800-526-2664 or 305-294-2661, fax 305-292-1007; reservations@gardenshotel.com; www.gardens hotel.com. *Cost:* doubles from $165 (low season), from $295 (high season). **BEST TIMES:** Nov–Easter. Fantasy Fest (www.fantasyfest. net) is 10 days of masquerading and fairs at the end of Oct, culminating with the Grand Parade the final Sat.

A Sybaritic South Seas Fantasy

LITTLE PALM ISLAND

Little Torch Key, Florida, U.S.A.

Sometimes you just don't have time to fly to the South Pacific. But when the pressing need for a shot of Robinson-Crusoe-goes-tropical calls, the Gauguin-like experience of Little Palm Island fulfills all expectations. A sleek

1930s-style motor launch brings guests to the hotel's private 5-acre island in the lower

Florida Keys, where the first impression is one of exotic perfection. There are fourteen thatched-roof bungalows, sitting on stilts and shaded by rustling palm trees, populated by an international mix of pampered guests lolling in rope hammocks or scattered about the rare-for-the-Keys sandy white beaches like so many washed up sea shells. The tropic-style accommodations are rustic (there are outdoor showers) but grand (indoor bathrooms have Jacuzzis), and TVs and telephones are purposefully absent to help guests get away

The island is accessible only by boat or seaplane.

with getting away. Little Palm Island is a special place, and it's not hard to imagine it as it was until the 1960s: an elite fishing camp favored by Presidents Roosevelt, Truman, and Kennedy, among others. The hotel will gladly arrange a number of interesting off-island excursions, like a day trip to historic and picturesque Key West or nearby Looe Key National Marine Sanctuary, where snorkelers and divers can explore the last living coral reef in North America. There are plenty of other activities available, but most guests choose to do nothing more than indulge in sacred inactivity, nursing a Rumrunner or Gumby Slumber and watching another Technicolor sunset while awaiting the next remarkable meal.

WHAT: island, hotel. **WHERE:** 120 miles southwest of Miami, 29 miles northeast of Key West. Launch departs from Little Torch Key. Tel 800-3-GET LOST or 305-515-4004, fax 305-872-4843; reservations@littlepalmisland.com, www.littlepalmisland.com. **COST:** doubles from $595 (low season), from $1,690 (high season); includes boat transfer from Little Torch Key, beach and watercraft amenities (meals extra). **BEST TIMES:** Jan–May for weather; Jun–Oct for fishing.

Perennial Hot Spot for Miami's Glamour Scene

THE DELANO

Miami Beach, Florida, U.S.A.

The dust has long settled since Miami's 1990s explosion of designer-hotel openings and renovations, but today the boldly stylish trailblazer of the lot, the Delano, still percolates at the epicenter of Miami's social scene.

Opened in 1995, the yin-yang collaboration of hotelier Ian Schrager and designer Philippe Starck immediately attracted the style-conscious of the world to this spare, all-white, tropical 1947 oceanfront landmark (named after President Franklin Delano Roosevelt in the patriotic spirit of that postwar time). To

see why, enter the movie-set–worthy dark-wood lobby through 30-foot diaphanous white curtains and prepare for your jaw to drop. Designed in a manner even minimalists would consider minimalist, the hotel possesses an elegant simplicity full of surreal twists and turns, all of it both refreshing and confounding

Delano's unique pool and "water salon"

to its roster of international fashionables or anyone fed up with the neighborhood's ubiquitous Art Deco theme. The style is carried over to the white and light guest rooms, but emphasis is on the public areas—the lobbies, restaurants, and bars. The fantasy swimming pool is the cool-pool of choice in South Beach and one of the hotel world's most famous, with classical music piped in underwater and café chairs and tables set up in the ankle-shallow end. And even now that Madonna is no longer a partner, the casually formal Blue Door restaurant is still a coveted booking.

WHAT: hotel, restaurant. **WHERE:** 1685 Collins Ave. Tel 800-697-1791 or 305-672-2000, fax 305-532-0099; delano@ianschrager hotels.com; www.delanohotel.com. **COST:** doubles from $345 (low season), from $655 (high season); full oceanfront view from $475 (low season), from $865 (high season). Dinner at Blue Door $80. **BEST TIMES:** Jan–Apr for the best weather.

A South Beach Institution

JOE'S STONE CRAB

Miami Beach, Florida, U.S.A.

"**B**efore SoBe, Joe be," touts Miami Beach's (and possibly the nation's) number-one crab institution, referring to its decades of renown prior to the rebirth of its trendy neighborhood, South Beach. Word spread quickly when the family-run place first opened in 1913, and the line to get in has been long ever since. On the menu, the stone crab: A delicacy of sweet meat that is as much a symbol of Miami as the palm tree or the state seal, and especially delectable because of its limited-season availability (mid-October to mid-May). At Joe's, they come in four different sizes (from medium to jumbo) and the standard order is an imposing mound of crabs, served with drawn butter or a piquant and creamy mustard sauce, coleslaw, creamed spinach, and cottage-fried sweet potatoes. For dessert, the Key lime pie is the real thing. Freshness and quality are paramount, but if you can't indulge in person, Joe's will FedEx you your fix, overnight. That helps explain why they sell about 200 tons during the average crab season, with 1 ton alone served on a good day in the 450-seat indoor restaurant, manned by a formally attired staff. Tender and sweet, Joe's crabs aren't cheap, even though they come from local waters—Damon Runyon once said they were sold by the karat. Go anyway and find out what all the hype is about—but be prepared to wait.

WHAT: restaurant. **WHERE:** 11 Washington Ave. Tel 305-673-0365, fax 305-673-0295; to place a shipping order, call 800-780-2722; for take-out, 305-673-4611; www.joesstonecrab.com. **COST:** dinner $60. **WHEN:** mid-Oct to mid-May. **BEST TIMES:** lines tend to be shortest around 5 P.M.

Art Deco Darling on the American Riviera

SOUTH BEACH

Miami Beach, Florida, U.S.A.

As Miami continues to nurture its role as an international crossroads, the hot-spot neighborhood of South Beach remains its vibrant, glamorous, multicultural core, open 24/7. Much of the neighborhood's visual allure derives from palm-lined Ocean Drive, along whose length (from 5th to 21st Streets and east to Alton Road) lies the largest concentration of tropical Art Deco architecture in the world, some 800 pastel treasures from the 1920s, 1930s, and 1940s. Now listed on the National Register of Historic Places, this electric concoction of teal, lavender, pink, and peach buildings houses outdoor cafés, shops, nightspots, condominium apartments, chic hotels, and world-class restaurants, but the real artwork here is the parade of people. If all the world is a stage, Ocean Drive is its casting

One of South Beach's many Art Deco hotels

couch, its sidewalks and eating places fairly choked with alarmingly good-looking people. It's all best appreciated from Ocean Drive's Café Cardozo (in the Cardozo Hotel at 13th and Ocean Drive), a kind of 24-hour reviewing stand that allows you to step out of the path of the year-round tourist crush and take in the sights.

To really escape the rollerbladers, buffer-than-thou poseurs, and Euro invaders, retreat to the cool oasis of the ultra-hip but classy Tides Hotel, a Deco queen from 1936. All of its oversize seaward-facing rooms are done in a quiet, good-taste style and have telescopes for "beach combing." The Tides's small but excellent lobby-level restaurant, La Marea is a total scene-and-cuisine experience.

WHAT: site, hotel, restaurant. **SOUTH BEACH:** at the southern end of Miami Beach, which is comprised of 17 islands in Biscayne Bay off the east coast of downtown Miami, a separate city. **ART DECO DISTRICT:** 90-minute guided walking tours of the Art Deco District are offered by the Miami Design Preservation League at the Art Deco Welcome Center, 1001 Ocean Drive. Tel 305-531-3484; www.mdpl.org. *Cost:* $20 per person. **THE TIDES HOTEL:** 1220 Ocean Dr. Tel 800-439-4095 or 305-604-5070, fax 305-503-3275; www.tidessouthbeach.com. *Cost:* doubles from $395 (low season), from $695 (high season). Dinner at La Marea $50. **BEST TIMES:** 2d weekend in Jan for annual Art Deco Weekend, with films, lectures, music, and street fairs. Contact the MDPL, above, for information.

A Grand Winter Escape, Italian Style

VILLA VIZCAYA

Miami, Florida, U.S.A.

Sometimes called the "Hearst Castle of the East," the Italian Renaissance–style Villa Vizcaya was completed in 1916 as the extravagant wintertime retreat of Chicago industrialist James Deering, known for his deep pockets

and keen European sensibility. A thousand continental artisans labored for five years to create the estate and its world-famous bayfront gardens in then-undeveloped Miami (whose population at the time was less than 10,000), incorporating a rich collection of antique doors, gates, paneling, ceilings, fireplaces, and decorative arts brought home from Europe by the owner and his architects. Deering's fascination with 15th- through 18th-century art and architecture is obvious in every detail of the lavish mansion, forty-two of whose seventy rooms are open to the public. It's a remarkable paean to late Renaissance architecture, authentic enough to convince visitors that it's been standing here overlooking Biscayne Bay for 400 years.

Of Vizcaya's current 28 acres (all that remains of the original 180), 10 are dedicated to formal gardens planned by Deering's Florentine-educated landscape artist. Adaptations were made to accommodate South Florida's brilliant

Italianate luxury on Biscayne Bay

light and subtropical climate, but the stone fountains, grottoes, statuary, and plant life still evoke a Mediterranean grandeur of centuries past and make a favorite spot for wedding photos. The waterfront teahouse, with its little footbridge, is a traditional proposal spot.

WHAT: site. **WHERE:** 3251 S. Miami Ave., 5 minutes south of downtown Miami in Coconut Grove. Tel 305-250-9133, fax 305-285-2004; www.vizcayamuseum.com. **COST:** admission to villa and gardens $15. **BEST TIMES:** Jun–Sept for flowering plants.

The Most Popular Resort Destination on Earth

WALT DISNEY WORLD RESORT

Orlando, Florida, U.S.A.

Still the pacesetter for theme parks around the globe, the brainchild of entertainment giant and genius animator Walt Disney is an ever-expanding universe of make-believe and escapism, celebrating magic, technology, nature, and, of course, Mickey Mouse. In the 30-plus years since it opened its doors, the 30,000-acre former cow pasture has developed into four distinct main theme parks, each of which nurtures its own personality. The Magic Kingdom (opened in 1971), the lighthearted fantasy world that revolves around Cinderella's Castle, is home to two of Disney World's most famous (and very different) attractions: It's a Small World and Space Mountain. Epcot (1982), the Experimental Prototype Community of Tomorrow, is an educational theme park where thrills are mostly of the mind, with attractions such as the very popular Spaceship Earth. At Disney-MGM Studios (1989), visitors walk right onto a "Hollywood that never was and always will be" movie set that blends nostalgia with high-tech wonders (don't miss the Twilight Zone Tower of Terror). The 500-acre Disney's Animal Kingdom (1998) is Disney World's largest and newest theme park, with more than 1,000 animals (from giraffes to lions) roaming in a natural, Serengeti-like setting. Three themed water parks fill out the Worldly options.

There are countless less expensive (and less fantastical) hotel options in the Orlando area, but make the magic last by staying in one of the Disney-owned and -run hotel/

resorts. The benefits are numerous, including sheer logistics: They're close to the principal attractions and are linked by complimentary boats, buses, or monorail. Of Disney's luxury options, the re-created gabled vintage of the Victorian-style Disney's Grand Floridian Resort and Spa is one of the most elegant and least contemporary in atmosphere, evoking the breezy days of a turn-of-the-century summer resort.

WHAT: site, hotel. **WALT DISNEY WORLD:** 45 minutes from Orlando International Airport. For general park and lodging information, tel 407-939-6244; www.disneyworld.com. *Cost:* 1-day tickets $75 adults, $63 children; 4-, 5-, 6- or 7-day passes (admission to water parks separate), $216–$224 adults, $184–$189 children. **DISNEY'S GRAND FLORIDIAN RESORT AND SPA:** on the Seven Seas Lagoon. Tel 407-824-3000, fax 407-824-3186; www.disneyworld.com. *Cost:* doubles from $399 (low season), from $550 (high season). **BEST TIMES:** the greatest numbers descend during any school holiday (Thanksgiving is less busy than Christmas) and summer vacation; slowest months are Jan and Sept–Nov; early morning arrival means beating the midafternoon crush.

Medici Pleasure Palace by the Sea

THE BREAKERS

Palm Beach, Florida, U.S.A.

"**E**urope is a place where people come from," wrote Henry Morrison Flagler more than 100 years ago. "Nobody should actually go there." The self-made American developer, railroad magnate, oil baron,

and partner of John D. Rockefeller in the creation of Standard Oil, built the magnificent Breakers in 1896, importing master European artisans to create his twin-towered, Medici villa–inspired extravaganza. Today, the ultra-affluent enclave of Palm Beach has other

top-drawer mega-resorts to be sure, but the 140-acre Breakers was the first to envision Florida's then wild and alligator-infested swamplands as the playground destination of choice for the North's most socially prominent families. Rebuilt after a fire in 1926, it is possibly the most remarkable beachfront hotel on the eastern seaboard, having secured its priceless sliver of real estate way back when competition was nonexistent. A heroic $145-million lily-gilding renovation has recently put it back on the map. Vaulted ceilings, frescoes,

Originally called the Palm Beach Inn, the hotel was renamed when guests began to request rooms "down by the breakers."

Venetian chandeliers, 15th-century Flemish tapestries, and a friendly, snap-to staff of 1,300 combine with a cool Floridian palette of seafoam greens, aqua, and seashell pinks to create the ultimate warm-weather resort. Gorgeously manicured, fountain-splashed grounds are shaded by more than 3,000 regal palms (representing thirty species) and include two 18-hole golf courses (one of which was Florida's first) and twenty-one Har-Tru tennis courts. Meandering pathways lead down to a half-mile of private beach, the breezy location of the hotel's Beach Club and Mediterranean-style 20,000-square foot indoor/outdoor spa.

WHAT: hotel. **WHERE:** 1 South County Road, 70 miles north of Miami. Tel 888-BREAKERS or 561-655-6611, fax 561-655-3577; www.thebreakers.com. **COST:** doubles from $320 (low season), from $630 (high season); full oceanfront/ocean-view doubles from $540 (low season), from $1,250 (high season). **BEST TIMES:** Nov–May.

Bonanza Beaches for the Shell Happy

SANIBEL AND CAPTIVA ISLANDS

Florida, U.S.A.

Linked in name and image—and in real life, by a bridge—Sanibel and Captiva are part of the hundred littoral islands basking in the sun off the west coast of Florida in the Gulf of Mexico. They share a reputation as one

of the world's best shelling locales, with palm-stenciled sunsets, tarpon fishing that's unparalleled in North America, and what is left of laid-back Old Florida. This may be the only warm-weather vacation spot where tourists pray for a storm, since a good northwest wind will fill the sandy white beaches with shells from some of the 400 species of marine life that have made

these two small islands world-class treasure troves. So eager have the shell-happy been that taking live shells away is now banned. But shell collectors doing the "Sanibel Stoop" or "Captiva Crouch" at low tide are welcome to claim uninhabited shells, such as angel's wings, jewel boxes, king's crowns, or lion's paws, although many choose to leave their finds behind, explaining it's the memories they enjoy collecting, not the shells themselves. The island's shell culture culminates with Sanibel's Bailey-Matthews Shell Museum, the only museum in the country dedicated solely to shells.

Those bothering to look up will find further confirmation that nature is king at Sanibel's J. N. "Ding" Darling National Wildlife Refuge, where foot- and bicycle trails and kayak and canoe routes crisscross the nearly 7,000-acre preserve; this is bird-watching at its finest.

A young shell hunter

If you're not feeling detached enough from the mainland and its everyday demands, visit Captiva and Sanibel's three most interesting neighbors in Pine Island Sound, car-free islands accessible only by boat. Cayo Costa State Park is an uninhabited barefoot Eden with deserted beaches whose shelling is arguably the best around. Cabbage Key, a 100-acre, down-home, real-life Margaritaville, is said to have inspired Jimmy Buffett's classic "Cheeseburger in Paradise." And genteel turn-of-the-century-looking Useppa Island is a Gatsby-esque (and

privately owned) enclave that was once the refuge of Teddy Roosevelt and his tarpon-fishing friends, and today warmly welcomes day-trippers and overnighters for excellent seafood lunches at the Collier Inn. Catch-and-release tarpon fishing originated here, though today the capital of the sport is nearby Boca Grande (on what is sometimes referred to as Gasparilla Island).

WHAT: island, site, hotel. **SANIBEL AND CAPTIVA ISLANDS:** linked by a causeway to Fort Myers and the mainland, 135 miles south of Tampa, 150 northwest of Miami. For general information, contact Lee County Visitor Bureau, tel 800-237-6449; www.leeislandcoast.com. **BAILEY-MATTHEWS SHELL MUSEUM:** 3075 Sanibel-Captiva Rd, Sanibel Island. Tel 239-395-2233; www.shellmuseum.org. **J. N. "DING" DARLING NATIONAL WILDLIFE REFUGE:** 1 Wildlife Dr., Sanibel. Tel 239-472-1100; dingdarling.fws.gov. *Cost:* $5 per car. **COLLIER INN:** tel 239-283-1061, fax 239-283-0290; www.useppa.com. *Cost:* doubles from $165 (low season), from $195 (high season). Dinner $35. **BEST TIMES:** Nov–May for weather and bird-watching; any time during low tide after a storm for shelling; May through mid-Jul for tarpon season. Best to avoid hurricane season, Jun–Oct.

The Queen of New Southern Cooking

ELIZABETH ON 37TH

Savannah, Georgia, U.S.A.

Elizabeth (a.k.a. "Miz Terry's place") has been Savannah's most famous restaurant since it opened in 1981. Housed in an elegant turn-of-the-century Beaux Arts mansion on the periphery of the Historic District, the taste-

fully decorated restaurant blends in with its Victorian neighbors, as impressive visually as its dining experience is gastronomically. In 1995, executive chef Elizabeth Terry was voted as the best chef in the Southeast by

the James Beard Foundation, and in the years since she's continued to thrill loyalists with her refined interpretation of classic, old-fashioned Southern recipes, favoring fresh seafood from along the coast and herbs from her own garden. She modestly calls her creations "comfort food," something of an understatement for dishes such as grouper Celeste with a crisp sesame-almond crust served with peanut sauce, and Savannah red rice with local shrimp and clams, spicy sausage, and grilled okra.

If by some error in judgment you don't make it to Elizabeth's for dinner, join those who stop by just for the sumptuous and imposing desserts. Savannah cream cake is Elizabeth's version of trifle—angel food cake, sherry, and cream with berry sauce. There's also a wonderful peach and blueberry cobbler topped with shortbread. The dessert-and-coffee scene is Savannah's very own *dolce*

vita. Elizabeth's husband, Michael Terry (who will also answer to "Mr. Elizabeth"), long ago gave up a challenging legal career to help navigate his wife's talent and fame, while happily nurturing his own passion for the grape. In 1998, the couple took on brothers Gary and Greg Butch (both longtime employees) as business partners; ask either for an unerring wine recommendation.

WHAT: restaurant. **WHERE:** 105 E. 37th St. Tel 912-236-5547, fax 912-232-1095; www.elizabethon37th.net. **COST:** dinner $50, 7-course tasting menu $70. **WHEN:** daily, dinner only. **BEST TIMES:** reserve a table on Sun for a quieter pace; weekends are booked weeks in advance.

Quintessential Comfort Food

MRS. WILKES'S BOARDING HOUSE

Savannah, Georgia, U.S.A.

There's no sign outside this venerable institution, but that doesn't stop the lines forming every morning at 10:45. When the lunch bell rings at 11:30, the hungry crowd shuffles inside to fill large communal tables, which soon

disappear under the brimming family-style platters and bowls of Georgia's heartiest all-you-can-eat feast—a rare culinary holdout from an era that Savannahians hold dear. Mrs. Wilkes opened the place in 1943 and presided over it for almost 60 years (she died in the fall of 2002). Today it's run by three generations of her comfort-food-savvy family, serving old-time traditional favorites that are as unpretentious as the restaurant's basement setting. The menu is constantly changing to keep things fresh for the many regular patrons, but fortunate travelers can always expect to find Mrs. Wilkes's famous fried or baked chicken and cornbread dressing. With luck, they'll also get to try her okra gumbo, peppery

crab stew spiked with sherry, sweet potato soufflé, and the low-country specialty, Savannah red rice. The old "boarding-house reach" is common practice here, and heaping your plate with seconds and thirds is expected—the Wilkes family intends to send you on your way happy. While you're there, though, be sure to strike up a conversation with the folks at your table—it's the camaraderie as much as the food that makes the experience unforgettable.

WHAT: restaurant. **WHERE:** 107 W. Jones. Tel 912-232-5997 (reservations not accepted); www.mrswilkes.com. **COST:** $16. **WHEN:** all-you-can-eat lunch, Mon–Fri. Arrive at 10:45 for lunch.

Strolling Through a Romance Novel Set in the Old South

SAVANNAH'S HISTORIC DISTRICT

Georgia, U.S.A.

An urban masterpiece, Savannah is America's best walking city, with its largest historical district: 2½ square miles holding more than 1,000 lovingly restored colonial homes and commercial buildings, all punctuated by 21 of the city's original 24 green-leafed 1-acre squares. America's first planned city, Savannah was laid out in 1733 on a perfect grid by its founder, British general James Oglethorpe, in the name of King George II. "White gold" (King Cotton) subsequently filled the port city's coffers with real gold, and handsome mansions prospered, those that survived the centuries eventually coming under the protection of the Historic Savannah Foundation, born in 1955 (visit their stately 1820 Davenport House, 321 E. York Street). In 1864, General William Tecumseh Sherman ended his "march to the sea" here, sparing the city at Lincoln's behest—and then offering it to the president as a Christmas gift.

To fully appreciate Savannah's seductive charms today, stay in one of the dozens of inns or bed-and-breakfasts that have been opened in some of the city's most impressive historic homes. Competition is stiff, but most agree that the genteel Gastonian is a front-runner. Encompassing two Italianate town houses and a carriage house dating from the 1860s, it has been painstakingly and magnificently restored using authentic Savannah colors and Scalamandre wallpaper of original patterns. Guest rooms have working fireplaces, most with four-poster canopied beds (with pralines left on your pillow) and lavish baths. It's a challenge to walk off the Gastonian's legendary Southern breakfast, which includes melon soup, home-baked cherry muffins, and scrambled eggs.

WHAT: site, hotel. **HISTORIC DISTRICT:** contact the Savannah Visitors Center for a list of events and tours, tel 877-SAVANNAH or 912-944-0455; www.savannahvisit.com. **THE GASTONIAN:** 220 E. Gaston St. Tel 800-322-6603 or 912-232-2869, fax 912-232-0710; innkeeper@gastonian.com; www.gastonian.com. *Cost:* doubles from $205 (low season), from $230 (high season). **BEST TIMES:** Savannah Tour of Homes and Gardens (www.savannahtourofhomes.org) takes place over 4 days, usually late Mar, when the azaleas begin to bloom. Annual Spring tour of Historic Gardens takes place mid-May.

Evening cordials are served in the Gastonian's parlor.

History, Aristocrats, and Splendid Isolation

THE GOLDEN ISLES

Georgia, U.S.A.

Once winter resorts for American aristocracy, Georgia's barrier islands hosted vacationing Rockefellers, Vanderbilts, Goodyears, Pulitzers, and Astors. Things are a little bit more egalitarian today, but the tinge of riches still lingers. Reachable only by ferry, Cumberland is the largest, most tranquil, and most pristine of the islands, a low-profile getaway that only attracts the world's attention once in a blue moon—as when, in 1996, the late John F. Kennedy Jr. and Carolyn Bessette secretly married and honeymooned here. More than 90 percent of the 35-square-mile island is protected as national seashore, and the National Park Service limits the number of day visitors to 300. This gives wide berth to white-tailed deer, wild horses, turkeys, sea turtles, 323 species of birds, and you. There are no cars and just one hostelry, the white-columned, twenty-room Greyfield Inn, built in 1901 by Thomas Carnegie (brother and business partner of steel magnate Andrew) and his wife Lucy, and run as an inn since 1964 by the Carnegies' great-great-grandchildren. It's luxurious (with original furniture, portraits, and mementos from the family's gilded past), but in a quirky, welcoming, and grandmotherly way.

Beginning in 1886, 9-mile-long Jekyll Island began earning a reputation as a ritzy wintertime Newport. Today, a state-protected park takes up a blessedly undeveloped two-thirds of the island, where 20 miles of paved bicycle paths allow a do-it-yourself tour of Jekyll's designated landmark homes, beach-hugging boardwalk, and cool forests. The turreted, Queen Anne–style Jekyll Island Club Hotel, which functioned as Jekyll's social headquarters until WW II, is the rambling centerpiece of a 240-acre historic district, and retains the aura of an Edwardian millionaire's club. Accommodations in the Club's annex (and in four other buildings) are available for today's non–robber baron guests.

The quiet good taste and good manners of the legendary Cloister resort and spa on Sea Island have drawn presidents, Forbes 500 types, and pedigreed families for decades, some for the golf—its fifty-four inspiring holes are commonly rated among America's finest—and some for romance: George and Barbara Bush are one of more than 36,000 (and counting) couples who have honeymooned here. The main building, a classic Spanish-missionary-style structure designed in the 1920s by Addison Mizner (already famous for his development of Palm Beach), sits amid immaculately tended grounds filled with flowering plants, palmetto palms, and oaks dripping with Spanish moss. At the hotel's pinky-white 5-mile swath of sandy beach, horseback riding is but one of many ways to pass the perfect day.

As with Cumberland, you'll need to hop a boat to get to private, 10,000-acre Little St. Simons Island and its Lodge, the only accommodation on the island. The island has been owned by the same family since 1908. Thirty lucky guests (at most) are encouraged to explore—solo, or with one of the staff naturalists—the unspoiled beauty of ancient, moss-draped forests, labyrinthine waterways, and 7 miles of pristine beach by foot, horseback, bike, canoe, or kayak. There's excellent fly-fishing, birding, and turtle tracking, or you can simply sit on the porch at the rustic Lodge

Cumberland Island's Greyfield Inn is set on 200 private acres.

with a drink and a good book. The food is fresh, simple, delicious, and evocative of the Southern childhood you never had.

WHAT: island, hotel. **CUMBERLAND ISLAND:** a hotel ferry runs daily from Fernandina Beach (Amelia Island), Florida, year-round. *Greyfield Inn:* tel 904-261-6408, fax 904-321-0666; seashore@greyfieldinn.com; www.grey fieldinn.com. *Cost:* doubles from $395, includes all meals, tours, and various amenities. **JEKYLL ISLAND:** 75 miles south of Savannah, 60 miles north of Jacksonville, Florida;

connected by causeway to the mainland at Brunswick. *Jekyll Island Club Hotel:* 371 Riverview Dr. Tel 800-535-9547 or 912-635-2600, fax 912-635-2818; reservations@jekyll club.com, www.jekyllclub.com. *Cost:* doubles from $169 (low season), from $199 (high season). **SEA ISLAND:** 80 miles south of Savannah, 70 miles north of Jacksonville; connected by causeway to Brunswick. *The Cloister:* tel 912-638-3611, fax 912-638-5159; www.seaisland.com. *Cost:* doubles from $450. **THE LODGE ON LITTLE ST. SIMONS ISLAND:** a boat for lodge guests runs twice daily from St. Simons Island. Tel 888-733-5774, fax 912-634-1811; lodge@littlestsimonsisland.com; www.littlest simonsisland.com. *Cost:* doubles, from $450, includes all meals, activities, and various amenities. Exclusive full-island reservations from $7,700 per night. **BEST TIMES:** fall months for best weather; Jan for Sea Island's Bridge Festival; Aug for Jekyll Island's Beach Music Festival; Dec for Jekyll Island's "Christmas Island" festival or Sea Island's Big Band Festival (10 days mid-Dec).

Cowboys, Moonscapes, and Amazing Stargazing

BIG ISLAND

Hawaii, U.S.A.

T he Big Island of Hawaii—the most primal of the spectacular 1,500-mile Hawaiian archipelago—is a unique place of contrasts and superlatives. It's the largest island in the Pacific and the youngest and one of the least

touristed in Hawaii, a place of black-lava deserts and dense tropical rain forests. It's home to five volcanoes (including Kilauea and Mauna Loa, two of the world's most active) and eleven of the earth's thirteen primary climate types—if you wanted to, you could ski and surf in a single day. At 93 miles long and

76 miles wide, the Big Island is big indeed—twice the size of the other islands combined and approximately the size of Connecticut, with some 250 miles of encircling roads that require seven hours to drive. King Kamehameha the Great was born here in 1758, uniting the island kingdom between 1785 and 1810 and

inviting foreign traders to settle on the islands; today, kings of commerce come to play golf on world-class courses known for their beauty.

From the black-sand beach at its mouth, the lush Waipio Valley sweeps back 6 miles between thickly jungled walls that reach almost a mile high. Once considered the sacred "Valley of the Kings," its cool rivers, tumbling waterfalls, and wild horses encourage the feeling that this is the valley that time forgot. Nearby, ½-mile-high Waimea (also called Kamuela) is the island's upcountry, where about 50,000 head of cattle graze on the 225,000 acres of 200-year-old Parker Ranch, one of the largest privately owned cattle ranches in the United States. Those with a mind to can hire one of the ranch's 400 horses and explore the area's magnificent terrain in the hoofprints of Hawaii's famous "paniolo" cowboys.

Below is the black-lava Kohala Coast, exceptional for the dazzling white-sand stretch of Kaunaoa Beach and the close-by Hapuna Beach State Park, stellar exceptions to the young island's beach-challenged reputation. This is the location for the perfectly situated 60-acre Mauna Kea, the trail-blazing super-resort that started it all and set the standard. Built in 1965 by Laurance Rockefeller, it's welcoming, understated, and surprisingly lush considering its desert-like location. It's also home to an 18-hole Robert Trent Jones Sr. golf course, one of the state's oldest, best, and most photographed. Throughout the resort, a 1,600-piece collection of Pacific and Asian art is on display.

The Kohala Coast ends where the serrated Kona ("leeward side") Coast begins. Its oceanfront town of Kailua-Kona has generally been known for superb snorkeling beaches (such as Kahaluu) and especially for big-game fishing—its Pacific blue marlin, called "granders" here, can weigh up to 1,000 pounds. Less-than-extravagant accommodations are the norm, with the prime exception being the

exquisite Four Seasons Resort Hualalai, a spare, breezy, plantation-chic oasis with low-rise bungalows and secluded swimming areas. Open only to resort guests, the 18-hole Jack Nicklaus–designed Hualalai Golf Course lies atop an 1801 lava flow produced by its now extinct namesake volcano.

For a traditional luau, head to the tiki-torch-lit Kona Village, whose Friday-night lagoon-side luau is the island's oldest and most authentic, managing to hold on to the spirit of Old Hawaii and escape corniness.

Panoramic views from the Mauna Kea golf course

The retreat's clutch of rustic thatched-roofed *hales* (cottages) are fashioned after the cultures of the Polynesian peoples, from Hawaiians to Fijians and Samoans, and have interior decor to match. Regardless of where you stay on the western coast, watch for summering humpback whales (December to April) and the sunset's legendary "green flash," both best seen from the Kona area.

The island's real show, where Mother Nature pulls out all the stops, is at Hawaii Volcanoes National Park, home of Pele, the volcano goddess. Mount Kilauea (meaning "spreading, much spewing") has been erupting since 1983, adding hundreds of acres to the island in the longest continuous eruption ever recorded. From the rustic Volcano House, the only hotel within the park, you can access the 11-mile summit Crater Rim Drive (which takes you around the Kilauea Caldera) and the Chain of Craters Road, a 28-mile drive from the Visitors Center down 4,000 feet to the coast. Both lead you past a surreal moonscape of raw power, hissing fumaroles, and both oozing and petrified lava flows. On the snowcapped peak of neighboring Mauna Kea ("White Mountain"), the highest point in all of Hawaii, ten nations have built state-of-the-art telescopes: thanks to unusually clear skies, it is possible from this lofty perch to view 90 percent of the heavens—though the oxygen-starved might prefer an only slightly compromised view from their hotel's beach hammock.

WHAT: island, site, hotel, restaurant. **HAWAII (BIG ISLAND):** direct flights from Los Angeles and San Francisco, 30-minute connecting flights from Honolulu. Big Island Visitors Bureau, tel 800-648-2441; www.bigisland.org. **MAUNA KEA:** Kohala. Tel 888-977-4623 or 808-882-7222, fax 808-882-5700; www.princeresortshawaii.com. *Cost:* doubles from $450. **FOUR SEASONS RESORT HUALALAI:** Kona. Tel 888-340-5662 or 808-325-8000, fax 808-325-8100; www.fourseasons.com/hualalai. *Cost:* doubles from $725. **KONA VILLAGE:** Kailua-Kona. Tel 800-367-5290 or 808-325-5555, fax 808-325-5124; www.konavillage.com. *Cost:* doubles from $660, includes all meals for 2. Luau for nonguests $100. **BEST TIMES:** weather changes little, but avoid the hottest (Sept) and rainiest (Dec–Feb) months. Weekend after Easter for the weeklong Merrie Monarch Hula Festival (Hilo), the state's premier contest for ancient and modern hula (advance-purchase tickets a must; contact Visitors Bureau); late Sept–early Oct for Aloha Week; May for Ironman Triathlon and Big-Game Fishing Tournament.

The Garden (of Eden) Isle

KAUAI

Hawaii, U.S.A.

The greenest and oldest island in the Hawaiian archipelago, lush and timeless Kauai is essentially a single massive volcano that rises 3 miles from the earth's floor, and has provided a scene-stealing vision of Paradise for many a Hollywood movie and TV show, including *Jurassic Park, Blue Hawaii, King Kong,* and *Fantasy Island.* With just 5 percent of the state's population, Kauai's people are known as the friendliest in the fiftieth state, and tend to live a rural and unrushed old-time Hawaiian lifestyle, in which natural beauty and not overly plush Maui-style resort life is the focus.

About 30 miles at its widest (you can drive around it in two hours), the relatively small island is two-thirds impenetrable, but what a wallop that final third delivers. The island's beauty peaks at the north shore, possibly the most beautiful spot in all Hawaii. Its Na Pali ("The Cliffs") Coast is said to be some of the fastest eroding land on earth, with deep folds and sawtooth 3,000-foot-high seacliffs unbreached by roads, though hiking trails lead down to the coast's exquisite beaches and secluded sea caves. Helicopter tours are available, but the best way to experience the stunning 15-mile stretch of thickly jungled shore at the foot of these craggy palisades is by inflatable boat, kayak, or (for experienced hikers) via the strenuous Kalalau Trail.

The St. Regis Princeville Resort is one of the state's largest and most challenging golf destinations, offering two different Robert Trent Jones Jr.–designed courses: the Makai Course, with its three 9-hole loops, and the 18-hole Prince Course, named Hawaii's number-one course by *Golf Digest*. It comprises a series of tiers leading down a seaside bluff, and is every bit as beautiful as the forested cliffs and Hanalei Bay it overlooks.

The Na Pali Cliffs rise 3,000 feet from the sea.

Kauai lays claim to Hawaii's most dazzling beaches, among which Hanalei's 2-mile strip—Kauai's surfing central—is the finest and the most famous. This is where Mitzi Gaynor washed Rossano Brazzi right out of her hair in the 1957 classic *South Pacific,* and also the fairy-tale home where Puff the Magic Dragon frolicked in the autumn mists. Poipu Beach, at the center of the island's southern coast, is another of the island's legendary beauty spots, famous for its diving opportunities and for glam resorts such as the 50-acre Grand Hyatt Kauai Resort and Spa, with its lavishly landscaped and environmentally sensitive grounds, open-air spa, and Robert Trent Jones Jr.–designed championship golf course. Nearby Kapaa, whose population of 5,000 makes it the largest town on the island, offers another winning beach on the island's Royal Coconut Coast.

Waimea, known chiefly as the place where British captain James Cook first dropped anchor in Hawaii in 1778, is another strollable town. Located at the mouth of the 14-mile-long Waimea Canyon, it was dubbed the "Grand Canyon of the Pacific" by Mark Twain. Belvederes look out over the 2-mile wide, 3,000-foot-deep gorge, painted in rich ocher, russet, and amber. The only accommodations to speak of on the west coast are Waimea Plantation Cottages, a collection of fifty workers' homes from the early 1900s that have been restored and relocated here within a lovely beachside coconut grove. Enveloped in an old-time plantation atmosphere (sugarcane remains one of the island's major agricultural products), they still feel like homes.

Mount Waialeale stands at the center of the nearly round island, its 5,148-foot summit said to be one of the wettest spots on earth with an average annual rainfall of 444 inches, leaving it perpetually hidden by clouds. The rest of the island receives far less precipitation (with parts getting only 35 inches per year), though on average it gets more than the rest of Hawaii. As a result, the island is known in Hawaiian lore as the birthplace of the rainbow. It's so extravagantly covered with flowers and dense hothouse vegetation that it seems like one large botanical garden, earning it the nickname of the "Garden Isle."

WHAT: island, hotel. **KAUAI:** 100 miles northwest and a 30-minute connecting flight from Honolulu. Daily direct flights from Los Angeles. Kauai Visitors Bureau, tel 800-262-1400 or 808-245-3971, fax 808-246-9235; www.kauaidiscovery.com. **ST. REGIS PRINCEVILLE RESORT:** tel 808-826-9644; www.princeville.com. *Cost:* doubles from $500. **GRAND HYATT KAUAI RESORT AND**

SPA: 1571 Poipu Rd. Tel 800-55-HYATT or 808-742-1234, fax 808-742-1557; info@ kauaipo.hyatt.com; www.kauai.hyatt.com. *Cost:* doubles from $440. **WAIMEA PLANTATION COTTAGES:** tel 800-992-4632 or 808-338-1625, fax 808-338-2338; www.waimea-plantation.com. *Cost:* oceanfront cottages from $365. **BEST TIMES:** mid-Sept for the Aloha Festivals and the Kauai Mokihana Festival featuring hula competitions.

A Pineapple Island's Yin and Yang

LANAI

Hawaii, U.S.A.

Hawaii's most secluded and intimate island, tiny unhyped Lanai was once the state's largest pineapple plantation, with field after field of red-dirt Dole pineapple groves producing 8 percent of the world's crop. The island's new role as a tourist destination was sealed in the 1990s when it was taken over by Los Angeles entrepreneur David Murdock, who suspended pineapple planting and instead built two superplush hotels, 8 miles and many worlds apart on the otherwise empty island. Indoors, guests are spoiled to an unashamed degree, while the outdoors remains unspoiled, with not a tourist shop in sight, nor any helicopters overhead to interrupt the fantasy.

The elegant Lanai at Manele Bay is a Polynesian- and Mediterranean-inspired seaside destination with waterfalls, fishponds, and dense tropical gardens. It quietly occupies the headland of idyllic Hulopoe Bay, whose crystal waters and perfect palm-shaded white-sand beach, excellent for swimming and snorkeling, is frequently visited by spinner dolphins and humpback whales. The natural drama extends to its Jack Nicklaus–designed Challenge at Manele golf course, located on the cliffs above Hulopoe and with some of the most riveting ocean views in all Hawaii. The resort's private-club atmosphere and panoply of amenities have made it a magnet for high-profile and celebrity guests such as Bill Gates, who chose the Manele Bay Hotel to tie the knot—on the golf course, no less.

The Manele Bay Hotel's counterpart in Lanai's wooded upland—the classy, colonial-style Lodge at Koele—is a handsome mix of Old Hawaii plantation, gentleman's hunting estate, and British country house, where guests can enjoy the croquet fields, lawn bowling, and the daily ritual of 3 o'clock tea. Rustic and rugged in a stylish, sophisticated, English country manor way, it's set at 1,700 feet among towering pine- and eucalyptus-covered hills, with views of green pastures, grazing horses, and the errant wild turkey. The Lodge's oversized rooms are gorgeously appointed, some with woodburning fireplaces, a touch you don't

Golfers on the Challenge at Manele's 12th hole are easily distracted by the stunning view.

expect in Hawaii. The resort's championship golf course, the Experience at Koele, was designed by Greg Norman and is regularly ranked among the nation's must-plays. In fact, the Manele and Koele courses are both so highly ranked that golfers frequently fly in from Honolulu or Maui for the day.

The sibling resorts share an exotic sense of remoteness, as if this distant, undeveloped island had not yet entered the 21st century, despite its modern, up-to-the-minute amenities. Their old-world graciousness encourages guests to linger and socialize over cocktails, on the tennis courts, or during tee-time. Lanai has few cars, no traffic lights, and only one real road (30

miles of which is paved), but guests can explore it by foot or bike or four-wheel-drive. Guests may use the facilities at both properties.

WHAT: island, hotel. **LANAI:** 9 miles west of Maui (25-minute flight from Maui, 30-minute flight from Honolulu). For tourist information, contact Destination Lanai, tel 800-947-4774 or 808-565-7600; www.visitlanai.com. **LANAI AT MANELE BAY:** tel 800-321-4666 or 808-565-7700; www.fourseasons.com/manelebay. *Cost:* doubles from $345. **LODGE AT KOELE:** tel 800-321-4666 or 808-565-4000, fax 808-565-4561; www.islandoflanai.com. *Cost:* doubles from $295. **BEST TIMES:** Pineapple Festival in Jun.

The Island-and-Golf-Lover's Destination of Choice

MAUI

Hawaii, U.S.A.

Who cannot agree with the local saying "Maui no ka oi"? Maui *is* the best. The "Valley Isle" is named after the Polynesian demigod who, after having plucked all the Hawaiian islands up out of the sea,

decided to make this—the most beautiful one—his home. Nothing beats the views of and from the hulking mass of 10,023-foot Haleakala (House of the Sun), whose dormant volcanic crater is the largest in the world—so big that the island of Manhattan could fit inside. Visitors follow a must-do tradition and make a 3 A.M. ascent through cool upcountry landscape to its lofty peak to watch the sunrise (which Mark Twain called "the sublimest spectacle I ever witnessed"), then bicycle down 38 miles of switchbacks along the Haleakala Crater Road, passing through three different climate zones along the way. On a clear day you'll take in stirring views of the island's lush sugarcane and pineapple plantations, some of its 42 famous miles of beach, and four of the Neighbor Islands—Molokai, Lanai, Kahoolawe, and Hawaii. Off the island's southwest coast you

might also catch the shadow of some of the thousands of North Pacific humpback whales that come to these algae-rich waters to breed and calve after summering in Alaska—the largest such concentration anywhere.

Besides the Crater Road to Haleakala's summit, the island's other famous road show (and one of the Pacific's most scenic) is the narrow, corkscrew Hana "Highway" on the lush, isolated northeastern coast. By unofficial count, there are 617 curves, 54 one-lane bridges, dozens of waterfalls, and distracting vistas aplenty. Beginning at the laid-back former sugar-plantation town of Paia (which along with nearby Hookipa Beach has become world famous for windsurfing and kitesurfing), the 50-mile drive takes two to three hours as it climbs and drops before reaching the quiet, old-fashioned, eye-blink town of Hana, home to a high percentage of Hawaiians and a stronghold of the local culture. There isn't much to the town except the unique Hotel Hana-Maui, the island's most exclusive hideaway, founded in 1946 by an American businessman and today affiliated with (and recently renovated by) California's famous Post Ranch Inn. A cluster of cliffside cottages on 66 green acres that slope down to a rugged seacoast, it's within walking distance of two other gorgeous beaches, the palm-fringed Hamoa Bay and Kaihalulu, the only volcanic red-sand beach in the Pacific.

From north to south on Maui's beach-blessed western coast, you'll find world-class golf courses. Kapalua encompasses five bays and is bordered by a working pineapple plantation, while Kaanapali is the oldest and largest and Wailea the showiest, with beautiful views of Maui's sister islands. Makena is home to the Hawaii State Open. If the pros had to choose, they'd likely pick the Plantation, the newest of Kapalua's three courses, and the palm-lined fairways of Wailea's Gold Course, the showpiece of its three courses. You can play all the courses from a base at any of the area's three best hotels. The Grand Wailea Resort Hotel & Spa boasts 780 rooms, an opulent 50,000-square-foot spa, and an astounding water park with waterfalls, white-water rapids, slides, and nine pools—an ideal choice for spa lovers with kids. Only slightly smaller, the classically elegant Ritz-Carlton Kapalua has 548 rooms and impeccable service amid a setting of historic plantation splendor. The Four Seasons Resort

Maui at Wailea boasts pampering service and top-ranked restaurants including Spago.

Maui's western coast is also home to the picturesque 19th-century whaling village of Lahaina, which now concentrates on excursions to watch the whales the locals once tried to harpoon. Once the royal seat of the island, today it's a delightfully walkable town, its restored Victorian buildings housing art galleries, trendy cafés and restaurants, and souvenir shops galore. At the town's Old Lahaina Luau, traditional hula and authentic Hawaiian fare sets the experience apart from what you'll catch in Waikiki.

WHAT: island, hotel, restaurant. **MAUI:** 25 minutes by air from Honolulu. Maui Visitors Bureau, tel 800-525-6284 or 808-244-3530, fax 808-244-1337; www.visitmaui.com. **HOTEL HANA-MAUI:** Hana. Tel 800-321-HANA or 808-248-8211, fax 808-248-7202; reservations @hotelhanamaui.com; www.hotelhanamaui. com. *Cost:* doubles from $495. **GRAND WAILEA RESORT HOTEL & SPA:** Wailea. Tel 800-888-6100 or 808-875-1234, fax 808-874-2442; www.grandwailea.com. *Cost:* doubles from $755. **RITZ-CARLTON KAPALUA:** Kapalua. Tel 800-262-8440, fax 808-669-1566; www.ritzcarlton. com. **FOUR SEASONS RESORT MAUI AT WAILEA:** tel 800-332-3442 or 808-874-8000, fax 808-874-2244; www.fourseasons.com/maui. **OLD LAHAINA LUAU:** 1251 Front St., Lahaina. Tel 800-248-5828 or 808-667-1998; www.old lahainaluau.com. *Cost:* $95. **BEST TIMES:** Jun for the sunniest and driest weather; Nov–Jun for whale-watching (peaking Jan–Mar).

Waikiki and Beyond

OAHU

Hawaii, U.S.A.

Oahu means "gathering place," and from the early days when Hawaiian royalty chose Waikiki Beach as the location of their first modest homes, to the mid-20th century when Pearl Harbor was a base for the American

Pacific Fleet, to today, when the sandy 2½-mile crescent has grown into the world's most famous city beach, Oahu has been a magnet. Kalakaua, the last Hawaiian king, ruled here from the Victorian-style Iolani Palace, the only royal residence on U.S. soil. Following WW II, builders usurped every last grain of then-empty Waikiki Beach, resulting in today's side-by-side cornucopia of tropical resort hotels. The beach is famous for its generally mild surfing and world-class people-watching, all set against the dramatic backdrop of Diamond Head, Hawaii's most famous landmark.

The sumptuous, intimate Halekulani (House Befitting Heaven) is the premier hotel in the Hawaiian Islands and one of the best in the United States, a 5-acre oasis of elegance that opened in 1917. For the most romantic (and expensive) dining in town, visit its world-class La Mer restaurant, whose superb preparation of fresh fish and island ingredients reinterprets the tenets of classic French cuisine. Downstairs, the hotel's less formal oceanfront Orchids dining room is probably the city's best, with a Sunday brunch that offers more than 200 delicious dishes served buffet style, and draws as many Hawaiian families as visitors. The hotel's beachside House Without A Key restaurant has long been a favorite sunset rendezvous—most nights an old-time trio, the Islanders, plays and sings classic Hawaiian tunes like "Hilo Hattie" beneath a century-old kiawe tree while a hula dancer mesmerizes.

There's plenty of yesterday's charm at the Royal Hawaiian, the "Pink Palace of the Pacific," a beloved institution since its founding in 1927. It long ago nabbed the broadest stretch of beach in all of Waikiki, and today remains true to its time, though carefully updated. Its beachside bar serves the best mai tai in town and its famous Monday luau is a classic.

Being in the very heart of Waikiki is what Oahu has always been about. Its plethora of restaurants bespeaks the city's exciting ethnic diversity and its place at the crossroads of the Pacific. Alan Wong's is the shrine of Hawaiian regional cuisine, the place where the most original practitioner of the city's gastronomic scene shows off his magic with native ingredients in an otherwise unremarkable office building. Another wonder chef is Roy Yamaguchi, Hawaii's biggest success story, with a string of eponymous restaurants that stretches from Guam to Pebble Beach. Some of them may stray, but this original site—loud, hectic, and fun—has never faltered since opening in 1988. Then there's the unassuming Ono Hawaiian Foods, a favorite local dive featuring island dishes you've never heard of—from kalua pig wrapped in laulau (taro) leaves to sweet haupia pudding made of coconut milk—as well as that old-time Hawaiian favorite, Spam.

In western Oahu, forty minutes and worlds away from the hubbub of Waikiki, the Ihilani Resort and Spa proves to be the best escape from big-city clamor, with a roster of five-star amenities, a spa inspired by ancient Hawaiian healing therapies, an oceanfront setting, and inimitable, inspirational sunsets—and that's not to mention its adjoining Ko Olina Golf Club, one of Oahu's best.

Honolulu reminds you that Oahu is the most densely populated of the islands (with nearly ten times the density of Maui, the second most crowded), and the U.S.S. *Arizona* Memorial in Pearl Harbor reminds you of the city's place in 20th-century history. But the Oahu experience can also mean the deserted beaches, spiky cliffs (*pali*), and lush vegetation located only minutes outside of Honolulu. Surfers agree that the monster waves of the island's legendary North Shore, from Haleiwa to Kahuku (including Waimea Bay, Sunset Beach, and the Banzai Pipeline) guarantee some of the world's best surfing during the "winter" months of November to March. The waves calm down substantially in the summer. For less extreme sports, try Hanauma Bay (Curved Bay), a gorgeous palm-studded crescent that offers the best snorkeling in all the Hawaiian islands. (Tip: arrive early.) Idyllic

Lanikai, a scenic twenty-minute drive from Honolulu, and its neighbor Kailua (a world-class windsurfing spot) are considered among the best beaches in America for their exquisite turquoise waters and powdery white sand, and for the jaw-dropping scenery along cliff-hugging Kalanianaole Highway, which takes you there.

WHAT: island, hotel, restaurant, experience. **OAHU:** Honolulu is about 5 hours by plane from the West Coast. Oahu Visitors Bureau, tel 877-525-6248; www.visit-oahu.com. **HALEKULANI:** 2199 Kalia Rd. Tel 800-367-2343 or 808-923-2311; www.halekulani.com. *Cost:* ocean-view doubles from $420. Dinner at La Mer $95; dinner at Orchids $75; Sun brunch at Orchids $45. **ROYAL HAWAIIAN:** 2259 Kalakaua Ave. Tel 800-325-3535 or 808-923-7311; www.royal-hawaiian.com. *Cost:* ocean-view doubles from $820. **ALAN WONG'S:** 1857 South King St. Tel 808-949-2526. *Cost:* dinner $60. **ROY'S:** 6600 Kalanianaole Hwy., Hawaii Kai (8 miles east of Waikiki). Tel 808-396-7697. *Cost:* dinner $40. **ONO HAWAIIAN FOODS:** 726 Kapahulu Ave. Tel 808-737-2275. *Cost:* lunch $15. *When:* closed Sun. **JW MARRIOTT IHILANI RESORT AND SPA:** Ko Olina. Tel 800-626-4446 or 808-679-0079; www.ihilani.com. *Cost:* doubles from $495. **BEST TIMES:** biggest Hula Festivals are the King Kamehameha Hula Competition (Jun) and the Prince Lot Hula Festival (Jul); the Aloha Festival (in Oahu, mid- to late Sept); Triple Crown Pro-Surfing Championship (Nov–Dec) at Sunset Beach; Dec–Feb is rainy season.

A Pine-Forest–Enshrouded Gem

LAKE COEUR D'ALENE

Idaho, U.S.A.

Glacier-gouged, forest-shrouded, and surrounded by the jagged Bitteroot Mountains on the western flank of the Rockies, Coeur d'Alene is one of the Pacific Northwest's most beautiful locations, a gem among the many lakes that accentuate Idaho's scenic northern Panhandle. Meandering bike trails and 8½ miles of groomed hiking paths lead through pine-scented forests to Tubbs Hill, which offers the best views of the lake, most of whose 128-mile shoreline has been blessedly protected from development. Keep an eye out for birds, as the lake area is also home to the nation's largest population of ospreys, as well as to their cousin, the American bald eagle.

Sitting stage center on 6 beachfront acres of the lake's northern shore is the area's primo hotel, the Coeur d'Alene Resort. Many of the rooms have balconies and windows that frame the lake's Alp-like beauty and overlook the floating boardwalk that wraps around the resort's busy marina. The hotel offers most of the lake-related diversions you can imagine, as well as a golf course (there are twenty-nine within an hour's drive) whose fourteenth hole is situated on the world's first movable, floating green. Daytime and dinner cruises aboard the *Mish-n-Nock* and its fellow fleet members explore the lake's placid steely blue waters, home to an abundance of Chinook salmon and trout. Fishing charters continue up the shadowy St. Joe River in quest of the feisty cutthroat trout. This history-rich area of the lake's southeast corner is silver country, dotted with peaceful late-19th-century mining towns that recall the heyday of what was once the continent's largest silver-producing region.

Wallace, a still-lively, time-stuck place listed on the National Register of Historic Places, is 35 miles away.

WHAT: site, hotel. **LAKE COEUR D'ALENE:** 350 miles east of Seattle. **COEUR D'ALENE**

RESORT: 115 S. 2nd St. Tel 800-688-5253 or 208-765-4000; fax 208-664-7276; resortinfo @cdaresort.com; www.cdaresort.com. *Cost:* lake-view rooms $129 (low season), $179 (high season). **BEST TIMES:** Jul–Sept for weather.

The Great Outdoors
Meets the Great Indoors

HENRY'S FORK LODGE

Island Park, Idaho, U.S.A.

Idaho is one of the most revered destinations in America for fishing, with 2,000 lakes, 16,000 miles of streams, and 39 species of game fish. And for trout, the state's famed Snake River is absolutely the place to be, particularly at Henry's Fork. The best fly-fishing in the world is only a strong cast away from any of the rocking chairs that line the long, open sun-porch of Henry's Fork Lodge, certainly one of the most tasteful wilderness inns anywhere. Sitting on an overlook above a secluded stretch of Henry's Fork, the handsome cedar lodge was built with the sophisticated angler in mind, in an unfussy "refined rustic" style that's all about comfort, simplicity, and informality. Guest rooms are wood-paneled (most with fireplaces of local volcanic stone), with log-hewn beds and down comforters. The focus, though, is all on the great outdoors. The lodge is just 2 miles from Henry's Fork's most famous stretch, Railroad Ranch, and is an easy drive from fishing waters at Yellowstone Park and along the lower Madison. Nonfishing spouses have hiking, swimming, boating, and de-stressing to keep them busy. Everyone heads back to the lodge for a won-derful low-key but elegant dinner, prepared by the hotel's European-trained chef.

WHAT: hotel, experience. **WHERE:** southeast Idaho, 68 miles from nearest airport at Idaho Falls, 40 miles to the western reaches of Yellowstone Park. Tel 208-558-7953, fax 208-558-7956; info@henrysforklodge.com; www.henrysforklodge.com. **COST:** 3-night minimum $400 per person, per night, includes all meals. **WHEN:** open during fishing season, mid-May to mid-Oct.

Henry's Fork of the Snake River

America's Great River Odyssey

MIDDLE FORK CANYON OF THE SALMON RIVER

Stanley, Idaho, U.S.A.

" I t's the journey that counts," wrote Montaigne, "not the arrival." True enough for the adrenaline-pumping trip on the Salmon River's churning 100-mile, 100-rapids Middle Fork, which runs through 20,000 square

miles of untamed backcountry, the largest federally protected territory in the lower forty-eight. Along with rafting through the Grand Canyon, this is *the* quintessential American river adventure. Deep-rolling class IV to V rapids carry you through spectacular rocky gorges, past sandy beaches for overnight camping, and natural hot springs to soak paddle-weary bones. Sightings of bear, river otter, Rocky Mountain bighorn sheep, elk, and large birds of prey are common, and rafters can also sneak in some superb fishing—Idaho's storied crystal-clear waters are rich with rainbow, cutthroat, and Dolly Varden trout. But the headliner is the undammed and unspoiled Salmon River itself, Idaho's longest and most scenic, called the River of No Return by Lewis and Clark because of its difficult passage.

Since Idaho has 3,100 white-water miles—more running water than any other state in the continental United States—several river outfitters offer over-the-top rafting trips on the Middle Fork. Most also offer trips through Hells Canyon (the deepest river-carved chasm in North America, deeper than the Grand Canyon) on the Snake River, and on the Main Salmon River, which has some fun class III rapids. Of the Middle Fork's scores of outfitters, few are as experienced as Rocky Mountain River Tours, operated by Boise's Dave and Sheila Mills since 1978. The outfit has an unimpeachable track record, employs the best guides, and at mealtimes lays out an unbe-

Dusk on the shores of the Salmon River

lievable gourmet spread. Campfire dinners include favorite recipes from Sheila's well-received *The Outdoor Dutch Oven Cookbook*, served under a canopy of brilliant stars.

WHAT: experience, site. **WHERE:** put-in is 43 miles from Stanley and 130 miles northeast of Boise, the closest airport. **HOW:** Rocky Mountain River Tours, tel 208-345-2400 (summer telephone 208-756-4808), dave@raft trips.com; www.rockymountainrivertours.com. **COST:** minimum trips of 4 days $995 per person, all-inclusive, includes pick-up in Stanley; 5- and 6-day trips offered. **WHEN:** trips offered late May–Sept. **BEST TIMES:** May and Jun for thrill seekers; Jul for good weather and great rapids; Aug for good rapids and warmer weather; Sept for calm, fun rapids, and best fly-fishing.

Queen of the Rockies: America's Classic Ski Destination

SUN VALLEY RESORT

Sun Valley, Idaho, U.S.A.

Before there was Vail or Aspen or Telluride, there was Sun Valley, America's original ski destination, created in 1936 by statesman Averell Harriman and today still considered the nation's finest. At the time,

Harriman was chairman of the board of Union Pacific Railroad, and created the resort as a way to fill his trains during the off-season winter months. He built its centerpiece, the luxurious Sun Valley Lodge, to encourage extended stays. From its infancy, the resort attracted a celebrity crowd (Norma Shearer married her ski instructor here), with the area's rugged Sawtooth Mountains (forty-two of whose peaks reach at least 10,000 feet) filling in easily whenever the Alps just seemed too far to go for the weekend. Today, the celebs arrive by private jet, and the world's speediest lifts and largest snowmaking system have picked up where the world's first alpine chairlift left off (cost back then: 25 cents). The 80-percent sunshine rate and laid-back, small-town atmosphere remain the same, though, allowing Sun Valley to retain its *numero uno* status among the country's ski spots. The resort's main ski mountain, the world-class peak affectionately known as Baldy, boasts a 3,400-foot vertical drop; of its sixty-five steep runs, 45 percent are intermediate level. The area also offers the country's best Nordic/cross-country skiing, and is just as popular as a playground destination in summer.

Much of the après-ski action takes place down the road in the old mining town of Ketchum, first put on the map when Ernest Hemingway set up camp here in 1939. His love of the area helped promote the top-rate fishing, hunting, riding, and hiking that the Big Wood

River Valley promises during summer months. Papa's still present, in more ways than one: He was buried here in 1961. His spirit lingers on at the classy and historic Pioneer Saloon, still the place for 32-once prime ribs and Idaho's best potatoes.

WHAT: site, experience, town, hotel, restaurant. **SUN VALLEY:** 150 miles east of Boise, 300 miles north of Salt Lake City; the closest airport is 11 miles south in Hailey. For ski information, tel 800-786-8259; www.sun valley.com. *When:* ski season is late Nov–Apr. **SUN VALLEY LODGE:** tel 800-786-8259 or 208-622-2001, fax 208-622-2030; reservations @sunvalley.com; www.sunvalley.com. *Cost:* doubles from $139 (low season), from $199 (high season). **PIONEER SALOON:** 308 N. Main St., Ketchum. Tel 208-726-3139, fax 208-726-5367; www.pioneersaloon.com. *Cost:* dinner $35. **BEST TIMES:** Feb–Mar for skiing.

Tucked into the base of Bald Mountain, one of the resort's many restaurants

A Remarkable Repository of Masterworks

ART INSTITUTE OF CHICAGO

Illinois, U.S.A.

Chicago, the quintessential American city, is the deserving home of one of the nation's top art institutions, with one of the world's largest collections—more than 225,000 works in all, distributed among ten exquisitely displayed departments. Two of American art's most recognizable paintings are here: Grant Wood's *American Gothic* (Wood's dentist posed for the pitchfork-holding farmer, the artist's sister for the spinster daughter at his side) and Edward Hopper's *Nighthawks*, his famously austere all-night diner scene. The world-class Surrealist collection includes Magritte's *Time Transfixed,* but the

Grant Wood's American Gothic

museum probably enjoys widest fame for its collections of French Impressionist and Postimpressionist art, unsurpassed in quality by any other American collection and including such celebrity pieces as Seurat's pointillist masterpiece *Sunday on La Grande Jatte—1884* and a series of Monet's *Stacks of Wheat* (once called *Haystacks;* six are on view at most times). Streams of schoolchildren and the appreciative hush of visitors are testament to Chicagoans' love for their museum, which has the largest membership of any U.S. art museum. Its century-old Renaissance-style building is one of countless reasons for Chicago's stature as the world capital of 19th- and 20th-century architecture. Top off a visit with a quick shopping spree in the impressive museum shop and a leisurely respite in the museum's alfresco Garden Restaurant (open June–September), or dine indoors at the museum's elegant Restaurant on the Park, surrounded by the verdant Grant Park, one of Chicago's loveliest outdoor spaces.

WHAT: site. **WHERE:** South Michigan Ave. at Adams St. Tel. 312-443-3600; www.artic. edu. **COST:** recommended donation $18; free Tues. **BEST TIMES:** Tues open until 8 P.M.

Better than Bangkok

ARUN'S

Chicago, Illinois, U.S.A.

More Paris than prairie, with more than 7,000 restaurants and a galaxy of stellar chefs, Chicago enjoys a growing reputation as a world-class eating destination. Among its top-of-the-line contenders is Arun's, a showcase for Thai food as creative haute cuisine—a concept that didn't exist before this place opened in the mid-1980s. Chef/owner Arun (who cleverly avoided using his surname—Sampanthavivat—for the restaurant's name) is considered by critics, chef colleagues, and adoring patrons alike to be both genius and artist for his elegant, sensitive interpretation of his native cuisine's delicate and complex flavors—but he didn't come to celebrity chefdom in the usual way. Born and raised on a rubber plantation in Thailand, Arun eventually made his way to Chicago to pursue a doctorate in Asian affairs, and while there was encouraged by friends to participate as partner and chef in a Thai restaurant, despite his complete lack of experience in the kitchen. The deal fell through but Arun forged ahead solo, and within a year the accolades had begun rolling in. Today, gracious and hospitable Mr. Sampanthavivat (who composes poetry during quiet moments) shuns lucrative opportunities to expand or open branches in other American cities or abroad, remaining in his original elegant if nondescript Irving Park address, where his siblings and mother fill out the forces in the kitchen. Other chefs come here regularly to be dazzled, and patrons who walk away suspecting they've experienced Thai food better than Bangkok's best (and minus the jetlag) aren't far off the mark.

WHAT: restaurant. **WHERE:** 4156 N. Kedzie Ave., Irving Park. Tel 773-539-1909; www.arunsthai.com. **COST:** 12-course prix fixe dinner $85. **WHEN:** dinner only; closed Mon.

At the Top of the Food Chain

CHARLIE TROTTER'S

Chicago, Illinois, U.S.A.

Is Charlie Trotter America's finest chef? Food fans are falling over each other to find out, making a reservation for one of his twenty-eight tables the toughest ticket in town. Known for an artistic, imaginative, and ever-changing presentation of modern American cuisine and legendary treatment of vegetables, Trotter's constant is his exquisite, famously complicated combinations of the highest quality ingredients, juxtaposed in ways never imagined by the average diner. It's not just food; it's art. Of the three set menus that change nightly, the restaurant's eight-to-ten-course tasting menus are the most famous, as exquisitely planned as every other detail in this coolly elegant, stately Lincoln Park townhouse, where more than forty china patterns will keep the eye busy. No less impressive is the massive and meticulously thought-out wine list, considered one of the country's best. The restaurant's most coveted table (with a waiting list of up to four months) is in the kitchen, where patrons can watch the master chef in action. It was here that Sweden's King Carl Gustaf XVI

Charlie Trotter suggests planning for a three-hour dining experience.

(an aspiring recreational chef himself) dined one evening, later inviting Trotter to share some of his culinary secrets—one reigning monarch to another.

WHAT: restaurant. **WHERE:** 816 W. Armitage Ave. Tel 773-248-6228, fax 773-248-6088; info@charlietrotters.com; www.charlietrotters.com. **COST:** grand tasting menu $165; vegetable tasting menu $135; kitchen table tasting menu $225. **WHEN:** open Tues–Sat, dinner only. Reservations accepted 4 months in advance.

The Most American Music in the Most American City

CHICAGO'S BLUES SCENE

Illinois, U.S.A.

After New York City, Chicago is America's most vital cultural capital, with music often coming to mind as its foremost contribution. The Chicago Symphony Orchestra is one of the nation's great cultural institutions (a glorious experience at its traditional venue or at the North Shore's summertime Ravinia Festival), and the Chicago Jazz Festival draws enormous crowds each August. But the music with which the city has been almost inseparable since the 1930s is the blues, one of the most truly American art forms.

A mixture of African and European musical traditions grown and nurtured in the South during the time of slavery, the blues came north with the African-American migration, moving from the rural Mississippi Delta to the hard streets of Chicago's South Side, where it was electrified and reshaped into a distinctly urban music, flourishing through the 1950s. Its star waned with the advent of Motown and rock 'n' roll, but is now on the rise again, the city's blues clubs crowded with audiences that span the generations and races.

Each May (or early June), the four-day Chicago Blues Festival presents shows on six stages in lakefront Grant Park, where music fans enjoy a breathtaking view of the storied Chicago skyline. It's America's largest blues festival, with more than seventy performances drawing audiences from around the world. Everyone who is anyone has performed here, including Ray Charles, B. B. King, Shirley King, Stevie Ray Vaughn, and Ruth Brown.

But you don't need a festival to hear great blues in Chicago. Any time of the year, you can go to the South Side, the place it all started and, with some exceptions, the place where the best blues clubs are still to be found. Local legend Buddy Guy (called the finest guitarist alive by Eric Clapton) makes an occasional appearance at his own eponymously named club on the south Loop, and there are plenty of other South Side clubs with performers that make the trip worthwhile despite the marginal neighborhood.

The Chicago Blues Festival draws more than half a million people.

WHAT: experience, event. **CHICAGO BLUES FESTIVAL:** Grant Park. For information, tel 312-744-3315; www.cityofchicago.org/special event. *Cost:* free admission. *When:* 4 days in late May or early Jun. **CHICAGO JAZZ FESTIVAL:** Grant Park. Same contact info as above. *Cost:* free admission. *When:* Labor Day weekend. **BUDDY GUY'S LEGENDS:** 754 S. Wabash Ave. Tel 312-427-1190; www.buddy guys.com.

Oak Park: A Living Museum of the Prairie School

FRANK LLOYD WRIGHT TOUR

Chicago, Illinois, U.S.A.

What Paris is to cuisine and Florence is to Renaissance art, Chicago is to late-19th- and 20th-century architecture, its downtown representing a complete chronology of the period's seminal powers, from Louis Sullivan to Mies van der Rohe. You must head to the nearby suburb of Oak Park, however, for a view of the early world of Frank Lloyd Wright, the self-taught wunderkind who founded the Prairie School of architecture. Drawing his inspiration from the horizontality of the Great Plains, he became America's most illustrious architect—and possibly the world's greatest (as Wright himself once claimed in an interview). No run-of-the-mill suburb, Oak Park reflects Wright's genius in its concentration of some two dozen private homes and buildings designed or renovated between 1889 and 1913. Together, the homes (and a few in neighboring River Forest) indicate what the young master would become.

Most of these homes—including the outstanding 1895 Moore-Dugal Home (333 Forest Avenue), the most widely recognized Wright-designed home in the world—are privately owned today by loving Wrightophiles who keep them up handsomely; they are generally not open to the public (except during the mid-May Wright Plus Tour), but viewing them from the outside is delight enough. For interiors, you have two main choices: the Frank Lloyd Wright Home and Studio and the Unity Temple. Twenty-three years old, the newly married Wright built his own house in

Wright Home and Studio

Oak Park in 1889, and in the years to come it would become a design laboratory, testing ground, work in progress, and home for his family, which would soon include six children. Wright designed most of the furniture here as well, so a visit promises many insights to the workings of his remarkable mind. The architect himself believed that his masterpiece was the Unity Temple, a Unitarian parish church that he designed in 1908, and of which he was a member. It was a cubist shrine in poured concrete that he called his "little jewel." Nearby is another famous Wright structure. The Cheney House is a private brick residence that the architect designed in 1903–1904, but a possibly more significant date for the house is 1909, when Wright left his wife and slipped away to Europe with Mrs. Cheney, creating one of the great scandals of the time.

WHAT: site, hotel. **OAK PARK:** 10 miles west of downtown Chicago. **FRANK LLOYD WRIGHT HOME AND STUDIO:** 951 Chicago Ave. at Forest Ave. Tel 708-848-1976; flwpr@wrightplus.org; www.wrightplus.org. *Cost:* admission $15. *When:* guided tours daily. **UNITY TEMPLE:** 875 Lake St. Tel 708-848-6225; www.unitytemple.org. **CHENEY**

HOUSE: 520 North East Ave. **HOW:** the Chicago Architecture Center, 224 S. Michigan Ave. (across from the Art Institute), offers more than 65 tours of downtown Chicago, including ones that highlight Wright's architecture in Oak Park. Tel 312-922-3432; www.architecture.org. *When:* Oak Park walking tours Sun; bus tours to Oak Park Sat and Tues mornings. **BEST TIMES:** 1 week in mid-May the Wright Plus Tour offers access to a number of privately owned Frank Lloyd Wright houses. Contact the Frank Lloyd Wright Preservation Trust, tel 708-848-1976; www.wrightplus.org.

Get Your Red Hots!

SUPERDAWG

Chicago, Illinois, U.S.A.

Think Chicago and you may think deep-dish pizza and Italian beef. But at the mention of hot dogs—well, no other American city gets so excited about the tradition of the humble "red hots," as they're called hereabouts. A savory icon of the city's hardscrabble working-class landscape, the Chicago dog is one of the great specialties in America's culinary hall-of-fame. Chicagoans are deeply divided about where to go for the dog to end all dogs, but there are several top contenders. The plump Vienna-brand beauties of tiny Byron's (1017 W. Irving Park Road) are buried underneath any combination of eleven toppings, while Gold Coast Dogs (418 N. State) offers an inspired specimen of a classic frankfurter and the best cheese fries in town.

But there is something special about the classic drive-in fun promised at Superdawg, open since 1948. Not only are the red hots flawless here, but so is the funky ambience, where you still order from outdoor "Order Matic" speakers and have your tray delivered by a carhop waitress who'll attach it to the side of your vehicle with a smile. Order your dinner with fries and the box reads, "Your Superdawg lounges inside contentedly cushioned . . . in Superfries, and comfortably attired in mustard, relish, onion, pickle, hot peppers." No one can explain why, of the two huge

Superdawg mascots Maurie and Flaurie

hot dogs with light-up eyes that dance atop the diner, the boy hot dog is dressed like Tarzan. Don't forget to order an ultrathick eat-it-with-a-spoon milk shake, and don't even think about putting ketchup on that 'dawg.

WHAT: restaurant. **WHERE:** 6363 N. Milwaukee Ave. at Devon and Nagle (on the far northwest edge of the city). Tel. 773- 763-0660. **COST:** Superdawg with fries $4.95. **WHEN:** daily lunch, dinner, and late night.

A Lifestyle Going, Going . . .

THE GREAT
AMISH COUNTRY AUCTION

Shipshewana, Indiana, U.S.A.

Horse and buggies start arriving before daybreak for the weekly Antique and Miscellaneous Auction in Shipshewana (population 542) in the heart of one of America's largest Amish and Mennonite communities.

The auction and market is as much a draw to view the goods for sale (dealers and bargain-hunters come from as far away as California and New York) as to enjoy those who come from nearby farms to buy. Farmers wearing wide-rimmed black hats and Old Testament beards are here to snatch up hand-powered tools, crockware, and kitchenware for their homes—even old wringer washing machines. Since its inception in 1922, the auction has grown in size and now fills the Auction Barn, whose eleven rings of auctioneers sell both valuable antiques and questionable collectables. Hang around and catch the Friday Horse and Pony Auction as well.

The farm region of Elkhart and LaGrange Counties, home to 17,000 Amish, can be experienced with a slow meander along the 100-mile Heritage Trail, beginning and ending in the town of Elkhart. Audio CD and cassette commentaries on the trail (available at Elkhart's Visitor Center) lead motorists down narrow country lanes, behind unhurried clip-clopping black buggies and past pristinely kept orchards and farms. Amish Acres in Nappanee (south of Shipshewana) features tours of a restored Amish farm and homestead made up of 18 structures from the 19th century. You can view much of it on

tractor-drawn wagon rides, enjoy musical theater in the round barn theater, or watch demonstrations of traditional crafts like quilt making and cider pressing. The highlight here is the Thresher's Dinner served family style in the barn: farm-size platters of fried chicken, roast turkey, or beef, plus mashed potatoes, corn bread, and fresh-grown vegetables. Desserts include the must-sample molasses-based shoofly pie.

WHAT: event, site, hotel, restaurant. **SHIPSHEWANA:** 130 miles east of Chicago, 150 miles north of Indianapolis. The Elkhart County Visitors Center is 22 miles west of Shipshewana. Tel 574-262-8161; www.Amish Country.org. **SHIPSHEWANA ANTIQUE AND MISCELLANEOUS AUCTION:** contact visitor center, above, for information. *When:* Wed,

A common sight in northern Indiana's Amish Country

year-round; Flea Market Tues–Wed, May–Oct; Shipshewana Horse and Pony Auction, Fri morning, year-round. **AMISH ACRES:** Nappanee. Tel 800-800-4942 or 574-773-4188; www.amishacres.com. Cost: dinner $18. When: closed Jan–Feb. **BEST TIMES:** avoid crowds by visiting in spring, early or late summer, and fall.

Carnival, Festival, and Feast:
America's Most Famous Ag-Extravaganza

IOWA STATE FAIR

Des Moines, Iowa, U.S.A.

Iowa's is the classic state fair, and one of the largest, a quintessentially American event that attracts a million revelers each August to the massive Iowa State Fairgrounds. Fortunately, not much has changed since local novelist

Phil Stong penned *State Fair* in 1932, inspiring Rodgers and Hammerstein's Broadway musical and three motion pictures. There's still hog- (and husband-) calling, cowchip tossing, the Super Bull contest, lots of make-it-and-take-it classes, and one of the symbols of the century-and-a-half-old fair: the beloved Butter Cow, sculpted annually since 1911 from 550 pounds of butter, which is recycled and reused for four to six years. There are real cows, too, of course—lots of them, competing among the more than 56,000 animal and vegetable entries. The Iowa fair, which celebrated its 150th birthday in 2004, is one of the world's largest livestock exhibitions and has the largest number of food categories (875 in 2002) of any state fair. The fair includes the freakish—in 1992, a jumbo squash weighed in here at 412 pounds, a watermelon at nearly 80—and the delicious: The pie department is an old-time favorite, with butterscotch, apricot, strawberry, pumpkin, apple, rhubarb-strawberry, and countless other subdivisions. Food, when it comes right down to it, is everyone's reason for coming to the fair. Among the more than 150 food stands, the culinary icon is the deep-fried corn dog on a stick. Outsize turkey drumsticks are another popular item, as are lamb burgers and pork everything—Iowa is home to 240 million hogs. Two-handful gizmos and grinders (local variations of the sloppy Joe) are followed by sugar-dusted funnel cakes, caramel-dipped apples, and cotton candy. It's all good old-fashioned American fun, and calories be damned.

WHAT: event. **WHERE:** at the same fairgrounds on the east side of town since 1886. Tel 800-545-FAIR; info@iowastatefair.org; www.iowastatefair.org. **COST:** admission $7. **WHEN:** 11 days mid-Aug.

The Iowa State Fair's Sky Glider opened in 1975.

America's Great Homegrown Spirit

THE BOURBON TRAIL

Bardstown, Kentucky, U.S.A.

Rich, amber-colored bourbon, a kind of whiskey distilled almost exclusively in nine Kentucky distilleries (down from twenty-two before Prohibition), is the intoxicating product of native corn and limestone-rich local spring water. About 95 percent of the world's bourbon comes from the state, and each brand boasts its own unique taste and character, defined mostly by the charred new-white-oak barrels where it must be aged a minimum of two years (though most are aged at least four). A whiskey renaissance that began in the 1980s has garnered bourbon newfound attention and respect, with exclusive small-batch premium bourbons helping to elevate the drink's image; they usually boast a higher strength than the normal 90 proof, and are generally aged six to eight years.

Seven Kentucky distilleries are open to the public. Bardstown is the de facto capital of Bourbon country, with distilleries such as Barton's and Heaven Hill right in town; Jim Beam is just 12 miles west and Maker's Mark 17 miles south (and 65 miles south of Louisville). The latter, now a national historic landmark and the nation's oldest working distillery (dating back to 1805), is tucked away on more than 1,000 pastoral acres; its product has been available nationwide only since 1982. World-famous Wild Turkey and Four Roses are 40 miles east of Bardstown near Lawrenceburg, and in nearby Versailles is Labrot & Graham, dating back to 1812: Its elixir has been the subject of praise by everyone from Mark Twain to Walt Whitman.

Bourbon buffs should not miss the annual Kentucky Bourbon Festival, a five-day event full of live music, dancing, historic tours, tastings, great food (including many bourbon-flavored specialties—and not just desserts), and a huge dose of Kentucky hospitality.

Labrot & Graham continues to distill bourbon in traditional copper-pot stills.

WHAT: experience, event. **DISTILLERY TOURS:** information on distilleries open to the public is available at the Bardstown Tourism Bureau, tel 800-638-4877 or 502-348-4877; www.bardstowntourism.com. *When:* distilleries open for tours daily, year-round. **KENTUCKY BOURBON FESTIVAL:** Bardstown. Tel 800-638-4877; www.kybourbonfestival.com. *When:* 6 days in mid-Sept. **BEST TIMES:** Sept–Oct, especially during the Bourbon Festival.

BLUEGRASS COUNTRY

Lexington, Kentucky, U.S.A.

C entral Kentucky's bluegrass country is one of America's most genteel and elegant landscapes, spread over fifteen counties and 4,000 square miles and chockablock with Tara-style manor houses and classic white or black

oak-plank fences. It is also the undisputed international center of thoroughbred horse breeding. Horses live better here than most aristocracy, in cupola-topped barns and handsome stables that look more like French villas or deluxe hotels, with hand-forged gates, stained-glass windows, crystal chandeliers, and impeccable housekeeping.

Central Kentucky's nutrient-dense bluegrass is believed to account in part for its thoroughbreds' success.

Two of America's most scenic byways, the Old Frankfort Pike and the Paris Pike, meander through the region under canopies of century-old trees and past more than 400 stately farms, their emerald fields dotted with mares and foals. Many of the grandest farms are home to past Derby winners (semi-retired four-legged gold mines now employed as fabulously well paid studs), and most are open for behind-the-scenes visits. North of Lexington, the 1,000-acre Kentucky Horse Park, a working horse farm, educational theme park,

and extensive horse museum, is perhaps the best place anywhere to get a feel for the American horse life. And while Louisville's Churchill Downs may be the site of the storied Kentucky Derby, the Keeneland Race Course in Lexington is actually the South's most beautiful. Show up in time to watch workout sessions from dawn to 10 A.M., and follow up with breakfast and gossip at the amiable Track Kitchen, a Keeneland tradition.

If horses in these parts are so pampered, shouldn't visiting humans be as well? They are, at the red brick Greek-Revival Beaumont Inn, which began its career as a finishing school for young ladies in 1845. In the heart of bluegrass country, the plantation-style inn is justifiably known far and wide for its Kentucky country-ham dinners (hickory-smoked and cured for two years in the inn's backyard ham house), served with biscuits, corn pudding, and armloads of Southern hospitality. Don't leave the table without sampling the inn's unforgettable four-layered General Robert E. Lee orange-lemon cake.

WHAT: site, hotel, restaurant. **BLUEGRASS COUNTRY:** Lexington is the best starting point. The Visitors Bureau has maps outlining self-guided drives throughout the area. Tel 800-845-3959 or 859-233-7299; www.visitlex.com. **KENTUCKY HORSE PARK:** 4089 Iron Works Pkwy. (4 miles north of Lexington). Tel 800-678-8813; www.kyhorsepark.com. *Cost:* admission $15. *When:* closed Mon–Tues Nov to mid-Mar. **KEENELAND RACE COURSE:** 4201 Versailles Rd., Lexington. Tel. 800-456-

3412 or 859-254-3412, fax 859-255-2484; www.keeneland.com. *Cost:* admission $2.50. *When:* 16 races in both Apr and Oct; auctions and special events at other times. **BEAUMONT INN:** 638 Beaumont Inn Dr., Harrodsburg (30 miles southwest of Lexington). Tel 859-734-3381, fax 859-734-6897, reservations tel 800-352-3992; www.beaumontinn.com. *Cost:* doubles $95 (low season), $120 (high season).

Dinner $24. *When:* inn open mid-Jan–Dec; restaurant open lunch and dinner, Wed–Sun. **BEST TIMES:** Apr and Oct for thoroughbred racing; Jun for the Kentucky Horse Park's Egyptian Event (a unique Egyptian Arabian horse show; www.pyramidsociety.org) and for its annual Festival of the Bluegrass weekend; Jul and Sept for sales at Keeneland (open to the public).

The United States's Premier Horse Race

THE KENTUCKY DERBY

Louisville, Kentucky, U.S.A.

"This Kentucky Derby, whatever it is," wrote novelist John Steinbeck, "a race, an emotion, a turbulence, an explosion—is one of the most beautiful and violent and satisfying things I have ever experienced."

Billed with little exaggeration as "the greatest two minutes in sports," the Kentucky Derby is the oldest continuously held sporting event in America and one of the most prestigious races in the world. Although horse racing in Kentucky dates back to 1789, Louisville's Churchill Downs didn't officially open as the home of the Derby until almost 100 years later (when the purse for the famed race was just $1,000). The ten days of festivities begin in mid-April, the nicest time of the year in the Bluegrass State, when the dogwoods are in full, magnificent bloom. Thunder Over Louisville, the largest annual fireworks display in the country, sets the events in motion, followed by the Pegasus Parade, the Great Hot Air Balloon Race, live concerts, and steamboat races, all washed down with rivers of mint juleps. For lodging between events, well-heeled Derby veterans have checked into the Seelbach Hotel since its 1905 opening. Its comfortable grandeur so impressed hotel guest F. Scott Fitzgerald that he set a scene from *The Great Gatsby* here.

Horse fans not attending "The Run for the Roses" can enjoy "Dawn at the Downs," beginning the Saturday before the Derby and continuing Monday through Thursday of Derby Week. The track is opened to the public from 7 A.M. to 10 A.M., and visitors can enjoy a Kentucky-style buffet breakfast while watching celebrity equines (and an occasional Derby contender) go through their training. If you happen to miss Derby season completely, you can relive the excitement of past races at the Kentucky Derby Museum, where the

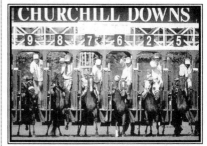

Thoroughbreds can maintain a speed of 45 miles per hour for more than one mile.

careers of its many champions are documented inspiringly.

WHAT: event, hotel. **CHURCHILL DOWNS/ KENTUCKY DERBY:** 700 Central Ave., Louisville (90 miles west of Lexington). Tel 502-636-4400; www.churchilldowns.com. *Cost:* standing-room-only general admission to Kentucky Derby sold the day of the race (with no access to reserved seating areas) $40; call for reserved-seating prices. *When:* derby held the first Sat in May; (written requests for ticket applica-

tions must be received before Nov of previous year). **SEELBACH HOTEL:** 500 4th Ave. Tel 800-333-3399 or 502-585-3200, fax 502-585-9239. *Cost:* doubles $159 (low season); Derby weekend prices upon request. **KENTUCKY DERBY MUSEUM:** at Churchill Downs. Tel 502-637-7097; www.derbymuseum.org. *Cost:* admission $8. *When:* open daily. **BEST TIMES:** late Apr and early May for the Derby; late Apr through 1st week of Jul for spring racing meet; final week of Oct–Nov for fall meet.

A Gumbo of Pleasures in America's Most Un-American City

THE FRENCH QUARTER

New Orleans, Louisiana, U.S.A.

N'Awlins is a fascinating city of contradictions, a sultry melting pot of indigenous French, Spanish, Creole, and Southern styles that perfectly blends decadence and elegance, Old South conservatism and rowdy debauchery, extroversion and sleepiness, gentility and tawdriness. It's hard to imagine a more impulsive or seductive city (this is where Rhett Butler brought Scarlett O'Hara for their honeymoon) or a more palatable one—the food scene is one of the country's most remarkable (see restaurant entry that follows) and music is everywhere.

The myriad pleasures of the Big Easy are jam-packed within the lively grid of streets that make up the Vieux Carré (French Quarter), the heavily touristed yet also heavily residential heart of the city, a compact ninety-square-block neighborhood of narrow cobbled streets first laid out by the French and Spanish in the 1720s. Gloriously faded 18th- and 19th-century landmark buildings house swanky stores selling museum-quality antiques, alongside others hawking alligator paté and voodoo paraphernalia all hours of the day. Out on the streets you'll risk sensory overload from the musicians, magicians, psychics, human sculptures, and tap dancers (who use bottle caps on their shoes). Jackson Square, facing the Mississippi River, is the epicenter of activity—you can take it all in from the alfresco, twenty-four-hour Café du Monde on the square's shady edge, famous for its beignets (deep-fried doughnuts dusted in powdered sugar) and chicory-charged coffee, a curious custom left over from Civil War days.

WHAT: site. **WHERE:** between the Mississippi River and Rampart St. to the north, and from Canal St. to Esplanade Ave. on the west and east. Jackson Square is between Decatur and Chartres Sts., at Madison. Café du Monde is at 800 Decatur. For information see www.frenchquarter.com. **BEST TIMES:** early spring for Mardi Gras; early Apr for the French Quarter Festival, held over a 3-day weekend; late Apr for Jazz Fest—though almost every weekend year-round promises a festival of one kind or another. Best months weather-wise are Feb and Mar, Oct, and Nov.

From Dives to Haute Creole Palaces

THE NEW ORLEANS RESTAURANT SCENE

New Orleans, Louisiana, U.S.A.

In the Crescent City, food is a religion, a place where the funkiest neighborhood spot is as much worth visiting as the grandest haute traditional restaurant. Emeril Lagasse (a transplanted Massachusetts man who's now über-Louisianan) may have pumped up the city's food-media image in recent years, but he hardly started from scratch. New Orleans has always been up there with New York and San Francisco on the list of American foodie-traveler hot spots.

In the city where jazz was born, the Jazz Brunch at Commander's Palace is a weekend tradition cherished by New Orleanians as well as tourists. Housed in a frothy blue-and-white Victorian mansion in the fabled Garden District, Commander's is the very embodiment of New Orleans graciousness, with cuisine that's decidedly Creole. Whether you're in the Garden Room favored by the locals or in the shade of the open courtyard's massive oak tree, order the signature turtle soup au sherry, the crispy pecan-crusted gulf fish, and the famous bread pudding soufflé wading in bourbon cream sauce that evaporates as it hits the tongue.

In the French Quarter, dining at Galatoire's has been a New Orleans tradition for the better part of a century, even though its egalitarian no-reservations policy (for the main dining room only) means that celebrities, visitors, and local patrons alike sometimes have to line up along Bourbon Street, the men dressed in jackets to conform to the restaurant's vintage dress code, no matter what the temperature. Inside, the timeless decor of brass fixtures, gleaming mirrors, polished wood, black, white, and green tiled floors, and a dozen ceiling fans hasn't changed much over the years, nor has the menu. Tuxedoed waiters bear appetizers of Shrimp Remoulade or Oysters Rockefeller, and entrées such as Galatoire's famous Lamb Chops Béarnaise, Trout Marguery, or grilled Pompano straight from the Gulf waters. The food is surpassed only by the floor show, which peaks on Fridays at lunchtime: Everyone is drinking, table-hopping, and recounting loud stories; the chatter crescendos, corks pop, "Happy Birthday" is sung at least once. Even newcomers soon get into the spirit of camaraderie and genteel long-lunch decadence.

Sometimes you just want to avoid white-linen locales, and when that urge strikes, nothing will do but to head for the Acme Oyster House, the town's most venerated dive since its founding in 1910. Down-home, unpretentious, forever full and jumping, it promises a Big Easy evening of elbow-to-elbow bonhomie with locals, luminaries, and Joe and Jane from Chicago, all of whom come for the reliably excellent food, washed down by the local Dixie or Abita beer, served ice-cold. In addition to its award-winning fresh and salty raw oysters and fried-oyster-filled po'boys (sandwiches made with crusty French bread), there is also a full menu of local delicacies prepared to perfection: gumbo poopa, creole jambalaya, and the seasonal crawfish étouffée. The enormous mirror behind the marble-topped raw bar reflects the roll-up-your-sleeves-and-wolf-down-those-oysters action, with a team of five shuckers bantering nonstop while opening about 5,000 oysters a day.

Other holy highlights for food-worshippers include Mother's on the Quarter's edge, where one bite of the fried seafood po'boy will explain why you might find a line that often stretches out the door. Owned and operated by Jerry and John Amato, this authentic home-style eatery has been open for over half a century. The weathered and funky Napoleon House is another winner, serving a muffuletta sandwich that's said to be the best in town. The fame of their Pimm's cup is not to be ignored either. A few other contenders: Emeril's own bastion at Nola; the high-altar haute of tradition-bound Antoine's; the more contemporary globe-hopping menu at Bayona.

WHAT: restaurant. **COMMANDER'S PALACE:** 1403 Washington Ave. Tel 504-899-8221; www.commanderspalace.com. *Cost:* Jazz brunch $39, dinner $40. *When:* dinner daily, lunch Mon–Fri, brunch Sat–Sun.

GALATOIRE'S: 209 Bourbon St. Tel 504-525-2021; www.galatoires.com. *Cost:* dinner $45. *When:* lunch and dinner daily, except Mon. **ACME OYSTER HOUSE:** 724 Iberville St. Tel 504-522-5973; www.acmeoyster.com. *Cost:* 12 oysters on the half shell $7, dinner $15. *When:* lunch, dinner daily; oysters available year-round (ignore the myth of eating oysters during "r" months only). **NAPOLEON HOUSE:** 500 Chartres St. Tel 504-524-9752. *Cost:* dinner $30. *When:* lunch and dinner daily. **NOLA:** 534 St. Louis St. Tel 504-522-6652; www.emerils. com. *Cost:* dinner $35. *When:* lunch and dinner Mon–Sat, dinner only on Sun. **ANTOINE'S:** 713 St. Louis St. Tel 504-581-4422; www.antoines. com. *Cost:* dinner $65. *When:* lunch and dinner Mon–Sat. **BAYONA:** 430 Dauphine St. Tel 504-525-4455; www.bayona.com. *Cost:* dinner $45. *When:* lunch and dinner Wed–Sat, dinner only on Mon–Tues. **MOTHER'S:** 401 Poydras St. Tel 504-523-9656; www.mothersrestaurant.net. *Cost:* po'boys $6.50–$11. **BEST TIMES:** year-round, though for oysters you should go during the cooler months (Oct–May), when they're fatter and saltier.

Let the Good Times Roll

MARDI GRAS

New Orleans, Louisiana, U.S.A.

Mardi Gras would be heaven without the multitudes of half-lit party-goers, but it would also not be Mardi Gras, so those of the "laissez les bons temps roulez" mentality should make a beeline for America's

biggest, funnest, and most show-stopping party. Months of intense preparation go into the creation of elaborate two- and three-story floats and costumes to match, crescendoing to a funky marching-band beat during the twelve-day lead-up to Mardi Gras itself. (Mardi Gras, which means "Fat Tuesday," is the day before Ash Wednesday, which ushers

in the forty days of the Catholic Lenten period, leading up to Easter.) This is New Orleans's exuberant feast before the famine, a dizzy intertwining of its centuries-old Caribbean and European cultural roots, as much a commercial show to reap tourism dollars as a revered local tradition around which otherwise conservative New Orleanians orchestrate their year. This is their party, but the world is invited.

If you're willing to get out there early, you may be able to stake out a spot along the parade routes of St. Charles Avenue and Canal Street, amid a sea of carnivalistas chanting "Throw me something, mister!"—the festival mantra, which every New Orleanian learns at Mama's knee. Uncounted tons of "throws"—plastic doubloons, trinkets, and ticky-tack beaded necklaces—are tossed by float-borne revelers in the fifty-some parades that begin in earnest two weeks prior to Fat Tuesday; the biggest and best—featuring the famous floats—take place day and night beginning the previous Thursday.

WHAT: event. **WHERE:** for information, tel 800-672-6124; www.mardigras.com; www. neworleanscvb.com. **WHEN:** Mardi Gras is a movable holiday, tied to Easter. Official opening day for the Carnival season is Twelfth Night or Epiphany, Jan 6. There are dozens of masked balls on the nights leading up to Fat Tues, most of them thrown by private clubs or "krewes." It is difficult but not impossible to buy tickets to a select few of them. Contact the tourism office for details.

Celebrating a Unique Union of Music and Culture

NEW ORLEANS JAZZ AND HERITAGE FESTIVAL

New Orleans, Louisiana, U.S.A.

The Big Easy's annual Jazz and Heritage Festival, one of America's great parties, has been giving Mardi Gras a run for its money lately. During ten days, 4,000 musicians perform on eleven stages of splendid dissonance, offering jazz, Cajun, Latin, zydeco, R & B, country and western, rock, gospel, and African-Caribbean music—with exuberant brass bands marching tirelessly through it all. Today's jazz and soul luminaries (including such New Orleans natives as Wynton Marsalis, Harry Connick Jr., and the Neville Brothers) wouldn't miss this shindig. Neither should you. The best of Louisiana's culinary heritage shares the spotlight, from shrimp po'boys to crawfish monica, alligator piquante, and jambalaya. Dessert? Try the endless variations of pralines, pecan pie, and sweet potato pone.

WHAT: event. **WHERE:** Fair Grounds Race Track. For information, tel 504-522-4786; www.nojazzfest.com. **COST:** tickets $40 in advance, $50 at the gate for all-day Heritage Fair admission; prices for evening concerts vary. **WHEN:** 10 days beginning late Apr.

An acoustic blues performance contributes to the rich sounds of the New Orleans Jazz Festival.

The Mother Lode of Jazz in the City That Birthed It

PRESERVATION HALL

New Orleans, Louisiana, U.S.A.

The music we now know as jazz was born in late-19th-century New Orleans, birthed from a confluence of European marching band music and African rhythms and brought up by dance and party musicians such as cornetist Buddy Bolden, drummer Papa Jack Laine, and pianist Jelly Roll Morton, who performed in the high-class bordellos of the legendary Storyville district. Locally born Louis "Satchmo" Armstrong gave the music a new and clear voice in the 1920s and 1930s. Though the city's importance as a musical center faded during the subsequent big band, be-bop, and postbop eras, by the late 1980s local trumpeter Wynton Marsalis and his family had succeeded in repopularizing the traditional New Orleans sound.

New Orleans's once frequent marching jazz funerals are becoming increasingly rare, but dozens of music venues are scattered throughout the city, in the French Quarter and beyond. For traditional jazz, visit the dark and spartan Preservation Hall, beloved by purists, showcasing classic New Orleans jazz. With a worn, wooden floor, no food or drinks, and only a few wooden benches for seating, the place is a diamond in brown-paper-bag clothing, a world-famous institution since it opened in 1961. The musical pilgrimage continues at the legendary Tipitina's (501 Napoleon Avenue) where jazz, Cajun, country, and R & B keep the dance floor full in what once was a gambling hall and whorehouse; then on to Snug Harbor (626 Frenchman Street), the best place to find contemporary jazz and R & B, with regular appearances by some big names. The best zydeco is Thursday night at the Mid-City Bowling Lanes, a.k.a. Rock 'n' Bowl (4133 S. Carrollton Avenue); other evenings are given over to Cajun, R & B, and jazz. And then there are those days when it may seem that the sax player in front of the cathedral in Jackson Square is the best thing you've heard all week—and it's free.

WHAT: site. **WHERE:** 726 St. Peter St. Tel 800-785-5772 or 504-522-2841 (day), 504-523-8939 (night), fax 504-558-9192; www.preservationhall.com. **COST:** admission $10. **WHEN:** doors open at 8 P.M. daily.

Serene Civility in the French Quarter

SONIAT HOUSE

New Orleans, Louisiana, U.S.A.

Considered by many to be the most beautiful hotel in town, the genteel, thirty-three-room Soniat House is quintessential New Orleans, decorated with lacy ironwork and located on a central French Quarter block that somehow seems far from the noise and honky-tonk. The 19th-century Creole mansion was built by a prosperous plantation owner and is today an incongruous though harmonious mélange of choice period pieces and modern-day comforts and amenities, including paintings on loan from the New Orleans Museum. The attractive rooms offer four-poster beds, toile de Jouy bedspreads, skylights, Oriental carpets, and thoughtfully chosen French and Louisiana antiques. Many of the guest rooms

overlook the romantic interior courtyard, lush with red hibiscus and palmetto palms. You can choose to have your breakfast there, listening to the rippling fountain while you savor the just-out-of-the-oven buttermilk biscuits with homemade preserves and sip steaming cups of chicory-charged coffee.

WHAT: hotel. **WHERE:** 1133 Chartres St. Tel 800-544-8808 or 504-522-0570, fax 504-522-7208; www.soniathouse.com. **COST:** doubles from $240.

Nature Unvarnished on Mount Desert Island

ACADIA NATIONAL PARK

Maine, U.S.A.

Mount Desert Island (from the French word meaning "bare," and pronounced like the English word *dessert*) is Maine's national treasure, a 12-by-14-mile domain of walks, sights, inns, and eating places that are as captivating today as when the Rockefellers, Astors, Fords, Vanderbilts, and their fellow "rusticators" founded a summer colony here in the early 20th century. The families later bequeathed much of the island to the government, which in 1929 set aside 60 percent of it as Acadia National Park, throwing a few neighboring islands in for good measure to create a park that's 35,000 total acres of craggy grandeur. It's got extraordinary oceanside drives along surf-battered bluffs, off-island whale-watching, and lobster shacks that promise ambrosial sustenance-with-a-view.

The timeless serenity of the island is tested by the ever increasing number of visitors—its centerpiece draw, for instance, the swooping 20-mile Park Loop Road, attracts big crowds (and for good reason)—but motorized tourism is nothing new. In 1917, when John D. Rockefeller Jr. became unhappy with the arrival of the noisy automobile on the island, he began work on the 57-mile network of

Acadia is dotted with more than twenty ponds and lakes.

graceful, bridge-linked carriage roads that are today some of the nation's loveliest car-free walking and bicycling roads. They become a splendid network of cross-country ski trails off-season. All across the island, about 120 total miles of hiking trails offer great views and high drama, at the expense of only moderate effort. Most people, however, will need a car to observe the park tradition of watching sunrise from Cadillac Mountain, at 1,530 feet the highest peak on the U.S. Atlantic coast, the spot where America catches its first rays of the morning sun.

Plan to arrive at Jordan Pond House on the Park Loop Road in time for late afternoon tea and popovers on the restaurant's front lawn, another island tradition dating back more than 100 years. Rusticate overnight at the island's Claremont Hotel and Cottages, sitting grandly on 6 shorefront acres since 1869. Rock away on the hotel porch with poetry-inspiring views of the Somes Sound, guarded on both sides by Acadia's mountains. The same idyllic view is enjoyed by window-front tables in the dining room, where a hearty breakfast stokes early risers for that trip up Cadillac Mountain.

WHAT: island, site, hotel. **MOUNT DESERT ISLAND:** connected to the mainland by a causeway, 36 miles southeast of Bangor. **ACADIA NATIONAL PARK:** general information, tel 207-288-3338; www.nps.gov/acad. *Cost:* admission. *When:* open daily year-round, though Park Loop Rd. is closed Dec–mid-April. **CLAREMONT HOTEL:** Southwest Harbor, near the mouth of Somes Sound. Tel 207-244-5036; www.theclaremonthotel.com. *Cost:* doubles from $120 (low season), from $185 (high season). **BEST TIMES:** Jul–Aug for the best weather and whale-watching (though it's also the busiest period); spring and fall foliage times are also lovely.

The Greatest Sailing on the Eastern Seaboard

MAINE WINDJAMMER ASSOCIATION

Camden, Maine, U.S.A.

S parkling Penobscot Bay, a standout among Maine's 3,500 miles of pristine and craggy coast (the largest stretch of shoreline in the forty-eight contiguous states), is dotted with some 3,000 islands and has been a maritime

center since the 17th century. Little wonder, then, that its waters are home to the nation's largest fleet of traditional wooden schooners, historic late-19th- and early-20th-century ships that specialize in three- to six-day

Passengers can choose to help the crew sail the ship.

sailing adventures, always within sight of the pine- and spruce-covered coastline and the fabulous yet low-key shingled "cottages" built 100 years ago for the summering rich. Going where the wind carries you through America's quintessential cruising grounds means celebrating paint-by-numbers sunsets, passing lighthouses right out of Andrew Wyeth paintings, and enjoying impromptu stops at tiny deserted islands to enjoy a feast of lobsters, plucked live moments before from a passing fisherman's boat. Accommodations aboard ship are generally small and spare, and nightlife is nonexistent except for counting the shooting stars, but you can just about finish that bestseller by the light of the moon.

WHAT: experience. **WHERE:** cruises set sail from Camden, Rockland, and Rockport. Camden is 60 miles southwest of Bangor, 190 miles north of Boston. **HOW:** a number of agencies in the Penobscot Bay area organize cruises. The Maine Windjammer Association represents the largest number of ships: 12 total (all privately owned and operated), 9 of which are designated National Historic Landmarks. Tel 800-807-WIND; windjam@ acadia.net; www.sailmainecoast.com. **COST:** average all-inclusive per person from $425 for 3 days. **WHEN:** departures mid-May to mid-Oct. **BEST TIMES:** Jul and Aug.

A Maine Mainstay

THE WHITE BARN INN

Kennebunkport, Maine, U.S.A.

The summer retreat of the first president George Bush (and sometimes of the second, though W. more commonly heads to his ranch in Texas), picture-perfect Kennebunkport is the setting for The White Barn, one of New England's most special inns. The converted 19th-century farm is comprised of four buildings dating to the 1820s, including a gatehouse, carriage house, May's Cottage (where the inn's original owner once lived), and the main building, a classic autumn-gold clapboard with white trim. Spread among these buildings, twenty-five meticulously appointed European-style guest rooms are done up with four-posted, canopy, and sleigh beds, and modern amenities including Jacuzzis. A pool offers an alternative to sandy Gooch's Beach, within walking distance but with water that's almost always too cold for swimming.

A highlight of any stay is the inn's restaurant, widely considered the best dining room north of Boston. Rustic and refined blend seamlessly in a setting of two lofty barns (one relocated here from the surrounding countryside), with creaky floorboards and locally crafted antiques, all glowing with candlelight. Succulent lobster appears in many guises on the menu, sometimes center-stage as an entrée and sometimes as a base for chunky minestrone soup. For a more casual feast, try the old-fashioned Mabel's Lobster Claw, near the Bushes' secluded compound on Ocean Avenue.

The White Barn Inn's rustic dining room looks onto a lush garden.

Sit outside on a little porch with your simple feast of seafood or their legendary lobster roll, and be sure to save room for the homemade peanut butter ice cream.

WHAT: hotel, restaurant. **THE WHITE BARN INN:** 37 Beach Ave. (Kennebunkport is 20 miles south of Portland). Tel 207-967-2321, fax 207-967-1100; www.whitebarninn.com. *Cost:* doubles $310 (low season), $440 (high season). Dinner $95. **MABEL'S LOBSTER CLAW:** 124 Ocean Ave. Tel 207-967-2562. **BEST TIMES:** spring–fall; the town's very New Englandy holiday celebration, the Christmas Prelude festival (www.christmasprelude.com), is held the 1st week of Dec.

Where Crustacean Is King

MAINE
LOBSTER FESTIVAL

Rockland, Maine, U.S.A.

For centuries considered food for the poor (its looks couldn't have helped much), the lobster is now unanimously considered the food of the gods, which would make Maine a veritable lobster Valhalla. Its claim to fame, the *Homarus americanus*, is generally considered the finest-eating crustacean in the sea, so sweet and succulent that one could almost dispense with the obligatory melted butter. Maine and lobster are all but synonymous (for a while the state even used the lobster on its license plates), and with good reason: The average annual catch along the state's indented coastline generally exceeds 36 million pounds—more than half the national total. Rockland, on Penobscot Bay, is the capital of the lobster universe, hosting an annual Lobster Festival that for more than fifty years has

Homo sapiens *enjoying* Homarus americanus

offered days full of live music, seafood-cooking and lobster-eating contests, the coronation of a Sea Goddess, and enough Americana to last till the following year at least.

Even if you're not in-state for the festivities, heavenly lobster dinners can be had almost any time at any of a thousand shacks, huts, pounds, and farms found scattered among Maine's coastal towns—it seems like every town that can float a fishing boat has one. Simple preparations are the best and most Yankee way to go—steamed or boiled, though the lobster roll (usually served on a hot dog bun with chunks of meat right from the shell) is a favorite and much less laborious and sloppy alternative. As for where to dine, you can't beat dockside, amid the perfume of the salt air, the sound of the ocean, and the screech of seagulls nose-diving for your unattended french fries.

WHAT: event, restaurant. **WHERE:** 61 miles from Bangor, 78 miles from Portland, 190 miles from Boston. The Lobster Festival is held in Harbor Park, overlooking Penobscot Bay. Tel 800-LOB-CLAW or 207-596-0376; www.mainelobsterfestival.com. **WHEN:** for 5 days (Wed–Sun) in late Jul/early Aug. **BEST TIMES:** lobster "season" is year-round. Lobsters shed their shells in early summer, when the soft-shell (or "shedder") variety is caught and served; it's easier to eat and is preferred by many, though hard-shell lobsters offer more meat.

Crab Town's Epicenter

OBRYCKI'S

Baltimore, Maryland, U.S.A.

O f the more than 2 million pounds of spindly-legged blue crabs annually harvested in Maryland's nearby Chesapeake Bay, a great number of them are merrily consumed in Crab Town, otherwise known as Baltimore.

At the center of this crab frenzy is Obrycki's, a friendly family-run institution where the freshest and the best-prepared crabs have been served since 1944. Don't come for atmosphere (think 250 bibbed mallet-wielding crab pickers at untidy brown-paper-covered tables anchored with pitchers of home-brewed beer), but do come for the freshest crabmeat. You can choose among trays of freshly steamed crabs coated with a piquant secret blend of spices (more peppery than Baltimore's own Old Bay spice), or crab cakes, savory cream of crab soup, deviled crab balls, crab meat cocktail, crab marinara linguini . . . you get the idea. It's hard to imagine, but you just might have room for dessert, and nothing tops off the night better than Obrycki's justly famous éclair supreme. Crab picking is hard work, but if you have any energy left over, take a stroll around Baltimore's 200-year-old, recently spiffed-up Inner Harbor area and its centerpiece National Aquarium.

WHAT: restaurant. **WHERE:** east of Inner Harbor at 1727 E. Pratt St., in the Fells Point neighborhood. Tel 410-732-6399; www.obryckis.com. **COST:** 12 steamed crabs $26 (small) to $62 (jumbo); average crab dinner $40; you can also have crabs shipped. **WHEN:** open mid-Mar to mid-Nov; mail order available year-round. **BEST TIMES:** Jun–Jul for soft-shell crabs, Aug–Oct for hard-shell.

Americana Charm on the Eastern Shore

CHESAPEAKE BAY

St. Michael's, Maryland, U.S.A.

T he Chesapeake Bay's ragged eastern shoreline is a weave of waterways with fingers of centuries-old farmland sloping to the water's edge. Small waterside towns were founded here in the 17th and 18th centuries as

shipbuilding hubs and trading ports, and today remain largely unspoiled and popular as low-key boating destinations. The triangle formed by St. Michael's, Oxford, and Easton is an enclave of well-preserved pre-Revolutionary and Federalist homes, all within 12 miles of each other. Quiet and quaint towns that are a delight to explore by foot, they offer vignettes of gracious homes with inviting porch swings, venerable magnolia trees, historic inns, and many antique stores. St. Michael's is the most visited, with the highly regarded Chesapeake

Bay Maritime Museum at Navy Point dedicated to preserving the bay's cultural heritage.

The principal pastime of visitors to the Chesapeake Bay ("Great Shellfish Bay" in the language of the Susquehanna Indians) is reveling in the area's celebrated crabs, which James Michener called "the best food under the sun" in his epic novel *Chesapeake*. Together with Atlantic blue crab, clams, shad, and rockfish (known elsewhere as striped bass), wild duck and wild goose remind restaurantgoers that this is also hunting country. Of the once-common oyster there are few left to dredge, and the two-sailed skipjack sloops have taken instead to offering cruises lasting anywhere from a few hours to a few days.

Further south is Crisfield, "The Crab Capital of the World." Boats leave regularly from here for the time-warped islands Tangier and Smith, whose watermen have been making a simple living from the Chesapeake Bay since the 1600s.

When price is not an issue, make your base at the exquisite Inn at Perry Cabin, the area's most luxurious. Built in the early 19th century, the river- and dockside Colonial Revival estate was purchased and impeccably refurbished in 1999, and is today part of the exclusive Orient-Express Hotels group.

WHAT: town, site, hotel. **ST. MICHAEL'S:** 70 miles east of Washington D.C., 90 miles southwest of Philadelphia. **THE INN AT PERRY CABIN:** tel 800-237-1236 or 410-745-2200, fax 410-745-3348; info@perrycabin.com; www.perrycabin.com. *Cost:* from $360. Dinner $50. **BEST TIMES:** in mid-Jun for St. Michael's Antique and Classic Boat Festival; in Aug for Crisfield's Crab Festival; in early Nov for Easton's 3-day Waterfowl Festival. Crabs-wise, Jun–Jul for soft-shell crabs, Aug–Oct for hard-shell.

A Patriotic Amble Through America's Most Historic City

THE FREEDOM TRAIL

Boston, Massachusetts, U.S.A.

Boston is compact, navigable, and steeped in history, making it one of America's finest and most interesting walking cities. Everything is within easy reach if you tour on foot via the 3-mile, self-guided Freedom Trail.

Beginning at Boston Common (a onetime cow pasture that is today the nation's oldest park), it follows a signposted, red-striped trail to eighteen Revolutionary War–era landmarks, including churches, graveyards, monuments, houses of government, and the U.S.S. *Constitution*, also known as Old Ironsides. The vessel was first launched in 1797, received its nickname during the War of 1812, and is still afloat today. It's the oldest commissioned warship in the U.S. Navy, and never lost a battle. The trail also takes in Faneuil Hall, Boston's original marketplace and once the colony's meeting hall and public forum. Vibrant and jam-packed, it's home today to the venerable Durgin Park, an unchic but much-loved eating institution. Visit the clapboard Paul Revere House, built in 1680 and purchased by patriot-silversmith Paul "one-if-by-land-

Paul Revere and his horse

two-if-by-sea" Revere and his family in 1770. It's the oldest dwelling in Boston and one of the finest 17th-century residential buildings to be found anywhere in America. Also along the route is the Old State House, Boston's oldest public building (1713) and the British government headquarters in the colonies.

WHAT: experience. **WHERE:** start at the Visitors Information Bureau on the Tremont St. side of Boston Common. For information, tel 888-SEE-BOSTO; www.thefreedomtrail.org or www.BostonUSA.com. **COST:** admission to some of the sites. **BEST TIMES:** May–Oct, and Jul for Harborfest.

Unique Creation of One Woman's Personal Taste

ISABELLA STEWART GARDNER MUSEUM

Boston, Massachusetts, U.S.A.

Beantown is a gem of a museum town. The city's heavyweight, the Museum of Fine Arts, is one of the finest in the nation, particularly prized for its unrivaled collection of Asian and Japanese art. Among the more intimate museums, however, the small, exquisite Gardner Museum is a standout, housing an idiosyncratic collection of European, Asian, and American art that's large enough to exhaust any museumgoer. In the 1890s, the fiercely individualistic and wealthy Mrs. Gardner called upon art historian Bernard Berenson to help her amass one of America's most important private collections, which she opened to the public in 1903 with more than 2,500 objects, including works by Giotto, Raphael, Rembrandt, and the only Piero della Francesca fresco outside Italy. The museum's highlight is arguably Titian's *Europa*, long considered one of the finest

The museum's Dutch Room

Italian paintings in America. A John Singer Sargent portrait of Gardner presides over the museum today, but that's not the only way in which her influence remains known: Provisions of her will specify that the collection be held in permanent trust for the "education and enjoyment of the public forever." What that means is that the museum's home—an ersatz 15th-century-style Venetian palazzo built in 1900, and known as Fenway Court when Mrs. Gardner lived here—remains exactly as "Mrs. Jack" left it when she died in 1924: a haphazardly plotted mosaic of eclectic Victorian clutter, its art galleries surrounding a four-story skylit courtyard filled with blooming flowers and statuary and ringed with tall windows on every level.

WHAT: site. **WHERE:** 280 The Fenway. Tel

617-566-1401; www.gardnermuseum.org. **COST:** $12 admission weekdays. **WHEN:** open Tues–Sun. **BEST TIMES:** courtyard loveliest at Christmas when filled with poinsettias and holly bushes, and in Apr when the narcissus are in bloom. The museum hosts the city's best series of chamber music concerts Sept–Jun in the Tapestry Room.

A Hallowed Haunt of Impeccably Fresh Fish

LEGAL SEA FOODS

Boston, Massachusetts, U.S.A.

D espite Boston's recent culinary hype, and despite a new generation of chefs that dismisses the city's old-guard establishments as boring or bland, Bostonians cherish tradition and the tried-and-true, and that's where

Legal Sea Foods comes in. It's not the trendiest nor the most chic of Boston's countless fish and shellfish eateries, but if you want freshness and quality, you'll find it here—right out of the sea and onto your plate. (The restaurant's motto: If it isn't fresh, it isn't Legal!) The family-owned institution has been around since 1950, first as a small fish market in Cambridge, then (in 1968) as a sawdust-floored restaurant. Things are a mite fancier today at the twenty-six Legal locations, but the menu has not changed radically. Its rich but not too thick New England clam chowder is arguably the best in town (constant queues stand testimony), and so are the fried clams. Whatever looked like a winner at the morning's market turns up on the day's menu—broiled, baked, stir fried, grilled, fried, steamed, or in a casserole, with raw oysters and littleneck and cherrystone clam first courses among the most requested offerings. (Don't worry: The restaurant is fanatical about testing its seafood for freshness and purity.) Astonishingly helpful and friendly staff are visibly proud to work at one of Boston's landmark restaurants, and the renown of their Boston cream pie does its part to bring in the crowds, too.

WHAT: restaurant. **WHERE:** Legal Sea Foods, 100 Huntington Ave., Copley Plaza. Tel 617-266-7775, fax 617-266-6304; www.legalseafoods.com. **COST:** dinner $30.

The World Series of Flea Markets

BRIMFIELD OUTDOOR ANTIQUES SHOW

Brimfield, Massachusetts, U.S.A.

T hree times a year, the 120-acre location of America's largest and most famous antiques market teems with more than 6,000 dealers and some 130,000 visitors who come to forage through history's marketplace. This is serious business for major-league swappers and shoppers who are on a mission to pitch or buy that perfect pre-Revolutionary silver tureen or brass postal scale. Twenty-three separate fields along Route 20 resemble a colorful Bedouin camp, brimming with tented dealers who come from all over America, bringing only their choicest pieces to this show. Major designers, decorators, and store owners come with empty U-Hauls at the ready, prepared for war.

Brimfield is not for wimps. The show's first days are for serious hunters and gatherers, and at 4:30 A.M. on opening day (Tuesday), the wheeling and dealing is furious and fevered. Saturday and Sunday are strictly for casual hobbyists who have no idea what they've missed, content to pick through any remaining unwantables, seeking the odd treasure among the trinkets. They'll usually buy something—anything—rather than go home empty-handed. The good news? Most dealers don't want to take merchandise back home, and will consider best-offer requests. Oh, and an insider's tip: It almost always rains during the May show, and snow is not unheard of.

WHAT: event. **WHERE:** 80 miles west of Boston, 170 miles north of New York City. Tel 413-283-6149; www.quaboag.com. **WHEN:** for 6 days (Tues–Sun), 3 times a year, beginning the 2d Tues in May, 2d Tues after Jul 4th, and 1st Tues in Sept after Labor Day.

Nature, Pristine and Wild

CAPE COD NATIONAL SEASHORE

Massachusetts, U.S.A.

A 40-mile strip of sea-pounded sand dunes, Cape Cod National Seashore has enjoyed federal protection only since 1961 (thanks to longtime summer son John F. Kennedy), but in fact precious little has changed

since Henry David Thoreau roamed the area in the 1850s, describing it as a place where "a man can stand and put all America behind him." From Chatham (at the peninsula's "elbow") in the south to artsy, end-of-the-line Provincetown (its "fist") at the northernmost tip, the solitary seashore of wide, open beaches, lighthouses, big waves, and rippling dune grass is one of America's most magnificent—over 43,000 acres of dramatic high dunes, the ubiquitous sea, and an ever-changing play of light. In autumn, one of the area's sweetest seasons, the Outer Cape is a flyway for more than 300 migratory species.

Once nothing more than a sandy Indian footpath, the Old King's Highway (a.k.a. Route 6A) is today a winding two-lane road

The parabolic dunes of Cape Cod

relatively free of strip malls and neon signs. It runs from the northern reaches of the Cape (oddly called the Lower Cape), through towns such as Truro and Eastham, which many consider to be the purest distillation of the Cape Cod spirit.

Chatham, a classic New England town, has long been an outpost for the discreetly wealthy: Witness the 25-acre, stately seaside resort of Chatham Bars Inn, a venerable monument to another time. Built as a hunting lodge in 1914, the historic hotel boasts an impressive list of amenities, and is much loved for its white-gloved but friendly staff, its

cottages, its wide porch lined with wicker rockers overlooking the beach, and for a Wednesday night New England clam and lobster bake under the stars.

WHAT: site, hotel. **CHATHAM:** 90 miles from Boston, 270 miles north of New York City. **CHATHAM BARS INN:** Shore Road. Tel 800-527-4884 or 508-945-0096, fax 508-945-6785; www.chathambarsinn.com. *Cost:* doubles from $195 (low season), from $455 (high season). **BEST TIMES:** spring and fall are lovely and uncrowded. Water reaches its warmest late Aug. Thanksgiving and Christmas are favorites for family stays at the inn.

Nirvana on the Clam Shell

WOODMAN'S OF ESSEX

Essex, Massachusetts, U.S.A.

Woodman's is the ultimate Massachusetts clam shack, and (so they say) the hallowed birthplace of the fried clam. Is it true? Well, maybe. What's true is that you'll never find this American delicacy tasting any

better elsewhere. Located north of Boston in an old shipbuilding town at the heart of the clam belt, Woodman's is a sprawling, ramshackle place full of wooden booths and picnic benches always packed with clam lovers, who often line the roadside on Saturday nights, waiting to get in. It is known far and wide for its plump, crunchy wonders—whole clams (the menu also offers clam strips) dipped in milk, robed in cornmeal, and dropped into 350-degree boiling lard. And Eureka! Harvested mostly by local clammers, they're the very essence of New Englandness, the area's haute cuisine. If one can believe the family myth, Chubby Woodman taught Howard Johnson how to fry 'em, and today Chubby's grandchildren do the frying, serving an average of 2,000 people on a busy summer day. Though it has expanded room by room since first opening in 1914, Woodman's still can't accommodate the throngs, so most

regulars just elbow in, shout their order through the confusion, and then eat outside off the hoods of their cars. Cardboard plates are piled precipitously high with crunchy delicacies, plus onion rings or french fries. Martinis and beer can be ordered in plastic Dixie cups.

Visitors and locals line up for clams at Woodman's.

Those who eat here regularly might opt for Woodman's equally excellent lobster roll or unbeatable clam chowder, but for first-timers, the fried clams are required eating. Fruity, sweet, buttery, and smooth—you'll never have them this good again.

WHAT: restaurant. **WHERE:** Essex is 25 miles north of Boston. 121 Main St. Tel 800-649-1773 or 978-768-2559; www.woodmans. com. **COST:** fried clam dinner $19. **BEST TIMES:** clams are sweeter when waters are colder, late fall into winter.

A Cultural Haven in the Lovely Berkshires

TANGLEWOOD MUSIC FESTIVAL

Lenox, Massachusetts, U.S.A.

The tranquil summertime home of the Boston Symphony Orchestra for the past sixty-plus years, 210-acre Tanglewood estate and its hilly Berkshires environs represent a cultural smorgasbord for arts lovers, offering a summer-long series that began small in 1934 and has grown into the country's most famous and prestigious summer music festival. Weekday evenings see performances by internationally acclaimed artists, but the real Tanglewood experience is at the popular weekend concerts, when the lush Great Lawn fills with music lovers and their elaborate picnic dinners, settling in for a lovely evening under the stars. The season culminates on Labor Day with the annual Tanglewood Jazz Fest.

High culture keeps these gentle hills alive. The Mount, Pulitzer-prize-winning novelist Edith Wharton's summer home in Lenox, is the site of lectures and other events. The popular Shakespeare & Co. performances, held here since 2001, now have a new home at 70 Kemble Street. Visitors can stay at the nearby Gables Inn, which was Wharton's home before she built The Mount. Dance enthusiasts gravitate to Jacob's Pillow, the country's oldest modern dance festival. Begun in 1933 on a 150-acre park on Route 20 in rural Becket (15 miles from Tanglewood), it may feature classic ballet one night and hip-hop, modern jazz, or Spanish flamenco the next.

Match high culture with high hospitality by checking into the elegant Blantyre country-house hotel, an 100-acre spread with one of the last "summer cottage" castles remaining from the area's late-19th-century gilded era. The pampering once reserved for the owner of the Tudor estate is now regaled upon each privileged guest, right down to the perfect gourmet picnic hamper for that concert at Tanglewood.

WHAT: event, hotel. **TANGLEWOOD MUSIC FESTIVAL:** Lenox is 120 miles west of Boston, 150 miles north of New York City. Box office, tel 888-266-1200; www.tanglewood.org or www.berkshires.org. *Cost:* tickets $18–$99; lawn seats $9. *When:* end of Jun–Labor Day weekend. **BLANTYRE:** Blantyre Rd., Lenox (2 miles from downtown). Tel 413-637-3556, fax 413-637-4282; welcome@blantyre.com; www.blantyre.com. *Cost:* doubles from $550, suites from $750. *When:* open year-round. **BEST TIMES:** aside from the festival, Jul and Aug for weather; late Sept–Oct is wonderful for foliage.

New England Charm Afloat

MARTHA'S VINEYARD

Massachusetts, U.S.A.

Christened in 1602 by British explorer Bartholomew Gosnold for his daughter, 20-by-10-mile Martha's Vineyard is no longer covered with wild grapes, but it still promises island enchantment, New England mystique, and a low-profile lifestyle. In terms of both landscape and towns, it's more diversified than mostly flat Nantucket, its neighbor 28 miles away. Its rolling sand dunes and cranberry bogs are more reminiscent of Cape Cod, though in general the island is less developed. Oak Bluffs is a time-warp fantasy, offbeat and fun for its hodgepodge of some 300 candy-colored Victorian cottages. West Tisbury offers a Saturday Farmers' Market (the largest of its kind in New England) as well as the Norman Rockwell–style Alley's General Store, "Dealers in Almost Everything," the island's oldest business, in operation since 1858. Among all this Americana, the island boasts a high celebrity quotient, with VIPs taking advantage of the traditional respect for privacy and safety (homes and cars are still left unlocked here). Pretty Edgartown's gracious Charlotte Inn enjoys a sophisticated in-town setting—not the place for flip-flops and hammock lounging. Old-fashioned, elegant, and service proud, it is a cluster of five 18th- and 19th-century houses decorated in an English country manner and linked by formal gardens. Much of the inn's island-wide fame can be attributed to its stellar Italian restaurant, Il Tesoro, where refined dining takes place in an elegant plant-filled conservatory lit romantically by candles, and indulgent complimentary continental breakfasts are awash in morning sunshine and the smell of fresh cranberry pancakes.

WHAT: island, hotel, restaurant. **MARTHA'S VINEYARD:** 5 miles south of Falmouth (Cape Cod); daily year-round ferry departures from Woods Hole on Cape Cod arrive at Vineyard Haven, and seasonally at Oak Bluff. **THE CHARLOTTE INN:** 27 S. Summer St., Edgartown. Tel 508-627-4151; www.charlotte inn.net. *Cost:* doubles from $295. Dinner at Il Tesoro $50. *When:* hotel open year-round; restaurant open daily (weekends only, off-season). **BEST TIMES:** May–Oct.

A Remote World, All Its Own

NANTUCKET

Massachusetts, U.S.A.

The island's Wampanoag Indian name means "faraway land," and Nantucket seems like just that. Thirty miles off the Massachusetts coast but seemingly thousands, the 49-square-mile island floats in its own insular world of time and space. There's a feeling of adventure as you arrive by ferry from nearby Cape Cod to this pristine enclave of 18th- and 19th-century clapboard homes. Approximately 12,000 residents live on the island year-round, but that number easily swells to 55,000 during the summer. The proud local community bucks all trends to keep alive the island's famously distinctive character: a salty Yankee quaintness blended with New England Old Guard gentility, the quiet impression of old money, and a zealous, deep-rooted appreciation for the island's history and integrity.

Spread out among the island's beaches and moors is one of the finest protected historic districts in America, with some of the most restrictive building ordinances. More than 800 homes and Quaker sea captains' mansions were built between 1740 and 1840, when Nantucket was the world's whaling capital—it is not by chance that Melville's Captain Ahab and First Mate Starbuck hailed from Nantucket. The weathered, pink-rose-covered homes have earned the island the nickname The Little Grey Lady of the Sea.

The most resplendent of them all, and standing in romantic end-of-the-road isolation on a windswept spit of land 8 miles from charming Nantucket Town, is The Wauwinet, the island's finest inn. The classic cedar-shingled sanctuary dates to 1860, a rambling hostelry on a 26-mile stretch of shoreline protected as a wildlife refuge. Its casual yet somewhat luxurious, antique-filled country/beach ambience carries over to the inn's excellent and always popular restaurant, Topper's, where specialties such as smoked seafood chowder and seared Nantucket Bay scallops celebrate the island's front yard bounty.

WHAT: island, hotel, restaurant. **NANTUCKET:** ferries depart from Hyannis (60 miles southeast of Boston) many times daily, year-round, taking 2 hours to reach the island. **THE WAUWINET:** 120 Wauwinet Rd. Tel 800-426-8718 or 508-228-0145, fax 508-228-7135; www.wauwinet.com. *Cost:* doubles from $380 (low season), from $680 (high season). Prix fixe dinner at Topper's $85. *When:* hotel and restaurant open early May–late Oct. **BEST TIMES:** May, Jun, and Sept.

Time Travel on the Quintessential American Holiday

THANKSGIVING AT PLIMOTH PLANTATION

Plymouth, Massachusetts, U.S.A.

Thanksgiving evokes images of Norman Rockwell family reunions, tables groaning under feasts of turkey and the trimmings, and historic associations of the Pilgrims and the Indians. Although a number of cities claim to have hosted the original Thanksgiving, Americans will always associate the first permanent settlement of Plymouth as the site of the documented 1621 dinner the Pilgrims celebrated with ninety male representatives of their Wamponoag neighbors, a year after the settlers had fled religious persecution in England. Today at Plimoth Plantation you can find out what really happened when you visit the Pilgrims at the 1621 Village and the Wamponoag people at Hobbamock's Homesite. The museum holds several dinners centered around the Thanksgiving holiday. In October and November, visitors can participate in dinners hosted by costumed interpreters portraying 17th-century English colonists. At the period dinner, visitors sit down to a "groaning board" filled with surprisingly tasty fare including seethed mussels, sauced turkey, roasted chine of pork, fricassee of fish, stewed pompion (a sweet pudding of Indian corn), and other early New England favorites. Particu-

The Mayflower II *is only 106 feet long.*

larly for families with children, the Plimoth Plantation experience is not complete without a visit to Plymouth Rock and the *Mayflower II,* a full-scale re-creation of the original 106-foot-long ship that landed first at the site of present-day Provincetown on Cape Cod, then headed across to Plymouth in December 1620. Though looming large in the nation's history, the ship is actually startlingly small considering the rough sixty-six-day voyage it undertook in transporting 102 passengers and their supplies to a new life in the then recently named "New England."

WHAT: site, event. **WHERE:** 40 miles southeast of Boston. Tel 508-746-1622, fax 508-746-4978; kcurtin@plimoth.org; www. plimoth.org. **COST:** admission $28. Dinners are extra and vary in cost; reservations required. **WHEN:** open daily, Apr–Thanksgiving weekend; Victorian Thanksgiving Feast offered Thanksgiving Day only; 1627 Pilgrim Dinner on selected dates in Oct and Nov (reservations accepted after Aug 1).

A Living Relic of the Gilded Age

MACKINAC ISLAND'S GRAND HOTEL

Michigan, U.S.A.

T he first thing ferry passengers spot as they approach Mackinac Island is the rambling white Grand Hotel, perched larger than life, high atop a hill sheathed in emerald green lawns and untold thousands of blooming flowers.

There are other hotels on this small time-locked island (whose name is pronounced "Mack-in-awe"), but Grand Hotel—the prototypical Great Lakes resort, which local authorities tout as the largest summer resort in the world (with some 380 rooms)—sets the tone. Don't let anyone talk you out of it. Family run with a Midwestern friendliness, the immense white Greek Revival palace lives resolutely

and proudly in the past. It was built in 1887 during the post–Civil War Gilded Age, when rates were $3 a night for vacationing Midwestern moguls, and the hotel still indulges its modern-day guests as if they were moguls themselves. Its stately, 660-foot-long pillared veranda, surely one of the world's largest porches, is perfect for watching magical sunsets play on the Mediterranean-blue waters of the lakes. The hotel's gracious turn-of-the-century feel, seldom found in the United States, permeates the entire 3-mile island, 85 percent of which is protected as a state park. In a state where the auto industry rules, cars are banned here, and travel is by bicycle or horse carriage only (there are more than 500 horses on the island). Hollywood has made use of the hotel and its time-weathered ambience, using it as the backdrop for the 1980 cult-classic film *Somewhere in Time* and Esther Williams's 1949 *This Time for Keeps*. The hotel named its 220-foot, 500,000-gallon pool after the actress. Swimming laps (or getting about by bicycle) will help burn up the calories you gain

Grand Hotel's grand front porch

sampling the local dense fudge, an island specialty. Even the potentially banal vanilla and chocolate are ultra-delicious, and that's not even mentioning the cranberry, maple syrup, and turtle alternatives.

WHAT: island, hotel. **WHERE:** Mackinac Island sits in the strait connecting Lakes Michigan and Huron. Daily passenger ferries leave from St. Ignace (on the upper or north peninsula) and Mackinaw City (lower or south peninsula) May–Oct. Mackinaw City is 280 miles north of Detroit. Tel 800-33-GRAND or 906-847-3331, fax 906-847-3259; www.grandhotel.com. **COST:** lake-view doubles from $235 (low season), from $255 (high season), per person, includes breakfast and 5-course dinner. **WHEN:** open mid-May through Oct. **BEST TIMES:** mid-May for the Grand Opening Weekend; mid-Jun for the 10-day Lilac Festival; Jul 4th for an old-fashioned celebration; the last 2 weeks of Oct for the Big Band Dance Extravaganza and *Somewhere in Time* weekends.

Paddling Through Paradise

BOUNDARY WATERS CANOE AREA WILDERNESS

Ely, Minnesota, U.S.A.

Bordering Canada, northern Minnesota's BWCAW is the largest U.S. wilderness preserve east of the Rockies, and is North America's best canoeing destination, giving the expression "lake district" new meaning.

It's a pristine labyrinth of 1 million acres and seemingly as many lakes, with more than 1,500 miles of mapped canoe routes running through it but not a single road. Since it's almost entirely off-limits to motorboats as well, it's easy to imagine the area as it was in the 17th century, when the craze for fur pelts brought the "voyageurs"—French, Dutch, and British trappers and traders—to this neck

of the woods. Today, it's outdoorsmen who come, drawn by crystal-clear waters rich with North America's greatest variety of game fish (including smallmouth bass, walleye, northern pike, and lake trout) and deer- and moose-filled wilderness that's guaranteed to wipe away the stresses of the modern world. If the U.S. wilderness isn't big enough for you, combine it with its equal-sized Canadian neighbor across the border, Ontario's Quetico Provincial Park.

The small, friendly town of Ely is the gateway for canoeists who arrive from all over the country, and home base for outfitters ready to send them off for an afternoon or a week, equipped with everything from soup to nuts. A final nod to civilization (and infinitely

A relaxing day on the water

more appreciated after a few shower-free nights in the wilderness) is the Burntside Lodge, an early-20th-century lakefront resort. A series of handsome log cabins nestled in wooded privacy, solidly built of local materials by expert local craftsmen, the

Burntside is especially sought out for its kitchen and wine list, whose unpretentious excellence is unmatched—and unexpected—in the area.

WHAT: site, experience, hotel. **BOUNDARY WATERS:** Ely is 100 miles northwest of Duluth. *How:* Williams and Hall Wilderness Guides and Outfitters, tel 800-322-5837 or 218-365-5837, fax 218-365-6369; canoe@williamsandhall.com, www.williamsandhall.com. *Cost:* plan on approximately $110 per person per day for an all-inclusive outfitting package. *When:* May–Sept. **BURNTSIDE LODGE:** Ely. Tel 218-365-3894; info@burntside.com; www.burntside.com. *Cost:* 1-bedroom cabins from $150 (low season), from $185 (high season). Dinner $25. *When:* hotel opens early May, restaurant opens just before Memorial Day; both open through Sept. **BEST TIMES:** fairest weather Jul–Aug; best bass fishing Jun–Jul (Jul generally best for all types).

Antebellum Life in the Old South

THE NATCHEZ TRACE

Natchez, Mississippi, U.S.A.

Any trek through the Deep South must include a visit to Natchez, once a bustling Mississippi River port and the fourth wealthiest city in America (after New York, Boston, and Philadelphia), today a veritable living museum of pre–Civil War architecture. Built between 1790 and 1861, when the cotton and sugarcane trade poured riches into the city's coffers, the city's opulent antebellum plantation homes and stylish town houses offer glimpses of the grand pre–Civil War lifestyle of wealthy white Mississippians. Ironically, their preservation is due to the city's occupation by the Union Army at the start of the war, which spared Natchez from significant physical damage.

More than 500 architectural treasures remain intact today, many still occupied and lovingly preserved by descendants of the original owners.

In the spring, azaleas, camellias, fragrant magnolias, and brilliant annuals make the Springtime Natchez Pilgrimage, begun in 1932, the year's highlight. More than thirty private homes (many with important gardens) are open to the public, their owners and hostesses dressed in antebellum attire, disarming visitors with their hospitality and charm. About half these homes are open to visitors year-round, a good number of them functioning as bed-and-breakfasts. The most luxurious is Monmouth, the former 1818 Greek Revival residence of a pre–Civil War Mississippi governor. Ask for his room, which contains his four-poster bed and a dresser where he stashed his many wigs, and opens onto views of the famous 26-acre gardens and the family graveyard.

WHAT: town, experience, hotel, event. **NATCHEZ:** 115 miles southwest of Jackson, 172 miles northwest of New Orleans. **NATCHEZ PILGRIMAGE TOURS:** tel 800-647-6742 or 601-446-6631; www.natchezpilgrimage.com. *When:* Spring Pilgrimage, 5 weeks in Mar–Apr; Fall Pilgrimage, 2 weeks in Oct. **MONMOUTH:** 36 Melrose Ave. Tel 800-828-4531 or 601-442-5852; www.monmouthplantation.com. *Cost:* doubles from $195. 5-course dinner $50. **BEST TIMES:** Mar–May and Oct–Nov. Catch the Confederate Pageant (a.k.a. the Historic

Monmouth was home to General John A. Quitman.

Natchez Pageant) held during Spring Pilgrimage only, when a cast of hundreds of costumed volunteers transports an audience through music and dance to the days of the Old South (Fri, Sat, Mon, and Wed throughout pilgrimage).

A Nationally Acclaimed Culinary Landmark

ARTHUR BRYANT'S BARBECUE

Kansas City, Missouri, U.S.A.

In KC, barbecue is king, beloved of native sons like Charlie Parker and Count Basie, and just as hot. You can queue up at any one of about ninety joints for short ribs and burnt ends (the crispy, coveted scraps of beef brisket),

but legendary Arthur Bryant's is near-unanimously considered to be the best barbecue joint in town, or maybe *anywhere*. There's no decor to speak of—never was when "King" Arthur ran the place (from 1931 till his death in 1980), never was when barbecue fan Give-'em-Hell Harry Truman dined here, and isn't now either. But that just means there's nothing to distract you from the signature half-pound of slow-cooked brisket slapped on plain old white bread, with a gritty herbs- and spices-flavored barbecue sauce and the best skin-on french fries in America.

Other capitals of the barbecue world specialize in particular styles, but KC (yes, even the locals call it that) prides itself on its anything-goes attitude toward the choice of meats (chicken, beef, pork, mutton, sausage) and the variety of sauce ingredients (tomatoes, vinegar, sugar, honey, maple syrup, mustard, garlic).

For a full-tilt barbecue experience, come during the two-month American Royal Livestock Horse Show and Rodeo, held every autumn since 1899. There are parades, steer auctions, and hog pageants throughout the 180-acre former stockyards area, but all that pales when compared to the barbecue competitions, in which more than 3,000 contestants from all over the United States set up camp and fire up their meat, each tent emitting an aroma more tantalizing than the last.

Your Own Private Ski Resort

BIG SKY

Montana, U.S.A.

Montana is like a shell game: While most people head here in summer, the real prize might very well be hidden in winter at Big Sky, which boasts 3,600 spectacularly skiable acres, (almost) uniformly excellent conditions, vaulting Rockies views, and an average of only two skiers per acre—meaning lift lines are pretty much unheard of. Much of the annual 400-inch snowfall is the bone-dry talc that local skiers reverently call "cold smoke," and while there's extreme white-knuckle skiing for sure (an aerial tram to the 11,166-foot summit of the Matterhorn-like Lone Peak offers skiers a 4,350-foot vertical drop, the second steepest in the nation after Snowmass, Colorado), a good 50 percent of the resort's 150-plus trails are perfect for the intermediate.

Big Sky abuts Yellowstone National Park, 18 miles away in southwestern Montana, where horizontal skiing can be enjoyed in an almost surreal setting of untracked snow and steam sent up by geysers that summertime visitors cannot imagine. More than 45 miles of exceptional cross-country trails are the uncontested draw at the much-ballyhooed Lone Mountain Ranch, an elegant four-seasons lodge (an official Orvis fly-fishing resort in the summer months) with an acclaimed restaurant and convenient shuttles that keep guests connected to the Big Sky area. To appease your inner 19th-century lady or gentleman, give in to the ranch's snowy horse-drawn sleigh ride through the woods to a lantern-lit cabin and an unforgettable old-time evening of fine food and a thoroughly delightful singalong.

WHAT: experience, hotel, restaurant. **WHERE:** 45 miles south of Bozeman, 50 miles north of West Yellowstone access to national park. For ski conditions, tel 406-995-5900. For reservations and information, tel 800-548-4486, fax 406-995-5001; www.bigskyresort. com. *When:* ski season is mid-Nov to mid-Apr. **LONE MOUNTAIN RANCH:** tel 800-514-4644 or 406-995-4644, fax 406-995-4670; reservations@lmranch.com; www.lmranch.com. *Cost:* $2,475 per person, per week (winter);

Open slopes at Lone Mountain

$3,145 (summer), includes all meals and all activities. Sleigh ride dinner $85 for nonguests. *When:* ranch and restaurant open mid-Jun to mid-Sept; mid-Dec through Mar. **BEST TIMES:** Jan–Mar for alpine skiing; Jan–Feb for cross-country.

Big Sky, Big Country, Big Fish

THE COMPLETE FLY FISHER

Wise River, Montana

"**I**n our family, there was no clear line between religion and fly fishing" reads the opening line of Norman McLean's classic Montana novel *A River Runs Through It,* and the same can probably be said of most folks in this state, the spiritual home of fly fishers everywhere. People come from all over the world to try its world-class streams, which offer more fish per mile than anywhere else. The whole trout family is represented here (brown, rainbow, brook, cutthroat, and grayling), and the scenery isn't too bad either.

The legendary Big Hole River and its sibling the Beaverhead have few rivals for quality fly-fishing and remarkable mountain scenery. The area's most famous lodge—numbered among the top fishing lodges on the planet by John Randolf, the publisher and editor of *Fly Fisherman* magazine—is the Complete Fly Fisher. Its location on the Big Hole and proximity to the Wise, Beaverhead, Bitterroot, Clark Fork, and Missouri rivers means excellent fishing, and its small size (fourteen guests is the limit) fosters camaraderie and a family-like atmosphere. Almost everyone seems to be a return guest, back for another week of catching rainbow and wild brown trout in quantities unsurpassed elsewhere, but even novices can pull in the big ones, with the help of the lodge's skilled instructors. Owners David and Christine Decker promise not just a wonderful time, but even a subtle change of perspective.

Dining on the lovely riverside porch is taken as seriously as fishing, and is far more sophisticated than you'd expect in this pristine wilderness, surpassing the fare many guests find back home. Special requests are taken, but why bother when Chef Lori Dooner consistently comes through with creations

Fishing for the big one on Big Hole River

such as sea bass baked in parchment with a citrus vanilla vinaigrette, followed by a mean chocolate crème brûlée.

WHAT: experience, hotel. **WHERE:** 40 miles south of Butte. Tel 866-832-3175 or 406-832-3175, fax 406-832-3169; comfly@montana.com; www.completeflyfisher.com. **COST:** 5-day stays $4,500 per angler, double occupancy, includes everything from meals to a guide and equipment. Shorter stays can be arranged. **WHEN:** open May 15–Oct 15. **BEST TIMES:** Jun–Aug for weather; May and Sept–Oct offer productive angling in a solitary setting.

Ice-Sculpted Majesty

GLACIER NATIONAL PARK

Montana, U.S.A.

Glacier Park's soul-inspiring landscape was carved by the movement of massive glaciers millennia ago, and so awesome is its beauty that the Blackfoot Indians consider the area sacred ground. "If it isn't God's backyard," said comedian Robin Williams, "He certainly lives nearby." Frequently called Little Switzerland or the American Alps, the park's dramatically glaciated terrain is prime hiking territory, with more than 700 miles of maintained trails that pass through vibrant wildflower-carpeted meadows. There are good opportunities for glimpsing abundant wildlife—moose, mountain goats and bighorn sheep, deer, elk, wolverines, wolves, more than 300 of the threatened grizzly bear (the largest concentration in the contiguous United States), and hundreds of the not so endangered black bear.

Less strenuous sightseeing is to be had along the spectacular two-hour, 50-mile-long Going-to-the-Sun Road, which roughly bisects the million-acre wilderness. Crossing glacially sculpted mountains, it takes you from the park's lowest elevations to the summit of the Continental Divide at the 6,646-foot Logan Pass (the highlight of the trip), passing fjordlike lakes, as many as a thousand seasonal waterfalls, and dense evergreen forests along the way. There are 37 named glaciers within the park, but that's down from about 150 in the mid-1800s. At this rate, experts believe the park's namesake glaciers will all but disappear by 2030. A favored means of seeing the park—the rollback canvas-topped Red Buses—first drove these routes in the 1930s, and are now back in service after an environmentally sensitive renovation by the Ford Motor Company.

Of the many massive, ponderosa-style lodges built here in the early 1900s to lure the first vacationers, the Swiss-style Many Glacier Hotel is perhaps the most beautifully sited and popular. Sitting regal and isolated amid alpine grandeur on the banks of Swiftcurrent Lake, it is rustic, charming, and laden with tradition. The rooms are spartan, but if you've secured one of the fifty with a balcony, the breathtaking views of Grinnell Point make up for the lack of amenities. More comfortable if less picturesque accommodations can be found at the park's Lake McDonald Lodge.

WHAT: site, hotel. **GLACIER NATIONAL PARK:** in the northernmost reaches of America's Rockies, at the Canadian border. The park's west entrance in West Glacier is 25 miles northeast of Kalispell, the closest airport. Going-to-the-Sun Road runs from West

A hiker's paradise in the "American Alps"

Glacier in the west to St. Mary in the east. Park information, tel 406-888-7800; www.nps. gov/glac. *Cost:* $10 per person or $15 per car. *When:* park open year-round, but much of Going-to-the-Sun Rd. is only open early

Jun–mid-Oct. **MANY GLACIER HOTEL/LAKE MCDONALD LODGE:** tel 406-892-2525, fax 406-892-1375; info@glacierparkinc.com, www. glacierparkinc.com. *Cost:* from $142. *When:* late May–late Sept. **BEST TIMES:** summer.

Home on the Range in the Mild Wild West

TRIPLE CREEK RANCH

Darby, Montana, U.S.A.

This may have been the Wild West, but today there's civilization to be found in these parts. Triple Creek is called a ranch but it's really a luxury resort, where urban types wistful for the *City Slickers* experience can

rough it Rich-and-Famous style in the beauty of the Rocky Mountains. Tucked into the southwest corner of Montana at the foot of Trapper Peak, Triple Creek shows off "The Last Best Place" state to its breathtaking finest. Its nineteen hand-hewn log cabins are scattered amid 440 acres of towering ponderosa pines fronted by several million acres of wilderness in the Bitterroot Valley, close to both Yellowstone and Glacier National Park. Such solitude is luxury enough, but what comes as a surprise—in addition to first-class amenities where accommodations and dining are concerned—is the unexpected sophistica-

Roughing it in style at Triple Creek Ranch

tion of the superpersonalized service, offered by an exceptionally friendly staff.

Spring brings mountain biking, hiking, and trail riding through high-country meadows carpeted with lilies-of-the-valley, fairybells, and dogtooth violets. Winter months promise 300 inches of snowfall and short lift lines at the nearby Lost Trail Powder Mountain ski area, in the Bitterroot Mountains. Those with a mind for less strenuous diversion can take a luxurious moonlit soak in the hot tub on their private deck; plan a drive into the poetically named town of Wisdom; order a custom-made hat down the road in Darby, a town straight out of a Western movie; or just stay put and enjoy

a hot buttered rum in front of a crackling fire while the kitchen staff works its magic. Like just about everyone else at Triple Creek, they're always willing to go the extra mile to make your meal two steps beyond exceptional.

WHAT: hotel. **WHERE:** 75 miles south of Missoula's airport. 5551 West Fork Stage Route. Tel 800-654-2943 or 406-821-4600, fax 406-821-4666; info@triplecreekranch.com; www. triplecreekranch.com. **COST:** from $650 per couple, includes meals and most on-ranch activities. **WHEN:** closed Nov. **BEST TIMES:** Feb, Jun, and Sept–Oct. Late Jul for Darby's Strawberry Festival; Labor Day weekend for the Ravalli County Fair.

A Most Sophisticated Lady

BELLAGIO

Las Vegas, Nevada, U.S.A.

An imposing Italianate palazzo modeled after its storied namesake on Lake Como, Bellagio is a trailblazer that sits a step above the neon and shtick that is Las Vegas. Which is not to say that every aspect at every turn is not grandiose and over the top—it's just *tastefully* over the top. With some 3,000 guest rooms filling its thirty-six floors, it's one of the world's largest hotels, with one of the largest casinos in town (along with the MGM Grand and the Riviera), and it's the most expensive ever built in Vegas so far, with a $1.6 billion price tag. That marble you see everywhere would do a Medici proud.

Until just a few years ago, everyone came to this town for the gambling (they still leave behind $7.7 billion yearly), but today its top-drawer restaurants are a competitive magnet too, and nowhere is the allure greater than under Bellagio's roof. Bookending the hotel's gamut of eateries are the hardly humble Buffet (loosen your belt buckle for the famous Sunday über-extravaganza dinner) and the heavily awarded Picasso, with eleven original Picassos gracing the walls. A host of alternatives lies in between: Aqua, the sleek, jazzy seafood restaurant; Le Cirque, an exquisite miniature of its legendary Manhattan cousin; Prime, a glamorous 1930s-style chophouse operated by Jean-Georges Vongerichten; and on and on and on. After dessert, catch the more than 1,000 dancing fountains choreographed to show tunes in an 8-acre artificial lake; enjoy a nocturnal dip in the Mediterranean-style pool area, with its six pools; or take in the indescribable underwater performance by the world-renowned Cirque du Soleil (in the hotel's custom-built $60 million theater), which is guaranteed to leave you in a state of wonderment. Afterward, Bellagio's Light nightclub will still be humming, proving that one needn't leave the hotel's premises from check-in till check-out. Oh, and this being Las Vegas, there are also two wedding chapels in the hotel, open twenty-four hours a day.

WHAT: hotel, restaurant. **WHERE:** 3600 Las Vegas Blvd. South. Tel 888-987-6667 or 702-693-7111; www.bellagio.com. **COST:** doubles from $199. **BEST TIMES:** Apr or Oct for the nicest weather and minimal crowds.

Where Megawatt Crass Marries Nouveau Class

THE LAS VEGAS STRIP

Nevada, U.S.A.

The 3½-mile stretch of Las Vegas Boulevard known as the Strip is the world capital of glitter, festooned with pleasure palaces, quick-hitch wedding chapels, and cheap, all-you-can-eat prime rib buffets—and, of course, it's alive with gambling, anytime, any kind, and everywhere. This is where Bugsy Siegel laid down the law and the Rat Pack laid down the style; where Howard Hughes hid out and where Elvis made his last stand; but, maybe sadly, maybe not, all that is changing. In an attempt to promote itself as a family destination, Vegas is still hell-bent on attaining bourgeois respectability, trading in its seedy Sin City image in favor of a luxury future that's more about indulgence than naughtiness.

That said, visitors will still find their fill of female impersonators and splashy dinner shows (starring Debbie Reynolds, Wayne Newton, and Celine Dion), and can still visit prime stops such as the ultra-camp Liberace Museum (off the Strip on 1775 E. Tropicana Avenue), and the busy Little Chapel of the Flowers (1717 Las Vegas Boulevard South), which, along with the twenty-five other Strip chapels, accounts for some 100,000 marriages every year.

Among those holdouts, though, you'll also find the new breed of themed megahotels (such as the Venetian, Paris, Mandalay Bay, and New York, New York) which continue Vegas's bigger-than-life tradition, appropriating world icons and pumping them up to exaggerated proportions.

More is still more as Vegas moves upscale, so it's no surprise that among its 225 hotels and motels are 19 of the world's 20 largest, including the MGM Grand, the champ with more than 5,000 rooms. It's all dazzling and unabashedly artificial, a 24/7 place where only the money is real and if the crowds in the casino are too big at 2 A.M., that just means one thing: It's time to go shopping. You gotta love this place.

WHAT: town, site. **WHERE:** 289 miles east of Los Angeles. Las Vegas Tourist Bureau, tel 800-777-8342; www.lvtb.com. **BEST TIMES:** Jun–Aug are extremely hot. On the other hand, this is when room rates are low, and Vegas is one big air-conditioned town anyway.

North Country Isolation for a Grande Dame

THE BALSAMS

Dixville Notch, New Hampshire, U.S.A.

Even if you can find your way off The Balsams' 15,000 acres of mountains and meadows, you'll be hard-pressed to come up with an incentive to do so. This lavish 1866 grand resort hotel sits on a remarkably isolated spot

12 miles south of the Canadian border, amid a landscape its owners describe as "the Switzerland of America," on the banks of Lake Gloriette, in a U-shaped mountain pass surrounded by 800-foot cliffs. The trek to The Balsams' remote location has stopped no one, it seems, since the rambling 203-room red-roofed classic fills each season. Guests welcome its rigorous old-world decorum and fashionably old-fashioned image, one that encourages guests to adhere to a dress code in the dining

room, where dinner is a romantic return to earlier times. The lunch buffet is more informal, judging from the 100-foot-long table loaded with a bounty and diversity that rivals that of any cruise ship. The hotel's wraparound verandas further reinforce the impression of being on a luxury liner to nowhere. Countless recreational activities explain The Balsams' popularity as a family resort, and three-generation vacations are commonplace. Summer promises 65 miles of trails for hiking and mountain biking and 27 holes of golf, no less impressive than the winter season's 250 inches of snow covering 95 kilometers of cross-country skiing and snowshoe trails, and three lifts serving sixteen downhill trails. For spectacular foliage viewing, you needn't even leave your room, much less the grounds, especially if you've booked into the Tower Suite, whose 360-degree panorama is hard to beat.

WHAT: hotel. **WHERE:** 210 miles north of Boston, 390 miles north of New York City, on Rt. 26. Tel 800-255-0600 or 603-255-3400; guestservices@thebalsams.com; www.thebalsams.com. **COST:** doubles from $175 per person, double occupancy (low season), from $275 (high season); Tower Suite from $775; rates include breakfast, dinner, and unlimited use of facilities. **WHEN:** open late May to mid-Oct, mid-Dec to Apr. **BEST TIMES:** Feb–Mar and Jul–Aug.

Golden Ponds and Yankee Towns

THE LAKES REGION

New Hampshire, U.S.A.

Beginning at the Maine border and spreading west, New Hampshire's Lakes Region consists of 273 lakes and ponds, a pristine wilderness where unspoiled Yankee towns, rustic summer camps, and charming cottage communities hug the water's edge. On the eastern shore of 72-square-mile Lake Winnipesaukee ("Smiling Waters," the largest in the state), the town of Wolfeboro bills itself as the "oldest summer resort in America" on the basis of a colonial governor's country home, which was built here in the 1760s. The town is the departure point for a three-hour cruise aboard the 230-foot *Mount Washington*, which explores the quiet beauty of the area.

Hollywood chose the smaller Squam Lake as its location of the classic 1981 film *On Golden Pond*. Because the lakefront land is privately owned by families who pass down modest lodges from generation to generation, the lake itself is off-limits to the public, unless they book at the Manor on Golden Pond, an English-style country estate built in 1907 on 14 acres (2 of which are lakefront) as the refined summer home of a prosperous European businessman. Chandeliers, leaded glass, hand-carved oak woodwork, and fireplaces in most rooms and cottages showcase the original owner's to-the-manor-born

aspirations. A cozy pub and the ritual of afternoon tea top off an ambience that is quintessentially British, and the Manor's restaurant is considered one of the best in the Squam Lake area. Repair to the corner Buckingham Room for ultimate pampering, courtesy of a king-sized canopy bed and private veranda with lake views. Although primarily a summer destination (with leaf-peepers filling the house till late October), the Manor becomes a winter wonder-

Kayaking on Lake Winnipesaukee, or "Smiling Waters"

land when decked out for Christmas or during any of the snowy months, when Nordic and alpine skiing are never more than a shush away.

WHAT: site, hotel, restaurant. **WHERE:** 110 miles north of Boston, 310 miles north of New York City. **THE MANOR ON GOLDEN POND:** Rt. 3 at Shepard Hill Rd., Squam Lake. Tel 800-545-2141 or 603-968-3348,

fax 603-968-2116; info@manorongoldenpond.com; www.manorongoldenpond.com. *Cost:* doubles from $210 (low season), from $255 (high season); Buckingham Room $290 (low season), $355 (high season). Dinner $60, chef's tasting menu $75. **BEST TIMES:** late Sept–late Oct for fall foliage, but a fine destination year-round.

The Appalachian Trail and the White Mountains

MOUNT WASHINGTON

North Conway, New Hampshire, U.S.A.

The Appalachian Trail, the most famous hiking trail in the world, wends its way down along the U.S. eastern coast from the north woods of Maine to Springer Mountain in Georgia, a distance of more than 2,100 miles.

Estimated to be some 5 million steps long, it passes through fourteen states, with the longest section in Virginia (545 miles), the greatest elevation in Tennessee's Great Smokies (6,643 feet), and, by most accounts, one of the most beautiful and challenging parts running through New Hampshire. About half of New Hampshire's section of the AT (as hikers like to call it) falls within the White Mountain National Forest, a rugged, sprawling recreational playground of 661,000 acres that has drawn lovers of the great outdoors since the 19th century, particularly hikers. The famous AT is only one of many trails that link up to an elaborate 1,200-mile network that ranges from the easy to the extraordinary.

The granddaddy of the White Mountains (so named because their granite peaks are so frequently covered by snow) is Mount Washington, the highest in the northeast at 6,288 feet, and fabled for harsh and unpredictable weather that can rival that of Antarctica. The area's most popular excursion is the innovative 1869 Mount Washington Cog Railroad, which chugs 3½ dramatic miles to Mount Washington's peak. It can also be reached on

foot or by car (allow one hour each way by car on the 8-mile road, and check your brakes first). Another favorite local excursion is the justly famous Kancamagus Highway (a.k.a. the Kanc), which stretches 33 miles from Lincoln in the west to North Conway in the east. During fall foliage season it's the quintessential scenic New England drive.

It's hard to compete with so much natural drama, but the majestic Mount Washington Hotel boasts 1,500 acres of its own. Its man-made centerpiece is a rambling 200-room leviathan that's been welcoming visitors since 1902, and makes for a perfect rest stop. Stake out a rocker on its 900-foot veranda for the chance to revel in the beauty of the Presidential Range without having to lace up your hiking boots.

WHAT: site, experience, hotel. **MOUNT WASHINGTON:** 165 miles north of Boston, 330 miles north of New York City. Mount Washington Valley Chamber of Commerce, in North Conway. Tel 877-948-6867; www.mtwashingtonvalley.org. **COG TRAIN:** 800-922-8825; www.thecog.com. *When:* cog train and motor road to Mount Washington summit late Apr–Oct, weather permitting. *Cost:* $60 round trip. **MOUNT WASHINGTON HOTEL:** Bretton Woods (6 miles from cog train). Tel 800-314-1752; resortinfo@mount washingtonresort.com; www.mountwashington resort.com. *Cost:* from $169 per person, includes breakfast, dinner, and use of all facilities. **BEST TIMES:** Jun, Jul; late Sept to mid-Oct for fall foliage; mid-Dec for the hotel's Victorian Christmas weekend.

A Victorian-Era Time Capsule on the Shore

CAPE MAY

New Jersey, U.S.A.

Cape May's unique claim to fame is the juxtaposition of its Victorian country-town atmosphere and its location, directly on the Jersey shore. As America's premier seaside resort in the mid-1800s, it attracted summering residents such as P. T. Barnum and Robert E. Lee, who came for the salty air and cool breezes. More than 600 Victorian structures that survived a fire in 1879 and a century of development after are neatly contained within the town's 2½-square-mile Historic District, where they've been transformed into shops, cafés, and gas-lit inns. Bicycles and horse-drawn buggies are the perfect way to tour the grand dowagers that proudly face the ocean along Beach Avenue, resplendent in gingerbread excess and colors that are visually surprising but (minus a few exceptions) historically accurate. Don't overlook the backstreets, where just as much Victorian froufrou abounds, confirming the town's "more is more" architectural philosophy.

The town boasts more than sixty historic bed-and-breakfasts, which range from boardinghouse basic to unashamed luxury. The Mainstay Inn was among the town's first bed-and-breakfasts, and remains one of its undisputed gems. A dignified Italianate manor one block from the ocean, it was built in 1872 as a gentlemen's exclusive gambling club, with 14-foot ceilings, 8-foot chandeliers, and a 12-foot mirror in the grand entrance hall. Luxury was paramount then as it is now, with airy rooms appointed with museum-quality antiques aug-mented by the necessary 21st-century amenities. Cape May is still an important commercial fishing port, providing fresh seafood that's built the town's reputation as one of the most impressive culinary enclaves on the eastern seaboard. For daytime activities, the invincibly kitsch seaside resort of Wildwood and its famous amusement-crammed boardwalk is only a twenty-minute drive, and, if you're feeling lucky, Atlantic City is a roll of the dice away. Or just stay put in Cape May, and keep very still: The 400 species of migrating birds that pass through annually have helped make Cape May one of the country's top three places for bird-watching.

WHAT: town, hotel. **CAPE MAY:** 45 miles south of Atlantic City, 165 miles south of New York City. For visitor information, tel 609-884-5508, fax 609-884-2054; www.capemay chamber.com. **MAINSTAY INN:** 635 Columbia Ave. Tel 609-884-8690; www.mainstayinn. com. *Cost:* doubles from $175 (low season), from $295 (high season). **BEST TIMES:** early spring and late fall for bird-watching (birding hotline, tel 609-884-2736); late Apr/early May for the annual Spring Festival and mid-Oct for Victoria Week, both of which offer tours of exceptional Victorian mansions not usually open to the public.

The World's Most Photographed Event

ALBUQUERQUE'S BALLOON FIESTA

New Mexico, U.S.A.

I t's just before sunrise, and more than 750 huge hot-air balloons are spread out across 70 acres, straining to take off. The camaraderie of international balloon enthusiasts escalates until the much-awaited 7 A.M. mass ascension,

which fills the early-morning sky with balloons of every color, size, and shape, including some seventy "special" balloons shaped like everything from Harley Davidson motorcycles to cows jumping over the moon. You can hitch a ride to the sky yourself by signing on with the festival's official balloon-ride concession. Aloft, the unearthly silence is punctuated only by erratic bursts of helium gas being released as you watch the early desert sun warm the Sandia Mountains. But things are pretty exciting back on earth, too, especially for photo enthusiasts; the Balloon Fiesta has been called the "world's most photographed event," filling the skies of New Mexico's largest city for nine days each October and the pages of America's glossy magazines for months after. If the nighttime balloon glow doesn't light the sky enough for you, the city's celebratory fireworks will.

WHAT: event, experience. **BALLOON FIESTA:** Balloon Fiesta Park. Tel 505-821-1000; www. balloonfiesta.com. **BALLOON RIDES:** contact Rainbow Ryders, Inc., tel 800-725-2477 or 505-823-1111; flightinfo@rainbowryders.com; www. rainbowryders.com. *Cost:* $160; from $375 during fiesta. **WHEN:** 9 days in early Oct.

A mass ascension fills the early-morning sky.

Rediscovering the Mother Road

ROUTE 66

Albuquerque, New Mexico, U.S.A.

N at King Cole told us to get our kicks on Route 66, untold numbers of dust bowl refugees traveled "the mother road" in search of opportunity, and in the Beatnik era countless freedom-seekers—inspired by the novels of Jack Kerouac and by the long-running 1960s *Route 66* TV series—took off down the tarmac in the romantic belief that footloose adventure could be had for the price of a tank of gas. Commissioned in 1926 and paved in 1937, Route 66 once ran for 2,448 miles through eight states, from Chicago to Santa Monica, California, providing an east-west Yellow Brick Road for America before it was chucked aside in favor of the new interstates built in the 1950s, '60s, and '70s. But how do you kill a route that was always as much idea as blacktop? It's not easy, and today 85 percent of the rural, mostly two-lane highway still exists, though modern-day pilgrims have to go looking for it.

It's in Albuquerque that one of the longest stretches of America's quintessential Main Street can still be traced. Alternate stretches elsewhere in the state take you back past ghost-town remnants of other decades—filling stations, diners, trading posts, barbecue pits, truck stops, and motels galore. The classic Route 66 motel, a new-at-the-time concept that found its niche and flourished along the legendary byway, can still be experienced at a few stuck-in-time examples that do a brisk nostalgia business. Some of the most famous, all built during the highway's nascent days, are Albuquerque's El Vado, Tucumcari's Blue Swallow Motel (across the road from Tepee Curios), and the El Rancho in Gallup, a location-ideal Western film capital from 1929 through 1964—you could very well be checking into Kirk Douglas's room.

WHAT: experience, hotel. **ROUTE 66:** for information and maps, call the National Historic Route 66 Federation, tel 909-336-6131; www.national66.org. **EL VADO MOTEL:** 2500 Central S.W. (Highway 66), Albuquerque. Tel 505-243-4594. *Note:* At press time, the motel was temporarily closed. **BLUE SWALLOW MOTEL:** 815 Route 66 Blvd., Tucumcari (175 miles east of Albuquerque). Tel 575-461-9849; www.blueswallowmotel.com. *Cost:* doubles from $66. **EL RANCHO:** 1000 E. Highway 66, Gallup (136 miles west of Albuquerque). Tel 505-863-9311; www.elranchohotel.com. *Cost:* doubles from $85.

A Natural Subterranean Wonder

CARLSBAD CAVERNS NATIONAL PARK

Carlsbad, New Mexico, U.S.A.

One of the world's most spectacular cave systems, Carlsbad Caverns National Park encompasses more than 100 known caves, including Carlsbad Cavern, renowned for its aptly named Big Room, with an area the size of six football fields and a 225-foot ceiling, and Lechuguilla Cave, one of the world's largest caves. Hundreds of millions of years in the making, the caves were known to Native Americans as far back as the 10th century (as proved by their pictographs, which can be seen on the entrance walls), but were not discovered by settlers until just 100 years ago.

Wide-eyed visitors on self-guided visits descend deep into the earth's belly below the Chihuahuan Desert, accompanied by the constant sound of dripping and the sweet smell of bat guano, to see the surreal formations and fragile mineral deposits that resemble everything from draperies and strings of pearls to rococo sculptures, bunches of grapes, and tum-

Surreal formations in Carlsbad Caverns

nature (albeit with 3 miles of paved walkways that lead visitors 800 feet down into the earth). Perhaps not frightening, but eerie, yes, and fascinating, definitely. And it's not just the caves' geology that fascinates, but its zoology as well. In summertime, the colony of Mexican free-tailed bats can number in the hundreds of thousands. And what a show they put on, taking off en masse every evening at dusk and filling the sky for miles in search of desert insects. It can take forty-five minutes for them all to exit the caves, a process reversed at dawn, when they all return.

bling waterfalls. Despite the 30 million visitors since the caves became a national park in 1923, this still remains an experience of raw

WHAT: site. **WHERE:** 285 miles southeast of Santa Fe, 143 miles northeast of El Paso. Tel 575-785-2232; www.nps.gov/cave. **COST:** admission $6. **BEST TIMES:** mid-May to Oct for the bats (who spend the winter in Mexico). The average year-round temperature in the caves is 56°F.

Attention Train Buffs: All Aboard!

THE CUMBRES & TOLTEC SCENIC RAILROAD

Chama, New Mexico, U.S.A.

A throwback to the late-19th-century network of trains that hauled gold, silver, coal, and timber across the southern Rockies, the refurbished Cumbres & Toltec today has the distinction of being North America's

longest, highest, and arguably best narrow-gauge steam railroad. Clattering and clunking along 64 miles of track between Chama, New Mexico, and Antonito, Colorado, the Cumbres & Toltec crisscrosses the New Mexico–Colorado border eleven times daily, passing the ever-changing vistas of God's country—sky-scraping peaks, verdant slopes, high valleys gouged by ancient glaciers, and bald eagles soaring majestically overhead. The train makes high-altitude stops at water stations inaccessible to cars, but the high point—literally—is the crossing of the

10,015-foot Cumbres Pass, the highest point reached by any passenger train in the United States. There is one open car for those who don't mind taking home a little soot and cinders at the end of the 6½-hour journey; in the autumn, there's no better way to go.

WHAT: experience. **WHERE:** from Chama, 130 miles north of Albuquerque, to Antonito, Colorado. Tel 888-286-2737; info@cumbres toltec.com; www.cumbrestoltec.com. **COST:** from $90 per person, includes lunch. **WHEN:** daily, May–Oct. **BEST TIMES:** fall for foliage.

ROSWELL

New Mexico, U.S.A.

They say that on July 8, 1947, an unidentified flying object crashed at the Hub Corn Ranch, some 20 miles north of the desert town of Roswell, leaving wreckage strewn across an area half a mile long. An official government-issued press release at first reported that "the incident" did involve a spaceship, perhaps two. Four hours later, the U.S. military retracted the story, saying it was a weather balloon, and in 1997 it changed its story again, saying it was a spy balloon. Allegedly, the bodies of four aliens were taken in secret to the nearby military base for autopsy and have never been seen since.

Every July marks the anniversary of America's real-life X-files mystery, when Roswell hosts the UFO Festival, a mix of fun, fantasy, and fact that draws the quirky, the curious, hard-core spaceheads, self-proclaimed alien abductees and UFOlogists, and generalized lovers of the absurd. There are lectures on alien breeding by "world-famous" specialists, a flying saucer (read: pancake) eating contest, the Intergalactic Food and Fashion Show, and a trade show that sells alien-emblazoned everything. The festive hoopla does its best to distract from the earnestness of the International UFO Museum and Research Center. It's all pretty much out of this world.

WHAT: town, event, site. **ROSWELL:** 200 miles southeast of Albuquerque. Roswell Visitors Bureau, tel 575-624-6700; www.roswell-nm.gov. **ROSWELL UFO FESTIVAL:** tel 888-767-3378; info@ufofestivalroswell.com; www.ufofestivalroswell.com. **INTERNATIONAL UFO MUSEUM AND RESEARCH CENTER:** 114 N. Main St. Tel 575-625-9495; info@roswellufomuseum.com; www.roswellufomuseum.com. *Cost:* admission $5. **BEST TIMES:** Jul 4th weekend for the 4-day UFO Festival.

INN OF THE ANASAZI

Santa Fe, New Mexico, U.S.A.

Neighboring the Palace of the Governors, the oldest public building in America, this unusual inn reaches back even further for its inspiration— to the region's 1,000-year-old indigenous culture, the Anasazi (Navajo for "ancient ones"). This is Santa Fe's most sophisticated hotel, but it functions more like an intimate, impeccably run inn, decorated with colorful rugs and hand-crafted baskets, textiles, and carvings that represent the area's Native, Latino, and Anglo cultures, and incorporating rough-hewn ceiling beams, kiva fire-places, and elements of Anasazi pottery and stonework into the overall southwestern design. Few hotels are in such perfect harmony with their environment, both architecturally and spiritually, and the result is never short of per-fection. Making it even more difficult to leave the premises is the Anasazi Restaurant, which features organically grown native foods pur-chased from local farmers or the Pueblo Indians whenever possible. The menu honors Native American and southwestern cuisines, with a little bit of cowboy thrown in. Elegant but earthy, the restaurant established itself as one of the area's best as soon as it opened.

WHAT: hotel, restaurant. **WHERE:** 113 Washington Ave. Tel 888-767-3966 or 505-988-3030, fax 505-988-3277; anasazi@ rosewoodhotels.com; www.innoftheanasazi. com. **COST:** doubles from $249. Prix fixe dinner $50. **BEST TIMES:** Sept and Oct for glorious fall weather.

Where the Desert Sunset Almost Steals the Show

THE SANTA FE OPERA

Santa Fe, New Mexico, U.S.A.

Founded in 1957 and going from strength to strength ever since, the Santa Fe Opera has earned a reputation for presenting innovative, varied, and risk-taking programs, with a repertoire that combines classics, rarely heard works,

and frequent American and world premieres. In addition to promising well-known interna-tional talents, the company is also known for discovering tomorrow's great voices. But is it the music or the setting that's the real draw? Performances are given in an ingenious indoor-outdoor amphitheater that's carved into a hillside, its glorious setting maximizing the drama of the encroaching Sangre de Cristo Mountains and inspiring both the performers and the sophisticated audience, many of whom have traveled far to get there. Black-tie opening nights are launched with an elegant tailgate party in the opera parking lot, catered by the city's best restaurants.

WHAT: event. **WHERE:** 7 miles north of Santa Fe on U.S. 84. For tickets, contact the Santa Fe Opera Box Office, tel 800-280-4654 or 505-986-5900; www.santafeopera.org. **WHEN:** late Jun–late Aug.

Taking the Waters Under the Stars

TEN THOUSAND WAVES

Santa Fe, New Mexico, U.S.A.

Take the atmosphere of a traditional Japanese hot-springs *onsen* and move it outdoors, add the panorama of the beautiful Sangre de Cristo Mountains and the perfume of piñon pines and juniper bushes, toss in the juvenile thrill of baring it all in the great outdoors, and you get Ten Thousand Waves, a one-of-a-kind wellness retreat. Check your modesty at the front desk at this oasis of pools, comprised of seven private tubs and two communal baths. Deep relaxation is the guiding principle here, and while many come for the waters alone, most also explore the menu of body treatments offered: salt glows, herbal wraps, something called the Nightingale Facial, and a variety of massage styles—from a simple sandalwood-scented rubdown to Four Hands One Heart, where two therapists work on you at once.

Opened in 1981, the Waves (as locals like to call it) is a little bit New Age, a little bit Zen, and a little bit high desert, all melded together in the simple elegance of Japanese and southwestern aesthetics. The eight guest suites in the Houses of the Moon are serene retreats all, with tatami mats and extra-thick futons. Overnight guests enjoy the option of soaking under a brilliant galaxy of stars. It's hard to believe you're so far from the Orient, despite what the sign in the courtyard reminds you: "Tokyo, 10,070 km."

WHAT: hotel. **WHERE:** 3451 Hyde Park Rd. (3.5 miles from downtown Santa Fe). Tel 505-982-9304; info@tenthousandwaves.com; www.tenthousandwaves.com. **COST:** doubles from $200, includes free use of communal tub; day guests pay $30 per person per hour in private tub; $20 per person in communal tub. **BEST TIMES:** winter for an outdoor hot tub experience during a light snowfall; summertime months through Sept, when the gardens are at their peak.

Extravagant Isolation, Forever Wild

THE ADIRONDACKS

New York, U.S.A.

The largest park in the continental United States—larger than Yosemite or the entire state of Massachusetts—the 6-million-acre Adirondacks State Park is legally protected to remain "forever wild." A whiff of aristocratic cachet remains from when 19th-century masters of the universe with names like Whitney, Vanderbilt, and Rockefeller chose this roadless wilderness to build their "Great Camps," servants in tow—one camp had a maid just to get rid of cobwebs. Surrounded by primeval forests, mountains, and more than 2,500 lakes and ponds, the lakefront compounds blended luxury and rustic charm, using native, minimally worked logs (with bark still attached), branches (the more twisted and gnarled the better), and decorative twigwork in what's become known as the Adirondack style.

Less than two dozen of these great camps have survived, many of them still owned by the families that built them, others operating as summer camps or educational institutions. A precious few operate as hotels, the most magnificent being the Point, a nine-building compound built in 1932 by William Avery Rockefeller, great-nephew of John D. Located on 8-mile-long Upper Saranac Lake and once known as Camp Wonundra, its common areas and eleven lavish guest rooms exude the spirit of another age with baronial chiseled stone fireplaces and gleaming spruce-paneled walls. The atmosphere of a house party prevails with candlelight meals and exceptional wine lists (black tie is optional on Wednesdays). Forced into extravagant isolation by the lack of telephones, faxes, and televisions, happy campers spend idyllic days canoeing, fishing, or exploring the hiking trails that thread through the grounds and out into the parkland.

If you pine for the Point but your budget doesn't, opt for the Lake Placid Lodge, built in 1882 on the western banks of the lake and owned and operated by the same proprietors that run the Point. The village of Lake Placid (site of the 1932 and 1980 Winter Olympics) offers numerous skiing and skating amenities in season. To experience the area's serene beauty from the water, book an afternoon aboard the elegant *Lady of the Lake*, a 40-foot, thirty-passenger Fay & Bowen built in 1929, just one of two such vessels in the United States.

The Adirondacks offer 6 million acres to explore.

WHAT: site, hotel. **ADIRONDACKS PARK:** 250 miles north of New York City. Adirondack Regional Tourism Council, tel 518-846-8016; www.adirondacks.org. **THE POINT:** Saranac Lake. Tel 800-255-3530 or 518-891-5674, fax 518-891-1152; www.thepointresort.com. *Cost:* from $1,300–$2,600 per night, year-round, includes all meals and activities for 2. *When:* hotel and restaurant closed Apr. **LAKE PLACID LODGE:** Whiteface Inn Rd., Lake Placid. Tel 877-523-2700 or 518-523-2700, fax 518-523-1124; www.lakeplacidlodge.com. *Cost:* doubles from $400, cabins from $750. **BEST TIMES:** Jun–Aug for the nicest weather; Sept–Oct for fall foliage and a number of small country festivals. Snowy months have their own special beauty.

Of Borscht and Buddha

THE CATSKILLS

New York, U.S.A.

With a mountain-wilderness beauty disproportionate to its modest size, parts of the Catskills region have been an on-again, off-again vacation destination for 200 years. Sullivan County was once the center of the summer Borscht Belt universe, with its primarily Jewish bungalow colonies, all-you-can-eat buffets, mambo nights, and sprawling family resorts like Browns, the Concord, and Grossingers, where Mel Brooks and Sid Caesar got their start. The most authentic and rural part of the area is Delaware County, still very much a farming community whose "cow country" authenticity is an irresistible lure for city sophisticates.

Today it's Ulster County that appeals most to urbanites looking for a Walden Pond escape, combining rich Hudson River heritage and a beautiful mountain interior of deep forests and hidden waterfalls. Riverside towns like Kingston and Saugerties offer history, but Woodstock is the Catskills' most famous, popularly known for the 1969 rock concert that bore its name—even though the festival was actually held 50 miles away, in Bethel. Today's Woodstock is part tie-dyed (with a number of ashrams and Buddhist retreat centers), part film-and-fashion crowd, and part Hamptons escapees, but that's just part of the Bohemian continuum that started in the early 1900s, when artists and writers, alternative thinkers, and the independent-minded started settling here.

Those who bond with nature while hip-high in cold mountain springs will want to make a pilgrimage to the Beaverkill River, the birthplace of American fly-fishing and perhaps the most famous trout stream in the United States. It is the raison d'être for the Beaverkill Valley Inn, built in 1893, and once owned by Laurance Rockefeller (Nelson's nephew). From here, anglers are only a quick cast away from the revered Wulff Fly Fishing School.

For those who prefer their great outdoors embellished with all the refined comforts of the great indoors, the Emerson Resort and Spa is far and away the Catskills' best destination, offering specialties from Ayurvedic head massages to a detoxifying algae wrap. Twenty-four beautifully appointed rooms fill out the inn's 1874 Victorian mansion, while celebrated French-influenced meals focus on local Hudson Valley fare complemented by an award-winning wine list.

For a dose of the old Catskills, the past lives on at Mohonk Mountain House, the only remaining example of a type of lodging once prevalent in the area. Seven stories high and sprawling at the edge of a deep glacier-gouged lake, it's a glorious hodge-podge of Victorian turrets, gables, and crenellated stone towers, built by two Quaker brothers in 1869 and still run by the same family today (the Smileys). It's set on 2,200 private acres of woodland abutting the 6,400-acre Mohonk Preserve in the Shawangunk Mountains and boasts 85 miles of quiet trails and carriage roads, plus nearly 130 gazebos. A 1-mile hike to Sky Top Tower rewards climbers with a breathtaking 360-degree view of Catskills beauty and six states.

WHAT: site, hotel, restaurant, experience. **THE CATSKILLS:** 100 miles northwest of New York City; www.visitthecatskills.com. **BEAVERKILL VALLEY INN:** Lew Beach. Tel 845-439-4844; innkeeper@beaverkillvalley inn.com; www.beaverkillvalley.com. *Cost:* doubles from $145 (low season), from $225 (high season), includes meals. **WULFF FLY FISHING SCHOOL:** tel 845-439-4060, www. royalwulff.com. **EMERSON RESORT AND SPA:** Mount Tremper (12 miles from Woodstock). Tel 877-688-2828; info@emersonresort.com; www.emersonresort.com. *Cost:* doubles from $365 (weekday), from $400 (weekend), includes use of spa facilities; spa treatments extra. **MOHONK MOUNTAIN HOUSE:** 1000 Mountain Rd., New Paltz. Tel 800-772-6646 or 845-255-1000; www.mohonk.com. *Cost:* doubles from $510, includes meals. **BEST TIMES:** mid-Sept for the 4-day Woodstock Film Festival, which screens more than 125 independent films (www.woodstockfilm festival.com); almost every week for one of Mohonk Mountain House's themed weekends; mid-Oct for peak fall foliage.

Baseball, Opera, and Bucolic Charm

COOPERSTOWN

New York, U.S.A.

A quiet, tree-lined village amid upstate New York's woodlands, Cooperstown sits proudly stuck in time on the southern tip of placid Otsego Lake, a lake so crystal clear it is the source of the town's drinking water.

According to dubious legend, it was here, in 1839, that Abner Doubleday laid out the dimensions of a diamond and originated the game of baseball—a distinction that's made the town a pilgrimage site for baseball lovers and home of the National Baseball Hall of Fame and Museum. Set in a modest, three-story brick building on the four-block-long Main Street, its collection runs the gamut from Joe DiMaggio's locker and Brooks Robinson's glove to Roger Maris's and Mark McGwire's home-run bats and Babe Ruth's "Called Shot" bat from the 1932 World Series. In all, some 36,000 objects make up the idiosyncratic collection.

But Cooperstown isn't just about baseball. Every July and August since 1975, it's been home to the prestigious Glimmerglass Opera, an acclaimed summer festival that blends classic repertory with operatic rarities, performed by a renowned cast. An intimate, acoustically perfect 900-seat house has walls that open to let in the country air and views of surrounding farmland. Popular 19th-century novelist James Fenimore Cooper, son of the New Jersey transplant who founded Cooperstown in 1786, referred to Otsego Lake as "Glimmerglass," and thus the name.

An unassuming and informal small town with a population hovering at about 2,500, Cooperstown is the site of a handsome cluster of early 19th-century architecture. Like most attractions here, the sprawling, Federal-style Hotel Otesaga was commissioned in 1909 by the Clark Family, heirs to the Singer sewing machine fortune and the town's benefactors (now in their fifth generation) since the mid-19th century. Much has been made of its 400 windows, unrivaled lakefront setting, and venerable 18-hole Leatherstocking Golf Course, one of the oldest and most scenic in the United States.

WHAT: town, site, experience, hotel. **COOPERSTOWN:** 65 miles west of Albany, 225 miles northwest of New York City. Cooperstown Chamber of Commerce, tel 607-547-9983; info1@cooperstownchamber.org; www.cooperstownchamber.org. **BASEBALL HALL OF FAME:** 25 Main St. Tel 888-HALL-OF-FAME or 607-547-7200; www.baseball halloffame.org. *Cost:* admission $16.50. **GLIMMERGLASS OPERA:** St. Hwy. 80. Tel 607-547-2255; www.glimmerglass.org. *Cost:* tickets $48–$130. *When:* Jul–Aug. **HOTEL OTESAGA:** 60 Lake St. Tel 800-348-6222 or 607-547-9931, fax 607-547-9675; www.ote saga.com. *Cost:* doubles from $410 (low season), from $465 (high season), includes dinner. *When:* open mid-Apr to mid-Nov. **BEST TIMES:** late Jul/early Aug for the Baseball Hall of Fame induction ceremonies, and Christmastime, when the town is particularly beautiful.

An Oceanside Colony Where the Elite Meet and Greet

EAST HAMPTON

New York, U.S.A.

O n weekends and during summer months, the seaside towns of eastern Long Island are inundated with the beautiful people, their Jaguars and BMWs clogging the narrow roads in a conga line between hot spots. East Hampton is a peculiar mix of rustic charm and urban taste, local year-rounders and vacationing celebs, and simple seaside pleasures protected for the seriously rich. During the off-season, though, you can still glimpse patches of the "real" Hamptons, with the colonial dignity, gorgeous homes, long sweeps of beaches abutted by grassy dunes, and casual-chic eateries. "Going to the country" it's not—you'll run into as many Manhattanites at Sag Harbor's silent-era movie house or its Bay Street Theatre, or at Bridgehampton's 1920s-soda-fountain Candy Kitchen as you would on Madison Avenue—but along with polo fields, there are still potato fields, vineyards, and pumpkin patches, and roadside farm stands that ask you to kindly leave correct change in the can after you load up on fresh local produce.

The towns of the Hamptons blend and merge with one another and share a centuries-old history, but they differ greatly in character today. Southampton is perhaps best known, the grande dame of old money and sweeping estates. But the homes in East Hampton are no less staggering, comprising some of the most coveted real estate in America. Founded in 1648 and "discovered" by society as an escape resort in the late 1800s, it was later the destination of artists like Willem de Kooning and Jackson Pollock (and, more recently, Eric Fischl and Julian Schnabel), who came for the big sky and golden light. Today East Hampton is arguably the East End's most fashionable and preferred town and beach, confirmed by a new wave of 1990s summerers from the West Coast's film industry and Manhattan's fashion world.

Creature comforts are taken seriously and restaurants have grown to be as fine as any of their New York City peers, with people watching and reservation waiting lists to match. You'll do less begging for a table off-season at classics like longtime favorite Nick & Toni's, which has long been the star-sighting venue of choice. Its menu is as impressive as the celebrity clientele. Health-conscious (and not) foodies have put the much more informal Babette's on the map, where everyone shows up sooner or later.

For the marriage of excellent food and perfect accommodations in a historically appropriate setting, book way in advance at the stately Maidstone Arms, an elegantly cozy 19th-century white clapboard inn overlooking the town pond, swans and all. During a wintery midweek stay, you might even have the nineteen-room charmer to yourself—or at least it will feel that way.

WHAT: town, restaurant, hotel. **EAST HAMPTON:** 90 miles east of New York City. East Hampton Chamber of Commerce, tel 631-324-0362; www.easthamptonchamber. com. **NICK & TONI'S:** 136 N. Main St. Tel 631-324-3550; www.nickandtonis.com. *Cost:* dinner $70. **BABETTE'S:** 66 Newton Ln. Tel 631-329-5377. *Cost:* lunch $30. **MAIDSTONE ARMS INN:** 207 Main St. Tel 631-324-5006, fax 631-324-5037; www.maidstonearms.com. *Cost:* doubles from $225 (low season), from $450 (high season). **BEST TIMES:** off-season, mid-Sept to late May (autumn weekends and early spring can still be relatively busy); Jul and Aug for nicest weather.

World-Class Wines and Small-Town American Charm

FINGER LAKES

New York, U.S.A.

The Iroquois attributed these long, skinny, and relatively narrow finger-like lakes to the Great Spirit, who laid his hands in blessing on this particularly beautiful area of upstate New York. Unless the Great Spirit had eleven fingers, though, it's more likely that an advancing glacier carved them out eons ago. Most are deep—Cayuga and Seneca, the two largest, are 400 and 632 feet deep respectively and about 37 miles long—and picturesquely framed by steeply sloping banks. The parallel lakes cover an area no more than 100 miles across in a bucolic setting where farm stands still work on the honor system, and the sleepy Main Streets of 19th-century towns like Geneva, Skaneateles, and Hammondsport invite strolling and antique-hunting. Sightseeing boats crisscross the lakes, and you're welcome to jump aboard the 48-foot postal boat that services Lake Skaneateles, one of the last water routes for mail delivery in the country.

With soil and topography that mimic the best of the German wine-growing districts, the Finger Lakes' "boutique" vineyards—the earliest dating to the 1860s and today numbering over seventy—have edged their way to prominence on a national if not yet international level, and their white wines, especially their Rieslings and Chardonnays, are recognized as some of the country's best. For the finest experiences, try the pioneering Dr. Konstantin Frank's Vinifera Wine Cellars, located in Hammondsport overlooking Lake Keuka (considered by many to be the prettiest of the lakes), and Dundee's Hermann J. Wiemer Vineyard.

Seneca Lake is the location of Geneva on the Lake, a 1910 hotel inspired by a rural Roman villa that had captivated the owner. A parterre garden leads to the lakeside pool, which is a godsend when the lake's waters are too cold for a dip. At ice-blue Lake Skaneateles—the highest of the Finger Lakes and among the cleanest in the country—the Mirbeau Inn and Spa is a francophile's dream of mud wraps and Vichy-water scrubs, with an exceptional restaurant and lily ponds straight out of a Monet painting. Newly opened but resembling a 200-year-old country estate, it is intimate and manages to feel right at home in a region that otherwise exudes small-town American charm.

Trinity Episcopal Church on the Seneca-Cayuga Canal

WHAT: site, experience, hotel. **FINGER LAKES REGION:** 20 miles southwest of Syracuse airport; 215 miles west of Albany, 300 miles northwest of New York City. Contact Finger Lakes Tourism, tel 800-548-4386; info@fingerlakes.org; www.fingerlakes.org. **DR. KONSTANTIN FRANK'S VINIFERA WINE CELLARS:** 9749 Middle Rd., Hammondsport. Tel 800-320-0735 or 607-868-4884, fax 607-868-4884; info@drfrankwines.com; www.drfrankwines.com. **HERMANN J. WIEMER VINEYARD:** 3962 Rt. 14, Dundee. Tel 800-371-7971 or 607-243-7971, fax 607-348-1498; www.wiemer.com. **GENEVA ON THE LAKE RESORT:** 1001 Lochland Rd. (Rt. 14), Geneva. Tel 800-343-6382 or 315-789-7190; info@genevaonthelake.com; www.genevaonthelake.com. *Cost:* lake-view doubles from $120 (low season), from $235 (high season). **MIRBEAU INN AND SPA:** 851 W. Genesse St., Skaneateles. Tel 877-647-2328 or 315-685-1927; www.mirbeau.com. *Cost:* doubles from $230 (low season), from $300 (high season). Dinner $70.

Where "America the Beautiful" Began

HUDSON VALLEY

New York, U.S.A.

In 1609, Dutch explorer Henry Hudson sailed up the river that now bears his name, looking for passage to the Orient's riches. He didn't find it, but he did uncover what turned out to be one of the most scenic waterways in the world.

Although not very long at 314 miles, the Hudson River is one of the nation's most commercially important and most historic—the Hudson Valley has been home to literary figures such as Washington Irving (his "Rip Van Winkle," and "Legend of Sleepy Hollow" were set here) and was the site of ninety-two Revolutionary War battles between New York City and Saratoga. Known to Native Americans as the "two-way river" because salty ocean tides are felt as far north as Albany, the Hudson and its towns were among the country's first tourist destinations. Take a drive on back roads past manicured horse farms, dairy farms, and pick-your-own orchards, then stop for lunch and antiquing in 18th- and 19th-century riverside towns such as Nyack, Cold Spring, Kingston, and Hudson, the latter with its 1869 lighthouse-cum-bed-and-breakfast.

Industry has obscured some of the natural beauty that inspired Thomas Cole, Frederic Church, and other landscape painters of the 19th-century Hudson River School—the first truly American art movement—but much along the waterline remains surprisingly unsullied. Church would find the vast views from Olana, his 1872 hilltop Moorish mansion, little changed. Arrive in time for sunset to see why Church claimed that this was "the center of the world." This open, rolling, farm country landscape is also home to one of America's oldest inns, Rhinebeck's Beekman Arms, first opened in 1776. Book in advance at its award-winning restaurant, the country outpost of New York City chef Larry Forgione, an alum of nearby Hyde Park's prestigious Culinary Institute of America. Widely known in international food circles as "the other CIA," it was founded in 1946 and remains the nation's first and foremost, housed in a former seminary with four student-staffed restaurants open to the public.

Hyde Park is also home to Springwood, Franklin D. Roosevelt's 290-acre lifelong home, whose river views inspired the man who would serve four terms as president of the United States. The FDR Presidential Library and Museum is also on the site, and a fifty-four-room Vanderbilt mansion lies nearby.

The valley has drawn artists and art lovers over time. Just north of West Point (the nation's oldest military academy and certainly its most beautifully sited), the hillside Storm King Art Center, one of the country's leading outdoor sculpture parks, invites picnicking among its 500 acres of landscaped grounds. More than 120 internationally recognized artists are represented from the post-1945 period, with works that are often monumental in size.

Across the river in the east bank town of Beacon (home of folksinger Pete Seeger), the valley's newest arts addition is Dia:Beacon, a branch of the New York City–based foundation that opened in May 2003. Occupying a dignified 1929 building that was formerly an industrial printing facility, it exhibits major (and often oversized) works from the 1960s to the present, including pieces by Donald Judd, Andy Warhol, Richard Serra, and Cy Twombly.

WHAT: site, hotel, restaurant. **HUDSON VALLEY:** Hudson Valley Tourism, tel 800-232-

4782 or 845-291-2136; www.travelhudson valley.com. **OLANA:** RD2, outside Hudson, a mile south of the Rip Van Winkle Bridge. Tel 518-828-0135; www.olana.org. **BEEKMAN ARMS:** 6387 Mill St., Rhinebeck. Tel 845-876-7077; www.beekmandelamaterinn.com. *Cost:* doubles from $115 (low season), from $130 (high season). Dinner $35. **CULINARY INSTITUTE OF AMERICA:** Campus Dr., Hyde Park. Tel 845-451-6608; www.ciachef.edu. **FDR'S HOME, SPRINGWOOD:** Hyde Park. Tel 800-337-8474 or 845-486-1966; www.nps.

gov/hofr. *Cost:* entrance to park and gardens free; guided tour of the FDR home and Presidential Museum $14. **WEST POINT:** Highland Falls. Tel 845-938-2638; www.usma.edu. **STORM KING ART CENTER:** Old Pleasant Hill Rd., Mountainville. Tel 845-534-3115; www.stormking.org. *Cost:* admission $10. *When:* Apr–early Nov. **DIA:BEACON:** Beacon. Tel 845-440-0100; info@diaart.org; www.dia beacon.org. **BEST TIMES:** May for spring beauty; summer for a variety of festivals and events; Oct for fall foliage.

---

*"If you're bored in New York,
it's your own fault."—MYRNA LOY*

NEW YORK CITY

New York, U.S.A.

This is Metropolis. This is Gotham City. This is the one all the other cities wish they were—"the only real city-city," as Truman Capote put it. Its skyscrapers loom above canyonlike streets where some 8 million New Yorkers go about their daily business—walking fast, talking fast, and taking no lip, yet sharing that pride and sense of community that was displayed so unforgettably when terrorists targeted their home on September 11, 2001. They say it's the capital of the world . . . and maybe it is.

THE TOP TEN SIGHTS

AMERICAN MUSEUM OF NATURAL HISTORY —There are dinosaurs in here! Plus about 36 million other things, from moon rocks to the Brazilian Princess Topaz, the world's largest cut gem at 21,005 carats. Don't miss the Hall of Biodiversity or the dioramas of animal and village life. Its most recent addition, the futuristic Rose Center for Earth and Space, is a four-story sphere encased in glass that holds the new Hayden Planetarium, the largest and most powerful virtual reality simulator in the world, sending visitors through the Milky Way and beyond. **WHERE:** Central Park West at 79th St. Tel 212-769-5100; www.amnh.org.

A popular resident of the American Museum of Natural History

CENTRAL PARK—Laid out between 1859 and 1870 on a design by Frederick Law Olmsted and Calvert Vaux, Central Park's 843 acres are an urban miracle, an oasis of green surrounded on all sides by high-rise buildings. Highlights include Bethesda Fountain, the romantic Loeb Boathouse Restaurant, the Wollman Memorial Ice Rink, the Sheep Meadow (an enormous lawn that's blanket-to-blanket with sunbathers in summer), the carousel with fifty-eight hand-carved horses, and the Conservatory Garden, a gem of a refuge near the park's northeast corner. In summer, visitors can take in free performances by the Metropolitan Opera and the New York Philharmonic; Summer Stage concerts by a spectrum of international pop, reggae, world-music, and other artists; and performances of Shakespeare in the Park. **WHERE:** between 59th and 110th Sts. (south to north) and Fifth Ave. and Central Park West (east to west). Tel 212-310-6600; www.centralparknyc.org.

EMPIRE STATE BUILDING—Though not the most beautiful of New York's skyscrapers (the Chrysler Building on 42nd Street usually wins that title), the Empire State Building is undoubtedly its most iconic, soaring up 1,454 feet from 34th Street and bathed at night in lighting chosen to reflect the season. Completed in 1931—two years before King Kong made his fateful climb—it reigned as the tallest building in the world until the Twin Towers of the World Trade Center went up in 1970 and 1972, but it's always been the city's romantic tall building of choice, as evidenced by Cary Grant and Deborah Kerr's enduring *Affair to Remember.* Visitors can find their own romance at the 86th floor's open-air observatory, with views up to 80 miles in all directions. **WHERE:** Fifth Ave. at 34th St. Tel 212-736-3100; www.esbnyc.com.

FRICK MUSEUM—Built in 1914, this lovely French-style mansion houses an intimate collection of mostly European art. For a description, see the "Museum Mile" entry on page 686.

LINCOLN CENTER—Since 1962, when the first of its eight theaters opened, the 15-acre Lincoln Center complex has been the centerpiece of New York's performing arts scene, with twelve resident companies that include the New York City Ballet, the American Ballet Theatre, the New York Philharmonic, and the Metropolitan Opera, widely considered to be the best in the world. In summer, dance bands from swing to salsa perform in the central Josie Robertson Plaza as part of the center's Midsummer Night Swing series. Look up from your dancing to view *Source of Music* and *Triumph of Music,* two enormous Marc Chagall murals hanging behind the Metropolitan Opera House's glass facade. **WHERE:** Broadway and 64th St. Tel 212-875-5456; www.lincolncenter.org.

METROPOLITAN MUSEUM OF ART—The largest and one of the finest museums in the western hemisphere. For a description, see the "Museum Mile" entry on page 686.

MUSEUM OF MODERN ART—After being closed for renovation for two and a half years, MoMA reopened in November 2004 to much fanfare. Remodeled and enlarged according to a design by Yoshio Taniguchi, the 630,000-square-foot museum is nearly twice the size of the original building.

Founded in 1929 to promote new approaches to artistic expression, MoMA is today home to the world's finest collection of works from the late 19th century to the present, including van Gogh's *Starry Night,* Picasso's 1907 *Les Demoiselles d'Avignon,* Matisse's *Dance (First Version),* and Jackson Pollock's *One (Number 31, 1950).* Other highlights include the 3,000 objects of the Architecture and Design collection (from appliances and tableware to cars and heli-copters); the Film and Media collection, with its 4 million stills and 19,000 films; and the photography collection, with works by Man

Ray, Walker Evans, Dorothea Lange, and Ansel Adams, among others. Overloaded art gazers can find respite in either the peaceful open-air Abby Aldrich Rockefeller Sculpture Garden—filled with Giacometti, Picasso, Rodin, and others—or in the two casual cafés or the much-lauded restaurant, The Modern, run by Chef Gabriel Kreuther. **WHERE:** MoMA, 11 W. 53rd St. Tel 212-708-9400; www.moma.org.

ROCKEFELLER CENTER AT CHRISTMAS—Yes, it's a group of office buildings, but what office buildings they are, and what a grand public space they surround. Built in the 1930s by John D. Rockefeller, the complex is a masterpiece of streamlined modern architecture, full of Art Deco relief work and sculpture that harks back to Greek mythology while paying homage to American optimism in the face of the Great Depression. The center looks its best at Christmastime, when a 75- to 90-foot Norway spruce is displayed as the city's official Christmas tree. Set below it is a tiny but incredibly romantic ice-skating rink. Take a spin, then head to Radio City Music Hall (corner of Sixth Ave. and 50th St., tel 212-247-4777; www.radio city.com.), the complex's Deco masterpiece, for the annual Christmas Spectacular, a grand, Broadway-esque stage show starring the Rockettes. **WHERE:** between 48th and 50th Sts. (south to north) and Fifth and Sixth Aves. (east to west); tel for Rockefeller Center: 212-632-3975; www.rocke fellercenter.com.

Lady Liberty

STATUE OF LIBERTY AND ELLIS ISLAND—Symbols of the American melting pot, both located in New York

Harbor. See the "Historic Downtown New York" entry on page 684 for a full description.

TIMES SQUARE/42ND STREET—Once the entertainment capital of America, full of gorgeous movie palaces, glamorous showgirls, and the kind of Guys-and-Dolls gangsters made famous by Damon Runyon, Times Square had by the 1970s degenerated into a swamp of drugs and peep shows, its streets filled with hustlers and lowlifes. That all changed in the 1990s, when the city invited Disney and a number of other business giants to collaborate in the revitalization of the area. Today, it's like Disney World without Cinderella's castle, a family-entertainment and business district that shows little trace of its seedy past. The "Great White Way's" old movie palaces have been restored, Broadway theater has survived intact, and neon to rival Las Vegas's sets tourists' heads spinning. On New Year's Eve, this is party central—upwards of half a million people brave the single-digit weather conditions, waiting for the ball to drop and the hoopla that follows. **WHERE:** technically between 42nd and 48th Sts. (south to north) along Broadway and Seventh Ave., but the vibe stretches west to Ninth Ave. and north to 54th St.

OTHER MUST-DO'S

BIG ONION WALKING TOURS—Long before New York became known as the Big Apple, it was the Big Onion—a place from which you could peel off layer after layer without ever reaching the core. Big Onion Walking Tours offers visitors a glimpse of many of those layers, past and present, with neighborhood tours visiting Greenwich Village, Harlem, and many others; historic tours; and specialty tours exploring labor, gay life, and many other strata of the Apple/Onion. All guides hold advanced degrees in American history from Columbia or New York University. **WHERE:** walking tours are held year-round, and depart from various meeting spots around the city. Tel 212-439-1090; www.bigonion.com.

BRONX ZOO—Opened in 1899, the Bronx Zoo is home to more than 6,000 animals, mostly in settings designed to mimic their natural habitats. At 265 acres it's the largest metropolitan zoo in the United States, with exhibits that include Himalayan Highlands complete with rare snow leopards; the 6.5-acre Congo Gorilla Forest, which includes one of the largest breeding groups of lowland gorillas in captivity; and Wild Asia, whose monorail takes you through a plain populated by Asian elephants, tigers, and rhinoceroses. Nearby, the New York Botanical Garden is a 250-acre oasis of another sort, home to twenty-seven outdoor gardens and the largest Victorian conservatory in America—New York's own Crystal Palace. **BRONX ZOO:** Fordham Rd. and the Bronx River Parkway, the Bronx. Tel 718-367-1010; www.bronxzoo.com. **BOTANICAL GARDEN:** 200th St. and Kazimiroff Blvd., the Bronx. Tel 718-817-8700; www.nybg.org.

BROOKLYN BOTANIC GARDENS—Founded in 1910, the BBG is the most popular garden in New York. Covering 52 acres adjacent to Prospect Park (which was designed by Frederick Law Olmsted and Calvert Vaux after their success with Central Park), the BBG has more than 12,000 species of plants arranged in more than twenty gardens and collections, including the Cranford Rose Garden, the English-style Shakespeare Garden, the Japanese Hill-and-Pond Garden, and the Cherry Esplanade, one of the finest sites outside Japan for seeing cherry blossoms bloom in spring. **WHERE:** 1000 Washington Ave., Brooklyn. Tel 718-623-7200; www.bbg.org.

THE BROOKLYN BRIDGE—Completed in 1883 after fourteen years of construction, this massive suspension bridge may or may not be the eighth wonder of the world (as period PR claimed), but it's undeniably one of the architectural gems of New York,

a monumental yet graceful icon that connects lower Manhattan with the 19th-century neighborhood of Brooklyn Heights. For a real back-in-time sensation, walk across the boardwalk-like walkway, which runs through the center of the bridge between huge stone pylons and a spiderweb of steel support cables. For some of the best urban views in the world, take the subway to Brooklyn Heights, explore for a while, then walk back to Manhattan across the bridge. **WHERE:** from the A or C subway stop at High St. (first stop in Brooklyn), walk to Cadman Plaza East, on the east side of narrow Cadman Plaza Park. Just north of the park you'll find the stairway to the bridge walkway under an overpass. **BROOKLYN HEIGHTS:** bounded by Old Fulton St. and Atlantic Ave. (north and south) and Court St./Cadman Plaza West and the East River (east and west). From the High St. subway station (see above), head west to the Promenade.

THE CLOISTERS—Near the northern tip of Manhattan, atop a riverside cliff within beautiful Fort Tryon Park, the Cloisters is a branch of the Metropolitan Museum of Art devoted to the art and architecture of medieval Europe. Its complex incorporates actual structures from the 12th through the 15th centuries brought from Europe and reassembled, including sections of five medieval French cloisters. Inside, the museum's collection covers some 5,000 works, including its famous Unicorn Tapestries and various manuscripts, metalwork, stained glass, and other pieces typical of the medieval period. **WHERE:** Fort Tryon Park near W. 190th St. Tel 212-923-3700; www.metmuseum.org.

GRAND CENTRAL TERMINAL—Chances are you'll be passing through anyway (since numerous subway lines stop here), but if not, make a special trip, because Grand Central is one of the best places in the city to catch the spirit of early 20th-century New York and America—the days when public buildings were still capable of filling the heart with civic pride. Grand Central's triumphant Beaux Arts exterior is adorned with statues of Hercules, Minerva, and Mercury; its huge main concourse is covered by a ceiling that mimics the vault of the sky (complete with constellations); its arched, tiled passageways are as graceful as the aisles of a mosque; and lofty windows illuminate its marble interior with the kind of light you usually only see in pictures. For a classic experience of the station, have lunch at the Oyster Bar on the lower level. In business since 1913, it serves 4,000 pounds of fresh seafood daily, including its famous New England clam chowder and dozens of different kinds of oysters. **WHERE:** 42nd St. at Park Ave. www.grandcentralterminal.com. **OYSTER BAR:** tel 212-490-6653; www.oysterbarny.com.

HARLEM SPIRITUALS TOUR—Since the 1990s, visitors (especially European ones) have been increasingly common at Harlem's traditional Sunday morning services, home to the near-ecstatic black gospel tradition that was born during days of slavery and came north with the African American migration of the early 20th century. Best bets are Mother A.M.E. (African Methodist Episcopal) Zion (140 W. 137th St.; tel 212-234-1544), founded in 1797 and with a history that connects it to the Underground Railroad; the Abyssinian Baptist Church (132 W. 138th St.; tel 212-862-7474), renowned for its choir; and the New Mount Zion Baptist Church (171 W. 140th St.; tel 212-283-0788), under the direction of much-loved pastor Carl L. Washington Jr. First-time visitors may want to check out the bus tours organized by Harlem Spirituals (690 Eighth Ave.; tel 212-391-0900), which depart from midtown.

A GAME AT YANKEE STADIUM—"The House that Ruth Built" is less than a half hour from midtown by subway and an essential element of the full NYC experience. Check the Yankees website for the game schedule, buy

Try to see the legendary Yankees in their own stadium.

tickets in advance or at the gate (cheap bleacher seats for the rowdiest crowd), and then hop on the number 4, D, or (weekdays only) B train to the 161st St. stop, which you can't miss because it's where everybody else is getting off, too. The hot dogs here are probably the most expensive in the world, but hey, you only live once. **WHERE:** 161st St. and River Ave., the Bronx. Ticket information, tel 718-293-4300; newyork.yankees.mlb.com.

WHERE TO STAY

THE FOUR SEASONS—Soaring fifty-two stories above one of the city's most sought-after shopping streets, the I. M. Pei–designed Four Seasons is the destination for the recognizable and those who follow in their Prada footprints. Sky-high room rates may limit your visit to the cool, sleek lobby, almost templelike in its vast quietude, and the Fifty Seven Fifty Seven Bar and the restaurant of the same name, midtown's venue for power breakfasts and lunches. **WHERE:** 57 E. 57th St. Tel 800-332-3442 or 212-758-5700, fax 212-758-5711; www.fourseasons.com/newyorkfs. *Cost:* high.

THE INN AT IRVING PLACE—The Inn at Irving Place is a boutique jewel, a little-known refuge of no pomp but great charm. The twelve-room inn was created when two 1834 town houses were joined and meticulously decorated in a manner reminiscent of the elegant style of a bygone New York. Edith Wharton would be very much at home in this dignified and gracious atmosphere. **WHERE:** 56 Irving Place (at E. 17th St.). Tel 800-685-1447 or 212-533-4600, fax 212-533-4611; www.innatirving.com. *Cost:* moderate.

THE PLAZA—The fabled Plaza still steals the show for its location, where Fifth Avenue hustle gives over to Central Park's quiet green. Since 1907, this storied châteaulike hotel (now also home to luxury condominiums) has been made famous by a Who's Who guest list—from Eloise to Cary Grant. Some say unless you secure a park-view room, your dollars may be better spent elsewhere, but a Bloody Mary in the Oak Room, the dark and clubby bar overlooking Central Park, should be on everyone's list. **WHERE:** W. 59th St. at Fifth Ave. Tel 888-850-0909 or 212-759-3000; www.theplaza.com. *Cost:* high.

ST. REGIS HOTEL—Built by Jacob Astor in 1904 as his private residence, this grand Beaux Arts building is only more impressive today, welcoming overindulged guests of a similar ilk with top-hatted doormen, glistening crystal chandeliers, Louis XV furnishings, and polished service. One of New York's favorite drinking dens is here—the wonderfully atmospheric King Cole Bar, named after the mural by Maxfield Parrish. **WHERE:** 2 E. 55th St. Tel 800-325-3589 or 212-753-4500; www.starwoodhotels.com. *Cost:* high.

EATING & DRINKING

BOULEY—New York is filled with top-notch restaurants steered by world-rank chefs—of these, Bouley (163 Duane Street; tel 212-964-2525; www.davidbouley.com) is the most comfortable and casual. Although Gallic to the max, owner-chef David Bouley absorbs foreign influences and flavors and transforms them into inspired, extraordinary creations. Just a block away, the Bouley Bakery and Bouley Market (120 West Broadway, tel 212-219-1011; www.davidbouley.com) occupy three floors of a small West Broadway building, with its top-floor Upstairs restaurant serving seasonal à la carte dishes from the open kitchen.

CARNEGIE DELICATESSEN—Immortalized in the Woody Allen film *Broadway Danny Rose*, the Carnegie is a kosher-style New York deli from the old school, its air redolent of pastrami and Henny Youngman jokes. Tables are set elbow-to-elbow and the seasoned waiters like to tease tourists as part of their shtick, but when they tell you that you won't be hungry till next week after eating one of their calorie-busting meals, they aren't kidding. Locals always ask to share, and never leave without a doggy bag. Save room for the cheesecake. **WHERE:** 854 Seventh Ave. (at 55th St.). Tel 800-334-5606; www.carnegiedeli.com.

DANIEL—Regarded by fellow chefs and devoted patrons as one of the country's most brilliant French-trained talents, Daniel Boulud is trail-blazing the future of haute cuisine. Refined fantasy describes both the decor of his eponymous restaurant and its poetic menu, which features technically complicated, perfectly executed, and artistically presented dishes. You can revel in Boulud's inventive spirit more cheaply at his neighborhoody Café Boulud (20 E. 76th St.; tel 212-772-2600) and the newer DB Bistro Moderne (55 W. 44th St.; tel 212-391-2400), justly famous for its sumptuous hamburger. **WHERE:** 60 E. 65th St. Tel 212-288-0033; www.danielnyc.com.

THE FOUR SEASONS—No restaurant personifies New York's power elite more than the Four Seasons. Virtually unchanged since it was designed in 1959 by Philip Johnson in Mies van der Rohe's landmark Seagram's Building, it is the place to come and be pampered by top-notch service. Out-of-towners fill the place for dinner, but a certain set of New York power brokers use the place as their lunchtime cafeteria. The food more than holds its own against all the hype. **WHERE:** 99 E. 52nd St. Tel 212-754-9494; www.fourseasonsrestaurant.com.

THE ITALIANS—New York City has come a long way since eating Italian meant a bowl of uninspired spaghetti swimming in oregano-doused tomato sauce at a mom-and-pop place in Little Italy. Among the new generation, television personality Mario Batali's Babbo (110 Waverly Pl.; tel 212-777-0303; www.babbonyc.com) is the best known, introducing curious New Yorkers to lamb's tongue, calf's brains, ravioli stuffed with beef cheek, among other delicacies. For more hesitant palates, there are less exotic and equally delicious southern Italian classics on the menu. Save the cost of an airplane ticket to Tuscany and spend a warm and cozy evening at Beppe (45 E. 22nd St.; tel 212-982-8422), a rustic room with exposed brick walls, beamed ceilings, and a wood-burning fireplace. Cesare Casella hails from the hills of Lucca, where the full flavors of grilled mushrooms and roasted meats leap off the plate, as they do here, fused with the aphrodisiacal aroma of wild rosemary and herbs. You'll be hard pressed to find fault with any of the pan-Italian specialties at Vincent Scotto's Gonzo (140 W. 13th St.; tel 212-645-4606), but don't leave without sampling one of the superior varieties of grilled pizzas, hailed by many as the best in town. The massive, perfectly charred *bistecca alla fiorentina* is the most authentic this side of Florence.

JEAN-GEORGES—Obscure flavors, innovative combinations, unsung ingredients, and dazzling presentations continue to captivate the savvy devotees who have followed Jean-Georges Vongerichten since he first fascinated palates at Jo Jo. From the simplest to the most complex, each masterpiece confirms that here reigns one of America's most creative culinary forces. **WHERE:** 1 Central Park West. Tel 212-299-3900; www.jean-georges.com.

LE BERNARDIN—French-born Eric Ripert, a permanent fixture among the city's line-up of all-star chefs, heads the kitchen at Le Bernardin, an elegant temple that first revolutionized seafood cooking in the 1980s. Whether lightly sauced, barely cooked, or simply raw, his ever-changing dishes surprise even the most jaded palates. **WHERE:** 155 W. 51st St. Tel 212-554-1515; www.le-bernardin.com.

NOBU—One of the most copied sushi restaurants in the world, this peerless Tribeca hot spot deserves much of the credit for initiating New Yorkers to the mysteries of raw fish. The master sushi chefs keep the celebrity-strewn dining room in thrall with fragrant, deftly prepared, and utterly fresh seafood. Next door is the aptly named Next Door Nobu, whose no-reservations policy and only slightly less extreme prices don't compromise the evening's delight one bit. **WHERE:** 105 Hudson St. Tel 212-219-0500.

PETER LUGER STEAKHOUSE—A veritable Parthenon of Porterhouse, Peter Luger's is possibly the country's finest steak restaurant, drawing happy carnivores to its tavernlike, old New York premises beneath the Williamsburg Bridge since 1887. Each perfect butter-tender prime beef steak is hand-picked and dry aged on site. If you ask for the menu, they'll know you're a first-timer. **WHERE:** 178 Broadway, Williamsburg, Brooklyn. Tel 718-387-7400; www.peterluger.com.

UNION SQUARE CAFÉ—This New American–style bistro offers a lunch or dinner experience that's one of the nicest you're likely to come by—if you can get in. At the helm of the well-oiled operation is the amiable Danny Meyer, who wrote the manual on genuinely warm service, good value, and unfussy, Mediterranean-based comfort food. This surefire formula explains the sustained popularity of the city's next-most-loved venue, the elegantly handsome Gramercy Tavern (42 E. 20th St.; tel 212-477-0777), another Meyer brainchild created in collaboration with supertalented chef Tom Colicchio. **WHERE:** 21 E. 16th St. Tel 212-243-4020.

Where the City Began

HISTORIC DOWNTOWN NEW YORK

New York, U.S.A.

This is the New York you remember from all those black-and-white 1930s movies: narrow streets, looming skyscrapers, suited businesspeople, Cary Grant, and cabbies with that quintessential New Yawk accent. Today, of course, the cabbies are mostly from Bangladesh, but the rest is pretty much the same— minus Cary Grant.

The Dutch colony of Nieuw Amsterdam was set up on these acres in the 1620s, and in 1626, the colony's governor, Peter Minuit, made his legendary $24 purchase of Manhattan island from the Indians at or near what is now Bowling Green Park, a tiny triangle of green at the very base of Broadway. At the tip of the island, Battery Park gives a wonderful view of New York Harbor. It is also the jumping-off point for ferry service to two great symbols of America: the Statue of Liberty and Ellis Island.

Lady Liberty (whose official name is *Liberty Enlightening the World*) was designed by Frédéric-Auguste Bartholdi and engineer Alexandre-Gustave Eiffel, and was presented as a gift from France to the United States in 1885 as a symbol of friendship and of the two countries' shared notions of liberty. Erected on a granite pedestal on Bedloe's Island (now Liberty Island), the statue was dedicated on October 28, 1886, and received a remarkably effective face-lift in time for her centennial.

Slightly north of Liberty Island, Ellis Island was the processing station for roughly 12 million immigrants between 1892 and 1954. Today, approximately 40 percent of Americans have an ancestor who entered the country through the island. A six-year renovation in the 1980s rescued the island from disuse, turning it into a moving memorial and interpretive center where Americans can research their heritage and retrace their ancestors' arrival, entering through the same baggage room and registry room. Those who don't want to visit the monuments but want a good view of Liberty and the Manhattan skyline can hop on the Staten Island Ferry, which runs every half hour to and from New York's outermost borough.

Back in Manhattan, enter the maze of streets north of Battery Park and listen for the sound of Big Money's heartbeat beating firmly on and around legendary Wall Street. Named for an actual wall erected by the Dutch to ward off Indian attacks, it's been the center of commerce in the New World for more than two centuries. The New York Stock Exchange, housed in a handsome Beaux Arts building designed by George Post in 1903, is the center of the action, the largest securities market in the world.

Wall Street is also home to Trinity Church, at one time the tallest structure on the New York skyline at 281 feet. Built in 1846 by William Upjohn, the Episcopal church is now dwarfed by practically everything around it, but still functions as a house of worship and as a peaceful refuge. On Mondays and Thursdays it hosts a free midday concert series.

Five blocks north is St. Paul's Chapel; built in 1766 in the Georgian Classic-Revival style, it's New York's only remaining pre-Revolutionary church, with a graveyard full of 18th- and early 19th-century notables. George Washington worshipped here after his inauguration as president in 1789, but the church recently became better known for the work it did following September 11, 2001, when it became a twenty-four-hour relief center for recovery workers. In the days after the attacks, the church's iron fence was festooned with notes, missing-persons posters, firemen's hats and baseball caps, banners, origami cranes (symbolizing peace), and other items dedicated to the more than 2,500 casualties. The memorial has now been removed and archived by the church and hopefully will be displayed in the future at a site to be determined.

At this writing, the hallowed 16-acre site of the World Trade Center itself (directly behind St. Paul's) was about to become a construction site. The winning design, picked from a grueling fifteen-month competition, was submitted by the firm of New York resident Daniel Libeskind, best known for the Jewish Museum in Berlin. A special memorial, "Reflecting Absence," will be created by designers Michael Arad and Peter Walker, selected from more than 5,000 applicants. Rebuilding is fully in evidence at the adjacent World Financial Center, whose glass Winter Garden dome, destroyed by falling debris, has been completely repaired, with restaurants back in business and a free concert series on tap. The outdoor plaza behind the center is a fine spot in warm weather, fronting the Hudson.

Moving uptown on Broadway, you'll pass the lovely Woolworth Building, which in 1913 was the tallest building in the world and home to the (now-defunct) five-and-dime chain. Designed by Cass Gilbert in the neo-Gothic style, it resembles an extremely tall, narrow Notre Dame, full of lacy stone traceries, gargoyles, turrets, and spires. The building is not open to the general public, but you can step inside briefly to view the cathedral-like lobby.

Just across the street is the south end of City Hall Park, a newly restored public space surrounded by municipal government buildings: the surprisingly small City Hall (off-limits to visitors); the stately Beaux Arts Hall of Records, housing the complete legal and realty history of Manhattan back to the 1600s; the Municipal Building, an enormous adjunct to City Hall; and the Tweed Courthouse, built during the reign of legendary New York politician William "Boss" Tweed. Construction of the courthouse, budgeted originally at $250,000, eventually exceeded $14 million, of which Tweed and his cronies allegedly pocketed more than 60 percent.

WHAT: site. **FINANCIAL DISTRICT:** at the southern tip of Manhattan island, tel 212-484-1222; www.nycgo.com. **STATUE OF LIBERTY:** www.nps.gov/stli. For ferry information, tel 877-523-9849; www.statue cruises.com. *Cost:* from $12. *When:* frequent ferries depart from Battery Park daily. **ELLIS ISLAND:** tel 212-363-3200; www.ellisisland. org. Ferry information as listed above. **STATEN ISLAND FERRY:** tel 718-815-BOAT; www. siferry.com. Departs from the Whitehall Terminal at Whitehall St. and South St. *Cost:* free. **NEW YORK STOCK EXCHANGE:** 20 Broad St. Tel 212-656-3000; www.nyse.com. **TRINITY CHURCH:** Wall St. and Broadway. Tel 212-602-0800; www.trinitywallstreet.org. *Cost:* concerts free, but a small contribution is suggested. *When:* see website for noonday concerts schedule. **ST. PAUL'S CHAPEL:** Broadway between Vesey and Fulton Sts. Tel 212-233-4164; www.saintpaulschapel.org. **WORLD FINANCIAL CENTER:** West St. at Vesey St. Tel 212-417-7000; www.world financialcenter.com.

5,280 Feet of Culture

MUSEUM MILE

New York, New York, U.S.A.

Fronting Central Park on Manhattan's well-moneyed Upper East Side, Fifth Avenue was once chockablock with millionaires' mansions, but is now home to riches of another kind. Far removed from midtown's hustle and bustle,

the twenty-two blocks between 82nd and 104th Streets contain one of the greatest concentrations of museums in the world, with several others just a few more blocks to the south.

The Metropolitan Museum of Art is the largest museum in the western hemisphere and one of the finest, with a collection of more than 2 million works from around the world, from the Stone Age to the 21st century. Founded in 1870 and moved to its present location in 1880, the museum has expanded to such a degree that its original Gothic Revival building is now completely surrounded by additions. Highlights include the Roman and Greek galleries; the Costume Institute; the collections of Byzantine and Chinese art; the collection of European paintings, with works by Tiepolo, Cézanne, Vermeer, and Monet; the Arms and Armor collection; the Egyptian collection, with its mummies, sphinx, and the amazing Temple of Dendur, a complete 1st century B.C. Egyptian temple presented as a gift of the Egyptian government. Also notable is the Frank Lloyd Wright room, set up to mirror the former living room of Francis W. Little. The museum's Roof Garden Café is a favorite summertime haunt for New Yorkers with its great view of Central Park, while a classical concert series is held in many of the museum's finest rooms September to June.

For more Wright, walk uptown to the Solomon R. Guggenheim Museum. Designed by Wright as a spiral wider at the top than at the base, the structure reflects the architect's use of organic form. Take the elevator to the

The spiral Solomon R. Guggenheim Museum

top and walk downhill through the uninterrupted gallery to ground level, viewing a collection that spans the period from the late 19th century to the present, including Mr. Guggenheim's original collection of nonobjective art; Peggy Guggenheim's collection of Surrealist and abstract paintings and sculptures; and works covering the Impressionist, Post-Impressionist, early Modern, German Expressionist, Minimalist, Environmental, and other modern and contemporary schools.

A little farther uptown, the Museum of the City of New York is a must for Gotham aficionados, with its collections of prints and photographs, paintings and sculpture, decorative arts, costumes, toys, and memorabilia that trace the city's history from a small Dutch colony to the capital of the world. The Theater Collection is one of the world's best, covering New York theater from the late 18th century to the present, with original set and costume renderings, photos, and original scripts, costumes, props, posters, and window cards. The Marine

Collection concentrates on New York's maritime history, with 100 scale models of historic ships and as many paintings of New York harbor through the years. On the fifth floor, John D. Rockefeller's 19th-century bedroom and dressing room are preserved intact, moved here from his house at 4 West 55th Street.

At 91st Street, the Cooper-Hewitt National Museum of Design occupies the former mansion of another famous New York tycoon, Andrew Carnegie. Part of the Smithsonian Institution, it's the only museum in the United States devoted solely to historic and contemporary design, with collections of product design and decorative arts, drawings, prints and graphic design, textiles, and wall coverings. The museum's libraries and archives are open to the public by appointment.

One block north, the Jewish Museum celebrates 4,000 years of Jewish culture through painting, sculpture, drawings, photos, and archaeological and everyday artifacts—some 28,000 pieces in all. The permanent exhibition, *Culture and Continuity: The Jewish Journey,* tells the story of the Jewish experience from ancient times to today through art, archaeology, ceremonial objects, video, and interactive media.

Technically not part of Museum Mile, the Whitney Museum of American Art and the Frick Collection are so close (and so important) that it's silly to quibble. The Whitney is home to possibly the finest collection of 20th-century American art in the world. Founded by Gertrude Vanderbilt Whitney in 1930 to showcase the works of neglected American artists, the museum holds an ever-growing collection that currently numbers more than 14,000 works. Highlights of the collection include works by Edward Hopper, Alexander Calder, Georgia O'Keeffe, Reginald Marsh, Claes Oldenburg, Alex Katz, and Stuart Davis. The museum's stern granite building, described as "an inverted Babylonian ziggurat" by one critic when it went up in 1966, was designed by Hungarian-born, Bauhaus-trained architect Marcel Breuer.

The Frick occupies the other end of the art spectrum, concentrating on European masters. It is housed in a lovely re-created French-style 18th-century mansion, built in 1914 by steel and railroad magnate Henry Clay Frick. The interior mirrors its time, looking like what it once was: the home of an inordinately rich man with a penchant for art. Much loved by New Yorkers for its intimacy and the relative absence of crowds, the museum features beautiful decorations at Christmastime. Works by Rembrandt, Vermeer, Holbein, Velázquez, Titian, El Greco, Bellini, and Goya are highlights.

Other museums on the Mile include El Museo del Barrio, the only museum in New York dedicated to Latino history and culture; the National Academy Museum, with its collection of 19th- and 20th-century American art; the Goethe House German Cultural Center, which hosts exhibitions by German artists; and the Neue Galerie New York, devoted to early-20th-century German and Austrian art and design.

WHAT: site. **METROPOLITAN MUSEUM:** 1000 Fifth Ave. at 82nd St. Tel 212-535-7710; www.metmuseum.org. *Cost:* suggested donation $20. *When:* Tues–Sun. **GUGGENHEIM MUSEUM:** 1071 Fifth Ave. at 89th St. Tel 212-423-3500; www.guggenheim.org. *Cost:* admission $18. *When:* Fri–Wed. **MUSEUM OF THE CITY OF NEW YORK:** 1220 Fifth Ave. at 103rd St. Tel 212-534-1672; www.mcny.org. *Cost:* admission $10. *When:* Tues–Sun. **COOPER-HEWITT MUSEUM:** 2 E. 91st St. at Fifth Ave. Tel 212-849-8400. www.cooperhewitt.org. *Cost:* admission $15. *When:* daily. **JEWISH MUSEUM:** 1109 Fifth Ave. at 92nd St. Tel 212-423-3200; www.jewishmuseum.org. *Cost:* admission $12. *When:* closed Wed. **WHITNEY MUSEUM:** 945 Madison Ave. at 75th St. Tel 212-570-3600; www.whitney.org. *Cost:* admission $15. *When:* Wed–Sun. **FRICK MUSEUM:** 1 E. 70th St. at Fifth Ave. Tel 212-288-0700; www.frick.org. *Cost:* admission $18. *When:* Tues–Sun. **EL MUSEO DEL BARRIO:** 1230 Fifth Ave. at 104th St. Tel 212-831-7272; www.elmuseo.org. *Cost:* admission $6. *When:*

Wed–Sun. **NATIONAL ACADEMY MUSEUM:** 1083 Fifth Ave. at 89th St. Tel 212-369-4880; www.nationalacademy.org. *Cost:* admission $10. *When:* Wed–Sun. **GOETHE INSTITUT:** 1014 Fifth Ave. at 82nd St. Tel 212-439-8700; www.goethe.de/newyork. *Cost:* free. *When:* library Tues–Sun; gallery Sun–Fri. **NEUE GALERIE:** 1048 Fifth Ave. at 86th St. Tel 212-628-6200; www.neuegalerie.org. *Cost:* admission $15. *When:* Thurs–Mon.

A 19th-Century Queen of Spas

SARATOGA SPRINGS

New York, U.S.A.

For the better part of two centuries, the name Saratoga Springs evoked a privileged life of horse racing, polo matches, fancy hats, and genteel garden parties, attracting aficionados of both the track and of mineral-water cures. A high-society magnet and oasis of Victorian elegance, the "Queen of Spas" was a summer playground for the rich thanks to its naturally carbonated springs, which can still be visited. The town's rich mix of architecture and gardens from the 1800s and early 1900s were spared from demolition in the 1960s when local preservationists decided to rejuvenate their historic treasure instead.

Saratoga Springs hosts numerous cultural events. It is the summer home for the New York City Ballet (three weeks in July), followed by the Philadelphia Orchestra (three weeks in August), both of which perform at the open-air Saratoga Performing Arts Center (SPAC). Big-name artists from opera to pop fill out the summer season. You can also stroll the inspiring gardens of the 100-year-old Yaddo, the famed artists' colony, just down the road. But it is undoubtedly the elegant Saratoga Race Course, America's oldest and loveliest sports venue, that is the flower-decked town's main attraction, along with the social scene that still flourishes because of it. A who's who of thoroughbreds and jockeys has long made Saratoga's summer the nation's best racing season, during which some 1,800 horses compete. Today's main course was built in 1864, and boasts a lovely Victorian grandstand. Across the street from the track, the National Museum of Racing and Hall of Fame is a repository of Triple Crown trophies, diamond-encrusted whips, and interactive events for adults and children.

The Adelphi Hotel, built in 1877, is classic Saratoga, a mint-condition time capsule of high Victorian architecture and charm, with rooms full of period antiques and vintage photos of old Saratoga. Its opulent lobby and the adjacent Café Adelphi are done up in a plush Belle Epoque style, and serve as a gathering place for local residents and performers from the summer arts community.

WHAT: town, experience, site, hotel. **SARATOGA:** 200 miles north of NYC; 30 miles north of Albany. Saratoga County Chamber of Commerce, tel 518-584-3255; www.saratoga.org. **SARATOGA RACE COURSE:** Union Ave. Tel 518-584-6200; www.saratogaracetrack.com. **NATIONAL MUSEUM OF RACING AND HALL OF FAME:** 191 Union Ave. Tel 518-584-0400; www.racingmuseum.org. *Cost:* admission $7. **ADELPHI HOTEL:** 365 Broadway. Tel 518-587-4688, fax 518-587-0851; www.adelphihotel.com. *Cost:* doubles from $145 (low season), from $220 (high season). *When:* open mid-May to late Oct. **BEST TIMES:** racing season (late Jul–Labor Day weekend).

The Biggest, Most Glorious Home in America

THE BILTMORE ESTATE

Asheville, North Carolina, U.S.A.

George Washington Vanderbilt III fancied himself as American royalty, and so in 1887 he aspired to model his country estate in the Blue Ridge Mountains after the châteaux of France's Loire Valley—perhaps even Versailles. Some say he outdid them, taking six years, 1,000 men's labor, 11 million bricks, and who knows how much of his fortune to create Biltmore, whose driveway is measured in miles and whose floor plan stretches across acres. Of the 250 rooms—some with soaring 70-foot ceilings—there are 34 bedrooms and 43 bathrooms. Amenities unheard of at the turn of the century include ten telephones, hot and cold running water, elevators, and refrigeration. Each of the sixty-four lucky houseguests who could be accommodated at the dinner table used as many as fifteen utensils during the seven-course meals, and even today, the staff numbers 650. Of the 1,600 prints and paintings gathered by Vanderbilt in his meanderings are works by Renoir, Dürer, and Sargent. Frederick Law Olmsted, the landscape genius who gave New York City its Central Park, left his mark on the estate's original 125,000 acres (of which a mere 8,000 stunning acres remain today). Flowers bloom year-round—50,000 tulips in the Walled Garden herald the arrival of spring—but it is the extravagance of Biltmore's Christmastime celebration that truly amazes visitors: Candlelight tours and concerts take place in timeless salons and halls decked with thirty-five magnificent trees and 10,000 feet of evergreen swags.

When it opened nearby in 1913, rave reviews proclaimed the Grove Park Inn Resort and Spa to be "the finest resort in the world," and for decades it hosted the overflow of high-society houseguests from nearby Biltmore, plus American presidents, industrialists like Henry Ford, and such celebrities as Zelda and F. Scott Fitzgerald. A top-to-toe renovation restored the glamour and rustic elegance of the inn's golden days, from the cavernous Great Hall to the outstanding Horizons Restaurant and Sunset Terrace, whose 3,000-foot vantage offers expansive, unrivaled views of the Blue Ridge Mountains.

The hotel's overall decor was inspired by the great rough-hewn lodges of the country's national parks. Enormous, locally quarried granite boulders (some weighing as much as 10,000 pounds) are used in the rock walls, and the oak woodwork speaks of devoted craftsmanship. As part of the renovation, much of the custom-made, handcrafted furniture and artisan-made fixtures sold off over the years were tracked down and brought back to their original Appalachian home, making the inn once more the largest private holder of American Arts and Crafts furniture, and helping cement its restored reputation as a world-class destination.

WHAT: site, hotel. **BILTMORE ESTATE:** One Approach Road (on Highway 25), Asheville. Tel 800-411-3812; www.biltmore. com. *Cost:* admission $55. **GROVE PARK INN RESORT AND SPA:** 290 Macon Ave., Asheville. Tel 800-438-5800 or 828-252-2711; info@groveparkinn.com; www.groveparkinn. com. *Cost:* doubles from $199 (low season); from $345 (high season). **BEST TIMES:** mid-Apr to mid-May for the Festival of Flowers; Nov 11–Dec 31 for the holiday season.

The Nation's Most Popular Park

GREAT SMOKY MOUNTAINS NATIONAL PARK

North Carolina, U.S.A.

T he Cherokee called this area of western North Carolina Shaconage ("mountains of blue smoke") owing to the "smoke" or vapor that clung to the mountain peaks then as now, caused not by fire but by evaporation

and transpiration. Today, the 800-square-mile Great Smoky Mountains National Park attracts more than twice as many visitors as any other of America's 300-some national parks (even the Grand Canyon runs a distant second). It boasts sixteen peaks that rise above 6,000 feet, and none within a 36-mile stretch that's lower than 5,000 feet. Visual drama abounds, and the diversity of the park's terrain accounts for a dramatic variety of flora, including more than 120 tree species (compared, for

America's most visited national park

instance, to Yellowstone's 20) and more than 1,600 flowering plants, which clothe the mountains and meadows from early spring to late autumn. About half of the park's 800 miles of marked trails allow visitors to explore the way the early mountain settlers did: by horse. (Four stables in the park rent horses for guided rides.)

At an elevation of 5,000 feet, The Swag Country Inn (named for a dip between two mountains) claims to be the highest country inn in the eastern United States, and has its own private hiking entrance to the park. Six original, hand-hewn Appalachian cabins and structures were brought from elsewhere, reassembled on the inn's 250 wooded mountaintop acres, and appointed with fireplaces, early American crafts, and homemade quilts for a rustic feel, while hot tubs and other luxuries add a dash of the ritz. From the inn's

lofty perspective one understands how such magnificent landscape has long inspired religious communities and the local poet Joyce Kilmer, who wrote the simple ode "I think that I shall never see / a poem lovely as a tree."

WHAT: site, hotel. **GREAT SMOKY MOUNTAINS NATIONAL PARK:** straddles 70 miles of the North Carolina–Tennessee line. The main North Carolina entrance to the park is at Cherokee. Tel 865-436-1200; www.nps. gov/grsm. *Cost:* admission free. **THE SWAG COUNTRY INN:** 13 miles from Waynesville (20 miles east of park's car entrance at Cherokee). Tel 800-789-7672, fax 828-926-2036; letters@theswag.com; www.theswag. com. *Cost:* doubles from $510, includes all meals for 2. *When:* open May to mid-Nov. **BEST TIMES:** May for spring flowers; Oct for brilliant fall foliage.

The World's Longest System of Barrier Islands

THE OUTER BANKS

Duck, North Carolina, U.S.A.

S ome of the most unusual and beautiful beaches on America's Atlantic coast can be found in North Carolina's Outer Banks, a string of skinny barrier islands that stretches 150 miles from the Virginia border to the southernmost point at Cape Lookout and Beaufort, a charming mainland town first settled in 1710. The candy-striped Cape Hatteras Lighthouse is the most famous structure on the Outer Banks and the tallest of America's lighthouses. Tricky winds and tides necessitated its construction, having sunk more than 650 ships and given the area its notoriety as the Graveyard of the Atlantic. Those same winds and tides now make it a windsurfers' heaven.

The Outer Banks were the legendary haunt of many infamous 18th-century pirates, including the notorious Blackbeard, whose alleged buried booty remains undiscovered. Easier to find is the dignified and extremely comfortable Sanderling Inn, which sits just north of the whimsically monikered town of Duck, on the edge of the 3,400-acre Pine Island Audubon Sanctuary, surrounded by 12 sea-to-sound acres of untouched real estate. Known as the Outer Banks's most luxurious refuge, the inn is also ecosensitive, offering tours that explore its exquisitely fragile habitat, which includes the East Coast's highest sand dunes and the Outer Banks's famous wild horses. You can stroll endlessly on miles of lonely, windblown beach, all the while looking forward to what awaits you later at the inn's restaurant, adjacent to the main house in a restored 1899 United States Lifesaving Station and famous for its excellent menu, themed to the sea, and with a Southern slant. Expect attention-getters like roasted oysters with peppers and jack cheese, fricassee of shrimp, and Carolina duckling with black cherry sauce.

WHAT: island, hotel, restaurant. **OUTER BANKS:** Chamber of Commerce, tel 252-441-8144; chamber@outer-banks.com; www.outer bankschamber.com. **SANDERLING INN:** 1461 Duck Rd., Duck. Tel 800-701-4111 or 252-261-4111; www.thesanderling.com. *Cost:* doubles from $159 (low season), from $350 (high season). Dinner $75, tasting menu $95. **BEST TIMES:** Mar–Apr and Sept–Oct for weather, though the hurricane factor should not be dismissed during the fall months.

The Cape Hatteras Lighthouse, America's tallest

Cleveland Rocks

ROCK AND ROLL
HALL OF FAME AND MUSEUM

Cleveland, Ohio, U.S.A.

Cleveland has long been famous as home to the esteemed Cleveland Orchestra, but among the other catalysts in the city's emergence as a cultural—even trendy—destination was the 1995 opening of the

Rock and Roll Hall of Fame (a.k.a. the Rock Hall), a bold seven-story glass-and-porcelain I. M. Pei structure located on the shores of Lake Erie. Inside, hands-on interactive displays, archives, and thought-provoking videos and films pay tribute to the artists, songwriters, producers, disc jockeys, and others who launched the genre in the 1950s and sustain it today. More than 100,000 bits of memorabilia and poignantly personal artifacts belonging to music royalty are on display, including Jim Morrison's Scouts uniform, Janis Joplin's 1965 Porsche, and ZZ Top's Eliminator. You'll also see the Everly Brothers' report cards, and scribbled lyrics by Jimi Hendrix together with his much-tortured Stratocaster guitars. There's also Buddy Holly's high school diploma, plus stage cos-

tumes worn by Chuck Berry, Iggy Pop, and the Temptations. Special exhibits aim at showcasing a mix of music, history, and sociology.

The Rock and Roll Hall of Fame's most visible annual event, the induction ceremony, continues to be held in the music-industry meccas of New York and Los Angeles. So why Cleveland? Could be because Alan Freed, a Cleveland radio disc jockey, coined the term "rock 'n' roll" in 1952, the same year that Cleveland hosted the Moondog Coronation Ball, the first rock 'n' roll concert. This and a boatload of other pop-culture trivia flood the Rock Hall, full of energy, high- and low-tech eye candy, and music, lots of music. **WHAT:** site. **WHERE:** 1100 Rock and Roll Boulevard. Tel 800-493-7655 or 216-781-7625; www.rockhall.com. **COST:** admission $22.

Where Beef Reigns

CATTLEMEN'S STEAKHOUSE

Oklahoma City, Oklahoma, U.S.A.

The Cattlemen's sits smack dab in the middle of the Oklahoma National Stockyards, the largest livestock trading center on earth, full of saddleries and Western-wear clothing stores. This is red meat country, and Cattlemen's

is the consummate Western steakhouse, unpretentious but luxuriously delicious, lauded as

paradise for lovers of good red meat (and with just as excellent fish dishes, though most patrons never discover them). Slowly aged and quickly broiled over hot charcoals, the corn-fed sirloin steak is so tender you can cut it with a butter knife—filet mignon will seem lackluster by comparison, as will the accompanying unremarkable salad and baked potato and bread, which come with a perfunctory pat of margarine.

If you want to go local with the spur-wearing cowboys, dig into a plate of lamb fries—sliced and fried testicles of young lambs, a dish that makes most out-of-towners shudder. Content with your ultimate hedonistic meal, sit back and enjoy the 1910 decor, full of murals, cattle-branding irons, and other Old West paraphernalia.

WHAT: restaurant. **WHERE:** 1309 S. Agnew Ave. Tel 405-236-0416, fax 405-235-1969; www.cattlemensrestaurant.com. **COST:** dinner $23.

Nature's Rugged Artistry

THE OREGON COAST

Oregon, U.S.A.

The Beaver State's boulder-strewn shoreline is 362 miles of perfection, with craggy, ocean-carved sandstone lining some stretches and other areas where forest runs right down to the water's edge, sheltering peaceful

farmland and picturesque towns. Follow Route 101 for one of the most awe-inspiring drives in America, beginning at Astoria, near the Washington border at the mouth of the Columbia River, where you'll see massive basalt sea stacks such as 235-foot Haystack Rock (on Cannon Beach). The route runs south toward Brooking Harbor, passing a wide-open, tumultuous seascape full of galloping waves and 600-foot sand dunes—some of the highest in the United States, often draped in fog and rolling mist.

Enjoy a stroll on one of Oregon's dramatic beaches.

One of the classiest hotels of the coast is the Salishan Lodge and Golf Resort, on Siletz Bay. Big yet environmentally sensitive to its 760-acre private pine and cedar groves, its reputation is built primarily around its championship-caliber golf course and a restaurant that knows its way around the Northwest's specialty seafood-and-game cuisine. Its acclaimed wine cellar is so prodigious it offers guided tours.

Newport's quirky Sylvia Beach Hotel (named for the American owner of the Shakespeare and Co. bookstore in Paris during the 1920s and 1930s) is the coastline's most notable refuge, a gourmet treat perched on a bluff above surf-pounded beach. Its 1912 green-shingled building has twenty guest rooms decorated to evoke the spirit and work of various authors. Ask for any of the "classic" rooms—Agatha Christie, Colette, Mark Twain —which come with fireplaces, balconies, and views of the pounding Pacific. The hotel's Tables of Content restaurant is ranked one of the best in the state.

In the extreme south of the state, 30 miles north of the California border, Gold Beach lies at the mouth of the wild Rogue River, one of many that empty into the Pacific, creating a seacoast rich in bays and coves. Seven miles upstream is the Tu Tu Tun Lodge, a handsomely appointed fisherman's retreat with an acclaimed restaurant featuring the bounty of the nearby river, ocean, and forests. The Rogue River's run of Spring Chinook salmon, one of the finest eating fish, is world famous, as is its steelhead trout season (August–October).

WHAT: experience, hotel, restaurant. **SALISHAN LODGE AND GOLF RESORT:** in Gleneden Beach (90 miles south of Portland). Tel 800-452-2300 or 541-764-2371; www.

salishan.com. *Cost:* doubles from $169 (low season), from $199 (high season). Dinner $40. **SYLVIA BEACH HOTEL:** Newport (120 miles southwest of Portland). Tel 888-795-8422 or 541-265-5428; www.sylviabeachhotel.com. *Cost:* "Novel" rooms from $100, "classic" rooms from $195. Family-style dinner $24. **TU TU TUN LODGE:** Gold Beach (300 miles southwest of Portland). Tel 800-864-6357 or 541-247-6664, fax 541-247-0672; www.tututun.com. *Cost:* doubles from $125 (low season), from $235 (high season). Dinner $53. *When:* restaurant open May–Oct. **BEST TIMES:** May or June for the Cannon Beach Sandcastle Contest; Oct–Dec and Mar–May for prime whale watching. Summer and early fall see little of Oregon's notorious rainfall; winter months mean excellent storm watching, a favorite pastime.

A Panoply of Elizabethan Diversions

OREGON SHAKESPEARE FESTIVAL

Ashland, Oregon, U.S.A.

The Tony Award–winning Oregon Shakespeare Festival is America's largest and longest celebration of the Bard, running eight months out of the year in this sunny, picturesque town, where theater lovers stroll around in "Will Power" T-shirts and boast of having crammed six plays into one weekend. Inaugurated in 1935, the festival's repertory group has since grown into one of the nation's largest professional theater companies, with more than seventy actors performing up to 200 roles each season.

In addition to the eleven plays presented annually—four by Shakespeare and seven by various classic and contemporary playwrights, each with a run of four to eight months—there are also backstage tours, lectures and discussions led by actors and scholars, alfresco concerts featuring a mix of period and world music and dance. Particularly evocative are summer-night performances at the open-air Elizabethan Stage, the most important of the festival's three official venues, built in 1959.

Few small cities of this size (20,000, minus theatergoers and artists in residence) can boast the number and variety of lauded restaurants and charming accommodations found in Ashland. The aptly named Peerless Hotel (once a railroad-workers' boarding house, today offering Frette linens and Aveda toiletries) has six lovingly appointed rooms. These take a backseat to the restaurant next door, whose acclaimed wine cellar guarantees the perfect complement to a menu that showcases the bounty of the Pacific Northwest. It's the best table in town.

WHAT: event, town, hotel, restaurant. **ASHLAND:** in the Rogue River Valley, 15 miles north of the California border, 300 miles north of San Francisco, 285 miles south of Portland. **OREGON SHAKESPEARE**

FESTIVAL: tel 541-482-4331; boxoffice@ osfashland.org; www.osfashland.org. *Cost:* tickets $20–$90. **PEERLESS HOTEL AND RESTAURANT:** tel 541-488-1082 (restaurant, tel 541-488-6067); www.peerlesshotel.com. *Cost:* doubles from $90 (low season), from $200 (high season). Dinner $32. *When:* restaurant, dinner only, Tues–Sat (low season), Tues–Sun (high season). **BEST TIMES:** Jun–early Nov.

Terra Incognita in the American West

THE LEWIS AND CLARK TRAIL

Columbia River Gorge, Oregon, U.S.A.

In the winter of 1803–1804, President Thomas Jefferson sent two Virginians, Meriwether Lewis and William Clark, to lead the search for a navigable route through the American West to the Pacific Ocean, estimating that they'd be

home within a year. He underestimated the task by about sixteen months, as Lewis and Clark endured a veritable American odyssey, blazing a 3,700-mile trail through a land previously known only to Indians and trappers.

Fed by Larch Mountain's underground springs, Multnomah Falls plummets a total of 620 breathtaking feet.

Many sites along the Lewis and Clark National Historic Trail (which runs from Wood River, Illinois, to the Pacific Coast) have been established by the National Park Service, and from January 2003 till 2006 will take part in Lewis and Clark's bicentennial, giving "lewisandclarkers" the chance to follow in the footsteps of the great explorers, their thirty-three-man "Corps of Discovery," and Sacagawea, their Shoshone guide and interpreter, who gave birth to a son ("Pomp") along the way. Segments of the trail can be explored by foot, horse, bicycle, car, or boat, and patches remain where the landscape appears virtually unchanged since the explorers' journey. The notorious Lolo Trail through the

Bitterroot Mountains on the border of Idaho-Montana remains almost as tough going today as then, when Lewis and Clark described it as the hardest test of the expedition.

A lot of attention has understandably been focused on the expedition's final and arguably most scenic leg: Oregon's 80-mile-long Columbia River Gorge, where thundering waterfalls such as the Multnomah (the second highest in the United States) drop from steep basalt cliffs on both sides of the Columbia River. The natural beauty of this geological wonder convinced Congress to designate it the nation's first national scenic area in 1986. At its end awaits the "great waters" of the mighty Pacific. "Ocian in view! O! the joy!" wrote William Clark on November 7, 1805. They soon headed back east to report the details of their most excellent adventure to the president.

WHAT: experience. **WHERE:** contact the Lewis and Clark Trail Heritage Foundation in Great Falls, Montana, for information, maps, and their 40 active chapters linked to the trail. Tel 888-701-3434; discovery@lewisandclark. org; www.lewisandclark.org. Also see the National Park Service website, www.nps.gov/ lecl. **HOW:** Lindblad Expeditions offers expeditions on the Columbia and Snake Rivers aboard a 70-passenger ship departing from Portland, accompanied by historians and naturalists of note. Tel 800-EXPEDITION or 212-765-7740; www.expeditions.com. *Cost:* 4 nights from $1,990 per person, double occupancy, all-inclusive. *When:* multiple departures in spring and fall. **BEST TIMES:** spring and fall.

Nature's Theater in the Round

CRATER LAKE NATIONAL PARK

Oregon, U.S.A.

The 6-mile-wide caldera in which Crater Lake sits was created more than 7,000 years ago by catastrophic explosions that caused a volcano to collapse on itself and slowly fill with water. Today it's America's deepest lake

Crater Lake's Wizard Island is said to be named for its resemblance to a wizard's hat.

(at 1,932 feet) and is the centerpiece of the only national park in Oregon. Scenic 33-mile Rim Drive encircles the 21-square-mile lake at an average elevation of 7,000 feet, offering awe-inspiring views for motorists, bicyclists, and hikers. Just as inspiring are the views looking up from boat tours on the lake's hauntingly mirror-still waters—both at the rim and to the peak of cone-shaped Wizard Island, a volcano in miniature. For a more thorough exploration of the Cascade Range's unearthly lava-field landscape, few drives can match the 140-mile Volcanic Legacy Scenic Byway, which starts at the park and heads south to

Klamath Falls, near the California border. Crater Lake Lodge was begun in 1909 but never properly finished due to budget constraints. Refurbished and re-created in 1995 with historical details and a rustic aesthetic (think massive bark-covered ponderosa pine pillars and walls, reproduction Stickley furniture, and huge fireplaces), it's now a gem among the national park system's great lodges. The Great Hall boasts a 60-foot span of picture windows, and though the rooms have no telephones or televisions, about half are endowed with that spectacular view of the cobalt-blue lake to compensate.

WHAT: site, hotel. **CRATER LAKE NATIONAL**

PARK: in southwestern Oregon, a riveting 256-mile drive south of Portland, 85 miles northeast of Medford. Rim Visitors Center, tel 541-594-3000; www.nps.gov/crla. *Cost:* admission $10 per car in high season; 1-hour guided boat tours $27. *When:* park open year-round; Rim Road generally open late Jun to Oct, depending upon snowfall; boat tours July to mid-Sept. **CRATER LAKE LODGE:** tel 541-830-8700, fax 541-830-8514; www.craterlake lodges.com. *Cost:* lake-view doubles from $195. *When:* hotel open mid-May to mid-Oct. **BEST TIMES:** Jul and Aug for nicest weather; wildflowers peak briefly in mid-Jul.

The Way Napa Used to Be

WILLAMETTE VALLEY

Oregon, U.S.A.

A t the end of the historic Oregon Trail, close to 10,000 acres of rolling vineyards unfold in the northern Willamette ("That's Will-AM-ette, dammit!") Valley, less than an hour's drive south of Portland. Much like Napa Valley in its early days, it's a lush agricultural area and one of two wine-producing regions that have helped make the state the envy of vintners from France to California. The northern Willamette is home to an estimated 260 (and growing) wineries, both small artisanal operations and more commercial enterprises that rival anything in the Napa Valley. A meander along bumpy roads promises gracious inns, picturesque barns, innovative restaurants, and farm stands around every bend. North to south on scenic Route 99W through the heart of the valley, you'll find the small towns of Newberg, home of Rex Hill Vineyards, whose wines and museum both warrant a stop, and Beaverton, home of Ponzi Vineyards, one of the state's first oenological visionaries, and the Argyle Winery, which produced some of the first Oregon wine served at the White House.

Dayton is worth an overnight stop. If you park your bag at the inviting Wine Country Farm B&B and Cellars, you'll enjoy sweeping views of the estate's wine-producing hills from the 1910 farmhouse, plus firsthand access to their popular wine-tasting rooms. You'll also have the chance to sample the one-of-a-kind menu at the Joel Palmer House, created by the celebrated Jack Czarnecki, a truffle and mushroom hunter and chef whose award-winning restaurant is a regular pilgrimage site for visiting foodies.

WHAT: site, hotel, restaurant. **WILLAMETTE VALLEY:** Oregon Wine Board, tel 503-228-8336; www.oregonwine.org. Yamhill Chamber of Commerce, tel 866-548-5018; www.oregon winecountry.org. **REX HILL VINEYARDS:** 30835 N. Highway 99W, Newberg. Tel 800-739-4455; www.rexhill.com. **PONZI VINEYARDS:** Beaverton. Tel 503-628-1227; www.ponzi wines.com. **ARGYLE WINERY:** Dundee.

Tel 888-4-ARGYLE; www.argylewinery.com. **WINE COUNTRY FARM B&B AND CELLARS:** Breyman Orchards Rd., Dayton. Tel 800-261-3446 or 503-864-3446; jld@winecountryfarm. com; www.winecountryfarm.com. *Cost:* doubles from $150. **JOEL PALMER HOUSE:** 600 Ferry St., Dayton. Tel 503-864-2995; www.joel palmerhouse.com. *Cost:* dinner $40. *When:* dinner Tues–Sat. **BEST TIMES:** most vineyards open to the public spring–fall; International Pinot Noir Celebration, tel 800-775-4762; www.ipnc.org.

A Shrine to the Civil War's Bloodiest Battle

GETTYSBURG NATIONAL MILITARY PARK AND CEMETERY

Gettysburg, Pennsylvania, U.S.A.

I n the first three days of July 1863, the Union and Confederate armies clashed on these grounds in a battle that has come to be seen as the turning point of the American Civil War. It was the bloodiest battle ever fought on American soil,

with more than 50,000 men killed, wounded, or captured—almost a third of those who fought on both sides. Four months after the battle, Abraham Lincoln gave his famous address at the dedication of the battlefield's National Cemetery, which held the bodies of 3,555 soldiers. Today the 6,000-acre grounds are protected as a national park, with more than 1,700 statues, monuments, and cannons marking 40 miles of scenic avenues that wend past the battlefield's most legendary sites, including Robert E. Lee's temporary head-quarters, Cemetery Hill, and the field on which General George Pickett made his cli-mactic and ill-fated charge against the Union lines, sustaining more than 5,000 casualties in a mere fifty minutes.

Gettysburg Civil War Heritage Days take place during the week surrounding July Fourth, when several skirmishes are reenacted by some 20,000 volunteer participants, many dressed in Confederate gray and Union blue, portraying infantry, cavalry, and fife-and-drum corps. On a lighter note, the week is filled with many diver-

The Pennsylvania Monument in the Gettysburg National Military Park

sions: band concerts, lectures and tours given by prominent Civil War scholars, vendors in costume selling authentic memorabilia, and a reenactment of a Civil War marriage.

WHAT: site, event. **WHERE:** 30 miles south of Harrisburg; 210 miles southwest of

New York City. Park Visitors Center, 97 Taneytown Rd. Tel 717-334-1124; www.nps.gov/gett. **Cost:** admission free. **Best times:** Jul 4th week for Civil War Heritage Days; end of May for the country's oldest Memorial Day festivities.

Where the Plain People Live

Pennsylvania Dutch Country

Lancaster County, Pennsylvania, U.S.A.

Amid the blur and traffic of Lancaster County's tourist gridlock, it's still possible to get a glimpse of the Plain People (the Pennsylvania Dutch), numbering some 70,000 divided between the strict Old Order Amish,

the more liberal Mennonites and Brethren (who are less opposed to making money on the tourism their neighbors attract), and more than a dozen other Anabaptist splinter sects. The Old Order—numbering some 25,000 here, making it the nation's second oldest and largest Amish settlement—wear aprons, suspenders, bonnets, and broad-brimmed straw hats, and travel by foot, horse-drawn black buggies, and scooters (but no bikes!). These are modest, religious, and hardworking folk, whose pristine patchwork farms spread across this bucolic corner of "God's Land," which looks much as it did when the German and Swiss first arrived in the early 1700s.

The "English" (that means you, and all other outsiders) are encouraged to respect the privacy of these insular but kind people and their simple lifestyle, but that doesn't mean you can't take a nice, aimless meander down the area's backcountry roads, which take you past one-room schoolhouses, neat fields cultivated by mule-driven plows, quaintly named towns like Bird-in-Hand and Paradise, and farmhouses and roadside stalls selling crafts, metalwork and woodwork, and cider and home-baked goods, including shoofly pie.

To keep mind and body in the Pennsylvania Dutch mood, book ahead at the Historic Smithton Inn, welcoming guests since 1763, when it was built as a stagecoach stop. Its eight lovely rooms have canopied beds covered with colorful handmade quilts and fireplaces. It's located adjacent to the Ephrata Cloister, an historic site. Composed of more than twenty beautifully restored buildings, it was once home to a Quaker-like monastic sect whose population reached 300 in its 1750 heyday.

What: site, hotel. **Where:** the Amish heartland is east of Lancaster, 60 miles west of Philadelphia, 160 miles southwest of New York City. Pennsylvania Dutch Visitors Bureau, Lancaster, tel 800-PA-DUTCH or 717-299-8901; www.padutchcountry.com. **Historic Smithton Inn:** 900 West Main St., Ephrata (11 miles north of Lancaster). Tel 877-755-4590 or 717-733-6094; www.historicsmithtoninn.com. *Cost:* doubles from $115 (low season), from $125 (high season). **Best times:** a number of farm markets operate throughout the area (but never on Sun, a day widely reserved for rest). Don't miss Roots in E. Petersburg (Tues), the Green Dragon Market in Ephrata (Fri) and the oldest, Lancaster's Central Market (Tues and Fri, but best on Tues).

One Man's Priceless Treasure Trove

BARNES FOUNDATION

Philadelphia, Pennsylvania, U.S.A.

Few miss Philadelphia's Museum of Art—with 300,000 artworks it is America's third largest and consistently ranked as one of the finest—but it's hard to understand why the word isn't out about the Barnes Foundation's collection, which is one of the world's premier private art collections, with over 6,000 pieces valued in excess of $6 billion filling some 23 galleries. The Foundation's centerpiece is its collection of French Modern and post-Impressionist paintings, with 181 works by Renoir alone, 69 by Cézanne, 60 by Matisse, and 44 by Picasso. You'll find many other major European artists represented here as well, including van Gogh, Degas, Corot, Seurat, Monet, Manet, Goya, and El Greco. African art and quirky items such as rustic door hinges and other hardware are arranged cheek by jowl with the masters to emphasize shared form or design. Limited access is the result of local township restrictions which means that the galleries are never crowded (though it also means you should book weeks in advance during busy periods). The gallery's beautiful 12-acre arboretum is one of the city's best-kept secrets.

The foundation is named for Dr. Albert Barnes, who was born poor and educated in Philadelphia's public schools, but went on to become a patent-medicine millionaire by the age of forty and a brilliant if idiosyncratic collector by the time of his death in 1951, at age seventy-nine. Dr. Barnes's spirit is still palpable in his limestone French-inspired mansion, where his famously quirky collection remains in its original arrangement, as provided in his will.

WHAT: site. **WHERE:** in the Main Line suburb of Merion, about 10 miles from downtown Philadelphia. 300 N. Latches Ln. Tel 610-667-0290; www.barnesfoundation.org. **COST:** admission $12, includes gardens. Free docent tours twice daily. **WHEN:** ticket reservations must be made in advance (during peak months this can mean 60 days in advance). Open Fri–Sun, Sept–May; Wed–Sun, Jun–Aug. **BEST TIMES:** gardens are most colorful spring and fall, but this means gallery tickets are hardest to come by. Ticket availability is easiest in Jul and Aug.

The World's Largest Indoor Floral Extravaganza

PHILADELPHIA FLOWER SHOW

Philadelphia, Pennsylvania, U.S.A.

The country's oldest and most prestigious flower show, held almost every year since 1829 and produced by the Pennsylvania Horticultural Society, is also its best, an extravaganza that transforms every inch of 10 acres of the Philadelphia Convention Center into a fantasy garden of bursting buds and blooming trees. Sixty major exhibits are enough to take your breath away, while 2,500 amateur exhibits in 580 competitive classes give the pros a run for their money. More than 200 judges from across the nation bestow awards on the penultimate night of the weeklong event, which is filled out with seminars, how-to demonstrations (pruning, replanting, bonsai and topiary training, fertilizer debates), and a hard-to-resist marketplace. Proceeds from the show—usually more than $1 million—are poured back into the city's community gardens and beautification projects. At last count, more than 2,000 gardening projects enjoyed the Horticultural Society's attention, and are integral to keeping Philadelphia the "Greene Countrie Town" envisioned by its founder, William Penn.

WHAT: event. **WHERE:** Pennsylvania Convention Center, 12th and Arch Sts. Pennsylvania Horticultural Society, tel 215-988-8810; www.theflowershow.com. **COST:** $20. **WHEN:** 1 week in early Mar.

A Culinary Playground for Princes and Paupers

PHILLY FOOD

Philadelphia, Pennsylvania, U.S.A.

N o longer just a stopping point between Washington, D.C., and New York, Philadelphia has lately resumed its place among America's great cities, boasting a vibrant restaurant scene that's begun to draw foodies from all over the East Coast. Philadelphia's culinary heights were staked out more than thirty years ago by Georges Perrier, chef-owner of the haute-cuisine classic Le Bec-Fin, since 1970 the East Coast's (and possibly America's) finest French restaurant. Its elegant atmosphere, reminiscent of a turn-of-the-century Parisian salon, oozes opulence, while its

Le Bec-Fin's chef-owner Georges Perrier in his bustling kitchen

downstairs bistro, the more intimate Le Bar Lyonnais (the "baby Bec"), offers a similarly excellent but less expensive menu that leans toward simplicity and lightness.

If you don't book weeks in advance, you might not find a reservation at any of Monsieur Perrier's outposts on Walnut Street (thanks to him, now known as Restaurant Row), but that'll just give you an opportunity to slum it with that other Philadelphia classic, the cheesesteak. A mountain of grilled, shaved beef smothered in greasy onions and topped by gobs of molten Cheez Whiz (the cheese choice is a divisive issue: provolone or American cheese toppings are also acceptable), it's a guaranteed calorie-monster wherever you find it. A trinity of venerated places all claim to be the home of Philly's best: Jim's Steaks (also known for turning out a mean hoagie, the local version of the submarine sandwich); the venerated Pat's King of Steaks, where—if you can believe the hype—Pat Olivieri invented the cheesesteak in 1932 (his grandnephew runs the place today); and, just across the street, is Pat's nemesis since 1966, Geno's. Though bright compared to Pat's Depression-era authenticity, it offers essentially the same menu, fueling a friendly decades-long argument about whose is the best.

WHAT: restaurant. **LE BEC-FIN AND LE BAR LYONNAIS:** 1523 Walnut St. Tel 215-567-1000; www.lebecfin.com. *Cost:* 6-course prix fixe at Le Bec-Fin $150; dinner at Le Bar Lyonnais, $45. *When:* lunch Mon–Fri, dinner Mon–Sat. **JIM'S STEAKS:** 400 South St. Tel 215-928-1911; www.jimssteaks.com. *Cost:* $6–$9. *When:* lunch and dinner daily. **PAT'S KING OF STEAKS:** 1237 Passyunk Ave. Tel 215-468-1546; www.patskingof steaks.com. *Cost:* $5–$9. *When:* open daily, 24 hours. **GENO'S:** 1219 S. Ninth at Passyunk Ave. Tel 215-389-0659; www. genosteaks.com. *Cost:* $5–$9. *When:* open daily, 24 hours.

The Birthplace of American Government

INDEPENDENCE NATIONAL HISTORICAL PARK

Philadelphia, Pennsylvania, U.S.A.

The City of Brotherly Love has what is arguably the most important historic district of any American city, an L-shaped seventeen-block swath created by an act of Congress in 1948 and encompassing more than fifteen buildings

Independence Hall is often recognized as the birthplace of the United States.

and monuments, all anchored by the Georgian-style red-brick Independence Hall. Built in 1732 as the Pennsylvania State House, it was here that the Declaration of Independence was voted on and signed on July 4, 1776, where the Articles of Confederation were adopted in 1778, and where patriots drafted the U.S. Constitution in 1787. Original copies of the Declaration and the Constitution are on display in the building's West Wing, and the leafy Independence Mall is adjacent. Just next door is the Federal-style Congress Hall, where the U.S. Senate and U.S. House of Representatives met from 1790 to 1800 (when Philadelphia ceded its role as the nation's capital to the newly built Washington, D.C.) and where the Bill of Rights, the first ten amendments to the Constitution, was adopted. Nearby is the 2,080-pound Liberty Bell, forged in an English foundry in 1752 and for more than two centuries one of the world's most important symbols of freedom.

Acting as a sort of gateway to the historic district of the region, the new, state-of-the-art Independence Visitor Center offers orientation films, an information desk, and ticketing for area attractions.

WHAT: site. **WHERE:** Independence Visitor Center, 6th and Market Sts. Tel 800-537-7676; www.independencevisitorcenter.com. **COST:** admission to Independence Hall is free, but tickets are required and can be reserved through the National Park Service. **HOW:** There are dozens of walking tours of the city, including Independence National Park, early Mar–late Oct, Thanksgiving and Christmas through New Year's. For a list of offerings, visit www.independencevisitor center.com. **BEST TIMES:** expect lines Jun–Aug. An event-packed, 10-day July 4th celebration includes fireworks, exhibits, concerts, and activities around town.

Bermuda of the North

BLOCK ISLAND

Rhode Island, U.S.A.

Both sophisticated and unpretentious, Block Island is a barefoot-and-bicycle kind of place, with rolling green hills and dramatic 200-foot bluffs that remind many of Ireland, and led the Nature Conservatory to call the island "one of the last great places in the Western Hemisphere." Despite its popularity with New Englanders, this 10-square-mile gem keeps its profile low and guards its quiet sense of privacy, happy to remain free of the social hobnobbing and fuss that come with Martha's Vineyard–style affluent chic. There are few historic sites to see (since the island has pretty much sidestepped history), but there are 365 freshwater ponds (some no larger than a swimming pool), 5 wildlife refuges (a full third of the island is protected), 32 miles of hiking trails, 17 miles of beach that varies from sandy to rocky, gorgeous cliffside biking trails, and lovely century-old lighthouses. Situated on the Atlantic flyway, it's also a great spot for bird-watching, with more than 150 species stopping annually on their migration.

Dubbed "the Bermuda of the North" during its Victorian-era heyday, the island still boasts a number of dignified, porch-fringed buildings that hark back to that quieter yesteryear. The Hotel Manisses is a big 1870s charmer that exudes traditional coziness and surprises with its standout restaurant, and the breakfast layout at their sister 1661 Inn (located nearby) is legendary. If you prefer small and romantic, book well in advance at the 100-year-old Blue Dory Inn, a few steps from the sea at the head of famous Crescent Beach.

WHAT: island, hotel, restaurant. **BLOCK ISLAND:** 12 miles south of mainland Rhode Island. Block Island Ferry leaves from Newport and Pt. Judith; New London, Connecticut; and Montauk, New York. Tel 401-783-4613; www.blockislandferry.com. Block Island Tourism Council, tel 800-383-2474. **HOTEL MANISSES AND 1661 INN:** 1 Spring St. Tel 800-626-4773; www.block islandresorts.com. *When:* Hotel Manisses open early Apr to mid-Nov; 1661 Inn open year-round. *Cost:* Manisses doubles from $75 (low season), from $220 (high season); 1661 doubles from $90 (low season), from $340 (high season). All rates include tour of island. Dinner at Manisses $40. **THE BLUE DORY**

INN: Dodge St. Tel 800-992-7290 or 401-466-5891. *Cost:* doubles from $95 (low season), $195 (high season). **BEST TIMES:** before or after the Memorial Day-to-Labor Day peak period; in Aug for the nicest weather; Sept and Oct for bird watching.

Castle-Size Cottages in a City by the Sea

CLIFF WALK

Newport, Rhode Island, U.S.A.

The American seaside vacation and the expression "conspicuous consumption" were both born in Newport in the 19th century, when high-society families with names like Vanderbilt and Astor descended here each summer to escape the urban heat for a few weeks. When you've got it, flaunt it, and at Newport that's exactly what they did, turning the island into America's regatta capital and building massive, European château–inspired "summer cottages" on the rocky coastline, putting the gilding on the Gilded Age with their over-the-top opulence. A bracing constitutional along Cliff Walk, a national historic trail that stretches 3½ miles 30 feet above the wild Atlantic shoreline, offers a convergence of natural and man-made beauty, displaying 150 years of American architectural heritage. The showstopper is undoubtedly the Breakers, a seventy-room, twenty-three-bedroom Italian Renaissance–style palazzo with 40-foot ceilings. Built in 1895 for Cornelius Vanderbilt II, it is the largest of them all, the product of two years' of labor by some 2,000 workers, including a platoon of artisans brought in from Europe. Less grand—with a mere forty rooms—Rosecliff is another favorite, built in 1902 by architect Stanford White after the Grand Trianon at Versailles.

The city's eight square miles are impressively chockablock with 17th- and 18th-century architecture, eighty examples of which were restored by tobacco heiress Doris Duke, who died in 1993. Countless inns, bed-and-breakfasts, and hotels dot the area, and while

The Breakers's architect took inspiration from some of Italy's 16th-century palaces.

none match the opulence of "the cottages," you can indulge yourself pretty well at the Castle Hill Inn and Resort. Gloriously sited on a secluded 40-acre peninsula fifteen minutes from Cliff Walk at the mouth of Narragansett Bay, this Victorian inn promises exceptional seafood dinners, a legendary brunch, and access to a private beach. Newport is also home to the grandfather of jazz festivals, the JVC Jazz Festival Newport, held at historic Ft. Adams. First staged in summer 1954, it's still the world's most famous.

WHAT: site, hotel, restaurant, event. **NEWPORT:** 130 miles northeast of New York City. Entrance to Cliff Walk at Memorial Blvd. Visitors Bureau, tel 800-976-5122 or 401-849-8048; www.gonewport.com. **THE MANSIONS:** Preservation Society of Newport County, tel 401-847-1000; www.newportmansions.org. *Cost:* $18 Breakers only; $23 for 2 mansions; $31 for 5 mansions. *When:* all 11 mansions maintained by the Preservation Society are open daily mid-May to mid-Oct; in off-season, at least 1 mansion is open daily; at Christmas, 3 are open. **CASTLE HILL INN AND RESORT:** 590 Ocean Dr. Tel 888-466-1355 or 401-849-3800; info@castlehillinn.com; www.castlehillinn.com. *Cost:* doubles from $299 (low season), from $495 (high season). **BEST TIMES:** a packed summer schedule includes classical music performed in many of the mansions during the prestigious Newport Music Festival (2 weeks in mid-Jul; www.newportmusic.org). The Newport Folk Festival is usually the 1st weekend in Aug, followed by the JVC Jazz Festival Newport, 2d weekend in Aug (for both, www.festivalnetwork.com). The New York Yacht Club Regatta takes place over a weekend between late Jun and mid-Jul.

Where the Old Times Aren't Forgotten

BEAUFORT AND THE LOW COUNTRY

South Carolina, U.S.A.

The honeycombed coastline south of Charleston stretches for some 200 miles, dissolving into peninsulas, channels, and dozens of marshy subtropical "sea islands" that make up South Carolina's Low Country, a rural and slow land peopled by the descendants of slaves and planters. Kiawah and neighboring Seabrook are well-known, well-heeled island-resorts, while the pristine, 5,000-acre Hunting Island, once a private hunting resort, is now blessedly protected as a nature reserve.

On St. Helena Island, the Penn Center was established in 1862 as the first school in the South for freed slaves, and today serves as a museum and nerve center of the area's Gullah community—descendants of Angolan Mende, Kisi, Malinke, and Bantu slaves who have managed to preserve a great many elements of African culture due to the Sea Islands' isolation. Test the simple cuisine at St. Helena's Gullah Grub Café or the well-known Shrimp Shack (whose unique shrimp burgers explain the lines). Both are on the Sea Island Parkway.

Well-manicured Hilton Head Island, the last sea island on the way to Savannah and one of the most popular (and developed) resort areas in eastern America, offers 25 championship golf courses and some 300 tennis courts, with 13 of the courses and 145 courts open to the public.

The small waterfront town of Beaufort (pronounced *Byew*-fert), a kind of Charleston in miniature, is the gateway to the Sea Islands and the most practical and popular base from which to explore the coastal area. Known for its many wide-verandaed antebellum houses, the once prosperous town has enjoyed something of a renaissance due to its popularity with Hollywood film crews, who've filmed *The Big Chill, Forrest Gump, Prince of Tides,* and many others here. Many of the celeb actors who've come through have parked their bags at the Rhett House Inn, one of the most charming accommodations in the Low Country. Only a short walk from the restored waterfront and the town's main drag (lined with antique stores, art galleries, innovative restaurants, and book stores), the inn is the quintessence of Southern hospitality. It supplies guests with complimentary bicycles for a peddle around the back streets, with their mammoth magnolia and gnarled oak trees, grand pre–Civil War homes, and graveyards filled with Confederate dead. Plan your visit around Beaufort's July Water Festival, a paean to local color, Low Country cuisine (think shrimp), and music.

WHAT: town, hotel, restaurant. **BEAUFORT:** 70 miles south of Charleston (St. Helena Island is 10 miles east of Beaufort). Beaufort Chamber of Commerce, tel 800-638-3525 or 843-524-3263; www.beaufortsc.org. **RHETT HOUSE INN:** 1009 Craven St. Tel 888-480-9530; www.rhetthouseinn.com. *Cost:* doubles from $175 (low season), from $215 (high season). **BEST TIMES:** Apr–Jun and mid-Sept to Jan for weather; mid- to late May for Beaufort's Gullah Fest; early Jul for the 10-day Beaufort Water Festival; Annual Shrimp Festival, 2d weekend in Oct.

Nothing Could Be Finer

THE HEART OF CHARLESTON

South Carolina, U.S.A.

America's most intact colonial city, sultry and gracious Charleston seduces visitors with its languid mystery and European charm, its historic architecture and friendly residents, and lately its exciting arts and restaurant scene—heralds of the city's new golden age.

Founded in 1670, Charleston took less than a century to become one of the richest cities in colonial America. The British laid much of it to waste during the Revolution, and just one century later the city became the symbol of Southern resistance when the first shots of the Civil War were fired at Union-occupied Fort Sumter, which guards Charleston Harbor. Take a crash course in the city's heritage with a visit to the Charleston Museum, the country's oldest (founded in 1773), located in the very heart of the Historic District at 360 Meeting Street. For a more personal take on the city, the annual springtime Festival of Houses and Gardens offers a rare glimpse into more than 150 magnificent private homes and walled gardens.

The Preservation Society hosts a similar event in the fall. For a historic overnight, check into the gorgeous 2 Meeting Street Inn. Boasting one of the city's most impressive facades, this 1890 Queen Anne Victorian gem is even more

Victorian charm on a corner of Charleston's Battery Street

resplendent indoors, with oak-paneled 12-foot ceilings, stained-glass windows by Louis Tiffany, and just nine guest rooms decorated with English antiques.

Ask for the turreted Spell Room, the original master suite, which offers access to the second-floor veranda, where you can enjoy afternoon tea or a hearty Southern breakfast. Breakfast in the garden is no less alluring, amid the magnolias and azalea bushes, and shaded by Japanese cherry trees and centuries-old oaks.

WHAT: town, event, hotel. **CHARLESTON:** Charleston Visitors Bureau, tel 800-744-0006 or 843-853-8000; www.charlestoncvb.com.

FESTIVAL OF HOUSES AND GARDENS: Historic Charleston Foundation (HCF), tel 843-722-3405; www.historiccharleston.org. *Cost:* tickets $45 for 8–10 homes. *When:* 1 month beginning mid-Mar. **PRESERVATION SOCIETY CANDLELIGHT TOUR OF HOMES:** tel 843-722-4630; www.preservationsociety. org. *Cost:* tickets $40 for 8–10 homes. *When:* late Sept, early Oct. **2 MEETING STREET INN:** 2 Meeting St. Tel 843-723-7322; www.two meetingstreet.com. *Cost:* doubles from $220. **BEST TIMES:** Mar–Jun and Sept–Dec for the most pleasant weather; mid-Mar for the peak blooming season of camelias, azaleas, and roses.

Mouth-Watering Dining from the Old South and the New

LOW COUNTRY CUISINE

Charleston, South Carolina, U.S.A.

Taken by the spell of Charleston? Wait till you taste the food. The extraordinary mingling of the French, Spanish, African, and Caribbean cultures that took root here during centuries of sometimes tumultuous history has left an imprint on the local cuisine, which incorporates traditional Low Country ingredients such as shrimp, oysters, rice, okra, field greens, and tomatoes. The elegant Magnolias, housed in the city's original 1739 Custom's House, is an immensely popular standout in Charleston's dynamic restaurant scene, offering tried-and-true classic recipes along with inspired interpretations like fried green tomatoes and shellfish over grits.

You can't really begin to appreciate the high style of the New South until you've experienced the homey excellence of the no-frills Old South. And for that, the family-run Bowen's Island is a must, serving some of the best roasted oysters and fresh shrimp on the eastern seaboard for more than fifty years. Some call it a dive, others call it heaven, but "atmospheric" would best describe this joint, with its rickety chairs, concrete floors, graffiti-covered walls, church-pew booths, and the smell and sound of the sea just outside. You can try the Low Country specialty of shrimp and grits or a "big ol' seafood platter," but most folks head for a separate room, where there's a sign that reads Oyster Eaters Only. Back there, shovelfuls of roasted oysters induce euphoria while Elvis plays on the 1946 jukebox.

WHAT: restaurant. **MAGNOLIAS:** 185 E. Bay St. Tel 843-577-7771; www.magnolias-blossom-cypress.com. *Cost:* dinner $45. *When:* daily lunch, dinner. **BOWEN'S ISLAND:** 1870 Bowen's Island Rd. Tel 843-795-2757; www.bowenislandrestaurant.com. *Cost:* dinner $15. *When:* dinner only, Tues–Sat. **BEST TIMES:** late Jan/early Feb for the Low Country Oyster Festival.

An Eclectic All-Purpose Arts Explosion

SPOLETO FESTIVAL USA

Charleston, South Carolina, U.S.A.

Founded as the American counterpart to the Festival dei Due Mondi (Festival of Two Worlds) in Spoleto, Italy, Spoleto Festival USA has grown over its twenty-six-year history to become a well-entrenched feature of the

American cultural landscape, presenting a diverse mix of world-class performers in opera, dance, theater, and music, and frequently hosting American and world premieres. Founded in 1977 by the American-born composer Gian Carlo Menotti, the festival has done much to revitalize the cultural scene of its home city (which, in 1735, was the first American city to stage an opera), and today takes over utterly each year, offering productions of music, dance, and theater at a dozen principal venues (all within easy walking distance of each other) as well as at every street corner, garden, church, concert hall, and park. The festival's more spirited and irreverent spinoff, Piccolo Spoleto, offers some 700 events of its own, most of them inexpensive or free.

The Festival Finale takes place under stars and fireworks at the 18th-century Middleton Place plantation, 14 miles from Charleston, on the Ashley River. It is tradition for concert-goers to lavish time and money on picnic dinners for the event (local celebrity judges wander from blanket to blanket awarding prizes), and many arrive early to enjoy America's first landscaped gardens, laid out in 1741.

WHAT: event. **WHERE:** tel 843-579-3100; www.spoletousa.org. **COST:** tickets $15–$130; Festival Finale $30. **WHEN:** begins Memorial Day weekend and runs for 17 days. **BEST TIMES:** 2d and 3d weekends, when tickets and hotel accommodations are more easily available.

An Alternate Reality, Sculpted by Nature

THE BADLANDS

South Dakota, U.S.A.

General Alfred Sully described it as "hell with the fires burned out," and to the Lakota Sioux and 19th-century French trappers and explorers, it was the Mako Sica and "les mauvaises Terres"—the bad lands. Frank

Lloyd Wright wrote that "what I saw gave me an indescribable sense of mysterious otherwhere—a distant architecture, ethereal, only touched with a sense of Egyptian, Mayan drift and silhouette." For 500,000 years, erosive

forces have eaten deep into the soft soil of Badlands National Park and carved out an alien landscape of cones, ridges, gorges, gulches, pinnacles, and precipices, with some formations more than 1,000 feet high, all painted in the shifting colors of layered mineral deposits. Take the 40-mile Badlands Loop, which provides an ample eyeful of nature's theatricality, especially at dawn, dusk, and just after a rainfall, when the interplay of light and shadow is most poetic.

By the way, it's predicted that within 500,000 years the Badlands will have been eroded away to nothing. Better go see them now.

WHAT: site. **WHERE:** 80 miles east of Rapid City. Ben Reifel Visitor Center, Highway 240, Interior. Tel 605-433-5361; www.nps.gov/badl. **COST:** admission $10 per

The forces of erosion have created an unearthly landscape.

car. **BEST TIMES:** winter, when you won't find another soul here.

Sacred Land of Heroes:
Mount Rushmore, Crazy Horse, and General Custer

THE BLACK HILLS

South Dakota, U.S.A.

Named for the dense shade of their ponderosa pines, the Black Hills of South Dakota have for centuries been considered sacred by the Lakota Sioux, once the most powerful tribe in the West. Today, because of the passions of a few artists, the land itself has become hallowed in another way.

It took the obsessed Danish-American sculptor Gutzon Borglum, his son Lincoln, and some four hundred workers fourteen years (from 1927 to 1941) to complete an artistic and engineering project so monumental that no one believed it possible: carving and blasting the six-story faces of George Washington, Thomas Jefferson, Teddy Roosevelt, and Abraham Lincoln out of stony Mount Rushmore. A little trivia: Washington's eyes are each 11 feet wide, and his nose is 26 feet long. Mr. Lincoln, for his part, sports a mole that measures 16 inches across.

Just 17 miles away, the gigantic Crazy Horse Memorial is slowly taking shape. Also carved into granite, this memorial, when com-pleted somewhere around 2050, after a century's labor, will depict Native America's greatest warrior chief astride his steed, dwarfing Mount Rushmore at 563 feet tall. The horse's nostril alone will be large enough to hold a five-room house.

From Crazy Horse, head east on the beautiful 14-mile Needles Highway (Highway 87), past jagged, billion-year-old granite spires, to Sylvan Lake and then north to Spearfish Canyon Scenic Byway, whose landscape you'll easily recognize as the epic

Scaling an outcrop in the Black Hills

backdrop used by Kevin Costner in his film *Dances with Wolves*. Alternatively, you can park your bags in the homey State Game Lodge that served as Calvin Coolidge's Summer White House. Of the historic inn's seven rooms, you can still book the room the thirtieth president and his wife occupied during three months in 1927. The lodge is one of three found within Custer State Park, whose 18-mile Wildlife Loop Road bisects unfenced meadows where herds of 1,500 shaggy buffalo roam.

WHAT: site, hotel, experience. **MOUNT RUSHMORE:** 25 miles southwest of Rapid City. Orientation Center, Keystone. Tel 605-574-2523; www.nps.gov/moru. *Cost:* admission free, parking fee $10. **CRAZY HORSE MEMORIAL:** 17 miles southwest of Mount Rushmore. Tel 605-673-4681; www.crazyhorsememorial.org. *Cost:* $10. **CUSTER STATE PARK:** 20 miles south of Mount Rushmore. Tel 605-255-4515; www.custerstatepark.info. *Cost:* admission $15 per car. **STATE GAME LODGE:** tel 888-875-0001; www.custerresorts.com. *Cost:* doubles from $160, Coolidge Room $310. *When:* open early May–early Oct. **BEST TIMES:** Jun–Aug at 9 P.M. and Sept at 8 P.M. for the daily illumination ceremony of Mount Rushmore; in late Sept or early Oct for the annual Buffalo Round-Up in Custer State Park.

Party!!!

STURGIS MOTORCYCLE RALLY

Sturgis, South Dakota, U.S.A.

For one week every summer, the small town of Sturgis (pop. 6,400) hosts the largest motorcycle rally in America, these days attracting well over half a million people. Begun in 1938 by the local Jackpine Gypsies and about 200 friends they invited for flat track races, the Black Hills Motor Classic (a.k.a. simply "Sturgis") grew over the years into a wild bacchanal that drew gangs of self-styled outlaws and caused locals to lock their doors for the duration. In the late 1980s the city partnered with the Jackpine Gypsies to civilize the event, and today law, order, and organization prevail—there's even a $90 fine for indecent exposure. Baby strollers are now a not uncommon sight and a good number of leather-clad CEOs and lawyers are in evidence among the hardcore rebels and their biker chicks. Wannabe or diehard, everyone partakes in the hill climbs and concerts, and notches up who knows how many hours admiring each other's gleaming bikes. Slightly sanitized or no, the saloons and tattoo parlors still do a brisk business. Main Street is the place to be—every bike buff should check out the Sturgis Motorcycle Museum and Hall of Fame, then head on over to the Roadkill Café for some Chicken That Didn't Quite Cross the Road or the daily special, Guess That Mess.

WHAT: event, restaurant. **STURGIS:** 24 miles north of Rapid City. Sturgis Chamber of Commerce, tel 605-720-0800; www.sturgis motorcyclerally.com. *When:* the 1-week rally is held early Aug. **NATIONAL MOTORCYCLE MUSEUM AND HALL OF FAME:** 999 Main St. Tel 605-347-2001; www.sturgismuseum.com. *Cost:* admission $5. **ROADKILL CAFÉ:** 1023 First St. Tel 605-347-4502. *Cost:* dinner $12. *When:* open Jun–Aug; daily, lunch and dinner.

There's No Place Like Home

GRACELAND
AND THE ELVIS TRAIL

Memphis, Tennessee, U.S.A.

The most visited home in America after the White House (when the latter is open for tours, that is), Elvis Presley's Graceland Mansion is hokey and something of a hoot, but it's also intriguing, entertaining, and at times very moving. From the day he moved in with his mama and daddy in 1957, Graceland was Elvis's escape and refuge, a place where he could kick back in an atmosphere that to him said "home"—crystal chandeliers, shag carpets, gilt mirrors, stained-glass windows, peacock-blue and gold curtains and all. The spirit of one of the 20th century's most musically and culturally influential figures is everywhere present, and as nostalgia trips go, it's an essential stop: Times have changed, but Graceland hasn't, remaining frozen in 1977, the year when Elvis was laid to rest in the Meditation Garden outside.

Highlights of the tour include Elvis's famous 1955 pink Cadillac Fleetwood (among twenty-one other vehicles), displays of his flashy stagewear, the incredible Jungle Room (just as over-the-top as you might guess from the name), and the 80-foot Hall of Gold, lined with gold and platinum albums and singles that represent more than 1 billion records sold worldwide—more than any other entertainer or group in the

The King in his glory days

history of the recorded voice. Across from Graceland's gates is the Heartbreak Hotel, a shrine to kitsch.

A side trip to the Sun Records studio is also obligatory on the Memphis go-round. Elvis cut his first record, *That's All Right*, here in 1954. A spirited tour of the studio brings alive the day when Elvis—influenced by the mid-South's mix of black blues, white country, and gospel and spiritual music—crossed over and gave birth to rock 'n' roll. This was only the latest musical innovation to come out of Memphis, where in 1909 the young trumpeter W. C. Handy, "Father of the Blues," introduced his version of Delta blues to the Beale Street music scene, and from there to the world. Today, a few blocks of Beale are neon-lit with clubs and juke joints that stay hopping with generally good music until the wee hours.

WHAT: site, hotel. **GRACELAND MANSION:** 3734 Elvis Presley Blvd. Tel 800-238-2000 or 901-332-3322; www.elvis.com/graceland. *Cost:* $28. **ELVIS PRESLEY HEARTBREAK HOTEL:** 3677 Elvis Presley Blvd. Tel 877-777-0606, fax 901-332-1000; www.elvis.com/epheart breakhotel. *Cost:* from $115. **SUN RECORDS STUDIO:** 706 Union Ave. Tel 800-441-6249; www.sunstudio.com. **BEST TIMES:** Jan 8 for Elvis's birthday; the week around Aug 16 (the anniversary of the King's death) for Elvis Presley Week; early May for the 3-day Beale Street Music Festival.

Pork Capital of America

MEMPHIS'S RIB JOINTS

Memphis, Tennessee, U.S.A.

There's more to Memphis than Elvis. Its barbecue has long been a hallmark of soul food, linked with the city's blues history since the beginning. This is succulent pork barbecue, not the beef commonly used elsewhere, and it's pretty much the rule that the best meals in town are also the sloppiest. Of the hundreds of barbecue joints in Memphis, a number are world-famous multigenerational institutions in business for more than fifty years and with no-frills decor that's just as old. The short list of major leaguers includes the Rendezvous, or 'Vous, where 10,000 meals a week are served in a boisterous college-beer-dive atmosphere. The ribs here aren't smoked but grilled, and are dry-rubbed with spices after (and sometimes before) they're done—a style of barbecue found mainly in Memphis. The place is hidden in an alley near the city's grand old Peabody Hotel, which is worth a visit just to see the famous twice-daily parade of trained ducks, who waddle across the neo-Renaissance lobby to the music of John Philip Sousa.

The dry rub can be used on chicken, the signature dish of Cozy Corner, also famous for barbecued bologna and deliciously charred rib ends. For an equally beloved variation, try the wet ribs at Jim Neely's Interstate Bar-B-Que, slathered with a thick, sweet-and-tangy basting sauce of the finger-lickin' kind. The same sauce also shows up on a curiously delicious house specialty, barbecued spaghetti.

For barbecue nirvana, show up at the cutthroat World Championship Barbecue Cooking Contest, part of the city's annual Memphis in May bash. More than 300 teams from around the world congregate to grill on the waterfront, using their own secret recipes for the uniquely American art of barbecue.

WHAT: restaurant, event. **RENDEZVOUS ROOM:** 52 S. Second St. Tel 901-523-2746. *Cost:* dinner $25. *When:* dinner only Tues–Sat, lunch and dinner Fri–Sat. **COZY CORNER:** 745 North Pkwy. Tel 901-527-9158. *Cost:* dinner $15. *When:* closed Sun, Mon. **INTERSTATE BAR-B-QUE:** 2265 S. Third St. Tel 901-775-2304. *Cost:* $10. *When:* lunch and dinner daily. **MEMPHIS IN MAY:** Barbecue Cooking Contest is held in Tom Lee Park. Tel 901-525-4611; www.memphisinmay.org. *Cost:* tickets $7. *When:* 3 days in mid-May.

A City That Lives and Breathes Music

NASHVILLE'S MUSIC SCENE

Nashville, Tennessee, U.S.A.

Known as "Music City U.S.A." since the Grand Ole Opry first started its weekend radio broadcasts back in 1925, Nashville is the hometown of the now globalized country music industry and has the landmarks to prove it.

The spanking new home of the Country Music Hall of Fame is a repository of innumerable objects and artifacts, from Elvis's 1960 "solid gold" Cadillac to Minnie Pearl's straw hat with dangling price tag, Willie Nelson's sneakers, and other enshrined memorabilia. Three theaters show clips of country's greatest performers, but why not head right to the source, the Grand Ole Opry, surviving as a down-home Southern family tradition even after its controversial 1974 move from the old Ryman Auditorium to new digs on Opryland Drive. Every weekend, modern names and legendary old-timers perform traditional country, bluegrass, gospel, honky-tonk, and rockabilly. From back-porch to big-time, you'd be hard pressed to find an award winner who hasn't performed here, from Hank Williams to Vince Gill, Patsy Cline to Trisha Yearwood, George Jones to Garth Brooks.

Elsewhere in town, the diminutive Bluebird Café still takes its music seriously, showcasing new and old talent in one of the city's most famous venues. On the once-again vibrant club strip of Lower Broadway across from the Ryman Auditorium, the funky Tootsie's Orchid Lounge has offered live music since 1960. You can mingle with the biggest and the best at the Loveless Café, as famous for its breakfast of country ham and eggs with feather-light buttermilk biscuits as it is for the Grand Ole Opry performers who have made it a favorite haunt for more than forty years. Or come in June, when music lovers descend on Nashville for the four-day party of music mania called the International Country Music Fan Fair.

WHAT: site, event. **COUNTRY MUSIC HALL OF FAME:** 222 Fifth Ave. South. Tel 800-852-6437 or 615-416-2001; www.countrymusichall offame.com. *Cost:* $20. **GRAND OLE OPRY:** 2804 Opryland Dr. Tel 800-733-6779; www. opry.com. *Cost:* tickets $38–$53. *When:* Fri and Sat; shows added in summer months. **BLUE-BIRD CAFÉ:** 4104 Hillsboro Rd. Tel 615-383-1461; www.bluebirdcafe.com. **TOOTSIE'S ORCHID LOUNGE:** 422 Broadway. Tel 615-726-0463; www.tootsies.net. **LOVELESS CAFÉ:** Rt. 5, Highway 100. Tel 615-646-9700; www.loveless cafe.com. **INTERNATIONAL COUNTRY MUSIC FAN FAIR:** tel 800-262-3378; www.fanfair.com. *Cost:* 4-day Fan Fair packages from $110.

High Style in the Smokies

BLACKBERRY FARM

Walland, Tennessee, U.S.A.

T he exclusive but comfortably laid-back Blackberry Farm sits on its own 4,200 acres 4 miles from Great Smoky Mountains National Park. Although there's plenty to do here, it's hard to resist the hotel's long veranda

and its flotilla of rocking chairs, commanding one of the most riveting views you're ever going to find. Those in the mood for company can join the 8 million visitors a year who visit the national park (the most visited in America), but there's also the option of exploring the Orvis-endorsed lodge's extensive network of private walking, mountain-biking, and bridle trails (where you'll rarely run into another soul) or taking a spa treatment in the original 1870s farmhouse. The rustic mountain environment offsets the romantic hotel's homey but luxe elegance, effortless sophistication, and impeccable service. This combination—together with the work of gifted chef John Fleer, who creates the best meals in Tennessee—help explain Blackberry Farm's reputation as a "Ritz-Carlton in the woods."

Blackberry Farm's welcoming porch

WHAT: hotel, restaurant. **WHERE:** 1471 W. Millers Cove Road, Walland. 30 miles south of Knoxville, 195 miles east of Nashville, 12 miles from closest entrance to the Great Smoky Mountains National Park (at Townsend). Tel 800-273-6004 or 865-984-8166, fax 865-681-7753; info@blackberry farm.com; www.blackberryfarm.com. **COST:** doubles from $695, includes breakfast, gourmet picnic lunch, and 5-course candlelight dinner. **BEST TIMES:** Oct and Nov for a frenzy of colored foliage.

A Citywide Party in the Live Music Capital of the World

SOUTH BY SOUTHWEST

Austin, Texas, U.S.A.

Casual, young, and fun-loving, Austin promotes itself as the Live Music Capital of the World. The city is defined by many things, but music reigns here, both as a business and a pastime. More than 100 live-music venues offer everything from rockabilly to Tejano, and it's not unusual to catch impromptu appearances by local talents Willie Nelson, Lyle Lovett, the Dixie Chicks, and the Fabulous Thunderbirds. Sixth Street, lined with Victorian buildings, is the city's year-round music nerve center. Rock 'n' roll, blues, jazz, country, and R & B emanate and blend from clubs that spill down every side street. There's the world-renowned Antone's, an institution for names both world-known and obscure; the Backyard, an old-time spot that presents big-name shows outdoors; the Broken Spoke, Texas's premier dance hall and the last word in Texas two-step; and Stubb's BBQ and Threadgill's, both loved for their combination of great food and great music—Threadgill's (a former gas station turned diner) is where Janis Joplin got her start in 1962. The city's annual musical climax is the famous South by Southwest Music and Media Festival, known as SXSW, a showcase for more than 1,000 fledgling musicians who come from all over the world hoping to be discovered by industry bigwigs. It's a ten-day trade show for the music, film, and interactive media industries, but music lovers looking for the new and edgy enjoy four jam-packed days and nights of music.

WHAT: town, restaurant, event. **ANTONE'S:** 213 West 5th St. Tel 512-320-8424; www.antones.net. **THE BACKYARD:** 13101 Hwy 71 West. Tel 512-263-4146; www.thebackyard.net. **BROKEN SPOKE:** 3201 S. Lamar. Tel 512-442-6189; www.brokenspokeaustintx.com. **STUBB'S BBQ:** 801 Red River. Tel 512-480-8341; www.stubbsaustin.com. *Cost:* BBQ plate $12. *When:* open daily. **THREADGILL'S:** Tel 512-472-9304, south@threadgills.com; www.threadgills.com. *When:* live music Thurs–Sun. **SOUTH BY SOUTHWEST:** tel 512-467-7979; www.sxsw.com. *Cost:* admission and cover charges vary. *When:* 10 days in mid-Mar, with music for 4 days at mid-festival.

Living the Life of an Oil Tycoon

THE MANSION ON TURTLE CREEK

Dallas, Texas, U.S.A.

The Mansion on Turtle Creek, Dallas's only five-star hotel, appears consistently on the very, very short list of America's top accommodations. Check in here and you'll feel just like Sheppard King, the Texan oil and cotton baron for whom this Italian Renaissance–style pink-stucco mansion was first built in the 1920s. King lost his shirt in the Depression, paving the way for his home to be converted into a luxury hotel where the stratospherically rich can revel in the privilege and refinement of a bygone era, with impeccable snap-to service that still retains a healthy dollop of Texas conviviality. A more contemporary tower of guest rooms and suites was added to the hotel later.

Just as famous as the hotel is its eponymous restaurant, which first appeared on the gastronomic radar when the daring, Kentucky-born Dean Fearing (known for having helped pioneer Southwestern cuisine) took up residence.

Many cookbooks and awards later, Fearing has left the restaurant but his signature dishes remain. The hotel's 24-hour room service menu is the same as that of the restaurant, but it's worth the effort to leave your exquisitely appointed room to spend an evening in the gorgeous restaurant and adjoining bar, housed in the original mansion. The award-winning 12,000-bottle wine cellar is in the former owner's silver vault.

WHAT: hotel, restaurant. **WHERE:** 2821 Turtle Creek Blvd. Tel 888-767-3966 or 214-559-2100, fax 214-528-4187; www.mansiononturtlecreek.com; restaurant, tel 214-443-4747. **COST:** doubles from $250. Dinner $100. **WHEN:** restaurant, lunch and dinner daily.

Back Roads and Bluebonnets

HILL COUNTRY

Fredericksburg, Texas, U.S.A.

Deep in the heart of Texas is a place that local boy President Lyndon B. Johnson called "a special corner of God's real estate," an area of grassy pastures, limestone bluffs, and oak-studded landscape rich in meandering streams, rivers, and lakes. With a rustic beauty that swells and dips but never reaches peaks of more than 1,900 feet, Texas's Hill Country, roughly the size of Connecticut and an anomaly in generally flat Texas, was settled in the mid-1800s by mostly German immigrants, whose ethnic influence can still be felt in and around the area's prettiest town,

Fredericksburg, named after Prince Frederick IV of Prussia. More cosmopolitan than cowpoke these days, its wide Main Street is lined with chic shops, antique stores, art galleries, scores of old-world inns and bed-and-breakfasts (one reason for the town's popularity), and small German eateries that make it as easy to get Wiener schnitzel as chicken-fried steak.

Outside of Fredericksburg, the 13-mile Willow City Loop rambles through some of the area's most beautiful scenery, unmatched during wildflower season, when Texas's rolling hills are blanketed with a sea of purplish bluebonnets (the state flower), swaths of fiery orange-red Indian paintbrushes, and more colors than you find in an Impressionist's palette. No state boasts more wildflowers than Texas—some 5,000 species, a full quarter of those existing in North America. The state's huge success with its wildflower propagation and highway beautification projects is in large part due to Lady Bird Johnson, so any wildflower lover's first stop should be Austin's unique 180-acre Lady Bird Johnson Wildflower Research Center, founded by its namesake in 1982, on her seventieth birthday. The center gives a fascinating insight on the preservation and restoration of the native flora of Lady Bird's birth state and of all North America.

The town of Bandera bills itself as the Cowboy Capital of the World, as much for the number of plain-to-luxurious dude ranches as for the world-champion ropers (eight at last count) who call it home. Kerville, a town high above the Guadalupe River, boasts the Cowboy Artists of America Museum. Those looking to go tubing down the tumbling Guadalupe usually stop by Gruene first, whose bare-bones 1878 Gruene Hall (the oldest continuously operating dancehall in Texas) and its weekly two-step sessions make every drop-in visitor a dancin' fool.

WHAT: site, town. **HILL COUNTRY:** anchored at its four corners by Austin, San Antonio, Llano, and Bandera. **FREDERICKSBURG:** 70 miles west of Austin, 65 miles northwest of San Antonio. Fredericksburg Convention and Visitors Bureau, tel 888-997-3600 or 830-997-6523, fax 830-997-8588; www.fredericksburg texas.com. **LADY BIRD JOHNSON WILDFLOWER CENTER:** 4801 La Crosse Ave., in southwest Austin. Tel 512-232-0100, fax 512-232-0156; www.wildflower.org. *Cost:* $7. *When:* open daily mid-Mar though Apr, Tues–Sun May–mid-Mar. **BEST TIMES:** wildflower season is early spring (mid-Mar to Apr for bluebonnets) to early fall. Oktoberfest is commonly celebrated 1st weekend in Oct in any of the German-American towns.

Small and Sophisticated, Texas's Biggest Cultural Surprise

THE MENIL COLLECTION

Houston, Texas, U.S.A.

The Menil Collection can be found in a leafy residential neighborhood southwest of the petro-dollar skyline of downtown Houston. Widely esteemed as one of the greatest and most eclectic private museums in the United States, it is a magnificent assemblage of some 15,000 objects (a revolving number are on display) amassed by the late Paris-born Dominique de Menil and her husband John. Sometimes described as American Medicis, the de Menils (whose fortunes derived from the oil-services firm Schlumberger, Ltd., founded by Dominique's father and uncle) were legendary as Houston's patron of the arts. Dominique outlived her husband by twenty-five years (she died in 1997 at eighty-nine) and it is her expansive spirit that's so evident in this individualistic and poetic collection.

Opened in 1987 in a simple but elegant low-rise building designed by the Italian architect Renzo Piano, the museum achieves a low-key atmosphere (there is a bookstore, but no audio guides, and admission is free), suffused with natural but skillfully filtered Texan light. Viewing art here is a very intimate experience, just what Dominique de Menil intended.

Often compared to the other small gems of America's museum scene—the Barnes Foundation outside of Philadelphia, the Frick in New York City—the Menil is in many ways broader than them all. At its heart is the justly famous Surrealism collection, with works by

Sublime art in an intimate environment

Man Ray, Duchamp, and Ernst, and one of the world's best collections of Magritte. The Menil is also rich in other 20th-century European artists such as Picasso, Matisse, Giacometti, and Rodin. Across the street, an annex built in 1995 (also designed by Piano) comprises nine galleries of the work of the American artist Cy Twombly, another favorite of the de Menils.

WHAT: site. **WHERE:** 1515 Sul Ross St. Tel 713-525-9400; www.menil.org. **COST:** admission free. **WHEN:** open Wed–Sun.

A Lively Oasis in This Multicultural Town

RIVER WALK

San Antonio, Texas, U.S.A.

Way back when, Mark Twain and Will Rogers both rated San Antonio as one of America's most outstanding cities—sharing the bill only with San Francisco, Boston, and New Orleans. Today Twain would recognize

the city's historic showpiece, the Alamo, but not its second most visited attraction, the River Walk (or Paseo del Rio), a lively and delightfully scenic flagstone esplanade bordering both banks of the lazy, narrow San Antonio River. Wending for 3 miles beneath giant cypress and palm trees, tropical foliage, and flowering bushes one level below the busy streets of downtown San Antonio, River Walk originated as a functional WPA project completed in 1941, was rejuvenated just a decade ago, and is now lined with cafés, restaurants, shops, and hotels.

At the oldest and nicest horseshoe bend is the Mansión del Rio Hotel, the crown jewel of the River Walk. Occupying a Spanish-influenced 19th-century boys' school and college, it was reborn as an elegant respite of cool courtyard fountains and old-world ambience, with most rooms overlooking the river. Its Las Canarias Restaurant, named after the city's original colonists from Spain's Canary Islands, is River Walk's most distinguished. For more casual fare, enjoy a prickly-pear margarita and smoked shrimp enchiladas or guacamole made fresh at your table at Boudro's, always popular with both visitors and locals. River Walk is a special pleasure at night and on weekends, but two periods are particularly wonderful: the Christmas season, when 80,000 twinkling lights illuminate its vintage facades and bridges and light the way for traveling barges of carolers; and late April, when the whole city stops for the Fiesta San Antonio, ten days of events, fireworks, and entertainment highlighted by three parades—the Battle of Flowers Parade and two barge parades on the river.

WHAT: site, hotel, restaurant. **SAN ANTONIO:** San Antonio Convention and Visitors Bureau, tel 800-447-3372 or 210-207-6700; www.san antoniovisit.com. **MANSIÓN DEL RIO HOTEL:** 112 College St. Tel 888-444-6664 or 210-518-1000, fax 210-226-0389; www.lamansion.com. *Cost:* doubles from $299. Dinner $45. **BOUDRO'S:** 421 E. Commerce St. Tel 210-224-8484; www.boudros.com. *Cost:* dinner $30; 2-hour barge cruises (by reservation only) $40, includes 5-course dinner. *When:* lunch and dinner daily. **FIESTA SAN ANTONIO:** tel 877-723-4378 or 210-227-5191; www.fiesta-sa.org. **BEST TIMES:** 10 days in late Apr for the Fiesta San Antonio; beginning early Dec for the Fiesta de las Luminarias, when thousands of candles anchored in sand-filled paper bags line the river; in early May for the 5-day Tejano-Conjunto Festival, which celebrates the music and dance of the Texas–Mexico border.

Nature Unrestrained

BRYCE CANYON NATIONAL PARK

Utah, U.S.A.

Bryce Canyon isn't a canyon at all, but a magical amphitheater that millions of years of rain, snow, and ice hollowed out of the pink and white limestone cliffs. Like a cave without a roof, its eerily shaped, stalagmite-like "hoodoo" pinnacles and pillars rise up out of the ground, unique for their brilliant, mineral-tinted colors and top-heavy shapes—the result of their harder upper levels staying firm as the low-er levels eroded away. The Paiute Indians believed these rocks to be early residents who were turned to stone for their evil deeds, frozen in time forever by a vengeful god. Like Rorschach blobs or cloud formations, the delicately sculpted spires can take on many guises depending on the viewer—one man's giraffe is another man's Elvis—though there's no mistaking the arches, bridges, and peepholes that fill out the scene. To tap into the deepest spirit of the place, go to Sunset Point at its namesake hour and watch the sky imitate the colors of the stone.

The fantasy canyon was named after Mormon settler Ebeneezer Bryce, who tried his best to raise cattle in these harsh environs

Bryce Canyon's natural sculpture

in the 1870s, famously commenting that it was "a helluva place to lose a cow." Fifty years later, Bryce Canyon Lodge was built to house visitors to this gem-sized park, at 56 square miles about as big as the Grand Canyon's broom closet. Constructed of large ponderosa-pine timbers and native stone, its cozy cabins encircle the Main Lodge, where you can get a pretty good meal.

WHAT: site, hotel. **BRYCE CANYON NATIONAL PARK:** 260 miles south of Salt Lake City. Visitors Center, tel 435-834-5322; www. nps.gov/brca. *Cost:* $25 per car. **BRYCE CANYON LODGE:** tel 435-834-8700; www.brycecanyon lodge.com. *Cost:* motel rooms from $130; cabins from $175. *When:* open Apr–Oct. **BEST TIMES:** summer, when the park's 8,000-foot altitude keeps temperatures cool.

Adventure Central

MOAB AND RED ROCK COUNTRY

Utah, U.S.A.

Set amid a spectacular desert terrain so far from anywhere that Butch Cassidy found it a perfect place to hide out, Moab has become the hot spot for international mountain bikers. Add to that river runners, four-wheel-drive enthusiasts,

hikers, rock climbers, and adrenaline junkies in general and you've explained Moab's sudden great-outdoors popularity. Settled by Mormons in 1855 (and named for the biblical town on the Jordan River), Moab became a uranium boomtown when that kind of thing was in vogue, but had gone bust by the 1980s, when ex-miners and the community had the bright idea of affixing big knobby tires to a sturdy bike and taking off into the vast and ruggedly beautiful terrain of nearby Canyonlands and Arches National Parks (think *Thelma and Louise* and *Indiana Jones and the Last Crusade*). Canyonlands, the largest national park in Utah, with entrances 35 miles southwest and 30 miles northwest of Moab, contains hundreds of miles of dirt prospectors' roads cutting through a surreal, colorful landscape of buttes, mesas, spires, balanced rocks, soaring arches, and deep gorges. Arches National Park, 5 miles northeast of Moab, is a photographer's paradise, home to more than 2,000 natural arches formed by the elements. Each park contains approximately 20 miles of paved scenic road.

One of the area's countless natural arches

Just outside Moab, the 10-mile Slickrock Trail offers a sadistically challenging roller-coaster ride through a moonscape of eroded sandstone, with rewarding views over the Colorado River below.

Local outfitters organize multiple-day camping trips or arrange for off-road vehicles to follow your biking party for the day, guaranteeing food, relief, unlimited water (particularly important in the brutal desert heat), Band-Aids, and portable showers. Scenic rafting and kayaking are wonderful along Moab's calm stretch of the Colorado River, and class II and IV rapids are only a day trip away. Whatever your choice of adventure, book in advance: Moab's secret has been out since the 1990s, and even the slew of new hotels and B & Bs keep up with the demand for rooms. Return bikers in the know always settle in just off Main Street at the new Gonzo Inn, with its retro 1970s decor.

WHAT: site, hotel. **WHERE:** 238 miles southeast of Salt Lake City. In Moab, Visitors Center, tel 800-635-6622 or 435-259-8825;

www.discovermoab.com. **GONZO INN:** 100 W. 200 South. Tel 800-791-4044 or 435-259-2515, fax 435-259-6992; www.gonzoinn.com. *Cost:* doubles from $160. **BEST TIMES:** Mar–late May and mid-Sept to early Nov for the best biking weather (also the biggest crowds); the week before Easter Sunday for the Jeep Safari; mid-Oct for the 4-day Fat Tire Festival.

The Classic Western Skyline

MONUMENT VALLEY

Utah, U.S.A.

You've been here before. You recognize it all. You grew up seeing this ancient wonder as the perfect backdrop for dozens of classic Western films and television series, as well as innumerable car commercials, billboards, and fashion shoots. It started with John Ford's 1939 masterpiece *Stagecoach*, which elevated then B-movie actor John Wayne onto Hollywood's A list. *Fort Apache, The Searchers,* and others followed, making this stark landscape of wind-sculpted buttes, eroded, sometimes 1,000-foot-high mesas, and craggy red-rock monoliths into the indelible symbol of the Old West. And the Navajos made Ford an honorary member.

From the beginning, Goulding's Lodge has been the epicenter of Monument Valley's movie career, providing film crews (and random visitors) with the only accommodations of note in this remote 2,000-square-mile area. Because Monument Valley sits on sacred Navajo land, visitors must be accompanied by local Navajo guides when traveling anywhere beyond the scenic, self-guided 17-mile unpaved loop that runs through the park. A few hours spent with a Navajo guide is the guaranteed highlight of any visit. Bouncing around the park's dirt roads to remote backcountry, pictographs, Anasazi ruins, and natural arches, you also gain insight into the heritage of the Navajo Nation, the largest American Indian tribe, with about 300,000 members. Comprising mostly high desert area (often over 5,000 feet), the 17-million-acre Navajo reservation is bigger than all of New England and includes not only Monument Valley but also the Four Corners area, the only place in the United States where four states—Utah, Colorado, Arizona, and New Mexico—come together.

WHAT: site, hotel. **MONUMENT VALLEY:** straddling the Utah-Arizona border, 240 miles from Phoenix. Official entrance to the park is just west of U.S. 163, 150 miles south of Moab, 395 miles south of Salt Lake City. Monument Valley Visitors Center, tel 435-727-5870; www.navajonationparks.org. *Cost:* admission $5 per person. **GOULDING'S LODGE:** 6 miles from park entrance. Tel 435-727-3231; gouldings@gouldings.com; www.gouldings.com. *Cost:* doubles from $75 (low season), from $180 (high season). Navajo-guided tours vary from 3½ hours to a full day, starting at $50. **BEST TIMES:** sunset, or aim for a full moon; spring and fall, when weather is cool (due to high altitude) and crowds are smaller.

The Greatest Snow on Earth—Just Like the License Plate Says

PARK CITY AND THE WASATCH RANGE

Utah, U.S.A.

With fourteen great ski resorts within an hour's drive of Salt Lake City and an enviable annual snowfall of 500 inches in some areas, it's no mystery why Utah was chosen to host the 2002 Winter Olympics.

Powder hounds and black diamond skiers may head to Alta and neighboring Snowbird for challenging steeps and deeps and some of the lightest snow imaginable. But those who want an exquisite, pampering hotel experience along with well-groomed slopes prefer chic but unpretentious Deer Valley, one of three ski destinations (together with Park City Mountain and The Canyons) whose trails and bowls funnel into Park City, a century-old mining town. *The* social beehive during Salt Lake City's winter games, the town continues to be a lively après-ski magnet in an otherwise sedate area. In Deer Valley, the Stein Eriksen Lodge was founded by its charismatic 1952 Olympic gold medalist namesake, who still plays host and ski director. Ranked as one of the world's finest ski-in/ski-out lodges, its mid-mountain location, cozy public areas and guest rooms (most with fireplaces), luxurious Scandinavian decor, and impeccable service set the gold standard.

Just out of the Park City loop, the ski hideaway Sundance (named by founder Robert Redford for his character in 1969's *Butch Cassidy and the Sundance Kid*) is both resort and, since 1981, home base of the famous film festival of the same name, North America's premiere showcase for independent film. Most of the festival's events and screenings now take place in Park City, but a good number continue to be held in Sundance Village, Redford's environmentally conscious picture-perfect community of rustic but stylish cottages, snuggled unobtrusively amid 6,000 acres of pines and aspens, blending nature with the arts. Screenings, classes, and events are held year-round, and in winter there's cross-country and alpine skiing, the latter on 8,250-foot Airhead Summit, home to the only mountaintop lodge in all of Utah, with magnificent views from Bearclaw Cabin.

WHAT: town, site, hotel, experience, event. **PARK CITY:** 30 miles east of Salt Lake City. State-wide ski conditions are listed at www.skiutah.com. **DEER VALLEY:** visitors information tel 800-424-3337 or 435-649-1000; www.deervalley.com. **STEIN ERIKSEN LODGE:** tel 800-453-1302 or 435-649-3700, fax 435-645-6429; www.steinlodge.com. *Cost:* doubles from $420 (low season), from $830 (high season). **SUNDANCE SKI RESORT/ SUNDANCE VILLAGE:** 40 miles southwest of Park City. Tel 800-892-1600 or 801-225-4107, fax 801-226-1937; www.sundance resort.com. *Cost:* studios from $225 (low season), from $400 (high season). **SUNDANCE FILM FESTIVAL:** tel 801-328-3456 or 310-360-1981; www.sundance.org. *Cost:* each screening $15; multiple-screening passes from $200. *When:* 10 days in late Jan. **BEST TIMES:** mid-Jun through Aug for the Music in the Mountains Festival; 1st week of Aug for the Park City Arts Festival; Jan–early Mar for the best ski conditions. The Utah Symphony plays outdoors in Deer Valley every Sat evening, Jun–Aug.

The Glorious Sound of Music

MORMON TABERNACLE CHOIR

Salt Lake City, Utah, U.S.A.

S inging has been an important part of the Mormon religion ever since Brigham Young led his followers west in wagon trains, making sure that musicians were along to keep the pioneers' morale high and their eyes on God.

The first Mormon choir sang in what is now Salt Lake City soon after Young and his ragged following arrived in 1847. Twenty years later, the now famous domed Mormon Tabernacle was inaugurated on the very same spot.

The acoustically perfect 6,500-seat structure is regularly filled with members of the Church of Jesus Christ of Latter Day Saints and with visitors, many of whom have become familiar with the 360-member choir and its 11,623-pipe organ through recordings or its weekly radio show. The peripatetic choir fills theaters and opera houses around the globe, and while they sound nothing less than professional, they're in fact a strictly volunteer organization, made up of professors, insurance agents, secretaries, and homemakers. Every Sunday morning choir performance is emotional and rafter raising, but the annual Christmas concert pulls out all stops with a well-known guest singer, a full orches-

tra, and that infectious holiday spirit. The Tabernacle is located in the heart of the city in Temple Square, as revered by Mormons as the Vatican is by Catholics. Anchoring this 35-acre compound is the granite, six-spired Salt Lake Temple, symbol of a movement that entered the 20th century as the most persecuted creed in America, and begins the 21st as one of its most robust, with close to 12 million members, half of them outside the United States. Unfortunately, the temple is open only to church members.

WHAT: site, event. **WHERE:** Temple Square Guest Services and Visitors Center, 50 North Temple St. Tel 801-240-4872; www.lds.org. **COST:** tours, entrance to the Tabernacle, and choir performances are free. **WHEN:** Tabernacle open daily. Tours every 15 minutes. Choir rehearsals Thurs 8 P.M., performances Sun 9:30 A.M. **BEST TIMES:** Dec for the 2 Christmas concerts.

On the Bottom Looking Up

ZION NATIONAL PARK

Utah, U.S.A.

T he 19th-century Mormon settlers saw the vertical monoliths, precipitous 2,000- to 3,000-foot canyon walls, and sculptured rocks, and decided this was the promised land, the "natural temples of God." And so, they named it Zion. If that sounds like hyperbole, wait until you see it. The 229-square-mile park's vertical topography—particularly the dramatic chasm of Zion Canyon, whose Technicolor sandstone cliffs have graced millions of postcards—means most park visitors see it all from the cottonwood-lined bottom of the canyon, carved out by the Virgin River over millions of years. Any vista will explain Zion's nickname, "the land of rainbow canyons," referring to the iron oxide and other minerals in the sandstone that leave a wash of red, pink, purple, yellow, and orange, remarkable at any time of the day.

Fifty miles of paved roads make Zion easy to explore by car or via the park's shuttle buses, but get out and hike to see why early visitors named awe-inspiring sites such as the Great White Throne and the West Temple. More than 100 miles of paths range from the strenuous (the trek to Angels Landing is unmatched for its views) to the strollable. The popular Riverside Walk leads to the Narrows, where the multicolored canyon walls tower above an only 20-foot-wide canyon floor, forcing trekkers to wade through the river's cool shallow waters. The surprisingly easy Canyon Overlook Trail is known for spectacular views, and the popular Emerald Pools Trail leads through forests to three basins fed by small waterfalls and kept a deep, rich green by the presence of algae. Zion Lodge, the park's historic accommodation, is the best place to stay if you can nab one of the cabins designed in the 1920s, which were stripped of their 1970s decor courtesy of a thorough redo in 1998.

WHAT: site, hotel. **ZION NATIONAL PARK:** Springdale is the gateway town—320 miles south of Salt Lake City, 120 miles northwest of the north rim of the Grand Canyon. Tel 435-772-3256; www.nps.gov/zion. *Cost:* $25 per car. **ZION LODGE:** tel 888-297-2757 or 303-297-2757, fax 303-297-3175; www.zionlodge.com. *Cost:* cabins from $175; motel rooms available from $160. **BEST TIMES:** spring and fall, when temperatures are best for hiking. Avoid peak summer temperatures that can reach more than 100 degrees. Zion Canyon's Scenic Drive is accessible by free shuttle bus Apr–Oct, when private cars are not allowed.

Zion's sandstone cliffs are some of the highest in the world.

An Archetypal New England Town for Sportsmen and Shoppers

MANCHESTER VILLAGE

Vermont, U.S.A.

In the heart of a picturesque valley ringed by the Green Mountains, the maple-shaded streets of this charming New England town have lured visitors since before Abe Lincoln's family started spending summers here.

Manchester Village's stately white mansions, marble sidewalks, and smart shops continue to draw visitors for its idyllic setting, year-round sports opportunities, and raft of high-end factory outlets. For golf, the prime local destination is the white-columned, Federal-style (and very Anglo) Equinox Resort and its championship golf course, part of the revered Gleneagles group based in Scotland. Established as a premier summer resort in the 1860s, the 2,300-acre property has been a favorite of U.S. presidents from Taft to Eisenhower. For sport of another kind, Equinox is also home to the first American branch of the Scottish-based British School of Falconry, and is just down the road from the original Manchester headquarters of famous fly-fisherman and fishing outfitter Charles Orvis. Orvis's present-day company offers day trips to trout-rich Battenkill. Afterward, repair back to Equinox's wonderfully atmospheric Marsh Tavern to compare fishing tales. Built in 1769, the tavern was where Vermont's famous Green Mountain Boys met during the Revolutionary War. For your night's sleep, the most charming of Equinox's 183 beautifully appointed rooms are in the Charles Orvis Inn, an early 19th-century residence that was once Orvis's home.

The Federal-style Equinox Resort has been a favorite with U.S. presidents.

WHAT: town, hotel, experience, restaurant. **MANCHESTER VILLAGE:** within 30 miles of both Stratton and Bromley ski resorts, 209 miles north of New York City. **EQUINOX RESORT:** Rt. 7A. Tel 800-362-4747 or 802-362-4700; www.equinoxresort.com. *Cost:* doubles from $209, Charles Orvis Inn suites from $609. Dinner at Marsh Tavern $35. **ORVIS COMPANY:** tel 800-548-9548 or 802-362-3450; www.orvis.com. *Cost:* fly-fishing school $470 (2 days) and $235 (1 day), includes equipment, lunch, workshops, and on-stream experience with a guide at the Battenkill (4 students per guide). *When:* Apr–early Oct. **BEST TIMES:** Jul of even-numbered years for the Antiques Festival; May to mid-Sept for the best fishing conditions.

Fall Foliage Nirvana and the Quintessential Vermont Inn

NORTHEAST KINGDOM

Vermont, U.S.A.

In 1949, a former U.S. senator from Vermont, struck by the timeless beauty and isolation of his state's three most northeastern counties (Orleans, Essex, and Caledonia), dubbed them the Northeast Kingdom, and when foliage flames each autumn, they could very well be the most beautiful place in America. Here, thickly forested hills of sugar maple, beech, and ash give way to sleepy hamlets, one-church villages, and gorgeous lakes—particularly the fjord-like Lake Willoughby, often compared to Switzerland's Lake Lucerne. The unofficial gateway to the region is St. Johnsbury ("St. J"), but look on your map for alternative spots like Peacham (pop. 611), probably Vermont's finest Kodak corner during foliage season. Keep driving until you get lost, through wide-open valleys of tidy farmlands where cows once outnumbered their proudly insular Yankee owners. Harsh winters and sheer isolation have kept development and tourism farther south, and when fall's riotous palette of red, orange, yellow, and gold cloaks these hills, you might feel as if you've happened upon a very well-kept secret. Back roads and lanes make this a paradise for cyclists as well, either on your own or on an organized inn-to-inn tour.

In the peaceful time-forgotten village of Lower Waterford (whose population hovers around 50), the Rabbit Hill Inn has a tradition of hospitality dating to 1795. The Federal-style white-colonnaded inn sits on 15 unspoiled acres with a commanding view of the White Mountains to the south. Its 19 guest rooms are individually decorated (suites have gas fireplaces and two-person whirlpool baths), and dinner is an elegant three-course affair of refined dishes, like agnolotti of braised pheasant and ricotta, followed by herb-crusted Alaskan halibut. Breakfast is every bit as romantic, served by candlelight and as ample as it is scrumptious. Walk it all off on the 7 miles of meandering cross-country trails near the inn.

WHAT: site, hotel, experience. **ST. JOHNSBURY:** 328 miles north of New York City, 75 miles east of Burlington. Northeast Kingdom Chamber of Commerce, tel 800-639-6379 or 802-748-3678; www.nekchamber.com (with a foliage update). **RABBIT HILL INN:** Lower Waterford. Tel 800-762-8669 or 802-748-5168; www.rabithillinn.com. *Cost:* from $195 (low season), from $230 (high season). **BEST TIMES:** peak fall foliage time is generally late Sept–early Oct. Northeast Kingdom Fall Foliage Festival, 1 week beginning last Sun in Sept, with events (church breakfasts to dairy farm tours) in a different town every day.

An Invitation to a Vanderbilt Estate

SHELBURNE FARMS

Shelburne, Vermont, U.S.A.

On a bluff overlooking 100-mile-long Lake Champlain and the Adirondacks beyond, the Inn at Shelburne Farms sits on 1,400 acres designed by the great landscape architect Frederick Law Olmsted, who laid out New York City's Central Park. You're lord of the manor at the redbrick, Queen Anne–style country mansion, built in 1899 as the largest home in Vermont by Lila Vanderbilt and her husband William Seward Webb. Step into another era of oak paneling, twenty-four massive fireplaces, turrets, towers, family portraits, and twenty-four guest rooms appointed with period and original family-heirloom antiques—you might even be sleeping in William Henry Vanderbilt's enormous mahogany bed. The inn's candle-lit restaurant, grand but cozy, offers a menu that might include roasted rack of New England lamb with apple-sorrel relish, complemented by organic produce direct from Shelburne Farm's market garden. The farm was conceived by the Webbs and embellished by their great-grandchildren as a nonprofit environmental educational center. In addition to being a rural marvel (with a hands-on Children's Farmyard that's every kid's fantasy), it produces an excellent Cheddar cheese, compliments of the Brown Swiss cows grazing within sight. You can sample it to your heart's content.

A 3-mile drive from the "Big House," the 45-acre Shelburne Museum comprises a general store, a round barn, a covered bridge, a lighthouse, and thirty-three other historic structures that re-create a 19th-century town. Long known as New England's Smithsonian, the museum contains what may be the finest collection of Americana in the country, featuring textiles and quilts, dolls and toys (some 2,000), weather vanes, horse-drawn vehi-cles—well over 100,000 artifacts in all, plus a collection of works by Rembrandt, Degas, Monet, Manet, and Cassatt.

WHAT: hotel, restaurant, site. **THE INN AT SHELBURNE FARMS:** 7 miles south of Burlington, 296 miles north of New York City. Tel 802-985-8498, fax 802-985-1233; www.shelburnefarms. org. *Cost:* doubles from $255 (low season), from $305 (high season). Dinner $45; admission to farm $6. *When:* open mid-May–mid-Oct. **SHELBURNE MUSEUM:** tel 802-985-3346; www.shelburnemuseum.org. *Cost:* admission $20. *When:* daily; open mid-April–late Oct. **BEST TIMES:** 5 weeks in Jul–early Aug for the Vermont Mozart Festival; 3d weekend in Sept to the 2d weekend in Oct for foliage; 3d weekend in Sept for the Harvest Festival.

Where the Hills Are Alive

STOWE MOUNTAIN RESORT

Stowe, Vermont, U.S.A.

Beginning at the Massachusetts border and continuing north for 200 scenic miles along the rugged spine of the Green Mountains, the winding two-lane Route 100 is Vermont's country road and main street. During wintry months it's also called the skier's highway, connecting some nine major alpine ski destinations. At the road's northernmost reach, toward the Canadian border, lies Stowe Mountain Resort, the queen of Northeast ski resorts and one of the oldest in the United States, created in the 1930s. Killington and Okemo may have surpassed Stowe in slickness, technology, and size, but the resort's challenging slopes and authentic 200-year-old Vermont town setting—with the prerequisite white-steepled church and old-fashioned general store—retain their popularity as one of the country's most romantic and beautiful ski getaways. There's much here to keep beginners and intermediate skiers occupied, but it is Stowe's mythically steep Front Four trails on the face of Mount Mansfield—Starr, Goat, National, Liftline—that are the highlights of the show, for expert skiers only.

Four interconnected cross-country ski areas provide 93 miles of groomed trails and another 62 miles of backcountry terrain, the most extensive of the four crisscrossing the 2,700-acre resort of the Trapp Family Lodge, the country's first-ever cross-country ski center, created in 1968. This is where the Austrian family of *Sound of Music* fame settled in 1942 after crossing over the Alps to escape the Nazis. The quality of Tyrolean coziness, old-world service, and the promise of a mean wiener schnitzel and spaetzle in the lodge's noted restaurant make this chalet-style lodge one of the loveliest around. Maria Von Trapp, who died here in 1987, has left her legacy in the hands of her youngest son, the ever-youthful Johannes, and daughter Rosmarie, who leads Tuesday and Friday evening singalongs.

WHAT: site, experience, hotel. **STOWE MOUNTAIN RESORT:** 45 miles east of Burlington, 330 miles north of New York City. Stowe Area Association, tel 800-24-STOWE or 802-253-7321; www.stowe.com. **TRAPP FAMILY LODGE:** 5 miles from Stowe at 700 Trapp Hill Rd. Tel 800-826-7000 or 802-253-8511; info@trapp family.com; www.trappfamily.com. *Cost:* doubles $175 (low season), $485 (high season). **BEST TIMES:** 1 week late Jan for the famous Stowe Winter Carnival; Jan–Feb for the best alpine and cross-country skiing; Mar for the deepest snow base, as well as for maple syrup making.

The King of the East Coast Mountains, and Royal Inns

KILLINGTON AND WOODSTOCK

Vermont, U.S.A.

The Aspen of the East Coast, Killington isn't the classic and romantic Vermont ski destination (for that, you must head to Stowe), but it's the first to open (late October) and the last to close (May). It also boasts a vertical drop just inches less than Aspen's, has some of the most high-tech snow-making equipment, and is within driving distance of the major cities of the Northeast. Unless you're a twenty-something board enthusiast, though, Killington's big-and-brash aesthetic might wear thin after a few great runs. If so, escape to nearby, Christmas-card-perfect Woodstock, a cosmopolitan small town that claims the title of oldest ski resort in America, and site of the first ski tow. Laurance Rockefeller married the granddaughter of a railroad baron and Woodstock conservationist in 1934, and together they spent the next sixty years making Woodstock the "prettiest small town in America," according to *Ladies' Home Journal.* Among other things, they built the rustic but genteel Woodstock Inn and Resort on the village green in 1969, incorporating the 1793 Richardson's Tavern. It operates the Woodstock Ski Touring Center, with almost 40 miles of groomed cross-country trails, and the misleadingly named Suicide Six, with down-hill slopes and twenty-three trails. Amenities at the inn itself are top-drawer, but with 142 rooms it cannot promise intimacy. For that, drive down the road to exclusive Twin Farms, New England's most luxurious resort inn. Secluded amid 300 stunning acres of woodlands and expansive meadows, the former 18th-century sanctuary (which Nobel Prize–winning novelist Sinclair Lewis gave to his wife as a wedding present in 1928) offers incredible art, clairvoyant service, unforgettable meals and wines, and fifteen individually designed guest rooms, with working fireplaces and a decor of eclectic treasures collected from around the world—all for a daily price just under the GNP of some small countries.

WHAT: town, hotel, experience. **KILLINGTON:** 80 miles south of Burlington, 280 miles north of New York City. **WOODSTOCK:** 20 miles east of Killington. Woodstock Chamber of Commerce, tel 802-457-3555; www.woodstockvt.com. **WOODSTOCK INN AND RESORT:** tel 800-448-

7900 or 802-457-1100, fax 802-457-6699; www. woodstockinn.com. *Cost:* doubles from $159 (low season), from $359 (high season). **TWIN FARMS:** 10 miles north of Woodstock. Tel 800-894-6327 or 802-234-9999, fax 802-234-9990; www.twinfarms.com. *Cost:* $1,300–$3,000, includes all meals, and use of all on-site recreation and equipment. *When:* closed Apr (mud season). **BEST TIMES:** mid-Dec for Woodstock's Wassail Weekend; Jan–Feb for the best ski conditions.

A World-Class Spa and Historic Hot Springs

THE HOMESTEAD

Hot Springs, Virginia, U.S.A.

Follow in the footsteps of Thomas Jefferson to the rustic Jefferson Pools for a sybaritic and therapeutic soak in mineral-rich 98-degree waters—an experience akin to bathing in warm Perrier. The historic baths are maintained by the nearby 500-room Homestead resort, a grand ole Georgian belle redolent of European spas like Baden-Baden. Dinners in the formal dining room are jacket-and-tie affairs, as befits a place where, in the olden days, a succession of Colonial heroes, presidents, and millionaires came to take the restorative waters, sometimes staying for months. In addition to coming to "take the cure," today's younger set comes to enjoy the extensive sports facilities scattered across 15,000 acres of pristine Allegheny Mountains and valleys, including 100 miles of riding and hiking trails, a movie-set 1903 indoor pool fed by the natural hot springs, four miles of streams stocked with rainbow trout, six tennis courts, nine ski trails, and three undulating championship golf courses that have hosted seven USGA championships. Throw in bowling, a little falconry, and a soak at the end of the day in the ancient, on-site 104-degree natural mineral springs, the highlight of the resort's state-of-the-art 34,000-square-foot spa.

WHAT: hotel. **WHERE:** 210 miles from Washington, D.C., 117 miles from Charlottesville. Tel 800-838-1766 or 540-839-1766, fax 540-839-7656; www.thehomestead.com. **COST:** from $275 per person, double occupancy, includes all activities. **BEST TIMES:** spring for flowers, fall for brilliant foliage; the Thanksgiving and Christmas holidays for traditional celebrations.

In Pursuit of Life, Liberty, and Luxury

MONTICELLO

Virginia, U.S.A.

America's most famous historic home, Monticello ("little mountain") was the dream house and final resting place of Thomas Jefferson—statesman, visionary, principal author of the Declaration of Independence, and

America's only architect-president, who said of the house, "I am as happy nowhere else." Overlooking the 2,000 remaining acres of the Jefferson family's original 5,000-acre plantation, the house serves as a kind of autobiography of the president who was known as a writer but chose not to pen the story of his life. The three-story Palladian-style structure was entirely of his own design, begun in 1769 when he was just twenty-six, influenced by his time in France as U.S. minister from 1785 to 1789, and only finished twenty years later, in the last year of his presidency. Out in the fields, orchards, and landscaped gardens, Jefferson raised numerous kinds of peas (his favorite food) and in 1807 planted one of the earliest crops of European grapevines in the New World. Inside, the thirty-three-room house (of which only the eleven first-floor rooms are open to the public) is scattered with Jefferson memorabilia, left as if the owner had just stepped out for a stroll.

Virginia's love affair with Thomas Jefferson continues at nearby Charlottesville's top-ranked University of Virginia, the beloved "academical village" he founded and whose buildings he designed. You can take a guided tour of the small but sophisticated city's prestigious campus, visiting the colonnades, serpentine brick walls, and Pantheon-inspired rotunda that in 1976 inspired the American Institute of Architects to designate Jefferson's campus the outstanding achievement in American architecture. Edgar Allan Poe fans can peek into the building at 13 West Range, where the author

lived for one year as an undergraduate in 1826, until his stepfather cut off the gambler's funds. To prolong your Jeffersonian moment, check into the Federal-style Clifton Inn, built in 1799 on what was then Jefferson family property by Jefferson's son-in-law, who used it as a trading post and then as his home.

WHAT: site, hotel, restaurant. **MONTICELLO:** 2 miles southeast of Charlottesville, 125 miles southwest of Washington, D.C. Tel 434-984-9822; www.monticello.org. *Cost:* $13 (low season), $20 (high season), includes guided house tour. **CLIFTON INN:** Clifton Inn Dr., Charlottesville. Tel 888-971-1800 or 434-971-1800; www.cliftoninn.net. *Cost:* doubles from $245. Dinner $45. **BEST TIMES:** Jul 4th for the Monticello Independence Day Celebration and Naturalization Ceremony, when those qualified are sworn in as U.S. citizens amid festivities celebrating both the signing of the Declaration of Independence and Jefferson's death exactly 50 years later, on Jul 4, 1826.

Thomas Jefferson died at Monticello on July 4, 1826.

The Beauty of the Daughter of the Stars

SHENANDOAH VALLEY

Virginia, U.S.A.

S tretching for 200 miles between the Allegheny Mountains to the northwest and the Blue Ridge Mountains to the southeast, the Shenandoah Valley has long inspired. Washington Irving found it "equal to the promised land in fertility, and far superior to it in beauty," while Herbert Hoover, riding horseback along the crest of the Blue Ridge, was said to have remarked, "These mountains are made for a road." That finally came to pass in 1939 with the completion of the 105-mile Skyline Drive, which bisects long, skinny Shenandoah National Park's wild backcountry, offering views that the appreciative Hoover called "the greatest in the world."

Devastated by the Civil War and scarred by early settlers, the land was reclaimed by the government in the 1930s and today is a haven for bird watchers and hikers, as well as motorists. Like the hardwood forests of New England, the Blue Ridge Mountains are home to sycamores, hickories, oaks, and maples that in autumn put on a breathtaking display of color—peaking later than almost all foliage on the East Coast. Autumn weekends on the two-lane Skyline Drive mean bottleneck traffic, but you can escape by parking at any of the seventy-five balcony-like scenic overlooks, many of which act as trailheads. The 2,100-mile Maine-to-Georgia Appalachian Trail roughly parallels the drive for 101 miles, and hikers can pick up short segments of it among the park's 500-mile network of trails. Skyland Resort, Shenandoah's oldest resort (founded in 1894), sits at the drive's highest point, offering stunning views and an unfussy restaurant serving "mountain cooking" staples such as fresh trout and country ham.

Can't get enough? Where Skyline Drive ends at Waynesboro, the equally spectacular (some say more so) Blue Ridge Parkway picks up, following the dips and curves of the mountain crest south through Virginia to Tennessee's Great Smoky Mountains.

WHAT: site, experience, hotel. **SKYLINE DRIVE:** begins at Front Royal (90 miles southwest of Washington, D.C.) in the north and runs to Waynesboro in the south. **SHENANDOAH NATIONAL PARK:** tel 540-999-3500; www. nps.gov/shen. *Cost:* $10 per car. **SKYLAND RESORT:** tel 888-896-3833 or 540-743-5108, fax 540-743-7883; www.visitshenandoah.com. *Cost:* doubles from $95 with valley views. *When:* open late Mar–Nov. **BEST TIMES:** mid-May for the annual Wildflower Weekend; Oct for the vibrant fall foliage; 2d weekend in Oct for Front Royal's Festival of Leaves.

A Gourmet Sanctuary
in the Blue Ridge Mountains

THE INN AT LITTLE WASHINGTON

Washington, Virginia, U.S.A.

Is this really the most romantic country house in the world? You'll be hard-pressed to find one that has garnered as many awards and accolades for its wonderful combination of restaurant, accommodations, and setting.

Built in 1749 at the foothills of the Blue Ridge Mountains and in the middle of Virginia hunt country, today "Little" Washington has a population of just 180, unless you count the politicos who limo in from "Big" Washington, D.C., and who revere this as a sort of heavenly escape from the stress of running America. Patrons like these are accustomed to the best. They leave smitten, singing The Inn's praises—it has been called a gastronome's nirvana, a work of art. The cuisine defies a pigeonhole, appearing at times nouvelle, regional, country or haute American. Both the fourteen perfectly appointed guest rooms and the meals are infused with a theatrical flair, but with an appropriate level of restraint. George Washington did not sleep here. His loss.

WHAT: hotel, restaurant. **WHERE:** Middle and Main Sts., Washington (67 miles west of Washington, D.C.). Tel 540-675-3800, fax 540-675-3100; www.theinnatlittlewashington. com. **COST:** doubles from $410 (low season), from $655 (high season). Dinner from $150.

Lauded as one of the country's premier gourmet getaways

A Re-created Day in the Life of a Royal Capital

COLONIAL WILLIAMSBURG

Williamsburg, Virginia, U.S.A.

Meticulously re-creating the crucial period of 1750–1775—the end of the colonial era—this amazingly detailed open-air living history museum is peopled by blacksmiths, carpenters, saddle makers, wig makers,

apothecaries, "slaves" (who made up more than half the town's population in the 18th century), freemen, gentry, and merchants, all dressed in period garb and ready to engage visitors in impromptu conversation. Named after William III, Williamsburg served as Virginia's capital from 1699 to 1780. In 1926, John D. Rockefeller Jr. initiated and financed (to the tune of $68 million) a top-to-bottom restoration so scrupulous and historically accurate that today it's impossible to tell which of the 500 buildings were restored and which were totally reconstructed. Standouts are the Georgian-style Governor's Palace, with extensive topiary gardens and holly maze; the Capitol; the Courthouse, fronted by pillories and stocks; and the George Wythe House, once the home of Thomas Jefferson.

Educational programs and engaging lectures take place around town, and Colonial Williamsburg's Fife and Drums parades really get the patriotic juices flowing. You might come face to face with Thomas Jefferson, Martha Washington, or the rabble-rousing Patrick Henry, plus a wide cast of townspeople going about their daily lives and completely immersed in their characters. Four historic dining taverns in town promise period atmosphere and menus that include regional favorites—just don't expect haute gourmet. Josiah Chowning's is probably the most authentic of the bunch, while Christiana Campbell's once served a hungry George Washington—the real one.

The elegant 1937 Williamsburg Inn is the showpiece of the nonprofit Colonial Williamsburg Foundation's lodging choices. For less extravagant but more authentic accommodations, the inn also manages twenty-eight restored Colonial Houses scattered about the cobbled streets of the Historic Area.

WHAT: site, hotel. **COLONIAL WILLIAMSBURG:** 150 miles south of Washington, D.C., 150 miles southeast of Charlottesville. Tel 800-HISTORY or 757-220-7645; www.colonialwilliamsburg.org. *Cost:* admission $37 for 1 day. **WILLIAMSBURG INN:** 136 East Francis St. Tel 800-447-8679 or 757-229-1000, fax 757-220-7096. *Cost:* doubles from $390 (low season), from $490 (high season). **COLONIAL HOUSES:**

Fifers and drummers were an integral part of Virginia's 18th-century military.

check in at 302-B East Francis St. Tel 800-447-8679 or 757-229-1000. *Cost:* double rooms from $150 (low season), from $200 (high season). **BEST TIMES:** school vacation periods mean big crowds. The Christmas holidays kick off the 1st week of Dec, featuring strolling carolers, candlelight concerts, and other events.

Where Seattle Goes to Decaffeinate

SAN JUAN ISLANDS

Puget Sound, Washington, U.S.A.

T ucked between the Washington coast and Canada, and with the Olympic Mountains and the Fuji-like volcanoes of the Cascades serving as its dramatic backdrop, Puget Sound is one of the most naturally majestic and distinctive corners of the Pacific Northwest. In its northern reaches, the archipelago of the San Juan Islands has remained relatively undeveloped despite its beautiful scenery and proximity to Seattle, whose rainy climate it does not share. The archipelago is made up of hundreds of islands if you count the rocky outcroppings, but just forty are inhabited. Sportsmen come from around the world to sail or kayak, fish for salmon and trout, decompress, or cycle on more than 500 miles of rolling country roads. Three pods of mischievous orcas, about ninety total, call these cold waters home—this was where they filmed *Free Willy*—as do many seals and dolphins. Bald eagles are a common sight overhead.

The three most visited islands in the chain are the relatively flat San Juan, the most populous and commercial (come here for some of America's best whale-watching, and for its fine Whale Museum); Orcas, the largest (57 square miles), hilliest, and most scenically varied; and the tranquil and bucolic Lopez, a legendarily friendly island.

Many consider Orcas the most beautiful, and among its many inns and bed-and-breakfasts the Turtleback Farm Inn is unique in many respects. It's a working farm set on 80 private acres of sheep- and cow-grazing meadows, woods, and duck ponds, with a green clapboard farmhouse that dates back to the late 1800s. Every night is romantic in any of its eleven elegant, uncluttered guest rooms, and every morning is special thanks to a prizewinning breakfast so memorable that it's featured regularly in food magazines (as well as in the inn's own *Turtleback Cookbook*).

WHAT: island, hotel. **SAN JUAN ISLANDS:** passenger ferries leave from Seattle during summer; passenger and car ferries from Anacortes, 90 miles north of Seattle year-round. The boat ride from Anacortes to Lopez (the closest of the islands) is 45 minutes. San Juan Islands Visitor Information, tel 888-468-3701 or 360-378-9551; www.visitsanjuans. com. **TURTLEBACK FARM INN:** Crow Valley Rd., Orcas. Tel 800-376-4914 or 360-376-4914; www.turtlebackinn.com. **COST:** doubles from $100 (low season), from $115 (high season), includes breakfast. **BEST TIMES:** mid-May through Aug for whale watching; mid-Aug for the 4-day San Juan (Island) County Fair. Jun and Sept get smaller crowds, though they can also see more rain. Avoid Nov, the rainiest month.

A Waterfront Microcosm of Seattle

PIKE PLACE MARKET

Seattle, Washington, U.S.A.

Seattle is virtually surrounded by water, so any visit to this growing Pacific Rim metropolis should begin on the waterfront, within earshot of the gulls and foghorns, among the harbors that have always been its lifeblood.

On Elliott Bay in the area of the Sea Aquarium, the exuberant Pike Place Market has been a Seattle institution since 1907, making it the oldest continuously operating farmer's market in the United States. A tourist trap loved by locals and visitors alike, it sprawls across seven city blocks and fills sixteen multilevel buildings with 600 vendors speaking dozens of different languages. Amazingly, it has remained largely unchanged through much of its colorful life, with wise-cracking fishmongers still screaming "Fish up!" or "Low-flying fish!" before tossing their catch like so many footballs for the amusement of passersby. The variety of the seafood is astonishing—witness local specialties like just-caught Dungeness crab, coho salmon, halibut, diver-caught pink scallops from the nearby San Juan Islands, spot prawns (Northwest shrimp), and clams and oysters chilling on mountains of shaved ice.

The city that gave the world Starbucks promises a caffeine fix at every turn (the original Starbucks opened in 1971 and is found here in the market) as well as jewelry, tchotchkes, crusty fresh-baked bread, a

A fishmonger at the Pike Place Market shows his fresh wares.

meadow's worth of cut flowers, and the chance to graze your way around the globe. Paired with local produce, the bounty of these waters (once destined only for distant markets) and the city's ever-growing Asian population make for a remarkably sophisticated dining scene.

Though you'll never go hungry at Pike Place or anywhere else in Seattle, the fifteen-minute taxi ride to the city's best-known waterside restaurant, Ray's Boathouse, is worth every penny. It's a Seattle classic—shorts and sandals upstairs on the popular summertime deck, and a more refined eatery downstairs, all with the city's best view of Shilshole Bay. This is your Seattle Moment: watch the sun go down over Puget Sound and the towering Olympic Mountains while enjoying straightforward, unfussy, incredibly fresh fish such as the grilled black cod marinated in sake.

WHAT: site, restaurant. **PIKE PLACE MARKET:** info booth and principal entrance at First Ave. and Pike Pl. **RAY'S BOATHOUSE:** 6049 Seaview Ave. Tel 206-789-3770; rays@rays.com; www.rays.com. *Cost:* dinner $45. *When:* lunch and dinner daily. **BEST TIMES:** Jun–Sept for clear skies; late May for the 1-weekend Pike Place Market Street Festival.

A Shrine to American Heroes

THE NATIONAL MALL AND ITS MONUMENTS

Washington, D.C., U.S.A.

"Hanging out at the mall" takes on a decidedly different meaning at Washington, D.C.'s version, an emerald-green esplanade that serves as America's Main Street and Town Square. The place where protesters protest, where locals take their dogs to romp, and where interns spend their lunch hours sunbathing, it's also the vital first stop on any visitor's tour of Washington.

To the surprise of many visitors—who bring the kids out of a sense of patriotism or to further their education—the seat of American government, with all its monumental trappings, is also a beautiful city. Founded in 1791, it was the first planned capital city in the world, purpose-built from marshy woodland. Today its green, 2-mile-long National Mall is lined with the city's most important monuments and museums, with the U.S. Capitol at the eastern end, the Lincoln Memorial at the western end, and the stark Washington Monument in between.

The Washington Monument was the first constructed on the Mall, and was completed in 1884, thrusting skyward 555 feet and offering spectacular 360-degree views from its peak. Its image is mirrored in a slender reflecting pool that stretches westward to the steps of the neoclassical Lincoln Memorial, from which the somber Civil War president gazes out, the powerful words of his Gettysburg Address engraved behind him, leaving few unmoved. This area of the Mall is particularly beautiful when illuminated at night or when its thousands of cherry blossom trees (presented to the nation by the Japanese in 1912) burst into bloom.

South of the Washington Monument on the banks of the Tidal Basin, the serenely classical Jefferson Memorial appears like a temple. The 19-foot bronze statue of the third president stands beneath the graceful columned rotunda, surrounded by passages from the Declaration of Independence. Erected in 1997, the Franklin Delano Roosevelt Memorial is the Mall's most recent presidential addition, comprising four outdoor galleries (one for each of the president's terms in office) and a series of statues depicting Roosevelt, his wife Eleanor, and his famous dog Fala. Near the Lincoln Memorial, the V-shaped Vietnam Memorial is perhaps the most moving of all. A simple black granite wall set into the earth, it's inscribed with the names of the 58,209 American men and women who gave their lives in America's longest war, or remain missing as a result. The WWII Memorial is the Mall's most recent addition.

The grassy Ellipse, north of the Washington Monument, links the Mall to the White House, one of the world's most famous residences. Most (sometimes all) of the White House's 132 rooms (and 32 bathrooms) are off limits, and don't even ask about seeing the Oval Office. (Check with the tourist office for visiting possibilities; if tours are available, tickets are required.) Somewhere in every tourist's jam-packed itinerary, time should also be made to tour the Capitol, the Library of Congress, and the National Archives. So much to see, so little time . . .

If your invitation for a night in the Lincoln Bedroom hasn't come through, settle for a room at the 1927 Italian Renaissance–style Hay-Adams Hotel, directly across Pennsylvania Avenue, with White House views from some of the more expensive rooms. Since 1928, it's been a home away from home for diplomats and visiting heads of state. Or head for the spot where Washingtonians bring out-of-town friends: the rooftop bar of the Hotel Washington, for the city's best view of the White House and Treasury.

WHAT: site, experience, hotel. **WASHINGTON MALL:** for tourist information, tel 202-485-9880, www.nps.gov/nama. Also the Washington, D.C., Convention and Tourism Corporation, tel 800-422-8644 or 202-789-7000; www.washington.org. *Cost:* admission free to all monuments. **HAY-ADAMS HOTEL:** 800 16th St. NW. Tel 800-853-6807 or 202-638-6600, fax 202-638-2716; www.hayadams.com. *Cost:* doubles from $299. **HOTEL WASHINGTON:** Pennsylvania Ave. at 15th St. Tel 202-661-2400; www.hotelwashington.com. *Cost:* doubles from $370. **BEST TIMES:** late Mar/Apr for Cherry Blossom Festival; late spring and fall for the best weather.

Repository of American Heritage

THE SMITHSONIAN AND BEYOND

Washington, D.C., U.S.A.

Once referred to as "the nation's attic," the Smithsonian Institution is the largest museum and research complex in the world, with eighteen museums (sixteen of them in Washington) and over 142 million works of art and other specimens—and admission is free. The Institution's National Air and Space Museum is one of the most visited museums in the world, a must-see for kids of all ages and the parents they drag behind. Don't miss Charles Lindbergh's *Spirit of St. Louis*, the Apollo spacecrafts, or the always great IMAX films. The Freer Gallery of Art and the Arthur

The National Air and Space Museum's Milestones of Flight Gallery

M. Sackler Gallery (to which it is connected by an underground tunnel) display one of the finest collections of Asian art in the world. The National Museum of African Art boasts a vast collection of both traditional and contemporary art from the entire continent of Africa, while the National Museum of Natural History draws crowds for its looming dinosaurs and the huge 45½-carat Hope Diamond. The cylindrical Hirshhorn Museum and Sculpture Garden, built around a gift of some 11,500 works from its namesake collector, is like a joyous crash course in 20th-century art. The list of the Smithsonian's properties goes on and on.

Among Washington's trove of fifty-some museums, many are gathered in front of the Capitol building, where the grassy Mall unfurls. Among them, the showpiece is the National Gallery of Art, one of the world's greatest museums and one of the American Big Three (along with the Metropolitan in New York and the Art Institute of Chicago). Jazzed up in 1978 by an I. M. Pei addition (his best-known American work), the sedate building houses a beautifully displayed selection of Dutch and Flemish masters, French Impressionists, and a poetic portrait of Ginevra de' Benci (1474), the only oil by Leonardo da Vinci in the Western hemisphere. For quality and quantity of masterworks, this would be a good place to spend your day.

Farther afield from the Mall, the Phillips

Collection was the country's first museum of modern art, housed in a beautiful neo-Georgian mansion that was once the home of its namesake collector. To the south, the Corcoran Gallery is home to the best collection of 19th-century art in the world. Undoubtedly the most powerful and sobering experience in town is the Holocaust Memorial Museum, dedicated to the victims of Nazi genocide between 1933 and 1945. And where else but Washington would you find the International Spy Museum, which demystifies many espionage secrets from throughout the ages and around the globe.

For those in search of the city's more intimate, unsung gems, there is Dumbarton Oaks, with its wonderful collections of Byzantine and Pre-Columbian works housed in a gorgeous mansion among elaborate, terraced gardens. In the northwest, overlooking Rock Creek Park, the Hillwood Museum and Gardens was once the forty-room Georgian home of Marjorie Merriweather Post, the cereal heiress and socialite. Today, it brims with her immense collection of decorative objects from France and imperial Russia, including icons and Fabergé eggs.

WHAT: site. **SMITHSONIAN INSTITUTION:** Smithsonian Information Center, 1000 Jefferson Dr. (on the Mall). Tel 202-633-1000; www.smithsonian.org. *Cost:* admission free. Also the Washington Visitors Bureau, tel 800-422-8644 or 202-789-7000; www.washington.org. **NATIONAL GALLERY OF ART:** on the Mall between 3rd and 9th Sts. at Constitution Ave. NW. Tel 202-737-4215; www.nga.gov. *Cost:* admission free. **PHILLIPS COLLECTION:** 1600 21st St. NW, at Q St. Tel 202-387-2151; www.phillipscollection.org. *Cost:* weekdays free; $10 for weekends, special exhibits. **THE UNITED STATES HOLOCAUST MEMORIAL MUSEUM:** south of the Mall and Independence Ave. SW, between 14th St. and Raoul Wallenberg Pl. Tel 202-488-0400; www.ushmm.org. *Cost:* admission free, but timed passes required for permanent exhibition; www.tickets.com, tel 800-400-9373. **INTERNATIONAL SPY MUSEUM:** 800 F St. NW. Tel 866-SPY-MUSEUM or 202-EYE-SPY-U; www.spymuseum.org. *Cost:* admission \$15. **DUMBARTON OAKS:** 1703 32nd St. NW. Tel 202-339- 6401; www.

doaks.org. *Cost:* museum admission free; gardens \$8 Mar–Oct (free Nov–Feb). **HILLWOOD MUSEUM AND GARDENS:** 4155 Linnean Ave. NW. Tel 877-HILLWOOD or 202-686-5807, fax 202-966-7846; www.hillwoodmuseum.org. *Cost:* reservations and \$12 deposit required.

Running the Rivers of the Mountain State

WEST VIRGINIA'S WHITE-WATER RAFTING

West Virginia, U.S.A.

With some of the largest thrills-per-rapid ratios anywhere in North America, West Virginia's rivers are regularly ranked among the top ten white-water runs in the world, passing through a landscape so rugged

(and so similar to that of Idaho and Colorado) that it's often referred to as the West of the East. Most outfitters suggest getting your feet wet in the poorly named New River (actually the second oldest river in the world after the Nile), which has as many calm stretches as white water pools. A 53-mile stretch at the upper part of the river's full 230-mile length has been named as a national scenic river, and in summer is so calm you could even bring Grandma along.

In the south-central part of the state, amid deep gorges and rough, wooded Appalachian terrain, the intimidating Gauley River is the state's most challenging—narrower, longer, and twice as steep as the New River. During "Fall Release," when the dam is opened for twenty-three days in early September to lower man-made Summersville Lake, the powerful river is the place to be for steep drops with names like Heaven Help You and Pure Screaming (you get the idea) and nonstop back-to-back class IV and V rapids. Your adrenaline will still be pumping long after your river ride is over.

WHAT: experience. **WHERE:** 310 miles southwest of Washington, D.C. For general information and a list of the 30-some licensed outfitters in the state, contact the West Virginia Division of Tourism, tel 800-225-5982; www. callwva.com. **HOW:** Wildwater Expeditions, Lansing. Tel 800-982-7238 or 304-658-4007; www.wvaraft.com. **WHEN:** New River, April–late Oct; Gauley, 6 consecutive weekends beginning the week after Labor Day. **COST:** 1-day New River trips from \$79; 1-day Gauley trips from \$110. Multiple-day camping trips available.

West Virginia boasts some of the world's best white-water rafting.

Southern Comfort

THE GREENBRIER

White Sulphur Springs, West Virginia, U.S.A.

Like West Virginia's wealth of river-rafting venues, the Greenbrier also owes its fame to water—in this case the sulfur-rich springs that long ago made it the summer capital of the Old South. It continues to attract pilgrims eager to "take the cure," including twenty-six U.S. presidents, from James Monroe on through George Bush the Younger. Begun as a cluster of cabins in the 1800s and later transformed into a stately, pillared, 600-plus-room hotel, the Greenbrier stands grandly amid 6,500 acres in a scenic valley of the Allegheny Mountains and promises more than fifty activities. Golf is the leading attraction, with three 18-hole golf courses that are regarded as among the best in the world. The Golf Digest Academy, opened in 1999, promises to share the secrets of "The Slammer" Sam Snead, while a 30,000-square-foot spa and ten tennis courts assure that nongolfers will hardly feel neglected.

The Greenbrier's 1,800 employees are part of the hotel's elegance and decorum. Expect musicians at teatime in the spacious, marble-floored lobby and later at dinner, where a jacket-and-tie dress code prevails beneath sparkling UFO-sized crystal chandeliers. However, Dorothy Draper's trademark postwar decor isn't necessarily what you'd expect, featuring a bold mix of stripes and flowers and an unconventionally bright color palate. All in all, it can make the hotel look like Buckingham Palace on psychedelics, and may not be for everybody—and that's if the high prices don't get you first (a consequence of many amenities not being included in the room rates). The hotel will always be associated with wealth, power, and prestige—so much so that it has its own underground fallout shelter, built during the Eisenhower administration and intended to house members of Congress in the event of nuclear war. The size of two football fields, the bunker was finally declassified after the *Washington Post* reported its existence in 1992, and is now open for tours. Weirdly enough, its spacious kitchen and cafeteria is now the site of the Greenbrier's Culinary Arts Center, which offers courses year-round.

WHAT: hotel. **WHERE:** 250 miles southwest of Washington, D.C. Tel 800-624-6070 or 304-536-1110; www.greenbrier.com. **COST:** $275 per person (low season), $400 per person (high season), includes breakfast, dinner, and use of some facilities. **BEST TIMES:** during holiday periods for the festive atmosphere; during Oct foliage time, which coincides with the local T.O.O.T. (Taste of Our Town) festival, held in nearby Lewisburg on the 2d weekend in Oct.

The stately Greenbrier in the Allegheny Mountains

The Great Lakes' Best-Kept Secret

APOSTLE ISLANDS

Bayfield, Wisconsin, U.S.A.

M isnamed by French missionaries who thought these islands numbered twelve instead of twenty-two, the heavily forested Apostles begin just a mile off the Lake Superior coastline and spread out for 600 square miles,

with the outermost lying some 20 miles offshore. Of their number, only one is residential, with the other twenty-one (plus a slice of the Bayfield Peninsula) comprising the Apostle Islands National Lakeshore, an area of unspoiled wilderness amid the world's largest spring-fed body of water—so huge (363 by 160 miles) that you can see its outline from the moon.

Nature is central here, with opportunities for barefoot beachcombing, bird watching (the islands become a refuge for some 100 migratory bird species in fall), nostalgic exploration of the six lighthouses, and kayaking in and around numerous coves and caves, from duck-your-head grottoes to cathedral-sized caverns.

All kinds of inter-island excursions can be arranged in the gateway village of Bayfield (pop. 686), including fishing and boating trips and drop-offs for hikers and campers (there are more than 50 miles of trails, as well as

official campsites on Stockton and seventeen of the other islands). Back on terra firma, the best place to recuperate from your camping holiday is the Old Rittenhouse Inn, a lovingly renovated, antiques-filled Victorian home that offers first-rate lake views and excellent dinners starring the lake's daily catch.

WHAT: island, hotel. **APOSTLE ISLANDS:** Bayfield is 90 miles east of Duluth, Minnesota, 350 miles northeast of Minneapolis-St. Paul. For national park information, tel 715-779-3397; www.nps.gov/apis. *When:* boat excursions arranged in town from mid-May–mid-Oct. **OLD RITTENHOUSE INN:** 301 Rittenhouse Ave. Tel 800-611-4667 or 715-779-5111; www.rittenhouseinn.com. *Cost:* doubles from $115. Prix fixe dinner $55. *When:* hotel open year-round; restaurant open year-round for dinner; open for lunch mid-May to mid-Oct. **BEST TIMES:** Jul and Aug for warm weather and calm waters; Sept for the annual Lighthouse Celebration.

Some Serious R&R&R: Rest, Relaxation, and Romance

CANOE BAY

Chetek, Wisconsin, U.S.A.

O nce a Seventh Day Baptist retreat, this secluded resort in Wisconsin's heavily forested Indianhead Region was re-created for the exclusive enjoyment of just nineteen couples, with no kids, no motorboats, no phones

An ideal spot for couples to rest and recharge

in the rooms, and no activities director to disturb the serenity. Exquisite lakeside rooms and cottages—each with fieldstone fireplace and double whirlpools—recall the genius of Wisconsin native Frank Lloyd Wright and blend perfectly with their woodland surroundings. It was, in fact, John Rattenbury, Wright's protégé and collaborator on New York City's Guggenheim Museum, who in 2000 designed the inn's hilltop Rattenbury Cottage, which elevates the property's naturalistic yet sophisticated style to another level.

More than 4 miles of scenic trails wind throughout the inn's 280 forested acres, where a panoply of wildlife—deer, pheasants, loons, and geese—lives around the shore of three hidden lakes. Most guests take breakfast in bed, go canoeing in pristine waters, reserve an in-room massage, then make an appearance at dinner, enjoying each day's new menu (and a selection from the 700-bottle wine list) in a candlelit restaurant with floor-to-ceiling windows that bring you face-to-face with the magic of Lake Wahdoon's sunsets.

WHAT: hotel. **WHERE:** 28 Rt. 8 (120 miles east of Minneapolis, 350 miles northwest of Chicago). Tel 800-568-1995 or 715-924-4594, fax 715-924-2078; www.canoebay.com. **COST:** doubles from $350 (low season), Rattenbury Cottage from $875. Prix fixe chef's menu $75. **BEST TIMES:** Jun–Aug to partake in the lake's offerings; first half of Oct for peak fall foliage.

The Golf Shrine of the Midwest

THE AMERICAN CLUB

Kohler, Wisconsin, U.S.A.

The American Club is a classy, top-rank all-around vacation resort, especially if your sport of choice is golf. Of the Club's mega-golf complex, Blackwolf Run's two 18-hole courses (Meadow Valleys and River) were naturally sculpted by glacier runoff tens of thousands of years ago, then refined by world-renowned course architect Pete Dye, who proclaimed upon their opening in 1988 that "there could not be a better natural setting for golf." Dye also designed the two built-from-scratch Whistling Straits courses whose undulating, windy links unfold along the Lake Michigan shoreline—the critically acclaimed Straits and The Irish, opened in 1998 and 2000 respectively and host of the PGA Tournament in 2004, a rare honor for such a new course. Each is a walking course and requires a caddy. The visionary behind the American Club,

Herbert Kohler Jr. (of designer plumbing products fame) wanted the course to emulate the great Ballybunion, and the result is so successful you could easily believe you're on the coast of Ireland.

In 1981, Kohler was responsible for transforming a redbrick, Tudor-style 1918 rooming house into the American Club's hub. Built originally for the workers employed at the bathroom fixtures factory across the street, it is now a grand, ivy-covered manor house of uncommon luxury, with mammoth in-suite bathrooms. Those seeking pampering after or instead of their round of golf can partake of fifty-five treatments at the new, state-of-the-art, 16,000-square-foot Kohler Waters Spa, which, naturally, showcases the family's plumbing legacy. (Incidentally, *everything* around here is named Kohler, as the family has dominated the area since opening its company in 1873.) Afterward, head for the hotel's refined Immigrant Restaurant and Winery, featuring six different ethnic-themed rooms designed to reflect the groups who once lived and worked here. Wisconsin's heritage of dairy farming and German immigrant cuisine are acknowledged on the menu at the hotel's publike Horse and Plow, with its signature three-cheese soup and grilled Sheboygan sausage sampler—plus a choice of at least eighty regional bottled beers and twelve Wisconsin beers on tap.

WHAT: experience, hotel, restaurant. **WHERE:** 444 Highland Dr. (55 miles north of Milwaukee, 135 miles north of Chicago). For hotel and to book tee times, tel 800-344-2838 or 920-457-8000, fax 920-457-0299; www. destinationkohler.com. *Cost:* doubles from $180 (low season), from $285 (high season). Dinner at the Immigrant Restaurant $75; at the Horse and Plow $30. **BEST TIMES:** golf season is generally May–Oct, with Aug the best of the best for weather (but you'll need to book 6 weeks in advance).

A Governor Suite at the American Club

*The World's Largest Outdoor Rodeo and Western Collection—
The "Daddy of 'Em All"*

CHEYENNE FRONTIER DAYS

Cheyenne, Wyoming, U.S.A.

The Cowboy State's capital city was once nicknamed Hell on Wheels, and during the annual ride-'em-cowboy Frontier Days celebration you'll understand why. It was first held in 1897, a mere fifteen years after William Frederick Cody, better known as Buffalo Bill, created the rodeo tradition with his traveling Wild West Show. Today's event is a ten-day carnival of rodeos, wild-horse races, marching bands, big-name country and rock concerts, inter-tribal Indian dancing, a chuck-wagon cook-off, free pancake breakfasts (at which more than 75,000 flapjacks and 475 gallons of syrup are consumed), and a parade that's been led by some memorable names over the years—Buffalo Bill himself in 1898, and an enthusiastic Teddy Roosevelt in 1910. Rodeo is a major sport these days, with big-name sponsors and growing television coverage, so it's no surprise that Frontier Days brings upward of 500,000 visitors to Cheyenne every year, many decked out in their finest Western wear.

A magnet for cowboys and cowboy wannabes

More than 1,800 of the toughest cowboys from across the nation compete in standing-room-only events such as bull riding, calf roping, steer wrestling (also called bulldogging), and the classic saddle and bareback bronc riding, with a purse of $1 million being split up among the winners.

In addition to Cheyenne's events, the Professional Rodeo Cowboys Association sanctions about 680 rodeos yearly, including those in Houston (March); Cody, Wyoming (July 4th); Pendleton, Oregon (September); and the year's finals in Las Vegas (December).

WHAT: event. **WHERE:** at the 83-acre Frontier Park Arena (12 miles from the Colorado border, 100 miles north of Denver). Cheyenne Frontier Days, tel 800-227-6336 or 307-778-7222; www.cfdrodeo.com. **COST:** rodeo tickets $12–$26; concert tickets $28–$79. **WHEN:** 10 days in late Jul. **BEST TIMES:** Wed for an aerial performance by the U.S. Thunderbirds Air Force drill team.

A Surreal, Almost Spiritual Geologic Wonder

GRAND TETON NATIONAL PARK

Wyoming, U.S.A.

L ess lofty and snowy than many other American mountain ranges, the dozen peaks of the Teton Range still win America's geologic beauty pageant as the most photogenic of them all. Often referred to as the Grand Tetons

(though "Grand Teton" properly refers only to the highest of the twelve), they are so divinely proportioned that early 19th-century French-Canadian trappers gave them their lasting nickname—which translates, straightforwardly enough, as "the big breasts." Craggy, glacier chiseled, and rising up to 7,000 feet above the flat floor of Wyoming's Jackson Hole Valley (itself about 6,400 feet above sea level), they're the youngest mountains in the Rockies and comprise a relatively small park area of 310,000 acres—one-sixth the size of

neighboring Yellowstone. Not even the slightest foothill blocks your full frontal view, making it easy for even nonpros to get that Ansel Adams photo shot.

At the foot of the range, glacial advance gouged a string of deep, cold, sapphire-blue lakes, of which Jenny Lake is one of the most beautiful and therefore most popular and visited. From here you can set off on the impressive Cascade Canyon Trail or to the cascading Hidden Falls and impressive Inspiration Point. With 230 miles of trails,

Grand Teton National Park is made for hikers. The largest lake, Jackson Lake, is 15 miles long, with cruises to Elk Island and along its western shore, where the mountains begin. Guided float trips let you meander down a calm stretch of the Snake River from Deadman's Bar to Moose. The 45-mile loop drive from Moose via Moran Junction presents much of the same spectacular scenery, but without leaving terra firma.

The popular Jenny Lake Lodge, one of the nicest and best-sited of the park's accommodations—and one of the most expensive in the entire national park system—originated as a dude ranch accommodating the Eastern effete who came to rough it for a few weeks. The elegant lodge is often booked a year in advance for those who don't care to rough it at all. Above all else, don't miss dinner in the lodge's timbered dining hall.

WHAT: site, hotel. **GRAND TETON NATIONAL PARK:** headquarters and Visitor Center is at Moose, 12 miles north of Jackson, 7 miles south of Yellowstone National Park. Tel 307-739-3300; www.nps.gov/grte. *Cost:* admission $25 per car (includes entrance into

Yellowstone), valid for 7 days. **JENNY LAKE LODGE:** contact the Grand Teton Lodge Company, tel 800-628-9988 or 307-733-4647. *Cost:* $585 double occupancy for cabins, includes breakfast, 5-course dinner, horseback riding, and use of bicycles. *When:* open early May–early Oct. **BEST TIMES:** Jul–Aug are warmest and busiest, with more than 900 varieties of wildflowers in full bloom; Jun–Sept for moose sightings; Jun (for early wildflowers) and Sept (for fall foliage) are less crowded.

Often voted America's most beautiful mountains

The East Goes West

AMANGANI

Jackson, Wyoming, U.S.A.

H otel junkies who collect the special properties of the world the way some souvenir hunters do swizzle sticks know all about Amangani, the long-awaited first North American property of Asia-based Aman Resorts.

An elegant vision perched at 7,000 feet on the edge of the East Gros Ventre Butte, it became an instant celebrity-magnet the minute it opened, living up both to its hype and its name, a mixture of Sanskrit and Shoshone that means "peaceful home." The Amangani's Asian sib-

lings are known for pampering service, minimalist decor that celebrates the exotic and ethnic, and a sense of Asian serenity. Here the design of the three-story complex of stone, glass, and wood is cool and modern, and both reflects and blends with the natural surroundings. Its spare lobby is marked by a 36-foot ceiling and a two-story glass wall that brings the outside in with larger-than-life westward views of Jackson Hole's mountain meadows and the snow-capped peaks of the Snake and Teton Ranges (a view that's also available from each of the forty suites). Sunsets here are a religious experience, but days aren't so far behind, whether you drink in the valley panoramas from the cliff-side year-round heated pool, allow yourself to be wrapped and kneaded at the adjacent spa, or partake of the four-season smorgasbord of outdoor diversions. **WHAT:** hotel. **WHERE:** 5 miles west of Jackson, 12 miles from Grand Teton National Park, and adjacent to Spring Creek Ranch (see following entry). Tel 877-734-7333 or 307-734-7333, fax 307-734-7332; www.aman resorts.com. **COST:** doubles from $565 (for room only). **BEST TIMES:** late May for Old West Days weekend; Jul 4th for Jackson's "Music in the Hole" Concert.

Smack in the Middle of American Grandeur

JACKSON HOLE

Jackson, Wyoming, U.S.A.

Aformer fur-trading cow town at the foot of "America's Alps," Jackson has evolved into a delightful tourist town that borders on the cosmopolitan. The feared faux glamour they call "Aspenization" has so far been kept at bay, and the town's plank boardwalks, old storefronts, and folksy small-town friendliness remain. Drop by time-worn hangouts like Bubba's Bar-B-Que (on Broadway) and the Million Dollar Cowboy Bar on the town square, where lots of local folk fill the house (and whose collection of Wild West Americana is worth a look-see). Jackson's location in the deep, scenic 48-mile-long Jackson Hole ("hole" is what settlers called a high, enclosed mountain valley) puts it within viewing range of some of America's most astounding scenery and prolific wildlife, while the valley's twisting Snake River, one of the country's cleanest, is well known to anglers and rafters.

Summer finds a steady stream of park goers here to visit Grand Teton and Yellowstone, but in winter all attention turns to the area's three major ski resorts, particularly the Jackson Hole Mountain Resort. Twelve miles from Jackson, it has one of America's greatest vertical drops (4,139 feet), some of its most varied terrain and longest runs, and a fearsome reputation for being extreme, cold, and tough. The deranged find pleasure on the vaunted east face of 10,450-foot Rendezvous Mountain, but half the resort's seventy-six named runs and 2,500 acres of awesomely skiable terrain are perfect for intermediates and even novices. Across the mountain, the snow

Spring Creek Ranch offers gorgeous views from every angle.

quality at Grand Targhee (45 miles from Jackson, connected by shuttle bus) is regularly voted best in the nation, with 500 inches of powder falling annually—a full 15 feet more than Jackson Hole.

On a spectacular expanse of 25,000 acres set aside by the government in 1912, the National Elk Refuge is the winter home for thousands of migrating elk, the largest herd in North America. You'll first start to hear them bugle in the fall during mating season, and from mid-December through March you can get up-close glimpses of them via a horse-drawn sleigh ride offered by the Fish and Wildlife Service in Jackson Hole.

If you stay in any of the elegant log cabins scattered about the 1,000-acre grounds of the Spring Creek Ranch, the only thing that can compete with the view is the ranch's acclaimed restaurant, The Granary, whose award-winning menu (think elk medallions and buffalo ten-derloin) is especially perfect when the outdoor deck is open during warm weather.

WHAT: town, site, experience, hotel, restaurant. **JACKSON:** 275 miles northeast of Salt Lake City. The airport, 10 miles from town, is located within Grand Teton National Park. Jackson Hole Chamber of Commerce, tel 307-733-3316; www.jacksonholechamber.com. **JACKSON HOLE MOUNTAIN RESORT:** tel 888-333-7766; www.jacksonhole.com. *When:* ski season is Dec to mid-Apr. **SPRING CREEK RANCH:** 5 miles west of Jackson at 1800 Spirit Dance Rd. Tel 800-443-6139 or 307-733-8833, fax 307-733-1524; www.spring creekranch.com. *Cost:* doubles from $170 (low season), from $340 (high season). Dinner at the Granary $55. **BEST TIMES:** Jan–Mar and Jul–Aug at the ski resort for the Grand Teton Music Festival; early Sept for the 9-day Fall Arts Festival; Feb–Mar for downhill skiing.

Dude Ranch Extraordinaire

BITTERROOT RANCH

Riverton, Wyoming, U.S.A.

In the embrace of a remote valley surrounded by the Shoshone National Forest and a 52,000-acre game and fish wildlife refuge, Mel and Bayard Fox own and operate this 1,300-acre horse ranch, breeding and training their Arabian beauties exclusively for the use of their twenty-eight guests, who bunk in hand-hewn log cabins scattered along the river that runs through the ranch. Horse-loving visitors will think they've died and gone to heaven. The availability of more than 100 prize specimens means guests can change horses frequently so mounts remain fresh and ready to go throughout the season. Within minutes, guests are totally immersed in a wilderness setting, in the competent hands of guides who know it intimately. Terrain is extremely varied: Riders pass from sagebrush plains and grassy meadows to rocky gorges that give way to forested mountains and alpine clearings.

WHAT: hotel, experience. **WHERE:** 26 miles northeast of Dubois. Airport transfers from Jackson or Riverton can be arranged. Tel 800-545-0019 or 307-455-3363, fax 307-455-2354; www.bitterrootranch.com. **COST:** from $1,785 per person per week (Sun–Sun), double occupancy, all-inclusive. **WHEN:** Jun–Sept. **BEST TIMES:** Jun and Jul, when wildflowers bloom in colorful profusion; Sept, when the aspen turn a glorious gold.

America's Preeminent Wildlife Preserve

YELLOWSTONE NATIONAL PARK

Wyoming, U.S.A.

Founded in 1872, America's (and the world's) oldest national park is best known for its geothermal features—remnants of its tumultuous volcanic past that Rudyard Kipling described as "the uplands of Hell." Visitors

flock to the Upper Geyser Basin in the southern half of the park to see 150 geysers, which together with the park's 10,000 bubbling mud pools, hissing fumaroles, and steaming hot springs act as pressure valves, releasing the heat and steam below. Yellowstone has 300 geysers total (about half of all the geysers in the world), but of them all Old Faithful is the superstar, sending a spray up to 184 feet into the air every 68 to 98 minutes. It's the world's most famous geyser, synonymous with Yellowstone in the minds of people everywhere.

The Old Faithful Inn was built on this site in 1904 and is still the largest log building in existence. Its creature-comforts-in-the-midst-of-utter-wilderness style set the fashion for all

the great lodges of the national park system. Unless you've booked a year in advance, it's not likely that you'll find room at this rustic, landmark inn, but at least peek in to see its awesome six-story lobby and massive four-sided fireplace and chimney made from 500 tons of volcanic rock. The restaurant's food is not remarkable, but the nearly face-to-face views of Old Faithful are. Among the park's nine properties, the more elegant Hotel on Lake Yellowstone is the oldest, completed in 1891.

Geothermal curiosities aren't the only thing Yellowstone has to offer: The second largest of America's national parks outside of Alaska, its natural diversity and abundant wildlife are some of the greatest on earth. The

Old Faithful is only one of Yellowstone's 300 geysers, but it is certainly the most beloved.

Grand Canyon of the Yellowstone River provides some of the park's most breathtaking views. Twenty-four miles long and up to 1,200 feet deep, it begins with the dramatic Lower Falls, which cascade 308 feet (nearly twice as high as Niagara Falls) into the river below. Bear and bison roam the Hayden Valley, the park's largest meadowland, alongside the 25,000 elk, 1,000 moose, and 148 bird species that call the 2.2-million-acre park home. Bald eagles soar overhead, and even the gray Rocky Mountain wolf—which the park did its best to eradicate in the 1930s—has returned, reintroduced in 1995.

Ninety-nine percent of the park's visitors never stray more than 3 miles from the road into the wilderness, and thus miss out on 1,200 miles of hiking trails and some of the most pristine wilderness in America. However, if you lack the time and/or inclination to hike, the figure-eight, 142-mile Grand Loop tour can't be beat, linking up with each of the park's five entrances and coming within sight of most major attractions.

WHAT: site, hotel. **YELLOWSTONE NATIONAL PARK:** in northwest Wyoming. There are 5 entrances located at the park's north, east, northeast, south, and west borders. Tel 307-344-7381; www.nps.gov/yell. *Cost:* $25 per car (includes entrance to Grand Teton National Park), good for 7 days. *When:* North and northeast entrances remain open year-round; others open early May–early Nov only. **OLD FAITHFUL INN:** central reservations for all Yellowstone Park lodges and some campsites, tel 307-344-7311; www.travelyellowstone.com. *Cost:* doubles from $125. *When:* open mid-May to mid-Oct. **BEST TIMES:** May through mid-Jun, Sept to mid-Oct (crowds are at their worst Jul–Aug); snowy winter months can be magical (2 park lodges remain open) and cross-country skiing is exceptional.

CANADA

Rocky Mountain High, Canada-Style

BANFF, JASPER, AND YOHO NATIONAL PARKS

Alberta, Canada

West of Edmonton and running north-south for more than 300 combined miles, Banff, Jasper, and Yoho national parks combine with several smaller parks to form the Rocky Mountain Parks World Heritage Site, one of the largest protected areas in the world. Alberta's three national parks alone draw almost 7 million visitors a year collectively. Beauty is the reason: rugged mountains and alpine meadows, spectacular waterfalls, glaciers and ice fields, deep canyons, and cold-water lakes that look like mirrored holes into another universe. At home in this landscape, elk, caribou, bighorn sheep, and black and grizzly bears frequently appear—a boon for camera-toting wildlife enthusiasts—while a number of grand hotels built by the Canadian Pacific Railway in the late 19th century number among the most beautiful, classic accommodations in North America.

Banff was Canada's very first national park, incorporated as a tiny 10-square-mile parcel in 1885 and now grown into a 2,656-square-mile giant that's Canada's number-one destination. Its most famous sites are Lake Louise and Moraine Lake, both surrounded by towering, snow-capped mountains that reflect in their otherworldly jade-green waters (the product of mineral-rich silt washing down from the surrounding glaciers). Louise has the greater name recognition due to its large ski area, its resort village, and its famous Fairmont Chateau Lake Louise, a sumptuous, turreted Edwardian dream that's probably the greatest of the Rocky Mountain hotels.

An ice castle at majestic Fairmont Chateau Lake Louise

Moraine Lake, 8 miles east of Louise, is the beauty spot of choice for those seeking a less commercialized experience, with a hiking trail that skirts the lake's north shore beneath soaring 10,000-foot peaks. To the southeast, Johnston Canyon offers another excellent hiking opportunity, with a trail that passes between 100-foot cliffs, tunnels through living rock, crosses wooden footbridges, and comes within spraying distance of seven waterfalls on its way to a series of emerald pools known as the Inkpots.

South of here is the town of Banff, a surprisingly stylish place considering its wilderness location. The Fairmont Banff Springs Hotel stands in princely splendor south of the town's Bow River—another testament to the Canadian Pacific, with remarkable views, a great spa, a world-class golf course, and indulgent service.

Heading north, the Icefields Parkway links Lake Louise with Jasper National Park, along the way passing through a northern fantasy of hanging glaciers, deep river valleys and waterfalls, subalpine forests, and the Columbia Icefield, one of the largest accumulations of ice south of the Arctic Circle, covering nearly 116 square miles.

Jasper, Canada's largest national park in the Rocky Mountains, has rugged scenery and a less touristed vibe. Hiking opportunities abound, with popular trails snaking through narrow Maligne Canyon and beyond, and rafting trips available on the Athabasca and Sunwapta rivers. Fishermen enjoy angling on Maligne Lake (the largest of the Rockies' glacier-fed lakes), while the Miette Hot Springs offer soaks in outdoor pools, surrounded by forest and mountains.

West of Banff and Jasper, Yoho National Park—whose name derives from a Cree expression of wonder and reverence—is much smaller, covering about 507 square miles, with more than 250 miles of well-kept hiking trails. Its history is bound up with the Canadian Pacific, which in 1909 blasted a pair of tunnels right through the mountains. Today, you can watch trains enter and leave at the Lower Spiral Tunnels Viewpoint, 10 miles east of the town of Field, which sits approximately at the park's centerpoint. Here, at the park's visitor center, you can learn about the nearby Burgess Shale fossil digs, in which creatures from the Cambrian-era sea that covered this region have been discovered on the mountaintops. Organized hikes to the site depart from town.

Seven miles northwest of Field, glacier-fed Emerald Lake is one of Yoho's most popular destinations, a perfect mountain-rimmed spot for hiking, canoeing, and horseback riding. The area's Emerald Lake Lodge offers the park's best accommodations in twenty-four two-story chalets. Another 3 miles will take you to Takakkaw Falls, Canada's second highest, with a drop of 1,250 feet.

WHAT: site, hotel, experience. **BANFF NATIONAL PARK:** 80 miles/129 km west of Calgary. Tel 403-762-1550; www.pc.gc.ca/pn-np/ab/banff. *Cost:* $10 per person. **FAIRMONT CHATEAU LAKE LOUISE:** tel 800-441-1414 or 403-522-3511, fax 403-522-3834; chateau lakelouise@fairmont.com; www.fairmont.com/lakelouise. *Cost:* from $250 (low season), from $415 (high season). **FAIRMONT BANFF SPRINGS HOTEL:** Spray Ave., Banff. Tel 800-441-1414 or 403-762-2211, fax 403-762-5755; www.fairmont.com/banffsprings. *Cost:* from $235 (low season), from $415 (high season). **JASPER NATIONAL PARK:** 256 miles/412 km northwest of Calgary. Tel 780-852-6176; www.pc.gc.ca/jasper. *Cost:* $10 per person. **YOHO NATIONAL PARK:** 130 miles/209 km west of Calgary. Tel

250-343-6783; www.pc.gc.ca/pn-np/bc/yoho. Cost: $10 per person. **EMERALD LAKE LODGE:** tel 800-663-6336 or 403-410-7411, fax 403-410-7406; www.emeraldlakelodge. com. *Cost:* doubles from $165 (low season),

from $330 (high season). **BEST TIMES:** Jan–Mar for best skiing at Banff; late Jan/early Feb for Winterfest; mid-Jul to mid-Aug for the Banff Arts Festival; Sept–Oct for fall foliage; busiest months are Jul and Aug.

Riding Canada's Steel Spine

THE CANADIAN ROCKIES BY TRAIN

Alberta, Canada

Unlike its neighbor to the south, Canada has maintained a viable tradition of rail travel ever since the 1885 completion of the coast-to-coast Canadian Pacific Railway; an engineering marvel and "act of insane recklessness," it united the nation and saved isolated British Columbia from becoming an American territory. "If we can't export the scenery," declared William Van Horne, the first president of the CPR, "we'll import the tourists."

The rail's route through the Canadian Rockies has been touted as one of the world's most spectacular train rides, and rail fans shouldn't exhale until they've checked it off their list. Along a 2,250-mile stretch west of Alberta, a Texas-size province with the population of Philadelphia, the route passes hundreds of relatively young (in geological terms) 60-million-year-old peaks and spires, their granite and glacier-capped profiles edgy and dog-toothed. The views keep crescen-doing until you reach the monarch of the Canadian Rockies, Mount Robson, jutting 12,972 feet into the British Columbian sky.

Train enthusiasts have several options for exploring this inspiring and generally roadless country. The Rocky Mountaineer, the largest privately owned passenger rail service

in North America, is deservedly popular for its two-day, all-daylight train ride (night accommodations are off-train) east- or west-bound between Vancouver (BC) and Jasper, Banff, or Calgary (Alberta). Glass-domed observation cars promise horizon-to-horizon views of the passing show, and a good deal of attention is given to dining.

The same continent-straddling five-province rail tour can also be made by the national public train. VIA Rail's Art Deco–style cars make the 2,774-mile trip between Toronto and Vancouver in three days but also offer the option of an open ticket,

The Rocky Mountaineer offers stunning views.

allowing you to disembark and explore any of Canada's urban and rural treasures independently, then resume your trip at a later date. Corridor service links Toronto with the line's easternmost point in Halifax, Nova Scotia, completing the entire awesome, one-of-a-kind, 4,000-mile cross-country adventure.

What: experience. **Rocky Mountaineer Railway Tours:** tel 800-665-7245 or 604- 606-7245; www.rockymountaineer.com. *Cost:* 2-day tour from $550 all-inclusive, double occupancy; longer rail tours available. *When:* mid-Apr to mid-Oct. **Via Rail Canada:** tel 888-842-7245; www.viarail.ca. *Cost:* Toronto–Vancouver from $$1,350 (low season), from $1,795 (high season) per person double-occupancy for 3-day/4-night trip; shorter trips offered.

A Quiet Spot on the Road to Nowhere

The Gulf Islands and the Hastings House

British Columbia, Canada

The Gulf Islands archipelago—a string of some 100 partially submerged mountain peaks lying in the Strait of Georgia, between Vancouver Island and mainland British Columbia—is Canada's answer to Washington's

The serene rocky shores of the Gulf Islands

popular San Juans, though nowhere near as busy. Vancouver and Victoria weekenders cherish the quiet, low-key atmosphere and the old ways of the local towns and villages, which dot twenty-five of the archipelago's islands. Take a kayak out for a spin here and you're more likely to bump into a seal or Dall's porpoise than another tourist.

Of the five most visited southern Gulf Islands, Salt Spring is the most popular and also the largest, with 82 miles of ragged coastline and a population of 9,000. The main town of Ganges sits on a protected cove filled with bobbing sailboats, and is becoming known for its small but growing colony of artists and craftspeople, some internationally known.

Incongruously perched above the town amid 30 acres of flowering English gardens, towering Douglas firs, and water views is one of western Canada's most exclusive hideaways, the Tudor-style Hastings House. Despite its swank English-estate-cum-elegant-country-inn decor, the Hastings House embraces the Gulf Islands' casual lifestyle except at dinner, when men are requested to wear jackets. It offers some of the best dining west of Vancouver, prepared with ingredients plucked from the inn's gardens and orchards and pulled from the islands' fish-rich waters and fertile farmland.

What: island, hotel, restaurant. **Gulf Islands:** Tourism Vancouver Island, tel 250-

754-3500, fax 250-754-3599; info@tourism vi.ca; www.vancouverisland.travel. **BC Ferries:** ferries depart from Victoria and other locations. Tel 250-386-3431; www.bcferries.com. **Hastings House:** 160 Upper Ganges Rd., Salt Spring Island. Tel 800-661-9255 or 250-537-

2362, fax 250-537-5333; info@hastingshouse. com; www.hastingshouse.com. *When:* mid-Mar to mid-Nov. *Cost:* doubles from $355 (low season), from $445 (high season). Dinner $100. **Best times:** Apr–Oct for weather and Sat markets.

High-Altitude Heaven Just a Hover Away

Heli-Skiing and Heli-Hiking

British Columbia, Canada

B ritish Columbia's remote southeast corner is the largest contiguous wilderness area in the Americas and a year-round wonderland just begging to be explored—but how, as the area is almost completely devoid of roads?

Canadian Mountain Holidays solved that problem beginning in 1965, ferrying in outdoor enthusiasts aboard its fleet of helicopters. Today, it remains one of the most reputable heli-adventure outfitters in the world, and in southeastern BC also operates twelve lodges perched at about 4,000 feet in the Cariboo, Bugaboo, Monashee, and Purcells mountain ranges. In the winter months, each lodge promises its forty-some heli-skiing guests exclusive access to 14,000 square miles of virgin snow—about 300 times more than even the largest of North America's ski resorts can offer, and without a chairlift (or chairlift line) in sight. Only strong, intermediate to advanced skiers need apply: In the course of one mind-boggling week, helicopters set them down for eight to fifteen different runs per day, all on snow uncrossed by any other human's tracks. The preferences and skills of the individual—and the expert guides and pilots' consideration of weather and snow conditions—will determine the day's adventure, all bookended by mountain-man breakfasts and epicurean dinners, with a massage to round things out.

As soon as the snows melt, expectations turn to hiking and trekking through a primordial world full of wildflowers, massive glaciers, rivulets, and monumental views of dozens of snow-capped, mile-high peaks. Some heli-hiking ambles are gentle enough to accommodate four-generation-family groups; others require a degree of technical skill and even some mountaineering experience—the possibilities are endless.

What: experience. **Where:** trips originate in Calgary. Land transportation (a 4- to 6-hour bus trip from Calgary, followed by a 15-minute helicopter ride to any of the 12 mountain lodges) included in price. **How:** Canadian Mountain Holidays (CMH), Banff, Alberta. Tel 800-661-0252 or 403-762-7100; info@cmhinc.com; www.cmhski.com or www. cmhhike.com. **Cost:** 7-day ski trips all-inclusive (with equipment) from $5,985. Of the various hiking packages offered, the 3-night trip is the most popular, from $2,295 all-inclusive. All prices based on double occupancy. **When:** ski trips Dec–May; hiking trips early Jul–late Sept. **Best times:** Dec and May for low-season ski trip rates; early Jul to mid-Aug for hikes among the wildflowers.

Majesty on the Edge of the Map

NIMMO BAY RESORT

British Columbia, Canada

There are no roads leading to Nimmo Bay, an eighteen-guest wilderness resort that sits on the remote, undeveloped, and largely unsung western coast of Canada. Instead, a sleek helicopter ferries you in from neighboring

After a day of adventure, guests can come home to an oceanfront chalet.

Vancouver Island, passing over the Inside Passage's Queen Charlotte Strait, where you might spot Alaska-bound cruise ships, killer whales, or a school of porpoises. You are deposited at Nimmo Bay Resort, a pocket-size enclave of luxury carved sensitively into what must be the middle of nowhere. Begin your day with a little beach-combing, caving, ocean kayaking, or river rafting. Or, choose among a series of thrilling "heli-adventures" courtesy of the resort's private pilot—ascending 6,000 feet up and over ancient rain forests for a gourmet mountaintop picnic and a nice glacier hike; flying to a small Kwakiutl Indian village whose totem poles tell the story of ancestors who settled these shores many centuries ago; or heading to the area's pristine, nameless rivers and streams for catch-and-release fishing, with wild salmon tipping the scales at 50 to 60 pounds and cutthroat trout and Dolly Varden char regularly weighing in at 5 pounds.

For all the sensory overload, the overwhelming encounter with nature, and the adrenaline-pumping experiences, perhaps the best part of every day's adventure is to return to the resort's nine chalets, built on stilts on this tidal, fjordlike bay. The dining here competes with Vancouver's best—think hours-old "drunken" salmon in a secret-recipe marinade, followed by a dessert of frozen white and dark chocolate truffles. The evening is topped off with a good soak in the open-air hot tub, located at the foot of a mountainside waterfall. When they created this bliss-in-the-wilderness sanctuary more than twenty years ago, the Murray family was written off as a bunch of eccentric dreamers. No one's laughing now.

WHAT: hotel, experience. **WHERE:** 350 miles/563 km north of Seattle, 200 miles/322 km north of Vancouver. Helicopter service from Vancouver Island's Port Hardy to Nimmo Bay arranged by hotel (included). Tel 800-837-4354 or 250-956-4000, fax 250-956-2000; heli@nimmobay.com; www.nimmobay.com. **COST:** numerous helicopter packages available. 3-night package $6,525 and up per person, all-inclusive. **WHEN:** open May–Oct. **BEST TIMES:** Aug–Oct for fishing; May–Jul for most other activities.

Double the Peaks, Double the Pleasure

WHISTLER-BLACKCOMB SKI RESORT

British Columbia, Canada

Confirmation that getting there really is half the fun, the spectacular 75-mile Sea-to-Sky coastal road linking Vancouver and Whistler-Blackcomb is probably the most beautiful approach to any ski resort in the world.

With the exception of Alberta, no other Canadian province comes close to matching British Columbia's mountain beauty and grandeur, as both the highway and a day on the slopes will confirm. The giant twin peaks of Whistler and Blackcomb, linked at their base by the European-style, pedestrian-only Whistler Village, are not only North America's biggest ski destinations but are regularly ranked as the best—and their two-for-one lift tickets just sweeten the deal.

There are countless superlatives here: the greatest vertical drop (more than 5,000 feet) of any ski resort on the continent, 7,000 acres of skiable terrain (that's 2,000 acres more than the largest U.S. resort), more than 200 marked trails, 12 massive alpine bowls, an unfathomable 30 feet of snowfall per year, and a ski season that runs from late November through May (with summer skiing on Blackcomb mid-June through August). It would all seem overwhelming if not for an unparalleled high-speed lift system and a smiling and efficient staff (from waitresses to ski instructors). In fact, the very size of Whistler-Blackcomb allows the million-plus annual visitors to disappear on their personal favorite runs—it never really feels crowded. The only possible downside is the weather, which is unpredictable in the extreme: With the resort base a mere 2,200 feet above sea level, it's often raining down below, though almost always clearing as you head peakward. Go high.

Although 55 percent of the trails on both mountains are tagged for intermediates, Whistler-Blackcomb has acquired something of a cult reputation with advanced and extreme skiers—and winning the 2010 Olympics bid indicates the quality of the terrain. Runs are both extensive (the longest is 7 miles) and dramatically set, with renowned views from the chairlift. Insatiable skiers can also take advantage of guided heli-skiing.

Whistler-Blackcomb boasts more slope-side lodging than any other resort in North America. Its only ski-in/ski-out property, however, is the swank Fairmont Chateau Whistler Resort, a friendly, gabled fortress dominating the ski area at the base of Blackcomb Mountain and embodying the style of the grand old Canadian Pacific railroad hotels. With 560 rooms it's not exactly intimate, and it isn't cheap (especially for the fit-for-royalty suites), but it's *the* place to ski and be seen. Its famous buffet brunch, served on Sundays, is reason enough to check in, as are superlative spa treatments that are nirvana for après-ski weariness. As the seasons turn, Chateau Whistler effortlessly segues into a summertime playground, with its 18-hole Robert Trent Jones Jr. course regularly ranked as Canada's best, and three other courses lying within striking distance.

WHAT: experience, hotel. **WHISTLER-BLACKCOMB:** visitor info tel 866-218-9690 or

604-932-3434; www.whistlerblackcomb.com. *Cost:* 3-day lift tickets from $175. **FAIRMONT CHATEAU WHISTLER RESORT:** 4599 Chateau Blvd. Tel 800-441-1414 or 604-938-8000; www.fairmont.com/whistler. *Cost:* from $179 (low season), from $395 (high season); brunch $36. **BEST TIMES:** avoid Fri night exodus from Vancouver on the Sea-to-Sky/Highway 99; also avoid fringe seasons of Dec and Apr if you want to ski the whole mountain.

The Canadian West, Inspired by the East

SUN YAT-SEN CLASSICAL CHINESE GARDEN

Vancouver, British Columbia, Canada

C anada has always prided itself on its vibrant multiculturalism, a fascinating mosaic of peoples and customs that finds its apogee in Vancouver. Canada's third largest city has been looking to Asia since Chinese immigrants arrived with the 1858 gold rush (and later to work on the transcontinental railroad). The massive influx of the 1980s and 1990s, when many left Hong Kong in anticipation of mainland China's takeover, spurred the city's transformation into the Pacific Rim melting pot of today.

The traditions of Asia found fertile ground in this former outpost of the British Empire. In a wonderful vision of urban renewal, the Sun Yat-Sen Classical Chinese Garden rises from a former parking lot on the edge of Vancouver's Chinatown, the third largest Asian enclave outside the Orient, topped only by those of San Francisco and New York. It was the first (and is reputed to be the most authentic) full-scale classical Chinese garden ever built outside of China, begun in 1985 by more than fifty skilled traditional artisans and gardeners brought in from Suzhou, China's famous Garden City. The finished product is a pocket-sized otherworld, a walled oasis of harmony where careful attention is paid to a classical balance between yin and yang: contrasting light and shadow, large and small, smooth and rough—the exquisite re-creation of a typical 14th-century Ming garden. Almost everything was brought from China, including the pagoda roof tiles, the naturally sculpted rocks, the worn pebbles that create the mosaics covering the winding pathways, and the bronze, bat-shaped door handles.

WHAT: site. **WHERE:** 578 Carrall St., on the outskirts of Chinatown. Tel 604-662-3207; www.vancouverchinesegarden.com. **COST:** admission $10. **WHEN:** open daily, May–Oct; closed Mon, Nov–Apr.

The classical Chinese garden's careful balance of elements—water, rocks, plants, and architecture—promotes harmony and tranquility.

Paying Homage to the Pacific's Bounty

TOJO'S AND GRANVILLE ISLAND

Vancouver, British Columbia, Canada

Save yourself the cost of an airline ticket to Tokyo and head for Tojo's, a bright and popular restaurant that is named for its revered chef-owner, an amiable innovator responsible for some of the best sushi Canadian dollars can buy.

The dining rooms' window tables with their stunning views over False Creek and the North Shore mountains beyond are the obvious choice, but they're not what you want. Instead, head for the coveted ten-seat *omakase* ("in the chef's hands") sushi counter, where the beaming and energetic Tojo performs his magic with the precision of a surgeon and the faintest Vegas swagger. Specialties reflect the changing seasons, but tuna and salmon are perennial favorites, consumed at the rate of 300 pounds and 200 pounds, respectively, every week. The waters around Vancouver are rich with king, coho, sockeye, chum, and pink salmon, and Tojo gets his hands on the very best of the lot, maintaining an unwavering commitment to fresh local ingredients. Everything is always handmade, never prepared in advance.

Foodies should also head to Granville Island (a now-gentrified former industrial area beneath the Granville Street Bridge) and spend the morning at Granville Market, one of North America's best, brimming with seafood, meats, and wines from the province's vineyards—the finest British Columbia has to offer. Its food court reflects the cross-pollination of Canada's most ethnically diverse city.

WHAT: restaurant, site. **TOJO'S:** 1133 West Broadway. Tel 604-872-8050, fax 604-872-8060; www.tojos.com. *Cost:* $65; *omakase* from $55. *When:* open Mon–Sat. **GRANVILLE PUBLIC MARKET:** for more information, tel 604-666-5784; www.granvilleisland.com.

When You Just Can't Get Enough of Nature

PACIFIC RIM NATIONAL PARK

Vancouver Island, British Columbia, Canada

Head out from the charming, ever-so-British city of Victoria on Vancouver Island's southern tip and civilization quickly dwindles, replaced by the magnificent Pacific Northwest landscape. The snaking two-lane highway weaves past silver-blue lakes and cuts through high mountain passes and dense old-growth forests whose towering spruce, hemlock, and cedar trees are some of the largest and oldest in North America. On the island's rugged and sparsely populated western coast, Pacific Rim National Park Reserve is hallowed ground for ecotourists, its famous West Coast Trail hailed by the Sierra Club as one of the most spectacular and challenging hikes on the continent.

In summer, intermediate and experienced hikers arrive from all over the world to follow the 47-mile stretch. Novices can take in the island's grandeur walking some of the national park's less demanding segments, or strolling along the 7-mile curve of Long Beach, some 500 yards wide at low tide and the park's sandy centerpiece. The area's rocky shoreline was once known by mariners as the Graveyard of the Pacific for the ferocious winter storms that hit these craggy headlands, but yesterday's tragedy is today's tourist attraction, providing a number of historic shipwrecks for scuba divers to explore. Diverse marine life is also a major draw: Clayoquot Sound and the archipelago of the Broken Group Islands in Barkley Sound are unbeatable for sea lions, bald eagles, and large numbers of whales.

Even winter is mesmerizing, with howling winds, sheets of rain, and crashing 20-foot Pacific waves that have spawned the curious pastime of winter storm watching on the exposed western coast around Tofino, the quirkily charming village that serves as the end of the Trans-Canadian Highway and as unofficial gateway to the park. Four miles south of town sits the stylishly stalwart Wickaninnish Inn, a surprisingly luxurious outpost in these remote parts, providing possibly the continent's best front-row seats for witnessing nature's fury. Each of the handsome rooms has floor-to-ceiling windows and private balconies close enough to the sea that you can hear the waves while you relax beside the fireplace, or in the windowside hot tub. Guests can dine at the inn's Pointe Restaurant, whose 240-degree views vie with the chef's Northwest specialties for sheer drama.

WHAT: island, site, hotel. **PACIFIC RIM NATIONAL PARK RESERVE:** tel 250-726-7721; www.pc.gc.ca/pn-np/bc/pacificrim. *Cost:* $8.50 per car; West Coast Trail hiking permit $110. *When:* West Coast Trail is open May–late Sept. **WICKANINNISH INN:** in Tofino, a 5-hour drive from Victoria, which is connected to Vancouver by ferry and air. Tel 800-333-4604 or 250-725-3100; www.wickinn.com. *Cost:* doubles from $260 (low season), from $435 (high season). Dinner $90. **BEST TIMES:** Jun and Jul for warm weather and long days. Nov–Feb is often stormy. The Pacific Rim Whale Festival takes place for 2 weeks in Mar, when some 20,000 whales migrate north past the island's west coast.

Revel in ocean views at the Wickaninnish Inn.

Gourmet Luxury Havens on the Edge of North America

SOOKE HARBOUR HOUSE AND THE AERIE RESORT

Vancouver Island, British Columbia, Canada

With its stunning diversity of Pacific seafood, high annual rainfall, and mild coastal climate that produces some of the best growing conditions in North America, Vancouver Island was a culinary revolution waiting to happen. It's no surprise, therefore, that two now internationally known restaurant/inns should have opened their doors only a short and scenic drive from Victoria, BC's intimate and very British capital.

On a lonely wooded promontory overlooking a cozy cove and the Strait of Juan de Fuca beyond, Sinclair and Fredrica Philips's neat white clapboard Sooke Harbour House has long been acclaimed as one of North America's foremost hotel-restaurants for authentic regional cuisine. Served amid panoramic views and lit by candle chandeliers, delicious repasts are complemented by an award-winning list of more than 2,000 wines, 40 of them served by the glass. Lovingly tended gardens reach down to the water's edge, with 400 varieties of rare and unusual herbs, edible flowers, and organic vegetables that are used liberally and innovatively in the menu's ever-changing, one-of-a-kind dishes. All of the rooms have fireplaces and most have whirlpools for two positioned to enjoy the gorgeous views. Delicious packed lunches encourage guests to explore the area's natural attractions.

Less homelike and more formal (and thus the special-occasion destination of many couples), the Aerie Resort offers stiff competition with its premium-quality kitchen and jaw-dropping setting, high atop Mallahat Summit at 1,200 feet, overlooking Finlayson Arm and southern Vancouver Island. Chef Castro Boateng and his house-proud staff make sure that any stay is a special occasion, offering old-world hospitality, meticulous attention to detail, and a wonderful mix of comfort and elegance. Meals combine elements of classic French cuisine with a cornucopia of Pacific Northwest possibilities, flavored with a dash of decadence to match the setting.

WHAT: hotel, restaurant. **SOOKE HARBOUR HOUSE:** 1528 Whiffen Spit Rd., Sooke (23 miles/37 km west of Victoria). Tel 800-889-9688 or 250-642-3421, fax 250-642-6988; www.sookeharbourhouse.com. *Cost:* doubles from $165 (low season), from $256 (high season), includes breakfast. Dinner $65. *When:* open year-round, dinner nightly. **AERIE RESORT:** 600 Ebedora Ln., Malahat (20 miles/32 km north of Victoria). Tel 800-518-1933 or 250-743-7115, fax 250-743-4766; www.aerie.bc.ca. *Cost:* from $125 (low season), from $179 (high season), includes breakfast and lunch. Dinner $75.

Sailing Among Orca

STUBBS ISLAND WHALE WATCHING

Vancouver Island, British Columbia, Canada

Quaint Telegraph Cove, a cluster of wooden houses built precariously on stilts on the northeastern tip of Vancouver Island, has a population that hovers around eleven, but it's the residents offshore that people come to bond with. Separating Vancouver Island from the pine-covered coast of British Columbia, Johnstone Strait is seasonal home to the world's largest concentration of orcas (killer whales).

Roughly 200 orcas inhabit these waters from late June throughout the winter months. Stubbs Island Whale Watching operates two 60-foot Coast Guard–certified vessels, both with heated areas inside, viewing decks, and hydrophones that allow passengers to eavesdrop on the whales' haunting melodies and other communications. With a curiosity that matches the visitors' own, the powerful, silent whales may approach the boat, which has become familiar to them over the company's twenty-three years of cruising (the success rate of sightings is 90 percent). Individually named and identified by their scars, their white "saddle patch" markings, and the shapes of their flukes, the whales slice through these calm waters, diving and surfacing as visitors ooh and ahh. Who's watching whom?

WHAT: experience. **WHERE:** 250 miles/ 402 km northwest of Victoria. Stubbs Island Whale Watching, tel 800-665-3066 or 250-928-3185, fax 250-928-3102; stubbs@island. net; www.stubbs-island.com. *Cost:* from $75 for 3½-hour trip. *When:* late May to mid-Oct, with daily cruises Jun–Sept. **BEST TIMES:** Jul–Sept.

Repositories of Native History, Art, and Culture

ROYAL BRITISH COLUMBIA MUSEUM AND THE MUSEUM OF ANTHROPOLOGY

Victoria and Vancouver, British Columbia, Canada

Regularly ranked as one of the top ten museums in North America, Victoria's Royal British Columbia is as much fun for kids as for adults and as intriguing to locals as to foreigners. Visitors can walk through the province's history from the Ice Age (the 10-foot woolly mammoth is a guaranteed hit with children) to its mining and fishing heritage, with lifelike dioramas showing the wealth of wildlife and flora from the mountains to the deltas to the temperate rain forests. A new state-of-the-art climate exhibit uses satellite imagery, live webcams, and graphic and text displays to explore weather patterns and changes. Perhaps most intriguing is the First Peoples Gallery, which details the history of the region's several distinct coastal nations before and after the arrival of Europeans, with displays of hand-carved masks, ceremonial garb and headdresses, decorative accessories and textiles, and iconic totem poles. Directly behind the museum is Thunderbird Park, the largest display of totem poles anywhere. On-site

From the First Peoples Gallery at the Royal British Columbia Museum

wood-carvers occasionally demonstrate their age-old methods.

In Vancouver, the province's largest city, museum meisters will assure you that the Museum of Anthropology's collection of native art and culture is no less stellar, making for a worthwhile thirty-minute trip west of Granville Island to the campus of the University of British Columbia. Housed in an award-winning building by Arthur Erickson, it's best known for the cedar sculpture *The Raven and the First Men* by Haida artist Bill Reid. The jury's out

regarding who wins the totem pole contest— both museums' collections are remarkable.

WHAT: site. **ROYAL BRITISH COLUMBIA MUSEUM:** 675 Belleville St., Victoria. Tel 888-447-7977 or 250-356-7226; www.royal bcmuseum.bc.ca. *Cost:* admission $25. **MUSEUM OF ANTHROPOLOGY:** University of British Columbia, 6393 NW Marine Drive, Vancouver. Tel 604-822-5087; www.moa. ubc.ca. *When:* daily mid-May–mid-Oct; closed Mon, mid-Oct–mid-May. *Cost:* $10; reduced admission on Tues evenings.

Kings of the Tundra

POLAR BEAR SAFARI

Cape Churchill, Manitoba, Canada

Africa has the Serengeti Plain, South America has the Amazon Basin, and North America has Cape Churchill on the Hudson Bay—the polar bear capital of the world. One of the largest of all terrestrial predators,

with some weighing fifteen hundred pounds, polar bears are generally elusive creatures, yet they gather at Cape Churchill yearly before Hudson Bay freezes, allowing them to venture off to hunt seals on its dramatic ice floes. Spectators watch from tundra buggies as the bears frolic and play in family groups, the newborn cubs just black noses and eyes against the white of the snow. The flora and wildlife of the arctic tundra create a beautiful backdrop for nature lovers, while the spectacular display of the aurora borealis lights up the brittle-cold night skies.

Thousands of polar bears gather at Cape Churchill.

WHAT: experience. **WHERE:** approximately 630 miles/1,014 km north of Winnipeg. **HOW:** Natural Habitat Adventures, tel 800-543-8917 or 303-449-3711; www.nathab.com. **COST:** 6- and 7-day trips from $4,595 per person, includes charter flights from Winnipeg to Cape Churchill. **WHEN:** mid-Oct to mid-Nov.

A Tidal Roller Coaster

BAY OF FUNDY

New Brunswick, Canada

Fundy is a place of absolute wonder where the world's highest tides rise as much as 48 feet in six hours—more than twenty-two times greater than the average in open seas. Fundy National Park, established in 1948, protects 80 square miles of the land along the bay's west coast, where the tides and cold waters are responsible for coastal spruce and fir forests, salt and freshwater wetlands, and a rocky, cave-pocked shore where the hard, rapid tides have carved huge boulders into fantasy shapes. So dramatic is the difference between low and high tide that, at Alma Beach, visitors can walk almost three-quarters of a mile across the tidal flats to the water's edge—then kayak that whole distance a few hours later, when 100 billion tons of water have rushed back in, producing a roar at midtide known as "the voice of the moon." You can see plant fossils millions of years old in the ancient sandstone rocks at the water's edge, while offshore, at low tide, bird watchers can view thousands of migratory shorebirds as they feed on crustaceans trapped by the waters' retreat.

Around Alma, the park has a manicured look, with gardens, stone walls, and numerous sports options, including golf and tennis, while offshore you can choose between whale watching (the bay hosts the largest population of endangered right whales anywhere), kayaking, and canoeing. Hiking opportunities abound, with 78 miles of trails traversing the park's 8 miles of bayside coast and its hilly inland, whose rolling plateau is cut by deep valleys and fast-flowing streams.

Those wanting scenery with less challenge can take the Fundy Coastal Drive from St. Stephen to Aulac, passing through not only natural beauty but some lovely towns as well, including the 19th-century village of St. Andrews with its distinguished Fairmont Algonquin Hotel. Built in 1889 to lure wealthy vacationers away from the city heat, the Algonquin is a manor-style gem, with a red-tile roof and bay views from the upper floors. If you'd prefer something smaller, the Kingsbrae Arms is consistently rated as one of the area's best accommodations. Built in 1897, it has just eight units, all decorated with upscale good taste and offering lovely views of the bay. Next door, the Kingsbrae Garden offers 27 acres of flowers and views.

Forty miles northeast of the national park, the Hopewell Rocks ("The World's Most Famous Flowerpots") are a group of immense boulders topped by trees and made concave at the bottom by centuries of tidal erosion. They're

The Kingsbrae Arms in the historic town of St. Andrews

the most photographed Bay of Fundy landmarks by far. Local Mi'kmaq legend has it that the boulders were once men, who were enslaved by angry whales and turned to stone when they tried to escape.

WHAT: site, experience, hotel. **BAY OF FUNDY:** between New Brunswick and Nova Scotia. Visitor information, tel 800-561-0123; www.bayoffundytourism.com. **FUNDY NATIONAL PARK:** Route 114, New Brunswick. Visitors centers on the eastern entrance at Alma and the western at Wolfe Lake. Tel 506-887-6000; www.pc.gc.ca/fundy. *Cost:*

$7 per person. **FAIRMONT ALGONQUIN:** 184 Adolphus St., St. Andrews. Tel 800-441-1414 or 506-529-8823, fax 506-529-7162; alg. reservations@fairmont.com; www.fairmont. com/algonquin. *Cost:* doubles from $115 (low season), from $235 (high season). **KINGSBRAE ARMS:** 219 King St., St. Andrews. Tel 506-529-1897, fax 506-529-1197; reservations@ kingsbrae.com; www.kingsbrae.com. *Cost:* doubles from $535. *When:* closed Dec–Feb. **BEST TIMES:** early Aug for St. Stephen's Chocolate Festival; late Sept–early Oct for the foliage and the best whale watching.

The Land That Time Forgot

GROS MORNE NATIONAL PARK

Newfoundland, Canada

What's in a name? Located along Newfoundland's rugged western coast, the "big mournful place" is in fact an area of stunning natural beauty, a fantasy landscape of rough, rocky mountains, stark fjords, deep glacial lakes, coastal bogs, and wave-carved cliffs. Add a dash of mist and it's easy to picture what life was like here 1,000 years ago, when Leif Eriksson and thirty-five Viking seagoers established North America's first European colony at L'Anse aux Meadows, about 80 miles north of the park.

In geologic terms, though, a thousand years may as well be a day—which is especially obvious in the Tablelands area of the Gros Morne. Like thickset versions of the American West's buttes and plateaus, Tablelands' hills are bare, rusty, flattened, and eroded by time, dotted here and there with patches of hardscrabble greenery but otherwise looking exactly like what they are: prehistory made manifest. About 570 million years ago, the rocks that form this area were part of the earth's mantle, driven to the surface from under the crust during the continental breakup, when the lands that became Africa

and North America butted against each other. It's like seeing the earth's skeleton. Hiking is the best way to experience the area. The 2½-mile (round-trip) Tablelands Trail stretches from Trout River Gulch to Winterhouse Brook Canyon and concentrates on the Tablelands' stark geology, while the longer Green Gardens Trail offers 6- and 9-mile options that descend from the barrens through boreal forest to a fertile sea coast, where beautiful meadows sit atop volcanic, cave-pocked cliffs.

Landlocked Trout River Pond, located right along the park's southern border, is another scenic highlight, running for 9 miles between steep, stark hills. The area's old Newfie fishing villages are also worth a stop, as is the Discovery Centre just outside Woody Point, with exhibits on geology, plant and animal life, and the area's human history.

North of Bonne Bay, the coastal road (Route 430) follows a broad, boggy plain, with the dramatic Long Range Mountains rising to the east. Gros Morne, the highest of those mountains at 2,644 feet, rewards in-shape hikers with spectacular views of the park, the bay, and the Gulf of St. Lawrence. Less than a half-hour's drive north of Rocky Harbour—the area's main town and the location of the park's visitors center—Western Brook Pond is the park's most popular stop, with a combination of hikes and boat trips exploring and interpreting this landlocked glacial fjord's landscape and wildlife.

WHAT: site. **WHERE:** on Newfoundland's west coast. Commercial airlines fly into Deer Lake, 20 miles/32 km from the park entrance at Wiltondale. Park Information Center, tel 709-458-2417; www.pc.gc.ca/grosmorne. **COST:** $8.50 per person. **WHEN:** Discovery Centre, campgrounds, and most services open late May through mid-Oct; visitors center open year-round; Gros Morne Mountain open to hikers mid-May to mid-Oct. **BEST TIMES:** spring, when the rhododendrons are in bloom; Sept and early Oct for the fall foliage; Feb–Mar for cross-country skiing; Jul–Aug for wildlife.

A Piece of Scotland Gone West

CAPE BRETON ISLAND AND THE CABOT TRAIL

Nova Scotia, Canada

Connected to the rest of Nova Scotia by a narrow causeway, Cape Breton Island is as Scottish as it gets on this side of the Atlantic, a place where the cultural influence of the original French settlement was subsumed long ago

as thousands of Scottish farm families streamed in between 1770 and 1850. The land's similarity to the auld sod must certainly have been a draw, with its mountains and plunging shoreline cliffs, but it's sheer pride that keeps the Gaelic traditions alive today, manifested in music, art, and even a bit of language.

Both natural beauty and island culture get their due on the 184-mile Cabot Trail, named for Italian-born explorer Giovanni Caboto (a.k.a. John Cabot), who sailed from Bristol, England, after hearing about Columbus's earlier journey, and made landfall on Cape Breton Island in 1497.

Following the picturesque, craggy coastline around Cape Breton Highlands National Park, the trail is one of the most scenic drives in North America, passing Acadian fishing villages, pristine valleys, and viewing points from which you can often spot finback and minke whales feeding in the waters below. Most breathtaking of all is the 27-mile stretch from Chéticamp north to Pleasant Bay, with its remarkable views of the western coast. You can drive the Cabot Trail in a day, but you'd be doing yourself a disservice. Instead, pull off for a hike on any of the 590-square-mile park's more than thirty trails (most of which are quite mild) or stop at any of the Cabot Trail's tiny fishing villages, such as Pleasant Bay, population 350.

On the east coast, the town of Ingonish is home to the Keltic Lodge, a gleaming white, red-roofed, Tudor-style resort situated on a spit of land so narrow it feels like an island. The views are a knockout, as is the nearby Highland Links golf course, ranked among the best in Canada. North of here, small, idyllic

Mary Ann Falls is probably the most visited waterfall on the island. To the south, at South Gut St. Ann's (where the Cabot Trail begins officially), the Gaelic College of Celtic Arts and Crafts hosts an annual Gaelic Mod, a day of traditional Gaelic language and song with workshops, a codfish supper, and a *ceilidh* (pronounced kay-lee) with traditional music and dancing. Its Great Hall of Clans museum depicts the history of the Scots on Cape Breton. In October, the nine-day Celtic Colours International Festival is celebrated island-wide with dozens of concerts, lectures, and workshops on Gaelic folklore, weaving, and the playing of the pipes.

WHAT: site, hotel, event. **CAPE BRETON ISLAND:** 175 miles/266 km northeast of Halifax. Nova Scotia Department of Tourism, tel 800-565-0000 or 902-425-5781; www.

novascotia.com. **CAPE BRETON HIGHLANDS NATIONAL PARK:** entrances at Chéticamp and Ingonish. Tel 902-224-2306 or 902-285-2691; www.pc.gc.ca/pn-np/ns/cbreton *Cost:* $6.50 per person. **KELTIC LODGE:** Middle Head Peninsula, Ingonish Beach. Tel 800-565-0444 or 902-285-2880, fax 902-285-2859; www.kelticlodge.ca. *Cost:* $150 (low season), from $255 (high season). **GAELIC COLLEGE OF CELTIC ARTS AND CRAFTS:** overlooking St. Ann's Bay. Tel 902-295-3411; www.gaelic college.edu. *When:* Jun–Sept; Gaelic Mod mid-Aug. **CELTIC COLOURS INTERNATIONAL FESTIVAL:** tel 877-285-2321 or 902-562-6700; www.celtic-colours.com. *Cost:* ticket costs vary. *When:* mid-Oct. **BEST TIMES:** Jul for best weather; Aug for Gaelic Mod; summer for the Cabot Trail Loop; Oct for Celtic Colours International Festival and fall foliage.

Nature's Thunderous Beauty

NIAGARA FALLS

Ontario, Canada

Straddling the U.S.-Canada border, Niagara Falls draws its waters from four of the five Great Lakes and flings them down twenty stories at the rate of 42 million gallons a minute. Almost a mile wide in total, the falls are divided by islands into three sections: the 1,060-foot American Falls (which includes a small section called Bridal Veil Falls) and the larger, 2,600-foot Horseshoe Falls on the Canadian side, which gets the most visitor attention.

Western society first became aware of the falls in 1678 when Jesuit missionary Louis Hennepin became curious about the thunderous roar he heard in the distance and followed it to its source, becoming Niagara's first tourist. Almost three centuries later, Marilyn Monroe and James Cotton headed this way in the falls' namesake film, becoming their iconic honeymooners. An

Since their formation, the falls have moved approximately 7 miles upriver.

uncounted number of real-life couples had the same idea, making Niagara the undisputed honeymoon capital of the continent for most of the 20th century, peaking in the 1950s and

1960s. Today, Coney Island–esque reminders of that era abound in the innumerable cheap honeymoon motels and tourist stops, but surrounding its carnival core, the Niagara area has attractions painted with a wider brush.

The Canadian side is much more happening, both in terms of falls views and general revelry —full of nightclubs, restaurants, upscale hotels, and the 2.5-million-square-foot Niagara Fallsview Casino Resort, which in addition to gaming offers lovely rooms with incredible views of the falls. Just north of the falls, the Niagara Parkway offers an entirely different world, dotted with beautiful gardens. At the end of this road lies the lovely little 19th-century town of Niagara-on-the-Lake, one of the prettiest in Canada and the heart of the Niagara wine region. All of the area's top wineries are open to the public, including Peller Estates; Inniskillin Wines (whose barn may—no one's 100 percent sure—have been designed by Frank Lloyd Wright); Château des Charmes, the first Canadian winery to win gold at Bordeaux's prestigious VinExpo; and Vineland Estates Winery, housed in a former Mennonite homestead.

But back to the point—or rather, the falls. The classic way to view them, and also the best, is from aboard the *Maid of the Mist*, a sturdy 600-passenger boat that's the tenth in a same-name line of crafts, taking passengers right into the spray at the base of Horseshoe Falls since 1846. You'll be very glad of the plastic raincoats they issue at boarding.

To get a different though still drenching view, take the Journey Behind the Falls tour, which descends via elevator through 150 feet of rock to a series of man-made tunnels that provide a view from behind the cascading water. On the U.S. side, the Cave of the Winds tour leads visitors to the base of the American Falls, while the thirty-passenger *Flight of Angels* tethered helium balloon takes you up 400 feet for a ten-minute view of the majesty below.

WHAT: site, experience. **NIAGARA FALLS:** 400 miles/644 km from New York City, 90 miles/145 km from Toronto. Niagara Falls Tourism, tel 800-563-2557 or 905-356-6061; www.niagarafallstourism.com. **NIAGARA FALLSVIEW CASINO:** Tel 888-325-5788; www.fallsviewcasinoresort.com. **NIAGARA WINE ROUTE:** Wine Council of Ontario, tel 800-263-2988 or 905-684-8070, ext. 12; www.winesof ontario.org. **MAID OF THE MIST:** departs from the docks just below the Rainbow Bridge. Tel 905-358-5781; www.maidofthemist.com. *Cost:* $14. *When:* Apr–Oct. **JOURNEY BEHIND THE FALLS:** from Table Rock House, next to Horseshoe Falls. Tel 905-354-1551. **CAVE OF THE WINDS:** Goat Island. Tel 716-278-1730; www.niagarafallslive.com/cave_of_the_winds. htm. *Cost:* $11. *When:* May–Oct. **FLIGHT OF ANGELS:** 310 Rainbow Blvd. S. Tel 716-278-0824 or 716-278-0825; falls@iaw.com. *Cost:* $20. *When:* May–Oct. **BEST TIMES:** Apr–Nov for Niagara-on-the-Lake's annual George Bernard Shaw Festival (www.shawfest.com).

Celebrating the Canadian Winter

WINTERLUDE AND SKATING ON THE RIDEAU CANAL

Ottawa, Ontario, Canada

The defining physical attribute of Canada is its northern climate, so why not embrace it? That's exactly what Canada's capital city does each February during Winterlude, Ottawa's paean to snow and ice, begun in 1979.

Well over half a million visitors show up every year for the celebration, which includes figure-skating performances, snowshoe races, a winter triathlon (skiing, skating, and running), snow golf, fireworks, a hot stew cookoff, and dogsled races, among many other events. In Gatineau's Jacques-Cartier Park (north of Ottawa, across the river), Snowflake Kingdom is the world's largest snow playground, while Ottawa's Confederation Park is the site for the Crystal Garden International Ice-Carving Competition, with pros the first week and amateurs the next. The Canada Snow Sculpture Competition at Major's Hill Park displays giant works prepared by professional snow sculptors from each province and territory.

It's no surprise that the country with the world's best hockey players also boasts the world's longest skating rink, the Rideau Canal, built in the 19th century as a military route linking Montreal and points west. During the winter, 5 miles of its length are groomed for skating and serve as Winterlude's main drag, the site of most of the races. During the rest of the winter it's busiest on business days, with managerial types skating to work with their attaché cases, schoolchildren zipping along carrying lunch boxes, Olympic wannabes getting in shape, and bureaucrats gliding by on their way to the nearby Parliament building. On weekends the pace is more leisurely,

Snow sculptures annually grace Mayor's Hill Park.

with skaters making frequent stops for hot chocolate and beavertails (deep-fried dough balls covered with cinnamon sugar) or maple syrup on shaved ice.

If you're looking for a place to stay, the imposing Château Laurier remains the finest hotel in the nation's capital, if not all of eastern Canada. Built in 1912, at the site where the Rideau Canal meets the Ottawa River, the Laurier offers a historical castle-like setting, handsome furnishings, old-world service, and one of the most European hotel experiences this side of the Atlantic.

WHAT: event, hotel. **WINTERLUDE:** held all around the city. Information, 800-465-1867 or 613-239-5000; www.winterlude.ca. *Cost:* most events and activities are free, but some sporting events and shows charge admission. *When:* 3 weeks in Feb. **FAIRMONT CHÂTEAU LAURIER:** 1 Rideau St. Tel 613-241-1414; www.fairmont.com/laurier. *Cost:* doubles from $215.

Canadian Art—Past, Present, and Future

ART GALLERY OF ONTARIO

Toronto, Ontario, Canada

The Art Gallery of Ontario (AGO) is one of the finest museums in North America, with a collection that encompasses both Canadian and international art. Founded in 1900 by a group of Toronto citizens, it currently holds more than 36,000 works, dating from the 11th century to the present. The museum's European collection includes works by Tintoretto, Bruegel, Rembrandt, Renoir, Degas, Picasso, Gauguin, and van Gogh, while its contemporary collection includes

Andy Warhol's *Elvis I* and *II* and works by Robert Smithson, Gerhard Richter, Claes Oldenburg, and Franz Kline. But you're in Canada, after all, so head for the Canadian collection, which represents more than half the museum's holdings. The chronologically ordered galleries focus on the breadth of Canadian art history, beginning prior to Confederation and continuing to the present day—including 19th-century portraits and landscapes; scenes of early Canadian life by artist Cornelius Krieghoff; a showpiece late-19th-century salon, whose stunning red walls feature masterpieces by Canadian icons such as Paul Peel and Lucius O'Brien; and a comprehensive installation of paintings by Tom Thomson and the Group of Seven, early 20th-century Canadian artists whose work celebrates the country's national splendor. The AGO also boasts an extensive collection of Inuit art, including signature works by sculptors Shorty Killiktree, George Tataniq, Paulassie Pootoogook, and Oviloo Tunillee.

In 1974, British sculptor Henry Moore was moved when the citizens of Toronto pitched in to purchase his sculpture *The Archer* for their new City Hall, after legislators had refused to provide funds. As a result, he donated more than 800 works—bronzes, woodcuts, lithographs, etchings, plasters, and drawings—representing the world's largest collection of his art.

The news these days, though, is about the future. In 2002 the museum announced that not only its collection but also the building itself were about to undergo radical changes. Kenneth Thomson, a leading Canadian art collector and businessman, donated nearly 2,000 works, including Rubens's *Massacre of the Innocents*; masterpieces by Canadian artists Paul Kane, Tom Thomson, Cornelius Krieghoff, and Lawren Harris; and a stunning collection of rare European art objects dating from the Middle Ages to the mid-19th century. To accommodate the additions and bring the museum into the 21st century, a physical redesign and expansion was led by renowned Toronto native Frank Gehry, the architectural genius behind the Guggenheim Museum Bilbao. The project broke ground in early 2005, and the transformed building made its debut in November of 2008.

Connoisseurs should also visit the impressive Royal Ontario Museum (which is undergoing a major expansion), with its remarkable collection of Chinese art, a wing dedicated to European decorative arts, a working paleontology lab and many dinosaur skeletons, a Canadian heritage gallery, and a whole lot more—some 6 million pieces in all. Kids love the Bat Cave, a walk-through diorama replica of Jamaica's St. Clair cave, with 3,000 very lifelike bats flitting about.

WHAT: site. **ART GALLERY OF ONTARIO:** 317 Dundas St. West. Tel 416-979-6648; www.ago.net. *Cost:* $13 (free Wed). *When:* closed Mon. **ROYAL ONTARIO MUSEUM:** 100 Queen's Park. Tel 416-586-8000; www.rom.on.ca. *Cost:* admission $22 (free Fri evenings).

A Temple of Northern Chic

FOUR SEASONS TORONTO

Ontario, Canada

T he New York of Canada—and also the Boston, Chicago, Cleveland, and L.A., to judge by the American cities it's stood in for in the movies— Toronto is a power-trip urban center, full of skyscrapers, limos, and buzz.

Head northwest of the high-end retail district of Yonge and Bloor, however, and you find yourself in a different vibe entirely, with pretty Victorian shopping streets full of art galleries, cafés, big-name designer boutiques, and chic restaurants. This is Yorkville, once an independent village, then the Haight-Ashbury of the North, now the gentrified home of all things haute Toronto.

If you were, say, Robert De Niro, and planned to spend some time here, you'd book a suite at the Four Seasons, the Toronto-based luxury chain's flagship hotel and a favorite of visiting celebs—especially during the 10-day Toronto International Film Festival, one of the film world's most important, when room reservations become as coveted as Oscars. The marble-floored lobby and other public areas are designed with a mix of clean modern lines and classic parlor style. The spacious guest rooms and suites follow the same aesthetic, with a quiet, restrained elegance that's more gentle embrace than bear hug. Book a corner room to enjoy the wonderful balconies; a north-facing room for the most wide-open views; or a south-facing room on an upper floor for views of the city skyline, with its 1,815-foot Canadian National (CN) Tower, the world's tallest freestanding structure.

The hotel's main restaurant, Studio Cafe, is a dining institution. Overseen by chef Claudio Rossi, the menu focuses on Italian and Mediterranean dishes made from top-shelf ingredients.

Overlooking Yorkville Avenue, the hotel's La Serre lounge is Toronto's number one power bar. Thick red cushioned chairs set the mood for high-end business schmoozing, and Cuban cigars and single-malt scotch help close the deal.

Celebrity digs at the Toronto Four Seasons

WHAT: hotel, restaurant. **WHERE:** 21 Avenue Rd. Tel 800-268-6282 or 416-964-0411, fax 416-964-2301; www.fourseasons.com/toronto. **COST:** doubles from $265 (low season), from $355 (high season). Dinner at Studio Cafe $65. **WHEN:** dinner only, Mon–Sat. **BEST TIMES:** Jun, Jul, and Sept for the best weather; early to mid-Sept for the film festival (tel 416-968-3456; www.tiffg.ca.

Bucolic Birthplace of Canada and Anne of Green Gables

PRINCE EDWARD ISLAND

Canada

Pastoral as a picture book, with tiny towns set among rolling green hills, Prince Edward Island (PEI) is surrounded by the cold North Atlantic and crisscrossed by red-dirt roads, the visible clue to the island's deep red sandstone bedrock. A primarily agricultural island, it's both the smallest and most densely populated province of Canada—the latter statistic hard to believe when you look around and see only cattle and (maybe) a lone tractor in the distance. It makes you appreciate how *under-populated* much of the country is. From the sea, fishermen pull the island's other major crops: lobsters, clams, scallops, and oysters. In the town of Summerside, the mid-July Lobster Carnival features feasts, fiddling contests, and games, while North Rustico's Fisherman's Wharf restaurant has tanks able to hold 40,000 pounds of lobster next to the kitchen, May through October.

PEI's bucolic lifestyle was nurtured by isolation, and even now—with the island connected to the mainland by the 8-mile Confederation Bridge (built in 1997)—the feel is more cow pasture than rat race. Scenic red roads are perfect for driving or cycling, and three officially designated routes are designed to showcase the island's best features. The Kings Byway concentrates on the east coast, winding through dozens of small, rural hamlets and green fields, and letting onto gorgeous ocean views. Lady Slipper Drive, around the west coast, is even more rural, passing lighthouses, villages, and (among other things) a group of houses in Cap-Egmont made entirely of recycled bottles.

Blue Heron Drive is probably the most traveled (and most commercial) route, as it passes through the north shore's PEI National Park, which includes the home of L. M. Montgomery and her novel *Anne of Green Gables*. The park is situated on a spectacular stretch of coast along the Gulf of St. Lawrence, and boasts 25 miles of beaches, sand dunes, and red sandstone cliffs, plus ponds, woodlands, and wildlife. Cavendish, the area's most-visited town, is on the touristy side, with every other shop dedicated to Ms. Montgomery and her creation. Montgomery was born here in 1874, and set her novel among the area's rich beauty. Translated now into some fifteen languages, the book has fan clubs around the world and draws 350,000 visitors annually to Green Gables House (inspiration for the novel's Cuthbert Farm) and other sites. For accommodations, there are cabins right next to Gables House at the Green Gables Bungalow Court,

One of Cap-Egmont's Bottle Houses

but Dalvay by the Sea Heritage Inn is a more evocative choice. Commissioned in 1895, this seaside Victorian mansion has been a summer resort since the 1930s, offering a TV-and-phone-free environment; simple, bright rooms; and chef Keith Wilson's excellent cuisine, with influences from the Mediterranean, Northern Africa, and the Asia-Pacific Rim.

South of Cavendish and the park, Charlottetown is the Philadelphia of Canada, the place where the Fathers of Confederation met in 1864 to discuss unifying the country. Province House was the site of the meeting, and today you can visit the Confederation Chamber and several other rooms, all restored to appear as they did in the 19th century.

Old Charlottetown has cobblestone, gaslit streets lined with 18th-century mansions, many now converted to inns and bed-and-breakfasts. The waterfront area, where their merchant-builders made their money, has seen its warehouses converted into seafood restaurants, shops, and nightspots. Most of PEI's original settlers came from Ireland, Scotland, England, and France, and today you can hear their descendants playing Celtic and Acadian traditional music at a number of places in town, including the Irish Hall and the Olde Dublin Pub.

WHAT: island, event, restaurant, experience, site, hotel. **PRINCE EDWARD ISLAND:** 8 miles/ 13 km across the Confederation Bridge from New Brunswick. PEI Tourism, tel 888-463-4734; www.peiplay.com. **SUMMERSIDE LOBSTER CARNIVAL:** tel 902-436-4925; lobstercarnival

@pei.aibn.com. *When:* mid-Jul. **FISHERMAN'S WHARF RESTAURANT:** Rt. 6, North Rustico. Tel 877-289-1010 or 902-963-2669, fax 902-963-3291; fishwharf@pei.aibn.com; www.fishermanswharf.ca. *When:* open daily mid-May to mid-Oct. *Cost:* dinner $16. **PRINCE EDWARD ISLAND NATIONAL PARK:** tel 902-672-6350; http://www.parkscanada.gc.ca/pn-np/pe/pei-ipe. *Cost:* $2. **GREEN GABLES HOUSE:** 2 Palmers Ln., Cavendish. Tel 902-963-3370; www.gov.pe.ca/greengables. **ANNE OF GREEN GABLES MUSEUM AT SILVER BUSH:** Rt. 20, Park Corner. Tel 800-665-2663 or 902-886-2884; www.annesociety.org/anne. *Cost:* admission $1.50. **DALVAY BY THE SEA:** off Rte. 6, Tracadie. Tel 902-672-2048, fax 902-672-2741 (summer), 902-672-1408 (winter); www.dalvaybythesea.com. *Cost:* doubles from $130; cottages from $265. *When:* open Jun–Sept. **BEST TIMES:** summer for the best weather; mid-Sept to late Oct for fall foliage; early Mar for seal watching.

Wilderness Grandeur in the Newport of the North

CHARLEVOIX

Quebec, Canada

Covering 6,177 square miles in Quebec's Laurentide region, Charlevoix is an area of astonishing natural beauty, its mountains bearded with fir, cedar, and spruce forests and its St. Lawrence River shoreline dotted with small villages and resorts that were once the vacation province of wealthy American families and international celebs like Mary Pickford, Charlie Chaplin, and the king of Siam. A young William Howard Taft visited here in 1892, remarked that its air "exhilarates like Champagne, without the effects of the morning after," and made it his vacation destination for the rest of his life. The French-Canadian villages known collectively as Murray Bay were the nexus of the "Newport of the North" and enjoyed a lively heyday from the 1870s into the 1950s. The arrival of the railroad made guests' own arrival easier, if somewhat less romantic, than aboard the Canadian Steamship Line's old *bateaux-blancs.*

Today the gilding is still on the lily, though guests no longer have to dress up in evening wear for dinner at the clifftop Manoir Richelieu, a 405-room resort opened in 1899 and once frequented by the most footloose of the summer swells. A 1998 renovation brought back much of its early majesty, reflecting Charlevoix's blend of quiet countryside charm, wilderness grandeur, and world-class resort life. For miles around, mountain and forest coexist with a sparse year-round population of around 30,000, a number that swells to two and a half times that size in summer, yet makes little impact on the area's backcountry solitude and wildlife. Ecotourism is the word of the day, with myriad opportunities for hiking, biking, kayaking, and canoeing at two nearby national parks, Parc des

Charlevoix boasts mountain, forest, and river views.

Grands Jardins, 20 miles inland from Baie St.-Paul (home to a vigorous arts scene), and Les Hautes-Gorges of the Rivière Malbaie, an hour's drive north of St.-Aime-des-Lacs. Twenty miles north from Murray Bay, the waters where the St. Lawrence and Saguenay rivers meet are home to beluga, minke, humpback, rorqual, and blue whales in summer. For the less wilderness-minded, Fairmont Le Manoir Richelieu's golf club offers a world-class 18-hole, par-71 course on a bluff above the river near La Malbaie.

Also in La Malbaie, La Pinsonnière is the area's finest hostelry. It's a gleaming white, twenty-six-room country inn offering personal service and refined elegance, with flower-bedecked terraces, in-room fireplaces, and oversized whirlpool bathtubs in its best suites. Topping it all, though, is the hotel's famous restaurant. Chef Jeannot Lavoie prepares an ever-changing menu of innovative cuisine and oversees an award-winning wine cellar that contains more than 12,000 bottles.

WHAT: site, hotel, restaurant. **MURRAY BAY:** 50 miles/80 km northeast of Quebec City. **FAIRMONT LE MANOIR RICHELIEU:** 181 Rue Richelieu, La Malbaie. Tel 800-441-1414 or 418-665-3703, fax 418-665-7736; manoir richelieu@fairmont.com; www.fairmont.com/richelieu. *Cost:* doubles from $135 (low season), from $180 (high season). **LA PINSONNIÈRE:** 124 Rue St. Raphaël, La Malbaie. Tel 800-387-4431 or 418-665-4431, fax 418-665-7156; pinsonniere@relaischateaux.com; www.lapinsonniere.com. *Cost:* doubles from $255 (low season), from $310 (high season). Dinner $50. **BEST TIMES:** Jun–Aug for outdoor activities and whale-watching; Dec–Feb for skiing and snowmobiling.

Québecois Comfort, Just North of the Border

LAKE MASSAWIPPI

Quebec, Canada

Wedged between the St. Lawrence River and the borders of Maine, New Hampshire, and Vermont, Quebec's Eastern Townships mix Québecois charm with a healthy dose of Anglo-Saxon culture, courtesy of the British loyalists who settled here in the 1770s and 1780s after fleeing the newly independent United States of America. The land is some of Quebec's most beautiful, with tiny Victorian villages and resorts nesting among fields, orchards, lakes, and majestic mountains. It's a popular holiday destination for Québecois, with numerous opportunities for outdoor sports in summer and winter and an autumn that defies description.

Ten-mile-long Lake Massawippi sits in the southeastern part of the Townships, less than a half hour's drive from the U.S. border, and is its most desirable resort area, especially around the northern end's North Hatley, a tiny town full of galleries, restaurants, and shops. Wealthy Americans began summering along the lakeshore in the early 20th century to escape the Southern heat, building grand homes that have in many cases been converted into fine inns.

Hovey Manor is one of these. Built in 1899 by Henry Atkinson, an Atlanta electricity baron who arrived every summer accompanied by eighteen servants and ten horses, it was designed in the style of George Washington's Mount Vernon, with a broad, white-columned veranda. Outside, its 25 hillside acres feature English-style gardens sloping down to two small lake beaches. Inside, the inn is still appointed with many of Atkinson's original antique furnishings. The inn's award-winning restaurant (and wine list) delight year-round with dinners accompanied by classical music.

In the Eastern Townships' Brome Missisquoi district, the landscape is not just for viewing, it's for savoring. This lovely area of rolling hills and valleys serves as the breadbasket of Quebec, and more than 60 winemakers, farmers, maple syrup producers, beekeepers, cheese makers, cider brewers, and other producers of fresh local food products open their properties to visitors.

Throughout the region, sheltered valleys produce microclimates where wine grapes and orchards flourish. A marvelous way to take in the scenery and enjoy the fine regional cuisine is aboard the Orford Express, a vintage excursion train that offers 3.5-hour sightseeing and culinary trips that travel past farms, vineyards, orchards, and lakes—the very countryside whose bounty appears on the menu. Board the train in Sherbrooke, take a seat in the observation car or one of three dining cars, and dine your way across the Eastern Townships.

At the southern end of Missawippi, in the town of Ayer's Cliff, Auberge Ripplecove (owned by Jeffrey Stafford, brother of Hovey Manor owner Steven Stafford), sits directly on the lake,

a testament to its beginnings as a 1940s fishing resort. In its modern incarnation, Ripplecove is the most hotel-like of the Massawippi inns, focusing in summer on golf, watersports, tennis, hiking, and horseback riding, and in winter on alpine and cross-country skiing. The thirty-five rooms are uniformly warm, cozy, and charmingly decorated, about half with fireplaces, balconies, and whirlpools.

WHAT: site, hotel, restaurant. **LAKE MASSAWIPPI:** 100 miles/161 km southeast of Montreal, less than 20 miles/32 km from the Vermont border. Eastern Townships Tourism, tel 800-355-5755 or 819-820-2020; www.easterntownships.org. **HOVEY MANOR:** Chemin Hovey, North Hatley. Tel 800-661-2421 or 819-842-2421, fax 819-842-2248; www.manoirhovey.com. *Cost:* from $115 (low season), from $140 (high season), includes dinner. **ORFORD EXPRESS:** tel 866-575-8081 or 819-575-8081; www.orfordexpress.com. *Cost:* from $57. *When:* early May–Oct. **AUBERGE RIPPLECOVE:** 700 Chemin Ripplecove, Ayer's Cliff. Tel 800-668-4296 or 819-838-4296, fax 819-838-5541; info@ripplecove.com; www.ripplecove.com. *Cost:* doubles from $220 (low season), from $265 (high season), includes dinner. Dinner $35. **BEST TIMES:** 1st week of Oct for peak fall foliage.

Fireworks, Film, Jazz, and a Good Laugh

MONTREAL'S SUMMER FESTIVALS

Quebec, Canada

Part iconoclastic Francophone outpost in otherwise *anglais*-speaking North America, part skyscraping internationalist city, Montreal is also a festival town *par excellence*, boasting several major festivals and a number of smaller events that fill the summer months.

By far the most important of the lot is the Montreal International Jazz Festival, which brings together some 2,000 world-class musicians from twenty different countries (from Tony Bennett to Buju Banton, Gonzalo

Music lovers gather at the Place des Arts for the annual Montreal Jazz Festival.

Rubalcaba to Archie Shepp) and attracts an audience of about a million and a half aficionados. In the entertainment district around the Place des Arts, Montreal's grand concert hall, ten outdoor stages present 350 free concerts, while 150 indoor concerts are held in venues around town. Held annually since 1979, it's the world's largest jazz fest, with a little (OK, a lot) for everybody.

Throughout June and July, the city's skies are lit up every week by the Montreal International Fireworks Competition (Le Mondial SAQ), in which the world's best pyrotechnicians—veritable artistes of the big boom—fire their biggest, newest, and most revolutionary creations into the Montreal night to the accompaniment of a musical score. Founded in 1985 at La Ronde, Quebec's largest amusement park (located on Ile Ste.-Helene in the St. Lawrence River), the event draws around 2½ million spectators annually, who view the action from the park, the Jacques Cartier Bridge, and both banks of the St. Lawrence.

In late August and early September, the World Film Festival brings together more than 400 films from all over the globe, including an average of 250 world premieres. Founded in 1977, the festival aims to encourage cultural diversity and understanding between peoples, and each year highlights films of a different country, from the United States to Hungary, Israel, Iran, and Korea.

On the lighter side, mid-July's Just for Laughs (Juste pour Rire) Festival promotes the idea that humor can be reinvented, with artists stretching the boundaries of the form. Founded in 1983, when sixteen French-speaking comedians performed for a total crowd of about 5,000, the festival has grown to host approximately 2,000 artists annually, performing for a million and a half laughers at more than thirty venues along Rue St.-Denis, and to a worldwide audience via TV feeds. Other standouts of Montreal's summer lineup include Les FrancoFolies de Montreal, celebrating French music from around the world; the Montreal Celtic Festival, celebrating Celtic music, dance, storytelling, art, and traditional food and drink; and the Festival Nuits d'Afrique, promoting music of the African diaspora with indoor and outdoor concerts.

WHAT: events. **GENERAL FESTIVAL INFORMATION:** Tourism Montreal, tel 877-266-5687 or 514-873-2015; www.tourism-montreal.org. All festivals held at various venues around town, with varying ticket prices. **MONTREAL INTERNATIONAL JAZZ FESTIVAL:** tel 888-515-0515 or 514-871-1881; www.montrealjazzfest. com. *When:* 10 or 11 days in late Jun/early Jul. **MONTREAL INTERNATIONAL FIREWORKS COMPETITION:** from La Ronde park, Ile Ste.-Helene. Tel 514-397-2000; www.international desfeuxloto-quebec.com. *When:* Jun–Jul, usually on weekends. **WORLD FILM FESTIVAL:** tel 514-848-3883; www.ffm-montreal.org. *When:* 12 days in late Aug–early Sept. **JUST FOR LAUGHS FESTIVAL:** tel 888-244-3155 or 514-845-3155; www.hahaha.com. *When:* 11 days in mid-Jul. **LES FRANCOFOLIES DE MONTREAL:** tel 800-361-4595 or 514-790-1245; www.franco folies.com. *When:* 10 days in late Jul–early Aug. **MONTREAL CELTIC FESTIVAL:** tel 514-481-3471; www.montrealcelticfestival.com. *When:* 4 days in mid-Aug. **FESTIVAL NUITS D'AFRIQUE:** tel 514-499-9239; www.festivalnuitsdafrique. com. *When:* 11 days in mid-Jul.

VIEUX MONTRÉAL

Montréal, Quebec, Canada

In 1535, Jacques Cartier arrived in a village called Hochelaga, populated by about a thousand Iroquois, and claimed it for France, renaming it Mont Réal (Royal Mountain) in honor of his king. Actual change didn't come, though, until 1642, when a group of missionaries led by Paul de Chomedey arrived and set up shop, intent on converting the Iroquois to Christianity. Within thirty years the mission had grown into a settlement of about 1,500, becoming in the process a major trading center and base for trappers and explorers. By 1759, when the British took the region from France, the population had grown to 5,000, inhabiting about 95 acres on the St. Lawrence River. Today, this area is known as Vieux Montréal or Old Montreal, and despite almost 250 years of British rule and the influence of *anglais*-speaking Canada and the United States all around, it remains a bastion of French diaspora culture—in its architecture, its cuisine, and its general attitude toward life.

By the 1960s, the area's predominately 18th- and 19th-century buildings and cobblestone streets had fallen into disrepair, but a popular restoration program saved it from ruinous modernization. The move has certainly paid off: Today, it's a hot spot of nightlife, café culture, and tourism, and preserves its atmosphere so well that it's commonly used by American and Canadian film producers as a stand-in for Europe. Don't miss the Rue St.-Paul, with its Victorian street lamps, or appealing public squares such as the Place d'Armes and the Place Jacques-Cartier. The latter is the epicenter of Montreal summer life, with its street performers, cafés, flower merchants, and a line of horse-drawn *calèches* waiting to put the *vieux* in your experience of Vieux Montréal. Nearby are some of the city's most beautiful and historic sites, including the 1824 Basilica of Notre Dame, with its stunningly rich interior; the Sulpician Seminary, Montreal's oldest building, dating to 1685; and the Art Deco Prévoyance Building, giving the city a dose of Big Apple with its resemblance to the Empire State Building. Along the riverfront, the Vieux Port has been transformed from a gritty warehouse district into a 1.2-mile promenade full of parks, exhibition spaces, skating rinks, and playgrounds. It's also the jumping-off point for various boating activities on the river.

For perfect 18th-century Montreal accommodations, check in at the Auberge Les Passants du Sans Soucy, a former fur warehouse built in 1723, now converted into a delightful bed-and-breakfast whose nine rooms—with their stone walls, beamed ceilings, polished wood floors, and traditional Québecois furniture—are veritable time machines. For a quick bite, head north of the old quarter to L'Express, one of the most popular spots in town for French bistro cuisine. For something more elaborate, Toque! offers an ever-changing menu that uses only the freshest (and sometimes rarest) ingredients. It mixes modern French with a tiny dash of Asian influence, and arrives at what has almost unanimously been considered the best meal in town since chef/owner Normand LaPrise opened the place in 1993.

WHAT: site, hotel, restaurant. **VIEUX MONTRÉAL:** bounded on the north by Rue St.-Antoine, on the south by the St. Lawrence

River, and on the east and west by Rue Berri and Rue McGill. **AUBERGE LES PASSANTS DU SANS SOUCY:** 171 Rue St.-Paul Oueste. Tel 514-842-2634, fax 514-842-2912; www.le sanssoucy.com. *Cost:* doubles from $105 (low season), from $140 (high season). **L'EXPRESS:** 3927 Rue St.-Denis. Tel 514-845-5333. *Cost:*

$22. *When:* daily breakfast, lunch, and dinner. **TOQUE!:** 900, Place Jean-Paul-Riopelle. Tel 514-499-2084. *Cost:* $65. *When:* dinner only, Tues–Sat. **BEST TIMES:** Feb/Mar for the High Lights winter festival (www.montreal highlights.com); summertime for many other festivals (see separate entry, page 771).

Snow King of the Canadian East

MONT TREMBLANT RESORT

Quebec, Canada

In 1938, Philadelphia millionaire Joe Ryan visited 3,001-foot Mont Tremblant, liked what he saw, bought it, and built the second real ski resort in North America, after Sun Valley. The highest peak in the Laurentians,

Tremblant derives its name (Trembling Mountain) from an Algonquin Indian legend in which the angry god Manitou gave the mountain a good shake whenever humans disturbed nature in any way.

Mont Tremblant slopes down to the pedestrian village and the shores of Lake Tremblant.

Perhaps Vancouver-based Intrawest (owner of Whistler/Blackcomb and other North American ski resorts) had the god's wrath in mind, then, when in the early 1990s they spent $800 million on a massive rebuilding project that specifically sought to blend man-made structures with nature, to provide intimate glimpses of the mountain and surrounding country at every turn. The resulting Mont Tremblant Resort has been called the best in eastern North America, with more than 46 miles of trails (broken up into ninety-two runs) attracting skiers from across North America and farther afield. Fully 50 percent of its trails are classified expert-grade, including the daunting double-black-diamond Dynamite, with its 42-degree incline, the steepest in eastern Canada. The 3¾-mile Nansen Trail is its opposite number, a gentle slope that takes in the resort's entire 2,131-foot drop.

At the base of the mountain's five high-speed lifts lies Mont Tremblant village, a pedestrian-only area designed to resemble Quebec City's historic district, right down to its cobbled streets, wrought-iron balconies, tin roofs, and old-fashioned signage. More than eighty bars, restaurants, and shops line the ground floors of the quaint, brightly painted buildings, while the top floors are filled with privately owned condos managed and rented by Intrawest. Le Shack, located on the St.-Bernard Plaza, is Tremblant's largest and most popular après-ski spot, with a continental menu, rustic decor, sports on the big screen, and a relaxed, completely nonglitzy feel that's shared by the whole resort. Scene seekers need not apply.

The resort's activities center offers a range of nonski activities, including dogsledding and evening sleigh rides that come complete with storytelling and hot chocolate. The resort's own La Source Aquaclub offers heated indoor pools, a eucalyptus steam bath, whirlpools, and a full fitness center.

The area's best hotel is the ski-in/ski-out Fairmont Mont Tremblant, located on a crest above the village. Pleasantly scaled, homey, and harmoniously integrated into its natural setting, the hotel has the feel of a country inn, its north-woods decor drawing from the tradition of Quebec's 19th-century Provençal-style residences and its lobby warmed by the requisite huge stone fireplace. In summer, Tremblant transforms into a destination for canoeing, hiking, mountain biking, fishing, and climbing, with miles of trails and two world-class 18-hole golf courses, the par-71 Le Diable and the par-72 Le Géant.

WHAT: experience, hotel, restaurant. **MONT TREMBLANT RESORT:** 75 miles/121 km north of Montreal. Tel 88-TREMBLANT, or 819-681-2000; www.tremblant.ca. *When:* skiing Nov–late Apr. **FAIRMONT MONT TREMBLANT:** 3045 Chemin de la Chapelle. Tel 819-681-7000, fax 819-681-7099; fairmont tremblant@fairmont.com; www.fairmont.com/ tremblant. *Cost:* doubles from $180 (low season), from $225 (high season). Breakfast and dinner package from $250. **BEST TIMES:** Dec–Mar for best ski conditions.

Bon Hiver, Vieux Québec

CARNAVAL IN THE HEART OF NEW FRANCE

Quebec City, Quebec, Canada

Perched on a rocky promontory above the St. Lawrence River, Quebec City was settled in 1608 by Samuel de Champlain and built up over the years into a perfect simulacrum of old France. It's all here: cobbled streets, slate-roofed stone houses, a 95-percent French-speaking population, patisseries, *vin rouge,* and fresh baguettes. North America's only walled city, Vieux Québec (Old Quebec) is divided into the Haute-Ville and Basse-Ville (upper and lower cities), designations that are now simply geographic, but were once economic and strategic—the lower city filled with warehouses and other necessities of the river trade, the upper with homes built on the heights as protection against the English. As it turned out, the altitude wasn't much of a help: In 1759, British general James Wolfe took the city after a two-month siege, losing his own life in the process but ensuring England's hegemony on the continent. The Québécois still haven't gotten over the shock, and the more nationalistic among them harbor dreams of partition from Canada and the establishment of an independent country.

To get the full flavor of the place, go in February for the seventeen-day Carnaval de Québec, when the Québecois make peace with their climate. Once a sort of northerly Mardi Gras where a drink called caribou (a mixture of brandy, vodka, sherry, and port) laid many a strong man low, Carnaval is now a family-friendly event.

At the famous Dufferin Terrace, a pedestrian-only rampart that offers the city's best views, adults and children sail down icy chutes on toboggans, while on the Plains of Abraham—the fields where the French and British fought it out—horse-drawn sleighs transport all comers back to a simpler time. Elsewhere, teams from around the world compete in snow-sculpting events, and brave souls participate in canoe races across the ice-choked St. Lawrence. At log-cabin "sugar shacks," revelers looking like the Michelin Man in their layers of down and fleece line up for maple taffy, while others strip down to their Speedos for a quick dip in the Snow Bath.

To warm up less bravely at the end of the day, nothing is more Quebec than a stay at the Château Frontenac, the very symbol of the city, dominating the skyline from the top of Cap Diamard, the highest point in town. Designed in the style of a Loire Valley château and looking as if it's stood here forever, it is, in fact, only a little over a century old, built in 1893 by Canadian Pacific railroad baron William Van Horne, who hoped to lure tourists with the promise of hotel luxury. Outside, it's all stone-and-brick turrets, green copper roofs, and dormered windows, while inside, its labyrinthine corridors lead through various wings built over a hundred-year span with total stylistic consistency. Book an odd-numbered room in the main tower for a view of the St. Lawrence, or an even-numbered room for a panorama of the city's rooftops—probably the most European vista this side of Paris. Various suites and the eighteenth-floor "honeymoon rooms" help relieve the Carnaval chill with Jacuzzi tubs. To dispel the chill in a different way, try a martini in front of the fireplace at the hotel's Bar St.-Laurent, overlooking the Terrasse Dufferin.

WHAT: event, hotel. **QUEBEC CITY:** 145 miles/233 km northeast of Montreal, 450 miles/724 km northeast of Toronto. Tourism Quebec, tel 877-266-5687; www.bonjour quebec.com. **CARNAVAL DE QUÉBEC:** tel 866-422-7628; www.carnaval.qc.ca. *When:* 17 days in early Feb. **LE CHÂTEAU FRONTENAC:** 1 Rue des Carrières. Tel 866-540-4460 or 418-692-3861, fax 418-692-1751; chateau frontenac@fairmont.com; www.fairmont.com/frontenac. *Cost:* doubles $250 (low season), from $290 (high season).

LATIN AMERICA

MEXICO AND CENTRAL AMERICA

SOUTH AMERICA AND ANTARCTICA

Windows to Paradise

LAS VENTANAS AL PARAISO

Los Cabos, Baja, Mexico

Located at the tip of the 1,000-mile long Baja Peninsula, near where the Pacific Ocean meets the Sea of Cortez, Las Ventanas al Paraiso evokes an ends-of-the-earth solitude, cushioned between sea and desert

sands, with the rough-hewn mountains beyond. Once geographically isolated, Los Cabos—a 25-mile corridor that joins the two desert towns of Cabo San Lucas and San José del Cabo—has undergone rapid development in the past decade, with Cabo San Lucas in particular becoming known for wild, *cerveza*-drenched spring breaks (check out the town's Cabo Wabo, where every night is tequila night) and hippie-happy social dropouts.

Las Ventanas, opened in 1997 on 12 acres along the much calmer corridor, has brought the ultimate note of refinement to this scene, from the breezy luxury suites (the largest in Mexico) to the seaside drop-edged pool, the championship 18-hole Robert Trent Jones Jr. golf course, and an indoor-outdoor spa that offers everything from a torchlit couples' massage and cactus-cleansing wraps

to—no kidding—a stress-reducing rubdown for your poodle. The smiling and eager staff second-guesses every whim, and guests who venture off the property can take advantage of the area's ruggedly beautiful scenery and world-class diving and big game fishing. Sunsets are completely intoxicating, even if you didn't attend the afternoon's tequila tasting.

WHAT: hotel. **WHERE:** Two hours by air from L.A. **LAS VENTANAS:** tel 52/624-144-2800, in the U.S., 888-ROSEWOOD; las ventanas @rosewoodhotels.com; www.lasventanas.com. **COST:** doubles from $595 (low season), from $775 (high season). **BEST TIMES:** Dec–Mar for watching the thousands of gray (and other) whales that arrive from the Arctic; May–Sept for greater availability and reduced rates (along with hotter weather); fall months for big game fishing tournaments.

Who's Watching Whom?

WHALE WATCHING IN BAJA

San Ignacio Lagoon, Baja, Mexico

At San Ignacio Lagoon, a magical place halfway down the Pacific Coast of the Baja Peninsula, whales regularly rise out of the sea to touch and be touched by humans. In one of the most remarkable annual migrations nature offers, Pacific gray whales make the 5,000-mile trip from the chilly feeding grounds of the Arctic to the safety of the warm, shallow waters of the Baja Peninsula for their breeding and calving season (the calves are about 15 feet long and weigh 1,500 pounds at birth). Several thousand whales may visit San Ignacio every winter, and there are sometimes up to 400 in the lagoon at one time. *Las amistosas* (the friendly ones) is the local nickname of the whales, which regularly approach the small *panga* fishing boats to be

Greeting a whale

stroked and touched by awed whale-watchers, in a genial gesture that has stumped scientists for more than twenty years, since it was first recorded. Nearly driven into extinction in the 19th and 20th centuries, the gray whales now return in greater numbers every year and were removed from the endangered species list in 1994. Baja's Pacific lagoons and fifty uninhabited islands, often referred to as Mexico's Galápagos, are renowned for their exceptional marine and bird life. Hundreds of dolphins accompany the gray whales, while humpbacks, finbacks, and Brydes whales make regular appearances along with blue whales, the largest animals on the planet.

WHAT: experience. **HOW:** Baja Expeditions in San Diego sets up a temporary safari-style camp and runs 5-day trips. Tel 800-843-6967 or 858-581-3311, fax 858-581-6542; travel@baja ex.com; www.bajaex.com. **COST:** $2,295 per person, double occupancy, all-inclusive land/air from San Diego. **WHEN:** late Jan–Mar.

An Anthropologist's Dream in the Heart of the Mayan Highlands

NA BOLOM

San Cristóbal de las Casas, Chiapas, Mexico

People-watching is the most exciting pastime in this blissfully untouched, high-altitude colonial city. More than thirty different Indian tribes—descendants of the ancient Mayas, known for their woven textiles and

other highly sophisticated crafts—trek into town to fill the daily *mercado*, especially on Saturday. Here near-extinct languages like Tzotzil or Tzeltal and beautiful headdresses and embroidered costumes decorated with tassels and ribbons distinguish one tribe from another.

No trip to San Cristóbal is complete without a visit to Na Bolom, home of the much-

respected archaeologist Frans Bloom, which he shared with his wife, ethnologist-journalist-photographer Gertrude Bloom, until her death in 1994. The 19th-century hacienda functions as a museum, cultural gathering point, and guesthouse. It is the headquarters for continuing research on the area's constellation of highland villages, where the cultural and religious traditions of the local people thrive. Communal dinners at the hacienda, in a salon filled with art and artifacts, guarantee an interesting mix of visiting scholars and like-minded travelers. Spending a night or more at the guest house may well be the highlight of your journey to this little-traveled corner of Mexico.

WHAT: town, hotel. **SAN CRISTÓBAL DE LAS CASAS:** southeastern Mexico near the Guatemala border. Daily 1-hour flights from Mexico City arrive at Tuxtla Gutiérrez airport, 90 minutes by car and approximately $60 by taxi. **NA BOLOM:** Avenida Vicente Guerrero no. 33. Tel 52/9-678-1418; reservations@nabolom.org; www.nabolom.org. *Cost:* doubles $70. Dinner $12. *When:* center and guest house open year-round; museum closed Mon. **BEST TIMES:** mid-Feb to mid-Mar.

Selling local wares

Most Haunting of the Ancient Mayan Cities

PALENQUE

Chiapas, Mexico

In a dense virgin jungle at the foothills of the Usumacinta Mountains lies one of the most extraordinary ruins of the Mayan culture. Occupying a high, strategically situated plateau, Palenque blossomed during the middle to late Classic Period of the 6th to 9th centuries A.D. as a center of art, religion, and astronomy. It was one of the first Mayan sites to be discovered and remains one of the most majestic and best preserved. Its elegant architecture, descriptive stucco carvings, calligraphy, and decorative friezes reached great artistic heights, and much has been left in situ. Other artworks are displayed in a small museum recently opened near the entrance to the grounds, or in the National Museum of Anthropology in Mexico City. Only a fraction of the monuments have been excavated, the foremost the Templo de las Inscripciones (Temple of the Incriptions), a stepped pyramid that holds the extraordinary tomb of Palenque's ruler, King Pacal, who died in A.D. 683 (his burial mask, made of 200 fragments of jade, is in the museum in Mexico City). The perfect complement to the Palenque experience is the lodging at Chan-Kah Ruinas. Its simple stone and wooden bungalows are spread out over 50 acres of primordial jungle like a timeless Mayan village. Your wake-up call comes at dawn when the tropical birds begin their chorus.

WHAT: site, hotel. **PALENQUE:** 94 miles/150 km northeast of San Cristóbal de las Casas, within the Parque Nacional Palenque. **CHAN-KAH RUINAS:** Carretera Palenque. Tel 52/916-345-1134, fax 52/916-345-0820; reservaciones@chan-kah.com.mx; www.chan-kah.com.mx. *Cost:* doubles $120.

A Breathtaking Train Ride Through a Rugged Wilderness

COPPER CANYON

Chihuahua, Mexico

This little-known, inaccessible region of the Sierra Madre contains one of the greatest canyon complexes in the world, inhabited by one of the most isolated peoples, the Tarahumara Indians. Las Barrancas del Cobre,

the Copper Canyon, is actually a network of deep gorges, five river systems, six major intertwined canyons, and 200 minor ones that are cumulatively four times larger (and often deeper) than the Grand Canyon in Arizona. Remote and largely unexplored, it is best seen from a window seat aboard Ferrocarril Mexicano's Chepe train, which travels the Chihuahua al Pacifico Railway. Perhaps the most scenic train ride in North America, it is 400 miles and thirteen Wild West hours from Chihuahua to Los Mochis on the Pacific coast, snaking through pine-forested highlands and wild ravines. To experience the real grandeur of this rugged wilderness, take advantage of the stops. At 7,300 feet, the midway station of Creel offers entry into the heart of the back country, either with organized treks or through a stay at the Copper Canyon Sierra Lodge, where native guides can be hired. The endless maze of hiking

trails through the highlands and lowlands of this enormous canyon land and the opportunity to interact with the shy and beguiling Tarahumara make your stay here unique. There's no electricity at the Sierra Lodge, but a toqued chef prepares surprisingly good local dishes, and the vast views are what you dreamed of.

The silver-mining village of Batopilas was once one of the wealthiest cities in Mexico; it now sits forgotten on the riverbank at the bottom of the canyon, amid lush subtropical foliage and flowers. Sierra Lodge can arrange for accommodation there, enabling you to take the most thrilling, cliff-hanging road trip you're ever likely to take: a 6,000-foot descent into the mouth of the canyon that takes six to eight spine-tingling hours. Those who think they've seen it all should opt for the "suicide seats" atop the lodge's Chevy van, a veritable roller coaster.

WHAT: site, experience, hotel. **CHIHUAHUA:** 230 miles/370 km south of the Texas border. **CHEPE TRAIN:** tel 52/614-439-7211 or 52/614-439-7212; chepe@ferromex.com.mx; www.chepe.com.mx. *Cost:* 7-day tour from $130, meals extra. **COPPER CANYON SIERRA LODGE:** in the U.S., contact Copper Canyon Sierra Lodges, tel 800-648-8488; info@coppercanyonlodges.com; www.coppercanyonlodges.com. *Cost:* doubles from $95, includes meals, guides, and side trips; 7-day excursions from Los Mochis $1,285 per person, all-inclusive. **BEST TIMES:** Feb–Apr and Oct–Dec.

Riverside lodge in Batopilas

A Colonial Showcase Resonates with Dance and Song

CERVANTES ARTS FESTIVAL

Guanajuato, Mexico

With its historic architecture and old-world courtliness, Guanajuato is the picture-perfect location for the Cervantes Arts Festival, an annual affair that keeps alive the image of the errant knight Don Quixote, tilting at windmills and fighting to preserve the romantic side of the Spanish soul. On any given day, the narrow cobblestone lanes resonate with the music of the *estudiantinas*—local university students dressed as strolling 16th-century troubadours and armed with mandolins and guitars, evoking the Andalusia of centuries ago. The multiweek Festival Internacional Cervantino is considered one of the most important celebrations in Latin America, and it floods the city's and state's many venues with well-known performing artists from around the world. Anything being performed in the Teatro Juárez, the center of Guanajuato's cultural life, is worth seeing, if only to admire the theater's ornate metalwork, gilt carving, and thick velvet. The opulent turn-of-the-century theater—considered by Enrico Caruso to be one of the finest in the Americas—is located on the Jardín de la Unión, the former mining capital's main square and ultimate gathering place for the festival's more spontaneous alfresco performances. The venerable Posada Santa Fé, the oldest and most charming inn in town, has a number of rooms that overlook the plaza and the festival's movable concert; its outdoor café downstairs promises front-row seats and some of the best regional food in town.

WHAT: event, hotel. **GUANAJUATO:** 225 miles/362 km northwest of Mexico City. **FESTIVAL INTERNACIONAL CERVANTINO:** tel 52/55-5615-9403; www.festivalcervantino. gob.mx. To order and pay for tickets in advance with credit card, call Ticketmaster in Mexico City at 52/5-325-9000; www.ticket master.com.mx. *When:* first 3 weeks in Oct. **POSADA SANTA FÉ:** Jardín de la Unión 12. Tel 52/473-732-0084, fax 52/473-732-4653; www.posada-santafe.com. *Cost:* doubles from $80.

A Celebrated Artists' Colony and a National Monument

SAN MIGUEL DE ALLENDE

Guanajuato, Mexico

Mexican and international artists and writers are drawn 6,200 feet above sea level to the mountaintop town of San Miguel de Allende by the glory of its Old Mexico charm and the purity of its seductive light. Among its many attributes are restored mansions of noble families, 18th-century churches, the always lively laurel tree–shaded El Jardín square, outdoor cafés, and excellent restaurants. In addition, a still-active and centuries-old trade in traditional Mexican artisanship helps make San Miguel a vigorous cultural center. Founded in 1542 by wealthy Spanish cattle barons and retaining an aura of prosperity that came later from the Guanajuato region's lucrative silver mines, this casual but sophisticated town draws a mix of well-heeled Mexico City weekenders, intelligentsia, international tourists, and a growing community of American residents. Much of its fame has been secured by the long-term success of the Casa de Sierra Nevada, San Miguel's most refined hotel (and one of Mexico's finest inns). Built in 1580 and transformed into the sumptuous home of the Archbishop of Guanajuato in the late 1700s, it is comprised of seven colonial-era manor houses. A welcoming staff gives new meaning to the expression "Mi casa es su casa." Each distinctive suite has its own personality and decor: Some have wood-burning fireplaces and their own courtyard patio or private garden, while many enjoy full

views from the unique mountaintop vantage point for which San Miguel is known.

WHAT: town, hotel. **SAN MIGUEL DE ALLENDE:** 180 miles/290 km from Mexico City. **CASA DE SIERRA NEVADA:** Calle Hospicio 35. Tel 52/415-152-7040, in the U.S., tel 888-341-5995; mail@casadesierra nevada.com; www.casadesierranevada.com. *Cost:* doubles from $250. **BEST TIMES:** Fiesta de San Miguel, the town's patron saint, is celebrated on Sept 29 and is the year's highlight; festivities include dancing, food, fireworks, and the Pamplonada (running of the bulls).

Eighteenth-century churches form part of the cityscape.

Among the Most Romantic Views on Earth

ACAPULCO BAY

Guerrero, Mexico

Much of Acapulco's sultry reputation as Hollywood's south-of-the-border beach club has been shattered by a groundswell of tourism, but the heart-stopping beauty of the bay is eternal. With physical endowments

that have often been compared to those of Rio de Janeiro, Acapulco also features unbeatable sunsets over its 7-mile horseshoe-shaped bay and the Pacific Ocean. Avoid the package tourists and revel in unparalleled water views

by checking in at the Hotel Las Brisas, the legendary hilltop grande dame that has shared Acapulco's fame and high profile for more than three decades. Every day is a honeymoon here: Secluded fuchsia- and bougainvillea-draped casitas boast private pools filled with floating hibiscus flowers and breathtaking views of the bay. The hotel's Bella Vista alfresco restaurant is aptly named. Most guests never leave Las Brisas's 750 tropical acres on the lush mountainside, but those who do jump in

Poolside at Las Brisas

one of the hotel's hallmark pink-and-white-striped jeeps and head 6 miles north to the nearby fishing village of Pie de la Cuesta, a laid-back spot where a hammock and the roar of the surf evoke a long-ago Acapulco.

WHAT: site, hotel. **ACAPULCO:** 240 miles/386 km south of Mexico City. **HOTEL LAS BRISAS:** Carretera Escénica, 8 miles/13 km south of Acapulco. Tel 52/744-469-6900, fax 52/744-469-5332; in the U.S. and Canada, tel 866-221-2961; brisas@brisas.com.mx; www.brisas.com.mx. *Cost:* casitas from $245 (low season), $280 (high season). **BEST TIMES:** beach weather year-round; some rain Jun–Sept.

The Charm of Old Mexico in a Hilltop Silver Capital

TAXCO

Guerrero, Mexico

Silver-hungry tourists make a beeline for this delightful colonial-era hill town, whose zigzag streets are lined with more than 250 silver shops. The shop-till-you-drop group won't be disappointed by the quantity

and refined quality of Taxco's silver objects and jewelry, but sightseers will also find a charming town of red-roofed, whitewashed houses piled on top of one another. Cobblestone streets lead to the Plaza Borda, the main square, named after the town's 18th-century benefactor, a miner who inaugurated Taxco's second silver boom (the first happened with the 16th-century arrival of the conquistadores). In gratitude for the bounty (since depleted) that made him wealthy, the French-born Borda financed the construction of a Baroque twin-towered church, Iglesia de Santa Prisca, in the square. It is considered one of the most elaborate examples of the extravagant churrigueresque architecture in Mexico—no expense was spared either for the exquisitely carved pink-stone facade or for the interior, where twelve gilded altarpieces

vie for attention. The church and plaza are at the heart of Taxco's renowned Semana Santa (Holy Week) processions, the most compelling in Mexico—self-flagellating, black-hooded, bare-torsoed penitents are only part of the lavish spectacle that involves the entire town. For more local character, it's an easy walk from the main zocalo to the welcoming Hotel Los Arcos. Housed in a converted 17th-century monastery, it brims with simplicity, serenity, and colonial charm.

WHAT: town, hotel. **TAXCO:** 111 miles/179 km southwest of Mexico City, 185 miles/298 km northeast of Acapulco. **HOTEL LOS ARCOS:** Juan Ruíz de Alarcon 4. Tel 52/762-622-1836; fax 52/762-622-7982; www.hotellosarcos.net. *Cost:* doubles from $45. **BEST TIMES:** Semana Santa, or Holy Week (usually Mar or Apr).

An Idyllic Getaway Times Two

ZIHUATANEJO

Guerrero, Mexico

While most of the world can barely spell (or pronounce) Zihuatanejo—let alone locate it on a map—the experienced set long ago designated the colorful, centuries-old fishing village (nicknamed Zihua) one of

Mexico's treasures. Two of its charming and highly distinctive hotels are regarded as among Mexico's top getaways. The unbeatable location of the small and romantic Villa del Sol on one of the loveliest beaches in Mexico (with the recent addition of three spacious beachside suites that feature private terraces, rimless pools, and sunset-perfect views of Zihuatanejo Bay) has long been showered with accolades and awards. Its breezy informality belies the precision of its clockwork service, which owes to the German owner's labor-of-love involvement. Who'd know from the luxury of its quiet and tropical serenity, disturbed only by birdsong and surf, that it is almost always full? Bright, hand-painted tiles are used throughout the cozy but elegant hotel, and local crafts have been collected on forays throughout the country. Swaths of sheer mosquito netting drape the canopied king-size beds and everywhere is the discreet attention to detail, design, and decor more commonly found in a private home.

Book an equal number of nights at the earth-colored, multilevel La Casa Que Canta (House That Sings), cantilevered on a rocky hillside above the gorgeous Playa La Ropa. Zihuatanejo's other must-see hotel, the Casa is made from molded adobe to resemble a traditional pueblo, with a mood that is both romantic and relaxed, and owes much to the exquisite taste of the hotel's French owners (who see to it that your bed is strewn with fresh flower petals every morning). The Casa's rimless, aptly named "infinity pool," where the blues of the sky, horizon, and Pacific Ocean all blend together in one magnificent tableau, is something magical at sunset. Each of the sea-view suites, many with open-air living rooms, private pools, and thatched-roof terraces, is named after a popular Mexican ballad (hence the hotel's whimsical name), each with a mood of its own. An aesthetic and visual extravaganza, filled as it is with brightly painted Michoacán handicrafts and surrounded by stunning views, the hotel became an immediate favorite with the international art-and-film crowd. The hotel's restaurant features locally caught seafood excellently prepared and served alfresco on a *palapa*-thatched terrace, with a starry sky served up for dessert.

WHAT: town, hotel. **ZIHUATANEJO:** 4.5 miles/7 km down the coast from Ixtapa; 150 miles/241 km northwest of Acapulco, a 3- to 4-hour drive on a scenic coastal road. Several daily 50-minute flights from Mexico City. **VILLA DEL SOL:** Playa La Ropa. Tel 52/755-

Peaceful days at the Villa del Sol

555-5500, fax 52/755-554-2758; in the U.S., tel 866-905-9560; hotel@villasol.com.mx; www.hotelvilladelsol.net. *Cost:* doubles from $355 (low season) to $500 (high season); suites from $570 (low season) to $875 (high season); beach suites from $780 (low season) to $1200 (high season). **LA CASA QUE**

CANTA: 1 mile/1.5 km outside of town center on the Camino Escénico. Tel 52/755-555-7000, fax 52/755-554-7900; in the U.S., tel 888-523-5050; guestservice@lacasaquecanta.com; www.lacasaquecanta.com. *Cost:* suites from $490; with private pools from $820. **BEST TIMES:** Dec–Apr.

Where the Gods Were Born

TEOTIHUACÁN AND THE NATIONAL MUSEUM OF ANTHROPOLOGY

Mexico City, Mexico

No one knows who built or inhabited Teotihuacán, a monumental city of pyramids, palaces, and temples. It is thought to have been settled around 100 B.C. and to have had more than 100,000 residents (some estimates say twice that) by A.D. 500. For the first six centuries A.D., Teotihuacán was possibly the most influential seat of political, religious, and cultural power in Central America. The Aztecs, who arrived later, believed that the cosmos was created here. So close to Mexico City and yet so far away, Teotihuacán covers more than 8 square miles and in its time was larger than contemporary Rome, making it then the biggest city in the world. By 700 it was mysteriously abandoned; some scholars believe it may have come to a sudden and violent end, possibly through arson.

A stroll down the pyramid-lined Avenue of the Dead, from the Pyramid of the Sun to the Pyramid of the Moon, underlines the symmetry and majesty of its architecture, all laid out in accordance with celestial movements—a meeting place of the gods, the heavens, the earth, and mankind.

A new state-of-the-art museum on the site helps eliminate much of the ruins' mystery, although many of the artifacts excavated here are on display at the Museo Nacional de Antropología in Mexico City. A trip to this museum is guaranteed to bring alive Mesoamerica's pre-conquest era in all its brilliance and splendor. One of the finest anthropological and archaeological museums anywhere, its collections are housed in an award-winning building reminiscent of the timeless grandeur of an Aztec temple. The Aztec calendar sun stone (the museum's pièce de résistance), elaborately feathered Aztec headdresses, exquisite pieces of gold or alabaster, and the simple instruments that were used in everyday life can be just as evocative as a crumbling ruin at the end of a jungle trek.

WHAT: site. **TEOTIHUACÁN:** 33 miles/53 km northeast of Mexico City. **MUSEO NACIONAL DE ANTROPOLOGÍA:** Paseo de la Reforma 1 Gante, in Parque Chapultepec, Mexico City. Tel 52/5-553-6268; www.mna.inah.gob.mx. *Cost:* admission $3; free on Sun. *When:* Tues–Sun.

A Home to Time-Honored Native Arts

MICHOACÁN

Mexico

Michoacán, wildly beautiful and perhaps the most artistic and culture-rich state in all Mexico, is the land of the indigenous Tarascans, a native people known for their brilliantly colored handicrafts and folk art, music and dance, and for their melodic Purépecha language. On the shores of Lake Pátzcuaro—at 7,250 feet, one of the world's highest—they founded the picturesque town of Pátzcuaro in 1324. Today the epicenter of Michoacán's *hecho a mano* craft culture, this is the best place to start your tour of the area. On Friday, market day, Indian women, many in brilliantly colored traditional dress, stream in from the neighboring villages, each one known for a different craft. Pátzcuaro itself is known for high-quality serapes and handwoven textiles (as well as homemade tamales), nearby Santa Clara del Cobre for hand-hammered copperware. There are also straw-work items and ceramics from Tzintzuntzán, furniture and native embroidery from Erongaricuaro, and exquisite lacquerware from Uruapán (which has a lively Sunday market). It is not by chance that Michoacán is one of Mexico's principal artisan centers. In the early 1600s a Spanish bishop arrived in the state capital, Morelia, intending to organize the indigenous settlements into a craft collective of sorts and to teach each town a different trade; much of his basic vision remains intact. An easy overview can be had without even leaving Morelia: Its Casa de Artesanías in the Plaza de San Francisco is a state-run showcase for the best regional folk art and craftwork.

The most European of Mexico's cities, the stately, colonial Morelia is also the perfect backdrop for the Villa Montaña. Set high in the Santa Maria hills amid exuberant foliage and panoramic views of the rose-stone city below, the villa is a regional craft- and antique-filled Mexican hostelry with a polished French veneer (due, no doubt, to its aristocratic European owners). Separate villas, a maze of patios and cobbled walkways create the atmosphere of a small, self-contained village with the original estate building at its core. Here the villa's sweeping views vie with the acclaimed kitchen for your attention, and every cityscape includes the graceful silhouette of Morelia's twin-towered cathedral—the second-largest in the Americas and one of the most beautiful in Mexico.

Overlooking Morelia from the Santa Maria hills

WHAT: town, hotel. **PÁTZCUARO:** 30 miles/48 km southwest of Morelia. All towns mentioned are within a half-hour drive of Pátzcuaro. Morelia is 190 miles/306 km west of Mexico City (40 minutes by air). **VILLA MONTAÑA:** tel 52/443-314-0231, fax 52/443-315-1423; in the U.S., tel 800-925-1737; hotel@villamontana.com.mx; www.villamontana.com.mx. *Cost:* doubles from $210. **BEST TIMES:** the enormously popular Día de los Muertos (Day of the Dead) is celebrated Nov 1 throughout Mexico, but the nighttime candle-lit vigils on the island of Janitzio in Lake Pátzcuaro are particularly famous.

A Phenomenon of Mother Nature

MONARCH BUTTERFLY MIGRATION

Michoacán, Mexico

In an astounding migratory pilgrimage that takes place every autumn, 300 million orange-and-black-winged Monarch butterflies from the eastern United States and Canada brave gales and downpours to make the arduous 2,000-mile trip south to winter in Mexico. High-altitude areas (over 8,000 feet) covered with fir trees northwest of Mexico City, which the Monarchs seem to prefer, have been made into natural reserves. By December, as many as 100 million will gather on these slopes, covering every tree in the vicinity. They are so numerous you can hear their wings beating; the combined weight of their tiny bodies clustered in dense layers on top of one another can actually break limbs from the trees. When they fly, the sky appears completely covered with orange and yellow confetti. Exceptionally cold weather in the winter months of 2002 resulted in the death of an enormous number of these wintering beauties, but local officials were surprised to see how quickly the population repropagated and recouped its losses.

WHAT: event. **WHERE:** Michoacán, in the fir forests of Central Mexico. **HOW:** Natural Habitats, tel 800-543-8917 or 303-449-3711, fax 303-449-3712; www.nathab.com. **COST:** $2,869 per person for a 6-day trip, all-inclusive, land only. **WHEN:** early Jan–early Mar.

In the City of Eternal Spring, a Treasured Inn

LAS MAÑANITAS

Cuernavaca, Morelos, Mexico

Las Mañanitas is considered a standard-bearer for luxury hotels in Mexico, the very definition of indulgence. Few do not know about it, and for good reason: At 5,000 feet above sea level, with a perfect climate the Aztecs called "eternal spring" and a smiling staff of 150 who live to pamper forty privileged guests, what's not to love? The atmosphere is sumptuous and relaxed, like the well-heeled city of Cuernavaca itself. Peacocks, cranes, and flamingos roam about the emerald lawns and flowering gardens as if in an open-air zoo, while parrots and rare blue macaws roost overhead. The city's ancient Aztec name of Cuauhnahuac, the Place of the Whispering Trees, might apply to the gardens here, bursting with flowers and Edenlike in their groomed perfection. Most of the twenty suites open onto the gardens'

Blue macaws swoop through the gardens.

cool, tropical glory, and much of life at Las Mañanitas takes place there —tea, cocktails, waiting for dinner, lingering for the joy of lingering, snoozing. If the hotel is full, guest-wannabes are in for a double disappointment if they intend to drop in for lunch or dinner instead. The justifiably acclaimed restaurant plays a key role in the inn's fame as an ideal getaway, and many weekend guests come for the dining experience alone. Book way in advance for either and cross your fingers.

WHAT: hotel, restaurant. **WHERE:** 50 miles/ 80 km south of Mexico City (the highway is known for heavy traffic). Calle Ricardo Linares 107. Tel 52/777-314-1466, fax 52/777-318-3672; lasmananitas@lasmananitas.com.mx; www.lasmananitas.com.mx. **COST:** doubles from $225, garden suites from $335. **BEST TIMES:** ideal climate year-round.

A Cultural Field Day—and Not Just for Shopping

OAXACA'S SATURDAY MARKET AND CAMINO REAL

Oaxaca, Mexico

With the mother lode of attractive crafts shops and galleries in this lovely colonial city, any day is a shopper's field day. Oaxaca has been called the most Mexican city in the republic, but on Saturday—

as hundreds of Indian merchants stream in from the surrounding villages in their traditional dress, hawking food and handmade and painted crafts—it becomes Mexico's largest and most intriguing Indian experience. (Oaxaca has the country's largest Indian population: Two out of three citizens are Indians, representing sixteen ethnic groups who speak nine languages and fifty-two dialects.) The Central de Abastos (Supply Center) is the market for handicrafts, with hand-painted pottery and forests of polka-dotted wooden cats and comical fantasy animals that must be bargained for, as well as embroidered *huipiles* (blouses) and *rebozos* (shawls), whose designs vary with their village of origin.

Oaxaca's remarkable blend of old-world Spanish affluence (exemplified by the magnificent Baroque Church of Santo Domingo and its gold-ornamented Rosario Chapel) and deep-rooted native tradition are gloriously at play in the 16th-century Convent of Santa Catarina de Siena. One of Mexico's colonial treasures, with various incarnations as a school, the mayor's office, and even a city jail, it has recently been converted into Camino Real, one of Mexico's most attractive hotels. The former convent can be found within an area officially declared a District of National Monuments, comprising twenty-six colonial-era churches—within the historic hotel's thick, cool walls, guests can enjoy a host of ancient frescoes, hushed flagstone loggias, jasmine-scented patios, and Los Lavaderos, a cupola-covered water fountain surrounded by twelve stone laundry basins. The former refectory has become the hotel's acclaimed restaurant, El Refectorio; sample the distinctive mole sauce, a local specialty found here in numerous interpretations.

WHAT: town, event, hotel, restaurant. **OAXACA:** 340 miles/547 km south of Mexico City; daily 55-minute flights from Mexico City (about $130 one-way). The Abastos market is at the southern edge of the town—just follow the crowd. **CAMINO REAL:** Calle Cinco de Mayo 300. Tel 52/951-516-0611, fax 52/951-516-0732; oax@caminoreal.com; www.

camino-real-oaxaca.com. *Cost:* doubles from $250. Dinner at El Refectorio $15. **BEST TIMES:** Oaxaca is famous for its celebration of the traditional holidays, particularly El Día de los Muertos (the Day of the Dead), Nov 1; Semana Santa (Holy Week) before Easter; and Christmas and New Year's. Unique to Oaxaca are the Guelaguetza Dance Festival in late Jul and the Food of the Gods Festival in early Oct.

Mayan Engineering Genius and Toltec Grandeur

CHICHÉN ITZÁ

Yucatán, Mexico

The most famous, spectacular, and, consequently, most frequently visited of Mexico's Mayan sites, the magnificent metropolis of Chichén Itzá was the principal ceremonial center of the Yucatán. If you are lucky enough to be here on the spring or autumnal equinox (March 21 or September 21), you will marvel at the mastermind who positioned the temple of El Castillo de Kulkulcán: The play of late-afternoon light and shadow creates a moving serpent (representing the ancient leader-turned-deity Kulkulcán) that, over the course of thirty-four minutes, slithers down 365 steps to the giant's head at the base of the pyramid's principal facade before disappearing into the earth. The 7-square-mile site at Chichén Itzá (2 square miles of jungle have been cleared) was inhabited for about 800 years, beginning as early as A.D. 432 during the Mayan Classic Period and ending with the arrival of the Toltec people. No more than thirty of its buildings have been explored, leaving hundreds untouched.

Beat the bus caravans of day-trippers by staying at the romantic Hotel Mayaland, set in 100 private acres at the edge of the ruins. Many of the rooms have views of the cylindrical El Caracol observatory. The flowering gardens and pools help pass the hottest part of the day; the only way to visit the ruins at night is with tickets for the sound-and-light show (which is a lot more entertaining than one might imagine).

WHAT: site, hotel. **WHERE:** 1½-hour drive from Mérida, 2½ hours from Cancún. **HOTEL MAYALAND:** through Mayaland Tours in Mérida. Tel 52/998-887-2450, fax 52/998-884-4510; in the U.S., tel 800-235-4079; info@mayaland. com; www.mayaland.com. *Cost:* doubles from $100. **BEST TIMES:** spring or autumnal equinox.

A highlight of the Yucatán's Mayan heritage

A Secluded Outpost on the Riviera Maya

MAROMA

Yucatán, Mexico

Maroma is a small jewel of a resort on a fragile coast, 30 miles down the road but light-years away from the pumped-up bulk of its coastal neighbor Cancún. Maroma's Mexican architect-owner envisioned it as a marriage between development and ecological preservation. Nestled on its own mile-long strip of wild Caribbean beach near the important Mayan ruins at Tulum, Maroma is a half-Moorish, half-Mayan enclave in 400 private acres covered with mangroves, jungle, and coconut palms. While Cancún continues to grow out of control, Maroma entertains no plans to grow at all. It is the most ambitious (and certainly the most luxurious) small-is-beautiful hotel in the area. From round, breezy, thatched-roof terraces and multicolored hammocks big enough for two, views of the turquoise sea are enough to stop hardened travelers in their tracks. Good food, good wine and margaritas, spa services, and finding the perfect spot on a wide, empty beach make up the average, perfect day. Those looking for glittering nightlife must head for downtown Cancún, but most guests at Maroma are seeking refuge from anything that resembles a crowd.

WHAT: hotel. **WHERE:** 30 miles/48 km south of Cancún. Tel 52/987-28200, fax 52/987-28220; reservations@maromahotel.com; www.maromahotel.com. **COST:** doubles from $765. **BEST TIMES:** Jul–Aug, Oct, and Dec–May.

Colonial Splendor Amid Ancient Mayan History

HACIENDA KATANCHEL

Mérida, Yucatán, Mexico

This masterfully restored 17th-century hacienda was built on the grounds of a pre–Classic Period Mayan settlement whose 3rd-century ruins can be toured with the hotel's resident scholarly guides. Its ancient Mayan mystique is apparent even in its name: Katanchel translates to "Where one asks the arc in the sky"—a Mayan reference to the Milky Way, which confirms the site as an ancient astronomical observatory. The hacienda's 740 acres were abandoned for decades after a cattle-ranch-turned-sisal-plantation reverted to jungle growth. Today it is a sanctuary for exotic wildlife and a prolific bird population, one of the hacienda's principal attractions. Katanchel's strategic location offers more than a dozen different day-trip options to lesser-known Mayan ruins, colonial towns, and natural sites. Accommodations are in former workers' dwellings scattered about the property, since restored and transformed into luxury pavilions surrounded by fragrant gardens. Most have private plunge pools filled with spring water from a mineral-rich underground source that's pumped by silent turn-of-the-century windmills.

Traditional Yucatán dishes made from organically grown ingredients are reinterpreted and served in a palatial salon that was once a sisal-processing factory. Katanchel's dynamic Mexican owners have brought ecotourism to new heights of luxury and excitement here; the hacienda is both their home and showcase.

WHAT: hotel. **WHERE:** 15 minutes east of Mérida, 2½ hours west of Cancún. Tel 52/999-923-4020, fax 52/999-923-4000;

anibal@haciendakatanchel.com; www.hacien dakatanchel.com. **COST:** suites from $300. **BEST TIMES:** Oct–Mar.

Katanchel: ecotourism at its most luxurious

Breathtaking View of a Colonial Pink City

CABLE CAR OVER ZACATECAS

Zacatecas, Mexico

The only thing more delightful than wending one's way through the byways of Mexico's colonial "Pink City" is to sail above it in the only *teleférico* cable car in the world that traverses an entire city. The effect is heady, since this once highly prosperous silver-mining city is already perched at 8,200 feet above sea level: Is it the altitude or views of the pictur-esque jumble of Baroque monuments below and the encircling hills beyond? By the 18th century, the mines of Zacatecas had made it one of the New World's richest cities. The city's former wealth is reflected in both the ubiqui-tous use of pink quarry stone, called *cantera*

A unique perspective on the Pink City

rosa, and the extravagantly decorated cathe-dral, one of Mexico's most outstanding Baroque buildings, whose silhouette monopolizes the view. Other stunning architectural sites greet travelers around every corner, some of them housing first-rate art collections. Two excellent museums are named for the Coronel brothers, both much-admired Zacatecan artists. Another architectural marvel is arguably Mexico's most unusual hotel, the Quinta Real, housed in the oldest bullring in the Americas. Many of the rooms have balconies overlooking the 17th-century *plaza de toros* (bullring), where echos of *¡Olé!* still resonate. Stop by, if only for a drink, in the hotel's bar, which occupies some of the former bull pens.

WHAT: experience, town, hotel. **ZACATECAS:** 375 miles/603 km north of both Mexico City and Guadalajara. The city has a small airport. **CABLE CAR:** runs from Cerro del Grillo to the craggy summit of the Cerro de la Bufa, where an 18th-century chapel dedicated to the Virgin, the city's patron saint, houses a portrait said to have miraculous powers. *Cost:* $4 round-trip. **HOTEL QUINTA REAL:** 434 Avenida Rayon. Tel 52/492-922-9104 or 52/492-922-9157, fax 52/492-922-8440; in the U.S., tel 866-621-9288; reservaciones @quintareal.com; www.quintareal.com. *Cost:* doubles from $205.

Fascination with the Afterlife: The Return of the Dead

EL DÍA DE LOS MUERTOS

Mexico

While many Americans view death with fear, anger, and anxiety, Mexicans maintain a vital bond between living and deceased family members, recognizing the Day of the Dead as a time to celebrate life while remembering those who have passed on. It is believed that the souls of the dead return for one week each year to visit friends and family and partake of the pleasures they knew and loved in life. The origins of this festive celebration predate the Aztecs, and the native tradition survived the arrival of the Spanish missionaries by mingling with the imposed observance of the Catholic Church's All Souls Day. Some rituals for El Día de los Muertos have remained unchanged over the centuries, and much preparation goes into the making of *ofrendas* of fruit, flowers, special pastries, and handicrafts for the dead, who are thought to begin to arrive on November 1. Special foods (and the occasional bottle of tequila) are laid out for the breakfast and dinner of departed loved ones. The cemeteries are full of people cleaning, painting, and decorating the tombs and graves of their ancestors. Family altars incorporate photographs, simple or elaborate flower arrangements with orange marigolds, or sometimes nothing more than a plain candle.

WHAT: event. **WHERE:** the Day of the Dead is celebrated in every pueblo and cemetery throughout Mexico. **HOW:** in the U.S., Sun Travel offers an annual trip to Oaxaca. Tel 800-369-2649 or 915-532-8900, fax 915-533-6887; www.suntvl.com. **COST:** $1,225 per person, double occupancy, for 5-night land-only package from Mexico City. **WHEN:** yearly departure around Oct 28.

First-Class Diving Along the World's Second Longest Barrier Reef

BARRIER REEF

Ambergris Caye, Belize

It is incongruous that along the coast of a little-known country the size of Massachusetts is a teeming barrier reef, the longest in the western hemisphere and second in area only to the Great Barrier Reef in Australia. More than 200 offshore islets and cays sit either directly on or just off the 185-mile-long reef, the two largest being Caye Caulker and Ambergris Caye. The latter is the most popular, its charming laid-back town of San Pedro the reef's most important jumping-off point for more than forty snorkeling and dive sites. Off the southern tip of Ambergris, the Hol Chan Marine Reserve offers one of the best day or night dives for sheer variety of marine life, including forty kinds of grouper, a forest of coral, and sponge as dense and varied as the mainland's jungle mantle. But if diving off Ambergris is great, then diving off the only three coral atolls in the Caribbean is unforgettable. Ringlike Lighthouse Reef is the most accessible, owing to a new airstrip built on the cay, and is nearest to two of the reef's most stellar dives: the fabled Blue Hole (in 1970 Jacques Cousteau called it "one of the four must-dive locations on this blue planet") and Half Moon Caye National Park. Lighthouse Reef also has spectacular wall dives, with superlative visibility often reaching 200 feet.

Once the entrance to a cave system, the Blue Hole is 1,000 feet across and more than 400 feet deep.

At Lighthouse Reef Resort, 90 percent of the guests come for the diving, the rest for the remoteness and serenity.

WHAT: site, experience, hotel. **AMBERGRIS CAYE AND LIGHTHOUSE REEF:** both are scenic 20-minute hops by air from Belize City. **LIGHTHOUSE REEF RESORT:** in the U.S., tel 800-423-3114, fax 863-439-2118; larc1@worldnet.att.net. *Note:* At press time, Lighthouse Reef Resort was temporarily closed for renovations. **BEST TIMES:** Mar–May.

Winning Combination of Texas Ranch and Belize Jungle

MOUNTAIN EQUESTRIAN TRAILS

Cayo, San Ignacio, Belize

Even if you don't ride, this beautiful place in the Maya Mountains will make you reconsider. Although some treks can be made by foot or four-wheel drive, many fascinating jungle destinations are accessible only on horseback. At Mountain Equestrian Trails (MET), your machete-wielding Mayan guide knows his backyard intimately. As he whacks back the dense brush along 60 miles of narrow, winding trails, he'll point out hidden wildlife and recount jungle lore on the way to breathtaking locations that include remote Mayan ruins and underground cave systems.

Unnamed waterfalls, hidden streams, and natural pools are perfect for a refreshing swim and a lunch break of homemade empanadas. Situated at 800 feet above sea level in the jungles of the Maya Mountains, some of the MET's trails head for twice that altitude on the Mountain Pine Ridge Forest Reserve. About 70 percent of this tiny former British colony is covered by forest; it is home to 700 species of trees and 250 kinds of orchids. Back at the ranch, owned by a hospitable American family, the simple but handsome thatched cabanas have no electricity, but are romantically lit by the flicker of kerosene lamps and resident fireflies. The showers are hot, the bacon is crisp, and the homemade banana pancakes are delicious. Extraordinary scenery and the clear mountain air should have even the formerly horse-phobic jumping back in the saddle for another day's journey of discovery.

WHAT: experience, hotel. **WHERE:** 72 miles/115 km west of Belize City. Pickup by MET can be arranged. Tel 501/669-1124; in the U.S., tel 800-838-3918, fax 941-488-3953; aw2trav2bz@aol.com; www.metbelize.com. **COST:** doubles $135. Half-day ride with lunch $60 per person. **BEST TIMES:** Jan–May (dry season).

Sleep Where the Ancient Maya Slept

CHAN CHICH LODGE

Orangewalk, Belize

S pending a night in this one-of-a-kind jungle-enveloped lodge is like being a guest of the Mayan spirits in an ancient world. Set within a Mayan plaza dating to the Classic Period (A.D. 300–900), itself surrounded by the pristine

vine-tangled wilderness of the 250,000-acre Rio Bravo Conservation area, the Chan Chich Lodge gives new meaning to the expression "off the beaten track." The ruin-studded location teems with birds and howler monkeys, while well-tended trails snake around grass-

Lie in your hammock or stroll among the ruins.

covered mounds concealing temples, pyramids, tombs, and residences dating back more than 1,500 years. Organized jeep and horseback trips to neighboring, less-excavated cities provide further insight into the rich Mayan heritage. The lodge's thatched-roof bungalows, built of local woods, resemble Mayan homes, but are elegant and luxurious inside, although TV- and telephone-free. Wraparound verandas strung with hammocks invite low-impact afternoons, when listening to the tropical birds may be all the gods meant for their guests to do.

WHAT: hotel. **WHERE:** 150 miles/241 km northwest of Belize City; 4-hour drive or 30-minute charter plane over virgin jungle. Tel/fax 501/234-419; in the U.S., tel 800-343-8009, fax 508-693-6311; info@chanchich.com; www.chanchich.com. **COST:** doubles $205 (low season), $215 (high season). Full board $70 per person per day. **WHEN:** year-round. **BEST TIMES:** Jan–May (dry season). Afternoon rains from mid-Jun to mid-Aug guarantee lots of animal and bird activity.

For That Real Jungle Experience

CORCOVADO NATIONAL PARK

Puerto Jimenez, Osa Peninsula, Costa Rica

With one of the world's best systems of reserves and national parks, Costa Rica's thirty-five wildlife refuges protect more than 25 percent of the country's territory; choosing where to head first is a visitor's

toughest choice. Covering one third of the remote Osa Peninsula that juts into the Pacific Ocean, in what *National Geographic* called "the most biologically intense place on earth," the Corcovado National Park is difficult to reach. You may, at times, feel like the only human interloper on the trails (there are no roads) meandering through its 100,000 acres. Corcovado is one of the country's largest and wildest parks, safeguarding virgin rain forest, deserted beaches, jungle-rimmed rivers, and a large, inaccessible swampland. Within its broad range of habitats live more than 140 species of mammals, from tapirs to ocelots and cougars. It has the largest remaining population of scarlet macaws, which—together with the 375 other species of birds in the park that occupy more than 850 kinds of trees—vie with four species of monkeys to be heard amid the wildlife cacophony.

Open-air living at Lapa Rios

At the park's southern border, the Corcovado Lodge Tent Camp is the highlight of a Costa Rica trip for many ecotourists. There's no electricity, shared baths only, and drinking water comes from a crystal-clear stream that runs by the twenty platformed tents. A unique "canopy tour" hoists awed guests up eight stories by pulley into the dense jungle canopy. Neither the canopy tour nor the Tent Camp is for everyone: Where the road from civilization ends, it is a forty-five-minute walk along a pristine beach for arriving guests, while luggage is transported by horse cart.

If roughing it is not to your taste, then consider Lapa Rios, a bungalow hideaway perched

350 feet above the Pacific in its own lush 1,000-acre nature reserve on the outskirts of Corcovado. Its American owners have created an intimate setup where guests can learn all about the encroaching rain forest. But school was never this much fun, or fascinating, or luxurious. Spread over three panoramic ridges above the Golfo Dolce in a self-contained corner of the Osa Peninsula, Lapa Rios's wondrous exposures of ocean and forest are evident everywhere from open-air observation platforms, the bar-restaurant, and the fourteen simple guest rooms appointed in polished tropical woods. Days revolve around nature, beginning with an early-bird tour that lets you share the sunrise with the indigenous bird species (Lapa Rios means "Rivers of the Macaws") and ending with shaman-guided medicinal treks and night nature walks.

WHAT: experience, site, hotel. **CORCOVADO**

NATIONAL PARK: 231 miles/368 km southwest of San José on the Osa Peninsula. 9 hours by car or 80 minutes by domestic flight or light-aircraft charter from San José. CORCOVADO LODGE TENT CAMP: operated by Costa Rica Expeditions in San José. Tel 506/257-0766, fax 506/257-1665; tp@expeditions.co.cr; www.costaricaexpeditions.com. *Cost:* from $120 per person. Package rates available. *Best times:* Jan–Apr (dry season). LAPA RIOS: tel 506/735-5130, fax 506/735-5179; info@laparios.com; www.laparios.com. *Cost:* $245 per person, includes all meals. Guided tours extra. BEST TIMES: Jan–Apr is high season, though many also like the "green" or rainy season of May–Sept.

Where Vibrant Rain Forest Plunges to the Sea

MANUEL ANTONIO NATIONAL PARK

Quepos, Puntarenas, Costa Rica

Of Costa Rica's dozens of national parks, Manuel Antonio has long been one of the jewels, an idyllic combination of exuberant forest, white-sand beaches, and rich coral reefs. The guardians of this beautiful wilderness are now attempting to harness its popularity by limiting the number of ecotourists and diverting some to other, less-visited parks. Manuel Antonio is one of Costa Rica's smallest parks, and one of the last remaining habitats for the red-backed squirrel monkey. Few parks boast a coastal location, but here there is snorkeling, skin diving, surfing, and fishing galore. After a visit to the rain forest gets you hot and sweaty, nothing beats jumping into the refreshing ocean . . . unless you're lucky enough to have booked at La Mariposa, dramatically sited on a cliff above the sea. Its six split-level Mediterranean-style villas are enveloped in a riot of hibiscus and bougainvillea and flawlessly integrated into the hillside. Astounding 360-degree panoramas may distract one from the excellent meals served in the open-air dining room. So captivating are the full-circle vistas that guests linger long after the brilliant colors of the sunset dissipate and the margaritas disappear. Some never make it down to Manuel Antonio, happy in their bird's nest above it all.

WHAT: site, hotel. **MANUEL ANTONIO NATIONAL PARK:** 3½ hours by car south of San José (hotel transfer one-way $150) or 20 minutes by air to Quepos. *When:* Tues–Sun. **HOTEL LA MARIPOSA:** tel 506/ 777-0355, fax 506/777-0050; in the U.S., tel 800-572-6440; info@hotelmariposa.com; www.hotelmariposa.com. *Cost:* doubles from $150 (low season), $215 (high season). **BEST TIMES:** Dec–Mar and Jun–Aug are dry months.

Delights for all five senses at Hotel La Mariposa

Costa Rica in a Nutshell

CHACHAGUA RAIN FOREST HOTEL

La Fortuna, San Carlos, Costa Rica

This beautifully situated cattle ranch is one of Costa Rica's most favored rain forest getaways. Located in the Tilaran Mountain range, one of the most biologically diverse areas in this verdant country, the Chachagua's 50-acre spread nestles up against the Children's International Rain Forest, which in turn joins the Monteverde Cloud Forest Reserve: Potential for bird and wildlife viewing here is tremendous. Arenal Volcano and Lake are an easy four-wheel drive away; there is spelunking, white-water rafting, and rappeling for those who aspire to do it all, and the Tabacón Hot Springs for those who don't. In this working cattle ranch, a stable of fine horses is on standby, and resident naturalists act as your guides. At the end of every perfect day, your handsomely appointed bungalow awaits by a mountain-clear stream. Chachagua could only be the brainchild of an owner dedicated to detail and creature comforts; the kingpin behind this smoothly run operation is the charismatic Carlos Salazar, who—with a lifetime of experience in the hotel industry—enjoys himself as much as all his international guests put together. Let him loose in the kitchen (much of the fruit and produce is grown on the ranch), and dinner becomes an event. Let him loose in the dining room, and he'll convince you that nothing less than a lifetime in Costa Rica will do.

WHAT: hotel, experience. **WHERE:** an easy 2-hour drive northwest of San José. Tel 506/2468-1010, fax 506/2468-1020; info@ chachaguarainforesthotel.com; www.chachagua rainforesthotelcom. **COST:** doubles from $85 (low season), from $95 (high season). **BEST TIMES:** Nov–Mar.

Colonial Monuments, Poetic Decay

ANTIGUA

Guatemala

Gorgeously set in a green mountain- and volcano-rimmed valley, Antigua is one of the oldest and loveliest cities in the Americas. The remnants of its colonial past are a charming and poignant legacy of a time when the city reigned as Spain's capital for all of the middle Americas, until the epic earthquake of 1773. Today's strict preserva-tion ordinances protect what remains of its 16th- to 18th-century Spanish Renaissance and Baroque churches, monasteries, and homes. Some have been reconstructed, while others have collapsed, probably forever. With its leisurely small-town pace, Antigua has become the darling of artistically inclined expats, wealthy weekend homeowners from Guatemala City, and more than thirty programs that teach Spanish as a second language. Amid the fashionable cafés and shops and poetically decaying weed-choked ruins stands the most beautiful rescued building of all, the Casa de Santo Domingo, Antigua's showpiece hotel. It is set among the romantic remains of what was Antigua's richest and most powerful monastery, built in 1642, 100 years after the city's founding.

WHAT: town, hotel. **ANTIGUA:** 15 miles/ 25 km from Guatemala City. **CASA DE SANTO DOMINGO:** 3a Calle Oriente 28. Tel 502/ 7820-1221, fax 502/7820-1222; reservas @casasantodomingo.com.gt; www.casasanto domingo.com.gt. *Cost:* doubles from $200 (low season), $235 (high season). **BEST TIMES:** Semana Santa (Holy Week) is the most lavishly celebrated in Central America; feast day of the local patron, Nuestra Señora de la Merced (Our Lady of Mercy), is Jul 25.

Ancient Beauty, Ancient Ways

LAKE ATITLÁN

Panajachel, Altiplano, Guatemala

The Altiplano, Guatemala's western highlands, is the country's most beautiful region, and perfect-blue Lake Atitlán—mirroring three Fuji-like volcanoes—is the image that most readily comes to mind and stays there.

Around the lake (itself a collapsed volcano cone), descendants of the ancient Maya still live off the ash-rich land, their simple maize-farming methods unchanged over time. Small towns top the olive green hills and promise interesting day trips, particularly when market day enlivens the village squares. The lakeside town of Panajachel retains something of its 1970s hippie heyday, when it was nicknamed Gringotenango. It is still the best jumping-off point for the other, more traditional lakeside towns on the western and southern shores, whose indigenous charm remains intact despite decades of tourism. The most visited, Santiago Atitlán still clings to the traditional lifestyle of its proud Tzutujil Maya; the women wear their colorfully hand-embroidered *huipiles* (blouses), and the Friday market is justly famed as a center for hand-woven textiles. Don't miss staying at the Posada de Santiago, nestled between two dormant volcanoes by a lagoonlike offshoot of the lake. It offers six small garden-surrounded stone bungalows that brim with local flavor, plus a well-known kitchen that does the same.

WHAT: site, hotel. **LAKE ATITLÁN:** Panajachel, the lake's main town, is 92 miles/ 147 km west of Guatemala City. Ferries leave Panajachel for Santiago Atitlán regularly. **POSADA DE SANTIAGO:** tel/fax 502/721-7167; posdesantiago@guate.net; www.atitlan. com. *Cost:* doubles from $65. **BEST TIMES:** Nov–Apr and Jul–Aug.

The volcano-rimmed lake is an oasis of serenity.

Incomparable Ghost Metropolis of the Maya

TIKAL

El Petén, Guatemala

In an empire that once encompassed Mexico, Belize, Honduras, El Salvador, and Guatemala, Tikal was the most resplendent of all Mayan cities. Its towering pyramids and acropoli were the highest structures in the western hemisphere, and by its heyday in the 7th century A.D. (it is believed to have been mysteriously abandoned around A.D. 900), an estimated 50,000–100,000 people (some accounts say twice that) lived in the 6-square-mile ceremonial city. Now Guatemala's most famous and impressive Mayan ruin, its centerpiece is the Great Plaza, flanked by tall, well-restored temples that were once covered in stucco and painted bright colors. At 186 feet and 212 feet respectively, Temple V and Temple IV are the highest on the grounds, and ideal for watching the sunset. Tikal lies in the middle of the vast, forest-covered Tikal National Park, so wildlife viewing and temple visiting to the cries of toucans and howler monkeys go hand in hand.

Special passes are granted to visit the Great Plaza after-hours when the moon is full, but Tikal is magical at any time of day. You can wake up and fall asleep to the sounds of macaws by staying on the park grounds in the modest bungalows of the Jungle Lodge, initially built to accommodate those who came to excavate.

WHAT: site, hotel. **TIKAL:** 1-hour drive northeast of Flores, whose airport services 1-hour flights to Guatemala City. (Car transfers between Flores and Jungle Lodge arranged by hotel, $17 round-trip.) **JUNGLE LODGE:** tel 502/2477-0570, fax 502/2476-0294; www. junglelodgetikal.com. *Cost:* doubles $215. **BEST TIMES:** Nov–Apr.

A Centuries-Old Trading Town Never Dies

MARKET AT CHICHICASTENANGO

Quiche, Guatemala

Guatemala's largest market takes place in Chichicastenango, one of the country's most colorful and accessible highland towns. Crafts from all over the country are sold here, and "Chichi's" famous twice-weekly market has become a popular tourist attraction. This has been an important trading town since well before the Spanish conquest, and Indian village life is still reflected by the vendors and the stalls with mouthwatering food set up to allay their hunger. The tourist stalls are traditionally set up around the outer edges of the market for better visibility, so head for the inner nucleus around the fountain, where the Indian population trades and barters. And pay a visit the night before, when Indian families from more than sixty surrounding villages set out their wares and exchange news and goods before settling in to sleep under the stars. Of the two market days, Sunday is when the traditional religious brotherhoods called *cofradías* often stage processions or ceremonies in the whitewashed 16th-century Church of Santo Tomás, where Catholic and Mayan rituals are practiced side by side. One of the country's most charming hotels, the Hotel Mayan Inn, is located here: The Quiche-Maya staff dress in traditional costume, and each room is its own museum, individually appointed in local crafts and textiles.

WHAT: event, town, hotel. **CHICHICASTENANGO:** 1½-hour drive from Panajachel, 3½ hours (92 miles/146 km) from Guatemala City. *When:* market opens Thurs and Sun at dawn. **HOTEL MAYAN INN:** tel 502/756-1176, fax 502/756-1212; info@mayaninn.com.gt; www.mayaninn.com.gt. *Cost*: doubles $135. **BEST TIMES:** feast day of the local patron, St. Thomas, is celebrated Dec 13–21, followed by special Christmas processions.

The Way the Caribbean Used to Be

ROATÁN

Bay Islands, Honduras

The lovely coral reefs off the unspoiled Bay Islands are an extension of Belize's barrier reefs—world-famous as the largest after Australia's Great Barrier Reef. But the unparalleled marine life here may seem even more beautiful, due to less tourism and less development. Of the three principal Bay Islands (four lesser islands and sixty small cays stretch 70 miles in a northeasterly arc), Roatán is the largest and most popular. With the only paved road in this mini-archipelago, it's also the most "developed." The reefs fringing these mountainous islands are home to the greatest diversity of corals, sponges, and invertebrates in the Caribbean—heaven to legions of divers, including scuba snobs who come here to avoid the overtrafficked and the done-to-death. As an escapist destination, these Islas de la Bahía are as lush and alluring as a tourist poster, attracting nondiving travelers as well. Many come to Roatán's Institute for Marine Sciences (RIMS), a research and educational facility working with dolphins, where training demonstrations are open to the public. Located on the peripheral grounds of Anthony's Key Resort, the island's best-sited and best-all-around hotel, RIMS offers guests the chance to swim, snorkel, or

Friendly dolphins at RIMS

dive with bottlenose dolphins in the open ocean or inside the lagoon.

WHAT: experience, site, hotel. **ROATÁN:** 35 miles/56 km off the northern coast of Honduras, connected by daily flights to Honduras's principal cities. **ANTHONY'S KEY RESORT:** on the northwest corner of Roatán,

Tel 504/445-1003, fax 504/445-1140; in the U.S., contact Bahia Tours, tel 800-227-3483 or 954-929-0090; info@anthonyskey.com; www.anthonyskey.com. *Cost:* from $449 per person for 4-night leisure package. Diving and snorkeling packages extra. **BEST TIMES:** Jan–Mar (dry season).

The Greatest Engineering Show on Earth

PANAMA CANAL

Panama City to Colón, Panama

Built across the narrowest point between the Atlantic and Pacific Oceans, the epic Panama Canal remains one of the greatest engineering achievements of the 20th century. The ingenious network of dams and locks linking two oceans took more than 75,000 workers more than ten years to build. Centuries of bankruptcy, mismanagement, and malaria delayed the project a number of times after the idea was first presented in 1524 by King Charles V of Spain. The first ship sailed through in 1914. Today ships line up on each side, waiting their turn to enter the canal, which operates around the clock. Most cruise ships offer on-board lecturers, who describe the three sets of double locks and how they function during the eight-hour, 50-mile crossing. Large ships worldwide are built with the Panama Canal's locks in mind (1,000 feet long and 110 feet wide), so no one has gotten stuck so far. Ships are charged according to size, the average commercial ship paying approximately $30,000. Individuals can no longer swim across, as Richard Halliburton did in 1928; he was charged 36 cents.

WHAT: site, experience. **WHERE:** stretching 50 miles/80 km northwest from Panama City on the Pacific side to Colón, Panama, on the Atlantic side. **HOW:** countless cruise ships cross the canal. Lindblad Expeditions uses the small, 62-passenger MV *Sea Lion* to tra-verse the Panama Canal and then continue along the Pacific coast of Costa Rica. In the U.S., tel 800-425-2724 or 212-765-7740, fax 212-265-3770; www.expeditions.com. **COST:** from $4,660 per person, per week. **BEST TIMES:** Dec–Apr (dry season).

One of many cargo vessels that travel down the Panama Canal daily

A Glimpse of Living History

ARCHIPELAGO DE SAN BLAS

Panama

Living a timeless existence on a scattering of small, idyllic tropical islands along the Caribbean coast of Panama, the Cuna Indians are a self-governing island community that Panama has encouraged to live according to their ancient ways. They are a colorful and proud people, and their autonomous and matriarchal province is a throwback to the Caribbean before the onset of mass tourism. The Cuna jealously guard their traditional economic and governance systems, music, dance, and dress. The men's attire is more Western than that of the women, who wear vividly colored skirts and gold necklaces, bracelets, earrings, and often nose rings and a black line tattooed down the length of their nose. They are known for elaborate hand-stitched *molas*, cloths made from many layers of colorful fabrics—the most popular of Panamanian handicrafts. The San Blas Archipelago comprises 365 islands, although the Cuna say there are many more than that—some are nothing more than a palm tree on an uninhabited spit of white sand.

WHAT: island. **WHERE:** off the Caribbean coast of Panama near Colombia. **HOW:** the largest in the island group, El Porvenir, has a small airport; daily 30-minute flights from Panama City cost about $110 round-trip. From El Porvenir, cargo ships make weekly runs to about 50 of the islands and accept paying passengers who don't mind the rudimentary cabins and simple meals.

SOUTH AMERICA AND ANTARCTICA

Chic in Life and Death

ALVEAR PALACE AND RECOLETA CEMETERY

Buenos Aires, Argentina

Buenos Aires's Barrio Norte is the chic address for Argentina's fashionable elite. Located in the heart of the elegant Recoleta district, it features the old-world landmark Alvear Palace, one of the most charming and stylish of South America's grand luxe hotels. Far more European than Argentine in ambience and design, its original Louis XVI materials and furnishings were brought directly from

France for its inauguration in 1932. The property has a decidedly French flair, most deliciously exemplified by its restaurant, La Bourgogne. Admire the alluring urban panorama from the hotel's roof garden, or make a rendezvous in the Lobby Bar, the city's meeting place of choice; then head out to any of the Recoleta's museums, boutiques, or eating spots. Or visit the nearby historic 10-acre cemetery where generations of Argentina's elite are buried: patriarchs, presidents, poets, and, yes, Evita repose here. You can roam around by yourself under century-old magnolias amid the ornate splendor of more than 7,000 tombs and mausoleums of the powerful and influential *porteño* (resident) families, but a guided tour can better fill in the backgrounds of Argentina's famous and infamous.

Of the seventy sites that have been declared national monuments, search out Evita's

nondescript black marble grave, inscribed with the world-famous epitaph: "Don't cry for me, Argentina, I remain quite near to you."

WHAT: hotel, site. **ALVEAR PALACE:** 1891 Avenida Alvear. Tel 54/11-4808-2100, fax 54/11-4804-0034; info@alvearpalace.com; www.alvearpalace.com. *Cost:* doubles from $435. Dinner at La Bourgogne $90. **RECOLETA CEMETERY:** Calle Junín across from Plaza Alvear. **BEST TIMES:** Sept–Oct, Apr–May.

Relax with a drink at the elegant Lobby Bar.

A Shrine to Argentina's National Dish

LA CABAÑA LAS LILAS

Buenos Aires, Argentina

Times are tough in Argentina and they say the average citizen is consuming less than his normal 130 pounds of beef per year (which is more than twice as much as Americans eat.) You'd never know it, though, at La Cabaña

Las Lilas, one of the most famous steakhouses in the world, which grills up some 90 tons of steak annually. Founded in 1905 and occupying a converted warehouse in the docks area of Puerto Madero, wood-paneled Las Lilas is the king of the capital's *parilladas* (grills), and the destination of choice for government-invited VIPs brought here to experience the

quintessential national specialty. Argentine steers are raised on a grain- and hormone-free diet that produces meat less marbled with fat and therefore lower in cholesterol. It is unrivaled elsewhere in the southern hemisphere, or perhaps anywhere in the world, a fact of which Argentineans are justifiably proud.

Although Las Lilas specializes in steak raised on its own 17,000-acre *estancia*, an alternative house specialty is the *parillada*, a mixed barbecue of things not commonly coveted back home, including sweetbreads, kidneys, and brains. Best to stick with the steak and accompany it with Argentina's excellent red malbec wines from Mendoza.

WHAT: restaurant. **WHERE:** Alicia Moreau de Justo 516, Puerto Madero. Tel 54/11-4313-1336; restaurant@restlaslilas.com.ar; www.laslilas.com.ar. *Cost:* $50.

Tango—the King of the Night

LAS TANGUERÍAS DE BUENOS AIRES

Argentina

The tango is Argentina's celebration of machismo, domination, and tormented love, and it is the very air the *porteños* (residents of Buenos Aires) breathe. This anguished lament, transformed into an intricate and exquisite dance, is the most authentic of Argentine creations. The tango's popularity has waxed and waned since the heady days of the 1920s, when the suave and darkly handsome singer Carlos Gardel drove the country wild before dying tragically in a 1935 plane crash. Tracking down the tango in Buenos Aires is both easy and impossible: it is everywhere and nowhere.

Tango—the vertical expression of a horizontal desire

A recent resurgence of tangomania confirms that this indigenous popular music has survived the era of rock 'n' roll, and some of the large dance halls, such as El Viejo Almacén and Casa Blanca, still put on an emotion-packed nightly show with the country's finest tango dancers, singers, and musicians. To see tango in its natural habitat—the classic small, smoky, dimly lit tango bar, where things don't start happening till the far side of midnight—the casual Bar Sur is the place to go. On Sundays at the weekly flea market at the Plaza Dorrego, a number of amateur tanguistas perform spontaneous shows on street corners—minus the flash and maybe with less polish, but from the soul.

WHAT: experience, site. **EL VIEJO ALMACÉN:** 799 Avenida Balcarce, San Telmo. Tel 54/11-4307-6689; www.viejoalmacen.com. *Cost:* $50 per person, includes drinks. *When:* show times Sun–Thurs 10 P.M., Fri and Sat 9:30 P.M. and 11:45 P.M. **CASA BLANCA:** 668 Avenida Balcarce, San Telmo. Tel 54/11-4331-4621 or 54/11-4343-5002. *Cost:* $40 per person, includes drinks. *When:* show times Mon–Fri 10 P.M., Sat 9 P.M. and 11 P.M. **BAR SUR:** 299 Calle Estados Unidos, San Telmo. Tel 54/11-4362-6086; info@bar-sur.com.ar; www.bar-sur.com.ar. *Cost:* $15 (drinks not included but there's free pizza!). *When:* Mon–Sat 8 P.M.–4 A.M.

The Stylish Theater and Après-Theater Scene

TEATRO COLÓN AND GRAN CAFÉ TORTONI

Buenos Aires, Argentina

Buenos Aires is the capital of the nonstop night, and much of its vibrant cultural life is due to its 300 theaters. Its most stately, the Teatro Colón, was conceived as a performers' venue of choice and completed in 1908 as a winter-season destination. It boasts impeccable acoustics, and has attracted such luminaries as Anna Pavlova, Maria Callas, Enrico Caruso, and Luciano Pavarotti, with Mikhail Barishnikov calling it "the most beautiful of the theaters I know." An enormous, majestic building that houses its own symphony and opera and ballet companies, its six-tiered interior is a tour de force of gilt and red plush, and the object of intense national pride. If your stay falls between performances, content yourself with a fascinating tour of the rehearsal halls, dance studios, and costume, wig, and set design workshops—all located in an amazing three-floor underground warren that employs more than 1,000 people. Don't be dismayed by the box office's "Agotado!" signs announcing sold-out performances: A grand Versailles-style antechamber called the Salón Dorado (Gold Room) hosts free chamber concerts almost every weekday afternoon.

After any show at the Teatro Colón, there's only one place to go: the Gran Café Tortoni, the city's grandest and oldest café. You might think you're in Paris rather than Buenos Aires. At this historic meeting spot, Einstein exchanged views with the intelligentsia, and Josephine Baker enjoyed being seen in the city's most sophisticated and cultural venue. Although a multitude of *confiterías*—each with its own flavor, history, and clientele—grace every street corner (they are the traditional place for *porteños* to begin and end the day), none celebrates the Belle Epoque like Tortoni, with its original 19th-century decor of stylish woodwork, decorated tiles, deep-red leather chairs, and painted skylights. No excuse is needed to linger solo or in good company over a *café con leche* or a *sidra*, a slightly alcoholic cider for which Tortoni has long been known.

WHAT: event, site, restaurant. **TEATRO COLÓN:** Avenida Cerrito 618. Tel 54/11-4378-7344; info@teatrocolon.org.ar;

The theater's grand exterior is matched by its stately performance hall.

www.teatrocolon.org.ar. *Cost:* tickets from $10–$50. *When:* season is Feb–Nov. **GRAN CAFÉ TORTONI:** 825 Avenida de Mayo near Plaza de Mayo. Tel/fax 54/11-4342-4328; tortoni@cafetortoni.com.ar; www.cafetortoni. com.ar. *When:* 8 A.M.–3 A.M. daily. Tango every evening except Tues; jazz late Fri and late Sat.

Of Gauchos, Pampas, and Polo Lessons

ESTANCIA LA PORTEÑA

San Antonio de Areco, Buenos Aires, Argentina

The verdant, flat pastures of the endless pampas and the culture of the nomadic gaucho cowboys are perhaps the images most associated with Argentina. The aristocratic life of the country's cattle-ranch *estancias* complete the romantic picture, and guests at the Estancia La Porteña can easily imagine that lordly life of another era as they immerse themselves here in Argentine history, myth, and literature. La Porteña is owned and run by Ricardo Güiraldes, international polo star and great-nephew of the celebrated Argentine novelist of the same name, whose books about gaucho life (including *Don Segundo Sombra*) made icons of these crusty real-life ranch hands. The colonial-style La Porteña is a 500-acre bed-and-breakfast whose owner's passion for polo (no one plays it like the Argentinians) and his team of eighty polo ponies have transformed the ranch into a destination for wealthy amateur players from around the world. Nonplayers may prefer to ride through trail-laced woods or to visit nearby San Antonio de Areco, whose renowned museum is dedicated to the novelist Güiraldes and the gaucho legend. This quiet village is known for the talented work of its gaucho-inspired silversmiths and artisans. Back at your 19th-century digs, they'll be preparing the evening's typical *asado* feast, centered around steaks unlike any you've ever tasted, grilled over an open fire.

WHAT: experience, hotel. **WHERE:** 70 miles/113 km northwest of Buenos Aires. **HOW:** contact Estancias Travel, tel 54/11-4315-8084, fax 54/11-5326-1056; info@estancias travel.com; www.estanciastravel.com. **COST:** $155 per person, includes all meals and drinks. **BEST TIMES:** Aug–Apr.

A 19th-Century Countryside Joy

ESTANCIA LA BENQUERENCIA

San Miguel del Monte, Buenos Aires, Argentina

When it comes to the *estancia* experience, Argentina's embarrassment of choices can flummox the first-time visitor. Take heart: For sheer character, beauty, picturesque setting, and Argentine hospitality, the 19th-century Estancia La Benquerencia is the best choice within easy reach of the nation's capital. This 6,000-acre working cattle ranch and its oat and wheat fields will make Buenos Aires seem remote, while the gracious welcome of Marta and Guillermo Staudt puts guests immediately at ease. Originally a public park, Benquerencia is now known for its meticulously preserved landscape and gardens; guests enjoy wandering around under huge pines, willows, and eucalyptus trees.

Better yet, take one of the horses bred and trained at the ranch and let a gaucho guide you the length and breadth of the estancia, unless you'd rather travel in one of Sr. Staudt's beautiful horse-drawn antique carriages. Large groups and receptions are frequently booked for the day or weekend, but you'll find them easy to avoid, given the *estancia*'s vast terrain and the numerous distractions it offers.

WHAT: experience, hotel. **WHERE:** 75 miles/121 km south of Buenos Aires. Tel 54/1-2714-3087. **HOW:** contact Estancias Travel, tel 54/11-4312-2355, fax 54/11-4313-5883; info@estanciastravel.com; www.estancias travel.com. **NOTE:** At press time, public access was restricted. Check before visiting. **BEST TIMES:** Aug–Apr.

---

*Nostalgic Iberian Grandeur in the
Heart of the Pampas*

ESTANCIA ACELAÍN

Tandil, Buenos Aires, Argentina

Estancia Acelaín gives visitors the chance to glimpse, even relive, the opulent seignorial lifestyle of the great cattle and grain barons, whose manor homes still dot the Argentine countryside. Built in 1922 by Enrique Larreta, a prolific Hispanophile author and one of the country's wealthiest *estancieros*, Acelaín was designed in the style of Moorish Spain, where Larreta spent his honeymoon in the early 1900s. Larreta's literary masterpiece, *The Glory of Don Ramiro*, is set in 16th-century southern Spain and explains the origins of the *estancia*'s imaginative decor, architecture, and landscaping redolent of—if not imported directly from—that place and time. His own prodigious collection of Spanish furniture and art from the 11th to the 17th centuries still graces the *estancia*. Perched on a promontory, the house overlooks the lush, fragrant Andalusian gardens that are the pride and joy of the current owners, Larreta's descendants and avid horticulturalists.

Woodlands make up but a part of the 1,600-acre Edenic parkland, which abuts 15,000 acres of grainfields and grazing lands for cattle; both woodland and park offer guests countless idylls, by horse, on foot, or in your favorite hammock.

WHAT: experience, hotel. **WHERE:** 34 miles/55 km northwest of Tandil, which is 241 miles/388 km from Buenos Aires. 45-minute flight from Buenos Aires ($115 round-trip). **HOW:** contact Estancia Acelaín, tel 54/22-9340-6101; safaris@cerroindio.com.ar; www.cerroindio.com. **COST:** doubles from $145, includes all meals and use of facilities, horses. **BEST TIMES:** Apr–May and Sept–Oct for weather; May–Aug for best hunting at the *estancia*'s Cerro Indio lodge.

An Oasis of Vines and Wines

ESTANCIA LOS ALAMOS

Mendoza, Argentina

Like the nearby city of Mendoza, the Estancia Los Alamos is a verdant oasis surrounded by vineyards and orchards. Here, in the middle of the Cuyo—the country's most arid region—and on the remains of what was once a half-million-acre cattle ranch, 12,000 irrigated acres are given over to extensive vineyards, olive groves, vegetable plots, and fruit orchards. Built in the early 1800s as a frontier fort, the sprawling white adobe main house has been home to the Bombal family since 1866. It later became known as something of a literary salon and country retreat for such luminaries as Jorge Luis Borges. Today

Rooms recall the estancia's *days as a retreat for artists and visitors.*

the good life still prevails at what seems a mixture of European manor hotel and U.S. dude ranch. You can visit nearby vineyards on horseback or by jeep, descend class IV rapids through a beautiful rimrock canyon, or just lounge by the *estancia*'s shaded pool. Lunches at 2:30 and suppers at 11:30 are anchored by pisco sours on the patio or late-afternoon tea. By day's end you'll know why the *mendocinos* call their home *La Tierra de Sol y Buen Vino*, the Land of Sun and Good Wine.

WHAT: experience, hotel. **WHERE:** 600 miles/965 km southwest of Buenos Aires. 2-hour daily flights to Mendoza. **HOW:** tel 54/26-2744-2350, fax 54/26-2742-6858; info@pagosargentinos.com; www.pagos argentinos.com. **COST:** $360 per person, double occupancy, includes all meals, open bar, all facilities, and numerous activities. **BEST TIMES:** Feb–Apr and Oct–Dec. Mendoza's biggest event is the weeklong Fiesta Nacional de la Vendimia (harvest festival), late Feb–Mar.

Nature's Mightiest Show of Sound and Fury

IGUAZÚ FALLS

Puerto Iguazú, Misiones, Argentina

Ironically one of the world's lesser-known great waterfalls, Iguazú manages nonetheless to steal the thunder of the others. In fact, it is wider than Niagara (proud South Americans call Niagara "a trickle in God's mind" compared to their greatest cataract). More than 1,700 cubic meters of water per second plunge over 200-foot cliffs here, creating 275 separate falls (as many as 350 during rainy season) in a wide horseshoe that forms northern Argentina's natural border with Brazil. The magnificence of the widest waterfall in the world can be viewed from both the Argentine and Brazilian sides. (Helicopter rides are only available from the Brazilian side, with special flights added during the full moon.) Iguazú, the original tribal name—"Big Water"— has outlived the official name bestowed in 1541 by the Portuguese explorer Alvaro Nuñez Cabeza de Vaca: Saltos de Santa Maria. A won-

The Iguazú Falls horseshoe is approximately 2 miles long.

derful network of spray-drenched walkways takes travelers through dense tropical jungle and alongside and over the falls for the best close-up experience. More than 80 percent of the falls lie within the Argentine border, including the over-whelming Garganta del Diablo (Devil's Throat) —the single most impressive cascade. But a fre-quently departing ferry or bus to the Brazilian side allows visitors to decide for themselves if the view can possibly be any better from there. If you long to fall asleep to the thunder of the falls, the Hotel das Cataratas in Brazil is your choice. If awakening to an awesome panorama from your hotel window is your pleasure, go for the Sheraton Internacional in Argentina.

WHAT: site, hotel. **IGUAZÚ FALLS:** Argentine-Brazilian border in the Parque Nacional Iguazú. Daily 2-hour flights from Buenos Aires. **SHERATON INTERNATIONAL IGUAZÚ RESORT:** tel 54/37-5749-1800, fax 54/37-5749-1848; in the U.S., tel 800-325-3535; reservas.iguazu@ sheraton.com; www.sheraton.com. *Cost:* doubles with view of falls from $365. **HOTEL DAS CATARATAS:** tel 55/45-2102-7000; reservas@ hoteldascataratas.com; www.hoteldascataratas. com. *Cost:* doubles from $345. **BEST TIMES:** access to certain catwalks may be limited during the high-water months of Apr–Jun, but the forests are filled with butterflies; Aug–Nov are optimum for climbing around the falls.

Patagonia: A Field and Stream Lover's Dream

ESTANCIAS QUEMQUEMTREU AND HUECHAHUE

San Martín de los Andes, Nequen, Argentina

Although the Estancia Quemquemtreu, a privately owned 250,000-acre working cattle ranch, is but a speck on the vast stretch of Patagonia, it's on every angler's dream map. Reverse-season fishing in a remote corner

of the world known for some of the hemi-sphere's best trout fishing draws sportsmen from all parts of the globe. A private stream

runs through the *estancia*, but it's the ranch's proximity to three of the region's best-stocked rivers that sweetens the deal. With only five

Riding the Patagonian landscape

guest rooms at the ranch, you'll be virtually alone wading those streams, taking in the big sky and big spaces that evoke the frontier days of the unspoiled American West. Streamside lunches, traditional barbecues, and wildlife viewing are framed by the awesome granite peaks of the Andes that separate Argentina from Chile to the west. In addition to raising 25,000 head of cattle, Quemquemtreu is a working polo ranch, and guests are welcome to watch some of the country's best players practice and train the ranch's forty resident polo ponies.

For a real cowboy experience in Patagonia, stay at the Estancia Huechahue, a more "intimate" 15,000-acre Anglo-Argentine cattle ranch at the foot of the Andes, where the stables of fine criollo horses can make a gaucho out of even the most unconvinced gringo rookie. The expanses of northern Patagonia are best appreciated on horseback, and riders can explore sparsely populated and wonderfully varied terrain, including barren, rolling hills, picturesque lakes, and dense forests, high ridges where the condors nest, and the valleys and narrow rock gorges below. Guests can roll up their sleeves and participate in rounding up, herding, and branding the *estancia*'s livestock, or do nothing more strenuous than attend the day's delicious *asado* lunch. There are optional rides to the ranch's summer pastures, higher in the mountains across the Atlantic-Pacific watershed. Or trade in your mount for a jeep and head for the charming lakefront city of San Martín de los Andes, a slice of the Swiss Alps transplanted to Patagonia. The region becomes a popular alpine and cross-country skiing area in the winter months of July and August.

WHAT: experience, hotel. **SAN MARTÍN DE LOS ANDES:** 2-hour flight southwest of Buenos Aires. **ESTANCIA QUEMQUEMTREU:** 90 minutes by car south of San Martín de los Andes. Tel/fax 54/29-7242-4410; info@quemquemtreu.com; www.quemquemtreu.com. *Cost:* $770 for 2 per day, all inclusive. **BEST TIMES:** Nov–Apr for fishing; Jan–Feb to observe polo practice. **ESTANCIA HUECHAHUE:** 45 miles/72 km east of San Martín. Tel 54/29-7249-1303; info@huechahue.com.ar; www.huechahue.com. *Cost:* $360 per person per day, all-inclusive. **WHEN:** Nov–Apr. **BEST TIMES:** peak summer months, Dec–Jan.

One of Mother Nature's Greatest Monuments

PERITO MORENO AND GLACIERS NATIONAL PARK

El Calafate, Patagonia, Argentina

A barren, stunning landscape that is home to some 300 glaciers, Glaciers National Park seems like another planet—and is almost as arduous to get to. While most of Earth's glaciers are receding, Perito Moreno—the park's centerpiece—is still growing; its imposing 3-mile-wide wall of ice rises 200 feet above the surface of Lago Argentino. Boats dodge the bobbing icebergs in the lake—the country's largest body of water and one of the loveliest because of its many fjords—for an up-close look at Perito Moreno as the 30,000-year-old, 20-mile advancing river of ice snakes its way down from the Andean cordillera.

The park is an area of harsh weather extremes and terrain to match, but you needn't explore the End of the World in the same conditions chronicled by Darwin. Luxury exists in the southern fringe of Patagonia's endless steppes at the handsome Hostería Alta Vista. This 155,000-acre working sheep farm that dates back to 1910 has made a gracious transition from private home to antiques-filled seven-room inn, with wrought-iron beds and luxurious custom linens. Guests can visit caves adorned with prehistoric paintings or ride horseback to the grounds' upper pastures, where the views of Moreno Glacier (yet another local phenomenon) and the peaks of the glacier park are exceptional.

WHAT: site, hotel. **GLACIERS NATIONAL PARK:** southern Patagonia. Daily 3-hour flights to Rio Gallegos from Buenos Aires, then connections by air (50 minutes) or car (3 hours) to El Calafate. **HOSTERÍA ALTA VISTA:** 20 miles/32 km from El Calafate. Tel 54/11-2902-499902; altavista@cotecal.com.ar; www.hosteriaaltavista.com.ar. *Cost:* doubles from $615, includes full board and activities—horseback riding, guided walks, cave visits. *When:* Oct–Apr. **BEST TIMES:** Mar–Apr for brilliant fall foliage; Dec for sheep shearing some of the hotel's 22,000 sheep.

Fine dining at the Hostería Alta Vista

In the Switzerland of South America

BARILOCHE

Rio Negro, Argentina

D etractors bemoan the loss of much of the old-world character of this developing ski resort in the heart of Argentina's Lake District, but no one criticizes its enviable location in one of the continent's most scenic areas.

Modeled after an Alpine village, Bariloche is full of chalets and gingerbread-style shops; and restaurants serve up Austrian-German cuisine—this is chocolate and fondue country. If you prefer natural beauty to man-made quaintness, head out of town and follow the signs for any of three driving tours that begin

and end in Bariloche: The mountain and lake scenery is uniquely beautiful in each of the four seasons. The three-hour *Circuito Chico* (Short Circuit) is a lovely afternoon's excursion, while the lengthier 150-mile *Circuito Grande* makes for a full day of gorgeous landscape. Both drives include excellent views of

Patagonia's Nahuel Huapí National Park, where you'll find some of the world's most dramatic peaks. And tucked away here in Argentina's largest and oldest national park is the Llao Llao Hotel, uniquely situated on 40 spectacular private acres. The hotel is in perfect harmony with its Andean location: There are ethnic fabrics, open fireplaces, and gleaming cypress logwork, all in an elegant hunting-lodge atmosphere—and everywhere, those views. Built in 1937 on the island-studded glacial Lake Nahuel Huapí (where Argentina's record salmon weighed in at 35 pounds), the Llao Llao has recently been resuscitated after having been closed for fifteen years. Privatized and impeccably renovated, it is once again one of the stellar hotel-resorts of South America, with a new 18-hole golf course and lakeside tennis courts for guests who visit at the height of the summer, and nearby Bariloche's sixteen ski runs for those who come in the austral winter. The cable car ride to the 7,000-foot peak of the Cerro Catedral is breathtaking in any season.

Rustic comfort in the lobby of the Llao Llao

WHAT: town, experience, hotel. **BARILOCHE:** Lake District, 2 hours from Buenos Aires by plane. **CIRCUITOS GRANDE AND CHICO:** can be booked through local tourist agencies or undertaken independently. **LLAO LLAO HOTEL & RESORT, GOLF SPA:** 15 miles/24 km from Bariloche. Tel 54/29-4444-8530, fax 54/29-4444-5781; info@llaollao.com.ar; www.llaollao.com. *Cost:* doubles from $220 (low season), from $385 (high season). **BEST TIMES:** Jun–Aug for skiing; summer is Dec–Mar.

A Breathtaking Train, a Relaxing Respite

EL TREN A LAS NUBES AND ESTANCIA EL BORDO DE LAS LANZAS

Salta, Argentina

Salta's stunning countryside is dotted with pre-Columbian ruins, artisan villages, and deep, mineral-streaked, polychrome *quebradas* (ravines) carved by rivers running down the snow-draped Andes. Through this eerily eroded area by the Argentina-Chile border, the seasonal El Tren a las Nubes (Train to the Clouds) makes an unforgettable high-altitude, high-adrenaline trip that is on the must-do list of all train buffs. The fifteen-hour trip—not for the faint of heart—leaves from Salta, one of the best-preserved colonial cities in Argentina. A magnificent engineering achievement, the track was finished only in 1948; it includes a harrowing series of switchbacks and tunnels, and crosses dozens of iron bridges and viaducts. The highlight is the 200-foot-high viaduct that crosses the La Polvorilla desert canyon before the train's turnaround point in San Antonio de los Cobres, an old Indian mining town 13,000 feet above sea level. The return trip may induce a case of scenery overload—a good time for a siesta.

Recharge any frayed nerves at the area's premier *estancia*, El Bordo de las Lanzas. After the revered General Martín Miguel de Güemes led local gauchos in several successful battles against the Spanish royalists in the early 1800s, he would rest up at this *estancia*—even then a nurturing hideaway. Bordered by Chile and Bolivia and framed by the foothills of the Andes, the northwestern Salta Province is a center for farming and livestock, and the *estancia*'s 11,000 acres are dedicated to sugarcane, tobacco, sunflowers, and raising zebu cattle and the famous paso peruano horses that are available for guests' use. Big, traditional meals based on regional specialties, using beef and ingredients from the estate, are proudly hosted by the gregarious Arias family of twelve, who make sure that their elegant 18th-century landmark estate provides the finest *estancia* experience in the region.

WHAT: experience, hotel. **EL TREN A LAS NUBES:** 15-hour round-trip leaves 7 A.M. daily from Salta (book ahead). *How:* contact La Veloz Turismo, tel 54/38-7401-2000, fax 54/38-7401-2001; info@laveloturismo.com.ar; www.veloturismo.com.ar. *Cost:* $130 per person, includes lunch on board. *When:* Mar–Dec. **ESTANCIA EL BORDO DE LAS LANZAS:** 15 miles/24 km south of Jujuy airport (2-hour Buenos Aires–Jujuy flight about $300 round-trip). Tel 54/38-7490-370; www.turismoelbordo.com. *Cost:* $360 per person, double occupancy, includes all meals and use of horses. **BEST TIMES:** Apr–May, Oct–Nov. Semana Salta (Salta Week) in Jun is a popular gaucho festival.

The Little Mother of Lake Titicaca

COPACABANA

Bolivia

This is the original Copacabana—not the beach in Rio de Janiero, but a sunny little town on the southern shores of Lake Titicaca (considered to be the cradle of the Inca civilization, the "womb of the world"). One of the most important Roman Catholic pilgrimage sites in South America, Copacabana's 400-year-old cathedral houses the shrine of the Indian Virgin, the Black Madonna, who is the beloved patron of Bolivia. The famous dark wood statue was believed to have been responsible for a spate of miracles since being carved by the native artist Tito Yunpanqui in 1592. Early Spanish Catholic influences are evident in the shrine's majestic gilded altar and the gem-encrusted robe worn by the gold-crowned statue of the Virgin. Set between two hills, the whitewashed church offers good views of the lake and town, but for the best vista, hike the extra mile to the replica of Calvary Hill, El Cerro Calvario, especially at sunset.

WHAT: town. **WHERE:** 4 hours by car and hydrofoil, crossing at Huatjata, north of La Paz on the coast of Lake Titicaca. **HOW:**

1-day and multiple-day trips from La Paz include Copacabana, the ideal departure point for the islands of Titicaca. Crillon Tours, tel 591/22-337-533, fax 591/22-116-482; in the U.S., tel 888-TITICACA; www.titicaca.com. **BEST TIMES:** the highlight of a number of feast days dedicated to the Virgin is the Fiesta de la Virgen de Copacabana, celebrated the first 2 days of Feb, when Aymara dancers arrive from all over Bolivia and Peru. Throngs of the faithful walk from La Paz during Holy Week, culminating in a spectacular candlelight procession on Good Friday.

A Witchcraft Market That Promises Peculiar Finds

MERCADO DE HECHICERÍA

La Paz, Bolivia

La Paz's daily Witchcraft Market is a fascinating place to visit: Herbal tea fusions and homeopathic folk cures as old as the Andes themselves abound, and there are coca leaves, figurines, snakeskins, and slabs of llama lard to be burned in offerings to the gods, amulets to guarantee a long and happy sex life, and other strange things. Integral to the native Kallawaya traditions of magic and healing is the local Aymara belief that their world is populated with benevolent and malevolent spirits—and many that can swing either way, depending on how they're treated. The market has lately begun to accommodate the growing number of gringo curiosity seekers, and booths selling colorful alpaca sweaters and woven textiles understandably do a brisker business than the vendors pushing dried llama fetuses. But the proud *chola* women (a reference to the native Bolivian dress) still sit among their witchcraft goods like queens, unfailingly wearing two braids fastened behind them and bowlers adopted from the British many generations ago.

WHAT: event. **WHERE:** Calle Linares, between Calle Santa Cruz and Calle Sagárnaga. **BEST TIMES:** Apr–Oct.

Journey into the Heart of Discovery

SAILING UP THE AMAZON

Amazonia, Brazil

The vast kingdom of the Amazon has fascinated explorers for centuries. Adventurers today can unpack in any of the rainforest lodges within an hour or two of Manaus, the populous yet middle-of-nowhere capital of Amazonas, Brazil's largest state. But to travel by river boat through its very heart is one of life's great adventures. The dimensions of the river—once known as "The River Sea"—are truly awesome. As it gathers its strength from more than 1,000 tributaries and drains into an area nearly the size of the contiguous United States, the Amazon's flow is ten times greater than that of the Mississippi. Iberostar's 75-cabin *Grand Amazon* sets off from Manaus, located some 800 miles upriver from the coastal city of Belém (see below). Its four- and five-night cruises include experienced naturalist guides who approach each trip with sensitivity and expertise, sharing it with like-minded passengers who make the vessel their floating home. You can expect daily exploration of remote jungle tributaries and visits to riverside villages, pristine islands, and jungle clearings behind the rain forest's "green wall." Of the many highlights is the "meeting of the waters," where the dark, tealike Rio Negro meets the cappuccino-colored Salimoes River where they flow side by side for several miles; this, according to Brazilians, is where the Amazon begins. Face-to-face encounters with any of the countless living species (science has yet to catalog some 85 percent of

Floating through the river's lush aquatic vegetation

them) illustrate the river's fascinating and fragile ecosystem.

WHAT: experience. **HOW:** Iberostar *Grand Amazon* leaves year-round from Manaus. Tel 55/92-2126-9900; www.iberostar.com.br. **COST:** 4- and 5-night river cruises from $350 per person per night (double occupancy), includes all meals and excursions. **BEST TIMES:** Jun–Sept are the driest months.

Colorful Mayhem at the Mouth of the Amazon

VER-O-PESO MARKET AND LÁ EM CASA

Belém, Amazonia, Brazil

Belém is the jumping-off point for most river trips up the Amazon, and its exuberant daily market Ver-o-Peso (whose name comes from the colonial-era sales pitch—literally, "See the weight!") is a jumbled, seemingly endless sprawl of exotic goods. The hypnotic confusion and heady smells of dried herbs, medicinal roots, concentrated essences of the jungle's spices and flowers, and miracle elixirs and potions hold visitors in thrall. Snakeskins, turtle soap, and dolphin eyes may be contraband articles, but they still make an occasional appearance along with other items linked to macumba superstition and voodoo folklore: aphrodisiacs, amulets, alligator-tooth charms, lizard powder, dried boa constrictor heads, and other unrecognizable things you may not want to know about. The humid air carries the aroma of mouthwatering food being prepared by native women, who cook for the hundreds of vendors in Brazil's largest outdoor marketplace amid a cacophony of cursing, flirting, touting, and bargaining. The market's main attraction is its cornucopia of the river's most unusual species of fish

Morning is the best time to experience the bustle of the Ver-o-Peso market.

uble chef-owner, Paulo Martins, carries the torch by giving his guests the best the river has to offer. The region's premier dish is *pato no tucupi*, duck in an herb sauce made from the juice of the ubiquitous manioc root, here raised to a culinary art form; only the locals seem to hanker for the minced turtle meat or frog legs. More than twenty years ago, Chef Martins's mother Doña Ana went upstream to the family farm to learn from the Indian elders; the family has been entertaining fortunate visitors ever since.

(piranha!), meat (armadillo!), fruit, and vegetables, many of them guaranteed to show up the same day at Lá Em Casa, Belém's best restaurant for native *cozinha brasileira*.

It was at Belém that the native people first showed the colonials the wonder of the Amazon's bounty. Today, Casa's warm and vol-

WHAT: site, restaurant. **VER-O-PESO MARKET:** in the port area along the Avenida Castilho França, facing the pier. **LÁ EM CASA:** Tv. Dom Pedro I 546. Tel 55/91-3242-4222; restaurante@laemcasa.com; www.laemcasa.com. *Cost:* dinner $20. *When:* lunch and dinner Mon–Sat; Sun dinner only.

The Ultimate Tree House

THE ARIAÚ JUNGLE TOWER

Manaus, Amazonia, Brazil

Perched high above the heart of the Amazon jungle, the greatest rain forest on earth, the Ariaú Jungle Tower is enveloped in the voluptuous beauty of dense treetop canopy where the Rio Ariaú and the Rio Negro meet.

A network of seven cylindrical towers, miles of connecting trapezelike catwalks, and two lookout towers made of thatched roofs and polished tropical woods, the hotel compound is supported by stilts that rise up to 130 feet. Some of the towers, such as Tarzan's Houses, are 110 feet aboveground, with 360-degree views of the Amazon's thousand shades of green. Electric generators and indoor plumbing ensure the luxury of ceiling fans and minibars, and the restaurant bakes its own hearty breads and does delicious things with fresh local ingredients and fish plucked from the river. But the real luxury is the hotel's seamless immersion in the Amazon and its mind-boggling profusion of plant and animal species, a living round-the-clock theater. The hotel's guided explo-

One of the viewing towers

rations by canoe, riverboat, or on foot are a celebration of the rain forest, the ultimate laboratory for life on earth.

WHAT: hotel. **WHERE:** 35 miles/60 km or 3 hours by boat upstream from Manaus, which is connected by daily flights to all principal cities in Brazil. **HOW:** tel 55/92-2121-5000, fax 55/92-3233-5615; treetop@ariautowers. com.br; www.ariautowers.com.br. In the U.S., contact Brazil Nuts, tel 239-593-0266, fax 239-593-0267; info@brazilnuts.com; www.brazilnuts.com. **COST:** 3-night/4-day package from $540 per person, double occupancy, includes transfers from Manaus, all meals, guides, and excursions. **BEST TIMES:** Jul–Nov.

A Wetland Wonderland

PANTANAL AND THE CAIMAN ECOLOGICAL REFUGE

Mato Grosso do Sul, Brazil

The largest wetland in the world, Pantanal is an oasis of water and wildlife whose numbers and variety are staggering. It is the meeting place of rivers, the last intact ecological paradise, home to a wealth of wildlife elsewhere hunted to extinction—and most South Americans don't even know about it. Spoonbills, chaco chachalacas, coatis, jabiru, rheas—chances are you've never heard the names of many of these exotic creatures, let alone seen them. Others (wolves, anteaters, tapirs, jaguars, deer, armadillos) you may have seen before, though not of this size: Here they grow to be the largest of their kind on the continent. Most of the South Dakota–size area is privately owned by huge *fazendas* (cattle ranches). Cows and caimans live side by side in a curious alliance, while the spirit of the *pantaneiros*, cowboys of the Pantanal, prevails. The Caiman Ecological Refuge—a combination cattle ranch and ecotourism destination—is the perfect home base for exploring the teeming Pantanal. Although the refuge's 131,000-acre range is but a sliver of the fascinating Pantanal pie, the possibilities for round-the-clock field excursions are nearly limitless. Expert professional guides take you on foot, by boat, by pickup truck, or by horseback through and around the intricate web of rivers, canals, and

One of many avian inhabitants

lagoons. Nature's spectacle continues at night, when millions of fireflies create Christmas-like effects, and the eerie sounds of the hunt are everywhere. Wild vistas under an open sky are shared by the ranch's 20,000 head of cattle and other visitors to the refuge.

Life on this working *fazenda* centers around the main *pousada*, a handsome, even elegant, Mediterranean-style building that was originally the manor house of the owner's family. Together with three other buildings scattered across the vast grounds, it accommodates guests who come for total immersion in this unique wildlife reserve, giving them air-conditioning, a pool, and some great home cooking thrown in for good measure.

WHAT: experience, site, hotel. **PANTANAL:** southwestern Brazil. *How:* International Expeditions, tel 205-428-1700, fax 205-428-1714; nature@ietravel.com; www.ietravel.com. **CAIMAN ECOLOGICAL REFUGE:** 147 miles/237 km (45-minute flight) from Campo Grande airport. Tel 55/11-3706-1800, fax 55/11-3706-1808; caiman @caiman.com.br; www.caiman.com.br. *Cost:* from $315 per person (double occupancy), all inclusive. **BEST TIMES:** Apr–Sept (dry season).

The Jewel of Brazilian Baroque

OURO PRETO

Minas Gerais, Brazil

This historical and perfectly preserved 18th-century town tucked into the mountains of the interior state of Minas Gerais is one of the world's greatest enclaves of Baroque architecture. Like a stage set of decorative wrought-iron balconies, pastel-colored mansions, and steep cobblestone streets (complete with the clatter of mule-drawn carts), the modestly sized Ouro Preto is home to thirteen Baroque churches that hark back to Brazil's gold boom, when this region was a major source of the world's supply. The artist whose name and work is synonymous with Ouro Preto is Aleijadinho. Deformed at the age of forty and so debilitated that his assistants had to tie his chisels to his hands, he would go on to become Brazil's premier Baroque sculptor, with Ouro Preto as his showcase. The church of São Francisco de Assis was Aleijadinho's last and most masterful solo project. Almost all the sculptures in the church are his, including those carved directly onto the ceiling. Competing for attention is the lavish church of Nossa Senhora de Pilar, Brazil's second richest church, with more than 1,000 pounds of gold used in homage to the Madonna.

WHAT: town. **WHERE:** 210 miles/338 km from Rio; 1 hour by plane from Rio to Belo Horizonte, then by car or bus. **BEST TIMES:** Nov–Apr.

Time Stands Still in a Colonial Hamlet

TIRADENTES

Minas Gerais, Brazil

When Ouro Preto became this once-affluent province's 19th-century capital following an earlier gold boom, Tiradentes missed out on the development, remaining remote and rural—much as it is today. Situated between the picturesque Rio das Mortes and the Atlantic forest at the foot of the mighty Serra São José mountain, its nine winding streets and seven impressive Baroque churches would still be recognized by those who knew Tiradentes in its 18th-century splendor. A smattering of contemporary art studios, galleries, and small restaurants have arrived as the town has become a favored weekend getaway for escapees from Rio and Belo Horizonte. The charming inn Solar da Ponte is an Anglo-Brazilian collaboration that has become a beloved home away from home for a diverse roster of international guests. This small *pousada* captures the spirit of a rustic but elegant country home in an 18th-century village with warm hospitality and old-world charm. There are freshly cut flowers from the garden in each of the spacious guest rooms, which have been beautifully decorated with the traditional regional handcrafts and designs for which the Minas Gerais region is known.

WHAT: town, hotel. **TIRADENTES:** 141 miles/ 225 km from Ouro Preto; 116 miles/185 km from Belo Horizonte; 214 miles/340 km from Rio de Janeiro. **SOLAR DA PONTE:** Praça das Mercês. Tel 55/323-355-1255, fax 55/323-355-1201; www.solardaponte.com.br. *Cost:* doubles $165. **BEST TIMES:** Nov–Apr.

Dolphin Ballets and Fragile Ecology

FERNANDO DE NORONHA

Pernambuco, Brazil

O ne of the last great, little-known, little-visited destinations for ecotourists, the mini-archipelago of Fernando de Noronha offers an unusual Galapágos-like experience. As a closely guarded national marine park, whose untroubled waters ensure a pristine ecosystem with year-round visibility of more than 300 feet, it's small wonder that the twenty-one-island paradise is considered one of the world's greatest sites for scuba and snorkeling. Add to that the community of more than 600 whitebelly spinner dolphins who have chosen to make the Baía dos Dolfinhos (Dolphin Bay) their home since the 1700s; their famous gravity-defying acrobatics can be viewed by boat excursions or from the bay's escarpments (though visitors are no longer allowed to swim with them). The volcanic main island's 1,600 friendly human residents are as unpolluted by outside contact as the local flora and fauna. Many of them are descended from penal inmates who were imprisoned here in the 18th and 19th centuries. TV is nonexistent, and rudimentary accommodations are often in bunker-type barracks built during the island's brief stint as an American military base during WW II.

WHAT: island. **WHERE:** connected by daily flights from Recife or Natal, both in northeast Brazil. **HOW:** because of a restricted visitors' quota, it is best to book a package deal in advance. The local Atlantis Divers agency is run by the Hotel Genipabu in mainland Natal. Tel

An opportunity to interact with the sea life

55/84-225-2063, fax 55/84-225-2071; hotel @genipabu.com.br; www.genipabu.com.br/ english. In the U.S., contact Marnella Tours, tel 866-993-0033 or 919-782-1664, fax 919-782-1665; www.marnellatours.com. **WHERE**

TO STAY: try a *pousada familiar* (family lodging). Prices for a double from $125 (low season), from $160 (high season). Many of these are listed at www.amazonadventures. com/noronha.htm. **BEST TIMES:** Nov–Apr.

Incredible Mountains of Roller-Coaster Adventure

SURFING THE SAND DUNES OF NATAL

Rio Grande do Norte, Brazil

Beaches are Natal's real claim to fame, and Genipabu is its finest. Located on the easternmost tip of the South American continent, Natal has become the hot spot of Brazil's northeastern area. Miles and miles of enormous white sand dunes and some of the world's most beautiful beaches can be found 15 miles north of Natal in and around Genipabu, where sunset strolls, donkey or horseback rides, sand surfing, or roller-coaster-style rides in four-wheel-drive beach *bugues* (buggies) are pastimes of choice. Beach buggies can be rented by the intrepid, but no one knows the shifting sands and adrenaline-busting turns and Indy-500 potential of the dunes like the local professional *bugueiros* drivers. They can also whisk you away to the secluded lagoons, palm-fringed lakes, or a well-earned celebration at a funky beach hut selling fried shrimp and cold beer after you've survived one of their rides. To keep in the spirit of this exotically beautiful dunescape, stay at the delightful Hotel Genipabu. It sits on a bluff above Genipabu Beach and offers great views of the fabled sand dunes.

WHAT: site, experience, hotel. **GENIPABU:** 15 miles/24 km north of Natal, which is 710 miles/1,142 km from Salvador de Bahia, (daily flights). **HOTEL GENIPABU:** Praia de Genipabu. Tel 55/84-225-2063, fax 55/84-225-2071; hotel@genipabu.com.br; www.genipabu.com.br/english. *Cost:* doubles $50. **BEST TIMES:** Nov–Apr.

Barefoot Casual Chic in Brazil's Party Beachtown

BÚZIOS

Rio de Janeiro, Brazil

Búzios is about gorgeous beaches and gorgeous nightlife. People looking for a quiet hideaway head to Parati; those looking for the St.-Tropez of South America flock here. Búzios—Portuguese for "shells"—remains a fishing village at heart, despite the vacationers from nearby Rio, who put this place on the map long before it was immortalized by Brigitte Bardot in the 1960s. The small amoeba-shaped peninsula of a town offers twenty-some-odd beaches, and the day's most pressing decision is which crescent cove to visit. Nights are filled with a variety of live-music bars and jazz clubs, whose denizens dance till dawn. The cobbled Rua das Pedras is lined with chic, expensive stores, casual but excellent restaurants, and open-air bars that invite lingering. Colonial-style inns, or *pousadas*, blend luxe with coziness for their sophisticated clientele. The castaway-minded hop aboard a schooner that shuttles them to Nas Rocas, a private island retreat for those who prefer to view the action from across a moonlit bay.

WHAT: town, hotel. **BÚZIOS:** 105 miles/ 169 km north of Rio de Janeiro. **NAS ROCAS:** tel 55/246-29-1303, fax 55/246-29-1289; www.nasrocas.com.br. *Note:* At press time, Nas Rocas was temporarily closed for renovation. **BEST TIMES:** Sept–Feb.

An 18th-Century Time Warp on the Costa Verde

PARATI

Parati, Rio de Janeiro, Brazil

As the gold rush of the 18th century died down, so did Parati's importance as the flourishing port for galleons carrying precious cargo from inland Minas Gerais to Portugal's royal court: The town went into hibernation,

encapsulating its colonial heyday until its eventual rediscovery in the 1950s. Located on the coast midway between Rio and São Paulo, its precious time-warped beauty is one of the few things on which the cariocas and paulistas (São Paulo residents) agree. Visitors and locals navigate the waterfront cobblestone streets (closed to traffic) by foot or by bicycle, while small family-run shops confirm the suspicion that this is a town where the locals still thrive on fishing and farming. There's no action and no beach to speak of, but you can still admire the fine houses and the few elaborate churches that wealthy merchants built for themselves (along with two churches exclusively for their slaves and servants). One of the first inns to jump on the tourist bandwagon is still the town's most charming: Pousada Pardieiro's rustic simplicity is offset by a stylish selection of artwork, objets, and such discerning touches as chilled Champagne in your minibar and a pool for further refreshment. Parati's location on the lush, jungle-clad Costa Verde makes it the perfect jumping-off place for boat excursions to any of the 365 outlying islands and the deserted beach idylls they promise.

WHAT: town, hotel. **PARATI:** 150 miles/ 241 km southwest of Rio de Janeiro; 189 miles/300 km northeast of São Paulo. **POUSADA PARDIEIRO:** Rua do Comércio 74. Tel 55/243-371-1370, fax 55/243-371-1139; pp@pousadapardieiro.com.br; www.pousada pardieiro.com.br. *Cost:* doubles from $310. **BEST TIMES:** Nov–Jun.

Take a trip back in time while visiting Parati.

The World's Most Lavish Party

CARNAVAL!

Rio de Janeiro, Brazil

S ay "Carnival" and the world thinks Rio de Janeiro. Each year, the whole city becomes a stage, hosting one of the great free-for-all productions of street theater and embodying the exuberant Brazilian spirit. Carnaval, as it

is spelled in Portuguese, is constantly being created and re-created, sexually charged and fueled by creative passion and, to some degree, the ever-growing commercial need to entertain tourists from everywhere. There are three distinct ways to experience it, not all of which are expensive or require advance planning. The major events are the grand parades of the eighteen lavishly costumed samba "schools" (actually teams) and their floats on

Extravagant costumes are a matter of course during Carnaval.

the Sunday and Monday before Ash Wednesday. The televised parades begin at 6 P.M. and last till dawn, filling the 70,000-seat Sambódromo with music, passion, and unbridled frenzy as the samba teams compete for the year's championship. Certain bleachers are reserved for foreign visitors. Elsewhere, indoor samba balls (often black tie or in full costume) are held in upper-crust clubs and hotels, the most exclusive being at the Copacabana Hotel. But perhaps the most authentic experience of all is to join the tag-along bands that snake through the beachside neighborhoods of Copacabana, Ipanema, and Leblon. They wander noisily until there is no audience left—only to reappear later on another corner.

WHAT: event. **HOW:** most hotels will help arrange for tickets to the parade or private balls; www.rioconventionbureau.com.br. **WHEN:** usually in Feb. Begins in the weeks before Ash Wednesday, culminating the Thurs–Tues before Ash Wednesday.

Rio's Elegant Beachside Landmark

COPACABANA PALACE HOTEL

Rio de Janeiro, Brazil

T he neoclassical-facaded Copacabana Palace is one of South America's most legendary hotels, and perhaps its greatest. Inspired by the French Riviera's grande luxe Negresco in Nice and the Carlton in Cannes, it exudes a light, airy Mediterranean feel unique in this chaotic city-resort. And following an extravagant tiara-to-toe renovation, it is once again the most stylish place in Rio. Overlooking the famous beach from which it takes its name, "the Copa" is a veritable pleasure palace: The semi-Olympic-size pool is the best in town for a dip or a high-octane poolside caipirinha break, and the daily tea service has become something of a cultural experience (reservations necessary!). Inside, the cool marble halls are lined with sepia photos of the Who's Who that have signed the Golden Book since the Copa first opened in 1923. Here was the backdrop for *Flying Down to Rio;* the 1933 film that was the first to pair Fred Astaire with Ginger Rogers also helped launch the hotel as the favorite vaca-tion spot of Hollywood stars. Ask for suite 751, home to Carmen Miranda for four months. The myth of yesteryear lives on in the ornate Golden Room; its famous glass dance floor is lit from below and is the exquisite location for the most exclusive black-tie Carnaval ball in Rio.

WHAT: hotel. **WHERE:** Avenida Atlântica 1702. Tel 55/21-2548-7070, fax 55/21-2235-7330; in the U.S., tel 800-237-1236; www.copacabanapalace.com.br. **COST:** doubles from $480, deluxe beach view doubles $585. Higher rates and minimum-stay requirements during Carnaval and Christmas–New Year's period. Carnaval's Magic Ball tickets $500–$1,500, black-tie or luxury fantasy only, includes dinner buffet and open bar. **BEST TIMES:** Nov–Mar.

The Feast of Iemanjá, Afro-Brazilian Goddess of the Sea

NEW YEAR'S EVE AT COPACABANA BEACH

Rio de Janeiro, Brazil

The New Year's Eve celebrations (*Reveillon*) along Rio's fabled Copacabana Beach begin December 29 with the exotic, mysterious, and, quintessentially Brazilian homage to Iemanjá, the beloved African goddess of the sea and central deity. Conflated with the Virgin Mary over the centuries and a central figure in many Afro-Brazilian spirit cults, she welcomes thousands of her white-clad followers who begin to gather before dusk on Rio's many beaches, particularly Copacabana. *Macumbeiros* baptize initiates while others chant and create candlelit sand altars. *Cariocas* (Rio's residents) launch small handmade boats carrying their gifts of flowers, perfume, lipstick, mirrors, and lit candles—anxious to see if Iemanjá will accept them and fulfill their wishes (the boats are washed out to sea and sink into the depths) or reject them (the waves return them to shore). On December 31 the crowds return, swelling to well over one million and dancing barefoot in the sand to live samba bands while a one-hour fireworks display fills the midnight sky. Many of the swank high-rise hotels lining Avenida Atlântica host extravagant parties with tickets impossible to find (or afford). Book a room months in advance at the JW Marriott and you won't need to head far—the beach party unfolds right across the street and goes on until all hours.

WHAT: event, hotel. **JW MARRIOTT:** Avenida Atlântica 2600. Tel 55/21-2545-6500; www.marriott.com. *Cost:* New Year's Eve rates from $380.

An Unmatched Urban Tableau

CORCOVADO

Rio de Janeiro, Brazil

The mesmerizing 360-degree panorama from atop Corcovado Mountain showcases Rio de Janeiro's beauty in all its heart-stopping glory. This unique, overpowering tableau of curving white beaches, skyscrapers, gray granite mountains, lush rain forest, and the island-studded Bay of Guanabara encouraged Rio's nickname, Cidade Maravilhosa (Marvelous City). Corcovado's summit is crowned by the 120-foot-high soapstone figure of Christ, his arms outstretched to a 75-foot expanse; the very symbol of the city, it was completed (nine years late) in 1931 to commemorate the 1922 centennial of Brazilian independence. Almost twice as high as its rival, 1,300-foot Pao de Açúcar (Sugarloaf Mountain), Corcovado offers a view of the gumdrop-shaped Sugarloaf, and confirms that no other major metropolis is as blessed with physical and natural beauty as Rio. The passenger train to the summit makes its steep 2.3-mile, twenty-minute ascent through lush Tijuca National Park, the largest urban park in the world—an 8,151-acre forest of plate-size blue morpho butterflies and refreshing waterfalls.

WHAT: site. **WHERE:** reachable by taxi or car along a winding road, but the more interesting cog-train cuts through the encroaching jungle; Cosme Velho Train Station (every cabdriver knows this one), 513 Rua Cosme Velho; www.corcovado.com.br. **COST:** $20. **WHEN:** trains leave every 30 minutes daily. **BEST TIMES:** on a clear day, leave in the late afternoon to catch the drama of dusk from the summit.

The Best Show in Town

IPANEMA BEACH

Rio de Janeiro, Brazil

In 1960 two starving local musicians, the now-famous Antonio Carlos Jobim and Vinicius de Moraes, wrote a song about a beautiful girl from Ipanema Beach. They could not have known they would turn this sandy strip into a shrine as inherent to the local character as Sugarloaf Mountain is to the city's unmistakable profile. Rio's twenty-three beaches make up a 45-mile stretch of white sand, but Ipanema is its most sophisticated and elite, for those endowed with gorgeous bodies, dental-floss swimwear, and attitudes to match. Bordering the city's upper-class neighborhoods, it is the beach of choice for the chic and fashion-conscious, who use it for daily preening, strutting, socializing, volleyball games, flirting, jogging, being seen, and generally showing off. Ipanema is a window, a stage, a microcosm, a study of the exuberant carioca ethos of rhythm and style. After a day here, sunburned visitors walk away with some insight into an unhurried and gregarious way of life that springs from the city's sensual and age-old love of beaches. It is a party for friends and family—not as rambunctious or boisterous as the street-festival atmosphere at Copacabana, but a party nonetheless, and outsiders need no invitation.

WHAT: site. **WHERE:** stretching north and northwest from Copacabana Beach. **BEST TIMES:** Nov–Mar (summer).

Culinary Excess Raised to Exalted Heights

RODIZIO AND FEIJOADA IN RIO

Rio de Janeiro, Brazil

Cariocas eat as they dress and party—with an enviable sense of abandon, calories be damned. It is this national love of excess that has made rodizio and feijoada the centerpieces of traditional national cuisine. Cariocas have a special affection for their steakhouse-style churrascarias, and Marius, for years the best place in town for rodizio, is an all-you-can-eat carnivorous festival, where succulent barbecued meat is the primary draw. Rodizio, or "rotation," refers not to the preparation of the meats but the type of service: A troop of waiters carrying skewers of sizzling charbroiled meat circulates in search of empty plates upon which to slice off every imaginable cut of beef, chicken, lamb, and pork. (Pace yourself: The filet mignon always seems to arrive last.) Churrascarias are not the place for animal-rights activists or vegetarians, although Marius's long list of side dishes includes great onion rings, french fries, and dozens of salads. It's amazing to watch the young and hungry who pack this beloved institution of gluttony, seemingly unconcerned that Ipanema and thong bathing suits await them. Perhaps they stop eating twenty-four hours in advance, since they all find room to order the huge crystal goblets filled with Marius's excellent desserts. Rodizio is a fun way to spend Friday night with all of your friends, but the great national banquet of hearty feijoada stew is best eaten with your boisterous family at the house of your Brazilian grandmother, who has spent all morning Saturday preparing it. For those who must resort to reliable alternatives, the elegant Galani, in the Caesar Park Hotel in Ipanema, has long been considered the best

Succumb to feijoada at Galani.

spot in Rio. They offer a delectable spread of this folkloric stew, based on black beans and traditionally reserved for lunch Saturday—presumably so one could then sleep it off all day Sunday. Light it's not (nor particularly attractive); the great Brazilian poet Vinicius de Moraes said that a feijoada is not complete unless there is an ambulance ready at the front door. More an event than a meal, feijoada is a fun dish, served up in huge black pots containing dried meats, bacon, salted pork, ribs, and different kinds of sausages. All of this is accompanied by white rice, farofa (manioc flour), kale, and oranges.

Hotel restaurants like Galani will usually hold off on certain pig parts (ear, tail, and trotter) unless otherwise requested.

WHAT: restaurant. **MARIUS:** three locations, the best one in the Leme neighborhood, overlooking the beach on Avenida Atlântica 290. Tel 55/21-2543-6363; www.marius.com.br. *Cost:* dinner $40. *When:* open daily from noon until the last customer leaves. **GALANI:** Caesar Park Hotel, Avenida Vieira Souto 460, in the Ipanema Beach area. Tel 55/21-2525-2525, fax 55/21-2521-6000; www.caesar-park.com. *Cost:* feijoada lunch $20. *When:* feijoada served Sat only, noon to 4:30 P.M.

Proud Heart and Soul of an Afro-Brazilian City

CIDADE ALTA

Salvador da Bahia, Brazil

The Pelourinho district, the architectural enclave and highlight of Salvador's hilltop Cidade Alta (Upper City), has been reclaimed, restored, and transformed into the cultural heart of a city long famous for the richness of its Afro-Brazilian heritage and colonial history. A wealth based on the unseemly but lucrative importation of African slaves peaked in the early 18th century, when most of Pelourinho's remarkable gold-drenched Baroque churches were completed. They are some of South America's most outstanding, clustered around what is now Pelourinho Square, whose name means "the pillory" or "whipping post" (one of the myriad reminders of the city's historical and emotional ties to Africa and slavery). The home of Salvador's affluent European descendants until the beginning of the 20th century, Pelourinho then descended into squalor and physical collapse. But a massive restoration begun in 1992 secured its return as a haunt of

poets and artists and a showplace for Bahian craftsmanship. Easter egg–colored landmark buildings now house a number of minor but interesting museums, art galleries, and cafés and restaurants.

Settle in for breakfast at the Hotel Catharina Paraguaçu.

When Casa da Gamboa, Salvador's most famous restaurant, opened a branch in Pelourinho, it further established the neighborhood's role as a cultural and culinary outpost. There are some large international beachside hotels, but they don't come close to the character and architectural flavor of the Hotel Catharina Paraguaçu, a pink colonial mansion with rooftop views of the Rio Vermelho beach that's just a taxicab ride away from Pelhourinho.

WHAT: site, restaurant, hotel. **CASA DA GAMBOA:** Rua João de Deus 32. Tel 55/71-3321-3393; contato@casadagamboa.com; www.casadagamboa.com. *Cost:* dinner $30. *When:* lunch and dinner Mon–Sat; Sun lunch only. **HOTEL CATHARINA PARAGUAÇU:** Rua João Gomes 128. Tel/fax 55/71-3334-0089; contato@hotelcatharinaparaguacu.com.br; www.hotelcatharinaparaguacu.com.br. *Cost:* doubles $95 (low season), $105 (high season). **BEST TIMES:** Nov–Jan.

Bahia's Special Heritage

THE FESTIVALS OF SALVADOR

Salvador da Bahia, Brazil

There's no dismissing the carnal, seething, pulsating extravaganza that is Rio's Carnaval, but these days many travelers are heading north to Salvador da Bahia for a more authentic, participatory, and no less indefatigable pre-Lenten celebration. The infectious rhythm of Rio's samba is replaced here by African-based axé music that engulfs the 8-mile Carnaval route snaking from Ondina to Pelourinho.

Through the euphoric crowds, motorized *trio elétricos* floats carry bands and some of Brazil's greatest musical superstars (many of whom hail from Bahia and its environs). Carnaval preparations start months in advance, so off-season visitors can absorb some of the city's myth and magic at the weekly rehearsals of Olodum, Salvador's most innovative *bateria* (Carnaval percussion group).

With more than twenty festivals and processions highlighting each year's calendar, you are likely to happen upon any one of them, especially if you arrive in December, January, or February. The year kicks off on December 31 and January 1 with the Festa de Nosso Senhor dos Navigantes, when the coastal city's population celebrates the "god of navigators." Next, Lavagem da Igreja do Bonfim (eight days starting the second Thursday in January) means African hymns and the local women washing the steps of the Church of Bonfim. Then, on February 2, Iemanjá, the African-Brazilian protectoress and mother of the sea (and counterpart to Catholicism's Virgin Mary), is honored with the Festa de Iemanjá. Exploring the spirituality and religious character of Bahia's African-based but purely Brazilian *condomblé* ceremonies is also possible almost any night in the city's neighborhood *terreiros:* ask around, but be discreet and respectful.

WHAT: event. **WHERE:** Casa do Olodum rehearsals are like spontaneous jam sessions and are not to be missed. Rua Gregorio de Matos 22, Pelourinho. Tel/fax 55/71-3321-4154; www.olodum.com.br. **WHEN:** Olodum rehearsals take place most Sun; Carnaval is almost always in Feb, culminating Thurs–Tues prior to Ash Wednesday. Festin Bahia is a 3-day international music festival held every Aug or Sept.

*Refined but Rustic Hospitality
at a 16th-Century Working Ranch*

HACIENDA LOS LINGUES

San Fernando, Central Valley, Chile

Nestled in a fertile valley at the foot of the Andes, the 9,000 acres that comprise the Hacienda Los Lingues have been in the family of Germán Claro Lira since 1545. Today one of the most prestigious horse-breeding and agricultural farms in South America, Los Lingues ships both its lush fruits and surefooted Acuelo Thoroughbreds worldwide. Lush gardens and flower-decked patios with splashing fountains, intimate dinners in the formal dining room embellished with family heirloom silver and antique crystal, and creaky-floored guest rooms appointed with 17th-century carved beds and white lace curtains are all part of the lovingly preserved colonial ambience.

Cattle roping is left to the pros.

Days are meant for lazing about on shaded verandas while consuming a string of pisco sours, Chile's national drink. Riders will want to saddle up and explore the rolling property on one of the ranch's horses, which are cousins of the Austrian Lipizzaners, first brought to Europe by the Moors and introduced to South America by Spanish conquistadores.

WHAT: hotel. **WHERE:** 75 miles/121 km or 1½ hours south of Santiago via the Pan-American Highway. Reservation hotline, tel 56/2-431-0510, fax 56/2-431-0501; informaciones @loslingues.com; www.loslingues.com. **COST:** doubles from $225. **BEST TIMES:** Oct–Apr.

At Home with Internationally Acclaimed Vintners

THE WINE ROADS OF CHILE

Central Valley, Chile

Chilean wines are taking the world by storm, and oenophiles are keen to head straight to the viticultural source. Chile's winemaking originated with the Spanish conquistadores and missionaries who cultivated the grape for sacramental purposes, but the wines really came into their own when noble French cuttings were planted in the mid-19th century. The principal vineyards lie in the provinces of

Aconcagua, Valparaiso, and Santiago, where a series of beautiful valleys, formed during the Ice Age, are rich with fertile soil. Chile escaped the plagues that later blighted France's vines: Together with Australia, it is the only country still planted with its original rootstock, and its ungrafted vines now last three to four times longer than their European counterparts.

The third largest wine exporter to the United States, after France and Italy, Chile boasts a list of star vintners led by Viña Concha y Toro, the largest and best known in the United States; the Viña Cousiño Macul, the country's oldest; and Viña Santa Rita, world famous for its Cabernets. Travelers to the region fill their days with tastings and gourmet lunches at vineyard restaurants, visits to local produce markets, and an obligatory stop at La Sebastiana, the exquisite coastal home (one of three) of Chile's Nobel Prize–winning poet, the late Pablo Neruda. Visiting Chile without paying homage to Neruda, the locals say, is like going to church and not praying to God.

WHAT: experience. **HOW:** 9-day trips to the Central Valley vineyards and back to Santiago arranged in the U.S. by Myths and Mountains, tel 800-670-6984 or 775-832-5454; travel@mythsandmountains.com; www.mythsandmountains.com. *Cost:* from $3,995 per person, double occupancy, all-inclusive, land only. Customized trips for minimum of 2 people arranged in the U.S. by Maxim Tours, tel 800-655-0222 or 973-927-0760, fax 973-927-1417; info@maximtours.com; www.maximtours.com. *Cost:* from $735 per person for 2 nights, all-inclusive, land only. **WHEN:** departures year-round. **BEST TIMES:** Mar for the harvest.

Island of a Thousand Mysteries

EASTER ISLAND

Chile

A tiny windswept piece of land called Rapa Nui continues to captivate and mystify a curious world long after its "discovery" by the Dutch West India Company in 1722, on Easter Sunday. Surrounded by a million square miles of Pacific Ocean, it's the world's most remote inhabited island—over 1,200 miles from its nearest populated neighbor,

The iconic stone figures of Easter Island

Pitcairn Island. Called the "Navel of the World" by early settlers, Easter Island is an ancient open-air 50-square-mile museum of natural history, home to some of archaeology's most valuable treasures. It is most often identified today with its famous *moai*, more than 600 huge, eerie, elongated stone figures that stare eyeless at the distant horizon. Many are 30 to 50 feet tall and weigh up to 250 tons. They were carved from the island's volcanic tufa, transported for miles, then raised onto great stone altars called *ahu*.

Believed to date from somewhere between the 9th and 17th centuries A.D., these silent figures are best viewed outdoors in all their primitive splendor at Ahu Tongariki, the largest excavated and restored religious monument in Polynesia. Were they conceived and carved by Polynesian people who first landed on the island around A.D. 500, or by pre-Incan stone carvers from Peru? The answer remains elusive.

A cluster of modest hotels can be found in and around Hanga Roa, the small town where virtually the island's entire population lives. But in 2007, the newest of the eco-sensitive Explora hotels made an appearance, its spaceship-like profile gracing a gentle hilltop four miles from town. Guests can expect fiery sunsets and unmatched views of the mighty Pacific. Meals are memorable and the twice-daily excursions led by passionate guides are timed so that guests feel like they are the only ones on the island.

WHAT: island. **WHERE:** 2,350 miles/3,781 km west of Santiago, Chile, 4½ hours by air on flights that typically continue on to Tahiti. It can also be reached by some cruise lines. **HOW:** A 4-day tour leaving weekly from Santiago year-round can be arranged in the U.S. through Maxim Tours, tel 800-655-0222 or 973-927-0760, fax 973-927-1417; info@maximtours.com; www.maximtours.com. *Cost:* from $515 per person, all-inclusive, land only. **EXPLORA RAPA NUI:** In the U.S., tel 866-750-6699 or 310-913-6747. In Santiago, tel 56/2-206-6060, fax 56/2-228-4655; www.explora.com. *Cost:* from $760 per person, per day, all-inclusive (includes 2 excursions daily); 3-day minimum. **BEST TIMES:** Nov–Mar.

The Best Downhill Skiing Down Under

PORTILLO

Chile

Upside-down seasons make a jaunt down to South America's best ski resort a great way to escape the sweltering summer heat up north. Here the western hemisphere's highest peaks boast the finest deep-powder snow,

no lift lines or slope traffic, Chilean hospitality, breathtaking scenery, and ice skating on Laguna del Inca (Inca Lake).

This glitzy ski resort, the site of the 1966 World Alpine Ski Championships (and off-season training destination of the northern hemisphere's pros), nestles high above the tree line at 9,233 feet, in a bowl surrounded by some of the most spectacular peaks of the Chilean/Argentine Andes (from here you can catch a glimpse of Argentina's Mount Aconcagua just over the border, the highest in South America at 22,834 feet). Twelve lifts give access to 2,200 acres, some at an elevation of 10,000 feet, while helicopters make thousands of additional acres accessible for unrivaled powder skiing. Some slopes are notoriously impossible, such as the almost-45-degree-angle Roca Jack, while others accommodate beginners and less-adept skiers. The bright yellow Hotel Portillo is the only game in town and offers a price range for every budget.

WHAT: experience, hotel. **WHERE:** 88 miles/132 km northwest of Santiago; 2-hour bus and car transfer arranged by Hotel Portillo, tel 56/2-2630-606, fax 56/2-2630-595; in the U.S., tel 800-829-5325; info@skiportillo.com; www.skiportillo.com. **COST:** 1-week all-inclusive rates from $890 per person. **WHEN:** mid-Jun to early Oct. **BEST TIMES:** Jul and Aug (Ski Carnival is in Aug).

A Unique Perspective on Patagonia's Otherworldly Channels

CRUISING
THE CHILEAN COAST

Puerto Montt, Patagonia, Chile

Two-thirds of the way down its coastline, Chile crumples into archipelagos of thousands of islets covered with flourishing vegetation that give way to eerie ice fields. This spectacular filigreed coast is home to startling land- and seascapes as well as icy channels opened by seismic and glacial activity millions of years ago that can only be fully appreciated by ship. The Chilean coastal cruise can be experienced two ways.

One choice is aboard the 110-passenger *Skorpios III*, the most luxurious of the small fleet of red-and-white ships that belong to the Kochifas family, the pioneers who opened this area to international tourism in the late 1970s. Its stops include the island of Chiloë, one of only three inhabited islands in a region where humankind has barely left a mark. Then it's south to the Strait of Magellan and the breath-taking San Rafael Glacier, the ship's ultimate destination in Chile's deep south. The mile-wide, 9-mile-long glacier rivets one's attention as its 200-foot ice spires calve off to thunderous roars. The impression is of being among the ice floes of the Antarctic; in fact, the San Rafael is the glacier closest to the Equator.

Alternatively, passengers can opt to ply the southernmost reaches of Chilean Patagonia aboard the *Mare Australis* or *Via Australis*, through an area boasting more glaciers than Alaska and more fjords than Norway, Denmark, and Sweden put together. In an area off-limits to most of the larger American and European ships, the compact 114-passenger vessels thread these waterways, skirting the island of Tierra del Fuego in the ghostly wake of Charles Darwin's ship, the *Beagle*. The utter silence of these labyrinthine seas inspires the same awe that must have overcome Magellan in 1520 when he stumbled upon these then-uncharted waters at the bottom of the world.

WHAT: experience. **TURISMO SKORPIOS:** departures from Puerto Montt, 630 miles/ 1,014 km south of Santiago. Tel 56/2-2477-1900, fax 56/2-232-2269. In the U.S., tel 305-484-5357; skoinfo@skorpios.cl; www. skorpios.cl. *Cost:* 8-day sailings from $2,000 per person, all-inclusive. *When:* departures every Sat, Sept–May; Dec–Feb is high season. **CRUCEROS AUSTRALIS:** departures from Punta Arenas, 1,400 miles/2,253 km south of Santiago; daily 4½-hour flights from Santiago (about $310 round trip). Tel 56/2-442-3115, fax 56/2-203-5173. In the U.S., tel 877-678-3772 or 305-695-9618, fax 305-534-9276; www.australis.com. *Cost:* from $$1,930 (low season), from $2,350 (high season) for 4-night cruise. Cruceros Australis also offers 3-night cruises from Ushuaia from $1,440 (low season) and $1,750 (high season). *When:* Sept–Apr.

Exploring the ice fields with Turismo Skorpios

Wilderness and Civilization at the End of the Earth

TORRES DEL PAINE NATIONAL PARK

Patagonia, Chile

This remote outpost in the heart of Chile's Patagonia is one of nature's last virtually untrammeled wildernesses. Located just north of Punta Arenas, it is a solitary region of overwhelming beauty that was not mapped until the 1930s. The 600,000-acre network of deep aquamarine lakes, rushing rivers, groaning glaciers, pampas, and fjords is best known for the Cuernos del Paine—spectacular 10,000-foot towers of rose-colored granite that are part of the Cordillera Paine mountain range. The 12-foot wingspan of the fabled Andean condor occasionally appears against the sky in this surreal landscape; it is one of more than 100 different species of native birds, from the ostrichlike rhea to wild flamingos and black-necked geese. The orange-and-white guanaco, a cousin of the llama, and the mountain puma, among others, also make their home here. Little wonder that Charles Darwin and Jules Verne were among those who fell under the spell of this region at the end of the world. Here the plenitude of air, light, time, and space crystallize the sense of disconnection from life as you know it. Maximize the experience with a stay at the Hotel Salto Chico, located on the shores of the glacial Lake Pehoe in the Torres del Paine National Park. At first glance, the hotel is unremarkable: The plain white clapboard structure does not try to compete with nature. But indoors it is light, airy, outfitted with natural fibers and local woods—and everywhere are huge windows framing views of the park's singularly beautiful granite towers. You may be 250 miles from the closest town, but the bed linens are from Barcelona, the china from England, the guests from every corner of the world. And while the good life is alluring and the outdoor Jacuzzi-with-a-view borders on the sublime, the real luxury is being in the heart of the park. Guests can choose from a menu of sixteen excursions at different ability levels covering more than 150 miles of trails and roads (at least five excursions are offered daily). Even the sedentary traveler can tour the area, from a four-wheel-drive jeep or motor launch. Other expeditions include hiking, trekking, mountain biking, and horseback riding. Then it's back to home base, to dine in jeans and flannel shirts on king crab and excellent Chilean wines.

Granite peaks tower over Hotel Salto Chico.

WHAT: site, hotel. **WHERE:** a 4½-hour flight from Santiago to Punta Arenas, then a 6-hour car transfer to hotel. **HOTEL SALTO CHICO:** reservations in Santiago, tel 56/2-206-6060; www.explora.com. **COST:** 4 nights, double occupancy, from $2,660 including 3 meals a day, guides, and transfers to and from Punta Arenas. **BEST TIMES:** each season has its own beauty; Jan temperatures average 40–55° F; Jul is 25–40° F and windy.

El Dorado Lives

GOLD MUSEUM

Bogotá, Colombia

Although less than 15 percent of the Museo del Oro's 30,000 gold artifacts are on display, the sophisticated workmanship of the viewable items as well as the sheer magnitude of the collection are astonishing. It is the only

A piece of Colombia's rich history

collection of its kind in the world. You won't doubt the legends of El Dorado as you view masterpiece after unique masterpiece, representing all the major pre-Columbian cultures in the region at the time of the Spanish conquest. Tastefully displayed is a choice array of golden figurines—birds, masks, frogs, insects, and are those earthlings? Is it Bogotá's altitude (8,640 feet above sea level) or the scope and beauty of the museum's collection that leaves you breathless?

WHAT: site. **WHERE:** 15-82 Carrera 6, Parque Santander. Tel 57/1-343-2222, fax 57/1-284-7450; www.banrep.gov.co/museo. **WHEN:** Tues–Sun. **COST:** admission $3.

Ciudad Vieja: An Open-Air Living Museum

CARTAGENA DE INDIAS

Colombia

When the Spanish came looking for the kingdom of El Dorado in 1533, they landed at Cartagena. Today this gem of colonial architecture has been beautifully restored, particularly within its authentic and lively 16th- and 17th-century Ciudad Vieja (Old City). Overhanging wooden balconies, flowering patios, narrow back streets, stately mansions housing fine restaurants, café- and palm-lined plazas, and centuries-old churches are enclosed and protected by the city's elaborate *murallas*, 7 miles of thick walls and an impregnable chain of outer forts. An outstanding piece of military engineering built to protect Colombia's most important city from pirate attacks, they are the only such fortifications in South America.

The early-17th-century Convento de Santa Clara is an architectural treasure; after a stint as a charity hospital, it was recently converted (under the watchful eye of UNESCO) into the city's finest hotel. The painstaking restoration exposed long-hidden murals and secret doors; ceramics and cannon shot from pirate attacks also surfaced, evidence of the site's intriguing history. Guests can dine in the former refectory of the Clarisa nuns or stroll through the flowering gardens in the quiet of what once was an arched cloister. the nuns' spartan rooms are now luxuriously appointed, but the inspiring views remain unchanged: the tiled roofs of the historic Ciudad Vieja against the indigo Caribbean sea.

WHAT: town, site, hotel. **CARTAGENA:** 60 miles/97 km from Barranquilla, on the northern coast. **HOTEL SANTA CLARA:** Calle del Torno. Tel 57/5-650-4700, fax 57/5-664-8040; H1871-RE@sofitel.com; wwwsofitel.com. In the U.S.,

The arched breezeways of the former convent

contact Sofitel, tel 800-763-4835. **COST:** doubles from $250 (low season), $300 (high season). **BEST TIMES:** Dec–Apr (dry season). Cartagena celebrates its independence from Spain on Nov 11. Annual Caribbean Music Festival held second half of Mar.

Evolutionary Miracles Above and Under Water

GALÁPAGOS ISLANDS

Ecuador

Amodern-day traveler's rules of thumb: Visit the most fragile places first; stay on the trails; disturb nothing. Nowhere does this apply more than to the fifty-eight fascinating islands and cays of the Galápagos archipelago,

essentially unknown until Charles Darwin's arrival 150 years ago. Here, straddling the Equator 600 miles off the coast of Ecuador, Darwin developed his theory of evolution among an amazing roster of all-but-tame wildlife that thrived in an eerie, moonlike landscape. The islands—each remarkably individual in its topography, flora, and fauna—are still home to the highest proportion of endemic species in the world; 400-pound land tortoises, marine iguanas, blue-footed boobies, and thirteen species of finches are peculiar to these islands. The Galápagos and their inhabitants continue to enchant nature buffs and adventurers who visit the twelve large (and dozens of smaller)

islands; cruising the pristine and gorgeous waters separating what has been called a living laboratory of evolution. The animals have no instinctive fear of man—if anything, their curiosity will surpass your own.

The Galápagos Islands also offer an experience that is as stunning underwater as it is topside. This enchanted archipelago hosts an astonishing variety of marine life: Scuba divers will see penguins (the hemisphere's northernmost community lives here, thanks to the cooling Humboldt Current), marine iguanas, or dolphins—even the odd migrating whale. Certain departures of the fully equipped *Reina Silvia* live-aboards head for the remote and completely uninhabited islands of Wolf and

Darwin. There, expect to be surrounded by the enormous schools of pelagics that populate these waters—hundreds of hammerheads and manta rays for which the Galápagos are famous.

Landlubbers can now forgo a stay on a pitching boat in favor of the pristine islands' first luxury resort, the Royal Palm Hotel, occupying a 400-acre site on the island of Santa Cruz. The resort's private boat ships guests off for wildlife-viewing day trips, but delivers them back to terra firma in time for a spa treatment before their candlelight dinner.

WHAT: site, experience, hotel. **HOW:** for land tours, Inca Floats in the U.S., tel 510-420-1550, fax 510-420-0947; www.incafloats.com. *Cost:* from $4,295 per person for 11-day trip, land/cruise. *Best times:* mid-Apr through early Jun. For diving tours, contact Caradonna Caribbean Tours; in the U.S., tel 800-328-

2288, fax 407-682-6000; sales@caradonna.com; www.caradonna.com. *Cost:* 7-nights from $4,295 per person, includes boat, meals, and diving. *When:* weekly departures year-round. **THE ROYAL PALM HOTEL:** tel 593/5-527-408; info@royalpalmgalapagos.com; www.royalpalmgalapagos.com. *Cost:* from $375. **BEST TIMES:** Nov–Jun.

A school of hammerheads is always a thrilling sight.

Civilization in the Heart of the Amazon

SACHA LODGE

Napo River, Ecuador

Set on its own spread of 3,000 acres, amid hundreds of species of birds, fish, and mammals, the Sacha Lodge provides a unique base from which to explore the world's largest and most biologically diverse rain forest, located in the steamy tropical lowlands of the Ecuadorian Amazon. Local Quechua- and English-speaking naturalists will lead you on daily, varied jungle walks—getting you back to the lodge's stunning lakeside location in time for some great (if basic) Ecuadorian cuisine. Dugout canoes take guests on river and lake safaris, past local communities of Quechua Indians and salt licks that attract hundreds of vivid parrots and parakeets in a whirl of color and noise. The breadth of the virgin property encompasses a variety of habitats, and a 135-foot observation tower has made the forest canopy accessible as well. From the tower you can discover a world of treetop bromeliads and orchids and the exotic birds they attract; the view stretches to the snow-topped peak of Sumaco, an extinct volcano 100 miles away. All this, and hot showers and electricity, too.

WHAT: experience, hotel. **WHERE:** on the Napo River. **HOW:** tel 593/2256-6090, fax 593/2223-6521; www.sachalodge.com. In the U.S., contact Andean Treks, tel 800-683-8148 or 617-924-1974; www.andeantreks.com. **COST:** 3-night/4-day land package $690 per person, double occupancy, includes all meals, guides, excursions. Quito–Coca round-trip airfare $120. **BEST TIMES:** Jan–Mar.

The Continent's Most Famous Market Town

OTAVALO

Ecuador

The oldest, best-known, and most important Indian market in South America takes place every Saturday high in the Andes. For 4,000 years, Otavalo's market has served as the social and economic heartbeat of the northern highlands; today it is Ecuador's most popular destination after the Galápagos Islands. The otherwise sleepy town awakens at dawn to a cacophony of chickens, cows, and sheep and the trading of hemp, saddles, vegetables, grain, and textiles—bartering being the traditional livelihood of brightly dressed Otavaleños who have converged from near and far away. There are tourist trinkets galore—pottery, weavings, jewelry, carved wooden animals—but visitors really come for the authentic local atmosphere, and the Indian population is here to swap livestock, provisions, and news. Early birds will want to arrive before the animal market bedlam winds down around 8 A.M., and before the bedlam of daytrippers winds up with the arrival of buses that roll in from Quito around 10 A.M. Spend Friday night at the nearby Hacienda Cusin, a 17th-century colonial plantation reincarnated as a first-class rural inn, or stay fifteen minutes (and as many light-years) away at La Mirage, a lush flower- and vine-draped oasis perched high on an

A highlands merchant sets up her wares.

Andean hillside. Just two hours by car from Quito, and one of the most casually elegant country hideaways on the continent, this contemporary inn was built to look like a traditional, centuries-old hacienda. La Mirage combines the best of local culture and artistry with the owners' love of European aesthetics and luxury; the result is a high-altitude, impeccably run haven. Horses from the inn's working farm transport you through ancient Indian towns, unspoiled high country, and a volcanic lake. Dining at La Mirage is as memorable for the view of the snow-capped Cotacachi and Imbabura mountains as it is for the excellent menu, enhanced by local Ecuadorian wines and served by beautiful young Otavalo Indian girls in traditional embroidered dress. After dinner, guests wander through luxuriant gardens back to their suites, where fireplaces have thoughtfully been lit to dispel the nighttime Andean chill.

WHAT: site, town, hotel. **OTAVALO:** 80 miles/120 km north of Quito. **HACIENDA CUSIN:** San Pablo del Lago, Imbabura. Tel 593/6291-8013, fax 593/6291-8003; in the U.S., tel 800-670-6984; hacienda@cusin. com.ec; www.haciendacusin.com. *Cost:* doubles (room only) $120; suites (all meals) $300. **LA MIRAGE:** Avenida 10 de Agosto, Cotacachi. Tel 593/6291-5237; in the U.S. and Canada, tel 800-327-3573; www.mirage. com.ec. *Cost:* doubles from $300. **WHEN:** Sat is most important market day. **BEST TIMES:** Jun 24–Jul 6 celebrates the patron saints of Cotacachi, and Indians come from all around.

Rail Journey Along the Avenue of the Volcanoes

THE RIOBAMBA EXPRESS

Riobamba, Ecuador

T he old market town of Riobamba, four hours south of Quito, is itself a destination worthy of a trip, but the rail ride that begins there and continues on to Guayaquil or Cuenca quadruples the fun. Travel on

antique refitted trains is an option, though perhaps not as memorable as the autoferro bus-on-rails, where you can sit on top of the train to take in the dramatic view of the highlands, the active Cotopaxi volcano, and Mount Chimborazo. The rails follow the Avenue of the Volcanoes before reaching the legendary Nariz del Diablo (Devil's Nose), a hair-raising engineering marvel that follows a series of switchback turns before delivering you to Riobamba safe and sound.

Riobamba's important Saturday Indian market sprawls across the town's eleven squares; you can identify the various communities of Indians who converge here by the different hats the women wear. The city's unrivaled Museo de Arte Religioso displays a remarkable collection of art and gold objects in a restored convent and cloisters.

WHAT: experience, town. **HOW:** Metropolitan Touring. In Quito, tel 593/2-988-200, fax 593/2-334-1439; info@metropolitan-touring.com; www.metropolitan-touring.com. In the U.S., Adventure Associates, tel 877-500-9402, fax 972-783-1286. **COST:** from $690 per person for multiday hotel/train packages. **WHEN:** departures from Quito Tues, Thurs, and Sat.

An Island of Serenity in Peru's White City

MONASTERIO DE SANTA CATALINA

Arequipa, Peru

M uch of colonial Arequipa—known as La Ciudad Blanca (the White City) for its elaborate 16th- and 17th-century Spanish homes—is hidden behind imposing walls. Nothing prepares the wanderer who stumbles

upon this lovely city's greatest secret, the cloistered world of the Monasterio de Santa Catalina, a miniature city within a city that was opened to the public only in 1970. The few elderly Dominican nuns still living there have moved to the northern corner of the convent, but the rest of the grounds may be visited. For centuries this quiet, self-contained community was home to well-to-do women who never left the premises, as the cemetery will testify. Covering an entire city block, the original convent was built in 1580 and soon gained a reputation as a sort of exclusive club, where young girls of aristocratic families arrived for an education, a safe haven, or a spiritual vocation (some with maids, slaves, large dowries, and fancy lifestyles to maintain). Of the maximum 450 women living there, only a third were actually nuns until the late 1800s, when circumstances redirected life back to the religious. Today, as you meander through the convent's twisting streets, admire pastel-painted buildings, stop in the tiny plazas, and visit the simple living quarters, you are taken back to an earlier, more refined age.

WHAT: site. **WHERE:** Avenida Santa Catalina 300, close to Arequipa's beautiful Plaza de Armas. Daily flights connect Arequipa to Lima and Cuzco. **WHERE TO STAY:** La Posada del Puente, Avenida Bolognesi 101, is the nicest hotel in town, with flowering gardens and river views. Tel 51/54-253-132, hotel@posadadelpuente.com; www.posadadel puente.com. *Cost:* doubles $125. **BEST TIMES:** at 7,590 feet above sea level, Arequipa enjoys eternal springtime. Aug 15 is the city's founding day, with parades, celebrations, and concerts in the convent.

At the Center of the Inca Universe

CUZCO

Peru

Cuzco is the archaeological capital of the Americas, a unique destination steeped in an age-old culture and surrounded by the beauty and mysticism of the Andes. In the native Quechua language, *qosqo*—the origin of

the name Cuzco—meant "the earth's navel," the birthplace and center of the Incan empire. And everything in this colonial city 11,000 feet above sea level leads back to the Plaza de Armas, the navel's navel. Called Huacaypata by the Inca, the plaza was the heart of the capital, which was founded in the 12th century by Manco Capac. The Old City that spreads in a ten-block radius around it is a colonial repository of the years following Pizarro's arrival in 1532, and the Spaniards' invasion and eventual destruction of the Incan civilization—once the western hemisphere's greatest empire.

The Plaza de Armas is ringed by the ornate Baroque cathedral—one of the most splendid examples of religious colonial architecture in the Americas—and churches, mansions, and colonnades built upon the ruins of razed Incan palaces and temples that were stripped of their ornamentation of gold,

silver, and precious stones. Vestiges of their sloping foundations of mammoth, impeccable masonry (fitted without mortar) are often still visible, with some as high as two stories.

Try to be in Cuzco on June 24 to celebrate Inti Raymi (the Incan Sun Festival), the greatest of all Incan celebrations and one of the most spectacular Andean festivals in South America today. It coincides with the Christian feast day of St. John, which is also the Day of Cuzco and the Peruvian Day of the Indian. The original pageantry of this ancient holiday is reenacted in the main plazas and throughout the streets of Cuzco, with parades, processions, dances, and folk music, plus special ceremonies at Coricancha, the former Incan Sun Temple that is now largely enclosed by the Church of Santo Domingo.

In Cuzco, stay at the historically layered Hotel Monasterio, housed in the self-enclosed 17th-century San Antonio de Abad seminary and built on the remains of the palace of the ancient Inca Emperor Amaru Qhala. One of the most important seminaries in Latin America from the 1700s to the late 1960s, its colonial origins remain visible in its patios, vaulted arches, stone water fountains, and artwork. Today it offers guests a rare combination of luxury and history. The comfortable rooms, former monks' cells, have been enlarged, and their antique furniture, carved wooden beds, and marbled baths create a setting that is a far cry from the monastic.

WHAT: site, town, event, hotel. **CUZCO:** 1-hour flight from Lima; daily service from most major cities in Peru. Considered an obligatory stop for those setting out for Machu Picchu and other Inca sites in the Urubamba Valley. **INTI RAYMI:** contact Southwind Adventures in the U.S., tel 800-377-9463 or 303-972-0701, fax 303-972-0708; info@southwind adventures.com; www.southwindadventures. com. *Cost:* $3,255 per person for 10-day trip, land only. **HOTEL MONASTERIO:** Calle Palacio 136-140. Tel 51/8460-4000, fax 51/8460-4001; in the U.S., tel 800-237-1236; info@ peruorientexpress.com.pe; www.monasterio. orient-express.com. *Cost:* doubles from $530. **BEST TIMES:** Apr–Oct (dry season).

The Pristine Preserves of the Amazon Forest

MANU NATIONAL PARK

Peru

At nearly 4½ million acres, Manu National Park is one of South America's largest wilderness preserves and perhaps the most important tropical park in the world. Protecting an entire virgin watershed, the park encompasses radically different ecological zones, ranging from Andean peaks of more than 13,000 feet down through the cloud forest and into the endless lowland rain forests below 1,000 feet. No other reserve on earth can compare to it in terms of sheer biodiversity. There are an estimated 20,000 plant species, more than 1,000 species of birds (more than in all of the United States and Canada), and 13 species of monkeys, from capuchin and spider to mustachioed emperor tamarin.

The park's unlogged, unhunted, nearly untouched state has left the animal inhabitants remarkably unafraid of human beings; visitors here find excellent wildlife and bird viewing of species that have vanished elsewhere in the Amazon.

Admittedly, Manu is difficult to get to; tours involve limited and rustic accommodations, some camping, and travel by motorized dugout canoe. Visitors need to obtain permission to enter the park, and reputable, experienced guides are a must. Manu is not for the unadventurous, but what an adventure it is!

WHAT: site, experience. **WHERE:** southeastern corner of Peru. Tours leave from Cuzco by charter flight or a 1½-day drive on mostly unpaved roads. **HOW:** in the U.S., contact Southwind Adventures, tel 800-377-9463 or 303-972-0701, fax 303-972-0708; info@ southwindadventures.com; www.southwind adventures.com. *Cost:* $4,685 per person for 12-day excursion, double occupancy, land only. Shorter trips organized by Manu Expeditions in Cuzco, tel 51/84-225-900; www.manu expeditions.com. *Cost:* $1,345 (4 days), $1,655 (6 days), and $2,255 (9 days), all-inclusive, land only. **WHEN:** May–Oct.

Desert Designs That Stir the Imagination

THE NAZCA LINES

Nazca, Peru

Peru's arid desert coast is the setting for the mysterious, ancient Nazca lines, a series of geometric forms and straight lines in the earth that depict stylized human and animal shapes. Covering an astounding 193 miles, they can be fully appreciated only from the air. Some are simple, perfectly formed triangles, trapezoids, or straight lines running for miles across the desert; others represent giant animals, such as a 540-foot-long lizard, a 270-foot-long monkey with a tightly curled tail, or a condor with a 390-foot wingspan. The geoglyphs are faithful to the shapes and figures found on Nazcan textiles and ceramics. It is believed that the lines were "etched"—by removing rocks and topsoil to reveal the lighter soil underneath—between 2,000 and 3,000 (some archaeologists say even 5,000) years ago. Who constructed these lines and why? And how, if they can be discerned only from high above? Far-fetched theories explain them as extraterrestrial landing sites (as speculated in Erich von Daniken's book *Chariots of the Gods*), astronomical calendars used for agricultural purposes, or land art that held secret messages for the gods who looked down at them. So far, this extraordinary pre-Inca cultural artifact remains veiled in mystery.

WHAT: site. **WHERE:** Ica, the nearest city, is 170 miles/274 km south of Lima. **HOW:** AeroCondor's 45-minute flight-seeing tours can be booked through any of the local hotels in Ica or Nazca, 85 miles/137 km south. *Cost:* from $160. 1-day tours from Lima, including lunch at Las Dunas, $390 through AeroCondor. **WHERE TO STAY:** Las Dunas is the nicest hotel, an Arabian-style palm-studded village resort with its own airstrip for easy Nazca excursions. In Ica, tel/fax 51/5625-6224; dunas@invertur.com.pe; www.lasdunashotel.com. *Cost:* doubles from $120 (weekdays) to $145 (weekends). **BEST TIMES:** Jan–Mar.

The Islands and Festivals of South America's Largest Lake

LAKE TITICACA

Puno, Peru

As some will remember from geography class, the legendary 3,200-square-mile Lake Titicaca is—at 12,500 feet above sea level—the highest navigable lake in the world. But only those who have visited it know of the luminescence of the light and the ever-changing play of color on its water. Titicaca's singular beauty supports the ancient myth that Manco Capac and his sister-consort, Mama Ocllo, founders of the Incan Empire, emerged from these magical Andean waters.

The Uros Indians created the lake's eponymous floating islands centuries ago to escape conflicts with the land-inhabiting Inca. Their descendants still live on the springy forty-odd islands of indigenous tortora reeds, which are also used to make both their homes and their boats. The two natural islands of Taquile and Amantani are hilly and peopled by hospitable Indians, whose bright-colored traditional dress and handwoven textiles are an irresistible draw for sightseers and shoppers. There are no cars or bicycles here, or even roads, but the gently terraced hills bespeak the islands' proud agricultural traditions. Schedule your trip to Puno for February or November, when local celebrations turn this city upside down.

The mythical founding of the lakeside city of Puno is the reason for November's fascinating Semana de Puno festivities, whose ornate and imaginative costumes, wild dancing, masks, music, and instruments are rooted in the Incan culture. February 2, Candlemas or the feast of the Virgen de la Candelaria, may ostensibly figure on the Roman Catholic calendar, but witness the famous *diablada* (devil's dance) and the *kallahuaya* (medicine man's dance) before deciding for yourself if it's a Christian or pagan celebration. As many as 300 folkloric dances are performed in the streets of Puno throughout the year. If things are quiet when you arrive, ask the local tourist office for directions to the area's nearest fiesta. You won't regret the trip.

WHAT: site, event. **WHERE:** in southern Peru, and shared by Bolivia and Peru. Puno is Peru's principal departure city for visits to the islands. Nearest airport is at Juliaca, about 475 miles/764 km southeast of Lima. **HOW:** any of the local travel agencies or hotels can book an excursion to the islands. Most tours include some of the floating islands before heading to Taquile, 1 hour from shore. **WHERE TO STAY:** on its own island connected to Puno by a causeway, the Libertador Lake Titicaca is the nicest place in town; rooms are unremarkable but many have lake views. Tel 51/54-367-780, fax 51/54-367-879; info@libertador.com.pe; www.libertador.com.pe. *Cost:* doubles $250. **BEST TIMES:** Candlemas is celebrated Feb 2 and the week that surrounds it. Puno Week is Nov 1–7; Puno Day is Nov 5.

Unmatched Biodiversity: Where the Amazon Begins

PERUVIAN AMAZON

Peru

The confluence of the Ucayali and Marañón Rivers is the legendary inception of the mighty Amazon, 2,000 miles from where it ultimately empties into the Atlantic. Brazil might have most of the Amazon fame, but Peru is one of the best places to see it. Iquitos, the largest town in the region, was established by the Jesuits in the 1750s, and grew as a rubber tree plantation hub in the late 1800s. It's the jumping off point for exploration of the river and the vast 5-million-acre wildlife-rich Pacaya-Samiria National Reserve.

American-based International Expeditions has more than 3 decades of experience in the region and takes visitors on the river aboard the 28-passenger *La Amatista,* newly built in the style of the grand 19th-century riverboats. Seven- to 10-day expeditions take you deep into the jungle and to stops along the way to visit small towns, many of which the company helps to keep self-sustaining. Attentive naturalist guides point out the prolific wildlife of the primeval environs both on board and on land. More species of primates have been recorded in this region than anywhere else in the New World, and the Ucayali River also boasts a large population of both gray and pink river dolphins that often follow alongside the boat. Small excursion boats take off for narrow passages, flooded forest, and blackwater lakes, dropping passengers off for guided stops at little-visited riverside settlements and hikes through virtually uninhabited portions of the Amazon jungle. A new company, Aqua Expeditions, uses the luxury cruiser *Aqua* for shorter expeditions into the jungle, with an unprecedented emphasis on comfort. Guests explore the jungle, and return to be pampered by master Peruvian chef Pedro Schiaffino, then retire to 230-square-foot cabins with enormous, panoramic windows opening onto the river.

Pre- or post-cruise, unpack on land at any of Explorama's five lodges in the 250,000-acre Amazon Biosphere Reserve, all within 3 hours by boat from Iquitos. The Ceiba is their newest, and the most luxurious, with 72 air-conditioned rooms, and a large pool to refresh the weary. They also offer more rustic cabins off the main building, and a canopy walkway along the river. Nearby, head to the nonprofit Swiss Family Robinson–style camp called the Amazon Center for Environmental Education and Research (ACEER), a treetop system of ladders, cables, and netting. Visitors ascend some thirteen stories, or 125 feet, to experience the rain forest's diversity from an ingenious multi-level system of aerial platforms and hanging pathways. From here you might spy one of the estimated two-thirds of the rain forest species that live in (and never descend from) the canopy—many of which still remain to be identified

WHAT: experience, hotel. **IQUITOS:** 1,153 miles/1,860 km northeast of Lima. Peru's largest jungle city cannot be reached by land. **INTERNATIONAL EXPEDITIONS:** Tel 800-633-4734 or 205-428-1700; www.ietravel.com. Cost: $3,148 per person for 10-day trips (7 days sailing) originating in Iquitos, includes most meals and tours. *When:* weekly departures year-round. **AQUA EXPEDTIONS;** Tel 51/65-601-053; In the U.S. and Canada, tel. 866-603-3687; www.aquaexpeditions.com. *Cost:* $5,250 per person for 7-night expedition originating in Iquitos, includes all meals, tours, and transfers. **EXPLORAMA TOURS AND LODGES:** Tel 51/65-252-530; www.explorama.com. In the U.S., tel 800-707-5275 or 781-581-0844. *Cost:* $695 per person for 4-night Ceiba Lodge expeditions; originates in Iquitos and includes Canopy Walkway Special. **BEST TIMES:** Rain forest temperature changes only marginally. May–Dec is least rainy (when land excursions are easier); Jan–Feb is the most rainy (with better animal viewing).

Through a Sacred Valley to the Lost City of the Incas

MACHU PICCHU

Urubamba Valley, Peru

On a continent endowed with magnificent pre-Columbian archaeological sites, this is the supreme showpiece. Machu Picchu's strategic and isolated high-altitude setting coupled with its mysterious significance in the ancient Inca universe make this "lost city" one of the world's most beautiful and haunting destinations. Abandoned by the Inca and reclaimed by the jungle, the 100-

acre complex of temples, warehouses, houses, irrigation terraces, and stairs remained hidden from outsiders until American explorer Hiram Bingham was led to it in 1911 by a ten-year-old local boy. It somehow had been entirely overlooked and unaccounted for in the Spanish conquistadores' otherwise meticulous records. Speculation about the age and significance of Machu Picchu (Old Mountain) continues, although current thinking suggests it was a retreat for Inca nobility most likely built in the 15th century.

On a clear day, the very fit should consider the hike to Huayna Picchu (Young Mountain), where the near-vertical scramble to the summit is breathtaking in more ways than one. The truly athletic can arrive at Machu Picchu's 500-year-old Gate of the Sun after a three- to five-day trek along the Inca Trail. The Inca built many mountain trails, but this was their "royal highway" through the 100-mile-long Urubamba (or Sacred) Valley, the cradle of the Incan civilization. The trail affords an awesome journey through the scenic splendor of the valley—the bread basket and favored vacation spot for the nobles of Cuzco. The 35-mile Inca Trail crosses two passes—the higher just over 13,500 feet—and requires that travelers be tolerant of thin air in order to fully appreciate the drama of the scenery, the wealth of Incan outposts, fortresses, and mysterious, terraced ruins, as well as the colorful Andean villages all along the way. The trip is well worth the effort. The Sunday market in Pisac draws vendors and tourists from all parts; even more memorable is a trip to the network of linked hilltop Incan strongholds. Ollantaytambo, with its well-preserved, formidable fortress, is the valley's other most-visited spot—an authentic Incan town that has retained its original street names, layout, irrigation system, and houses.

For years Machu Picchu suffered from a lack of good hotels while backpacker crash sites abounded. Today, the town of Machu Picchu Pueblo (also known as Aguas Calientes) at the base of the peak, and the train's final stop, provides many options. Luxury accommodations have arrived steps from the train station with the Inkaterra Pueblo Hotel, 85 whitewashed casitas set amidst 12 terraced acres harmoniously designed to look like an Andean village. Up at the entrance to the ruins, the Orient-Express–managed Sanctuary Lodge is all about luxe high-altitude comfort and an unmatched location.

WHAT: site, experience. **MACHU PICCHU:** 3-hour deluxe and tourist PeruRail trains leave Cuzco daily; the last climb is done by bus. *Cost:* round-trip tickets on tourist train are about $96. Round-trip tickets on deluxe train $590, includes dinner. For reservations, reservas@perurail.com; www.perurail.com. **INCA TRAIL:** in the U.S., contact Wilderness Travel, tel 800-368-2794 or 510-558-2488; fax 510-558-2489; www.wildernesstravel. com. *Cost:* 10-day trips departing from Lima, includes 5 days trekking, from $4,595. *When:* departures Apr–Dec. **INKATERRA MACHU PICCHU PUEBLO HOTEL:** Cuzco office, tel 51/84-245-314. In the U.S., 800-442-5042; www.inkaterra.com. **COST:** from $610, includes all meals. **MACHU PICCHU SANCTUARY LODGE:** Cuzco office, tel 51/1610-8300; reservas@peru orientexpress.com.pe; www.orientexpress.com. *Cost:* doubles from $950, includes meals for two. **BEST TIMES:** dry months of Jun–Sept, but expect crowds.

Machu Picchu, towering over the world below

One of the Continent's Least-Known Treasures

COLONIA DEL SACRAMENTO

Uruguay

Situated on the littoral west of Montevideo and surrounded by rolling gaucho country, Colonia is the unappreciated gem of Uruguay. The sycamore-shaded cobbled streets of the Barrio Histórico, this small town's colonial

core, is one of the loveliest and more carefully restored urban areas on the continent. Founded by the Portuguese, coveted by the British, Spanish, and later the Brazilians, Colonia is a charming collection of whitewashed buildings, tile-and-stucco homes, and Uruguay's oldest church. There are a number of small museums and good restaurants—but altogether little indication of the 21st, or even 20th, century. For the moment. On weekends Argentines from nearby Buenos Aires breeze in on the hydrofoil for the day. A stay at the charming 19th-century Hotel

Plaza Mayor will draw you gently into the past; its flowering patio and indigenous-looking guest rooms are what discerning travelers hope for.

WHAT: town, hotel. **COLONIA DEL SACRAMENTO:** 113 miles/182 km west of Montevideo; 45 minutes by hydrofoil from Buenos Aires, Argentina. **HOTEL PLAZA MAYOR:** Calle del Comercio 111. Tel 598/522-3193 or 598/522-5316, fax 598/522-5812; hmayor@adinet.com.uy; www.posasaplaza mayor.com. *Cost:* doubles with Jacuzzi from $140. **BEST TIMES:** Mar–Apr and Sept–Nov.

Uruguay's Glamorous Summer Scene

PUNTA DEL ESTE

Uruguay

"Punta" is the quintessential jet-set mecca for South America's elite, a former colonial town whose top-drawer restaurants and clubs vie with the continent's finest. Revered for its long stretches of white sandy

beach and elegant designer boutiques, this is a fashionable see-and-be-seen summer destination, where sun worship is the primary activity. To escape its rash of high-rise condos and stellar prices, some travelers now opt for the neighboring areas of Punta Ballena and Barra de Maldonado. Day trips to the offshore Isla Gorriti and Isla de Lobos offer another temporary escape from the gorgeous thonged crowds. La Posta del Cangrejo, one of

Uruguay's loveliest hotels, in the slightly less-congested Barra de Maldonado, offers informal Mediterranean-style luxury. Despite its oceanside location, there is something of an elegant farmhouse ambience in the white stucco walls, terra-cotta floors, and hand-stenciled guest rooms with canopied beds. Barefoot relaxation is encouraged by a staff truly fond of their special hotel.

WHAT: town, hotel. **PUNTA:** 2-hour drive

east of Montevideo. **LA POSTA DEL CANGREJO:** 6 miles/9 km east of Punta. Tel 598/42-770-021; www.lapostadelcangrejo.com. *Cost:* doubles with ocean view $150 (low season), $400 (high season). **WHEN:** Nov–Apr, busiest mid-Dec to late Jan.

Earth's Highest Waterfalls Deep in the Lost World

ANGEL FALLS

Puerto Ordaz, Gran Sabana, Venezuela

American bush pilot Jimmy Angel was searching for a fabled mountain of gold when he "discovered" these wondrous falls—the highest in the world—in 1935. At 3,212 feet, and with an uninterrupted drop of more than 2,600 feet, they are fifteen times taller than Niagara Falls and one and a half times higher than the Empire State Building. Angel Falls springs from the summit of Auyan Tepuy, one of the area's mysterious tabletop *tepuys* (from a Pemón Indian word meaning "mountain") that interrupt the jungles and savanna. La Gran Sabana is populated by more than 100 of these massive sandstone mesas. They are some of the oldest and—with heights reaching 9,000 feet—some of the most impressive rock formations on earth, located within the Canaima National Park. Sir Arthur Conan Doyle was inspired here to write about dinosaurs and other Jurassic creatures in his classic *The Lost World*. On the park's lagoon side, Campamento Canaima is a rustic but comfortable jungle lodge of thatched-palm cabanas that offers flight-seeing tours and trips to the base of the falls by jeep, foot, and motorized dugout canoe.

WHAT: site, experience, hotel. **ANGEL FALLS:** from Caracas, by light aircraft 1½ hours to Puerto Ordaz. *How:* in the U.S., contact Southwind Adventures, tel 800-377-9463; info@southwindadventures.com; www.south windadventures.com. *Cost:* $3,725 per person, double occupancy, 9 days (4 nights camping), land only. *When:* departures Jun–Nov. **CAMPAMENTO CANAIMA:** tel 58/2-976-0530; www.hoturvensa.com.ve. *Cost:* 1 night $307 per person, includes round-trip airfare from Caracas, hotel, meals, and flight-seeing trip to falls. **BEST TIMES:** Oct–May for hiking; mid-May to mid-Dec for navigating the rivers to the base of the falls. Jan–May is dry season—the falls are a thin ribbon; Jun–Dec, falls are voluminous but frequently covered by clouds.

The Caribbean's Oldest and Largest Marine Park

ISLAS LOS ROQUES

Los Roques, Venezuela

Venezuela's offshore islands are so little known that few but Venezuelans talk about them—and they rave. Islas los Roques form a remarkable archipelago of forty largish islands (three alone are inhabited—sparsely) and more than 250 islets and cays, all surrounded by healthy coral reefs that promise snorkeling and diving in conditions that haven't existed elsewhere in the Caribbean for decades. Schools of fish numbering in the thousands, massive forests of soft coral, unending stretches of virgin hard coral, perpendicular drop-offs, caverns, and pinnacles are what Islas los Roques—the Caribbean's oldest and largest (850 square miles) marine national park—are known for. Nondivers will find talcum-soft beaches with no trace of a footprint and some 300 bird species, including the largest concentration of scarlet ibises on earth. You can land by helicopter or small aircraft on the ambitiously named Gran Roque, a traffic-free island whose main

fishing village is all of three blocks long. The lack of high-dollar resorts is made up for by a cluster of modest "posada" guest houses. Many of them are owned by a small Italian expat community, and promise simple barefoot living with a dash of la dolce vita and some pretty great food. Ask and they can arrange a boat drop-off for snorkeling and diving, or a castaway lunch on a deserted beach.

WHAT: experience, island. **WHERE:** 100 miles/161 km from La Guaira; round-trip from Caracas about $85. **WHERE TO STAY:** Posada Movida, tel 58/237-221-1016; www.posada movida.com. *Cost:* $110 per person (low season); $165 per person (high season), all meals included. **BEST TIMES:** Apr–Dec.

The White Continent

ANTARCTICA

Antarctica—Terra Australis Incognita, "the unknown land of the south"— is the surreal continent at the bottom of the world, a destination of ethereal beauty and unequivocal grandeur. Its limitless landscape of ice,

sea, and sky comes in a million shades of blue. One of the modern world's most magical destinations and one of nature's last, most remote strongholds, Antarctica affords an opportunity for adventure, excitement, and discovery rarely accessible to the average traveler. The nearly total absence of human presence fosters nonaggressive wildlife that welcome you into their habitat. A visit to a penguin rookery, whose tuxedoed residents number in the tens of thousands, is a once-in-a-lifetime experience. Different itineraries are possible: You can sail the Antarctic Peninsula or circumnavigate the entire continent, with options to travel by Zodiac launch amid the towering icebergs to neighboring islands, or with ports of call on South Georgia Island and the Falklands. Though dozens of cruise ship com-

panies ply these frigid waters, the first and best of the seaborne expedition ships is the *Explorer*, the "little red ship" that invented Antarctic cruising. This shallow-drafted icebreaker carries a veteran crew that includes geologists, zoologists, polar explorers, historians, ecologists, and oceanographers who help bring the incredible within reach.

WHAT: experience. **WHERE:** transfer from Santiago, Chile, to Ushuaia, Argentina, for embarkation. **HOW:** in the U.S., contact Abercrombie & Kent, tel 800-554-7016 or 630-725-3400; www.abercrombiekent.com. **COST:** from $8,895 per person, all-inclusive, double occupancy, for cruises of 14 days or more. Air transfers extra. **WHEN:** Nov–Feb (austral summer), when temperatures average a balmy 28°F.

THE
CARIBBEAN,
BAHAMAS,
AND
BERMUDA

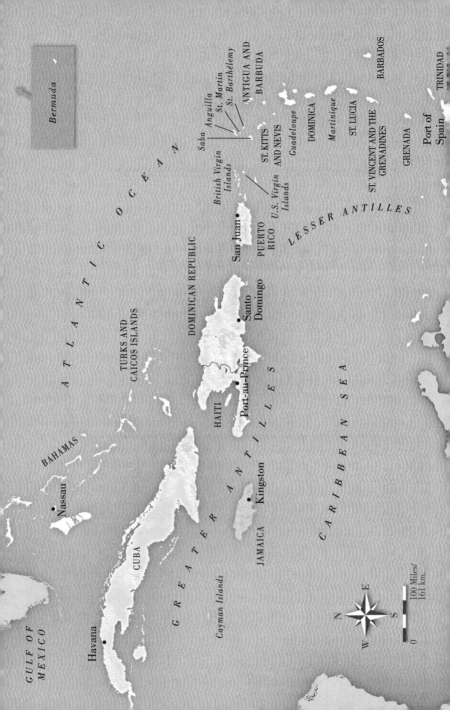

GULF OF
MEXICO

Havana

CUBA

Cayman Islands

JAMAICA

Kingston

CARIBBEAN SEA

HAITI

Port-au-Prince

DOMINICAN REPUBLIC

Santo
Domingo

BAHAMAS

Nassau

TURKS AND
CAICOS ISLANDS

ATLANTIC OCEAN

GREATER ANTILLES

San Juan

PUERTO
RICO

U.S. Virgin
Islands

British Virgin
Islands

Saba

Anguilla

St. Martin

St. Barthélemy

ANTIGUA AND
BARBUDA

ST. KITTS
AND NEVIS

Guadeloupe

DOMINICA

Martinique

ST. LUCIA

ST. VINCENT AND THE
GRENADINES

BARBADOS

GRENADA

Port of
Spain

TRINIDAD

LESSER ANTILLES

Bermuda

100 Miles/
161 km.

0

N
S
E
W

Swank Luxury Oases and an 18th-Century Great House

CAP JULUCA AND THE MALLIOUHANA HOTEL

Anguilla, Lesser Antilles (British West Indies)

Maybe it is the special clarity of the light that heightens the mirage effect of Cap Juluca's Moorish turrets, arches, and domes. Like a sensual Saharan casbah nestled within 179 flowering acres near Anguilla's southernmost point, and braced by a magical, mile-long curve of sugary white sand—one of the island's most beautiful—the ultraromantic hotel Cap Juluca employs an artist's palette of intense primary colors: green gardens, white-washed villas draped in brilliant bougainvillea, and everywhere the deep azure sea and sky. It can be almost too much for the winter-weary eyes of newly arrived guests. The oversized rooms are minimally but exotically appointed; many have enormous bathrooms with tubs for two and adjoining private sunning patios. Be sure to head out for dinner at the hotel's acclaimed Pimm's Restaurant, the only time and place guests wear anything more elaborate than a swimsuit and a suntan. At sunset Cap Juluca is the most glamorous vision west of Fez.

Not far to the north, the bluff-top Malliouhana Hotel boasts exquisite decor; a two-to-one staff-to-guest ratio; attentive, hands-on involvement by the gracious father and son British owners; and, perhaps most significantly, one of the most extensive wine lists in the western hemisphere, with 25,000 bottles and 1,500 selections, including more than 60 varieties of Champagne. The dining pavilion sits above the gorgeous sweep of Meads Bay and faces west for unequaled sunset viewing. The kitchen and menu are supervised and designed by the acclaimed French chef Alain Laurent. The classic French cuisine with an island accent is a marvel, particularly when one considers it is created on an unspoiled island where traffic lights are still a fairly new concept.

Farther north, in the area known as the Valley, Koal Keel is a romantic alternative to Anguilla's beachfront eateries. The open-air restaurant can be found in what used to be the garden of a sultry, sensual, and breezy 1780 plantation house, now beautifully restored. It's one of the oldest and prettiest West Indian homes on the island, with cool, heavy stone walls providing the theatrical backdrop to your meal, aglow with candlelight and the palpable aura of centuries past. This hillside charmer has created its own interpretation of delicious Euro-Caribbean cuisine. Try ginger-barbecued lamb, scrumptious lobster crepes, or delicate callaloo soup made with chard, coconut milk, and crab. Even if you drop in just for tea, you'll be hooked.

WHAT: hotel, restaurant. **CAP JULUCA:** southwestern coast, 15 minutes from the air-

Malliouhana Hotel

port. Tel 264/497-6666, fax 264/497-6617; in the U.S., tel 888-858-5822; www.capjuluca.com. *Cost:* doubles from $425 (low season) to $995 (high season); suites from $695 (low season) to $1,595 (high season); villas with private pools available. *When:* closed Sept–Oct. **MALLIOUHANA HOTEL:** northwest shore, at Meads Bay, 7 miles/11 km from the airport.

Tel 264/497-6111, fax 264/497-6011; in the U.S., tel 800-835-0796; reservations@malliouhana.com; www.malliouhana.com. *Cost:* doubles from $415 (low season), from $860 (high season). *When:* closed Sept–Oct. **KOAL KEEL:** the Valley. Tel 264/497-2930; www.koalkeel.com. *When:* dinner only; closed Sun. *Cost:* dinner $45. **BEST TIMES:** Nov–Apr.

---

*A Beach Among Beaches,
and a Full-Scale Party on a Desert Island*

SHOAL BAY AND GORGEOUS SCILLY CAY

Anguilla, Lesser Antilles (British West Indies)

Anguilla is a flat, scrubby island that's light on interior scenery, but its confectionery 12-mile perimeter has some of the most picture-perfect white-sand beaches anywhere. These have conspired with incredibly clear water and undisturbed reefs to make Anguilla a favorite haunt for beach-and-a-book sun seekers looking for the Caribbean's least-developed islands. Among Anguilla's thirty-some beaches, Shoal Bay ranks as anyone's dream. Although your footprints won't be the only ones left in the sand, particularly in the high season or on weekends, escapists need merely walk a few feet into the diamond-clear water to submerge themselves in another world, where schools of iridescent

fish and magnificent coral gardens are the only crowds to contend with. Should hunger strike, Uncle Ernie's is the archetypal shanty beach bar, where a beer and barbecued chicken, ribs, or catch of the day doesn't get any better—unless it's Sunday afternoon, when an island band manages to enhance the flavor.

For a more full-on party atmosphere, head out to Gorgeous Scilly Cay, which is on its own coral-sand islet. This popular watering hole/beach-shack restaurant can really get wound up on weekends, when day-trippers from St. Martin descend and a local band warms up; on weekdays it's more like a Robinson Crusoe fantasy. King Gorgeous (a.k.a. owner Eudoxie Wallace) entertains swimsuited diners with tall tales and powerfully delicious rum punches while preparing an alfresco feast of simple grilled lobster or crayfish marinated in his secret and justly legendary curry-based sauce. Most diners come for the better part of the day, snorkeling and swimming before and after lunch. The

Gorgeous Scilly Cay

ballfield-size cay now accommodates a helipad for the St. Martin set, but from Anguilla you can take King Gorgeous's ready-when-you-are motor launch. Just stand at the pier at Island Harbour and wave, and someone will be by to fetch you.

WHAT: site, restaurant. **SHOAL BAY:** a 2-mile/3-km strip on the northeast coast of Anguilla is divided into Lower Shoal Bay to the west and Upper Shoal Bay to the east. **UNCLE ERNIE'S:** on Upper Shoal Bay; tel 264/497-3907. *When:* lunch and dinner daily. **GORGEOUS SCILLY CAY:** off the northeastern coast; complimentary 2-minute motor launch from Island Harbour. Tel. 264/497-5123; www.scillycayanguilla.com. *Cost:* lunch $50. *When:* lunch only, Wed–Fri. **BEST TIMES:** Nov–Apr.

A Nautical Kentucky Derby and a Top-Drawer Resort

ANTIGUA SAILING WEEK AND CURTAIN BLUFF

English Harbour and Vicinity, Antigua, Lesser Antilles

In 1784, a young Horatio Nelson arrived in Antigua, home base for the British fleet during the Napoleonic Wars. He'd still recognize the landlocked harbor—its restored dockyard, now a national park, is one of few British Georgian-style naval dockyards left in the world, and still serving sailing vessels. Once a year, the yachting world descends on this otherwise quiet outpost for a kind of Henley Royal Regatta, Caribbean-style. Some 200 boats from 25 countries show up for a week's worth of serious racing and beautiful-people-watching, filling English Harbour and Nelson's Dockyard with blue-blooded sailors, curious landlubbers, and a fair share of pomp and circumstance. Look for the seventeen stately pillars, originally supports for a very large loft where sails were repaired, and a number of colonial naval buildings that are now used as galleries, saloons, shops, and inns.

The unofficial headquarters for the sailing week hubbub, and the architectural center-piece of the Dockyard, is the Admiral's Inn, a Georgian brick building dating back to 1788. Known as the Ads, it's the island's most interesting historic hotel, housed in a former engineers' office and pitch and tar store, wearing the ambience of an old ship. The well-tanned yachting crowd comes here to cool off in the shady terrace bar/restaurant, from which they can keep an eye on their multimillion-dollar craft. The food is first rate, as is the Joiner's Loft upstairs, the nicest and largest of the inn's dozen or so rooms, with a view of the busy harbor.

The beach at Curtain Bluff

If you want a quiet retreat from the scene, the Curtain Bluff resort, about 3 miles west, occupies one of the prettiest spots in Antigua, flanked by two beaches. Pounding surf on the windward side lulls guests to sleep at night, while the lagoon-smooth leeward beach serves as the launching place for the hotel's host of water activities. Amid impeccably manicured grounds lush with orchids and palms, spacious suites climb the headland bluff step-fashion, culminating with the Terrace Room, whose size and views offer royal accommodations. A genteel, old-money, country-club air prevails; well-heeled return guests don't count their pennies or calories. Exceptionally fine food, a stellar wine cellar, and dancing under the stars create a celebratory mood. And if the island is regarded as one of the Caribbean's foremost tennis enclaves, it is in no small part due to Curtain Bluff's inimitable founder and hands-on owner, Howard Hulford, who sponsors and hosts the prestigious Antigua Tennis Week every May.

WHAT: event, hotel. **SAILING WEEK:** Nelson's Dockyard is in English Harbour on the southern coast of Antigua; www.sailingweek.com. *When:* end of Apr. **ADMIRAL'S INN:** English Harbour. Tel 268/460-1027, fax 268/460-1534; www.admiralsantigua.com. *Cost:* doubles from $100 (low season), from $145 (high season); Joiner's Loft, from $160 (low season). *When:* closed mid-Aug to mid-Oct. **CURTAIN BLUFF:** on the south coast 3 miles/5 km west of English Harbour. Tel 268/462-8400, fax 268/462-8409; in the U.S., tel 888-289-9898; www.curtainbluff.com. *Cost:* beachfront doubles from $645 (low season), from $995 (high season), all-inclusive; Terrace Room $825 (low season), $1,425 (high season). *When:* mid-Oct–mid-May. **BEST TIMES:** Nov–Apr.

*World-Class Reef-Diving
and Bonefishing in Florida's Backyard*

ANDROS ISLAND

Bahamas

Much of Andros, the Bahamas' largest island, is uninhabited, connected by a series of shallow canals and cays called "bights"—Andros is, in fact, mostly water. Aside from the occasional tourist, most visitors here are divers or fishermen. At 142 miles, Andros's barrier reef is the third longest in the world after those in Australia and Belize, with a wall that begins around 70 feet from shore and plunges 6,000 feet to a narrow underwater canyon known as the Tongue of the Ocean (TOTO). A unique system of more than fifty blue holes, as these watery caves are called (first made famous by Jacques Cousteau), offers endless opportunities to explore in tunnels filled with shipwrecks and sea life.

All this is just 1 mile offshore from the Bahamas' oldest dive resort, the comfortable, family-run Small Hope Bay Hotel. If you don't know how to dive or snorkel, they'll teach you at your own pace and at no extra cost, but non-diving guests are just as happy flopping into the inviting hammocks positioned here and there among the tall coconut palms. No one puts on airs at this easygoing beachfront colony—no one even puts on shoes very often, except perhaps at dinner, a hearty, convivial affair that might include fresh conch fritters and chowder, lobster, and hot home-

Diving Andros's reef

baked johnny bread. If you'd rather catch your own seafood, Andros's gin-clear waters are the bonefishing capital of the world, with large numbers of trophy-size bonefish (often topping 12 pounds) providing some of the most exciting light-tackle fishing there is. It's not hard to find a specialist to help you perfect your saltwater angling technique and to guide you to the vast flats in and around the bights, where you'll often be the only one in sight.

WHAT: island, experience, hotel, site. **WHERE:** 30 miles/48 km (15 minutes by air) southwest of Nassau. A private 1-hour flight from Ft. Lauderdale is offered by Small Hope Bay Lodge ($120 per person each way). **SMALL HOPE BAY LODGE:** tel 242/368-2014, fax 242/368-2015; in the U.S. and Canada, tel 800-223-6961; SHBinfo@SmallHope.com; www.smallhope.com. *Cost:* daily, per person from $235 (low season), from $260 (high season), includes all drinks, meals, introductory dive lessons, and sports facilities. Dive packages available. **BEST TIMES:** Nov–Apr for weather. Nov and May are best fishing months; also Jun, Mar, and Apr, in that order.

Cottages in the Carnival Colors of Junkanoo

COMPASS POINT

Love Beach, New Providence Island, Bahamas

The kaleidoscopic, Crayola colors of Compass Point's trendy cabanas and clapboard cottages evoke Junkanoo, the Afro-Bahamian carnival, and lend a playful theme-park-for-adults spirit to an island known more for Nassau's casinos, mammoth resorts, and cruise-ship travelers. Compass Point's cottages offer hints of Nassau's bustle, but have more of an outer islands vibe, with their own sandy cove offering privacy and access to justly famous Love Beach, located just steps away. For one of the island's best eating experiences, guests need merely brush off the sand and amble to the hotel's alfresco restaurant, one of the few in Nassau with an ocean view. Compass Point's visually lively, upbeat spirit is evident in its Bahamian-Californian cuisine as well, a cutting-edge fusion that produces winners like maki rolls (made with queen conch, mango, and cucumber) or roast lobster tail seasoned with Thai herbs. It's the in spot for diners to watch the sun's nightly performance, and each other.

WHAT: hotel. **WHERE:** near Love Beach, on the western shores of Ol' Town Nassau, 10 minutes from the airport. Tel 242/327-4500,

A Compass Point cottage

fax 242/327-3299; in the U.S., tel 800-OUT-POST; www.compasspointbeachresort.com. **COST:** double cabanas from $245. Dinner $35. **BEST TIMES:** the streets of downtown Nassau are invaded during the elaborate parades of Junkanoo Dec 26–Jan 1.

Spectacular Sailing in a Marine Preserve

THE EXUMA CAYS

The Exumas, Bahamas

Swooping in over the long, spiny chain of the Exuma's 365 cays—which start about 30 miles southeast of Nassau and extend for 120 miles—offers a first glimpse of these mostly undeveloped islands considered by many to be the crown jewels of the Bahamas. It looks like an exquisite sand painting rising up out of the sea, with elaborate channels and sandbars surrounded by waters in aquamarine, jade, amethyst, and every other shade of blue in the palette.

Once you've landed, explore the Exuma Cays Land and Sea Park, a 176 square-mile, breathtakingly beautiful "no-take" marine preserve where coral gardens flourish. Established in 1959 and accessible only by boat (your own or a tour company's), this is the oldest land and sea park on the planet. But while the land is pretty, providing habitat for turtles, iguanas, and sea birds, it is the sea that truly dazzles, offering some of the best kayaking, boating, snorkeling, and diving in all the Bahamas.

Set near the middle of the Exumas, Staniel Cay Yacht Club is the perfect home base, providing easy access to the park and other attractions like Thunderball Grotto (an underwater cave named for the James Bond movie shot there) and friendly pigs you can swim with (they live on Big Major Spot and greet boaters, who often bring them food). While it sounds swanky, the yacht club is just nine cottages in fun colors right on the water, an 18-slip marina for boaters, and a 3,000-foot landing strip for flights from Nassau and Fort Lauderdale.

WHERE: 30 miles southwest of Nassau. **VISITOR INFO:** Tel 800-688-4752; www.myoutislands.com. **EXUMA CAYS LAND AND SEA PARK:** 22 miles northwest of Staniel Cay. www.exumapark.com. **STANIEL CAY YACHT CLUB:** 75 miles south of Nassau. Tel 242/355-2024; www.stanielcay.com. *Cost:* rooms from $145 (low season) from $210 (high season).

Enchanting Creatures, Face-to-Face

DOLPHIN DIVE

Little Bahama Banks, Bahamas

There's a magical place northeast of Grand Bahama Island where a pod of wild spotted dolphins congregates regularly—without the enticement of food or reward—to play and swim and interact with people, apparently more charmed by their human playmates than fearful. There's no way to predict exactly when or where they'll show up, so you'll have to team up with a reputable operator who's familiar with the dolphins, their habitat, and their habits. Captain Scott of Dream Team is the most experienced, having photographed, identified, and named more than a hundred dolphins. Scott seems to have an uncanny intuition for finding them, and treats them like old friends. His 65-foot live-aboard, the *Dolphin Dream,* scores an 85 percent success rate, sometimes with several encounters a day, lasting from a few emotional moments to a couple of adrenaline-packed hours. The water over the Little Bahama Banks—shallow, calm, and with excellent visibility—is perfect for nondiving snorkelers and swimmers, who can enjoy themselves here even after the dolphins get bored and disappear.

WHAT: experience. **WHERE:** departures from West Palm Beach. **HOW:** Dream Team, tel 888-277-8181, fax 561-840-7946; info@ dolphindreamteam.com; www.dolphindream team.com. 12 passengers can be accommodated aboard the *Dolphin Dream.* **COST:** all-inclusive weeklong trips $1,595 per person (low season), $1,795 (high season), based on 8 passengers. **WHEN:** Apr–Aug.

A Pastel Village on a Gorgeous Beach

PINK SANDS

Harbour Island, Eleuthera Island Group, Bahamas

As the Bahamas' first capital, before Nassau, Harbour Island is rich in history, but today it is best known for the 3-mile-long cover of pale pink sand. It's a private fantasy beach with water as clear as a swimming pool,

rimmed by the classic seashell-pink-and-white Bahamian cottages of the Pink Sands Hotel. Spread out over 16 green acres, the Pink Sands, once a venerable and slightly stodgy favorite of old-money families, has been transformed into a glamorous destination for a younger and decidedly cooler crowd. The elegant informality of the place is deceptively unassuming, in keeping with the personality of Harbour Island, an offshore cay of Eleuthera. Lacy gingerbread houses and white picket fences remind some of Nantucket, but don't think stuffy: There's whimsy in Pink Sands' strong pastels and chic decor, and the restaurant's Caribbean-Asian cuisine is one of the most exciting in the far-flung Out Islands.

WHAT: hotel. **WHERE:** 20-minute flight from Nassau to Eleuthera; water-taxi transfers to Harbour Island. Tel 242/333-2030, fax 242/ 333-2060; in the U.S., tel 800-OUTPOST; www.islandoutpost.com. **COST:** 1-bedroom cottage from $600 (low season), from $750 (high season), includes breakfast and dinner. **WHEN:** Nov–Aug. **BEST TIMES:** Nov–May.

A Mini-Archipelago Lures Boaters, Diners, and Anglers

SAILING THE ABACOS

The Abacos, Bahamas

Known as "the sailing capital of the world," the Abacos is one of the Caribbean's stellar sailing destinations. Off the eastern coast of the boomerang-shaped Great Abaco island is a collection of 25 cays, each with its own distinct character, some uninhabited and others charming settlements that date to the American Revolution. It's one big barrier reef, and the pleasure is in leisurely threading your way from one cay to the next, dropping anchor for a little snorkeling, swimming, fishing, diving, or island exploration, then sleeping on board before sailing off to the next.

Launch from Great Abaco's Marsh Harbour. If you don't have your own boat (or even know how to sail), this is the place to get one, with or without a crew. Before you set off on your yacht crawl, stop by the Jib Room. A popular harbor-view lunch spot, this place is really jumping on the nights it serves dinner—baby back pork ribs on Wednesdays and sizzling New York strip steaks on Saturday.

Sail the islands in any particular order, but some, like Elbow Cay, are not to be missed. Best known for its 120-foot-tall, peppermint-striped lighthouse built in 1838, Elbow Cay is home to the Abaco Inn (also accessible by ferry), which offers cheerful rooms nestled among the sand dunes and coconut palms. Its restaurant offers some of the best seafood in the Abacos and desserts by Miss Belle, whose fresh-squeezed key lime, coconut, and chocolate silk pies are legendary. At the very tip of Elbow Cay is Tahiti Beach, a gorgeous curve of sand with utterly placid, clear turquoise waters.

The longest of the Abaco cays, Great Guana stretches nearly seven miles tip to tip but has just 100 full-time residents. Its lovely beach runs the entire length of the island.

If it's golf you're after, Treasure Cay Hotel Resort & Marina on Treasure Cay (a peninsula on the eastern shore of Great Abaco) has a top-notch Dick Wilson–designed 18-hole course. On Green Turtle Cay, New Plymouth, a palm-filled historic village settled in 1783, is best known for Miss Emily's Blue Bee Bar (a shack really), home of the famous Goombay Smash.

The Abacos is also world-renowned for its fishing. Here avid anglers will find yellowtail and grouper on the reefs, marlin and tuna in the deeps, and fast, canny bonefish in the Marls, 400 square miles of lush mangrove islands and sandy cays on the western side of Great Abaco.

WHERE: Marsh Harbour is 60 miles northeast of Nassau. **VISITOR INFO:** Tel 800-688-4752; www.myoutislands.com. **HOW:** The Moorings can set you up with a boat, with or without a crew. Tel 888-952-8420 or 242-367-4000; www.moorings.com. **JIB ROOM:** Marsh Harbour Marina. Tel 242-367-2700; www.jibroom.com. *Cost:* dinner $25. **ABACO INN:** White Sound, Elbow Cay. Tel 800-468-8799 or 242-366-0133; www.abacoinn.com. *Cost:* from $90 (low season), from $160 (high season). Dinner $50. *When:* closed mid-Aug–mid-Oct. **TREASURE CAY HOTEL RESORT & MARINA:** 16 miles northwest of Marsh Harbour. Tel 800-327-1584 or 954-525-7711; www.golfbahamas.com. *Cost:* from $150 (low season), from $170 (high season). **MISS EMILY'S BLUE BEE BAR:** Green Turtle Cay. Tel 242-365-4181. *Cost:* Goombay Smash, $6. **BEST TIMES:** Nov–May for weather; Apr–June for the Bahamas Billfish Championship; July for Bahamas Cup and Regatta Time; May–Aug for blue marlin fishing.

A Palladian Estate Where Everyone Gets the Royal Treatment

SANDY LANE

St. James, Barbados, Lesser Antilles

Sandy Lane is one of the resort world's classiest acts, its house-proud Bajan staff treating every guest with the same degree of service they gave Queen Elizabeth when she visited. Although independent since 1966, Barbados has retained a *veddy* British atmosphere, and life at this former sugarcane plantation is redolent of the old cultural ties, with many Brits (including some royals) filling the guest register. Things are done on a grand scale, from the snow-white Rolls-Royce greeting you at the airport to complimentary Champagne at breakfast and vast marbled bathrooms the size of most hotel guest rooms. An army of gardeners carefully tends the 320-acre grounds, and the

The beach at Sandy Lane

hotel's own championship 18-hole, par-72 golf course is but one of a host of complimentary recreational activities (which also include tennis, deep-sea fishing, and scuba diving). Plan to spruce up for dinner—the dress code is enforced more by the guests than by management—and plan to follow your meal with dancing under the stars on the Starlight Terrace. Could it be more swank?

WHAT: hotel. **WHERE:** west coast of Barbados, 18 miles/29 km from the airport. Tel 246/444-2000, fax 246/444-2222; in the U.S., tel 866-444-4080; reservations@sandy lane.com; www.sandylane.com. **COST:** garden-view doubles from $1,000 (low season) to $1,400 (high season); ocean-view doubles from $1,500 (low season) to $2,300 (high season). **BEST TIMES:** Nov–Apr.

La Dolce Vita and a Beach That Goes On Forever

K-CLUB

Codrington, Barbuda, Lesser Antilles

This is the kind of deserted, champagne-colored, talcum-powder strand that can bring tears to the eyes of true beach aficionados. When Mariuccia Mandelli, arbiter elegantiarum and mastermind behind the Milan-based

Krizia design empire (the "K" in K-Club), decided to create her sybaritic Eden, only the best location would suffice, and she found it on Barbuda, an island so quiet it has no paved roads. There is every proof that no expense was spared—ask any of the fashion world's elite, who come here to flop, hassle-free and with nothing more than the ultimate beach and a book to distract them. Ms. Mandelli's incomparable style animates every niche of the 230-acre resort, from the imaginative doorknobs to the linen and place settings in the elegantly simple restaurant. Excellent homemade pastas

and the innovative, Mediterranean-inclined menu might make you forget for a minute that you're not on the Riviera. Like everything else, the restaurant is open to the cooling trade winds and turquoise ocean view.

WHAT: hotel. **WHERE:** a 15-minute flight from Antigua can be arranged by the K-Club for about $400 per passenger, round-trip. Tel 268/460-0300, fax 268/460-0305; www.kclub barbuda.com. **COST:** from $950 (low season), from $1,400 (high season), meals included. **WHEN:** mid-Nov to May. **BEST TIMES:** Nov–Apr.

Tee-Time Heaven

GOLFING IN BERMUDA

Bermuda (British Overseas Territory)

Bermuda's diminutive 21-square-mile dimensions belie its riches, including more golf courses per square mile than anywhere else in the world. Six public and two private golf clubs offer spectacular scenery,

challenging courses (seven are championship standard), and wind—plenty of wind—plus a British tradition of excellence not easy to find outside Scotland. Riddell's Bay, established in 1922, is the island's oldest, most picturesque club. Belmont, challenging and undulating, opened a year later. Port Royal also figures on any visiting golfer's shortlist, with a much-photographed sixteenth hole. But the ne plus ultra (and private) Mid Ocean Club is undoubtedly the island's finest, with a fabulous fifth hole regularly included in surveys of the world's top fifty.

Some of the better hotels can facilitate booking tee times at these enclaves, among them the venerable Cambridge Beaches Hotel, only 2½ miles from the Port Royal Club. The century-old grand dame of Bermuda's cottage communities, Cambridge Beaches occupies a beautifully landscaped peninsula edged with private coves and pink sand beaches. High tea is observed punctiliously, and the

formal Tamarisk Restaurant serves some of Bermuda's best food.

WHAT: experience, hotel. **GOLF CLUBS:** west of Hamilton, 10–30 minutes from Cambridge Beaches Hotel. Contact the government-run golf association to book at any of the public clubs, tel 441/295-9972, or call directly: Riddell's Bay, tel 441/238-1060, fax 441/238-8785; Newstead Belmont Hills, tel 441/236-6060, fax 441/236-2296; Port Royal, tel 441/234-0974, fax 441/234-3562; Mid Ocean Club, tel 441/293-0330, fax 441/293-8837. **CAMBRIDGE BEACHES HOTEL:** on the island's extreme western edge, in Somerset. Tel 441/234-0331, fax 441/234-3352; in the U.S., tel 800-468-7300; www.cambridgebeaches. com. *Cost:* garden-view doubles from $305 (low season), from $470 (high season), includes breakfast, tea, and dinner; water-view doubles from $385 (low season), from $590 (high season). **WHEN:** golf clubs open year-round. **BEST TIMES:** May–Nov for golfing.

Pink Sand and Turquoise Waters

THE SOUTHSHORE BEACHES

Bermuda (British Overseas Territory)

This time the tourist literature doesn't exaggerate: The sand of Bermuda's beaches—especially in the late-afternoon sun—really is rosy pink, the result of granules of crushed coral washed ashore from the island's band

Elbow Beach, where the sand really is rosy

of protective reefs. Though it's known as an island, Bermuda is actually a fishhook-shaped archipelago made up of seven major islands and about 143 smaller ones, interconnected by bridges and causeways. That's a lot of blushing pink coastline.

Of the world's resort islands, Bermuda enjoys the highest rate of return visitors, many of whom come back, at least in part, to bask on the dozens of small, hidden beaches they didn't have time for on their last trip. Typically, southshore beaches are more scenic than those on the north side. Postcard-perfect

Horseshoe Bay is one of the most popular and the most photographed—which means lots of cooler-toting families and teenage beach-blanket parties. Lovely as it is, on weekends you're better off going to nearby Elbow Beach. For utter serenity from sunrise to sunset, search out Warwick Long Bay—lengthy, soft, and truly pink. Really.

WHAT: site. **WHERE:** roughly 24 coral-dust beaches spread along the coast south of Hamilton. **WHERE TO STAY:** although no hotels are built directly on Bermuda's beaches, Elbow Beach Hotel is as beachfront as you can get. Tel 441/236-3535, fax 441/236-8043; in the U.S., tel 800-223-7434; ebbda_reservations@mohg.com; www.mandarinoriental.com. Cost: ocean-view double rooms from $309 (low season), from $495 (high season). **BEST TIMES:** May–Oct for weather. Four days in early Oct for the Bermuda Music Festival.

Famous Underwater Forests of Coral Reefs and 24-Hour Diving

BONAIRE MARINE PARK

Bonaire, Lesser Antilles (Netherlands Antilles)

An island almost completely surrounded by teeming coral reefs, Bonaire is one big dive site. More than eighty diving spots are scattered off the 24-mile shoreline, and no other island boasts so many

first-rate sites so close to shore (just walk in!) nor such a conservation-sensitive dive industry and enlightened, forward-thinking government. The latter's unprecedented creation of the island-encircling Bonaire Marine Park in 1979 has resulted in some of the world's finest, and healthiest, hard- and soft-coral reef diving, with 80-plus kinds of colorful coral and more than 355 species of fish at last count. Since spear guns were replaced by underwater cameras in the

1970s, the fish here have become among the most numerous and friendly in the Caribbean. Bonaire is an exceptionally dry island, with minimal freshwater runoff, so that underwater visibility is among the Caribbean's clearest—the diving is great year-round.

Captain Don's Habitat is the nerve center for visiting scuba divers. Californian Captain Don is a salty island legend and was instrumental in the dive industry's early days of conservation. His

Captain Don's Habitat

1970s pit-stop beachfront bungalows have evolved into some of the island's best accommodations, and his five-star, full-service PADI diving center is considered the finest in the Caribbean.

WHAT: site, experience, hotel. **BONAIRE MARINE PARK:** surrounds boomerang-shaped Bonaire and the small, uninhabited island of Klein Bonaire, off the main island's western leeward coast; tel 599/717-8444; www.bmp.org. **CAPTAIN DON'S HABITAT:** Kaya Gobernador N. de Brot 103, 1.5 miles/2.5 km north of Kralendijk and the airport; complimentary transfer arranged by hotel. Tel 599/717-8290; in the U.S., tel 800-327-6709; info@habitatbonaire.com; www.habitatdiveresorts.com. *Cost:* doubles from $149 (low season), from $190 (high season). *When:* open year-round. **BEST TIMES:** Jan–Oct for diving.

Your Own Private Wildlife Preserve

GUANA ISLAND

British Virgin Islands, Lesser Antilles (British West Indies)

For latent hermits or people who want nature all to themselves, Guana's 850 virginal acres will never feel crowded, even with an occasional full house of thirty guests. It's the Galápagos of the Caribbean, a wildlife sanctuary that's said to have the richest variety of flora and fauna of any island its size in the region. A hundred species of birds—roseate flamingos, black-necked stilts, herons, egrets, and the endangered masked booby—make Guana a paradise for bird-watchers. In the 18th century, Guana was dominated by a sugarcane and cotton plantation owned by two American Quaker families, and today that classic simplicity is still evident in the stylish but restrained accommodations at the island's only lodge. The panoramic sweep from the whitewashed ridge-top cottages is spectacular. Reached only by boat, the hilly island, with its twenty nature trails and seven beaches, is virtually private and for guests' use alone (yacht "drop-ins" are discouraged); two of the beaches are accessible only by the hotel's private launch. Why not invite twenty-nine friends and rent the whole island?

WHAT: island, hotel. **WHERE:** 10 minutes by hotel launch from Tortola ($25 per person). Tel 284/494-2354, fax 284/495-2900; in the U.S., tel 800-544-8262 or 212-482-6247; reservations@guana.com; www.guana.com. **COST:** doubles from $695 (low season), from $1,450 (high season), all-inclusive. Full island rental $21,000 per day (low season), $31,750 per day (high season). **WHEN:** closed Sept–Oct. **BEST TIMES:** Dec–Apr.

Room with a view at Guana's only hotel

Superb Style, Splendid Isolation, and Some Really Big Boulders

LITTLE DIX BAY AND THE BATHS

Virgin Gorda, British Virgin Islands, Lesser Antilles (British West Indies)

For decades, word of mouth celebrated the 500-acre resort of Little Dix Bay and the exquisite location it commanded on a perfect half-mile crescent of white-sand beach on Virgin Gorda, the "Fat Virgin." Together with its sister property, Caneel Bay, Little Dix was created by Laurance Rockefeller in the 1960s for his blue-blood circle of old-money friends and family. Despite a change in ownership, it remains a classic, still known for its laid-back luxury, relaxed pampering, and a low-key, unpretentious ambience. The native stone and hardwood cottages nestle amid the lush but impeccably manicured grounds, a veritable Garden of Eden maintained by no less than twenty full-time gardeners. Even breakfast is romantic in the dining area—four intercon-nected, open-sided, thatch-roofed pavilions sitting right on the hotel's marvelous beach. Dinners are both genial and exciting, the work of an ambitious and sophisticated kitchen the Rockefellers would have been proud of.

About a mile south is the island's most noted natural site, The Baths, where huge, time-sculpted granite boulders—some as big as small houses—create spellbinding pools, shallow coves, and interconnected grottoes that are heaven for snorkelers, swimmers, and those who merely appreciate natural beauty. Stacked along the beach in jumbled piles, these prehistoric rocks are most impressive when approached by sea. The site is on every visitor's list, so to avoid the boatloads of in-and-out tourists and cruise ship passengers, come early or late, or wander along the less-visited coastline on either side, where the massive boulders continue.

WHAT: hotel, site. **LITTLE DIX BAY:** tel 284/495-5555, fax 284/495-5661; in the U.S., tel 212-758-1735; www.littledixbay.com. *Cost:* doubles from $395. **THE BATHS:** approached by Lee Rd., on the southwest coast. **BEST TIMES:** Jan–Mar.

A Visionary's Version of Heaven

NECKER ISLAND

British Virgin Islands, Lesser Antilles (British West Indies)

Guests have some pretty celebrated footprints to fill when booking this private island. Owner and creator Richard Branson—the British multi-millionaire founder of Virgin Airways—spared no expense when he designed and built his fantasy escape on this previously uninhabited, reef-surrounded, 74-acre island. An airy, twenty-two-room Balinese villa commands a 360-degree seascape and reflects the rich architectural and crafts traditions of Indonesia. The place is so romantic, it has inspired a number of impromptu weddings, including Branson's. Guests readily don the colorful sarongs left for their use and never bother to unpack. In fact, they wear little clothing at all, and shoes rarely make an appearance. When the Bransons aren't in residence, Necker can be rented in its fabulous entirety, which includes a staff of thirty-one. The private holiday island is popular with Hollywood celebs and European aristos, but couples can book individually during "Celebration Weeks," held four times yearly. It's expensive, but duplicating heaven on earth often is.

WHAT: island, hotel. **WHERE:** off north coast of Virgin Gorda; complimentary 10-minute launch from Virgin Gorda or 30-minute launch from Tortola can be arranged by hotel. In the U.S. and Canada, tel 877-577-8777 or 212-994-3070, fax 212-997-9051.

Romantic style with every comfort

COST: Celebration Weeks during designated periods, from $25,400 per couple per week, all-inclusive. Rent the whole island with up to 14 guests for $26,500 per day; can accommodate up to 26 guests at $53,000 per day. **BEST TIMES:** Nov–Apr.

Cruising Capital of the World

SAILING THE BRITISH VIRGIN ISLANDS

Lesser Antilles (British West Indies)

The craggy peaks of a submerged chain of volcanoes form the British Virgin Islands, scattered across miles of incomparably blue sea. The islands have been considered prime cruising grounds since the 1600s, when pirates would find the perfect hiding place among their endless coves. Today, seven out of ten visitors come here for a sailing vacation, and those three unsuspecting landlubbers don't know what they're missing. Sixty-plus islands, islets, and cays offer sailors the chance to drop anchor in inviting, deserted coves, walk empty beaches, visit Tortola's Cane Garden Bay at sunset, or dive the wreck of the 310-foot RMS *Rhone*, a royal mail steamer that sank in a hurricane near Salt Island in 1867.

The Moorings, a world-famous yacht operation, has its Caribbean headquarters in Tortola. The seventy-two-slip charter dock and seventy-slip visitors' dock are a tourist destination in themselves. Stroll the boards and meet some of the most interesting boat lovers and owners in the world. Most of these yachts probably sell for more than the home you left behind, many in the millions. The Moorings' hotel, the Mariner Inn, is a beloved boaters' hangout that accommodates Moorings customers before and after rentals of bareboat and crewed sailing vacations.

Nearby—although way up at 1,300 feet above sea level—the lofty Skyworld restaurant provides an amazing 360-degree view of these sailing waters, plus one of the most innovative menus in the area. Order the conch fritters, which even the locals admit are the best on the island, and Skyworld's signature steak, prepared with port and peaches—you'll start looking for available island real estate in the morning. Throw caloric caution to the wind and go for the "chocolate suicide" dessert, made with dark and white chocolates.

About 2 miles west, Bomba's Shack is the island's oldest, most memorable, and most uninhibited watering hole, and one of the Caribbean's most famous bars. The colorful makeshift decor—driftwood and flotsam nailed together, with a sand floor and walls festooned with old license plates, postcards, abandoned rubber tires, and paper leis—helps camouflage a powerful sound system that gets

things jumpin' even before Bomba's Punches (made with homemade rum) kick in. Crowds of yachties and folk from all over Tortola and the neighboring islands fill the beach and rock on to live music until the wee hours during "full moon parties," and on Wednesday and Sunday nights aficionados gather for the all-you-can-eat barbecue of Creole specialties.

WHAT: experience, hotel, restaurant. **THE MOORINGS:** Road Town, Wickham's Cay, Tortola. Tel 284/494-2332, fax 284/494-9747; in the U.S., tel 888-952-8420; www.moorings.com. Weekly bareboat rentals from $1,560 for 4 people. Various sizes of bareboats accommodate 4 to 8 people. Daily rates available. Rates for crewed yachts per person double occupancy in a private stateroom from $1,595 weekly. **MARINER INN:** tel 284/494-2333; www.bvimarinerinnhotel.com. *Cost:* from $160 (low season), from $220 (high season). **SKYWORLD:** above Road Town on Ridge Rd., Tortola. Tel 284/494-3567. *Cost:* dinner $35. *When:* open for lunch Tues–Sun; dinner by reservation only. Closed Sept. **BOMBA'S SHACK:** at Cappoon's Bay, on Tortola's northwestern coast. Tel 284/495-4148; www.bombasurfsideshack.com. *Cost:* barbecue $15. **BEST TIMES:** Nov–Apr.

An Island as Virgin as When Columbus Landed

SANDCASTLE

White Bay, Jost Van Dyke, British Virgin Islands, Lesser Antilles (British West Indies)

R oll up your trousers and wade ashore to this modern-day alternative to the real world. The tiny island of Jost Van Dyke boasts one of the area's most stunning beaches. Four simple waterfront bungalows and two

air-conditioned rooms make up the colony of Sandcastle, which has an island dog and cat on staff, no electricity except in the kitchen, and solar-heated showers. Wear to dinner what you wore to breakfast, and spend the day

moving from one hammock to another with a Painkiller in hand: The bar's signature drink (now famous throughout the islands) can vary from mild to lethal. Pity the yachties who row in just for the day, although the highlight of their sailing vacation is usually a candlelit four-course dinner at the Soggy Dollar. It's the focal point of the hotel—and the island—and deservedly beloved in yachting circles.

This 3- by 4-mile island, whose main street is a sandy lane, is also home to Foxy's Tamarind Bar, a legendary yachtsman's haunt that's a lovely half-hour stroll down the beach and over the hill into Great Harbor.

WHAT: island, hotel, restaurant. **WHERE:** regular 30-minute ferry service ($25 round-trip) or 20 minutes by hotel's private boat ($75), from West End, Tortola. Water taxi service (from $225 one-way) from Red Hook, St. Thomas. **SANDCASTLE:** tel 284/495-9888,

A Sandcastle welcome

fax 284/495-9999. *Cost:* doubles from $190 (low season), from $265 (high season). Packages available. Dinner $40. *When:* closed Sept. **BEST TIMES:** Nov–Apr.

The Ultimate Dive, and Divine Dining After

BLOODY BAY WALL AND PIRATE'S POINT RESORT

Little Cayman, Cayman Islands (British West Indies)

The Caymans, a three-island British Crown Colony, sit atop an ancient undersea mountain chain. On the surface, the translucent turquoise waters are serene, but below you'll find dramatic walls and sheer drop-offs only feet from shore, like an underwater Grand Canyon. It's one of the best dive sites in the world, with an astounding diversity of underwater life residing among coral-encrusted reefs and walls.

Little Cayman has unparalleled underwater views.

Off Grand Cayman is the famous Stingray City, considered one of the best shallow dive/snorkeling sites in the world, where the winged marine creatures are hand-fed by divers like so many park pigeons. The numero uno dive site in the area, though, is the 1,200-foot plunging coral garden known since pirate days as Bloody Bay Wall, located off Little Cayman's north shore. Little Cayman is the Caribbean's largest bird sanctuary and has one of its smallest human populations, numbering around 100. It's the last bastion of wilderness in the Cayman Islands, famous for its 20,000 red-footed boobies and for Texas-born Gladys Howard—a student of famed cookbook writer and chef extraordinaire Julia Child—who caters to guests' every diving and dining need at her small beachside inn, Pirate's Point Resort. Aside from working miracles with fish caught in her front yard and produce flown in daily, Gladys also offers a custom-built dive boat with a staff of qualified diving instructors.

WHAT: experience, hotel, restaurant. **PIRATE'S POINT RESORT:** Little Cayman,

85 miles/137 km northeast of Grand Cayman. Tel 345/948-1010; www.piratespointresort.com. *Cost:* 7-day stay from $1,795 per person, double occupancy (low season), from $1,995 (high season), includes all meals and diving. **BEST TIMES:** water temperatures range from 78°F in Feb to 86°F in Aug. Visibility is always excellent.

A Little-Known Highlight of the World Circuit

CUBA'S JAZZ FESTIVAL

Havana, Cuba, Greater Antilles

Music, at times profoundly African in rhythm and origin, is a deep-reaching and complex ingredient of the Cuban soul, so it's no surprise that when musicians from around the world show up each February for

Cuba's Jazz Festival, they marvel at the number of exceptionally talented local musicians sharing the bill with them and performing throughout the city. Held since the early 1980s, the annual festival spotlights many of Cuba's revered grassroots stars, but the local audience is starved for the cross-pollination of American music. The result is a week of transcultural jam sessions, spontaneous concerts, and late-night parties that bring disparate

classes and nationalities together with the common language of music. Disorganized and sprawling but endlessly rich, with a carnival-like atmosphere, the festival takes place in dozens of Havana's theaters, bars, and clubs, with performances around the clock.

WHAT: event. **WHERE:** venues throughout Havana. **HOW:** in the U.S., contact Marazul, tel 201-319-1054, fax 201-840-6719; www.marazul charters.com. **WHEN:** 1 week mid-Feb.

The Capital's Historic Quarter and Its Most Glamorous, Nostalgic Hotel

LA HABANA VIEJA AND THE HOTEL NACIONAL

Havana, Cuba, Greater Antilles

Anchored by the gracious Plaza de la Catedral, Havana's 2-square-mile Old Quarter is one of the most envied in the Americas, a partially renovated architectural ensemble of monuments, fortresses, cobblestone streets, and grandiose, ostentatious townhouses that once belonged to an affluent bourgeoisie. Close to 150 buildings dating from the 16th and 17th centuries have been handsomely preserved while others have been left to crumble. It's one of the many conflicting impressions made by this once magnificent capital, still the largest city in the Caribbean. Paradoxically, the very revolution responsible for the island's decades-long withdrawal has helped keep the city's finest

Poolside lounging at the historic Hotel Nacional

architecture intact by banning private investments and real estate speculation—there's not an incongruous modern structure to be found among the arcades and palm-shaded courtyards of the old Spanish core. Foreseeing a great future in tourism, this niche of the city has been tidied up and is once again a mirror of the colonial Havana that was the richest city in the Caribbean, when the treasures of

the New World flooded through on their way to the royal courts of Spain. Even its dilapidated corners have a charmed feel about them, a sunwashed melancholy that mixes with a sense of peeling and decaying glory.

If Havana seems stuck in the past, nowhere is it felt more glamorously or nostalgically than at the Hotel Nacional, located in the Vedado district, west of the Old Quarter, and overlooking the Malecón, Havana's great 4-mile waterfront drive. Featuring eclectic Art Deco architecture, this landmark was spruced up not long ago to recapture the glory of its 1930s youth, restoring the opulent beauty of its Moorish arches and hand-painted tiles. In 1950s Havana, mobster Meyer Lansky operated one of Cuba's most glamorous casinos here; his Vegas cronies lounged at the palm-shaded pool, playing penny-ante poker. Today they've been replaced by VIP guests, the foreign press corps, boycott-busting American tycoons pretending not to be doing business, and cigar-smoking, rum-sipping Europeans on their way to one of the island's coastal resorts.

WHAT: site, hotel. **HOTEL NACIONAL:** Calle 21 at Calle O. Tel 53/7-833-3564; www. hotelnacionaldecuba.com. **HOW:** in the U.S., contact Marazul, tel 201-840-6711, fax 201-319-1054; www.marazulcharters.com. *Cost:* doubles from $175. **BEST TIMES:** Nov–Apr.

Where Papa's Spirit Lives On

HEMINGWAY'S HANGOUTS

Havana, Cuba, Greater Antilles

Ernest Hemingway spent most of the 1940s and 1950s in Havana. Today his spirit is alive and well at La Bodeguita del Medio ("The Little Bar in the Middle") and the slightly more formal La Floridita, two legendary watering holes in the historic Habana Vieja district that provided him with much of the inspiration and local color found in *The Old Man and the Sea* and *Islands in the Stream*. Both of these haunts were established long before Papa showed up, and neither has changed much since he checked out. A visit is de rigueur, to test-sample two of Cuba's classic rum-based cocktails, of which Hemingway imbibed vast quantities: La Bodeguita's refreshing mojito (originally a farmers' drink, as common as beer; the rich added shaved ice and club soda) and La Floridita's frozen daiquiri, which Papa is said to have helped perfect (there are reports that the author could down as many as fifteen

Papa's Specials and still walk out the door). Havana isn't known for the refinement of its cusine, but La Bodeguita offers some of the best available in its upstairs room, serving such Creole specialties as lechón asado (roast suckling pig). Hemingway's home, La Vigía, is 9.5 miles outside Havana in the village of San Francisco; it has been left untouched and is open to the public. He lived here until returning to Idaho in 1960, where he committed suicide a year later.

WHAT: restaurant. **LA FLORIDITA:** Calle Monserrate 557 at Obispo. Tel 53/7-867-1299. *When:* daily lunch and dinner. **LA BODEGUITA DEL MEDIO:** Calle Empedrado 207. Tel 53/7-567-1374. *When:* daily lunch and dinner.

A Walk on the Wild Side Through Primal Island Rain Forest

MORNE TROIS PITONS NATIONAL PARK

Dominica, Lesser Antilles

With few beaches to tout, Dominica is the perfect island destination for naturalists and ecotourists, who come to explore Morne Trois Pitons National Park, an ungovernable refuge of huge ferns, ancient trees,

wild orchids, and bright anthuriums. Much of Dominica's fame as the Caribbean's "Nature Island"—and the only landfall Columbus would recognize if he were to return tomorrow—derives from this wild and gorgeous jungle movie set of a park, a 25-square-mile slice of nature that looks and feels more like Hawaii than the Caribbean.

Waterfalls (like the one feeding the fern-bedecked Emerald Pool grotto) hide among lush, steep-sided peaks that are among the Caribbean's highest, the centerpiece being the three-pronged mountain after which the park is named. Those who want a little less

Shangri-la and a little more sulfur and brimstone can make the trek to Boiling Lake, the earth's largest flooded fumarole. Located in the southern part of the park, it's one of the Caribbean's most vigorous walks. The volcanic field called the Valley of Desolation lives up to its name, with steaming vents and boiling mud cauldrons.

The Victorian-era Springfield Plantation Guest House is located close to the Emerald Pool. It's modest but full of character, and offers home-style Creole cooking plus gorgeous rain forest views. For a more Tarzan-and-Jane experience, try the Papillote Wilderness Retreat. Located deep in the rain forest on the border of the Morne Trois Pitons Park, it's a popular destination for nature-loving visitors. Guinea hens, geese, and peacocks stroll about freely, and the remarkable 12-acre botanical garden of bamboo, bromeliads, and begonias is the owner's pride and joy.

Visitors can take a dip into a bubbling hot-spring pool or cool mountain river, join one of the guided walks along paths that crisscross the inn's lush property, or take the escorted fifteen-minute hike to nearby hot-and-cold Trafalgar Falls, a remarkable 200-foot twin cataract.

At the Retreat's plant-filled, thatched-roof terrace restaurant, meals are both unfussy and excellent. If you're lucky, flying fish or the succulent bouk shrimp caught in one of the island's 365 rivers will be on the menu. Or opt for crapaud—"mountain chicken" in local jargon—just remember that it's a land frog. Rooms are simple and basic, but the accessibility of the rain forest's landscape is the lure here.

WHAT: site, hotel, restaurant. **MORNE TROIS PITONS:** easiest access from mountain village of Laudat, 7 miles/11 km east of Roseau. **SPRINGFIELD PLANTATION GUEST HOUSE:** Imperial Highway (9 miles/14 km from Emerald Pool, 2 miles/3 km from entrance to National Park). Tel 767/449-3026; www.springfield-dominica.org. *Cost:* doubles $120, dinner included. **PAPILLOTE WILDERNESS RETREAT:** 20 minutes by car northeast of Roseau. Tel 767/448-2287, fax 767/448-2285; papillote@cwdom.dm, www.papillote.dm. *Cost:* doubles from $115; $40 additional per person, includes all meals. *When:* hotel and restaurant closed Sept–Oct. **BEST TIMES:** Jan–Jul for dry season.

A Sportsman's Fantasy Come True

CASA DE CAMPO

La Romana, Dominican Republic, Greater Antilles

Sprawled across a former sugar plantation eleven times the size of Monaco, Casa de Campo is one of the world's best golf and sporting destinations, justly famous for its two top-notch 18-hole, Pete Dye–designed courses—

one inland and the other, the masterpiece "Teeth of the Dog," skirting the ocean. Active guests spend their vacation lobbing on any of the thirteen clay-composition tennis courts, frolicking in numerous swimming pools, occupying themselves with a slew of water sports available on one of the island's best beaches, or taking advantage of shooting ranges or the equestrian center, with its 150 horses and as many polo ponies. Bicycles, mopeds, and golf carts zip guests across 7,000 well-planned acres that include Altos de Chavón, a painstaking re-creation of a 16th-century hill

Gallop along the beach.

town that doubles as a flourishing cultural center and as home to the resort's colony of artists and artisans. Dominican-born fashion designer Oscar de la Renta was involved in the early stages of the resort's interior design. The vast villagelike complex includes sequestered private villas whose owners read like a who's who of international CEOs and sports-loving magnates.

WHAT: hotel. **WHERE:** 45 minutes by car east of Santo Domingo, on the southeast coast, with its own international airport. Tel 809/523-3333, fax 809/523-8548; in the U.S., tel 800-877-3643 or 305-856-5405; www. casadecampo.com. **COST:** doubles from $180 (low season), from $375 (high season); 2-, 3-, and 4-bedroom villas available. **BEST TIMES:** Nov–Apr.

Sailing into the Crater of a Volcano,
Lounging on a Fabled Beach

ST. GEORGE'S HARBOUR AND GRAND ANSE BEACH

St. George's, Grenada, Windward Islands

This postcard-perfect horseshoe-shaped port—actually the crater of an inactive volcano—is one of the most scenic in the Caribbean, flanked by early 18th-century forts and hugged by one of the area's most authentic and raffishly charming West Indian cities, St. George's. Rainbow-colored homes with "fish scale" roofs climb the steep green hills behind. The crescent-shaped waterfront district, the Carenage, is the colorful commercial hub of the naturally landlocked inner harbor, whose pedestrian walkways still belong to the Grenadians, even when the cruise ships are in town. Stop by the daily open-air market (especially on busy Saturday mornings) to listen to the turbaned ladies sell their fragrant cloves, bay leaves, cinnamon, and nutmeg—there's a reason Grenada is called the Isle of Spice. If the vibrant aroma makes your head swim, grab a chair and a Carib beer by the large open windows on the second floor of the Nutmeg—an informal restaurant that is the city's most popular meeting spot—where you can watch the harbor traffic. The curried

lambi (conch) is a longtime specialty, and the nutmeg ice cream is remarkable.

St. George's is not recommended for action-seekers or casino devotees, but beach lovers need look no further than nearby Grand Anse, south of town. This 2-mile curve of fine white sand is the most famous of the island's forty-five beaches, with a gentle surf that's perfect for a wide variety of water sports—

Spice Island Beach Resort hugs the white sand beach.

which is where the sixty-six stylish beach suites of Spice Island Beach Resort come in handy. As an alternative, you can opt for one of the ultra-secluded suites with private fresh-water pools. For some of the island's most creative cuisine, the Blue Horizons Cottage Hotel just across the road steals the show. Here, from the airy terrace of La Belle Creole restaurant, sunset views accompany family-recipe classics like chilled lobster mousse, cream of tannia soup, or veal à la Creole. For dessert, there's nothing sweeter than a stroll under the stars along Grenada's prettiest beach.

WHAT: site, hotel, restaurant. **THE NUTMEG:** the Carenage, St. George's. Tel 473/440-2539. *Cost:* lunch $25. *When:* lunch and dinner daily. **GRANDE ANSE:** midway between St. George's and the airport; 15 minutes and $15 by taxi from either. **SPICE ISLAND BEACH RESORT:** tel 473/444-4258, fax 473/444-4807; in the U.S., tel 845-628-1701; www.spicebeachresort.com. *Cost:* beachfront suites from $850 (low season), from $1,200 (high season), all-inclusive; private pool suites from $1,080 (low season) to $1,370 (high season), all-inclusive. Dinner at La Belle Creole $40. **BEST TIMES:** Dec–May.

---

*The Grenadines's Most Popular Watering Spot
and a Quiet Hillside Plantation*

BEQUIA

Grenadines, Lesser Antilles

Tiny Bequia is the largest and northernmost of the Grenadines and once enjoyed the distinction of being the region's best whaling station, back in the days of *Moby-Dick*. Today it maintains its seafaring heritage, and

Ships dot Bequia's Harbor.

most of its 5,000 inhabitants are employed as fishermen, sailors, or master boat builders. Nothing much happens on the island except on Thursday night, when the Frangipani hotel's open-air barbecue is *the* place to be. Live steel-drum music and a table groaning with island specialties make for a popular

event, drawing a mix of hotel guests, locals, and the yacht set. The latter use this casual and raffish gingerbread guesthouse as their communications and nerve center, a convenient hub located right on wonderfully picturesque Admiralty Bay, where their craft are moored. The small Frangi, as locals call it, exudes the ambience of an old West Indies wicker-decked inn. It was built almost a century ago as the home of a sea captain who disappeared with his crew in the Bermuda Triangle while his schooner sailed on.

If it's the promise of island serenity that's drawn you here, head for Firefly Bequia, a hillside plantation perfect for those whose ideal vacation is spent lounging in a balcony hammock, listening to cows mooing and palm fronds rustling while catching up on your reading—and maybe turning your head occasionally to catch the glorious views. This bucolic, 250-year-old working plantation provides an exquisite state of suspended animation for island purists who like to hide out amid the cooling breezes and the music of crickets and tree frogs. Eight luxurious guest rooms nestle in a profusion of frangipani and scarlet cordia, and it's a short, pleasant stroll to the deserted beach at Spring Bay and a 1-mile walk to Admiralty Bay. In the evenings, candlelit dinners at the Firefly's excellent restaurant feature ingredients fresh from the grounds or just netted in the nearby waters.

WHAT: island, hotel, restaurant. **BEQUIA:** 8.5 miles/14 km south of St. Vincent. Although a small airport has been built (15

minutes from Port Elizabeth), most guests still arrive from St. Vincent by boat. **FRANGIPANI:** 5-minute walk from the main dock; yachts anchor right by the front door. Tel 784/458-3255, fax 784/458-3824; reservations@frangipanibequia.com; www.frangipanibequia.com. *Cost:* simply furnished doubles with shared coldwater baths from $60 (low season), from $75 (high season); garden and deluxe rooms with en suite baths from $120 (low season), from $190 (high season). Thurs night barbecue $40. *When:* closed Aug to mid-Oct. **FIREFLY PLANTATION BEQUIA:** Tel 784-458-3414, fax 784-457-3305; www.fireflybequia.com. *Cost:* from $395 (low season), from $495 (high season). **BEST TIMES:** Dec–May.

---

*Plantation Civilization and
the Place Where Every Night's a Party*

THE COTTON HOUSE AND BASIL'S BEACH BAR

Mustique, Grenadines, Lesser Antilles

The privately owned Grenadine island of Mustique looks almost too perfect—rustic villages, a few dirt roads, lush green hills. Little wonder the rich and royal have built their vacation homes here, but unless you've

The Great Room at Cotton House

wangled an invitation from one of them, you'll have to settle for equally coveted accommodations at the elegant but comfortable Cotton House, the island's only hotel. Renovated not long ago and once again in the world's top rank, it's the oldest structure on Mustique, an 18th-century plantation house formerly used to store cotton, sugar, and rum. Guests are urbane and sophisticated, often celebrated, and everyone seems at home amid the quiet panache of a restrained, cool-and-breezy decor. Much of the transformation, directed by the late British theatrical designer Oliver Messel, is still evident, and the ambience remains palpably British, as if you're at a long, informal, but civilized house party. An international cadre of private villa owners come and go, dropping in for afternoon tea in the Hemingwayesque Great Room; picking up visiting friends for a picnic at nearby, mythically beautiful, and almost always empty Macaroni Beach; or carting them off to experience the daily sunset spectacle (and a few Hurricane Davids) at Basil's Beach Bar. Drinking the night away here may be something of a ritual, but Basil's, which stands on piers facing the turquoise waters of Britannia Bay, also happens to be a great place for seafood and fresh fish. You don't need to be British or Hollywood royalty to enjoy the fresh-grilled, bought-right-off-the-boat lobster or homemade ice cream—or the charm of Basil S. Charles, the Caribbean's answer to

Casablanca's Rick. Show up on Wednesday night for one of the rocking, sometimes raucous jump-up barbecues—or on New Year's Eve, for which the barbecues are just a very mild preview.

WHAT: hotel, restaurant. **MUSTIQUE:** 15 miles/24 km south of St. Vincent. **COTTON HOUSE:** 0.5 mile/1 km from the airport. Tel 784/456-4777, fax 784/456-5887; in the U.S., tel 310-440-4225, fax 310-440-4220; www.cottonhouseresort.com. *Cost:* doubles from $700 (low season), from $1,280 (high season), includes all meals. **BASIL'S BEACH BAR:** Royal St., Britannia Bay. Tel 784/488-8405, fax 784/456-5825, basils@vincysurf.com; www.basilsbar.com. *Cost:* lobster dinner $40. **BEST TIMES:** Nov–Apr; 2-week Blues Festival, late Jan–early Feb.

Island Resort or Resort Island?

PETIT ST. VINCENT

Grenadines, Lesser Antilles

Those who really, *really* want to get away from it all should drop anchor at this privately owned 113-acre luxury island resort. Encircled by white-sand beaches, covered with palm trees, and washed by the impossibly clear waters of the fabled Grenadine archipelago, it's one man's castaway fantasy, which he chooses to share with just forty privacy-seeking guests. Of course, they pay handsomely to stay in the quiet, natural setting without sacrificing service or remarkable dining, and they also pay for what's missing: television, telephones, air-conditioning, faxes, casinos, beach vendors—even room keys. Large breeze-cooled stone cottages are situated for maximum views and privacy. Room service works like a charm: Raise the red flag and the staff gives you a wide berth; raise the yellow flag, stick your request in your mailbox—a mango daquiri, extra suntan lotion, dinner on your private terrace—and it arrives in record time. Weary CEO types in need of a retreat love it here. So do couples who

Empty beaches encircle privately owned Petit St. Vincent.

appear to be very much in love—if they make an appearance at all. Single guests will probably stay that way and should consider PSV only if they like their own company or that of an epic novel. Guests who have become dangerously relaxed or are suffering a bout of cabin fever can arrange for a day's snorkeling at nearby Tobago Cays, also part of the Grenadines island chain—it's one of the loveliest uninhabited corners left in the Caribbean.

WHAT: island, hotel. **WHERE:** charter flights from Barbados to Union Island arranged by hotel ($190 per person one-way). From Union, hotel provides 30-minute connecting boat ride. Tel 954/963-7401, fax 954/963-7402; in the U.S., tel 800-654-9326; info@psvresort.com; www.psvresort.com. **COST:** cottages $675 (low season), $1,020 (high season), includes all meals and activities. **WHEN:** closed Sept–Oct. **BEST TIMES:** Nov–Apr.

Natural Glamour, Not Commercial Clamor

SAILING THE GRENADINES

Grenadines, Lesser Antilles

Revered by yachtsmen and sailor wannabes, the thirty-two islands and hundreds of dotlike cays that form the archipelago of the Grenadines are one of the most beautiful yachting destinations in the world. Strung like a necklace of gems across 40 miles of pristine waters between St. Vincent and Grenada, they're blessed with powdery white-sand beaches and coral reefs that are among the most amazing outside the Pacific. Many islands are uninhabited and accessible only by boat. Some have tiny populations, mostly descended from African slaves (such as privately owned Mayreau, with 180 residents), while others, like Bequia, are larger and are quietly awakening to tourism, offering a limited sampling of inns and a barefoot, small-town ambience.

A springtime regatta

Daily schooners, ferries, and passenger-carrying mail boats sail south from St. Vincent (locally known as "the mainland"), servicing the half-dozen populated Grenadines. But the ideal way to go, for those in search of a different, picnic-perfect, beach-ringed isle every day, is to charter a crewed yacht (or, for those who know their main from their genoa, a self-skippered bareboat) through The Moorings in Grenada, and sail north.

WHAT: experience. **WHERE:** The Moorings' jumping-off places for the Grenadines are their 50-slip marina at True Blue Bay, on Grenada's southeast coast, and at Marigot Bay in St. Lucia. In the U.S., tel 888-952-8420 or 727-535-1446, fax 727-530-9747; www.moorings.com. **COST:** weekly bareboat rentals from $2,230 (low season), from $5,180 (high season). Various sizes of bareboats accommodate 5 to 8 people. Daily rates available. Daily rates for crewed yachts run from $1,750 (low season), from $2,595 (high season), per person, based on double occupancy in a private stateroom. **BEST TIMES:** Nov–Apr, although sailors may have preferences determined by wind conditions, etc.

Island Cooks Celebrate an Art Form

FÊTE DES CUISINIÈRES AND GUADELOUPE'S FINEST RESTAURANTS

Grande-Terre, Guadeloupe, Lesser Antilles (French West Indies)

One of the culinary epicenters of the Caribbean, Guadeloupe celebrates its marriage of African, French, and West Indian cuisine during the annual Fête des Cuisinières. Honoring St. Laurent, patron saint of cooks, the colorful festival is launched with a gala parade of hundreds of the island's women chefs, lavishly dressed in traditional madras costumes and starched white linen aprons,

carrying and balancing baskets of the island's exotic bounty on their heads as they wend their way through the streets of the island's main hub, Pointe-à-Pitre. The parade ends with the day's only solemn moment: high Mass at the 19th-century Cathédrale de St.-

Women chefs on parade

Pierre et St.-Paul. A five-hour cook-off feast follows, with music, song, and dance.

Even if you miss the late-summer event, there's always a gourmet experience waiting to be found in Guadeloupe's 200 restaurants, which, together with Martinique's, prepare some of the best food in the Caribbean. Those with a smattering of high-school French can manage the menus, where the names of dishes may be familiar, such as *crabe farci* (spicey stuffed land crab—more meaty than sea crabs) or *écrevisse* (freshwater crayfish), though the spicy Creole preparations might be a surprise. The long list of island specialties may be mostly unrecognizable: *colombo* (a rich curry stew with chicken or goat), *calalou* (a spinach-like soup), *accras* (cod fritters), *lambi* (conch), *chatrou* (octopus), and the much loved though oddly named *blaff* (a stew of fish and shellfish poached in a spicy broth).

A waterside view and an island drink—whether a cold locally brewed Corsair beer or the potent Ti-punch, an aperitif made from island rum mixed with sugarcane syrup and lime—will top off any meal or enhance a lazy afternoon at the beach.

The majority of visitors to Guadeloupe come from France, and both they and the islanders take their eating seriously. Some of the best French dining on the island can be found at La Vielle Tour, in a setting that's somewhat formal for Guadeloupe. For lively full-on Creole ambience, the colorful West Indian decor of the Iguane Café sets the tone. Begin with one of the two dozen rum punches, then enjoy the culinary repertoire. The talented chef's penchant for original cuisine explains the intriguing mix of Asian and Indian influences.

WHAT: event, restaurant. **FÊTE DES CUISINIÈRES:** at various venues in Pointe-à-Pitre. *Cost:* tickets for the 5-hour banquet cost about $30 and can be acquired through your hotel or the local tourism office (tel 590/590-

82-09-30). *When:* held every year on the 2d Sat in Aug. **LA VIELLE TOUR:** Rte. de Montauban, Gosier. Tel 590/84-23-23. *Cost:* Dinner $60. *When:* closed Thurs. **IGUANE CAFÉ:** Rte. de la Pointe des Châteaux, St. François. Tel 590/88-61-37. *Cost:* Dinner $55. *When:* dinner Wed–Mon; lunch and dinner Sun. **BEST TIMES:** Dec–May.

Where You Can Hear the Sugarcane Grow

GUADELOUPE'S OFFSHORE ISLES

Lesser Antilles (French West Indies)

G uadeloupeans are understandably loath to divulge the destination of their weekend getaways. When hard pressed, they'll admit they escape to the small offshore archipelago of Iles des Saintes (also known as Les Saintes)

and the larger Marie Galante, whose innocent, rustic charm is reminiscent of St. Barts twenty years ago, with few cars and a rural character. The pastoral allure of Marie Galante is unmatched in the Caribbean; scores of tended plantations, windmills, and oxcarts attest to the importance of sugarcane and rum (said to be the best in the Caribbean) on an island where tourism is given little heed. The long, golden Petite Anse beach is a favorite weekend spot for picnics—bring your own or enjoy a deliciously simple meal at any of the

handful of Creole shacks. Terre-de-Haut, the largest of the Saintes, is only slightly more tourist-oriented, with its pastel cottages and winding trails. The charmingly kitschy inn L'Auberge des Petits Saints aux Anacardies is the most distinctive of the island's small inns, eccentrically cluttered with antiques and curious souvenirs fancied by the world-trekking owners. It has an airy veranda, and the ocean-view restaurant offers a surprisingly sophisticated wine list and menu, considering its delightful middle-of-nowhere spirit.

View of Marigot Bay

WHAT: island, hotel. **MARIE GALANTE:** 20 miles/32 km south of "mainland" Guadeloupe's Grande-Terre; 20 minutes by plane ($100 round-trip) or longer by daily ferry service ($40 round-trip). **ILES DES SAINTES:** 15 minutes ($40 round-trip) or 50 minutes by daily ferry service ($40 round-trip) from Grande-Terre. **L'AUBERGE DES PETITS SAINTS AUX ANACARDIES:** La Savanne, Terre-de-Haut, Iles des Saintes. Tel 590-590-99-50-99, fax 590-590-99-54-51; info@petitssaints.com; www.petitssaints.com. *Cost:* doubles from $90 (low season), from $112 (high season). Dinner $35. **BEST TIMES:** Nov–Apr.

A Civilized Anachronism

JAMAICA INN

Ocho Rios, Jamaica, Greater Antilles

It is by choice that the venerable Jamaica Inn never changes: The most beloved of the island's Old Guard, it's the classic privately owned inn all the others try to emulate. If you can, book the White Suite, which stands on its own promontory on one of the island's prettiest beaches. It was the favored accommodation of Winston Churchill, who loved the light here for his watercolor painting (and no doubt the establishment's exemplary service and timeless grace as well). The guest rooms are tastefully furnished with Jamaican antiques, but it's their spacious balustraded balconies that really make them special, furnished like open-air living rooms with sofa, writing table, rocking chair, and gorgeous ocean views. Breakfast on your balcony is a must, as is dinner by candlelight, but be sure to step out at least once for the mise-en-scène of dining on the romantic, lantern-lit terrace restaurant under the stars to the sound of the swaying palms and the nightly live band. The affluent patrons seem to enjoy dressing up for dinner during the high-season; there's a smooth transition from the daytime's relaxed comfort to the evening's retro, old-fashioned elegance.

Enjoy sea breezes on your private balcony.

WHAT: hotel. **WHERE:** 64 miles/96 km east of Montego Bay on the north coast, 2 miles/3 km east of Ocho Rios. Tel 876/974-2514, fax 876/974-2449; in the U.S., tel 800-837-4608; reservations@jamaicainn.com; www.jamaicainn.com. **COST:** doubles from $255 (low season) to $500 (high season); White Suite $735 (low season), from $1,600 (high season). **BEST TIMES:** Dec–Apr.

The Party of Parties

JAMAICA'S REGGAE FESTIVAL

Jamaica, Greater Antilles

Jamaica is the birthplace of reggae, its heartbeat, soul, and inspiration. Born of the Rastafarian religion, and with a deep-rooted spirituality evolved from centuries-old slave songs, the music is a blend of African-influenced percussion, contemporary pop instrumentation, and lyrics that give voice to everything from religious to political and social commentary.

The annual Sumfest festival showcases star performers jamming nonstop from dusk till dawn, and highlights the music's most influential mouthpiece, something of a national folk hero, the late Bob Marley. Sumfest runs for approximately five days at the beginning of August, usually in Montego Bay, when hotels are booked to overflowing and the hot summer nights reverberate with music that includes hip-hop, rap, soca, and calypso.

WHAT: event. **WHERE:** Summerfest Productions, Montego Bay, tel 876/953-2933; www.reggaesumfest.com. **COST:** individual events from $15; concerts from $40; festival-long passes from $105. Inquire about hotel packages that include entry to festival events.

A Beachside Introduction to the World of Jerk

PORK PIT

Montego Bay, Jamaica, Greater Antilles

J amaica is the world's largest exporter of spice, and there's no shortage of "jerk pits" on the island, each one using its own blend of spices to season meat, sausage, fish—whatever—which is then cooked slowly over pimento wood.

Upmarket restaurants have adopted the dish, modifying the heat for uninitiated tasters, but rolling up your sleeves and tucking your greasy hands into the spicy fare with all the trimmings—sweet baked yams, "festival" (deep-fried cornbread) fritters, and the requisite Red Stripe beer—is half the fun. The shady, open-air Pork Pit, a longtime local institution in Montego Bay, serves the best barbecued pork, chicken, and ribs on the island. The place is always jumping, and the beach crowd knows to arrive around noon, when the fiery jerk is ready to be lifted from its bed of coals and fragrant wood and slapped down on the communal picnic tables. Tip: If there's a choice of mild or hot, go with the mild.

WHAT: restaurant. **WHERE:** 27 Gloucester Ave. at Kent Ave., near Walter Fletcher Beach in Montego Bay. Tel 876/940-3008. **COST:** barbecue $11. **WHEN:** daily for lunch and dinner.

High Style, Low Attitude, and Sunset Served on the Rocks

ROCK HOUSE AND RICK'S

Negril, Jamaica, Greater Antilles

W hen Negril, on the western tip of Jamaica, 50 miles from Montego Bay, was still the do-as-you-please capital of the Caribbean and best-kept secret of every flower child of the 1970s, the Rock House had already staked out its premier location atop a rocky waterfront promontory just outside town. Don't bother looking for yesterday's bohemian mecca along Negril's developed but still lovely 7-mile beach: Yuppies now fill the large, all-inclusive sybaritic resorts, and the beat is young, partying, and uninhibited. Well removed from such

A dining terrace at the Rock House

freewheeling commercialism, the thatched-roof Rock House offers the natural charm and seclusion of the Negril of yore. The new owners have re-created the thatched-villa hotel, mixing and matching the tropical soul of the South Seas with the laidback Caribbean escapism that first put Negril on the map. The hotel's no-hassle, no-hustle atmosphere blends seamlessly with its simple style-sensitive design: Utilizing rich local woods, it harmonizes with the overwhelming beauty of the cliffside setting and junglelike surroundings. Splash and snorkel

in the sheltered waters of the aptly named Pristine Cove, which is yours alone, or enjoy Negril's legendary sunsets from the Zen-like pool that seems suspended in air at what must be Jamaica's westernmost point.

Negril's famous sunsets have long been the draw at Rick's, the most famous bar on the island, located atop the rocky cliffs south of Negril's beach and inspired by the film *Casablanca*. Everyone still bursts into applause when the sun sinks, but what's the inspiration—the sky's Technicolor hues or the fresh-fruit daiquiris? Everyone has a grand time at this island hangout, watching divers jump off cliffs into the sea more than 100 feet below in homage to the setting ball of fire, a daily ritual that's part pagan, part frat party. Rick's is also a restaurant, serving some great fresh fish and lobster, but once you're embalmed with overproof rum and intoxicated by the sky's crescendo of orange and pink, dinner may seem anticlimactic.

WHAT: hotel, restaurant. **ROCK HOUSE:** West End Rd., 2.5 miles/4 km west of Negril. Tel 876/957-4373, fax 876/957-0557; info@rockhousehotel.com; www.rockhousehotel.com. *Cost:* from $125 (low season), from $160 (high season). **RICK'S CAFÉ:** West End Rd. Tel 876/957-0380; www.rickscafejamaica.com. *When:* open daily, lunch and dinner. **BEST TIMES:** Nov–Dec, Apr–May.

On Top of the World in the Blue Mountains

STRAWBERRY HILL

Irish Town, Jamaica, Greater Antilles

If life is a beach, then heaven is Strawberry Hill's perch in the Blue Mountains. It's not for lovers of the sea and sand, but rather for those who relish sitting on their private verandas at 3,000 feet, watching the late afternoon's swirling mist settle on the green hills and lush gardens while the tree frogs begin their night-time serenade. This is your own private Jamaica, with twelve colonial-inspired cottages sprawled across 26 acres, their rooms evoking 19th-century planters' daily lives with their mahogany four-poster beds, wispy mosquito netting, plank floors, and ceiling fans—not to mention carefully camouflaged high-tech amenities and a soothing, minimalist design sense. Strawberry Hill's locally born chef turns out exotic, full-flavored reinventions of traditional Jamaican dishes. You'll soon understand why the Caribbean's most idyllic property is not even near a beach.

The afternoon mist at Strawberry Hill

WHAT: hotel. **WHERE:** 50 minutes from Kingston airport. Tel 876/944-8400, fax 876/ 944-8408; in the U.S., tel 800-OUTPOST, reservations@islandoutpost.com; www.island outpost.com/strawberryhill. **COST:** doubles from $495. **BEST TIMES:** Dec–Mar.

Island Fusion Cuisine—C'est Magnifique!

THE FLAVORS OF MARTINIQUE

Martinique, Lesser Antilles (French West Indies)

Unspoiled corners of this mountainous island look much as they did when Napoleon's empress, Josephine, was growing up here on the family sugar plantation in the late 18th century. It is the same islandscape that inspired Paul Gauguin long before his better known journey to Tahiti. A low-profile contrast to the more common Anglo or American experience offered by much of today's Caribbean, Martinique's Frenchness and island *charme* is an alluring component in what the tourism authorities promote as a sliver of "France in the tropics." It is of little wonder then that local gastronomy—namely the fusion of classic French with Indian and African influences distinguished by a dash of Creole—plays a major role in the island's character and heritage, as a stroll through the local Spice Market in Fort-de-France will confirm. (A few euros will buy you a sampling of delicious homemade manioc ice cream, a tribute to the island's slave ancestry, when root vegetables were relied upon as dietary staples.) Set on a hilltop offering gorgeous views of the Atlantic, the chic and artistic Hôtel Plein Soleil is a front-runner in Martinique's vital food scene. Sixteen brightly colored rooms accommodate those who come for the food prepared by the well-known chef, local-born and French-trained Nathanael Ducteil, who specializes in surprising creative twists to classic fare.

WHAT: hotel, restaurant. **HÔTEL PLEIN SOLEIL:** 3 miles north of Le François, 20 miles east of Fort-de-France. Tel 596/38-07-77; www.pleinsoleil.mq. *Cost:* from $190 (low season), from $260 (high season). Dinner $50. **BEST TIMES:** Dec–Jul; late Feb/early Mar for Vaval (Carnival), one of the Caribbean's best.

Where Beach and Golf Both Rank Number One

FOUR SEASONS RESORT

Pinney's Beach, Nevis, Lesser Antilles

Is it any surprise that the Caribbean's best golf course is on a formerly British island? The Four Seasons Resort on small, slow-moving Nevis is a golfer's dream, combining an exceptional (and never crowded) championship course designed by Robert Trent Jones Jr., with luxury resort accommodations, superlative service, and a location on the island's most beautiful powdery white-sand beach. The 18-hole, 6,766-yard course was carved out of mountainous terrain, leading up to an awesome par-5 fifteenth hole: At 550 feet, overlooking

The fifteenth hole is a par-5 stunner.

the sea, its breathtaking backdrop is a dormant volcano capped in clouds. The course's plantation-like main house was designed to reflect the island's traditional British character (Admiral Horatio Nelson and Fanny Nisbet were married at the Montpelier Plantation back in 1787), and is surrounded by 350 acres of exquisite grounds, abutting the water at gorgeous Pinney's Beach, a 3-mile, reef-protected stretch that knows few rivals. If you feel like slumming it, Sunshine's Bar and Grill, a shack plunked down right on the beach, serves a mean Painkiller.

WHAT: hotel. **WHERE:** Pinney's Beach, Charlestown. Private launch from St. Kitts airport can be arranged. Tel 869/469-1111, fax 869/469-1112; www.fourseasons.com. **NOTE:** At press time, the Four Seasons Resort was temporarily closed. **BEST TIMES:** Jan–Mar.

Blazing the Path to Luxury

THE HORNED DORSET PRIMAVERA

Rincón, Puerto Rico, Greater Antilles
(U.S. Commonwealth)

Sitting on Puerto Rico's unspoiled western coast, where green mountains tumble down into the sea, this elegant and curiously named Spanish neocolonial hacienda is the sumptuous getaway of choice for the smart set, weekend runaways from nearby San Juan, and international travelers who want to explore beyond San Juan. Named after an inn the owners maintain in upstate New York, the hotel and its celebrated restaurant have established and maintained an unprecedented standard for luxury boutique hotels in Puerto Rico. The nurturing ambience is one of quiet pampering and plushness, as if this were the aristocratic home of a Spanish grandee whose coddled house guests rest, relax, and lounge between one superb meal and the next. The surrounding gardens, a virtual arboretum of exotic blooms, were lovingly created by the former owner, a research botanist. Situated above a secluded beach, the hotel offers a beautiful palm-flanked freshwater pool, too.

WHAT: hotel, restaurant. **WHERE:** route 429, 100 miles/150 km west of San Juan. Tel 787/823-4030; in the U.S., tel 800-633-1857; www.horneddorset.com. **COST:** from $360 (low season), from $595 (high season). Dinner $70, tasting menu $110. **BEST TIMES:** Nov–Apr.

Character and Life Amid Architectural Treasures

OLD SAN JUAN

Puerto Rico, Greater Antilles (U.S. Commonwealth)

El Viejo San Juan, the seven-square-block landmark zone of the island's capital, is a perfectly preserved microcosm of Spanish colonial architecture and a remarkable walk back through history. In fact, were it not for the chaotic traffic jams that are its liaison with reality, this 475-year-old theater set would look almost too beautiful to be authentic. Its narrow streets are paved with cobbles of adoquine (a blue stone used as ballast on Spanish galleons) and its 16th-century fortresses, particularly the impregnable six-level El Morro, which rises 150 feet above the sea, still strike one as engineering marvels. This showcase of protected old-world landmarks is also chockablock with fashionable bistros, designer shops, art galleries, churches, and colonial town houses with flowering wrought-iron balconies.

The elegant El Convento is the only hotel in the heart of Old San Juan, recently refurbished after serving for more than two centuries as a Carmelite convent and later as a dance hall, a Howard Johnson's, and even a flophouse. Understandably, it serves as the official government guest house for visiting heads of state. This is where the spirit of Old San Juan lives, and visitors who stay at the self-contained glitzy hotel-villages on the city's outskirts are missing the point.

WHAT: site, hotel. **EL CONVENTO:** 100 Cristo St. Tel 787/723-9020, fax 787/721-2877; in the U.S., tel 800-468-2779; www.elconvento.com. **COST:** doubles from $160 (low season), from $250 (high season). **BEST TIMES:** Nov–Apr.

El Convento: history, beauty, and luxury

Small-Island Life and a Fragile Bioluminescent Bay

VIEQUES

Puerto Rico, Greater Antilles (U.S. Commonwealth)

Puerto Rico's small sister island Vieques is not for everyone, but its uneventful lifestyle, a throwback to the old days in the Spanish Virgin Islands, can feel heaven-sent. The sixty-two-year presence of the U.S. Navy (who pulled out in 2003) kept the island and its forty-odd beaches from being developed (so far), making it a perfect escape for wound-up mainlanders and San Juanitos, who travel here (and to neighboring island Culebra, whose beaches are even more renowned) for natural beauty and the restorative pleasures of doing next to nothing. Wild descendants of the *paso fino* horses left by the Spanish centuries ago roam freely. Some have been tamed, and horseback riding across the hills and dunes of the island is one of its finest pleasures.

More psychedelic pleasure is to be had at Mosquito Bay, one of the few bioluminescent bays left in the world. The concentration of dinoflagellates (called pyrodiniums—"whirling fire") creates a liquid green light when the water is agitated. The phenomenon is best viewed during nighttime tours, when boat propellers cause the billions of microorganisms that live near the surface to illuminate. Troll your hand overboard and leave a sparkling trail of shooting stars behind you, or dive in for an even more magical experience.

Vieques's limited accommodations were funky and eccentric until the arrival of the Hacienda Tamarindo, named for the ancient tamarind tree that anchors the villa's open patio. Set atop a windswept hill, the hacienda's breezy rooms are open to the refreshing trade winds and sweeping views of the Caribbean. An eclectic mix of art, antiques, and collectibles accumulated by the American owners—Viequans by adoption—testify to their former life as interior designers.

WHAT: island, experience, hotel. **VIEQUES:** 6 miles/8 km east of Puerto Rico. **HACIENDA TAMARINDO:** near Esperanza, 5 miles/7.5 km from the ferry and the airport. Tel 787/741-0420, fax 787/741-3215; hactam@aol.com; www.haciendatamarindo.com. *Cost:* doubles from $190. **MOSQUITO BAY:** Island Adventures organizes 1 or 2 departures every evening from Casa del Frances hotel in Esperanza. Tel 787/741-0720; biobay@biobay.com; www.biobay.com. *Cost:* $23 per person. **BEST TIMES:** Nov–Apr for weather; dark, moonless nights for Mosquito Bay.

One of forty-some untrammeled beaches

*Underwater Alps, and
Room in the Clouds at Day's End*

SABA

Lesser Antilles (Netherlands Antilles)

With just 1,200 inhabitants, diminutive Saba is neither chic nor fancy. But those with a thing for mountains—above or below the water—consider it a regular heaven on earth. Trekkers take to 3,000-foot Mount Scenery—the forest-clad tip of an extinct volcano, whose walls plunge into the blue-green sea—and if it looks like the backdrop of *King Kong*, that's because it was. The classic movie was partially filmed here. Rare and uncommon creatures appear below the water as well, and in quantity, but divers are just as surprised by what they don't see as by what they do; with little tourism, Saba and its offshore waters remain uncrowded and uncorrupted.

Saba Marine Park encircles the small island, the result of a farsighted

A diver looking at corals in the waters around Saba

government that chose to safeguard a pristine ecosystem rather than be forced to repair a damaged one later on. Coral-encrusted rocks, boulders, reefs, and a marked snorkeling trail draw less-experienced divers, but it's the spectacular pinnacles and offshore seamounts that make Saba a world-class diving destination. Challenging sites have atmospheric names that say it all: Shark Shoal, Twilight Zone, Outer Limits, and Third Encounter.

Since gumdrop-shaped Saba's 5 square miles are mostly vertical, it makes sense to spend the night in the clouds, at Shearwater Resort. At 2,000 feet, the views from the hotel's pool are heart-stopping, taking in the immense sea, Saba's five neighboring islands, and sometimes the clouds themselves. Like everything else on the island—from one of the world's shortest commercial airstrips to The Road (there's only one, with switchbacks up

one side of the island and down the other)—the hotel is an extraordinary feat of engineering if only because of the difficulty of bringing construction materials to the site. Getting there can be hair-raising. Nevertheless, the Shearwater is the perfect aerie in which to catch up with your reading or your thoughts, and its level of taste and sophistication is a happy surprise.

WHAT: island, experience, site, hotel. **SHEARWATER RESORT:** 3 miles/5 km from the airport. Tel 599/416-2498, fax 599/416-2482; in the U.S., tel 800-504-9861; info@shearwater-resort.com; www.shearwater-resort.com. *Note:* Shearwater Resort, formerly called Willard's of Saba, will reopen under new ownership in 2010. **HOW:** Sea Saba Dive Center, tel 599/416-2246; www.seasaba.com. *Cost:* from $98 a day for two dives. **BEST TIMES:** Dec–Apr; diving is good year-round.

An Unmatched Setting, Part Villa Life, Part Island Lore

EDEN ROCK

St.-Jean's Bay, St. Barthélemy, Lesser Antilles
(French West Indies)

Jutting dramatically from a quartzite promontory between two perfect white-sand beaches and surrounded on three sides by water, this much-photographed, castlelike landmark was built as the home of onetime St. Barts mayor Rémy de Haenen. The first pilot to land on the island (in 1947) and father of the island's tourism industry, he found this spot, recognized it as a piece of paradise, and named his house accordingly. Many of Eden Rock's nine tasteful guest rooms seem to be suspended over St.-Jean's Bay— St. Barts's best swimming beach —with the sound of crashing waves serving as back-

Eden Rock: almost an island

ground music, and behemoth mosquito-net-swathed four-poster beds standing so high you'll need a stepstool to jump aboard. The atmospheric terrace bar/restaurant has long been a legendary rendezvous for whiling away the late-afternoon hours before an artful and ambitious meal at the hotel's stylish Eden Beach Restaurant.

WHAT: hotel, restaurant. **WHERE:** 2 miles/3 km east of Gustavia, 6 miles/10 km from the airport. Tel 590/590-29-79-99, fax 590/590-27-88-37; in the U.S., tel 877-563-7105; info@edenrockhotel.com; www.edenrockhotel.com. **COST:** doubles from $695 (low season), from $970 (high season), 3-night minimum required. Dinner $115. **BEST TIMES:** Nov, Jan, and Mar.

La Vie Parisienne, Caribbean Style

GUSTAVIA HARBOUR & MAYA'S

St. Barthélemy, Lesser Antilles (French West Indies)

The storybook-quaint harbor of Gustavia is so tiny that cruise ships have to anchor offshore, but that doesn't stop the private yachts of St. Barts's veteran habitués from flocking here. Chic, rich, and very Parisian (and only about half the size of Manhattan), St. Barts continues to be the celebrity favorite of the Caribbean, and from the terrace of the Hotel Carl Gustaf, the charming harbor and surrounding green hills seem like a dollhouse set for an operetta. Gustavia is St. Barts's only town and seaport, and the Carl Gustaf sits above it like a regal eagle's nest, its charming bar and open-air restaurant enjoying the uppermost level and premier vantage point.

Linger here for a magnificent *coucher de soleil*, escape the cruise ship passengers bent on duty-free perfume bargains, and enjoy the piano bar's changing cocktail du jour. Those with deep pockets can check in and enjoy the unencumbered panorama round-the-clock from any of the fourteen red-roofed cottages that climb the bougainvillea-covered hillside, each with its own plunge pool. The hotel's *raffiné* hilltop dining room serves the most haute of haute cuisine, and happy diners can watch the glittering night lights that twinkle across the lilliputian harbor.

For at least one sunset during your stay, consider venturing down from your hillside hideaway and visiting Maya's, the island's most de rigueur dining venue. It's a laid-back place serving excellent Creole specialties prepared by the Martinique-born chef/owner, who eschews extraneous flourishes, preparing her dishes with artful simplicity. The restaurant's waterfront terrace is the perfect spot for sundowner cocktails, as well as for watching the island's cast of glamorous celebs and beau monde.

High view of the sheltered harbor of Gustavia

WHAT: site, hotel, restaurant. **HOTEL CARL GUSTAF:** tel 590/590-29-79-00, fax 590/590-27-82-37; www.hotelcarlgustaf.com. *Cost:* cottage suites from $865 (low season), from $1,400 (high season). Dinner $95. **MAYA'S:** Anse de Public, northwest of Gustavia. Tel 590/590-27-75-73; mayas-restaurant@orange.fr. *Cost:* dinner $70. *When:* dinner only; closed Sun. Open Nov–mid-Jun and mid-Jul–Aug. **BEST TIMES:** Nov, Jan, and Mar.

Relaxed Sophistication in the Grand Manner

THE GOLDEN LEMON

Dieppe Bay Town, St. Kitts, Lesser Antilles

This cloud-crowned volcanic island so enchanted Christopher Columbus that he named it after himself—it was only later that locals unofficially shortened the name from St. Christopher's to St. Kitts. With its less

lively sister island, Nevis, it was once part of the British Commonwealth, but today it's the smallest country in the United Nations and is proclaimed by local tourism officials as "the Secret Caribbean." Word is out, however, about the Golden Lemon, a handsome 17th-century great house that sits beneath the spectacular, 3,800-foot volcanic peak of Mount Liamuiga at the island's northern

end. Famed for its eclectic and highly original interiors, the hotel is the domain of an American design-magazine editor and connoisseur who used the historic island property as his blank canvas, combining local crafts, European antiques, crystal chandeliers, white rattan furniture, and stunning fabrics in a spirited but impeccably tasteful mix. Understandably, it's a design-conscious international clientele that fills the beautifully appointed villas (all of which have private plunge pools) and guest rooms, and shows up for the poolside Sunday buffet brunch, which is served in the shade of a breadfruit tree.

WHAT: hotel. **WHERE:** near Dieppe Bay Town, a fishing village 14 miles/23 km north of Basseterre and 12 miles/19 km from the airport. Tel 869/465-7260, fax 869/465-4019; info@goldenlemon.com; www.goldenlemon.com. **COST:** doubles in Great House from $175 (low season), $325 (high season, includes breakfast and dinner); villas with plunge pools from $200 (low season), $495 (high season, includes breakfast and dinner). Sunday brunch $25, dinner $55. **WHEN:** mid-Oct–Jul. **BEST TIMES:** Jan–Mar.

Caribbean Life as It Used to Be

RAWLINS PLANTATION

Mount Pleasant, St. Kitts, Lesser Antilles

St. Kitts and Nevis are loved by Caribbean aficionados for their tastefully restored plantation inns-cum-restaurants, and Rawlins Plantation is one of the most captivating, allowing guests to savor a vanishing way of life amid old-fashioned West Indies charm and gracious surroundings. The main house, with its wide veranda overlooking carefully clipped lawns and flower-splashed gardens, was built on the original 17th-century foundations of an old sugar works, and offers what's arguably the best dining on the island, an imaginative blend of Kittian and French cuisine designed by the talented owner/chef. Many ingredients are grown on the plantation. A wondrous West Indian buffet lunch draws both the local elite and nonislanders. The regulars come to relive the nostalgic planter's life—or is it the sensational chocolate terrine with a light passion fruit sauce?

WHAT: hotel, restaurant. **WHERE:** on the northern coast outside of St. Paul's, 15 miles/24 km from Basseterre. Tel 869/465-6221; info@rawlinsplantation.com; www.rawlinsplantation.com. **COST:** doubles $220 (low season), $330 (high season), includes breakfast, dinner, and afternoon tea. Buffet lunch $30, dinner $65. **WHEN:** mid-Oct–late Aug. **BEST TIMES:** Jan–Mar.

A Villa and a View Beyond Extraordinary

ANSE CHASTANET

Soufrière, St. Lucia, Lesser Antilles

Located on a 600-acre estate in the southwestern corner of this lush island, Anse Chastanet is way beyond romantic, with octagonal hillside gazebos hidden amid verdant foliage and bursts of color, harmonizing beautifully with the natural surroundings: Some of the handsome suites are built around trees, others are minus a wall to let the magnificent outdoors in. The secluded palm-fringed beach 125 steps below has its own excellent five-star scuba center and school, and some of the Caribbean's best snorkeling and diving is just a few feet offshore. Joining the inn's many unrivaled attributes (the kitchen is known across the island) is the amazing view of Gros Piton and Petit Piton, twin 2,619- and 2,461-foot pointed volcanic peaks that rise from the surf just to the south, looking like the jagged mountains of Bali Ha'i, adding something of a South Pacific touch to the island. It's a vista that silences with its power and mystique, visible from your wonderfully secluded porch, which is perfect for reading and snoozing once you break away from the view. There are nearby rain forest treks, a drive-in volcano to visit, and Diamond Falls, which tumbles in six stages through sulfur springs that

Twin peaks rise from the surf.

color the waters like a rainbow— but make sure you're back in time for sunset.

WHAT: hotel, site. **WHERE:** just north of Soufrière. Tel 758/459-7000; in the U.S., tel 800-223-1108; www.ansechastanet.com. **COST:** doubles from $300 (low season), from $450 (high season, includes breakfast and dinner). **BEST TIMES:** Nov–Apr, the first week of May for the St. Lucia Jazz Fest.

Caribbean Magic with a Moroccan Flair

LA SAMANNA

Baie Longue, St. Martin, Lesser Antilles (French West Indies)

La Samanna offers service, food, and ambience so special that most guests never venture beyond the tony, sybaritic enclave's 55 impeccably groomed beachfront acres. Though located on the French side of an island split

between France and the Netherlands, the feel is evocative of the Mediterranean and Morocco, with whitewashed villas and patios, hand-painted tiles adding splashes of color, and bold fabrics in hues drawn from the sea and sky. The hotel's glorious Baie Longue Beach, the island's nicest, stretches for what seems like miles, promising untrammeled beauty and privacy. And in the evenings, a dramatic tented bar and terrace surrounded by bougainvillea and alla-manda is the spot for elegant candlelit dinners, and the chance to sample from the hotel's

prodigious wine cellar. Rates are high but pretension is low, and "name" patrons adorn the guest book but then disappear for a memorable stay that can be filled with every imaginable sport, or nothing more than a good book.

WHAT: hotel. **WHERE:** 3 miles/5 km from the airport, northwest of Mullet Bay. Tel 590/590-87-64-00, fax 590/590-87-87-86; in the U.S., tel 800-854-2252; www.lasamanna. com. **COST:** deluxe doubles from $395 (low season), from $995 (high season). **WHEN:** closed Sept–Oct. **BEST TIMES:** Dec–Apr.

Weird and Wonderful Underwater Sights

DIVING WITH TOBAGO'S MANTA RAYS

Speyside, Tobago, Lesser Antilles

The lovely little island of Tobago is gaining popularity as a world-class dive site as divers flock here for the chance to swim and interact with monster manta rays in waters where visibility can reach 150 feet on a good day.

"Expect the unexpected," they'll tell you, and your expectations will still be surpassed: A dozen or so giant manta rays measuring from 6 to 10 feet across live in the Batteaux Bay area, some staying year-round because of the thick clouds of plankton, on which they and myriad other creatures feed. Some divers may have to settle for a sighting of these graceful, majestic creatures, but most will be able to interact. The friendly mantas encourage divers to hold on for a free ride, returning to them time and again—a practice that once earned them the

Swim with the giant rays.

nickname "Tobago taxis." Today's more sensitive approach is to interact by merely swimming in their magical presence. Tobago, Trinidad's sleepy country cousin, is one of those diving destinations that can reward topside curiosity as well. Its Amazon-type forests are some of the oldest protected on our planet.

WHAT: experience. **WHERE:** the fishing village of Speyside on the northeast coast is the most convenient point for top dive sites. Beachside Manta Lodge is one of the newest of the dedicated dive resorts, with its own PADI facility. **HOW:** Tobago Dive Experience, tel 868/660-5268; in U.S., tel 866-486-2246; info@mantalodge.com; www.mantalodge.com. **COST:** doubles from $110 (low season), from $150 (high season). Dive packages available. **BEST TIMES:** Nov–mid-Dec, Jan–Apr.

Eden's Aviary

ASA WRIGHT NATURE CENTER AND LODGE

Arima, Trinidad, Lesser Antilles

Sitting on this former plantation's screened-in veranda is like sitting in an enormous aviary. From your ringside seat you can see as many as thirty different species of bird, including toucans, squirrel cuckoos, tufted coquettes, and half a dozen varieties of hummingbirds —and that's before breakfast! Birders are obviously in seventh heaven here, but this nature and wildlife sanctuary, located on 700 acres 1,200 feet up in the island's northern rain forest, is a fascinating destination for naturalists, hikers, or the just plain curious as well, since Trinidad and sister island Tobago are home to a cornucopia of exotic flora and fauna unknown elsewhere in the Caribbean.

Day guests are welcome to visit, but overnight residents in the simple guest rooms of the large, airy 1908 plantation house or in cottages scattered around the grounds get in on all the activity at dawn and dusk. Trained guides take guests on a network of rain forest trails in search of the more than 160 species of birds—not to mention innumerable varieties of mammals, reptiles, butterflies, and flowering plants that make you feel you've found the Garden of Eden.

WHAT: hotel. **WHERE:** Spring Hill Estate, in the Arima Valley, 20 miles/32 km from Port of Spain. Contact Caligo Ventures. Tel 305/292-0708; in the U.S., tel 800-426-7781; info@caligo.com; www.caligo.com. **COST:** from $125 per person, double occupancy, includes all meals. **BEST TIMES:** Jan–May for weather.

A Riotous Celebration Where Calypso Is King

CARNIVAL

Port of Spain, Trinidad, Lesser Antilles

C arnival is the quintessential expression of Creole culture, and Trinidad's is acknowledged throughout the Caribbean as the mother of all carnivals, with Port of Spain at its heart. Bands and masqueraders begin their

preparations a year in advance, and before Christmas things really start to hum. The final two-day explosion of color, music, and unbridled excess officially begins at 4 A.M. on Carnival Monday with the Jour Ouvert (Opening Day) parade, and comes to a head on Shrove Tuesday (Mardi Gras), the day before Ash Wednesday, which ushers in the solemn pre-Easter period of Lent. Tens of thousands take to the streets in extravagant and elaborate costumes, with groups as large as 3,000 following DJ trucks blaring out the island's indigenous calypso music. Introduced to the Caribbean at the end of the 18th century by the Roman Catholic French planters, the celebration shifted from its European emphasis after the emancipation of slaves in 1838, when the largely African urban underclass took to the streets. Raucous rivalries evolved into the heated steel-band competitions of today, in which "pan" bands 100 musicians strong perform nonstop in a riotous celebration of King Carnival. Each band has a headquarters, or panyard, where rehearsals and preliminary playoffs are worth searching out.

To heighten your island experience, visit Veni Mange ("come and eat"), where Allyson Hennesy—the talk-show Julia Child of Trinidad—and her friendly and flamboyant sister, Rosemary Hezekiah, prepare the best lunch on the island, overseeing both the kitchen and a gallery of local art set in a typical Creole home. The offspring of parents who were of English, Venezuelan, African, and Chinese descent, the charming, ebullient sisters will guide you through a quintessentially Trinidadian feast that might start with traditional callaloo-pumpkin soup (which, according to legend, can make a man propose marriage if it's prepared well) and end with homemade soursop ice cream or coconut mousse. Come on Wednesday's Caribbean Night, the only day the sisters serve dinner.

WHAT: event, restaurant. **CARNIVAL:** contact the Board of Tourism, tel 868/6275-7034, fax 868/638-7962, or the National Carnival Commission, tel 868/627-1357, www.ncctt. org/cms. *Cost:* grandstand tickets $25. *When:* week before Lent. **VENI MANGE:** 13 Lucknow St., St. James (3 miles/5 km west of city center). Tel 868/624-4597; venimange@gmail. com; www.venimange.com. *Cost:* lunch $25. *When:* open for lunch Mon–Fri; dinner Wed only. **BEST TIMES:** Dec–Apr.

An Unrivaled Underwater Nature Trail

BUCK ISLAND

St. Croix, U.S. Virgin Islands, Lesser Antilles (U.S. Territory)

The snorkeling is legendary at this uninhabited satellite island off St. Croix, where an elkhorn coral reef lies in crystal-clear waters (think 100-foot visibility) at an average depth of 13 feet. Off Buck's northeast end, a meandering snorkeler's trail is marked with explanatory plaques so you'll surface knowing the difference between one forest of sculpture-shaped coral and another. The reef abounds with more than 250 species of fish, including queen angelfish, parrotfish, iridescent blue tangs, sergeant majors, and a host of other colorful creatures who remain remarkably nonplussed in your presence. Much of the reef is protected as an underwater national park.

WHAT: experience, site. **WHERE:** 1.5 miles/ 2.5 km off the northeast coast of St. Croix. **HOW:** a half-dozen tour operators offer snorkeling boat tours. Big Beard's Adventure Tours offers full-day tours on a glass-bottomed boat (allowing even the water-phobic to enjoy), as well as half-day snorkeling trips, both departing from Christiansted, St. Croix; includes beach barbecue. Tel 340/773-4482; fax 340/719-2245; in the U.S., tel 866-773-4482; info@bigbeards.com; www.bigbeards. com. **COST:** full day $100, half day $70. **BEST TIMES:** Nov–Mar.

A Rockefeller's Escape

CANEEL BAY

St. John, U.S. Virgin Islands, Lesser Antilles (U.S. Territory)

Consider the numbers: 170 lush, landscaped acres surrounded by a 9,000-acre national park on the Caribbean's least-developed island; 170 plush, secluded rooms; 7 private, pristine beaches lapped by 5,600 acres of underwater national park; and 400 smiling staffers to make sure your vacation is supreme. Laurance Rockefeller was so stunned by St. John's natural beauty when he visited in 1952 that he bought up a large part of the island, created an exquisite getaway for his blue-chip cronies, and donated the rest to the U.S. government for the creation of the United States's twenty-ninth national park. Luxury here is low-key but five-star every inch of the way: five-course breakfasts served on your open balcony to the music of ocean breezes and birdsong; tennis on first-class courts; snorkeling with 100-foot visibility amid some of the Caribbean's most dramatic undersea landscapes; strolls along footpaths shaded by eighty different species of palm trees, past flowering plants with names like Flamboyant, Cup-of-Gold, and Angel's Trumpet. Your most challenging decision during your invariably too-short stay: Which beach today?

WHAT: hotel. **WHERE:** closest airport is on St. Thomas. Hotel can arrange transfer by car and boat ($100/passenger). Tel 340/776-6111, fax 340/693-8280; in the U.S., tel 888-ROSEWOOD; www.caneelbay.com. **COST:** doubles from $325 (low season), from $600 (high season). **BEST TIMES:** Nov–Apr.

An Eco-Friendly Resort on a Protected Island

HARMONY STUDIOS AND THE REEF BAY TRAIL

Cruz Bay, St. John, U.S. Virgin Islands, Lesser Antilles (U.S. Territory)

For environmentally conscious vacationers who like their paradise injected with a little intellectual and moral challenge, this ecotourism phenomenon is peerless. Harmony Studios (and the appendage of the no-frills, permanent-tent colony of Maho Bay camps), set in the midst of St. John's verdant national parkland, was the first resort to be built almost entirely of recycled materials and designed to operate exclusively on solar and wind power. But it offers no telltale signs of its building materials' humble origins: rubber tires, bottle glass, waste plastic, newsprint, and discarded lightbulbs. The resort's two hillside sites were excavated by hand, built on stilts, and linked by an intricate labyrinth of elevated steps and wooden walkways, leaving the environment undisturbed. Rather than dominate the beautiful, pristine tract of parkland that leads down to its own white-beached aqua cove, Harmony blends with it, leaving guests to feel like privileged interlopers in paradise. This is not everyone's idea of a dream vacation, but with some of the highest occupancy rates in the Caribbean, they must be doing something right.

In large part due to the foresight of conservationist Laurance Rockefeller back in the 1950s, more than two-thirds of St. John is protected virgin forest, with three dozen well-marked hiking trails winding through more than 9,000 tropical acres. The Reef Bay Trail, starting not far from Harmony Resort from a spot on Centerline Road, is one of the most popular. It's all downhill, beginning at 800 feet above sea level and winding past spectacular views, ancient graffiti-like petroglyphs, and the ruins of 18th-century Danish plantation houses before ending about three hours later on the southern shore.

What: hotel, site. **Harmony Studios and Maho Bay Camp:** at Maho Bay, 8 miles/ 12 km northeast of Cruz Bay. Tel 340/776-6240, fax 340/776-6504; in the U.S., tel 800-392-9004 or 212-472-9453, fax 212-861-6210; mahobay@maho.org; www.maho.org. *Cost:* Harmony Studios doubles from $130 (low

season), $225 (high season). Maho Bay Camps doubles from $80 (low season), $135 (high season). **Reef Bay Trail:** begins 5 miles /8 km east of Cruz Bay. *When:* open daily. Every Mon, Thurs, and Fri, a Park Service naturalist leads an organized walk, for which there's a nominal fee. Contact the Cinnamon Bay Campground, www.cinnamonbay.com, to reserve a spot. **Best times:** Nov–Apr.

Virgin Sands

MAGENS BAY BEACH

St. Thomas, U.S. Virgin Islands, Lesser Antilles (U.S. Territory)

Much has been made of the fact that *National Geographic* magazine voted Magens Bay one of the world's most beautiful beaches. You're bound to second that, especially if you visit this mile-long, horseshoe-shaped strip of white sand when it's uncrowded (most visitors to the island are either in a duty-free shopping frenzy in Charlotte Amalie or vegetating at their hotel's private beach).

The thick fringe of palms that lines the bay's calm blue waters makes the admission charge the best $3 you'll spend in your life.

What: site. **Where:** north coast of St. Thomas, 3 miles/5 km north of the capital, Charlotte Amalie; www.magensbayvi.com. **Cost:** admission $3. **When:** open year-round. **Best times:** Nov–Apr.

Preparing for a kayaking trip at Magens Bay, St. Thomas

SPECIAL INDEXES

NOTE: In these indexes, readers will find entries for the following categories:

For additional information, please refer to the General Index starting on page 918.

ANCIENT WORLDS

PYRAMIDS, RUINS, AND LOST CITIES

CULINARY EXPERIENCES

See also DINING
IN GENERAL INDEX

FESTIVALS AND SPECIAL EVENTS

GLORIES OF NATURE

GARDENS, PARKS AND WILDERNESS PRESERVES, AND NATURAL WONDERS

GARDENS

NATURAL WONDERS

GORGEOUS BEACHES AND GETAWAY ISLANDS

BEACHES AND SEASHORES

GREAT HOTELS AND RESORTS

LIVING HISTORY

CASTLES AND PALACES, HISTORICAL SITES

CASTLES AND PALACES

UNRIVALED MUSEUMS

ROADS, ROUTES, AND BYWAYS

Scenic Drives

Train Trips

GENERAL INDEX

NOTE: In the General Index, readers will find proper names listed alphabetically, as well as categories such as accommodations and dining. Please note that items in SMALL CAPS refer to main topics.

Other topics are covered in the Special Indexes found on pages 895–917. The Special Indexes include the following categories: ACTIVE TRAVEL AND ADVENTURE; ANCIENT WORLDS: PYRAMIDS, RUINS, AND LOST CITIES; CULINARY EXPERIENCES; FESTIVALS AND SPECIAL EVENTS; GLORIES OF NATURE: GARDENS, PARKS AND WILDERNESS PRESERVES, AND NATURAL WONDERS; GORGEOUS BEACHES AND GETAWAY ISLANDS; GREAT HOTELS AND RESORTS; LIVING HISTORY: CASTLES AND PALACES, HISTORICAL SITES; UNRIVALED MUSEUMS; ROADS, ROUTES, AND BYWAYS; SACRED PLACES

H

HERMANUS, Western Cape, S.Af., 387

Hermitage, South Island, N.Z., 538

HERMITAGE MUSEUM, St. Petersburg, Rus., 310

HERON ISLAND, Queensland, Aus., 524–525

Het Loo palace, Otterlo, Nth., 246

HET MAURITSHUIS, The Hague, Nth., 247

Heuriger Experience, Vienna, Austria, 97

Hexham, Northumberland, Eng., 27–28

Hidcote Gardens, The Cotswolds, Eng., 13

Hide, Hwange, Zim., 393

HIGH ATLAS, Moro., 356–357

HIGHLAND GAMES, Scot., 45–46

HIGHLAND SING-SING FESTIVAL, Mount Hagen, Pap.NG., 555–556

Highlands, Scot., 44–45

hiking and trekking. *See under* Active Travel and Adventure, 895

HILL COUNTRY OF TEXAS, U.S., 715–716

HILL TRIBES OF NORTHERN THAILAND, Chiang Mai, Thai., 500–501

Hillwood Museum and Gardens, Washington, D.C., U.S., 736

Hilton Head Island, South Carolina, U.S., 705

Hilton Hotel, Budapest, Hung., 296

Hilton Nuweiba Coral Resort, Nuweiba, Egypt, 349

HISTORIC DOWNTOWN NEW YORK CITY, U.S., 684–685

Historic Savannah Foundation, Georgia, U.S., 610

Historic Smithton Inn, Pennsylvania, U.S., 699

historical sites. *See under* Living History, 910. *See also* archaeological sites

Historische Wurstküche, Bavaria, Ger., 158

Ho Chi Minh City, Viet., 509–510

Ho Chi Minh Mausoleum, Hanoi, Viet., 508

Hoan Kiem Lake, Hanoi, Viet., 508–509

Hofbräuhaus am Platzl, Bavaria, Ger., 157

Hofburg (Imperial Hapsburg Palace), Vienna, Austria, 95

HOGMANAY, Scot., 51–52

Hog's Breath Inn, California, U.S., 578

Hohe Tauern National Park, Austria, 93

Hohenschwangau Castle, Bavaria, Ger., 152, 154

HOI AN, Viet., 511

Hol Chan Marine Reserve, Belz., 795

holidays (by region). *See also* festivals

Europe, Western

Bastille Day, Paris, Fr., 117

Christmas in Vienna, Austria, 96

Feria de Abril, Andalusia, Sp., 259

Fête des Gardians, Provence-Alpes-Côte d'Azur, Fr., 130

Semana Santa (Holy Week) in Seville, Andalusia, Sp., 258

Mexico

El Día de los Muertos, 794

Middle East

Christmas in Bethlehem, Israel, 399–400

South America

New Year's Eve at Copacabana Beach, Brazil, 825

United States

Rockefeller Center at Christmas, New York, 679

Thanksgiving at Plimoth Plantation, Massachusetts, 651–652

HOLLYWOOD, California, U.S., 575–576

Hollywood Boulevard Walk of Fame, California, U.S., 576

Holocaust Memorial Museum, Washington, D.C., U.S., 736

Holyrood Palace, Edinburgh, Scot., 50

HOME RANCH, Colorado, U.S., 586–587

Homer, Alaska, U.S., 564

HOMESTEAD, Virginia, U.S., 728

Homestead, Western Australia, Aus., 531

Homestead Resort, Virginia, U.S., 728

Honduras, 802–803

Hong Kong, China, 423

Honours of Scotland (Scottish crown jewels), 50

Hookipa Beach, Hawaii, U.S., 617

Hopewell Rocks, New Brunswick, Can., 760

HORNED DORSET PRIMAVERA, Rincón, Prt.Rc., 882–883

Horse and Plow, Wisconsin, U.S., 740

horseback riding. *See under* Active Travel and Adventure, 895

HORSESHOE BAY BEACH, Matangi Island, Fiji, 541–542

Hostal del Cardenal, Castile La Mancha, Sp., 265

HOSTELLERIE DE CRILLON LE BRAVE, Provence-Alpes-Côte d'Azur, Fr., 133

Hostería Alta Vista, Patagonia, Argen., 813

Hosteria La Mirage, Otavalo, Ecu., 838

hotel accommodations. *See* accommodations, overnight

Hotel Aido Mori, Venice, It., 234

Hotel Aliki, Dodecanese, Gr., 175

Hotel Amigo, Brussels, Bel., 101

Hotel Bel Air, California, U.S., 576

Hôtel Bernard Loiseau, Burgundy, Fr., 109

Hotel Bora Bora, Fr.Poly., 548

Hotel Cala di Volpe, Sardinia, It., 207

Hotel Carl Gustaf, St. Barts, L.Ant., 886–887

Hotel Catharina Paraguaçu, Salvador de Bahia, Brazil, 829

HOTEL CONTINENTAL, Oslo, Nor., 329–330

HÔTEL D'ANGLETERRE, Copenhagen, Dnm., 312–313

Hotel Danieli, Venice, It., 234

Hotel Das Cataratas, Misiones, Argen., 811

HÔTEL DE CRILLON, Paris, Fr., 120

Hôtel de la Cité, Languedoc-Roussillon, Fr., 124

HÔTEL DE PARIS, Monte Carlo, Monaco, 147

Hôtel de Ville, Brussels, Bel., 101

Hôtel de Ville, Lorraine, Fr., 125

HOTEL DEL CORONADO, California, U.S., 580–581

Hotel Derlon, Maastricht, Nth., 249

Hôtel des Invalides/Napoleon's Tomb, Paris, Fr., 116

Hotel Deuring Schlössle, Austria, 90

HÔTEL DU CAP EDEN-ROC, Provence-Alpes-Côte d'Azur, Fr., 129–130

Hôtel du Palais, Aquitaine, Fr., 104

PHOTO CREDITS

Unless otherwise specified, copyright on the works reproduced lies with the respective photographers, agencies, and museums. Despite extensive research, it has not always been possible to establish copyright ownership. Where this is the case, we would appreciate notification.

BACK COVER: Portrait of author by Dwight Gast.

TABLE OF CONTENTS: p. x (top) Olaf Malver; p. xi (top) Elkhart County Convention & Visitors Bureau; p. xii (top) Joe Petrocik.

MAPS: p. 2, p. 344, p. 398, p. 418, p. 514, p. 562, p. 778, p. 850 5W INFOGRAPHIC

EUROPE: p. 22 (top) Simon Bracken/Lonely Planet Images, (bottom) Lee Foster/Lonely Planet Image; p. 24 Simon Bracken/Lonely Planet Images; p. 55 Alan Majchrowicz/age fotostock; p. 56 (top) Peter Thompson/age fotostock; p. 57 Ann Cecil/Lonely Planet Images; p. 67 Vidler Steve/age fotostock; p. 68 Eoin Clarke/Lonely Planet Images; p. 88 (bottom) Gareth McCormack/Lonely Planet Images. *Western Europe*: p. 93 Mark Honan/Lonely Planet Images; p. 94 Karl Forster; p. 118 Veronica Garbutt/Lonely Planet Images; p. 123 (top) Henri de Toulouse-Lautrec, Eldorado, Aristide Bruant, 1892, collection Musée Toulouse-Lautrec, photo © Musée Toulouse-Lautrec-Albi-Tarn-France, (bottom) Michel Hartin; p. 129 Neil Setchfield/Lonely Planet Images; p. 130 Manfred Gottschalk/Lonely Planet Images; p. 142 Aman Resorts; p. 144 Derek Hudson 1995; pgs. 152, 153, 155, 157, 158 German National Tourist Office; p. 159 Courtesy Berlin Philharmonic; pgs. 160, 161, 165, 166, 168 German National Tourist Office; p. 171 Neil Setchfield/Lonely Planet Images; pgs. 172, 173, 174, 175 (top), 176, 177 Greek National Tourist Organization; p. 185 Stephen Saks/Lonely Planet Images; p. 192 Jon Davison/Lonely Planet Images; p. 193 Russell Mountford/Lonely Planet Images; p. 200 Geoff Stringer/Lonely Planet Images; p. 202 Jon Davison/Lonely Planet Images; p. 206 Italian Government Tourist Board; pgs. 213, 216 Martin Hughes/Lonely Planet Images; p. 222 John Hay/Lonely Planet Images; p. 227 Margot Granitsas/The Image Works; p. 246 Zaw Min Yu/Lonely Planet Images; p. 253 (bottom) Catarina Gomes Ferreira, Carlos Azevedo, Margarida Ramalho; pgs. 256, 257 Tourist Board of Spain; p. 258 Jenny Jones/Lonely Planet Images; pgs. 259, 262 (bottom), 264, 267, 270 Tourist Board of Spain; p. 272 Elliot Daniel/Lonely Planet Images; p. 284 ARCO/HenryP/age fotostock; pgs. 290–293, 295 Czech Tourist Authority; pgs. 300–302 Polish National Tourist Office; p. 303 (both) Romanian National Tourist Office; pgs. 322–323 Finnish Tourist Board; p. 325 Grant Dixon/Lonely Planet Images; pgs. 327, 329–332 Norwegian Tourist Board; p. 335 Udo Haafke/TuristRådet, Tyskland; p. 336 Marc Oliver Schulz/TuristRådet, Tyskland; p. 337 Bengt Wanselius.

AFRICA: p. 348 (bottom) Louis Usie; p. 353 Anders Blomqvist/Lonely Planet Images; p. 354 John Elk III/Lonely Planet Images; p. 367 Ariadne Van Zandbergen/Lonely Planet Images; p. 369 (top) EQUITOUR; p. 381 Image Courtesy South Africa Tourism; p. 386 The Print Collector/age fotostock; p. 390 Patricia Schultz.

THE MIDDLE EAST: pgs. 402 (bottom), 403–404 Courtesy of the Israel Ministry of Tourism; p. 407 Anthony Ham/Lonely Planet Images; p. 408 (bottom) Chris Mellor/Lonely Planet Images; p. 410 (both) Saudi Arabia Embassy; p. 413 John Elk III/Lonely Planet Images; p. 415 Government of Dubai, Department of Tourism and Commerce Marketing.

ASIA: p. 419 Diana Mayfield/Lonely Planet Images; p. 430 Jean Robert/Lonely Planet Images; p. 434 Japan National Tourist Organization; p. 435 Bob Charlton/Lonely Planet Images; p. 437 (both) Japan National Tourist Organization; p. 438 P. Bussian; p. 441 Alison Wright/Lonely Planet Images; p. 444 Lindsay Brown/Lonely Planet Images; p. 446 Bill Wassman/Lonely Planet Images; p. 455 Chris Beall/Lonely Planet Images; p. 456 Patrick Ben Luke Syder/Lonely Planet Images; p. 458 Nepal Tourism Board; p. 462 (top) Tiger Mountain; p. 464 (top) INCA; pgs. 465, 467, 468, 472 Eric Harvey Brown; p. 474 Martin Moos/Lonely Planet Images; p. 477 (top) Robert Houser; p. 479 (bottom) Marilyn Staff/Bolder Adventures, Inc; p. 487 Asia Transpacific Journeys; p. 496 Glenn Beanland/Lonely Planet Images; p. 501 Bolder Adventures, Inc/Asia Transpacific Journeys; p. 502 Kevin Orpin; p. 504 Anders Blomqvist/Lonely Planet Images; p. 506 Guy Coburn; p. 507 Olaf Malver.

AUSTRALIA, NEW ZEALAND, AND THE PACIFIC ISLANDS: p. 515 Ross Barnett/Lonely Planet Images; p. 518 Richard I'Anson/Lonely Planet Images; p. 523 (top) Leonard Douglas Zell/Lonely Planet Images; p. 527 Richard I'Anson/Lonely Planet Images; pgs. 535, 538 Eric Harvey Brown; p. 539 A.J. Hackett; p. 547 Peter Hendrie/Lonely Planet Images; p. 551 Manfred Gottschalk/Lonely Planet Images.

THE UNITED STATES OF AMERICA AND CANADA: p. 561 Ryan Fox/Lonely Planet Images; p. 568 Russ Finley; p. 575 Tom Bonner/J. Paul Getty Trust; p. 576 Richard Cummins/Lonely Planet Images; p. 577 Lee Foster/Lonely Planet Images; p. 588 Robert Royem Photography; p. 591 Courtesy of Vail Resorts; p. 593 George Ruhe; p. 594 Charles W. Morgan/Mystic Seaport; p. 595 Litchfield Hills Visitors Bureau; p. 598 Kennedy Space Center Visitor Complex; p. 604 Neil Setchfield/Lonely Planet Images; p. 605 Jon Davison/Lonely Planet Images; p. 608 Sanibel Island/Lee Island Coast Visitor and Convention Bureau; p. 612 George W. Gardner; p. 613 Hawaii Visitors & Convention Bureau/Kirk Lee Aeder; p. 615 Hawaii Visitors & Convention Bureau/Robert Coello; p. 616 Sheila Donnelly & Associates; p. 621 Emily Riddell/Lonely Planet Images; p. 622 Dave Mills; p. 623 Courtesy of Sun Valley Resort; p. 624 Susan Reich/Richard Thomas/The Art Institute of Chicago; p. 626 City of Chicago, Mayor's Office of Special Events; p. 627 Jon Miller, Hedrich-Blessing; p. 629 Elkhart County Convention & Visitors Bureau; p. 632 Courtesy of the Lexington Convention and Visitors Bureau; p. 637 Thomas Downs/Lonely Planet Images; p. 639 National Park Service; p. 642 Rockland Festival Corp.; p. 644 Greater Boston Convention and Visitors Bureau; p. 645 David Bohl; p. 647 Kim Grant/Lonely Planet Images; p. 648 Kim Grant/Lonely Planet Images; p. 652 Plimoth Plantation, Plymouth Massachusetts; p. 656 Stephen Saks/Lonely Planet Images; p. 658 Glacier National Park; p. 667 Mark Newman/Lonely Planet Images; pgs. 671, 675 New York State Department of Economic Development; p. 677 Kim Grant/Lonely Planet Images; p. 681 Angus Oborn/Lonely Planet Images; p. 686 Donald C. & Priscilla Alexander Eastman/Lonely Planet Images; p. 690 John Elk III/Lonely Planet Images; p. 691 Outer Banks Visitors Bureau; p. 693 Brent Winebrenner/Lonely Planet Images; p. 695 Richard Cummins/Lonely Planet Images; p. 696 Ryan Fox/Lonely Planet Images; p. 701 David Fields; p. 702 Lee Foster/Lonely Planet Images; p. 704 Kim Grant/Lonely Planet Images; p. 706 Rick Gerharter/Lonely Planet Images; p. 709 (bottom) Corey Rich/Lonely Planet Images; p. 709 (top) Carol Polich/Lonely Planet Images; p. 711 Elvis Presley Enterprises, Inc.; p. 719 Chris Mellor/Lonely Planet Images; p. 724 Kim Grant/Lonely Planet Images; p. 729 Alison Wright/Lonely Planet Images; p. 732 Colonial Williamsburg Foundation, Williamsburg, VA; p. 733 Shannon Nace/Lonely Planet Images; p. 736 Rick Gerharter/Lonely Planet Images; p. 737 Stephen J. Shaluta/West Virginia Division of Tourism; p. 738 David E. Fattaleh/West Virginia Division of Tourism; p. 740 Layne Kennedy; p. 746 Carol Polich/Lonely Planet Images; p. 749 John F. Marriott/Getty Images; p. 750 Michael Laanela/Lonely Planet Images; p. 752 photo by Neil Rabinowitz; p. 754 Ross Barnett/Lonely Planet Images; p. 756 Rob Melnychuk; p. 759 Nicholas Reuss/Lonely Planet Images; p. 765 Cheryl Conlon/Lonely Planet Images; p. 768 Thomas Huhti/Lonely Planet Images; p.769 Yves Marcoux/Getty Images; p. 772 Jeremy Gray/Lonely Planet Images; p. 774 Mark Lightbody/Lonely Planet Images.

LATIN AMERICA: p. 777 Krzystof Dydnski/Lonely Planet Images; p. 780 Cherie Pittillo; p. 781 Richard I'Anson/Lonely Planet Images; pgs. 784, 793 (bottom) Mexico Tourism Board; p. 795 Greg Johnston/Lonely Planet Images; p. 800 Richard I'Anson/Lonely Planet Images; p. 802 Darrell Jones; p. 803 Alfredo Maiquez/Lonely Planet Images; p. 806 Alfredo Maiquez/Lonely Planet Images; p. 811 Krzystof Dydnski/Lonely Planet Images; p. 817 Holger Leue/age fotostock; p. 818 (top) Robyn Jones/Lonely Planet Images; p. 823 John Maier Jr./Lonely Planet Images; p. 824 John Maier Jr./Lonely Planet Images; p. 831 T.C. Swartz/TCS Expeditions; p. 838 Lee Foster/Lonely Planet Images; p. 845 Wes Walker/Lonely Planet Images.

THE CARIBBEAN, BAHAMAS, AND BERMUDA: p. 855 Cookie Kinkead (Island Outpost); p. 866 (bottom) Stephen Frink/Getty Images; p. 873 (top) Wayne Walton/Getty Images; p. 876 Joe Petrocik; p. 877 Greg Gawlowski/Lonely Planet Images; p. 884 Steve Simonsen/Lonely Planet Images; p. 885 Mark Webster/Lonely Planet Images; p. 887 Wayne Walton/Lonely Planet Images; p. 890 Douglas Spranger; p. 894 Lee Foster/Lonely Planet Images.